Decedents' Estates

Decedents' Estates

Cases and Materials

FOURTH EDITION

Raymond C. O'Brien
PROFESSOR OF LAW
THE CATHOLIC UNIVERSITY OF AMERICA
COLUMBUS SCHOOL OF LAW

Michael T. Flannery
ASSOCIATE DEAN FOR ACADEMIC AFFAIRS
JUDGE GEORGE HOWARD, JR. DISTINGUISHED PROFESSOR OF LAW
UNIVERSITY OF ARKANSAS AT LITTLE ROCK
WILLIAM H. BOWEN SCHOOL OF LAW

CAROLINA ACADEMIC PRESS
Durham, North Carolina

ISBN   978-1-5310-1835-1
e-ISBN 978-1-5310-1836-8
LCCN   2019950692

Carolina Academic Press
700 Kent Street
Durham, North Carolina 27701
Telephone (919) 489-7486
Fax (919) 493-5668
www.cap-press.com

Printed in the United States

I have sometimes thought that the emphasis on facts and procedure instead of generally applicable substantive rules provided us with a vertical rather than a horizontal legal education.
Justice John Paul Stevens
THE MAKING OF JUSTICE 54 (2019)

For
Nicholas James Williams
because there is so much more than chintz
ROB

For
John F. Dobbyn
the kindest person I will ever know
MTF

Summary of Contents

Contents

Table of Cases

Table of Authors

Preface

The evolution of decedents' estates continues. The first edition of this casebook was published in 2006 but was written mostly in 2005. The changes during this time have been significant. With the publication of the fourth edition, we illustrate societal changes, including same sex marriage, an increasing number of individuals utilizing assisted reproduction technology, and the continuing increase in the percentage of nonmarital cohabiting couples. While these changes seem to be issues related solely to family law, they impact inheritance, elective share, and often the distribution of trust benefits. Indeed, the interaction between family law and inheritance prompted a revision of the Uniform Parentage Act (2017), which now is gender neutral, contains updates on surrogacy developments, and requires Artificial Reproductive Technology (ART) clinics to ask gamete donors if they want identifying information to be shared with the resulting children when he or she reaches 18 years of age.

Societal and judicial developments also have found expression in recent legislation. For instance, the trustee's ability to "decant" one trust into another is now codified in the Uniform Trust Decanting Act (2015). Likewise, delineating the duties of a "trust protector" is now formulated in the Uniform Directed Trust Act (2017). In an effort to better promote uniformity in the power to adjust between income and principal so as to maintain impartiality, there is an updated Uniform Fiduciary Income and Principal Act (2018). Also, corresponding with estate administration in the digital age, there is now a Revised Uniform Fiduciary Access to Digital Assets Act (2015).

An increasing number of states have adopted the Uniform Trust Code (2000), which testifies to the greater use of trusts nationally and internationally. Working in tandem with the Code are the Uniform Probate Code — revised in 2008 — the Uniform Powers of Appointment Act (2013), the Uniform Fraudulent Transfer/Voidable Transaction Act (2014), and the Uniform Premarital and Marital Agreements Act (2012). The Uniform Trust Code offers a series of default rules whenever the terms of the trust are absent or ambiguous.

Uniform legislation has an effect on ancient practices adjusting to modern usage. For example, these codes specify that wills can become valid through notarization alone, proposed expansive non-biological heirship, and a new formulation of a spouse's elective share. Self-settled asset protection trusts flourish among the states, as do decanting statutes. An increasing number of older Americans use charitable remainder unitrusts and dynasty trusts, prompted, in part, by a substantial increase in the federal estate tax exemption.

Undoubtedly, the increasing longevity of Americans and the concomitant wealth in these older clients prompt legal issues pertaining to standards of capacity, as well as choice and payment options for long-term care. Attorneys must be cognizant of interfamily dynamics, undue influence, fraud, tortious interference with expectancies, and delusion. As with the first three editions of this casebook, our goal is to offer cases that magically transfer the professor and the student into a factual human situation that explores both the law and personal options.

As we continue into the Twenty-First Century, any course on decedents' estates is best characterized by the creation of *inter vivos* trusts, the continuing proliferation of non-probate transfers, the easing of the "harsh formalism" of ancient formulae, the disclaimer of inheritance and contest through prenuptial agreements, and the casting of lifelines as an ever-increasing generation of older persons plans for incapacity. The once all-pervasive power of the Rule Against Perpetuities continues to wane, and no one would have predicted that academics would tinker with the share of a pretermitted heir, discount the word "survivor," or rationalize the introduction of clear and convincing extrinsic evidence to change the plain meaning of words.

Some elements in decedents' estates remain the same. For example, taxation of estates remains among a few states, no matter what the federal outcome. Taxation has always been the tail that wags the dog, and this concern remains at the state level and at the federal level among the super-rich. The human desire to make a difference in life remains the same, evidencing itself in gifts to charity, educational trusts for children, spousal trusts, and a myriad of trusts to provide "care, comfort and support" for everyone and everything, including pets and mausoleums. Remaining the same, too, is the public policy of any government that seeks to provide an orderly, efficient, and fair administration of wealth transfer.

A final inevitability factor, expressed in each of the three previous editions of this casebook, is the reality that, at some point in time, each person seeking to transfer wealth will become a decedent. No matter what legal changes have occurred, strategies have been adopted, or taxes have been imposed and paid, each person is amassing a decedent's estate that will one day transfer. Even though we are conscious observers of the scene and realize that *inter vivos* transfers and planning options are the focus of the modern course material, the focus is on meeting the needs of future decedents. In assembling the material for the book, choosing cases and problems, writing the Notes, and incorporating code provisions, we have made a purposeful effort to concentrate on the modern adaptations of *inter vivos* planning, but we are ignoring neither our indebtedness to what has gone before, nor the things that have remained the same. We hope that the reader will recognize and appreciate this balance in the following themes.

First, our primary concern is to make this book a good teaching vehicle. To facilitate this, we continue to place a Tool Bar at the start of each chapter, hoping that this will allow for a brief introductory summary before entering the thicket of material. Often, students miss the forest for the trees, and we hope that the Tool Bar will assist in providing a comprehensive overview from which the reader will be able to start, make reference throughout, and refer to as a summary at the conclusion. We have painstakingly chosen cases with fact patterns that invite interest, creativity, and debate. We believe that good cases make good classes!

A second theme of the book is informational. While we do provide questions and problems in the Notes, far more often we explain, elaborate on the case, and highlight what we think is important. Furthermore, students and professors have embraced the Internet, which is even available during class. Therefore, the casebook has more than a few Internet addresses. We hope you will utilize the international references provided, furnishing a glimpse into such arenas as spousal rights and fiduciary administration in foreign countries. Finally, we offer a device we have used to teach some of the material—what we refer to as the Analytical Principle. This is a tool that consists of time frames and points of reference. We use it to explain complicated issues such as lapse, powers of appointment, class gifts, vesting, and the Rule Against Perpetuities. We explain it in Chapter Six: Utilizing Future Interests, but its applicability will be shown in Chapter Seven: Creation, Classification, and Utilization of Trusts. Because we believe it offers students a visual connection with the material discussed, we believe it can assist in understanding. We hope that it provides you with a good resource.

A third theme is our purposeful inclusion of excerpts from articles authored by practitioners of decedents' estates. Many law schools and state bar associations are demanding that new attorneys have a familiarity with the law that makes them what is termed "practice ready." Current and insightful suggestions from women and men practicing at some of the finest law firms and investment companies in the nation provide a glimpse into practice throughout this casebook.

The final theme inculcated throughout the chapters is statutory construction analysis. Too often students become imbued with a lopsided appreciation for the common law to the detriment of statutory interpretations. To address this, included within the casebook are various code provisions, such as a number of state and uniform statutes, many from community property states. Of course, individual cases will discuss various state statutes in the context of decisions rendered. Admittedly, often cases were included because of the extensive discussion generated by the state's statute. Although the statutes may lack the factual context, including the drama of decisional law, they are the indisputable first step in any analysis.

The casebook is divided into eight chapters. Chapter One: An Introduction, introduces students to the issues that will arise in the succeeding chapters. Initially, we provided "A Family Affair," which concerns a family confronting death, parent incapacity, multiple forms of wealth transfer, and how the government, attorneys, and the family's own decisions will interconnect. The family portrayed confronts a reoccurring dilemma in modern society—how to plan for incapacity and transmit wealth to others. How to address this issue invites what is to come in all the succeeding chapters. But the first chapter is where students are likely to be introduced to the significance of non-probate transfers in the transmission of wealth, the struggle between state and federal tax entities, the overwhelming effort to avoid either gift or estate taxes, and the possibility that attorneys may be held liable for negligence. Eventually, when we end the book with Chapter Eight: Planning for Incapacity, we will revisit the issues introduced in this first chapter. In the last chapter, we will also introduce Medicare, Medicaid, Social Security, and the challenge of how to pay for long-term care for yourself or those you love. Increasingly, as is demonstrated in the first chapter, the goal of estate planning is to plan for many years of incapacity and assisted living.

Chapter Two: Intestate Succession, is traditional, statutory, and yet very modern. If you were to die without making any arrangements for the transfer of your wealth, how would you want your property disbursed? Every state has an intestate statute defining heirs; this is both traditional and statutory. But extensive consideration is given to the changing definition of the American family; the 2015 introduction of same sex marriage is one illustration; another is the increasing utilization of assisted reproductive technology by persons wishing to become parents. After establishing the pattern of distribution of wealth, the material in chapter two explores how, when there is neither a Last Will and Testament nor a valid non-probate substitute, spouses, issue, and parentage status affect the distribution of wealth under intestate statutes. Science has increased opportunities for parenthood and heirs. Who is an issue of whom? This is very modern. The most recent revisions to the Uniform Parentage Act, in tandem with the Uniform Probate Code, have introduced new elements. Although the concepts discussed in this chapter will have applicability to other forms of wealth transfer, this chapter provides the opportunity for students to discuss simultaneous death, assignment of expectancies, and disclaimers.

Chapter Three: The Last Will and Testament details the traditional and modern application of the rules meant to safeguard a testator's last wishes. We will examine the different types of wills and then explore the formalities and intentionalities needed to execute each. These rules have deep historical significance, but technology, the preference for transfers other than wills, and a less rigorous society have tempered the strict application of formalities. Instead, today, the rules are complemented with doctrines of substantial compliance and primary intent. All of the pomp and circumstances of days-gone-by, with witnesses and lots of signatures in stuffy law offices, now may be reduced to a simple notary public signature. Progress? This is the chapter in which we seek to balance the old against the new, the evolution of presence at execution, how much influence is undue, and, in an aging population, how do we define testamentary capacity? The cases illustrate the vagaries of the human condition. Once we have mastered valid execution of the will, with all of its competing interests, we discuss revocation and revival of revoked wills. This chapter is the subject matter of bar examinations.

Chapter Four: The Meaning of Words offers the opportunity to make a "fortress out of the dictionary." The law has accepted facts of independent significance and also incorporation by reference. Likewise, extrinsic evidence may be admitted for latent and patent ambiguities. However, legal lists and exoneration are evolving, as are ademption and accessions. Likewise, the law regarding contracts to make wills is fairly settled, but commentators have suggested, and offered legislation, proposing changes to the rules addressing mistaken plain meaning and the distribution of property when there has been a lapse in persons or property. Comparing the age-old rules with the new exigencies is like pouring new wine into old bottles, precipitating good class participation. This chapter offers a chance to explore textualism and evolution.

Chapter Five: Restraints on Transfer of Wealth challenges the premise discussed in Chapter One—that persons have a right under the Constitution to pass their property to others at death. In chapter five, students learn that there are restraints upon that right. For example, you cannot create a trust that promotes lawlessness, and you cannot mistakenly overlook your issue, marital or nonmarital. Since your spouse is also your economic partner, she or he is entitled to part of the wealth amassed during marriage—something that you cannot disparage without that spouse's consent. Constitutional law is a good preparation for these restraints. This chapter adds another restraint—the bureaucratic process that describes the cumbersome restraint upon wealth transferring through the probate process. The costs, forms, delays, taxes, administration, and contests can be a bureaucratic nightmare. Finally, because spouses have a right to property amassed during marriage, we discuss elective share. The statutory and judicial models to provide for augmenting the estate for election by a surviving spouse equivalent are meant to promote dialogue about public policy's deficiencies and the need for change. Indeed, the 2008 revision to the elective share provisions of the Uniform Probate Code, which seeks to integrate marital property considerations into distribution of property at death, offers good discussion opportunities.

Chapter Six: Utilizing Future Interests provides an explanation of the words, phrases, and constructions that have divided "vested" from "possession" for hundreds of years. Anticipating the next chapter, devoted exclusively to trusts, this chapter provides definitions, cases, and the Analytical Principle, which may be used to chart the interests that pass under anti-lapse statutes, class gifts, powers of appointment, vesting, and the Rule Against Perpetuities. Rather than study the material in a vacuum, the cases and statutes illustrate what is necessary to use future interests in estate planning instruments. Much of this material was discussed in property classes, for better or for worse, so what we provide here is the practical application of those words and phrases, applicable to trusts and what goes into them.

Chapter Seven: Creation, Classification, and Utilization of Trusts is the longest chapter in the casebook, but we thought the breadth and length was justified to assemble all of the trust material in one place. Grouping permits a comprehensive approach to the topic. It is essential to understand the five elements of a trust. Because of the modern importance of trusts, there are many statutes included in the chapter: the Uniform Trust Act, Uniform Trust Decanting Act, Uniform Directed

Trust Act, and the Uniform Fiduciary Income and Principal Act, to name a few. The cases we include complement the statutes, and we emphasize fiduciary responsibility with excerpts from leading practitioners in the field. Too often, courses on decedents' estates neglect to illustrate types of trusts common to estate planning. Instead, we discuss ten distinctive trusts and five non-probate contractual arrangements that provide modern utilization, placing the material firmly in the context of what occurs each day in law offices and wealth management firms throughout the United States. Likewise, modification and termination of trusts have historical roots and, therefore, have rules, but more modern statutes have made substantial inroads, offering a discussion as to preference and, more importantly, professional responsibility.

Trust administration has become a career for many attorneys. Chapter seven offers cases and materials considering what constitutes prudent performance, the duty of loyalty, and how to maintain impartiality between income and remainder beneficiaries. How should a trustee invest, repair, sell, or administer the trust property? These issues are discussed under powers of the trustee, and appropriate statutory guidelines are provided. Likewise, we provide commentary from practitioners and scholars in the field.

Finally in chapter seven, we discuss three legal constructions that rest upon the validity of trusts. These constructions are class gifts, powers of appointment, and the Rule Against Perpetuities. With class gifts and powers of appointment, it is possible to present the rules pertaining to definition, scope, and validity, especially with the introduction of the Uniform Powers of Appointment Act (2018). However, the Rule Against Perpetuities offers a considerable challenge because of its changing status among the states. Speculation suggests that the Rule began to lose its binding force when states sought to ameliorate its harshness with doctrines such as wait and see, second look, and cy pres. These are all explained in the material provided. However, when states, and eventually the Uniform Probate Code, adopted the Uniform Statutory Rule Against Perpetuities, extending wait and see to ninety years, it was possible to imagine eliminating the Rule completely. Some states have done so. We provide illustrative state statutes abolishing the Rule. We provide sufficient material to offer a discussion on the impact of the Rule's abolition, including dynasty trusts or perpetual trusts.

Chapter Eight: Planning for Incapacity offers an opportunity to return to the Family Affair presented in the first chapter, and then to discuss options in light of what was learned between then and now. For example, the utility of a will, the consequences of intestate succession, the necessity of clear language, the avoidance of unreasonable restraints upon beneficiaries, and the use of trusts to provide for care and support. With that done, practicality demands assessment of resources and, specifically, payments from entitlement programs such as Social Security, Medicare, and Medicaid. So as to provide for personal dignity and privacy, and to ease the burden on family members, there are state forms and cases concerning durable powers, health care decision delegation, and the powers of conservators and guardians. The facts of these cases command headlines, and we seek to provide context through famous lives, such as Brooke Astor. Increasingly, we believe that the issues presented in this chapter will dominate the lives discussed in the issues presented in previous chapters. None of us get out alive, and between now and then, we need to plan for incapacity and death.

As you use this book, we welcome your comments and suggestions. We wish to express our deep appreciation to many who contributed to this enterprise. Especially, we are grateful to our student research assistant, Thomas J. Garrity III, for his prompt and expert editorial assistance in the preparation of this casebook.

January 2020

RAYMOND C. O'BRIEN
obrien@law.edu

MICHAEL T. FLANNERY
mxflannery@ualr.edu

Acknowledgments

We especially thank the National Conference of Commissioners on Uniform State Laws for its permission to reprint excerpts from its copyrighted text of the Uniform Probate Code, the Uniform Directed Trust Act, the Uniform Trust Decanting Act, the Uniform Fiduciary Income and Principal Act, the Revised Uniform Fiduciary Access to Digital Assets Act, the Uniform Trust Code, the Uniform Parentage Act, the Uniform Simultaneous Death Act, the Uniform Prudent Investor Act, the Uniform Statutory Rule Against Perpetuities, the Revised Uniform Anatomical Gift Act, the Uniform Health Care Decisions Act, and the Uniform Custodial Trust Act.

Note on Editing

Some text, footnotes, and citations have been edited to make the cases we have included more manageable and relevant to the teaching tools applicable to a three- or four-credit course. The footnotes that are included contain the original footnote numbers from the original source. All omissions are indicated with an appropriate ellipses symbol to indicate that material has been omitted.

Decedents' Estates

Chapter 1

An Introduction

I. A Family Affair

Once upon a time, in an average American city, in a modest three bedroom rambler with a sizable mortgage, there lived a married couple with their three children. Tim and Gina were married ten years ago; this was Tim's second marriage and the first for Gina. Tim and his first wife divorced, but prior to this, he and his wife had two children. Upon the divorce, Tim was awarded physical custody of their two children and they share joint legal custody. Tim's former wife lives nearby and often sees the children during the week and on weekends. One child is seventeen and the other is twelve. Tim and Gina have one son of their own, a seven year-old boy named Gabriel, but Gina never adopted Tim's two children from his first wife.

The family kitchen is the gathering place for the family. Tim looks older than his forty-two years indicate as he sits at the kitchen table. He is a high school principal and met his wife, Gina, at the high school, where she still works as a teacher. She is forty years old. The three children, Rachel (17), Kevin (12), and Gabriel (7), are either watching television or playing video games.

The family has just returned from the funeral and burial of Gina's father, who died after a lengthy struggle with Alzheimer's disease. He is survived by his wife of fifty years and their two daughters, Gina and Rosetta. Rosetta is a stock broker, unmarried, and lives and works in a large metropolitan area about a thousand miles away. She volunteered to take her recently-widowed mother back to the home that she had shared with her now-deceased husband so that she could rest after the ordeal of the last few days. In Rosetta's absence, Gina and Tim discuss the changes that they have observed in Gina's mother. Gina is concerned that her mother no longer may be able to live by herself in the home in which Gina and Rosetta were raised. The mother has fallen a few times and there could have been other times of which Gina is unaware.

"Tim, what do you think of the idea of us fixing the basement, putting in a bathroom, and bringing my mother here to live with us? We could make it pretty, perhaps get one of those devices that would allow my mother to sit down while going up the stairs, and we could carpet everything for her. She and Dad must have some savings to help pay for the changes, there's the house, and there must be Social Security income. I am sure that Rosetta would help us pay for the renovations too."

"Why can't she continue to live in her own house?" Tim replies. "I'm not so certain she is going to let you move her out of her house into our basement. That woman has a mind of her own. I know!"

"But we need to do something," Gina responded. "Have you seen how mother has lost so much weight? I don't think she's eating and I know for a fact that she isn't drinking enough water. At the funeral, she couldn't remember the names of people she has known all of her life. And Tim, I certainly never thought I would say this about my mother, but she just smelled. I don't think she is bathing or taking care of herself. Dad's struggle with Alzheimer's and now his death have taken a toll on her. I watched her walk and, frankly, she's frail and she teeters sometimes."

"She's still a pistol in my book! No way she's leaving her own home," Tim replies. "How about if we hire someone to look in on her from time-to-time. Maybe Medicare will pay for it. We need to go on line and check for a service that looks in on people. I think your mother is stubborn in spite of having some hygiene issues."

"Medicare is so complicated. I wouldn't know anyone to call. I really don't know much about Medicaid or Social Security. And even if we could afford to pay for someone to come to her home, I don't think my mother would like having a stranger in her house. You just don't know what will happen. You read so many crazy things today. Mother has always been a very private person. She will put up a fuss if we tell her that we are going to have a nurse or a caretaker spending a lot of time in her house."

"Yes," Tim agreed, "but she will be all alone here when we are at work and the kids are in school. I have an idea, maybe we can move her into one of those assisted living places."

"Are you crazy? I read where assisted living can cost more than $9,000 a month! She can't have long-term care insurance, so that money has to come out of her income—or our income! Maybe I can spin it to her that she's coming here for a visit. Spending time with the kids, she may adjust to the change and be happy to live in the basement. I am home early in the afternoon and I don't teach during the summers. I can be with her then too."

"Honey, I'm trying to be supportive here, but I think you are going to have a tough time making your mother move out of her house. And then you are going to resent the fact that we are homebound taking care of her 24/7. I just think we need to explore all of our options. Let's talk to Rosetta too. Maybe we ought to see how much money your parents have before we start making plans. Do you have any idea?"

"When dad began declining rapidly, we looked for any papers that we thought were important. Our parents never discussed with us anything about their property, and there was no mention made of any Last Will and Testaments, health care directives, or durable powers of attorney. But we did find the deed to their house, and it is listed as tenancy by the entirety, whatever that means. We think their house is paid for too. Rosetta looked at comparable Internet listings nearby and thinks the house is probably worth around $300,000. We may need to fix it up a bit if we plan to sell it at that price. I don't think anything has been done to it in thirty years. We also found a life insurance policy on my dad, payable to my mother for $10,000, and there must be joint savings and checking accounts. My guess is that they probably have $15,000 in those combined accounts at the bank. Their car is only two years old and is titled in my father's name, alone; no lease, he owned it. My mother never worked outside the house, but Rosetta discovered that my father's Social Security check comes to $1,500 a month; mother must get some of that. But Rosetta and I have found no Will or other documents signed by mom.

They have been contributing to an individual retirement account (IRA) because Rosetta and I found some papers about this, but I do not know how much it is worth. The papers said that the IRA is in mutual funds, and we have the phone number of the broker listed. Also, the forms we found say the IRA is payable to my father's "estate," and there is no alternate listed. We also found forms for a Fidelity

Destiny Mutual Fund account, into which my father paid $25.00 a month starting before my parents were married. I know the number of shares he owns from the summary he received each month. When Rosetta looked it up on her laptop, we read that his shares are worth about $600,000, at least. But it is very strange because the beneficiary of the Fidelity Destiny account is listed as 'The Society for the Prevention of Cruelty to Animals (SPCA).' Why would he do that?"

"I guess he loved animals," Tim quipped.

"Maybe," Gina said, "but he had the account for a very long time and probably never thought about it. I know that he and mother liked to feed the birds and the squirrels." "What else did you find?" Tim asked.

"There are his clothes, some cuff links, a Cartier watch, books, fishing equipment, and a Washington Senators baseball signed by all of the players and dated 1961. The Senators was the baseball team before the Nationals. I doubt my mother knew he had it, let alone what it may be worth, but Rosetta found it when we were searching for clothes in which to bury him. Oh! I almost forgot. We found a Last Will and Testament dated nearly sixty years ago—long before my father and mother were married and, of course, before Rosetta and I were born. It has his signature and the signatures of three witnesses. The ink has faded, and we cannot read the names, but we can read the Will itself. It lists as the sole beneficiary of everything 'The Society for the Prevention of Cruelty to Animals.' Who does that? I'm amazed."

"Me too," Tim replied. "Does that mean that animals get everything? Do we have to call them? In fact, what do we do? Have you asked your sister about this? Where do we start with any of this?"

Gina thought for a moment and said, "First, I think we need to make a list of the assets we know about, and that will be our starting point."

- Marital home: held as tenants by the entirety ($300,000).

- Life Insurance policy: payable to surviving spouse ($10,000).

- Jointly-held savings and checking accounts: ($15,000).

- Automobile: titled in decedent husband's name, alone.

- Social Security based on decedent husband's employment: ($1,500 monthly).

- Individual Retirement Account (IRA): payable to decedent husband's estate.

- Fidelity Destiny Account: payable to SPCA ($600,000).

- Clothes, watch, cufflinks, baseball, and fishing equipment: (unknown value).

- Last Will and Testament: sole beneficiary is the SPCA.

The fact pattern provided by Tim and Gina illustrates what occurs in an increasing number of homes in the United States. Recall the family dynamics: a middle-aged husband and wife; a prior marriage with stepchildren and half-siblings; the death of an older parent; and the child's sudden realization that she must now administer her father's unknown estate and provide for the long-term care of her once strong and dominant mother. The methods for transferring wealth and planning for incapacity are issues discussed throughout this casebook,. The task of the professional attorney is to anticipate the issues arising in A Family Affair and maximize options and the overall intent of the client.

There are three methods by which wealth is transferred in the United States. Two of these three methods involve a state's probate process, by which the state administers the distribution of a decedent's assets through active involvement. These two methods are testate succession (the probate of a valid Last Will and Testament) and intestate succession (distribution of assets according to an objective, state statutory structure). However, the majority of American wealth passes through a third method that does not involve probate but, instead, involves will substitutes or non-probate transfers. For now, we will look at each of these three methods of wealth transfer — the Last Will and Testament, intestate succession, and non-probate transfers — in reference to the property about which Tim and Gina are concerned — the father's estate.

A. Will Substitution: Non-Probate Transfers

Reviewing the assets left by Gina's father, we can see that he had many will substitutes:

(1) The marital home is titled as tenants-by-the-entirety, causing the house to transfer to the surviving spouse automatically, without the need for probate;

(2) The life insurance policy is a payable-on-death (POD) contract that permits the policy-designated contract beneficiary to take the proceeds without going through probate;

(3) The joint savings and checking accounts will permit the surviving joint tenant to take without the necessity of probate;

(4) The individual retirement account (IRA) is another non-probate contract device, but note that it is payable to the father's estate; the proceeds will eventually pass through probate;

(5) The Fidelity Destiny mutual fund account is another form of (POD) contract passing outside of probate, paid directly to the SPCA.

It is important to note again that will substitutes, or non-probate transfers, form the bulk of wealth transfers in the United States. Non-probate transfers trump the other two forms of wealth transfers. Issues arise throughout this casebook as to whether non-probate assets should be available for payment of decedents' debts, whether a Last Will and Testament should trump a designated beneficiary, whether the named beneficiary should be revoked if he or she is divorced from the decedent at time of death, and, pertinent for the facts in A Family Affair, whether the decedent's surviving spouse should share in non-probate assets paid to a third party.

B. Testate Succession: Probate and a Valid Last Will and Testament

Gina's father had a Last Will and Testament, and the person named as the Personal Representative in his Will is obligated to submit the Will, together with a death certificate, a written petition for probate, and the appropriate fees, to the county offices where the decedent was domiciled at death. Probate is a lengthy process. We will discuss its parameters *infra*. The Personal Representative has the initial burden of establishing the decedent's intentionality to execute the Will and that the prescribed formalities were performed. Most of the states have adopted various provisions proposed by the Uniform Probate Code, which makes formalities more uniform among the states. During the last fifty years, the states have relaxed the heretofore strict requirements associated with formalities by adopting substantial compliance statutes.

If a Will is validly executed in one state, but the decedent dies domiciled in another state, does the subsequent state have to give Full Faith and Credit to the validly-executed Will from the prior state? Should the length of time between the execution of a Will and the date of death provide a mechanism for revoking that Will? Note that the father married and had two daughters after he executed the Will. Should marriage, birth of children, or oral intentions be sufficient to revoke a validly executed Will? Note that in the facts of A Family Affair, a significant portion of the decedent's estate passes to persons other than his surviving spouse.

Whatever assets of the decedent that do not pass as non-probate transfers pass under any valid Will. The facts reveal that the father's automobile, titled in his name alone, and all of his personal property (clothes, watch, cuff links, baseball, and fishing equipment) will pass under the terms of his Last Will and Testament. Please note that his Will, executed prior to his marriage, names the Society for the Prevention of Cruelty to Animals (SPCA) as the sole beneficiary. What rights would Gina's mother have to these assets passing to the SPCA?

C. Intestate Succession: Probate and a State's Statutory Formula

A decedent's assets will transfer first through will-substitutes. If these are unavailable, they will pass through any valid Last Will and Testament. Finally, if neither of these is available, then the decedent's property will transfer through the intestate statute of the state in which the decedent was domiciled. Every state has its own intestate statute, with each state drafting its intestate statutes based on that state legislature's understanding of public policy in that state. As we will see in this casebook, state statutes can vary. Notice how the Uniform Probate Code differs from Maryland's statute.

When drafting their respective statutes, all states begin with the share of the estate to which a surviving spouse is entitled. A few states provide a share of the decedent's estate to the parents of the decedent, but all states regard issue—children and their descendants—as worthy of a share unless, according to most states, the surviving spouse is the parent of all surviving issue. Also, all states favor consanguinity over affinity; blood is thicker than relationships by marriage. Many states limit inheritance to family members within a certain degree of consanguinity. If no one is available within that degree, then the decedent's property escheats to the state. Unlike many foreign nations, there is no subjectivity in state intestate statutes. Persons with whom the decedent may have been in love, or protected, or simply wished to benefit after death, are omitted from intestate consideration unless that intended person is able to take under oral contract, a valid trust, or equity considerations. Intestacy should be the last resort for any decedent with wealth and family. It is not a good default option. Under intestate succession, any federal or state tax advantages are often lost, and any estate planning is surrendered to the generalities of a state's public policy goals. Note that under A Family Affair, because Gina's father died with both non-probate transfers and a presumptively valid Last Will and Testament, intestacy is avoided. Gina's and Rosetta's first goals must be to provide their mother with the documents necessary to safeguard her assets, provide for her eventual incapacity, and minimize the taxes and costs associated with dying.

II. Estate Planning Considerations

A. Taxation

A. Taxation: When Gina's father died, his estate became responsible for the following taxes:

(1) FEDERAL AND STATE INCOME TAXES: Any decedent is responsible for income earned from the start of the taxable year up to the death of the decedent's death. There is a uniform federal obligation, and nearly all of the states have a concomitant state income tax obligation.

(2) FEDERAL ESTATE TAX: Taxation of an estate at the federal level begins by computing the value of a decedent's gross estate (*see* I.R.C. §§ 2033-2044) minus permitted deductions (*see* I.R.C. §§ 2053, 2055, 2056 & 2058). Each decedent's estate is granted an exemption amount, currently at $11,400,000 (2019), indexed for inflation, so it changes each year ($11,180,000 in 2018). The maximum tax rate for those estates over the exemption amount is 40% (2019).

(3) STATE ESTATE TAX: In 2001, Congress changed the structure of the federal estate tax, prompting almost all of the states to repeal their own state estate taxes. For those states retaining the estate tax, careful estate planning consideration must be given to state exemptions, compared to the generous federal exemption of $11,400,00 (2019). Note, for example, the state estate tax exemptions for those states retaining the estate tax:

Connecticut: $3.6 million (2019) (CONN. GEN. STAT. ANN § 12-391(g)(5)).

District of Columbia: $5.6 million (2019) (D.C. CODE §§ 47-3701(14)(C), 47-3702(a-1) & 47-3703(b-1)).

Hawaii: $5.49 million (2019) (HAW. REV. STAT. §§ 236E-6 & -8).

Illinois: $4 million (2019) (35 ILCS 405/2).

Maine: $5.7 million (2019) (36 ME. REV. STAT. § 4102(5)).

Maryland: $5 million (2019) (MD. CODE ANN., TAX GEN. § 7-309(b)).

Massachusetts: $1 million (2019) (MASS. GEN. LAWS, ch. 65C, § 2A(a)).

Minnesota: $2.7 million (2019) (MINN. STAT. ANN. § 289A.10 subd. 1).

New York: $5,740,000 million (2019) (N.Y. TAX LAW § 952(c)(2)(a)).

Oregon: $1 million (2019) (OR. REV. STAT. § 118.010(4)).

Rhode Island: $1,561,719 (2019) (R.I. DIV. OF TAXATION: ADV. NO. 2018-44).

Vermont: $2.75 million (2019) (32 VT. STAT. ANN. § 7442a).

Washington: $ 2,193,000 (2019) (WASH. DEP'T REV., ESTATE TAX TABLES).

(4) STATE INHERITANCE TAX: Very few states impose an inheritance tax. The tax depends on the value of the property received and the relationship of the decedent to the beneficiary of the property. The closer the beneficiary is to the decedent in terms of consanguinity, the lower the inheritance tax will be. *See, e.g.,* Iowa (IOWA CODE ANN. §§ 450.1 to 450.97 (2019)); Kentucky (KY. REV. STAT. § 140.010 (2019)); Maryland (MD. CODE ANN., TAX-GEN. § 7-309(b)(5) (2019)); Nebraska (NEB. REV. STAT. § 77-2001) (2019)); New Jersey (N.J. STAT. ANN. §§ 54:33-1 to 54:37-8 (2019)); Pennsylvania (72 PA. CONS. STAT. ANN. §§ 9101 to 9188) (2019)).

(5) FEDERAL GIFT TAX: Any transfer of property for less than full and adequate consideration is considered a taxable gift (I.R.C. § 2501(a)). Currently, Congress provides a tax exemption of $15,000 (2019) for each donee, gifted by any donor, for each taxable year; married couples can gift up to $30,000 (2019) per donee in each taxable tax year (I.R.C. § 2503(b)).

(6) STATE GIFT TAX: Only Connecticut currently imposes a state gift tax (CONN. GEN. STAT. ANN. §§ 12-640 and 12-642 (2019)).

(7) GENERATION-SKIPPING TRANSFER TAX (GST): The GST is a federal tax that originated in the Tax Reform Act of 1986 as an effort to ensure that taxes could be collected at least once in each generation. (I.R.C. § 2612). The tax is imposed whenever there is a taxable transfer to any person who is two or more generations below the transferor's generation. Because the federal exemption amount applies — $11,400,000 (2019) — significant assets may be excluded from the federal GST. Nonetheless, a few states that impose a separate estate tax impose a GST. *See* Hawaii (HAW. REV. STAT. § 236E-17 (2019)); Massachusetts (MASS. GEN. LAWS. ch. 65C, § 4A (2019)); Vermont (32 VT. STAT. ANN. § 7460(b) (2019)). *See generally* Alyssa A. DiRusso, *The Generation-Skipping Transfer Tax and Sociological Shifts in*

Generational Length: Proposing a Generation-Inflation Index for Taxation, 41 ACTEC L. J. 307 (2015–2016).

B. Public Policy

Whenever wealth is transferred, there are restrictions on what may occur. In addition to intentionalities and formalities, public policy and federal supremacy circumscribe the intent of the transferor. The following issues are pertinent to Gina's situation, but similar issues may arise in other estate contexts:

(1) SPOUSAL CLAIMS: Much of Gina's father's estate will pass through his Last Will and Testament, benefitting the Society for the Prevention of Cruelty to Animals (SPCA). Yet he had a spouse of more than fifty years who presumptively contributed to his estate. Also, his Fidelity Destiny account, worth more than $600,000, likewise, will pass as a will substitute to the Society for the Prevention of Cruelty to Animals rather than to his spouse of fifty years. If the father and his spouse had divorced, these assets would have been considered as marital property and subject to the spouse's claim for division of marital property. Should public policy provide for a spouse's share at death in proportion to what the spouse could have claimed at divorce? *See* Raymond C. O'Brien, *Integrating Marital Property into a Spouse's Elective Share*, 59 Cath. U. L. Rev. 617 (2010).

(2) FEDERAL BENEFITS: Gina's father was entitled to Social Security benefits because he had earned a sufficient number of qualifying quarters (*see* Social Security Administration, Automatic Determinations, http://www.ssa.gov/OACT /COLA?OC.html). Upon his death, federal law shifts benefits to any surviving spouses, qualifying divorced spouses, unmarried minor children, parents of minor children who are dependent on eligible persons, or disabled children (*see* Social Security Administration, *Social Security Handbook*, http://www.ssa.gov/OP_Home /handbook/handbook-toc.html). Federal law preempts state laws contradicting federal eligibility rules and procedures. Thus, a decedent may not assign these benefits to anyone other than designated recipients under the Social Security laws. *See* Raymond C. O'Brien, *Equitable Relief for ERISA Benefit Plan Designation Mistakes*, 67 Cath. U. L. Rev. 433 (2018).

(3) FREEDOM OF DISPOSITION: Should wealth permit a testator unbridled discretion at death? May decedents erect exorbitant monuments to themselves, incentivize others to commit crimes, or create unreasonable demands on heirs to acquire their inheritance? Fastidious estate planning may permit settlors and testators to control the conduct of heirs and beneficiaries, but at what point should public policy prohibit conditions that offend modern sensibilities? Issues to consider include: disinheritance of children because of religious, sexual orientation, or marital preferences; the expenditure of significant funds on animals, burial vaults, or cryopreservation; and limits on the length of private trusts in the age of dynastic trust provisions meant to last for centuries beyond the death of the settlor or testator.

III. Government's Role

A. Constitutional Guarantee

Hodel v. Irving

Supreme Court of the United States, 1987
481 U.S. 704, 107 S. Ct. 2076

O'CONNOR, Justice.

The question presented is whether the original version of the "escheat" provision of the Indian Land Consolidation Act of 1983 * * * effected a "taking" of appellees' decedents' property without just compensation.

* * *

Towards the end of the 19th century, Congress enacted a series of land Acts which divided the communal reservations of Indian tribes into individual allotments for Indians and unallotted lands for non-Indian settlement. This legislation seems to have been in part animated by a desire to force Indians to abandon their nomadic ways in order to "speed the Indians' assimilation into American society," *Solem v. Bartlett*, 465 U.S. 463, 466, 104 S.Ct. 1161, 1164, 79 L.Ed.2d 443 (1984), and in part a result of pressure to free new lands for further white settlement. *Ibid.* Two years after the enactment of the General Allotment Act of 1887, ch. 119, 24 Stat. 388, Congress adopted a specific statute authorizing the division of the Great Reservation of the Sioux Nation into separate reservations and the allotment of specific tracts of reservation land to individual Indians, conditioned on the consent of three-fourths of the adult male Sioux. Act of Mar. 2, 1889, ch. 405, 25 Stat. 888. Under the Act, each male Sioux head of household took 320 acres of land and most other individuals 160 acres. 25 Stat. 890. In order to protect the allottees from the improvident disposition of their lands to white settlers, the Sioux allotment statute provided that the allotted lands were to be held in trust by the United States. *Id.*, at 891. Until 1910, the lands of deceased allottees passed to their heirs "according to the laws of the State or Territory" where the land was located, *ibid.*, and after 1910, allottees were permitted to dispose of their interests by will in accordance with regulations promulgated by the Secretary of the Interior. 36 Stat. 856, 25 U.S.C. § 373. Those regulations generally served to protect Indian ownership of the allotted lands.

The policy of allotment of Indian lands quickly proved disastrous for the Indians. Cash generated by land sales to whites was quickly dissipated, and the Indians, rather than farming the land themselves, evolved into petty landlords, leasing their allotted lands to white ranchers and farmers and living off the meager rentals. Lawson, Heirship: The Indian Amoeba, reprinted in Hearing on S. 2480 and S. 2663 before the Senate Select Committee on Indian Affairs, 98th Cong., 2d Sess., 82–83 (1984). The failure of the allotment program became even clearer as successive generations came to hold the allotted lands. Thus 40-, 80-, and 160-acre parcels became splintered into multiple undivided interests in land, with some parcels having hundreds, and many parcels having dozens, of owners. Because the land was held in trust and often could not be alienated or partitioned, the fractionation problem grew and grew over time. * * *

Ownership continued to fragment as succeeding generations came to hold the property, since, in the order of things, each property owner was apt to have more than one heir. In 1960, both the House and the Senate undertook comprehensive studies of the problem. See House Committee on Interior and Insular Affairs, Indian Heirship Land Study, 86th Cong., 2d Sess. (Comm.Print 1961); Senate Committee on Interior and Insular Affairs, Indian Heirship Land Survey, 86th Cong., 2d Sess. (Comm.Print 1960–1961). These studies indicated that one-half of the approximately 12 million acres of allotted trust lands were held in fractionated ownership, with over 3 million acres held by more than six heirs to a parcel. *Id.*, at pt. 2, p. X. Further hearings were held in 1966, Hearings on H.R. 11113, *supra*, but not until the Indian Land Consolidation Act of 1983 did the Congress take action to ameliorate the problem of fractionated ownership of Indian lands.

Section 207 of the Indian Land Consolidation Act—the escheat provision at issue in this case—provided:

> "No undivided fractional interest in any tract of trust or restricted land within a tribe's reservation or otherwise subjected to a tribe's jurisdiction shall descedent [sic] by intestacy or devise but shall escheat to that tribe if such interest represents 2 per centum or less of the total acreage in such tract and has earned to its owner less than $100 in the preceding year before it is due to escheat." 96 Stat. 2519.

Congress made no provision for the payment of compensation to the owners of the interests covered by § 207. The statute was signed into law on January 12, 1983, and became effective immediately. * * *

The Congress, acting pursuant to its broad authority to regulate the descent and devise of Indian trust lands, *Jefferson v. Fink*, 247 U.S. 288, 294, 38 S.Ct. 516, 518, 62 L.Ed. 1117 (1918), enacted § 207 as a means of ameliorating, over time, the problem of extreme fractionation of certain Indian lands. By forbidding the passing on at death of small, undivided interests in Indian lands, Congress hoped that future generations of Indians would be able to make more productive use of the Indians' ancestral lands. We agree with the Government that encouraging the consolidation of Indian lands is a public purpose of high order. The fractionation problem on Indian reservations is extraordinary and may call for dramatic action to encourage consolidation. * * *

But the character of the Government regulation here is extraordinary. In *Kaiser Aetna v. United States*, 444 U.S. [164,] 176, 100 S.Ct. [383,] 391 (1979), we emphasized that the regulation destroyed "one of the most essential sticks in the bundle of rights that are commonly characterized as property—the right to exclude others." Similarly, the regulation here amounts to virtually the abrogation of the right to pass on a certain type of property—the small undivided interest—to one's heirs.

In one form or another, the right to pass on property—to one's family in particular—has been part of the Anglo-American legal system since feudal times. See
United States v. Perkins, 163 U.S. 625, 627–628, 16 S.Ct. 1073, 1074, 41 L.Ed. 287
(1896). The fact that it may be possible for the owners of these interests to effectively
control disposition upon death through complex *inter vivos* transactions such as
revocable trusts is simply not an adequate substitute for the rights taken, given the
nature of the property. Even the United States concedes that total abrogation of the
right to pass property is unprecedented and likely unconstitutional. Tr. of Oral Arg.
12–14. Moreover, this statute effectively abolishes both descent and devise of these
property interests even when the passing of the property to the heir might result
in consolidation of property—as for instance when the heir already owns another
undivided interest in the property. * * * Cf. 25 U.S.C. §2206(b) (1982 ed., Supp.
III). Since the escheatable interests are not, as the United States argues, necessarily
de minimis, nor, as it also argues, does the availability of *inter vivos* transfer obviate
the need for descent and devise, a *total* abrogation of these rights cannot be upheld.
But cf. *Andrus v. Allard*, 444 U.S. 51, 100 S.Ct. 318, 62 L.Ed.2d 210 (1979) (upholding
abrogation of the right to sell endangered eagles' parts as necessary to environmental protection regulatory scheme).

In holding that complete abolition of both the descent and devise of a particular
class of property may be a taking, we reaffirm the continuing vitality of the long line
of cases recognizing the States', and where appropriate, the United States', broad
authority to adjust the rules governing the descent and devise of property without implicating the guarantees of the Just Compensation Clause. See, *e.g.*, *Irving
Trust Co. v. Day*, 314 U.S. 556, 562, 62 S.Ct. 398, 401, 86 L.Ed. 452 (1942); *Jefferson
v. Fink*, 247 U.S., at 294, 38 S.Ct., at 518. The difference in this case is the fact that
both descent and devise are completely abolished; indeed they are abolished even in
circumstances when the governmental purpose sought to be advanced, consolidation of ownership of Indian lands, does not conflict with the further descent of the
property. * * *

Affirmed. * * *

Notes

Today, the factual matter discussed in *Hodel* is addressed through the American Indian Probate Reform Act (AIPRA), 25 U.S.C. §2206 (2012), which supplants
state probate procedures with a federal scheme that seeks to keep land within the
decedent's line of descent and avoid fractionalism by providing individuals and
tribes greater opportunity to consolidate fractioned land and eliminate restrictions
on what an individual or tribe may do with their lands. For further discussion of
a decedent's right to transfer assets at death, see Chapter Five: Restraints on the
Transfer of Wealth, *infra*. For commentary on the contest between private property
and public policy, see Krithika Ashok, Paul T. Babie, and John V. Orth, *Balancing
Justice Needs and Private Property in Constitutional Takings Provisions: A Comparative Assessment of India, Australia, and the United States*, 42 Fordham Int'l L.J. 999,
1036 (2019) (concluding that the U.S. Supreme Court tends to side more frequently

with the holder of private property; individual rights have a priority). For full commentary on economic inequality, the role of taxation, and the redistribution of wealth, see Felix B. Chang, *Asymmetries in the Generation and Transmission of Wealth*, 79 Ohio St. L.J. 73, 116 (2018) (concluding that the gravity of rising economic inequality and the inability of wealth transfer taxes to counteract inequality suggests that trusts and estates' legal rules must step in, even if it fosters inconsistencies in doctrines shared with business law).

B. Procedural Responsibilities

Tulsa Professional Collection Services, Inc. v. Pope

Supreme Court of the United States, 1988
485 U.S. 478, 108 S. Ct. 1340

Justice O'CONNOR delivered the opinion of the Court. * * *

Oklahoma's Probate Code requires creditors to file claims against an estate within a specified time period, and generally bars untimely claims. * * * Such "nonclaim statutes" are almost universally included in state probate codes. See Uniform Probate Code § 3-801, 8 U.L.A. 351 (1983); Falender, Notice to Creditors in Estate Proceedings: What Process is Due?, 63 N.C.L.Rev. 659, 667–668 (1985). Giving creditors a limited time in which to file claims against the estate serves the State's interest in facilitating the administration and expeditious closing of estates. See, *e.g., State ex rel. Central State Griffin Memorial Hospital v. Reed*, 493 P.2d 815, 818 (Okla.1972). Nonclaim statutes come in two basic forms. Some provide a relatively short time period, generally two to six months, that begins to run after the commencement of probate proceedings. Others call for a longer period, generally one to five years, that runs from the decedent's death. See Falender, *supra*, at 664–672. Most States include both types of nonclaim statutes in their probate codes, typically providing that if probate proceedings are not commenced and the shorter period therefore never is triggered, then claims nonetheless may be barred by the longer period. See, *e.g.*, Ark.Code Ann. §§ 28-50-101(a), (d) (1987) (three months if probate proceedings commenced; five years if not); Idaho Code §§ 15-3-803(a)(1), (2) (1979) (four months; three years); Mo.Rev.Stat. §§ 473.360(1), (3) (1986) (six months; three years). Most States also provide that creditors are to be notified of the requirement to file claims imposed by the nonclaim statutes solely by publication. See Uniform Probate Code § 3-801, 8 U.L.A. 351 (1983); Falender, *supra*, at 660, n. 7 (collecting statutes). Indeed, in most jurisdictions it is the publication of notice that triggers the nonclaim statute. The Uniform Probate Code, for example, provides that creditors have four months from publication in which to file claims. Uniform Probate Code § 3-801, 8 U.L.A. 351 (1983). See also, *e.g.*, Ariz.Rev.Stat.Ann. § 14-3801 (1975); Fla.Stat. § 733.701 (1987); Utah Code Ann. § 75-3-801 (1978).

The specific nonclaim statute at issue in this case, Okla.Stat., Tit. 58, § 333 (1981), provides for only a short time period and is best considered in the context of

Oklahoma probate proceedings as a whole. Under Oklahoma's Probate Code, any party interested in the estate may initiate probate proceedings by petitioning the court to have the will proved. § 22. The court is then required to set a hearing date on the petition, § 25, and to mail notice of the hearing "to all heirs, legatees and devisees, at their places of residence," §§ 25, 26. If no person appears at the hearing to contest the will, the court may admit the will to probate on the testimony of one of the subscribing witnesses to the will. § 30. After the will is admitted to probate, the court must order appointment of an executor or executrix, issuing letters testamentary to the named executor or executrix if that person appears, is competent and qualified, and no objections are made. § 101.

Immediately after appointment, the executor or executrix is required to "give notice to the creditors of the deceased." § 331. Proof of compliance with this requirement must be filed with the court. § 332. This notice is to advise creditors that they must present their claims to the executor or executrix within two months of the date of the first publication. As for the method of notice, the statute requires only publication: "[S]uch notice must be published in some newspaper in [the] county once each week for two (2) consecutive weeks." § 331. A creditor's failure to file a claim within the 2-month period generally bars it forever. § 333. The nonclaim statute does provide certain exceptions, however. If the creditor is out of State, then a claim "may be presented at any time before a decree of distribution is entered." § 333. Mortgages and debts not yet due are also excepted from the 2-month time limit. * * *

H. Everett Pope, Jr., was admitted to St. John Medical Center, a hospital in Tulsa, Oklahoma, in November 1978. On April 2, 1979, while still at the hospital, he died testate. His wife, appellee JoAnne Pope, initiated probate proceedings in the District Court of Tulsa County in accordance with the statutory scheme outlined above. The court entered an order setting a hearing. * * * After the hearing the court entered an order admitting the will to probate and, following the designation in the will, * * * named appellee as the executrix of the estate. * * * Letters testamentary were issued, * * * and the court ordered appellee to fulfill her statutory obligation by directing that she "immediately give notice to creditors." * * * Appellee published notice in the Tulsa Daily Legal News for two consecutive weeks beginning July 17, 1979. The notice advised creditors that they must file any claim they had against the estate within two months of the first publication of the notice. * * *

Appellant Tulsa Professional Collection Services, Inc., is a subsidiary of St. John Medical Center and the assignee of a claim for expenses connected with the decedent's long stay at that hospital. Neither appellant, nor its parent company, filed a claim with appellee within the 2-month time period following publication of notice. In October 1983, however, appellant filed an Application for Order Compelling Payment of Expenses of Last Illness. * * * In making this application, appellant relied on Okla.Stat., Tit. 58, § 594 (1981), which indicates that an executrix "must pay . . . the expenses of the last sickness." Appellant argued that this specific statutory command made compliance with the 2-month deadline for filing claims unnecessary.

The District Court of Tulsa County rejected this contention, ruling that even claims pursuant to §594 fell within the general requirements of the nonclaim statute. Accordingly, the court denied appellant's application. * * *

Mullane v. Central Hanover Bank & Trust Co., supra, 339 U.S., at 314, 70 S.Ct., at 657, established that state action affecting property must generally be accompanied by notification of that action: "An elementary and fundamental requirement of due process in any proceeding which is to be accorded finality is notice reasonably calculated, under all the circumstances, to apprise interested parties of the pendency of the action and afford them an opportunity to present their objections." In the years since *Mullane* the Court has adhered to these principles, balancing the "interest of the State" and "the individual interest sought to be protected by the Fourteenth Amendment." * * * The focus is on the reasonableness of the balance, and, as *Mullane* itself made clear, whether a particular method of notice is reasonable depends on the particular circumstances. * * *

The Fourteenth Amendment protects this interest, however, only from a deprivation by state action. Private use of state-sanctioned private remedies or procedures does not rise to the level of state action. See, *e.g., Flagg Bros., Inc. v. Brooks,* 436 U.S. 149, 98 S.Ct. 1729, 56 L.Ed.2d 185 (1978). Nor is the State's involvement in the mere running of a general statute of limitations generally sufficient to implicate due process. See *Texaco, Inc. v. Short,* 454 U.S. 516, 102 S.Ct. 781, 70 L.Ed.2d 738 (1982). See also *Flagg Bros., Inc. v. Brooks, supra,* 436 U.S., at 166, 98 S.Ct., at 1738. But when private parties make use of state procedures with the overt, significant assistance of state officials, state action may be found. See, *e.g., Lugar v. Edmondson Oil Co.,* 457 U.S. 922, 102 S.Ct. 2744, 73 L.Ed.2d 482 (1982); *Sniadach v. Family Finance Corp.,* 395 U.S. 337, 89 S.Ct. 1820, 23 L.Ed.2d 349 (1969). The question here is whether the State's involvement with the nonclaim statute is substantial enough to implicate the Due Process Clause.

Appellee argues that it is not, contending that Oklahoma's nonclaim statute is a self-executing statute of limitations. Relying on this characterization, appellee then points to *Short, supra.* Appellee's reading of *Short* is correct—due process does not require that potential plaintiffs be given notice of the impending expiration of a period of limitations—but in our view, appellee's premise is not. Oklahoma's nonclaim statute is not a self-executing statute of limitations. * * * It is true that nonclaim statutes generally possess some attributes of statutes of limitations. They provide a specific time period within which particular types of claims must be filed and they bar claims presented after expiration of that deadline. Many of the state court decisions upholding nonclaim statutes against due process challenges have relied upon these features and concluded that they are properly viewed as statutes of limitations. See, *e.g., Estate of Busch v. Ferrell-Duncan Clinic, Inc.,* 700 S.W.2d, at 89; *William B. Tanner Co. v. Estate of Fessler,* 100 Wis.2d 437, 302 N.W.2d 414 (1981).

As we noted in *Short,* however, it is the "self-executing feature" of a statute of limitations that makes *Mullane* and *Mennonite* inapposite. See 454 U.S., at 533, 536, 102 S.Ct., at 794, 796. The State's interest in a self-executing statute of limitations is in providing repose for potential defendants and in avoiding stale claims. The State has no role to play beyond enactment of the limitations period. While this enactment obviously is state action, the State's limited involvement in the running of the time period generally falls short of constituting the type of state action required to implicate the protections of the Due Process Clause.

Here, in contrast, there is significant state action. The probate court is intimately involved throughout, and without that involvement the time bar is never activated. The nonclaim statute becomes operative only after probate proceedings have been commenced in state court. The court must appoint the executor or executrix before notice, which triggers the time bar, can be given. Only after this court appointment is made does the statute provide for any notice; § 331 directs the executor or executrix to publish notice "immediately" after appointment. Indeed, in this case, the District Court reinforced the statutory command with an order expressly requiring appellee to "immediately give notice to creditors." The form of the order indicates that such orders are routine. Finally, copies of the notice and an affidavit of publication must be filed with the court. § 332. It is only after all of these actions take place that the time period begins to run, and in every one of these actions, the court is intimately involved. This involvement is so pervasive and substantial that it must be considered state action subject to the restrictions of the Fourteenth Amendment.

Where the legal proceedings themselves trigger the time bar, even if those proceedings do not necessarily resolve the claim on its merits, the time bar lacks the self-executing feature that *Short* indicated was necessary to remove any due process problem. Rather, in such circumstances, due process is directly implicated and actual notice generally is required. * * * In sum, the substantial involvement of the probate court throughout the process leaves little doubt that the running of Oklahoma's nonclaim statute is accompanied by sufficient government action to implicate the Due Process Clause. * * *

In assessing the propriety of actual notice in this context consideration should be given to the practicalities of the situation and the effect that requiring actual notice may have on important state interests. *Mennonite, supra,* 462 U.S., at 798–799, 103 S. Ct., at 2711–2712; *Mullane,* 339 U.S., at 313–314, 70 S.Ct., at 656–657. As the Court noted in *Mullane,* "[c]hance alone brings to the attention of even a local resident an advertisement in small type inserted in the back pages of a newspaper." *Id.,* at 315, 70 S.Ct., at 658. Creditors, who have a strong interest in maintaining the integrity of their relationship with their debtors, are particularly unlikely to benefit from publication notice. As a class, creditors may not be aware of a debtor's death or of the institution of probate proceedings. Moreover, the executor or executrix will often be, as is the case here, a party with a beneficial interest in the estate. This could diminish an executor's or executrix's inclination to call attention to the potential expiration of a creditor's claim. There is thus a substantial practical need for actual notice in this setting.

At the same time, the State undeniably has a legitimate interest in the expeditious resolution of probate proceedings. Death transforms the decedent's legal relationships and a State could reasonably conclude that swift settlement of estates is so important that it calls for very short time deadlines for filing claims. As noted, the almost uniform practice is to establish such short deadlines, and to provide only publication notice. See, *e.g.,* Ariz.Rev.Stat.Ann. § 14-3801 (1975); Ark. Code Ann. § 28-50-101(a) (1987); Fla.Stat. § 733.701 (1987); Idaho Code § 15-3-803(a) (1979); Mo.Rev.Stat. § 473.360(1) (1986); Utah Code Ann. § 75-3-801 (1978). See also Uniform Probate Code § 3-801, 8 U.L.A. 351 (1983); *Falender,* at 660, n. 7 (collecting statutes). Providing actual notice to known or reasonably ascertainable creditors, however, is not inconsistent with the goals reflected in nonclaim statutes. Actual notice need not be inefficient or burdensome. We have repeatedly recognized that mail service is an inexpensive and efficient mechanism that is reasonably calculated to provide actual notice. * * * Here, as in *Mullane,* it is reasonable to dispense with actual notice to those with mere "conjectural" claims. 339 U.S., at 317, 70 S.Ct., at 659. * * *

Whether appellant's identity as a creditor was known or reasonably ascertainable by appellee cannot be answered on this record. Neither the Oklahoma Supreme Court nor the Court of Appeals nor the District Court considered the question. Appellee of course was aware that her husband endured a long stay at St. John Medical Center, but it is not clear that this awareness translates into a knowledge of appellant's claim. We therefore must remand the case for further proceedings to determine whether "reasonably diligent efforts," *Mennonite, supra,* 462 U.S., at 798, n. 4, 103 S.Ct., at 2711, n. 4, would have identified appellant and uncovered its claim. If appellant's identity was known or "reasonably ascertainable," then termination of appellant's claim without actual notice violated due process. * * *

It is so ordered.

Justice BLACKMUN concurs in the result.

Chief Justice REHNQUIST, dissenting. * * *

Notes

Virginia Code Annotated (2019)

§ 64.2-443. Jurisdiction of probate of wills.

A. The circuit courts shall have jurisdiction of the probate of wills. A will shall be offered for probate in the circuit court in the county or city wherein the decedent has a known place of residence; if he has no such known place of residence, then in a county or city wherein any real estate lies that is devised or owned by the decedent; and if there is no such real estate, then in the county or city wherein he dies or a county or city wherein he has estate.

B. Where any person has become, either voluntarily or involuntarily, a patient in a nursing home, convalescent home, or similar institution due to advanced age or impaired health, the place of legal residence of the person shall be rebuttably presumed to be the same as it was before he became a patient.

§ 64.2-514. Duty of every personal representative.

Every personal representative shall administer, well and truly, the whole personal estate of his decedent.

§ 64.2-550. Proceedings for receiving proof of debts by commissioners.

. . .

B. The personal representative shall give written notice by personal service or by regular, certified, or registered mail at least 10 days before the date set for the hearing to any claimant of a disputed claim that is known to the personal representative at the last address of the claimant known to the personal representative. The notice shall inform the claimant of his right to attend the hearing and present his case, his right to obtain another hearing date if the commissioner of accounts finds the initial date inappropriate, and the fact that the claimant will be bound by any adverse ruling. The personal representative shall also inform the claimant of his right to file exceptions with the circuit court in the event of an adverse ruling. The personal representative shall file proof of any mailing or service of notice with the commissioner of accounts.

. . .

§ 64.2-508. Written notice of probate, qualification, and entitlement to copies of inventories, accounts, and reports to be provided to certain parties.

A. Except as otherwise provided in this section, a personal representative of a decedent's estate or a proponent of a decedent's will when there is no qualification shall provide written notice of qualification or probate, and notice of entitlement to copies of wills, inventories, accounts, and reports, to the following persons:

    1. The surviving spouse of the decedent, if any;

    2. All heirs at law of the decedent, whether or not there is a will;

    3. All living and ascertained beneficiaries under the will of the decedent, including those who may take under § 64.2-418, and beneficiaries of any trust created by the will; and

    4. All living and ascertained beneficiaries under any will of the decedent previously probated in the same court.

B. Notice under subsection A need not be provided (i) when the known assets passing under the will or by intestacy do not exceed $5,000 or (ii) to the following persons:

    1. A personal representative or proponent of the will;

    2. Any person who has signed a waiver of right to receive notice;

    3. Any person to whom a summons has been issued pursuant to § 64.2-446;

    4. Any person who is the subject of a conservatorship, guardianship, or committeeship, if notice is provided to his conservator, guardian, or committee;

5. Any beneficiary of a trust, other than a trust created by the decedent's will, if notice is provided to the trustee of the trust;

6. Any heir or beneficiary who survived the decedent but is deceased at the time of qualification or probate, and such person's successors in interest, if notice is provided to such person's personal representative;

7. Any minor for whom no guardian has been appointed, if notice is provided to his parent or person in loco parentis;

8. Any beneficiary of a pecuniary bequest or of a bequest of tangible personal property, provided in either case the beneficiary is not an heir at law and the value of the bequest is not in excess of $5,000; and

9. Any unborn or unascertained persons.

C. The notice shall include the following information:

1. The name and date of death of the decedent;

2. The name, address, and telephone number of a personal representative or a proponent of a will;

3. The mailing address of the clerk of the court in which the personal representative qualified or the will was probated;

4. A statement as follows: "This notice does not mean that you will receive any money or property";

5. A statement as follows: "If personal representatives qualified on this estate, they are required by law to file an inventory with the commissioner of accounts within four months after they qualify in the clerk's office, to file an account within 16 months of their qualification, and to file additional accounts within 16 months from the date of their last account period until the estate is settled. If you make written request therefor to the personal representatives, they must mail copies of these documents (not including any supporting vouchers, but including a copy of the decedent's will) to you at the same time the inventory or account is filed with the commissioner of accounts unless (i) you would take only as an heir at law in a case where all of the decedent's probate estate is disposed of by will or (ii) your gift has been satisfied in full before the time of such filing. Your written request may be made at any time; it may relate to one specific filing or to all filings to be made by the personal representative, but it will not be effective for filings made prior to its receipt by a personal representative. A copy of your request may be sent to the commissioner of accounts with whom the filings will be made. After the commissioner of accounts has completed work on an account filed by a personal representative, the commissioner files it and a report thereon in the clerk's office of the court wherein the personal representative qualified. If you make written request therefor to the

commissioner before this filing, the commissioner must mail a copy of this report and any attachments (excluding the account) to you on or before the date that they are filed in the clerk's office"; and

6. The mailing address of the commissioner of accounts with whom the inventory and accounts must be filed by the personal representatives, if they are required.

D. Within 30 days after the date of qualification or admission of the will to probate, a personal representative or proponent of the will shall forward notice by delivery or by first-class mail, postage prepaid, to the persons entitled to notice at their last known address. If the personal representative or proponent does not determine that the assets of the decedent passing under the will or by intestacy exceed $5,000 until after the date of the qualification or admission of the will to probate, notice shall be forwarded to the persons entitled thereto within 30 days after such determination.

E. Failure to give the notice required by this section shall not (i) affect the validity of the probate of a decedent's will or (ii) render any person required to give notice, who has acted in good faith, liable to any person entitled to receive notice. In determining the limitation period for any rights that may commence upon or accrue by reason of such probate or qualification in favor of any entitled person, the time that elapses from the date that notice should have been given to the date that notice is given shall not be counted, unless the person required to give notice could not determine the name and address of the entitled person after the exercise of reasonable diligence.

F. The personal representative or proponent of the will shall record within four months in the clerk's office where the will is recorded an affidavit stating (i) the names and addresses of the persons to whom he has mailed or delivered notice and when the notice was mailed or delivered to each or (ii) that no notice was required to be given to any person. The commissioner of accounts shall not approve any settlement filed by a personal representative until the affidavit described in this subsection has been recorded. If the personal representative of an estate or the proponent of a will is unable to determine the name and address of any person to whom notice is required after the exercise of reasonable diligence, a statement to that effect in the required affidavit shall be sufficient for purposes of this subsection. Notwithstanding the foregoing provisions, any person having an interest in an estate may give the notice required by this section and record the affidavit described in this subsection. If this subsection has not been complied with within four months after qualification, the commissioner of accounts shall issue, through the sheriff or other proper officer, a summons to such fiduciary requiring him to comply, and if the fiduciary does not comply, the commissioner shall enforce the filing of the affidavit in the manner set forth in §64.2-1215.

G. The form of the notice to be given pursuant to this section, which shall contain appropriate instructions regarding its use, shall be provided to each clerk of the circuit court by the Office of the Executive Secretary of the Supreme Court and each clerk shall provide copies of such form to the proponents of a will or those qualifying on an estate.

IV. Attorney's Role

Simpson v. Calivas

Supreme Court of New Hampshire, 1994
650 A.2d 318

HORTON, Justice.

The plaintiff, Robert H. Simpson, Jr., appeals from a directed verdict, grant of summary judgment, and dismissal of his claims against the lawyer who drafted his father's will. The plaintiff's action, sounding in both negligence and breach of contract, alleged that the defendant, Christopher Calivas, failed to draft a will which incorporated the actual intent of Robert H. Simpson, Sr. to leave all his land to the plaintiff in fee simple. * * *

In March 1984, Robert H. Simpson, Sr. (Robert Sr.) executed a will that had been drafted by the defendant. The will left all real estate to the plaintiff except for a life estate in "our *homestead* located at Piscataqua Road, Dover, New Hampshire" (emphasis added), which was left to Robert Sr.'s second wife, Roberta C. Simpson (stepmother). After Robert Sr.'s death in September 1985, the plaintiff and his stepmother filed a joint petition in the Strafford County Probate Court seeking a determination, essentially, of whether the term "homestead" referred to all the decedent's real property on Piscataqua Road (including a house, over one hundred acres of land, and buildings used in the family business), or only to the house (and, perhaps, limited surrounding acreage). The probate court found the term "homestead" ambiguous, and in order to aid construction, admitted some extrinsic evidence of the testator's surrounding circumstances, including evidence showing a close relationship between Robert Sr. and plaintiff's stepmother. The probate court, however, did not admit notes taken by the defendant during consultations with Robert Sr. that read: "House to wife as a life estate remainder to son, Robert H. Simpson, Jr. . . . Remaining land . . . to son Robert A. [sic] Simpson, Jr." The probate court construed the will to provide Roberta with a life estate in all the real property. After losing the will construction action—then two years after his father's death—the plaintiff negotiated with his stepmother to buy out her life estate in all the real property for $400,000.

The plaintiff then brought this malpractice action, pleading a contract count, based on third-party beneficiary theory, and a negligence count. * * *

In order to recover for negligence, a plaintiff must show that "there exists a duty, whose breach by the defendant causes the injury for which the plaintiff seeks to recover." *Goodwin v. James*, 134 N.H. 579, 583, 595 A.2d 504, 507 (1991). The critical issue, for purposes of this appeal, is whether an attorney who drafts a testator's will owes a duty of reasonable care to intended beneficiaries. We hold that there is such a duty.

As a general principle, "the concept of 'duty' . . . arises out of a relation between the parties and the protection against reasonably foreseeable harm." *Morvay v. Hanover Insurance Co.*, 127 N.H. 723, 724, 506 A.2d 333, 334 (1986). The existence of a contract between parties may constitute a relation sufficient to impose a duty to exercise reasonable care, but in general, "the scope of such a duty is limited to those in privity of contract with each other." *Robinson v. Colebrook Savings Bank*, 109 N.H. 382, 385, 254 A.2d 837, 839 (1969). The privity rule is not ironclad, though, and we have been willing to recognize exceptions particularly where, as here, the risk to persons not in privity is apparent. * * *

Because this issue is one of first impression, we look for guidance to other jurisdictions. The overwhelming majority of courts that have considered this issue have found that a duty runs from an attorney to an intended beneficiary of a will. R. Mallen & J. Smith, *Legal Malpractice 3d.* §26.4, at 595 (1989 & Supp.1992); *see, e.g., Stowe v. Smith*, 184 Conn. 194, 441 A.2d 81 (1981); *Needham v. Hamilton*, 459 A.2d 1060 (D.C.1983); *Ogle v. Fuiten*, 102 Ill.2d 356, 80 Ill.Dec. 772, 466 N.E.2d 224 (1984); *Hale v. Groce*, 304 Or. 281, 744 P.2d 1289 (1987). A theme common to these cases, similar to a theme of cases in which we have recognized exceptions to the privity rule, is an emphasis on the foreseeability of injury to the intended beneficiary. As the California Supreme Court explained in reaffirming the duty owed by an attorney to an intended beneficiary:

> When an attorney undertakes to fulfil the testamentary instructions of his client, he realistically and in fact assumes a relationship not only with the client but also with the client's intended beneficiaries. The attorney's actions and omissions will affect the success of the client's testamentary scheme; and thus the possibility of thwarting the testator's wishes immediately becomes foreseeable. Equally foreseeable is the possibility of injury to an intended beneficiary. In some ways, the beneficiary's interests loom greater than those of the client. After the latter's death, a failure in his testamentary scheme works no practical effect except to deprive his intended beneficiaries of the intended bequests.

Heyer v. Flaig, 70 Cal.2d 223, 74 Cal.Rptr. 225, 228–29, 449 P.2d 161, 164–65 (1969). We agree that although there is no privity between a drafting attorney and an intended beneficiary, the obvious foreseeability of injury to the beneficiary demands an exception to the privity rule. * * *

The general rule that a nonparty to a contract has no remedy for breach of contract is subject to an exception for third-party beneficiaries. *Arlington Trust Co. v. Estate of Wood*, 123 N.H. 765, 767, 465 A.2d 917, 918 (1983). Third-party beneficiary status necessary to trigger this exception exists where "the contract is so expressed as to give the promisor reason to know that a benefit to a third party is contemplated by the promisee as one of the motivating causes of his making the contract." *Tamposi Associates, Inc. v. Star Market Co.*, 119 N.H. 630, 633, 406 A.2d 132, 134 (1979). We hold that where, as here, a client has contracted with an attorney to draft a will and the client has identified to whom he wishes his estate to pass, that identified beneficiary may enforce the terms of the contract as a third-party beneficiary. *See Stowe v. Smith*, 441 A.2d at 84; *Ogle v. Fuiten*, 102 Ill.2d at 359, 80 Ill.Dec. at 775, 466 N.E.2d at 227; *Hale v. Groce*, 744 P.2d at 1292.

Because we hold that a duty runs from a drafting attorney to an intended beneficiary, and that an identified beneficiary has third-party beneficiary status, the trial court erred by dismissing the plaintiff's writ. * * *

Reversed and remanded.

Notes

The holding in the *Simpson* decision is now the majority approach among the states. The Supreme Court of New Hampshire permits an intended beneficiary—a plaintiff not in privity with the drafting attorney—to enforce the terms of a testator's contract as a third-party beneficiary. But the parameters of who qualifies as an intended beneficiary remain opaque. *See* Kaitlyn C. Kelly, Note and Comment, *Put Privity in the Past: A Modern Approach for Determining When Washington Attorneys are Liable to Nonclients for Estate Planning Malpractice*, 91 WASH. L. REV. 1851 (2016). Also, there is the suggestion that malpractice by attorneys should be distinguishable. *See* Kevin H. Michels, *Third-Party Negligence Claims Against Counsel: A Proposed Unified Liability Standard*, 22 GEO. J. LEGAL ETHICS 143 (2009) (proposing an "ethical differentiation" standard: an attorney should owe a duty of care to a nonclient if: (1) such duty is recognized under the nexus standards of negligence law that are applicable to all tortfeasors; and (2) no attorney-ethics obligation contradicts the nexus-based duty).

Problem

Decedent retained an attorney at a major law firm in the state to draft a Last Will and Testament. The decedent stated that he had cancer and did not want to die intestate. Specifically, the decedent told the attorney that he wanted to leave all of his estate to one of his two siblings, but definitely not the other sibling, from whom he was bitterly estranged. The attorney drafted the will and brought it to the decedent's nursing home, where the decedent was receiving care. When they discussed the will together, the attorney recommended that there be an alternate taker named, in case the beneficiary brother should predecease. The decedent agreed, and the attorney left to make the change to the unexecuted will. Three days later, the attorney returned to the decedent with the revised instrument but would not allow the decedent to execute the will because the attorney concluded that the decedent lacked testamentary capacity at that time. Three weeks later the decedent died without having executed the will. Because he died intestate, his estate was divided between his two brothers, including the brother from whom the decedent was estranged. The favored brother then sued the decedent's attorney for malpractice, asserting that it was negligent not to have the will executed promptly. How should a court rule on the plaintiff's petition? *See Sisson v. Jankowski*, 809 A.2d 1265 (N.H. 2002).

V. Client's Role

When initiating estate planning, the twenty-first century American client is likely to live longer than his or her predecessors, own a wider ranges of assets, be attracted to a diversity of wealth transfer devices because of reasons of speed and secrecy, and have far more options when planning for retirement or long-term care.

A. The Aging of America

Population Reference Bureau
Fact Sheet: Aging in America

https://www.prb.org/aging-unitedstates-fact-sheet/
Jan. 13, 2016

The number of Americans ages 65 and older is projected to more than double from 46 million today to over 98 million by 2060, and the 65-and-older age group's share of the total population will rise to nearly 24 percent from 15 percent. According to the AARP, approximately 52 percent of people turning 65 years-of-age will develop disabilities that will require Long Term Care for a period of approximately two years. *Fact Sheet Long-Term Support and Services,* www.aarp.org/cont/dam/aarp/ppi/2017-01/Fact%20Sheet%20 Long-Term%20Support%20and%20Services.pdf.

The older population is becoming more racially and ethnically diverse. Between 2014 and 2060 the share of the older population that is non-Hispanic white is projected to drop by 24 percentage points, from 78.3 percent to 54.6 percent.

Older adults are working longer. By 2014, 23 percent of men and about 15 percent of women ages 65 and older were in the labor force, and these levels are projected to rise further by 2022, to 27 percent for men and 20 percent for women.

Average U.S. life expectancy increased from 68 years in 1950 to 79 years in 2013, in large part due to the reduction in mortality at older ages.

B. Portfolio of Assets

Brad Davidson
Unique Asset Administration

154 TRUSTS & ESTS. 12 (July 2015)

It may surprise readers . . . to know that stocks, bonds, and mutual funds represent half—but only half—of the investments owned by wealthy Americans. The other half consists of real estate, closely held business interests, mineral interests, collectibles and other "unique assets." * * *

[Unique assets] are investments that don't trade on a generally recognized exchange. The most common unique asset types include: real estate, farms and ranches, timber, mineral interests, closely held businesses, loans and note, life insurance, tangible assets and collectibles, private equity, and alternate investments.

Sometimes, these investments are owned directly but more often they're owned indirectly, in the form of securities, such as: non-publically traded securities, warrants and options, general partnership interests, limited partnership interests, asset holding companies, real estate investment trusts, royalty trust interests, promissory notes, debt instruments, and preferred interests.

C. Diversity of Wealth Transfer Devices

R. Hugh Magill
The Changing Face of American Wealth
150 TRUSTS & ESTS. 47 (May 2011)

As we plan for individuals and families, several aspects of our approach bear reexamination. First, many of the will and trust forms on which we base our estate-planning documents don't reflect the diversity of family structures that exist in the United States today. Indeed, many of these forms were initially developed decades ago, and while they have undergone modifications to accommodate countless changes in federal tax and local tax law, few include sufficient alternatives to allow planners to readily adapt the forms to the unique objectives and needs of our client "families."

Consider the myriad innovations in trust design over the last 30 years, including the many tax-qualified trusts (for example, qualified terminal interest property (QTIP), qualified replacement property, qualified personal residence and qualified domestic trusts), the trusts developed after changes in state trust law (for example, dynasty, asset protection and administrative trusts), trusts developed for special asset circumstances (for example, irrevocable life insurance, special purpose and directed trusts) and trusts developed for tax-advantaged wealth transfer (for example, grantor retained annuity, defective grantor and super-charged credit shelter trusts). Yet few trusts have been broadly developed to accommodate unique family circumstances (the few exceptions that come to mind include special needs and incentive trusts). Many of our common will and trust forms inadequately address issues such as beneficial interests in non-spousal relationships, discretionary interests for stepchildren and inheritance rights for children of artificial reproductive technology.

D. Planning for Incapacity

Lawrence A. Frolik & Bernard Krooks
Planning for Later in Life

154 Trusts & Ests. 21 (July 2015)

The first rule of planning for later life is for clients to face up to the realities of growing older. Like much of life, you have to hope for the best and plan for the worst. Everyone ages in their own way, but the reality of growing older is the inevitable decline in physical ability and the effects of normal aging on mental capacity.

Michael Gilfix
Addressing Financial Elder Abuse

153 Trusts & Ests. 34 (Sept 2014)

Over the course of two months, my colleagues and I discovered that three of our clients were the victims of financial elder abuse. All three clients showed signs of modest cognitive decline, but all had capacity and insisted on remaining independent and in control of their affairs. Even in retrospect, while some signs of potential exposure were arguably evident, intervention was unavailable for many reasons, including the constraint imposed by the attorney-client relationship and client denials. . . . At what point should protective intervention be allowed—and by whom? At what point should it be encouraged?

CDC, National Center for Chronic Disease Prevention and Health Promotions
Alzheimer's Disease

(June 21, 2018)

Alzheimer's disease, a type of dementia, is an irreversible, progressive brain disease that affects an estimated 5.7 million Americans. It is the sixth leading cause of death among all adults and the fifth leading cause for those aged 65 or older.

The causes of Alzheimer's disease and other dementias are not completely understood, but researchers believe they include a combination of genetic, environmental, and lifestyle factors. In more than 90% of people with Alzheimer's, symptoms do not appear until after age 60. The incidence of the disease increases with age and doubles every 5 years beyond age 65.

Russell N. Adler, Peter J. Strauss & Regina Kiperman
America's Long-Term Care Crisis

152 Trusts & Ests. 44 (July 2013)

Fifty percent of individuals over 85 will need assistance with daily functioning, and their home care can cost from $55,000 to $75,000 a year and up to $180,000 annually for nursing home care.

Brian Andrew Tully
Wealth or Health?

157 Trusts & Ests. 34 (July 2018)

As Medicare doesn't have [Long Term Care] benefits, there are three ways in which an elderly client can pay for his chronic care: (1) private payment with personal funds that can exceed $7,000 per month for home care or $16,000 per month for nursing home care in the New York metro area, (2) a robust [Long Term Care] insurance policy that has both home care and nursing care benefits, or (3) by becoming financially eligible through divestiture for the Medicaid program.

On average, according to AARP, 52 percent of individuals who turn 65 years of age today will develop a severe disability that will require [Long Term Care] services for a period of approximately two years.

Karen Clegler Hansen
The Modern Family

152 Trusts & Ests. 18 (Aug. 2013)

[Twenty-one] percent of middle-aged adults provided financial support in 2012 to a parent over age 65, with most viewing it as their responsibility; . . . 78 percent of middle-aged adults believe that they'll be responsible for caring for an aging family member; . . . 4.6 percent of adults are diagnosed as having a serious mental illness.

Chapter 2

Intestate Succession

I. Public Policy of Succession

When specific intent is lacking, the law may provide for what an individual wishes. Intestate succession is one way this is accomplished. It is a statutory method by which the property of a decedent that does not pass by Last Will and Testament or by non-probate transfer may be transmitted to others. With very few exceptions, the "others" are always family members identified by blood, marriage, or adoption. But with the advent of non-marital cohabitation between adults, greater utilization of assisted reproductive technology, stepchildren, and special needs dependents, intestate succession statutes may not adequately accommodate what an individual may or may not want done with his or her property. A will or non-probate transfer is always available, yet is not always utilized by the decedent; the intestate statute is simply a last resort. This last resort will be applicable in the following situations:

(1) When there is no Last Will and Testament and no non-probate transfers to pass the property to named others.

(2) There is a Last Will and Testament, but the terms of the declaration do not make provision for all of the property owned by the decedent at death.

(3) The Last Will and Testament is revoked or found to be invalid as a result of contest, and no other Last Will and Testament is probated.

(4) The decedent directs in a Last Will and Testament that property pass according to the intestate statutes in effect in the state in which he or she is domiciled at the date of his or her death.

(5) A non-probate instrument, such as an insurance policy or a retirement account, is payable to "heirs," as compared to "estate." Language such as this would mean the property would not pass according to the terms of a valid Last Will and Testament, but according to the intestate statutes in effect at the date of the decedent's death.

The state traditionally presumes that a relative should inherit under an intestate statute if no provision is made otherwise in a will or non-probate transfer. The closer the relative is to the decedent in terms of kinship or "blood," the more likely that relative will inherit from the decedent. Likewise, if the relative is a distant third cousin, thrice removed, the relative has less claim to the decedent's wealth. Lengthy emotional ties seldom merit the status of blood relationships. Interesting questions arise:

(1) *Intestate Limit.* Should the state place a blood line limit on the extent to which the property of a decedent may descend? Thus, should the state be able to limit inheritance to relatives closer to the decedent in blood relationship and eliminate completely those of more distant degree? Existing limits occur because the state wishes to provide for speedy administration of the estate and more distant relatives may be difficult to find. Plus, more distant relatives are often "laughing heirs," affected more by the joy of inheritance than grief over the death of the deceased relative. But where does the property go if the state eliminates heirs? Answer: To the state. Is there a conflict of interest? Does Internet and computer prowess provide for greater speed in locating heirs, thereby mitigating the state's rational basis for restriction of heirs?

(2) *Special Needs.* Intestate succession allows no provision for heirs that may have special needs. Handicap and youth are two examples. Does the statute thereby detract from the decedent's poorly expressed intent, which may have been to benefit these individuals more than others? How may public policy remedy this oversight?

(3) *Barring Inheritance.* What role should public policy play in preventing heirs from taking property of the decedent? For example, what of the spouse who has abused the other spouse, but the marriage remained intact? If the death did not occur because of the abuse, but the abuse can still be proven, should this, alone, be sufficient reason to bar intestate inheritance? Is the same true of adultery? Desertion? Or, if a child has not spoken to a parent for a long term of years, should the child still be able to inherit from that parent through intestate succession? What if a step-child were closer to the decedent by caring for and loving the decedent until the moment of death? Should the step-child receive nothing and the birth child receive everything, simply by taking into account blood and not affection?

(4) *Spousal Inheritance.* What role should a spouse play in intestate inheritance? Is it safe to assume that a decedent intended for his or her spouse to inherit everything? Should the parent of a decedent be able to say that he or she "deserves a return on the investment of raising the child" and benefit from intestate succession? Is it safe to assume that the surviving spouse will care for the children of the decedent, himself or herself, and that, thus, the children should receive nothing from intestate succession? Should other collateral relatives of the decedent—persons such as siblings or grandparents—have any claim to the intestate estate? Should there be a public policy claim?

(5) *Spousal Protections.* Should there be some connection in testate succession to what the spouse could have received had there been a divorce? Should the spouse's intestate share be equivalent to what the spouse would have received under a theory of "economic partnership" existing during the time of the couple's marriage? What should be the relationship between what the spouse would receive under the intestate provisions and what the spouse could receive if there were a valid Last Will and Testament but the spouse "elected" against it, taking a forced statutory share?

(6) *Tax Considerations.* Federal and state taxes imposed at death provide a number of deductions, credits, and exemptions that may significantly lessen the adverse impact of taxation at death. For example, under the Internal Revenue Code, § 2056 provides an unlimited marital deduction for any property passing to a valid spouse of the decedent at the decedent's death. Many estate plans rely upon a formula that permits a decedent to utilize the then-applicable federal estate tax exemption—$11,400,000 in 2019—to disburse assets to children or other private individuals, and then the remainder to his or her spouse. In addition, the decedent may utilize a Qualified Terminable Interest Property (QTIP) trust, thereby restricting the surviving spouse's ability to freely dispose of the property. Because any testamentary or *inter vivos* estate plan is attentive to taxation, there would be no federal estate tax due upon that person's death. On the other hand, if a person dies intestate with his or her assets passing according to the state's intestate statute, any tax advantage

may be lost, along with the ability to restrict the surviving spouse's options. In addition to marital estate planning, utilizing a Will or *inter vivos* trust will result in tax savings when administering special assets, engaging in charitable gift-giving, or administering a family business upon the death of a manager. *See generally* Shelly Kreiczer-Levy, *Big Data and the Modern Family*, 2019 Wis. L. Rev. 349 (arguing that current intestate statutes privilege the nuclear family to the exclusion of modern forms of associations and relationships); Raymond C. O'Brien, *Assessing Assisted Reproductive Technology*, 27 Cath. U. J. L. & Tech. 1 (2018) (describing the evolution of parenthood structures implicating intestacy, including surrogacy and mitochondrial replacement that could create more than two biological parents); E. Gary Spitko, *Intestate Inheritance Rights for Unmarried Committed Partners: Lessons for U.S. Law Reform from the Scottish Experience*, 103 Iowa L. Rev. 2175 (2018) (illustrating the Scottish approach that allows unmarried committed partners to share in a deceased partner's intestate estate).

II. Establishing a Pattern

Each state has its own intestate statutory scheme. Nonetheless, each will have a pattern in common with other states. The pattern will start with a surviving spouse; it will proceed, then, to issue; then to parents; and, eventually, it will proceed to more distant relatives. As an example of intestate distribution, the Uniform Probate Code has four divisions: (1) the definition of the intestate estate, Unif. Prob. Code § 2-101; (2) the share of the surviving spouse, Unif. Prob. Code § 2-102; (3) the share of heirs other than the surviving spouse, Unif. Prob. Code § 2-103; and (4) when there are no takers, Unif. Prob. Code § 2-105. The amount that each person will receive will likely differ from state-to-state, but the pattern is a consistent one among the states. If the pattern were reduced to a diagram, it would appear as such:

```
P=P                              Terms:  (X) decedent
 |                                       S spouse
(X)=S                                    I issue
 |                                       P parents
 I
```

If (X) is dead, signified by the closed parentheses, how would the intestate estate be distributed? Assuming that S is truly a spouse of the decedent or able to take as a spouse through an alternative state statute, S is likely to receive a fixed monetary amount and then a percentage of the remainder. It is very important to ascertain if S and X were validly married because only marriage or a status such as a civil union may qualify a person to occupy this pivotal position in the intestate pattern. After the surviving spouse has taken this fixed amount and percentage, what is left goes to the issue or, if none, to the parents, equally. The word "issue" is an inclusive term and is meant to include children and their issue (*e.g.*, grandchildren and great-grandchildren), should any of the children predecease the decedent.

Sometimes the statute will replace the word "issue" with "descendent" but the two are synonymous. Thus, the word "issue" is more inclusive than children and it is meant to incorporate issue of the body, marital and non-marital, and, to a degree, adopted issue. Should the surviving spouse be pregnant at the death of her deceased husband, the child-in-gestation would qualify as an issue as well; a child in gestation would qualify to inherit. And, as will be discussed, the 2008 revision to the Uniform Probate Code establishes a parent-child relationship: (1) between the child and a "functioning" parent, UNIF. PROB. CODE § 2-115(4); (2) for a stepchild or any child in the process of being adopted when the adopting parent dies, UNIF. PROB. CODE § 2-118(b); and (3) for a child conceived by assisted reproduction, other than a child born to a gestational carrier, UNIF. PROB. CODE § 2-120. Of great interest is the Code's provision allowing a child *posthumously conceived* to be treated as a child of the decedent donor of egg or sperm, if the child is in utero not later than 36 months after the individual's death, or if the child is born not later than 45 months after the individual's death. *See* UNIF. PROB. CODE § 2-120(k). The Code's provisions are progressive and pertinent to technological changes.

Issue of the decedent will always take to the exclusion of more remote heirs. These more remote heirs may include the parents of the decedent. Parents are termed "ancestors" and occupy a privileged status in the testate scheme, but not when issue survive. Thus, if (X) dies without a spouse but with parents and issue, the issue take the entire intestate estate. But if (X) dies with a spouse and issue, the spouse will take the bulk of the estate, or sometimes the entire intestate estate, and the issue take only a portion. The parents would take nothing because issue will always trump ancestors and collaterals, which includes parents.

If there are no issue surviving the decedent, but there are parents and a spouse, then the spouse will take a significant portion of the estate, and the parents will take a minor percentage. As a practical matter, when a spouse receives the "first $300,000," for example, this is usually the entire intestate estate because the vast amount of property has usually passed by non-probate transfer. But it is possible for a parent to inherit from a deceased child through the intestate statute, and the question arises: "Is this what the decedent intended?" It is arguable that the spouse should always inherit, and a parent should inherit only in rare circumstances. Finally, if only the spouse survives the decedent, and there are no issue, no ancestors, and no collaterals, the spouse takes the entire estate. Thus, the spouse occupies a pivotal role in the distribution of an intestate estate. Interestingly, the marriage could be of short or long duration.

What if there is no spouse, no issue, and no ancestors? What if the decedent is survived by only collaterals — siblings, nephews, nieces, and other, more distant relatives? How should the property be distributed then? State statutes will vary, but, again, there is a pattern among them. First, only relatives by blood or adoption take; seldom do relatives by marriage take. The spouse is the only one to inherit because of marriage, and, in this situation, there is no living spouse. Thus, the statute will look to blood relatives. Second, the statutes are likely to limit inheritance to those persons inheriting through the parents of the decedent, not those related through the grand-parents. Siblings and their issue (should they be deceased as well) take to the exclusion of aunts, uncles, and first cousins. Because these latter persons descend from the grandparents and not the parents, often, they are too remote for the statute to include them. To establish with precision the relationship between a decedent and a distant collateral heir, some states utilize a Table of Consanguinity to determine degrees of kinship. The degree of kinship is important for establishing limits upon who can inherit, but the degrees do not establish the pattern of distribution. Indeed, the degree of kinship concept is more important in connection with "laughing heir" provisions.

Table of Consanguinity

Degrees of relatedness
are shown in parentheses.

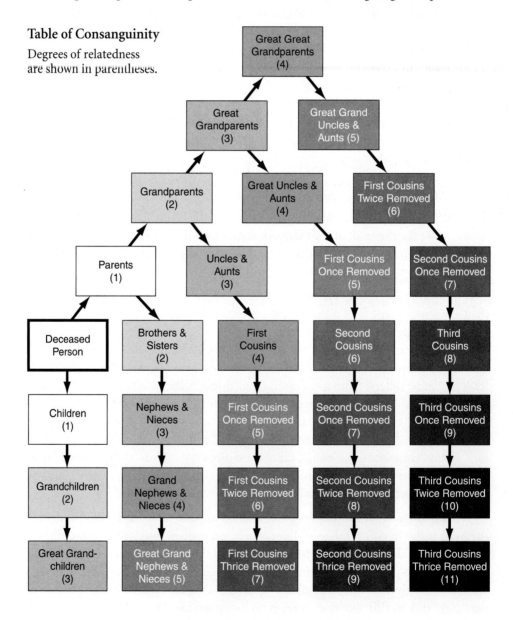

Laughing heir provisions limit more distant relatives from taking from a decedent under the state presumption that more distant relatives will respond to the death of the decedent with more glee over sudden inheritance than remorse over the death of a relative. Such statutes have a firmer basis when they seek to make intestate administration more manageable by limiting heirs and confining inheritance to those more likely to have supported the decedent. The constitutionality of these statutes is debatable, however, when examined in the context of computer tracking of persons and state presumptions concerning remorse.

Once a pattern of intestate distribution has been established, beginning with a spouse, issue, ancestors, and collaterals, and even possible escheat to the state if none of the preceding is found, it is beneficial to look at two statutes that represent the pattern described. Remember to begin with the spouse and then work your way through to establish the amount each person would take. Note that the state statute is more representative of statutes in existence today. The Uniform Probate Code, including 2008 amendments, proposes a uniform system of probate and administration that is often the model for state legislation. Nonetheless, laws relating to wills, intestacy, trusts, and property have a long history, and there are many variations among the states. Many states have retained different approaches, which will prove illustrative. Also, as probate becomes international, foreign statutes are included to provide perspective. But the Uniform Probate Code provides a common model from which to proceed.

Uniform Probate Code (2019)

§ 2-101. Intestate Estate.

(a) Any part of a decedent's estate not effectively disposed of by will passes by intestate succession to the decedent's heirs as prescribed in this Code, except as modified by the decedent's will.

(b) A decedent by will may expressly exclude or limit the right of an individual or class to succeed to property of the decedent passing by intestate succession. If that individual or a member of that class survives the decedent, the share of the decedent's intestate estate to which that individual or class would have succeeded passes as if that individual or each member of that class had disclaimed his [or her] intestate share.

§ 2-102. Share of Spouse.

The intestate share of a decedent's surviving spouse is:

(1) the entire intestate estate if:

(A) no descendant or parent of the decedent survives the decedent; or

(B) all of the decedent's surviving descendants are also descendants of the surviving spouse and there is no other descendant of the surviving spouse who survives the decedent;

(2) the first [$300,000], plus three-fourths of any balance of the intestate estate, if no descendant of the decedent survives the decedent, but a parent of the decedent survives the decedent;

(3) the first [$225,000], plus one-half of any balance of the intestate estate, if all of the decedent's surviving descendants are also descendants of the surviving spouse and the surviving spouse has one or more surviving descendants who are not descendants of the decedent;

(4) the first [$150,000], plus one-half of any balance of the intestate estate, if one or more of the decedent's surviving descendants are not descendants of the surviving spouse.

[ALTERNATIVE PROVISION FOR COMMUNITY PROPERTY STATES]

§ 2-102A. Share of Spouse.

* * *

(a) The intestate share of a surviving spouse in separate property is:

(1) the entire intestate estate if:

(A) no descendant or parent of the decedent survives the decedent; or

(B) all of the decedent's surviving descendants are also descendants of the surviving spouse and there is no other descendant of the surviving spouse who survives the decedent;

(2) the first [$300,000], plus three-fourths of any balance of the intestate estate, if no descendant of the decedent survives the decedent, but a parent of the decedent survives the decedent;

(3) the first [$225,000], plus one-half of any balance of the intestate estate, if all of the decedent's surviving descendants are also descendants of the surviving spouse and the surviving spouse has one or more surviving descendants who are not descendants of the decedent;

(4) the first [$150,000], plus one-half of any balance of the intestate estate, if one or more of the decedent's surviving descendants are not descendants of the surviving spouse.

(b) The one-half of community property belonging to the decedent passes to the [surviving spouse] as the intestate share.

§ 2-103. Share of Heirs other than Surviving Spouse.

(a) Any part of the intestate estate not passing to the decedent's surviving spouse under Section 2-102, or the entire intestate estate if there is no surviving spouse, passes in the following order to the individuals designated below who survive the decedent:

(1) to the decedent's descendants by representation;

(2) if there is no surviving descendant, to the decedent's parents equally if both survive, or to the surviving parent if only one survives;

(3) if there is no surviving descendant or parent, to the descendants of the decedent's parents or either of them by representation;

(4) if there is no surviving descendant, parent, or descendant of a parent, but the decedent is survived on both the paternal and maternal sides by one or more grandparents or descendants of grandparents:

(A) half to the decedent's paternal grandparents equally if both survive, to the surviving paternal grandparent if only one survives, or to the descendants of the decedent's paternal grandparents or either of them if both are deceased, the descendants taking by representation; and

(B) half to the decedent's maternal grandparents equally if both survive, to the surviving maternal grandparent if only one survives, or to the descendants of the decedent's maternal grandparents or either of them if both are deceased, the descendants taking by representation;

(5) if there is no surviving descendant, parent, or descendant of a parent, but the decedent is survived by one or more grandparents or descendants of grandparents on the paternal but not the maternal side, or on the maternal but not the paternal side, to the decedent's relatives on the side with one or more surviving members in the manner described in paragraph (4).

(b) If there is no taker under subsection (a), but the decedent has:

(1) one deceased spouse who has one or more descendants who survive the decedent, the estate or part thereof passes to that spouse's descendants by representation; or

(2) more than one deceased spouse who has one or more descendants who survive the decedent, an equal share of the estate or part thereof passes to each set of descendants by representation.

§ 2-105. No Taker.

If there is no taker under the provisions of this Article, the intestate estate passes to the [state].

§ 2-106. Representation.

(a) [**Definitions.**] In this section:

(1) "Deceased descendant," "deceased parent," or "deceased grandparent" means a descendant, parent, or grandparent who either predeceased the decedent or is deemed to have predeceased the decedent under Section 2-104.

(2) "Surviving descendant" means a descendant who neither predeceased the decedent nor is deemed to have predeceased the decedent under Section 2-104.

(b) [**Decedent's Descendants.**] If, under Section 2-103(1), a decedent's intestate estate or a part thereof passes "by representation" to the decedent's descendants, the estate or part thereof is divided into as many equal shares as there are (i) surviving descendants in the generation nearest to the decedent which contains one or more surviving descendants and (ii) deceased descendants in the same generation who left surviving descendants, if any. Each surviving descendant in the nearest generation is allocated one share. The remaining shares, if any, are combined and then divided in the same manner among the surviving descendants of the deceased descendants as if the surviving descendants who were allocated a share and their surviving descendants had predeceased the decedent.

(c) [**Descendants of Parents or Grandparents.**] If, under Section 2-103(3) or (4), a decedent's intestate estate or a part thereof passes "by representation" to the descendants of the decedent's deceased parents or either of them or to the descendants of the decedent's deceased paternal or maternal grandparents or either of them, the estate or part thereof is divided into as many equal shares as there are (i) surviving descendants in the generation nearest the deceased parents or either of them, or the deceased grandparents or either of them, that contains one or more surviving descendants and (ii) deceased descendants in the same generation who left surviving descendants, if any. Each surviving descendant in the nearest generation is allocated one share. The remaining shares, if any, are combined and then divided in the same manner among the surviving descendants of the deceased descendants as if the surviving descendants who were allocated a share and their surviving descendants had predeceased the decedent.

Maryland Code, Estates and Trusts (2019)

§ 3-102. Share of Intestate Estate Inherited by Surviving Spouse.

(a) The share of a surviving spouse shall be as provided in this section.

(b) If there is a surviving minor child, the share shall be one-half.

(c) If there is no surviving minor child, but there is surviving issue, the share shall be the first $40,000 plus one-half of the residue.

(d) If there is no surviving issue but a surviving parent, and the surviving spouse and the decedent had been married for less than 5 years, the share shall be the first $40,000 plus one-half of the residue.

(e) If there is no surviving issue but a surviving parent, and the surviving spouse and the decedent had been married for at least 5 years, the share shall be the whole estate.

(f) If there is no surviving issue or parent, the share shall be the whole estate.

* * *

§ 3-103. Shares of surviving issue.

The net estate, exclusive of the share of the surviving spouse, or the entire net estate if there is no surviving spouse, shall be divided equally among the surviving issue, by representation as defined in § 1-210 of this article.

§ 1-210. Division per stirpes.

(a) When provision is made for representation in this article, the shares shall be determined in accordance with subsections (b) and (c) of this section.

(b)(1) In the case of issue of the decedent, the property shall be divided into as many equal shares as there are children of the decedent who survive the decedent and children of the decedent who did not survive the decedent but of whom issue did survive the decedent.

(2) Each child of the decedent who did survive the decedent shall receive one share and the issue of each child of the decedent who did not survive the decedent but of whom issue did survive the decedent shall receive one share apportioned by applying to the children and other issue of each nonsurviving child of the decedent the pattern of representation provided for in this subsection for the children and other issue of the decedent and repeating that pattern with respect to succeeding generations until all shares are determined.

(c)(1) In the case of issue of a parent, grandparent, or great-grandparent of the decedent, the property shall be divided into as many equal shares as there are lineal descendants of either, or of both, of the pair of parents, grandparents, or great-grandparents, as the case may be, of the nearest degree of relationship to the decedent of whom any survived the decedent and who did so survive, and lineal descendants of the same degree who did not survive the decedent but of whom issue did survive the decedent.

(2) Each lineal descendant of the nearest degree surviving the decedent shall receive one share and the issue of each deceased lineal descendant of that degree who left issue surviving the decedent shall receive one share apportioned in the manner of representation set forth for issue of the decedent in subsection (b) of this section.

§ 3-104. Absence of any surviving issue.

(a) If there is no surviving issue, the personal representative shall distribute, as prescribed in this section:

   (1) If there is a surviving spouse, the net estate exclusive of the share of the surviving spouse; or

   (2) If there is no surviving spouse, the entire net estate.

(b) Subject to §§ 3–111 and 3–112 of this subtitle, the net estate shall be distributed:

   (1) To the surviving parents equally;

   (2) If only one parent survives, to the survivor; or

   (3) If neither parent survives, to the issue of the parents, by representation.

(c)(1) If there is no surviving parent or issue of a parent, the net estate shall be distributed:

   (i) One-half:

      1. To the surviving paternal grandparents equally;

      2. If only one paternal grandparent survives, to the survivor; or

3. If neither paternal grandparent survives, to the issue of the paternal grandparents, by representation; and

(ii) One-half:

1. To the surviving maternal grandparents equally;

2. If only one maternal grandparent survives, to the survivor; or

3. If neither maternal grandparent survives, to the issue of the maternal grandparents, by representation.

(2) In the event that neither of one pair of grandparents and none of the issue of either of that pair survives, the one-half share applicable shall be distributed to:

(i) The other pair of grandparents;

(ii) The survivor of the other pair of grandparents; or

(iii) The issue of either of the other pair of grandparents, in the same manner as prescribed for their half share.

(d)(1) If there is no surviving parent or issue of a parent, or surviving grandparent or issue of a grandparent, the net estate shall be distributed one-quarter to:

(i) Each pair of great-grandparents equally;

(ii) All to the survivor; or

(iii) If neither survives, all to the issue of either or of both of that pair of great-grandparents, by representation.

(2) In the event that neither member of a pair of great-grandparents nor any issue of either of that pair survives, the quarter share applicable shall be distributed equally among the remaining pairs of great-grandparents or the survivor of a pair or issue of either of a pair of great-grandparents, in the same manner as prescribed for a quarter share.

(e)(1) In this subsection, "stepchild" means the child of any spouse of the decedent, if the spouse was not divorced from the decedent.

(2) If there is no surviving blood relative entitled to inherit under this section, the net estate shall be divided into as many equal shares as there are:

(i) Stepchildren of the decedent who survive the decedent; and

(ii) Stepchildren of the decedent who did not survive the decedent but of whom issue did survive the decedent.

(3)(i) Each stepchild of the decedent who did survive the decedent shall receive one share.

(ii) The issue of each stepchild of the decedent who did not survive the decedent but of whom issue did survive the decedent shall receive one share apportioned by applying the pattern of representation set forth in § 1–210 of this article.

§ 3-105. Absence of heirs.

(a)(1)(i) The provisions of this subsection are applicable if there is no person entitled to take under §§ 3-102 through 3-104 of this subtitle.

(ii) The provisions of this subsection do not apply to any portion of a decedent's estate that is comprised of land that is the subject of an application for a certificate of reservation for public use under Title 13, Subtitle 3 of the Real Property Article.

(2)(i) If an individual was a recipient of long-term care benefits under the Maryland Medical Assistance Program at the time of the individual's death, the net estate shall be converted to cash and paid to the Department of Health and Mental Hygiene, and shall be applied for the administration of the program.

(ii) If the provisions of subparagraph (i) of this paragraph are not applicable, the net estate shall be converted to cash and paid to the board of education in the county in which the letters were granted, and shall be applied for the use of the public schools in the county.

(b)(1) After payment has been made to the Department of Health and Mental Hygiene or to the board of education, if a claim for refund is filed by a relative within the fifth degree living at the death of the decedent or by the personal representative of the relative, and the claim is allowed, the claimant shall be entitled to a refund, without interest, of the sum paid.

(2) A claim for refund under this subsection may not be filed after the later of:

(i) 3 years after the death of the decedent; or

(ii) 1 year after the time of distribution of the property.

United Kingdom Inheritance (Provision for Family and Dependents) Act 1975 (2014)

1. Application for Financial Provision from Deceased's Estate.

(1) Where after the commencement of this Act a person dies domiciled in England and Wales and is survived by any of the following persons: —

[(a) the spouse or civil partner of the deceased;

(b) a former spouse or former civil partner of the deceased, but not one who has formed a subsequent marriage or civil partnership;] * * *

[(ba) any person (not being a person included in paragraph (a) or (b) above) to whom subsection (1A) [or (1B)* * *] below applies;] * * *

(c) a child of the deceased;

(d) any person (not being a child of the deceased) [who in relation to any marriage or civil partnership to which the deceased was at any time a party, or otherwise in relation to any family in which the deceased at any time stood in the role of a parent, was treated by the deceased as a child of the family;] * * *

(e) any person (not being a person included in the foregoing paragraphs of this subsection) who immediately before the death of the deceased was being maintained, either wholly or partly, by the deceased;

that person may apply to the court for an order under section 2 of this Act on the ground that the disposition of the deceased's estate effected by his will or the law relating to intestacy, or the combination of his will and that law, is not such as to make reasonable financial provision for the applicant.

[* * * indicates footnote omitted.]

III. The Surviving Spouse

Always make certain that the claimant is actually a surviving spouse. Nearly every person in America has seen the television episode of *Cheers* when Carla mourns the death of her husband at his wake but soon learns she is not the only "spouse" in attendance. In an age when people have multiple marriages and non-marital cohabitation, the intestate process invites multiple claimants to whatever the decedent passes to others without a Last Will and Testament or non-probate transfers. A person may become a spouse through one of the following ways:

(1) *Statutory Marriage*. Available in every state, a valid statutory marriage requires certain formalities, such as proper capacity to enter into the marriage, a license, and solemnization. Once the couple is married, the marriage is valid everywhere, unless contrary to strong public policy. On June 26, 2015, the Supreme Court of the United States held that the right to marry is a fundamental right inherent in the liberty of the person, and under the Due Process and Equal Protection Clauses of the Fourteenth Amendment, couples of the same sex may not be deprived of that right and liberty. Obergefell v. Hodges, 135 S. Ct. 2584 (2015). As a result of this decision, the Fourteenth Amendment requires states to recognize same-sex marriages validly performed out of state, and there is now no lawful basis by which a state may refuse marriage licenses to persons otherwise able to marry, simply because the marriage is between two persons of the same sex.

(2) *Common Law Marriage*. Far fewer states allow for the status of marriage when a couple, meeting all of the statutory requirements except for a license and officiant, hold themselves out as married for a period of time. If the couple does, in fact, meet the requirements, the marriage is official and will be recognized in other states, unless it is contrary to strong state public policy. *See, e.g., In re* Marriage of Derryberry, 853 N.W.2d 301 (Iowa Ct. App. 2014) (finding that common law marriage exists in nine states and explaining elements necessary to contract common law marriage in Iowa).

(3) *Putative Spouse*. This is a curative device, not the establishment of a marriage for purpose of marital rights of inheritance or election. Inheritance and similar remedies occur only because of equity. *See* Cortes v. Fleming, 307 So. 2d 611, 613

(La. 1973). When a marriage is annulled due to a major impediment, but one of the parties entered into the marriage in good faith, thinking that the marriage was valid, that innocent spouse is a putative spouse.

> A majority of states recognize the doctrine when dividing property acquired during marriage, applying equitable principles. . . . However, absent fraud, the doctrine generally does not apply to awards of spousal support. While some states have extended the doctrine to permit spousal support awards, they have done so under the authority of state statutes.

Williams v. Williams, 120 Nev. 559, 97 P.3d 1124 (2004). Alabama became the latest state to abolish prospective common law marriages celebrated in the state. *See* ALA. Code § 30-1-20 (2019).

New York Domestic Relations Law (2019)

§ 170 An action for divorce may be maintained by a husband or a wife to procure a judgement divorcing the parties and dissolving the marriage on . . . the following ground: * * *

(6) The husband and wife have lived separate and apart pursuant to a written agreement of separation, subscribed by the parties thereto and acknowledged or proved in the form required to entitle a deed to be recorded, for a period of one or more years after the execution of such agreement and satisfactory proof has been submitted by the plaintiff that he or she has substantially performed all the terms and conditions of such agreement. Such agreement shall be filed in the office of the clerk of the county wherein either party resides. In lieu of filing such agreement, either party to such agreement may file a memorandum of such agreement, which memorandum shall be similarly subscribed and acknowledged or proved as was the agreement of separation and shall contain the following information: (a) the names and addresses of each of the parties, (b) the date of marriage of the parties, (c) the date of the agreement of separation and (d) the date of this subscription and acknowledgment or proof of such agreement of separation.

In re Estate of McKown

Missouri Court of Appeals, 2008
274 S.W.3d 496

JAMES EDWARD WELSH, Judge.

Elaine F. McKown appeals the circuit court's judgment denying her election of surviving spouse, application of surviving spouse for exempt property, and application of surviving spouse for homestead allowance against the estate of Larry R. McKown. Elaine McKown asserts that the circuit court erred in finding that a Kansas decree of separate maintenance barred her from claiming statutory allowances or from otherwise inheriting property in Larry McKown's estate. We reverse the circuit court's judgment.

The evidence established that Elaine McKown and Larry McKown were married on June 9, 1968. On November 1, 1995, the District Court of Johnson County, Kansas, entered a decree of separate maintenance in regard to Elaine and Larry McKown's marriage. The district court found that Elaine and Larry McKown were incompatible with one another and that they "should be granted an Absolute Decree of Separate Maintenance one from the other on the grounds of incompatibility." The decree stated, "[T]he parties state to the Court that an oral settlement agreement has been reached as to the disposition of all rights, duties and obligations of the parties[.]" In regard to the property, the decree ordered:

> 10. The marital real estate of the parties located at 7500 Norwood Drive, Prairie Village, Kansas, 66208, shall be set aside as the sole and separate property of [Elaine McKown], free and clear of any interest of [Larry McKown] and [Larry McKown] shall execute a Quit-Claim Deed releasing any interest that he has in such real estate to [Elaine McKown]. [Elaine McKown] shall be responsible for maintaining the mortgage obligation on such real estate and shall pay all costs associated with the property henceforth.

> 11. The lake lot property located at Pomme de Terre and legally described as Lot 17, Stamp Development, a Subdivision of Hickory County, Missouri, is set aside to [Larry McKown] as his sole and separate property and [Elaine McKown] shall execute a Quit-Claim Deed or any other document necessary to relinquish any right, title, claim or interest she may have in said property.

> 12. The pension and profit sharing at General Motors and any other retirement benefits which may have accrued as a result of [Larry McKown's] employment with General Motors shall be set aside to him as his sole and separate property free and clear of any right, title, interest or claim on the part of [Elaine McKown] therefore.

> 13. Each party shall be given their own personal property and clothing. All other personal property has been divided and each party hereto shall keep and maintain as his or her sole and separate property all that property which is in his or her possession at the time of the granting of this Decree of Separate Maintenance and neither shall make any further claim upon the other for any personal property.

After the court issued the decree of separate maintenance, Elaine McKown and Larry McKown lived separate and apart. They never dissolved their marriage.

On August 7, 2002, Larry McKown executed his Last Will and Testament, in which he acknowledged that Elaine McKown was his spouse but noted that they had "a separate maintenance agreement of record in Johnson County, Kansas." Under the terms of his will, Larry McKown left his estate to his mother, Gwendolyn McKown, so long as she survived him. If Gwendolyn McKown did not survive Larry McKown, which she did not do, the will directed that Larry McKown's estate would go to his sister, Lutricia Rapue.

On May 7, 2007, Larry McKown died. On June 20, 2007, Larry McKown's last will and testament was admitted to probate. The Inventory and Appraisement filed with the court indicated that Larry McKown's estate consisted of real property located in Bates County, Missouri, having a value of $30,000 and subject to a deed of trust in the amount of $17,950; a 1994 Ford Taurus having a value of $1,000; household goods and furnishings having a value of $500; and General Motors life insurance proceeds in the amount of $96,905.95.

On October 11, 2007, Elaine McKown filed with the circuit court an election of surviving spouse, an application of surviving spouse for exempt property, and an application of surviving spouse for homestead allowance. On January 28, 2008, the circuit court held a hearing on the claims of the creditors of the estate and on Elaine McKown's election to take against the will and her applications for exempt property and homestead allowance. On February 8, 2008, the circuit court entered its judgment denying Elaine McKown's election of surviving spouse, application of surviving spouse for exempt property, and application of surviving spouse for homestead allowance. After considering the Kansas decree of separate maintenance, the circuit court found that "all rights of the parties exchanged in the separate maintenance order included allowances, exempt property, homestead allowance, and right to take against the will," and that "all claims of the surviving spouse were previously settled by the settlement agreement . . . as set forth in the Decree of Separate Maintenance from the State of Kansas." Elaine McKown appeals.

In her sole point on appeal, Elaine McKown contends that the circuit court erred in finding that the Kansas decree of separate maintenance barred her from claiming statutory allowances or from otherwise inheriting property in Larry McKown's estate. We agree.

We must give the Kansas decree of separate maintenance the same force and effect it would have in Kansas. *In re Marriage of Sumners,* 645 S.W.2d 205, 210 (Mo.App.1983). In Kansas, while a divorce completely dissolves the marital relationship of the parties, a decree of separate maintenance "permits the continuation of the relation in a legal sense." *Linson v. Johnson,* 1 Kan.App.2d 155, 563 P.2d 485, 488 (1977) (*Linson I*), *aff'd by Linson v. Johnson,* 223 Kan. 442, 575 P.2d 504 (1978) (*Linson II*). * * * Accordingly, a surviving spouse subject to a decree of separate maintenance is a "surviving spouse" under Kansas law of intestacy and may inherit from the deceased spouse's estate, notwithstanding the decree of separate maintenance. *Linson I,* 563 P.2d at 491. The surviving spouse's right to inherit from a deceased spouse's estate, however, may be limited by the division of property in the decree of separate maintenance. *Id.* If the decree of separate maintenance indicates "any clear intent of the trial court at that time to terminate rights of inheritance by either of [the] parties in the estate of the other," the surviving spouse is barred from asserting a right to inherit from a deceased spouse's estate. *Id.; Linson II,* 575 P.2d at 505. Indeed, in affirming *Linson I,* the Kansas Supreme Court instructed:

[W]here separate maintenance [is] decreed, . . . to cut off the right of inheritance of the survivor of the first of the parties to die[, the trial court must] provide in the decree that title to the real property awarded each of the parties be vested free and clear of any right, title, interest, lien, claim or estate of the other party.

When a decree of separate maintenance is entered, and the property is divided . . . , *the decree must be specific and clearly indicate* an intent on the part of the trial court, when the decree is entered, to terminate the rights of inheritance by either of the parties to the marriage in the estate of the other.

Linson II, 575 P.2d at 505–06 (emphasis added).

In *Linson I,* in the decree of separate maintenance, the trial court awarded "all right, title and interest" in two parcels of real property to the parties as tenants in common. *Linson I,* 563 P.2d at 487. The court determined the decree of separate maintenance did not indicate a clear intent to terminate the parties' inheritance rights in the estate of the other. *Id.* at 491. The court concluded that the surviving spouse was entitled pursuant to Kansas law "to make an election to take what she is entitled to by the laws of intestate succession and her right to inherit from the estate of her deceased husband was not barred by the decree of separate maintenance [.]" *Id.*

In this case, the Kansas decree of separate maintenance said that the parties had reached "an oral settlement agreement . . . as to the disposition of all rights, duties and obligations of the parties," that Larry McKown's retirement benefits shall be his "sole and separate property free and clear of any right, title, interest or claim" on the part of Elaine McKown, and that neither party "shall make any further claim upon the other for any personal property." The language of the decree of separate maintenance, however, did not "specific[ally] and clearly indicate an intent on the part of the trial court . . . to terminate the rights of inheritance by either of the parties to the marriage in the estate of the other" as instructed by the Kansas Supreme Court in *Linson II. Linson II,* 575 P.2d at 506. Although the decree awarded Larry McKown his retirement benefits as his sole and separate property "free and clear of any right, title, interest or claim," the Kansas trial court did not specifically and clearly indicate an intent to terminate Elaine McKown's rights of inheritance in Larry McKown's estate. *Id.* Nor did the other language employed by the Kansas trial court in the decree cut off Elaine McKown's rights of inheritance in Larry McKown's estate. Elaine McKown's right to inherit from Larry McKown's estate, therefore, was not barred by the decree of separate maintenance.

Moreover, in *Linson I,* the court noted that, in the case before it, all parties agreed "as to the right of a surviving spouse to inherit his or her interest in property acquired after a decree of separate maintenance." *Linson I,* 563 P.2d at 491. In support of this proposition, the court cited *In re Estate of Fults,* 193 Kan. 491, 394 P.2d 32 (1964). In that case, the court held that a decree of separate maintenance did not prohibit a surviving spouse from asserting her rights under the statutes of descent and distribution as to property acquired by her husband between the date of the decree of separate maintenance and the date of his death. *Id.* at 37. In so holding, the *Fults* court cited *Hardesty v. Hardesty*, 115 Kan. 192, 222 P. 102 (1924) and noted that "a court cannot reach out and appropriate future property" in a decree of separate maintenance. *Fults*, 394 P.2d at 36.

The circuit court in this case determined, however, that "*all claims* of [Elaine McKown] were previously settled by the settlement agreement of [Larry McKown and Elaine McKown] as set forth in the Decree of Separate Maintenance from the State of Kansas." Such a declaration by the circuit court pertained to not only the property in the decree of separate maintenance but also to any property acquired by Larry McKown between the date of the decree of separate maintenance and the date of his death. Because, however, the Kansas trial court did not specifically and clearly indicate its intent to terminate Elaine McKown's rights of inheritance in Larry McKown's estate, the decree of separate maintenance does not prohibit Elaine McKown's from asserting her rights to property acquired by Larry McKown between the date of the decree of separate maintenance and the date of his death. *Id.* at 37. * * *

The circuit court erred in concluding that the decree of separate maintenance terminated Elaine McKown's right to take against the will and terminated her claims for exempt property and homestead allowance. We, therefore, reverse the circuit court's judgment and remand with instructions to allow Elaine McKown to pursue her claims as a surviving spouse of Larry McKown in regard to any property in Larry McKown's estate.

All concur.

Notes

There are multiple situations in which pending spousal rights at death conflict with pending divorce matters. *See, e.g.*, Kay v. Kay, 200 N.J. 551, 985 A.2d 1223 (2010) (holding that when spouse dies during course of divorce, estate of decedent may continue divorce litigation to establish claim to marital property of decedent); Karpien v. Karpien, 146 N.M. 188, 207 P.3d 1165 (2009) (holding that if one spouse dies during pendency of divorce action, surviving spouse is not entitled to probate benefits because of state statute allowing court to resolve pending marital property issues); Oldham v. Oldham, 147 N.M. 329, 222 P.3d 701 (2009) (holding that if, during pendency of divorce action, spouse dies, surviving spouse may not be appointed as personal representative of estate due to conflict of interest), *aff'd in part, rev'd in part on other grounds*, 247 P.3d 736 (2011); Carr v. Carr, 120 N.J. 336, 576 A.2d 872 (1990) (surviving spouse can continue divorce action against estate of decedent to recover marital assets allegedly diverted by decedent).

Tax Considerations: State and federal benefits accrue because of marital status. A few examples of these advantages are the following:

(1) *Retirement Rollover.* If an employee is entitled to a distribution under a qualified retirement plan and is entitled to rollover treatment, then the surviving spouse of that employee is entitled to rollover treatment into an account in the surviving

spouse's name, under the same terms and conditions that would have applied to the employee. I.R.C. § 402(c)(9).

(2) *Jointly Held Property.* Whenever property is held jointly by spouses, it does not matter who furnished the consideration for the property—one half of the property is included in the gross estate of the first spouse to die. There is a presumption of joint ownership. I.R.C. § 2040(b).

(3) *Marital Deduction.* An unlimited estate tax deduction is allowable for property passing from the decedent to a surviving spouse. I.R.C. § 2056. The surviving spouse must be a United States citizen, and the passing property must not be a terminable interest. A terminable interest is any interest that terminates or fails because of the lapse of time or the occurrence of an event. I.R.C. § 2056(b)(1). Nonetheless, the marital deduction is allowed for a qualified terminable interest (QTIP), as long as the spouse has the right to all of the income for life, payable no less frequently than annually. I.R.C. § 2056 (b)(7).

(4) *Widow(er)'s Allowance.* Whenever a court orders statutory support for a surviving spouse during the administration of an estate, the support qualifies as a deduction for the estate if paid pursuant to a court order or decree under local law. I.R.C. Reg. § 1.661(a)-2(e).

(5) *Gifts Between Spouses.* There is no gain or loss when property is transferred between spouses, or to a former spouse as an incident to divorce. The transferor's basis for the property is carried over to the transferee. I.R.C. § 1041.

(6) *Gift Tax.* As of 2019, each donor is allowed a $15,000 annual exclusion for each gift made to a donee. But spouses who consent to split their gifts may transfer up to a total of $30,000 per donee. I.R.C. §§ 2046, 2518.

IV. Share of Heirs Other Than a Surviving Spouse

If the spouse and issue survive the decedent, the spouse will take all, or a significant portion of, the intestate estate. The remaining portion will descend to issue of the decedent. Likewise, if there is no spouse surviving, all of the intestate estate will descend to the issue, or if no issue, then to the decedent's parents. If there is no surviving spouse, no surviving issue and no surviving parents, then the remaining portion will descend to the collateral heirs. Issue and collateral heirs—we will later refer to them as "classes"—are open-ended, which means that persons who qualify could predecease the decedent or additional ones could be born after the death of the decedent. For now, we are not concerned over those who may be born in the future. They will receive nothing; only those alive and ascertainable at the death of the decedent will be able to take a portion of the intestate estate.

The class of persons involved—both issue and collaterals—may consist of a mixed group. Some may be closer to the decedent in degree of kinship than others. How, then, should the estate be divided when the decedent leaves one child and

three grandchildren from a predeceasing child? How should the estate be distributed when the decedent leaves no spouse, no issue, and no parents, but two sisters
and three nephews from a predeceasing brother? In other words, how should the
estate be divided when the degrees of kinship vary and, yet, every claimant is within
the statutory limit? Before these questions may be answered, certain terminology
must be understood: *per capita* and *per stirpes* distribution. *Per capita* distribution
means that a person receives in and of himself or herself from a decedent—he or
she takes by his or her own head and not through another. When the term *per stirpes*
is used, it refers to when a person takes "by representation" or through another. The
following chart will provide an example for distribution among issue:

A. Issue

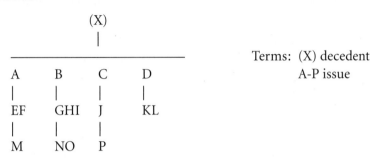

Terms: (X) decedent
        A-P issue

If (X) dies without a surviving spouse, but with issue, the issue would take before
any parent would take. Thus, in the presence of issue, we are not concerned with
distribution to parents or more distant collaterals. The four issue identified in the
above chart are: A-B-C-D. Each is a child and each would take equally because each
survived the decedent. Also, each would take per capita from the decedent because
each is taking himself or herself. But now add additional facts: If B-C-D all predecease (X), A would be the only surviving child. Should A take all of (X)'s estate? No.
Children of B-C-D survive: G-H-I-J-K-L. Even though they are grandchildren, they
are still issue and are entitled to take under the intestate statute. But each would
take through a predeceasing parent (B-C-D) and, because they take by representation or through another, the grandchildren would take per stirpes. Finally, if H and
J were to predecease (X), each of them is survived by an issue as well, and that issue
(N-O-P) would be able to share in (X)'s intestate estate, per stirpes, through H and
J. Because the statute provides for representation among issue, it is conceivable that
per stirpes distribution could continue through multiple generations.

B. Collaterals

```
    _____
    A      B     (X)    C      D
    |      |            |      |
    EF     GHI          J      KL
    |      |            |
    M      NO           P
```

Terms: (X) decedent
        A-P collaterals

As with the example concerning issue, (X) is predeceasing without a spouse. Remember that collaterals are not issue. Rather, collaterals are more distant relatives, such as brothers and sisters, and, as shown in the diagram, nephews and nieces; therefore, the presence of parents matters. Here, there are no ancestors—parents—so we are not concerned with them taking and, thereby, excluding the collaterals. Thus, how should the estate be divided? The answer is simple: the same as with issue. Thus, if A-B-C-D survive, each would take equally and per capita because each would take himself or herself. But if B-C-D predeceased (X), then A would be the only surviving sibling, and the nephews and nieces of (X) would take per stirpes through their predeceasing parent.

Once we understand how the system works in relationship to per capita and per stirpes, we must ask how much each of the parties would take if we were to make a percentage distribution. There are four methods by which we may arrive at the percentage of each of the intestate takers. The state in which you practice will apply one of these four methods. Furthermore, a person may utilize one of these methods in a valid Last Will and Testament or trust to distribute property to heirs. States may also borrow from the four methods when implementing statutory distribution under statutes such as anti-lapse—a concept we will discover later in the course. For now, it is important to master the four methods of distribution.

C. Methods of Distribution

1. Old Uniform Probate Code (1969)

Most often referred to as the "modern" form of distribution, this method would go to the first horizontal line where there is a survivor and make a per capita distribution there, then make a per stirpes distribution at each succeeding line. The important element in the old UPC scheme is the combination of per capita and per stirpes distribution. For example, if we look at the previous chart, where (X) has died and is survived by collateral heirs, if B-C-D predecease (X), we would still start at this first horizontal line because A is still alive. A would receive one-quarter share because B-C-D, even though predeceasing, are survived by issue. There are four vertical lines of succession, and each would be entitled to receive a portion. Under this example, A would receive one-quarter share per capita and the remaining three-fourths would be divided among the other three vertical lines.

However, because B has predeceased and is survived by G-H-I, each of them would receive one-third of B's one-fourth, or one-twelfth each. Also, if H had predeceased and was survived by N and O, then N and O would have to divide per stirpes the one-twelfth share of H. Therefore, N and O would each receive a one-twenty-fourth share in the estate. The same manner of distribution would occur with C and D, but please note that J would do best among all of the nephews and nieces of (X) because J is the lone survivor of C, and B was survived by G-H-I. Thus, even though J and G-H-I are in the same degree of kinship to (X), J will receive one-fourth of the estate and G-H-I will receive one-twelfth. Because of the per stirpes method of distribution, whereby an heir is taking through another heir, there is a disparity among persons similarly related and of equal degree of kinship to the decedent. To rectify this disparity, the New Uniform Probate Code was adopted.

2. New Uniform Probate Code (2008)

§ 2-103. Share of Heirs Other Than Surviving Spouse.

(a) Any part of the intestate estate not passing to a decedent's surviving spouse under Section 2-102, or the entire intestate estate if there is no surviving spouse, passes in the following order to the individuals who survive the decedent:

(1) to the decedent's descendants by representation;

(2) if there is no surviving descendant, to the decedent's parents equally if both survive, or to the surviving parent if only one survives;

(3) if there is no surviving descendant or parent, to the descendants of the decedent's parents or either of them by representation;

(4) if there is no surviving descendant, parent, or descendant of a parent, but the decedent is survived on both the paternal and maternal sides by one or more grandparents or descendants of grandparents:

(A) half to the decedent's paternal grandparents equally if both survive, to the surviving paternal grandparent if only one survives, or to the descendants of the decedent's paternal grandparents or either of them if both are deceased, the descendants taking by representation; and

(B) half to the decedent's maternal grandparents equally if both survive, to the surviving maternal grandparent if only one survives, or to the descendants of the decedent's maternal grandparents or either of them if both are deceased, the descendants taking by representation;

(5) if there is no surviving descendant, parent, or descendant of a parent, but the decedent is survived by one or more grandparents or descendants of grandparents on the paternal but not the maternal side, or on the maternal but not the paternal side, to the decedent's relatives on the side with one or more surviving members in the manner described in paragraph (4).

(b) If there is no taker under subsection (a), but the decedent has:

(1) one deceased spouse who has one or more descendants who survive the decedent, the estate or part thereof passes to that spouse's descendants by representation; or

(2) more than one deceased spouse who has one or more descendants who survive the decedent, an equal share of the estate or part thereof passes to each set of descendants by representation.

§ 2-106. Representation.

(a) [Definitions.] In this section:

(1) "Deceased descendant," "deceased parent," or "deceased grandparent" means a descendant, parent, or grandparent who either predeceased

the decedent or is deemed to have predeceased the decedent under Section 2-104.

(2) "Surviving descendant" means a descendant who neither predeceased the decedent nor is deemed to have predeceased the decedent under Section 2-104.

(b) [Decedent's Descendants.] If, under Section 2-103(1), a decedent's intestate estate or a part thereof passes "by representation" to the decedent's descendants, the estate or part thereof is divided into as many equal shares as there are (i) surviving descendants in the generation nearest to the decedent which contains one or more surviving descendants and (ii) deceased descendants in the same generation who left surviving descendants, if any. Each surviving descendant in the nearest generation is allocated one share. The remaining shares, if any, are combined and then divided in the same manner among the surviving descendants of the deceased descendants as if the surviving descendants who were allocated a share and their surviving descendants had predeceased the decedent.

(c) [Descendants of Parents or Grandparents.] If, under Section 2-103(3) or (4), a decedent's intestate estate or a part thereof passes "by representation" to the descendants of the decedent's deceased parents or either of them or to the descendants of the decedent's deceased paternal or maternal grandparents or either of them, the estate or part thereof is divided into as many equal shares as there are (i) surviving descendants in the generation nearest the deceased parents or either of them, or the deceased grandparents or either of them, that contains one or more surviving descendants and (ii) deceased descendants in the same generation who left surviving descendants, if any. Each surviving descendant in the nearest generation is allocated one share. The remaining shares, if any, are combined and then divided in the same manner among the surviving descendants of the deceased descendants as if the surviving descendants who were allocated a share and their surviving descendants had predeceased the decedent.

Notes

The new Uniform Probate Code § 2-103 and § 2-106 are similar to the old provision in many respects, but it has one major difference: there is a per capita distribution at each level of distribution; there is no per stirpes distribution. Go to the first horizontal level where there is a survivor and make a per capita distribution, then make a per capita distribution at each succeeding level. The utilization of per capita distribution at each level is the distinctive element. We can look to the previous chart for an example. Upon (X)'s death, if A is the lone survivor of the four collaterals (A-B-C-D), we begin at that level. A would receive a one-fourth share since A is a survivor and each of the predeceasing collaterals (B-C-D) is survived by issue. Thus, A would take his one-fourth share and be content. But three-fourths remains. In the old UPC, we would distribute that per stirpes among the descending heirs from B-C-D. This is not the case under the new UPC. Instead, we will take the remaining three-fourths and divide it per capita among the heirs at this second level: G-H-I-J-K-L. Each of them would receive one-sixth of three-fourths, or one-eighth each. Obviously, this method of computation would be far better for G-H-I than it would be for J. You may recall that J was receiving one-fourth under the old UPC. Yet the system does have the advantage of treating equally each of the nephews and nieces who are related to (X) by the same degree of kinship.

It is worthwhile to continue with the new UPC distribution to illustrate the per capita distribution at each level. We have seen that G-H-I-J-K-L each will receive one-eighth of the estate. The mathematics is relatively easy to this point. But what would happen if H and J had predeceased (X)? H is survived by N and O, and J is survived by P. All three (N-O-P) are related to (X) equally and, thus, under the new UPC, all three should share in the estate of (X) equally and per capita. To make this happen, we simply combine the share that H and J would have taken if each had survived. Because each would have taken one-eighth, we combine the two and arrive at one-quarter. This one quarter is then divided equally among the three heirs: N-O-P. Thus, each receives one-third of one-quarter for a share of one-twelfth each. Of course, N-O-P would take this one-twelfth share per capita.

The 2008 revision to the 1990 Uniform Probate Code continues the objective of providing equal shares to those equally related to the decedent. To achieve this, the 2008 revision permits a per capita division at each level, rather than a per stirpes distribution, as in the 1969 Code and a feature of many state statutes. The Commissioners revising the Code adopted what they thought to be the preference of a majority of clients when polled on the issue. More than 70% of clients preferred the per capita at each generation model. *See* UNIF. PROB. CODE § 2-106, cmt. The 2008 Code revision includes another distinctive feature—one that we have seen in Maryland Code § 3-104, *supra*, providing for distribution to stepchildren—persons heretofore excluded because they were not within the decedent's bloodline. Now, under Uniform Probate Code § 2-103, if there are no takers within the decedent's bloodline, but the decedent had one or more spouses who are predeceased but survived by descendants, then the decedent's estate passes to those former spouses' descendants by representation.

The following method of distribution—Strict Per Stirpes—is based on the English model, which seeks to pass property "by stocks" and, thus, to keep property within a bloodline, regardless of equality among those related to the decedent.

3. Strict Per Stirpes

This method of distribution is similar to the 1969 UPC, except the necessity of starting with a survivor is eliminated. Thus, under the strict method, you go to the first horizontal line, regardless of whether there is a survivor there. Once there, you make a per capita or per stirpes distribution throughout. For example, if we go back to our previous chart, we can say that A has survived (X), but not so with B-C-D. Each of them has predeceased and is survived by descendants. Just as in the 1969 UPC, we would give A one-fourth of the estate per capita and distribute one quarter per stirpes to each of the descendants of B (G-H-I), C (J), and D (K-L). Each would receive an amount identical to what would occur if we were distributing the property under the 1969 UPC method.

However, if the entire first horizontal line has predeceased (X), i.e., all of A-B-C-D are dead at (X)'s death, should we begin to make distribution at this point? The old and new UPC would say no; instead, go to the first line where there is a survivor and start there. But this is not how distribution would begin under the strict method of distribution. Here, you would go to the first horizontal line and distribute the property per stirpes, regardless of survivorship. Looking at our previous chart, if A-B-C-D are all predeceased, then the one-fourth distribution that each would have received if each were living will be divided among each of their respective heirs. Assuming that everyone is alive at the second horizontal line, the intestate estate would be divided among the following: E and F would each receive one-eighth, or one-half of A's one-fourth distribution; G-H-I would each receive one-twelfth, or one-third of B's one-fourth distribution; J would do the best with one-fourth, which is C's one-fourth distribution; and K and L would take one-eighth, or one-half of D's one-fourth distribution.

If fairness is a consideration, then it centers on the fact that the dead have the ability to determine the amounts the living will receive. It can be argued that this is always a factor whenever per stirpes is used. But in the strict method, it is possible to foist per stirpes upon the living through a line of persons who are all dead, not just some of them, as with the 1969 UPC. In times past, the blood line measured through strict descent may have proven a justification for the strict per stirpes method. *See, e.g.,* Md. Est. & Trusts Code §§ 3-103 & 1-210 (2019), *see supra*; Ga. Code Ann. § 53-2-1 (2019).

4. Next of Kin

The final method of distribution could be described as a completely per capita system. It is applied by going to the first level where there is a survivor of the closet degree of kinship and giving all of the intestate estate to that person or group of persons equally. No heir takes through another. Thus, if we go to the previous chart, suppose that A and B survive (X), and that J-K-L survive as well. How should the estate be divided if every other heir has predeceased? The answer under the method of next of kin distribution is that A and B would divide the entire estate. Sadly, J-K-L would receive nothing. The value of this method is that it provides for a fast and easily identifiable distribution of the estate among heirs, it lessens the chance of laughing heirs, and it provides for equality among persons of the same degree of kinship.

Problem

When decedent died intestate in 1981, she left no spouse, issue, parents, siblings, issue of siblings, or grandparents. However, she had survivors on her father's side — an uncle and first cousins who were the issue of seven predeceased aunts and uncles. The uncle is related in the third degree of kinship; the first cousins are related in the fourth degree of kinship. On her mother's side, she was survived by first cousins (fourth degree) and first cousins once removed (fifth degree) who were the issue of predeceasing first cousins. The uncle argued that he was next of kin and should take all of the property passing through the father's side. Also, the first cousins on the mother's side argued that they should take all of the property passing through the mother's side because the first cousins once removed were related within the fifth degree. The state statute provided that "No representation shall be allowed among collaterals beyond the degree of brothers' and sisters' grandchildren."

If you were the probate judge asked to distribute the estate of the intestate decedent, how would you decide on the petition of the uncle as to the paternal share? How would you decide on the petition of the first cousins as to the maternal share? *See In re* Estate of Martineau, 126 N.H. 250, 490 A.2d 779 (1985).

D. The Last Resort: Escheat to the State

Board of Education of Montgomery County v. Browning

Court of Appeals of Maryland, 1994
333 Md. 281, 635 A.2d 373

MURPHY, Chief Judge.

This case involves the concept of equitable adoption, and in particular, whether a person, if equitably adopted, may inherit by intestate succession from the sister of an equitably adoptive parent.

* * *

Eleanor G. Hamilton, a resident of Montgomery County, died intestate in August, 1990, leaving an estate valued at $394,405.57. At the time of her death, Hamilton had no known living blood relatives. Appellee Paula M. Browning was appointed Personal Representative of the Estate of Eleanor G. Hamilton on May 21, 1991.

Paula was born out of wedlock on October 4, 1919. Her natural father, Lawrence E. Hutchison, legally adopted Paula on October 10, 1921. In March of 1922, Hutchison married Marian Estelle Gibson. Paula grew up in the Hutchison's household in the District of Columbia; Marian, however, never formally adopted Paula. Marian, who died in 1986, was the sister of the decedent Eleanor Hamilton.

Because Eleanor apparently died without any heirs, the Board of Education of Montgomery County claimed that it was entitled to Eleanor's estate pursuant to the Maryland escheat laws. * * * Believing that she was a legal heir of Eleanor, Paula filed a complaint for declaratory judgment and a motion for summary judgment in the Circuit Court for Montgomery County. In her complaint, Paula named the Board of Education as defendant because the Board had a potential claim to the proceeds of Eleanor's estate through the escheat laws. Paula sought a declaration that she was the equitably adopted child of Marian; and as such was entitled to inherit the Estate of Eleanor G. Hamilton, Marian's sister.

In support of her motion for summary judgment, Paula submitted an affidavit in which she stated that she maintained a normal child-parent relationship with Lawrence and Marian Hutchison throughout her life. She also stated that Lawrence and Marian told her when she was a child, and later when she was an adult, that she had been adopted by them; moreover, Paula stated that Marian specifically told her in 1984 that Marian had adopted her. In 1992, when she was asked to produce proof of adoption for the instant litigation, Paula discovered that she had not been legally adopted by Marian. In her affidavit, Paula also stated that no other heirs had presented or filed claims regarding Eleanor's estate.

The Board of Education of Montgomery County, pursuant to Maryland Rule 2-322(b), filed a motion to dismiss for failure to state a claim upon which relief can be granted. The Board maintained that Paula's complaint failed to allege facts which would enable a court to declare that she was the equitably adopted child of Marian. The Board further averred that, even if Paula were adjudged to be the equitably adopted daughter of Marian, she could not, as a matter of law, inherit from the estate of her equitably adoptive mother's sister. The Board therefore argued that because Eleanor Hamilton died without a will and without any legal heirs, it was entitled to her estate under the Maryland law of escheat, as set forth in Maryland Code (1991 Repl.Vol., 1993 Cum.Supp.) § 3-105(a) of the Estates and Trusts Article. Specifically, the Board asked the circuit court to grant its motion to dismiss and declare that: (1) Paula is not entitled to inherit from Eleanor's estate; and (2) the estate escheats to the Board of Education of Montgomery County.

After a December, 1992 hearing, the court concluded that the Board of Education had conceded that Paula was the equitably adopted child of Marian. * * * The court therefore framed the sole remaining issue as follows: "whether Paula Browning, as the equitably adopted daughter of Marian Hutchison, may inherit as a collateral heir to the estate of Marian Hutchison's sister, Eleanor G. Hamilton."

Relying on First Nat. Bank in Fairmont v. Phillips, 176 W.Va. 395, 344 S.E.2d 201 (1985), upon the fact that the Board of Education was the only other party interested in the Hamilton estate, and on the close relationship between Paula and her equitably adoptive mother, the court determined that Paula could inherit from the estate of her equitably adoptive mother's sister. Thus, the court denied the Board's motion to dismiss and granted Paula's motion for summary judgment. The Board appealed to the Court of Special Appeals. We granted certiorari prior to consideration of the appeal by the intermediate appellate court to decide the significant issue presented in this case. 331 Md. 178, 626 A.2d 967.

* * *

Before us, the Board reasserts its view that an equitably adopted child may not inherit from her equitably adoptive parent's sibling. On the other hand, Paula argues that the lower court correctly ruled, as a matter of law, that a child may inherit by intestate succession from the sister of an equitably adoptive parent thereby defeating an escheat to the State.

The Board also contends that the lower court improperly granted Paula's motion for summary judgment because the court failed to consider the elements of equitable adoption and the evidence fell far short of the clear and convincing proof necessary to establish an equitable adoption. We need not address this argument, however, because even assuming *arguendo* that Paula was equitably adopted by Marian, we conclude that Paula may not inherit from her equitably adoptive parent's sister. Therefore, the trial court should have granted the Board's motion to dismiss and declared that the Estate of Eleanor G. Hamilton escheats to the Board of Education of Montgomery County.

When analyzing a motion to dismiss pursuant to Maryland Rule 2-322(b), we must accept as true all well-pleaded facts and allegations in the complaint. Faya v. Almaraz, 329 Md. 435, 443, 620 A.2d 327 (1993). Dismissal is only proper if the facts and allegations viewed in the light most favorable to the plaintiff fail to afford the plaintiff relief if proven. *Id.*; Berman v. Karvounis, 308 Md. 259, 264–65, 518 A.2d 726 (1987); Sharrow v. State Farm Mutual, 306 Md. 754, 768, 511 A.2d 492 (1986). Moreover, "any ambiguity or uncertainty in the allegations bearing on whether the complaint states a cause of action must be construed against the pleader." Figueiredo-Torres v. Nickel, 321 Md. 642, 647, 584 A.2d 69 (1991) (quoting Sharrow, *supra*, 306 Md. at 768, 511 A.2d 492).

For purposes of our analysis, we accept as true the factual allegations of Paula's complaint for declaratory judgment and motion for summary judgment. Thus, we will assume that Paula is the equitably adopted daughter of Marian Hutchison, Eleanor Hamilton's sister.

* * *

In the instant case, Paula seeks to inherit not from her putative mother, Marian Hutchison, but rather from Marian's sister. We agree with those cases that stand for the proposition that an equitably adopted child may not inherit *through* an equitably adoptive parent. Under both contractual and estoppel notions, the equities that clearly exist in favor of permitting an equitably adopted child to inherit from an equitably adoptive parent do not exist when that child seeks to inherit from a sibling of the child's adoptive parents. The governing law has been well summarized as follows:

> "The determinative factor, of course, is the relation of the child to the deceased in whose estate he seeks to participate. While he may recover against the estate of a defaulting promisor, the equities in his favor do not extend so far as to allow recovery against the estate of a foster parent's relative, one who has made no promise and — having done no wrong — has equities in his favor as well."

Note, *supra*, 58 Va.L.Rev. at 740.

Paula suggests that those cases which hold that an equitable adoptee may not inherit *through* an equitably adoptive parent are inapposite to the case at bar because in each of those cases, a legal heir of the decedent, as well as the equitably adopted child, claimed an interest in the estate, whereas in the instant case, only the Board of Education has filed a claim against the Estate of Eleanor Hamilton. Paula maintains that a party, who is not an heir, such as the Board of Education, can not defeat her claim to the Hamilton estate.

Paula's counsel conceded during oral argument before us that if an heir existed, Paula would have no interest in Eleanor's estate. Consequently, the crux of Paula's argument is that the doctrine of equitable adoption permits an equitably adopted child to inherit from the adoptive parent's sibling when the only other party seeking to inherit is the local Board of Education through the escheat laws.

This rationale was rejected by a federal district court in In re Estate of McConnell, 268 F.Supp. 346 (D.D.C.1967), aff'd, 393 F.2d 665 (D.C.Cir.1968). There, the federal district court, applying Florida law, was faced with the question of whether the natural children of the equitably adoptive parents could inherit from the equitable adoptee as "half-sisters" thereby defeating an escheat to the District of Columbia. The court held that no Florida or District of Columbia case "touching on equitable adoption is a precedent for a decree by this Court approving distribution of the estate of a deceased adoptee to the heirs of an adoptive parent who did not legally consummate the adoption." *Id.* at 349. Accordingly, the court found that the "half-sisters" had no interest in the estate and the estate escheated to the District of Columbia.

Although Paula correctly points out that escheats are not favored by law, see *e.g.*, United States v. 198.73 Acres of Land, More or Less, 800 F.2d 434, 435 (4th Cir.1986); In re Estate of Wallin, 16 Ariz.App. 34, 490 P.2d 863, 864 (1971); Estate of Supeck, 225 Cal.App.3d 360, 366, 274 Cal.Rptr. 706, 710 (1990); State v. Public Service Electric & Gas Co., 119 N.J.Super. 264, 291 A.2d 32, 35 (1972); Rippeth v. Connelly, 60 Tenn.App. 430, 447 S.W.2d 380, 382 (1969), Maryland law is crystal clear that if no legal heir exists, the decedent's property escheats to the local Board of Education. See Maryland Code (1991 Repl.Vol., 1993 Cum.Supp.) § 3-105 of the Estates and Trust Article. * * * In the instant case, therefore, because Paula may not inherit from her equitably adoptive mother's sister, and Eleanor Hamilton died without heirs, her estate escheats to the Board of Education.

We therefore conclude that an equitably adopted child may not inherit from her adoptive parent's sibling. Consequently, the entry of summary judgment in favor of Paula was inappropriate in this case. Furthermore, the circuit court erred in denying the Board's motion to dismiss. Because Paula may not inherit from Eleanor's estate, it escheats to the Board of Education of Montgomery County.

JUDGMENT OF THE CIRCUIT COURT FOR MONTGOMERY COUNTY REVERSED. CASE REMANDED TO THAT COURT WITH DIRECTIONS TO ENTER A DECLARATORY JUDGMENT NOT INCONSISTENT WITH THIS OPINION. COSTS TO BE PAID BY APPELLEE.

ELDRIDGE, J., * * * [dissenting opinion is omitted.]

Notes

People are living longer and are less likely than their ancestors to have children. The incidents of elder persons dying without a valid Last Will and Testament or operative non-probate transfers are greater; thus, state statutes providing for escheat are more likely. Nonetheless, many statutes seek to avoid escheat if possible. *See, e.g.,* Unif. Prob. Code § 2-104(b) ("This section [Simultaneous Death] does not apply if its application would cause the estate to pass to the state under Section 2-105 [Escheat]."). The Massachusetts statute that follows is illustrative of what happens to intestate property when there are no heirs:

Massachusetts General Laws (2019)

Ch. 190B, § 2-105 No Taker.

If there is no taker under the provisions of this article, the intestate estate passes to the commonwealth; provided, however, if such intestate is a veteran who died while a member of the Soldiers' Home in Massachusetts or the Soldiers' Home in Holyoke, the intestate estate shall inure to the benefit of the legacy fund or legacy account of the soldiers' home of which the intestate was a member.

V. Heirs: Changing Definition of Family

Since inheritance is based on family, it stands to reason that the laws concerning inheritance should be affected by changes in the definition of the family. Historically, the definition of family was a matter of "form," and this consisted of a married couple, without the inclusion of divorce, stepchildren, protracted paternity disputes, and few adoptions. Today's families are more aptly characterized as "functional," with modern deference given to individual liberty, and, thus, far more combinations of what may be the intention of an intestate decedent. For example, the probate court may find that, at the time of his death, the decedent had two children by his second wife and three other non-marital children, each under the age of eighteen. His second wife could have a child from a previous marriage—a step-child to the decedent—and the decedent could have been supporting the child since his marriage to the child's mother. Adoption, the marvels of the new biology, and the ability to provide heirs long after the death of the decedent, contribute to the dilemmas facing legislatures and courts when seeking to discern the definition of family. The following are examples of current issues.

A. Non-Marital Relationships

"The number of Americans living with an unmarried partner reached 18 million in 2016, up 29% since 2007. Roughly half of cohabiters are younger than 35—but cohabitation is rising most quickly among Americans ages 50 and older." *See* Renee Stepler, *Number of U.S. Adults Cohabiting with a Partner Continues to Rise, Especially among Those 50 and Older*, Pew Research Center, FactTank, Apr. 6, 2017, at http:// www.pewresearch.org/fact-tank/2017/04/06/number-of-u-s-adults-cohabiting -with-a-partner-continues-to-rise-especially-among-those-50-and-older/. A few commentators have suggested that increasing numbers and generated equitable concerns suggest that nonmarital cohabitants who meet certain objective criteria should have access to entitlements heretofore reserved to married partners. *See, e.g.,* Lawrence W. Waggoner, *Marriage is on the Decline and Cohabitation is on the Rise: At What Point, If Ever, Should Unmarried Partners Acquire Marital Rights?*, 50 FAM. L. Q. 215 (2016) (suggesting a Uniform De Facto Marriage Act). But the objectivity needed to qualify these nonmarital cohabitants for marital entitlements, including spousal inheritance, continues to elude legislatures. *See* Adam J. Hirsch, *Inheritance on the Fringes of Marriage*, 2018 U. ILL. L. REV. 235 (2018).

Although their numbers continue to rise, American nonmarital cohabitants do not qualify for statutory intestate inheritance and related spousal marital entitlements at dissolution and at death. But nonmarital cohabitants may pursue claims against a deceased partner's estate through three methods: (1) they can marry prior to the death of one partner — an option now available to same sex partners; (2) they can enter into enforceable written or oral contractual agreements during lifetime but enforceable after death, but some states such as Minnesota and New Jersey require these agreements to be in writing to be enforceable; or (3) they can utilize equitable remedies such as equitable (promissory) estoppel. The following decision references the requirement of clear and convincing agreements between the parties and the option of equitable (promissory) estoppel.

Byrne v. Laura

California Court of Appeal, 1997
52 Cal. App. 4th 1054, 60 Cal. Rptr. 2d 908

HANLON, J.

Appellant Gladys A. Byrne (Flo) sued respondents Charon A. Laura, et al., the administrator and heirs of the estate of Donald F. Lavezzo (respondents are hereafter referred to collectively as the Estate) to enforce her *Marvin* agreement (Marvin v. Marvin (1976) 18 Cal.3d 660 [134 Cal.Rptr. 815, 557 P.2d 106]) with the decedent (hereafter referred to as Skip). * * * The Estate cross-complained against Flo for damages for removing personal property from the home she had shared with Skip before his death, and for unpaid rent based on her occupancy of the home after his death.

The Estate's motion for summary adjudication was granted as to all of Flo's causes of action other than her quantum meruit claim, the Estate dismissed its claim for conversion without prejudice, and the case proceeded to trial before the court on Flo's quantum meruit claim and the Estate's claim for unpaid rent. The trial court found that there had been no agreement between Skip and Flo to compensate Flo for her services, and that, even if there had been such an agreement,

Flo had been adequately compensated for any services she provided. Judgment was entered against Flo for $2,400 for unpaid rent, and in favor of the Estate on all of Flo's causes of action.

On appeal from the judgment, Flo contends that the court erred in granting the summary adjudication motion, and that she was entitled to a trial on her causes of action other than the one for quantum meruit. We reverse the judgment on the claims that were summarily adjudicated and on the Estate's claim for unpaid rent.

* * *

Evidence presented on the motion for summary adjudication included declarations and deposition testimony from Flo, Flo's daughter Denise, Flo's niece, a neighbor of Skip's who had known Skip and Flo since the 1930's and '40's, and two couples, the Maffeis and Simpsons, who had known Flo and Skip since their days together in high school.

Skip and Flo were childhood sweethearts who were engaged to be married when Flo was 18, but Flo broke off the engagement and they married other people. Skip was divorced from his wife in 1974, and Flo's husband died in January of 1987. Skip and Flo began dating in August of 1987, and he proposed marriage to her that December. She declined his proposal because her handicapped children, Lori and Michele, would lose insurance coverage from her deceased husband's employer if she remarried.

Skip and Flo began living together in January of 1988. She moved from San Mateo into his house in San Francisco, and they resided there together until Skip's death in 1993. When Flo was asked why she moved in with Skip, she said, "[b]ecause I loved him and we wanted to be together." The Maffeis and Simpsons said that Skip adored Flo, and called her "the queen."

When Flo moved into Skip's home in San Francisco, she brought furniture and linens from her rented house in San Mateo and commingled her belongings with Skip's. The couple eliminated some of the items Skip had in the home, purchased new furniture together, and opened a joint savings account. Flo cleaned up the house, and saw to the installation of new drapes, carpets, and appliances.

Flo said that, when she moved in, Skip told her that it "was our home, and that anything that he had was mine, and I told him . . . whatever I had was his." Skip also told their friends that his possessions in the house belonged to Flo. The Simpsons recalled going over to the house for dinner, Mrs. Simpson "commenting on different pretty hand-painted Italian dishes that maybe were [Skip's] mom's," and Skip saying "well, they belong to the queen, and everything in this house is hers." Skip also said that his car was Flo's, and he apparently put their names on the license plate. When Mr. Simpson "commented about the license plate on the car," Skip said, "well, its our car, you know. It's Flo and Skip."

Skip promised Flo when she moved in, and many times thereafter, that he would take care of her for the rest of her life in exchange for her services as a homemaker.

Skip repeatedly reassured Flo that she did not have to worry because he would take care of her and she would "have a roof over [her] head." Skip also assured Flo's niece and her daughter Denise, and told the Maffeis and Simpsons, that he intended to take care of Flo.

During the first four years they lived together, Skip continued working as a plumber in San Francisco, and Flo continued working part time at a school cafeteria in San Mateo. Flo did all of the couple's cooking, cleaning, laundry, and shopping. She handled their entertaining, and took care of Skip if he got sick. Their neighbor, Blanche Maffei, recalled that when she jokingly asked Skip, "'How's married life?' he answered, 'Wonderful! Flo takes very good care of me.'" They "cohabited," in Flo's words, "as husband and wife."

Flo contributed all of her earnings toward the household, and Skip paid for Flo's living expenses, including paying her monthly credit card balances and giving her grocery and spending money on a regular basis. Skip paid to set up a conservatorship for Flo's handicapped daughters, and made Flo the beneficiary of his retirement benefits. Flo was not relying solely on Skip's pension benefits to provide for her future. She said that Skip was a very private person, and that she did not "think it was my place to ask him how much money he had." But she trusted Skip, and believed him when he indicated that he had sufficient funds in the form of savings, stocks, and bonds to afford them both a comfortable retirement.

Skip retired in March of 1992. Flo continued working, but then began suffering from angina, and underwent double bypass surgery in September of 1992. Flo returned to work after a period of disability, and then retired in May of 1993. In the months when Flo did not work, Skip wrote her a check for $500, in addition to giving her money for anything she needed. Flo said she retired because "Skip wanted [her] to stay home and to retire and spend more time with him." "[H]e relied on [her] staying home so that [they] could have a good life together. . . ."

Skip renewed his marriage proposals to Flo on many occasions while they lived together, but she continued to decline them out of concern over the insurance for her handicapped daughters. On June 15, 1993, Skip and Flo were out to dinner with the Maffeis and Simpsons, and while Flo was away from the table, Skip said that he wanted them all to take a cruise to Hawaii, where he was going to surprise Flo and arrange a marriage ceremony. Skip gave the Simpsons a wedding ring for Flo, and asked them to keep it for him. They planned to spend the July 4th holiday at the Simpsons' place in the country finalizing the dates and details of the cruise and wedding.

However, Skip died unexpectedly on June 29, 1993.

Flo said that she and Skip promised each other and agreed that all of the property they owned when they began living together and later acquired "would be jointly held and mutually owned by us and remain the property of the survivor of us." Skip repeatedly told Flo that everything he had was hers, and Flo's daughter and niece and the Maffeis and Simpsons all recalled statements by Skip to the effect that everything he had was Flo's and would someday belong to her. Skip repeatedly assured Flo that he was going to put everything, including the house, stocks and bonds, in her name. Just a week before he died, he reiterated to her that he was going to put all of his property into a living trust for her benefit.

However, according to Flo, Skip "was a procrastinator, and he'd always say 'Well, I'm going to change everything into your name, the house,' et cetera, through all the years that we lived together. But he was the type of person that didn't move too quickly on things. He procrastinated all his life. * * * So finally, like I said, the week before he died, we sat down and talked and got to the issue that we were going to do the living trust or a will because he said as of then, he didn't have anything legal. So this was something that he had to do."

Skip left an estate worth over $1.2 million. The property consisted of: $844,023.99 in stocks and bonds; $134,689.66 in various bank accounts; the house, appraised at $246,000; furnishings in the house valued at $3,000; and a 1988 Camaro valued at $5,500. Skip also left a will dated December 10, 1975, leaving all of his property to his parents or, if they did not survive him, to Claire Suy.

All of the named beneficiaries under the will had predeceased Skip. The Simpsons said that Skip never talked about family other than his parents, and as far as they knew he had no other relatives. Yolanda Maffei said that Skip "had nobody else in his life but Flo." She said that before he got together with Flo, "Skip was very much alone and very much lonesome. We one time had him for Christmas when nobody else did."

Flo said she was in a state of shock after Skip died. She considered everything of Skip's to be hers, but she did not have an attorney at the time, and did not know what her legal rights might be. She purchased the Camaro Skip had driven, and moved out of the home after she was asked to leave, taking some property in the home with her.

Flo filed a creditor's claim against Skip's estate alleging that she was the "sole and exclusive owner" of all of his property. After the claim was rejected, she filed a complaint against the Estate, which, in addition to the cause of action for quantum meruit, included causes of action for: "damages for failure to pay debt on rejected claim"; "specific performance of express oral agreement"; "imposition of constructive trust"; "temporary restraining order, preliminary injunction and permanent injunction"; "breach of oral contract"; and "declaratory relief."

The Estate moved for summary adjudication of these claims on the ground that Skip's promises were too uncertain to enforce, or, alternatively, that enforcement of the promises was barred by statutes of frauds, and there was insufficient evidence to support an estoppel to rely on a statute of frauds defense. In response, Flo argued that the evidence was sufficient to support her claims for breach of contract, and that the evidence established an *inter vivos* gift to her of all of Skip's property. In reply, the Estate argued inter alia that Flo's testimony and her actions in the wake of Skip's death negated any claim of a valid *inter vivos* transfer of any of Skip's assets.

The court determined that all of Skip's promises boiled down to an agreement to create a joint tenancy. When the court indicated that it was inclined to grant the motion for summary adjudication on the basis of this finding, and acknowledged that the Estate had not advanced an argument about joint tenancy until its reply brief on the motion, Flo requested an opportunity to submit further evidence and authorities on the point. The request was denied and the court proceeded to file its order on the motion.

* * *

The summary adjudication of Flo's claims cannot be sustained on the narrow grounds cited by the law and motion court. The ruling against Flo rested entirely on the finding of fact that she and Skip had an oral joint tenancy agreement, and the conclusion of law that equity does not allow for the enforcement of such an agreement. However, all of the promises and conduct in evidence cannot be characterized solely as an agreement for a joint tenancy, and to the extent that the agreements at issue are subject to a statute of frauds, there is a triable issue of fact as to whether the Estate is equitably estopped to assert the statute as a defense. The summary adjudication of Flo's claims must therefore be reversed.

* * *

In support of her creditor's claim in the probate proceeding, Flo declared that "at all times" she had "relied upon Skip's promises and his assurances that he would take care of me for the rest of my life." She submitted declarations from the Maffeis, and her niece and daughter, who likewise reported that Skip had said that he would take care of Flo for the rest of her life. Similar testimony was given in depositions after the rejection of the creditor's claim, and presented in opposition to the motion for summary adjudication. Skip's repeated promises to care for Flo for the rest of her life created a triable issue of fact as to the existence of a contract for her support.

Support agreements between cohabitants are enforceable under the *Marvin* case. (Marvin v. Marvin, *supra*, 18 Cal.3d at pp. 665, 674–675, 685, fn. 26; Friedman v. Friedman (1993) 20 Cal.App.4th 876, 889 [24 Cal.Rptr.2d 892]; Marvin v. Marvin (1981) 122 Cal.App.3d 871, 876 [176 Cal.Rptr. 555].) Skip's promise of support is indistinguishable from that of the defendant in *Marvin*, who allegedly "agreed to 'provide for all of plaintiff's financial support and needs for the rest of her life.'" (Marvin v. Marvin, *supra*, 18 Cal.3d at p. 666.) *Marvin* held that this agreement supported a cause of action for breach of an express contract (id. at pp. 667, 675), and there is no basis for a different conclusion in Flo's case. No issue is raised of any breach of contract on Flo's part. The record indicates that she fully performed the role of a loving spouse during all of the time they lived together.

A *Marvin* agreement is enforceable against an estate when one of the parties to the agreement dies. (See Estate of Fincher (1981) 119 Cal.App.3d 343, 348–350 [174 Cal.Rptr. 18]; Hogoboom & King, Cal. Practice Guide: Family Law 3 (The Rutter Group 1996) ¶ 20:55, p. 20-11, rev. #1, 1995.) There is no evidence that Skip breached his promise of support during his lifetime. To the contrary, it appears that Skip gave

Flo money to buy anything she needed and sought to provide her with a comfortable life while they lived together. Thus, Skip's caring for Flo during his lifetime is further evidence of the existence of a contract for support. However, the *estate* breached that contract by rejecting Flo's claim and thereby failing to provide her with means of support after Skip died. Accordingly, we conclude that it was error to grant the motion for summary adjudication of Flo's cause of action for "Damages for Failure to Pay Debt on Rejected Claim."

The Estate's various arguments with respect to Flo's case generally and her claim of support in particular do not alter this conclusion. The Estate's threshold contention is that, because Flo does not contest the outcome of the trial of her quantum meruit claim, she has waived any challenge to the grant of summary adjudication of her contract causes of action. This argument is premised on the assertion, advanced without authority, that Skip's various promises were not "severable." The Estate reasons that, because there was only one contract between Skip and Flo, and the finding after trial was that "the" contract did not exist, that finding precludes any recovery for breach of contract.

However, the claim that Skip agreed out of love and concern to care for Flo for the rest of her life is manifestly different from a claim that he had agreed to compensate her for the value of her services as if she had been his maid. As the Estate itself emphasized at the end of its closing argument at trial, "[t]he concept of quantum meruit is *not* some future I'll always be taken care [of]; it is payment for services rendered." A trier of fact could conclude that Skip had agreed to support Flo apart from any understanding about payment for her household services.

Skip's promises to care for Flo were likewise distinct from his statements about giving her his property, and those promises could be construed by a trier of fact as an agreement for support apart from any entitlement Flo might have to specific assets. Support and property division are separate issues in marital dissolutions (Fam. Code, §§ 2500 et seq., 4300 et seq.), and they are also separate issues for cohabitants. (See Marvin v. Marvin, *supra*, 18 Cal.3d at pp. 674–675 [distinguishing between agreement for support and agreement for sharing of property].) In granting summary adjudication, the court focused entirely on the evidence of Skip and Flo's property arrangement, and improperly ignored the evidence of a contract for Flo's support.

The Estate contends that the support claim must be rejected because it has been "newly-minted" to circumvent the summary adjudication ruling. However, while it is generally improper to assert a new theory for the first time on appeal, it is the Estate, not Flo, that has changed its position by arguing, contrary to its theory at trial, that all of Flo's contract claims were subsumed in her quantum meruit cause of action. Flo has asserted from the time she filed her creditor's claim that there was an agreement for her support, and although she has not specifically related the support agreement to the cause of action for rejection of her creditor's claim as we have done here, she has consistently and correctly maintained that the motion for summary adjudication could not be granted in light of that agreement. There are no grounds for concluding that Flo has waived her claim for support.

The Estate argues that the oral promise of support is not enforceable under Probate Code section 150, subdivision (a), which provides that a "contract to make a will or devise" must be in writing. However, this statute is inapplicable. An agreement for support, even for a lifetime, is by its terms neither a "contract to make a will," nor a contract to make a "devise," as that word is defined in the Probate Code to mean "a disposition of real or personal property by will." (Prob. Code, § 32.) No disposition by will was expressly agreed upon or necessarily implicit in the promise of support because Flo could have predeceased Skip, and in that event the contract could have been fully performed during Skip's lifetime. The fact that Skip died, and thus that the amounts owed were payable from his estate, did not transform the agreement into a promise to make a will or devise. If that were the result, then every contractual claim against an estate would involve a will or devise. * * *

The Estate contends that Skip's promises to Flo are too uncertain to enforce. However, "the modern trend of the law favors carrying out the parties' intention through the enforcement of contracts and disfavors holding them unenforceable because of uncertainty." (Hennefer v. Butcher (1986) 182 Cal.App.3d 492, 500 [227 Cal.Rptr. 318].) * * * Marvin endorsed "a policy based upon the fulfillment of the reasonable expectations of the parties to a nonmarital relationship." (Marvin v. Marvin, supra, 18 Cal.3d at p. 684.) If Flo's evidence is credited, as it must be for purposes of summary adjudication (Waisbren v. Peppercorn Productions, Inc. (1995) 41 Cal.App.4th 246, 252 [48 Cal.Rptr.2d 437]), then it is certain that Skip expected to provide for Flo's support. Denial of that expectation as a matter of law would be contrary to the policy enunciated in Marvin. Moreover, as Flo observes, her understandings with Skip were no more uncertain than the "general and nonspecific" Marvin agreement which was enforced in Alderson v. Alderson (1986) 180 Cal.App.3d 450, 463 [225 Cal.Rptr. 610], where "[t]he parties never bothered to actually spell out the terms of their agreement or the consideration therefor."

It is unclear how much support Skip intended by his promises to take care of Flo, but uncertainty about "'the precise act . . . to be done'" may be resolved in light of extrinsic evidence. (Crescenta Valley Moose Lodge v. Bunt (1970) 8 Cal.App.3d 682, 689 [87 Cal.Rptr. 428].) Flo received about $96,500 from Skip's retirement benefits, and she has testified that Skip told her "'I'm putting you down as beneficiary on my retirement because I want to take care of you.'" Based on this evidence, the Estate can argue that Flo has already been "taken care of" in the manner Skip intended. On the other hand, Skip provided Flo with a certain standard of living before he died, which included a rent-free residence and money to cover all of her other needs. Flo could argue on the basis of that conduct for a level of support consistent with the lifestyle she and Skip had enjoyed. Flo could also argue for all or half of Skip's assets by way of support, based on his statements to her "that he was able to retire early because he was very careful in what he did [with his money], and that I didn't have to worry about retiring because what he had would take care of us for the rest of both of our lives, that we would not be limited, that we would be able to not go overboard, but do things that we would enjoy doing together."

These conflicting interpretations and any others supported by reasonable inferences from the evidence must be resolved by a trier of fact. "The fundamental goal
of contractual interpretation is to give effect to the mutual intention of the parties"
(Bank of the West v. Superior Court (1992) 2 Cal.4th 1254, 1264 [10 Cal.Rptr.2d 538,
833 P.2d 545]), and "questions of 'intent' and 'purpose' are ordinarily questions of
fact" (Redke v. Silvertrust (1971) 6 Cal.3d 94, 103 [98 Cal.Rptr. 293, 490 P.2d 805]).
Where, as here, the agreement is reasonably susceptible of different interpretations,
summary adjudication is an inappropriate means of resolving the ambiguity. (See
Walsh v. Walsh (1941) 18 Cal.2d 439, 444 [116 P.2d 62]; Faus v. Pacific Elec. Ry. Co.
(1960) 187 Cal.App.2d 563, 570 [9 Cal.Rptr. 697]; see also Castaneda v. Dura-Vent
Corp. (9th Cir. 1981) 648 F.2d 612, 619.) * * * The judgment on the cause of action
based on the rejection of Flo's creditor's claim must therefore be reversed.

* * *

Equitable estoppel to rely on a statute of frauds is certainly a question of fact in
Flo's case. Flo has stated that she relied on Skip's assurances that she would receive his
property and that he would document this understanding. The reliance supporting
an equitable estoppel need not necessarily be reliance on representations that a writing will be executed (Monarco v. Lo Greco, *supra*, 35 Cal.2d at pp. 625–626), but Flo's
evidence that she relied on such representations constitutes a classic case for application of the doctrine. (See Wilk v. Vencill (1947) 30 Cal.2d 104, 107 [180 P.2d 351]; 5
Witkin, Cal. Procedure (4th ed. 1997) Pleading, § 743, p. 200.) A trier of fact could
find that Flo had "seriously" changed her position in reliance on Skip's promises by
moving in with him, performing the duties of a spouse, and retiring from her job at
his insistence. (See Porporato v. Devincenzi (1968) 261 Cal.App.2d 670, 673, 678–679
[68 Cal.Rptr. 210] [in reliance on decedent's oral promise to devise home to plaintiff,
plaintiff remained in San Francisco and did not seek employment].) A trier of fact
could also conclude that Flo would be "unconscionably" injured, under the circumstances, if the lack of a writing precluded any recovery. (Id. at p. 679.) Since equitable
estoppel is a triable issue of fact in Flo's case, it was error to summarily adjudicate her
claim for damages for breach of the property agreement.

The law and motion court could reach a contrary result only by first construing
the property agreement to be for the creation of a joint tenancy, and then applying Estate of Seibert (1990) 226 Cal.App.3d 338 [276 Cal.Rptr. 508], which holds
that joint tenancy agreements are not subject to the doctrine of equitable estoppel.
The *Seibert* court found no case which had applied the doctrine to a joint tenancy,
and concluded on that basis alone that the writing requirement for joint tenancies
constituted "a more formidable 'statute of frauds' than the ordinary requirement
pertaining to contracts having to do with real property." (Id. at p. 343.)

Seibert's reasoning is unpersuasive for a number of reasons. First, we fail to see
why an agreement for a joint tenancy in real property should be treated differently
for equitable purposes than any other conveyance of land, and the court does not
explain the distinction. Second, it is not true that there is no precedent for equitable enforcement of an unwritten joint tenancy. While we have not undertaken

an exhaustive survey of the subject, we have found at least one case in which an implied contract for a joint tenancy in real property was enforced on the basis of an equitable estoppel. (See Grant v. Long (1939) 33 Cal.App.2d 725, 739–742 [92 P.2d 940].) Third, even if there were no precedent for application of equitable estoppel in connection with a joint tenancy, that alone would not be a sufficient reason to conclude that the doctrine could not be so applied. Equitable estoppel is a "firmly rooted legal principle in this state" (Juran v. Epstein (1994) 23 Cal.App.4th 882, 894 [28 Cal.Rptr.2d 588]), which generally applies to *all* statutes of frauds. (Phillippe v. Shapell Industries, *supra*, 43 Cal.3d at pp. 1272–1273 (dis. opn. of Kaufman, J.); Hall v. Hall (1990) 222 Cal.App.3d 578, 585 [271 Cal.Rptr. 773].) Exceptions to this general rule may be drawn on the basis of a substantial public policy (Phillippe v. Shapell Industries, *supra*, at pp. 1265–1269 [consumer protection statute]) or a clear directive from the Legislature (see Juran v. Epstein, *supra*, at p. 896). However, neither of these grounds for an exception is identified in *Seibert*, and it is not apparent that either applies to joint tenancies.

The absence of an enforceable joint tenancy would not be fatal to Flo's claim for damages for breach of the property agreement in any event. As we have noted, joint tenancy is only one of several means by which Skip could have effected his promise to give Flo his property. It is not clear that Skip had resolved to employ a joint tenancy. Skip and Flo did not use the words "joint tenancy" to describe their property agreement, Skip did not have any particular form of agreement drawn up, and it appears from his statements shortly before his death that he may have been more inclined to use a trust than a joint tenancy. The evidence was at least susceptible of different interpretations, and did not support the court's finding as a matter of law that the agreement was for a joint tenancy. Indeed, a different finding was compelled under the court's reasoning.

"A contract must receive such an interpretation as will make it lawful, operative, definite, reasonable, and capable of being carried into effect, if it can be done without violating the intention of the parties." (Civ. Code, § 1643.) Thus, "[i]t is a fundamental rule of contractual construction that where two interpretations are reasonably permissible, courts will adopt that which renders a contract valid and effectual." (Service Employees Internat. Union, Local 18 v. American Building Maintenance Co. (1972) 29 Cal.App.3d 356, 359 [105 Cal.Rptr. 564].) While there may be little precedent for the use of equitable estoppel to enforce an oral joint tenancy, it is settled that the doctrine may be employed to enforce an oral trust in land where the beneficiary has "irrevocably change[d] his position in reliance upon the trust." (Rest.2d Trusts, § 50; see Jose v. Pacific Tile & Porcelain Co. (1967) 251 Cal. App.2d 141, 144–145 [58 Cal.Rptr. 880]; Mulli v. Mulli (1951) 105 Cal.App.2d 68, 73 [232 P.2d 556]; Haskell v. First Nat. Bank (1939) 33 Cal.App.2d 399, 402 [91 P.2d 934].) Thus, there is no question that if Skip intended to put his property in trust, Flo would have a triable claim to an estoppel against a statute of frauds defense.

Insofar as it appears from the evidence, Skip could just as well have intended to use a trust as a joint tenancy. Both interpretations are "reasonably permissible." If an oral joint tenancy were in fact absolutely unenforceable, then the rule of construction in favor of enforcement would dictate that the contract be interpreted to be for the creation of a trust, rather than a joint tenancy. * * * Such an interpretation would not "violate" Skip's intentions. According to Flo's evidence, he would have wanted her to have a chance to enforce their property agreement.

The evidence, in sum, cannot properly be construed so as to negate a claim to damages for breach of the property agreement on a theory of equitable estoppel. There are two triable issues of fact: (1) whether there was such an agreement; and (2) whether Flo should be allowed to enforce it through equitable estoppel. The form of the arrangement Skip may have intended—joint tenancy, will, or trust—is irrelevant.

The Estate contends finally that Flo cannot establish an estoppel because she fulfilled her part of the bargain with Skip out of love for him and not just out of a desire for his property. This argument is premised on a statement in the *Seibert* case that, in order to enforce "a joint tenancy commitment through estoppel . . . [the plaintiff] would be required to demonstrate not only that she relied upon the alleged promise from the decedent, but that she entered into acts or performance which was 'not only referable, but unequivocally [*sic*] referable, to the particular oral agreement sought to be enforced.'" (Estate of Seibert, *supra*, 226 Cal.App.3d at p. 343.) *Seibert* reasoned that estoppel could not be invoked in that case because the actions taken by the plaintiff in alleged reliance on her oral joint tenancy agreement with the decedent could "just as easily [have been] explained by her renewed interest in him generally, resulting from their resumption of a conjugal relationship." (*Ibid.*) Since it is undisputed that Flo performed her part of the agreement with Skip because she loved him and not solely because she wanted his property, the Estate submits that *Seibert*'s reasoning precludes any finding of estoppel in Flo's case.

However, *Seibert* is insupportable insofar as it suggests that equitable estoppel must be predicated on "performance 'unequivocally referable' to the contract." This portion of *Seibert* conflates the doctrines of equitable estoppel and part performance. When a plaintiff seeks to avoid a statute of frauds on the ground of part performance, it has sometimes been said that the performance must be "unequivocally referable" to the agreement to be enforced. (See Note, Part Performance, Estoppel, and the California Statute of Frauds (1951) 3 Stan.L.Rev. 281, 286.) "It is doubtful that acts are ever unequivocally referable to a contract," and this requirement has not been consistently applied even in part performance cases. (*Ibid.*) The doctrines of part performance and equitable estoppel are, in any event, separate grounds for avoiding a statute of frauds. (Id. at pp. 281–283; see, *e.g.*, Paul v. Layne & Bowler Corp., *supra*, 9 Cal.2d at pp. 564–565 [considering, in turn, part performance and equitable estoppel].) *Seibert* itself, prior to the passage at issue, referred to "cases establishing part performance *and* detrimental reliance as grounds for enforcing an oral agreement." (Estate of Seibert, *supra*, 226 Cal.App.3d at p. 342, italics added.) The sole authority cited by *Seibert* in support of its analysis, 35 California Jurisprudence Third, Frauds, Statute of, §85, pages 121–122, concerns part performance, not equitable estoppel (as to the latter, see 35 Cal.Jur.3d, *supra*, § 95 et seq., p. 134 et seq.). Equitable estoppel is a broader doctrine than part performance. (Note, *supra*, 3 Stan.L.Rev. at p. 297.) All that is required for an equitable estoppel is a "serious" change of position and "unconscionable" injury. (Monarco v. Lo Greco, *supra*, 35 Cal.2d at p. 623.) Performance unequivocally referable to the agreement is not an indispensable part of the equation. (See Carlson v. Richardson, *supra*, 267 Cal. App.2d at pp. 208–209.)

If such a requirement were engrafted onto the equitable estoppel doctrine, then the doctrine would be abrogated in the context of *Marvin* agreements, because the sentiments which led the parties to cohabit would prevent a finding that their actions toward each other were motivated solely by their property agreements. *Marvin* noted that most cohabitation agreements are oral, and that cases had "expressly rejected defenses [to such agreements] grounded upon the statute of frauds." (Marvin v. Marvin, *supra*, 18 Cal.3d at p. 674, fn. 9, citing Cline v. Festersen (1954) 128 Cal. App.2d 380, 386–387 [275 P.2d 149] [equitable estoppel prevented reliance on statute of frauds].) In light of *Marvin*'s endorsement of "equitable remedies to protect the expectations of the parties to a nonmarital relationship" (Marvin v. Marvin, *supra*, at p. 684, fn. 25), the court's observations on the enforcement of oral cohabitation agreements can only be interpreted as an approval of the use of equitable estoppel by cohabitants in appropriate cases. Love does not vitiate Flo's equitable estoppel claim.

* * *

Flo's causes of action for declaratory relief, specific performance, constructive trust, and injunctive relief are also viable. * * *

Marvin held that rights under a cohabitation agreement may be established by way of an action for declaratory relief. (Marvin v. Marvin, *supra*, 18 Cal.3d at p. 675.)

Flo may properly elect to pursue specific performance of the property agreement with respect to assets such as the residence and family heirlooms for which damages may be an inadequate remedy. (Civ. Code, § 3387 [real property]; Rest.2d Contracts, § 360, com. b, at pp. 171–172 [personal property with sentimental value].) Since performance by Skip cannot be compelled, the action is one for "quasi-specific" performance. (See Porporato v. Devincenzi, *supra*, 261 Cal.App.2d at p. 674.) Such an action requires: (1) a contract that is sufficiently definite to be enforced; (2) a contract that is just and reasonable; (3) performance by the plaintiff; (4) failure to perform by the defendant; (5) adequate consideration; (6) an inadequate legal remedy; and (7) if the contract is oral and subject to a statute of frauds, a means such as estoppel of avoiding the statute. (Id. at pp. 674–675.) A trier of fact could find that all of these elements are present in Flo's case. Proof of a *Marvin* agreement for an interest in property contrary to record title must be made by "clear and convincing" evidence. (Tannehill v. Finch (1986) 188 Cal.App.3d 224, 228 [232 Cal.Rptr. 749].) A trial is needed to determine whether evidence of the property agreement in Flo's case is "sufficiently strong to command the unhesitating assent of every reasonable mind." (*Ibid.* [internal quotation marks omitted].)

A constructive trust can be imposed on the estate's assets to provide for quasi-specific performance of the property agreement. (Estate of Brenzikofer (1996) 49 Cal.App.4th 1461, 1466–1467 [57 Cal.Rptr.2d 401]; Porporato v. Devincenzi, *supra*, 261 Cal.App.2d at p. 674.)

Distribution under the will can be enjoined pending the trial of Flo's claims. (Estate of Anderson (1977) 68 Cal.App.3d 1010, 1016 [137 Cal.Rptr. 727]; Estate of Murphy (1964) 225 Cal.App.2d 224, 229 [37 Cal.Rptr. 205].)

The judgment against Flo for rent based on her occupancy of the home after Skip's death must be reversed pending the trial of her entitlement to that property.

* * *

The judgment against appellant on the quantum meruit cause of action is affirmed. The balance of the judgment is reversed. Appellant shall recover her costs on appeal.

Anderson, P. J., and Poché, J., concurred.

[Respondents' petition for review by the Supreme Court was denied May 28, 1997.]

Notes

At the death of a spouse, the surviving spouse has significant federal and state benefits under intestacy, testacy, and any election against will substitutes. Plus a lawful spouse has a preferred tax status and has a right to support, homestead, and automatic standing to contest any will. Courts are reluctant to encroach upon these and other spousal statutory entitlements, even if the equities of a factual situation are compelling. Likewise, if dissolution of the nonmarital cohabitation occurs during the lifetime of both parties, courts are reluctant to apply marital classifications to nonmarital cohabitants when dividing property acquired during the union.

One exception, occurring at death, is illustrated by the Supreme Court of Washington in Olver v. Fowler, 168 P.3d 348 (Wash. 2007). The facts involved a couple who lived together for fourteen years and had two children together, yet they never officially married. Both partners and one of their children were killed simultaneously in an automobile accident, leaving one child surviving. Everything the couple owned was titled in the name of one of the partners, but state intestate statutes controlled the disposition of all their jointly acquired property. The administrator of the estate of the partner, in whose name nothing was titled, sued the estate of the other in equity, arguing that the property acquired during the partner's union should be considered as marital property and apportioned accordingly, since each party owned fifty percent in accordance with Washington community property standards. A majority of the Washington court agreed with the petitioner's argument and held accordingly, but there was a strong dissent that argued equitable division should only be available to nonmarital cohabitants at an *inter vivos* dissolution, not at death. For discussion, see Michael T. Flannery, *The Division of Assets*

Owned by Decedents Who Were Engaged in a "Committed Intimate Relationship": Olver v. Fowler. LexisNexis Expert Commentary (Apr. 2008).

When faced with facts similar to the Washington decision, in Matter of Estate of Hatten, 440 P.3d 245 (Alaska 2019), the Supreme Court of Alaska held that because Alaska is a common law state, unlike Washington, which is a community property state, ownership in property occurs at death and not during lifetime. Therefore, the property acquired by nonmarital cohabitants during lifetime creates no interest in anyone other than the title holder. Therefore, because ownership is established at death only, the state's intestate and testate laws apply, and it is not within the jurisdiction of the courts to modify the plain language of state legislation. Alaska's probate statutes make no provision for nonmarital cohabitants, therefore, a nonmarital cohabitant does not qualify as an heir, no matter how long the cohabitation occurred.

Problem

Plaintiff and defendant lived together for about ten years, sharing an intimate relationship. During that time, the plaintiff took care of their child and, at times, the defendant's child from a previous relationship. In addition, the plaintiff regularly maintained the home and contributed financially by performing one of the defendant's daily newspaper delivery routes. While the plaintiff took care of the children and the home, the defendant had the time to develop his water softener business. From the income generated through the defendant's employment, the defendant purchased a home and furnishings and titled it in the defendant's name alone. Nonetheless, the parties referred to the property acquired during their cohabitation as "ours" and treated it as such. Although it is true that the plaintiff benefited from the resources and the home provided by the defendant, the defendant substantially benefited from the services provided by the plaintiff throughout their ten year relationship.

Shortly after their ten year anniversary, the defendant ordered the plaintiff from the home and provided no financial support thereafter. The couple never married and never executed a written agreement stipulating provisions for support or division of property. In a suit by the plaintiff against the defendant for support and division of property acquired during the ten year relationship, how would you formulate an argument on the plaintiff's behalf? *See* Turner v. Freed, 792 N.E.2d 947 (Ind. Ct. App. 2003).

B. Relatives by the Half-Blood

In the age of increasing numbers of divorce and remarriage, the possibility of relatives by the half-blood increases as well. For example, suppose Joe and Lisa marry and have three children. Then Lisa dies or divorces Joe. Joe is left to raise the children by himself until he meets Patty. Joe and Patty marry and they have two children, Michael and Rachel. Joe and Patty have no additional children. The five children—three from Joe's first marriage and two from his second marriage—grow up to treat each other as members of the same family; each has the same name, each is on the same insurance policy, and each is treated as a sibling at school, although Patty never adopted the three children from Joe's marriage to Lisa. If both Joe and Patty are killed in an automobile accident and they are survived by all five children, the inheritance statutes would treat Joe as being survived by five children because all five of the children were his. But Patty would be survived by only two children because the other three are legally the children of Lisa. What if Michael or Rachel should die a year later without any spouse, issue, or parent surviving? The intestate estate would have to be divided among the siblings. Would it make a difference that Michael and Rachel had *two* parents in common and either of them had only *one* parent in common with the other three siblings? Michael and Rachel would be half-bloods to the other three children but whole bloods to each other.

The Uniform Probate Code makes no distinction between half and whole bloods. Thus, if Michael died and was survived by his sister, Rachel, and the other three children of Joe and Lisa, with whom he had only one common parent, each of the survivors would take a fourth of his estate. Just because Rachel and Michael were related by the whole blood, Rachel would take no greater amount from the estate than would the half-bloods. *See* Unif. Prob. Code § 2-107 (2018) (providing that relatives of the half-blood inherit the same share they would inherit if they were of the whole blood). But some states provide that whole blood siblings take twice as much as half-blood siblings. *See, e.g.,* Va. Code Ann. § 64.2-202 (2019) ("Collaterals of the half blood shall inherit only half as much as those of the whole blood."); Fla. Stat. § 732.105 (2019) (half blood kindreds inherit only half as much as those of the whole blood). *See generally* Ralph Calhoun Brashier, *Half-Bloods, Inheritance, and Family*, 37 U. Mem. L. Rev. 215 (2007).

C. Relatives by Adoption

1. Statutory Stranger Adoption

During ancient times—for Greeks, Persians, and Romans—adoptions were meant to satisfy the needs of the adopting party, usually to provide for inheritance of title or wealth. But currently adoptions in the United States seek to provide for the best interest of the adoptee, usually a child in need of a permanent relationship. All of the American states have adoption statutes, making the process entirely statutory; the requirements of the statutes are mandatory to effectively adopt a child. *See, e.g.,* Brown v. Harper, 761 S.E.2d 779 (S.C. Ct. App. 2014), *aff'd*, 766 S.E.2d 375 (S.C. 2014) (holding that state's long history of strict construction of adoption statutes could not be cured through substantial compliance). The Constitution requires each state to give Full Faith and Credit to any final adoption judgement of another state's court, regardless of the reasoning underlying the judgement, as long as that state court has proper jurisdiction to decide the matter. *See* V.L. v. E.L., 136 S. Ct. 1017, 1020 (2016); Sanders v. Yanez, 190 Cal. Rptr. 3d 495 (Cal. Ct. App. 2015) (holding that adoption of adult in another state was entitled to recognition in California even though rights and duties under California law would be less expansive).

There is no common law adoption, although many states employ an equity device called "equitable adoption" or "virtual adoption." But it is important to note that this is not strictly adoption as that term is officially used, but rather a process of doing equity so that a person can receive an intestate share from an "equitable parent" under certain conditions. *See, e.g., In re* Marriage of Mancine, 9 N.E.3d 550 (Ill. Ct. App. 2014) (holding that equitable adoption is a concept in probate to determine inheritance and has no application in the context of statutory adoption). Equitable adoption will be discussed, *infra*.

Statutory adoption occurs through a two-step process. The first step is the termination of the birth parent's parental rights in his or her child through the parent's surrender of the child, the involuntary termination of the parent's rights because of abuse, neglect, or abandonment, or because termination of the parent's rights is necessary to avoid detriment to the child. Once termination of the biological parent's rights occurs, the second step is for the state to recognize a new parent-child relationship with the adoptive parent or parents. In the not-too-distant past, the state would issue the child a new birth certificate and seal the record of the adoption so that the child and the birth parent would be deprived of future contact. This process was done to promote the child's best interest, permitting the child to grow up in a new household, free from the interference of the birth parents. Nonetheless, during the latter part of the last century, there arose a movement fostering "open adoption." Adopted persons argued that they were a stigmatized group because only they were forbidden to view records surrounding their births; advances in health care techniques strengthened their arguments, permitting them to view their adoption records. States began enacting legislation permitting access, and at least half of the states have some form of registry that permits persons directly involved in an adoption to solicit information concerning their birth. *See* Joan H. Hollinger, *Aftermath of Adoption: Legal and Social Consequences*, in 2 ADOPTION LAW AND PRACTICE 13–35 (Joan Heifetz Hollinger, ed. Matthew Bender, 1998). Some states provide that, if an adopted person requests birth records, the state will search for the birth parents and request their consent to release the records. If the birth parents do not consent, then the adopted person may still petition the court to open the adoption records. But there are still restraints on an adoptee's right to information in a sealed adoption record. *See, e.g., In re* Adoption of S.J.D., 641 N.W.2d 794 (Iowa 2002) (holding that an adult adoptee's right to free speech does not include the right to receive private information absent statutory good cause).

Uniform Probate Code (2019)

§ 2-116. Effect of Parent-Child Relationship.

Except as otherwise provided in Section 2-119(b) through (e), if a parent-child relationship exists or is established under this [subpart], the parent is a parent of the child and the child is a child of the parent for the purpose of intestate succession.

§ 2-117. No Distinction on Marital Status.

Except as otherwise provided in Section 2-114, 2-119, 2-120, or 2-121, a parent-child relationship exists between a child and the child's genetic parents, regardless of the parents' marital status.

§ 2-118. Adoptee and Adoptee's Adoptive Parent or Parents.

(a) [Parent-Child Relationship Between Adoptee and Adoptive Parent or Parents.] A parent-child relationship exists between an adoptee and the adoptee's adoptive parent or parents.

(b) [Individual in Process of Being Adopted by Married Couple; Stepchild in Process of Being Adopted by Stepparent.] For purposes of subsection (a):

(1) an individual who is in the process of being adopted by a married couple when one of the spouses dies is treated as adopted by the deceased spouse if the adoption is subsequently granted to the decedent's surviving spouse; and

(2) a child of a genetic parent who is in the process of being adopted by a genetic parent's spouse when the spouse dies is treated as adopted by the deceased spouse if the genetic parent survives the deceased spouse by 120 hours.

* * *

§ 2-119. Adoptee and Adoptee's Genetic Parents.

(a) [Parent-Child Relationship Between Adoptee and Genetic Parent.] Except as otherwise provided in subsections (b) through (e), a parent-child relationship does not exist between an adoptee and the adoptee's genetic parents.

* * *

(c) [Individual Adopted by a Relative of a Genetic Parent.] A parent-child relationship exists between both genetic parents and an individual who is adopted by a relative of a genetic parent, or by the spouse or surviving spouse of a relative of a genetic parent, but only for the purpose of the right of the adoptee or a descendant of the adoptee to inherit from or through either genetic parent.

(d) [Individual Adopted After Death of Both Genetic Parents.] a parent-child relationship exists between both genetic parents and an individual who is adopted after the death of both genetic parents, but only for the purpose of the right of the adoptee or a descendant of the adoptee to inherit through either genetic parent.

* * *

Virginia Code Annotated (2019)

§ 63.2-1243. Adoption of certain persons eighteen years of age or over.

A petition may be filed in circuit court by any natural person who is a resident of this Commonwealth

(i) for the adoption of a stepchild eighteen years of age or over to whom he has stood in loco parentis for a period of at least three months;

(ii) for the adoption of a close relative, as defined in § 63.2-1242.1, eighteen years of age or older;

(iii) for the adoption of any person eighteen years of age or older who is the birth child of the petitioner or who had resided in the home of the petitioner for a period of at least three months prior to becoming eighteen years of age; or

(iv) for the adoption of any person eighteen years of age or older, for good cause shown, provided that the person to be adopted is at least fifteen years younger than the petitioner and the petitioner and the person to be adopted have known each other for at least one year prior to the filing of the petition for adoption.

Proceedings in any such case shall conform as near as may be to proceedings for the adoption of a minor child under this chapter except that:

(a) No consent of either parent shall be required; and

(b) The consent of the person to be adopted shall be required in all cases.

Any interlocutory or final order issued in any case under this section shall have the same effect as other orders issued under this chapter; and in any such case the word "child" in any other section of this chapter shall be construed to refer to the person whose adoption is petitioned for under this section. The entry of a final order of adoption pursuant to this section which incorporates a change of name shall be deemed to meet the requirements of § 8.01-217.

Monty S. v. Jason W.

Supreme Court of Nebraska, 2015
290 Neb. 1048, 863 N.W.2d 484

HEAVICAN, C.J.

Teresa S. gave birth to an infant son in July 2013. Two days later, Teresa and Monty S., Teresa's husband and the child's biological father, each signed a consent and relinquishment, indicating that each gave up any parental rights to the child and further that they consented to the child's adoption by Jason W. and Rebecca W. . . . Teresa and Monty subsequently filed a motion for habeas corpus seeking return of the child. The couple alleged that the consents and relinquishments they signed were invalid. Following a trial, the district court concluded, on grounds not argued by Teresa and Monty, that their consents and relinquishments were invalid. Rebecca and Jason appeal. We affirm. . . .

The parties in this case were friends. Rebecca was unable to have children, and a foster child that had been placed with Rebecca and Jason had been moved to a placement with biological relatives. Teresa and Monty "felt sorry" for Rebecca and discussed the possibility that Teresa might serve as a surrogate for the couple. Rebecca and Jason ultimately agreed, and it was decided that Teresa and Monty would conceive a child and, at the time of its birth, give that child to Rebecca and Jason for private placement adoption.

The parties agree that from the beginning, and certainly throughout Teresa's pregnancy and the days immediately following the child's birth, the intent was that Teresa and Monty would be a part of the child's life. The parties mostly agree that no discussions beyond this general agreement took place; it was an understanding, and not a detailed plan, that a relationship would exist. . . . Teresa testified that in her view, an "open" adoption was one in which the "adoptive parents [were] open to allowing the biological parents to be a part of his life and that his records would never be sealed." The record suggests that this was the general definition of the term as understood by all the parties. . . . Monty testified that he and Teresa were not informed that "open" adoptions were essentially unenforceable in Nebraska. This was confirmed by the testimony of the attorney conducting the meeting, as well as by Rebecca and Jason. Teresa and Monty also testified that had they known that they would not be able to maintain contact with the child, they would not have signed the relinquishment forms.

Teresa gave birth to the child in July 2013. The child went to Rebecca and Jason's home from the hospital. Two days after the child's birth, both couples and the child rode together to a meeting at the office of Rebecca and Jason's attorney. During that meeting, Teresa and Monty each signed separate documents relinquishing their parental rights and consenting to the adoption by Rebecca and Jason. At this meeting, Rebecca tore up the nonconsent forms presented to Teresa and Monty and announced that they were unnecessary because the adoption was to be "open." Nonconsent forms are signed by biological parents to signify the intent that adoption records be sealed. Where the forms are not signed, such records are not sealed.

On May 12, 2014, Teresa and Monty filed a petition for habeas corpus, seeking return of the child. Teresa and Monty alleged that their consents and relinquishments were invalid for a number of reasons, including fraud, duress, and the failure to present the nonconsent adoption forms prior to signing the relinquishments. . . . The district court rejected all of Teresa and Monty's allegations. Nevertheless, relying upon McCormick v. State,[1] the district court invalidated the relinquishments, concluding that the parties' plan for an "open" adoption invalidated the relinquishments as conditioned upon the retention of some parental rights. . . . Following a best interests hearing, custody of the child was placed with Teresa and Monty. Rebecca and Jason appeal. . . . On appeal, Rebecca and Jason assign, reordered, that the district court erred in (1) excluding evidence of post relinquishment visits by Teresa and Monty and why those visits were discontinued and (2) holding that the consents were conditioned upon the retention of parental rights and were therefore invalid. . . .

---

1. *McCormick v. State*, 218 Neb. 338, 354 N.W.2d 160 (1984).

A decision in a habeas corpus case involving custody of a child is reviewed by an appellate court de novo on the record.[2] The burden is on the natural parent challenging the validity of a relinquishment of a child for adoption to prove that the relinquishment was not voluntarily given.[3] In the absence of threats, coercion, fraud, or duress, a properly executed relinquishment of parental rights and consent to adoption signed by a natural parent knowingly, intelligently, and voluntarily is valid[4]. . . .

We first turn to Rebecca and Jason's contention that the district court erred in not admitting certain evidence of the reasons why Rebecca and Jason ceased to allow Teresa and Monty visitation with the child. That evidence generally showed that Rebecca and Jason initially had the full intent of allowing Teresa and Monty to be a part of the child's life until Teresa's visits became so frequent that they began to interfere with Rebecca and Jason's relationships with the child. . . . Assuming without deciding that this evidence was relevant to Rebecca and Jason's defense that their actions did not amount to fraud or misrepresentation, and thus should have been admitted, we find any such error to be harmless. In fact, the district court did not find any fraud or misrepresentation in the signing of the relinquishments. Rather, it found that the open adoption agreement itself acted as coercion and invalidated the relinquishments. Because Rebecca and Jason prevailed on the fraud and misrepresentation issues, they suffered no prejudice by the failure of the district court to admit this evidence. . . . There is no merit to this assignment of error. . . .

We now turn to whether the relinquishments in this case were invalid. This case presents a private adoption. In this situation, the child is relinquished directly into the hands of the prospective adoptive parents without interference by the state or a private agency[5]. . . . A natural parent who relinquishes his or her rights to a child by a valid written instrument gives up all rights to the child at the time of the relinquishment.[6] A valid relinquishment is irrevocable.[7] The only right retained by the natural parents is the "right to commence an action seeking . . . to be considered as a prospective parent if the best interests of the child so dictate. The natural parent's rights are no longer superior to those of the prospective adoptive family."[8] . . . Where the relinquishment of rights by a natural parent is found to be invalid for any reason, a best interests hearing is nevertheless held: "The court shall not simply return the child to the natural parent upon a finding that the relinquishment was not a valid instrument."[9] . . . Such relinquishments are generally upheld. We have held repeatedly that a change of attitude subsequent to signing a relinquishment

---

2. *Brett M. v. Vesely*, 276 Neb. 765, 757 N.W.2d 360 (2008).
3. *Hohndorf v. Watson*, 240 Neb. 368, 482 N.W.2d 241 (1992).
4. *Id.*
5. *Yopp v. Batt*, 237 Neb. 779, 467 N.W.2d 868 (1991).
6. *Id.*
7. *Id.*
8. *Id.* at 791, 467 N.W.2d at 877.
9. *Id.* at 791–92, 467 N.W.2d at 878.

is insufficient to invalidate the relinquishment.[10] Rather, as we noted above, in the absence of threats, coercion, fraud, or duress, a properly executed relinquishment of parental rights and consent to adoption signed by a natural parent knowingly, intelligently, and voluntarily is valid.[11]

Neb.Rev.Stat. § 43-111 (Reissue 2008) provides that after a decree of adoption has been entered in a private adoption case, the natural parents of an adopted child shall be relieved of all parental duties and responsibilities for the child and shall have no rights over the child. . . . In this case, the district court explicitly found that there were no threats, fraud, or duress involved in the execution of Teresa and Monty's relinquishments. But the district court, relying on this court's decision in McCormick v. State,[12] concluded that the relinquishments were conditioned upon the retention of some parental rights and were therefore invalid. . . . *McCormick* involved the parental rights of Richard and Joan McCormick to their son. The State had filed for termination of those rights. Just prior to the final hearing on the State's motion to terminate, a meeting took place between the McCormicks, their counsel, the guardian ad litem, and their caseworker. It was explained to the McCormicks that if they signed a relinquishment of their parental rights, there was a possibility that an "open" adoption could be arranged if cooperative adoptive parents were found. This idea was originally suggested by the caseworker. The McCormicks were told by their counsel that it was likely the court would terminate their parental rights if the hearing were held.

The McCormicks signed the relinquishments. Despite the conversation regarding the "open" adoption, the McCormicks were not permitted visitation with their son after they signed the relinquishments. The McCormicks filed a motion for a writ of habeas corpus, which was denied. The McCormicks appealed. The court found that the McCormicks' relinquishments were coerced by the promise of the open adoption. We noted that "[a] relinquishment conditioned upon the retention of some parental rights is invalid."[13] . . . *McCormick* was decided in 1984. By 1988, the Legislature had passed 1988 Neb. Laws, L.B. 301, which provided for exchange-of-information contracts in cases involving children in temporary foster care. The legislative intent states:

> The Legislature finds that there are children in temporary foster care situations who would benefit from the stability of adoption. It is the intent of the Legislature that such situations be accommodated through the use of adoptions involving exchange-of-information contracts between the department and the adoptive or biological parent or parents.[14]

---

10. *Yopp v. Batt, supra* note 5.
11. *Id.*
12. *McCormick v. State, supra* note 1.
13. *Id.* at 344, 354 N.W.2d at 163.
14. Neb. Rev. Stat. § 43-155 (Reissue 2008).

An exchange-of-information contract is defined by statute as a "two-year, renewable obligation, voluntarily agreed to and signed by both the adoptive and biological parent or parents as well as the department."[15] And Neb.Rev.Stat. § 43-158 (Reissue 2008) provides:

> When the department determines that an adoption involving exchange of information would serve a child's best interests, it may enter into agreements with the child's proposed adoptive parent or parents for the exchange of information. The nature of the information promised to be provided shall be specified in an exchange-of-information contract and may include, but shall not be limited to, letters by the adoptive parent or parents at specified intervals providing information regarding the child's development or photographs of the child at specified intervals. . . . Nothing in [these] sections . . . shall be interpreted to preclude or allow court-ordered parenting time, visitation, or other access with the child and the biological parent or parents.

Neb.Rev.Stat. § 43-160 (Reissue 2008), also enacted by L.B. 301, seems directed at this court's decision in *McCormick*: "The existence of any agreement or agreements of the kind specified in section 43-158 shall not operate to impair the validity of any relinquishment or any decree of adoption entered by a court of the State of Nebraska."

By 1993, the exchange-of-information contract had been supplemented with the communication or contact agreement set forth in Neb.Rev.Stat. § 43-162 (Reissue 2008). That section provides:

> The prospective adoptive parent or parents and the birth parent or parents of a prospective adoptee may enter into an agreement regarding communication or contact after the adoption between or among the prospective adoptee and his or her birth parent or parents if the prospective adoptee is in the custody of the Department of Health and Human Services. Any such agreement shall not be enforceable unless approved by the court pursuant to section 43-163.

While there is not a single definition of an "open" adoption, in our view, it is clear that these statutorily-provided-for agreements would fit within the general understanding of such an adoption. . . . The enactment of the exchange-of-information contracts and communication or contact agreements shows us that the Legislature clearly responded to this court's decision in *McCormick*. However, it did so in a limited way: as is noted above, these contracts are available only in foster care situations. Not included in these statutes or covered by other statutes are private adoptions such as the one presented by these facts.

---

15. Neb. Rev. Stat. § 43-156 (Reissue 2008).

Adoption was unknown to the common law and is a creature of statute.[16] As such, adoptions are permissible only when done in accordance with statute. While the Legislature responded to the *McCormick* holding in the foster-adopt situation, thus legitimizing the practice in that context, it has left *McCormick* untouched insofar as it applies to private adoptions. Thus, the central holdings of *McCormick*—that the effect of an open adoption acts as the retention of some parental rights and, further, that the retention of some parental rights renders a relinquishment invalid—remain intact. . . . In this case, the record is clear, and the parties do not dispute, that an open adoption was planned. But this retention of parental rights, however slight, is sufficient to invalidate Teresa's and Monty's relinquishments.

We are not unsympathetic to the plight of adoptive and biological parents as they navigate through the highly emotional process of adoption. And it may be that in some situations, benefit could result from open arrangements such as those endorsed by the Legislature in the foster-adopt situation. At the same time, it is not this court's place to make such policy judgments. Until the Legislature acts to approve of these open adoption arrangements in a private adoption context, this court will not recognize them and will instead continue to hold that relinquishments signed with the promise of such an open adoption are invalid.

Rebecca and Jason's second assignment of error is without merit. . . .

The decision of the district court is affirmed.

Affirmed.

McCormack, J., participating on briefs.

Notes

The *Monty S.* decision involves a private surrogacy agreement between two couples that would have allowed for a private adoption between the two couples. The donee infertile couple (Jason W. and Rebecca W.) had no biological connection with the child born to the donor couple (Teresa and Monty S.). Because the donor couple used their own genetic materials—egg and sperm—this was a "genetic surrogacy." State courts and the Uniform Parentage Act impose additional requirements on genetic surrogacy agreements, as compared to gestational surrogacy agreements. *See* Unif. Parentage Act § 813(a) (2017) (mandating validation by an appropriate court prior to beginning the genetic assisted reproductive procedure related to the agreement). Compare this to gestational surrogacy, when the surrogate does not use her own genetic material but does in fact carry the child to term. For a discussion of surrogacy, see, *e.g.*, Raymond C. O'Brien, *Assessing Assisted Reproductive Technology*, 27 Cath. U. J. L. & Tech. 1 (2018). Courts are far more prone to enforce gestational surrogacy agreements then genetic gestational agreements. *See, e.g.*, P.M. v. T.B., 907 N.W.2d 522, 525 (Iowa 2018) (holding that gestational surrogacy agreements violate neither statutory nor public policy prohibitions). One profile of modern

---

16. *Wulf v. Ibsen*, 184 Neb. 314, 167 N.W.2d 181 (1969).

surrogates in the United States describes them as married, Christian, middle-class, with two or three biological children, working a part-time job, living in a small town or suburb, with at least some education from a higher institution, usually a bachelor's degree. Leslie Morgan Steiner, *Who Becomes a Surrogate?*, The Atlantic, Nov. 25, 2013, at https://www.theatlantic.com/health/archive/2013/11/who -becomes-a-surrogate/281596. For additional discussion of surrogacy, *see infra, In re Paternity of F.T.R.*, 833 N.W.2d 634 (Wis. 2013).

2. Statutory Stepparent Adoption

Nearly half of all adoptions in the United States involve stepparents. As an illustration of stepparent adoption, suppose that two persons give birth to a child and then divorce, or perhaps were never married at all when their child was born and paternity was established. If one of the parents to that child is awarded physical custody of the child and then later marries a third party, the stepchild becomes part of a growing family as the custodial birth parent and his or her spouse give birth to additional children. As their family grows, the new spouse remains a stepparent to the child of his or her spouse, which could create a strain on the family. As a result, often the custodial parent and the stepparent spouse go to the other biological parent of the child and ask if the stepparent may adopt the child. Usually the reason is so that the child will have a legal relationship with his or her biological/custodial parent's spouse. If permission is obtained, stepparent adoption will occur, whereby the child may share a form of "open adoption" and inheritance rights with all three parents.

The Comment to Uniform Probate Code § 2-119, *infra*, provides an illustration of stepparent adoption—one that involves what occurs when there is a post-divorce remarriage. Thus, assume that A and B were married and had two children, X and Y. Subsequently, A and B divorced and B was awarded physical custody of the two children. Then B married C and C wanted to adopt the two children of A and B. If A provides his or her consent, then C will be able to adopt X and Y. What will be the effect for inheritance purposes? Under Unif. Prob. Code § 2-119(b)(1), X and Y are treated as B's children, but also, under § 2-2-118(a), as C's children for purposes of inheritance. Please note that under § 2-119(b)(2), X and Y are treated as A's children for purposes of inheritance from and through A, but neither A nor any of A's relatives can inherit from or through X and Y after the stepparent adoption takes place. The Uniform Probate Code always maximizes a child's benefits, and we see that illustrated here.

There are a few rules. First, prior to a stepparent adoption, there must be a valid marriage between the custodial parent and the potential adoptive parent. *See* S.J.L.S. v. T.L.S., 265 S.W.3d 804 (Ky. Ct. App. 2008) (holding that a valid marriage is necessary for statutory stepparent adoption). Second, any biological parent of the child must give consent to the stepparent adoption, but once the adoptee is no longer a minor, parental consent is no longer necessary. *See, In re K.A.H.*, No. 14AP-831, 2015 WL 2452282 (Ohio Ct. App. May 21, 2015) (holding that father's consent to stepparent adoption of minor was required, even though he had little contact and provided no support for his children); *In re* Adoption of R.M.Z., No. 23-511, 2009 WL 3404008 (Ohio Ct. App. Oct. 23, 2009) (holding that consent is required of a biological parent, even though the parent had not paid child support or communicated with the child for one year prior to the adoption petition).

Uniform Probate Code (2019)

§ 2-119. Adoptee and Adoptee's Genetic Parents.

* * *

(b) [Stepchild Adopted by Stepparent.] A parent-child relationship exists between an individual who is adopted by the spouse of either genetic parent and:

(1) the genetic parent whose spouse adopted the individual; and

(2) the other genetic parent, but only for the purpose of the right of the adoptee or a descendant of the adoptee to inherit from or through the other genetic parent.

* * *

Problem

During a period of nonmarital cohabitation, twin boys were born to a couple in 1994. After the mother filed a paternity petition in 1995 and established her male partner as the father of the boys, she obtained an order of child support. Thereupon the father left the area and did not return until 1997. Upon his return, he filed to secure visitation rights to the boys but exercised that right only two or three times. The father made infrequent payments of child support, resulting in significant arrearages. Only in 2003, when he obtained steady employment, did he begin to make regular child support payments.

In 2004, the twins' mother married, and in 2006, the mother's husband, the stepparent of the twins, filed a petition to adopt the twins under the state's stepparent adoption statute. The petition alleges that it is in the best interest of the twins to be adopted by the stepparent because the natural father of the twins has not had meaningful contact with the boys for nine years, and payment of child support has been sporadic at best. The biological father refuses to consent, arguing he is getting better with contact and support. If you were the judge asked to rule upon the stepparent adoption petition, how would you rule? *See In re* Adoption of G.L.V., 286 Kan. 1034, 190 P.3d 245 (2008).

3. Establishing Parenthood with and without Artificial Reproductive Technology (ART)

Uniform Probate Code (2019)

§ 2-120. Child Conceived by Assisted Reproduction Other than Child Born to Gestational Carrier.

* * *

(b) [**Third-Party Donor.**] A parent-child relationship does not exist between a child of assisted reproduction and a third-party donor.

(c) [**Parent-Child Relationship with Birth Mother.**] A parent-child relationship exists between a child of assisted reproduction and the child's birth mother.

(d) [**Parent-Child Relationship with Husband Whose Sperm Were Used During His Lifetime by His Wife for Assisted Reproduction.**] Except as otherwise provided in subsections (i) and (j), a parent-child relationship exists between a child of assisted reproduction and the husband of the child's birth mother if the husband provided the sperm that the birth mother used during his lifetime for assisted reproduction.

(e) [**Birth Certificate: Presumptive Effect.**] A birth certificate identifying an individual other than the birth mother as the other parent of a child of assisted reproduction presumptively establishes a parent-child relationship between the child and that individual.

(f) [**Parent-Child Relationship with Another.**] Except as otherwise provided in subsections (g), (i), and (j), and unless a parent-child relationship is established under subsection (d) or (e), a parent-child relationship exists between a child of assisted reproduction and an individual other than the birth mother who consented to assisted reproduction by the birth mother with intent to be treated as the other parent of the child. Consent to assisted reproduction by the birth mother with intent to be treated as the other parent of the child is established if the individual:

> (1) before or after the child's birth, signed a record that, considering all the facts and circumstances, evidences the individual's consent; or

> (2) in the absence of a signed record under paragraph (1):

>> (A) functioned as a parent of the child no later than two years after the child's birth;

>> (B) intended to function as a parent of the child no later than two years after the child's birth but was prevented from carrying out that intent by death, incapacity, or other circumstances; or

>> (C) intended to be treated as a parent of a posthumously conceived child, if that intent is established by clear and convincing evidence.

ALI Principles of the Law of Family Dissolution (2003)

§ 2.03c) [**De Facto Parent**] A de facto parent is an individual other than a legal parent or a parent by estoppel who, for a significant period of time not less than two years,

> (i) lived with the child and,

> (ii) for reasons primarily other than financial compensation, and with the agreement of a legal parent to form a parent-child relationship, or as a result

of a complete failure or inability of any legal parent to perform caretaking functions,

    (A) regularly performed a majority of the caretaking functions for the child, or

    (B) regularly performed a share of the caretaking functions at least as great as that of the parent with whom the child primarily lived.

In re Guardianship of Madelyn B.

Supreme Court of New Hampshire, 2014
166 N.H. 453, 98 A.3d 494

HICKS, J.

The appellant, Susan B., appeals orders of the 10th Circuit Court—Derry Family Division (*Sadler*, J.) that: (1) terminated her guardianship over the person of Madelyn B., a child; (2) dismissed her verified parenting petition; and (3) denied her motion to intervene in adoption proceedings involving Madelyn B. The appellee, Melissa D., is Madelyn B.'s biological mother. We reverse in part, vacate in part, and remand.

Susan's pleadings allege, in part, the following: She and Melissa met in 1997 and soon became romantically involved. They held a commitment ceremony on August 16, 1998, and "considered [them]selves to be as fully committed to one another as any married couple." Melissa took Susan's last name as her own. We note that, at that time, same-sex marriage was prohibited in New Hampshire, and did not become legal until 2010. *Compare* RSA 457:1, :2 (1992) (amended 2009) *with* RSA 457:1, :1-a, :2 (Supp.2013). . . . Susan and Melissa intended to raise a family together, and they jointly bought a house in which to raise their family. When Melissa sought to become pregnant using an anonymous sperm donor, they searched for a donor who shared Susan's Irish heritage. After the initial course of fertility treatments failed, Susan sought insurance coverage for another course of treatments. Melissa became pregnant and, in 2002, gave birth to Madelyn. Susan and Melissa decided to give Madelyn Susan's middle and last names. . . . Susan and Melissa were both named as Madelyn's parents in the birth announcements sent to friends and family and printed in the local newspaper, as well as in a "dedication ceremony" held in the Unitarian Universalist Church when Madelyn was a year old. Susan was listed as Madelyn's parent in her preschool documents and in her medical records. Susan was involved in the daily care of Madelyn, and Susan and Melissa jointly made all decisions involved in raising Madelyn, including decisions regarding health care, education, and religion. . . . An attorney for Susan and Melissa advised them that Susan could not legally adopt Madelyn, and that "a guardianship was the best available option to protect [Susan's] parental relationship with her." Susan was appointed Madelyn's guardian on March 15, 2002. Melissa also amended her will to appoint Susan as Madelyn's guardian should Melissa die while Madelyn was a minor.

In November 2008, when Madelyn was six years old, Susan and Melissa's relationship ended. Melissa and Madelyn moved in with Eugene D., whom Melissa later married. Susan and Melissa agreed upon a schedule for regular visitation. Susan saw Madelyn every weekend, had overnight visits every other week, and continued to be actively involved in Madelyn's life. Susan paid weekly child support and, in addition, helped with the cost of Madelyn's extracurricular activities. She also provided Madelyn with food, clothing, and gifts. . . . In February 2013, Melissa stopped cashing Susan's child support checks. Susan avers that she nevertheless continued to send them. On March 2, 2013, when Susan attempted to pick up Madelyn for her weekly visitation, she was informed that Madelyn no longer wanted a relationship with her. At a meeting the two had later to discuss the situation, Melissa "claimed that [Madelyn] no longer wanted to see Susan." Melissa did not return Susan's subsequent phone calls, and Susan was unable to contact Madelyn directly through online social media because Madelyn's settings had been changed.

On April 2, 2013, Melissa filed a motion to terminate Susan's guardianship over Madelyn, asserting that the guardianship was "no longer necessary because Madelyn no longer wishes to have a relationship with Susan." On April 4, Melissa filed an *ex parte* emergency motion to terminate the guardianship alleging that Susan had been "showing up at Madelyn's school, contacting family members and behaving in such a way that both Madelyn and [Melissa] fear [for Madelyn's] safety." The court suspended the guardianship that day "pending response to [r]equest to terminate . . . and subsequent order," and ordered "[n]o hearing to be scheduled pending further order." Susan, representing herself, filed an objection on April 5. On April 12, the court terminated the guardianship on the grounds that it was "no longer necessary to provide for Madelyn's essential physical and safety needs and termination would not adversely affect Madelyn psychologically." The court found that the guardianship had been created to give Susan the "right and duty" to care for Madelyn if Melissa were not available to do so. It further found that following the termination of Susan and Melissa's relationship and Melissa's subsequent marriage, Melissa's "husband is the logical choice to care for Madelyn in Melissa's absence as they are now the family unit." . . . On April 18, Susan, represented by counsel, moved for an immediate hearing. Melissa objected, noting, "We have begun the process of my husband, Madelyn['s] stepfather, adopting her." The court denied the motion and Susan's subsequent motion to reconsider.

On April 29, 2013, Susan moved to intervene in the pending adoption proceeding. On the same day, she filed a verified parenting petition seeking temporary and final orders on child support and a parenting plan, as well as a determination that she "is a legal parent to," or "stands *in loco parentis* to [,] Madelyn." The court denied the motion to intervene, and dismissed Susan's verified parenting petition, finding that she "is not [a] parent." (Quotation and bolding omitted.) The court denied Susan's subsequent motion for reconsideration of the order denying her motion to intervene and for an order "providing [her] with notice and the right to request a hearing to prove her legal parentage of Madelyn." . . . On appeal, Susan argues, in part, that the family division erred by: (1) terminating the guardianship without a hearing or opportunity to conduct discovery; (2) ruling that the legal standard for termination of a guardianship had been satisfied; (3) dismissing her parenting petition; and (4) denying her motion to intervene in the adoption case. Melissa counters that the guardianship was created to allow Susan to provide health insurance for Madelyn and to further "the daily practicalities of child-rearing." She argues that since "Madelyn's sustenance is being adequately met by her new family," the guardianship is no longer necessary.

We first address Susan's parenting petition claim because it is dispositive of her other claims at this stage of the proceedings. Susan characterizes the trial court's *sua sponte* dismissal of her verified parenting petition as a dismissal for failure to state a claim upon which relief can be granted. *See Kennedy v. Titcomb*, 131 N.H. 399, 402, 553 A.2d 1322 (1989) (noting that "[a] trial court has the discretion to dismiss an action *sua sponte* where the allegations contained in a writ do not state a claim upon which relief can be granted"). In essence, the trial court ruled that Susan's petition failed to state a claim on any of her asserted bases for claiming to be a parent of Madelyn. *Cf. In the Matter of J.B. & J.G.*, 157 N.H. 577, 580, 953 A.2d 1186 (2008) (holding that petitioner could maintain his action seeking "parental rights and responsibilities under RSA chapter 461-A," notwithstanding his lack of biological relationship to the child, "so long as he alleges sufficient facts to establish his status as a parent by other means"). . . . . "[I]n reviewing the trial court's order of dismissal [for failure to state a claim], [we] must determine whether the plaintiff's writ contains facts which are sufficient to constitute a cause of action. [We] must rigorously scrutinize the complaint to determine whether, *on its face*, it asserts a cause of action." *Kennedy*, 131 N.H. at 401, 553 A.2d 1322 (quotation and citation omitted). "[W]e assume the truth of the facts alleged by the plaintiff and construe all reasonable inferences in the light most favorable to the plaintiff." *Farm Family Cas. Ins. Co. v. Town of Rollinsford*, 155 N.H. 669, 670, 927 A.2d 1234 (2007).

Susan first argues that the family division erred in dismissing her parenting petition because she sufficiently alleged a claim under RSA 168-B:3, I(d)'s "holding out" provision. *See* RSA 168-B:3, I(d) (2002). Because this argument raises an issue of statutory interpretation, our review is *de novo*. *See Town of Newbury v. N.H. Fish & Game Dep't*, 165 N.H. 142, 144, 70 A.3d 461 (2013).

> We are the final arbiter of the intent of the legislature as expressed in the words of the statute considered as a whole. When examining the language of the statute, we ascribe the plain and ordinary meaning to the words used. We interpret legislative intent from the statute as written and will not consider what the legislature might have said or add language that the legislature did not see fit to include. We also interpret a statute in the context of the overall statutory scheme and not in isolation.

> *Id.*

(quotations and citations omitted).

RSA 168-B:3, I, provides, in relevant part:

> I. Notwithstanding any other provision of law, a man is presumed to be the father of a child if:
>
> . . .
>
> (d) While the child is under the age of majority, he receives the child into his home and openly holds out the child as his child.

RSA 168-B:3, I (2002). Susan asserts that "[a]lthough the statute uses 'father' and male pronouns, this Court must construe the holding out provision to apply to mothers as well, in accordance with statutory rules of construction, the original intent and purpose of the statute, and constitutional guarantees of equal protection."

The legislature has instructed that in construing all statutes, "words importing the masculine gender may extend and be applied to females," RSA 21:3 (2012), "unless such construction would be inconsistent with the manifest intent of the legislature or repugnant to the context of the same statute," RSA 21:1 (2012). We have previously declined to employ that instruction as liberally as is urged here. In *Chretien v. Company*, 87 N.H. 378, 180 A. 254 (1935), we held that "a statute requiring that words denoting the masculine gender shall include females will not authorize us to read the word widow as including widower." *Chretien*, 87 N.H. at 379, 180 A. 254 (quotation omitted); *cf. id.* at 378–79, 180 A. 254 (noting also, however, that the statutory instruction to construe masculine terms to include women would allow the words "'workman' and 'his'" to include a female worker). In reaching that conclusion, we noted, after surveying similar cases from other jurisdictions, that "[n]o case has been found where so liberal a construction has been adopted as would supply 'widower' for 'widow.'" *Id.* at 380, 180 A. 254. . . . By contrast, other jurisdictions have interpreted the terms "paternity" and "father" to apply to women. In *Rubano v. DiCenzo*, 759 A.2d 959 (R.I.2000), for instance, the Supreme Court of Rhode Island noted:

> While the word "paternity" implies the "fathering" of a child, we are mindful of the Legislature's instruction that when statutes are construed "[e]very word importing the masculine gender only, may be construed to extend to and to include females as well as males." Thus, two women may certainly be "adults who shall be involved with paternity" of a child for purposes of this statute.

Rubano, 759 A.2d at 970 n. 13 (citation omitted) (interpreting statute granting family court jurisdiction over matters relating to adults involved with paternity of children born out of wedlock to apply to dispute between same-sex partners over visitation with child conceived by one, according to agreement between them, through artificial insemination).

Susan correctly notes that courts in other jurisdictions have applied the particular paternity presumption she asserts—the "holding out provision"—equally to mothers. *See, e.g., Chatterjee v. King*,— N.M.—, 280 P.3d 283, 293 (2012). We note that those jurisdictions had statutory provisions, more specific than ours, instructing that their paternity "presumptions are to be read in a gender-neutral manner insofar as practicable in an action to determine . . . the existence of a mother and child relationship." *Frazier v. Goudschaal*, 296 Kan. 730, 295 P.3d 542, 559 (2013) (Biles, J., concurring in part) (quotation omitted); *see Elisa B. v. Superior Court*, 37 Cal.4th 108, 33 Cal.Rptr.3d 46, 117 P.3d 660, 665 (2005) (holding that woman was presumed mother under Uniform Parentage Act's (UPA) provision presuming paternity based upon receiving the child into one's home and holding out child as one's own where UPA "expressly provides that in determining the existence of a mother and child relationship, insofar as practicable, the provisions of this part applicable to the father and child relationship apply" (quotation and brackets omitted)); *In re S.N.V.*, 284 P.3d 147, 151 (Colo.Ct.App.2011) (interpreting presumptive paternity provision of the UPA, in light of its statutory construction provisions, so that "[a] woman's proof of marriage to the child's father, or her proof of receiving the child into her home and holding the child out as her own, . . . may establish the mother-child relationship"); *Chatterjee*, 280 P.3d at 287.

We find these cases instructive, not only for our application of RSA 21:3, but also for our application of other canons of statutory construction. One such canon recognizes that "[o]ur goal is to apply statutes in light of the legislature's intent in enacting them, and in light of the policy sought to be advanced by the entire statutory scheme." *Sheehan v. N.H. Dep't of Resources & Economic Dev.*, 164 N.H. 365, 368, 55 A.3d 1031 (2012). RSA 168-B:3 is contained within a chapter entitled "Surrogacy." *See* RSA ch. 168-B (2002). The chapter's statement of purpose provides that "[t]he purpose of this act is to establish consistent state standards and procedural safeguards for the protection of all parties, and to determine the legal status of children born as a result of [surrogacy] arrangements." Laws 1990, 87:1, II. Specifically, the Legislature noted that the chapter ensures, among other things, that "the resulting child's status is legally certain in order that the child not be the chief remedial focus of litigation; and that adequate support be assured for the resulting child." *Id.* In furtherance of the chapter's stated purpose, RSA 168-B:7 provides: "If, under the provisions of this chapter, a parent-child relationship is created between 2 persons, the child shall be considered, for all purposes of law, the legitimate child of the parent." Further, RSA 168-B:8 declares that "[a]ny person who is determined to be the parent of a child under the provisions of RSA 168-B:2-5 shall support the child." RSA 168-B:8, I.

In addition, the chapter indicates an implicit legislative preference for the recognition of two parents. *See, e.g.*, RSA 168-B:2 (mother-child relationship), :3 (father-child relationship). "By recognizing the value of determining paternity, the Legislature implicitly recognized the value of having two parents, rather than one, as a source of both emotional and financial support, especially when the obligation to support the child would otherwise fall to the public." *Elisa B.*, 33 Cal.Rptr.3d 46, 117 P.3d at 669; *cf. In the Matter of Gendron & Plaistek*, 157 N.H. 314, 321, 950 A.2d 151 (2008) (noting, in the context of paternity determinations, that "stability and continuity of support, both emotional and financial, are essential to a child's welfare" (quotation omitted)); RSA 461-A:2, I (Supp.2013) (stating as premise of statutory policy that "children do best when both parents have a stable and meaningful involvement in their lives"). The *Chatterjee* court similarly noted:

> [T]he state has a strong interest in ensuring that a child will be cared for, financially and otherwise, by two parents. If that care is lacking, the state will ultimately assume the responsibility of caring for the child. This is one of the primary reasons that the original UPA was created, and it makes little sense to read the statute without keeping this overarching legislative goal in mind.

Chatterjee, 280 P.3d at 292 (citation omitted).

The policy goals of ensuring legitimacy and support would be thwarted if our interpretation of RSA 168-B:3 failed to recognize that a child's second parent under that statute can be a woman. *Cf. id.* at 287–88 (noting that "[b]ecause the [UPA's holding out] presumption is based on a person's conduct, not a biological connection," it "is reasonably capable of being accomplished by either a man or a woman"). Without that recognition, a child in a situation similar to Madelyn's could be entitled to support from, and be the legitimate child of, only her birth mother. *See* RSA 168-B:2, :7, :8. Two adults — Melissa and Susan — intentionally brought Madelyn into the world and held her out as their child; we cannot read RSA 168-B:3 so narrowly as to deny Madelyn the legitimacy of her parentage by, and her entitlement to support from, both of them. *Cf. In re Jessica W.*, 122 N.H. 1052, 1056–57, 453 A.2d 1297 (1982) (interpreting adoption statute liberally, "in accordance with the legislative intent to protect, not injure, adopted children," to allow unwed natural parents to utilize the stepparent exception to the general rule that "adoption severs the rights of the natural parent(s)," so that their child would "not have to be deprived of its relationship with its mother in order to be legitimized by its natural father through the adoption process"). We note that the intention of Melissa's husband to adopt Madelyn does not alter our view.

Consistent with the above-noted policy goals is the recognition that "[t]he paternity presumptions are driven, not by biological paternity, but by the state's interest in the welfare of the child and the integrity of the family." *In re Salvador M.*, 111 Cal.App.4th 1353, 4 Cal.Rptr.3d 705, 708 (2003). "The familial relationship between a nonbiological [parent] and an older child [over two years of age], resulting from years of living together in a purported parent/child relationship, is considerably more palpable than the biological relationship of actual paternity and should not be lightly dissolved." *Id.* (quotations omitted); *cf. Roberts v. Ward*, 126 N.H. 388, 392–93, 493 A.2d 478 (1985) (noting that "[p]sychiatrists and psychologists unanimously counsel that children should maintain and retain meaningful relationships and that to deny them continuing contacts is a deprivation" (quotation and ellipses omitted)).

Accordingly, in some cases, we have refused to allow a presumption of paternity to be rebutted by proof of biological paternity. In *Watts v. Watts*, 115 N.H. 186,

337 A.2d 350 (1975), for instance, we affirmed the denial of a divorcing husband's request for blood tests to dispute the paternity of children of the marriage. *Watts*, 115 N.H. at 189, 337 A.2d 350. We held that although, in general, common law and statutory paternity presumptions may be rebutted by blood tests, "those rules do not apply . . . where defendant has acknowledged the children as his own without challenge for over fifteen years." *Id.* Similarly, we have allowed a determination of paternity to stand despite a confirmed lack of biological connection. Thus, in *In the Matter of J.B. & J.G.*, we held that the petitioner—who was listed as the father on the child's birth certificate, had filed an affidavit of paternity, had a child support order entered against him, and had "consistently maintained contact with the child"—had "standing to seek full parental rights and responsibilities under RSA chapter 461-A" notwithstanding that paternity testing had confirmed he was not the child's biological father. *In the Matter of J.B. & J.G.*, 157 N.H. at 578, 581, 953 A.2d 1186. We rejected the contention of the respondent, the child's biological mother, that the petitioner could not be a "parent" under RSA chapter 461-A because he did not meet the dictionary definition of "one that begets or brings forth offspring." *Id.* at 580, 953 A.2d 1186. We reasoned:

> After considering the overarching statutory scheme in this area, as we must, we observe that the legislature has set forth too many alternative routes to establish parental status that do not require proof of biological ties for us to give the respondent's argument much weight. The petitioner's lack of a biological connection to [the child] is therefore not fatal to his request for parental rights and responsibilities under RSA chapter 461-A, so long as he alleges sufficient facts to establish his status as a parent by other means.

Id. (citations omitted). Accordingly, we conclude that the lack of a biological connection between Susan and Madelyn is not a bar to application of the holding out presumption. . . . Given our construction of RSA 168-B:3, I(d), we need not address Susan's constitutional arguments. *See Olson v. Town of Fitzwilliam*, 142 N.H. 339, 345, 702 A.2d 318 (1997) (noting that we decide cases on constitutional grounds only when necessary).

For all of the foregoing reasons, we hold that RSA 168-B:3, I(d) applies equally to women and men. We must now determine whether Susan has alleged sufficient facts to state a claim under that statute. We conclude that she has.

Assuming the truth of Susan's alleged facts, and construing all reasonable inferences in the light most favorable to her, *Farm Family Cas. Ins. Co.*, 155 N.H. at 670, 927 A.2d 1234, we conclude that she adequately pleaded that she received Madelyn into her home and openly held Madelyn out as her child. She and Melissa planned to have and raise children together. They prepared Madelyn's nursery together in the home they had jointly purchased because they "thought it would be a good place to raise a family." When Madelyn was born, Susan was in the delivery room. She alleges: "From the very beginning, Maddie, Melissa, and I were a family. Melissa was the 'Mommy,' and I was the 'Momma.' Together we were . . . Maddie's parents, and Maddie was our daughter. I loved Maddie as my daughter, treated her as my daughter, and saw her as my daughter." . . . Susan's allegations, taken as true, indicate that Melissa also regarded Susan as Madelyn's parent as evidenced by, among other things, giving Susan a greeting card commemorating the "Birth of Our Baby," and including her as "Momma," and her parents as Madelyn's grandparents, on Madelyn's family tree. The allegations also indicate that Susan appeared "to the world" to be Madelyn's parent. Madelyn shares Susan's last name. Susan was named as a parent, along with Melissa, in birth announcements and in a church ceremony. Susan was named as a parent in Madelyn's school and medical records, and was treated as a parent at Madelyn's preschool. . . . Taking Susan's allegations as true and drawing all reasonable inferences in her favor, we hold that she has stated a claim for presumed parentage under RSA 168-B:3, I(d). *Cf. Elisa B.*, 33 Cal.Rptr.3d 46, 117 P.3d at 670 (holding birth mother's same-sex partner was "a presumed mother . . . because she received the children into her home and openly held them out as her natural children"); *Chatterjee*, 280 P.3d at 296 (holding same-sex partner of adoptive mother asserted sufficient facts to give her standing to establish parentage "because her allegations satisfy the [statutory] hold out provision"). Accordingly, we reverse the family division's dismissal of Susan's verified parenting petition and remand. We direct the family division to schedule a prompt hearing on Susan's request for temporary orders. In light of our holding regarding Susan's parentage claim based upon the statutory holding out provision, we need not address her other asserted bases of parental rights, and we express no opinion with respect to them.

Consequently, we also vacate the family division's denial of Susan's motion to intervene in the adoption proceedings and stay those proceedings until the issue of Susan's parentage of Madelyn is finally determined. . . . Similarly, we vacate the family division's termination of Susan's guardianship over Madelyn and stay those proceedings until the issue of Susan's parentage of Madelyn is finally determined.

Reversed in part; vacated in part; and remanded.

DALIANIS, C.J., and CONBOY, LYNN, and BASSETT, JJ., concurred.

Notes

The New Hampshire court focuses its opinion on the phrase in its statute "openly holds the child out as his own" when establishing the presumption of parenthood. The statute also requires that this occurs when a child is still a minor. The Uniform Probate Code utilizes a similar standard when it requires a party "to function as a parent of the child." *See* UNIF. PROB. CODE § 2-120(f)((2)((B). But note that the Uniform Probate Code requires this function to occur no later than two years after the child's birth. A similar time requirement is absent from the American Law Institute's de facto parent provision at § 203(c), *supra*.

The legalization of same sex marriage has not eliminated the type of litigation illustrated in *Madelyn B. See, e.g., In re* J.W., 2019 WL 2847460 (N.H. 2019) (holding that state statute specifies that an unmarried cohabitant cannot adopt his partner's child unless the partner-parent surrenders his parental rights); Roe v. Patton,

No. 2:15-cv-00253-DB, 2015 WL 4476734 (D. Utah July 22, 2015) (holding that two females who had married and had a child through insemination with anonymous donor sperm had the same rights as males to have the names of both women placed on the resulting child's birth certificate). But same sex marriage does prohibit any discriminatory treatment. *See, e.g.,* Pavan v. Smith, 137 S. Ct. 2075, 2078 (2017) (states cannot deny to same sex married couples any of the constellation of benefits that are extended to opposite sex married couples).

Litigation is augmented by the rise in the number of nonmarital cohabiting parents. The Pew Research Center reports that since 1997, the first year for which data on cohabitation are available, the share of parents that are cohabiting has risen from 4% to 6%. The total number of single parents and nonmarital cohabiting parents is estimated to be more than 16 million in 2018, up from 4 million in 1968 and just under 14 million in 1997.

4. Equitable Adoption

Lankford v. Wright

Supreme Court of North Carolina, 1997
347 N.C. 115, 489 S.E.2d 604

FRYE, Justice.

The sole issue in this case is whether North Carolina recognizes the doctrine of equitable adoption. We hold that the doctrine should be recognized in this state, and therefore, we reverse the decision of the Court of Appeals.

Plaintiff, Barbara Ann Newton Lankford, was born to Mary M. Winebarger on 15 January 1944. When plaintiff was a child, her natural mother entered into an agreement with her neighbors, Clarence and Lula Newton, whereby the Newtons agreed to adopt and raise plaintiff as their child. Shortly thereafter, plaintiff moved into the Newton residence and became known as Barbara Ann Newton, the only child of Clarence and Lula Newton.

The Newtons held plaintiff out to the public as their own child, and plaintiff was at all times known as Barbara Ann Newton. Plaintiff's school records referred to plaintiff as Barbara Ann Newton and indicated that Clarence and Lula Newton were her parents. Plaintiff's high-school diploma also referred to plaintiff as Barbara Ann Newton. After Clarence Newton died in 1960, the newspaper obituary listed Barbara Ann Newton as his surviving daughter. Later, with Lula Newton's assistance, plaintiff obtained a Social Security card issued to her under the name of Barbara Ann Newton.

After plaintiff joined the Navy, plaintiff and Lula Newton frequently wrote letters to each other. In most of the letters, plaintiff referred to Lula Newton as her mother and Lula Newton referred to plaintiff as her daughter. Lula Newton also established several bank accounts with plaintiff, where Lula Newton deposited money plaintiff sent to her while plaintiff was in the Navy. On several occasions, plaintiff took leaves of absence from work to care for Lula Newton during her illness.

In 1975, Lula Newton prepared a will. When she died in 1994, the will was not accepted for probate because some unknown person had defaced a portion of the will. The will named plaintiff as co-executrix of the estate and made specific bequests to plaintiff. Since the will could not be probated, Lula Newton died intestate.

After Lula Newton's death, plaintiff filed for declaratory judgment seeking a declaration of her rights and status as an heir of the estate of Lula Newton. Defendants, the administrators and named heirs of Lula Newton, filed a motion for summary judgment. The trial court granted defendants' motion. The North Carolina Court of Appeals affirmed the order granting summary judgment, reasoning that plaintiff was not adopted according to N.C.G.S. §§ 48-1 to -38 and that North Carolina does not recognize the doctrine of equitable adoption. This Court granted plaintiff's petition for discretionary review, and we now conclude that the doctrine of equitable adoption should be recognized in North Carolina.

"It is a fundamental premise of equitable relief that equity regards as done that which in fairness and good conscience ought to be done." Thompson v. Soles, 299 N.C. 484, 489, 263 S.E.2d 599, 603 (1980). "Equity regards substance, not form," In re Will of Pendergrass, 251 N.C. 737, 743, 112 S.E.2d 562, 566 (1960), and "will not allow technicalities of procedure to defeat that which is eminently right and just," id. at 746, 112 S.E.2d at 568. These principles form the essence of the doctrine of equitable adoption, and it is the duty of this Court to protect and promote them.

Equitable adoption is a remedy to "protect the interest of a person who was supposed to have been adopted as a child but whose adoptive parents failed to undertake the legal steps necessary to formally accomplish the adoption." Gardner v. Hancock, 924 S.W.2d 857, 858 (Mo.Ct.App.1996). The doctrine is applied in an intestate estate to "give effect to the intent of the decedent to adopt and provide for the child." Id. It is predicated upon

> principles of contract law and equitable enforcement of the agreement to adopt for the purpose of securing the benefits of adoption that would otherwise flow from the adoptive parent under the laws of intestacy had the agreement to adopt been carried out; as such it is essentially a matter of equitable relief. Being only an equitable remedy to enforce a contract right, it is not intended or applied to create the legal relationship of parent and child, with all the legal consequences of such a relationship, nor is it meant to create a legal adoption.

2 Am.Jur.2d Adoption § 53 (1994) (footnotes omitted).

Adoption did not exist at common law and is of purely statutory origin. Wilson v. Anderson, 232 N.C. 212, 215, 59 S.E.2d 836, 839 (1950). Equitable adoption, however, does not confer the incidents of formal statutory adoption; rather, it merely confers rights of inheritance upon the foster child in the event of intestacy of the foster parents. * * * In essence, the doctrine invokes the principle that equity regards that as done which ought to be done. The doctrine is not intended to replace statutory requirements or to create the parent-child relationship; it simply recognizes the foster child's right to inherit from the person or persons who contracted to adopt the child and who honored that contract in all respects except through formal statutory procedures. As an equitable matter, where the child in question has faithfully performed the duties of a natural child to the foster parents, that child is entitled to be placed in the position in which he would have been had he been adopted. Likewise, based on principles of estoppel, those claiming under and through the deceased are estopped to assert that the child was not legally adopted or did not occupy the status of an adopted child.

Further, the scope of the doctrine is limited to facts comparable to those presented here. Thirty-eight jurisdictions have considered equitable adoption; at least twenty-seven have recognized and applied the doctrine. See, *e.g.*, First Nat'l Bank in Fairmont v. Phillips, 176 W.Va. 395, 344 S.E.2d 201 (1985). A majority of the jurisdictions recognizing the doctrine have successfully limited its application to claims made by an equitably adopted child against the estate of the foster parent. Geramifar v. Geramifar, 113 Md.App. 495, 688 A.2d 475 (1997). By its own terms, equitable adoption applies only in limited circumstances. The elements necessary to establish the existence of an equitable adoption are:

(1) an express or implied agreement to adopt the child,

(2) reliance on that agreement,

(3) performance by the natural parents of the child in giving up custody,

(4) performance by the child in living in the home of the foster parents and acting as their child,

(5) partial performance by the foster parents in taking the child into their home and treating the child as their own, and

(6) the intestacy of the foster parents.

See 2 Am.Jur.2d *Adoption* § 54 (1994). These elements, particularly the requirement of intestacy, limit the circumstances under which the doctrine may be applied. Specifically, the doctrine acts only to recognize the inheritance rights of a child whose foster parents died intestate and failed to perform the formalities of a legal adoption, yet treated the child as their own for all intents and purposes. The doctrine is invoked for the sole benefit of the foster child in determining heirship upon the intestate death of the person or persons contracting to adopt. Whether the doctrine applies is a factual question, and each element must be proven by clear, cogent, and convincing evidence. See, *e.g.*, First Nat'l Bank in Fairmont v. Phillips, 176 W.Va. 395, 344 S.E.2d 201.

In this case, the evidence in the record tends to show that the above elements can be satisfied by clear, cogent, and convincing evidence. The record demonstrates that the Newtons agreed to adopt plaintiff; that the Newtons and plaintiff relied on that agreement; that plaintiff's natural mother gave up custody of plaintiff to the

Newtons; that plaintiff lived in the Newtons' home, cared for them in their old age, and otherwise acted as their child; that the Newtons treated plaintiff as their child by taking her into their home, giving her their last name, and raising her as their child; and that Mrs. Newton died intestate several years after Mr. Newton died. These facts fit squarely within the parameters of the doctrine of equitable adoption and are indicative of the dilemma the doctrine is intended to remedy.

We note that our decision to recognize the doctrine of equitable adoption is not precluded by prior decisions of this Court as asserted by defendants and decided by the Court of Appeals. In Ladd v. Estate of Kellenberger, 314 N.C. 477, 334 S.E.2d 751 (1985), we specifically stated that "[w]e find no occasion to address the question of whether North Carolina recognizes the doctrine of equitable adoption." *Id.* at 479, 334 S.E.2d at 753. Likewise, in Chambers v. Byers, 214 N.C. 373, 199 S.E. 398 (1938), our holding was limited to whether the agreement at issue was an enforceable contract to make a will. Thus, neither *Ladd* nor *Chambers* foreclosed the possibility of future recognition of equitable adoption by this Court.

The dissent points out that a minority of jurisdictions have declined to recognize the doctrine of equitable adoption. However, we again note that an overwhelming majority of states that have addressed the question have recognized and applied the doctrine. More importantly, it is the unique role of the courts to fashion equitable remedies to protect and promote the principles of equity such as those at issue in this case. We are convinced that acting in an equitable manner in this case does not interfere with the legislative scheme for adoption, contrary to the assertions of the dissent. Recognition of the doctrine of equitable adoption does not create a legal adoption, and therefore does not impair the statutory procedures for adoption.

In conclusion, a decree of equitable adoption should be granted where justice, equity, and good faith require it. The fairness of applying the doctrine once the prerequisite facts have been established is apparent. Accordingly, we reverse the Court of Appeals' decision which affirmed the trial court's entry of summary judgment for defendants and remand to the trial court for further proceedings not inconsistent with this opinion.

REVERSED AND REMANDED.

MITCHELL, Chief Justice, dissenting.

In its opinion, the majority for the first time accepts the doctrine of equitable adoption for North Carolina. As applied by the majority in this case, the doctrine results in neither an adoption nor equity. Therefore, although I am convinced the majority is engaged in an honest but unfortunate attempt to do good in the present case, I must dissent.

"Equity" is that established set of principles under which substantial justice may be attained in particular cases where the prescribed or customary forms of ordinary law seem to be inadequate. 27A Am.Jur.2d *Equity* § 1 (1994). Equity "is a complex system of established law and is not merely a reflection of the judge's sense of what is appropriate." *Id.* § 2. It arose in response to the restrictive and inflexible rules of the common law, and not as a means of avoiding legislation that courts deemed unwise or inadequate.

For purposes of governing and regulating judicial action, equity courts over the centuries "have formulated certain rules or principles which are described by the term 'maxims.'" *Id.* § 108. It is these maxims which must control the equity jurisdiction of the courts if their judgments are to reflect anything other than the peculiar preferences of the individual judges involved.

> A court of equity has no more right than has a court of law to act on its own notion of what is right in a particular case; it must be guided by the established rules and precedents. Where rights are defined and established by existing legal principles, they may not be changed or unsettled in equity. A court of equity is thus bound by any explicit statute or directly applicable rule of law, regardless of its views of the equities.

Id. § 109 (footnotes omitted).

One maxim of equity, as the majority explains, is that equity regards as done that which in fairness and good conscience ought to be done. A court's notion of what is good or desirable does not determine what "ought to be done" in applying equity. The maxim of equity upon which the majority relies must yield to other controlling and established rules or maxims. One such maxim is that a court of equity, however benevolent its motives, is "bound by any explicit statute or directly applicable rule of law, regardless of its view of the equities." *Id.* Thus, no equitable remedy may properly be applied to disturb statutorily defined and established rights, such as those rights created by North Carolina statutes controlling intestate succession or those controlling legal adoption.

Notes

Equitable adoption is not adoption. Rather, it is an equity device, sometimes called "virtual adoption" or "adoption by estoppel," by which courts permit an intended heir to share in the intestate estate of a decedent. This is the extent of the benefits conferred by equitable adoption. *See, e.g., In re* Estate of Ford, 82 P.3d 747, 750 (Cal. 2004) ("In its essence, the doctrine of equitable adoption allows a person who was accepted and treated as a natural or adopted child and as to whom adoption typically was promised or contemplated but never performed, to share in inheritance of the foster parents' property."). But courts have refused to extend the benefits of equitable adoption beyond intestate succession from the decedent purported adopter. *See, e.g.,* Estate of Furia, 103 Cal. App. 4th 1, 5, 126 Cal. Rptr. 2d 384, 387 (2002) ("The doctrine of equitable adoption creates a contractual right to receive property, but it does not convey to the equitable child all the rights of an heir under the Probate Code."); *In re* Estate of Seader, 76 P.3d 1236 (Wyo. 2003) (holding that equitably adopted children cannot benefit from the state's anti-lapse statute).

The vast majority of states currently recognize the doctrine of equitable adoption. In 2013, the Illinois Supreme Court became one of the more recent courts to allow claims of equitable adoption. The state's highest court permitted a plaintiff to proceed with a claim against the estate of a man he considered to be his father, requiring clear and convincing evidence of intent to adopt and that the decedent acted consistently with that intent by forming a close and enduring family relationship with the plaintiff. DeHart v. DeHart, 986 N.E.2d 85 (Ill. 2013). By statute, some states expressly permit courts to apply the equity device. *See, e.g.,* UNIF. PROB. CODE § 2-122 ("This [subpart] does not affect the doctrine of equitable adoption."); CALIF. PROB. CODE § 6455 ("Nothing in this chapter affects or limits application of the judicial doctrine of equitable adoption for the benefit of the child or the child's issue."). But not all states permit the doctrine. *See, e.g., In re* Estate of Scherer, 336 P.3d 129 (Wyo. 2014) (equitable adoption is contrary to the state probate code provision that "foster children and their heirs do not inherit").

5. Statutory Adoption by Relatives

Uniform Probate Code (2019)

§ 2-119. Adoptee and Adoptee's Genetic Parents.

* * *

(c) [Individual Adopted by Relative of Genetic Parents] A parent-child relationship exists between both genetic parents and an individual who is adopted by a relative of a genetic parent, or by the spouse or surviving spouse of a relative of a genetic parent, but only for the purpose of the right of the adoptee or a descendant of the adoptee to inherit from or through either genetic parent.

* * *

Comment: F and M, a married couple with a four-year old child, X, were badly injured in an automobile accident. F Subsequently died. M, who was in a vegetative state and on life support, was unable to care for X. Thereafter, M's sister, A, and A's husband, B, adopted X. F's father, PGF, a widower, then died intestate. Under subsection (c), X is treated as PGF's grandchild (F's child).

D. Non-Marital Issue

Gretchen Livingston
The Changing Profile of Unmarried Parents
PEW RESEARCH CENTER (Apr. 25, 2018)

Not only are fewer Americans getting married, but it's also becoming more common for unmarried people to have babies. In 1970 there were 26 births per 1,000 unmarried women ages 15-44, while that rate in 2016 stood at 42 births per 1,000 unmarried women. Meanwhile birthrates for married women have declined from

121 births per 1,000 down to about 90. As a result, in 2016 four-in-ten births were to women who were either solo mothers or living with a nonmarital partner.

1. How Do You Establish Paternity and Maternity of a Child?

Uniform Parentage Act (2019)

§ 201. Establishment of Parent-Child Relationship.

A parent-child relationship is established between an individual and a child if:

(1) the individual gives birth to the child[, except as otherwise provided in [Article] 8];

(2) there is a presumption under Section 204 of the individual's parentage of the child, unless the presumption is overcome in a judicial proceeding or a valid denial of parentage is made under [Article] 3;

(3) the individual is adjudicated a parent of the child under [Article] 6;

(4) the individual adopts the child;

(5) the individual acknowledges parentage of the child under [Article] 3, unless the acknowledgment is rescinded under Section 308 or successfully challenged under [Article] 3 or 6; [or]

(6) the individual's parentage of the child is established under [Article] 7; [or]

(7) the individual's parentage of the child is established under [Article] 8.

§ 301. Acknowledgment of Parentage.

A woman who gave birth to a child and an alleged genetic father of the child, intended parent under [Article] 7, or presumed parent may sign an acknowledgment of parentage to establish the parentage of the child.

§ 204. Presumption of Parentage.

(a) An individual is presumed to be a parent of a child if:

(1) except as otherwise provided under [[Article] 8 or] law of this state other than this [act]:

(A) the individual and the woman who gave birth to the child are married to each other and the child is born during the marriage, whether the marriage is or could be declared invalid;

(B) the individual and the woman who gave birth to the child were married to each other and the child is born not later than 300 days after the marriage is terminated by death, [divorce, dissolution, annulment, or declaration of invalidity, or after a decree of separation or separate maintenance], whether the marriage is or could be declared invalid; or

(C) the individual and the woman who gave birth to the child married each other after the birth of the child, whether the marriage is or could be declared invalid, the individual at any time asserted parentage of the child, and:

> (i) the assertion is in a record filed with the [state agency maintaining birth records]; or

> (ii) the individual agreed to be and is named as a parent of the child on the birth certificate of the child; or

(2) the individual resided in the same household with the child for the first two years of the life of the child, including any period of temporary absence, and openly held out the child as the individual's child.

(b) A presumption of parentage under this section may be overcome, and competing claims to parentage may be resolved, only by an adjudication under [Article] 6 or a valid denial of parentage under [Article] 3.

2. Who May Bring an Action to Establish Paternity?

Uniform Parentage Act (2019)

§ 602. Standing to Maintain Proceeding.

Except as otherwise provided in [Article] 3 and Sections 608 through 611, a proceeding to adjudicate parentage may be maintained by:

(1) the child;

(2) the woman who gave birth to the child, unless a court has adjudicated that she is not a parent;

(3) an individual who is a parent under this [act];

(4) an individual whose parentage of the child is to be adjudicated;

(5) a child-support agency[or other governmental agency authorized by law of this state other than this [act]];

(6) an adoption agency authorized by law of this state other than this [act] or licensed child-placement agency; or

(7) a representative authorized by law of this state other than this [act] to act for an individual who otherwise would be entitled to maintain a proceeding but is deceased, incapacitated, or a minor.

3. How May the Court Protect the Best Interests of the Child?

Uniform Parentage Act (2019)

§ 608. Adjudicating Parentage of Child with Presumed Parent.

(a) A proceeding to determine whether a presumed parent is a parent of a child may be commenced:

(1) before the child becomes an adult; or

(2) after the child becomes an adult, but only if the child initiates the proceeding.

(b) A presumption of parentage under Section 204 cannot be overcome after the child attains two years of age unless the court determines:

(1) the presumed parent is not a genetic parent, never resided with the child, and never held out the child as the presumed parent's child; or

(2) the child has more than one presumed parent.

(c) Except as otherwise provided in Section 614, the following rules apply in a proceeding to adjudicate a presumed parent's parentage of a child if the woman who gave birth to the child is the only other individual with a claim to parentage of the child:

(1) If no party to the proceeding challenges the presumed parent's parentage of the child, the court shall adjudicate the presumed parent to be a parent of the child.

(2) If the presumed parent is identified under Section 506 as a genetic parent of the child and that identification is not successfully challenged under Section 506, the court shall adjudicate the presumed parent to be a parent of the child.

(3) If the presumed parent is not identified under Section 506 as a genetic parent of the child and the presumed parent or the woman who gave birth to the child challenges the presumed parent's parentage of the child, the court shall adjudicate the parentage of the child in the best interest of the child based on the factors under Section 613(a) and (b).

(d) Except as otherwise provided in Section 614 and subject to other limitations in this [part], if in a proceeding to adjudicate a presumed parent's parentage of a child, another individual in addition to the woman who gave birth to the child asserts a claim to parentage of the child, the court shall adjudicate parentage under Section 613.

§ 613. Adjudicating Competing Claims of Parentage.

(a) Except as otherwise provided in Section 614, in a proceeding to adjudicate competing claims of, or challenges under Section 608(c), 610, or 611 to, parentage of a child by two or more individuals, the court shall adjudicate parentage in the best interest of the child, based on:

(1) the age of the child;

(2) the length of time during which each individual assumed the role of parent of the child;

(3) the nature of the relationship between the child and each individual;

(4) the harm to the child if the relationship between the child and each individual is not recognized;

(5) the basis for each individual's claim to parentage of the child; and

(6) other equitable factors arising from the disruption of the relationship between the child and each individual or the likelihood of other harm to the child.

(b) If an individual challenges parentage based on the results of genetic testing, in addition to the factors listed in subsection (a), the court shall consider:

(1) the facts surrounding the discovery the individual might not be a genetic parent of the child; and

(2) the length of time between the time that the individual was placed on notice that the individual might not be a genetic parent and the commencement of the proceeding.

Alternative A

(c) The court may not adjudicate a child to have more than two parents under this [act].

Alternative B

(c) The court may adjudicate a child to have more than two parents under this [act] if the court finds that failure to recognize more than two parents would be detrimental to the child. A finding of detriment to the child does not require a finding of unfitness of any parent or individual seeking an adjudication of parentage. In determining detriment to the child, the court shall consider all relevant factors, including the harm if the child is removed from a stable placement with an individual who has fulfilled the child's physical needs and psychological needs for care and affection and has assumed the role for a substantial period.

Wingate v. Estate of Ryan

Supreme Court of New Jersey, 1997
149 N.J. 227, 693 A.2d 457

COLEMAN, J.

The issue raised in this appeal is whether the twenty-three-year limitations period found in N.J.S.A. 9:17-45(b) of the New Jersey Parentage Act ("Parentage Act"), codified at N.J.S.A. 9:17-38 to -59, applies to an intestacy action filed by a thirty-one-year-old claimant to prove parentage and heirship under N.J.S.A. 3B:5-10 of the Administration of Estates — Decedents and Others Act. That statute, commonly referred to as the Probate Code, is codified at N.J.S.A. 3B:1-1 to 3B:29-1. In 1991, the Legislature amended section 5-10 of the Probate Code to provide that a parent and child relationship "may be established as provided by the 'New Jersey Parentage Act,'" by persons born out of wedlock for purposes of proving heirship. L. 1991, c. 22, § 1.

Plaintiff Joanne Wingate filed a complaint under the Probate Code to establish that she and her son are heirs of John L. Ryan. The trial court denied defendants' motion for summary judgment to dismiss plaintiff's complaint for failure to file the claim by her twenty-third birthday. On defendants' appeal, the Appellate

Division reversed in a published opinion, holding that the twenty-three-year limitations period in the Parentage Act, N.J.S.A. 9:17-45(b), applied to plaintiff's claim. 290 N.J.Super. 463, 676 A.2d 144 (1996). We granted plaintiff's petition for certification, 146 N.J. 496, 683 A.2d 199 (1996), and now reverse. We hold that the limitations period under the Parentage Act does not apply to claims filed under the Probate Code.

*   *   *

Plaintiff Joanne Wingate was born on December 15, 1963. Plaintiff's mother, Rachel M. Parsio, was married to Willard Wingate at the time of plaintiff's birth. Parsio and Willard Wingate were divorced in 1970. Willard Wingate died in 1988. On February 6, 1995, decedent John J. Ryan died intestate. Until just before Ryan's death, plaintiff had believed that she was Willard Wingate's natural child. However, ten days before Ryan's death, plaintiff's mother informed her that Ryan was her natural father.

Decedent had a close relationship with Parsio and plaintiff. Parsio asserts that decedent purchased gifts for plaintiff on holidays and birthdays, and paid for substantial expenses, such as her braces and her wedding gown. According to Parsio, decedent acknowledged to her that he was plaintiff's biological father on several occasions, but decedent repeatedly refused to publicly acknowledge that fact because he and Parsio were not married, and such a revelation would cause embarrassment, particularly in light of his Catholic faith. Parsio claims that she did not reveal decedent's paternity because Ryan threatened to "cut off ties," including financial support, to her and plaintiff.

After filing her complaint on February 7, 1995, in the Chancery Division, Family Part, plaintiff obtained an order permitting blood and hair samples to be taken from decedent prior to embalming. Cellmark Diagnostics performed genetic testing on samples from decedent, Parsio, and plaintiff.

Cellmark's DNA fingerprint analysis revealed a match between decedent and plaintiff, the probability of which was one in twenty-three million for unrelated persons. DNA blood profiles revealed a 99.99% probability of decedent's paternity, as compared to that of a random Caucasian male. Cellmark's report concluded that decedent was plaintiff's natural father, and decedent's estate has not contested that conclusion.

Plaintiff filed an amended complaint on February 17, 1995, adding Helen Thomas, both individually as decedent's sister and as administratrix of decedent's estate, as a defendant. Defendants then filed a motion for summary judgment. The Family Part granted summary judgment to defendants dismissing the complaint, reasoning that plaintiff had failed to comply with the twenty-three-year limitations period under the Parentage Act, N.J.S.A. 9:17-45(b).

On plaintiff's motion for reconsideration, the Family Part vacated its summary judgment and transferred the matter to the Probate Part. The Appellate Division granted defendants' motion for leave to appeal and stayed further proceedings in the Probate Part pending disposition of the appeal. The Appellate Division reversed the trial court's denial of defendants' motion for summary judgment.

* * *

Our analysis must begin with the legislative enactments that will inform our ultimate decision. The Wills, Descent and Simultaneous Death Act was enacted in 1977 and amended in 1979. The predecessor to the provision that is pertinent to this case provided:

> If, for purposes of intestate succession, a relationship of parent and child must be established to determine succession by, through, or from a person.

> a. The relationships and rights of an adopted minor child shall be those as provided by section 14 of P.L.1977, c. 367 (C. 9:3-50), and the relationships and rights of an adopted adult shall be as provided in N.J.S. 2A:22-3.

> b. In cases not covered by a., a person born out of wedlock is a child of the mother. That person is also a child of the father, if:

> (1) The natural parents, before or after the birth of the child, participated in a ceremonial marriage or shall have consummated a common-law marriage where such marriage is recognized as valid in the manner authorized by the law of the place where such marriage took place, even though the attempted marriage is void; or

> (2) The paternity is established by an adjudication before the death of the father or is established thereafter by clear and convincing proof, except that the paternity established under this subparagraph is ineffective to qualify the father or his kindred to inherit from or through the child unless the father has openly treated the child as his, and has not refused to support the child.

* * *

In 1982, the Legislature revised the Wills, Descent and Simultaneous Death Act and renamed it an Act for the Administration of Estates—Decedents and Others, now commonly known as the Probate Code. L. 1981, c. 405. Pertinent to this case is N.J.S.A. 3B:5-10, which repealed N.J.S.A. 3A:2A-41 and became effective in 1982. The 1982 version of N.J.S.A. 3B:5-10 provided:

> If, for the purposes of intestate succession, a relationship of parent and child must be established to determine succession by, through or from a person, a child born out of wedlock is a child of the mother. That child is also a child of the father, if:

> a. The natural parents, before or after the birth of the child, participated in a ceremonial marriage or shall have consummated a common-law marriage where the marriage is recognized as valid in the manner authorized by the law of the place where the marriage took place, even though the attempted marriage is void; or

b. The paternity is established by an adjudication before the death of the father or is established thereafter by clear and convincing proof, except that the paternity established under this subsection is ineffective to qualify the father or his kindred to inherit from or through the child unless the father has openly treated the child as his, and has not refused to support the child.

N.J.S.A. 3B:23-19 of the Probate Code provides a general limitations period for claims brought under that statute. Claims by persons whose names or addresses are unknown must be brought "within a reasonable time and after reasonable notice . . . as may be prescribed by the court." N.J.S.A. 3B:23-19. N.J.S.A. 3B:23-20 provides that a person who fails to file a claim within the time required by the court pursuant to N.J.S.A. 3B:23-19 "shall be forever thereafter debarred from all right, title or claim to the decedent's estate."

The 1982 version of N.J.S.A. 3B:5-10(b) is identical to a provision in the Uniform Probate Code of 1969. Unif. Probate Code § 2-109(2)(ii), 8 U.L.A. 67 (1983). That section has alternative provisions, one for jurisdictions that have adopted the Uniform Parentage Act, and the other, followed by New Jersey, for those jurisdictions that have not adopted the Uniform Parentage Act. *Id.* at 67–68 cmt. Thus, when the Probate Code was modified in 1982, New Jersey had not yet adopted a Parentage Act. That, however, was changed the next year, creating inconsistent methods and standards of proof for establishing parentage under New Jersey's Probate Code and Parentage Act.

* * *

In 1983, the Legislature passed the Parentage Act, which is modeled after the Uniform Parentage Act of 1973. Assembly Judiciary, Law, Public Safety and Defense Committee Statement to Senate Bill No. 888—L. 1983, c. 17. The Legislature enacted the Parentage Act "to establish the principle that regardless of the marital status of the parents, all children and parents have equal rights with respect to each other and to provide a procedure to establish parentage in disputed cases." *Ibid.*

Procedurally, the Parentage Act establishes several presumptions of paternity in N.J.S.A. 9:17-43(a), and sets forth in section 43(d) the burden of proving paternity absent the existence of such a presumption. Claims to establish paternity must be filed timely: "[n]o action shall be brought under this act more than 5 years after the child attains the age of majority." N.J.S.A. 9:17-45(b). That section effectively imposes a twenty-three-year statute of repose for actions under the Parentage Act, running from the child's date of birth.

N.J.S.A. 9:17-45(b) is analogous to a provision of the Uniform Parentage Act that requires an action to be brought within three years of a child's majority. Unif. Parentage Act § 7, 9B U.L.A. 306 (1987). The comment to that Uniform Parentage Act section states that, "[i]n effect, . . . this Section provides for a twenty-one-year statute of limitations, except that a late paternity action does not affect laws relating to distribution and closing of decedents' estates or to the determination of heirship." *Ibid.* cmt. Because the Probate Code and the Parentage Act prior to 1991 provided different methods and standards for establishing parentage, steps were taken to resolve the conflicts.

* * *

The responsibility for attempting to reconcile the conflicting methods and standards of proof in the two acts fell on the New Jersey Law Revision Commission ("Commission"). N.J.S.A. 1:12A-8. In its 1987 annual report to the Legislature pursuant to N.J.S.A. 1:12A-9, the Commission reported that the methods and standards for proving parentage under the Probate Code and the Parentage Act were inconsistent. First Annual Report of the New Jersey Law Revision Commission 3 (1987) ("Law Revision Commission Report"). The focus of the report was limited to the inconsistent burdens of proof required by those two statutes. *Ibid.* The Commission noted that the Parentage Act specified several presumptions of paternity that could be rebutted by clear and convincing evidence. *Ibid.* If no presumption of parentage existed, then that issue would be determined by a preponderance of the evidence. N.J.S.A. 9:17-43(d). The Probate Code, on the other hand, required claimants to prove paternity by clear and convincing evidence for post-mortem claims under the 1982 version of N.J.S.A. 3B:5-10(b).

The Commission explained that "the version of the [Uniform] Probate Code chosen for N.J.S. 3B:5-10 was never intended to be enacted in jurisdictions which accepted the [Uniform] Parentage Act," and that the Legislature had enacted the version of the Uniform Probate Code provision that reflected the absence of a Parentage Act in New Jersey at that time. Law Revision Commission Report, *supra*, at 3–4. The Commission recommended that the Legislature amend the Probate Code to reflect New Jersey's adoption of the Uniform Parentage Act in 1983, and to allow children born out of wedlock to prove paternity for heirship purposes by using the more permissive standards of the Parentage Act. *Id.* at 4. The Commission stated that such an amendment would promote "the modern principle that the parent-child relationship extends equally, irrespective of the marital state of the parents." *Ibid.*

Consistent with the Commission's recommendation, in 1991 the Legislature revised N.J.S.A. 3B:5-10 to provide:

> If, for the purposes of intestate succession, a relationship of parent and child must be established to determine succession by, through, or from a person, in cases not covered by N.J.S. 3B:5-9, [for adoption,] a person is the child of the person's parents regardless of the marital state of the person's parents, and the parent and child relationship may be established as provided by the "New Jersey Parentage Act," P.L.1983, c. 17 (C. 9:17-38 et seq.).

* * *

The parties agree that in view of the 1991 amendment, plaintiff must follow the methods and standards of proof outlined in the Parentage Act. They also agree that the DNA test results establish that John Ryan is plaintiff's father. The parties disagree, however, on whether plaintiff's claim against the estate is time barred.

* * *

Plaintiff argues that the Probate Code's statute of limitations, N.J.S.A. 3B:23-19, applies to her claim. That section provides that "the court may require all those persons whose names or addresses are unknown, to appear or file their [intestacy] claims . . . within a reasonable time and after reasonable notice by publication or otherwise, as may be prescribed by the court." *Ibid.* Plaintiff contends that the 1991 amendment to the Probate Code was intended to incorporate only the favorable methods and standards of proof found in the Parentage Act without altering the limitations period for filing her claim under N.J.S.A. 3B:23-19.

Defendants argue that the Appellate Division was correct in applying the limitations provision of the Parentage Act, N.J.S.A. 9:17-45(b), because it is more specific and was enacted more recently than N.J.S.A. 3B:23-19. 290 N.J.Super. at 471, 676 A.2d 144 (citing 3A Norman J. Singer, Sutherland on Statutory Construction, § 70.03 (5th ed. 1992) ("When two or more statutes of limitation deal with the same subject matter, the statute which is more recent and specific will prevail over the older and more general one.")).

The critical question is whether the Legislature intended in 1991 to change the Probate Code's statute of limitations, N.J.S.A. 3B:23-19. To answer that question, we must interpret the amendment. We have consistently held that when interpreting a statute, "courts must seek to fulfill the statutory objective 'so far as the terms of the legislation and proper consideration of the interests of those subject to it will fairly permit.'" State v. Haliski, 140 N.J. 1, 9, 656 A.2d 1246 (1995) (quoting State v. Gill, 47 N.J. 441, 444, 221 A.2d 521 (1966)); Merin v. Maglaki, 126 N.J. 430, 435, 599 A.2d 1256 (1992). A court should interpret a statute in a way that advances "the sense and meaning fairly deducible from the context." Lesniak v. Budzash, 133 N.J. 1, 14, 626 A.2d 1073 (1993).

The first consideration when interpreting a statute is the statute's plain meaning. State v. Szemple, 135 N.J. 406, 421, 640 A.2d 817 (1994); *Merin, supra,* 126 N.J. at 434, 599 A.2d 1256; Town of Morristown v. Woman's Club, 124 N.J. 605, 610, 592 A.2d 216 (1991). If different interpretations exist, then the statute's meaning is not obvious or self-evident on its face. *Szemple, supra,* 135 N.J. at 422, 640 A.2d 817; GE Solid State, Inc. v. Director, Div. of Taxation, 132 N.J. 298, 307, 625 A.2d 468 (1993). When a statute is ambiguous, a court's function is to ascertain and to effectuate the Legislature's intent. Szemple, *supra,* 135 N.J. at 422, 640 A.2d 817 (citing Cedar Cove, Inc. v. Stanzione, 122 N.J. 202, 213, 584 A.2d 784 (1991)). Extrinsic aids, such as legislative history, committee reports, and contemporaneous construction, may be used to help resolve any ambiguity and to ascertain the true intent of the Legislature. *Ibid.*

The legislative history regarding the 1991 amendment includes the Senate Judiciary Committee's Statement that accompanied the proposed amendment. It provides:

'This bill is intended to resolve a potential conflict between N.J.S.A. 3B:5-10 part of New Jersey's Probate Code and the 'New Jersey Parentage Act,'

P.L.1983, c. 17 (C. 9:17-38 et seq.) with regard to the standard for the determination of the parentage of children born out of wedlock.

* * *

The Parentage Act which was enacted in 1983 sets procedures and standards for determining parentage of children born out of wedlock. *These procedures were intended to be applicable in all actions. In order to insure that a determination of parentage under the Parentage Act would also be applicable in probate matters, this bill would amend 3B:5-10 to provide that for purposes of intestate succession the parent-child relationship may be established as provided in the Parentage Act.*

* * *

As noted earlier, the 1991 amendment to N.J.S.A. 3B:5-10 was in response to the 1987 report submitted by the Law Revision Commission that emphasized the different burdens of proof for establishing parentage under the Parentage Act and under the Probate Code. The Parentage Act creates rebuttable presumptions of parentage under some circumstances. N.J.S.A. 9:17-43(a). In those circumstances, a putative father may overcome that presumption only by clear and convincing evidence. N.J.S.A. 9:17-43(b). Absent a designated presumption of parentage, the burden of proof is by a preponderance of the evidence. N.J.S.A. 9:17-43(d). In contrast, under the Probate Code prior to the 1991 amendment, a parentage action to prove heirship after the decedent's death required a claimant to establish heirship by clear and convincing proof. N.J.S.A. 3B:5-10(b).

What emerges from a review of the legislative history is an intent to change the Probate Code's provision, N.J.S.A. 3B:5-10, to create the same burden of proof existing under the Parentage Act. Consistent with that intent, the Senate Committee's Statement reveals that the only articulated purpose of the amendment was to resolve a potential conflict between the Probate Code and the Parentage Act regarding "the standard for the determination of the parentage of children born out of wedlock." Senate Judiciary Committee Statement to Senate Bill No. 1346—L. 1991, c. 22. The word "standard" most commonly refers to the burden of proof in a cause of action. *See* Del Tufo v. Township of Old Bridge, 147 N.J. 90, 98, 685 A.2d 1267 (1996) (using term "standard" to refer to burden of proof); see also SSI Med. Servs., Inc. v. State, 146 N.J. 614, 617, 685 A.2d 1 (1996) (same).

That conclusion is supported by the fact that the Commission discussed only the inconsistent burden of proof issue. The Commission recommended changing the burden of proof under the Probate Code because of the increased reliance on scientific tests under the Parentage Act to establish paternity. Hence, the Commission recommended that the Legislature

> accept the more clear and specific rules for the determination of parent-child relationships of the Parentage Act and its reflection of the modern

principle that scientific tests can be used to make an accurate determination of parentage in the majority of cases.

* * *

We conclude that the Legislature intended the 1991 amendment to N.J.S.A. 3B:5-10 to amend *only* the standard of proof. The Legislature was convinced that, given the reliable scientific tests used under the Parentage Act to establish parentage, it no longer made sense to require a higher burden of proof under the Probate Code to establish the identical fact. Consequently, the Legislature's use of the terms "standard for the determination of parentage of children," intended for the word "standard" to have its common meaning, namely, the burden of proof.

* * *

Apart from the legislative history revealing that the 1991 amendment intended to change only the burden of proof for establishing parentage under the Probate Code, the Parentage Act and the Probate Code are independent statutes designed to address different primary rights. The purpose of the Parentage Act is to establish "the legal relationship . . . between a child and the child's natural or adoptive parents, incident to which the law confers or imposes rights, privileges, duties, and obligations." N.J.S.A. 9:17-39. Child support is the major concern under the Parentage Act. The purpose of the Probate Code, on the other hand, is to determine the devolution of a decedent's real and personal property. N.J.S.A. 3B:1-3. The different purposes the two statutes serve, help to explain why the Legislature contemplated different periods of limitations for filing claims under those statutes.

It is well established in New Jersey that parents have a duty to support their children from the date of birth until the children are emancipated, which is presumed to occur upon the age of majority. Newburgh v. Arrigo, 88 N.J. 529, 543, 443 A.2d 1031 (1982). Because the right to support accrues on the date of birth and ends on emancipation, it is fair to apply N.J.S.A. 9:17-45(b) to claims for support.

Although plaintiff received financial and emotional support from decedent for many years before his death, decedent's parentage was not established before plaintiff reached her twenty-third birthday as required by N.J.S.A. 9:17-45(b). She was not told that decedent was her father until she was thirty-one-years old, at which time she was not in need of his support. Indeed, the law imposed no obligation for him to support her at that time. Consequently, application of the Parentage Act's statute of limitations to any support claim that she might have filed at the age of thirty-one would have been fair because (1) that period balances a claimant's right to support with the State's interest in requiring prompt filing of parentage actions, *see* Unif. Parentage Act § 7, 9B U.L.A. 306-07 cmt. (1987); and (2) a parent is relieved of the duty to provide support upon the child's emancipation. *Newburgh, supra,* 88 N.J. at 543, 443 A.2d 1031.

In contrast to children who file support claims, which accrue on the date of birth, potential heirs have no right to share in an estate until the death of the decedent.

By definition under the Probate Code, heirs are "those persons . . . who are entitled under the statutes of intestate succession to the property of a decedent." N.J.S.A. 3B:1-1. Applying N.J.S.A. 9:17-45(b) to actions under the Probate Code would create a statute of repose that commences on the birth of a potential heir, rather than a statute of limitations running from the decedent's death. Indeed, the Parentage Act provides that it does not affect the time within which an heirship claim must be filed. N.J.S.A. 9:17-45(f). That section provides further evidence that claims under the Probate Code and Parentage Act are subject to independent limitations periods. To hold otherwise would grant heirship immunity to parents of children who are born out of wedlock and do not establish parentage before reaching age twenty-three. That would terminate many claims before they accrue. E.A. Williams, Inc. v. Russo Dev. Corp., 82 N.J. 160, 167, 411 A.2d 697 (1980). To allow that to occur would be contrary to the Legislature's recognition in 1991 that "a person is the child of the person's parents regardless of the marital state of the person's parents." N.J.S.A. 3B:5-10.

Furthermore, the purpose of the 1991 amendment was to make it easier, not harder or impossible, for persons born out of wedlock to establish heirship. Before the 1991 amendment, a child's heirship could be established after the death of a parent, regardless of the age of the child. N.J.S.A. 3A:2A-41(b)(2) (repealed 1982). Absent some express contrary indication, it is highly unlikely that the Legislature would reduce the limitations period for filing heirship claims. A reduction in the limitations period would indeed be anomalous, given that our society has been moving gradually away from imposing legal disadvantages on children born out of wedlock who bear no responsibility for their parents' "irresponsible liaisons beyond the bonds of marriage." Weber v. Aetna Cas. & Sur. Co., 406 U.S. 164, 175, 92 S.Ct. 1400, 1406, 31 L.Ed.2d 768, 779 (1972). "[P]enalizing the illegitimate child is an ineffectual—as well as an unjust—way of deterring the parent." Id. at 175, 92 S.Ct. at 1407, 31 L.Ed.2d at 779. Finally, the comment to the limitations provision of the Uniform Parentage Act § 7, 9B U.L.A. 306 (1987), is persuasive. That comment states that, "[i]n effect, . . . this Section provides for a twenty-one-year statute of limitations, except that *a late paternity action does not affect laws relating to distribution and closing of decedents' estates or to the determination of heirship.*" *Ibid.* cmt. (emphasis added). Thus, the Uniform Parentage Act was not intended to affect the limitations period for actions to prove heirship. Because our Parentage Act is modeled after the Uniform Parentage Act, and for the other reasons stated, we hold that the Legislature did not intend its 1991 amendment to change the Probate Code's limitation on when claims can be filed thereunder for determination of heirship.

Our holding that the 1991 amendment changes only the standard for proving parentage for heirship purposes should have no effect on estate planning. It is inconceivable that since the amendment, fathers of children born out of wedlock have made their estate planning decisions based on whether post-mortem parentage claims for heirship purposes had to be established by a preponderance of the evidence or by clear and convincing evidence, as was required before the amendment. In the present case, the social opprobrium associated with having a liaison with a married woman is more likely to have influenced decedent not to include plaintiff in his estate planning by publicly acknowledging her as his daughter or by providing for her in a will.

* * *

We also reject the Appellate Division's reasoning that the twenty-three-year period of repose should be imposed in order to guard against spurious claims. 290 N.J.Super. at 476–77, 676 A.2d 144. The need to prevent fraudulent claims has been "substantially alleviated by recent scientific developments in blood testing dramatically reducing the possibility that a defendant will be falsely accused of being the illegitimate child's father." Mills v. Habluetzel, 456 U.S. 91, 104 n. 2, 102 S. Ct. 1549, 1557 n. 2, 71 L.Ed.2d 770, 781 n. 2 (1982) (O'Connor, J., concurring); *see also* Pickett v. Brown, 462 U.S. 1, 17, 103 S.Ct. 2199, 2208, 76 L.Ed.2d 372, 385 (1983) (stating that "the relationship between a statute of limitations and the State's interest in preventing the litigation of stale or fraudulent paternity claims has become more attenuated as scientific advances in blood testing have alleviated the problems of proof surrounding paternity actions"); State v. Marcus, 294 N.J.Super. 267, 279, 683 A.2d 221 (App.Div.1996) (noting general acceptance of DNA analysis by scientific community and courts); State v. Williams, 252 N.J.Super. 369, 380, 599 A.2d 960 (Law Div.1991) (stating that "[i]t is generally accepted that [DNA testing] can limit the spectrum of potential donors of a blood specimen to one out of every 10 million persons").

Another source has noted that

> [j]udicial recognition of the scientific acceptance of the foundations of DNA analysis is consistent with our conclusion that the methods of DNA analysis surveyed in this report are firmly grounded in molecular biology. When [DNA] profiling is done with due care, the results are highly reproducible. . . . [T]here seems little doubt in the courtroom, as in the laboratory, that properly conducted [DNA] profiling is a scientifically acceptable procedure. . . .

> [Committee on DNA Forensic Science, National Research Council, The Evaluation of Forensic DNA Evidence 176 (1996) (footnote omitted).] * * *

In another decision, the United States Supreme Court noted that "increasingly sophisticated tests for genetic markers permit the exclusion of over 99% of those who might be accused of paternity, regardless of the age of the child." Clark v. Jeter, 486 U.S. 456, 465, 108 S.Ct. 1910, 1916, 100 L.Ed.2d 465, 474 (1988) (emphasis added). Indeed, in the present case, the Cellmark report has revealed a 99.99% probability of decedent's paternity and a DNA fingerprint match with decedent, the probability of which is one in twenty-three million for unrelated people. In the face of such compelling evidence, few spurious claims will go undetected.

* * *

We hold that N.J.S.A. 3B:23-19 controls and that the 1991 amendment to N.J.S.A. 3B:5-10 did not change the Probate Code's statute of limitations. That statute allows an out-of-wedlock child of a deceased parent to file an heirship claim with the personal representative of the decedent's estate within the time the court has deemed reasonable for the filing of claims. Here, there can be no dispute over whether plaintiff filed her claim within a reasonable time. Ryan died on February 6, 1995, and plaintiff filed her claim on February 7, 1995.

* * *

The judgment of the Appellate Division is reversed. The matter is remanded to the Chancery Division, Probate Part to dispose of the complaint on the merits.

For reversal and remandment—Chief Justice PORITZ, and Justices HANDLER, POLLOCK, O'IIERN, GARIBALDI, STEIN and COLEMAN * * * .

Notes

The *Wingate* decision makes a distinction between petitions for child support from a putative father *during the lifetime* of the petitioner and father, and those petitions to take from the putative father's estate at *probate. See also,* Jenkins v. Johnson, 276 Va. 30, 661 S.E.2d 484 (2008) (distinguishing paternity petitions seeking support from those seeking intestate inheritance). Following the *Wingate* decision, the New Jersey legislature amended its statute to specify a two-year statute of limitations rather than the reasonableness standard established in *Wingate. See* N.J. STAT. ANN § 3B:23-19(c) (West 2019). Other states have similar statutes. *See, e.g., In re* Marriage of Ostrander, 27 N.E.3d 698 (Ill. Ct. App. 2015) (holding that statute of limitations bars any action to declare the non-existence of the parent-child relationship if brought later than two years after the petitioner obtains knowledge of the relevant facts).

Even if a petition is presented within the statutory period, courts often deny standing to persons challenging the paternity of a child. *See, e.g.,* R.J.S. v. Stockton, 886 N.E.2d 611 (Ind. Ct. App. 2008) (holding that parents of a man who died shortly before birth of their son's alleged non-marital child did not have "next friend" standing to seek an order establishing paternity); J.R.W. *ex rel.* Jemerson v. Watterson, 877 N.E.2d 487 (Ind. Ct. App. 2007) (after woman's husband filed a paternity affidavit stating he was the father of her child, even though he knew he was not, child's aunt and uncle were named guardians of the child, but custody was awarded to husband, whereupon aunt and uncle sought to deny the validity of the paternity affidavit but the court ruled they lacked standing to do so). However, a few courts have allowed standing to some claimants if there is a modicum of evidence to support or disprove an allegation of paternity, such as genetic testing. *See, e.g.,* R.R.C. v. D.G.C., 183 So. 3d 164 (Ala. Civ. App. 2015) (permitting a former husband to contest an order for child support after the husband obtained DNA evidence that he could not be the father of the child). The Unif. Parentage Act specifies who has standing at § 602 (Standing to Maintain Proceeding). The following decision illustrates the process of contest.

Reese v. Muret

Supreme Court of Kansas, 2007
283 Kan. 1, 150 P.3d 309

The opinion of the court was delivered by ROSEN, J:

This is a paternity action in the context of a probate case. Heather S. Reese (formerly Waldschmidt) (Heather) seeks a determination that she is the child of Wade Samuel Waldschmidt, Jr. (Sam). Sam's spouse, Sandra Waldschmidt (Sandra) opposed Heather's claim as a child in Samuel's intestate estate and filed a motion for genetic testing. Heather filed a paternity action pursuant to the Kansas Parentage Act, claiming that Sam was her presumptive father. Sandra intervened in the paternity action and moved for genetic testing. The district court denied Sandra's motions in both the probate and paternity actions, and she brings this appeal, claiming that *In re Marriage of Ross*, 245 Kan. 591, 783 P.2d 331 (1989), does not apply to genetic testing in paternity cases brought by adults for the purpose of determining inheritance.

Sam married Deloris Hibbs (Deloris) on June 1, 1970. On January 25, 1971, Deloris gave birth to a daughter named Heather Shea Waldschmidt (Heather). Heather's birth certificate named Sam as her father. Deloris and Sam divorced on July 12, 1972. The divorce pleadings acknowledged Heather as a child of the union. The district court ordered Sam to pay child support and granted Sam visitation with Heather.

In November 1972, Sam filed a motion to terminate his child support payments, alleging that Deloris "took the minor child of said parties and disappeared." Sam's motion further alleged that Deloris was unfit and that he should have custody of Heather. In December 1972, the district court entered an order terminating Sam's child support until Deloris could show just cause to have the child support reinstated. Deloris never reinstated Sam's child support obligation, but Sam's Aunt Irene provided financial assistance to Deloris and Heather.

After the divorce, Sam had little contact with Heather. Sam saw Heather at Waldschmidt family gatherings for Thanksgiving and Christmas but did not attempt to have a relationship with her. However, Heather was very close to members of Sam's family including his mother, Margaret; his brother, David; and his Aunt Irene. Heather was also close to her Waldschmidt cousins. Although Heather did not have a relationship with Sam, she always considered him to be her father.

Sam married Sandra Woodard in October 1976. According to Sandra, Sam said that Heather was not his child. Sam and Sandra had no children. They separated in September 1988 and divorced in 1990. Sandra moved back in with Sam in 1994, moved out again in 1995, and remarried him in 1996. After their remarriage, Sandra did not live with Sam, but visited him occasionally on weekends.

Before Sandra moved back in with Sam in 1994, he executed a will leaving everything to his sisters, Camille and Anna Jane. On December 10, 2002, Sam visited with an attorney about his estate. Sam told the attorney that he had a daughter. The attorney perceived that there was tension between Sam and Sandra regarding Sam's daughter, but Sam did not explain the situation. On or about December 13, 2002, Sam committed suicide.

On December 18, 2002, Heather petitioned the district court to appoint administrators for Sam's estate. Sandra responded to Heather's petition, denying that Heather was Sam's daughter and requesting the court to appoint her as the administrator for Sam's estate. Sandra also filed a petition in the probate action for genetic testing to determine whether Sam was Heather's biological father. The district court appointed an attorney, who was a disinterested third party, as the administrator of Sam's estate.

In response to Sandra's motion for genetic testing, Heather filed a paternity action pursuant to the Kansas Parentage Act, seeking a determination that Sam was Heather's father. The petition alleged that Sam was Heather's presumed father because she was born during her mother's marriage to Sam, Sam had acknowledged his paternity in the divorce pleadings, and Sam was ordered to pay child support on Heather's behalf. Sandra filed a motion to intervene and a motion for genetic testing. Over Heather's objection, the district court granted Sandra's motion to intervene pursuant to K.S.A. 60-224(b).

Heather objected to Sandra's motions for genetic testing. The district court then ordered a *Ross* hearing to determine whether it was in Heather's best interests to grant Sandra's motions. The parties agreed to submit the evidence for the *Ross* hearing based on stipulated depositions and exhibits rather than conducting an evidentiary hearing. Based on this evidence, the district court held that it was not in Heather's best interests to conduct genetic testing and denied Sandra's motion.

Sandra filed a motion for an interlocutory appeal in the paternity action and requested a ruling on her petition for genetic testing in the probate action. The district court denied Sandra's petition for genetic testing in the probate action and granted her request for an interlocutory appeal in the paternity action. Sandra filed a notice of appeal in both actions. The appeals were consolidated and transferred to this court on our motion pursuant to K.S.A. 20-3018(c).

The matter was originally set for oral argument on December 5, 2005. However, upon finding a copy of Sam's will in the record, we remanded the matter to the district court for a determination of the validity of Sam's will. Thereafter, Sam's sister, Camille Pond, petitioned the district court to admit a copy of Sam's will to probate. After an evidentiary hearing, the district court denied Camille's petition to probate Sam's will because she had failed to overcome the presumption that Sam had destroyed or revoked his original will. Following the district court's refusal to probate Sam's will, we reinstated Sandra's appeal. * * *

Sandra argues that the district court improperly applied the ruling of *Ross*, 245 Kan. 591, 783 P.2d 331, in determining whether to order genetic testing in a probate action and in a parentage action brought by an adult for the purposes of applying the probate code. According to Sandra, *Ross* is inapplicable to a probate case and inapplicable to adults. We analyze this issue as a question of law subject to de novo review because it involves stipulated facts and statutory interpretation. * * *

Because this action arises out of the administration of a decedent's estate, we will begin our analysis with the probate code, K.S.A. 59-101 *et seq.* K.S.A. 59-501 defines children for purposes of intestate succession, stating:

> "'Children' means biological children, including a posthumous child; children adopted as provided by law; and children whose parentage is or has been determined under the Kansas parentage act or prior law."

When Heather filed the petition to administer Sam's estate, she asserted her interest in Sam's estate as a biological child because none of the other possible definitions in K.S.A. 59-501 applied. As long as Heather's claim to Sam's estate was based on her being Sam's biological child, the genetic connection between Heather and Sam was in issue. Under this scenario, Sandra correctly argues that *Ross* is inapplicable to an intestate claim based on the biological definition of child because genetic testing is the only conclusive means of establishing biological parentage.

However, K.S.A. 59-501 does not limit the definition of children to biological offspring. Rather, the definition of children is much broader, requiring the probate court to treat any person as a child if such person's parentage is or has been determined under the Kansas Parentage Act. K.S.A. 59-501(a). Heather invoked the Kansas Parentage Act as the basis for her inheritance claim under K.S.A. 59-501 when she filed her petition to determine paternity under the Act. We note that K.S.A. 59-501(a) does not require a determination under the Kansas Parentage Act to occur prior to a probate proceeding. Rather, the legislature acknowledged that proceedings under the Kansas Parentage Act may occur simultaneously with probate proceedings by incorporating the phrase "whose parentage is or has been determined" in the definition of children. See K.S.A. 59-501(a).

The probate code treats a determination of parentage pursuant to the Kansas Parentage Act as conclusive. See K.S.A. 59-501(a). Once paternity is established in accordance with the Kansas Parentage Act, the probate code provides no mechanism for challenging that paternity determination. Because Heather eliminated the issue of biological parentage in the probate action by filing her paternity action and the probate code does not authorize genetic testing to challenge a paternity determination under the Kansas Parentage Act, there is no statutory basis for Sandra's motion for genetic testing in the probate case. Although Sandra correctly argues that *Ross* does not apply to an order for genetic testing under the probate code, the district court properly denied Sandra's motion because there was no statutory basis for the motion. * * *

Pursuant to the Kansas Parentage Act, a man is presumed to be the father of a child born while the man is married to the child's mother. K.S.A. 38-1114(a)(1). A child or a person on behalf of the child may file an action at any time to establish paternity when there is a presumption of paternity. K.S.A. 38-1115(a)(1). However, a presumption based on genetic test results must relate to genetic testing that occurs prior to the filing of the paternity action. See K.S.A. 38-1114(a)(5); *In re Estate of Foley,* 22 Kan.App.2d 959, 925 P.2d 449 (1996). The child, the child's mother, and the presumptive father are parties to the paternity action. K.S.A. 38-1117(a). K.S.A. 38-1118(a) requires the district court to order genetic testing when any party requests genetic testing. However, the *Ross* court tempered the statutory requirement of K.S.A. 38-1118(a), by requiring the district court to conduct a hearing prior to issuing an order for genetic testing to determine whether genetic testing is in the best interests of the child. *Ross,* 245 Kan. at 602, 783 P.2d 331. Since *Ross* was decided in 1989, the legislature has not amended the statute to reverse the limitation imposed by *Ross.*

In *Ross,* the child, R.A.R., was born during the marriage of his mother Sylvia to Robert. When Sylvia and Robert divorced, Sylvia alleged that Robert was R.A.R.'s father. Robert was granted joint custody and ordered to pay child support. Two years later, Sylvia filed a petition pursuant to the Kansas Parentage Act to establish Charles as R.A.R.'s biological father. Sylvia wanted Charles to be named R.A.R.'s father so he could consent to R.A.R.'s adoption by Sylvia's current husband. To establish Charles as R.A.R.'s biological parent, Sylvia requested an order compelling all of the parties to submit to genetic testing. The district court ordered the genetic testing pursuant to K.S.A. 38-1118(a) and admitted the results over Robert's and Charles's objections. Based on the results of the genetic testing, the district court determined that Charles was R.A.R.'s biological father and ordered him to pay child support. Nevertheless, the district court determined that it was in R.A.R.'s best interest to maintain his relationship with Robert, so the court continued the joint custody arrangement between Sylvia and Robert.

The *Ross* court reversed the district court's order for genetic testing and the order establishing Charles as R.A.R.'s biological father. 245 Kan. at 602, 783 P.2d 331. Noting that "the ancient presumption of the legitimacy of a child born in wedlock is one of the strongest presumptions known to the law," the *Ross* court held that the district court must conduct a hearing to determine whether it is in the child's best interests to perform genetic testing and determine the child's biological paternity as opposed to his presumptive paternity. 245 Kan. at 596, 602, 783 P.2d 331.

Sandra argues that *Ross* only applies to minor children. However, in *Ferguson v. Winston,* 27 Kan.App.2d 34, 35, 36, 996 P.2d 841 (2000), the Court of Appeals applied *Ross* to a paternity proceeding involving an adult child. In *Ferguson,* the child, Michael, was born to Debra while she was living with Dale. Debra and Dale married after Michael's birth, and Debra recognized Dale as Michael's father for a period of 14 years. During Debra and Dale's divorce proceedings, Debra asserted for the first time that Dale was not Michael's biological father. In response, Dale filed a paternity action pursuant to the Kansas Parentage Act, seeking a determination that Michael was his son. Michael became an adult during the pendency of the paternity proceedings but was not made a party to the action and was not represented by a guardian ad litem. Without conducting a *Ross* hearing, the district court ordered genetic testing and summarily determined that Dale was not Michael's biological father.

The *Ferguson* court reversed the district court's decision, concluding that the district court committed both legal and procedural errors. 27 Kan.App.2d at 36, 996 P.2d 841. The *Ferguson* court determined that Dale is Michael's presumptive father based on K.S.A. 38-1114. Because of the presumption that Michael is Dale's son, the *Ferguson* court held that the district court erroneously considered genetic test results obtained without the benefit of a *Ross* hearing to determine whether it was in Michael's best interests to shift paternity from the presumptive father to the biological father. 27 Kan.App.2d at 36–37, 996 P.2d 841. The *Ferguson* court also held that the district court erred when it treated the genetic test results as conclusive on the issue of paternity, stating:

> "If DNA evidence is conclusive on the issue of paternity, we could simply do away with the judicial process in paternity cases. If the DNA test is conclusive, the paternity of children will be left for resolution by the scientists, and judges will become superfluous in that regard. We do not perceive the law to require or to recommend that result, and we hold that DNA evidence is not conclusive on the issue of paternity. On remand, if the trial court decides the DNA evidence is in Michael's best interests, it must still consider any other evidence offered before making a final decision." 27 Kan. App.2d at 38, 996 P.2d 841.

The *Ferguson* court further concluded that the district court violated Michael's constitutional right to due process by proceeding without joining Michael as a party or protecting his interests by appointing a guardian ad litem on his behalf. 27 Kan. App.2d at 38–39, 996 P.2d 841. Ordering that Michael be joined as a party and represented by counsel on remand, the *Ferguson* court suggested that the district court and the parties give "special attention" to Michael's wishes. 27 Kan.App.2d at 40, 996 P.2d 841.

Sandra attempts to distinguish *Ferguson* by arguing that it did not involve a question of intestate succession. Sandra further argues that *Ferguson* does not apply because, unlike Michael, Heather was an adult when the action was filed. Sandra also points to Heather's representation by counsel and asserts that Heather waived her right to a *Ross* hearing when she filed the paternity action. Sandra focuses on the following excerpt from *Ferguson:*

> "The facts which underlie this action give it a somewhat bizarre tilt and certainly create questions as to the relevance of the entire proceedings. To begin with, there is an obvious question as to just why this is being litigated. Michael became an adult during the litigation, and it is apparent there were and are no issues of child custody or child support being litigated." 27 Kan. App.2d at 35, 996 P.2d 841.

Sandra's attempt to factually distinguish *Ferguson* overlooks the legal foundation of the *Ferguson* court's holding. Both the *Ross* and *Ferguson* courts were concerned with the purpose for determining a child's biological paternity when there was already a presumptive father. *Ross,* 245 Kan. at 601, 783 P.2d 331; *Ferguson,* 27 Kan. App.2d at 35–36, 996 P.2d 841. Like the *Ross* court, the *Ferguson* court focused on the legal presumption of paternity that existed prior to the commencement of the paternity action. *Ross,* 245 Kan. at 596, 602, 783 P.2d 331; *Ferguson,* 27 Kan.App.2d at 36, 996 P.2d 841. The *Ferguson* court expressed this focus by stating that the "relevance, in a legal sense, of who is Michael's biological father is questionable." 27 Kan.App.2d at 35–36, 996 P.2d 841.

We believe the *Ross* and *Ferguson* analysis applies in this case. The relevance of who is Heather's biological father is questionable given the strong presumption that Sam was her father. The presumption of Sam's paternity existed for many years prior to the filing of this paternity action. Although the *Ferguson* court found the facts in that case were "somewhat bizarre" because it was litigated even though there were no issues regarding support or custody and the child had become an adult, this case demonstrates a set of circumstances in which an adult child may be forced to establish paternity pursuant to the Kansas Parentage Act even though a strong presumption of paternity already exists. *Ross* and *Ferguson* support the protection of presumptive paternity over biological paternity when it is in the child's best interests. We believe that protection extends to both minor and adult children.

Extending *Ross* to adult children accomplishes the legislature's intent as stated in the plain language of the statutory scheme. K.S.A. 38-1114 establishes six presumptions of paternity. If two presumptions conflict, the court must determine which presumption is founded on "weightier considerations of policy and logic, including the best interests of the child" before deciding which presumption controls. K.S.A. 38-1114(c). If any one of the presumptions arise, that presumption is a sufficient basis for an order requiring a man to support a child. K.S.A. 38-1114(e).

Without a *Ross* hearing to determine whether genetic testing is in the child's best interests, genetic testing becomes conclusive on the issue of paternity regardless of whether any other presumptions apply. As a result, denying adult children the protection of a *Ross* hearing is tantamount to rewriting the Kansas Parentage Act because it eliminates all of the other paternal presumptions besides genetic testing. If the legislature intended for genetic testing to be conclusive for determining the paternity of an adult child, it could have included language limiting the remaining presumptions to minor children. However, the Kansas Parentage Act does not include such limiting language in the statutory scheme. See K.S.A. 38-1114. The *Ferguson* court recognized the legislature's intent to treat all children the same, regardless of age, when it specifically held that genetic testing is not conclusive on the issue of paternity and ordered the district court to consider all of the evidence available before deciding Michael's paternity if it determined that genetic testing was in Michael's best interests. *Ferguson,* 27 Kan.App.2d at 38, 996 P.2d 841.

Extending *Ross* to adult children also furthers the purpose of the Kansas Parentage Act by protecting an adult child's right to inherit from his or her presumptive parent. The *Ross* court noted that the purpose of the Kansas Parentage Act is to provide for the "equal beneficial treatment of children." 245 Kan. at 597, 783 P.2d 331. The Kansas Parentage Act requires courts to act in the child's best interests "when imposing legal obligations or conferring legal rights" on the parent/child relationship. 245 Kan. at 597, 783 P.2d 331. The *Ross* court construed the Kansas Parentage Act to recognize that "every child has an interest not only in obtaining support, but also in inheritance rights, family bonds, and accurate identification of his parentage." 245 Kan. at 597, 783 P.2d 331. While the court does not need to protect a child's right to support after emancipation, the need to protect a child's right to inherit, the child's family bonds, and the accurate identification of the child's parentage are not limited to the child's period of minority.

Finally, extending *Ross* to adult children recognizes the public policy that paternity is both broader and deeper than genetics. The recognition of family identity extends beyond the years of a child's minority. Every adult continues to be someone's son or daughter for purposes of family identification, family bonding, and inheritance. The parental relationship continues to exist regardless of whether the bonds are close, strained, or nonexistent. The presumptions of paternity set forth in K.S.A. 38-1114(a) were instituted to protect and maintain the concept of family identity. Intruding upon this concept can cause emotional damage to children of all ages, not only to minors. See *Ross,* 245 Kan. at 602, 783 P.2d 331 (noting that "[t]he shifting of paternity from the presumed father to the biological father could easily be detrimental to the emotional and physical well-being of *any* child" [emphasis added]); *Ferguson,* 27 Kan.App.2d at 39, 996 P.2d 841 (concluding that children have a fundamental liberty interest in maintaining familial relationships).

This case illustrates the importance of protecting the presumption of paternity. Although the ultimate issue in this case involves the division of a decedent's estate, the resolution of that issue turns on the legal designation of paternity for a child born with a presumptive father. Heather was born during Sam's and Deloris' marriage. Sam's name appears on Heather's birth certificate. Heather was identified with Sam's familial name and included in the membership of Sam's family. Although her relationship with Sam was externally distant, she always believed he was her father. Sandra is attempting to vitiate a legal parent and child relationship that had not been questioned while Sam was alive. Requiring the district court to conduct genetic testing without determining whether it is in Heather's best interest would allow Sandra to accomplish after Sam's death that which could not be accomplished during Sam's lifetime. We cannot support a policy which gives anyone an opportunity to legally undermine a child's lifelong understanding of his or her parental heritage after his or her presumptive parents are deceased.

Sandra relies on *Tedford v. Gregory,* 125 N.M. 206, 959 P.2d 540 (Ct.App.1998), for the proposition that courts should only consider the best interests of the child when the action involves a minor. In *Tedford,* an adult child filed a paternity action against her purported natural father even though the adult child had a presumptive father who had raised and supported her since her birth. The adult child filed the action seeking retroactive child support from the date of her birth. After ordering genetic testing, which revealed that the purported natural father was the adult child's biological father, the district court granted the adult child's paternity action and awarded her $50,000 in retroactive child support. Noting that case law in other jurisdictions was limited to actions involving minor children, the *Tedford* court upheld the district court's ruling, concluding that the best interest of the child standard did not apply to adult children in paternity actions. 125 N.M. at 211, 959 P.2d 540. The *Tedford* court reasoned that the putative father was not the proper party to assert the best interest of the child standard because the standard could not be invoked on behalf of someone other than the child. 125 N.M. at 212, 959 P.2d 540.

Applying the *Tedford* court's reasoning to this case does not support Sandra's argument for two reasons. First, *Tedford,* which is not controlling precedent, was decided before *Ferguson,* which is controlling precedent. Second, Heather invoked the application of the best interests standard. Under the *Tedford* court's reasoning, Heather is the proper party to invoke the standard. *Tedford* does not persuade us to allow anyone to bypass the best-interest standard simply because the child has reached the age of majority.

We cannot subvert the presumption of paternity in favor of biology without requiring a court to consider whether it is in the child's best interests regardless of the child's age. Interpretation of the relevant statutes, controlling precedent, and public policy support the district court's decision to hold a *Ross* hearing in Heather's paternity action. Sandra's appeal is limited to the legal application of *Ross* to an adult child's paternity action in the context of a probate case. Sandra does not contest the district court's determination that it is not in Heather's best interests to conduct genetic testing. Thus, we affirm the district court's well-reasoned opinion denying Sandra's motions for genetic testing in both the probate and paternity cases and remand the matter for further proceedings.

ALLEGRUCCI, J., not participating.

LOCKETT, J., Retired, assigned. * * *

Notes

The *Reese* decision illustrates the force of the presumptive status of paternity, *see also* Unif. Parentage Act § 204, *supra,* and the protection of the best interest of the child in question, no matter what the age, *see* Unif. Parentage Act §§ 602 (Standing to Maintain Proceeding) & 608 (Authority to Deny Motion for Genetic Testing), which illustrates how difficult it is to rebut the presumption of parentage. More recent decisions have reiterated the best interest of the child as the prime consideration and the need to have an independent determination (a *Ross* determination) of whether the best interest of the child would be served by any petition. *See, e.g., In re* Paternity of A.R.R., 860 N.W.2d 538 (Wis. Ct. App. 2015) (dismissing a man's action to establish his paternity of a married mother's child after finding that a judicial determination that he was the girl's biological father was not in her best interest). Some decisions utilize equitable estoppel in paternity cases, holding that there are circumstances when the non-biological father of a child may be held to be the legal father of the child, in spite of evidence to the contrary, if this supports the equities of the situation. *See* K.W. v. J.S., 459 S.W.3d 399 (Ky. Ct. App. 2015).

Larry Lee Hillblom Co-Founder of DHL

Mr. Hillblom died at the age of fifty-two, when his airplane crashed into the Pacific Ocean in 1995. Prior to his death, he amassed $600 million and had a valid Last Will and Testament that bequeathed his fortune to various charities. He was unmarried at the time of his death, and it was rumored that he had non-marital children, but he never acknowledged their existence. Nonetheless, weeks after his death, several young women emerged from Vietnam, the Philippines, and the Islands of Micronesia, claiming that Mr. Hillblom was the father of their children. To establish the paternity of Mr. Hillblom, attorneys for the children were unable to obtain direct DNA samples from him or his belongings. Nonetheless, after Mr. Hillblom's mother was paid $1 million and given a French villa, she provided her own blood to establish a DNA connection between the children and her son, Mr. Hillblom.

The children would take an intestate share of their father's estate as what is called "omitted" children or "pretermitted heirs." In a settlement reached by the attorneys for the children and the charities, four children received $50 million each, after taxes, and the bulk of the estate was paid to the charities. The case generated more than $40 million in legal fees, and the estate paid more than $150 million in taxes.

For further details concerning the facts and the settlement, see Robert Frank, *The Fatherlode: Settled Paternity Suit Makes Junior Hillblom One Very Rich Kid—Three Others Get $50 Million Each, Too, but Wealth Has Certain Drawbacks—Jetting in to Catch the Knicks,* WALL ST. J., Mar. 20, 2000, at A1. In 2009, a documentary entitled *Shadow Billionaire* was released about Mr. Hillblom's estate. *See Shadow Billionaire,* IMDb, http://www.imdb.com/title/tt1212449/ (last visited Aug. 30, 2015).

Problem

A man and woman were married for more than 27 years. Together they had three children. Their youngest child, Mark, was nineteen when the wife filed for divorce, which was granted. Subsequently, the former husband filed a petition to force genetic testing of Mark, whereas the former husband was convinced he was not the father of Mark and wanted to establish this and collect damages from the man he alleged to be the father for the financial support he provided Mark for nineteen years. The former husband provided evidence of an affair between his former wife and the putative father, as well as his own genetic testing, proving that he was not the biological father of Mark. Mark and the man's former wife oppose the petition to enforce genetic testing. Mark was an adult but suffered from alcohol and drug dependency issues and testified that genetic testing was not in his best interests at the present time. The former husband, on the other hand, argued that establishing parentage was in Mark's best interest and would allow everyone a fresh start and permit healing to develop. Under what circumstances should the court order genetic testing? *See* D.W. v. R.W., 212 N.J. 232, 52 A.3d 1043 (2012).

E. Parenthood and Assisted Reproductive Technology

With the birth of "Baby Louise" in 1978, human fertilization through artificial means became a part of the process by which children are born. Baby Louise was the first child conceived through in vitro fertilization. First developed in Great Britain, the procedure involved taking eggs from a woman's ovary and fertilizing them with sperm from the prospective father or donor. The fertilized egg was then artificially inserted into the mother, who carried the embryo to term. *See* Roy Reed, *Scientists Praise British Birth as Triumph: Early Insertion of Embryo Into Womb is Liked to Successful Gestation*, N.Y. Times, July 27, 1978, at A1, col. 2. The procedure has prompted many unanticipated legal issues, including establishment of parenthood and gestational surrogacy agreements.

Raymond C. O'Brien
Assessing Assisted Reproductive Technology
27 Cath. U. J. L. & Tech. 1 (2018)

From 2005 through 2014 the number of ART [Assisted Reproductive Technology] cycles performed in the United States has increased 26%, and the number of live births in 2014 was almost one and a half times higher than in 2005. Likewise, the number of infants born who were conceived using ART increased from 52,041 in 2005 to 68,791 in 2014. By 2014, the number of fertility clinics within the United States rose to 498 and the number of clinics submitting data was 458. ART cycles performed at these clinics rose to 208,604 in 2014, a substantial increase from the 190,773 recorded in 2013. The CDC reports that "[t]he number of clinics, cycles performed, live-birth deliveries, and infants born as a result of ART have all increased steadily since CDC began collecting this information in 1995." Indeed, by 2014 the "CDC estimates that ART accounts for slightly less than 2% of total US births."

1. Establishing Parenthood through Consent

In re Marriage of Buzzanca
Court of Appeal, Fourth District, 1998
61 Cal. App. 4th 1410, 72 Cal. Rptr. 2d 280

SILLS, P. J.

* * *

Jaycee was born because Luanne and John Buzzanca agreed to have an embryo genetically unrelated to either of them implanted in a woman—a surrogate—who would carry and give birth to the child for them. After the fertilization, implantation and pregnancy, Luanne and John split up, and the question of who are Jaycee's lawful parents came before the trial court.

Luanne claimed that she and her erstwhile husband were the lawful parents, but John disclaimed any responsibility, financial or otherwise. The woman who gave birth also appeared in the case to make it clear that she made no claim to the child.

The trial court then reached an extraordinary conclusion: Jaycee had *no* lawful parents. First, the woman who gave birth to Jaycee was not the mother; the court had—astonishingly—already accepted a stipulation that neither she nor her husband were the "biological" parents. Second, Luanne was not the mother. According to the trial court, she could not be the mother because she had neither contributed the egg nor given birth. And John could not be the father, because, not having contributed the sperm, he had no biological relationship with the child.

We disagree. Let us get right to the point: Jaycee never would have been born had not Luanne and John both agreed to have a fertilized egg implanted in a surrogate.

The trial judge erred because he assumed that legal motherhood, under the relevant California statutes, could *only* be established in one of two ways, either by giving birth or by contributing an egg. He failed to consider the substantial and well-settled body of law holding that there are times when *fatherhood* can be established by conduct apart from giving birth or being genetically related to a child. The typical example is when an infertile husband consents to allowing his wife to be artificially inseminated. As our Supreme Court noted in such a situation over 30 years ago, the husband is the "lawful father" because he *consented* to the procreation of the child. (See People v. Sorensen (1968) 68 Cal.2d 280, 284–286 [66 Cal. Rptr. 7, 437 P.2d 495, 25 A.L.R.3d 1093].)

The same rule which makes a husband the lawful father of a child born because of his consent to artificial insemination should be applied here—by the same parity of reasoning that guided our Supreme Court in the first surrogacy case, Johnson v. Calvert (1993) 5 Cal.4th 84 [19 Cal.Rptr.2d 494, 851 P.2d 776]—to both husband and wife. Just as a husband is deemed to be the lawful father of a child unrelated to him when his wife gives birth after artificial insemination, so should a husband *and* wife be deemed the lawful parents of a child after a surrogate bears a biologically unrelated child on their behalf. In each instance, a child is procreated because a medical procedure was initiated and consented to by intended parents. The only difference is that in this case—unlike artificial insemination—there is no reason to distinguish between husband and wife. We therefore must reverse the trial court's judgment and direct that a new judgment be entered, declaring that both Luanne and John are the lawful parents of Jaycee. * * *

John filed his petition for dissolution of marriage on March 30, 1995, alleging there were no children of the marriage. Luanne filed her response on April 20, alleging that the parties were expecting a child by way of surrogate contract. Jaycee was born six days later. In September 1996 Luanne filed a separate petition to establish herself as Jaycee's mother. Her action was consolidated into the dissolution case. In February 1997, the court accepted a stipulation that the woman who agreed to carry the child, and her husband, were not the "biological parents" of the child. * * * At a hearing held in March, based entirely on oral argument and offers of proof, the trial court determined that Luanne was not the lawful mother of the child and therefore John could not be the lawful father or owe any support.

* * *

John argues that the artificial insemination statute should not be applied because, after all, his wife did not give birth. But for purposes of the statute with its core idea of estoppel, the fact that Luanne did not give birth is irrelevant. The statute contemplates the establishment of lawful fatherhood in a situation where an intended father has no biological relationship to a child who is procreated as a result of the father's (as well as the mother's) *consent* to a medical procedure.

* * *

In the present case Luanne is situated like a husband in an artificial insemination case whose consent triggers a medical procedure which results in a pregnancy and eventual birth of a child. Her motherhood may therefore be established "under this part," by virtue of that consent. In light of our conclusion, John's argument that the surrogate should be declared the lawful mother disintegrates. The case is now postured like the Johnson v. Calvert case, where motherhood could have been "established" in either of two women under the Act, and the tie broken by noting the intent to parent as expressed in the surrogacy contract. (See Johnson v. Calvert, *supra*, 5 Cal.4th at p. 93.) The only difference is that this case is not even close as between Luanne and the surrogate. Not only was Luanne the clearly intended mother, no bona fide attempt has been made to establish the surrogate as the lawful mother. * * *

We should also add that neither could the woman whose egg was used in the fertilization or implantation make any claim to motherhood, even if she were to come forward at this late date. Again, as between two women who would both be able to establish motherhood under the Act, the *Johnson* decision would mandate that the tie be broken in favor of the intended parent, in this case, Luanne.

* * *

In the case before us, there is absolutely no dispute that Luanne caused Jaycee's conception and birth by initiating the surrogacy arrangement whereby an embryo was implanted into a woman who agreed to carry the baby to term on Luanne's behalf. In applying the artificial insemination statute to a gestational surrogacy case where the genetic donors are unknown, there is, as we have indicated above, no reason to distinguish *between* husbands and wives. Both are equally situated from the point of view of consenting to an act which brings a child into being. * * * Accordingly, Luanne should have been declared the lawful mother of Jaycee.

* * *

Even though neither Luanne nor John are biologically related to Jaycee, they are still her lawful parents given their initiating role as the intended parents in her conception and birth. And, while the absence of a biological connection is what makes this case extraordinary, this court is hardly without statutory basis and legal precedent in so deciding. * * * Fortunately, as the *Johnson* court also noted, intent to parent "'correlate[s] significantly'" with a child's best interests. (Johnson v. Calvert, *supra*, 5 Cal.4th at p. 94, quoting Schultz, op. cit. *supra*, Wis. L.Rev., at p. 397.)

That is far more than can be said for a model of the law that renders a child a legal orphan. * * *

Again we must call on the Legislature to sort out the parental rights and responsibilities of those involved in artificial reproduction. No matter what one thinks of artificial insemination, traditional and gestational surrogacy (in all its permutations), and — as now appears in the not-too-distant future, cloning and even gene splicing — courts are still going to be faced with the problem of determining lawful parentage. A child cannot be ignored. Even if all means of artificial reproduction were outlawed with draconian criminal penalties visited on the doctors and parties involved, courts will still be called upon to decide who the lawful parents really are and who — other than the taxpayers — is obligated to provide maintenance and support for the child. These cases will not go away.

Courts can continue to make decisions on an ad hoc basis without necessarily imposing some grand scheme, looking to the imperfectly designed Uniform Parentage Act and a growing body of case law for guidance in the light of applicable family law principles. Or the Legislature can act to impose a broader order which, even though it might not be perfect on a case-by-case basis, would bring some predictability to those who seek to make use of artificial reproductive techniques. As jurists, we recognize the traditional role of the common (i.e., judge-formulated) law in applying old legal principles to new technology. (See, *e.g.*, Hurtado v. State of California (1884) 110 U.S. 516, 530 [4 S.Ct. 111, 118, 28 L.Ed. 232] ["This flexibility and capacity for growth and adaptation is the peculiar boast and excellence of the common law."]; Rodriguez v. Bethlehem Steel Corp. (1974) 12 Cal.3d 382, 394 [115 Cal.Rptr. 765, 525 P.2d 669] ["in the common law system the primary instruments of this evolution are the courts, adjudicating on a regular basis the rich variety of individual cases brought before them"].) However, we still believe it is the Legislature, with its ability to formulate general rules based on input from all its constituencies, which is the more desirable forum for lawmaking.

That said, we must now conclude the business at hand.

(1) The portion of the judgment which declares that Luanne Buzzanca is not the lawful mother of Jaycee is reversed. The matter is remanded with directions to enter a new judgment declaring her the lawful mother. The trial court shall make all appropriate orders to ensure that Luanne Buzzanca shall have legal custody of Jaycee, including entering an order that Jaycee's birth certificate shall be amended to reflect Luanne Buzzanca as the mother.

(2) The judgment is reversed to the extent that it provides that John Buzzanca is not the lawful father of Jaycee. The matter is remanded with directions to enter a new judgment declaring him the lawful father. Consonant with this determination, today's ruling is without prejudice to John in future proceedings as regards child custody and visitation as his relationship with Jaycee may develop. * * * The judgment shall also reflect that the birth certificate shall be amended to reflect John Buzzanca as the lawful father.

(3) To the degree that the judgment makes no provision for child support it is reversed. The matter is remanded to make an appropriate permanent child support order. Until that time, the temporary child support order shall remain in effect. (See Jaycee B. v. Superior Court, *supra*, 42 Cal.App.4th at p. 730.)

Luanne and Jaycee will recover their costs on appeal.

Wallin, J., and Crosby, J., concurred.

[Respondent's petition for review by the Supreme Court was denied June 10, 1998.]

Notes

The *Buzzanca* decision permits a person to become a parent through consent. The statutory provision for this is taken from Unif. Parentage Act § 703, which provides that "An individual who consents under Section 704 to assisted reproduction by a woman with the intent to be a parent of a child conceived by the assisted reproduction is a parent of the child." Additional provisions of the Act specify the manner of the consent, the withdrawal of consent, and the status of parenthood in the event of divorce prior to the placement of the eggs, sperm, or embryos. *See* UNIF. PARENTAGE ACT §§ 704 to 708. These issues and others arose in part because of an earlier California decision—Kane v. Superior Ct., 37 Cal. App. 4th 1577, 44 Cal. Rptr. 2d 578 (1995) (holding that sperm, and presumably other human genetic materials, is property and could be bequeathed as property in spite of public policy objections). For further commentary on these issues, see, *e.g.,* Lynda Wray Black, *The Birth of a Parent: Defining Parentage for Lenders of Genetic Materials,* 92 NEB. L. REV. 799 (2014); Michael T. Flannery, *"Rethinking" Embryo Disposition Upon Divorce,* 29 J. CONTEMP. HEALTH L. & POLICY 233 (2013).

Raymond C. O'Brien
The Immediacy of Genome Editing and Mitochondrial Replacement
9 WAKE FOREST J. OF L. & PUB. POL'Y 419 (2019)

Today, as a result of recent scientific research and developments it is possible to edit a genome, that is, to "modify [ ] an embryo or the cells from which it is formed by techniques of genome editing, in order to ensure that a future child has the selected genetic variants." When we speak of genome editing we mean the process by which the genome sequence is changed through intervention of a DNA break or other DNA modification. Because of modern scientific ability to edit the genome, science began the study and diagram of the human genome variants, by which it could decipher the array of human characteristics, the propensities for disease in any given embryo, and how an individual may live in an environment that may precipitate reactions to various environmental factors.

2. Establishing Parentage through Surrogacy

In re Paternity of F.T.R.

Supreme Court of Wisconsin, 2013
349 Wis. 2d 84, 833 N.W.2d 634

ANNETTE KINGSLAND ZIEGLER, J.

This appeal is before the court on certification by the court of appeals, pursuant to Wis. Stat. § 809.61 (2009–10).1 David and Marcia Rosecky (the Roseckys) entered into a Parentage Agreement (PA or the agreement) with Monica and Cory Schissel (the Schissels) whereby the parties agreed that Monica Schissel (Monica) would become pregnant and carry a child for the Roseckys. The agreement provided that "[the Roseckys] shall be the legal parents of [the] Child," that the "Child's best interests will be served by being in [the Roseckys'] legal custody and physical placement," and that "[t]he parties will cooperate fully in any parentage proceedings to determine [the Roseckys] as [the][C]hild's legal parents, . . . including but not limited to termination of parental rights and adoption." Monica became pregnant through artificial insemination using her egg and David Rosecky's (David) sperm. On March 19, 2010, Monica gave birth to F.T.R. Shortly before F.T.R.'s birth, Monica informed the Roseckys she no longer wanted to give up her parental rights. She further sought custody and placement of F.T.R. David responded by seeking enforcement of the PA. The Columbia County Circuit Court, Judge Alan J. White, determined that the PA was not enforceable, and after a trial, awarded sole custody of F.T.R. to David, primary placement to David, and secondary placement to Monica. David appealed, seeking enforcement of the PA and sole custody and placement of F.T.R. The court of appeals certified to this court the question of "whether an agreement for the traditional surrogacy and adoption of a child is enforceable." . . .

Marcia and Monica were good friends for many years, having met in grade school. Each participated in the other's wedding. The Roseckys were godparents to the Schissels' youngest daughter. . . . In 2004, and again in 2008, Marcia was diagnosed with leukemia. After receiving treatments, she is currently in good health and the doctors consider the leukemia "a nonissue." However, her eggs are no longer viable and she is unable to have biological children. . . . In 2004, and again in 2008, Monica offered to act as a surrogate for the Roseckys. Monica testified that she wanted to help the Roseckys: "I was [Marcia's] friend. I offered to do this. . . . I orchestrated this whole thing. This whole thing was my doing. I offered. I carried. I said I would do it." In 2008, the Roseckys accepted Monica's offer. The parties discussed using a donor egg, but decided to use Monica's egg because they could be sure of Monica's family history, there was a higher chance of having multiples using a donor egg, and Monica preferred to use her own egg. Marcia expressed concern that Monica would have trouble giving up her biological child, but Monica reassured Marcia that she would allow the Roseckys to raise the child.

The parties had extensive conversations about the legal ramifications of the surrogacy before Monica became pregnant. The parties discussed and agreed that Monica and the child would have no legal relationship, Monica would not have formal custody and placement of the child, Monica would see the child through informal social visits, and the Roseckys would raise the child. Both parties retained counsel, and the attorneys reduced the agreement to writing. The parties negotiated terms in the agreement, and sent revised drafts back and forth. The parties acknowledge that the written agreement is an accurate reflection of the discussions they had before Monica became pregnant. Monica became pregnant in June 2009 through artificial insemination using her egg and David's sperm. . . . Toward the end of the pregnancy, the parties had a falling out. It suffices to say that there were several events resulting in hurt feelings and lack of trust among the parties. In any event, shortly before F.T.R. was born, Monica reneged on the PA and refused to terminate her parental rights. On March 19, 2010, Monica gave birth to F.T.R. and allowed F.T.R. to go home with the Roseckys from the hospital. . . .

On August 25, 2011, the circuit court awarded sole custody and primary placement of F.T.R. to David and secondary placement to Monica. The court awarded Monica six hours of placement every other weekend until F.T.R. turned two (March 2012), and at that time, Monica was awarded an overnight stay from Friday evening until Saturday evening every other weekend. The court did not consider the PA in any way, but instead relied solely on Wis. Stat. §767.41 to determine custody and placement. The court reasoned that under Wis. Stat. §767.41(4)(b), both families were entitled to placement unless "the court finds that physical placement with a parent would endanger the child's physical, mental or emotional health." By granting placement with Monica, the court rejected the expert testimony and the guardian ad litem's opinion that the tension between the parties and the separation from attachment figures could endanger F.T.R.'s mental or emotional health: "The possibility that difficulties may occur and that allowing the Schissels to play a role in the child's life is a risk. But risks are a part of life." . . .

Aside from the termination of parental rights provisions in the PA at issue, we conclude a PA is a valid, enforceable contract unless enforcement is contrary to the best interests of the child. While the traditional defenses to the enforcement of a contract could apply, none appear to render the entire PA in this case unenforceable.[4] . . .

Assisted reproductive technology (ART) has created ways for people to have children regardless of their reproductive capacity: "ART, in particular surrogacy arrangements, forces us to confront deeply held beliefs about what makes a 'mother' or a 'father,' . . . and perhaps most fundamentally, what makes a 'family.'" Darra L. Hofman, *"Mama's Baby, Daddy's Maybe:" A State-By-State Survey of Surrogacy Laws and Their Disparate Gender Impact*, 35 Wm. Mitchell L.Rev. 449, 450 (2009). . . .

---

4. Even though the TPR provisions in the PA are not enforceable, the remaining portions of the PA can be enforced if severing the unenforceable portion does not defeat the primary purpose of the bargain. *See Simenstad v. Hagen*, 22 Wis.2d 653, 662, 126 N.W.2d 529 (1964).

In general terms, surrogacy "is the process by which a woman makes a choice to become pregnant and then carry to full term and deliver a baby who, she intends, will be raised by someone else." Thomas J. Walsh, *Wisconsin's Undeveloped Surrogacy Law*, Wisconsin Lawyer, Mar. 2012, at 16. *See also Black's Law Dictionary* 1458 (7th ed. 1999) (defining "surrogate mother" as "[a] woman who carries a child to term on behalf of another woman and then assigns her parental rights to that woman and the father"). This opinion will refer to the woman who carries the baby as the "surrogate." . . . [footnote omitted]. An "intended parent" is "an individual, married or unmarried, who manifests the intent . . . to be legally bound as the parent of a child resulting from assisted or collaborative reproduction." American Bar Association Model Act Governing Assisted Reproductive Technology (ABA Model Act) § 102(19) (Feb. 2008). The Roseckys are the intended parents of F.T.R. . . . . There are two broad categories of surrogacies, traditional and gestational, but there are many permutations within those categories. In a traditional surrogacy, the surrogate is the genetic mother of the child and is artificially inseminated with the sperm of the intended father or a sperm donor. *See Walsh, supra*, at 16. In a gestational surrogacy, the surrogate is not genetically related to the child; instead, "sperm is taken from the father (or from a donor) and an egg is taken from the mother (or from a donor), fertilization happens outside the womb (called *in vitro* fertilization), and the fertilized embryos are then implanted into the surrogate mother's uterus." *Id.* The case before the court involves a traditional surrogacy, as Monica was artificially inseminated with David's sperm.

Parties contemplating a surrogacy will often enter into a surrogacy agreement. *Id.* at 18. This agreement typically outlines the parties' rights and responsibilities throughout the surrogacy process. Common provisions include contemplated medical procedures, contingencies in case of medical complications, compensation, parental rights and responsibilities, choice of law, and the parties' intent. . . .

The vast majority of states do not have statutory provisions addressing surrogacy. . . . [footnote omitted]. Many courts have encountered issues surrounding surrogacy, and the cases often involve ad hoc procedures attempting to effectuate the parties' intent by analyzing surrogacy issues under the state's statutes for TPR, adoption, custody and placement, and the like. *See generally* Rachel M. Kane, *Cause of Action for Determination of Status as Legal or Natural Parents of Children Borne by Surrogate or Gestational Carrier*, 48 COA 2d 687 (Jun. 2011). At oral argument, counsel for the Roseckys explained that surrogacy is a reality in Wisconsin and that Wisconsin attorneys attempt to effectuate the parties' intent in a surrogacy. Clearly, when the parties follow the agreement and everything goes as planned, the court's involvement is quite limited. For example, if the surrogate agrees to terminate her parental rights, the intended parents can adopt the child. *See* Wis. Stat. § 48.41 (voluntary consent to TPR); Wis. Stat. § 48.82 (persons eligible to adopt a minor child); Wis. Stat. § 48.91 (if prerequisites are met, court shall grant adoption if it is in the best interests of the child). A court will often adjudicate the intended biological parent as the biological parent of a child, as David was adjudicated to be F.T.R.'s father. The adjudicated parent may then seek custody and placement of the child. Counsel for David also noted that some Wisconsin circuit courts have used Wis. Stat. §69.14(1)(h) to make a determination of parentage for the intended mother and intended father. . . . [footnote omitted]. When the parties do not agree, however, the courts are forced to confront issues of the most difficult nature. . . .

In this case, Monica was presumed to be the mother of F.T.R. because she gave birth to him, David was adjudicated as the father of F.T.R., the circuit court determined that the PA was unenforceable, and Monica is unwilling to voluntarily terminate her parental rights. Under the current statutory schemes, Marcia is left without any parental rights unless and until Monica's parental rights are terminated and Marcia adopts F.T.R.:

> It is clear that the more complex surrogacy relationships do not easily fit into Wisconsin's statutory scheme. The statutes do not refer to compensation of surrogate mothers or sperm and egg donors. No provisions address the interests of the child created in this process or by in vitro fertilization. Thus, parties seeking relief in Wisconsin courts are provided no guarantee that relief can be had. Further, circuit court judges attempting to determine if relief is appropriate are given no guidance on how to apportion that relief.

Walsh, *supra*, at 19. Considering the facts of this case, none of the statutory schemes neatly answer the multiple legal issues presented. . . . In summary, the Wisconsin Statutes do not provide a specific answer as to whether the PA is enforceable, and they do not contain a statement of public policy against enforcement. . . .

Despite this being a unique contract, we turn to contract law for guidance. "Wisconsin courts have long recognized the importance of freedom of contract and have endeavored to protect the right to contract." *Watts v. Watts*, 137 Wis.2d 506, 521, 405 N.W.2d 303 (1987). A founding principle of freedom of contract is that "individuals should have the power to govern their own affairs without governmental interference." *Merten v. Nathan*, 108 Wis.2d 205, 211, 321 N.W.2d 173 (1982). Courts protect parties' "justifiable expectations and the security of transactions" by "ensuring that the promises will be performed." *Id.*

The elements of a contract are offer, acceptance, and consideration. *See Goossen v. Estate of Standaert*, 189 Wis.2d 237, 247, 525 N.W.2d 314 (Ct.App.1994); Michael B. Apfeld et al., *Contract Law in Wisconsin* §2.1 (3d ed.2012). Defenses to the enforcement of a contract include misrepresentation, mistake, illegality, unconscionability, void against public policy, duress, undue influence, and incapacity. *See* Apfeld et al., *supra*, at ch. 3. . . . Even if a contract contains an illegal provision, "Wisconsin has long accepted that a portion of a contract may be severable." *Markwardt v. Zurich Am. Ins. Co.*, 2006 WI App 200, ¶ 30, 296 Wis.2d 512, 724 N.W.2d 669. A severability clause, though not controlling, is entitled to great weight in determining if the remaining portions of a contract are severable. *See Town of Clearfield v. Cushman*, 150 Wis.2d 10, 24, 440 N.W.2d 777 (1989) (internal quotation omitted). If a contract contains an illegal clause, the remaining portions of the contract can be enforced if severing the illegal portions does not defeat the primary purpose of the bargain. *See Simenstad v. Hagen*, 22 Wis.2d 653, 662, 126 N.W.2d 529 (1964); *Baierl v. McTaggart*, 2001 WI 107, ¶¶ 15, 18, 245 Wis.2d 632, 629 N.W.2d 277.

In this case, there is no question that the PA contains the essential elements of a contract. Monica made an offer to the Roseckys that she would act as a surrogate. The Roseckys accepted Monica's offer. Consideration was provided.... The unique nature of this contract, however, cannot be understated.[10] Creating a child is not something that one can decide to do one day and decide not to do the next. Typical damages cannot make one whole. Nonetheless, this is a contract and we conclude that it is largely enforceable.... Specifically, we conclude that the interests supporting enforcement of the PA are more compelling than the interests against enforcement. Enforcement of surrogacy agreements promotes stability and permanence in family relationships because it allows the intended parents to plan for the arrival of their child, reinforces the expectations of all parties to the agreement, and reduces contentious litigation that could drag on for the first several years of the child's life.

We do not hold this opinion alone; the legislature has manifested its intent in the children's code, wherein it concluded that the best interests of the child are always paramount. *See* Wis. Stat. § 48.01. *See also* § 767.41(5) (stating that in custody and placement determinations, the court considers "all facts relevant to the best interest of the child"); § 54.15(1) (stating that in selection of a guardian for a proposed ward, the "best interests of the proposed ward shall control"); § 938.01(2)(f) (stating that in the Juvenile Justice Code, the court considers " each juvenile's best interest" in responding to "a juvenile offender's needs for care and treatment"). Furthermore, the legislature has legislated that "instability and impermanence in family relationships are contrary to the welfare of children." Wis. Stat. § 48.01(1)(a).... According to the expert testimony in this case, social science research also supports the conclusion that permanency and stability promote child welfare, whereas being exposed to contentious family relationships, an inevitable consequence of litigation, is harmful. As Dr. Waldron testified: "[O]ut of over 2,000 studies that have been done ... where there are separate caregivers, ... in every single one ... the higher the level of tension and conflict, the more detrimental it is to kids. . . . [T]hat is the number one predictor for child adjustment over time, [ ] whether or not there's tension and conflict between caregivers." Dr. Huebner also testified that, according to research, the tension between the Roseckys and Schissels could be harmful to

---

10. The guardian ad litem's brief summarizes why surrogacies are so unique:
   [T]his case exists at the intersection of several distinct and historically different areas of law and stands at the crossroads of ever-evolving artificial reproduction technology. The most critical fact that distinguishes this case from others is that [F.T.R.] was created so that the Roseckys could have a child of their own. This crucial fact distinguishes this case from an adoption, third-party placement, paternity or divorce case.

F.T.R. . . . . We find no public policy statement contrary to the enforcement of the PA in the Wisconsin Statutes or in Wisconsin cases.[11]

The portions of the PA requiring Monica to terminate her parental rights, however, are not enforceable under the language of the existing statutes. The PA stated that "[t]he parties will cooperate fully in any parentage proceedings to determine [the Roseckys] as [C]hild's legal parents, or in any other similar legal proceedings, including but not limited to termination of parental rights and adoption." It further stated:

> The parties intend to participate voluntarily in any legal proceedings necessary to have [the Roseckys] determined to be Child's legal parents. . . . It is the intent of the parties that regardless of any circumstances that may arise in the future, both [Marcia] and [David] shall be the legal parents of Child. The parties agree to sign all necessary documents and attend any scheduled court hearings either prior to or after Child's birth to achieve these goals.

As the circuit court correctly noted, the portions of the PA requiring a voluntary TPR do not comply with the procedural safeguards set forth in Wis. Stat. § 48.41 because Monica would not consent to the TPR and there is no legal basis for involuntary termination. *See* Wis. Stat. § 48.415. As a result, the TPR provisions of the PA are unenforceable. That fact, however, does not end the analysis.

We further conclude that the offending TPR provisions in the PA can be severed from the remainder of the contract without defeating the primary purpose of the agreement. The PA addresses severability:

---

11. To support their public policy arguments, the Roseckys, the Schissels, and the guardian ad litem point to cases and statutes from other jurisdictions. While it is true that many other jurisdictions have examined surrogacy issues, there is no clear majority rule:

> The vast majority of states are silent or near silent on the issues of whether, when, and how surrogacy agreements are enforceable, void, or voidable. Of those states that do have laws on the books regarding such agreements, the responses range from relying heavily on the Uniform Parentage Act or party intent to outright bans or even criminalization of surrogacy. In many of the states that are 'silent' on surrogacy, bills have been shot back-and-forth through the legislature but come to naught.

Hofman, *supra*, at 454. *See also* Mark Hansen, *As Surrogacy Becomes More Popular, Legal Problems Proliferate*, ABA Journal, Mar. 2011, at 55; Thomas J. Walsh, *Wisconsin's Undeveloped Surrogacy Law*, Wisconsin Lawyer, Mar. 2012, at 20. Case law in this area is similarly scattered. *See, e.g., Raftopol v. Ramey*, 299 Conn. 681, 12 A.3d 783, 793 (2011) (concluding that Connecticut Statute, which governs birth certificates when birth is subject to a surrogacy agreement, "allows an intended parent who is a party to a valid [surrogacy] agreement to become a parent without first adopting the children, without respect to that intended parent's genetic relationship to the children" (emphasis omitted)); *Johnson v. Calvert*, 5 Cal.4th 84, 19 Cal.Rptr.2d 494, 851 P.2d 776, 782 (1993) (concluding that when the intended mother/egg donor and the gestational carrier had equal claims to maternity under California law, "she who intended to procreate the child—that is, she who intended to bring about the birth of a child that she intended to raise as her own—is the natural mother under California law"); *Matter of Baby M.*, 109 N.J. 396, 537 A.2d 1227, 1246–50 (1988) (concluding that enforcement of a traditional surrogacy agreement violated various statements of public policy).

In the event any of the provisions of this Agreement are deemed to be invalid or unenforceable, such provisions will be deemed severable from the remainder of this Agreement and will not cause the invalidity or unenforceability of the remainder of this Agreement. Consistent with the provisions of this paragraph, if any provision is deemed invalid due to its scope or breadth, such provision will be deemed valid to the extent of the scope or breadth permitted by law.

Though a severability clause itself is not controlling, it is entitled to great weight in determining whether the remainder of a contract is enforceable. *See Town of Clearfield*, 150 Wis.2d at 24, 440 N.W.2d 777 [(1989)]. The primary purpose of this agreement is to ensure that the Roseckys will be the parents of F.T.R. and will have custody and placement. The PA contains provisions for custody and placement: "The parties believe strongly that Child's best interests will be served by being in [the Roseckys'] legal custody and physical placement, as it is necessary for Child to regard [the Roseckys] as the sole legal parents and [the Roseckys'] home as the sole parental home." The purpose of the PA can be carried out, after severing the TPR portions, by enforcing the custody and placement provisions of the PA. *See Simenstad*, 22 Wis.2d at 662, 126 N.W.2d 529.

As to the remaining portions of the PA, the current court record does not support any defense to the enforcement of the contract so as to render it unenforceable. There are no facts in the record to indicate, nor does Monica argue, that the contract should be void or voidable due to misrepresentation, mistake, duress, undue influence, or incapacity. *See* Apfeld et al., *supra*, ch. 3. Instead, the facts in the record appear to establish that the contract was entered into voluntarily and was well-planned, negotiated, and carefully executed. The circuit court made findings about the PA:

The contract, on its face, is clear and unambiguous. . . .

- The parties are each represented by counsel, and were at the time the agreement was drawn. The agreement itself covers virtually every eventuality which could possibly occur during the pregnancy.

- There is no claim here by [Monica] that she did not understand the contract when she signed it. Indeed, to a great extent, it appears it was her idea to act as a surrogate in the first instance.

- Had [Monica] gone through with the termination of her parental rights, this Court would have no problem upholding the agreement. . . .

Monica offered, not once but twice, to act as a surrogate for the Roseckys. Both the Roseckys and the Schissels had independent counsel, who assisted in drafting and revising the parties' agreement. The parties negotiated the terms of the agreement. When the Roseckys raised concerns about using Monica's egg, for fear that she would not be able to separate herself from the child, Monica reassured the Roseckys that she could separate herself from the child. Monica testified that she understood all of the terms of the contract and that she simply changed her mind as to the terms.

Instead of arguing that the contract is void due to duress, mistake, or similar reasons, Monica argues that the PA is void as against public policy. The essence of Monica's public policy argument is that a contract cannot cut off a biological parent from his or her child, and any contract that purports to do so violates a myriad of cases and statutes relating to divorce, custody, placement, adoption, and similar areas. A contract will not be enforced if it violates public policy. *Watts*, 137 Wis.2d at 521, 405 N.W.2d 303. A court may declare a contract void on public policy grounds only if it determines, after weighing the interests, that the interests in enforcing the contract are clearly outweighed by the interests in upholding the policy that the contract violates. *Id.*; Restatement (Second) of Contracts § 178 (1981). Public policy may be expressed by a statute, regulation, or judicial opinion. *See N. States Power Co. v. Nat'l Gas Co., Inc.*, 2000 WI App 30, ¶ 8, 232 Wis.2d 541, 606 N.W.2d 613. For the reasons stated above, we reject Monica's public policy arguments.

In summary, though the TPR portions of the PA cannot be enforced under Chapter 48 of the Wisconsin Statutes, the remainder of the PA is an enforceable contract. No Wisconsin Statute or case contains a specific statement of public policy contrary to the enforcement of this PA. We conclude that enforcement of surrogacy agreements promotes stability and permanence in family relationships because it allows the intended parents to plan for the arrival of their child, reinforces the expectations of all parties to the agreement, and reduces contentious litigation that could drag on for the first several years of the child's life. Aside from the termination of parental rights provisions in the PA at issue, the PA is a valid, enforceable contract unless enforcement is contrary to the best interests of F.T.R. We turn to consider the circuit court action concerning custody and placement. . . . Because we conclude that the PA is a valid, enforceable contract, the circuit court's exclusion of the PA and decision to render a custody and placement order without consideration of the PA constituted an erroneous exercise of discretion. . . . [footnote omitted]. [*Bohms v. Bohms*, 144 Wis. 2d 490,] 496, 424 N.W.2d 408 [(1988)]. We therefore reverse the circuit court's order and remand for a determination of custody and placement consistent with this opinion. . . .

We respectfully urge the legislature to consider enacting legislation regarding surrogacy.[13] Surrogacy is currently a reality in our Wisconsin court system. Legislation could "address surrogacy agreements to ensure that when the surrogacy process is used, the courts and the parties understand the expectations and limitations under Wisconsin law."[14] Walsh, *supra*, at 56. . . .

---

13. Assisted reproductive technology has turned "the science of making babies into a $3 billion-a-year industry." Hansen, *supra*, at 54. Though reliable data is scarce on the number of surrogacies that occur every year, one account estimates that about 22,000 babies have been born using surrogacy in the United States since the mid-1970s. *Id.* Anecdotal evidence from attorneys practicing in this area suggests that the number may be much higher. *Id.* (noting a California surrogacy attorney's account that her office handles about 150 surrogacies a year).

14. *See, e.g., Raftopol*, 12 A.3d at 801–03 (calling for legislative guidance and listing a myriad of legal issues presented by surrogacy); ABA Model Act (Feb.2008); Uniform Parentage Act (2002);

Aside from the termination of parental rights provisions in the PA at issue, we conclude a PA is a valid, enforceable contract unless enforcement is contrary to the best interests of the child. While the traditional defenses to the enforcement of a contract could apply, none appear to render the entire PA in this case unenforceable. . . . We also conclude that the circuit court erroneously exercised its discretion by excluding the PA and rendering its custody and placement decision without consideration of the PA. We reverse the circuit court's determination that the PA is unenforceable and remand for a hearing on custody and placement, wherein the terms of the PA are enforced unless enforcement is contrary to the best interests of F.T.R.

Order reversed and cause remanded for proceedings consistent with this opinion.

ABRAHAMSON, Chief Justice, BRADLEY, J., concur. . . .

Notes

As the Wisconsin Supreme Court admits in its decision in *In re Paternity of F.T.R.*, few states have enacted legislation addressing surrogacy, but the states addressing the issue make a distinction between gestational surrogacy and genetic surrogacy, with the latter coming under increased scrutiny if permitted at all. And yet, comments to the newly revised Uniform Parentage Act (2017) suggest that an increasing number of states are enacting surrogacy statutes, willing to permit the procedure, especially if it is a gestational surrogacy. *See* UNIF. PARENTAGE ACT § 904 cmt. This modicum of acceptance is, in part, due to the increasing number of persons utilizing surrogacy to become parents. *See* UNIF. PARENTAGE ACT art. 8 cmt. For commentary on surrogacy, see Adeline A. Allen, *Surrogacy and Limitations to Freedom of Contract: Toward Being More Fully Human*, 41 HARV. J. L. & PUB. POL'Y 753, 759, 769–70 (2018); Deborah S. Mazer, *Born Breach: The Challenge of Remedies in Surrogacy Contracts*, 28 YALE J.L. & FEMINISM 211, 218–19 (2017); see also New Jersey Gestational Carrier Agreement Act of 2018, 9 N.J. STAT. ANN §§ 17 to 60 (2018).

Uniform Parentage Act (2019)

SECTION 801. DEFINITIONS. In this [article]:

(1) "Genetic surrogate" means a woman who is not an intended parent and who agrees to become pregnant through assisted reproduction using her own gamete, under a genetic surrogacy agreement as provided in this [article].

(2) "Gestational surrogate" means a woman who is not an intended parent and who agrees to become pregnant through assisted reproduction using gametes that are not her own, under a gestational surrogacy agreement as provided in this [article].

(3) "Surrogacy agreement" means an agreement between one or more intended parents and a woman who is not an intended parent in which the woman agrees

---

750 Ill. Comp. Stat. Ann. § 47/1–47/75 (West 2012) ("Illinois Gestational Surrogacy Act").

to become pregnant through assisted reproduction and which provides that each intended parent is a parent of a child conceived under the agreement. Unless otherwise specified, the term refers to both a gestational surrogacy agreement and a genetic surrogacy agreement.

SECTION 802. ELIGIBILITY TO ENTER GESTATIONAL OR GENETIC SURROGACY AGREEMENT.

(a) To execute an agreement to act as a gestational or genetic surrogate, a woman must:

(1) have attained 21 years of age;

(2) previously have given birth to at least one child;

(3) complete a medical evaluation related to the surrogacy arrangement by a licensed medical doctor;

(4) complete a mental-health consultation by a licensed mental-health professional; and

(5) have independent legal representation of her choice throughout the surrogacy arrangement regarding the terms of the surrogacy agreement and the potential legal consequences of the agreement.

(b) To execute a surrogacy agreement, each intended parent, whether or not genetically related to the child, must:

(1) have attained 21 years of age;

(2) complete a medical evaluation related to the surrogacy arrangement by a licensed medical doctor;

(3) complete a mental-health consultation by a licensed mental health professional; and

(4) have independent legal representation of the intended parent's choice throughout the surrogacy arrangement regarding the terms of the surrogacy agreement and the potential legal consequences of the agreement.

SECTION 803. REQUIREMENTS OF GESTATIONAL OR GENETIC SURROGACY AGREEMENT: PROCESS. A surrogacy agreement must be executed in compliance with the following rules:

(1) At least one party must be a resident of this state or, if no party is a resident of this state, at least one medical evaluation or procedure or mental-health consultation under the agreement must occur in this state.

(2) A surrogate and each intended parent must meet the requirements of Section 802.

(3) Each intended parent, the surrogate, and the surrogate's spouse, if any, must be parties to the agreement.

(4) The agreement must be in a record signed by each party listed in paragraph (3).

(5) The surrogate and each intended parent must acknowledge in a record receipt of a copy of the agreement.

(6) The signature of each party to the agreement must be attested by a notarial officer or witnessed.

(7) The surrogate and the intended parent or parents must have independent legal representation throughout the surrogacy arrangement regarding the terms of the surrogacy agreement and the potential legal consequences of the agreement, and each counsel must be identified in the surrogacy agreement.

(8) The intended parent or parents must pay for independent legal representation for the surrogate.

(9) The agreement must be executed before a medical procedure occurs related to the surrogacy agreement, other than the medical evaluation and mental health consultation required by Section 802.

SECTION 804. REQUIREMENTS OF GESTATIONAL OR GENETIC SURROGACY AGREEMENT: CONTENT.

(a) A surrogacy agreement must comply with the following requirements:

(1) A surrogate agrees to attempt to become pregnant by means of assisted reproduction.

(2) Except as otherwise provided in Sections 811, 814, and 815, the surrogate and the surrogate's spouse or former spouse, if any, have no claim to parentage of a child conceived by assisted reproduction under the agreement.

(3) The surrogate's spouse, if any, must acknowledge and agree to comply with the obligations imposed on the surrogate by the agreement.

(4) Except as otherwise provided in Sections 811, 814, and 815, the intended parent or, if there are two intended parents, each one jointly and severally, immediately on birth will be the exclusive parent or parents of the child, regardless of number of children born or gender or mental or physical condition of each child.

(5) Except as otherwise provided in Sections 811, 814, and 815, the intended parent or, if there are two intended parents, each parent jointly and severally, immediately on birth will assume responsibility for the financial support of the child, regardless of number of children born or gender or mental or physical condition of each child.

(6) The agreement must include information disclosing how each intended parent will cover the surrogacy-related expenses of the surrogate and the medical expenses of the child. If health-care coverage is used to cover the medical expenses, the disclosure must include a summary of the health-care policy provisions related to coverage for surrogate pregnancy, including any possible liability of the surrogate, third-party-liability liens, other insurance coverage, and any notice requirement that could affect coverage

or liability of the surrogate. Unless the agreement expressly provides otherwise, the review and disclosure do not constitute legal advice. If the extent of coverage is uncertain, a statement of that fact is sufficient to comply with this paragraph.

(7) The agreement must permit the surrogate to make all health and welfare decisions regarding herself and her pregnancy. This [act] does not enlarge or diminish the surrogate's right to terminate her pregnancy.

(8) The agreement must include information about each party's right under this [article] to terminate the surrogacy agreement.

(b) A surrogacy agreement may provide for:

(1) payment of consideration and reasonable expenses; and

(2) reimbursement of specific expenses if the agreement is terminated under this [article].

(c) A right created under a surrogacy agreement is not assignable and there is no third-party beneficiary of the agreement other than the child.

3. Establishing Parentage through Posthumous Conception

Woodward v. Commissioner of Social Security

Massachusetts Supreme Judicial Court, 2002
760 N.E.2d 257, 435 Mass. 536

MARSHALL, C.J.

The United States District Court for the District of Massachusetts has certified the following question to this court. See S.J.C. Rule 1:03, as appearing in 382 Mass. 700 (1981).

> If a married man and woman arrange for sperm to be withdrawn from the husband for the purpose of artificially impregnating the wife, and the woman is impregnated with that sperm after the man, her husband, has died, will children resulting from such pregnancy enjoy the inheritance rights of natural children under Massachusetts' law of intestate succession?

We answer the certified question as follows: In certain limited circumstances, a child * * * resulting from posthumous reproduction may enjoy the inheritance rights of "issue" under the Massachusetts intestacy statute. These limited circumstances exist where, as a threshold matter, the surviving parent or the child's other legal representative demonstrates a genetic relationship between the child and the decedent. The survivor or representative must then establish both that the decedent affirmatively consented to posthumous conception and to the support of any resulting child. Even where such circumstances exist, time limitations may preclude commencing a claim for succession rights on behalf of a posthumously conceived child. Because the government has conceded that the timeliness of the wife's paternity action under our intestacy law is irrelevant to her Federal appeal, we do not address that question today.

The United States District Court judge has not asked us to determine whether the circumstances giving rise to succession rights for posthumously conceived children apply here. In addition, she has removed from our consideration the question whether the paternity judgment obtained by the wife in this case was valid. See note 6, infra. We answer only the certified question. See Canal Elec. Co. v. Westinghouse Elec. Corp., 406 Mass. 369, 370 n. 1, 548 N.E.2d 182 (1990); Cabot Corp. v. Baddour, 394 Mass. 720, 721, 477 N.E.2d 399 (1985).

* * *

The undisputed facts and relevant procedural history are as follows. In January, 1993, about three and one-half years after they were married, Lauren Woodward and Warren Woodward were informed that the husband had leukemia. At the time, the couple was childless. Advised that the husband's leukemia treatment might leave him sterile, the Woodwards arranged for a quantity of the husband's semen to be medically withdrawn and preserved, in a process commonly known as "sperm banking." The husband then underwent a bone marrow transplant. The treatment was not successful. The husband died in October, 1993, and the wife was appointed administratrix of his estate.

In October, 1995, the wife gave birth to twin girls. The children were conceived through artificial insemination using the husband's preserved semen. In January, 1996, the wife applied for two forms of Social Security survivor benefits: "child's" benefits under 42 U.S.C. § 402(d)(1) (1994 & Supp. V 1999), and "mother's" benefits under 42 U.S.C. § 402(g)(1) (1994).[3]

The Social Security Administration (SSA) rejected the wife's claims on the ground that she had not established that the twins were the husband's "children" within the meaning of the Act.[4] In February, 1996, as she pursued a series of appeals

---

3. At the time of his death, the husband was a fully insured individual under the United States Social Security Act (Act). Section 402(d)(1) of 42 U.S.C. provides "child's" benefits to dependent children of deceased parents who die fully insured under the Act. See 42 U.S.C. § 402(d)(1); 20 C.F.R. § 404.350. Section 402(g)(1) of 42 U.S.C. provides "mother's" benefits to the widow of an individual who died fully insured under the Act, if, inter alia, she has care of a child or children entitled to child's benefits. See 42 U.S.C. § 402(g)(1); 20 C.F.R. § 404.339 (2001). Thus, the wife's eligibility for Social Security survivor benefits hinges on her children's eligibility for such benefits.

4. The Act defines children, in pertinent part, as the "child or legally adopted child of an individual." See 42 U.S.C. § 416(e). The term "child" includes "natural child." See 20 C.F.R. § 404.355. The Act also establishes presumptions of dependency for certain classes of children, as well as other mechanisms for establishing dependency. As stated in the certification order, the wife's

appeal centers on only one possible basis for eligibility, which is that under SSA regulations the children are eligible if they would be treated as [the husband's] natural children for the disposition of his personal property under the Massachusetts law of intestate succession. See 42 U.S.C. §§ 402(d)(3) and 416(h)(2)(A); 20 C.F.R. § 404.355(a)(1); 20 C.F.R. § 404.361(a).

from the SSA decision, the wife filed a "complaint for correction of birth record" in the Probate and Family Court against the clerk of the city of Beverly, seeking to add her deceased husband as the "father" on the twins' birth certificates. In October, 1996, a judge in the Probate and Family Court entered a judgment of paternity and an order to amend both birth certificates declaring the deceased husband to be the children's father. In his judgment of paternity, the Probate Court judge did not make findings of fact, other than to state that he "accepts the [s]tipulations of [v]oluntary [a]cknowledgment of [p]arentage of [the children] . . . executed by [the wife] as [m]other, and [the wife], [a]dministratrix of the [e]state of [the husband], for father." See G.L. c. 209C, § 11. * * *

The wife presented the judgment of paternity and the amended birth certificates to the SSA, but the agency remained unpersuaded. A United States administrative law judge, hearing the wife's claims de novo, concluded, among other things, that the children did not qualify for benefits because they "are not entitled to inherit from [the husband] under the Massachusetts intestacy and paternity laws."[6] The appeals council of the SSA affirmed the administrative law judge's decision, which thus became the commissioner's final decision for purposes of judicial review. The wife appealed to the United States District Court for the District of Massachusetts, seeking a declaratory judgment to reverse the commissioner's ruling.

The United States District Court judge certified the above question to this court because "[t]he parties agree that a determination of these children's rights under the law of Massachusetts is dispositive of the case and . . . no directly applicable Massachusetts precedent exists."

* * *

We have been asked to determine the inheritance rights under Massachusetts law of children conceived from the gametes[7] of a deceased individual and his or her sur-

---

6. The administrative law judge reasoned that the children were not "ascertainable heirs as defined by the intestacy laws of Massachusetts," because they were neither born nor in utero at the date of the husband's death and "the statutes and cases contemplated an ascertainable child, one who had been conceived prior to the father's death." He also found that the children could not inherit as the husband's children under Massachusetts intestacy law because the evidence failed to establish that the husband, before his death, either acknowledged the children as his own or intended to contribute to their support. See G.L. c. 190, § 7. Further, the administrative law judge held that the SSA was not bound by the judgment of paternity because that judgment "is not only inconsistent with Massachusetts paternity laws but also constitutes a proceeding to which the [SSA] was not a party." See Soc. Sec. Rul. 83-37c; Gray v. Richardson, 474 F.2d 1370 (6th Cir.1973). In her certification order, the United State District Court judge affirmed that, as a matter of Federal law, the administrative law judge "was not compelled to give dispositive weight to the Probate Court judgment." She did not ask us to determine whether the paternity judgment is "inconsistent with Massachusetts paternity laws," as the administrative law judge concluded.

7. We use the term "gamete" here to denote "[a]ny germ cell, whether ovum or spermatozoon." Stedman's Medical Dictionary 701 (26th ed.1995).

viving spouse.[8] We have not previously been asked to consider whether our intestacy statute accords inheritance rights to posthumously conceived genetic children. Nor has any American court of last resort considered, in a published opinion, the question of posthumously conceived genetic children's inheritance rights under other States' intestacy laws.[9]

This case presents a narrow set of circumstances, yet the issues it raises are far reaching. Because the law regarding the rights of posthumously conceived children is unsettled, the certified question is understandably broad. Moreover, the parties have articulated extreme positions. The wife's principal argument is that, by virtue of their genetic connection with the decedent, posthumously conceived children must always be permitted to enjoy the inheritance rights of the deceased parent's children under our law of intestate succession. The government's principal argument is that, because posthumously conceived children are not "in being" as of the date of the parent's death, they are always barred from enjoying such inheritance rights.

Neither party's position is tenable. In this developing and relatively uncharted area of human relations, bright-line rules are not favored unless the applicable statute requires them. The Massachusetts intestacy statute does not. Neither the statute's "posthumous children" provision, see G.L. c. 190, § 8, nor any other provision of our intestacy law limits the class of posthumous children to those in utero at the time of the decedent's death. Cf. La. Civ.Code Ann. art. 939 (West 2000) ("A successor must exist at the death of the decedent").[10] On the other hand, with the act of

---

8. Although the certified question asks us to consider an unsettled question of law concerning the paternity of children conceived from a deceased male's gametes, we see no principled reason that our conclusions should not apply equally to children posthumously conceived from a deceased female's gametes.

9. We are aware of only two cases that have addressed, in varying degrees, the question before us. In Hecht v. Superior Court, 16 Cal.App.4th 836, 20 Cal.Rptr.2d 275 (1993), the California Court of Appeal considered, among other things, whether a decedent's sperm was "property" that could be bequeathed to his girl friend. Id. at 847, 20 Cal.Rptr.2d 275. In answering in the affirmative, the court noted, in dicta and without elaboration, that, under the provisions of California's Probate Code, "it is unlikely that the estate would be subject to claims with respect to any such children" resulting from insemination of the girl friend with the decedent's sperm. Id. at 859, 20 Cal.Rptr.2d 275. In Matter of Estate of Kolacy, 332 N.J.Super. 593, 753 A.2d 1257 (2000), the plaintiff brought a declaratory judgment action to have her children, who were conceived after the death of her husband, declared the intestate heirs of her deceased husband in order to pursue the children's claims for survivor benefits with the Social Security Administration. A New Jersey Superior Court judge held that, in circumstances where the decedent left no estate and an adjudication of parentage did not unfairly intrude on the rights of others or cause "serious problems" with the orderly administration of estates, the children would be entitled to inherit under the State's intestacy law. Id. at 602, 753 A.2d 1257.

10. The cases relied on by the administrative law judge do no more than affirm the general common-law rule that heirs are fixed as of the date of death, see National Shawmut Bank v. Joy, 315 Mass. 457, 467, 53 N.E.2d 113 (1944); Gorey v. Guarente, 303 Mass. 569, 576–577, 22 N.E.2d 99 (1939), and that children born after death within the probable period of gestation may inherit as issue of the deceased parent in exception to the general rule. See Bowen v. Hoxie, 137 Mass.

procreation now separated from coitus, posthumous reproduction can occur under a variety of conditions that may conflict with the purposes of the intestacy law and implicate other firmly established State and individual interests. We look to our intestacy law to resolve these tensions.

* * *

We begin our analysis with an overview of Massachusetts intestacy law. In our Commonwealth, the devolution of real and personal property in intestacy is neither a natural nor a constitutional right. It is a privilege conferred by statute. Merchants Nat'l Bank v. Merchants Nat'l Bank, 318 Mass. 563, 573, 62 N.E.2d 831 (1945). Our intestacy statute "excludes all rules of law which might otherwise be operative. It impliedly repealed all preexisting statutes and supersedes the common law." Cassidy v. Truscott, 287 Mass. 515, 521, 192 N.E. 164 (1934).

Section 1 of the intestacy statute directs that, if a decedent "leaves issue," such "issue" will inherit a fixed portion of his real and personal property, subject to debts and expenses, the rights of the surviving spouse, and other statutory payments not relevant here. See G.L. c. 190, § 1. * * * To answer the certified question, then, we must first determine whether the twins are the "issue" of the husband.

The intestacy statute does not define "issue." However, in the context of intestacy the term "issue" means all lineal (genetic) descendants, and now includes both marital and nonmarital * * * descendants. See generally S.M. Dunphy, Probate Law and Practice § 8.5, at 123 (2d ed. 1997 & Supp.2001), and cases cited. * * * See also G.L. c. 4, § 7, Sixteenth ("Issue, as applied to the descent of estates, shall include all the lawful lineal descendants of the ancestor"); Powers v. Wilkinson, 399 Mass. 650, 662, 506 N.E.2d 842 (1987). The term "'[d]escendants' . . . has long been held to mean persons 'who by consanguinity trace their lineage to the designated ancestor.'" Lockwood v. Adamson, 409 Mass. 325, 329, 566 N.E.2d 96 (1991), quoting Evarts v. Davis, 348 Mass. 487, 489, 204 N.E.2d 454 (1965).

Turning to "issue" who are the nonmarital children of an intestate, the intestacy statute treats different classes of nonmarital children differently based on the presumed ease of establishing their consanguinity with the deceased parent. A nonmarital child is presumptively the child of his or her mother and is entitled by virtue of this presumption to enjoy inheritance rights as her issue. G.L. c. 190, § 5. However, to enjoy inheritance rights as the issue of a deceased father, a nonmarital child, in the absence of the father's acknowledgment of paternity or marriage to the mother, must obtain a judicial determination that he or she is the father's child. G.L. c. 190, § 7. The general purpose of such a specific adjudication requirement is to ensure that wealth passes from and to the actual family. See generally 2 T.H. Belknap, Newhall's Settlement of Estates and Fiduciary Law in Massachusetts

---

527, 528–529, 1884 WL 10644 (1884). See also Waverley Trust Co., petitioner, 268 Mass. 181, 183, 167 N.E. 274 (1929). Our intestacy statute supersedes any Massachusetts common law in this area. * * *

§ 24:2, at 38–42 (5th ed.1997). We held, at a time when the means for establishing the paternity of a child were less certain than they are today, that such disparate treatment between the mother and the father of a child advanced the Legislature's interests in preventing fraudulent claims against the estate and in administering estates in an orderly fashion. See Lowell v. Kowalski, 380 Mass. 663, 668, 405 N.E.2d 135 (1980) ("distinction between rights to inherit from a natural father and rights to inherit from a natural mother may properly be based on the greater difficulty of proving paternity than of proving maternity").

The "posthumous children" provision of the intestacy statute, G.L. c. 190, § 8, is yet another expression of the Legislature's intent to preserve wealth for consanguineous descendants. That section provides that "[p]osthumous children shall be considered as living at the death of their parent." The Legislature, however, has left the term "posthumous children" undefined. The Massachusetts intestacy statute originally made no provision for after-born children. See, *e.g.*, St. 1805, c. 90 (approved Mar. 12, 1806). Then in Hall v. Hancock, 15 Pick. 255, 1834 WL 2638 (1834), in the context of a will contest, this court held that a child who was presumptively in utero as of the date of the decedent's death was a child "in being" as of the date of the decedent's death "in all cases where it will be for the benefit of such child to be so considered." *Id.* at 257, 258. Two years later, the Legislature enacted the "posthumous children" provision of the intestacy statute, bringing that devolution mechanism into conformity with our decision concerning wills. See Rev. St. 1836, c. 61, § 13. Despite numerous later amendments to our intestacy laws, the "posthumous children" provision has remained essentially unchanged for 165 years. * * *

The Massachusetts intestacy statute thus does not contain an express, affirmative requirement that posthumous children must "be in existence" as of the date of the decedent's death. The Legislature could surely have enacted such a provision had it desired to do so. Cf. La. Civ.Code Ann. art. 939 (effective July 1, 1999) (West 2000) ("A successor must exist at the death of the decedent"). See also N.D. Cent.Code Ann. 14-18-04 (Michie 1997) ("A person who dies before a conception using that person's sperm or egg is not a parent of any resulting child born of the conception"). We must therefore determine whether, under our intestacy law, there is any reason that children conceived after the decedent's death who are the decedent's direct genetic descendants—that is, children who "by consanguinity trace their lineage to the designated ancestor"—may not enjoy the same succession rights as children conceived before the decedent's death who are the decedent's direct genetic descendants. Lockwood v. Adamson, *supra*.

To answer that question we consider whether and to what extent such children may take as intestate heirs of the deceased genetic parent consistent with the purposes of the intestacy law, and not by any assumptions of the common law. See Cassidy v. Truscott, *supra* at 520–521, 192 N.E. 164. In the absence of express legislative directives, we construe the Legislature's purposes from statutory indicia and judicial decisions in a manner that advances the purposes of the intestacy law. Houghton v. Dickinson, 196 Mass. 389, 391, 82 N.E. 481 (1907).

The question whether posthumously conceived genetic children may enjoy inheritance rights under the intestacy statute implicates three powerful State interests: the best interests of children, the State's interest in the orderly administration of estates, and the reproductive rights of the genetic parent. Our task is to balance and harmonize these interests to effect the Legislature's over-all purposes.

* * * First and foremost we consider the overriding legislative concern to promote the best interests of children. "The protection of minor children, most especially those who may be stigmatized by their 'illegitimate' status . . . has been a hallmark of legislative action and of the jurisprudence of this court." L.W.K. v. E.R.C., 432 Mass. 438, 447–448, 735 N.E.2d 359 (2000). Repeatedly, forcefully, and unequivocally, the Legislature has expressed its will that all children be "entitled to the same rights and protections of the law" regardless of the accidents of their birth. G.L. c. 209C, § 1. See G.L. c. 119, § 1 ("It is hereby declared to be the policy of the commonwealth to direct its efforts, first, to the strengthening and encouragement of family life for the protection and care of children . . ."). Among the many rights and protections vouchsafed to all children are rights to financial support from their parents and their parents' estates. See G.L. c. 119A, § 1 ("It is the public policy of this commonwealth that dependent children shall be maintained, as completely as possible, from the resources of their parents, thereby relieving or avoiding, at least in part, the burden borne by the citizens of the commonwealth"); G.L. c. 191, § 20 (establishing inheritance rights for pretermitted children); G.L. c. 196, §§ 1–3 (permitting allowances from estate to widows and minor children); G.L. c. 209C, § 14 (permitting paternity claims to be commenced prior to birth). See also G.L. c. 190, §§ 1–3, 5, 7–8 (intestacy rights). * * *

We also consider that some of the assistive reproductive technologies that make posthumous reproduction possible have been widely known and practiced for several decades. See generally Banks, Traditional Concepts and Nontraditional Conceptions: Social Security Survivor's Benefits for Posthumously Conceived Children, 32 Loy. L.A. L.Rev. 251, 267–273 (1999). In that time, the Legislature has not acted to narrow the broad statutory class of posthumous children to restrict posthumously conceived children from taking in intestacy. Moreover, the Legislature has in great measure affirmatively supported the assistive reproductive technologies that are the only means by which these children can come into being. See G.L. c. 46, § 4B (artificial insemination of married woman). See also G.L. c. 175, § 47H; G.L. c. 176A, § 8K; G.L. c. 176B, § 4J; G.L. c. 176G, § 4 (insurance coverage for infertility treatments). We do not impute to the Legislature the inherently irrational conclusion that assistive reproductive technologies are to be encouraged while a class of children who are the fruit of that technology are to have fewer rights and protections than other children.

In short, we cannot, absent express legislative directive, accept the commissioner's position that the historical context of G.L. c. 190, § 8, dictates as a matter of law that all posthumously conceived children are automatically barred from taking under their deceased donor parent's intestate estate. We have consistently construed statutes to effectuate the Legislature's overriding purpose to promote the welfare of all children, notwithstanding restrictive common-law rules to the contrary. See, e.g., L.W.K. v. E.R.C., *supra* at 447, 735 N.E.2d 359; Adoption of Tammy, 416 Mass. 205, 210, 619 N.E.2d 315 (1993); Powers v. Wilkinson, 399 Mass. 650, 661–662, 506 N.E.2d 842 (1987); Powers v. Steele, 394 Mass. 306, 310, 475 N.E.2d 395 (1985); Hall v. Hancock, 32 Mass. 255, 15 Pick. 255 (1834). * * * Posthumously conceived children may not come into the world the way the majority of children do. But they are children nonetheless. We may assume that the Legislature intended that such children be "entitled," in so far as possible, "to the same rights and protections of the law" as children conceived before death. See G.L. c. 209C, § 1.

* * * However, in the context of our intestacy laws, the best interests of the posthumously conceived child, while of great importance, are not in themselves conclusive. They must be balanced against other important State interests, not the least of which is the protection of children who are alive or conceived before the intestate parent's death. In an era in which serial marriages, serial families, and blended families are not uncommon, according succession rights under our intestacy laws to posthumously conceived children may, in a given case, have the potential to pit child against child and family against family. Any inheritance rights of posthumously conceived children will reduce the intestate share available to children born prior to the decedent's death. See G.L. c. 190, § 3(1). Such considerations, among others, lead us to examine a second important legislative purpose: to provide certainty to heirs and creditors by effecting the orderly, prompt, and accurate administration of intestate estates. See generally S.M. Dunphy, Probate Law and Practice § 8.1, at 115 (2d ed.1997).

The intestacy statute furthers the Legislature's administrative goals in two principal ways: (1) by requiring certainty of filiation between the decedent and his issue, and (2) by establishing limitations periods for the commencement of claims against the intestate estate. In answering the certified question, we must consider each of these requirements of the intestacy statute in turn.

First, as we have discussed, our intestacy law mandates that, absent the father's acknowledgment of paternity or marriage to the mother, a nonmarital child must obtain a judicial determination of paternity as a prerequisite to succeeding to a portion of the father's intestate estate. Both the United States Supreme Court and this court have long recognized that the State's strong interest in preventing fraudulent claims justifies certain disparate classifications among nonmarital children based on the relative difficulty of accurately determining a child's direct lineal ancestor. See Lowell v. Kowalski, 380 Mass. 663, 668–669, 405 N.E.2d 135 (1980). See also Trimble v. Gordon, 430 U.S. 762, 771, 97 S.Ct. 1459, 52 L.Ed.2d 31 (1977).

* * *

We now turn to the second way in which the Legislature has met its administrative goals: the establishment of a limitations period for bringing paternity claims against the intestate estate. Our discussion of this important goal, however, is necessarily circumscribed by the procedural posture of this case and by the terms of the certified question. The certification record discloses that, after one unsuccessful insemination attempt, the wife conceived using her deceased husband's sperm approximately sixteen months after his death. The children were born approximately two years after the husband's death, and the paternity action (in the form of a "complaint for correction of birth record") was filed approximately four months after the children's birth. Both the SSA and the administrative law judge concluded that the wife and the children were not entitled to Social Security survivor benefits because, among other things, the paternity actions were not brought within the one-year period for commencing paternity claims mandated by the intestacy statute. See G.L. c. 190, § 7.

However, in his brief to this court, the commissioner represented that he had informed the United States District Court judge that the wife "had been advised that she need not address" the timeliness issue on appeal in light of a change in Federal regulations. Specifically, the SSA has amended its regulations to read:

> We will not apply any State inheritance law requirement that an action to establish paternity must be taken within a specified period of time measured from the worker's death or the child's birth, or that an action to establish paternity must have been started or completed before the worker's death. . . .

20 C.F.R. § 404.355(b)(2). * * * We understand the commissioner's representation to be a concession that the timeliness of the wife's Massachusetts paternity actions is not relevant to the Federal law question whether the wife's children will be considered the husband's "natural children" for Social Security benefits purposes, and that therefore whatever we say on this issue has no bearing on the wife's Federal action. We also note that the certified question does not specifically address the limitations matter and that, in their briefs to this court, the parties referred to the limitations question only peripherally. * * *

Nevertheless, the limitations question is inextricably tied to consideration of the intestacy statute's administrative goals. In the case of posthumously conceived children, the application of the one-year limitations period of G.L. c. 190, § 7 is not clear; it may pose significant burdens on the surviving parent, and consequently on the child. * * * It requires, in effect, that the survivor make a decision to bear children while in the freshness of grieving. It also requires that attempts at conception succeed quickly. Cf. Commentary, Modern Reproductive Technologies: Legal Issues Concerning Cryopreservation and Posthumous Conception, 17 J. Legal Med. 547, 549 (1996) ("It takes an average of seven insemination attempts over 4.4 menstrual cycles to establish pregnancy"). Because the resolution of the time constraints question is not required here, it must await the appropriate case, should one arise.

* * * Finally, the question certified to us implicates a third important State interest: to honor the reproductive choices of individuals. We need not address the wife's argument that her reproductive rights would be infringed by denying succession

rights to her children under our intestacy law. Nothing in the record even remotely suggests that she was prevented by the State from choosing to conceive children using her deceased husband's semen. The husband's reproductive rights are a more complicated matter.

In A.Z. v. B.Z., 431 Mass. 150, 725 N.E.2d 1051 (2000), we considered certain issues surrounding the disposition of frozen preembryos. A woman sought to enforce written agreements between herself and her former husband. The wife argued that these agreements permitted her to implant frozen preembryos created with the couple's gametes during the marriage, even in the event of their divorce. We declined to enforce the agreements. Persuasive to us, among other factors, was the lack of credible evidence of the husband's "true intention" regarding the disposition of the frozen preembryos, and the changed family circumstance resulting from the couple's divorce. See *id.* at 158–159, 725 N.E.2d 1051. Recognizing that our laws strongly affirm the value of bodily and reproductive integrity, we held that "forced procreation is not an area amenable to judicial enforcement." *Id.* at 160, 725 N.E.2d 1051. In short, A.Z. v. B.Z., *supra*, recognized that individuals have a protected right to control the use of their gametes.

Consonant with the principles identified in A.Z. v. B.Z., *supra*, a decedent's silence, or his equivocal indications of a desire to parent posthumously, "ought not to be construed as consent." See Schiff, Arising from the Dead: Challenges of Posthumous Procreation, 75 N.C. L.Rev. 901, 951 (1997). * * * The prospective donor parent must clearly and unequivocally consent not only to posthumous reproduction but also to the support of any resulting child. Cf. Paternity of Cheryl, 434 Mass. 23, 37, 746 N.E.2d 488 (2001) ("The law places on men the burden to consider carefully the permanent consequences that flow from an acknowledgment of paternity"). After the donor-parent's death, the burden rests with the surviving parent, or the posthumously conceived child's other legal representative, to prove the deceased genetic parent's affirmative consent to both requirements for posthumous parentage: posthumous reproduction and the support of any resulting child.

This two-fold consent requirement arises from the nature of alternative reproduction itself. It will not always be the case that a person elects to have his or her gametes medically preserved to create "issue" posthumously. A man, for example, may preserve his semen for myriad reasons, including, among others: to reproduce after recovery from medical treatment, to reproduce after an event that leaves him sterile, or to reproduce when his spouse has a genetic disorder or otherwise cannot have or safely bear children. That a man has medically preserved his gametes for use by his spouse thus may indicate only that he wished to reproduce after some contingency while he was alive, and not that he consented to the different circumstance of creating a child after his death. Uncertainty as to consent may be compounded by the fact that medically preserved semen can remain viable for up to ten years after it was first extracted, long after the original decision to preserve the semen has passed and when such changed circumstances as divorce, remarriage, and a second family may have intervened. See Banks, Traditional Concepts and Nontraditional

Conceptions: Social Security Survivor's Benefits for Posthumously Conceived Children, 32 Loy. L.A. L.Rev. 251, 270 (1999). * * *

Such circumstances demonstrate the inadequacy of a rule that would make the mere genetic tie of the decedent to any posthumously conceived child, or the decedent's mere election to preserve gametes, sufficient to bind his intestate estate for the benefit of any posthumously conceived child. Without evidence that the deceased intestate parent affirmatively consented (1) to the posthumous reproduction and (2) to support any resulting child, a court cannot be assured that the intestacy statute's goal of fraud prevention is satisfied.

As expressed in our intestacy and paternity laws, sound public policy dictates the requirements we have outlined above. Legal parentage imposes substantial obligations on adults for the welfare of children. Where two adults engage in the act of sexual intercourse, it is a matter of common sense and logic, expressed in well-established law, to charge them with parental responsibilities for the child who is the natural, even if unintended, consequence of their actions. Where conception results from a third-party medical procedure using a deceased person's gametes, it is entirely consistent with our laws on children, parentage, and reproductive freedom to place the burden on the surviving parent (or the posthumously conceived child's other legal representative) to demonstrate the genetic relationship of the child to the decedent and that the intestate consented both to reproduce posthumously and to support any resulting child.

* * *

The certified question does not require us to specify what proof would be sufficient to establish a successful claim under our intestacy law on behalf of a posthumously conceived child. Nor have we been asked to determine whether the wife has met her burden of proof. The record reveals that the administrative law judge repeatedly requested that the wife provide objective corroboration of her claim that the husband consented to father children after his death.[24] The administrative law judge's opinion indicates that he was willing to consider "additional declarations or

---

24. In pertinent part, the factual record contains a brief affidavit that the wife submitted to the Probate Court judge in her action to amend the children's birth records, a physician's letter that was submitted in that action, and a transcript of the wife's testimony before the administrative law judge. The wife's affidavit attests only that the husband's sperm was extracted and preserved "because my husband and I wanted to have children from our union." The two-sentence notarized physician's letter, addressed to the wife's attorney, was from the director of Reproductive Endocrinology and Fertility Services of Malden Hospital. He wrote that, on February 3, 1995, the wife "had a twin pregnancy" as a result of her insemination with the husband's "frozen/thawed semen" and that "[w]e were notified that she delivered twins in October, 1995." Before the administrative law judge the wife testified only that she and the husband had discussed with doctors whether she would "be able to have children, [the husband's] children" should the husband's bone marrow transplant not succeed. At the time, the couple had been told that the husband's leukemia treatments might render him sterile, if he survived. She further testified that the husband "agreed" with her that "if something should happen . . . I would still be able to have his children."

written statements from the decedent's family, [the wife's] family, financial records or records from the fertility institute that demonstrate any acknowledgment [of the children] made by [the husband]." Cf. Higgins v. Ripley, 16 Mass.App.Ct. 928, 450 N.E.2d 186 (1983); Wrenn v. Harris, 503 F.Supp. 223, 226–227 (D.Mass.1980). Perhaps because the law was unsettled at the time, the wife's counsel took the position that the paternity judgment and the birth certificates were sufficient, and that no further evidence was required. In the wife's Probate Court action, however, the judge held the husband to be the "father" of the children, but did not make any specific findings to support that determination. Nor did he determine whether the husband intended to support the wife's children. Moreover, although a birth certificate is prima facie evidence of the facts recorded therein, G.L. c. 46, § 19, under our laws, genetic and legal parentage are not always coterminous. See G.L. c. 210 (adoption statute).

It is undisputed in this case that the husband is the genetic father of the wife's children. However, for the reasons stated above, that fact, in itself, cannot be sufficient to establish that the husband is the children's legal father for purposes of the devolution and distribution of his intestate property. In the United States District Court, the wife may come forward with other evidence as to her husband's consent to posthumously conceive children. She may come forward with evidence of his consent to support such children. We do not speculate as to the sufficiency of evidence she may submit at trial.

* * *

We feel constrained to comment on the judgment of paternity and the issuance of the amended birth certificates. The Probate and Family Court judge should not have entered the paternity judgment, or ordered the husband's name added to the birth certificates, on the record the mother presented. The mother sought to establish her deceased husband's paternity of the twins by bringing a complaint to amend birth records against the clerk of the city of Beverly (who, according to the judgment of paternity, did not object to the action). Where an estate is at issue—which will always be the case where a parent is deceased—notice of the action to establish legal parentage should be given to every other interested party, including the potential heirs who would have taken but for the posthumous creation of the children. See Mass. R. Civ. P. 19(a)(2), 365 Mass. 765 (1974) (joinder of interested persons); Mass. R. Dom. Rel. P. 19 (West 2001) (same); Rodrigues v. Rodrigues, 286 Mass. 77, 83, 190 N.E. 20 (1934). See also Sondra S. v. Jay O., 126 Misc.2d 322, 327–328, 482 N.Y.S.2d 660 (Fam.Ct.1984) (proceeding to establish deceased father's paternity must be adversary proceeding, with notice given to all interested parties). In this case, no such notice was given. * * *

The record also discloses that the wife sought to bind the husband's estate for the benefit of her posthumously conceived children by filing stipulations of voluntary acknowledgment of parentage executed by herself as mother and by herself as administratrix of the husband's estate. See G.L. c. 209C, § 11. The Probate and Family Court judge should not have considered these stipulations, much less grounded his paternity judgment on them. Neither the statutory powers granted to administrators, see, *e.g.*, G.L. c. 195, § 5A, nor the Massachusetts intestacy and paternity laws permit such procedures to establish paternity. See, *e.g.*, G.L. c. 209C, § 11 (requiring voluntary acknowledgments of paternity to be signed by both parents).

* * *

For the second time this term, we have been confronted with novel questions involving the rights of children born from assistive reproductive technologies. See Culliton v. Beth Israel Deaconess Med. Ctr., 435 Mass. 285, 756 N.E.2d 1133 (2001). As these technologies advance, the number of children they produce will continue to multiply. So, too, will the complex moral, legal, social, and ethical questions that surround their birth. The questions present in this case cry out for lengthy, careful examination outside the adversary process, which can only address the specific circumstances of each controversy that presents itself. They demand a comprehensive response reflecting the considered will of the people.

In the absence of statutory directives, we have answered the certified question by identifying and harmonizing the important State interests implicated therein in a manner that advances the Legislature's over-all purposes. In so doing, we conclude that limited circumstances may exist, consistent with the mandates of our Legislature, in which posthumously conceived children may enjoy the inheritance rights of "issue" under our intestacy law. These limited circumstances exist where, as a threshold matter, the surviving parent or the child's other legal representative demonstrates a genetic relationship between the child and the decedent. The survivor or representative must then establish both that the decedent affirmatively consented to posthumous conception and to the support of any resulting child. Even where such circumstances exist, time limitations may preclude commencing a claim for succession rights on behalf of a posthumously conceived child. In any action brought to establish such inheritance rights, notice must be given to all interested parties.

The Reporter of Decisions is to furnish attested copies of this opinion to the clerk of this court. The clerk in turn will transmit one copy, under the seal of this court, to the clerk of the United States District Court for the District of Massachusetts, as the answer to the question certified, and will also transmit a copy to each party.

Notes

The *Woodward* decision is unique due to its emphasis upon the best interest of any child born through posthumous conception. The applicable Massachusetts intestacy statute was vague enough to permit such an emphasis. Increasingly, states are enacting legislation to acknowledge posthumous conception and resulting inheritance rights. "Today, more than a quarter of the states have enacted legislation specifically governing posthumous conception, but there has yet to be an approved model act." Raymond C. O'Brien, *Assessing Assisted Reproductive Technology*, 27 CATH. U. J. L. & TECH. 1, 35 (2018). As the enacted statutes illustrate, *infra*, genetic connection, time frames, and consent are all important considerations.

California Probate Code (2019)

§ 249.5. Posthumous conception; child of decedent deemed born in decedent's lifetime; conditions.

For purposes of determining rights to property to be distributed upon the death of a decedent, a child of the decedent conceived and born after the death of the decedent shall be deemed to have been born in the lifetime of the decedent, and after the execution of all of the decedent's testamentary instruments, if the child or his or her representative proves by clear and convincing evidence that all of the following conditions are satisfied:

(a) The decedent, in writing, specifies that his or her genetic material shall be used for the posthumous conception of a child of the decedent, subject to the following:

(1) The specification shall be signed by the decedent and dated.

(2) The specification may be revoked or amended only by a writing, signed by the decedent and dated.

(3) A person is designated by the decedent to control the use of the genetic material.

(b) The person designated by the decedent to control the use of the genetic material has given written notice by certified mail, return receipt requested, that the decedent's genetic material was available for the purpose of posthumous conception. The notice shall have been given to a person who has the power to control the distribution of either the decedent's property or death benefits payable by reason of the decedent's death, within four months of the date of issuance of a certificate of the decedent's death or entry of a judgment determining the fact of the decedent's death, whichever event occurs first.

(c) The child was in utero using the decedent's genetic material and was in utero within two years of the date of issuance of a certificate of the decedent's death or entry of a judgment determining the fact of the decedent's death, whichever event occurs first. This subdivision does not apply to a child who shares all of his or her nuclear genes with the person donating the implanted nucleus as a result of the application of somatic nuclear transfer technology commonly known as human cloning.

Uniform Probate Code (2019)

§ 2-120. Child Conceived By Assisted Reproduction Other Than Child Born to Gestational Carrier. * * *

(k) [When Posthumously Conceived Child Treated as in Gestation.] If, under this section, an individual is a parent of a child of assisted reproduction who is conceived after the individual's death, the child is treated as in gestation at the individual's death for purposes of Section 2-104(a)(2) if the child is:

(1) in utero not later than 36 months after the individual's death; or

(2) born not later than 45 months after the individual's death.

[Note that Unif. Prob. Code § 2-104(a)(2) requires the child to survive birth by 120 hours to inherit under this section].

Uniform Parentage Act of 2000

§ 708. Parental Status of Deceased Individual.

(a) If an individual who intends to be a parent of a child conceived by assisted reproduction dies during the period between the transfer of a gamete or embryo and the birth of the child, the individual's death does not preclude the establishment of the individual's parentage of the child if the individual otherwise would be a parent of the child under this [act].

(b) If an individual who consented in a record to assisted reproduction by a woman who agreed to give birth to a child dies before a transfer of gametes or embryos, the deceased individual is a parent of a child conceived by the assisted reproduction only if:

> (1) either:
>
>> (A) the individual consented in a record that if assisted reproduction were to occur after the death of the individual, the individual would be a parent of the child; or
>>
>> (B) the individual's intent to be a parent of a child conceived by assisted reproduction after the individual's death is established by clear-and-convincing evidence; and
>
> (2) either:
>
>> (A) the embryo is in utero not later than [36] months after the individual's death; or
>>
>> (B) the child is born not later than [45] months after the individual's death.

VI. Simultaneous Death

If a person wishes to transfer property to another at death, this may be done through a Last Will and Testament, a state statute of intestate succession, or a will substitute, which, for example, pays the benefits of a life insurance policy to another. In each of these three situations, the person wishing to transfer wealth must have intended that the recipient survive. But for how long? If the survivor lives for a very short period of time, he or she will have other plans for the wealth received, and, thus, the wealth could quickly go to persons the original decedent neither knew nor intended to benefit from his or her transfer. Thus, the law implies that any beneficiary should survive for at least a while in order to enjoy the inheritance. Otherwise, the purpose of the transfer is negated and, in addition, probate costs come too rapidly.

For example, if a married woman dies with a valid Last Will and Testament and leaves all of her property to her husband, this is both logical and appropriate. But if she and her husband are both victims of the same traffic accident, and the husband dies a day after his wife, he still survives. His estate would receive the property of the wife, and this property will pass according to his Last Will and Testament. His estate plan was to provide for his wife if she survived him, otherwise, for his property to pass to his own sisters and brothers. Because his wife did not survive, the property goes to his own sisters and brothers. Of course, this includes the property of the wife since he inherited it from her the day before. Her family will not share in her assets, it all will go to her husband's brothers and sisters.

Various approaches have been adopted to address what the law regards as the unfairness of passing property to a beneficiary who dies too quickly. In the most obvious case, if a decedent has a valid Last Will and Testament, the will may provide for a time in which the survivor must survive to take under the Last Will and Testament. For example: "Any beneficiary under this, my Last Will and Testament, must survive me by at least nine months. In the event that he or she does not survive me by this time, then I direct that his or her bequest or devise pass to the alternate taker or to the residuary clause." But if the decedent does not provide in a valid will for a time in which a beneficiary must survive, there are statutes that will provide some guidance. For example, the Uniform Simultaneous Death Act has been adopted in many states and provides that an heir must survive by at least 120 hours. However, it only applies if there is no proof of survivorship. To determine whether this is a good approach, the following case is illustrative.

Janus v. Tarasewicz

Illinois Appellate Court, 1985
135 Ill. App. 3d 936, 482 N.E.2d 418

O'CONNOR, Justice:

This non-jury declaratory judgment action arose out of the death of a husband and wife, Stanley and Theresa Janus, who died after ingesting Tylenol capsules which had been laced with cyanide by an unknown perpetrator prior to its sale in stores. Stanley Janus was pronounced dead shortly after he was admitted to the hospital. However, Theresa Janus was placed on life support systems for almost two days before being pronounced dead. Claiming that there was no sufficient evidence that Theresa Janus survived her husband, plaintiff Alojza Janus, Stanley's mother, brought this action for the proceeds of Stanley's $100,000 life insurance policy which named Theresa as the primary beneficiary and plaintiff as the contingent beneficiary. Defendant Metropolitan Life Insurance Company paid the proceeds to defendant Jan Tarasewicz, Theresa's father and the administrator of her estate. The trial court found sufficient evidence that Theresa survived Stanley Janus. We affirm.

The facts of this case are particularly poignant and complex. Stanley and Theresa Janus had recently returned from their honeymoon when, on the evening of

September 29, 1982, they gathered with other family members to mourn the death of Stanley's brother, Adam Janus, who had died earlier that day from what was later determined to be cyanide-laced Tylenol capsules. While the family was at Adam's home, Stanley and Theresa Janus unknowingly took some of the contaminated Tylenol. Soon afterwards, Stanley collapsed on the kitchen floor.

Theresa was still standing when Diane O'Sullivan, a registered nurse and a neighbor of Adam Janus, was called to the scene. Stanley's pulse was weak so she began cardiopulmonary resuscitation (CPR) on him. Within minutes, Theresa Janus began having seizures. After paramedic teams began arriving, Ms. O'Sullivan went into the living room to assist with Theresa. While she was working on Theresa, Ms. O'Sullivan could hear Stanley's "heavy and labored breathing." She believed that both Stanley and Theresa died before they were taken to the ambulance, but she could not tell who died first.

Ronald Mahon, a paramedic for the Arlington Heights Fire Department, arrived at approximately 5:45 p.m. He saw Theresa faint and go into a seizure. Her pupils did not respond to light but she was breathing on her own during the time that he worked on her. Mahon also assisted with Stanley, giving him drugs to stimulate heart contractions. Mahon later prepared the paramedic's report on Stanley. One entry in the report shows that at 18:00 hours Stanley had "zero blood pressure, zero pulse, and zero respiration." However, Mahon stated that the times in the report were merely approximations. He was able to say that Stanley was in the ambulance en route to the hospital when his vital signs disappeared.

When paramedic Robert Lockhart arrived at 5:55 p.m., both victims were unconscious with non-reactive pupils. Theresa's seizures had ceased but she was in a decerebrate posture in which her arms and legs were rigidly extended and her arms were rotated inward toward her body, thus, indicating severe neurological dysfunction. At that time, she was breathing only four or five times a minute and, shortly thereafter, she stopped breathing on her own altogether. Lockhart intubated them both by placing tubes down their tracheae to keep their air passages open. Prior to being taken to the ambulance, they were put on "ambu-bags" which is a form of artificial respiration whereby the paramedic respirates the patient by squeezing a bag. Neither Stanley nor Theresa showed any signs of being able to breathe on their own while they were being transported to Northwest Community Hospital in Arlington Heights, Illinois. However, Lockhart stated that when Theresa was turned over to the hospital personnel, she had a palpable pulse and blood pressure.

The medical director of the intensive care unit at the hospital, Dr. Thomas Kim, examined them when they arrived in the emergency room at approximately 6:30 p.m. Stanley had no blood pressure or pulse. An electrocardiogram detected electrical activity in Stanley Janus' heart but there was no synchronization between his heart's electrical activity and its pumping activity. A temporary pacemaker was inserted in an unsuccessful attempt to resuscitate him. Because he never developed spontaneous blood pressure, pulse or signs of respiration, Stanley Janus was pronounced dead at 8:15 p.m. on September 29, 1982.

Like Stanley, Theresa Janus showed no visible vital signs when she was admitted to the emergency room. However, hospital personnel were able to get her heart beating on its own again, so they did not insert a pacemaker. They were also able to establish a measurable, though unsatisfactory, blood pressure. Theresa was taken off the "ambu-bag" and put on a mechanical respirator. In Dr. Kim's opinion, Theresa was in a deep coma with "very unstable vital signs" when she was moved to the intensive care unit at 9:30 p.m. on September 29, 1982.

While Theresa was in the intensive care unit, numerous entries in her hospital records indicated that she had fixed and dilated pupils. However, one entry made at 2:32 a.m. on September 30, 1982, indicated that a nurse apparently detected a minimal reaction to light in Theresa's right pupil but not in her left pupil.

On September 30, 1982, various tests were performed in order to assess Theresa's brain function. These tests included an electroencephalogram (EEG) to measure electrical activity in her brain and a cerebral blood flow test to determine whether there was any blood circulating in her brain. In addition, Theresa exhibited no gag or cord reflexes, no response to pain or other external stimuli. As a result of these tests, Theresa Janus was diagnosed as having sustained total brain death, her life support systems then were terminated, and she was pronounced dead at 1:15 p.m. on October 1, 1982.

Death certificates were issued for Stanley and Theresa Janus more than three weeks later by a medical examiner's physician who never examined them. The certificates listed Stanley Janus' date of death as September 29, 1982, and Theresa Janus' date of death as October 1, 1982. Concluding that Theresa survived Stanley, the Metropolitan Life Insurance Company paid the proceeds of Stanley's life insurance policy to the administrator of Theresa's estate.

On January 6, 1983, plaintiff brought the instant declaratory judgment action against the insurance company and the administrators of Stanley and Theresa's estates, claiming the proceeds of the insurance policy as the contingent beneficiary of the policy. Also, the administrator of Stanley's estate filed a counterclaim against Theresa's estate seeking a declaration as to the disposition of the assets of Stanley's estate.

During the trial, the court heard the testimony of Ms. O'Sullivan, the paramedics, and Dr. Kim. There was also testimony that, while Theresa was in the intensive care unit, members of Theresa's family requested that termination of her life support system be delayed until the arrival of her brother who was serving in the military. However, Theresa's family denied making such a request.

In addition, Dr. Kenneth Vatz, a neurologist on the hospital staff, was called as an expert witness by plaintiff. Although he never actually examined Theresa, he had originally read her EEG as part of hospital routine. Without having seen her other hospital records, his initial evaluation of her EEG was that it showed some minimal electrical activity of living brain cells in the frontal portion of Theresa's brain. After reading her records and reviewing the EEG, however, he stated that the electrical activity measured by the EEG was "very likely" the result of interference from surrounding equipment in the intensive care unit. He concluded that Theresa was brain dead at the time of her admission to the hospital but he could not give an opinion as to who died first.

The trial court also heard an evidence deposition of Dr. Joseph George Hanley, a neurosurgeon who testified as an expert witness on behalf of the defendants. Based on his examination of their records, Dr. Hanley concluded that Stanley Janus died on September 29, 1982. He further concluded that Theresa Janus did not die until her vital signs disappeared on October 1, 1982. His conclusion that she did not die prior to that time was based on: (1) the observations by hospital personnel that Theresa Janus had spontaneous pulse and blood pressure which did not have to be artificially maintained; (2) the instance when Theresa Janus' right pupil allegedly reacted to light; and (3) Theresa's EEG which showed some brain function and which, in his opinion, could not have resulted from outside interference.

At the conclusion of the trial, the court held that the evidence was sufficient to show that Theresa survived Stanley, but the court was not prepared to say by how long she survived him. Plaintiff and the administrator of Stanley's estate appeal. In essence, their main contention is that there is not sufficient evidence to prove that both victims did not suffer brain death prior to their arrival at the hospital on September 29, 1982. * * *

Regardless of which standard of death is applied, survivorship is a fact which must be proven by a preponderance of the evidence by the party whose claim depends on survivorship. (In Re Estate of Moran (1979), 77 Ill.2d 147, 150, 32 Ill. Dec. 349, 395 N.E.2d 579.) The operative provisions of the Illinois version of the Uniform Simultaneous Death Act provides in pertinent part:

> If the title to property or its devolution depends upon the priority of death and there is no sufficient evidence that the persons have died otherwise than simultaneously and there is no other provision in the will, trust agreement, deed, contract of insurance or other governing instrument for distribution of the property different from the provisions of this Section:
>
> (a) The property of each person shall be disposed of as if he had survived.
>
> * * *
>
> (d) If the insured and the beneficiary of a policy of life or accident insurance have so died, the proceeds of the policy shall be distributed as if the insured had survived the beneficiary.

Ill.Rev.Stat.1981, ch. 110 1/2, par. 3-1.

In cases where the question of survivorship is determined by the testimony of lay witnesses, the burden of sufficient evidence may be met by evidence of a positive sign of life in one body and the absence of any such sign in the other. (In Re Estate of Lowrance (1978), 66 Ill.App.3d 159, 162, 22 Ill.Dec. 895, 383 N.E.2d 703; Prudential Insurance Co. v. Spain (1950), 339 Ill.App. 476, 90 N.E.2d 256.) In cases such as the instant case where the death process is monitored by medical professionals, their testimony as to "the usual and customary standards of medical practice" will be highly relevant when considering what constitutes a positive sign of life and what constitutes a criteria for determining death. (See In Re Haymer (1983), 115 Ill.App.3d 349, 71 Ill. Dec. 252, 450 N.E.2d 940.) Although the use of sophisticated medical technology can also make it difficult to determine when death occurs, the context of this case does not require a determination as to the exact moment at which the decedents died. Rather, the trial court's task was to determine whether or not there was sufficient evidence that Theresa Janus survived her husband. Our task on review of this factually disputed case is to determine whether the trial court's finding was against the manifest weight of the evidence. (See Fransen Construction Co. v. Industrial Commission (1943), 384 Ill. 616, 628–29, 52 N.E.2d 241; In Re Estate of Adams (1952), 348 Ill.App. 115, 121, 108 N.E.2d 32.) We hold that it was not.

In the case at bar, both victims arrived at the hospital with artificial respirators and no obvious vital signs. There is no dispute among the treating physicians and expert witnesses that Stanley Janus died in both a cardiopulmonary sense and a brain death sense when his vital signs disappeared en route to the hospital and were never reestablished. He was pronounced dead at 8:15 p.m. on September 29, 1982, only after intensive procedures such as electro-shock, medication, and the insertion of a pacemaker failed to resuscitate him.

In contrast, these intensive procedures were not necessary with Theresa Janus because hospital personnel were able to reestablish a spontaneous blood pressure and pulse which did not have to be artificially maintained by a pacemaker or medication. Once spontaneous circulation was restored in the emergency room, Theresa was put on a mechanical respirator and transferred to the intensive care unit. Clearly, efforts to preserve Theresa Janus' life continued after more intensive efforts on Stanley's behalf had failed.

It is argued that the significance of Theresa Janus' cardiopulmonary functions, as a sign of life, was rendered ambiguous by the use of artificial respiration. In particular, reliance is placed upon expert testimony that a person can be brain dead and still have a spontaneous pulse and blood pressure which is indirectly maintained by artificial respiration. The fact remains, however, that Dr. Kim, an intensive care specialist who treated Theresa, testified that her condition in the emergency room did not warrant a diagnosis of brain death. In his opinion, Theresa Janus did not suffer irreversible brain death until much later, when extensive treatment failed to preserve her brain function and vital signs. This diagnosis was confirmed by a consulting neurologist after a battery of tests were performed to assess her brain function. Dr. Kim denied that these examinations were made merely to see if brain death had already occurred. At trial, only Dr. Vatz disagreed with their finding, but even he admitted that the diagnosis and tests performed on Theresa Janus were in keeping with the usual and customary standards of medical practice.

There was also other evidence presented at trial which indicated that Theresa Janus was not brain dead on September 29, 1982. Theresa's EEG, taken on

September 30, 1982, was not flat but rather it showed some delta waves of extremely low amplitude. Dr. Hanley concluded that Theresa's EEG taken on September 30 exhibited brain activity. Dr. Vatz disagreed. Since the trier of fact determines the credibility of expert witnesses and the weight to be given to their testimony (Anderson v. General Grinding Wheel Corp. (1979), 74 Ill.App.3d 270, 281, 30 Ill.Dec. 354, 393 N.E.2d 9), the trial court in this case could have reasonably given greater weight to Dr. Hanley's opinion than to Dr. Vatz'. In addition, there is evidence that Theresa's pupil reacted to light on one occasion. It is argued that this evidence merely represents the subjective impression of a hospital staff member which is not corroborated by any other instance where Theresa's pupils reacted to light. However, this argument goes to the weight of this evidence and not to its admissibility. While these additional pieces of neurological data were by no means conclusive, they were competent evidence which tended to support the trial court's finding, and which also tended to disprove the contention that these tests merely verified that brain death had already taken place.

In support of the contention that Theresa Janus did not survive Stanley Janus, evidence was presented which showed that only Theresa Janus suffered seizures and exhibited a decerebrate posture shortly after ingesting the poisoned Tylenol. However, evidence that persons with these symptoms tend to die very quickly does not prove that Theresa Janus did not in fact survive Stanley Janus. Moreover, the evidence introduced is similar in nature to medical presumptions of survivorship based on decedents' health or physical condition which are considered too speculative to prove or disprove survivorship. (See In Re Estate of Moran (1979), 77 Ill.2d 147, 153, 32 Ill.Dec. 349, 395 N.E.2d 579.) Similarly, we find no support for the allegation that the hospital kept Theresa Janus on a mechanical respirator because her family requested that termination of her life support systems be delayed until the arrival of her brother, particularly since members of Theresa's family denied making such a request.

In conclusion, we believe that the record clearly established that the treating physicians' diagnoses of death with respect to Stanley and Theresa Janus were made in accordance with "the usual and customary standards of medical practice." Stanley Janus was diagnosed as having sustained irreversible cessation of circulatory and respiratory functions on September 29, 1982. These same physicians concluded that Theresa Janus' condition on that date did not warrant a diagnosis of death and, therefore, they continued their efforts to preserve her life. Their conclusion that Theresa Janus did not die until October 1, 1982, was based on various factors including the restoration of certain of her vital signs as well as other neurological evidence. The trial court found that these facts and circumstances constituted sufficient evidence that Theresa Janus survived her husband. It was not necessary to determine the exact moment at which Theresa died or by how long she survived him, and the trial court properly declined to do so. Viewing the record in its entirety, we cannot say that the trial court's finding of sufficient evidence of Theresa's survivorship was against the manifest weight of the evidence.

Because of our disposition of this case, we need not and do not consider whether the date of death listed on the victims' death certificates should be considered "facts" which constitute *prima facie* evidence of the date of their deaths. See Ill.Rev. Stat. 1981, ch. 111 1/2, par. 73-25; People v. Fiddler (1970), 45 Ill.2d 181, 184–86, 258 N.E.2d 359.

Accordingly, there being sufficient evidence that Theresa Janus survived Stanley Janus, the judgment of the circuit court of Cook County is affirmed.

Affirmed.

BUCKLEY, P.J., and CAMPBELL and O'CONNOR, JJ., concur.

Notes

The Illinois statute used in the *Janus* decision offers one approach to simultaneous death. It specifies that if there is insufficient preponderance of the evidence that a person survived the decedent—even by a few seconds—then that person died simultaneously. Of course, any Last Will and Testament or non-probate transfer could specify otherwise, but this is the default position that will be utilized if no other provision is made. The Uniform Probate Code offers another alternative, which may be found in Uniform Probate Code §§ 2-104 (regarding intestacy with an individual in gestation) and 2-702 (regarding testacy and non-probate transfers). Uniform Probate Code § 2-104 requires four things: (1) clear and convincing evidence of survivorship; (2) survivorship must be for a minimum of 120 hours; (3) if there is insufficient proof, but this would result in the property passing to the state under § 2-105, then the requirement of survivorship does not apply; and (4) when a child is posthumously conceived under § 2-120(k), to inherit, the child must survive by 120 hours after birth. The objective feature of 120 hours is a default feature, and settlors or testators may expand the time required, as long as the requirement does not conflict with any other rule of law, such as the Rule Against Perpetuities applicable to private trusts. Likewise, Uniform Probate Code § 2-702 applies simultaneous death requirements to non-probate transfers.

Uniform Probate Code (2019)

§ 2-702. Requirement of Survival by 120 Hours.

(a) [**Requirement of Survival by 120 Hours Under Probate Code.**] For the purposes of this Code, except as provided in subsection (d), an individual who is not established by clear and convincing evidence to have survived an event, including the death of another individual, by 120 hours is deemed to have predeceased the event.

(b) [**Requirement of Survival by 120 Hours under Governing Instrument.**] Except as provided in subsection (d), for purposes of a provision of a governing instrument that relates to an individual surviving an event, including the death of another individual, an individual who is not established by clear and convincing evidence to have survived the event by 120 hours is deemed to have predeceased the event.

(c) [Co-owners With Right of Survivorship; Requirement of Survival by 120 Hours.] Except as provided in subsection (d), if (i) it is not established by clear and convincing evidence that one of two co-owners with right of survivorship survived the other co-owner by 120 hours, one-half of the property passes as if one had survived by 120 hours and one-half as if the other had survived by 120 hours and (ii) there are more than two co-owners and it is not established by clear and convincing evidence that at least one of them survived the others by 120 hours, the property passes in the proportion that one bears to the whole number of co-owners. For the purposes of this subsection, "co-owners with right of survivorship" includes joint tenants, tenants by the entireties, and other co-owners of property or accounts held under circumstances that entitles one or more to the whole of the property or account on the death of the other or others.

(d) [Exceptions.] Survival by 120 hours is not required if:

(1) the governing instrument contains language dealing explicitly with simultaneous deaths or deaths in a common disaster and that language is operable under the facts of the case;

(2) the governing instrument expressly indicates that an individual is not required to survive an event, including the death of another individual, by any specified period or expressly requires the individual to survive the event by a specified period; but survival of the event or the specified period must be established by clear and convincing evidence;

(3) the imposition of a 120-hour requirement of survival would cause a nonvested property interest or a power of appointment to fail to qualify for validity under Section 2-901(a)(1), (b)(1), or (c)(1) or to become invalid under Section 2-901(a)(2), (b)(2), or (c)(2); but survival must be established by clear and convincing evidence; or

(4) the application of a 120-hour requirement of survival to multiple governing instruments would result in an unintended failure or duplication of a disposition; but survival must be established by clear and convincing evidence.

VII. Assignment of Expectancy

Scott v. First National Bank of Baltimore

Maryland Court of Appeals, 1961
224 Md. 462, 168 A.2d 349

HENDERSON, Judge.

This appeal is from a decree of an equity court declaring valid the assignment of a one-half expectancy from the estate of the assignor's father, then living, in favor of the assignor's daughter Virginia. The assignment was alluded to in Kelly v. Scott,

215 Md. 530, 532, 137 A.2d 704, although that case is not in point here, and the effect of that decision was modified by subsequent legislation. See Code (1960 Supp.), art. 16, sec. 135A (ch. 93, Acts of 1958).

The facts are not in dispute. Wilmer Scott became enamoured of another woman in 1947 and told his wife Grace he intended to leave her. The marital home was in Connecticut. On January 31, 1948, Wilmer and Grace entered into a separation agreement whereby she was to have custody of the child and he agreed to pay $250 per month for the support of Grace and Virginia, then just two years of age. In the event of Grace's remarriage he agreed to pay $150 a month for Virginia's support until she reached the age of twenty-one. Wilmer transferred to Grace his interest in their house at Rowayton, Conn., subject to a $10,000 mortgage which she assumed, his 1935 car, his modest bank account, his interest in a bank partnership trust, and a $10,000 service life insurance policy, provided Grace continue the payments. In a separate instrument he assigned under seal to Virginia one-half of his expectancy in his father's estate 'for the consideration of one dollar and other valuable considerations received to my full satisfaction from my wife * * * on behalf of my daughter'. Grace sued for divorce in August, 1948, and obtained a decree *a vinculo* on March 11, 1949, from the Fairfield County Court. The decree did not mention the assignment, although the decree for alimony and support incorporated the provisions set out in the separation agreement, but the agreement was not made a part of the decree. Evidently the separation agreement was exhibited to the court, but it was not shown that the assignment was so exhibited.

Wilmer married the other woman in 1949, but this marriage ended in a divorce and another alimony decree against him. In 1952 he married his present wife, by whom he has two children. Grace remarried in 1950. Wilmer did not comply with the support decree, indeed, he has made no payments at all since 1952. In March, 1959, Grace recovered a judgment for over $12,000 in back payments. On September 11, 1958, Wilmer's father died intestate. At the time of his death and since 1936 the father, Thomas A. Scott, had been mentally incompetent and committed to the Sheppard & Enoch Pratt Hospital in Baltimore, Maryland. He left surviving him two children, of whom Wilmer was one. His administrator, the First National Bank of Baltimore, filed an inventory showing a personal estate of about $490,000. It brought this proceeding by way of interpleader.

Wilmer was in financial straits at the time of the separation in 1948. He was earning about $300 a month and receiving $150 a month from the committee of his father, but he had numerous unpaid bills and unpaid small loans. Although he was an educated man he had difficulty in holding jobs, he claims, because of the fact that he suffered from epilepsy, although there was other testimony that it was due to his excessive drinking. Whatever cash he turned over to Grace was used to pay bills then unpaid. His history is one of improvidence and living beyond his means.

The parties agree and concede that the validity and effect of the assignment is to be determined under the law of Connecticut, where it was executed and delivered. That, of course, is the general rule applicable to foreign contracts dealing with personalty. See Restatement, Conflict of Laws § 332, and Baltimore & O. R. Co. v. Glenn, 28 Md. 287, 321. It is also agreed that at common law the transfer of a mere possibility or expectancy, not coupled with an interest, is void. Dart v. Dart, 1928, 7 Conn. 250; cf. Keys v. Keys, 148 Md. 397, 400, 129 A. 504. The parties further agree that under some circumstances, at least, equity will enforce the assignment of an expectancy after the death of the ancestor despite its invalidity at law. It is generally recognized that since the relief sought is in the nature of specific performance of a contract, equity will enforce the contract only where it is fair and equitable and supported by an adequate consideration. Keys v. Keys, *supra*; 6 Williston, Contracts (Rev. ed.) § 1681A; Pomeroy, Equity Jurisprudence (5th ed.) §§ 953a and 1287; 1 Bogert, Trusts § 112; 1 Scott, Trusts (2d ed.) § 86.1; Restatement, Property § 316. See also Notes, 17 A.L.R. 597, 44 A.L.R. 1465, and 121 A.L.R. 450, and Notes, 25 Colum.L.Rev. 215, and 35 No.Car.L.Rev. 127, 131. The appellant contends that the necessary consideration is lacking in the instant case. * * *

All of the authorities seem to agree that a gratuitous assignment is unenforceable, because there is no contract to enforce. 1 Scott, Trusts, *supra* at p. 655. Some courts, notably in Kentucky, refuse to enforce any agreements to assign an expectancy because of a public policy against sales to moneylenders and the danger of overreaching in the case of impoverished prospective heirs. Others enforce agreements to sell, provided the consideration amounts to a fair equivalent. Some of the commentators suggest that the adequacy of consideration is only one element in determining whether equity will enforce and that contracts to assign an expectancy should not be placed in any special category. See the Note, 25 Colum.L.Rev., *supra*. In this connection we may quote the language of Judge Hammond in Ledingham v. Bayless, 218 Md. 108, 115, 145 A.2d 434, 439, a case involving a contract to make a will, where it was said: 'As in other contracts, the parties may agree on the surrender or acquisition of any legal rights as consideration, and the adequacy of such consideration is material only as an element of fraud or undue influence or as one of the factors which a court will take into consideration in determining whether or not to grant specific performance.' Cf. Sidor v. Kravec, 135 Conn. 571, 66 A.2d 812. In 1 Scott, Trusts, *supra* at p. 654, the learned author states that the courts uniformly find adequate consideration present in the case of marriage settlements and separation agreements. We find nothing in the Connecticut cases cited to indicate that a property settlement in contemplation of divorce would be unenforceable because lacking in consideration amounting to equivalence. We think the cases cited point in the opposite direction.

We do not suggest that any weight should be attached to the seal or recited consideration. Nor do we suggest that love and affection alone would suffice, although there are cases that suggest a more liberal rule in the case of family settlements. See 6 Williston, Contracts, *supra*, and Warner v. Warner, 124 Conn. 625, 1 A.1d 911, 118 A.L.R. 1348. Of course, both parties in the instant case were concerned with the welfare of the child Virginia. Grace assumed the burden of the care and education of Virginia, over and above the rather small sum stipulated for her support. It is true that the divorce court could not be bound by the parties' agreement, insofar as it might affect the welfare of the child. But the wife may well have tempered her demands because of the assignment in order to insure that the child would receive a share of the expectancy which might otherwise be frittered away. She also assumed liability for the unpaid bills and loans and the mortgage. We find adequate consideration in these undertakings. There is no claim of fraud or overreaching and the chancellor found that the agreement was not unfair or inequitable under the circumstances. The bargain was at arm's length and the husband had an opportunity to seek independent advice. * * *

Decree affirmed, with costs.

Notes

A Florida court has held that the test to enforce an assignment of an expectancy is two-pronged: first, there must be sufficient consideration to support the assignment, but then, too, the assignment must be fairly entered into, without fraud, duress, or any breach of a fiduciary relationship. Diaz v. Rood, 851 So. 2d 843 (Fla. Dist. Ct. App. 2003). Assignment of expectancy often takes place in the context of nursing home care. If an individual qualifies for Medicaid assistance in payment of nursing home care, an entitlement most often achieved by spending down assets, the nursing home resident, or his or her guardian, will be required to assign any expectancy the resident may currently, or one day, receive. For example, in return for the "consideration" of government assistance in the payment of nursing home care, the resident will assign his or her Social Security check to the nursing home. In addition, if the resident should win the lottery, inherit a fortune, or receive a gift, the resident would be required to assign that lottery winning, inheritance, or gift to the nursing home. The consideration is the cost of the care received. To qualify for Medicaid, persons or their guardians often seek to disclaim assets; this procedure is discussed, *infra*. But courts have been very reluctant to allow the disclaimer. The assets should be counted in determining if a person reaches the poverty threshold necessary for Medicaid assistance. *See* Raymond C. O'Brien, *Selective Issues in Effective Medicaid Estate Recovery Statutes*, 65 Cath U. L. Rev. 27, 56–61 (2015); Raymond C. O'Brien & Michael T. Flannery, The Fundamentals of Elder Law, 361–81 (2015).

VIII. Disclaimer: Release and Renunciation

Disclaimer is an umbrella term that incorporates both release and renunciation. Both refer to the prospective beneficiary's ability and conduct in rejecting proposed benefits. Today, particularly under the Uniform Probate Code, disclaimer is possible in reference to benefits under a Last Will and Testament, intestacy, and even under non-probate transfers or will substitutes. If a potential beneficiary wishes to disclaim benefits during the lifetime of a donor or testator, he or she "releases" any claim. Because the claim is still a mere expectancy, consideration is required to provide substance. A common form of release today is a prenuptial agreement between two parties not to take from one another's estate. Particularly among older persons who are marrying for the second time, with children from prior unions, the mutuality of the release provides the consideration. *See* Uniform Premarital and Marital Agreement Act, 9C U.LA. 12 et seq. (Supp. 2015).

The applicability of disclaimer to testate, intestate, and non-probate transfers is important in an age when contract and individual concerns predominate. Examine the Uniform Probate Code for the applicability of disclaimer to all aspects of wealth transfer.

Uniform Probate Code (2019)

§ 2-1105. Power to Disclaim; General Requirements; When Irrevocable.

(a) A person may disclaim, in whole or part, any interest in or power over property, including a power of appointment. A person may disclaim the interest or power even if its creator imposed a spendthrift provision or similar restriction on transfer or a restriction or limitation on the right to disclaim.

(b) Except to the extent a fiduciary's right to disclaim is expressly restricted or limited by another statute of this State or by the instrument creating the fiduciary relationship, a fiduciary may disclaim, in whole or part, any interest in or power over property, including a power of appointment, whether acting in a personal or representative capacity. A fiduciary may disclaim the interest or power even if its creator imposed a spendthrift provision or similar restriction on transfer or a restriction or limitation on the right to disclaim or an instrument other than the instrument that created the fiduciary relationship imposed a restriction or limitation on the right to disclaim.

(c) To be effective, a disclaimer must be in a writing or other record, declare the disclaimer, describe the interest or power disclaimed, be signed by the person making the disclaimer, and be delivered or filed in the manner provided in Section 2-1112. In this subsection:

> (1) "record" means information that is inscribed on a tangible medium or that is stored in an electronic or other medium and is retrievable in perceivable form; and

> (2) "signed" means, with present intent to authenticate or adopt a record, to;

>> (A) execute or adopt a tangible symbol; or

>> (B) attach to or logically associate with the record an electronic sound, symbol, or process.

(d) A partial disclaimer may be expressed as a fraction, percentage, monetary amount, term of years, limitation of a power, or any other interest or estate in the property.

(e) A disclaimer becomes irrevocable when it is delivered or filed pursuant to Section 2-1112 or when it becomes effective as provided in Sections 2-1106 through 2-1111, whichever occurs later.

(f) A disclaimer made under this Part is not a transfer, assignment, or release.

§ 2-1107. Disclaimer of Rights of Survivorship in Jointly Held Property.

(a) Upon the death of a holder of jointly held property, a surviving holder may disclaim, in whole or part, the greater of:

(1) a fractional share of the property determined by dividing the number one by the number of joint holders alive immediately before the death of the holder to whose death the disclaimer relates; or

(2) all of the property except that part of the value of the entire interest attributable to the contribution furnished by the disclaimant.

(b) A disclaimer under subsection (a) takes effect as of the death of the holder of jointly held property to whose death the disclaimer relates.

(c) An interest in jointly held property disclaimed by a surviving holder of the property passes as if the disclaimant predeceased the holder to whose death the disclaimer relates.

§ 2-1113. When Disclaimer Barred or Limited.

(a) A disclaimer is barred by a written waiver of the right to disclaim.

(b) A disclaimer of an interest in property is barred if any of the following events occur before the disclaimer becomes effective:

(1) the disclaimant accepts the interest sought to be disclaimed;

(2) the disclaimant voluntarily assigns, conveys, encumbers, pledges, or transfers the interest sought to be disclaimed or contracts to do so; or

(3) a judicial sale of the interest sought to be disclaimed occurs.

(c) A disclaimer, in whole or part, of the future exercise of a power held in a fiduciary capacity is not barred by its previous exercise.

(d) A disclaimer, in whole or part, of the future exercise of a power not held in a fiduciary capacity is not barred by its previous exercise unless the power is exercisable in favor of the disclaimant.

(e) A disclaimer is barred or limited if so provided by law other than this [Part].

(f) A disclaimer of a power over property which is barred by this section is ineffective. A disclaimer of an interest in property which is barred by this section takes effect as a transfer of the interest disclaimed to the persons who would have taken the interest under this [Part] had the disclaimer not been barred.

Tax Considerations: While it may seem strange behavior to disclaim any monetary advantage, most disclaimers are motivated by federal, or perhaps state, tax considerations. For example, a parent with sufficient assets may wish to "disclaim" assets so that an issue, descendant, child, or grandchild may receive the asset instead. Disclaimer avoids any gift tax consequences associated with giving the asset to the child. Or in another example, disclaimer by anyone other than a spouse may have the effect of increasing the share that would go to the spouse and, thus, increase the marital deduction. These are valid considerations and motivations under the present federal tax code, and should the estate tax be repealed, they may remain as motivations under state regimes. Failure to advise clients of the tax ramifications of disclaimers has been considered as attorney malpractice. *See, e.g.,* Kinney v. Shinholser, 663 So. 2d 643 (Fla. App. 1995). So as to make the rules standard within the federal tax code, Congress has set forth the following provision:

Internal Revenue Code

§ 2518. Disclaimers.

(a) General Rule.

For purposes of this subtitle, if a person makes a qualified disclaimer with respect to any interest in property, this subtitle shall apply with respect to such interest as if the interest had never been transferred to such person.

(b) Qualified disclaimer defined.

For purposes of subsection (a), the term "qualified disclaimer" means an irrevocable and unqualified refusal by a person to accept an interest in property but only if—

(1) such refusal is in writing,

(2) such writing is received by the transferor of the interest, his legal representative, or the holder of the legal title to the property to which the interest relates not later than the date which is 9 months after the later of—

(A) the day on which the transfer creating the interest in such person is made, or

(B) the day on which such person attains the age of 21,

(3) such person has not accepted the interest or any of its benefits, and

(4) as a result of such refusal, the interest passes without any direction on the part of the person making the disclaimer and passes either—

(A) to the spouse of the decedent, or

(B) to a person other than the person making the disclaimer.

* * *

DePaoli v. C.I.R.

10th Circuit Court of Appeals, 1995
62 F.3d 1259

JENKINS, Senior District Judge.

This case arises out of the taxpayers' efforts to escape estate taxes by disclaiming a testamentary transfer of property. The Tax Court held the purported disclaimer invalid for estate tax purposes, subjecting the taxpayers to liability not only for estate taxes but also for a gift tax and an addition to tax under section 6651(a)(1) of the Internal Revenue Code. See 66 T.C.M. (CCH) 1493, 1993 WL 500190 (1993). The taxpayers appeal. We have jurisdiction under I.R.C. § 7482(a)(1) and reverse.

* * *

Quinto DePaoli, Sr., a resident of New Mexico, died in 1987. He was survived by his wife, Soila DePaoli, and his only son, Quinto DePaoli, Jr. Quinto Senior's will left his entire estate to Quinto Junior. The will was formally probated on December 30, 1987. On July 21, 1988, shortly before the estate tax return was due, Soila and Quinto Junior moved to have the probated will set aside. They claimed that the original will had been destroyed, that the will admitted to probate was actually a duplicate copy and that Quinto Senior had intended to make a new will leaving Quinto Junior the greatest amount he could receive without any tax liability (namely, $600,000) and leaving the bulk of the estate to Soila but that he had died before he could execute the new will. Quinto Junior acknowledged that he could claim a substantial part of the estate but agreed to receive only $600,000 to settle the will contest. The probate court granted the motion and ordered the estate distributed accordingly.

The federal estate tax return filed for Quinto Senior's estate indicated that the entire estate passed to Soila, less certain expenses and a $600,000 bequest to Quinto Junior. The bequest to Soila was classified as a deductible bequest to a surviving spouse. The return indicated that no property passed to the surviving spouse as a result of a qualified disclaimer under I.R.C. § 2518(b), and no written disclaimer was attached to the return. The return indicated that no tax was due, since the tax on the $600,000 taxable estate was within the unified credit available to the estate.

The Commissioner denied the entire marital deduction on the grounds that Quinto Senior's will, as probated, bequeathed all his property to his son and the agreement between Quinto Junior and Soila was invalid. The Commissioner also determined that the agreement between Quinto Junior and Soila constituted a taxable gift for gift tax purposes and assessed an addition to tax against Quinto Junior under I.R.C. § 6651(a)(1) for failing to file a gift tax return.[1]

The Tax Court upheld the Commissioner's determinations. The court held that Quinto Junior's agreement to forego all but $600,000 of his father's estate did not entitle the estate to the marital deduction because the portion of the estate passing to Soila passed to her from Quinto Junior and not from Quinto Senior. The court further held that the property passing to Soila constituted a taxable gift from Quinto Junior, making Quinto Junior liable for the federal gift tax. Finally, the court held that Quinto Junior's failure to file a gift tax return was not "due to

---

1. Section 6651(a)(1) imposes an addition to tax for failure to file a gift tax return "unless it is shown that such failure is due to reasonable cause and not due to willful neglect." I.R.C. § 6651(a)(1). The penalty ranges from 5 to 25 percent of the gift tax due, depending on how delinquent the taxpayer is. *Id.*

reasonable cause" and that Quinto Junior was therefore liable for an addition to tax under I.R.C. § 6651(a)(1). The Tax Court concluded that the deficiency in estate tax due was $1,633,250, the deficiency in gift tax due was $1,297,750 and the addition to tax was $324,438. Quinto Junior, the estate, and Quinto Senior's personal representatives (Soila and Rachel Craig) appealed.

* * *

The appellants claim that the Tax Court erred by denying the estate a marital deduction. They claim that, as a result of Quinto Junior's disclaimer of his property rights under Quinto Senior's will, Quinto Senior's property passed to his surviving spouse (Soila) as a matter of law and was therefore properly deducted.[2] The parties agree that this issue is subject to de novo review.

Estate taxes are imposed on the value of a decedent's taxable estate. I.R.C. § 2001. In determining the value of the taxable estate, the value of property that passes to a surviving spouse is deducted. *Id.* § 2056(a). If property passes from a decedent to someone other than the surviving spouse and that person makes a "qualified" disclaimer that results in the surviving spouse being entitled to the property, the disclaimed interest is treated as passing directly from the decedent to the surviving spouse and therefore qualifies for the marital deduction. See Treas.Reg. § 20.2056(d)-1(b).

To qualify, a disclaimer must meet certain requirements, chief of which, for purposes of this appeal, is that, as a result of the disclaimer, the interest passes to the surviving spouse "without any direction on the part of the person making the disclaimer." I.R.C. § 2518(b)(4). The Tax Court held that Quinto Junior's agreement to forego all but $600,000 of his father's estate was not a qualified disclaimer because his interest would not have passed to Soila without his direction.[3]

The requirement that the disclaimed property pass without any direction from the person making the disclaimer means that the disclaimer must result in a valid passing of the disclaimed interest to the surviving spouse by operation of state law. Federal law does not prescribe rules for the passing of disclaimed property interests,

---

2. Before the Tax Court, the petitioners also argued that they had properly claimed the marital deduction under former section 20.2056(e)-2(d) of the estate tax regulations because the decedent's property had passed to Soila in settlement of a will contest. The Tax Court rejected this argument, and the petitioners have not challenged that ruling on appeal.

3. The Commissioner does not claim and the Tax Court did not hold that the disclaimer failed to meet the requirements for a valid disclaimer under New Mexico law, contained in N.M.Stat.Ann. § 45-2-801 (Michie Repl.1989). The Tax Court doubted whether Quinto Junior intended to make a qualified disclaimer under federal law when he entered into the settlement agreement with Soila, since the estate tax return did not indicate that any property passed to Soila as a result of a qualified disclaimer. The court called the argument "patently an afterthought with weak factual support." See 66 T.C.M. (CCH) at 1495, 1993 WL 500190. However, the Commissioner concedes that the Tax Court did not reject the taxpayers' claim on that ground. It held only that the disclaimer was not a qualified disclaimer under I.R.C. § 2518(b)(4) because it directed that the disclaimed property pass to Soila. See Br. for Appellee at 22–23 n. 6. It is only that issue that we need address.

so any disclaimed property passing other than by operation of state law must be at the direction of the disclaimant. See Estate of Goree v. Commissioner, 68 T.C.M. (CCH) 123, 125–26, 1994 WL 379246 (1994); Estate of Bennett v. Commissioner, 100 T.C. 42, 67, 72–73, 1993 WL 19583 (1993).

Under New Mexico law, unless the decedent indicates otherwise in his will, any disclaimed property passes as if the disclaimant had predeceased the decedent. See N.M.Stat.Ann. § 45-2-801(C) (Michie 1989 Repl.).[4] Under New Mexico's anti-lapse statute, if a devisee who is related to the testator by kinship is treated as if he had predeceased the testator, the devisee's "issue" who survive the testator by 120 hours "take in place of" the devisee. Id. § 45-2-605. Thus, if Quinto Junior had "issue," his disclaimer would not have caused the disclaimed property to pass to his step-mother, Soila, by operation of law and therefore would not have been a qualified disclaimer under I.R.C. § 2518(b) entitling the estate to the marital deduction.

Quinto Junior has never been married but has two illegitimate children — Thomas Derrick DePaoli and Christopher Noel Contreras DePaoli. Derrick was five years old at the time of Quinto Senior's death, and Christopher was four. The Tax Court concluded that the property Quinto Junior disclaimed would not have passed to Soila absent his agreement that Soila take the property but would have passed to Derrick and Christopher. The petitioners claim that Quinto Junior's illegitimate children were not his "issue" within the meaning of the anti-lapse statute and there-fore would not have taken in his place as a result of his disclaimer.

The New Mexico Probate Code in effect at the time of Quinto Senior's death and Quinto Junior's disclaimer defines "issue" as "all of a person's lineal descendants of all generations, with the relationship of parent and child at each generation being determined by the definitions of child and parent contained in the Probate Code." N.M.Stat.Ann. § 45-1-201(A)(21). The Probate Code defines "child" as "any indi-vidual entitled to take as a child under the Probate Code by intestate succession from the parent whose relationship is involved" and excludes stepchildren, foster children and grandchildren. Id. § 45-1-201(A)(3). For purposes of intestate succes-sion, the Probate Code provides that a child born out of wedlock is considered a "child" of the father if, among other things, "the reputed father has recognized the child in writing by an instrument signed by him, which shows upon its face that it was so signed with the intent of recognizing the child as an heir." Id. § 45-2-109(B)(2).[5] The code makes declarations of deceased persons admissible to prove that such

---

4. Article II of the Uniform Probate Code (dealing with intestate succession) and section 1-201 (the general definitional section) were revised in 1990. In accordance with this revision, New Mex-ico substantially revised its probate code in 1993. Unless otherwise indicated, citations to the New Mexico Probate Code, N.M.Stat.Ann. ch. 45, are to the code in effect at the time of the events giv-ing rise to this action.

5. Under the Probate Code as it existed before 1993, an illegitimate child could also be con-sidered a child of his natural father for purposes of intestate succession if the child's natural par-ents participated in a marriage ceremony or if paternity was established by an adjudication. See N.M.Stat.Ann. § 45-2-109(B)(1) & (3). Neither of those conditions has been met here.

an instrument was lost or destroyed, as well as to prove the existence, contents and genuineness of such an instrument. The statute further provides, "Such declarations shall be corroborated by proof of general and notorious recognition of such child by the father." *Id.* § 45-2-109(B)(2). Finally, the code defines "heirs" as "those persons . . . who are entitled under the statutes of intestate succession to the property of a decedent." *Id.* § 45-1-201(A)(17). Under the statutes of intestate succession, the part of the intestate estate not passing to the surviving spouse passes "to the issue of the decedent." *Id.* § 45-2-103(A).

In other words, under New Mexico law as it existed in 1987 and 1988, an illegitimate child was considered "issue" of his natural father and therefore entitled to take in place of the natural father under the anti-lapse statute if the natural father recognized the child by a signed, written instrument that "shows upon its face" that the father signed it "with the intent of recognizing the child as an heir," *id.* § 45-2-109(B)(2), that is, as someone entitled to succeed to the father's property under the intestate succession statutes, see *id.* § 45-1-201(A)(17).

The Tax Court concluded that Quinto Junior had recognized his illegitimate children as his heirs when he filed his federal income tax returns for the years 1987 through 1990 listing each of them as his "son" and claiming dependency exemptions for them. The Internal Revenue Code defines "dependent" to include a "son or daughter of the taxpayer" and any other individual who "has as his principal place of abode the home of the taxpayer and is a member of the taxpayer's household" for the tax year. See I.R.C. § 152(a). The Tax Court reasoned that, if Quinto Junior had intended to take an exemption for his children without recognizing them as his heirs, he would have listed them simply as dependents or household members, as he did for the children's mother, Gloria Contreras.[6] The court concluded: "Because petitioner chose to identify Thomas and Christopher specifically as his 'sons,' instead of as just members of his household, we are persuaded that these returns, signed by petitioner under penalties of perjury, constitute a written instrument signed with the intent of recognizing the children as heirs." 66 T.C.M. (CCH) at 1497, 1993 WL 500190.[7]

The problem with the Tax Court's reasoning is that it equates "son" under the Internal Revenue Code with "heir" under the New Mexico Probate Code. The term "son" is ambiguous. See Lalli v. Lalli, 439 U.S. 259, 274 n. 11, 99 S.Ct. 518, 528 n. 11, 58 L.Ed.2d 503 (1978). It may refer to a natural child, an adopted child, a stepchild, a legitimate child or an illegitimate child. The Internal Revenue Code's definition of a child is broader than the Probate Code's. For example, a stepchild can be a "child"

---

6. Quinto Junior claimed an exemption for Ms. Contreras on his 1987 and 1990 income tax returns, identifying her as "Girlfriend" and "Fam[ily] Mem[ber]," respectively.

7. The Tax Court further held that Quinto Junior had not met his burden of proving that he had any contrary intention. In fact, the only direct evidence on this issue was Quinto Junior's own testimony. He testified that he had never acknowledged in writing the intent to recognize a child as an heir. Tr. at 6.

within the meaning of the Internal Revenue Code and therefore a dependent for purposes of the dependency exemption but is not a "child" and therefore an heir for purposes of intestate succession. Compare I.R.C. § 151(c)(3) (formerly § 151(e)(3)) with N.M.Stat.Ann. § 45-1-201(A)(3).

Similarly, an illegitimate child may be a child (and hence a dependent) under the Internal Revenue Code without being a child (and hence an heir) under the Probate Code. A son or daughter need not be legitimate for the father to qualify for a dependency exemption under the Internal Revenue Code. * * * By listing Derrick and Christopher as his "sons" on his tax returns, Quinto Junior may have recognized them as his children but did not necessarily recognize them as his "heirs."

The Commissioner argues that New Mexico law recognizes no distinction between a child and an heir, that all New Mexico law requires is that the natural father recognize his illegitimate child as his child, since a child is entitled to inherit under New Mexico's intestacy statutes and thus is an "heir." However, not all children are entitled to inherit by intestate succession under New Mexico law. A child must satisfy the statutory definition of "child" to be considered "issue" under the Probate Code. Cf. Coleman v. Offutt (In re Estate of Coleman), 104 N.M. 192, 194, 718 P.2d 702, 704 (Ct.App.1986) (an adopted son who satisfies the statutory definition of "child" is also "issue" of his father). For present purposes, an illegitimate child is not entitled to succeed to his or her fathers' property by intestate succession unless the father (1) "has recognized the child in writing," (2) "by an instrument signed by him," (3) "which shows upon its face that it was so signed with the intent of recognizing the child as an heir." N.M.Stat.Ann. § 45-2-109(B)(2). At best, Quinto Junior's tax returns only satisfy the first two requirements. They do not show "upon [their] face" that they were signed "with the intent of recognizing" Derrick and Christopher as Quinto Junior's heirs. The only intent evident from the returns is the intent to claim a dependency exemption, which, the Commissioner concedes, a taxpayer can claim without intending to make the dependent an heir (as Quinto Junior did when he filed his 1987 and 1990 returns claiming an exemption for his mistress).

In construing section 45-2-109(B)(2), we are required to give effect to all its provisions and not to render any part of the statute surplusage. See, e.g., Whitely v. New Mexico State Personnel Bd., 115 N.M. 308, 311, 850 P.2d 1011, 1014 (1993); Roberts v. Southwest Community Health Servs., 114 N.M. 248, 251, 837 P.2d 442, 445 (1992). The Commissioner's argument, which equates "heir" with "child," would read the phrase "which shows upon its face that it was so signed with the intent of recognizing the child as an heir" out of the statute. It would be enough if the father of an illegitimate child "recognized the child in writing by an instrument signed by him." We believe that the next phrase—"which shows upon its face that it was so signed with the intent of recognizing the child as an heir"—requires something different from recognition of parentage, namely, an intent to recognize the child as an heir, that is, as someone entitled to inherit from the father by intestate succession. In other words, we believe that section 45-2-109(B)(2), properly construed, requires both recognition of paternity and evidence of an intent that the child inherit.

For that reason, this case is distinguishable from the cases the Commissioner relies on. In each of those cases state law required only proof of paternity; it did not require evidence of an intent to recognize the child as an heir. The relevant statute in each case provided that an illegitimate child is an heir of "the person who, in writing, signed in the presence of a competent witness, acknowledges himself to be the father" of the child. See In re Estate of Jerrido, 339 So.2d 237, 239 (Fla.Dist. Ct.App.1976), cert. denied, 346 So.2d 1249 (Fla.1977); Glick v. Knoll (In re Estate of Glick), 136 Mont. 176, 346 P.2d 987, 987 (1959); Schalla v. Roberts (In re Estate of Schalla), 2 Wis.2d 38, 86 N.W.2d 5, 8 (1957). Moreover, in each of those cases, the court relied on governing case law to the effect that the form and purpose of the writing acknowledging paternity was immaterial. See *Jerrido*, 339 So.2d at 240 (relying on Florida case law holding that "the written acknowledgment of parent-hood need not assume any particular formality") (citations omitted); *Glick*, 346 P.2d at 989 (relying on Montana case law holding that a writing acknowledging paternity "is a sufficient compliance with the statute without regard to the purpose for which the instrument was executed") (citation omitted); *Schalla*, 86 N.W.2d at 9 (under the relevant statute, the written acknowledgment did not have to be made for the express purpose of establishing heirship). By contrast, the New Mexico stat-ute requires that the writing "show[ ] upon its face that it was . . . signed with the intent of recognizing the child as an heir." Where a statute prescribes the form a written acknowledgment must take, other courts have held that a tax return that identified the taxpayer's illegitimate child as his son or daughter did not constitute a sufficient written acknowledgment where the return did not strictly comply with all the requirements of the statute. See, *e.g.*, Smith v. Smith, 40 Conn.Supp. 151, 483 A.2d 629, 630–31 (1984); Distefano v. Commonwealth, 201 Va. 23, 109 S.E.2d 497, 500–01 (1959).

The parties have not provided any legislative history for section 45-2-109(B) (2),[8] and we have not found any New Mexico cases directly on point. However, we believe our construction of the statute is consistent with New Mexico law. The New Mexico Supreme Court has recognized a distinction between paternity and

---

8. The phrase "which shows upon its face that it was so signed with the intent of recognizing the child as an heir" is of obscure (though not illegitimate) parentage. The language dates back to at least 1915, see 1915 N.M.Laws ch. 69, § 1, and was carried over into subsequent revisions of the New Mexico Probate Code until the latest revision, in 1993. Although New Mexico borrowed its probate statutes from Kansas, which in turn adopted Iowa statutes, see State v. Chavez, 42 N.M. 569, 572–74, 82 P.2d 900, 903 (1938), the quoted language appears to be unique to New Mexico. The corresponding Iowa and Kansas statutes only required that the putative father recognize his illegitimate children as his children by "general and notorious" recognition "or else in writing." See McKellar v. Harkins, 183 Iowa 1030, 166 N.W. 1061, 1063 (1918) (quoting Iowa Code § 3385 (1897)); Estate of McKay v. Davis, 208 Kan. 282, 491 P.2d 932, 933 (1971) (quoting Kan.G.S. § 3845 (1915)). Under New Mexico law, proof of general and notorious recognition was required to corroborate a declaration of a deceased person regarding a written recognition, but alone it was not sufficient to make an illegitimate child an heir. See N.M.Stat.Ann. § 45-2-109(B)(2).

heirship.[9] In Gallup v. Bailey (In re Gossett's Estate), 46 N.M. 344, 129 P.2d 56 (1942), the court held that the so-called bastardy act, which required the putative father of an illegitimate child to support and maintain the child if the father had acknowledged paternity in writing, "has no application to the descent and distribution and inheritance of estates; in which case the writing must be made for the purpose of recognizing the child as an heir, but this is not so as to the Bastardy Act." 46 N.M. at 351–52, 129 P.2d at 61.

In Haskew v. Haskew (In re Haskew's Estate), 56 N.M. 506, 245 P.2d 841 (1952), the court considered whether the putative father of an illegitimate child had sufficiently recognized the child so as to make the child his heir. The statute in effect at the time provided that, absent written recognition, the father must have recognized the child as his child and "such recognition must have been general and notorious." There was no written recognition in that case. The court held that there was sufficient evidence that the father had recognized the child as his own, but there was not sufficient evidence that the recognition was general and notorious. See 56 N.M. at 507, 245 P.2d at 841. Thus, the illegitimate child was not entitled to inherit from his father, even though paternity had been established.

Quinto Junior's tax returns do not show on their face that he intended his illegitimate children to be his heirs, that is, to inherit from him under New Mexico's intestate succession statutes. Consequently, they were not his "issue" within the meaning of the anti-lapse statute and would not have succeeded to any disclaimed property under section 45-2-605.[10] Therefore, when Quinto Junior disclaimed an interest in his father's estate, that interest passed to his stepmother, Soila, by operation of law, making the disclaimer a "qualified disclaimer" within the meaning of I.R.C. § 2518(b). Because the property passing to Soila, the surviving spouse, passed as a result of a qualified disclaimer, the estate properly claimed the marital deduction. Moreover, because the property is deemed to have passed directly from Quinto Senior to Soila, the disclaimer did not make Quinto Junior liable for the federal gift tax. Finally, because Quinto Junior was not required to file a gift tax return as a

---

9. New Mexico is not alone in recognizing the distinction. See, *e.g.*, Wong v. Wong Hing Young, 80 Cal.App.2d 391, 181 P.2d 741, 743 (1947) (an admission of paternity sufficient under the probate code was not sufficient to impose a support obligation on the putative father under the civil code); In re Flemm, 85 Misc.2d 855, 381 N.Y.S.2d 573, 577 (Sur.Ct.1975) (recognizing that under prior New York law an order of filiation establishing paternity entitled an illegitimate child to the support of the putative father but did not entitle the child to inherit from the putative father).

10. Our holding that Derrick and Christopher could not have inherited from their father at the time of Quinto Senior's death does not necessarily mean that the children will be denied an inheritance. The New Mexico Legislature repealed section 45-2-109 when it revised the Probate Code in 1993. The current statute provides that, for purposes of intestate succession, a person is "the child of his natural parents, regardless of their marital status," provided the natural parent "has openly treated the child as his and has not refused to support the child." N.M.Stat.Ann. § 45-2-114(A) & (C) (Michie Repl.1993). Quinto Junior's tax returns may well be evidence that he has "openly treated" the children as his and "not refused" to support them. However, that issue is not before us, and we express no opinion on it.

result of the disclaimer, he is not liable for the addition to tax under I.R.C. § 6651(a) (1) for failing to file a gift tax return.[11]

We recognize that the parties' settlement, which provided the basis for their disclaimer argument, may be nothing more than a blatant attempt to avoid paying estate taxes. However, neither the probate court nor the Tax Court found anything wrong with the disclaimer other than its purported direction that the estate pass to Soila. The validity of the disclaimer is not properly before us. We have concluded that the effect of the disclaimer under the unique New Mexico probate statutes in effect at the time was to cause the estate to pass to Soila regardless of any direction on the part of Quinto Junior, thus making the estate eligible for the marital deduction under federal law. There is nothing wrong with trying to escape tax liability if the law allows a taxpayer to do so. See, e.g., Rothschild v. United States, 407 F.2d 404, 413 (Ct.Cl.1969); Prentis v. United States, 273 F.Supp. 449, 457 (S.D.N.Y.1964), aff'd in part, rev'd in part, 364 F.2d 525 (2d Cir.1966). Cf. Re Weston's Settlements, [1968] 3 All E.R. 338, 342 (C.A.1968) (per Lord Denning) ("no-one has ever suggested that [tax avoidance] is undesirable or contrary to public policy"; but although the avoidance of tax "may be lawful, . . . it is not yet a virtue"). We believe in this case the law allowed the estate to claim the marital deduction. That does not mean that the petitioners can successfully escape taxation altogether. It simply means that the Commissioner may have to wait until Soila dies to collect taxes on the estate.

REVERSED.

Problem

Decedent died survived by his wife, two children, and two grandchildren. Immediately after the decedent's death, the two children filed written disclaimers stating, "I hereby disclaim and renounce any interest in the estate and relinquish any clam I may have to it. Their attorney's letter accompanying the filing describes the disclaimers as "Disclaimers of the decedent's children in favor of the decedent's spouse." The decedent's personal representative subsequently distributed the proceeds of the estate to the decedent's spouse—the mother of the two children. Once the children realized that they had made a mistake and that, as a result of the disclaimers, the estate would go to the grandchildren and not their mother, they filed papers titled, "Revocation and Withdrawal of Disclaimer." A guardian ad litem was appointed to represent the grandchildren at the hearing to determine if the children could revoke their disclaimers. The court held that they could not revoke their disclaimers, and the two children appealed. What did the two children do incorrectly? Is there any remedy for the children? See In re Estate of Holden, 343 S.C. 267, 539 S.E.2d 703 (2000).

---

11. Our conclusion that the Tax Court erred in holding that the disclaimer did not meet the requirement of I.R.C. § 2518(b)(4) that the property pass "without any direction on the part of the person making the disclaimer" makes it unnecessary to reach the other issues the petitioners raise.

IX. Advancements

Under the common law, it was presumed that a parent intended equality among his or her children. Thus, if a parent died intestate, and children—sometimes issue—survived the parent, the intestate statute would make an equal distribution among the surviving children. But what if one or more of the children had received his or her "portion" during lifetime, in the form of tuition assistance, an expensive wedding, a car, or other significant gift? If, in relation to the deceased parent's estate, the child received something substantial during life, it was then presumed that this child had received what was his or her share of the intestate estate; therefore, this child was presumed to receive a proportionally less amount from the intestate statute. The child would rebut this by saying that the item that was received was a gift, free and simple, and was not intended to be part of the parent's intestate estate. Of course, it also may be a loan. There are three possibilities: advancement, gift, or loan. But the child would wish it to be a gift and, thus, would need to rebut the presumption that it was an advancement.

If, in fact, the parent intended an advancement, the amount of the advancement must be taken into consideration in calculating the amount the child will now receive. The advanced amount does not go through probate, but the value of the advancement at the time it was made comes into "hotchpot"—a fictitious amount, which includes the advancement and the intestate estate going to all of the children. Each child would then receive his or her share, and if the recipient of the advancement chooses to take from the intestate estate, the advanced amount is subtracted from what that child would have received. *See, e.g.,* Miss. Code Ann. § 91-1-17 (Advancement from Intestate) (2019).

Because the burden of proof is on the child, the child would have to produce evidence of the parent's desire to make this a gift or a loan. Because the parent is dead and it is the siblings who are litigating, the process is involved and factional. There are few winners. The Uniform Probate Code both enlarges the possibility of advancement in the context of intestate succession and, at the same time, reduces the possibility. Many states have followed the lead of the Code and now reject the presumption of advancement by requiring written proof of advancement, contemporaneously with the gift. *See, e.g.,* Va. Code Ann. § 64.2-417 (2019). Compare the common law rule with that of the Uniform Probate Code.

Uniform Probate Code (2019)

§ 2-109. Advancements.

(a) If an individual dies intestate as to all or a portion of his [or her] estate, property the decedent gave during the decedent's lifetime to an individual who, at the decedent's death, is an heir is treated as an advancement against the heir's intestate share only if (i) the decedent declared in a contemporaneous writing or the heir acknowledged in writing that the gift is an advancement or (ii) the decedent's contemporaneous writing or the heir's written acknowledgment otherwise indicates that the gift is to be taken into account in computing the division and distribution of the decedent's intestate estate.

(b) For purposes of subsection (a), property advanced is valued as of the time the heir came into possession or enjoyment of the property or as of the time of the decedent's death, whichever first occurs.

(c) If the recipient of the property fails to survive the decedent, the property is not taken into account in computing the division and distribution of the decedent's intestate estate, unless the decedent's contemporaneous writing provides otherwise.

Chapter 3

The Last Will and Testament

Tool Bar

A Little Background

The prominence of a Last Will and Testament has waned with the closing of the second millennium. Whereas, previously, a person of sufficient age, intent, and capacity needed to fulfill the commands of the Statute of Frauds (1677) and the Wills Act (1837) to bequeath and devise property to succeeding generations upon death, the third millennium has fully embraced a less formalistic mode of property transfer. Today, much of wealth is transferred at death through non-probate transfers or will substitutes. It is arguable that this has lowered the bar for Last Wills and Testaments. For example, today, the formalities of the Last Will and Testament may often be met with the clear and convincing proof of substantial compliance, and the rigidity of the demonstration of what was meant by a plain meaning word or phrase may be captured with clear and convincing proof of primary intent. These ameliorative devices result, in part, from the explosion of non-probate transfers.

Professor John H. Langbein was among the first to conclude that the Last Will and Testament no longer exclusively served the needs of a modern society. First, the non-probate or will substitute transfer used by so many people today reflects the need of modern people to be individualistic in making decisions on how to transfer wealth. The probate system, with its strict requirements, forced people into a monopoly that stultified initiative and often resulted in failure to achieve individually desired goals. On the other hand, using living trusts, insurance policies, joint bank accounts, rights of survivorship, and payable on death beneficiaries allows a vast array of options to property owners. These modern options are fast, inexpensive, and far more accurate. Also, modern wealth does not consist so much of real estate but, rather, of contract rights or wealth in the form of stocks, pension funds, intellectual property, and bank deposits. These may more speedily be transferred at death through alternatives to a Last Will and Testament. *See* John H. Langbein, *The Nonprobate Revolution and the Future of the Law of Succession*, 97 HARV. L. REV. 1108 (1984). Finally, the business of selling non-probate devices and plans has firmly established itself in older, wealthier communities, and is able to reach millions of potential customers through advertisements, web sites, and community associations.

Illustrating the continuing process of diminishing testamentary formalities in the execution of a Last Will and Testament, the 2008 revision of the Uniform Probate Code included a provision to allow a will to be valid even if it is not holographic, and even if there are no witnesses. Under Unif. Prob. Code § 2-502(a)(3)(B), the will is valid if it is "acknowledged by the testator before a notary public or other individual authorized by law to take acknowledgments." This new feature, in combination with already implemented doctrines, like harmless error, indicates a further abandonment of strict formalities for wills. Surely the future will witness the dawn of the electronic will and similar testamentary vehicles. *See Trusts and Estates—Electronic Wills—Michigan Court of Appeals Holds Electronic Document to be Valid under Harmless Error Rule.* In re *Estate of Horton, No. 339737 (Mich. Ct. App. July 17, 2018) (Per Curiam)*, 132 HARV. L. REV. 2082 (2019); David Horton, *Tomorrow's Inheritance: The Frontiers of Estate Planning Formalism*, 58 B.C. L. REV. 539 (2017) (suggesting that even in the digital age, formalism serves a useful purpose); REVISED UNIFORM FIDUCIARY ACCESS TO DIGITAL ASSETS ACT (2015) (providing a fiduciary with access and authority to manage electronic communications while safeguarding privacy of account holder); D. Casey Flaherty & Corey Lovato, *Digital Signatures and the Paperless Office*, 17 J. INTERNET L. 3 (2014) (illustrating how digital transfers have become ubiquitous); Scott S. Boddery, *Electronic Wills: Drawing a Line in the Sand Against Their Validity*, 47 REAL PROP. TR. & EST. L.J. 197 (2012).

In reviewing the following material, ask yourself if you think the traditional requirements surrounding the execution of a probate transfer, especially in the context of a Last Will and Testament, are necessary or effective, and if they serve the public interest. Remember that there is a public policy obligation to those persons who earned the wealth and who seek to transfer it at death. And there is a concomitant obligation to those expecting a transfer. We should also admit that third parties, such as creditors, taxing agencies, and family members have a stake in the transfer of wealth as well. It is easy to get lost in the rules and fail to ask about the point of it all.

I. Categories of Wills

A. Statutory and Form Wills

The Internet has expanded creative approaches to form wills, and software companies provide usable forms that may be modified to meet individual objectives. For examples, see *Will Forms for Your State*, https://www.uslegalforms.com /wills/ (accessed July 28, 2019); Legalzoom, Last Will and Testament, http://www .legalzoom.com/personal/estate-planning/last-will-and-testament-overview.html (last visited July 28, 2019); Legacy Writer, *Online Estate Planning Tools for Life*, http:// www.legacywriter.com/createyourwill_process.html (accessed July 28, 2019); Free Last Will and Testament, Law Depot, http://www.lawdepot.com/contracts/last -will-and-testament-usa/#.VZn6qef1gt8 (accessed July 28, 2019); Online Will, Nolo, http://www.nolo.com/products/online-will-nnwill.html (accessed July 28, 2019); Quicken WillMaker Plus 2015, Nolo, http://www.nolo.com/products/quicken -willmaker-plus-wqp.html (accessed July 28, 2019); Make Your Free Legal Will, Rocket Lawyer, http://www.rocketlawyer.com/document/legal-will.rl (accessed July 28, 2019). Downloaded from web services, these forms allow persons to individualize testamentary transfers, but they most often lack professional assistance, which invites mistakes and, often, invalidity. Questions then arise as to the liability of companies that provide the forms to potential heirs, who would have benefitted if the forms had met the statutory requirements for a valid testamentary transfer.

B. Nuncupative Wills

The practice of permitting property to pass by nuncupative (oral) wills is very restricted. The oral character permits confusion and litigation, yet, in a few states, personal property of a very limited amount may be transferred at death through an oral transfer. Most often, the state will require that the oral will transpire in connection with a last illness and that it be stated in the presence of at least three people, who must reduce the statement to writing within a specified time. *See, e.g., In re* Carlton's Estate, 221 So. 2d 184, 185 (Fla. 4th DCA 1969) (describing deathbed scene and man calling four persons to bedside to hear him recite his will); West's Fla. Stat. Ann. §732.502 (2019) (resident and nonresident nuncupative wills are invalid).

C. Holographic Wills

About half of the states allow for holographic wills. Many of these states adopt the common law requirement that the holograph be: (1) entirely in the handwriting of the decedent; (2) dated; and (3) signed; and (4) that there be some "death talk" indicating that it is meant to be a will and not something akin to a love letter. The listed requirements vary from state-to-state. *See generally* Emily Robey-Phillips, *Reducing Litigation Costs for Holographic Wills*, 30 Quinnipiac Prob. L.J. 314 (2017) (supporting holographic wills but recommending they be supported by a series of presumptions). Often, a state statute requires proof that the will is actually in the handwriting of the testator. *See, e.g.,* Va. Code Ann. §64.2-403 (requiring two disinterested persons to testify as to the handwriting of the testator). But very often the issue is whether the testator intended the document to be a will—a feature resolved by proving that there is "death talk." The following decision is illustrative.

Uniform Probate Code (2019)

§2-502. Execution; Witnessed or Notarized Wills; Holographic Wills.

* * *

(b) [**Holographic Wills.**] A will that does not comply with subsection (a) is valid as a holographic will, whether or not witnessed, if the signature and material portions of the document are in the testator's handwriting.

(c) [**Extrinsic Evidence.**] Intent that a document constitute the testator's will can be established by extrinsic evidence, including, for holographic wills, portions of the document that are not in the testator's handwriting.

In re Kimmel's Estate

Supreme Court of Pennsylvania, 1924
278 Pa. 435, 123 A. 405

SIMPSON, J.

One of decedent's heirs at law appeals from a decree of the orphans' court, directing the register of wills to probate the following letter:

'Johnstown, Dec. 12.

'The Kimmel Bro. and Famly We are all well as you can espec fore the time of the Year. I received you kind & welcome letter from Geo & Irvin all OK glad you poot your Pork down in Pickle it is the true way to keep meet every piece gets the same, now always poot it down that way & you will not miss it & you will have good pork fore smoking you can keep it from butchern to butchern the hole year round. Boys, I wont agree with you about the open winter I think we are gone to have one of the hardest. Plenty of snow & Verry cold verry cold! I dont want to see it this way but it will will come see to the old sow & take her away when the time comes well I cant say if I will come over yet. I will wright in my next letter it may be to ruff we will see in the next letter if I come I have some very valuable papers I want you to keep fore me so if enny thing hapens all the scock money in the 3 Bank liberty lones Post office stamps and my home on Horner St goes to George Darl & Irvin Kepp this letter lock it up it may help you out. Earl sent after his Christmas Tree & Trimmings I sent them he is in the Post office in Phila working.

'Will clost your Truly,

Father.'

This letter was mailed by decedent at Johnstown, Pa., on the morning of its date—Monday, December 12, 1921—to two of his children, George and Irvin, who were named in it as beneficiaries; the envelope being addressed to them at their residence in Glencoe, Pa. He died suddenly on the afternoon of the same day.

Two questions are raised: First. Is the paper testamentary in character? Second. Is the signature to it a sufficient compliance with our Wills Act? Before answering them directly, there are a few principles, now well settled, which, perhaps, should be preliminarily stated. * * *

It is difficult to understand how the decedent, probably expecting an early demise—as appears by the letter itself, and the fact of his sickness and inability to work, during the last three days of the first or second week preceding—could have possibly meant anything else than a testamentary gift, when he said 'so if enny thing hapens [the property specified] goes to George Darl and Irvin'; and why, if this was not intended to be effective in and of itself, he should have sent it to two of the distributees named in it, telling them to 'Kepp this letter lock it up it may help you out.'

The second question to be determined depends on the proper construction of section 2 of the Wills Act of June 7, 1917 (P. L. 403, 405; Pa. St. 1920, § 8308), which is a re-enactment of section 6 of the Wills Act of April 8, 1833 (P. L. 249), reading as follows:

'Every will shall be in writing, and, unless the person making the same shall be prevented by the extremity of his last sickness, shall be signed by him at the end thereof, or by some person in his presence and by his express direction.'

The letter now being considered was all in the handwriting of decedent, including the word 'Father,' at the end of it; and hence the point to be decided would appear to resolve itself into this: Does the word 'Father,' when taken in connection with the contents of the paper, show that it was 'signed by him?' When stated thus bluntly—in the very language of the statute—the answer seems free from doubt; but since we said in Brennan's Estate, 244 Pa. 574, 581, 91 Atl. 220, 222, that 'signing in the usual acceptation of the word and in the sense in which, presumably, it is used in the act is the writing of a name or the affixing of what is meant as a signature,' we must go further and determine whether or not the word 'Father' was 'meant as a signature.' * * *

Decree affirmed and appeal dismissed, the costs in this court to be paid by the estate of Harry A. Kimmel, deceased.

D. Notarized Wills

With its 2008 revision, the Uniform Probate Code introduced another category of wills—Notarized Wills. Uniform Probate Code § 2-502(a)(3)(B) permits a will to be valid if it is either: (1) acknowledged by the testator before a notary; or (2) acknowledged by a testator before any other individual authorized by law to take acknowledgments. Thus, there are no requirements for signatures by witnesses or writing by the testator, such as is required for a holograph. Hence, there is a significant relaxation of the formalities traditionally associated with valid Last Wills and Testaments. Arguably, the lessening of formalities enhances testamentary freedom of individuals. *See, e.g.,* Anne-Marie Rhodes, *Notarized Wills*, 27 QUINNIPIAC PROB. L.J. 419 (2014).

Uniform Probate Code (2019)

§ 2-502. Execution; Witnessed or Notarized Wills; Holographic Wills

Cmt.

Allowing notarized wills as an optional method of execution addresses cases that have begun to emerge in which the supervising attorney, with the client and all witnesses present, circulates one or more estate-planning documents for signature, and fails to notice that the client or one of the witnesses has unintentionally neglected to sign one of the documents. [citations omitted] This often, but not always, arises when the attorney prepares multiple estate-planning documents—a will, a durable power of attorney, a health-care power of attorney, and perhaps a revocable trust. It is common practice, and sometimes required by state law, that the documents other than the will be notarized. It would reduce confusion and chance for error if all of the documents could be executed with the same formality.

Lawrence W. Waggoner
The UPC Authorizes Notarized Wills
34 ACTEC J. 83 (2008)

For a variety of reasons, some individuals avoid professional advice and attempt to execute wills on their own. As long as it is clear that the decedent adopted the document as his or her will, * * * the law has no reason to deny validity on the ground of defective execution. The harmless-error rule is one curative measure for this problem. Allowing notarization as an optional method of execution is another. The public is accustomed to thinking that a document is made "legal" by getting it notarized. * * * To some, this conception is mistakenly but understandably carried over to executing a will. * * * A testator who goes to the trouble of going to a bank or even a package or a photocopy store * * * to get a home-drawn will notarized shows as much of a deliberate purpose to make the will final and valid as asking a couple of individuals to sign as witnesses. In effect, the UPC as amended treats the notary as the equivalent of two attesting witnesses. The case law invalidating a notarized will after death arises from the decedent's ignorance of the statutory requirements, not in response to evidence raising doubt that the will truly represents the decedent's wishes. * * *

Id. at 85.

In re Estate of Hall

Supreme Court of Montana, 2002
310 Mont. 486, 51 P.3d 1134

Justice JIM REGNIER delivered the Opinion of the Court. * * *

James Mylen Hall ("Jim") died on October 23, 1998. At the time of his death, he was 75 years old and lived in Cascade County, Montana. His wife, Betty Lou Hall ("Betty"), and two daughters from a previous marriage, Sandra Kay Ault ("Sandra") and Charlotte Rae Hall ("Charlotte"), survived him.

Jim first executed a will on April 18, 1984 (the "Original Will"). Approximately thirteen years later, Jim and Betty's attorney, Ross Cannon, transmitted to them a draft of a joint will (the "Joint Will"). On June 4, 1997, Jim and Betty met at Cannon's office to discuss the draft. After making several changes, Jim and Betty apparently agreed on the terms of the Joint Will. Jim and Betty were prepared to execute the Joint Will once Cannon sent them a final version.

At the conclusion of the meeting, however, Jim asked Cannon if the draft could stand as a will until Cannon sent them a final version. Cannon said that it would be valid if Jim and Betty executed the draft and he notarized it. Betty testified that no one else was in the office at the time to serve as an attesting witness. Jim and Betty, therefore, proceeded to sign the Joint Will and Cannon notarized it without anyone else present.

When they returned home from the meeting, Jim apparently told Betty to tear up the Original Will, which Betty did. After Jim's death, Betty applied to informally probate the Joint Will. Sandra objected to the informal probate and requested formal probate of the Original Will.

On August 9, 2001, Judge McKittrick heard the will contest. He issued the Order admitting the Joint Will to probate on August 27, 2001. Sandra appealed. * * *

Sandra argues that the judicial interpretation and construction of a will are questions of law. This appeal, however, does not involve interpreting or constructing a will. The dispositive issue is whether the District Court properly admitted the disputed will to probate. Determining whether a court properly admitted a will involves both questions of law and fact. *See In re Estate of Brooks* (1996), 279 Mont. 516, 519, 927 P.2d 1024, 1026. In *Brooks,* we described our standard as follows:

> We will not disturb a district court's findings of fact unless they are clearly erroneous. A court's findings are clearly erroneous if they are not supported by substantial credible evidence, the court has misapprehended the effect of the evidence, or our review of the record convinces us that a mistake has been committed. We review a district court's conclusions of law to determine whether the interpretation of the law is correct. [Citations omitted.]

Brooks, 279 Mont. at 519, 927 P.2d at 1026. * * *

In contested cases, the proponent of a will must establish that the testator duly executed the will. *See* § 72-3-310, MCA; *Brooks,* 279 Mont. at 519, 927 P.2d at 1026. For a will to be valid, two people typically must witness the testator signing the will and then sign the will themselves. *See* § 72-2-522(1)(c), MCA. If two individuals do not properly witness the document, § 72-2-523, MCA, provides that the document may still be treated as if it had been executed under certain circumstances. One such circumstance is if the proponent of the document establishes by clear and convincing evidence that the decedent intended the document to be the decedent's will. *See* § 72-2-523, MCA; *Brooks,* 279 Mont. at 522, 927 P.2d at 1027.

Sandra urges this Court not to use § 72-2-523, MCA, "to circumvent the statute requiring two witnesses to the execution of a will." Jim and Betty's failure to use witnesses, according to Sandra, was not an innocent omission on their part. She also expresses concern that the improperly witnessed Joint Will materially altered a long-standing agreement to divide the property. She primarily argues, however, that the Joint Will should be invalid as a matter of law because no one properly witnessed it.

Sandra's numerous arguments about why the will was improperly witnessed are irrelevant to this appeal. Neither party disputes that no witnesses were present at the execution of Jim and Betty's Joint Will as required by § 72-2-522, MCA. In the absence of attesting witnesses, § 72-2-523, MCA, affords a means of validating a will for which the Montana Legislature expressly provides. The only question before this Court, therefore, is whether the District Court erred in concluding that Jim intended the Joint Will to be his will under § 72-2-523, MCA. We conclude that the court did not err.

The District Court made several findings of fact that supported its conclusion. In particular, it noted that the Joint Will specifically revoked all previous wills and codicils made by either Jim or Betty. Furthermore, the court found that, after they had executed the Joint Will, Jim directed Betty to destroy the Original Will.

Sandra does not dispute any of the court's factual findings. She argues only that Betty testified that she and Jim had not executed the will even after they had signed it. In making this argument, she points to the following testimony:

Question: Do you know if [Jim] gave [Sandra and Charlotte] a copy of the new will?

Answer: I don't believe he did, no.

Question: Do you know why?

Answer: Well, I guess because we didn't have the completed draft without all the scribbles on it.

Question: So he thought that will was not good yet?

Answer: No, he was sure it was good, but he didn't give it to the girls. And we didn't give it to my son. We didn't give it to anybody.

Question: Why?

Answer: Because it wasn't completely finished the way Ross was going to finish it.

This testimony may suggest that Betty believed that the Joint Will was not in a final form because of "all the scribbles on it." Nevertheless, she immediately goes on to state that she believed the will was good. When asked if it were Jim's and her intent for the Joint Will to stand as a will until they executed another one, she responded, "Yes, it was." The court could reasonably interpret this testimony to mean that Jim and Betty expected the Joint Will to stand as a will until Cannon provided one in a cleaner, more final form. Sandra points to no other evidence that suggests that Jim did not intend for the Joint Will to be his will.

For these reasons, we conclude that the District Court did not err in admitting the Joint Will into final probate. Because Jim directed Betty to destroy the Original Will, we also conclude that the District Court did not err in finding that these acts were acts of revocation of the Original Will under §72-2-527, MCA.

Affirmed.

KARLA M. GRAY, TERRY N. TRIEWEILER, PATRICIA COTTER and JIM RICE, concur.

Notes

The *Hall* decision illustrates the manner in which courts have allowed a relaxation of testamentary formalities. In the *Hall* decision, the court used the concept of harmless error—a concept we will discuss further in connection with substantial compliance and Uniform Probate Code §2-503. Here, however, even though there was sufficient clear and convincing evidence to satisfy the court that the testator intended the will to be effective, the fact that the will was notarized by the attorney would have been sufficient, in itself, for validity under the new statute. For further commentary on the progression towards lessening formalities, see generally

Stephanie Lester, *Admitting Defective Wills to Probate, Twenty Years Later: New Evidence for the Adoption of the Harmless Error Rule*, 42 REAL PROP. PROB. & TRUST J. 577 (2007).

E. Witnessed Wills

When people think of a Last Will and Testament, they think of a process described in print, television, and the movies. That is, an attorney invites a well-dressed person into a dignified room and, in the presence of two or three disinterested persons, invites the lead character to admit that this document is his or her will and to signify this with a signature on the last page. This signing is then followed by inviting the witnesses to sign and then departing after the attorney makes a grand show of handing the completed document to the client. The entire procedure seems quite staged and, in fact, it is. And the procedure has a lengthy history.

The formalities and the procedure for the execution of a witnessed will derive from two English statutes: the Statute of Frauds (1677) and the Wills Act (1837). These two statutes form the basis of a procedure that dominated will attestation for decades but now may vary from state to state. It can be argued that, to be secure in due execution, a will should be executed in conformity with the strictest requirements (the Statute of Frauds and the Wills Act) to meet the requirements of any state within which the testator may one day die domiciled. Even though the Uniform Probate Code may be enacted in whole or in part, the requirements contained therein vary from those of the two, much earlier English statutes. Thus, examine the historical requirements of the English statutes and compare them to the California statute:

Statute of Frauds
29 Car. II, c. 3, §V (1677).

And be it further enacted by the authority aforesaid, that from and after the said four and twentieth day of June all devises and bequests of any lands or tenements, devisable either by force of the Statute of Wills, or by this Statute, or by force of the custom of Kent, or the custom of any borough, or any other particular custom, shall be in writing, and signed by the party so devising the same, or by some other person in his presence and by his express directions, and shall be attested and subscribed in the presence of the said devisor by three or four credible witnesses, or else they shall be utterly void and of none effect.

Wills Act
7 Wm. IV & 1 Vict., c. 26, §IX (1837).

And be it further enacted, that no will shall be valid unless it shall be in writing and executed in manner hereinafter mentioned; (that is to say), it shall be signed at the foot or end thereof by the testator, or by some other person in his presence and by his direction; and such signature shall be made or acknowledged by the testator in the presence of two or more witnesses present at the same time, and such witnesses shall attest and shall subscribe the will in the presence of the testator, but no form of attestation shall be necessary.

California Probate Code (2019)

§ 6110. Necessity of writing; other requirements.

(a) Except as provided in this part, a will shall be in writing and satisfy the requirements of this section.

(b) The will shall be signed by one of the following:

(1) By the testator.

(2) In the testator's name by some other person in the testator's presence and by the testator's direction.

(3) By a conservator pursuant to a court order to make a will under Section 2580.

(c)(1) Except as provided in paragraph (2), the will shall be witnessed by being signed, during the testator's lifetime, by at least two persons each of whom (A) being present at the same time, witnessed either the signing of the will or the testator's acknowledgment of the signature or of the will and (B) understand that the instrument they sign is the testator's will.

(2) If a will was not executed in compliance with paragraph (1), the will shall be treated as if it was executed in compliance with that paragraph if the proponent of the will establishes by clear and convincing evidence that, at the time the testator signed the will, the testator intended the will to constitute the testator's will.

Notes

Like the California Code above, the Uniform Probate Code relaxes the requirements of the English statutes in reference to witnesses and the testator's acknowledgment. *See also* UNIF. PROB. CODE § 2-502(a)(3) (allowing for witnesses to sign "within a reasonable time after either the signing of the will . . . or the testator's acknowledgment. . . ."). Whether or not any of the statute's formalities have been met is a matter for contest of the will. The requirements contained in the previous statutes may be divided into two separate grounds of contest: formalities and intentionalities. The statutes explicitly define the formalities required, yet there is a corresponding requirement that, at the time the formality was executed, the testator must possess proper intentionalities. These intentionalities will be discussed later in the context of contest of wills. For now, we examine each of the formalities recited in the previously identified statutes. While each state may or may not require each of these, each formality may decide whether or not the will may be probated.

II. Statutory Formalities

Irene Sherwyn Cooper
Rebutting the Presumptions of Due Execution and Testamentary Capacity

153 Trusts & Ests. 34 (Dec. 2014)

In every probate proceeding, the proponent of the will has the burden of proof on the issues of due execution and testamentary capacity . . . To prove the due execution of a will, the proponent must establish by a fair preponderance of the evidence that: (1) the testator signed at the end of the instrument or that someone else signed the instrument on the testator's behalf in his presence and at his direction; (2) the testator signed before or acknowledged his signature to at least two witnesses, each of whom signed the instrument at the testator's request and in his presence; (3) the attesting witnesses signed the instrument within 30 days of each other; and (4) the testator published the instrument as his will.

A. Presence

Stevens v. Casdorph

Supreme Court of Appeals of West Virginia, 1998
203 W. Va. 450, 508 S.E.2d 610

PER CURIAM: . . .

On May 28, 1996, the Casdorphs took Mr. Homer Haskell Miller to Shawnee Bank in Dunbar, West Virginia, so that he could execute his will.[1] Once at the bank, Mr. Miller asked Debra Pauley, a bank employee and public notary, to witness the execution of his will. After Mr. Miller signed the will, Ms. Pauley took the will to two other bank employees, Judith Waldron and Reba McGinn, for the purpose of having each of them sign the will as witnesses. Both Ms. Waldron and Ms. McGinn signed the will. However, Ms. Waldron and Ms. McGinn testified during their depositions that they did not actually see Mr. Miller place his signature on the will. Further, it is undisputed that Mr. Miller did not accompany Ms. Pauley to the separate work areas of Ms. Waldron and Ms. McGinn. . . . Mr. Miller died on July 28, 1996. The last will and testament of Mr. Miller, which named Mr. Paul Casdorph[2] as executor, left the bulk of his estate to the Casdorphs.[3] The Stevenses, nieces of Mr. Miller, filed the instant action to set aside the will. The Stevenses asserted in their complaint that Mr. Miller's will was not executed according to the requirements set forth in

---

1. Mr. Miller was elderly and confined to a wheelchair.
2. Paul Casdorph was a nephew of Mr. Miller.
3. Mr. Miller's probated estate exceeded $400,000.00. The will devised $80,000.00 to Frank Paul Smith, a nephew of Mr. Miller. The remainder of the estate was left to the Casdorphs.

W.Va.Code § 41–1–3 (1995).[4] After some discovery, all parties moved for summary judgment. The circuit court denied the Stevenses' motion for summary judgment, but granted the Casdorphs' cross motion for summary judgment. From this ruling, the Stevenses appeal to this Court. . . .

The Stevenses' contention is simple. They argue that all evidence indicates that Mr. Miller's will was not properly executed. Therefore, the will should be voided. The procedural requirements at issue are contained in W.Va.Code § 41–1–3 (1997). The statute reads:

> No will shall be valid unless it be in writing and signed by the testator, or by some other person in his presence and by his direction, in such manner as to make it manifest that the name is intended as a signature; and moreover, unless it be wholly in the handwriting of the testator, *the signature shall be made or the will acknowledged by him in the presence of at least two competent witnesses, present at the same time; and such witnesses shall subscribe the will in the presence of the testator, and of each other,* but no form of attestation shall be necessary. (Emphasis added.)

The relevant requirements of the above statute calls for a testator to sign his/her will or acknowledge such will in the presence of at least two witnesses at the same time, and such witnesses must sign the will in the presence of the testator and each other. In the instant proceeding the Stevenses assert, and the evidence supports, that Ms. McGinn and Ms. Waldron did not actually witness Mr. Miller signing his will. Mr. Miller made no acknowledgment of his signature on the will to either Ms. McGinn or Ms. Waldron. Likewise, Mr. Miller did not observe Ms. McGinn and Ms. Waldron sign his will as witnesses. Additionally, neither Ms. McGinn nor Ms. Waldron acknowledged to Mr. Miller that their signatures were on the will. It is also undisputed that Ms. McGinn and Ms. Waldron did not actually witness each other sign the will, nor did they acknowledge to each other that they had signed Mr. Miller's will. Despite the evidentiary lack of compliance with W.Va.Code § 41–1–3, the Casdorphs' argue that there was substantial compliance with the statute's requirements, insofar as everyone involved with the will knew what was occurring. The trial court found that there was substantial compliance with the statute because everyone knew why Mr. Miller was at the bank. The trial court further concluded there was no evidence of fraud, coercion or undue influence. Based upon the foregoing, the trial court concluded that the will should not be voided even though the technical aspects of W.Va.Code § 41–1–3 were not followed.

Our analysis begins by noting that "[t]he law favors testacy over intestacy." . . . [Citation to Record omitted], *In re Teubert's Estate,* 171 W.Va. 226, 298 S.E.2d 456 (1982). However, we clearly held in syllabus point 1 of *Black v. Maxwell,* 131 W.Va. 247, 46 S.E.2d 804 (1948), that "[t]estamentary intent and a written instrument,

---

4. As heirs, the Stevenses would be entitled to recover from Mr. Miller's estate under the intestate laws if his will is set aside as invalidly executed.

executed in the manner provided by [W.Va.Code § 41–1–3], existing concurrently, are essential to the creation of a valid will." *Black* establishes that mere intent by a testator to execute a written will is insufficient. The actual execution of a written will must also comply with the dictates of W.Va.Code § 41–1–3. The Casdorphs seek to have this Court establish an exception to the technical requirements of the statute. In *Wade v. Wade*, 119 W.Va. 596, 195 S.E. 339 (1938), this Court permitted a narrow exception to the stringent requirements of the W.Va.Code § 41–1–3. This narrow exception is embodied in syllabus point 1 of *Wade*:

> Where a testator acknowledges a will and his signature thereto in the presence of two competent witnesses, one of whom then subscribes his name, the other or first witness, having already subscribed the will in the presence of the testator but out of the presence of the second witness, may acknowledge his signature in the presence of the testator and the second witness, and such acknowledgment, if there be no indicia of fraud or misunderstanding in the proceeding, will be deemed a signing by the first witness within the requirement of Code, 41–1–3, that the witnesses must subscribe their names in the presence of the testator and of each other.

See Brammer v. Taylor, 175 W.Va. 728, 730 n. 1, 338 S.E.2d 207, 215 n. 1 (1985), ("[T]he witnesses' acknowledgment of their signatures . . . in the presence of the testator [and in the presence of each other] is tantamount to and will be deemed a 'signing' or 'subscribing' in the presence of those persons").

Wade stands for the proposition that if a witness acknowledges his/her signature on a will in the physical presence of the other subscribing witness *and the testator*, then the will is properly witnessed within the terms of W.Va.Code § 41–1–3. In this case, none of the parties signed or acknowledged their signatures in the presence of each other. This case meets neither the narrow exception of *Wade* nor the specific provisions of W.Va.Code § 41–1–3. . . .

Reversed.

WORKMAN, Justice, dissenting:

The majority once more takes a very technocratic approach to the law, slavishly worshiping form over substance. In so doing, they not only create a harsh and inequitable result wholly contrary to the indisputable intent of Mr. Homer Haskell Miller, but also a rule of law that is against the spirit and intent of our whole body of law relating to the making of wills.

There is absolutely no claim of incapacity or fraud or undue influence, nor any allegation by any party that Mr. Miller did not consciously, intentionally, and with full legal capacity convey his property as specified in his will. The challenge to the will is based solely upon the allegation that Mr. Miller did not comply with the requirement of West Virginia Code 41–1–3 . . . [footnote omitted] that the signature shall be made or the will acknowledged by the testator in the presence of at least two competent witnesses, present at the same time. The lower court, in its very thorough findings of fact, indicated that Mr. Miller had been transported to the bank by his nephew Mr. Casdorph and the nephew's wife. Mr. Miller, disabled and confined to a wheelchair, was a shareholder in the Shawnee Bank in Dunbar, West Virginia, with whom all those present were personally familiar. When Mr. Miller executed his will in the bank lobby, the typed will was placed on Ms. Pauley's desk, and Mr. Miller instructed Ms. Pauley that he wished to have his will signed, witnessed, and acknowledged. After Mr. Miller's signature had been placed upon the will with Ms. Pauley watching, Ms. Pauley walked the will over to the tellers' area in the same small lobby of the bank. Ms. Pauley explained that Mr. Miller wanted Ms. Waldron to sign the will as a witness. The same process was used to obtain the signature of Ms. McGinn. Sitting in his wheelchair, Mr. Miller did not move from Ms. Pauley's desk during the process of obtaining the witness signatures. The lower court concluded that the will was valid and that Ms. Waldron and Ms. McGinn signed and acknowledged the will "in the presence" of Mr. Miller.

In *Wade v. Wade*, 119 W.Va. 596, 195 S.E. 339 (1938), we addressed the validity of a will challenged for such technicalities . . . [footnote omitted] and observed that "a narrow, rigid construction of the statute should not be allowed to stand in the way of right and justice, or be permitted to defeat a testator's disposition of his property." 119 W.Va. at 599, 195 S.E. at 340–341. We upheld the validity of the challenged will in *Wade*, noting that "each case must rest on its own facts and circumstances to which the court must look to determine whether there was a subscribing by the witnesses in the presence of the testator; that substantial compliance with the statute is all that is required. . . ." *Id.* at 599, 195 S.E. at 340. A contrary result, we emphasized, "would be based on illiberal and inflexible construction of the statute, giving preeminence to letter and not to spirit, and resulting in the thwarting of the intentions of testators even under circumstances where no possibility of fraud or impropriety exists." *Id.* at 600, 195 S.E. at 341.

The majority's conclusion is precisely what was envisioned and forewarned in 1938 by the drafters of the *Wade* opinion: illiberal and inflexible construction, giving preeminence to the letter of the law and ignoring the spirit of the entire body of testamentary law, resulting in the thwarting of Mr. Miller's unequivocal wishes. In *In re Estate of Shaff*, 125 Or. 288, 266 P. 630 (1928), the court encountered an argument that the attesting witness had not signed the will in the presence of the testator. The evidence demonstrated that the witnesses had signed the document at the request of the testator, and the court reasoned:

> While it is the duty of the court[s] to observe carefully the spirit and intent of the statute, they will not adopt a strained and technical construction to defeat a will where the capacity and intention is plain and where by fair and reasonable intendment the statute may be held to have been complied with, and such is the case here.

Id. at 298, 266 P. 630.

We also specified, in syllabus point two of *Wade*, that "[w]hether witnesses to a will have subscribed the same in the presence of the testator and of each other, as required by statute, is a question of fact to be determined in each case from the circumstances thereof." Summary judgment is inappropriate where there is a dispute regarding the conclusions to be drawn from evidentiary facts. *Williams v. Precision Coil, Inc.*, 194 W.Va. 52, 59, 459 S.E.2d 329, 336. Thus, the majority could have legitimately concluded that summary judgment was inappropriate and that the issue of compliance with the statute was a question of fact to be determined by the jury. I could have accepted such reasoning far more readily than that employed by the majority in its swift eradication of Mr. Miller's legal right to convey his estate in the manner of his own conscious choosing. . . . The majority strains the logical definition of "in the presence" as used in the operative statute. The legal concept of "presence" in this context encompasses far more than simply watching the signing of the will, which is the technical, narrow interpretation of the word apparently relied upon by the majority. Where the attestation of the will by the witnesses occurred within the same room as the testator, there is, at the very minimum, prima facie evidence that the attestation occurred within the "presence" of the testator. *See* 20 *Michie's Jurisprudence*, Wills § 34 (1993); Annotation, What constitutes the presence of the testator in the witnessing of his will, 75 A.L.R.2d 318 (1961).

In re Demaris' Estate, 166 Or. 36, 110 P.2d 571 (1941), involved a challenge to a will signed by a very ill gentleman, witnessed in another room by a physician and his wife thirty minutes after the testator signed the will. The court grappled with the question of whether the witnesses had complied with the statutory requirement that the witnesses sign in the presence of the testator. *Id.* at 39–40, 110 P.2d at 572. The court rejected a strict interpretation of the language of the statute, recognizing that the purpose of requiring the presence of the witnesses was to protect a testator against substitution and fraud. *Id.* at 62, 110 P.2d at 581. Rather, the court determined that "presence" did not demand that the witnesses sign within the sight of the testator, if other senses would enable the testator to know that the witnesses were near and to understand what the witnesses were doing. *Id.* The court concluded that "the circumstances repel any thought of fraud and speak cogently of the integrity of the instrument under review. The signatures of all three persons are conceded. The circumstances of the attestation are free from dispute." 166 Or. at 74, 110 P.2d at 586. . . . To hold the will invalid on a strictly technical flaw would "be to observe the letter of the statute as interpreted strictly, and fail to give heed to the statute's obvious purpose. Thus, the statute would be turned against those for whose protection it had been written." 166 Or. at 76, 110 P.2d at 586.

The majority embraces the line of least resistance. The easy, most convenient answer is to say that the formal, technical requirements have not been met and that the will is therefore invalid. End of inquiry. Yet that result is patently absurd. That manner of statutory application is inconsistent with the underlying purposes of the statute. Where a statute is enacted to protect and sanctify the execution of a will to prevent substitution or fraud, this Court's application of that statute should further such underlying policy, not impede it. When, in our efforts to strictly apply legislative language, we abandon common sense and reason in favor of technicalities, we are the ones committing the injustice.

I am authorized to state that Justice MAYNARD joins in this dissent.

Notes

A review of the Statute of Frauds and the Wills Act reveals that the presence requirement for execution was originally a three-prong test: (1) the witnesses saw the testator sign; (2) the testator saw the witnesses sign; and (3) the witnesses saw each other sign. The test implied a requirement of *sight*: that any of those named could actually see the others if he or she were to look. Exceptions were often made for those who were sight impaired, and more modern jurisdictions have rejected the absoluteness of sight in favor of the conscious presence test. An example of the incorporation of conscious presence may be found in the Uniform Probate Code § 2-502(a)(2). This test does not require actual sight, but only that the persons involved comprehend the signing through a *consciousness* of the events taking place, even in different proximate locations. And even if the testator were to sign the will in an isolated moment, but later "acknowledge that signature or acknowledge the Will" as his or her own, then the sight or consciousness of that event would allow for a valid attestation of the will. *See* UNIF. PROB. CODE § 2-502(a)(3) (2009).

The Uniform Probate Code provides three means by which the Last Will and Testament described in *Stevens* could nonetheless have been valid: First, failure to comply with statutory formalities may be accommodated by finding that there is clear and convincing evidence that the testator intended this to be his or her Last Will and Testament and, hence, any deficiency is "harmless error." *See* UNIF. PROB. CODE § 2-503. This process will be discussed in further detail at D. Compliance Devices, *infra*. Second, conscious presence may suffice for sighted presence. *See* UNIF. PROB. CODE § 2-502(a)(2). And third, the Uniform Probate Code permits a testator to acknowledge the signature or the will. *See* UNIF. PROB. CODE § 2-502(a)(3)(A).

The lesson to be learned from the decision, however, is that the formalities should be performed precisely and recorded as such. While we may be sympathetic to the views of the dissent in *Stevens*, the majority approach illustrates the consequences of inattentiveness to professional responsibility.

A time sequence is implied, and at least one decision has held that the witnesses must sign while the testator is still alive. *See In re* Estate of Royal, 826 P.2d 1236 (Colo. 1992). Some states provide a number of days for witnesses to sign after a testator has signed: New York requires witnesses to sign within 30 days, and the Uniform Probate Code provides for signing within a reasonable time. *See* N.Y. EST. POWERS & TRUSTS L. § 3-2.1(a)(4) (McKinney 2019); UNIF. PROB. CODE § 2-502(a)(3) (2019).

B. Signature

In re Estate of Wait

Tennessee Court of Appeals, 1957
43 Tenn. App. 217, 306 S.W.2d 345

CARNEY, Judge.

The appellant, Sylvia Sunderland, executrix and principal beneficiary under the will of Georgie Miriam Wait, deceased, appeals from an order of the Probate Court of Shelby County, Tennessee, which refused to admit said will for probate. The appellees are the next of kin of the deceased, Georgie Miriam Wait, and will inherit the estate of Miss Wait if said will is not admitted to probate. The estate consists of approximately $22,000 in personalty and a house and lot located in Memphis, Tennessee.

Said paper writing was on three pages partly typewritten and partly filled in in pen and ink and is as follows:

'Last Will and Testament of Georgie Miriam Wait

* * *

'I, Georgie Miriam Wait, a resident of Memphis, Shelby County, State of Tennessee, being of sound and disposing memory do hereby make, publish and declare this to be my last will and testament, hereby revoking all other and former wills or codicils to wills by me at anytime heretofore made. I request and direct and it is my will as follows:

Item I

'I direct that all of my just debts, and the expense of my last illness and for my funeral and burial shall be paid from my estate by my Executor or Executrix as the case may be, hereinafter named, as soon after my death as may be practicable.

Item II

'I do hereby give and bequeath to Anne C. Wait, widow, of my deceased brother Jonathon Wait, the sum of one ($1.00) dollar.

Item III

'I do hereby give, grant, convey, devise and bequeath all the real property which I may own or to which I am or may be in any way entitled to my friend of many years—Sylvia Sunderland.

Item IV

'I do hereby give and bequeath all the rest, residue and remainder of my estate consisting of personalty only which I may own at my death or to which I am or may be entitled in any way to: To my cousins—Minnie Gill, Alice Wait and Mattie Bailey, I give $1.00 (one dollar) each, and the balance of my personalty including house furnishings to my dear friend Sylvia Sunderland.

Item V

'I do hereby appoint Sylvia Sunderland Executrix of my will, and dispense with, and ask that she be not required to give any bond as such.

'Witness my hand in the presence of Lessie M. Cunningham and Mrs. Dock White who are requested to sign this, my last will, as witnesses, at Memphis, Tennessee, on this the 30th day of March, 1956.

'x Georgie Miriam Wait

'The above Georgie Miriam Wait, did on this the 30th day of March, 1956, declare to us the foregoing instrument to be her last will and testament, and called on us to witness same, and did in our presence and sight, and each of us, sign her name thereto as and for her last will and testament, and we at her request, and in her presence and sight and of each other, sign our names as witnesses, this 30th day of March, 1956.

'Lessie M. Cunningham

'Mrs. Dock White'

Those parts of the will which were filled in in pen and ink have been underscored.

The beneficiary, Sylvia Sunderland, at the request of the testatrix, completed in pen and ink Items III and IV of the will and also wrote her name as executrix in the first paragraph of Item V of the will. The testatrix was old and feeble and could not write very well. The beneficiary, Miss Sunderland, was not present at the time of the attempted execution of the will on March 30, 1956.

It is to be noted that the attestation clause appears in all things regular and indicates that the will was executed and witnessed in conformity with the provisions of T.C.A. § 32-104.

However, it developed from the testimony of the attesting witnesses in the proceeding to probate the will in common form that the testatrix, Miss Wait, had not signed the will at the time the two attesting witnesses signed it but that she signed it a day or two later. It is the contention of the appellant that the testatrix showed the will to the attesting witnesses and declared the same to be her last will; that she touched the pen to the will at the place indicated for her signature and made a mark sufficient in law to constitute her signature under the statute and that thereupon the two attesting witnesses at her request and in her presence and in the presence of each other signed their names thereto as attesting and subscribing witnesses to said will.

The two attesting witnesses are in substantial agreement as to most of the circumstances surrounding the attempted signing of the will by the testatrix, Miss Wait. However, they do differ somewhat in just what the testatrix said at the time.

Both attesting witnesses were neighbors of the testatrix and testified that they were requested by Miss Wait to come to her home and to witness her will.

One of the attesting witnesses, Mrs. Dock White, testified that Miss Wait, the testatrix, was sitting at a table and that she placed a pen to the will on the table as if to sign and her hand was shaking and she said, 'Oh, I can't write; you all go ahead and sign it and I will sign it later when I can control my hand.'

Further, Mrs. White testified that she could not see whether Miss Wait had written anything or any part of her signature on the line because when Miss Wait handed the will over to the two witnesses she had placed a piece of paper over the line indicated for the signature of the testatrix. A few days later she was in the home of Miss Wait and the testatrix showed her the will which had been signed saying, 'At last I got to where I could control my hand and I signed this will.'

The other attesting witness, Mrs. Cunningham, corroborated the testimony of Mrs. White to the effect that the testatrix was sitting at the table and tried to write her name; that she was shaking and trying to write and that the pen was moving but that she did not know just exactly what, if anything, the testatrix had written at that time.

Mrs. Cunningham testified that she did not hear the testatrix say that she would sign the will later but that she did hear her say, 'I am so nervous I can't sign it' and that she asked the two witnesses to go ahead and sign the will which they did.

Both of the witnesses were positive in their testimony that while they could not testify that Miss Wait had actually written anything on the signature line because the paper was placed over this line, yet they could not say that she had not actually made a mark on the signature line.

The judge of the Probate Court held that the proof was insufficient to establish that Miss Wait had executed the will in accordance with the provisions of T.C.A. § 32-104; i.e. (1) That Miss Wait herself had not signed the will in the presence of the two witnesses; nor (2) did she acknowledge her signature already made; nor (3) did she direct that some other person sign her name for her.

It is the contention of appellant that since the witnesses testified that Miss Wait was actually attempting to execute a will and that she placed a pen to the paper that she thereby made some sort of a mark on the paper which was sufficient in law to constitute her legal signature.

Appellees contend, (1) that there was no evidence that Miss Wait intended to make a signature by mark; (2) that under the provisions of T.C.A. § 32-104 a signature by mark is not recognized and that therefore, the will would not be entitled to probate even if the proof were sufficient to show that the testatrix attempted to make a signature by mark on the paper writing.

Appellant relies upon the language of the Supreme Court in the case of Leathers v. Binkley, 196 Tenn. 80, 264 S.W.2d 561, 563, which was as follows:

> 'To protect the right of testamentary disposition of property, we must sustain a will as legally executed if it is possible to do so, Sizer's Pritchard on Wills, Secs. 384, 386 et seq.; 57 Am.Jur., Wills, Sec. 218. Compare: Ball v. Miller, 31 Tenn.App. 271, 214 S.W.2d 446.'

However, in our opinion, the facts in the *Leathers* case were substantially different from the case at bar. The attesting witnesses in that case testified that they did not remember whether they signed before or after the testator. In the present case both attesting witnesses affirmatively testified that the testatrix did not sign the will until after they had signed and that it was signed by her out of their presence. For that reason we think the decision in the *Leathers* case is not controlling of the case at bar.

In the case of Ball v. Miller, 1948, 31 Tenn.App. 271, 214 S.W.2d 446, the testatrix was in the hospital and had signed the will in the presence of two witnesses whom she had requested to witness her will. One of the witnesses, a doctor, had signed but before the other witness could sign, the testatrix suffered a coughing spell and the second attesting witness went to seek a nurse. The condition of the testatrix became considerably worse and the second attesting witness failed or neglected to sign the will before the death of the testatrix.

Prior to the execution of the Uniform Wills Act in 1941, now T.C.A. § 32-104, said will would have been entitled to probate as a will of personalty even though it would not have been sufficiently valid to devise real estate. The Court of Appeals, following the case of Fann v. Fann, 186 Tenn. 127, 208 S.W.2d 542, reannounced the rule that there is no difference in the requirements for the execution of a will bequeathing personalty and a will devising real estate. The Court of Appeals held in the *Ball* case that since only one witness had actually signed the will that it was not executed in compliance with the provisions of Code Section 8098.4, T.C.A. § 32-104, and therefore not entitled to probate as a will.

In the case of Eslick v. Wodicka, 1948, 31 Tenn.App. 333, 215 S.W.2d 12, the proof showed that the testator signed the will privately and subsequently acknowledged his signature before both attesting witnesses. The attesting witnesses signed the will out of the presence of each other though they later were jointly in the presence of the testator and he thanked both of them for acting as subscribing witnesses. At this subsequent meeting the testator did not have the will with him though it had been actually signed by each subscribing witness in the presence of the testator prior to the meeting. In the *Eslick* case the Court of Appeals held that the failure of the attesting witnesses to sign the will both in the presence of the testator and in the presence of each other as required by Code Section 32-104 was fatal to the validity of the will and that the subsequent acknowledgement of their signatures in the presence of the testator and in the presence of each other was not authorized by the statute and ineffective to validate the will.

We do not find it necessary or proper for this court to rule whether or not a testator may legally sign a will by mark. A careful reading of the testimony of the attesting witnesses indicates clearly to us that the testatrix may have made a mark of some sort, either an initial or one or more letters of her signature, on the will but she clearly indicated that she did not consider such mark or marks to constitute her signature. In our opinion neither the testatrix nor the attesting witnesses understood the requirements of the statute that the testatrix must (1) signify to the attesting witnesses that the instrument is his will and then take one of three courses: (a) Himself sign the will or (b) acknowledge his signature already made or (c) at the direction of the testator and in the testator's presence have someone else sign the name of the testator to the document.

The statute is very clear that regardless which one of the three courses is pursued the act must be done in the presence of two or more attesting witnesses. We think the evidence clearly shows that on the day in question the testatrix had not signed the will or attempted to sign the will before the attesting witnesses were called to her home.

Further, we think the evidence shows that she complied with a portion of the statute by signifying to the attesting witnesses that the paper writing was her will and that she then set about to sign the will by writing her usual signature thereon; that due to her physical infirmity her hand shook so that she decided to defer her signature until a later date and asked the attesting witnesses to go ahead at that time and sign their names to the will which they did; that the testatrix did not consider that she had signed the will until after the attesting witnesses had signed the will and had left her presence. At some later date her hand became more steady and she did actually sign the will but not in the presence of either attesting witness though at a later date she did acknowledge her signature to one of the attesting witnesses.

There is simply no proof on which the Probate Court or this Court could find that the testatrix intended any mark she may have made on the paper as her signature. On the contrary, we think the overwhelming proof is that she did not intend any such mark to be her signature but that she intended to and did actually sign the will at some later date after the attesting witnesses had already signed it and were out of her presence. This the statute does not permit.

Therefore, we feel constrained to hold that His Honor, the Judge of the Probate Court of Shelby County, correctly held that the purported will of Miss Wait was not executed in accordance with the requirements of Code Section 32-104 and therefore, it is not entitled to probate and the assignment of error is overruled.

A decree will be entered affirming the judgment of the lower court and taxing the appellant and her surety with the costs of this appeal.

AVERY P. J. (W. D.), and BEJACH, J., concur.

Notes

While the case demonstrates that presence and the requirement of a "full intended signature" overlap, there are additional requirements surrounding the signatures. For example, what should be the order of signing? Should the testator always sign first? Logic would appear to require this, but in the absence of statutory requirement, the issue seems moot. And the signature may be by "proxy;" such as allowed by the Unif. Prob. Code § 2-502(a)(2). A proxy signature occurs when the testator, for any reason, does not sign personally but, instead, asks another to sign the testator's name in the testator's presence. This is different from signature by assistance. There, the testator's hand is assisted by another, but the physical signing is done by the testator. Signing by proxy has particular requirements; it must be in the presence of the testator and at the direction of the testator. The Wills Act (1837) requires that the testator sign at the foot or end of the will. But what will happen if dispositions of property appear physically after the signature? Under the common law, any provision appearing after the signature would be denied probate as simply an unexecuted codicil. However, at least one state has interpreted the "end" as the "logical end" of the instrument and not the physical end, thus allowing dispositions to be probated that appear after the signature in terms of physical location, but that, logically, may be accommodated within the entire instrument through language or sequence numbering. *See* Stinson's Estate, 228 Pa. 475, 77 A. 807 (1910).

Taylor v. Holt

Tennessee Court of Appeals, 2003
134 S.W.3d 830

D. MICHAEL SWINEY, J. * * *

Steve Godfrey ("Deceased") prepared a document in January of 2002, purporting to be his last will and testament. The one page document was prepared by Deceased on his computer. Deceased asked two neighbors, Hershell Williams and Teresa Williams to act as witnesses to the will. Deceased affixed a computer generated version of his signature at the end of the document in the presence of both Hershell and Teresa Williams. Hershell and Teresa Williams then each signed their name below Deceased's and dated the document next to their respective signatures. In the document, Deceased devised everything he owned to a person identified only as Doris. Deceased died approximately one week after the will was witnessed.

Defendant, Deceased's girlfriend, who lived with Deceased at the time of his death, filed an Order of Probate attempting to admit the will to probate and requesting to be appointed the personal representative of the estate. Defendant also filed affidavits of both Hershell and Teresa Williams attesting to the execution of the will. The affidavits each state that the affiant was a witness to Deceased's last will and testament and that each had signed at Deceased's request in the presence of both Deceased and the other witness. The affidavits both also state: "That the Testator, Steve Godfrey personally prepared the Last Will and Testament on his computer, and using the computer affixed his stylized cursive signature in my sight and presence and in the sight and presence of the other attesting witness. . . ." Further, each affidavit states that the affiant "was of the opinion that the Testator, Steve Godfrey, was of sound mind" at the time the will was witnessed.

Plaintiff, Deceased's sister, filed a complaint alleging, *inter alia,* that she is the only surviving heir of Deceased, that Deceased died intestate, that the document produced for probate was void because it did not contain Deceased's signature, and that Doris Holt has no blood relation or legal relation to the Deceased and should not have been appointed administratrix of Deceased's estate. Defendant filed a motion to dismiss or in the alternative for summary judgment claiming that all of the legal requirements concerning the execution and witnessing of a will under Tennessee law had been met and filed the supporting affidavits of Hershell and Teresa Williams.

The Trial Court entered an order on December 23, 2002, granting Defendant summary judgment. The December order held that all of the legal requirements concerning the execution and witnessing of a will under Tennessee law had been met and held that Defendant was entitled to summary judgment as a matter of law. Plaintiff appeals. * * *

Tenn. Code Ann. § 32-1-104 addresses the requisite formalities for the execution and witnessing of a will in Tennessee and states:

> The execution of a will, other than a holographic or nuncupative will, must be by the signature of the testator and of at least two (2) witnesses as follows:
>
> (1) The testator shall signify to the attesting witnesses that the instrument is his will and either:
>
> (A) Himself sign;
>
> (B) Acknowledge his signature already made; or
>
> (C) At his direction and in his presence have someone else sign his name for him; and
>
> (D) In any of the above cases the act must be done in the presence of two (2) or more attesting witnesses.
>
> (2) The attesting witnesses must sign:
>
> (A) In the presence of the testator; and
>
> (B) In the presence of each other.

Tenn. Code Ann. § 32-1-104 (1984). * * * The definition of "signature" as used in the statute is provided by Tenn. Code Ann. § 1-3-105, which states: "As used in this code, unless the context otherwise requires: . . . 'Signature' or 'signed' includes a mark, the name being written near the mark and witnessed, or any other symbol or methodology executed or adopted by a party with intention to authenticate a writing or record, regardless of being witnessed." Tenn. Code Ann. § 1-3-105(27) (1999).

We begin by considering whether the Trial Court erred in finding that the computer generated signature on the will complied with the legal requirements for the execution of a will, and, thus, erred in granting Defendant summary judgment.

Plaintiff claims that the will was not signed. Plaintiff's brief argues "there is no indication of any type or nature that there was a mark of any type made by the testator." Plaintiff cites to *Sunderland v. Bailey (In Re: Estate of Wait)*, a 1957 case in which this Court found that "the testatrix may have made a mark of some sort, either an initial or one or more letters of her signature, on the will but she clearly indicated that she did not consider such mark or marks to constitute her signature."

Sunderland v. Bailey (In Re: Estate of Wait), 43 Tenn.App. 217, 306 S.W.2d 345, 348 (1957). The witnesses in *Estate of Wait* testified that the testatrix had stated to them when the will was witnessed that she could not sign the will at that time, but would sign it later. *Id.* at 347. The *Wait* testatrix actually signed the will a day or two after it was witnessed. *Id.*

The *Wait* testatrix stated to the witnesses that she did not consider any mark to be her signature and this is borne out by the fact that she later signed the will. The *Wait* Court did not "find it necessary or proper . . . to rule whether or not a testator may legally sign a will by mark." *Id.* at 348. Rather, the Court upheld the determination that the will was not entitled to probate based upon the fact that the will was not executed and witnessed in conformity with the statute. *Id.* at 349.

The situation in *Estate of Wait* is dissimilar to the instant case. In the case at hand, Deceased did make a mark that was intended to operate as his signature. Deceased made a mark by using his computer to affix his computer generated signature, and, as indicated by the affidavits of both witnesses, this was done in the presence of the witnesses. The computer generated signature made by Deceased falls into the category of "any other symbol or methodology executed or adopted by a party with intention to authenticate a writing or record," and, if made in the presence of two attesting witnesses, as it was in this case, is sufficient to constitute proper execution of a will. Further, we note that Deceased simply used a computer rather than an ink pen as the tool to make his signature, and, therefore, complied with Tenn. Code Ann. § 32-1-104 by signing the will himself.

Defendant made a properly supported motion for summary judgment claiming there were no disputed issues of material fact and that Defendant was entitled to judgment as a matter of law. Defendant supported this assertion with the affidavits of Hershell and Teresa Williams, the witnesses to the will, attesting to the circumstances surrounding the execution of the will. As Defendant made a properly supported motion, the burden shifted to Plaintiff to set forth specific facts establishing the existence of disputed, material facts which must be resolved by the trier of fact. Plaintiff failed to do this. Plaintiff produced a letter that Plaintiff's appellate brief claims "set out a very different picture of [Deceased's] feelings towards [Defendant]." However, this letter has absolutely no relevance as to whether the will was properly executed and witnessed. Plaintiff failed to set forth specific facts establishing the existence of disputed, material facts regarding the execution of the will which must be resolved by the trier of fact.

There are no disputed material facts and, as discussed above, Defendant is entitled to judgment as a matter of law because the will was executed and witnessed in conformity with the statute. Thus, we hold that the Trial Court did not err in holding that the legal requirements for the execution and witnessing of a will had been met.

The other issue Plaintiff raises concerns whether an alleged beneficiary under a will should be allowed to receive benefits from the estate even though the will refers to the beneficiary by first name, but fails to state the beneficiary's last name. The will devises everything Deceased owned to someone named Doris, but fails to give a last name for Doris. Plaintiff apparently raises an issue regarding whether the Doris named in the will is the Defendant.

The Trial Court based its decision to grant summary judgment upon whether the will in question met the statutorily prescribed elements to be a valid last will and testament. The Trial Court did not consider or decide whether the Doris named in the will is the Defendant as this issue is not germane to whether the will was properly executed and witnessed in conformity with Tennessee law. We agree. Defendant was entitled to summary judgment because the will was properly executed and witnessed in conformity with Tennessee law. The identification of the beneficiary has no bearing on the dispositive issue before the Trial Court of whether this was Deceased's validly executed and witnessed last will and testament. We affirm the grant of summary judgment. * * *

The judgment of the Trial Court is affirmed, and this cause is remanded to the Trial Court for such further proceedings as may be required, if any, consistent with this Opinion and for collection of the costs below. The costs on appeal are assessed against the Appellant, Donna Godfrey Taylor, and her surety.

Problem

By the time of the decedent's death, he had practiced law as a decedents' estates attorney for more than 25 years. His only heirs at law were the three children from his deceased brother, two of whom he had not seen in decades. The third child, a nephew, remained in contact and was designated to receive seventy-five percent of the decedent's estate under an alleged Last Will and Testament that the decedent left behind. The purported fourteen-page will was found after a due and diligent search within the clutter and debris of the decedent's home. It was typed on traditional legal paper with the printed name of the decedent and his law office in the margin of each page. There is no signature from the decedent or from any witness. However, in the upper right-hand corner, there is a notation in the decedent's handwriting stating that the original was mailed to the decedent's personal representative—a friend who was deceased at the time of the decedent's death. The original could not be found. After the date on the will, the decedent acknowledged to friends that he had a will, a durable power of attorney, and a health care directive. The nephew submitted the unsigned will for probate, and his two siblings filed objections, stating that it did not meet the state's signature requirements. Should the Last Will and Testament be admitted for probate? *See In re* Ehrlich, 427 N.J. Super. 64, 47 A.3d 12 (2012).

C. Witnesses

The Statute of Frauds (1677) requires three or four credible witnesses, but the Wills Act (1837) requires only two. Today, only Louisiana requires a will to be witnessed in the presence of a notary and two competent witnesses, thereby requiring three witnesses. *See* La. Rev. Stat. art. 1577(1) (West 2018). Are there any remedies here? A state may, by statute, accept a will for probate if it meets the requirements of the testator's domicile or place of execution. *See* Unif. Prob. Code § 2-506 (2019) (choice of law as to execution). With few exceptions, age of the witnesses is not specifically mentioned in statutes, but the witness must be able to testify in court as to the intentionalities of the testator, and the witness' youth will be a detriment.

Because the Statute of Frauds refers to credible witnesses, the issue of competence of the witnesses arises, most often in the context of self interest. If a witness receives something under the Last Will and Testament that he or she would not receive under intestate succession or an otherwise valid will, does that mean he or she is incompetent to serve as a witness because he or she is an interested party? Under the common law interest rules, the answer was, "Yes." But to deny probate to the entire will because of a lack of sufficient witnesses due to interest seems harsh to many legislatures. For a recent assessment of what states are doing in reference to interested witnesses, see Elizabeth R. Carter, *Tipping the Scales in Favor of Charitable Bequests: A Critique*, 34 Pace L. Rev. 983, 989 (2014). Thus, several states take an intermediate approach. Compare the Uniform Probate Code with the provisions of New York and California as examples.

Uniform Probate Code (2019)

§ 2-505. Who May Witness.

(a) An individual generally competent to be a witness may act as a witness to a will.

(b) The signing of a will by an interested witness does not invalidate the will or any provision of it.

N.Y. Est., Powers & Trusts L. (2019)

§ 3-3.2 Competence of attesting witness who is beneficiary; application to nuncupative will.

(a) An attesting witness to a will to whom a beneficial disposition or appointment of property is made is a competent witness and compellable to testify respecting the execution of such will as if no such disposition or appointment had been made, subject to the following:

> (1) Any such disposition or appointment made to an attesting witness is void unless there are, at the time of execution and attestation, at least two other attesting witnesses to the will who receive no beneficial disposition or appointment thereunder.

> (2) Subject to subparagraph (1), any such disposition or appointment to an attesting witness is effective unless the will cannot be proved without the testimony of such witness, in which case the disposition or appointment is void.

> (3) Any attesting witness whose disposition is void hereunder, who would be a distributee if the will were not established, is entitled to receive so

much of his intestate share as does not exceed the value of the disposition made to him in the will, such share to be recovered as follows:

(A) In case the void disposition becomes part of the residuary disposition, from the residuary disposition only.

(B) In case the void disposition passes in intestacy, ratibly * * * from the distributees who succeed to such interest. For this purpose, the void disposition shall be distributed under 4-1.1 as though the attesting witness were not a distributee.

* * *

Cal. Prob. Code (2015)

§ 6112. Witnesses; interested witnesses.

(a) Any person generally competent to be a witness may act as a witness to a will.

(b) A will or any provision thereof is not invalid because the will is signed by an interested witness.

(c) Unless there are at least two other subscribing witnesses to the will who are disinterested witnesses, the fact that the will makes a devise to a subscribing witness creates a presumption that the witness procured the devise by duress, menace, fraud, or undue influence. This presumption is a presumption affecting the burden of proof. This presumption does not apply where the witness is a person to whom the devise is made solely in a fiduciary capacity.

(d) If a devise made by the will to an interested witness fails because the presumption established by subdivision (c) applies to the devise and the witness fails to rebut the presumption, the interested witness shall take such proportion of the devise made to the witness in the will as does not exceed the share of the estate which would be distributed to the witness if the will were not established. Nothing in this subdivision affects the law that applies where it is established that the witness procured a devise by duress, menace, fraud, or undue influence.

In re Estate of Parsons

California Court of Appeal, First District, 1980
103 Cal. App. 3d 384, 163 Cal. Rptr. 70

GRODIN, J.

This case requires us to determine whether a subscribing witness to a will who is named in the will as a beneficiary becomes "disinterested" within the meaning of Probate Code section 51 by filing a disclaimer of her interest after the testatrix's death. While our own policy preferences tempt us to an affirmative answer, we feel constrained by existing law to hold that a disclaimer is ineffective for that purpose.

* * *

Geneve Parsons executed her will on May 3, 1976. Three persons signed the will as attesting witnesses: Evelyne Nielson, respondent Marie Gower, and Bob Warda, a notary public. Two of the witnesses, Nielson and Gower, were named in the will as beneficiaries. Nielson was given $100; Gower was given certain real property. Mrs. Parsons died on December 13, 1976, and her will was admitted to probate on the petition of her executors, respondents Gower and Lenice Haymond. On September 12, 1977, Nielson filed a disclaimer of her $100 bequest.[1] Appellants then claimed an interest in the estate on the ground that the devise to Gower was invalid.[2] The trial court rejected their argument, which is now the sole contention on appeal.

Appellants base their claim on Probate Code section 51, which provides that a gift to a subscribing witness is void "unless there are two other and disinterested subscribing witnesses to the will."[3] Although Nielson disclaimed her bequest after subscribing the will, appellants submit that "a subsequent disclaimer is ineffective to transform an interested witness into a disinterested one." Appellants assert that because there was only one disinterested witness at the time of attestation, the devise to Gower is void by operation of law.

Respondents contend that appellants' argument is "purely technical" and "completely disregards the obvious and ascertainable intent" of the testatrix. They urge that the property should go to the person named as devisee rather than to distant relatives who, as the testatrix stated in her will, "have not been overlooked, but have been intentionally omitted." They stress that there has been no suggestion of any fraud or undue influence in this case, and they characterize Nielson's interest as a "token gift" which she relinquished pursuant to the disclaimer statute. (Prob. Code, § 190 et seq.) Finally, respondents point to the following language of Probate Code section 190.6: "In every case, the disclaimer shall relate back for all purposes to the date of the creation of the interest." On the basis of that language, respondents conclude that Nielson "effectively became disinterested" by reason of her timely

---

1. The disclaimer was filed pursuant to Probate Code section 190.1, which provides in part: "A beneficiary may disclaim any interest, in whole or in part, by filing a disclaimer as provided in this chapter." The disclaimer here was filed within the statutory period set forth in Probate Code section 190.3, subdivision (a), which provides in part: "[A] disclaimer shall be conclusively presumed to have been filed within a reasonable time if filed as follows: [¶] (1) In case of interests created by will, within nine months after the death of the person creating the interest. . . ."

2. Appellants Phyllis Maschke and Roger, Donald, and Clifford Winelander are the assignees of their uncle Sydney Winelander, the decedent's first cousin once removed. Appellants Frances Areitio, Florence Rennaker, and Josephine, Henry, and Walter Marion are also the decedent's first cousins once removed.

Mrs. Parsons' will contained no residuary clause. If the devise to Gower fails, appellants and other next of kin of equal degree will inherit the property.

3. Probate Code section 51 reads as follows: "All beneficial devises, bequests and legacies to a subscribing witness are void unless there are two other and disinterested subscribing witnesses to the will, except that if such interested witness would be entitled to any share of the estate of the testator in case the will were not established, he shall take such proportion of the devise or bequest made to him in the will as does not exceed the share of the estate which would be distributed to him if the will were not established."

disclaimer. According to respondents, the conditions of Probate Code section 51 have therefore been satisfied, and the devise to Gower should stand.

* * *

This appears to be a case of first impression in California, * * * and our interpretation of Probate Code section 51 will determine its outcome. * * * We are required to construe the statute "so as to effectuate the purpose of the law." (Select Base Materials v. Board of Equal. (1959) 51 Cal.2d 640, 645 [335 P.2d 672].) To ascertain that purpose, we may consider its history. (Estate of Ryan (1943) 21 Cal.2d 498, 513 [133 P.2d 626].)

At common law a party to an action, or one who had a direct interest in its outcome, was not competent to testify in court because it was thought that an interested witness would be tempted to perjure himself in favor of his interest. (See Davis v. Davis (1864) 26 Cal. 23, 35.) Centuries ago, this principle concerning the competence of witnesses in litigation was injected into the substantive law of wills. (See Estate of Zeile (1910) 5 Coffey's Prob. Dec. 292, 294.) The statute of frauds of 1676 required that devises of land be attested and subscribed "by three or four credible witnesses, or else they shall be utterly void and of none effect." (29 Car. II, ch. 3, § 5.) The word "credible" was construed to mean "competent" according to the common law principles then prevailing, and "competent" meant "disinterested"—so that persons having an interest under the will could not be "credible witnesses" within the meaning of the statute. The entire will would therefore fail if any one of the requisite number of attesting witnesses was also a beneficiary. (Holdfast v. Dowsing (K.B. 1746) 2 Str. 1253 [93 Eng.Rep. 1164].) In 1752 Parliament enacted a statute which saved the will by providing that the interest of an attesting witness was void. (25 Geo. II, ch. 6, § I.) Under such legislation, the competence of the witness is restored by invalidating his gift. (Estate of Zeile, supra, 5 Coffey's Prob. Dec. at p. 294.) The majority of American jurisdictions today have similar statutes; and California Probate Code section 51 falls into this category. (Rees, American Wills Statutes (1960) 46 Va.L.Rev. 613, 629–633. See generally 2 Bowe-Parker: Page on Wills (3d rev. ed. 1960) Formalities of Execution, §§ 19.73–19.110, pp. 169–216; Evans, The Competency of Testamentary Witnesses (1927) 25 Mich.L.Rev. 238.)

The common law disabilities to testify on account of interest have long been abolished. (Evid. Code, § 700; Davis v. Davis, supra, 26 Cal. at p. 35; II Wigmore, Evidence (3d ed. 1940) Testimonial Qualifications, § 488, p. 525, fn. 2.) Having become a part of the substantive law of wills, Probate Code section 51, on the other hand, survives. (See Evans, supra, 25 Mich.L.Rev. at pp. 238–239; II Wigmore, supra, § 582, pp. 722–723.) Our task is to ascertain and effectuate its present purpose. * * * When a court seeks to interpret legislation, "the various parts of a statutory enactment must be harmonized by considering the particular clause or section in the context of the statutory framework as a whole." (Moyer v. Workmen's Comp. Appeals Bd. (1973) 10 Cal.3d 222, 230 [110 Cal.Rptr. 144, 514 P.2d 1224].) We therefore turn to the Probate Code.

In order to establish a will as genuine, it is not always necessary that each and every one of the subscribing witnesses testify in court. (Prob. Code, §§ 329, 372.) Moreover, Probate Code section 51 does not by its terms preclude any witness from testifying; nor does the section void the interest of a subscribing witness when "two other and disinterested" witnesses have also subscribed the will. It is therefore entirely conceivable and perfectly consistent with the statutory scheme that a will might be proved on the sole testimony of a subscribing witness who is named in the will as a beneficiary; and if the will had been attested by "two other and disinterested subscribing witnesses," the interested witness whose sole testimony established the will would also be permitted to take his gift, as provided in the instrument. (Prob. Code, §§ 51, 329, 372.) If Probate Code section 51 serves any purpose under such circumstances, its purpose must necessarily have been accomplished before the will was offered for probate. Otherwise, in its statutory context, the provision would have no effect at all.

The quintessential function of a subscribing witness is performed when the will is executed. (Prob. Code, § 50; Estate of LaMont (1952) 39 Cal.2d 566, 569 [248 P.2d 1].) We believe that Probate Code section 51 looks in its operation solely to that time. (See 2 Bowe-Parker: Page on Wills, *supra*, § 19.85, p. 185, and § 19.102, pp. 204–205; Evans, *supra*, 25 Mich.L.Rev. at p. 238.) The section operates to ensure that at least two of the subscribing witnesses are disinterested. Although disinterest may be a token of credibility, as at common law, it also connotes an absence of selfish motives. We conclude that the purpose of the statute is to protect the testator from fraud and undue influence at the very moment when he executes his will, by ensuring that at least two persons are present "who would not be financially motivated to join in a scheme to procure the execution of a spurious will by dishonest methods, and who therefore presumably might be led by human impulses of fairness to resist the efforts of others in that direction." (Gulliver & Tilson, Classification of Gratuitous Transfers (1941) 51 Yale L.J. 1, 11. See also 2 Bowe-Parker: Page on Wills, *supra*, § 19.74, p. 173.) No other possible construction which has been brought to our attention squares so closely with the statutory framework. * * * We cannot ignore what the statute commands, however, "merely because we do not agree that the statute as written is wise or beneficial legislation." (Estate of Carter (1935) 9 Cal.App.2d 714, 718 [50 P.2d 1057].) Any remedial change must come from the Legislature.

That portion of the judgment from which this appeal is taken is therefore reversed. * * *

Notes

As may be seen from the statutes that precede the *Parsons* decision, states either do not require that the witness be disinterested, *see, e.g.*, CAL. PROB. CODE § 6112 (West 2019), or they simply purge the benefit that the witness would receive if the will were probated. Nonetheless, the witness will be able to take whatever he or she would take under intestacy, and the statute allows the witness to count as to the validity of the will itself, *see, e.g.*, N.Y. Est., Powers & Trusts L. § 3-3.2. Even if purging does occur, only the "benefit" that the witness would receive is purged, not the entire bequest. Of course, if there are an excess number of witnesses, the witness will be able to take his or her full share without purging, since his or her signature was not required for validity. California provides a unique approach in that it creates a rebuttable presumption that the bequest was a result of undue influence, duress, fraud, or menace, unless the beneficiary is in a fiduciary capacity. *See* Cal. Prob. Code § 6112. If the witness is unable to rebut the presumption, the witness is still valid as a witness but he or she only takes what he or she would take from the decedent under intestate succession. Nonetheless, the witness still counts for validity. Even after this, a will contest may still be brought to argue that the witness — solely as a legatee — exercised undue influence, menace, fraud, or duress upon the decedent. These intentionalities will be discussed, *infra*.

D. Compliance Devices

1. Substantial Compliance

In re Alleged Will of Ranney

Supreme Court of New Jersey, 1991
124 N.J. 1, 589 A.2d 1339

POLLOCK, J. [delivered the opinion of the court.]

The sole issue is whether an instrument purporting to be a last will and testament that includes the signature of two witnesses on an attached self-proving affidavit, but not on the will itself, should be admitted to probate. At issue is the will of Russell G. Ranney. The Monmouth County Surrogate ordered probate of the will, but the Superior Court, Law Division, Probate Part, reversed, ruling that the will did not contain the signatures of two witnesses as required by N.J.S.A. 3B:3-2. The Appellate Division found that the self-proving affidavit formed part of the will and, therefore, that the witnesses had signed the will as required by the statute. 240 N.J.Super. 337, 573 A.2d 467 (1990). It reversed the judgment of the Law Division and remanded the matter for a plenary hearing on the issue of execution. We granted the contestant's petition for certification, 122 N.J. 163, 584 A.2d 230 (1990), and now affirm the judgment of the Appellate Division.

* * *

The following facts emerge from the uncontested affidavits submitted in support of probate of the will. On October 26, 1982, Russell and his wife, Betty (now known as Betty McGregor), visited the law offices of Kantor, Mandia, and Schuster to execute their wills. Russell's will consisted of four pages and a fifth page containing a self-proving affidavit, entitled "ACKNOWLEDGMENT AND AFFIDAVIT RELATING TO EXECUTION OF WILL." The pages of Russell's will were neither numbered nor attached before execution. After Russell and Betty had reviewed their wills, they and their attorney, Robert Kantor, proceeded to a conference room, where they were joined by Kantor's partner John Schuster III and by two secretaries, Laura Stout and Carmella Mattox, who was also a notary.

Consistent with his usual practice, Kantor asked Russell if the instrument represented Russell's will and if Russell wanted Schuster and Stout to act as witnesses. Russell answered both questions affirmatively, and signed the will on the fourth page:

> IN WITNESS WHEREOF, I have hereunto set my hand and seal this 26th day of October, One Thousand Nine Hundred and Eighty Two.
>
> /s/   Russell G. Ranney

/s/   Russell G. Ranney

No one else signed the fourth page of the will. Russell, followed by Schuster and Stout, then signed the self-proving affidavit on the fifth page. Both Schuster and Stout believed that they were signing and attesting the will when they signed the affidavit. Furthermore, both Kantor, who had supervised the similar execution of many wills, and Schuster believed that the witnesses' signatures on the "Acknowledgment and Affidavit" complied with the attestation requirements of N.J.S.A. 3B:3-2. Mattox, whose practice was to notarize a document only if she witnessed the signature, notarized all the signatures.

After execution of the will, Stout stapled its four pages to the self-proving affidavit. The fifth and critical page reads:

ACKNOWLEDGMENT AND AFFIDAVIT RELATING TO EXECUTION OF WILL

STATE OF NEW JERSEY

> ss.

COUNTY OF MONMOUTH

> RUSSELL G. RANNEY, JOHN SCHUSTER III, and LAURA J. STOUT, the Testator and the witnesses, respectively whose names are signed to the attached instrument, being first duly sworn, do hereby declare to the undersigned authority that the Testator signed and executed the instrument as his Last Will and Testament and that he signed willingly and that he executed it as his free and voluntary act for the purposes therein expressed; and that each witness states that he or she signed the Will as witnesses in the presence and hearing of the Testator and that to the best of his or her knowledge, the Testator was at the time 18 or more years of age, of sound mind and under no constraint or undue influence.
>
> /s/   Russell G. Ranney

RUSSELL G. RANNEY

/s/   John Schuster III

/s/   Laura J. Stout

Subscribed, sworn to, and acknowledged before me, by Russell G. Ranney, the Testator, and subscribed and sworn to before me by JOHN SCHUSTER III and LAURA J. STOUT, witnesses, this 26 day of October 1982.

/s/   Carmella Mattox

Notary

The acknowledgment and affidavit is almost identical to the language suggested by N.J.S.A. 3B:3-5 for a self-proving affidavit signed subsequent to the time of execution. The form for making a will self-proved at the time of execution, as occurred here, is set forth in the preceding section, N.J.S.A. 3B:3-4. Although the subject affidavit was executed simultaneously with the execution of the will, the affidavit refers to the execution of the will in the past tense and incorrectly states that the witnesses had already signed the will.

Immediately after the execution of Russell's will, Betty executed her will in the presence of the same witnesses. As with Russell's will, Schuster and Stout signed the page containing the self-proving affidavit, but did not sign the will. Betty's will contained somewhat different dispositive provisions, and each page bore a legend identifying it as one page of "a three page will." The acknowledgment and affidavit, which appeared on the fourth page of the document, bore the legend "attached to a three page will."

Russell's will gives Betty a life estate in their apartment in a building at 111 Avenue of Two Rivers in Rumson, the rental income from other apartments in that building, and the tuition and rental income from the Rumson Reading Institute, which was merged into the Ranney School after the execution of Russell's will. The will further directs that on Betty's death, the Avenue of Two Rivers property and the proceeds of the Institute are to be turned over to the trustees of the Ranney School. Additionally, Betty receives all of Russell's personal property except that necessary for the operation of the Institute.

The residue of Russell's estate is to be paid in trust to Betty, Kantor, and Henry Bass, Russell's son-in-law, who were also appointed as executors. Betty and Harland Ranney and Suzanne Bass, Russell's two children, are to receive thirty-two percent each of the trust income, and are to share equally the net income from the operation of Ransco Corporation. Nancy Orlow, Betty's daughter and Russell's step-daughter, is to receive the remaining four percent of the trust income. Russell's will provides further that after Betty's death the income from Ransco Corporation is to be distributed equally between Harland Ranney and Suzanne Bass, and on their deaths is to be distributed to the Ranney School.

Russell died on April 4, 1987, and the Monmouth County Surrogate admitted the will to probate on April 21, 1987. Kantor represented Betty during the probate proceedings, but on March 8, 1988, he was disbarred for reasons unrelated to this case. See In re Kantor, 486 U.S. 1030, 108 S. Ct. 2010 (1988). Subsequently, Betty retained new counsel and contested the probate of Russell's will. She did not, however, assert that the will was the product of fraud or undue influence. Nor did she contend that it failed to express Russell's intent. Her sole challenge was that the will failed to comply literally with the formalities of N.J.S.A. 3B:3-2. Suzanne R. Bass, Harland Ranney, Henry Bass, and the Ranney School urged that the will be admitted to probate.

Without taking any testimony, the Law Division heard the matter on the return date of Betty's order to show cause. The court was satisfied that the will was Russell's last will and testament, but felt constrained to deny probate because the attesting witnesses had not strictly complied with the requirements of N.J.S.A. 3B:3-2.

Although the Appellate Division "decline[d] to hold that the placement of the witnesses' signatures is immaterial," 240 N.J.Super. at 344, 573 A.2d 467, it ruled that the self-proving affidavit was part of the will and that the witnesses' signatures on the affidavit constituted signatures on the will, *id.* at 344–45, 573 A.2d 467. Treating Russell's will as if it contained a defective attestation clause, the court remanded for a hearing to determine whether Russell had executed the document as his will, whether Schuster and Stout had signed the self-proving affidavit in response to Russell's request to witness the will, and whether they had witnessed either Russell's signature or his acknowledgment of that signature. *Id.* at 345, 573 A.2d 467.

We disagree with the Appellate Division that signatures on the subsequently-executed self-proving affidavit literally satisfied the requirements of N.J.S.A. 3B:3-2 as signatures on a will. We further hold, however, that the will may be admitted to probate if it substantially complies with these requirements.

* * *

The first question is whether Russell's will literally complies with the requirements of N.J.S.A. 3B:3-2, which provides:

> [E]very will shall be in writing, signed by the testator or in his name by some other person in his presence and at his direction, and shall be signed by at least two persons each of whom witnessed either the signing or the testator's acknowledgment of the signature or of the will.

* * *

Other states have recognized that a will failing to satisfy the attestation requirements should not be denied probate when the witnesses have substantially complied with those requirements and the testator clearly intended to make a will. See, *e.g.*, In re LaMont's Estate, 39 Cal.2d 566, 569–70, 248 P.2d 1, 2–3 (1952) (signature of witness substantially complied with execution requirements even if witness thought he was signing as executor); In re Estate of Petty, *supra*, 227 Kan. at 702–03, 608 P.2d at 992–93 (witnesses' signatures on self-proving affidavit substantially comply with attestation requirements); Smith v. Neikirk, 548 S.W.2d 156, 158 (Ky.Ct.App.1977) (will substantially satisfies statutory requirements even though witness turned back on testator at moment of signing and another witness signed as notary); In re Will of Kiefer, 78 Misc.2d 262, 264, 356 N.Y.S.2d 520, 522–23 (Sur.1974) (will admitted to probate when only one of two witnesses signed); see also 2 Bowe & Parker, Page on Wills § 19.4 nn. 15–21 (1960) (collecting cases applying rule of substantial compliance).

Scholars also have supported the doctrine of substantial compliance. Langbein, Substantial Compliance with the Wills Act, 88 Harv.L.Rev. 489 (1975); Nelson & Starck, Formalities and Formalism: A Critical Look at the Execution of Wills, 6 Pepperdine L.Rev. 331, 356 (1979). At the 1990 annual conference, the Commissioners on Uniform State Laws added a section to the Uniform Probate Code explicitly advocating the adoption of the doctrine. Uniform Probate Code § 2-503 (National Conference of Commissioners on Uniform State Laws 1990). That section, 2-503, provides:

> Although a document * * * was not executed in compliance with § 2-502 [enumerating the wills formalities], the document * * * is treated as if it had been executed in compliance with that section if the proponent of the document * * * establishes by clear and convincing evidence that the decedent intended the document to constitute (i) the decedent's will * * *.

In the 1990 edition of the Restatement (Second) of Property (Donative Transfers) (Restatement), moreover, the American Law Institute encourages courts to permit probate of wills that substantially comply with will formalities. § 33.1 comment g (Tentative Draft No. 13) (approved by the American Law Institute at 1990 annual meeting). The Restatement concludes that in the absence of legislative action, courts "should apply a rule of excused noncompliance, under which a will is found validly executed if the proponent establishes by clear and convincing evidence that the decedent intended the document to constitute his or her will." *Ibid.* Thus, courts and scholars have determined that substantial compliance better serves the goals of statutory formalities by permitting probate of formally-defective wills that nevertheless represent the intent of the testator.

* * *

Substantial compliance is a functional rule designed to cure the inequity caused by the "harsh and relentless formalism" of the law of wills. Langbein, *supra*, 88 Harv.L.Rev. at 489; see also L. Waggoner, R. Wellman, G. Alexander & M. Fellows, Family Property Law: Wills, Trusts and Future Interests 32–35 (Tentative Draft 1990) (discussing genesis of substantial compliance doctrine). The underlying rationale is that the

> finding of a formal defect should lead not to automatic invalidity, but to a further inquiry: does the noncomplying document express the decedent's testamentary intent, and does its form sufficiently approximate Wills Act formality to enable the court to conclude that it serves the purposes of the Wills Act? [Langbein, *supra*, 88 Harv.L.Rev. at 489.]

Scholars have identified various reasons for formalities in the execution of wills. The primary purpose of those formalities is to ensure that the document reflects the uncoerced intent of the testator. *Id.* at 492; Mann, *supra*, 63 Wash.U.L.Q. at 49. Requirements that the will be in writing and signed by the testator also serve an evidentiary function by providing courts with reliable evidence of the terms of the will and of the testamentary intent. Gulliver & Tilson, Classification of Gratuitous Transfers, 51 Yale L.J. 1, 6–7 (1941). Additionally, attestation requirements prevent fraud and undue influence. *Id.* at 9–10; In re Estate of Peters, *supra*, 107 N.J. at 276, 526 A.2d 1005. Further, the formalities perform a "channeling function" by requiring a certain degree of uniformity in the organization, language, and content of wills. Langbein, *supra*, 88 Harv.L.Rev. at 494. Finally, the ceremony serves as a ritual that impresses the testator with the seriousness of the occasion. Gulliver & Tilson, *supra*, 51 Yale L.J. at 5. * * *

Concerned about inequities resulting from excessive adherence to formalism, the Commissioners on Uniform State Laws proposed the Uniform Probate Code. The goals of the Code were to simplify the execution of wills, Uniform Probate Code, art. 2, pt. 5, General Comment at 46 (1974), and to recognize the intent of the testator in the distribution of his property, *id.* at § 1-102(b)(2). Consequently, the Commissioners minimized the formalities of execution and diminished "the ceremonial value of attestation." Langbein, *supra*, 88 Harv.L.Rev. at 510–11. Responding to similar concerns in 1977, the New Jersey Legislature adopted a variation of the Uniform Probate Code that differed significantly from its pre-Code predecessor. 1977 N.J. Laws, ch. 412, § 1; see In re Estate of Peters, *supra*, 107 N.J. at 271, 526 A.2d 1005. Thus, N.J.S.A. 3B:3-2, like its identical 1977 counterpart, N.J.S.A. 3A:2A-4, does not require that witnesses sign in the presence of the testator and of each other. In re Estate of Peters, *supra*, 107 N.J. at 273, 526 A.2d 1005. The 1977 amendments also removed the interested-witness provisions, N.J.S.A. 3A:2A-7, with the result that a beneficiary who acts as a witness is no longer prevented from taking under a will, N.J.S.A. 3B:3-8. As a result of those amendments, moreover, unwitnessed holographic wills could be admitted to probate. N.J.S.A. 3A:2A-5. Under the current provision, N.J.S.A. 3B:3-3, a holographic will is valid whether or not witnessed, so long as the signature and material provisions of the will are in the handwriting of the testator. N.J.S.A. 3B:3-3. The approval of unwitnessed holographic wills, like the diminution of attestation requirements, reflects a more relaxed attitude toward the execution of wills.

Legislative history confirms that N.J.S.A. 3B:3-2 was enacted to free will execution from the ritualism of pre-Code law and to prevent technical defects from invalidating otherwise valid wills. Senate Judiciary Committee Public Hearing on Uniform Probate Code Bills at 20 (comments of Harrison Durand) (reduction of statutory formalities meant to prevent failure of testamentary plans); see In re Estate of Peters, *supra*, 107 N.J. at 272 n. 2, 526 A.2d 1005 (noting that former statute often resulted in wills being refused probate because some formality not followed). Generally, when strict construction would frustrate the purposes of the statute, the spirit of the law should control over its letter. New Jersey Builders, Owners & Managers Ass'n v. Blair, 60 N.J. 330, 338, 288 A.2d 855 (1972). Accordingly, we believe that the Legislature did not intend that a will should be denied probate because the witnesses signed in the wrong place.

The execution of a last will and testament, however, remains a solemn event. A careful practitioner will still observe the formalities surrounding the execution of wills. When formal defects occur, proponents should prove by clear and convincing evidence that the will substantially complies with statutory requirements.

See Uniform Probate Code, *supra*, §2-503; Restatement, *supra*, §33.1 comment g. Our adoption of the doctrine of substantial compliance should not be construed as an invitation either to carelessness or chicanery. The purpose of the doctrine is to remove procedural peccadillos as a bar to probate.

Furthermore, as previously described, ante at 1342–1343, a subsequently-signed self-proving affidavit serves a unique function in the probate of wills. We are reluctant to permit the signatures on such an affidavit both to validate the execution of the will and to render the will self-proving. Accordingly, if the witnesses, with the intent to attest, sign a self-proving affidavit, but do not sign the will or an attestation clause, clear and convincing evidence of their intent should be adduced to establish substantial compliance with the statute. For that reason, probate in these circumstances should proceed in solemn form. See N.J.S.A. 3B:3-23; R. 4:84-1. Probate in solemn form, which is an added precaution to assure proof of valid execution, may be initiated on an order to show cause, R. 4:84-1(b), and need not unduly delay probate of a qualified will.

* * *

The record suggests that the proffered instrument is the will of Russell Ranney, that he signed it voluntarily, that Schuster and Stout signed the self-proving affidavit at Russell's request, and that they witnessed his signature. Furthermore, Betty has certified that Russell executed the will and that she is unaware of the existence of any other will. Before us, however, her attorney questions whether Russell "actually signed" the will. If, after conducting a hearing in solemn form, the trial court is satisfied that the execution of the will substantially complies with the statutory requirements, it may reinstate the judgment of the Surrogate admitting the will to probate.

Following the judgment of the Appellate Division, this Court amended the Rules of Civil Procedure pertaining to probate practice. Those amendments resulted in the allocation of the probate jurisdiction of the Chancery Division to the Chancery Division, Probate Part. See R. 4:83.

The judgment of the Appellate Division is affirmed, and the matter is remanded to the Chancery Division, Probate Part.

For affirmance and remandment—Justices CLIFFORD, HANDLER, POLLOCK, O'HERN, GARIBALDI, and STEIN—6.

Opposed—None.

Uniform Probate Code (2019)

§2-503. Harmless Error.

Although a document or writing added upon a document was not executed in compliance with Section 2-502, the document or writing is treated as if it had been executed in compliance with that section if the proponent of the document or writing establishes by clear and convincing evidence that the decedent intended the document or writing to constitute:

(1) the decedent's will,

(2) a partial or complete revocation of the will,

(3) an addition to or an alteration of the will, or

(4) a partial or complete revival of his [or her] formerly revoked will or of a formerly revoked portion of the will.

§ 2-504. Self-Proved Will.

(a) A will that is executed with attesting witnesses may be simultaneously executed, attested, and made self-proved, by acknowledgment thereof by the testator and affidavits of the witnesses, each made before an officer authorized to administer oaths under the laws of the state in which execution occurs and evidenced by the officer's certificate, under official seal * * *.

(b) A will that is executed with attesting witnesses may be made self-proved at any time after its execution by the acknowledgment thereof by the testator and the affidavits of the witnesses, each made before an officer authorized to administer oaths under the laws of the state in which the acknowledgment occurs and evidenced by the officer's certificate, under official seal, attached or annexed to the will * * *.

(c) A signature affixed to a self-proving affidavit attached to a will is considered a signature affixed to the will, if necessary to prove the will's due execution.

2. Self-Proved Will

The attorney who supervised the execution of the Last Will and Testament in the *Ranney* decision utilized a statutory form known as a self-proved will. *See* UNIF. PROB. CODE § 2-504. Comments to the Uniform Probate Code provision state that a "self-proved will may be admitted to probate as provided in Sections 3-303, 3-405, and 3-406 without the testimony of any attesting witness. . . ." *See* UNIF. PROB. CODE § 2-504, cmt. But the true value of a self-proved Last Will and Testament lies in the provision of Unif. Prob. Code § 3-406(1), which states:

> In a contested case in which the proper execution of a will is at issue, the following rules apply: (1) If the will is self-proved pursuant to Section 2-504, the will satisfies the requirements for execution without the testimony of any attesting witness, upon filing the will and the acknowledgement and affidavits annexed or attached to it, unless there is evidence of fraud or forgery affecting the acknowledgement or affidavit.

Therefore, if the Last Will and Testament is validly self-proved and there is an absence of fraud or forgery, the *formalities* associated with the execution of the Will become irrebuttable. *Intentionalities*, such as undue influence, lack of testamentary capacity, or delusion, may still provide a sufficient ground for contest, but the formalities recited in the self-proved affidavit are irrebuttable.

An attestation clause in any Last Will and Testament may recite the formalities that were executed. But since there is no notary public, and if the state does not permit self-proved execution, the attestation clause provides only a rebuttable presumption that the formalities recited were actually performed. Likewise, only the formalities recited are rebuttable; any intentionalities may be litigated.

The following Uniform Probate Code provisions describe what occurs when a Will is not self-proved, or if a Will is validly self-proved in one state but must be probated in another. Note that there are many instances of international Last Wills and Testaments, and the Uniform Probate Code addresses the validity requirements for these.

Uniform Probate Code (2019)

§ 3-406. Formal Testacy Proceedings; Contested Cases.

In a contested case in which the proper execution of a will is at issue, the following rules apply:

(1) If the will is self-proved pursuant to Section 2-504, the will satisfies the requirements for execution without the testimony of any attesting witness, upon filing the will and the acknowledgment and affidavits annexed or attached to it, unless there is evidence of fraud or forgery affecting the acknowledgment or affidavit.

(2) If the will is notarized pursuant to Section 2-502(a)(3)(B), but not self-proved, there is a rebuttable presumption that the will satisfies the requirements for execution upon filing the will.

(3) If the will is witnessed pursuant to Section 2-502(a)(3)(A), but not notarized or self-proved, the testimony of at least one of the attesting witnesses is required to establish proper execution if the witness is within this state, competent, and able to testify. Proper execution may be established by other evidence, including an affidavit of an attesting witness. An attestation clause that is signed by the attesting witnesses raises a rebuttable presumption that the events recited in the clause occurred.

3. Changing Jurisdictions

Uniform Probate Code (2019)

§ 2-506. Choice of Law as to Execution.

A written will is valid if executed in compliance with Section 2-502 or 2-503 or if its execution complies with the law at the time of execution of the place where the will is executed, or of the law of the place where at the time of execution or at the time of death the testator is domiciled, has a place of abode, or is a national.

§ 2-1002. International Will; Validity.

(a) A will shall be valid as regards form, irrespective particularly of the place where it is made, of the location of the assets and of the nationality, domicile, or residence of the testator, if it is made in the form of an international will complying with the requirements of this [part].

(b) The invalidity of the will as an international will shall not affect its formal validity as a will of another kind.

(c) This [part] shall not apply to the form of testamentary dispositions made by two or more persons in one instrument.

§ 2-1003. International Will; Requirements.

(a) The will shall be made in writing. It need not be written by the testator himself. It may be written in any language, by hand or by any other means.

(b) The testator shall declare in the presence of two witnesses and of a person authorized to act in connection with international wills that the document is his will and that he knows the contents thereof. The testator need not inform the witnesses, or the authorized person, of the contents of the will.

(c) In the presence of the witnesses, and of the authorized person, the testator shall sign the will or, if he has previously signed it, shall acknowledge his signature.

(d) When the testator is unable to sign, the absence of his signature does not affect the validity of the international will if the testator indicates the reason for his inability to sign and the authorized person makes note thereof on the will. In these cases, it is permissible for any other person present, including the authorized person or one of the witnesses, at the direction of the testator to sign the testator's name for him, if the authorized person makes note of this also on the will, but it is not required that any person sign the testator's name for him.

(e) The witnesses and the authorized person shall there and then attest the will by signing in the presence of the testator.

§ 2-1007. International Will; Revocation.

The international will shall be subject to the ordinary rules of revocation of wills.

III. Intentionalities

Proper intent is a necessary complement to the testamentary formalities previously discussed. Contest of the will is always based in either a deficiency in formalities or intentionalities. Furthermore, this deficiency must exist at the moment of execution of the will. In an effort to avoid formalism pertaining to formalities, courts and legislatures adopted "harmless error" and its requirement of clear and convincing evidence. Additionally we have discussed choice of law statutes to accommodate formality deficiencies and self-proved affidavits to confer irrebuttability on formalities. Is there something comparable for intentionalities? Perhaps.

A few states have enacted statutes permitting pre-mortem probate, which would allow a testator to probate his or her will *prior to death* and make irrebuttable issues pertaining to fraud, undue influence, testamentary capacity, and intent that this be a will. For example, New Hampshire permits proof of a will during life whereby an individual may commence a judicial proceeding to determine the validity of his or her will during lifetime, subject only to the will's subsequent modification or revocation. The action must be commenced by the person and not by an entity or person with an interest in the estate. But each interested person must receive notice of the petition, and the burden of proof is upon the petitioner to establish the validity of the will. *See* N.H. Rev. Stat. § 552.18 (2019). Other states that have enacted pre-mortem statutes include: Alaska, Arkansas, Delaware, Hawaii, Nevada, North Carolina, North Dakota, and Ohio.

Increasingly states are attracted to the opportunity to prevent post-mortem litigation with pre-mortem probate. But not all commentators are favorable. *See, e.g.,* Jacob Arthur Bradley, Comment, *Antemortem Probate is a Bad Idea: Why Antemortem Probate Will Not Work and Should Not Work*, 85 Miss. L.J. 1431 (2017) (arguing that pre-mortem probate disregards the internal safeguards of probate). In 2009, New York City Bar's Committee on Trusts, Estates and Surrogate Courts opposed pre-mortem probate, in part, because it is viewed as a waste of judicial resources, stifling to persons not willing to offend the testator, and ineffective if testator becomes domiciled in another state. *See* Susan G. Thatch, *Ante-Mortem Probate in New Jersey—An Idea Resurrected?*, 39 Seton Hall Legis. J. 331, 346 (2015).

The following intentionalities involve medical testimony, judges and juries, bias, dashed expectations, sex and intrigue, and a sibling or two with more than one ax to grind. The practitioner's challenge is to best protect the intent of his or her client when drafting testamentary instruments.

A. Testamentary Intent

In re Estate of Beale

Supreme Court of Wisconsin, 1962
15 Wis. 2d 546, 113 N.W.2d 380

BROWN, Justice.

* * *

Appellant begins with the assertion that the 1959 will is an unnatural one in that it disinherited Beale's ten year old son. Then he states his proposition that 'proponents of an unnatural will have burden to give a reasonable explanation for its unnatural provisions.' The learned trial court filed a written decision which demonstrated the meticulous study which the court gave to the will itself and to the evidence adduced in the several hearings, and the court concluded that the will was not 'unnatural.' Thomas' inheritance was reduced by the 1959 will to a contingent remainder but whether this rendered the will an unnatural one seems to us to be immaterial in the absence of any contention by appellant that, because of testamentary incapacity, undue influence or other factors appearing in the evidence, the will does not express the testator's true desires and intent. There are present no such factors to impugn the conclusion that the 1959 will exactly stated Professor Beale's own wish and purpose in respect to provision for his son Thomas. As the provisions or the lack of them are within the permission of the law neither Beale nor anyone else has to justify them or please any other person. * * *

While appellant concedes, or at least does not dispute, that when Professor Beale signed the purported 1959 will he had testamentary capacity and was not subject to undue influence appellant vigorously denies that the 14 pages of the 1959 instrument were legally published and declared to be his will and legally signed and witnessed as such and, in the alternative, that these pages did not constitute his will at the moment of execution.

In this record there are a few indisputable facts. From them there are a number of conflicting inferences reasonably to be drawn.

It cannot be questioned that on June 16 or 17, 1959, Professor Beale dictated a 14 page Document in the form of a last will, revoking all prior wills; that his secretary typed the original will, with three carbon copies, and delivered all of them to him in loose-leaf form the afternoon of June 20th; that Beale was in New York City at the home of a friend, a professor of Columbia University, on the evening of June 21st and on that evening he exhibited 'a pile' of sheets of paper and declared to his three friends that this was his will and desired them to witness his will; that they saw him sign the sheet which was on top of the pile and that immediately thereafter, at his request, they signed as witnesses in his presence and in the presence of each other; that the place where they put their signatures was immediately below the usual testamentary clause declaring this to be Professor Beale's will; that none of the witnesses paid any detailed attention to the number of pages in the pile nor could they identify later any of the pages except the one where they had written their names; that when all four participants had signed, Beale put all papers in his briefcase and the meeting ended.

It is uncontradicted that on the next day, or shortly thereafter, Beale and his two sons left by plane for Moscow; that a few days after June 21st Mrs. Burleigh, Beale's secretary, received a letter from him on Columbia University note paper, bearing date June 21, 1959, mailed in New York or in London on a day not given; that the letter asked Mrs. Burleigh to make several changes in pages 12 and 13 of the will which she had previously typed, to carry out marginal penciled notes in Beale's handwriting on those pages; that enclosed with the letter were the original pages 12 and 13; that Mrs. Burleigh made the alterations as directed and mailed them back to him in Moscow; that these pages were later found in a sealed envelope addressed to Beale in Beale's handwriting and mailed from London, England to him at his Madison address.

There is nothing legally invalid in the execution of a will because the separate pages of the will have not been fastened together. It is a requirement, though, that all the pages be present at the time of execution. * * *

Appellant, however, has other shots in his locker, the first of which is that even if the entire 14 pages of the will, as originally typed, were before the testator and witnesses at the time of execution the fact that Beale so quickly chose to make changes in it must persuade the court that at the moment of execution Beale did not intend this to be his will, no matter what he may have declared. The burden is on appellant to show that although Beale had himself dictated this will in the very recent past and had declared it to his three friends to be his will, he had already changed his mind concerning it.

As before, the court might have drawn that inference but it was not compelled to do so. The trial court considered Beale's express declaration that this was his will as of that moment was entitled to the greater weight. That court said, in its written decision:

> 'The objectors contend that the proper *Animus Testandi* is lacking in this case. Such an objection cannot be sustained. It certainly cannot be said that a man who dictates a document consisting of fourteen pages which purports to be his last will and testament, takes the finished typewritten document from Madison, Wisconsin to New York City, secures three personal friends to witness the document, telling them it is his will, all of which takes place shortly before he is to take a long trip to a foreign land, lacks the necessary testamentary intent to make that document his last will. The necessary testamentary intent existed at the time the will was executed, and that is all that is required.'

The inference drawn by the trial court is reasonable and we must adopt its conclusion.

* * *

At least one more mystery appears worth mentioning, although in our view it presents no fact to affect the outcome:

A few days before Christmas, 1959, Beale, who had returned to Madison, directed Mrs. Burleigh to re-type the altered pages 12 and 13 on the same typewriter she had used when she first typed the will. We may guess that Beale wanted pages which did not show they had been tampered with, as was apparent on the two original sheets now showing erasures and re-typed corrections. We may guess, further, that Beale intended to insert in the will without discovery the new pages without republication and re-execution of the will. This is no more than guesswork and is of no consequence. Before Mrs. Burleigh typed the two new sheets Beale's death intervened on December 27, 1959. Whatever his purpose, nefarious or not, he did not accomplish it. Mrs. Burleigh had not begun this final typing when she was told that Professor Beale had died. She then typed the two pages as Professor Beale directed and gave them to Beale's son, Henry. There were then no marginal initials on them. These pages are in evidence and, although Professor Beale never in his life had them or saw them, his initials are now on the margin of each of these pages and, as Mrs. Burleigh testified, are in his handwriting.

We began with a consideration of the unnatural. At the end we are confronted by the supernatural. We consider ourselves fortunate that this weird addition to the facts turns out to be immaterial.

We conclude that the trial court's findings and conclusions are not against the great weight and the clear preponderance of the evidence and the judgment admitting the will to probate as the will existed when it was executed and as Mrs. Burleigh first typed it must be affirmed.

Judgment affirmed.

CURRIE, Justice (dissenting).

On the record here presented, the paramount issue is whether, at time of execution of the 1959 will, testator intended the then existing fourteen typewritten pages to be his will. As the majority opinion intimates, if it was testator's intent to keep the instrument ambulatory in character, so that from time to time he could substitute pages for any except the last, which bore the signature of himself and witnesses, then this instrument would not qualify as his last will and testament because the requisite testamentary intent would be lacking. The crucial piece of evidence on this issue is testator's letter of June 21, 1959, to Mrs. Burleigh forwarding for retyping the two pages on which he had made alterations. If this letter was written before testator and the witnesses affixed their signatures, it would carry great weight in establishing that testator had intended an ambulatory instrument.

The June 21st letter was written on Columbia University stationery. A reasonable inference is that he procured this stationery at the apartment of his friend, Professor Forcey, a member of the Columbia University faculty, and the host of the June 21st party given in honor of testator. However, Professor Forcey, who testified as a subscribing witness to the 1959 will, was asked no questions about furnishing stationery to testator or about whether he possessed any knowledge concerning the writing of the June 21st letter.

Forcey did testify that both Howard Kennedy Beale, Jr., and Henry Barton Beale were present with their father in the Forcey apartment at the June 21st party. Neither of these two sons of testator were called as witnesses at the trial. The general rule is that failure of a party to call a material witness within his control, or whom it would be more natural for such party to call than the opposing party, raises an inference against such party. Feldstein v. Harrington (1958), 4 Wis.2d 380, 388, 90 N.W.2d 566; 2 Wigmore, Evidence (3rd ed.), p. 162, et seq., secs. 285, 286. This rule is applicable in situations of family relationship, such as parent and child. Anno., 5 A.L.R.(2d) 893, 934. Thus, the failure to call either of these two sons as a witness raised an inference against the proponents of the 1959 will. However, the trial court's memorandum opinion does not comment upon the fact that these two older sons were not called to testify as to their knowledge with respect to the writing of the June 21st letter.

It may very well be that the *guardians ad litem* for all three sons interviewed the two older sons about the June 21st letter and found they possessed no knowledge or recollection with respect to their father writing it. However, this is a situation where the trial court might very well have drawn the opposite inference from that which it did. Additional testimony with respect to the June 21st letter might have tipped the scales the other way. This is very important considering the fact that a ten year old boy, who is a ward of the court, has been virtually disinherited by his father's will.

Under these circumstances I would exercise our discretionary power under sec. 251.09, Stats. to reverse and remand for the purpose of taking the testimony of the two older boys with respect to the June 21st letter.

I am authorized to state that DIETERICH, J., joins in this dissenting opinion.

Notes

The issue in *Beale* was whether the testator intended the assemblage of pages to be his Last Will and Testament or whether he intended it to be a draft of one that would follow. The difficulty of discerning the intent of a decedent is captured in will phrases such as: "I am going on a journey and may not return. If I do not, I leave everything to my adopted son." Eaton v. Brown, 193 U.S. 411, 24 S. Ct. 487 (1904). Did the testatrix intend this to be a term will, valid only for the length of her journey? Did the testatrix thus imply that if she does, in fact, return from the trip safely, the Last Will and Testament is no longer effective? Or was the trip merely an inducement for her to execute the will?

Problem

Decedent died leaving an executed Last Will and Testament that divided her estate differently from what she stated in the following letter, dated three years after the will was executed. The daughter who is named in the letter as beneficiary submitted the will as a holographic will, which is valid in that jurisdiction. Of course, the heirs under the executed will object, arguing that the letter is not a valid holograph. The letter reads:

"Dear Roselyn & Sid:

"Your letter really surprised me, do you think for one minute that I would be fool enough to leave anything to Steve & Susan? I will leave something for Judy because she is the only one who calls me and when she isn't too busy on a Sunday she comes to be with me for a couple of hours. Next Monday afternoon she wants to take me to Cherry Creek to lunch at a cafeteria. I haven't heard from or seen Steve & Susan since my Sams funaral [sic]. Whatever is left after I'm gone is all yours. So rest asured [sic] that I know where my belongings will go, to you and your family. Weather here is beautiful and mild in the 50s & 60s. I'm getting busy now with cleaning and preparing for Peasach. Shirley is having the first Seder and Bea has the second Seder as always. Nothing new here, my knee is fine, all is well, so I can't complain.

"Love to all, stay well all of you.

"Love, Mother."

How should the probate judge rule? Why? *See* Matter of Estate of Olachonsky, 735 P.2d 927 (Ill. Ct. App. 1987).

B. Testamentary Capacity

Barnes v. Marshall

Supreme Court of Missouri, 1971
467 S.W.2d 70

HOLMAN, Judge.

This action was filed to contest a will and two codicils executed by Dr. A. H. Marshall a short time before his death which occurred on July 29, 1968. The plaintiff is a daughter of the testator. The defendants are the beneficiaries of the alleged will. A number are relatives of testator, but many are religious, charitable, and fraternal organizations. A trial resulted in a verdict that the paper writings were not the last will and codicils of Dr. Marshall. A number of the defendants have appealed. We will hereinafter refer to the appellants as defendants. We have appellate jurisdiction because the will devises real estate and also because of the amount in dispute.

One of the 'Points Relied On' by defendants is that the verdict is against the greater weight of the credible evidence. Since this court will not weigh the evidence in a case of this nature this point, strictly speaking, would not present anything for review. However, in considering the argument under that point we have concluded that defendants actually intended to present the contention that plaintiff did not make a submissible case and that the trial court erred in not directing a verdict for defendants, and we will so consider the point. The petition charged that testator was not of sound mind and did not have the mental capacity to make a will. The transcript contains more than 1,100 pages and there are a large number of exhibits. We will state the facts as briefly as possible and we think they will clearly support our conclusion that the submission is amply supported by the evidence.

The will, executed April 30, 1968, made specific bequests of testator's home and office furniture and equipment. The remainder of the net estate was devised to trustees, with annual payments to be made from the income to various individuals, churches, charities, and fraternal organizations. Plaintiff, her husband and two children were to receive $5.00 each per year. The estate was appraised in the inventory at $525,400.

The Marshalls had three children: plaintiff who lived in St. Louis, Mary Taylor Myers who lived in Dexter, Missouri, and died in May 1965, and Anetta Ester Vogel who lived near Chicago and who died about a month after her father's death.

In stating the evidence offered by plaintiff we will deal specifically with five witnesses: three lay witnesses because of contentions concerning their testimony, hereinafter discussed, and the two medical witnesses because of the importance we attribute to their testimony. There were many other witnesses whose testimony we will endeavor to summarize in a general way.

Ward Barnes, husband of plaintiff, testified that he visited in the Marshall home frequently from the time of his marriage in 1930 until Dr. Marshall's death; that Mrs. Marshall was a very cultured, refined, patient, and accommodating woman;

that he spent a great deal of time with testator and soon learned that testator would dominate the conversation in accordance with a certain pattern; that testator told him that he discontinued his medical practice at the command of the Lord so that he might use his time in saving the nation and the world; that testator had told him 'that the Lord had revealed to him the secrets of heaven; that he was the only man on earth to whom the Lord had revealed these secrets; that he had told him that heaven was a glorious place and that when he went to heaven he would have a beautiful crown and a wonderful throne sitting next to Thee Lord. He said that there were three powers in heaven, the Lord, Thee Lord, and God, and he said that this throne that he would have would be on the right hand side of Thee Lord in heaven. He said that heaven was a wonderful place, Thee Lord had revealed to him that whatever pleasures man had on earth he would have in heaven. If it was whiskey, if it was gambling, if it was women, that these would be provided him.' He stated that testator had also told him that the Lord had given him a special power of calling upon the Lord to right the wrongs which people had done to him; that many times he related instances of various people whom he had 'turned over to the Lord' and the Lord had meted out justice at his instance by taking away the person's wealth, and usually that the person lost his health, had a long period of suffering, and eventually died; that when testator related stories about the men he had turned over to the Lord he would become highly emotional, would pound on the table with his fists, would call these men dirty profane names, his face would become flushed, and the veins in his neck would stand out; that testator had told him that he (testator) had run for Congress on two occasions and had run for President of the United States (although apparently never nominated by any party) on two or three occasions; that he had told him that 'if he were made President of the United States he would cancel all public debt, that he would call in all government bonds and discontinue the interest on all of these obligations, and that he would then print money and control the currency, and that he would kill the damn bankers and the crooks and the thieves that were robbing the people in political office and that the world would then be able to settle down and live in peace.' He stated that on one occasion testator took him to his office and showed him a number of young women who were mailing out material in the interest of his candidacy; that he had said it was costing him 'thousands of dollars to mail this material out, but the Lord had told him to do it and he had no right to go counter to what the Lord had told him to do.' He further stated that in one of his campaigns for President testator had purchased a new car and had many biblical quotations and sayings of his own printed all over the automobile; that he had observed him, campaigning from this car, at the corner of Grand and Lindell Boulevard in St. Louis.

Witness Barnes further testified that testator had told him that Mrs. Marshall had inherited a piece of land and that when it was sold he took part of the money and gave her a note for $3,500; that later Mrs. Marshall had pressed him for payment and had conferred with Moore Haw, an attorney, and that because of that testator had locked her out of the house; that Mrs. Marshall then filed a suit and caused him to pay her the $3,500; that eventually the Marshalls were reconciled and resumed their life together; that at the time Mrs. Marshall died he and plaintiff went immediately to Charleston and at testator's request plaintiff made the funeral arrangements; that testator went to his wife's bedroom and searched the room looking for money and called him and plaintiff in to help him; that he found only a few dollars and then became enraged, 'his fists clenched * * * his hands were shaking, his body was trembling; his face was red and he was — you could see he was in a terrible emotional state as he stood there shaking his fists and shouting. He said, 'I know she had more money than that. * * * Your mother made me pay and that scoundrel Moore Haw, the dirty, low down * * * made me pay that thirty-five hundred dollars,' and he said, 'I want my money back. I want you to give it to me." Witness further testified that of the $3,500 testator had paid his wife in 1941 Mrs. Marshall had given plaintiff $1,500; that from the time of his wife's death until his own death testator had frequently demanded that plaintiff send him $3,500 and stated that if she didn't he would cut her out of his will; that it was his opinion that from the time he first became acquainted with him until his death Dr. Marshall was not of sound mind.

Frank Eaves testified that he had known testator for about eight years before his death; that he was Plant Supervisor for Crenshaw Packing Company and that testator would come to the plant about once a week; that he had heard testator talk about having the Lord come down on people, making them suffer, and having them killed; that he said his furnace didn't work and he had the Lord put a curse on it and it had worked good ever since; that he said he 'talked directly to God and God told him things'; that when he would discuss subjects of that kind 'his face would get real red, his eyes would bug out, the vessels would stand out on his neck, he would slobber and shout, and pound on anything available'; that he would sometimes come in dressed in nothing but his nightgown and his house shoes; that on one occasion he came to the plant with nothing on but a housecoat; that he was talking about a rash on his body and opened his housecoat and exposed his private parts to the female secretary and others present. Mr. Eaves was of the opinion that testator was of unsound mind over the period he had known him.

William West testified that he was a drug clerk in the Myers Drug Store in Dexter; that he had known testator from 1951 until his death; that testator came in the drug store about once a month during that period; that he had heard testator say that he talked directly to the Lord and the Lord told him the things he was to do; that one of these was that he should save the world and should be prime minister of the United States; that he also talked about turning people over to the Lord for punishment and when he did so the Lord would mete out the punishment and the men would die, or lose their wealth or something of that nature; that when he would talk about such things he used loud abusive language, his face would be flushed, and he would pound the table; that at the funeral of testator's daughter, Mrs. Myers, he (the witness) started to assist Mrs. Marshall, who was then about 80 years old, out of her chair and Dr. Marshall 'slapped me on the arm and told me to keep my hands off of her'; that he was present when Mrs. Marshall was trying to get out of the car and in so doing exposed a portion of her leg and testator 'bawled her out for it.' Witness was of the opinion that testator, during the time he had known him, was of unsound mind.

Dr. Charles Rolwing testified that he first saw testator professionally in 1940; that at that time testator complained of heart trouble but he was unable to find any evidence of such; that he was of the opinion that he was then suffering from manic-depressive psychosis for which there is no cure and that it would gradually get worse; that he also attended testator from the first part of May 1968 until his death in July; that at that time he was suffering from a serious heart ailment; that he was at that time still suffering from manic-depressive psychosis; that he was of the opinion that on April 30, May 17, and May 24, 1968, testator was of unsound mind.

Plaintiff also presented the testimony of Dr. Paul Hartman, a specialist in psychiatry and neurology, who testified in response to a hypothetical question. This question hypothesized much of the evidence related by the other witnesses for plaintiff and utilizes ten pages of the transcript. In response thereto Dr. Hartman expressed the opinion that Dr. Marshall was of unsound mind on the dates he executed his will and codicils; that he would classify Dr. Marshall's mental disease as manic-depressive psychosis with paranoid tendencies; that it was his opinion that Dr. Marshall was incapable of generalized logical thinking.

In addition to the foregoing evidence plaintiff testified herself and offered more than a dozen other witnesses, all of whom related unusual conduct and statements of testator. Plaintiff also offered a large number of exhibits in the nature of letters from testator and various publications containing advertisements and statements written by testator. There was evidence that plaintiff had been a dutiful daughter, had been solicitous of testator and her mother, had visited them frequently and often would take prepared food which she knew they liked. A number of these witnesses testified that testator had told them of various men who had wronged him and that he had turned them over to the Lord who meted out punishment in the form of financial loss, illness, death, or all three; that when he would tell of these things he would speak loud, get excited, his face would become red, his eyes bulge out, and he would gesture violently; that testator was unreasonably jealous of his wife and often said that all women who wore short skirts, or smoked, were immoral.

There was testimony that on the Christmas before the death of his daughter, Mary Myers, the Myers and Barnes families ate Christmas dinner with the Marshalls, and after the dinner testator 'jumped on' Mary about her skirt being short and continued doing so until Mary became so upset that she and her husband had to leave.

A number of witnesses testified concerning the fact that testator would go to various public establishments dressed in his nightgown and bathrobe. An article written by testator and published in a local newspaper under date of June 4, 1942, under the heading of 'DR. MARSHALL SAYS,' contained the following: 'Providence they say always raises up a great leader in every crisis * * *. I am that great leader.

I am that prophet that Moses and all the other prophets have spoken about. I am the Messiah that the people of this world have been talking and praying about and believing and hoping that he would soon show up. I am the inspired prophet.'

In contending that plaintiff did not make a submissible case defendants point to the testimony of their witnesses to the effect that testator was of sound mind and was calm, quiet, and collected on the day the will was executed. The difficulty with that argument is that in determining this question 'we must disregard the evidence offered by defendants unless it aids plaintiffs' case, accept plaintiffs' evidence as true, and give them the benefit of every inference which may legitimately be drawn from it.' Sturm v. Routh, Mo.Sup., 373 S.W.2d 922, 923.

It is also contended that most of plaintiff's evidence dealt with testator's 'sickness, peculiarities, eccentricities, miserliness, neglect of person or clothing, forgetfulness, anger, high temper, unusual or peculiar political and religious views, jealousy, mistreatment of family, unusual moral views, and repeating of stories, which are not evidence of testamentary incapacity or of unsound mind.'

As we have indicated, we do not agree with defendants' contentions. We have stated a portion of the evidence and it need not be repeated here. It is sufficient to say that we think testator's stated views on government, religion, morals, and finances go beyond the classification of peculiarities and eccentricities and are sufficient evidence from which a jury could reasonably find he was of unsound mind. When we add the strong medical testimony to that of the lay witnesses there would seem to be no doubt that a submissible case was made.

Defendants also point out that there is evidence that a person suffering from manic-depressive psychosis has periods of normalcy between the abnormal periods of elation or depression and that testator was in a normal period at the time the will was executed. The mental condition of testator at the precise time the will was executed was a question for the jury to decide. The jury was obviously persuaded that he was not of sound mind and since there was evidence to support that verdict it is conclusive.

* * *

The next point briefed by defendants is that the court erred in permitting lay witnesses Ward Barnes, Frank Eaves, and William L. West to express an opinion that testator was of unsound mind. This for the reason that the facts related by those witnesses were not inconsistent with sanity and hence the necessary foundation was not established. The rule regarding the competency of lay witnesses to express an opinion on the issue as to whether a person is or is not of sound mind is that 'a lay witness is not competent to testify that, in the opinion of such witness, a person is of unsound mind or insane, without first relating the facts upon which such opinion is based; and, when the facts have been stated by such lay witness, unless such facts are inconsistent with such person's sanity, the opinion of such lay witness that the person under consideration was insane or of unsound mind, is not admissible in evidence and may not be received. * * * In this connection it has repeatedly been determined that evidence of sickness, old age, peculiarities, eccentricities in dress or oddities of habit, forgetfulness, inability to recognize friends, feebleness resulting from illness, and other facts or circumstances not inconsistent with the ability to understand the ordinary affairs of life, comprehend the nature and extent of one's property and the natural objects of his bounty, and which are not inconsistent with sanity, cannot be used as a basis for the opinion testimony of a lay witness that a person is of unsound mind or insane. * * * 'The rule is well settled that, ordinarily, before a lay witness will be permitted to give his opinion that a person is of unsound mind, he must first detail the facts upon which he bases such opinion, but if he expresses an opinion that such person is of sound mind, he is not required to detail the facts upon which he founds his opinion. The reason for the rule is obvious. An opinion that a person is of unsound mind is based upon abnormal or unnatural acts and conduct of such person, while an opinion of soundness of mind is founded upon the absence of such acts and conduct." Lee v. Ullery, 346 Mo. 236, 140 S.W.2d 5, l.c. 9, 10.

Because of this point we have heretofore detailed the testimony of these three witnesses in the factual statement and such need not be repeated here. We think it is obvious that each witness detailed sufficient facts upon which to base the opinion stated. Those facts went far beyond a mere showing of peculiarities and eccentricities. They were clearly inconsistent with the conclusion that testator was of sound mind. The facts detailed by these witnesses are quite different from those stated by the witnesses in Lewis v. McCullough, Mo.Sup., 413 S.W.2d 499, the case upon which defendants rely. * * *

The judgment is affirmed.

All concur.

Notes

In addition to mental capacity, the lack of testamentary capacity could occur because the testator was of insufficient age to execute a Last Will and Testament in that jurisdiction. Most states require that the testator be at least eighteen years-of-age. Lack of age and lack of the requisite mental capacity at the moment of execution would make the entire Last Will and Testament null and void. But the legal test for testamentary capacity is a minimal one. To make a valid will, it is sufficient that the testator "understands the nature of the business in which he is engaged and when making a will, has a recollection of the property he means to dispose of, the object or objects of his bounty, and how he wishes to dispose of his property." Milhoan v. Koenig, 196 W. Va. 163, 166, 469 S.E.2d 99, 102 (1996). This test may be met even when the testator is under guardianship or has been committed to a mental facility. *See, e.g., In re* Estate of Gentry, 32 Or. App. 45, 573 P.2d 322 (1978). Even if the testator lacks capacity, he or she may be within a "lucid interval" and, thus, possess capacity at the moment of execution but not otherwise. *See, e.g.,* Lee v. Lee, 337 So. 2d 713 (Miss. 1976); Daley v. Boroughs, 310 Ark. 274, 835 S.W.2d 858 (1992). Often it is the attorney who must make the initial and pivotal decision of whether the client possesses testamentary capacity; failure to inquire could raise professional responsibility consequences. *See, e.g.,* Logotheti v. Gordon, 414 Mass. 308, 607 N.E.2d 1015 (1993) (holding that "[a]n attorney owes to a client, or a potential client, for whom the drafting of a will is contemplated, a duty to be reasonably alert to indications that the client is incompetent or is subject to undue influence and, where indicated, to make reasonable inquiry and a reasonable determination in that regard"). Ethical ramifications arise from this responsibility. *See* Jan E. Rein, *Ethics and the Questionably Competent Client: What the Model Rules Say and Don't Say,* 9 STAN. L. & POL'Y REV. 241 (1998).

Most cases involving a lack of testamentary capacity, delusion, fraud, and undue influence involve a person who is older or, in some other way, seemingly more susceptible to issues of intentionality. Nonetheless, be mindful that "[t]he law does not withhold from the aged, the feeble, the weak-minded, the capricious, the notionate, the right to make a will, provided such person has a decided and rational desire as to the disposition of his property." Hill v. Deal, 185 Ga. 42, 46, 193 S.E. 858, 861 (1937). Clearly, the attorney who is asked to draft a will for a client has a duty to make a judgment regarding the ability of a client to properly state his or her wishes. This is a delicate task, but it seems that professional responsibility demands that any attorney have a process in place that would provide evidence for the attorney's belief that his or her client possessed capacity, was not acting under duress or undue influence, and was not being defrauded through the Last Will and Testament that the attorney prepared. For guidance in developing a plan, see Raymond C. O'Brien, *Attorney Responsibility and Client Incapacity,* 30 J. CONTEMP. HEALTH L. & POL'Y 59 (2013); Kristine S. Knaplund, *The Right of Privacy and America's Aging Population,* 86 DENV. U. L. REV. 439 (2009); Timothy P. O'Sullivan, *Family Harmony: An All Too Frequent Casualty of the Estate Planning Process,* 8 MARQ. ELDER'S ADVISOR 253 (2007); Jan E. Rein, *Ethics and the Questionably Competent Client: What the Model Rules Say and Don't Say,* 9 STAN. L. & POL'Y REV. 241 (1998). *See also* Celia R. Clark, *A Senior Trust,* 147 TRUSTS & ESTS. 29 (June 2008) (recommending that *inter vivos* "senior trusts" be created for vulnerable clients). "Senior trusts" would become irrevocable or unamenable when either the client dies or becomes disabled. The special trustee named in the trust instrument may then exercise discretion without concern for incapacity or removal by the settlor. The following are specific recommendations for the estate planning attorney to follow:

(1) Create a revocable trust or a joint tenancy rather than a Last Will and Testament. If notice is provided to the client's heirs at the time of creation, the statute of limitations should bar suits upon the subsequent death of the client;

(2) Couple any bequest to an heir with a "no contest" clause. Simply stated, if the clause is held to be effective, then the contestant risks losing the bequest if a contest is made and lost;

(3) Suggest to the client that he or she submit to using a Mini-Mental State Examination–short and easy questions that relate to the four issues involving testamentary capacity;

(4) Communicate with the client about what is happening and keep a record of what transpires;

(5) Consult with the client's physician with the client's permission;

(6) Videotape the execution of the Last Will and Testament;

(7) Select appropriate witnesses, persons who will be available and knowledgeable about the client's condition at the time of execution;

(8) Know the client so as to ascertain what the client wishes, not what the family wishes;

(9) Execute a series of Wills so if one is held invalid, a previous one with similar provisions could take its place; and

(10) Make a significant gift to an heir likely to contest on the day that the Will is executed. If the heir takes the check it will be difficult for the heir to argue that the client lacked capacity if on the same day, the client had the capacity to transfer assets adequately.

Lisa M. Stern, *An Ounce of Prevention*, 147 Trusts & Ests. 41 (Aug. 2008).

Once the proponent of the will can prove that the formalities have been performed, the persons seeking to challenge the testator's intentionalities at the time of execution has the burden to show that there was a lack of intentionalities. *See* Cal. Prob. Code § 8252(a) (West 2019); *Restatement (Third) of Property: Wills and Other Donative Transfers* § 8.1 cmt. F (2003). Once the contest is brought, a jury may play an instrumental role in any determination, but some states, like California, ban juries from will contest cases. *See* Cal. Prob. Code § 8252(b) (West 2019).

Sharon L. Klein, Sandra D. Glazier, Thomas M. Dixon & Thomas F. Sweeney
Confronting Undue Influence in Your Practice?
154 Trusts & Ests. 33, 37 (July 2015)

At the time of execution, speak with the individual in the presence of witnesses regarding his intentions and the contents of the documents. To the extent possible, avoid using leading questions that all for a 'yes/no' response. Also, ask questions in the presence of witnesses, which can establish capacity. One might even consider asking for witness memos and using professional witnesses (for example, attorneys, paralegals or financial advisors). If the planner is concerned about future power shifts further reducing the individual's ability to withstand influences, he may consider taking some prophylactic measures, such as including a corporate or other independent fiduciary as either a lifetime co-trustee or a trust protector to approve any amendment. Providing that a corporate trustee can only be removed and replaced by another corporate trustee might prevent an end-run around an estate plan by ensuring a neutral third party is always acting. Consider selecting a trust situs in a jurisdiction such as Delaware that permits notifying beneficiaries or heirs at law of a proposed plan while the grantor is alive. Such a pre-mortem notification procedure typically requires an immediate challenge to a proposed plan or otherwise bars a future challenge.

Uniform Probate Code (2019)

§ 3-407. [Formal Testacy Proceedings; Burdens in Contested Cases].

In contested cases, petitioners who seek to establish intestacy have the burden of establishing prima facie proof of death, venue, and heirship. Proponents of a will have the burden of establishing prima facie proof of due execution in all cases, and, if they are also petitioners, prima facie proof of death and venue. Contestants of a will have the burden of establishing lack of testamentary intent or capacity, undue influence, fraud, duress, mistake or revocation. Parties have the ultimate burden of persuasion as to matters with respect to which they have the initial burden of proof. If a will is opposed by the petition for probate of a later will revoking the former, it shall be determined first whether the later will is entitled to probate, and if a will is opposed by a petition for a declaration of intestacy, it shall be determined first whether the will is entitled to probate.

C. Delusion

In re Hargrove's Will

Supreme Court, Appellate Division, First Department, 1941
262 A.D. 202, 28 N.Y.S.2d 571, *aff'd* 288 N.Y. 604, 42 N.E.2d 608 (1942)

TOWNLEY, J.

The decree appealed from denies probate to the will of Ernest Temple Hargrove. This decree was based upon the verdict of the jury which by a vote of ten to two found the deceased lacking in testamentary capacity. The jury's finding was based upon its conclusion that the testator suffered from an insane delusion that two children born to his wife during their marriage were not his and that as a consequence the testator did not know the true objects of his bounty. The will made no provision for these children but left all of his property to Mrs. Clement Griscom 'as an inadequate acknowledgment of the lifelong kindness shown to me by my business associate and intimate personal friend, her late husband.'

With the exception of this claimed delusion about the paternity of his children there is no serious claim of mental deficiency. The testator appears to have been a very successful business man, capable of managing large interests with conspicuous success and equally successful in the management of many charitable and religious activities in which he became interested. He was active as president and head of the Griscom-Russell Company, manufacturers of heavy machinery, up to within a month of his death, on April 8, 1939. The instrument offered for probate was in his own handwriting and executed by him on December 17, 1923. Ten witnesses, all men of importance in New York city, testified that decedent was at all times of sound mind and a man of unusual intelligence and four of these witnesses were called by the contestants.

The only witnesses to the contrary were an alienist who had never seen him and the testator's divorced wife who had not seen him for thirty-one years prior to his death except for an accidental meeting in a book store twenty years prior to his death. As bearing on the credibility of the latter it is significant that she denied here that the testator prior to his death had ever accused her of being indiscreet, whereas she had obtained a Colorado divorce from the testator in which she alleged that about three years prior to the date of her complaint, the decedent had accused her of being indiscreet in her association with certain persons and that in November, 1905, he had also made similar charges. In that action the jury found the decedent guilty of the matters charged in the complaint.

The law is that assuming that decedent was mistaken in his belief that he was not the father of the children of his divorced wife, that fact would not necessarily establish testator's incapacity. The rule applicable to the determination of the question was clearly stated in Matter of White (121 N. Y. 406, 413) as follows: 'Delusion is insanity, where one persistently believes supposed facts, which have no real existence, except in his perverted imagination, and against all evidence and probability, and conducts himself, however logically, upon the assumption of their existence. That was so held in Seamen's Society v. Hopper [33 N. Y. 624]. But, if there are facts, however insufficient they may in reality be, from which a prejudiced, or a narrow or a bigoted mind might derive a particular idea, or belief, it cannot be said that the mind is diseased in that respect. The belief may be illogical, or preposterous, but it is not, therefore, evidence of insanity in the person. Persons do not always reason logically, or correctly, from facts, and that may be because of their prejudices, or of the perversity, or peculiar construction of their minds. Wills, however, do not depend for their validity upon the testator's ability to reason logically, or upon his freedom from prejudice.'

The question presented, therefore, is whether there is any rational basis, however slight, for the decedent's belief that he was not the father. The story of the married life of the Hargroves may be summarized as follows: The deceased married Aimee Neresheimer in 1899. For the next six years he traveled in Europe, Africa and Australia with her. A son was born in Brussels in February, 1902, and a daughter in Dresden in 1904. In 1905 the decedent and his children returned to the United States and took up a residence in Denver, Col. In Denver, the testator became interested in the business of his then father-in-law and in that connection met and became friendly with one Smith, a friend of his father-in-law and his attorney. In the latter part of 1906 the testator's wife asked him for a divorce, claiming incompatibility. This led to many conferences in which testator's father-in-law and Smith assumed to act as friendly advisers. An action for divorce on the ground of cruelty was brought. The entire proceeding from the service of process to the entry of judgment was accomplished in a single day. Within an hour after the entry of the decree Smith, whom decedent had consulted about his divorce, procured a divorce from his own wife and announced that he would marry the wife of the testator.

The conditions surrounding these decrees created a considerable scandal in Denver. Within a month Smith and the testator's wife were married at the alleged insistence of her father. The testator apparently did not discover the remarriage for some months. He then applied to have the divorce set aside on the ground of fraud and alleged that his wife prior thereto had been guilty of improper relations with Smith. This application was denied upon technical grounds. He thereafter left Denver and came to New York where he was befriended by Clement Griscom, became associated with him in business and died the president of his company. Mr. Griscom's wife is named as beneficiary in this will. Neither the divorced wife nor the children communicated with the deceased during the thirty-one years intervening before his death.

Decedent left an affidavit with his executor stating that his divorced wife had confessed to him that the children were not his and that he had satisfied himself that that was so. He spoke of this belief only to his intimate friends and then only when necessary. His entire conduct in this connection was that of a dignified considerate gentleman and there is nothing in connection therewith which justifies the belief that his opinion was based on an insane delusion. All of his reasons for his belief, of course, cannot be known. They relate to the intimate personal affairs incident to the marriage relation. When consideration is given, however, to his unfortunate experiences in connection with his divorce, the fact of his belief in his wife's infidelity certified to by her under oath in her divorce proceeding and confirmed by the formal affidavit left by him with his executor, it cannot be said that his belief on this subject was entirely without reason, although possibly mistaken.

Upon the foregoing facts the finding that the decedent lacked testamentary capacity cannot be sustained. The conclusion we have reached, however, must not be considered as involving any finding as to the legitimacy of the children involved. * * *

The decree so far as appealed from by the contestants should be affirmed. In so far as appealed from by the proponent, it should be reversed, with costs to said appellant payable out of the estate, and the will admitted to probate.

MARTIN, P. J., and CALLAHAN, J., concur.

GLENNON and DORE, JJ., dissent.

GLENNON, Justice (dissenting).

There is ample testimony in the record to support the verdict of the jury that Ernest Temple Hargrove, at the time of the execution of the paper offered for probate, was not of sound and disposing mind and memory. In the course of his charge to the jury, the surrogate clearly stated the issue between the parties to the will contest in the following language: 'You can well see that this question is a comparatively simple one. I do not mean by that that it may be simple for you to decide, but I think the issue is simple. It comes down to the issue as to whether or not Mrs. Neres did tell Mr. Hargrove that these children were not his, for of course, if she told him that, and she was the mother of these children, then of course he had ample basis in fact for his belief that these children were not his. However, if her testimony is truthful, that she never told him of this as he says she did, then if this was the mere creature of his imagination, you may find that he was suffering from an insane delusion on this subject.'

At the conclusion of the charge, counsel for the proponent said in part: 'With that addition, if your Honor please, the proponent is entirely satisfied with your Honor's charge.'

The evidence clearly shows that William Archibald Temple Hargrove, who was born in Brussels, Belgium, in February, 1902, is the legitimate son of Ernest Temple Hargrove, deceased, and the latter's former wife, Aimee Neres, and that Joan Leona Constance Hargrove, who was born on August 14, 1904, in Dresden, Germany, is the legitimate daughter of the same parents. At the outset it might be well to note that the son bears in part the given name of the decedent, whereas the daughter, as part of her name, was christened Constance, after the decedent's sister.

The decedent first became acquainted with Aimee Neres, nee Neresheimer, when she was about twelve years of age. At that time she lived with her parents in Bayside, Long Island.

When Mrs. Neres was fourteen years of age, in 1897, the decedent proposed marriage to her and took her to England, under the chaperonage of his sister Constance, to meet his parents. He repeated his proposal upon their return from England, but her father objected to the marriage at that time on account of her age and sent her to a convent in Canada, where she remained for a year and a half. When Mrs. Neres became sixteen years of age, the marriage took place.

They went to England on their honeymoon and thence to the Peace Conference at the Hague. In connection with his work, which we do not deem necessary to go into at this time, they traveled throughout the world. The testimony of Mrs. Neres indicates that their son was conceived in Australia and born in Brussels, while the daughter was conceived in Paris and born, as heretofore noted, in Dresden.

About 1905, they returned to the United States and went to Boulder, Col., to the home where Mrs. Neres' parents then resided and later they moved to Denver, where they took up a residence. We do not believe it necessary to refer at any length to the divorce which was obtained by Mrs. Neres in 1906, since the speed with which it was effected has been covered in the majority opinion.

In his application, sworn to by the decedent on December 12, 1907, to set aside the divorce which Mrs. Neres had obtained, the decedent said in part: 'That your petitioner then and there informed said Smith, as his said attorney, that such divorce proceedings would bring disgrace upon the children of said plaintiff and your petitioner, and that he, your petitioner, would resist such proceedings to the utmost, and asked said Smith to aid him in pacifying and conciliating said plaintiff in order to avoid said proposed action for divorce.'

It must be conceded that the children, to whom reference was made in the quoted sentence, were his son William and his daughter Joan, and still the decedent under date of February 20, 1920, made the following affidavit which appears in the record:

'ERNEST TEMPLE HARGROVE 10 Horatio Street New York

'Ernest Temple Hargrove of the city and county of New York, being duly sworn, deposeth and saith that he was married to a girl named Amy Neresheimer of Bayside, Long Island, toward the end of the year 1899, though he is not certain of this date; that he took this woman to Europe with him as his wife and that they also visited South Africa and Australia; that said woman gave birth to two children, the first a boy, born in Brussels, and the second a girl born near Dresden; that in 1894 or 1895, deponent took this woman with the two said children to Denver, Colorado, where her parents were then living; that deponent engaged in business with said woman's father, and with a Denver lawyer named Milton Smith; that within a year of their arrival in Denver, said woman declared her determination to obtain a divorce from deponent; that deponent, knowing she had no grounds for a divorce, thereupon requested said Milton Smith to speak to said woman and to tell her she could not obtain a divorce; that said Milton Smith, to the amazement of deponent, assured him that any woman could get a divorce in Colorado who for any reason whatever was dissatisfied with her husband, showing deponent law books and recent decisions to substantiate this statement; that said Milton Smith urged deponent, so as to avoid publicity and scandal, to concede said woman a divorce, stating to deponent that in all probability a reconciliation would take place in six months; that deponent was at last persuaded and that said woman obtained a decree of divorce within a few weeks thereafter; that within two weeks after said divorce had been obtained by her, deponent learned that Milton Smith had at the same time divorced his own wife, and that Milton Smith had at once married deponent's former wife; that deponent, realizing he had been tricked, was angry, and at an interview with his former wife insisted that she must confess the whole truth to deponent about the past; that said woman thereupon confessed that she had cohabited with a number of men, whose names she gave, after her marriage with deponent, and that two of these men, one a citizen of Chicago, whose name deponent has forgotten, and another a German doctor, whose name was Weidner, were respectively the fathers of her two children; said woman reminded deponent of certain facts, which at the time he had not understood, and which tended to prove that he himself could not have been the father of said children; that deponent shortly thereafter visited Chicago and accused said man, a citizen of Chicago, of being the father of the older of two said children; that said man confessed that he had cohabited with said woman and that said woman at that time had declared her intense desire to have a child by him and that they had cohabited together a number of times at her solicitation; that deponent later verified the other statements said woman made to him during said interview, and that deponent obtained absolute evidence that neither of said children was his; that deponent also investigated said woman's life prior to her marriage to him and learned that she had been common property in and around Bayside, Flushing, and other small towns on Long Island, prior to said marriage, and that she had been notorious as an immoral character; that deponent knows said woman to be grasping and unscrupulous, and that he makes this affidavit to facilitate the task of the executors of his will in the event that said woman or her children should dare to claim any share of deponent's estate in spite of the explicit terms of said will; and that deponent swears that said woman married deponent under false pretenses and by lying and by concealing vital facts, and that deponent has no children, by her or by any other woman.

'In testimony whereof, deponent hath hereunto subscribed his name and affixed his seal on this twentieth day of February in the year 1920.

'ERNEST TEMPLE HARGROVE.'

Since the jury had this exhibit before it, they must have realized that the alleged confession of Aimee Neres as to her intimacy with the citizen of Chicago, who might be styled as the forgotten man, and the German doctor, were the expressions of a mind afflicted with a delusion as to the paternity of his children who would be, under normal conditions, the natural objects of his bounty. If the vigorous denials of Aimee Neres as to these groundless charges of misconduct be cast aside, although the jury had the right to believe her denials and did so, we may ask when was the so-called confession obtained? Manifestly, it could not have been immediately subsequent to her marriage with Milton Smith since, as we have heretofore pointed out, in his affidavit of December, 1907, the decedent indicated that these, his two children, were then uppermost in his mind. Neither could it have been at the chance meeting in a book store in New York in September, 1921, where in the first instance the decedent failed to recognize his former wife and upon being apprised of her identity, the record shows that he fled. Furthermore, that meeting took place about a year after the affidavit of February 20, 1920, was sworn to.

The jury undoubtedly noted that part of the affidavit wherein the decedent referred to his investigations of Aimee Neres' life as a child and stated that she had been 'common property' in and around Bayside, Flushing, and other small towns on Long Island. The marriage it will be remembered took place when she was only sixteen years of age, very shortly after she left the school in Canada.

It seems almost absurd to believe that an intensely religious man, which concededly the decedent was, could have subscribed his name, affixed his seal and sworn to a document containing such outlandish statements if he was not suffering from an insane delusion concerning his children who normally would be the proper objects of his bounty.

We of the minority do not doubt for a moment that in other matters the decedent was capable of sound reasoning. He was, what might be termed, an outstanding success in the business world. Still we repeat that in so far as his children were concerned, he was suffering from an insane delusion. * * *

DORE, J., concurs.

Decree, so far as appealed from by the contestants, unanimously affirmed. Decree, so far as appealed from by the proponent, reversed, with costs to said appellant payable out of the estate, the will admitted to probate, and proceeding remitted to the Surrogate's Court in accordance with opinion.

Notes

Delusion is not the same as lack of testamentary capacity, although the two are closely related. While the lack of testamentary capacity at the time of the execution of the Last Will and Testament will invalidate the entire will, delusion will only invalidate the entire will if it can be shown that the delusion affected the entire disposition under that will. For an explanation of the difference between capacity and delusion, *see, e.g.*, Breeden v. Stone, 992 P.2d 1167, 1170–72 (Colo. 2000).

The New York court in *Hargrove's Will* held that there is no delusion if there is a rational basis for a testator's beliefs, permitting the questionable disposition to stand. However, as is indicated by the dissenting opinion, a delusion exists if any rational person, judging by the facts available, would have failed to come to the same conclusion. Thus, rather than viewing rationality through the eyes of the testator, it is preferable to examine the facts from the perspective of *any* rational person, not just the testator. This is a more objective approach and one suggested by the *Restatement*. *See Restatement (Third) of Property: Wills and Other Donative Transfers* §8.1 cmt. S (2003) ("An insane delusion is a belief that is so against the evidence and reason that it must be the product of derangement."); *see generally* Kevin Bennardo, *The Madness of Insane Delusions*, 60 Ariz. L. Rev. 601 (2018); Adam J. Hirsch, *Testation and the Mind*, 74 Wash. & Lee L. Rev. 285 (2017); Joshua C. Tate, *Personal Reality: Delusion in Law and Reality*, 49 Conn. L. Rev. 891 (2017); Thomas E. Simmons, *Testamentary Capacity, Undue Influence, Insane Delusions*, 60 San. Diego L. Rev. 175 (2015).

D. Undue Influence

It is safe to say that influence is a consistent factor in motivating a testator to devise or bequeath property to a beneficiary. The difficulty is in defining what is undue influence. As the American family becomes more "functional" and less "form" oriented in its definition, expectancy of inheritance becomes less precise, and more surprises occur in the distribution of assets upon death. Divorce, increasing numbers of stepchildren, and remarriage contribute to a rise in will contest litigation. Many of these contests originate from disappointment over asset distribution, and litigants assert undue influence. *See* Adam Hofri-Winogradow & Richard L. Kaplan, *Property Transfers to Caregivers: A Comparative Analysis*, 103 Iowa L. Rev. 1997 (2018); Ariela R. Dubler, *All Unhappy Families: Tales of Old Age, Rational Actors, and the Disordered Life*, 126 Harv. L. Rev. 2289 (2013) (reviewing Hendrick Hartog, Someday All This Will be Yours: A History of Inheritance and Old Age (2012)); Blair J. Berkley, *Canceling Deeds Obtained Through Fraud and Undue Influence*, 39 W. St. U. L. Rev. 129 (2012). Often a person with standing—for example, a blood relative—argues that the will is a product of the undue influence of another individual. The other person could be in a social, charitable, sexual, or supportive role with the testator, and the blood relative argues that this role provided the opportunity for undue influence and unjust enrichment.

In analyzing the next two cases, utilize these analytical steps to determine if the testator was unduly influenced by the beneficiary of the Last Will and Testament:

(1) Upon whom is the burden of proof placed — the proponent of the will (the beneficiary interest) or the contestant asserting undue influence?

(2) Does the burden of proof shift because of the presence of a confidential relationship between the testator and the beneficiary? Confidential relationships include attorney-client, doctor-patient, priest-penitent, and guardian-ward relationships, or a relationship of trust.

(3) If the burden shifts and a presumption of confidentiality is created, what is the level of proof needed to rebut that presumption and to allow the will's provision to be probated? If the burden does not shift, what is the level of proof needed to prove the undue influence?

(4) Are there suspicious circumstances that assist in creating a presumption of undue influence?

(5) Is the focus on the mind of the testator or on the conduct of the beneficiary?

(6) What is the remedy to be imposed if undue influence is established? Should all or a portion of the will be voided?

1. Family

Haynes v. First National State Bank of New Jersey

Supreme Court of New Jersey, 1981
87 N.J. 163, 432 A.2d 890

HANDLER, J.

This is a will contest in which the plaintiffs, two of the decedent's six grandchildren, seek to set aside the probate of their grandmother's will and two related trust agreements. The major issue presented is whether the will is invalid on the grounds of "undue influence" attributable to the fact that the attorney, who advised the testatrix and prepared the testamentary instruments, was also the attorney for the principal beneficiary, the testatrix's daughter, in whom the testatrix had reposed trust, confidence and dependency. A second question concerns the enforceability of a "non-contestability" or *in terrorem* clause in the testamentary documents under New Jersey common law since the decedent died before the effective date of the new probate code, N.J.S.A. 3A:2A-32, which invalidates such clauses in wills.

In an unreported opinion upholding the probate of the will and related trusts, the trial court held that the circumstances created a presumption of undue influence but that this presumption had been rebutted by defendants. It ruled further that the *in terrorem* clause was unenforceable. The case was appealed to the Appellate Division, which affirmed the trial court as to the lack of undue influence, sustaining the probate of the will and its judgment upholding the related trust agreements, but disagreed with the trial court's ruling that the *in terrorem* clause was unenforceable.

Plaintiffs then filed their petition for certification which was granted. 85 N.J. 99, 425 A.2d 264 (1980).

* * *

The issues raised by this appeal, particularly whether the contested will was invalid as a result of "undue influence," require a full exposition of the facts.

Mrs. Isabel Dutrow, the testatrix, was the widow of Charles E. Dutrow, an employee of Ralston Purina Co. who had acquired substantial stock in that corporation. Upon his death the stock, aggregating almost eight million dollars, was distributed to his widow and their two daughters, both outright and in trust.

Betty Haynes, one of the daughters of Charles and Isabel Dutrow, came with her two sons to live with her parents in the Dutrow family home in York, Pennsylvania in 1941 while Betty's husband was in military service during World War II. Following Charles Dutrow's death in 1945 and her own divorce, Betty and her sons continued to live with Mrs. Dutrow in York. The relationships between mother and daughter were extremely close, Mrs. Dutrow having deep affection for Betty, as well as her grandsons whom she practically raised. The two boys, however, left the York home sometime around 1968 to the considerable aggravation and disappointment of their grandmother.[1] But Betty remained with her mother until Betty's death in June 1973.

At the time of Betty's death, she had been living with her mother for more than 30 years. Mrs. Dutrow was then 84 years old and suffered from a number of ailments including glaucoma, cataracts and diverticulitis, and had recently broken her hip. Mrs. Dutrow, distraught over the death of her closest daughter and somewhat alienated from the Haynes children, decided to move in with her younger daughter, Dorcas Cotsworth, and Dorcas' husband, John, who had homes in Short Hills and Bay Head, New Jersey. This decision was a reasonable one, freely made by Mrs. Dutrow, who despite her age, physical condition and feelings of despair was and remained an alert, intelligent and commanding personality until the time of her death.

During her lifetime, Mrs. Dutrow executed a great many wills and trust agreements. All of these instruments, as well as those her husband had executed prior to his death, were prepared by the longstanding family attorney, Richard Stevens, of Philadelphia. By June 1967 Stevens had prepared five wills and several codicils for Mrs. Dutrow.

As of the time she moved in with the Cotsworths, Mrs. Dutrow's estate plan reflected a basic disposition to treat the Haynes and the Cotsworth family branches equally. During the last four years of her life, however, while living with daughter Dorcas, Mrs. Dutrow's will went through a series of changes which drastically

---

1. The Haynes children apparently undertook lifestyles which caused both their mother and grandmother great anguish: one son resisted military service and took refuge in Canada during the Vietnam war and both had live-in girlfriends whom they eventually married.

favored Dorcas and her children while diminishing and excluding the interests of the Haynes brothers. These changes, and their surrounding circumstances, bear most weightily upon the issue of undue influence.

Shortly after moving in with Dorcas, following a conference between her daughter and Stevens, the first of many will and trust changes was made by Mrs. Dutrow on July 25, 1973. Under the new provisions of the will, Mrs. Dutrow's residuary estate was to be divided into two equal trusts, one for Dorcas, the principal of which Dorcas could invade up to certain limits and the other a trust with income to each of the Haynes boys without a power of invasion. A new will and an *inter vivos* trust with almost identical provisions, including approximately 60,000 shares of Ralston Purina stock, were later executed on November 24, 1973 and December 4, 1973, respectively. Mrs. Dutrow also gave Dorcas 5,000 shares of stock outright to compensate her for the expense of having Mrs. Dutrow live with her.

During the time these instruments were being drawn, Dorcas and her husband, John Cotsworth, began actively to express their views about Mrs. Dutrow's estate plans to Stevens. In a meeting between Stevens, Mrs. Dutrow, and the Cotsworths on November 13, 1973 at the Cotsworth home in Short Hills, John Cotsworth gave Stevens two charts of Mrs. Dutrow's estate which Cotsworth had prepared. According to Stevens' testimony at trial, the import of the charts was to make "substantial outright gifts to the members of the Cotsworth family and smaller gifts to [plaintiffs, the Haynes children]." Stevens further testified that Mrs. Dutrow had told him at this meeting that the pressure upon her by the Cotsworths to change her will was enormous. On November 19, 1973, John Cotsworth wrote Stevens a long letter in which he summarized what he, Cotsworth, saw as Mrs. Dutrow's "objectives" with regard to her estate plans and then detailing in over five pages the calculations as to how these "objectives" could be achieved. An important aspect of his proposal was to deplete substantially the estate to simplify Mrs. Dutrow's "money worries." Cotsworth further noted at the beginning of this letter to Stevens that

> [o]ur joint obligation—you and the family—is to accomplish these objectives with minimum tax effects upon the total estate. Obviously you are in a far better position to work out the details than I am, but you appear reluctant to go as fast or as far as I have suggested for reasons that are not clear to us.

Then, on November 26, 1973, Cotsworth proceeded to consult Grant Buttermore, his own lawyer, regarding Mrs. Dutrow's estate plans. Buttermore had been the attorney for the Cotsworth family and the Cotsworth family business, the Berry Steel Corporation, for six to seven years and had provided substantial legal advice concerning the corporation. He had also prepared wills for both Mr. and Mrs. Cotsworth and some of their children. For all intents and purposes, Buttermore can be viewed as having been the family attorney for the Cotsworths.

On November 29, 1973, following the initial contact by her husband, Dorcas Cotsworth went to Buttermore concerning the trust agreement of November 24 that Stevens had prepared for her mother. As a result, Buttermore called Stevens while Dorcas was in his office and discussed the matter of Mrs. Dutrow's domicile. This subject, in addition to a proposal concerning "gifting" by Mrs. Dutrow, had earlier been broached to Buttermore by John Cotsworth. Both lawyers agreed that Mrs. Dutrow's domicile should be changed to New Jersey for tax purposes and Buttermore made the change on the instrument by hand. Later that day Buttermore wrote to Stevens to confirm the results of the call, as well as the fact that the Cotsworths were personally involved in Mrs. Dutrow's estate planning, viz:

> We are in the process of reviewing Mrs. Dutrow's estate with her and Mr. and Mrs. Cotsworth along the lines suggested by Mr. Cotsworth in his outline heretofore submitted to you.

Buttermore concluded this letter by relaying Mrs. Dutrow's request to Stevens to provide "a complete list of all [her] assets . . . in order that we may make a proper analysis."

Stevens immediately responded, writing separate letters to Buttermore and Mrs. Dutrow on November 30. He gave Buttermore a skeletal list of Mrs. Dutrow's assets with no detail. At the same time he also undertook to make some technical corrections of Mrs. Dutrow's will, which was executed, as noted, on December 4. In the letter accompanying the will, he mentioned his conversation with Buttermore and his "assumption" that Mrs. Dutrow wanted him to give Buttermore the information he was requesting.

The response to this communication was a letter written to Stevens on December 3, 1973 in Dorcas Cotsworth's handwriting on her personal stationary, and signed by Dorcas and Mrs. Dutrow, which contained the following:

> These are my mother's observations as she sits here besides me and she insists she is not being pressured. . . .
>
> Mother and I have discussed this so often—now she says get it over and let me forget it—as it worries her with everything undone. . . .
>
> Her desire and intent is to have Dorcas rewarded while alive—to have an Irrevocable Trust set up to let Dorcas have income and right to sprinkle money to Grandchildren when necessary. . . .
>
> When Dorcas dies then the per stirpes takes over. . . .
>
> Mother approves of Mr. Grant Buttermore knowing all details and keeping in this estate.

A meeting of Buttermore and John Cotsworth with Stevens was scheduled for December 13, 1973. Prior to this meeting Buttermore met with Mrs. Dutrow alone, as he testified was his customary practice, "so that I could get the intent directly from . . . the testatrix." During this two hour conference, according to Buttermore, he explained various legal and tax aspects of estate planning to Mrs. Dutrow. He also told her "that intent was much more important and controlled over the other two items, meaning taxation and liquidity." Buttermore also reviewed at length Mrs. Dutrow's assets and her present will and trusts. Among other things, Mrs. Dutrow, according to Buttermore's testimony, said that "her first priority was to make sure she had enough to last during her lifetime," for which purpose Mrs. Dutrow said she would need $26,000 per year. Buttermore also explained to Mrs. Dutrow that the practical effect of the per stirpes disposition of the November 24 trust agreement would be to enable the two plaintiffs, the Haynes brothers, ultimately to "receive twice as much as each of the other grandchildren," to which Mrs. Dutrow responded, according to Buttermore, "I didn't realize that."

Buttermore testified that he told Stevens at the December 13 meeting that Mrs. Dutrow "wanted to go to the per capita basis equally among the grandchildren." Stevens, according to Buttermore, was very skeptical that Mrs. Dutrow wanted to do this and asked Buttermore to doublecheck it with her. Buttermore replied that "[i]n my mind she'd already made that decision after our talk on December the eleventh."

On December 17 and 18, a concerned Stevens wrote Buttermore letters confirming the discussion of December 13, and on December 18, specifically adverted to the possibility of "undue influence." There is no indication in the record that Buttermore responded to Stevens on this matter.

Buttermore, in response to a call from Dorcas Cotsworth, again met alone with Mrs. Dutrow in Short Hills on January 11 to discuss a problem concerning some back dividends. While he was with her, Buttermore, at his own initiative, told her what had happened during his December 13 meeting with Stevens and John Cotsworth and reviewed with her Stevens' letter of December 17 concerning her estate plans. Following that exchange, Buttermore related, Mrs. Dutrow instructed *him* to "draw the papers." Although Stevens had previously asked Buttermore to write him in Vermont, where he was vacationing, if there were any further developments concerning Mrs. Dutrow's estate planning, Buttermore did not do so, apparently believing that Mrs. Dutrow, who complained of Stevens' absence, did not desire or need Stevens to be further involved. Thus, Buttermore, still the Cotsworths' attorney, also stepped in, exclusively, as Mrs. Dutrow's attorney for purposes of planning her estate.

Significantly, at this juncture, drastic changes in Mrs. Dutrow's estate planning materialized. According to Buttermore, he and Mrs. Dutrow then proceeded to discuss in detail her wishes for a new will and trust agreements. Mrs. Dutrow assertedly indicated that she wanted "to leave [her estate] equally . . . between the grandchildren," and did not care about the adverse tax consequence which Buttermore claimed he had explained to her. Buttermore also seemed to minimize the effect of the proposed change allegedly requested by Mrs. Dutrow by pointing out to her that altering the particular trust in question would not accomplish her goals; although all six grandchildren would inherit equally under the particular trust in question, the consequence of other trusts already in existence would be that the two Haynes grandchildren would "still be getting greater in the end" than Mrs. Cotsworth's children. During that meeting, Buttermore also apparently showed Stevens' letter of December 18 concerning undue influence to Mrs. Dutrow.

These discussions resulted in the near total severance of the Haynes children from their grandmother's estate. Assertedly, at Mrs. Dutrow's request, Buttermore promptly prepared two new trust agreements, which provided for the payment of income with full right of invasion of principal to Dorcas Cotsworth during her lifetime and that, upon Dorcas' death, "the then remaining balance in said trust shall be divided equally among settlor's grandchildren." In addition, Mrs. Dutrow's new will provided for the bequest of all her tangible personal property to Dorcas Cotsworth, "or if she does not survive me to my grandchildren who survive me, equally." These instruments were executed by Mrs. Dutrow on January 16, 1974.

On January 19 Buttermore sent Stevens copies of the new instruments along with a letter in which he explained that after going over everything "meticulously with Mrs. Dutrow," the new instruments had been prepared "along the lines we have discussed" and that, in Stevens' absence, Mrs. Dutrow had become "quite upset with the Fidelity Bank and decided that she wanted to immediately revoke" the existing trust agreements and will. Stevens testified to astonishment at the proposed distribution. He also expressed surprise about the provision in both trust agreements, which permitted Dorcas Cotsworth to withdraw the principal each year so that, if exercised, there might be nothing left when she died.

In early May 1974 Buttermore again met with Mrs. Dutrow to make some changes in the trust agreements. The most important change allowed the corporate trustee First National State Bank of New Jersey to distribute principal, "in its sole discretion," to Dorcas Cotsworth and any of Mrs. Dutrow's grandchildren (i.e., plaintiffs as well as Dorcas' children). This was in contrast to the original terms of this trust agreement, as executed by Mrs. Dutrow in January 1974, which allowed for such discretionary distribution by the bank only to Mrs. Cotsworth and her children, not to plaintiffs. According to Buttermore's testimony, this change was clearly Mrs. Dutrow's idea.

On April 24, 1975, Mrs. Dutrow amended the revocable trust agreement and added a codicil to her will in order to add *in terrorem* clauses to each instrument. Both the amendment and the codicil were prepared by Buttermore. At trial, Buttermore said that Mrs. Dutrow had decided to add the clause after reading that J. Paul Getty had included such a clause in his will to prevent litigation.

Buttermore next met with Mrs. Dutrow to discuss her estate on December 11, 1975. At this meeting, according to Buttermore's testimony, Mrs. Dutrow told him that she had decided to give her estate, other than special bequests or amounts, to Dorcas Cotsworth, to enable Dorcas to enjoy it during Dorcas' lifetime. Buttermore testified that he was "taken by surprise" by this proposal and tried to explain to Mrs. Dutrow that this change would result in additional taxes of between $700,000 and $800,000 when Dorcas died. But, according to Buttermore, Mrs. Dutrow insisted on making the change. The necessary amendments to the revocable trust agreement were prepared by Buttermore and executed by Mrs. Dutrow on January 9, 1976, providing for distribution of the principal to Dorcas upon Mrs. Dutrow's death, or, if Dorcas was not then living, equally among Mrs. Dutrow's grandchildren. A new will executed the same day provided, as had previous wills, that Dorcas would inherit all of Mrs. Dutrow's tangible personal property. The final change made by Mrs. Dutrow in her estate plans before she died in September 1977, was to amend the revocable trust to give $10,000 to each of her grandchildren at her death, apparently realizing that otherwise the Haynes children would likely not inherit anything.

The last testamentary document executed by the testatrix was a will dated April 8, 1976. It contained no further major changes in her dispositions. Mrs. Dutrow died on September 27, 1977 and her final will was admitted to probate by the Surrogate of Ocean County on October 12, 1977, with the First National State Bank of New Jersey as executor.

* * *

In any attack upon the validity of a will, it is generally presumed that "the testator was of sound mind and competent when he executed the will." Gellert v. Livingston, 5 N.J. 65, 71, 73 A.2d 916 (1950). If a will is tainted by "undue influence," it may be overturned. "Undue influence" has been defined as "mental, moral or physical" exertion which has destroyed the "free agency of a testator" by preventing the testator "from following the dictates of his own mind and will and accepting instead the domination and influence of another." In re Neuman, 133 N.J.Eq. 532, 534, 32 A.2d 826 (E. & A. 1943). When such a contention is made

> the burden of proving undue influence lies upon the contestant unless the will benefits one who stood in a confidential relationship to the testatrix and there are additional circumstances of a suspicious character present which require explanation. In such case the law raises a presumption of undue influence and the burden of proof is shifted to the proponent. [In re Rittenhouse's Will, 19 N.J. 376, 378–379, 117 A.2d 401 (1955)]

Accord, In re Blake's Will, 21 N.J. 50, 55–56, 120 A.2d 745 (1956); In re Davis, 14 N.J. 166, 169, 101 A.2d 521 (1953); In re Hopper, 9 N.J. 280, 282, 88 A.2d 193 (1952), 5 N.J. Practice (Clapp, Wills and Administration) § 62 (3rd ed. 1962).

The first element necessary to raise a presumption of undue influence, a "confidential relationship" between the testator and a beneficiary, arises

> where trust is reposed by reason of the testator's weakness or dependence or where the parties occupied relations in which reliance is naturally inspired or in fact exists. . . . [In re Hopper, *supra*, 9 N.J. at 282, 88 A.2d 193]

Here, the aged Mrs. Dutrow, afflicted by the debilitations of advanced years, was dependent upon her sole surviving child with whom she lived and upon whom she relied for companionship, care and support. This was a relationship sustained by confidence and trust. The determination of the trial court, in this case, that there was a confidential relationship between the testatrix and the chief beneficiary of her will is unassailable.

The second element necessary to create the presumption of undue influence is the presence of suspicious circumstances which, in combination with such a confidential relationship, will shift the burden of proof to the proponent. Such circumstances need be no more than "slight." In re Blake's Will, *supra*, 21 N.J. at 55–56, 120 A.2d 745; In re Rittenhouse's Will, *supra*, 19 N.J. at 379, 117 A.2d 401; Gellert v. Livingston, *supra*, 5 N.J. at 71, 73 A.2d 916; In re Week's Estate, 29 N.J.Super. 533, 540, 103 A.2d 43 (App.Div.1954).

In this case there were suspicious circumstances attendant upon the execution of the will. There was a confidential relationship between the testatrix and her attorney, who was also the attorney for the daughter and the daughter's immediate family. Furthermore, following the establishment of the confidential relationship of the daughter's attorney with the testatrix, there was a drastic change in the testamentary dispositions of the testatrix, which favored the daughter. These factors collectively triggered the presumption that there was undue influence in the execution of the will.

On this record, the trial court correctly posited a presumption of undue influence that shifted the burden of proof on this issue to the proponents of the will. The court concluded ultimately on this issue, however, that the proponents, the defendants, had overcome the presumption of undue influence. The trial judge determined that Mrs. Dutrow was of firm mind and resolve, that the final testamentary disposition, though markedly different from previous plans, was not unnatural or instinctively unsound and it represented her actual intent. Further, the court found the explanation for Mrs. Dutrow's final testamentary disposition to be candid and satisfactory.

The plaintiffs argue vigorously that the trial court's findings of fact and conclusions are not supported by sufficient evidence. They contend that in view of the strength of the presumption of undue influence created by the confidential relationships and the peculiarly suspicious circumstances of this case, there is an unusually heavy burden of proof required to disprove undue influence, which defendants failed to meet.

In this jurisdiction, once a presumption of undue influence has been established the burden of proof shifts to the proponent of the will, who must, under normal circumstances, overcome that presumption by a preponderance of the evidence. In re Week's Estate, *supra*, 29 N.J.Super. at 538–539, 103 A.2d 43. Accord, In re Estate of Churick, 165 N.J.Super. 1, 5, 397 A.2d 677 (App.Div.1978), aff'd o. b., 78 N.J. 563, 397 A.2d 655 (1979); In re Baker's Will, 68 N.J.Super. 574, 587, 173 A.2d 422 (App. Div.1971). See Gellert v. Livingston, *supra*, 5 N.J. at 71, 73 A.2d 916 (1950). See generally 5 N.J. Practice, *supra*, § 62. As stated by Judge Clapp in In re Week's Estate, *supra*:

> In the case of a presumption of undue influence, apparently because the presumption is fortified by policy, the proponent must, according to the language of the cases, prove, to the satisfaction of the trier of fact, that there was no undue influence. In connection with this presumption, unlike other presumptions, the courts do not speak as to the burden of going forward with the evidence. However, we conclude, the moment this presumption is erected, both the burden of proof . . . and the burden of going forward with

proof, shift to the proponent and are identical and coincident. To meet each
of these assignments, the proponent must establish by the same quantum
of proof that is, by a preponderance of the proof that there is no undue
influence. [29 N.J.Super. at 538–539, 103 A.2d 43 (citations omitted)]

In re Week's Estate, *supra*, recognized, however, that there were situations calling for a stronger presumption of undue influence and a commensurately heavier
burden of proof to rebut the presumption. While in that case the presumption of
undue influence was deemed to be rebuttable by a preponderance of evidence, the
court acknowledged other

> cases where the presumption of undue influence is so heavily weighted
> with policy that the courts have demanded a sterner measure of proof than
> that usually obtaining upon civil issues. That is the situation, for instance,
> where an attorney benefits by the will of his client and especially where he
> draws it himself. [29 N.J.Super. at 539, 103 A.2d 43.]

It has been often recognized that a conflict on the part of an attorney in a testimonial situation is fraught with a high potential for undue influence, generating a strong presumption that there was such improper influence and warranting a
greater quantum of proof to dispel the presumption. Thus, where the attorney who
drew the will was the sole beneficiary, the Court required "substantial and trustworthy evidence of explanatory facts" and "candid and full disclosure" to dispel the
presumption of undue influence. In re Blake's Will, 21 N.J. 50, 58–59, 120 A.2d 745
(1956). And, where an attorney-beneficiary, who had a preexisting attorney-client
relationship with the testatrix, introduced the testatrix to the lawyer who actually
drafted the challenged will, this Court has required evidence that was "convincing or impeccable," In re Rittenhouse's Will, *supra*, 19 N.J. at 382, 117 A.2d 401,
"convincing," In re Hopper, *supra*, 9 N.J. at 285, 88 A.2d 193, and, "clear and convincing," In re Davis, *supra*, 14 N.J. at 170, 101 A.2d 521. Accord, In re Baker's Will,
supra; see In re Estate of Lehner, 142 N.J.Super. 56, 360 A.2d 400 (App.Div.1975),
rev'd on other grounds, 70 N.J. 434, 360 A.2d 383 (1976); cf. In re Estate of Churick,
supra, 165 N.J.Super. at 5, 397 A.2d 677 (applying lower burden of proof where testator advised by independent attorney); In re Week's Estate, *supra* (same).

In imposing the higher burden of proof in this genre of cases, our courts have
continually emphasized the need for a lawyer of independence and undivided loyalty, owing professional allegiance to no one but the testator. In In re Rittenhouse's
Will, *supra*, 19 N.J. at 380–382, 117 A.2d 401, the Court questioned the attorney's
independence and loyalty in view of the attorney-beneficiary's role in bringing the
draftsman and the testatrix together, noting that the beneficiary had been "unable
to give a satisfactory explanation of the relationship" between himself, the draftsman and the testatrix, viz:

> [I]t would appear the testatrix did not independently choose [the drafts-
> man] as the scrivener of her will. It is fair to assume from the record that she
> was influenced to do so by [the beneficiary].

Similarly, in In re Davis, *supra*, 14 N.J. at 171, 101 A.2d 521, the Court observed:

> We wish to reiterate what has been said repeatedly by our courts as to the
> proprieties of a situation where the testatrix wishes to make her attorney
> or a member of his immediate family a beneficiary under a will. Ordinary
> prudence requires that such a will be drawn by some other lawyer of the
> testatrix' own choosing, so that any suspicion of undue influence is thereby
> avoided. Such steps are in conformance with the spirit of Canons 6, 11, of
> the Canons of Professional Ethics promulgated by this court.* * *

See also In re Hopper, *supra*, 9 N.J. at 282, 88 A.2d 193.

It is not difficult to appreciate the policy reasons for creating an especially strong
presumption of undue influence in cases of attorney misconduct. Such professional
delinquency is encompassed by our official rules governing the professional ethics
of attorneys. Our disciplinary rules cover all gradations of professional departures
from ethical norms, and, the existence of an ethical conflict exemplified in this
case is squarely posited under DR 5-105.* * * This ethical rule prohibits an attorney
from engaging in professional relationships that may impair his independent and
untrammeled judgment with respect to his client. This disciplinary stricture

> should be practically self-demonstrative to any conscientious attorney.
> There is nothing novel about the ethical dilemma dealt with by DR 5-105. A
> lawyer cannot serve two masters in the same subject matter if their interests
> are or may become actually or potentially in conflict. [In re Chase, 68 N.J.
> 392, 396, 346 A.2d 89 (1975)]

So pervasive and fundamental is the ethical reach of DR 5-105 that ethical violations of this disciplinary rule based upon conflicts of interest have been found
in a myriad of situations and in almost every walk of professional life. * * * Such
conflicts often arise where there is dual representation. E. g., In re Krakauer, 81 N.J.
32, 404 A.2d 1137 (1979); In re Dolan, 76 N.J. 1, 384 A.2d 1076 (1978). See "Developments of the Law—Conflicts of Interest in the Legal Profession," 94 Harv.L.Rev.
1244, 1292–1315 (1961). A conflict of interest, moreover, need not be obvious or
actual to create an ethical impropriety. The mere possibility of such a conflict at the
outset of the relationship is sufficient to establish an ethical breach on the part of
the attorney. In re Kushinsky, 53 N.J. 1, 5, 247 A.2d 665 (1968); In re Braun, 49 N.J.
16, 18, 227 A.2d 506 (1967); In re Blatt, 42 N.J. 522, 524, 201 A.2d 715 (1964); In re
Kamp, 40 N.J. 588, 595, 194 A.2d 236 (1963). Even where the representation of two
clients has become a routine practice on the part of the bar generally, when the
latent conflict becomes real, the attorney must fully disclose all material information and, if need be, extricate himself from the conflict by terminating his relationship with at least one party. Cf. Lieberman v. Employers Ins. of Wausau, 84 N.J.
325, 338–340, 419 A.2d 417 (1980) (conflict of interest on part of insurance defense
counsel who normally represented both the insured and the insurer).

Accordingly, it is our determination that there must be imposed a significant burden of proof upon the advocates of a will where a presumption of undue influence

has arisen because the testator's attorney has placed himself in a conflict of interest and professional loyalty between the testator and the beneficiary. * * * In view of the gravity of the presumption in such cases, the appropriate burden of proof must be heavier than that which normally obtains in civil litigation. The cited decisions which have dealt with the quantum of evidence needed to dispel the presumption of influence in this context have essayed various descriptions of this greater burden, viz: "convincing," "impeccable," "substantial," "trustworthy," "candid," and "full." Our present rules of evidence, however, do not employ such terminology. The need for clarity impels us to be more definitive in the designation of the appropriate burden of proof and to select one which most suitably measures the issue to be determined. See, e. g., In re Week's Estate, *supra*. Only three burdens of proof are provided by the evidence rules, namely, a preponderance, clear and convincing, and beyond a reasonable doubt. Evid.R. 1(4). The standard in our evidence rules that conforms most comfortably with the level of proofs required by our decisions in this context is the burden of proof by clear and convincing evidence. * * * In re Davis, *supra*, 14 N.J. at 170, 101 A.2d 521; cf. Sarte v. Pidoto, 129 N.J.Super. 405, 411, 324 A.2d 48 (App.Div.1974) (de facto use of a standard stricter than preponderance of the evidence entails proof by clear and convincing evidence under rules of evidence). Hence, the presumption of undue influence created by a professional conflict of interest on the part of an attorney, coupled with confidential relationships between a testator and the beneficiary as well as the attorney, must be rebutted by clear and convincing evidence.

Applying these principles to this case, it is clear that attorney Buttermore was in a position of irreconcilable conflict within the common sense and literal meaning of DR 5-105. In this case, Buttermore was required, at a minimum, to provide full disclosure and complete advice to Mrs. Dutrow, as well as the Cotsworths, as to the existence and nature of the conflict and to secure knowing and intelligent waivers from each in order to continue his professional relationship with Mrs. Dutrow. DR 5-105(C). Even these prophylactic measures, however, might not have overcome the conflict, nor have been sufficient to enable the attorney to render unimpaired "independent professional judgment" on behalf of his client, DR 5-105(B); see Lieberman v. Employers Ins. of Wausau, *supra*, 84 N.J. at 338–340, 419 A.2d 417. Any conflict, of course, could have been avoided by Buttermore simply refusing to represent Mrs. Dutrow. DR 5-105(A), (B); see In re Davis, *supra*, at 171, 101 A.2d 521. But, Buttermore was apparently insensitive or impervious to the presence or extent of the professional conflict presented by these circumstances. He undertook none of these measures to eliminate the dual representation or overcome the conflict.[7]

---

7. In this case, we recognize that Buttermore believed in good faith that he was taking proper precautions to overcome or avoid the consequences of the improper conflict and did not believe or perceive that his position involved an impermissible conflict of interest in light of these measures. He also expressed the view that frequently estate planning involves members of an entire family and therefore no conflict exists for an attorney who has professional relationships with members of the family, in addition to the testator. This position is, of course, inconsistent with our explicit

Consequently, a strong taint of undue influence was permitted, presumptively, to be injected into the testamentary disposition of Mrs. Dutrow.

Accordingly, the attorney's conduct here, together with all of the other factors contributing to the likelihood of wrongful influence exerted upon the testatrix, has engendered a heavy presumption of undue influence which the proponents of the will must overcome by clear and convincing evidence.

This determination that clear and convincing evidence must be marshalled to overcome the presumption of undue influence appropriately requires that the matter be remanded to the trial court for new findings of fact and legal conclusions based upon application of this burden of proof. We remand, recognizing that there is considerable evidence in the record as to Mrs. Dutrow's intelligence, independence and persistence, of her alienation, to some extent, from the Haynes children, and as to her natural intent primarily to benefit her children, rather than her grandchildren. Moreover, all of this evidence is based upon the credibility of witnesses, which we cannot independently evaluate. We are also mindful that the trial court found that the explanation for Mrs. Dutrow's testamentary disposition was candid and satisfactory.

Nevertheless, the trial court does not appear to have given full weight to the additional significant factor generating the heightened presumption of undue influence in this case, namely, that occasioned by the conflict of interest on the part of the attorney drafting the will, whose testimony was crucial to the outcome of this case. Most importantly, the court's conclusion was premised upon an application of the conventional standard of proof entailing only a preponderance of the evidence. We therefore cannot with any certitude predict that the trial court's findings of fact and resultant conclusions would be the same were he to reassess the evidence, imposing upon the proponents of the will the burden of proof of lack of undue influence by clear and convincing evidence. Consequently, the fair disposition, which we now direct, is to remand the matter to the trial court for a redetermination of facts and conclusions based upon the record.

* * *

The second issue involves the enforceability of the *in terrorem* clauses challenged by the plaintiffs. The trial court noted that under the State's common law, *in terrorem* clauses are enforceable when the contest is based upon an allegation of undue influence, even if probable cause and good faith are present. The trial judge nonetheless declared the clauses unenforceable because the new probate code, N.J.S.A. 3A:2A-32, admittedly not controlling in this case because of the date of Mrs. Dutrow's death, "provides that *in terrorem* clauses are unenforceable if probable cause exists"

---

holding that such conduct, as exemplified by the facts of this case, violates DR 5-105. Since this application of DR 5-105 to such situations has not been generally acknowledged, we do not think it fair that ethical sanctions be pursued retroactively in this case for such conduct, since there are no additional aggravating circumstances. See In re Smock, 86 N.J. 426, 432 A.2d 34 (1981).

and, following the lead of the new code on this point, the court refused to enforce the clauses, noting that its ruling was "in accord with the authoritative view and the modern trend."

On this latter issue, the Appellate Division found that there was no basis in law for the trial court's decision, and that although the new probate code, N.J.S.A. 3A:2A-32, changed the law with respect to wills, the change applied only to wills of decedents who died on or after September 1, 1978, nearly a year after Mrs. Dutrow's death. In addition, the Appellate Division found no indication that the new statute is meant to apply to trusts. Furthermore, the court said in support of reversal on this issue, "[e]nforcement of the *in terrorem* clause is particularly equitable here."

As noted earlier, on April 24, 1975, Mrs. Dutrow amended the revocable trust agreement and added a codicil to her will in order to add *in terrorem* clauses to each instrument. The clause in the amendment to the revocable trust agreement, almost identical to that in the will, provided:

> If any beneficiary under this trust shall contest the validity of, or object to this instrument, or attempt to vacate the same, or to alter or change any of the provisions hereof, such person shall be thereby deprived of all beneficial interest thereunder and of any share in this Trust and the share of such person shall become part of the residue of the trust, and such person shall be excluded from taking any part of such residue and the same shall be divided among the other persons entitled to take such residue. * * *

In 1977 the Legislature enacted N.J.S.A. 3A:2A-32 as part of the new probate code [Uniform Probate Code (U.L.A.) § 3-905 (1969)] * * *. This statute renders *in terrorem* clauses in wills unenforceable if probable cause for a will contest exists:

> A provision in a will purporting to penalize any interested person for contesting the will or instituting other proceedings relating to the estate is unenforceable if probable cause exists for instituting proceedings.

In Alper v. Alper, 2 N.J. 105, 65 A.2d 737 (1949), the Court said that the existence of probable cause to bring the challenge to the will should result in nonenforcement of an *in terrorem* clause "where the contest of the will is waged on the ground of forgery or subsequent revocation by a later will or codicil." However, where typical grounds of challenge were advanced "fraud, undue influence, improper execution or lack of testamentary capacity" the clause was deemed to be enforceable, notwithstanding probable cause, as a safeguard against deleterious, acrimonious and wasteful family litigation. *Id.* at 112–113, 65 A.2d 737. Accord, Provident Trust Co. v. Osborne, 133 N.J.Eq. 518, 521, 33 A.2d 103 (Ch.1943). See also In re Estate of Badenhop, 61 N.J.Super. 526, 535, 161 A.2d 318 (Cty.Ct.1960).

The new statute, N.J.S.A. 3A:2A-32, however, abolishes the distinction drawn by the Court in Alper between cases in which *in terrorem* clauses in wills shall be enforced, and those in which they shall not, stating quite simply that whenever there is probable cause to contest a will, the clause should not be enforced. While the statute applies neither to the will in this case, which was probated prior to the statute's effective date, nor to the trust agreement, since the statute applies only to wills, the statute is indicative of a legislative intent to create a policy less inhibitory to the bringing of challenges to testamentary instruments. There does not appear to be any logical reason why the purpose of the statute should not be presently recognized and be applied equally to trust instruments or should not be applied in the circumstances of this case.

There are public policy considerations both favoring and disfavoring the enforcement of *in terrorem* clauses. On the one hand, such provisions seek to reduce vexatious litigation, avoid expenses that debilitate estates and give effect to a testator's clearly expressed intentions. * * *

On the other hand, a majority of jurisdictions have declined to enforce *in terrorem* clauses where challenges to testamentary instruments are brought in good faith and with probable cause. * * *

Given this relative equipoise of considerations, it is entirely appropriate for the courts to be sensitive and responsive to the Legislature's perception of the public interest and policy in these matters. See Knight v. Margate, 86 N.J. 374, 431 A.2d 833 (1981); Kruvant v. Mayor & Council Tp. of Cedar Grove, 82 N.J. 435, 414 A.2d 9 (1980). The assessment, balancing and resolution of these concerns by the Legislature, now reflected in the statute law, is, of course, not binding upon the judiciary's decisional authority in a matter not governed by such enactments. Nevertheless, the legislative handling of the subject is, and should be, strongly influential in the judicial quest for the important societal values which are constituent elements of the common law and find appropriate voice in the decisions of the court expounding the common law. See Van Beeck v. Sabine Towing Co., 300 U.S. 342, 351, 57 S.Ct. 452, 456, 81 L.Ed. 685, 690 (1937).

We therefore decline to enforce an *in terrorem* clause in a will or trust agreement where there is probable cause to challenge the instrument. The trial court concluded that the plaintiffs in this case "proceeded in good faith and on probable cause." That finding is amply supported by evidence of record.

* * *

We have determined that *in terrorem* clauses in the will and trust instruments are not enforceable. We have also directed, for reasons set forth in this opinion, that the case be remanded for new findings of fact and legal conclusions with respect to the major issue of undue influence in the execution of the will.

Accordingly, the judgment below is reversed and the matter remanded. Jurisdiction is not retained.

CLIFFORD, J., dissenting in part [is omitted].

* * *

For reversal—Justices SULLIVAN, PASHMAN, CLIFFORD, SCHREIBER and HANDLER—5.

For affirmance—None.

2. Sexuality

In re Will of Moses

Supreme Court of Mississippi, 1969
227 So. 2d 829

SMITH, Justice:

Mrs. Fannie Traylor Moses died on February 6, 1967. An instrument, dated December 23, 1957 and purporting to be her last will and testament, was duly admitted to probate in common form in the Chancery Court of the First Judicial District of Hinds County. Thereafter, on February 14, 1967, appellant, Clarence H. Holland, an attorney at law, not related to Mrs. Moses, filed a petition in that court tendering for probate in solemn form, as the true last will and testament of Mrs. Moses, a document dated May 26, 1964, under the terms of which he would take virtually her entire estate. This document contained a clause revoking former wills and Holland's petition prayed that the earlier probate of the 1957 will be set aside.

The beneficiaries under the 1957 will (the principal beneficiary was an elder sister of Mrs. Moses) responded to Holland's petition, denied that the document tendered by him was Mrs. Moses' will, and asserted, among other things, that it was (1) the product of Holland's undue influence upon her, (2) that at the time of its signing, Mrs. Moses lacked testamentary capacity, and, (3) that the 1957 will was Mrs. Moses' true last will and testament and its probate should be confirmed. By cross bill, respondents prayed that Holland's apparent ownership of an interest in certain real estate had been procured by undue influence and that it should be cancelled as a cloud upon the title of Mrs. Moses, the true owner.

By agreement, the case was heard by the chancellor without a jury.

After hearing and considering a great deal of evidence, oral and documentary, together with briefs of counsel, the chancellor, in a carefully considered opinion, found that (1) the 1964 document, tendered for probate by Holland, was the product of undue influence and was not entitled to be admitted to probate, (2) the earlier probate of the 1957 will should be confirmed and, (3) Mrs. Moses had been the true owner of the interest claimed by Holland in the real estate and his claim of ownership should be cancelled as a cloud upon the title of Mrs. Moses.

Holland's appeal is from the decree entered denying probate to the 1964 document and cancelling his claim to an undivided one-half interest in the real estate.

A number of grounds are assigned for reversal. However, appellant's chief argument is addressed to the proposition that even if Holland, as Mrs. Moses' attorney, occupied a continuing fiduciary relationship with respect to her on May 26, 1964, the date of the execution of the document under which he claimed her estate, the presumption of undue influence was overcome because, in making the will, Mrs. Moses had the independent advice and counsel of one entirely devoted to her interests. It is argued that, for this reason, a decree should be entered here reversing the chancellor and admitting the 1964 will to probate. The question as to the land would then become moot as Holland would take it under the residuary clause of the 1964 will.

A brief summary of facts found by the chancellor and upon which he based his conclusion that the presumption was not overcome, follows:

Mrs. Moses died at the age of 57 years, leaving an estate valued at $125,000. She had lost three husbands in less than 20 years. Throughout the latter years of her life her health became seriously impaired. She suffered from serious heart trouble and cancer had required the surgical removal of one of her breasts. For 6 or 7 years preceding her death she was an alcoholic.

On several occasions Mrs. Moses had declared her intention of making an elder sister her testamentary beneficiary. She had once lived with this sister and was grateful for the many kindnesses shown her. Mrs. Moses' will of December 23, 1957 did, in fact, bequeath the bulk of her estate to this sister.

The exact date on which Holland entered Mrs. Moses' life is unclear. There is a suggestion that she had met him as early as 1951. Their personal relationship became what the chancellor, somewhat inaccurately, characterized, as one of 'dubious' morality. The record, however, leaves no doubt as to its nature. Soon after the death of Mrs. Moses' last husband, Holland, although 15 years her junior, began seeing Mrs. Moses with marked regularity, there having been testimony to the effect that he attended her almost daily. Holland was an attorney and in that capacity represented Mrs. Moses. She declared that he was not only her attorney but her 'boyfriend' as well. On August 22, 1961, a date during the period in which the evidence shows that Holland was Mrs. Moses' attorney, she executed a document purporting to be her will. This instrument was drawn by an attorney with whom Holland was then associated and shared offices, and was typed by a secretary who served them both. It was witnessed by Holland's associate and their secretary. In addition to other testamentary dispositions, this document undertook to bequeath to Holland 'my wedding ring, my diamond solitare ring and my three gold bracelets containing twenty-five (25) pearls each.' In it Holland is referred to as 'my good friend.' The validity of this document is not an issue in the present case.

After Mrs. Moses died, the 1964 will was brought forward by another attorney, also an associate of Holland, who said that it had been entrusted to him by Mrs. Moses, together with other papers, for safekeeping. He distinguished his relation with Holland from that of a partner, saying that he and Holland only occupied offices together and shared facilities and expenses in the practice of law. He also stated that he saw Mrs. Moses on an 'average' of once a week, most often in the company of Holland.

Throughout this period, Mrs. Moses was a frequent visitor at Holland's office, and there is ample evidence to support the chancellor's finding that there existed a continuing fiduciary relationship between Mrs. Moses and Holland, as her attorney.

In May, 1962, Holland and the husband of Holland's first cousin, one Gibson, had contracted to buy 480 acres of land for $36,000. Mrs. Moses was not, it appears, originally a party to the contract. Gibson paid the $5,000 earnest money but testified that he did not know where it had come from and assumed that it came from Mrs. Moses. At the time, Mrs. Moses had annuity contracts with a total maturity value of some $40,000 on which she obtained $31,341.11. This sum was deposited in a bank account called 'Cedar Hills Ranch.' She gave Holland authority to check on this account, as well as upon her personal account. About this time, Gibson disappeared from the land transaction. On June 7, 1962, the deal was closed. At closing, the persons present, in addition to the grantors and their agents and attorney, were Mrs. Moses and Holland, her attorney. Mrs. Moses had no other counsel. Holland issued a check on the Cedar Hills Ranch account (in which only Mrs. Moses had any money) for the $31,000 balance. Although none of the consideration was paid by Holland, the deed from the owners purported to convey the land to Holland and Mrs. Moses in equal shares, as tenants in common. On the day following, Holland issued another check on the Cedar Hills Ranch account (in which he still had deposited no money) for $835.00 purportedly in payment for a tractor. This check was issued by Holland to his brother. Eight days later Holland drew another check on this account for $2,100.00 purportedly for an undisclosed number of cattle. This check was issued to Holland's father.

The evidence supports the chancellor's finding that the confidential or fiduciary relationship which existed between Mrs. Moses and Holland, her attorney, was a subsisting and continuing relationship, having begun before the making by Mrs. Moses of the will of August 22, 1961, under the terms of which her jewelry had been bequeathed to Holland, and having ended only with Mrs. Moses' death. Moreover, its effect was enhanced by the fact that throughout this period, Holland was in almost daily attendance upon Mrs. Moses on terms of the utmost intimacy. There was strong evidence that this aging woman, seriously ill, disfigured by surgery, and hopelessly addicted to alcoholic excesses, was completely bemused by the constant and amorous attentions of Holland, a man 15 years her junior. There was testimony too indicating that she entertained the pathetic hope that he might marry her. Although the evidence was not without conflict and was, in some of its aspects, circumstantial, it was sufficient to support the finding that the relationship existed on May 26, 1964, the date of the will tendered for probate by Holland.

The chancellor's factual finding of the existence of this relationship on that date is supported by evidence and is not manifestly wrong. Moreover, he was correct in his conclusion of law that such relationship gave rise to a presumption of undue influence which could be overcome only by evidence that, in making the 1964 will, Mrs. Moses had acted upon the independent advice and counsel of one entirely devoted to her interest.

Appellant takes the position that there was undisputed evidence that Mrs. Moses, in making the 1964 will, did, in fact, have such advice and counsel. He relies upon the testimony of the attorney in whose office that document was prepared to support his assertion.

This attorney was and is a reputable and respected member of the bar, who had no prior connection with Holland and no knowledge of Mrs. Moses' relationship with him. He had never seen nor represented Mrs. Moses previously and never represented her afterward. He was acquainted with Holland and was aware that Holland was a lawyer.

A brief summary of his testimony, with respect to the writing of the will, follows:

Mrs. Moses had telephoned him for an appointment and had come alone to his office on March 31, 1964. She was not intoxicated and in his opinion knew what she was doing. He asked her about her property and 'marital background.' He did this in order, he said, to advise her as to possible renunciation by a husband. She was also asked if she had children in order to determine whether she wished to 'pretermit them.' As she had neither husband nor children this subject was pursued no further. He asked as to the values of various items of property in order to consider possible tax problems. He told her it would be better if she had more accurate descriptions of the several items of real and personal property comprising her estate. No further 'advice or counsel' was given her.

On some later date, Mrs. Moses sent in (the attorney did not think she came personally and in any event he did not see her), some tax receipts for purposes of supplying property descriptions. He prepared the will and mailed a draft to her. Upon receiving it, she telephoned that he had made a mistake in the devise of certain realty, in that he had provided that a relatively low valued property should go to Holland rather than a substantially more valuable property which she said she wanted Holland to have. He rewrote the will, making this change, and mailed it to her, as revised, on May 21, 1964. On the one occasion when he saw Mrs. Moses, there were no questions and no discussion of any kind as to Holland being preferred to the exclusion of her blood relatives. Nor was there any inquiry or discussion as to a possible client-attorney relationship with Holland. The attorney-draftsman wrote the will according to Mrs. Moses' instructions and said that he had 'no interest in' how she disposed of her property. He testified 'I try to draw the will to suit their purposes and if she (Mrs. Moses) wanted to leave him (Holland) everything she had, that was her business as far as I was concerned. I was trying to represent her in putting on paper in her will her desires, and it didn't matter to me to whom she left it * * * I couldn't have cared less.'

When Mrs. Moses returned to the office to execute the will, the attorney was not there and it was witnessed by two secretaries. One of these secretaries, coincidentally, had written and witnessed the 1961 will when working for Holland and his associate.

The attorney's testimony supports the chancellor's finding that nowhere in the conversations with Mrs. Moses was there touched upon in any way the proposed testamentary disposition whereby preference was to be given a nonrelative to the exclusion of her blood relatives. There was no discussion of her relationship with Holland, nor as to who her legal heirs might be, nor as to their relationship to her, after it was discovered that she had neither a husband nor children.

It is clear from his own testimony that, in writing the will, the attorney-draftsman, did no more than write down, according to the forms of law, what Mrs. Moses told him. There was no meaningful independent advice or counsel touching upon the area in question and it is manifest that the role of the attorney in writing the will, as it relates to the present issue, was little more than that of scrivener. The chancellor was justified in holding that this did not meet the burden nor overcome the presumption.

In Croft v. Alder, 237 Miss. 713, 724, 115 So.2d 683, 686 (1959) there was an extensive review of the authorities relating to the question here under consideration. This Court said:

> Meek v. Perry, 1858, 36 Miss. 190, 243, 244, 252, 259, is perhaps the leading case. It involved a will by a ward leaving a substantial amount of her property to her guardian. The Court held that the presumption of invalidity applies to wills as well as deeds. It was said the law watches with the greatest jealousy transactions between persons in confidential relations and will not permit them to stand, unless the circumstances demonstrate the fullest deliberation on the part of the testator and the most abundant good faith on the part of the beneficiary. Hence the law presumes the existence of undue influence, and such dealings are *prima facie* void, and will be so held 'unless the guardian show by *clearest proof*' that he took no advantage over the testator, and the *cestui's* act was a result of his own volition and upon the fullest deliberation. * * *

> Moreover, even where there is no presumption of undue influence, the burden of proof rests upon the proponents throughout and never shifts to the contestants, both on undue influence and mental incapacity. Cheatham v. Burnside, 1954, 222 Miss. 872, 77 So.2d 719. From its very nature, evidence to show undue influence must be largely circumstantial. Undue influence is an intangible thing, which only rarely is susceptible of direct or positive proof. As was stated in Jamison v. Jamison, 1909, 96 Miss. 288, 51 So. 130, '*the only positive and affirmative proof required is of facts and circumstances from which the undue influence may be reasonably inferred.*'* * *

> The able and respected attorney who prepared the will upon data furnished him by Barney, who stated he was acting for Mr. Alder, testified that, in his opinion, the testator was mentally competent and the instrument reflected testator's independent purpose. However, the record indicates that the witness had not conferred with Mr. Alder about the will prior to its drafting. Moreover, *his testimony does not negative the presumption of undue influence resulting from 'antecedent agencies' and prior actions by the principal beneficiary who was in the confidential relation.* In Jamison v. Jamison, 1909, 96 Miss. 288, 298, 51 So. 130, 131, it was said: 'The difficulty is also enhanced by the fact, universally recognized, that he who seeks to use undue influence does so in privacy. He seldom uses brute force or open threats to terrorize his intended victim, and if he does he is careful that no witnesses are

about to take note of and testify to the fact. He observes, too, the same pre-cautions if he seeks by cajolery, flattery, or other methods to obtain power and control over the will of another, and direct it improperly to the accom-plishment of the purpose which he desires. Subscribing witnesses are called to attest the execution of wills, and testify as to the testamentary capacity of the testator, and the circumstances attending the immediate execution of the instrument; but *they are not called upon to testify as to the antecedent agencies by which the execution of the paper was secured, even if they had any knowledge of them, which they seldom have.*' In re Coins' Will (Fortner v. Coins), 1959, [237 Miss. 322] 114 So.2d 759.

We do not think that the testimony of the attorney who attested the will, as to his observations at that particular time, can suffice to rebut the already existing presumption. *As stated in Jamison, he naturally would have had no knowledge of any precedent activities by Barney.* (emphasis added).

In *Croft, supra,* this Court quoted the rule as stated in 57 Am.Jur. Wills sec-tions 389, 390 as follows:

> * * * [A]lthough the mere existence of confidential relations between a tes-tator and a beneficiary under his will does not raise a presumption that the beneficiary exercised undue influence over the testator, as it does with gifts *inter vivos,* such consequence follows where the beneficiary 'has been actively concerned in some way with the preparation or execution of the will, or where the relationship is coupled with *some suspicious circum-stances, such as mental infirmity of the testator*;' * * * (emphasis added).

See also Young v. Martin, 239 Miss. 861, 125 So.2d 734, 126 So.2d 529 (1961).

Holland, of course, did not personally participate in the actual preparation or execution of the will. If he had, under the circumstances in evidence, unquestion-ably the will could not stand. It may be assumed that Holland, as a lawyer, knew this.

In *Croft, supra,* this Court said that the presumption of undue influence in the production of a will may arise from 'antecedent circumstances' about which its draftsman and the witnesses knew nothing. The rule, as stated in that case, is that undue influence will be presumed where the beneficiary 'has been actively con-cerned in some way with the preparation or execution of the will, or where the *rela-tionship* is coupled with some *suspicious circumstances,* such as mental infirmity of the testator.' (emphasis added).

Undue influence operates upon the will as well as upon the mind. It is not depen-dent upon a lack of testamentary capacity.

The chancellor's finding that the will was the product of Holland's undue influ-ence is not inconsistent with his conclusion that 'Her (Mrs. Moses) mind was capable of understanding the essential matters necessary to the execution of her will on May 26, 1964, at the time of such execution.' A weak or infirm mind may, of course, be more easily over persuaded. In the case under review, Mrs. Moses was in ill health, she was an alcoholic, and was an aging woman infatuated with a young lover, 15 years her junior, who was also her lawyer. If this combination of circumstances cannot be said to support the view that Mrs. Moses suffered from a 'weakness or infirmity' of mind, vis-a-vis Holland, it was hardly calculated to enhance her power of will where he was concerned. Circumstances in evidence, both antecedent and subsequent to the making of the will, tend to accord with that conclusion.

The sexual morality of the personal relationship is not an issue. However, the intimate nature of this relationship is relevant to the present inquiry to the extent that its existence, under the circumstances, warranted an inference of undue influence, extending and augmenting that which flowed from the attorney-client relationship. Particularly is this true when viewed in the light of evidence indicating its employment for the personal aggrandizement of Holland. For that purpose, it was properly taken into consideration by the chancellor.

In 94 C.J.S. Wills § 263 (1956) it is stated:

> The mere existence of illicit, improper, unlawful, or meretricious relations between the testator and the beneficiary or the beneficiary's mother is insufficient of itself to prove fraud or undue influence, although the existence of such relations is an important fact to be considered by the jury along with other evidence of undue influence, giving to other circumstances a significance which they might not otherwise have; and much less evidence will be required to establish undue influence on the part of one holding wrongful and meretricious relations with the testator.

In *Croft* and *Taylor*, *supra*, the beneficiary was present at or participated at some stage or in some way in the preparation or execution of the will. However, it is to be noted that it was the 'antecedent circumstances' which gave rise to the presumption of undue influence, and that this was not overcome by testimony of an independent lawyer-draftsman who testified that the will reflected the independent wishes of the testator who had been of sound mind and had known what he was doing.

The rule laid down in *Croft*, *supra*, would have little, if any, practical worth, if, under circumstances such as those established in this case, it could be nullified by a mere showing that the beneficiary was not physically present when the will was prepared and executed.

The rule that where a fiduciary relationship has been established, a presumption of undue influence arises, is not limited to holographs, nor confined to wills otherwise prepared by the testator himself. It encompasses with equal force wills written for the testator by a third person. There is no sound reason supporting the view that a testator, whose will has become subservient to the undue influence of another, is purged of the effects of that influence merely because the desired testamentary document is prepared by an attorney who knows nothing of the antecedent circumstances.

The chancellor was justified in finding that the physical absence of Holland during Mrs. Moses' brief visit to the office of the attorney who wrote the will did not suffice to abate or destroy the presumption of undue influence.

The chancellor was the judge of the credibility of the witnesses and the weight and worth of their testimony. Moreover, as trier of facts, it was for him to resolve conflicts and to interpret evidence where it was susceptible of more than one reasonable interpretation. It was also his prerogative to draw reasonable inferences from facts proved. As said in *Croft, supra,* '[T]he only positive and affirmative proof required is of facts and circumstances from which the undue influence may be reasonably inferred.' This Court, in passing upon the sufficiency of the evidence to support the factual findings of the chancellor, must accept as true all that the evidence proved or reasonably tended to prove, together with all reasonable inferences to be drawn from it, supporting such findings.

Viewed in the light of the above rules, it cannot be said that chancellor was manifestly wrong in finding that Holland occupied a dual fiduciary relationship with respect to Mrs. Moses, both conventional and actual, attended by suspicious circumstances as set forth in his opinion, which gave rise to a presumption of undue influence in the production of the 1964 will, nor that he was manifestly wrong in finding that this presumption was not overcome by 'clearest proof' that in making and executing the will Mrs. Moses acted upon her 'own volition and upon the fullest deliberation,' or upon independent advice and counsel of one wholly devoted to her interest.

* * *

As stated in *Croft, supra,* the rule that a presumption of undue influence arises when a fiduciary relationship is established applies with even greater stringency in cases of transactions *inter vivos.* In the land transaction, Holland attended as Mrs. Moses' attorney. She had no other advice or counsel. The chancellor correctly held that, under the circumstances, Holland, as her attorney, could take no interest adverse to Mrs. Moses in the land purchased by her. He took title to the half interest in the land as trustee for Mrs. Moses and not otherwise. His apparent claim of ownership of a half interest was properly cancelled and removed as a cloud upon the title of Mrs. Moses to the complete fee. Johnson v. Outlaw, 56 Miss. 541 (1879) and Cameron v. Lewis, 56 Miss. 601 (1879). See also Sojourner v. Sojourner, 247 Miss. 342, 153 So.2d 803, 156 So.2d 579 (1963) and Smith v. Dean, 240 S.W.2d 789 (Tex. Civ.App.) (1951).

For the foregoing reasons, the petition for rehearing is sustained, the original majority opinion is withdrawn, this opinion will be that of the Court, and the decree of the chancery court will be affirmed.

Petition for rehearing sustained, original opinion withdrawn, and decree of chancery court affirmed.

ETHRIDGE, C.J., and GILLESPIE, RODGERS and JONES, JJ., concur.

BRADY, PATTERSON, INZER and ROBERTSON, JJ., dissent.

ROBERTSON, Justice (dissenting):

I am unable to agree with the majority of the Court that Mrs. Moses should not be allowed to dispose of her property as she so clearly intended.

Since 1848 it has been the law of this state that every person twenty-one years of age, male of female, married or unmarried, being of sound and disposing mind, has the power by last will and testament or codicil in writing to dispose of all of his or her worldly possessions as he or she sees fit. §657 Miss.Code 1942 Ann. (1956).

In 1848 the Legislature also said:

> "Whenever any last will and testament shall empower and direct the executor as to the sale of property, the payment of debts and legacies, and the management of the estate, *the directions of the will shall be followed by the executor* * * *." §518 Miss.Code 1942 Ann. (1956). (Emphasis added).

The intent and purpose of the lawmakers was crystal clear: No matter what the form of the instrument, if it represented the free, voluntary and knowledgeable act of the testator or testatrix it was a good will, and the directions of the will should be followed. We said in Gillis v. Smith, 114 Miss. 665, 75 So. 451 (1917):

> "A man of sound mind may execute a will or a deed from any sort of motive satisfactory to him, *whether that motive be love, affection, gratitude, partiality, prejudice, or even a whim or caprice.*" 114 Miss. at 677, 75 So. at 453. (Emphasis added).

Mrs. Fannie T. Moses was 54 years of age when she executed her last will and testament on May 26, 1964, leaving most of her considerable estate to Clarence H. Holland, her good friend, but a man fifteen years her junior. She had been married three times, and each of these marriages was dissolved by the death of her husband. Holland's friendship with Mrs. Moses dated back to the days of her second husband, Robert L. Dickson. He was also a friend of her third husband, Walter Moses.

She was the active manager of commercial property in the heart of Jackson, four apartment buildings containing ten rental units, and a 480-acre farm until the day of her death. All of the witnesses conceded that she was a good businesswoman, maintaining and repairing her properties with promptness and dispatch, and paying her bills promptly so that she would get the cash discount. She was a strong personality and pursued her own course, even though her manner of living did at times embarrass her sisters and estranged her from them.

The chancellor found that she was of sound and disposing mind and memory on May 26, 1964, when she executed her last will and testament, and I think he was correct in this finding.

The chancellor found that there was a confidential relationship between Mrs. Moses and Holland, who had acted as her attorney in the past, and who was, in addition, a close and intimate friend, and that because of this relationship and some suspicious circumstances a presumption of undue influence arose.

In Croft v. Alder, 237 Miss. 713, 115 So.2d 683 (1959), this Court said:

> '57 Am.Jur., Wills, Secs. 389, 390, state that, although the mere existence of confidential relations between a testator and a beneficiary under his will does not raise a presumption that the beneficiary exercised undue influence over the testator, as it does with gifts inter vivos, such consequence follows where the beneficiary 'has been actively concerned in some way with the preparation or execution of the will, or where the relationship is coupled with some suspicious circumstances, such as mental infirmity of the testator;' or where the beneficiary in the confidential relation was active directly in preparing the will or procuring its execution, and obtained under it a substantial benefit. * * *' 237 Miss. at 723–724, 115 So.2d at 686. (Emphasis added).

There is no proof in this voluminous record that Holland ever did or said anything to Mrs. Moses about devising her property to anybody, much less him. It is conceded that in the absence of the presumption of undue influence that there is no basis to support a finding that Holland exercised undue influence over Mrs. Moses. This being true, the first question to be decided is whether the presumption of undue influence arises under the circumstances of this case.

It is my opinion that the presumption did not arise. The fact, alone, that a confidential relationship existed between Holland and Mrs. Moses is not sufficient to give rise to the presumption of undue influence in a will case. We said in *Croft*, *supra*:

> '[S]uch consequence follows where the beneficiary 'has been actively concerned in some way with the preparation or execution of the will, or where the relationship is coupled with some suspicious circumstances, *such as mental infirmity of the testator;*' or where *the beneficiary* in the confidential relation *was active directly in preparing the will or procuring its execution,* and obtained under it a substantial benefit.' 237 Miss. at 723–724, 115 So.2d at 686. (Emphasis added).

It was not contended in this case that Holland was in any way actively concerned with the preparation or execution of the will. Appellees rely solely upon the finding of the chancellor that there were suspicious circumstances. However, the suspicious circumstances listed by the chancellor in his opinion had nothing whatsoever to do with the preparation or execution of the will. These were remote antecedent circumstances having to do with the meretricious relationship of the parties, and the fact that at times Mrs. Moses drank to excess and could be termed an alcoholic, but there is no proof in this long record that her use of alcohol affected her will power or her ability to look after her extensive real estate holdings. It is common knowledge that many persons who could be termed alcoholics, own, operate and manage large business enterprises with success. The fact that she chose to leave most of her property to the man she loved in preference to her sisters and brother is not such an unnatural disposition of her property as to render it invalid.

* * *

In this case, there were no suspicious circumstances surrounding the preparation or execution of the will, and in my opinion the chancellor was wrong in so holding. However, even if it be conceded that the presumption of undue influence did arise, this presumption was overcome by clear and convincing evidence of good faith, full knowledge and independent consent and advice.

* * *

What else could she have done? She met all the tests that this Court and other courts have carefully outlined and delineated. The majority opinion says that this still was not enough, that there were 'suspicious circumstances' and 'antecedent agencies', but even these were not connected in any shape, form or fashion with the preparation or execution of her will. They had to do with her love life and her drinking habits and propensities.

It would appear that the new procedure will be to fine-tooth comb all the events of a person's life and if, in the mind of the judge on the bench at that particular time, there are any 'suspicious circumstances' or 'antecedent agencies' in that person's life even though they are in nowise connected with the preparation or execution of that person's will, such last will and testament will be set aside and held for naught. With all time-honored tests out the window, the trial judge will be in the dangerous predicament of embarking on an unknown sea, without chart or compass.

If full knowledge, deliberate and voluntary action, and independent consent and advice have not been proved in this case, then they just cannot be proved. We should be bound by the uncontradicted testimony in the record; we should not go completely outside the record and guess, speculate and surmise as to what happened.

I think that the judgment of the lower court should be reversed and the last will and testament of Fannie T. Moses executed on May 26, 1964, admitted to probate in solemn form.

BRADY, PATTERSON and INZER, JJ., join in this dissent.

Notes

Undue influence cases often appear as sensational headlines, movies, and books. *See, e.g.,* DAVID MARGOLICK, UNDUE INFLUENCE: THE EPIC BATTLE FOR THE JOHNSON & JOHNSON FORTUNE (1993) (describing the suit brought by the children of J. Seward Johnson against their stepmother, Barbara Piasecka, and the attorneys who played an instrumental role in the preparation of Mr. Johnson's will).

Attorneys and those serving in confidential relationships with testators must be especially careful in anticipating contest. *See, e.g.,* Disciplinary Counsel v. Galinas, 76 Ohio St. 3d 87, 666 N.E.2d 1083 (1996) (attorney suspended for drafting will that gave him interest in estate). California has a statute that invalidates any bequest to named individuals, including any attorney who drafts the will, unless the attorney is related by blood or affinity, within the third degree, to the testator. *See* CAL. PROB. CODE ANN. §21380 (as amended by 2019 Cal. Legis. Serv. Ch. 10 (A.B. 328)

(WEST) (filed June 26, 2019). *But see* Vaupel v. Barr, 194 W. Va. 296, 460 S.E.2d 431 (1995) (attorney-friend able to keep bequest). Religious organizations are vulnerable to contest because of the confidentiality that resides between pastor and parishioner. *See* Estate of Maheras, 897 P.2d 268 (Okla. 1995). Nursing homes are certain to become the subject of more litigation as increasing numbers of persons trust in their care. *See* Matter of Burke, 82 A.D.2d 260, 441 N.Y.S.2d 542 (N.Y. App. Div. 2 Dept. 1981). The California Probate Code provides a certificate of independent review and should be considered when any form of confidentiality is present. *See* CAL. PROB. CODE § 21384 (West 2019). *See also* NEV. REV. STAT. § 155.097 (2019) (providing that transfer is presumptively void if made to transferee who drafted transfer instrument); NEV. REV. STAT. § 155.0975 (2019) (allowing otherwise prohibited transfers if transfer instrument is signed by independent attorney who complies with certain requirements, including signing Certificate of Independent Review).

E. Fraud

In re Roblin's Estate

Supreme Court of Oregon, 1957
210 Or. 371, 311 P.2d 459

ROSSMAN, Justice.

This is an appeal by Charles Dana Roblin, contestant, from a decree of the Circuit Court for Marion County which dismissed proceedings he had instituted to contest the will of his father, Charles Ernest Roblin, and which ordered that the will be admitted to probate.

Charles Ernest and Ollie M. Roblin, both now deceased, were the parents of the appellant, Charles Dana Roblin, and of a daughter, Ruth Emily Shantz, proponent and respondent. For convenience we will refer to the elder Charles Roblin as Mr. Roblin and to the younger as Charles.

The family resided for many years in Salem. When Ruth Married Carl Shantz they took their residence in Milwaukie, Oregon. Charles became a peripatetic, but during summer months returned to Salem for extended visits in the family home. In 1950 Mr. Roblin left the family home and made his abode in a Salem hotel. Ruth testified that he left in aggravation over his wife's conduct in sending money to Charles and paying his bills. In 1951 Mr. Roblin suffered a stroke and shortly repaired to a nursing home in Salem.

In the fall of 1951, Ruth, at her father's instance, arranged for him to undergo an eye operation in Portland. In that period he resided with Ruth and her husband for seven months. After he had recovered from the operation he returned to the nursing home where Ruth visited him every two weeks. Mrs. Roblin also called upon him from time to time, being driven to the nursing home in the Roblins' car by Charles. The latter, however, did not enter the home. Upon an earlier occasion when he attempted to visit his father, the latter ordered him out of the room in no unmistakable language.

Mrs. Roblin executed a will on July 3, 1953, and died five days later. Her will bequeathed all of her property equally to both children. Its terms were operative on property appraised at $1,581. But Charles received, in addition to his half of that sum, property worth $12,301.06 which was not part of the estate proper. This greater amount represented accounts and chattels the title to which was in Charles and the mother jointly, and to which he survived.

On either the evening of July 8 or the morning of July 9, 1953, Ruth visited her father in the nursing home and informed him, perhaps in response to his inquiry, that her mother had left everything to Charles except a diamond ring. Immediately Mr. Roblin ordered Ruth to obtain for him a lawyer. Ruth suggested a Mr. Steelhammer who was her husband's cousin. The suggestion was acceptable to her father, he having known Mr. Steelhammer through their mutual membership in the Salem Elks Lodge. On the morning of July 9 Mr. Steelhammer went to the nursing home and conversed in privacy with Mr. Roblin, who directed him to prepare a will, leaving Charles one dollar only and the remainder to Ruth. The father also requested Mr. Steelhammer to prepare a petition for a conservatorship of the father's property with Ruth as conservator. That afternoon, Ruth, upon Mr. Steelhammer's request, drove him to the nursing home. When they arrived, the attorney alone met with the testator, who then executed his will, with Steelhammer and the operator of the home as witnesses. The will nominated Ruth as executrix and left to her everything except one dollar which was bequeathed to Charles. The petition for conservatorship was filed on July 20. Mr. Roblin died September 6, 1953, aged 83.

* * *

Courts set aside wills whose provisions reflect the testator's belief in false data arising from fraudulent misrepresentation made to him by a beneficiary. In re Estate of Rosenberg, 196 Or. 219, 246 P.2d 858, 248 P.2d 340.

> 'Fraud which causes testator to execute a will consists of statements which are false, which are known to be false by the party who makes them, which are material, which are made with the intention of deceiving testator, which deceive testator, and which cause testator to act in reliance upon such statements.'

I Page on Wills, 3d Ed. 347, § 176. Absent any one of the elements of that definition of fraud, no ground for contest is established.

The statement which we are considering, and the consequences of its utterance, must be measured against the elements of fraud which vitiates a solemnly executed will.

The statement must be false and known to be such by the maker. In fact, Ruth's mother did not leave everything, except a ring, to her brother. Ruth was to receive half of $1,581; the other half of which went to Charles along with the $12,301.06 in jointly held property to which Charles survived. After the expenses of administration and taxes were paid by that estate, Ruth received $61.90. Charles received from his mother $12,367.96. The disparity is so great that Ruth may be excused for having been piqued, as is Charles now.

We must distinguish between a belief in the literal truth and falsity of a statement and that type of belief in falsity that underlies the fraudulent misrepresentation. Ruth testified at trial that 'The only thing one could say, or I did say, was that Mother had left everything to Charlie.' In this context a belief in the falsity of an utterance must be defined with regard to the nature of man and his reactions to an unexpected disappointment. The testimony just quoted demonstrates that at the time of utterance, and indeed at the time of trial, after reflection, Ruth doubted not that the hyperbole fairly described the division of her mother's estate.

The speaker must intend to deceive, and succeed. We are unwilling to decide that even a conscious exaggeration necessarily imports an intent to deceive. Even people of high character often exaggerate in order to express their belief with clarity and force. The purpose in instances of that kind is not to deceive, but better to communicate the belief. We are convinced that the statement made by Ruth is an example of that process. The speaker may in perfect good faith omit what he considers to be a non-material qualification upon his broad statement, thinking that a recital of all the details merely obfuscates the main point.

The misrepresentation must cause the testator to act upon it. In other words, the will must be the fruit of the fraud. In the Roblin family, little family unity or mutuality of attitude toward life bound father and son together. We know that the father emphatically expressed a desire that Charles stay away from the nursing home so that the two would not meet. Evidently, the wanderlust of the son was a canker to the parent. The learned trial judge would have been justified in a conclusion that the statement made by Ruth did not cause her father to rely upon it in the execution of his will, but rather that the statement merely provided an occasion for the taking of a step which the disappointed parent may have independently taken even if the statement had never been uttered.

The testimony of Ruth and of Charles conflicts in that she states, and he denies, that all her information about the division of their mother's estate came from him. If one believes her account, which the judge below may have done, her statement to her father cannot be objectionable. In that event, she merely relayed information which Charles gave her.

Both parties testified on direct and on cross-examination at some length about the amount of money each had received from Mr. and Mrs. Roblin *inter vivos*. We deem this evidence irrelevant. The statement of Ruth which is objected to refers only to the disposition of her mother's property upon her death. It does not relate to the *inter vivos* gifts to the children, of which Ruth received the greater share. Consequently the truth or falsity of the statement stands independent of the history of *inter vivos* donations.

Agreeing, as we do, with the disposition of this matter by the judge below, we affirm his decree.

Affirmed.

Latham v. Father Divine

Court of Appeals of New York, 1949
299 N.Y. 22, 85 N.E.2d 168

DESMOND, J.

The amended complaint herein has, in response to a motion under rule 106 of the Rules of Civil Practice, been dismissed for insufficiency. Its principal allegations are these: plaintiffs are first cousins, but not distributees, of Mary Sheldon Lyon, who died in October, 1946, leaving a will, executed in 1943, which gave almost her whole estate to defendant Father Divine, leader of a religious cult, and to two corporate defendants in some way connected with that cult, and to an individual defendant (Patience Budd) said to be one of Father Divine's active followers; that said will has been, after a contest instituted by distributees, probated under a compromise agreement with the distributees, by the terms of which agreement, to which plaintiffs were not parties, the defendants just above referred to will receive a large sum from the estate; that after the making of said will, decedent on several occasions expressed 'a desire and a determination to revoke the said will, and to execute a new will by which the plaintiffs would receive a substantial portion of the estate', 'that shortly prior to the death of the deceased she had certain attorneys draft a new will in which the plaintiffs were named as legatees for a very substantial amount, totalling approximately $350,000'; that 'by reason of the said false representations, the said undue influence and the said physical force' certain of the defendants 'prevented the deceased from executing the said new Will'; that, shortly before decedent's death, decedent again expressed her determination to execute the proposed new will which favored plaintiffs, and that defendants 'thereupon conspired to kill, and did kill, the deceased by means of a surgical operation performed by a doctor engaged by the defendants without the consent or knowledge of any of the relatives of the deceased.'

Nothing is better settled than that, on such a motion as this, all the averments of the attacked pleading are taken as true. For present purposes, then, we have a case where one possessed of a large property and having already made a will leaving it to certain persons, expressed an intent to make a new testament to contain legacies to other persons, attempted to carry out that intention by having a new will drawn which contained a large legacy to those others, but was, by means of misrepresentations, undue influence, force, and indeed, murder, prevented, by the beneficiaries named in the existing will, from signing the new one. Plaintiffs say that those facts, if proven, would entitle them to a judicial declaration, which their prayer for judgment demands, that defendants, taking under the already probated will, hold what they have so taken as constructive trustees for plaintiffs, whom decedent wished to, tried to, and was kept from, benefiting.

We find in New York no decision directly answering the question as to whether or not the allegations above summarized state a case for relief in equity. But reliable texts, and cases elsewhere (see 98 A. L. R. 474 et seq.) answer it in the affirmative. Leading writers (3 Scott on Trusts, pp. 2371–2376; 3 Bogert on Trusts and Trustees, Part 1, §§ 473–474, 498, 499; 1 Perry on Trusts and Trustees [7th ed.], pp. 265, 371) in one form or another, state the law of the subject to be about as it is expressed in comment i under section 184 of the Restatement of the Law of Restitution: 'Preventing revocation of will and making new will. Where a devisee or legatee under a will already executed prevents the testator by fraud, duress or undue influence from revoking the will and executing a new will in favor of another or from making a codicil, so that the testator dies leaving the original will in force, the devisee or legatee holds the property thus acquired upon a constructive trust for the intended devisee or legatee.'

A frequently-cited case is Ransdel v. Moore (153 Ind. 393) where, with listing of many authorities, the rule is given thus (pp. 407–408): 'when an heir or devisee in a will prevents the testator from providing for one for whom he would have provided but for the interference of the heir or devisee, such heir or devisee will be deemed a trustee, by operation of law, of the property, real or personal, received by him from the testator's estate, to the amount or extent that the defrauded party would have received had not the intention of the deceased been interfered with. This rule applies also when an heir prevents the making of a will or deed in favor of another, and thereby inherits the property that would otherwise have been given such other person.' (To the same effect, see 4 Page on Wills [3d ed.], p. 961.)

While there is no New York case decreeing a constructive trust on the exact facts alleged here, there are several decisions in this court which, we think, suggest such a result, and none which forbids it. Matter of O'Hara (95 N. Y. 403), Trustees of Amherst College v. Ritch (151 N. Y. 282), Edson v. Bartow (154 N. Y. 199), and Ahrens v. Jones (169 N. Y. 555) which need not be closely analyzed here as to their facts, all announce, in one form or another, the rule that, where a legatee has taken property under a will, after agreeing, outside the will, to devote that property to a purpose intended and declared by the testator, equity will enforce a constructive trust to effectuate that purpose, lest there be a fraud on the testator. (In Williams v. Fitch, 18 N. Y. 546, a similar result was achieved in a suit for money had and received.) In each of those four cases first above cited in this paragraph, the particular fraud consisted of the legatee's failure or refusal to carry out the testator's designs, after tacitly or expressly promising so to do. But we do not think that a breach of such an engagement is the only kind of fraud which will impel equity to action. A constructive trust will be erected whenever necessary to satisfy the demands of justice. Since a constructive trust is merely 'the formula through which the conscience of equity finds expression' (Beatty v. Guggenheim Exploration Co., 225 N. Y. 380, 386; see 3 Bogert on Trusts and Trustees, Part 1, § 471; Lightfoot v. Davis, 198 N. Y. 261; Falk v. Hoffman, 233 N. Y. 199; Meinhard v. Salmon, 249 N. Y. 458; also, see, Warren in 41 Harv. L. Rev. 309 et seq.), its applicability is limited only by the inventiveness of men who find new ways to enrich themselves unjustly by grasping what should not belong to them. Nothing short of true and complete justice satisfies equity, and, always assuming these allegations to be true, there seems no way of achieving total justice except by the procedure used here.

The Appellate Division held that Hutchins v. Hutchins (7 Hill 104) decided by the Supreme Court, our predecessor, in 1845, was a bar to the maintenance of this suit. Hutchins v. Hutchins (*supra*) was a suit at law, dismissed for insufficiency in the days when law suits and equity causes had to be brought in different tribunals; the law court could give nothing but a judgment for damages (see discussion in 41 Harv. L. Rev. 313, *supra*). Testator Hutchins' son, named in an earlier will, charged that defendant had, by fraud, caused his father to revoke that will and execute a new one, disinheriting plaintiff. The court sustained a demurrer to the complaint, on the ground that the earlier will gave the son no title, interest or estate in his father's assets and no more than a hope or expectancy, the loss of which was too theoretical and tenuous a deprivation to serve as a basis for the award of damages (see, also, Simar v. Canaday, 53 N. Y. 298, 302, 303). Plaintiffs' disappointed hopes in the present case, held the Appellate Division, were similarly lacking in substance. But disappointed hopes and unrealized expectations were all that the secretly intended beneficiaries, not named in the wills, had in Matter of O'Hara, Trustees of Amherst College v. Ritch and Edson v. Bartow (*supra*) but that in itself was not enough to prevent the creation of constructive trusts in their favor. Hutchins v. Hutchins (*supra*), it seems, holds only this: that in a suit at law there must, as a basis for damages, be an invasion of a common-law right. To use that same standard in a suit for the declaration and enforcement of a constructive trust would be to deny and destroy the whole equitable theory of constructive trusts.

Nor do we agree that anything in the Decedent Estate Law or the Statute of Frauds stands in the way of recovery herein. This is not a proceeding to probate or establish the will which plaintiffs say testatrix was prevented from signing, nor is it an attempt to accomplish a revocation of the earlier will, as were Matter of Evans (113 App. Div. 373) and Matter of McGill (229 N. Y. 405, 411). The will Mary Sheldon Lyon did sign has been probated and plaintiffs are not contesting, but proceeding on, that probate, trying to reach property which has effectively passed thereunder (see Ahrens v. Jones, 169 N. Y. 555, 561, *supra*). Nor is this a suit to enforce an agreement to make a will or create a trust, or any other promise by decedent (Personal Property Law, § 31; see Frankenberger v. Schneller, 258 N. Y. 270; Bayreuther v. Reinisch, 264 App. Div. 138, affd. 290 N. Y. 553; Blanco v. Velez, 295 N. Y. 224). This complaint does not say that decedent, or defendants, promised plaintiffs anything, or that defendants made any promise to decedent. The story is, simply, that defendants, by force and fraud, kept the testatrix from making a will in favor of plaintiffs. We cannot say, as matter of law, that no constructive trust can arise therefrom.

The ultimate determinations in Matter of O'Hara and Edson v. Bartow (*supra*) that the estates went to testators' distributees do not help defendants here, since, after the theory of constructive trust had been indorsed by this court in those cases, the distributees won out in the end, but only because the secret trusts intended by the two testators were, in each case, of kinds forbidden by statutes.

We do not agree with appellants that Riggs v. Palmer (115 N. Y. 506) completely controls our decision here. That was the famous case where a grandson, overeager to get the remainder interest set up for him in his grandfather's will, murdered his grandsire. After the will had been probated, two daughters of the testator who, under the will, would take if the grandson should predecease testator, sued and got judgment decreeing a constructive trust in their favor. It may be, as respondents assert, that the application of Riggs v. Palmer (*supra*) here would benefit not plaintiffs, but this testator's distributees. We need not pass on that now. But Riggs v. Palmer (*supra*) is generally helpful to appellants, since it forbade the grandson profiting by his own wrong in connection with a will; and, despite an already probated will and the Decedent Estate Law, Riggs v. Palmer (*supra*) used the device or formula of constructive trust to right the attempted wrong, and prevent unjust enrichment.

The reference to a conspiracy in the complaint herein makes it appropriate to mention Keviczky v. Lorber (290 N. Y. 297). Keviczky, a real estate broker, got judgment on findings that a conspiracy by defendants had prevented him from earning a commission which he would otherwise have gotten. All sides agreed that he had not in fact performed the engagement which would have entitled him to a commission as such; thus, when the conspiracy intervened to defeat his efforts, he had no contractual right to a commission but only an expectation thereof which was frustrated by the conspirators. Thus again we see, despite the broad language of Hutchins v. Hutchins (*supra*) that it is not the law that disappointed expectations and unrealized probabilities may never, under any circumstances, be a basis for recovery.

This suit cannot be defeated by any argument that to give plaintiffs judgment would be to annul those provisions of the Statute of Wills requiring due execution by the testator. Such a contention, if valid, would have required the dismissal in a number of the suits herein cited. The answer is in Ahrens v. Jones (169 N. Y. 555, 561, *supra*): "The trust does not act directly upon the will by modifying the gift, for the law requires wills to be wholly in writing, but it acts upon the gift itself as it reaches the possession of the legatee, or as soon as he is entitled to receive it. The theory is that the will has full effect by passing an absolute legacy to the legatee, and that then equity, in order to defeat fraud, raises a trust in favor of those intended to be benefited by the testator, and compels the legatee, as a trustee ex maleficio, to turn over the gift to them."

The judgment of the Appellate Division, insofar as it dismissed the complaint herein, should be reversed, and the order of Special Term affirmed, with costs in this court and in the Appellate Division. [See 299 N. Y. 599.]

LOUGHRAN, Ch. J., CONWAY and FULD, JJ., concur with DESMOND, J.;

LEWIS and DYE, JJ., dissent and vote for affirmance upon the grounds stated by VAUGHAN, J., writing for the Appellate Division.

Judgment reversed, etc.

BILL DEDMAN AND PAUL CLARK NEWELL, JR.
EMPTY MANSIONS
xxii (2013)

[Huguette Clark died at the age of 104, unmarried and without issue. She owned palatial homes in New York, California and Connecticut, each staffed and maintained throughout the time she owned them, but she lived the last twenty years of her life in a simple hospital room in lower Manhattan despite being in excellent health.]

In May 2011, just two weeks before her 105th birthday, Huguette Clark died in Beth Israel Medical Center in Manhattan. Court records soon answered one mystery while raising another. Huguette had not signed 'a will' to distribute her fortune but had signed two wills with contrary instructions. Both had been signed in the spring of 2005, when she was nearly ninety-nine.

The first will left $5 million to her nurse and the rest of her fortune to her closest living relatives, who would have inherited anyway if she had signed no will at all. These heirs were not named in the document. Six weeks later, Huguette had signed a second will, leaving nothing to her relatives. She split her estate among her nurse, a goddaughter, her doctor, the hospital, her attorney, and her accountant, but directed that the largest share go to a new arts foundation at Bellosguardo, her California vacation home.

Thus began a court battle—with more than $300 million at stake—to determine Huguette's true intentions. Nineteen relatives, from her father's first marriage, challenged her last will, saying that Huguette was a victim of fraud, that she was mentally ill, and unable to understand what she had signed.

F. Tortious Interference with an Expectancy

Diane J. Klein
"Go West, Disappointed Heir": Tortious Interference with Expectation of Inheritance—A Survey with Analysis of State Approaches in the Pacific States
13 LEWIS & CLARK L. REV. 209 (2009)

What is "tortious interference with expectation of inheritance"? It is the wrongful interference with an inheritance (or legacy, *inter vivos* gift, or interest in trust) that another would have received, but for that interference. * * * Significantly, it is not an action against the decedent or the decedent's estate. Instead, the defendant might be a person who wrongfully induced or prevented the execution or revocation of a testamentary instrument. In many cases, a person injured by this type of conduct can obtain the intended legacy through a successful challenge in probate court. For example, if the wrongdoer employed undue influence or fraud to procure a will in his favor, a successful challenge to that will "undoes" the harm. In such cases, arguably, a separate tort remedy is neither necessary nor appropriate.

Id. at 212–13.

[S]tates that recognize the tort require the plaintiff either to have exhausted her remedies in probate court, or to demonstrate why seeking a remedy in probate court would be futile. * * * Generally this functions as a jurisdictional prerequisite, rendering the tort suit subject to a motion to dismiss for failure to exhaust probate remedies. As for elements of the tort, most states that have recognized it in recent years have adopted a version of it close to that found in Restatement (Second) of Torts § 774B. That section provides, "One who by fraud, duress or other tortious means intentionally prevents another from receiving from a third person an inheritance or gift that he would otherwise have received is subject to liability to the other for loss of the inheritance or gift." * * * The elements are then generally identified as, "(1) a valid expectancy; (2) intentional interference with that expectancy; (3) independently tortious conduct (such as undue influence, fraud, or duress); (4) reasonable certainty that absent the tortious interference the plaintiff would have received the expectancy; and (5) damages."

Id. at 214.

Schilling v. Herrera
Court of Appeal of Florida, 2007
952 So. 2d 1231

ROTHENBERG, Judge. * * *

Mr. Schilling, the decedent's brother, sued Ms. Herrera, the decedent's caretaker, for intentional interference with an expectancy of inheritance. Ms. Herrera moved to dismiss the complaint, arguing that Mr. Schilling failed to state a cause of action and that he was barred from filing his claim because he failed to exhaust his probate remedies. The trial court granted the motion to dismiss without prejudice.

Thereafter, Mr. Schilling filed an amended complaint asserting the same cause of action against Ms. Herrera. The amended complaint alleges that in December 1996, Mignonne Helen Schilling (the decedent) executed her Last Will and Testament, naming her brother and only heir-at-law, Mr. Schilling, as her personal representative and sole beneficiary, and in May 1997, she executed a Durable Power of Attorney, naming Mr. Schilling as her attorney-in-fact.

In December 1999, the decedent was diagnosed with renal disease, resulting in several hospitalizations. During this period, Mr. Schilling, who resides in New Jersey, traveled to Florida to assist the decedent. In January 2000, the decedent executed a Power of Attorney for Health Care, naming Mr. Schilling as her attorney-in-fact for health care decisions.

On January 12, 2001, when the decedent was once again hospitalized, Mr. Schilling traveled to Florida to make arrangements for the decedent's care. After being released from the hospital, the decedent was admitted to a rehabilitation hospital, then to a health care center, and then to the Clairidge House for rehabilitation. While at the Clairidge House, Ms. Herrera became involved in the decedent's care, and when the decedent was discharged from the Clairidge House on December 16, 2001, Ms. Herrera notified Mr. Schilling.

After being discharged from the Clairidge House, the decedent returned to her apartment, and Ms. Herrera began to care for her on an "occasional, as needed basis." In 2003, when the decedent's condition worsened and she was in need of additional care, Ms. Herrera converted her garage into a bedroom, and the decedent moved in. The decedent paid Ms. Herrera rent and for her services as caregiver.

When Mr. Schilling spoke to Ms. Herrera over the phone, Ms. Herrera complained that she was not getting paid enough to take care of the decedent, and on April 10, 2003, Mr. Schilling sent Ms. Herrera money. While living in the converted garage, the decedent became completely dependent on Ms. Herrera. In September 2003, without Mr. Schilling's knowledge, Ms. Herrera convinced the decedent to prepare and execute a new Power of Attorney, naming Ms. Herrera as attorney-in-fact, and to execute a new Last Will and Testament naming Ms. Herrera as personal representative and sole beneficiary of the decedent's estate.

Mr. Schilling visited the decedent in March of 2004. On August 6, 2004, the decedent died at Ms. Herrera's home.

On August 24, 2004, Ms. Herrera filed her Petition for Administration. On December 2, 2004, following the expiration of the creditor's period, Ms. Herrera petitioned for discharge of probate. On December 6, 2004, *after the expiration of the creditor's period and after Ms. Herrera had petitioned the probate court for discharge of probate, Ms. Herrera notified Mr. Schilling for the first time that the decedent, his sister, had passed away on August 6, 2004.* Shortly thereafter, in late December 2004, the Final Order of Discharge was entered by the probate court. Mr. Schilling alleges that prior to being notified of his sister's death on December 6, 2004, he attempted to contact the decedent through Ms. Herrera, but Ms. Herrera did not return his calls until the conclusion of probate proceedings and did not inform him of his sister's death, thereby depriving him of both the knowledge of the decedent's death and the opportunity of contesting the probate proceedings. Mr. Schilling further alleges that prior to the decedent's death, Ms. Herrera regularly did not immediately return his phone calls, and that Ms. Herrera's "intentional silence was part of a calculated scheme to prevent [Mr.] Schilling from contesting the Estate of Decedent, and was intended to induce [Mr.] Schilling to refrain from acting in his interests to contest the probate proceedings in a timely fashion, as [Mr.] Schilling was used to long delays in contact with [Ms.] Herrera, and did not suspect that the delay was intended to fraudulently induce [Mr.] Schilling to refrain from acting on his own behalf." Finally, Mr. Schilling alleges that he expected to inherit the decedent's estate because he was the decedent's only heir-at-law and because he was named as the sole beneficiary in the 1996 will; Ms. Herrera's fraudulent actions prevented him from receiving the decedent's estate, which he was entitled to; and but for Ms. Herrera's action of procuring the will naming her as sole beneficiary, he would have received the benefit of the estate.

After Mr. Schilling filed his amended complaint, Ms. Herrera filed a renewed motion to dismiss, arguing the same issues that she had raised in her previous motion to dismiss. The trial court granted the motion to dismiss with prejudice, finding that Ms. Herrera had no duty to notify Mr. Schilling of the decedent's death as Mr. Schilling did not hire Ms. Herrera to care for the decedent, and therefore, there was "no special relationship giving rise to a proactive responsibility to provide information. . . ." The trial court also found that Mr. Schilling was barred from filing a claim for intentional interference with an expectancy of inheritance because he failed to exhaust his probate remedies. * * *

A trial court's ruling on a motion to dismiss for failure to state a cause of action is an issue of law, and therefore, our standard of review is *de novo. Roos v. Morrison,* 913 So.2d 59, 63 (Fla. 1st DCA 2005); *Susan Fixel, Inc. v. Rosenthal & Rosenthal, Inc.,* 842 So.2d 204, 206 (Fla. 3d DCA 2003). This court "must accept the facts alleged in a complaint as true when reviewing an order that determines the sufficiency of the complaint." *Warren ex rel. Brassell v. K-Mart Corp.,* 765 So.2d 235, 236 (Fla. 1st DCA 2000); *see also Marshall v. Amerisys, Inc.,* 943 So.2d 276, 278 (Fla. 3d DCA 2006) ("In determining the merits of a motion to dismiss, the court is confined to the four corners of the complaint, including the attachments thereto, the allegations of which must be accepted as true and considered in the light most favorable to the nonmoving party.").

To state a cause of action for intentional interference with an expectancy of inheritance, the complaint must allege the following elements: (1) the existence of an expectancy; (2) intentional interference with the expectancy through tortious conduct; (3) causation; and (4) damages. *Claveloux v. Bacotti,* 778 So.2d 399, 400 (Fla. 2d DCA 2001)(citing *Whalen v. Prosser,* 719 So.2d 2, 5 (Fla. 2d DCA 1998)). The court in *Whalen* clearly explained that the purpose behind this tort is to protect the testator, not the beneficiary:

> Interference with an expectancy is an unusual tort because the beneficiary is authorized to sue to recover damages primarily to protect the testator's interest rather than the disappointed beneficiary's expectations. The fraud, duress, undue influence, or other independent tortious conduct required for this tort is directed at the testator. The beneficiary is not directly defrauded or unduly influenced; the testator is. Thus, the common law court has created this cause of action not primarily to protect the beneficiary's inchoate rights, but to protect the deceased testator's former right to dispose of property freely and without improper interference. In a sense, the beneficiary's action is derivative of the testator's rights.

Whalen, 719 So.2d at 6.

In the instant case, the trial court's ruling was based on the fact that the amended complaint fails to allege that Ms. Herrera breached a legal duty owed to Mr. Schilling. However, as the *Claveloux* court noted, there are four elements for a cause of action for intentional interference with an expectancy of inheritance, and breach of a legal duty is not one of the elements. This is consistent with the *Whalen* court's explanation that the "fraud, duress, undue influence, or other independent tortious conduct required for this tort *is directed at the testator. The beneficiary is not directly defrauded or unduly influenced; the testator is.*" *Id.* (emphasis added). We, therefore, review the amended complaint to determine if it sufficiently pleads a cause of action for intentional interference with an expectancy of inheritance.

In essence, the amended complaint alleges that Mr. Schilling was named as the sole beneficiary in the decedent's last will and testament; that based on this last will and testament, he expected to inherit the decedent's estate upon her death; that Ms. Herrera intentionally interfered with his expectancy of inheritance by "convincing" the decedent, while she was ill and completely dependent on Ms. Herrera, to execute a new last will and testament naming Ms. Herrera as the sole beneficiary; and that Ms. Herrera's "fraudulent actions" and "undue influence" prevented Mr. Schilling from inheriting the decedent's estate. Based on these well-pled allegations, we conclude that the amended complaint states a cause of action for intentional interference with an expectancy of inheritance. Therefore, the trial court erred, as a matter of law, in dismissing the amended complaint on that basis.

Mr. Schilling also contends that the trial court erred in finding that he was barred from filing a claim for intentional interference with an expectancy of inheritance as he failed to exhaust his probate remedies. We agree.

In finding that Mr. Schilling was barred from filing his action for intentional interference with an expectancy of inheritance, the trial court relied on *DeWitt v. Duce*, 408 So.2d 216 (Fla.1981). In *DeWitt*, the testator's will was admitted to probate after his death. Thereafter, the plaintiffs filed a petition for revocation of probate of the testator's will, but voluntarily dismissed the petition, choosing to take under the will instead of challenging the will in probate court. More than two years later, the plaintiffs filed their claim for intentional interference with an inheritance, arguing that the defendants exercised undue influence over the testator at a time when he lacked testamentary capacity, causing the testator to execute the probated will, which was less favorable to the plaintiffs and more favorable to the defendants than the testator's previous will. The trial court dismissed the action, finding that pursuant to section 733.103(2), Florida Statutes (1977), the plaintiffs were foreclosed from proving the facts necessary to establish a cause of action for intentional interference with an expectancy of inheritance. Section 733.103(2), Florida Statutes (1977), provides as follows: * * *

> In any collateral action or proceeding relating to devised property, the probate of a will in Florida shall be conclusive of its due execution; that it was executed by a competent testator, free of fraud, duress, mistake, and undue influence; and of the fact that the will was unrevoked on the testator's death.

The decision was appealed to a federal district court, and the federal court determined it would be better for the Florida Supreme Court to decide the issue, certifying the following question to the Florida Supreme Court:

> Does Florida law, statutory or otherwise, preclude plaintiffs from proving the essential elements of their claim for tortious interference with an inheritance where the alleged wrongfully procured will has been probated in a Florida court and plaintiffs had notice of the probate proceeding and an opportunity to contest the validity of the will therein but chose not to do so?

DeWitt, 408 So.2d at 216–17.

In answering the certified question in the affirmative, the Florida Supreme Court stated that "[t]he rule is that if adequate relief is available in a probate proceeding, then that remedy must be exhausted before a tortious interference claim may be pursued." *Id.* at 218. The Court, however, stated that an exception to this general rule is that "[i]f the defendant's fraud is not discovered until after probate, plaintiff is allowed to bring a later action for damages since relief in probate was impossible." *Id.* at 219. The Court also noted that "[c]ases which allow the action for tortious interference with a testamentary expectancy are predicated on the inadequacy of probate remedies. . . ." *Id.* In conclusion, the Florida Supreme Court held:

> In sum, we find that [plaintiffs] had an adequate remedy in probate *with a fair opportunity to pursue it*. Because they lacked assiduity in failing to avail themselves of this remedy, we interpret section 733.103(2) as barring [plaintiffs] from a subsequent action in tort for wrongful interference with a testamentary expectancy, and accordingly answer the certified question in the affirmative.

Id. at 221. Therefore, the Court's holding that the plaintiffs were barred from pursuing their claim for intentional interference with an expectancy of inheritance, was based on the fact that the plaintiffs had an adequate remedy in probate; the plaintiffs had a fair opportunity to pursue their remedy; and the plaintiffs' failure to pursue their remedy was due to their lack of diligence.

We find that *DeWitt* is factually distinguishable, and therefore inapplicable. A review of the amended complaint reflects that Mr. Schilling has alleged two separate frauds. The first alleged fraud stems from Ms. Herrera's undue influence over the deceased in procuring the will, whereas the second alleged fraud stems from Ms. Herrera's actions in preventing Mr. Schilling from contesting the will in probate court. We acknowledge that pursuant to *DeWitt*, if only the first type of fraud was involved, Mr. Schilling's collateral attack of the will would be barred. However, language contained in *DeWitt* clearly indicates that a subsequent action for intentional interference with an expectancy of inheritance may be permitted where "the circumstances surrounding the tortious conduct effectively preclude adequate relief in the probate court." *Id.* at 219.

278 · 3 · THE LAST WILL AND TESTAMENT

This issue was later addressed by the Fourth District in *Ebeling v. Voltz*, 454 So.2d 783 (Fla. 4th DCA 1984). In *Ebeling*, the plaintiffs filed an action against the defendant for intentional interference with an expectancy of inheritance, alleging that, although they knew of the probate proceeding, they did not contest the will in probate court because the defendant made fraudulent statements inducing them not to contest the will. The trial court granted the defendant's motion to dismiss, finding that pursuant to section 733.103, Florida Statutes (1983), the plaintiffs were barred from attacking the will. The Fourth District reversed, finding that "[e]xtrinsic fraud, or in other words, fraud alleged in the prevention of the will contest, as opposed to in the making of the will, would appear to be the type of circumstance that would preclude relief in the probate court." *Id.* The court noted that the fraud alleged in the complaint prevented the plaintiffs from pursuing the incapacity claim in the probate court, and therefore, the action "falls into the category of cases that *DeWitt* considers outside the purview of Section 733.103(2), Florida Statutes." *Id.*

In the instant case, we must accept the facts alleged by Mr. Schilling as true. He alleges in the amended complaint that when the decedent began to live in Ms. Herrera's home, pursuant to powers of attorney executed by the decedent, Mr. Schilling was the decedent's attorney-in-fact; throughout the decedent's numerous illnesses, Mr. Schilling made decisions regarding the decedent's care; Mr. Schilling traveled to Miami on numerous occasions to visit the decedent, whose condition progressively worsened; Mr. Schilling stayed in contact with Ms. Herrera while the decedent was living in her home; Mr. Schilling relied on Ms. Herrera to obtain information regarding the decedent; Mr. Schilling sent money to Ms. Herrera to pay for the decedent's care; after the decedent passed away, Mr. Schilling called Ms. Herrera numerous times, but she would not return his calls; and Ms. Herrera did not inform Mr. Schilling of his sister's death until after she petitioned for discharge of probate. As the facts in the amended complaint sufficiently allege that Mr. Schilling was prevented from contesting the will in the probate court due to Ms. Herrera's fraudulent conduct, we find that the trial court erred in finding that Mr. Schilling's claim for intentional interference with an expectancy of inheritance was barred. * * *

Accordingly, we reverse the order dismissing Mr. Schilling's amended complaint, and remand for further proceedings.

Notes

Tortious interference with an expectancy of an inheritance is a relatively new theory of tort liability. For comments on the subject, see Eike G. Hosemann, *Protecting Freedom of Testation: A Proposal for Law Reform*, 47 Mich. J.L. Reform 419 (2014); Angela G. Carlin, Shriners Hospital for Children v. Bauman: *Interplay Between a Will Contest and Tort of Intentional Interference With an Expectancy of Inheritance—Time for the Legislature to Enter the Game?*, 20 Ohio Prob. L.J. 19 (2009); Irene D. Johnson, *Tortious Interference With Expectancy of Inheritance of*

Gift—*Suggestions for Resort to the Tort*, 39 U. Tol. L. Rev. 769 (2008); Diane J. Klein, *A Disappointed Yankee in Connecticut (or Nearby) Probate Court: Tortious Interference With Expectation of Inheritance*—*A Survey With Analysis of State Approaches in the First, Second, and Third Circuits*, 66 U. Pitt. L. Rev. 235 (2004); Diane J. Klein, *The Disappointed Heir's Revenge, Southern Style: Tortious Interference With Expectation of Inheritance*—*A Survey With Analysis of State Approaches in the Fifth and Eleventh Circuits*, 55 Baylor L. Rev. 79 (2003).

IV. Revocation

Once a Last Will and Testament has been executed with proper formalities and intentionalities, it may be revoked under certain circumstances. Traditionally, the circumstances appear within statutes providing for the formalities of execution. Nonetheless, circumstances often occur that blur the fine lines delineated by the statutes, inviting court interpretation and construction. But in reviewing the material concerning revocation, we remain focused on the acts done by the testator or the testator's agent, and the intent evidenced by the testator at the time of the act.

A. Physical Act

Uniform Probate Code (2019)

§ 2-507 Revocation by Writing or by Act.

(a) A will or any part thereof is revoked:

(1) by executing a subsequent will that revokes the previous will or part expressly or by inconsistency; or

(2) by performing a revocatory act on the will, if the testator performed the act with the intent and for the purpose of revoking the will or part or if another individual performed the act in the testator's conscious presence and by the testator's direction. For purposes of this paragraph, "revocatory act on the will" includes burning, tearing, canceling, obliterating, or destroying the will or any part of it. A burning, tearing, or canceling is a "revocatory act on the will," whether or not the burn, tear, or cancellation touched any of the words on the will.

(b) If a subsequent will does not expressly revoke a previous will, the execution of the subsequent will wholly revokes the previous will by inconsistency if the testator intended the subsequent will to replace rather than supplement the previous will.

(c) The testator is presumed to have intended a subsequent will to replace rather than supplement a previous will if the subsequent will makes a complete disposition of the testator's estate. If this presumption arises and is not rebutted by clear and convincing evidence, the previous will is revoked; only the subsequent will is operative on the testator's death.

(d) The testator is presumed to have intended a subsequent will to supplement rather than replace a previous will if the subsequent will does not make a complete disposition of the testator's estate. If this presumption arises and is not rebutted by clear and convincing evidence, the subsequent will revokes the previous will only to the extent the subsequent will is inconsistent with the previous will; each will is fully operative on the testator's death to the extent they are not inconsistent.

Notes

The revocation of a valid Last Will and Testament must be distinguished from revocation of a valid *inter vivos* trust. The preceding Uniform Probate Code provision specifies three distinct methods for revoking a will: the two specified in §2-507, and one that we will discuss shortly—revocation by operation of law, addressed in §2-804. Each of these has its own formalities and, as in executing a will, require concomitant intentionality. Likewise, as we were able to *probate*, through the "harmless error" doctrine, a will that was deficient in formalities, so will we be able to *revoke*, through the "harmless error" doctrine, a will that is deficient in formalities. But later, when we discuss *inter vivos* trusts and we inquire as to whether it is possible to revoke, terminate, or modify a trust, a separate series of rules will apply. There is an overlap in some places, but in analyzing the formalities of revoking a will, prepare to make comparisons when we discuss *inter vivos* trusts. *See generally* Mark Glover, *Formal Execution and Informal Revocation: Manifestations of Probate's Family Protection Policy*, 34 Okla. City U. L. Rev. 411 (2009); Kent D. Schenkel, *Testamentary Fragmentation and the Diminishing Role of the Will: An Argument for Revival*, 41 Creighton L. Rev. 155 (2008); Alan Newman, *Revocable Trusts and the Law of Wills: An Imperfect Fit*, 43 Real Prop., Trust & Est. L.J. 523 (2008).

Thompson v. Royall

Supreme Court of Virginia, 1934
163 Va. 492, 175 S.E. 748

HUDGINS, J., delivered the opinion of the court.

The only question presented by this record, is whether the will of Mrs. M. Lou Bowen Kroll had been revoked shortly before her death.

The uncontroverted facts are as follows: On the 4th day of September, 1932, Mrs. Kroll signed a will, typewritten on five sheets of legal cap paper; the signature appeared on the last page duly attested by three subscribing witnesses. H. P. Brittain, the executor named in the will, was given possession of the instrument for safekeeping. A codicil typed on the top third of one sheet of paper dated September 15, 1932, was signed by the testatrix in the presence of two subscribing witnesses. Possession of this instrument was given to Judge S. M. B. Coulling, the attorney who prepared both documents.

On September 19, 1932, at the request of Mrs. Kroll, Judge Coulling, and Mr. Brittain took the will and the codicil to her home where she told her attorney, in the presence of Mr. Brittain and another, to destroy both. But instead of destroying the papers, at the suggestion of Judge Coulling, she decided to retain them as memoranda, to be used as such in the event she decided to execute a new will. Upon the back of the manuscript cover, which was fastened to the five sheets by metal clasps, in the handwriting of Judge Coulling, signed by Mrs. Kroll, there is the following notation:

> This will null and void and to be only held by H. P. Brittain, instead of being destroyed, as a memorandum for another will if I desire to make same. This 19 Sept 1932.
>
> M. LOU BOWEN KROLL.

The same notation was made upon the back of the sheet on which the codicil was written, except that the name, S. M. B. Coulling, was substituted for H. P. Brittain; this was likewise signed by Mrs. Kroll.

Mrs. Kroll died October 2, 1932, leaving numerous nephews and nieces, some of whom were not mentioned in her will, and an estate valued at approximately $200,000. On motion of some of the beneficiaries, the will and codicil were offered for probate. All the interested parties including the heirs at law were convened, and on the issue, *devisavit vel non,* the jury found that the instruments dated September 4th and 15, 1932, were the last will and testament of Mrs. M. Lou Bowen Kroll. From an order sustaining the verdict and probating the will this writ of error was allowed.

For more than one hundred years, the means by which a duly executed will may be revoked, have been prescribed by statute. These requirements are found in section 5233 of the 1919 Code, the pertinent parts of which read thus:

> No will or codicil, or any part thereof, shall be revoked, unless * * * by a subsequent will or codicil, or by some writing declaring an intention to revoke the same, and executed in the manner in which a will is required to be executed, or by the testator, or some person in his presence and by his direction, cutting, tearing, burning, obliterating, canceling, or destroying the same, or the signature thereto, with the intent to revoke.

The notations, dated September 19, 1932, are not wholly in the handwriting of the testatrix, nor are her signatures thereto attached attested by subscribing witnesses; hence under the statute they are ineffectual as 'some writing declaring an intention to revoke.' The faces of the two instruments bear no physical evidence of any cutting, tearing, burning, obliterating, canceling, or destroying. The only contention made by appellants is, that the notation written in the presence, and with the approval, of Mrs. Kroll, on the back of the manuscript cover in the one instance, and on the back of the sheet containing the codicil in the other, constitute 'canceling' within the meaning of the statute.

Both parties concede that to effect revocation of a duly executed will, in any of the methods prescribed by statute, two things are necessary: (1) The doing of one of the acts specified, (2) accompanied by the intent to revoke—the *animo revocandi.* Proof of either, without proof of the other, is insufficient. Malone v. Hobbs, 1 Rob. (40 Va.) 346, 39 Am.Dec. 263; 2 Minor Ins. 925. The proof established the intention to revoke. The entire controversy is confined to the acts used in carrying out that purpose. The testatrix adopted the suggestion of her attorney to revoke her will by written memoranda, admittedly ineffectual as revocations by subsequent writings, but appellants contend the memoranda, in the handwriting of another, and testatrix's signatures, are sufficient to effect revocation by cancellation. To support this contention appellants cite a number of authorities which hold that the modern definition of cancellation includes, 'any act which would destroy, revoke, recall, do away with, overrule, render null and void, the instrument.'

Most of the authorities cited, that approve the above, or a similar meaning of the word, were dealing with the cancellation of simple contracts, or other instruments that require little or no formality in execution. However there is one line of cases which apply this extended meaning of 'canceling' to the revocation of wills. The leading case so holding is Warner v. Warner's Estate, 37 Vt. 356. In this case proof of the intent and the act were a notation on the same page with, and below the signature of the testator, reading: 'This will is hereby cancelled and annulled. In full this the 15th day of March in the year 1859,' and written lengthwise on the back of the fourth page of the foolscap paper, upon which no part of the written will appeared, were these words, 'Cancelled and is null and void. (Signed) I. Warner.' It was held this was sufficient to revoke the will under a statute similar to the one here under consideration.

In Evans' Appeal, 58 Pa.St. 238, the Pennsylvania court approved the reasoning of the Vermont court in Warner v. Warner's Estate, *supra*, but the force of the opinion is weakened when the facts are considered. It seems that there were lines drawn through two of the three signatures of the testator appearing in the Evans will, and the paper on which material parts of the will were written was torn in four places. It therefore appeared on the face of the instrument, when offered for probate, that there was a sufficient defacement to bring it within the meaning of both obliteration and cancellation.

The construction of the statute in Warner v. Warner's Estate, *supra*, has been criticized by eminent textwriters on wills, and the courts in the majority of the states in construing similar statutes have refused to follow the reasoning in that case. * * *

The above, and other authorities that might be cited, hold that revocation of a will by cancellation within the meaning of the statute, contemplates marks or lines across the written parts of the instrument, or a physical defacement, or some mutilation of the writing itself, with the intent to revoke. If written words are used for the purpose, they must be so placed as to physically affect the written portion of the will, not merely on blank parts of the paper on which the will is written. If the writing intended to be the act of cancelling, does not mutilate, or erase, or deface, or otherwise physically come in contact with any part of written words of the will, it cannot be given any greater weight than a similar writing on a separate sheet of paper, which identifies the will referred to, just as definitely, as does the writing on the back. If a will may be revoked by writing on the back, separable from the will, it may be done by a writing not on the will. This the statute forbids.

* * *

The attempted revocation is ineffectual, because testatrix intended to revoke her will by subsequent writings not executed as required by statute, and because it does not in any wise physically obliterate, mutilate, deface, or cancel any written parts of the will.

For the reasons stated, the judgment of the trial court is affirmed.

Affirmed.

Notes

Even though Uniform Probate Code §2-507(a)(2) would seem to change the holding of the *Thompson* decision, the issue arises as to what must occur for the physical act to be sufficient for a revocation to occur. Must the act be on the same piece of paper as the will itself? Is a mere line sufficient, or is there a requirement of a level of proof, such as clear and convincing? Would physical acts done to a "copy" of the will, but not the will itself, be sufficient? *See, e.g., Restatement (Third) of Property* §4.1 cmt. f. (1999). Finally, if physical revocation of the entire will is allowed, and physical revocation of part of the will is allowed, how may we tell when the testator intended the act to revoke only part of the will and not the whole will? Sometimes the testator may partially obliterate a word or phrase and then write something next to it, intending that this be substituted for that which was in the original. Why will the subsequent addition be ineffective, and why will the physical act done to the original be effective or not?

Uniform Probate Code (2019)

§2-503. Harmless Error.

Although a document or writing added upon a document was not executed in compliance with Section 2-502, the document or writing is treated as if it had been executed in compliance with that section if the proponent of the document or writing establishes by clear and convincing evidence that the decedent intended the document or writing to constitute:

(1) the decedent's will,

(2) a partial or complete revocation of the will,

(3) an addition to or an alteration of the will, or

(4) a partial or complete revival of his [or her] formerly revoked will or of a formerly revoked portion of the will.

Harrison v. Bird

Supreme Court of Alabama, 1993
621 So. 2d 972

HOUSTON, Justice.

The proponent of a will appeals from a judgment of the Circuit Court of Montgomery County holding that the estate of Daisy Virginia Speer, deceased, should be administered as an intestate estate and confirming the letters of administration granted by the probate court to Mae S. Bird.

The following pertinent facts are undisputed:

Daisy Virginia Speer executed a will in November 1989, in which she named Katherine Crapps Harrison as the main beneficiary of her estate. The original of the will was retained by Ms. Speer's attorney and a duplicate original was given to Ms. Harrison. On March 4, 1991, Ms. Speer telephoned her attorney and advised him that she wanted to revoke her will. Thereafter, Ms. Speer's attorney or his secretary, in the presence of each other, tore the will into four pieces. The attorney then wrote Ms. Speer a letter, informing her that he had "revoked" her will as she had instructed and that he was enclosing the pieces of the will so that she could verify that he had torn up the original. In the letter, the attorney specifically stated, "As it now stands, you are without a will."

Ms. Speer died on September 3, 1991. Upon her death, the postmarked letter from her attorney was found among her personal effects, but the four pieces of the will were not found. Thereafter, on September 17, 1991, the Probate Court of Montgomery County granted letters of administration on the estate of Ms. Speer, to Mae S. Bird, a cousin of Ms. Speer. On October 11, 1991, Ms. Harrison filed for probate a document purporting to be the last will and testament of Ms. Speer and naming Ms. Harrison as executrix. On Ms. Bird's petition, the case was removed to the Circuit Court of Montgomery County. Thereafter, Ms. Bird filed an "Answer to Petition to Probate Will and Answer to Petition to Have Administratrix Removed," contesting the will on the grounds that Ms. Speer had revoked her will.

Thereafter, Ms. Bird and Ms. Harrison moved for summary judgments, which the circuit court denied. Upon denying their motions, the circuit court ruled in part (1) that Ms. Speer's will was not lawfully revoked when it was destroyed by her attorney at her direction and with her consent, but not in her presence, see Ala .Code 1975, §43-8-136(b); (2) that there could be no ratification of the destruction of Ms. Speer's will, which was not accomplished pursuant to the strict requirements of §43-8-136(b); and (3) that, based on the fact that the pieces of the destroyed will were delivered to Ms. Speer's home but were not found after her death, there arose a presumption that Ms. Speer thereafter revoked the will herself. * * *

[F]inding that the presumption in favor of revocation of Ms. Speer's will had not been rebutted and therefore that the duplicate original will offered for probate by Ms. Harrison was not the last will and testament of Daisy Virginia Speer, the circuit court held that the estate should be administered as an intestate estate and confirmed the letters of administration issued by the probate court to Ms. Bird.

If the evidence establishes that Ms. Speer had possession of the will before her death, but the will is not found among her personal effects after her death, a presumption arises that she destroyed the will. See Barksdale v. Pendergrass, 294 Ala. 526, 319 So.2d 267 (1975). Furthermore, if she destroys the copy of the will in her possession, a presumption arises that she has revoked her will and all duplicates, even though a duplicate exists that is not in her possession. See Stiles v. Brown, 380 So.2d 792 (Ala.1980); see, also, Snider v. Burks, 84 Ala. 53, 4 So. 225 (1887). However, this presumption of revocation is rebuttable and the burden of rebutting the presumption is on the proponent of the will. See *Barksdale, supra.*

Based on the foregoing, we conclude that under the facts of this case there existed a presumption that Ms. Speer destroyed her will and thus revoked it. Therefore, the burden shifted to Ms. Harrison to present sufficient evidence to rebut that presumption—to present sufficient evidence to convince the trier of fact that the absence of the will from Ms. Speer's personal effects after her death was not due to Ms. Speer's destroying and thus revoking the will. See Stiles v. Brown, *supra.*

From a careful review of the record, we conclude, as did the trial court, that the evidence presented by Ms. Harrison was not sufficient to rebut the presumption that Ms. Speer destroyed her will with the intent to revoke it. We, therefore, affirm the trial court's judgment.

We note Ms. Harrison's argument that under the particular facts of this case, because Ms. Speer's attorney destroyed the will outside of Ms. Speer's presence, "[t]he fact that Ms. Speer may have had possession of the pieces of her will and that such pieces were not found upon her death is not sufficient to invoke the presumption [of revocation] imposed by the trial court." We find that argument to be without merit.

AFFIRMED.

HORNSBY, C.J., and MADDOX, SHORES and KENNEDY, JJ., concur.

Notes

The decision raises an issue that arises in many cases—that of a lost will. While the case demonstrates the attempt at physical revocation, the will was actually revoked because the torn pieces were returned to the possession of the Testatrix and could not be found in her possession. The issue raised is the presumption of revocation by physical act brought on by the will, which is traceable to the possession of the Testatrix but which cannot be found. How should the presumption of a lost will be addressed if the person who would most benefit from its non-production had access to the will? Perhaps the best recourse is a shift in the burden of proof necessary to rebut the presumption. *See, e.g.,* Estate of Travers, 121 Ariz. 282, 589 P.2d 1314 (1978); Lonergan v. Estate of Budahazi, 669 So. 2d 1062 (Fla. Dist. Ct. App. 1996). Once the presumption of revocation has been rebutted, what will you admit to probate to prove the intentions of the testator? *See* Charles M. Davis, Comment,

A Lost Will, a Photocopy of the Original, and Two "Snakes in the Grass": Is It Time To Update Section 85 of the Texas Probate Code?, 40 Tex. Tech. L. Rev. 89 (2007).

B. Subsequent Instrument

In re Wolfe's Will

Supreme Court of North Carolina, 1923
185 N.C. 563, 117 S.E. 804

ADAMS, J.

* * *

A will may be revoked by a subsequent instrument executed solely for that purpose, or by a subsequent will containing a revoking clause or provisions inconsistent with those of the previous will, or by any of the other methods prescribed by law; but the mere fact that a second will was made, although it purports to be the last, does not create a presumption that it revokes or is inconsistent with one of prior date. * * *

The propounder admits that the instrument dated August 14th (herein for convenience referred to as the second will) is a part of the maker's testamentary disposition, but insists that it does not affect the validity of the instrument dated July 31st, herein designated as the first will. By reason of this admission the appeal presents the single question whether the two wills are so inconsistent that they cannot stand together and whether the first is revoked by the second.

It has often been held that in the construction of wills the primary purpose is to ascertain and give effect to the testator's intention as expressed in the words employed, and if the language is free from ambiguity and doubt, and expresses plainly, clearly, and distinctly the maker's intention, there is no occasion to resort to other means of interpretation. * * *

In the instant case, the language being clear and unequivocal, the chief controversy between the parties involves the meaning of the words "all my effects" as used in the second will. The propounder contends that they include only personal property; the respondents insist that the term embraces real as well as personal property, and that the second will revokes the first, the two being necessarily inconsistent.

The observation has been made that the individual cases construing "effects" are of value only for the purpose of illustration, each case being a law unto itself; but there seems to be a practical unanimity of judicial decision, with the exception of certain English cases, that the word "effects," used simpliciter or in a general or unlimited sense and unaffected by the context, signifies all that is embraced in the words "personal property," but is not sufficiently comprehensive to include real estate. "Effects," however, may include land when used as referring to antecedent words which describe real estate, or when used in written instruments in which the usual technical terms are not controlling * * *.

In the second will there are no words which ex vi termini import a disposition of real property; there is no residuary clause or clause of revocation; and in these circumstances, as the courts do not favor the revocation of wills by implication, there appears to be no sound reason for holding that the two instruments are so inconsistent as to be incapable of standing together and that the first is necessarily revoked by the second. It is true there is a presumption that the testator intended to dispose of all his estate, and under our construction the testator died intestate as to the land not devised to Mary Lillie Luffman, but, as said in Andrews v. Applegate, *supra*, such presumption, however strong, will not justify or warrant a construction incorporating in the second will any kind of property which cannot be brought within its terms.

Having admitted that the second will is a valid testamentary disposition of the property therein described, the propounder is entitled to have the jury determine whether the instrument dated July 31, 1911, is any part of the maker's will. The judgment and verdict are therefore set aside and a new trial is awarded.

New trial.

Notes

Subsequent instruments may revoke previous valid instruments explicitly or impliedly. A subsequent explicit revocation occurs when the valid subsequent instrument states that it explicitly "revokes all wills and codicils to wills executed by me." There could be a million previous wills, but if this last one is valid, it revokes all of them. Revocation by subsequent instrument occurs by implication when there is no explicit clause included, but when a specific item is given in the first will, and the same specific item is given in the second will, but to a different legatee, the second legatee trumps the first one. *See* Unif. Prob. Code § 2-507(a)(1) (2019).

C. Revocation by Operation of Law

Uniform Probate Code (2019)

§ 2-804. Revocation of Probate and Nonprobate Transfers by Divorce; No Revocation by Other Changes of Circumstances.

(a) [**Definitions.**] In this section:

(1) "Disposition or appointment of property" includes a transfer of an item of property or any other benefit to a beneficiary designated in a governing instrument.

(2) "Divorce or annulment" means any divorce or annulment, or any dissolution or declaration of invalidity of a marriage, that would exclude the spouse as a surviving spouse within the meaning of Section 2-802. A decree of separation that does not terminate the status of husband and wife is not a divorce for purposes of this section.

(3) "Divorced individual" includes an individual whose marriage has been annulled.

(4) "Governing instrument" means a governing instrument executed by the divorced individual before the divorce or annulment of his [or her] marriage to his [or her] former spouse.

(5) "Relative of the divorced individual's former spouse" means an individual who is related to the divorced individual's former spouse by blood, adoption, or affinity and who, after the divorce or annulment, is not related to the divorced individual by blood, adoption, or affinity.

(6) "Revocable," with respect to a disposition, appointment, provision, or nomination, means one under which the divorced individual, at the time of the divorce or annulment, was alone empowered, by law or under the governing instrument, to cancel the designation in favor of his [or her] former spouse or former spouse's relative, whether or not the divorced individual was then empowered to designate himself [or herself] in place of his [or her] former spouse or in place of his [or her] former spouse's relative and whether or not the divorced individual then had the capacity to exercise the power.

(b) [**Revocation Upon Divorce.**] Except as provided by the express terms of a governing instrument, a court order, or a contract relating to the division of the marital estate made between the divorced individuals before or after the marriage, divorce, or annulment, the divorce or annulment of a marriage:

(1) revokes any revocable

(A) disposition or appointment of property made by a divorced individual to his [or her] former spouse in a governing instrument and any disposition or appointment created by law or in a governing instrument to a relative of the divorced individual's former spouse,

(B) provision in a governing instrument conferring a general or nongeneral power of appointment on the divorced individual's former spouse or on a relative of the divorced individual's former spouse, and

(C) nomination in a governing instrument, nominating a divorced individual's former spouse or a relative of the divorced individual's former spouse to serve in any fiduciary or representative capacity, including a personal representative, executor, trustee, conservator, agent, or guardian; and

(2) severs the interests of the former spouses in property held by them at the time of the divorce or annulment as joint tenants with the right of survivorship [or as community property with the right of survivorship], transforming the interests of the former spouses into equal tenancies in common.

* * *

(d) [**Effect of Revocation.**] Provisions of a governing instrument are given effect as if the former spouse and relatives of the former spouse disclaimed all provisions revoked by this section or, in the case of a revoked nomination in a fiduciary or representative capacity, as if the former spouse and relatives of the former spouse died immediately before the divorce or annulment.

(e) [**Revival if Divorce Nullified.**] Provisions revoked solely by this section are revived by the divorced individual's remarriage to the former spouse or by a nullification of the divorce or annulment.

(f) [**No Revocation for Other Change of Circumstances.**] No change of circumstances other than as described in this section and in Section 2-803 effects a revocation.

* * *

Notes

When we discuss protection of spouses and children in Chapter Five, we examine pretermitted heir statutes (protection of issue, usually children) and pretermitted spouse statutes (protection of spouses). These state statutes are shown to further the public policy of the protection of children who were born after the execution of the will, or spouses who married the testator after the execution of the will. The statutes provide a presumption of intention; if the testator forgot these persons, the state will provide for them. Now we see in the Uniform Probate Code provision another attempt at assisting the testator's intent. That is, the statute provides that, if a testator divorces or the marriage is annulled after execution of the Last Will and Testament, any provision in the will for the former spouse, or a relative of the former spouse who is not a relative of the decedent, is revoked from the will. Note that this also applies to non-probate transfers, which is not a surprising development for the Uniform Probate Code. Of course, the provisions of the Code will not apply if the testator's intent has been stated otherwise in the will, a court order, or a pre- or post-nuptial agreement. The will remains valid; only the relevant provisions are stricken. If the couple has only separated, do the Code's provisions apply? Would the provisions apply if the couple legally separated and divided all of the marital assets, but have not yet received a final decree of divorce? *See, e.g., In re* Estate of Bullotta, 575 Pa. 587, 838 A.2d 594 (2003) (holding husband's estate to terms of settlement agreement that he and wife had reached before his death, even though divorce action abated upon death and parties could no longer divorce). Often the issue is whether one or both of the divorcing spouses intended to prevent revocation by operation of law and, thus, permit the former spouse to inherit after the decree of divorce. *See, e.g.,* Nichols v. Suiter, 78 A.3d 344 (Md. 2013) (holding that terms of separation agreement were insufficiently clear and convincing to prevent revocation by operation of law under state statute). For a commentary on the application of "revocation by operation of law" when application frustrates the intent of the testator, see Michael T. Flannery, *Revoking a Valid Will, Even When the Revocation Frustrates the Clearly-Established Intent of the Testator:* Langston v. Langston *(Ark.),* LexisNexis Expert Commentary, 2008 EMERGING ISSUES 2038 (Apr. 2008) (available at Lexis, Emerging Issues, Combined Area of Law library).

V. Revival

Like revocation, revival of any Last Will and Testament occurs because of statutory or common law procedures. What follows are the five methods for revival—some resulting from common sense, such as writing a new will or re-executing a revoked will—but each reflects an intent on the part of the testator to reapply the formalities and intentionalities necessary for a valid instrument.

A. Revoking the Revoking Will

Uniform Probate Code (2019)

§ 2-509. Revival of Revoked Will.

(a) If a subsequent will that wholly revoked a previous will is thereafter revoked by a revocatory act under Section 2-507(a)(2), the previous will remains revoked unless it is revived. The previous will is revived if it is evident from the circumstances of the revocation of the subsequent will or from the testator's contemporary or subsequent declarations that the testator intended the previous will to take effect as executed.

(b) If a subsequent will that partly revoked a previous will is thereafter revoked by a revocatory act under Section 2-507(a)(2), a revoked part of the previous will is revived unless it is evident from the circumstances of the revocation of the subsequent will or from the testator's contemporary or subsequent declarations that the testator did not intend the revoked part to take effect as executed.

(c) If a subsequent will that revoked a previous will in whole or in part is thereafter revoked by another, later, will, the previous will remains revoked in whole or in part, unless it or its revoked part is revived. The previous will or its revoked part is revived to the extent it appears from the terms of the later will that the testator intended the previous will to take effect.

Notes

Once a Last Will and Testament has been effectively executed in accordance with formalities and intentionalities, it may only be revoked in accordance with similar formalities and intentionalities. Thus, if a valid Last Will and Testament is revoked by a subsequently valid Last Will and Testament, is that revocation valid? The answer is, "Yes." But what if that second Last Will and Testament is then revoked—perhaps by physical act—and the first will, although revoked by subsequent instrument, has no other methods of revocation associated with it? May it then be probated? This is the issue of revoking the revoking will. The common law provided that the first will should be automatically revived as long as there were no other acts of revocation. States adopting this view analyze the issue as one in which the court should look at the date of the death of the testator and not what occurred prior to that time. Because the first will is valid as of that date, it should be probated. Other states adopt the position of the Uniform Probate Code, which provides that, before automatically reviving the first will, the court should look at the circumstances of revocation, the subsequent will, and the declarations of the testator. *See, e.g.,* Estate of Alburn, 18 Wis. 2d 340, 118 N.W.2d 919 (1963). Some states take the position that a revoked will cannot be revived unless it is re-executed. *See, e.g., In re* Eberhardt's Estate, 1 Wis. 2d 439, 85 N.W.2d 483 (1957). Finally, should it make a difference that the second will wholly or partially revoked the first will? According to the Uniform Probate Code § 2-509(b), it should.

B. Dependent Relative Revocation and Mistake

Carter v. First United Methodist Church of Albany

Supreme Court of Georgia, 1980
246 Ga. 352, 271 S.E.2d 493

NICHOLS, Justice.

The caveator, Luther Reynolds Carter, appeals from judgment entered in the superior court in behalf of the propounder, First United Methodist Church, admitting to probate, as the will of Mildred C. Tipton, an instrument bearing the date of August 21, 1963.

The 1963 instrument, typed and signed in the form of and purporting to be the last will and testament of Mildred C. Tipton, was found among Mrs. Tipton's other personal papers in her dining room chest after her death on February 14, 1979. It was folded together with a handwritten instrument dated May 22, 1978, captioned as her will but unsigned and unwitnessed, purporting to establish a different scheme of distribution of her property. Pencil marks had been made diagonally through the property disposition provisions of the 1963 document and through the name of one of the co-executors.

The superior court found that from time to time prior to her death, Mrs. Tipton had made it known to her attorney that she needed his services in order to change or revise her will, or to make a new will; that at one time she had written out some proposed changes on tablet paper to be suggested to her lawyer when he prepared a new will for her; and that she did not intend to revoke her will by scratching through some of its provisions and by writing out the proposed changes.

* * * The parties stipulated that the 1963 instrument offered for probate had been found among Mrs. Tipton's records and papers in a drawer of a chest in her dining room, and that the 1963 will was executed by Mrs. Tipton and attested by the witnesses to the will. * * *

The case was submitted to the trial court on stipulated facts, and under stipulation that the depositions of Mrs. Tipton's attorney and one of her friends, relating to her intentions, be admitted in evidence. There is no transcript, and the record is sparse as to facts. Each party seems to have felt that the burden of proof properly was to be placed upon the other party and, accordingly, neither made much effort to develop the facts. The issue resolves itself, however, if certain presumptions are placed into proper perspective with each other.

"As a general rule, the burden is on a person attacking a paper offered for probate as a will to sustain the grounds of his attack. But by express provision of our statute, where a will has been canceled or obliterated in a material part, a presumption of revocation arises, and the burden is on the propounder to show that no revocation was intended . . . Where the paper is found among the testator's effects, there is also a presumption that he made the cancellations or obliterations . . . It having been shown that the paper offered for probate in this case had been in the custody of the deceased up to the time of his death, the propounder was met with both of the presumptions above alluded to." McIntyre v. McIntyre, 120 Ga. 67, 70, 47 S.E. 501 (1904).

The deposition of Mrs. Tipton's attorney, introduced by stipulation in behalf of the propounder, establishes, without contradiction, that Mrs. Tipton had written out some changes in her will on tablet paper and repeatedly had attempted to get her attorney to change or to revise her will, or to make a new will. The parties stipulated that the two writings, the 1963 will and the 1978 manuscript, were found after her death among her personal effects. No evidence appears in the record, and no contention is made, that Mrs. Tipton did not make the marks on the 1963 will or write the 1978 instrument. The presumption that Mrs. Tipton made the pencil marks and wrote the memorandum of her intentions stands unrebutted. Langan v. Cheshire, 208 Ga. 107, 65 S.E.2d 415 (1951); Porch v. Farmer, 158 Ga. 55, 122 S.E. 557 (1924); Howard v. Hunter, 115 Ga. 357, 41 S.E. 638 (1902). The other presumption, that of absolute revocation, is the focal point of our remaining inquiry.

The statute to which McIntyre refers is Code Ann. § 113-404, which provides, in part, that an intention to revoke will be presumed from the obliteration or canceling of a material portion of the will. In Georgia, the drawing of pencil lines through provisions of a will is a sufficient "canceling". McIntyre, *supra*, at p. 70, 47 S.E. 501. The question of whether or not the canceled provision is "material" is one of law. Howard v. Cotten, 223 Ga. 118, 122, 153 S.E.2d 557 (1967). The caveator contends that the propounder introduced no evidence to rebut the statutory presumption of revocation, and the propounder contends that under the doctrine of dependent relative revocation, or conditional revocation, the facts proven give rise to a presumption in favor of the propounder (which the caveator failed to rebut) that Mrs. Tipton did not intend for her 1963 will to be revoked unless her new dispositions of her property became effective in law. The caveator thus contends that the propounder failed to rebut the presumption of absolute or unconditional revocation, and the propounder contends he rebutted that presumption by evidence giving rise to another presumption, that of conditional revocation, which the caveator failed to rebut.

The doctrine of dependent relative revocation (conditional revocation) has been stated by this court as follows:

"It is a doctrine of *presumed intention*, and has grown up as a result of an effort which courts always make to arrive at the real intention of the testator. Some of the cases appear to go to extreme lengths in the application of this doctrine, and seem to defeat the very intention at which they were seeking to arrive. The doctrine, as we understand it and are willing to apply it, is this: The mere fact that the testator intended to make a new will, or made one which failed of effect, will not alone, in every case, prevent a cancellation or obliteration of a will from operating as a revocation. If it is clear that the cancellation and the making of the new will were parts of one scheme, and the revocation of the old will was so related to the making of the new as to be dependent upon it, then if the new will be not made, or if made is invalid, the old will, though canceled, should be given effect, if its contents can be ascertained in any legal way. But if the old will is once revoked — if the act of revocation is completed — as if the will be totally destroyed by burning and the like, or if any other act is done which evidences an unmistakable intention to revoke, though the will be not totally destroyed, the fact that the testator intended to make a new will, or made one which can not take effect, counts for nothing. In other words, evidence that the testator intended to make or did actually make a new will, which was inoperative, may throw light on the question of intention to revoke the old one, but it can never revive a will once completely revoked." (Emphasis added.) McIntyre v. McIntyre, 120 Ga. 67, 71, 47 S.E. 501, 503 *supra*. The doctrine has been recognized and applied by the highest courts of many states. Annos. 62 ALR 1401, 115 ALR 721. It has been the subject of considerable discussion by the text writers. 1 Redfearn, Wills And Administration In Georgia (4th Ed.), p. 188, § 96; Chaffin, Studies In The Georgia Law of Decedent's Estates and Future Interests, pp. 184, 186.

Professor Chaffin is of the opinion that "*McIntyre* represents a sound approach to the doctrine of dependent relative revocation." He writes that in McIntyre, "The doctrine was correctly perceived to be a rule of presumed intention rather than a rule of substantive law. The court refused to set aside the revocation until evidence bearing on testator's intent, including his oral declarations, was examined in an effort to discern what he would have desired if he had been aware of the true facts." He also concludes, correctly, this court believes, that "Most courts have taken the position that dependent relative revocation is judged by a stricter standard in a situation involving revocation by subsequent instrument as opposed to physical act." He is strongly of the opinion that "if the purpose of the doctrine is to effect testator's intent, there is no point in distinguishing between revocation by physical act and by subsequent instrument." Chaffin, *supra*, pp. 186–187. This court agrees. In Georgia, the doctrine is one of presumed intention. The principle is the same whether the revocation is by physical act or by subsequent instrument. * * *

In the present case, the testatrix wrote the 1978 instrument which the parties have conceded (by the absence of their contentions) cannot be admitted to probate because it lacks some of the requisites of a will. The propounder says, in effect, if not in express words, that the testatrix would have preferred the property disposition clauses of the 1963 will over the only other alternative — intestacy. The caveator contends, in essence, that the testatrix would have preferred intestacy. How stands the record?

The fact that the old will, with pencil lines drawn by Mrs. Tipton through the property disposition provisions, was found among her personal papers folded together with the 1978 writing, that makes a somewhat different disposition of her property, is some evidence tending to establish that "the cancellation and the making of the new will were parts of one scheme, and the revocation of the old will was so related to the making of the new as to be dependent upon it." 120 Ga. at 71, 47 S.E. at 503. This evidence was sufficient to rebut the statutory presumption of revocation (Code Ann. § 113-404) and to give rise to a presumption in favor of the propounder under the doctrine of dependent relative revocation or conditional revocation. *McIntyre, supra.* The stipulation that these two instruments were found together thus shifted the burden of proof to the caveator to prove, in essence, that Mrs. Tipton would have preferred intestacy.

* * * The presumption against intestacy (or in favor of the continued validity of the 1963 will) stands unrebutted in the present case. * * *

Accordingly, the trial court, as finder of the facts, did not err in admitting the will to probate.

Judgment affirmed.

Notes

Dependent relative revocation is a traditional common law doctrine of failed intent. The *Restatement* applies this doctrine by providing that a partial or complete revocation is presumptively ineffective if the testator made the purported revocation in connection with an alternate attempted disposition that then fails because of mistake. Often the failure is occasioned by a false understanding of law or fact that is either recited in the will itself or proven by clear and convincing evidence. *See Restatement (Third) of Property: Wills and Other Donative Transfers* § 4.3 (1999).

More modern approaches would still require clear and convincing evidence of the mistake of fact or law and the intent of the transferor before permitting reformation. *See* Uniform Probate Code § 2-805; Uniform Trust Code § 415; *Restatement (Third) of Property (Wills and Other Donative Transfers* § 12.1. Note that a mistaken intent is separate from a mistaken formality, which may be corrected with clear and convincing evidence under Uniform Probate Code § 2-503. *See generally* Jane B. Baron, *Irresolute Testators, Clear and Convincing Wills Law,* 72 Wash. & Lee L. Rev. 3 (2015).

C. Republication by Codicil

If there is a valid codicil to a valid Last Will and Testament and the codicil is revoked, the Last Will and Testament remains valid and subject to probate. But if the will is revoked, then all codicils to that will are revoked as well. But what if there is a Last Will and Testament that had been valid, but then was revoked under any of the three methods available? Would a valid codicil be able to revive that Last

Will and Testament? The answer is, "Yes," as long as the codicil referred to the will and successfully overcame any facts that may make it appear that the revocation occurred after the execution of the codicil. *See generally In re* Estate of Stormont, 34 Ohio App. 3d 92, 517 N.E.2d 259 (1986). But what if the Last Will and Testament had never been valid to begin with because it lacked the proper testamentary formalities or intentionalities? Would the codicil be able to make the Last Will and Testament valid? *See Restatement (Third) of Property (Wills and Other Donative Transfers)* § 3.4 (1999) (treating a will as executed when its most recent codicil was executed).

D. Re-Execution and New Will

These last two means of revival complete the list of five but are added with the caution that re-execution of the revoked Last Will and Testament invites a level of confusion and negligence as to what may precipitate a charge of malpractice. Indeed, being properly attentive to all of the issues heretofore discussed, executing a new will seems to be the best course of action for client and attorney. *See generally* Espinosa v. Sparber, Shevin, Shapo, Rosen & Heilbronner, 612 So. 2d 1378 (Fla. 1993).

Chapter 4

The Meaning of Words

Tool Bar

Once a Last Will and Testament becomes effective through the accomplishment of the formalities and intentionalities mandated by the particular state, or once the non-probate transfer effectively creates an interest that is transferrable at death, the issue arises as to what the words contained within the will or the will substitute mean. To paraphrase the poet T.S. Eliot, when we think we have done our legal duty, we are still left "with the intolerable wrestle with words and meaning."[1] For example, if, in my will, I write: "Jennifer is to receive all that I have within my safe deposit box," what is Jennifer to receive if the contents of that box changes repeatedly between the time I execute the will and the date of my death? Or, in another

---

1. T.S. Eliot, *East Coker in* FOUR QUARTETS, at II (1940).

example, if I write: "Jimmy is to receive the motor vehicle that I own at the date of my death," and the vehicle is replaced between the time of execution and the date of my death, what is Jimmy to receive? Should the law be conscious of the need to balance certainty in fixing intent with changing circumstances, mistake, and ambiguity?

As you progress through the following material, concentrate on the fact that you have a valid instrument but are now asked to define what is encompassed by that instrument. Often that which is encompassed may not make sense when viewed in the context of surrounding circumstances. Was a mistake made by the decedent or by the attorney who drafted the instrument? If there is a mistake, what may the law do about it to help the decedent obtain the benefit of having his or her estate pass according to his or her wishes? And what may the law do to protect the legitimate expectations of actual and potential beneficiaries? There will be a struggle in the pages that follow between what has been termed "harsh and relentless formalism"[2] and what less formal evidence indicates was the true intent of the decedent. The task is not so much to pick one side or the other, but to identify the issue and make a firm resolve to do what is necessary to avoid this pitfall in the future drafting of similar instruments.

I. Incorporation by Reference

Uniform Probate Code (2019)

§ 2-510. Incorporation by Reference.

A writing in existence when a will is executed may be incorporated by reference if the language of the will manifests this intent and describes the writing sufficiently to permit its identification.

Clark v. Greenhalge

Supreme Judicial Court of Massachusetts, 1991
411 Mass. 410, 582 N.E.2d 949

NOLAN, Justice.

We consider in this case whether a probate judge correctly concluded that specific, written bequests of personal property contained in a notebook maintained by a testatrix were incorporated by reference into the terms of the testatrix's will.

We set forth the relevant facts as found by the probate judge. The testatrix, Helen Nesmith, duly executed a will in 1977, which named her cousin, Frederic T. Greenhalge, II, as executor of her estate. The will further identified Greenhalge as the principal beneficiary of the estate, entitling him to receive all of Helen Nesmith's tangible

---

2. John Langbein, *Substantial Compliance With the Wills Act,* 88 HARV. L. REV. 489 (1975).

personal property upon her death except those items which she "designate[d] by a memorandum left by [her] and known to [Greenhalge], or in accordance with [her] known wishes," to be given to others living at the time of her death.[2] Among Helen Nesmith's possessions was a large oil painting of a farm scene signed by T.H. Muckley and dated 1833. The value of the painting, as assessed for estate tax purposes, was $1,800.00.

In 1972, Greenhalge assisted Helen Nesmith in drafting a document entitled "MEMORANDUM" and identified as "a list of items of personal property prepared with Miss Helen Nesmith upon September 5, 1972, for the guidance of myself in the distribution of personal tangible property." This list consisted of forty-nine specific bequests of Ms. Nesmith's tangible personal property. In 1976, Helen Nesmith modified the 1972 list by interlineations, additions and deletions. Neither edition of the list involved a bequest of the farm scene painting.

Ms. Nesmith kept a plastic-covered notebook in the drawer of a desk in her study. She periodically made entries in this notebook, which bore the title "List to be given Helen Nesmith 1979." One such entry read: "Ginny Clark farm picture hanging over fireplace. Ma's room." Imogene Conway and Joan Dragoumanos, Ms. Nesmith's private home care nurses, knew of the existence of the notebook and had observed Helen Nesmith write in it. On several occasions, Helen Nesmith orally expressed to these nurses her intentions regarding the disposition of particular pieces of her property upon her death, including the farm scene painting. Helen Nesmith told Conway and Dragoumanos that the farm scene painting was to be given to Virginia Clark, upon Helen Nesmith's death.

Virginia Clark and Helen Nesmith first became acquainted in or about 1940. The women lived next door to each other for approximately ten years (1945 through 1955), during which time they enjoyed a close friendship. The Nesmith-Clark friendship remained constant through the years. In more recent years, Ms. Clark frequently spent time at Ms. Nesmith's home, often visiting Helen Nesmith while she rested in the room which originally was her mother's bedroom. The farm scene painting hung in this room above the fireplace. Virginia Clark openly admired the picture.

According to Ms. Clark, sometime during either January or February of 1980, Helen Nesmith told Ms. Clark that the farm scene painting would belong to Ms. Clark after Helen Nesmith's death. Helen Nesmith then mentioned to Virginia Clark that she would record this gift in a book she kept for the purpose of memorializing her wishes with respect to the disposition of certain of her belongings. * * * After that conversation, Helen Nesmith often alluded to the fact that Ms. Clark someday would own the farm scene painting.

---

2. The value of Ms. Nesmith's estate at the time of her death exceeded $2,000,000.00, including both tangible and nontangible assets.

Ms. Nesmith executed two codicils to her 1977 will: one on May 30, 1980, and a second on October 23, 1980. The codicils amended certain bequests and deleted others, while ratifying the will in all other respects.

Greenhalge received Helen Nesmith's notebook on or shortly after January 28, 1986, the date of Ms. Nesmith's death. Thereafter, Greenhalge, as executor, distributed Ms. Nesmith's property in accordance with the will as amended, the 1972 memorandum as amended in 1976, and certain of the provisions contained in the notebook.[4] Greenhalge refused, however, to deliver the farm scene painting to Virginia Clark because the painting interested him and he wanted to keep it. Mr. Greenhalge claimed that he was not bound to give effect to the expressions of Helen Nesmith's wishes and intentions stated in the notebook, particularly as to the disposition of the farm scene painting. Notwithstanding this opinion, Greenhalge distributed to himself all of the property bequeathed to him in the notebook. Ms. Clark thereafter commenced an action against Mr. Greenhalge seeking to compel him to deliver the farm scene painting to her.

The probate judge found that Helen Nesmith wanted Ms. Clark to have the farm scene painting. The judge concluded that Helen Nesmith's notebook qualified as a "memorandum" of her known wishes with respect to the distribution of her tangible personal property, within the meaning of Article Fifth of Helen Nesmith's will.[5] The judge further found that the notebook was in existence at the time of the execution of the 1980 codicils, which ratified the language of Article Fifth in its entirety. Based on these findings, the judge ruled that the notebook was incorporated by reference into the terms of the will. Newton v. Seaman's Friend Soc'y, 130 Mass. 91, 93 (1881). The judge awarded the painting to Ms. Clark.

The Appeals Court affirmed the probate judge's decision in an unpublished memorandum and order, 30 Mass.App.Ct. 1109, 570 N.E.2d 184 (1991). * * * We allowed the appellee's petition for further appellate review and now hold that the probate judge correctly awarded the painting to Ms. Clark.

A properly executed will may incorporate by reference into its provisions any "document or paper not so executed and witnessed, whether the paper referred to be in the form of . . . a mere list or memorandum, . . . if it was in existence at the time of the execution of the will, and is identified by clear and satisfactory proof as the paper referred to therein." Newton v. Seaman's Friend Soc'y, *supra* at 93. The

---

4. Helen Nesmith's will provided that Virginia Clark and her husband, Peter Hayden Clark, receive $20,000.00 upon Helen Nesmith's death. Under the terms of the 1972 memorandum, as amended in 1976, Helen Nesmith also bequeathed to Virginia Clark a portrait of Isabel Nesmith, Helen Nesmith's sister with whom Virginia Clark had been acquainted. Greenhalge honored these bequests and delivered the money and painting to Virginia Clark.

5. Article Fifth of Helen Nesmith's will reads, in pertinent part, as follows: "that [Greenhalge] distribute such of the tangible property to and among such persons *as I may designate by a memorandum left by me and known to him, or in accordance with my known wishes,* provided that said persons are living at the time of my decease" (emphasis added).

parties agree that the document entitled "memorandum," dated 1972 and amended in 1976, was in existence as of the date of the execution of Helen Nesmith's will. The parties further agree that this document is a memorandum regarding the distribution of certain items of Helen Nesmith's tangible personal property upon her death, as identified in Article Fifth of her will. There is no dispute, therefore, that the 1972 memorandum was incorporated by reference into the terms of the will. *Newton, supra.*

The parties do not agree, however, as to whether the documentation contained in the notebook, dated 1979, similarly was incorporated into the will through the language of Article Fifth. Greenhalge advances several arguments to support his contention that the purported bequest of the farm scene painting written in the notebook was not incorporated into the will and thus fails as a testamentary devise. The points raised by Greenhalge in this regard are not persuasive. First, Greenhalge contends that the judge wrongly concluded that the notebook could be considered a "memorandum" within the meaning of Article Fifth, because it is not specifically identified as a "memorandum." Such a literal interpretation of the language and meaning of Article Fifth is not appropriate.

"The 'cardinal rule in the interpretation of wills, to which all other rules must bend, is that the intention of the testator shall prevail, provided it is consistent with the rules of law.'" Boston Safe Deposit & Trust Co. v. Park, 307 Mass. 255, 259, 29 N.E.2d 977 (1940), quoting McCurdy v. McCallum, 186 Mass. 464, 469, 72 N.E. 75 (1904). The intent of the testator is ascertained through consideration of "the language which [the testatrix] has used to express [her] testamentary designs," Taft v. Stearns, 234 Mass. 273, 277, 125 N.E. 570 (1920), as well as the circumstances existing at the time of the execution of the will. Boston Safe Deposit & Trust Co., *supra* 307 Mass. at 259, 29 N.E.2d 977, and cases cited. The circumstances existing at the time of the execution of a codicil to a will are equally relevant, because the codicil serves to ratify the language in the will which has not been altered or affected by the terms of the codicil. See Taft, *supra* 234 Mass. at 275–277, 125 N.E. 570.

Applying these principles in the present case, it appears clear that Helen Nesmith intended by the language used in Article Fifth of her will to retain the right to alter and amend the bequests of tangible personal property in her will, without having to amend formally the will. The text of Article Fifth provides a mechanism by which Helen Nesmith could accomplish the result she desired; i.e., by expressing her wishes "in a memorandum." The statements in the notebook unquestionably reflect Helen Nesmith's exercise of her retained right to restructure the distribution of her tangible personal property upon her death. That the notebook is not entitled "memorandum" is of no consequence, since its apparent purpose is consistent with that of a memorandum under Article Fifth: It is a written instrument which is intended to guide Greenhalge in "distribut[ing] such of [Helen Nesmith's] tangible personal property to and among . . . persons [who] are living at the time of her decease." In this connection, the distinction between the notebook and "a memorandum" is illusory.

A second argument

A third argument

A final argument

The appellant acknowledges that the subject documentation in the notebook establishes that Helen Nesmith wanted Virginia Clark to receive the farm scene painting upon Ms. Nesmith's death. The appellant argues, however, that the notebook cannot take effect as a testamentary instrument under Article Fifth, because the language of Article Fifth limits its application to "a" memorandum, or the 1972 memorandum. We reject this strict construction of Article Fifth. The language of Article Fifth does not preclude the existence of more than one memorandum which serves the intended purpose of that article. As previously suggested, the phrase "a memorandum" in Article Fifth appears as an expression of the manner in which Helen Nesmith could exercise her right to alter her will after its execution, but it does not denote a requirement that she do so within a particular format. To construe narrowly Article Fifth and to exclude the possibility that Helen Nesmith drafted the notebook contents as "a memorandum" under that Article, would undermine our long-standing policy of interpreting wills in a manner which best carries out the known wishes of the testatrix. See Boston Safe Deposit & Trust Co., *supra*. The evidence supports the conclusion that Helen Nesmith intended that the bequests in her notebook be accorded the same power and effect as those contained in the 1972 memorandum under Article Fifth. We conclude, therefore, that the judge properly accepted the notebook as a memorandum of Helen Nesmith's known wishes as referenced in Article Fifth of her will.

The appellant also contends that the judge erred in finding that Helen Nesmith intended to incorporate the notebook into her will, since the evidence established, at most, that she intended to bequeath the painting to Clark, and not that she intended to incorporate the notebook into her will. Our review of the judge's findings on this point, which is limited to a consideration of whether such findings are "clearly erroneous," proves the appellant argument to be without merit. First Pa. Mortgage Trust v. Dorchester Sav. Bank, 395 Mass. 614, 621, 481 N.E.2d 1132 (1985). The judge found that Helen Nesmith drafted the notebook contents with the expectation that Greenhalge would distribute the property accordingly. The judge further found that the notebook was in existence on the dates Helen Nesmith executed the codicils to her will, which affirmed the language of Article Fifth, and that it thereby was incorporated into the will pursuant to the language and spirit of Article Fifth. It is clear that the judge fairly construed the evidence in reaching the determination that Helen Nesmith intended the notebook to serve as a memorandum of her wishes as contemplated under Article Fifth of her will.

Lastly, the appellant complains that the notebook fails to meet the specific requirements of a memorandum under Article Fifth of the will, because it was not "known to him" until after Helen Nesmith's death. For this reason, Greenhalge states that the judge improperly ruled that the notebook was incorporated into the will. One of Helen Nesmith's nurses testified, however, that Greenhalge was aware of the notebook and its contents, and that he at no time made an effort to determine the validity of the bequest of the farm scene painting to Virginia Clark as stated therein. There is ample support in the record, therefore, to support the judge's conclusion that the notebook met the criteria set forth in Article Fifth regarding memoranda.

We note, as did the Appeals Court, that "one who seeks equity must do equity and that a court will not permit its equitable powers to be employed to accomplish an injustice." Pitts v. Halifax Country Club, Inc., 19 Mass.App.Ct. 525, 533, 476 N.E.2d 222 (1985). To this point, we remark that Greenhalge's conduct in handling this controversy fell short of the standard imposed by common social norms, not to mention the standard of conduct attending his fiduciary responsibility as executor, particularly with respect to his selective distribution of Helen Nesmith's assets. We can discern no reason in the record as to why this matter had to proceed along the protracted and costly route that it did.

Judgment affirmed.

Notes

For a document to be incorporated by reference by a subsequent valid will, that document must be in existence, and nothing contained within that document may be changed after the will is executed. In one set of facts, a decedent incorporated by reference a blank form, and there was no evidence that the form had been completed prior to the execution of the will that incorporated it. Because of this omission, the Supreme Court of West Virginia rejected the incorporation of the document by the will, requiring proof that everything on the form was in existence at the time of execution of the will. *See* Cyfers v. Cyfers, 759 S.E.2d 475 (W. Va. 2014). Contrary to incorporation by reference, facts of independent significance and legal lists permit modification after the execution of the will.

Estate of Nielson

California Court of Appeal, 1980
105 Cal. App. 3d 796, 165 Cal. Rptr. 319

STANIFORTH, Acting P. J.

Arthur G. Nielson (contestant) opposed the admission to probate of the will of his deceased nephew, Lloyd M. Nielson (testator). At the close of contestant's evidence, the trial court granted the proponent's motion for judgment made pursuant to Code of Civil Procedure section 631.8, denied the contest and admitted the will to probate. The court found contestant had failed to meet his burden of proof to overcome the presumption of validity of the will. The court concluded there was no evidence to show that the testator had made the strikeover, interlineations appearing on the face of his 1969 will. * * *

Contestant appeals asserting his evidence had established the absence of any valid will and therefore testator's estate was required to pass by rules of intestate succession to the nearest heirs-at-law.

* * *

Testator executed a typewritten witnessed will dated February 25, 1969 (1969 will) disposing of the bulk of his estate to his mother. If the mother predeceased him, it would go to the Salvation Army of San Diego, the Braille Club of San Diego, the San Diego County Association for Retarded Children, and the National Anti-Vivisection Society (Chicago, Ill.) Paragraph sixth of the 1969 will indicated the testator intentionally omitted provision for any of his heirs.

This will was validly executed; however, on its face numerous lines have been drawn through the dispositive provisions to the above enumerated charities. Interlineated in their place were the handwritten words "Bulk of Estate-1.-Shrine Hospital for Crippled Children-Los Angeles. $10,000-2.-Society for Prevention of Cruelty to Animals (nearest chapter)." Appearing at the margin of these cancellations and interlineations were the testator's initials. Additionally, the date of the 1969 will was cancelled followed by the date "November 29, 1974." At both the top and bottom of this typewritten will were the handwritten words "*Revised* by Lloyd M. Nielson November 29, 1974."

Contestant asserts these deletions and interlineations (1) revoke the 1969 will and (2) were ineffective as a holographic will or codicil for failure to comply with Probate Code section 53.

Upon trial contestant testified he was the testator's closest living heir. He offered no testimonial evidence as to the authorship, the intent with which the deletions, interlineations were made on the will. The trial court found "[t]here was no evidence admitted concerning the handwriting of the interlineations which appear on the decedent's will of February 25, 1969 except for signature of the decedent and the signatures of the subscribing witnesses and their addresses." Accordingly, the trial court found "[t]hat the handwriting and interlineations . . . are of no force and effect except for signature of the testator. . . ."

* * *

Once the proponent of a will proves a prima facie case of due execution, the contestant has the burden of proving by competent evidence the issues raised by his contest. (Estate of Relph (1923) 192 Cal. 451, 459 [221 P. 361]; Estate of Darilek (1957) 151 Cal.App.2d 322, 325 [311 P.2d 615].)

Direct evidence, however, is not essential to prove the destruction, cancellation, alterations in a will were made by the testator. A presumption of cancellation can arise from circumstantial evidence alone. (Estate of Streeton (1920) 183 Cal. 284, 290 [191 P. 16]; Estate of Olmsted (1898) 122 Cal. 224, 230 [54 P. 745].)

For example, where the will is in the possession or under the control of a decedent until his last illness, the inference is the changes and alterations were made by the testator. (Estate of Stickney (1951) 101 Cal.App.2d 572, 575 [225 P.2d 649]; Estate of Hewitt (1923) 63 Cal.App. 440, 447 [218 P. 778].)

Furthermore, the handwriting on the will may speak for itself. Where the issue is the questioned authorship of a will, the trier of fact can determine the issue by comparison of the questioned writing with "genuine" or admitted handwriting of the testator without the aid of the oral testimony of any witness. (Evid. Code, § 1417; Estate of Johnson (1927) 200 Cal. 299, 304 [252 P. 1049]; Castor v. Bernstein (1906) 2 Cal.App. 703, 706 [84 P. 244].) Thus, no handwriting expert or testimony was necessary. The court—the trier of fact—had the testator's admitted handwriting before it in the proffered will. It was authorized by law to determine the authenticity of the "questioned handwriting by comparison" with the conceded handwriting of the testator.

Since the trial court erroneously concluded there was "no evidence" presented as to authorship of the deletions/interlineations on the face of the will, we must reverse and remand for further proceedings consistent with this opinion. (Cf., Heap v. General Motors Corp. (1977) 66 Cal.App.3d 824 [136 Cal.Rptr. 304].) For guidance of the trial court upon any retrial of this cause, we resolve these further contentions of error.

* * *

Upon the assumed premise the trial court will find the deletions and interlineations to be in the testator's handwriting, * * * contestant argues that a holographic will or codicil did not result from the testator's writings on the face of his formal witnessed will. Section 53 of the Probate Code provides:

> A holographic will is one that is entirely written, dated and signed by the hand of the testator himself. It is subject to no other form, and need not be witnessed. No address, date or other matter written, printed or stamped upon the document, which is not incorporated in the provisions which are in the handwriting of the decedent, shall be considered as any part of the will.

If the handwriting on the face of the formal will is "*entirely* [italics added] written, dated and signed by the hand of the testator," then the statutory requisites of section 53 are met. Contestant argues the handwriting was united with, integrated, incorporated into the type-written portions of the 1969 will, therefore no valid holograph resulted. The resolution of this contention requires an examination of several well-established rules relating to wills and particularly holographic wills or codicils.

First, there is no requirement that a holograph be written on a separate paper or denominated by the testator as a will or codicil. (Estate of Spitzer (1925) 196 Cal. 301, 307 [237 P. 739]; Estate of French (1964) 225 Cal.App.2d 9, 15 [36 Cal.Rptr. 908].)

Second, the mere presence of typewritten words on the paper upon which a holographic will or codicil is written, of which such words are no part, does not render the holograph invalid. (Prob. Code, § 53.)

> [A]s declared in Estate of Bower . . . 'the mere presence of printed matter on the paper is not fatal to the validity of an holographic will written thereon if such printed matter be not included or incorporated, directly or indirectly,

in the will as written by the hand of the decedent.' (Estate of Baker (1963) 59 Cal.2d 680, 683 [31 Cal.Rptr. 33, 381 P.2d 913]; see also Estate of Helmar (1973) 33 Cal.App.3d 109 [109 Cal.Rptr. 6].)

The Supreme Court in Estate of Baker, *supra*, tells us the test is not whether the handwritten portion of the document independently evidences the decedent's intent as to the disposition of his property and to matters essential to the validity of the will *but whether the handwritten portion evidences an intent to include any printed or typed matter* which, when read with the handwritten words, *is relevant* to the decedent's will.

The *Baker* court further indicated that unless the printed or typed matter is relevant to the "substance" of the decedent's will, it can be disregarded as surplusage. (Estate of Baker, *supra*, 59 Cal.2d 680, 683.) In *Baker, supra*, the place of execution of the will (Modesto, California) was not relevant to the decedent's testamentary intent or to the validity of the will, therefore, the printed words were held not to be incorporated into the handwritten portions of the will. (Id., at pp. 683–684; Estate of Christian (1976) 60 Cal.App.3d 975, 981 [131 Cal.Rptr. 841].)

A second set of relevant rules pertains to the reverse process, the incorporation by reference of *extrinsic documents* into an otherwise valid witnessed or holographic will.

In Estate of Smith (1948) 31 Cal.2d 563 [191 P.2d 413], the decedent had written a holographic revocatory clause across the face of a copy of an attested will (the original of which had been left with the decedent's attorney). The Supreme Court held the decedent had incorporated the attested will in the holographic clause, and said (p. 567):

> It has long been settled in this state that either a holographic or an attested testamentary instrument may refer to and incorporate another testamentary instrument executed with different statutory formalities or an informal or unattested document, so long as the reference is unmistakable or with the aid of extrinsic proof can be made so. (See 7 Witkin, Summary of Cal. Law (8th ed. 1974) Wills and Probate, § 144, p. 5660.)

"The papers incorporated by reference are used to construe and apply the will, and do not become part of the will in the same sense as those integrated. Hence the holographic will may be regarded as entirely in the testator's handwriting, as required by the statute." (7 Witkin, *supra*, p. 5661; Estate of Smith, *supra*, 31 Cal.2d 563, 567–568; see also Estate of Atkinson (1930) 110 Cal.App. 499, 502 [294 P. 425].)

The requisites of incorporation by reference are (1) the extrinsic paper must be in existence at the time the will makes reference to it; (2) the will must identify the paper by a sufficiently certain description, and extrinsic evidence is admissible as an aid to such identification; and (3) it must appear that the testator intended to incorporate the paper for the purpose of carrying out his testamentary desires. (Estate of Foxworth (1966) 240 Cal.App.2d 784, 788, 789 [50 Cal.Rptr. 237].)

Finally, a prior will is revoked by a subsequent will which contains an "express revocation or provisions wholly inconsistent" with its terms. (Prob. Code, § 72.) The revoking instrument must be executed with the same formalities required for the execution of a will. (Prob. Code, § 74.) Thus a formal will may be revoked by a valid holographic will or codicil.

Applying these statutes and judicial declarations to the document under scrutiny we conclude the following: First, if the handwriting on the face of the formal will were written, dated and signed by the testator, then it meets the statutory requisites of a holographic will (Prob. Code, § 53) unless "other written matter" was expressly or impliedly, directly or indirectly, incorporated into and relevant to the handwritten words. The word "incorporate" as used in section 53 means "formed or combined into one body or unit; intimately united, joined, or blended" (Webster's New World Dict. of the English Language (1966) p. 738) or "to unite with or introduce into something already existent" (Webster's Third New Internat. Dict. (1961) p. 1145.)

An examination of the document, in its entirety, leads to these conclusions: the typewritten words are not relevant to the substance of the holograph or essential to its validity as a will or codicil. Nor do the written or express words or physical ordering of relationships indicate any intention that the holograph unite, form or blend with the provisions of the typewritten will. Nor does the word-content of the holograph indicate any intent to integrate the handwriting with the typewritten will. We conclude no evidence from the face of this document tells us the author intended to "incorporate" directly or indirectly the typewritten will into the provisions which are in his handwriting so as to render the handwriting ineffective as a will or codicil and thereby defeat the author's declared testamentary intent. * * *

Judgment reversed and cause remanded for proceedings conformable to this opinion.

Henderson, J., * * * concurred.

II. Facts of Independent Significance

Uniform Probate Code (2014)

§ 2-512. Events of Independent Significance.

A will may dispose of property by reference to acts and events that have significance apart from their effect upon the dispositions made by the will, whether they occur before or after the execution of the will or before or after the testator's death. The execution or revocation of another individual's will is such an event.

Notes

Modern estate planning utilizes a device known as a pour-over trust. The device allows for a living person to create a legal arrangement — a trust — which may accomplish stated objectives either during the person's life or after the person's death. If the trust has no assets when it is created, it is called an unfunded trust. If there are assets at the time of creation, it is called a funded trust. If the trust is unfunded, the person may direct that his or her Last Will and Testament fund the trust at death, thus allowing for a "pour over" from the will to the trust. But this "pour-over" practice created a difficulty in the law because, if there were no funding at creation, then no valid trust was created since every trust must have a corpus. Thus, the will could not "pour over" into the trust since no trust was ever created. This sounds confusing; however, of even greater importance is the fact that this interfered with estate planning objectives. To rectify this dilemma and to facilitate the modern estate planning culture, statutes were enacted to enable unfunded *inter vivos* trusts to be created as events of independent significance, into which Last Wills and Testaments may "pour over" assets.

Uniform Probate Code (2019)

§ 2-511. Uniform Testamentary Additions to Trusts Act.

(a) A will may validly devise property to the trustee of a trust established or to be established (i) during the testator's lifetime by the testator, by the testator and some other person, or by some other person, including a funded or unfunded life insurance trust, although the settlor has reserved any or all rights of ownership of the insurance contracts, or (ii) at the testator's death by the testator's devise to the trustee, if the trust is identified in the testator's will and its terms are set forth in a written instrument, other than a will, executed before, concurrently with, or after the execution of the testator's will or in another individual's will if that other individual has predeceased the testator, regardless of the existence, size, or character of the corpus of the trust. The devise is not invalid because the trust is amendable or revocable, or because the trust was amended after the execution of the will or the testator's death.

(b) Unless the testator's will provides otherwise, property devised to a trust described in subsection (a) is not held under a testamentary trust of the testator, but it becomes a part of the trust to which it is devised, and must be administered and disposed of in accordance with the provisions of the governing instrument setting forth the terms of the trust, including any amendments thereto made before or after the testator's death.

(c) Unless the testator's will provides otherwise, a revocation or termination of the trust before the testator's death causes the devise to lapse.

III. Legal List

Uniform Probate Code (2019)

§ 2-513. Separate Writing Identifying Devise of Certain Types of Tangible Personal Property.

Whether or not the provisions relating to holographic wills apply, a will may refer to a written statement or list to dispose of items of tangible personal property not otherwise specifically disposed of by the will, other than money. To be admissible under this section as evidence of the intended disposition, the writing must be signed by the testator and must describe the items and the devisees with reasonable certainty. The writing may be referred to as one to be in existence at the time of the testator's death; it may be prepared before or after the execution of the will; it may be altered by the testator after its preparation; and it may be a writing that has no significance apart from its effect on the dispositions made by the will.

In re Last Will and Testament and Trust Agreement of Moor

Court of Chancery of Delaware, 2005
879 A.2d 648

STRINE, Vice Chancellor. * * *

Betty R. Moor ("Mrs. Moor") died on April 5, 2002, when she was a resident of Rehoboth Beach, Delaware. Mrs. Moor had executed a will (the "Will") on February 4, 1998 in Fort Lauderdale, Florida, where she resided at that time. The Will named Jerome A. Bauman and April Hudson as Mrs. Moor's executors. The second article of the Will provides for the attachment of a written statement disposing of tangible personal property. The third article—the residuary clause of the Will— directs that the remainder of Mrs. Moor's estate be conveyed to the trustees of the Betty R. Moor Revocable Trust, which she created in 1985, for distribution in accordance with that Trust.

In 2000, Mrs. Moor moved from Fort Lauderdale to Rehoboth Beach, Delaware. She executed two documents related to her Will while living in Delaware. On March 9, 2001, Mrs. Moor executed a personal property memorandum (the "Property Memo") that, as described in the second article of her Will, made several specific bequests of personal property to specific persons. On September 8, 2001, Mrs. Moor executed a codicil to her Will, the effect of which was to remove Jerome A. Bauman as executor and replace him with Richard S. McCann. April Hudson remained the other executor, and all of the other provisions of the 1998 Will were retained and ratified. * * *

The penultimate clause of Mrs. Moor's Property Memo is the source of the current dispute. That clause provides the following instruction: "Any items not listed in this WILL are to be auctioned, the capitol gain [sic] from the auction is to be dispersed to those stated in the aforesaid document." I will refer to that provision of the Property Memo as the "Capital Gain Clause" for ease of reference. The Property Memo was signed by Mrs. Moor and notarized by a single witness. In accordance with the Property Memo, eighteen items are to be distributed to five persons.

April Hudson and Richard McCann, as the executors of Mrs. Moor's estate and respondents in this action, concede that the Property Memo was signed by Mrs. Moor and that it reflects the best evidence of her testamentary intent. In accordance with that concession, they intend to distribute the eighteen items described in the Property Memo to the five individuals named as the intended recipients of those items. The executors also agree that Mrs. Moor's misuse of the term "capitol gain," which should be read as "capital gain," properly refers to net proceeds from the sale of her personal property. * * * Further, the executors concede that the Capital Gain Clause reflects the intent that the net proceeds from the sale of Mrs. Moor's personal property be divided among the five individuals named in the Property Memo.

What occasions this dispute is the executors' contention that the Capital Gain Clause, because it calls for the residue of Mrs. Moor's personal property to be sold and the cash proceeds from that sale distributed to the five named individuals, is unenforceable under the laws of the two states—Delaware and Florida—whose law might govern Mrs. Moor's Will.

The lack of clarity about the choice of law arises because Mrs. Moor was a resident of Florida when she made her Will, but a resident of Delaware when she signed the Property Memo and the Codicil to her Will. And, unlike other of Mrs. Moor's estate planning documents which contained express Florida choice of law provisions, her Will contained no choice of law provision. According to the executors, the choice of law question does not matter. The executors contend that whichever state's law applies, a personal property memorandum may not be used to direct executors to sell certain tangible personalty and convey the sale proceeds to specific beneficiaries. Furthermore, the executors claim that the Capital Gain Clause is equivalent to a bequest of cash, which cannot be accomplished under either Delaware or Florida law by use of a separate writing, such as Mrs. Moor's Property Memo. Bequests of cash, they contend, must be included in the body of a will.

Thus, the executors do not intend to honor the Property Memo in its entirety. They have already honored the provisions of the Property Memo calling for the distribution of discrete items to the intended recipients, but they intend to disregard the Capital Gain Clause, and to distribute the proceeds of the sale of the rest of Mrs. Moor's personal property—an amount totaling just over $167,000— to April Hudson, Mrs. Moor's niece and a respondent in this case, and Charles Carey, Mrs. Moor's friend and accountant, who are the residual beneficiaries of the Betty R. Moor Revocable Trust, consistent with the residuary clause of the Will,[2] rather than distribute the proceeds pro rata to the five individuals named in the Property Memo. The executors have formulated this intent not because they perceive there to be any ambiguity in the Capital Gain Clause, but because, they contend, distribution of cash is not permitted under the relevant statutes concerning bequests by separate writing.

The executors' intention not to respect the Capital Gain Clause has drawn objection from Mrs. Moor's stepson, Robert Cooper Moor, Jr. ("Cooper"), and her granddaughter, Marilyn Mercedes Moor ("Marilyn"). Both Cooper and Marilyn,

---

2. The Will directs that the residue of her estate be distributed in accordance with the Betty R. Moor Revocable Trust. Because all specific bequests in that Trust have been satisfied with the Trust's assets, the residue of the estate will be conveyed to Hudson and Carey.

the petitioners in this action, are among the five individuals named in the Property Memo who would share pro rata in the sale proceeds if the Capital Gain Clause was honored by the executors. Cooper and Marilyn argue that the Capital Gain Clause is enforceable, as it does not contravene the clear language of the relevant statutes. * * *

Parties' position

The resolution of this dispute turns entirely on a question of law. As suggested previously, answering that question is complicated to some degree by uncertainty as to what state's law applies to Mrs. Moor's Will. Rather than haggle over choice of law, the parties take the position that choice of law does not matter. The executors contend that, under either Delaware or Florida law, a testator may not, by separate writing, direct that specific personal property be sold and the proceeds of the sale be distributed to specific persons. For their part, Cooper and Marilyn argue that neither Delaware nor Florida law prevents a testator from disposing of personal property by directing that it be sold and the proceeds conveyed to particular persons.

I agree with the parties that there appears to be no material difference between the Delaware and Florida statutes bearing on this issue, and therefore, no definitive choice of law needs to be made. * * * Both states require that, in order to be valid, a will must be signed by two witnesses.[4] Both states also permit bequests of tangible personal property in a separate writing 1) if the separate writing is referred to in the will, and 2) if, as here, the separate writing is signed by the testator.[5]

The types of disposition that may permissibly be made by separate writing are limited under 12 *Del. C.* § 212, which states in part that: "A will may refer to a written statement or list to dispose of items of tangible personal property not otherwise specifically disposed of by the will, other than money, evidences of indebtedness, documents of title, and securities, and property used in trade or business." The analogous Florida statute, *Fla. Stat.* § 732.515, is substantially similar, stating in part that: "A written statement or list referred to in the decedent's will shall dispose of items of tangible personal property, other than property used in trade or business, not otherwise specifically disposed of by the will."

The executors argue that the Capital Gain Clause of Mrs. Moor's Property Memo exceeds the scope of these statutes by attempting to devise money gained from the sale of personal property, rather than the personal property itself. Both Delaware and Florida law, they say, forbid the use of a separate writing to dispose of intangible property, like cash and securities. Therefore, because the Property Memo was not executed in compliance with the requisite formalities applicable to the execution of wills—that is, because the Property Memo was signed by one witness instead of two—the Capital Gain Clause is void. I am not persuaded by this argument, for the following reasons.

---

4. *See* 12 *Del. C.* § 202; *Fla. Stat.* § 732.502.

5. *See* 12 *Del. C.* § 212; *Fla. Stat.* § 732.515. Under the Delaware statute, even an unsigned instrument will be held valid if it is handwritten by the testator. 12 *Del. C.* § 212.

Initially and most importantly, the executors' argument would read into the statutory text words of restriction that were not included by the relevant legislatures, contrary to the law of statutory construction in both Delaware and Florida.[6] Both the Delaware and Florida statutes use the broad term "dispose of" in reference to the power that a testator might exercise in a personal property memorandum. The executors contend that this capacious phrase can only be read as meaning "to devise directly to" rather than "to sell and distribute the sale proceeds to." But the term "dispose of" has been employed by the legislatures of both Delaware and Florida in other contexts to refer to an elastic range of activities.[7] Accordingly, I find no basis for interpreting the words of the pertinent statutes here in the cramped manner that the executors advocate. Under a literal reading of those statutes, Mrs. Moor "disposed of" her personal property by directing her executors to sell that property and distribute the proceeds to specific persons. Importantly, there is no contention that Mrs. Moor attempted, through the Capital Gain Clause, to devise by her Property Memo a species of property—intangible property—that Delaware or Florida law explicitly preclude from being devised through a separate writing. All of the property covered by the Capital Gain Clause was tangible, identified by the executors, and has, in fact, already been sold by them, generating a substantial amount of cash.

The executors seek to convince me that a more restricted definition of the term "dispose of" should be read into §212 because the relevant Delaware statute

---

6. *See, e.g., Stifel Fin. Corp. v. Cochran*, 809 A.2d 555, 560 (Del.2002) (refusing to "engraft a requirement that creates a further bar" where a specific legislative restriction was absent from a statute); *State v. Trimworks*, 1991 WL 15229, at *3 (Del.Super.Jan.25, 1991) ("[S]tatutory language which is clear on its face should not be given a more restrictive application than its plain language calls for."). *See also Bruner v. GC-GW, Inc.*, 880 So.2d 1244, 1246 (Fla.Dist.Ct.App.2004) (refusing to read restrictive language into a statute, noting that "[w]e are not at liberty to add words to statutes that were not placed there by the Legislature.") (quoting *Hayes v. State*, 750 So.2d 1, 4 (Fla.1999)).

7. In Delaware law, the term "dispose of" has been equated with, for example: break, mutilate, or destroy (3 *Del. C.* §3142(a)); transport, treat, store, or export (7 *Del. C.* §6309(i)); sell, convey, lease, exchange, or transfer (8 *Del. C.* §122(4)); remove, conceal, or encumber (11 *Del. C.* §892(1)); mortgage, pledge, or abandon (11 *Del. C.* §4358); assign, devise, bequeath, or encumber (13 *Del. C.* §311); issue or give (16 *Del. C.* §7102(2)); hypothecate (18 *Del. C.* §7501); leave, drop, or throw away (21 *Del. C.* §4189(e)); use (22 *Del. C.* §1307(a)); alienate or gift (25 *Del. C.* §4002). In Florida law, the term "dispose of" has been used even more broadly to mean, for example: destroy (*Fla. Stat.* §20.255(5)(a)); transfer custody or alter (*Fla. Stat.* §119.11(4)); sell, lease, mortgage, or transfer (*Fla. Stat.* §154.209(7)); use (*Fla. Stat.* §163.01(15)(b)(2)(a)); assign or convey (*Fla. Stat.* §215.56005(2)(c)(4)); release (*Fla. Stat.* §255.503(7)); hold or license (*Fla. Stat.* §282.102(12)); alienate (*Fla. Stat.* §320.643(1)(a)); exchange (*Fla. Stat.* §343.54(3)(e)); transport or inter (*Fla. Stat.* §382.026(7)); endorse, pledge, or hypothecate (*Fla. Stat.* §425.04(5)); distribute (*Fla. Stat.* §499.028(10)); create a security interest in (*Fla. Stat.* §607.0302(4)); own, vote, or lend (*Fla. Stat.* §607.0302(6)); compromise (*Fla. Stat.* §663.17(7)); deliver (*Fla. Stat.* §677.303(1)); dispense (*Fla. Stat.* §812.012(8)(a)); take, possess, or give away (*Fla. Stat.* §859.058); detain or traffic in (*Fla. Stat.* §865.10(2)); enforce, satisfy, settle or subordinate (*Fla. Stat.* §938.29(3)); or abandon (*Fla. Stat.* §949.07). These wide-ranging legislative usages of "dispose of" tend to inter the notion that the term means only "to devise directly to another," as the executors would have it.

explicitly prohibits a testator from disposing of *money* via a separate writing. They contend that to permit Mrs. Moor to direct her executors, in her Property Memo, to sell certain personal property for cash and distribute the proceeds would be to permit an end-run around the General Assembly's deliberate decision to exclude cash from the kinds of property that may be devised via separate writing. Likewise, the executors note that the relevant Florida statute does not permit a testator to convey intangible property (such as, they claim, money) * * * by a separate writing, and that it would be inconsistent with the intent of the Florida legislature to permit Mrs. Moor, through her Property Memo, to reduce personal property into a liquid pool of cash for distribution. Under both Delaware and Florida law, the executors say, testators must use the body of their wills to distribute intangible property, particularly pure financial assets like cash, negotiable instruments, and securities.

The executors ignore that the Florida statute differs from the Delaware statute in that it does not specifically exclude money from disposition by separate writing.[9] This reality somewhat belies the executors' contention that choice of law is not

---

9. The differences between the Delaware and Florida statutes track the evolution of the Uniform Probate Code § 2-513, from which both statutes were derived. The pre-1990 version of the Code, which Delaware adopted, precludes dispositions of "evidences of indebtedness, documents of title, and securities," while the post-1990 revision of the Code, which Florida adopted, deleted references to evidences of indebtedness, documents of title, and securities. Comments on the purpose of the 1990 revision of the Uniform Code clarify that the enumerated dispositions were deleted in order to remove a source of confusion from the pre-1990 version, noting that those items "are not items of tangible personal property to begin with." *See* Unif. Probate Code § 2-513, Revised 1990 Version, Comment (1997). Notably, unlike enumerated items that were deleted because they were clearly *not* tangible personal property, "money" was retained in the revised § 2-513. Comments on the revision specify that the section contemplates disposition by separate writing of "tangible personalty other than money." *See id.* As such, the Uniform Code seems to view money as tangible personalty that is treated differently from species of tangible personalty other than money.

The Florida legislature originally adopted language from § 2-513 that explicitly excluded "money" from devise by separate writing. In 2001, the legislature amended its version of § 2-513, *Fla. Stat.* § 732.515, deleting all reference to money or cash. *See* West's F.S.A. § 732.515. As such, the current statute does not explicitly exclude money from disposition by a separate writing. On the other hand, because the statute only permits disposition of "tangible property" by a separate writing, disposition of money is permitted only if money is considered under Florida law to be "tangible property." That is, if money is not tangible, it is excluded because it is not permitted.

Money is not consistently treated as being either tangible property or intangible property under Florida law. For example, *Fla. Stat.* § 192.001(11)(b) states that, as applicable to ad valorem taxes, " 'Intangible personal property' means money . . . ," while *Fla. Stat.* § 198.01(10) states that, as applicable to estate taxes, " 'Tangible personal property' means corporeal personal property, including money." Both definitions are limited in application to the statutes in which they appear, and there are no similar definitions applicable to statutes governing the construction of wills.

In light of that inconsistency in Florida law, and the absence of any legislative history explaining the intent behind the 2001 amendment of § 732.515, I am forced to resort to common sense. The Florida legislature deleted statutory language in § 732.515 that unequivocally proscribed dispositions of money. If the legislature viewed money as "intangible property" that should not be disposed of by a separate writing, its amendment had the effect of achieving exactly the same result—the exclusion of money dispositions by separate writing—by replacing unequivocally explicit statutory language with an ambiguous exclusion-by-failure-to-include. I am reluctant to attribute an

important to their argument. But even under the Delaware statute and under the assumption that Florida law is to the same effect, the executors' argument has at best a glancing surface logic—and even that disappears upon closer examination. The point of both the Delaware and Florida statutes is to provide testators with a more flexible means by which to devise their personal property.[10] That legislative intention was accomplished, as are most public policy judgments, by a compromise between competing values. The more rigorous formalities required of the body of a will itself were relaxed, permitting a testator to dispose of personal property by a simple, unwitnessed writing that becomes an annex to the will. By that tradeoff, both legislatures made the judgment that the flexibility and convenience of this method were, on balance, worth the enhanced possibility that such a writing might not reflect the uncoerced, free will of the testator.

There is, of course, risk in this sort of tradeoff. One can easily imagine persons who possess items of personal property—works of art, period piece furniture, sports memorabilia—that are more valuable than their cash and securities. Because a personal property memorandum may be executed without the procedural protections of a will, there is an increased chance that such a memorandum might be induced by designing persons. Under both the Delaware and Florida statutes at issue, the public policy judgment is that this increased chance is worth taking, even if that means, for example, that grandma's expensive Ellsworth Kelly[11] might be devised by a personal property memorandum cajoled out of her by a designing granddaughter.

With this public policy judgment having been made, I fail to see what purpose is served by acceding to the executors' demand to engraft a restriction on the term "dispose of" that does not arise naturally from the statutory text. To do so would do nothing to better protect testators from undue influence.

The executors concede that a testator may convey an expensive painting directly in a separate writing, thereby giving the recipient ownership and the right to sell the painting for cash profit. As a result, it is difficult to conceive of what public policy offense occurs if the testator instead directs her executors to sell the painting and to convey the sale proceeds to certain persons. In either case, the economic incentives for designing persons, and the corresponding economic risk to the testator and other possible objects of her testamentary good wishes, remain the same. And, in

---

oddly oblique and confusing approach to the effectuation of public policy to the Florida legislature. It seems more plausible that the Florida legislature intended to relax its enumeration of restricted dispositions, following the modern trend, as reflected in the revision of the Uniform Probate Code, "to permit the disposition of a broader range of tangible personal property." *See* Unif. Probate Code § 2-513, Revised 1990 Version, Comment (1997). But I need not and do not make any definitive interpretation of the Florida statute. Under either reading of the statute, the executors do not prevail.

10. *See* Unif. Probate Code § 2-513, Pre-1990 Version, Comment (1997) ("As part of the broader policy of effectuating a testator's intent and of relaxing formalities of execution, this section permits a testator to refer in his or her will to a separate document disposing of tangible personalty.").

11. American minimalist painter and sculptor, b.1923, Newburgh, N.Y.

either case, the crucial question should not turn on how many signatures were on the personal property memorandum, but on whether the personal property memorandum was the product of the testator's rational and uncoerced wishes.

In view of these realities, I conclude that accepting the executors' arguments would serve no public policy interest. Indeed, acceptance of their argument would contravene the public policies of Delaware and Florida, by overriding the clearly expressed intent of Mrs. Moor, as set forth in the Capital Gain Clause.[12] That Clause is contained in a Property Memo the executors otherwise concede is a product of Mrs. Moor's free will and clear mind, and that they otherwise intend to respect. To permit the executors to single out the Capital Gain Clause for invalidation would undermine Mrs. Moor's wishes by depriving her intended beneficiaries of her benevolence and bestowing a windfall on the residuary beneficiaries of her will.[13] * * *

For the foregoing reasons, the executors shall convey the net proceeds of the sale of the personal property covered by the Capital Gain Clause to the five individuals referred to in Mrs. Moor's Property Memo, with each beneficiary receiving 20 percent of the total.

This decision resolves the remaining issue in this case. The executors shall, upon notice as to form, present a conforming final order within five days.

Notes

Few can refute the flexibility that a legal list provides. Before or after execution of the Last Will and Testament, a testator may create a list and frequently change items of personal property—jewelry, art, furniture—without the necessity of writing a new will. True, the list must be signed and the will must refer to the list as being in existence or to come into existence, but a legal list provides far greater flexibility and is a by-product of the relaxation of testamentary formalities. But some questions remain: Would stocks, money market funds, and bonds be considered money or tangible personal property? Does a file on the computer constitute a written legal list? If the list provides for a personal item to go to X, and the will provides that it go to Y, who gets the item? If a legal list and a holographic will serve as sufficient writings, which would be better to employ?

States often modify the legal list statute proposed in the Uniform Probate Code. *See, e.g.,* CAL. PROB. CODE § 6132(g) (providing that any single item of tangible

---

12. *See Matter of Will of Carter,* 565 A.2d 933, 935 (Del.1989) ("In construing a will, the intent of the testator is paramount."); *Allen v. Dalk,* 826 So.2d 245, 247 (Fla.2002) ("The primary consideration in construing a will is the intent of the testator.").

13. Cooper also raised a general exception to the inventory of personal property items that were sold by the executors. He claimed that there should have been additional property included. But the executors responded to that objection through counsel by indicating that, to the best of their knowledge, the inventory was complete. In the face of that representation, Cooper failed to provide any evidence that Mrs. Moor actually possessed specific items of property at her death that he alleged were not included in the inventory. At oral argument, I therefore rejected his general exception as too vague and unsubstantiated for further pursuit.

personal property passing under a legal list cannot be valued in excess of $5,000, and the total of all items of tangible personal property passing under the legal list cannot exceed $25,000). Any item exceeding the limits imposed by the statute pass under the residuary clause of the decedent's will or through intestacy. The statute also defines tangible personal property as

> articles of personal or household use or ornament, including, but not limited to, furniture, furnishings, automobiles, boats, and jewelry, as well as precious metals in any tangible form, such as bullion or coins, and articles held for investment purposes. The term "tangible personal property" does not mean real property, a mobile home as defined in Section 798.3 of the Civil Code, intangible property, such as evidences of indebtedness, bank accounts and other monetary deposits, documents of title, or securities.

Id. at §6132(h)(1).

Problem

Decedent died survived by five adult children and a companion, with whom he lived in an intimate relationship for fourteen years. During the course of his life, the decedent wrote multiple Last Will and Testaments, some of which he signed, but the most recent he signed and dated two years before his death, and apparently he revoked any previous wills. Attached to this last will was a "Gift by Memorandum" paper that disposed of antiques, firearms, and automobiles to named children and friends. The language of the memorandum indicates that it was written and signed by the decedent prior to the execution of the will, which references that a memorandum may come about in the future. Also, there is a clause in the will that specifies:

> SIXTH: It is my intention to make a separate written instrument leaving items of tangible personal property to various people as allowed by Section 15–2–513 of the Idaho Code. All items not listed by me, or should no list be made by me, then all items of various personal property not specifically listed to go to specific persons shall pass to my longtime companion, including my personal effects, clothes, household furnishings, furniture, and appliances.

Decedent's surviving companion argues that the will supersedes and revokes the memorandum and that she takes all of the items of personal property owned by the decedent at death. How would you address her argument? *See* Wilkins v. Wilkins, 137 Idaho 315, 48 P.3d 644 (2002).

IV. Plain Meaning Versus Ambiguity

Often a testator may say one thing and mean another. Even when the language is clear on its face and it describes with clarity an object or person in existence, this may not be the object or person intended. Such legal disputes are often categorized as resulting from three possibilities: (1) plain meaning: where the words or phrases appear to describe with complete accuracy the testator's objective; (2) latent ambiguity: where the description, although accurate in its possibilities, may be open to more than one meaning or objective of the testator; and (3) patent ambiguity: where the description is clearly erroneous and cannot be what the testator had as an objective. Because of the court's reluctance to re-write the Last Will and Testament, rules have developed that insulate the court from attempts at judicial modification by plaintiffs. The following case invites consideration of how a court may respond to any dispute over ambiguity in what the testator has written.

A. Latent and Patent Ambiguity

In re Estate of Russell

Supreme Court of California, 1968
69 Cal. 2d 200, 444 P.2d 353

SULLIVAN, J.

Georgia Nan Russell Hembree appeals from a judgment (Prob. Code, § 1240 . . .) entered in proceedings for the determination of heirship (§§ 1080–1082) decreeing *inter alia* that under the terms of the will of Thelma L. Russell, deceased, all of the residue of her estate should be distributed to Chester H. Quinn.

Thelma L. Russell died testate on September 8, 1965, leaving a validly executed holographic will written on a small card. The front of the card reads:

'Turn the card March 18–1957 I leave everything I own Real & Personal to Chester H. Quinn & Roxy Russell Thelma L. Russell'

The reverse side reads:

My ($10.) Ten dollar gold Piece & diamonds I leave to Georgia Nan Russell. Alverata, Geogia [*sic*].'

Chester H. Quinn was a close friend and companion of testatrix, who for over 25 years prior to her death had resided in one of the living units on her property and had stood in a relation of personal trust and confidence toward her. Roxy Russell was testatrix' pet dog which was alive on the date of the execution of testatrix' will but predeceased her.[2] Plaintiff is testatrix' niece and her only heir-at-law.

In her petition for determination of heirship plaintiff alleges, inter alia, that 'Roxy Russell is an Airedale dog'; * * * that section 27 enumerates those entitled to

---

2. Actually the record indicates the existence of two Roxy Russells. The original Roxy was an Airedale dog which testatrix owned at the time she made her will, but which, according to Quinn, died after having had a fox tail removed from its nose, and which, according to the testimony of one Arthur Turner, owner of a pet cemetery, was buried on June 9, 1958. Roxy was replaced with another dog (breed not indicated in the record before us) which, although it answered to the name Roxy, was, according to the record, in fact registered with the American Kennel Club as 'Russel's [*sic*] Royal Kick Roxy.'

take by will; that 'Dogs are not included among those listed in . . . Section 27. Not even Airedale dogs'; that the gift of one-half of the residue of testatrix' estate to Roxy Russell is invalid and void; and that plaintiff was entitled to such one-half as testatrix' sole heir-at-law.

At the hearing on the petition, plaintiff introduced without objection extrinsic evidence establishing that Roxy Russell was testatrix' Airedale dog which died on June 9, 1958. To this end plaintiff, in addition to an independent witness, called defendant pursuant to former Code of Civil Procedure section 2055 (now Evid. Code, § 776). Upon redirect examination, counsel for Quinn then sought to introduce evidence of the latter's relationship with testatrix 'in the event that your Honor feels that there is any necessity for further ascertainment of the intent above and beyond the document.' Plaintiff's objections on the ground that it was inadmissible under the statute of wills and the parole evidence rule 'because there is no ambiguity' and that it was inadmissible under section 105, were overruled. Over plaintiff's objection, counsel for Quinn also introduced certain documentary evidence consisting of testatrix' address book and a certain quitclaim deed 'for the purpose of demonstrating the intention on the part of the deceased that she not die intestate.' Of all this extrinsic evidence only the following infinitesimal portion of Quinn's testimony relates to care of the dog: 'Q. [Counsel for Quinn] Prior to the first Roxy's death did you ever discuss with Miss Russell taking care of Roxy if anything should ever happen to her? A. Yes.' Plaintiff carefully preserved an objection running to all of the above line of testimony and at the conclusion of the hearing moved to strike such evidence. Her motion was denied.

The trial court found, so far as is here material, that it was the intention of the testatrix 'that CHESTER H. QUINN was to receive her entire estate, excepting the gold coin and diamonds bequeathed to' plaintiff and that Quinn 'was to care for the dog, ROXY RUSSELL, in the event of Testatrix's death. The language contained in the Will concerning the dog, ROXY RUSSELL, was precatory in nature only, and merely indicative of the wish, desire and concern of Testatrix that CHESTER H. QUINN was to care for the dog, ROXY RUSSELL, subsequent to Testatrix's death.'[4] The court

---

4. The memorandum decision elaborates on this point, stating in part: 'The obvious concern of the human who loves her pet is to see that it is properly cared for by someone who may be trusted to honor that concern and through resources the person may make available in the will to carry out this entreaty, desire, wish, recommendation or prayer. This, in other words, is a most logical example of a precatory provision. It is the only logical conclusion one can come to which would not do violence to the apparent intent of Mrs. Russell.'

The trial court found further: 'Testatrix intended that GEORGIA NAN RUSSELL HEMBREE was not to have any other real or personal property belonging to Testatrix, other than the gold coin and diamonds.' This finding also was elaborated on in the memorandum decision: 'In making the will it is apparent she had Georgia on her mind. While there is other evidence in the case about Thelma Russell's frame of mind concerning her real property and her niece, which was admitted by the Court, over counsel's vigorous objection, because it concerned testatrix' frame of mind, a condition relevant to the material issue of intent, nevertheless this additional evidence was not necessary to this Court in reaching its conclusion.' The additional evidence, referred to included an address

concluded that testatrix intended to and did make an absolute and outright gift to Mr. Quinn of all the residue of her estate, adding: 'There occurred no lapse as to any portion of the residuary gift to CHESTER H. QUINN by reason of the language contained in the Will concerning the dog, ROXY RUSSELL, such language not having the effect of being an attempted outright gift or gift in trust to the dog. The effect of such language is merely to indicate the intention of Testatrix that CHESTER H. QUINN was to take the entire residuary estate and to use whatever portion thereof as might be necessary to care for and maintain the dog, ROXY RUSSELL.' Judgment was entered accordingly. This appeal followed.

Plaintiff's position before us may be summarized thusly: That the gift of one-half of the residue of the estate to testatrix' dog was clear and unambiguous; that such gift was void and the property subject thereof passed to plaintiff under the laws of intestate succession; and that the court erred in admitting the extrinsic evidence offered by Quinn but that in any event the uncontradicted evidence in the record did not cure the invalidity of the gift.

We proceed to set forth the rules here applicable which govern the interpretation of wills.

First, as we have said many times: 'The paramount rule in the construction of wills, to which all other rules must yield, is that a will is to be construed according to the intention of the testator as expressed therein, and this intention must be given effect as far as possible.' (Estate of Wilson (1920) 184 Cal. 63, 66–67 [193 P. 581].) * * * The rule is imbedded in the Probate Code. (§ 101.)[6] Its objective is to ascertain what the testator meant by the language he used. * * *

When the language of a will is ambiguous or uncertain resort may be had to extrinsic evidence in order to ascertain the intention of the testator.[8] We have said that extrinsic evidence is admissible 'to explain any ambiguity arising on the face of a will, or to resolve a latent ambiguity which does not so appear.' (Estate of Torregano (1960) 54 Cal.2d 234, 246 [5 Cal.Rptr. 137, 352 P.2d 505, 88 A.L.R.2d 597],

---

book of testatrix upon which she had written: 'Chester, Don't let Augusta and Georgia have one penny of my place if it takes it all to fight it in Court. Thelma.'

6. Section 101 in pertinent part provides: 'A will is to be construed according to the intention of the testator. Where his intention cannot have effect to its full extent, it must have effect as far as possible.'

8. 'It is a fundamental and indisputable proposition that wherever doubt arises as to the meaning of a will, such doubt is resolved by construction and that construction is one of law. It is an application of legal rules governing construction either to the will alone or to properly admitted facts to explain what the testator meant by the doubtful language. In those cases where extrinsic evidence is permissible there may be a conflict in the extrinsic evidence itself, in which case the determination of that conflict results in a finding of pure fact. But when the facts are thus found, those facts do not solve the difficulty. They still are to be applied to the written directions of the will for the latter's construction, and that construction still remains a construction at law.' (Estate of Donnellan (1912) 164 Cal. 14, 19 [127 P. 166], per Henshaw, J.; accord: Estate of Platt (1942) 21 Cal.2d 343, 352 [131 P.2d 825]; see Parsons v. Bristol Dev. Co. (1965) 62 Cal.2d 861, 865 [44 Cal. Rptr. 767, 402 P.2d 839].)

citing § 105.)[9] A latent ambiguity is one which is not apparent on the face of the will but is disclosed by some fact collateral to it. (See 4 Page on Wills (Bowe-Parker Rev.) § 32.7, p. 255; Comment: Extrinsic Evidence and the Construction of Wills in California (1962) 50 Cal.L.Rev. 283, 284–291.)

As to latent ambiguities, this court in the *Donnellan* case said: 'Broadly speaking, there are two classes of wills presenting latent ambiguities, for the removal of which ambiguities resort to extrinsic evidence is permissible. The one class is where there are two or more persons or things exactly measuring up to the description and conditions of the will, . . . The other class is where no person or thing exactly answers the declarations and descriptions of the will, but where two or more persons or things in part though imperfectly do so answer.' (Estate of Donnellan (1912) 164 Cal. 14, 20 [127 P. 166].) * * * Extrinsic evidence always may be introduced initially in order to show that under the circumstances of a particular case the seemingly clear language of a will describing either the subject of or the object of the gift actually embodies a latent ambiguity for it is only by the introduction of extrinsic evidence that the existence of such an ambiguity can be shown. Once shown, such ambiguity may be resolved by extrinsic evidence. (Estate of Dominici (1907) 151 Cal. 181, 184 [90 P. 448]; Taylor v. McCowen (1908) 154 Cal. 798, 802 [99 P. 351]; Estate of Donnellan, *supra,* 164 Cal. 14, 20, 22–24; cf. Estate of Sargavak (1953) 41 Cal.2d 314, 320 [259 P.2d 897]; Estate of Carter (1956) 47 Cal.2d 200, 207–208 [302 P.2d 301].)

A patent ambiguity is an uncertainty which appears on the face of the will. (Estate of Womersley (1912) 164 Cal. 85, 87 [127 P. 645]; Estate of Willson (1915) 171 Cal. 449, 456–457 [153 P. 927]; Estate of Salmonski (1951) 38 Cal.2d 199, 214 [238 P.2d 966]; see generally 4 Page on Wills, op.cit. *supra,* § 32.7, p. 255; Comment: *supra,* 50 Cal.L.Rev. 283, 284–291.) 'When an uncertainty arises upon the face of a will as to the meaning of any of its provisions, the testator's intent is to be ascertained from the words of the will, but the circumstances of the execution thereof may be taken into consideration, excluding the oral declarations of the testator as to his intentions.' (Estate of Salmonski, *supra,* 38 Cal.2d 199, 214.) * * * This is but a corollary derived from an older formalism. Long before *Salmonski* it was said in Estate of Willson, *supra,* 171 Cal. 449, 456: 'The rule is well established that where the meaning of the will, on its face, taking the words in the ordinary sense, is entirely clear, and where no latent ambiguity is made to appear by extrinsic evidence, there can be no evidence of extrinsic circumstances to show that the testatrix intended

---

9. Section 105 provides: 'When there is an imperfect description, or no person or property exactly answers the description, mistakes and omissions must be corrected, if the error appears from the context of the will or from extrinsic evidence, excluding the oral declarations of the testator as to his intentions; and when an uncertainty arises upon the face of a will, as to the application of any of its provisions, the testator's intention is to be ascertained from the words of the will, taking into view the circumstances under which it was made, excluding such oral declarations.'

or desired to do something not expressed in the will.' * * * However, this ancient touchstone has not necessarily uncovered judicial material of unquestioned purity.

In order to determine initially whether the terms of *any written instrument* are clear, definite and free from ambiguity the court must examine the instrument in the light of the circumstances surroundings its execution so as to ascertain what the parties meant by the words used. Only then can it be determined whether the seemingly clear language of the instrument is in fact ambiguous. 'Words are used in an endless variety of contexts. Their meaning is not subsequently attached to them by the reader but is formulated by the writer and can only be found by interpretation in the light of all the circumstances that reveal the sense in which the writer used the words. The exclusion of parol evidence regarding such circumstances merely because the words do not appear ambiguous to the reader can easily lead to the attribution to a written instrument of a meaning that was never intended.' (Universal Sales Corp. v. California etc. Mfg. Co. (1942) 20 Cal.2d 751, 776 [128 P.2d 665] (Traynor, J., concurring).) 'The court must determine the true meaning of the instrument in the light of the evidence available. It can neither exclude extrinsic evidence relevant to that determination nor invoke such evidence to write a new or different instrument.' (Laux v. Freed (1960) 53 Cal.2d 512, 527 [2 Cal.Rptr. 265, 348 P.2d 873] (Traynor, J., concurring); see also Corbin, The Interpretation of Words and the Parol Evidence Rule (1965) 50 Cornell L.Q. 161, 164: '[W]hen a judge refuses to consider relevant extrinsic evidence on the ground that the meaning of written words is to him plain and clear, his decision is formed by and wholly based upon the completely extrinsic evidence of his own personal education and experience'; Corbin, op.cit. *supra*, pp. 189–190; Farnsworth, 'Meaning' in the Law of Contracts (1967) 76 Yale L.J. 939, 957–965; Holmes, The Theory of Legal Interpretation (1899) 12 Harv.L.Rev. 417, 420; Rest., Contracts, § 230, coms. a, b, § 235, cls. (a), (d), coms. a, f, § 238, cl. (a), com. a, § 242, com. a; 3 Corbin on Contracts (1960) § 535, pp. 17–21, § 536, pp. 27–30 et seq.; 4 Page on Wills, op.cit. *supra*, § 30.8, p. 59, § 32.1, pp. 232–233, § 32.2 pp. 236–237; 9 Wigmore on Evidence (3d ed. 1940) § 2470 et seq.; 4 Williston on Contracts (3d ed. 1961) § 610, pp. 499–503; § 610A, pp. 517–519, § 629, pp. 923–925; Witkin, Cal. Evidence (2d ed. 1966) § 730, p. 675 et seq.)

The foregoing reflects the modern development of rules governing interpretation, for in the words of Wigmore 'The history of the law of Interpretation is the history of a progress from a stiff and superstitious formalism to a flexible rationalism.' (9 Wigmore, op.cit. *supra*, § 2461, p. 187.) While 'still surviving to us, in many Courts, from the old formalism . . . [is] the rule that you *cannot disturb a plain meaning*' (9 Wigmore, op.cit. *supra*, p. 191, original emphasis) nevertheless decisions and authorities like those cited above bespeak the current tendency to abandon the 'stiff formalism of earlier interpretation' and to show the meaning of words even though no ambiguity appears on the face of the document.

There is nothing in these rules of interpretation which confines their application to contracts. Indeed quite the contrary. The rules are a response to 'problems which run through all the varieties of jural acts,' are therefore not necessarily solvable separately for deeds, contracts and wills, are not peculiar to any one kind of jural act, but involve a general principle applicable to all. (9 Wigmore, op.cit. *supra*, § 2401, pp. 6–7, § 2458, pp. 179–181, § 2463, § 2467.) Thus Wigmore says: 'In the field of *wills,* where there is none but the individual standard [* * *] of meaning to be considered, this principle is seen in unrestricted operation; . . .'[14] (§ 2470, p. 228.)

Accordingly, we think it is self-evident that in the interpretation of a will, a court cannot determine whether the terms of the will are clear and definite in the first place until it considers the circumstances under which the will was made so that the judge may be placed in the position of the testator whose language he is interpreting. (Cf. Code Civ. Proc., § 1860.) * * * Failure to enter upon such an inquiry is failure to recognize that the 'ordinary standard or 'plain meaning,' is simply the meaning of the people who did *not* write the document.' (9 Wigmore, op.cit. *supra*, § 2462, p. 191.)

Thus we have declared in a slightly different context that extrinsic evidence as to the circumstances under which a written instrument was made is "admissible to interpret the instrument, but not to give it a meaning to which it is not reasonably susceptible' (Coast Bank v. Minderhout, 61 Cal.2d 311, 315 [38 Cal.Rptr. 505, 392 P.2d 265]; . . .), and it is the instrument itself that must be given effect. (Civ. Code, §§ 1638, 1639; Code Civ. Proc., § 1856.)' (Parsons v. Bristol Dev. Co. (1965) 62 Cal.2d 861, 865 [44 Cal.Rptr. 767, 402 P.2d 839].) * * * 'If the evidence offered would not persuade a reasonable man that the instrument meant anything other than the ordinary meaning of its words, it is useless.' (Estate of Rule (1944) 25 Cal.2d 1, 22 [152 P.2d 1003, 155 A.L.R. 1319] (Traynor, J., dissenting), disapproved on other grounds, Parsons v. Bristol Dev. Co., *supra*, 62 Cal.2d 861, 866, fn. 2.) * * * On the other hand an ambiguity is said to exist when, in the light of the circumstances surrounding the execution of an instrument, 'the written language is fairly susceptible of two or more constructions.' (Hulse v. Juillard Fancy Foods Co. (1964) 61 Cal.2d 571, 573 [39 Cal.Rptr. 529, 394 P.2d 65]; Nofziger v. Holman (1964) 61 Cal.2d 526,

---

14. 'The truth had finally to be recognized that words *always* need interpretation; that the process of interpretation inherently and invariably means the ascertainment of the association between words and external objects; and that this makes inevitable a free resort to extrinsic matters for applying and enforcing the document. 'Words *must* be translated into things and facts.' Instead of the fallacious notion that 'there should be interpretation only when it is needed,' the fact is that there must always be interpretation. Perhaps the range of search need not be extensive, and perhaps the application of the document will be apparent at the first view; but there must always be a traveling out of the document, a comparison of its words with people and things. The deed must be applied 'physically to the ground.' Perhaps the standard of interpretation will limit our search; perhaps the obligation (as some Courts maintain) to enforce the ordinary standard as against the mutual or the individual standard . . . , or to enforce the mutual as against the individual standard . . . , will render certain data immaterial. But these restrictions are independent of the present principle. Once freed from the primitive formalism which views the document as a self-contained and self-operative formula, we can fully appreciate the modern principle that the words of a document are never anything but indices to extrinsic things, and that therefore *all the circumstances must be considered which go to make clear the sense of the words,* —that is, their associations with things.' (9 Wigmore, op.cit. *supra*, p. 227, original emphasis.)

528 [39 Cal.Rptr. 384, 393 P.2d 696]; Coast Bank v. Minderhout (1964) 61 Cal.2d 311, 315 [38 Cal.Rptr. 505, 392 P.2d 265], citing cases; see Pacific Gas & E. Co. v. G. W. Thomas Drayage etc. Co., ante, p. 40.)

As we have explained, what is here involved is a general principle of interpretation of written instruments, applicable to wills as well as to deeds and contracts. Even when the answer to the problem of interpretation is different for different kinds of written instruments, 'it appears in all cases as a variation from some general doctrine.' (9 Wigmore, op.cit. *supra*, § 2401, p. 7.) Under the application of this general principle in the field of wills, extrinsic evidence of the circumstances under which a will is made (except evidence expressly excluded by statute) * * * may be considered by the court in ascertaining what the testator meant by the words used in the will. If in the light of such extrinsic evidence, the provisions of the will are reasonably susceptible of two or more meanings claimed to have been intended by the testator, 'an uncertainty arises upon the face of a will' (§ 105) and extrinsic evidence relevant to prove any of such meanings is admissible (see § 106), * * * subject to the restrictions imposed by statute (§ 105). If, on the other hand, in the light of such extrinsic evidence, the provisions of the will are not reasonably susceptible of two or more meanings, there is no uncertainty arising upon the face of the will (§ 105; see Estate of Beldon (1938) 11 Cal.2d 108, 117 [77 P.2d 1052]; Estate of Pierce (1948) 32 Cal.2d 265, 272 [196 P.2d 1]; Estate of Carter, *supra*, 47 Cal.2d 200, 207) and any proffered evidence attempting to show an intention *different* from that expressed by the words therein, giving them the only meaning to which they are reasonably susceptible, is inadmissible. In the latter case the provisions of the will are to be interpreted according to such meaning. In short, we hold that while section 105 delineates the manner of ascertaining the testator's intention 'when an uncertainty arises upon the face of a will,' it cannot always be determined whether the will is ambiguous or not until the surrounding circumstances are first considered.

Finally, before taking up testatrix' will, we add a brief word concerning our proper function on this appeal. This function must subserve the paramount rule that the 'will is to be construed according to the intention of the testator.' (See fns. 5 and 6, ante, and accompanying text.) As we said in Parsons v. Bristol Dev. Co., *supra*, 62 Cal.2d 861, 865, it is 'solely a judicial function to interpret a written instrument unless the interpretation turns upon the credibility of extrinsic evidence.' (See fn. 8, ante.) Accordingly, 'an appellate court is not bound by a construction of a document based solely upon the terms of the written instrument without the aid of extrinsic evidence, where there is no conflict in the evidence, or a determination has been made upon incompetent evidence. [Citations.]' (Estate of Wunderle (1947) 30 Cal.2d 274, 280 [181 P.2d 874]; see Estate of Donnellan, *supra*, 164 Cal. 14, 19; Estate of Platt (1942) 21 Cal.2d 343, 352 [131 P.2d 825]; Parsons v. Bristol Dev. Co., *supra*, 62 Cal.2d 861, 865.)

We said in Estate of Beldon, *supra*, 11 Cal.2d 108, 111–112, "The making of a will raises a presumption that the testator intended to dispose of all his property. Residuary clauses are generally inserted for the purpose of making that disposition complete, and these clauses are always to receive a broad and liberal interpretation, with a view of preventing intestacy as to any portion of the estate of the testator, and this general rule is in harmony with the declaration of our code that the provisions of a will must be construed, if possible, so as to effect that purpose.' (O'Connor v. Murphy, 147 Cal. 148, 153 [81 P. 406].) But there is no room for application of the rule if the testator's language, taken in the light of surrounding circumstances, will not reasonably admit of more than one construction. . . . If [testator] used language which results in intestacy, and there can be no doubt about the meaning of the language which was used, the court must hold that intestacy was intended.' Therefore, if having ascertained in the instant case that the provisions of the will are not reasonably susceptible of two or more meanings, we conclude that the only meaning to which the words expressed by testatrix are reasonably susceptible results in intestacy, we must give effect to her will accordingly. (Estate of Beldon, *supra*, 11 Cal.2d 108, 112; Estate of Akeley (1950) 35 Cal.2d 26, 32 [215 P.2d 921, 17 A.L.R.2d 647] (Traynor, J. dissenting); Estate of Barnes (1965) 63 Cal.2d 580, 583–584 [47 Cal. Rptr. 480, 407 P.2d 656].)

Examining testatrix' will in the light of the foregoing rules, we arrive at the following conclusions: Extrinsic evidence offered by plaintiff was admitted without objection and indeed would have been properly admitted over objection to raise and resolve the latent ambiguity as to Roxy Russell and ultimately to establish that Roxy Russell was a dog. Extrinsic evidence of the surrounding circumstances * * * was properly considered in order to ascertain what testatrix meant by the words of the will, including the words: 'I leave everything I own Real & Personal to Chester H. Quinn & Roxy Russell' or as those words can now be read 'to Chester H. Quinn and my dog Roxy Russell.'

However, viewing the will in the light of the surrounding circumstances as are disclosed by the record, we conclude that the will cannot reasonably be construed as urged by Quinn and determined by the trial court as providing that testatrix intended to make an absolute and outright gift of the entire residue of her estate to Quinn who was 'to use whatever portion thereof as might be necessary to care for and maintain the dog.' No words of the will gave the entire residuum to Quinn, much less indicate that the provision for the dog is merely precatory in nature. Such an interpretation is not consistent with a disposition which by its language leaves the residuum in equal shares to Quinn and the dog. A disposition in equal shares to two beneficiaries cannot be equated with a disposition of the whole to one of them who may use 'whatever portion thereof as might be necessary' on behalf of the other. (See § 104; cf. Estate of Kearns (1950) 36 Cal.2d 531, 534–536 [225 P.2d 218].) (8) Neither can the bare language of a gift of one-half of the residue to the dog be so expanded as to mean a gift to Quinn in trust for the care of the dog, there being no words indicating an enforceable duty upon Quinn to do so or indicating to whom the trust property is to go upon termination of the trust. 'While no particular form of expression is necessary for the creation of a trust, nevertheless some expression of intent to that end is requisite.' (Estate of Doane, *supra*, 190 Cal. 412, 415; see § 104;

Estate of Marti (1901) 132 Cal. 666, 669 [61 P. 964, 64 P. 1071]; Estate of McCray (1928) 204 Cal. 399, 402 [268 P. 647]; Estate of Sargavak, *supra,* 41 Cal.2d 314, 319, citing cases.)

Accordingly, since in the light of the extrinsic evidence introduced below, the terms of the will are not reasonably susceptible of the meaning claimed by Quinn to have been intended by testatrix, the extrinsic evidence offered to show such an intention should have been excluded by the trial court. * * * Upon an independent examination of the will we conclude that the trial court's interpretation of the terms thereof was erroneous. Interpreting the provisions relating to testatrix' residuary estate in accordance with the only meaning to which they are reasonably susceptible, we conclude that testatrix intended to make a disposition of all of the residue of the estate to Quinn and the dog in equal shares; therefore, as tenants in common. (§ 29; Estate of Hittell (1903) 141 Cal. 432, 434–436 [75 P. 53]; Estate of Murphy (1909) 157 Cal. 63, 66–72 [106 P. 230, 137 Am.St.Rep. 110]; Estate of Kunkler (1912) 163 Cal. 797, 800 [127 P. 43]; Noble v. Beach (1942) 21 Cal.2d 91, 94 [130 P.2d 426].) As a dog cannot be the beneficiary under a will (§ 27; see 1 Page on Wills, op.cit. *supra,* § 17.21, p. 851) the attempted gift to Roxy Russell is void.[22] (§ 27; Estate of Burnison (1949) 33 Cal.2d 638, 646 [204 P.2d 330], affd. 339 U.S. 87 [94 L.Ed. 675, 70 S.Ct. 503]; Estate of Doane, *supra,* 190 Cal. 412.)

There remains only the necessity of determining the effect of the void gift to the dog upon the disposition of the residuary estate. That portion of any residuary estate that is the subject of a lapsed gift to one of the residuary beneficiaries remains undisposed of by the will and passes to the heirs-at-law. (§§ 92, 220; Estate of Hittell, *supra,* 141 Cal. 432, 437; Estate of Kunkler, *supra,* 163 Cal. 797, 800; Estate of Hall (1920) 183 Cal. 61, 63 [190 P. 364].) The rule is equally applicable with respect to a void gift to one of the residuary beneficiaries. (§ 220; see 96 C.J.S., Wills, § 1226; 53 Cal.Jur.2d, Wills, § 271, p. 531.) Therefore, notwithstanding testatrix' expressed intention to limit the extent of her gift by will to plaintiff (see Estate of Barnes, *supra,* 63 Cal.2d 580, 583) one-half of the residuary estate passes to plaintiff as testatrix' only heir-at-law (§ 225). We conclude that the residue of testatrix' estate should be distributed in equal shares to Chester H. Quinn and Georgia Nan Russell Hembree, testatrix' niece.

The judgment is reversed and the cause is remanded with directions to the trial court to set aside the findings of fact and conclusions of law; to make and file findings of fact and conclusions of law in conformity with the views herein expressed; and to enter judgment accordingly. Such findings of fact, conclusions of law and judgment shall be prepared, signed, filed and entered in the manner provided by law. Plaintiff shall recover costs on appeal.

---

22. As a consequence, the fact that Roxy Russell predeceased the testatrix is of no legal import. As appears, we have disposed of the issue raised by plaintiff's frontal attack on the eligibility of the dog to take a testamentary gift and therefore need not concern ourselves with the novel question as to whether the death of the dog during the lifetime of the testatrix resulted in a lapsed gift. (§ 92.)

Traynor, C. J., Peters, J., Tobriner, J., Mosk, J., and Burke, J., concurred.

McCOMB, J. (dissenting) [opinion omitted] * * *

Notes

The *Russell* decision is often cited as illustrating that the interpretation of words is an issue that resonates in contracts, deeds, and wills. Furthermore, the court's holding illustrates a progression in the law that now permits a court to examine the words used *in the light of the circumstances surrounding its execution*, so as to ascertain what the parties meant by the words used. Hence, even when the words appear plain on their face, the words may be evaluated in the context in which they were written. Such an approach was advocated as needed reform. *See* John Langbein & Lawrence Waggoner, *Reformation of Wills on the Ground of Mistake: Change of Direction in American Law?*, 130 U. Pa. L. Rev. 521, 524–29 (1982). The use of extrinsic evidence when interpreting plain meaning is recognized in the *Restatement. See Restatement (Third) of Property: Wills & Donative Transfers* § 11.1(a) (2019) ("[A]n ambiguity in a donative document [i]s an uncertainty in meaning that is revealed by the text or by extrinsic evidence other than direct evidence of intention contradicting the plain meaning of the text").

Such an approach will permit courts to reform unambiguous instruments if there is clear and convincing evidence. *See, e.g.*, Estate of Duke, 352 P.3d 863 (Cal. 2015) (holding that "an unambiguous will may be reformed to conform to the testator's intent if clear and convincing evidence establishes that the will contains a mistake in the testator's expression of intent at the time the will was drafted, and also establishes the testator's actual specific intent at the time the will was drafted."). In addition to correcting deficiencies in the formalities of will execution, *see* Unif. Prob. Code § 2-513, we may correct plain language in wills, *see Restatement (Third) of Property: Wills & Donative Transfers* § 12.1 (2015), and in trusts, *see* Unif. Trust Code § 415.

B. Plain Meaning Rule and Mistake

In re Pavlinko's Estate

Supreme Court of Pennsylvania, 1959
394 Pa. 564, 148 A.2d 528

BELL, Justice.

Vasil Pavlinko died February 8, 1957; his wife, Hellen, died October 15, 1951. A testamentary writing dated March 9, 1949, which purported to be the will of Hellen Pavlinko, was signed by Vasil Pavlinko, her husband. The residuary legatee named therein, a brother of Hellen, offered the writing for probate as the will of Vasil Pavlinko, but probate was refused. The Orphans' Court, after hearing and argument, affirmed the decision of the Register of Wills.

The facts are unusual and the result very unfortunate. Vasil Pavlinko and Hellen, his wife, retained a lawyer to draw their wills and wished to leave their property to each other. By mistake Hellen signed the will which was prepared for her husband, and Vasil signed the will which was prepared for his wife, each instrument being signed at the end thereof. The lawyer who drew the will and his secretary, Dorothy Zinkham, both signed as witnesses. Miss Zinkham admitted that she was unable to speak the language of Vasil and Hellen, and that no conversation took place between them. The wills were kept by Vasil and Hellen. For some undisclosed reason, Hellen's will was never offered for probate at her death; in this case it was offered merely as an exhibit.

The instrument which was offered for probate was short. It stated:

'I, *Hellen* Pavlinko, of * * *, do hereby make, publish and declare this to be *my* * * * [Italics thoughout [sic], ours] Last Will and Testament, * * *.'

In the first paragraph she directed her executor to pay her debts and funeral expenses. In the second paragraph she gave her entire residuary estate to 'my husband, Vasil Pavlinko * * * absolutely'. She then provided:

'Third: If my aforesaid husband, Vasil Pavlinko, should predecease me, then and in that event, I give and bequeath:

'(a) To my brother-in-law, Mike Pavlinko, of McKees Rocks, Pennsylvania, the sum of Two hundred ($200) Dollars.

'(b) To my sister-in-law, Maria Gerber, (nee Pavlinko), of Pittsburgh, Pennsylvania, the sum of Two Hundred ($200) Dollars.

'(c) The rest, residue and remainder of *my* estate, of whatsoever kind and nature and wheresoever situate, I give, devise and bequeath, absolutely, to *my brother*, Elias Martin, now residing at 520 Aidyl Avenue, Pittsburgh, Pennsylvania.

'I do hereby nominate, constitute and appoint my husband, Vasil Pavlinko, as Executor of this my Last Will and Testament.' It was then mistakenly signed: 'Vasil Pavlinko [Seal]'.

While no attempt was made to probate, as Vasil's will, the writing which purported to be his will but was signed by Hellen, it could not have been probated as Vasil's will, because it was not signed by him at the end thereof.

The Wills Act of 1947 provides in clear, plain and unmistakable language in § 2: 'Every will, * * * shall be in writing and shall be signed *by the testator* at the end thereof', 20 P.S. § 180.2, with certain exceptions not here relevant. The Court below correctly held that the paper which *recited* that it was the will of Hellen Pavlinko and intended and purported to give Hellen's estate to her husband, could not be probated as the will of Vasil and was a nullity.

In order to decide in favor of the residuary legatee, almost the entire will would have to be rewritten. The Court would have to substitute the words 'Vasil Pavlinko' for 'Hellen Pavlinko' and the words 'my wife' wherever the words 'my husband' appear in the will, and the relationship of the contingent residuary legatees would likewise have to be changed. To consider this paper—as written—as Vasil's will, it would give his entire residuary estate to 'my husband, Vasil Pavlinko, absolutely' and 'Third: If my husband, Vasil Pavlinko, should predecease me, then * * * I give and bequeath my residuary estate to my brother, Elias Martin.' The language of this writing, which is signed at the end thereof by *Vasil* Pavlinko, is unambiguous, clear and unmistakable, and it is obvious that it is a meaningless nullity. * * *

Once a Court starts to ignore or alter or rewrite or make exceptions to clear, plain and unmistakable provisions of the Wills Act in order to accomplish equity and justice in that particular case, the Wills Act will become a meaningless, although well intentioned, scrap of paper, and the door will be opened wide to countless fraudulent claims which the Act successfully bars.

Decree affirmed. Each party shall pay their respective costs.

MUSMANNO, Justice (dissenting).

Vasil Pavlinko and his wife, Hellen Pavlinko, being unlettered in English and unlearned in the ways of the law, wisely decided to have an attorney draw up their wills, since they were both approaching the age when reflecting persons must give thought to that voyage from which there is no return. They explained to the attorney, whose services they sought, that he should draw two wills which would state that when either of the partners had sailed away, the one remaining ashore would become the owner of the property of the departing voyager. Vasil Pavlinko knew but little English. However, his lawyer, fortunately, was well versed in his clients's native language, known as Little Russian or Carpathian. The attorney thus discussed the whole matter with his two visitors in their language. He then dictated appropriate wills to his stenographer in English and then, after they had been transcribed, he translated the documents, paragraph by paragraph, to Mr. and Mrs. Pavlinko, who approved of all that he had written. The wills were laid before them and each signed the document purporting to be his or her will. The attorney gave Mrs. Pavlinko the paper she had signed and handed to her husband the paper he had signed. In accordance with customs they had brought with them from the old country, Mrs. Pavlinko turned her paper over to her husband. It did not matter, however, who held the papers since they were complementary of each other. Mrs. Pavlinko left her property to Mr. Pavlinko and Mr. Pavlinko left his property to Mrs. Pavlinko. They also agreed on a common residuary legatee, Elias Martin, the brother of Mrs. Pavlinko.

Mrs. Pavlinko died first, but for some reason her will was not probated. Then Mr. Pavlinko died and Elias Martin came forth to claim his inheritance. The Register of Wills of Allegheny County refused to accept the Vasil Pavlinko will for probate. It now developed for the first time that, despite every care used by her attorney, a strange thing had happened. Mr. Pavlinko had signed his wife's will and Mrs. Pavlinko had signed her husband's will.

At the hearing before the Register of Wills, the will signed by Vasil Pavlinko was introduced as Exhibit No. 1 and the will signed by Hellen Pavlinko was introduced as Exhibit No. 2. The attorney, who had drawn the wills and had witnessed the signatures of the testator and testatrix, testified to what had occurred in his office; his secretary who had typed the wills and had witnessed the signatures, also testified to the events which spelled out the little mishap of the unintentional exchange of the wills.

The Orphans' Court of Allegheny County sustained the action of the Register of Wills. Elias Martin appealed to this Court, which now affirms the lower court and, in doing so, I submit, creates another enigma for the layman to ponder over, regarding the mysterious manner in which the law operates, it wonders to perform. Everyone in this case admits that a mistake was made: an honest, innocent, unambiguous, simple mistake, the innocent, drowsy mistake of a man who sleeps all day and, on awakening, accepts the sunset for the dawn.

Nothing is more common to mankind than mistakes. Volumes, even libraries have been written on mistakes: mistakes of law and mistakes of fact. In every phase of life, mistakes occur and there are but few people who will not attempt to lend a helping hand to the person who mistakes a step for a landing and falls, or the one who mistakes a nut for a grape and chokes, or the one who steps through a glass so clear that he does not see it. This Court, however, says that it can do nothing for the victim of the mistake in this case, a mistake which was caused through no fault of his own, nor of his intended benefactors.

Next to the love which the Pavlinkos bore to each other, they were devoted to Mrs. Pavlinko's brother, Elias Martin. They wholeheartedly agreed that after they had quitted the earth, this devoted kinsman of theirs should have all that they would leave behind them. No one disputes this brute fact, no one can dispute this granitic, unbudgeable truth. Cannot the law, therefore, dedicated as it is to the truth, and will all its wisdom and majestic power, correct this mistake which cries out for correction? May the law not untie the loose knot of error which begs to be freed? I know that the law is founded on precedent and in many ways we are bound by the dead hand of the past. But even, with obeisance to precedent, I still do not believe that the medicine of the law is incapable of curing the simple ailment here which has not, because of any passage of time, become aggravated by complications.

We have said more times than there are tombstones in the cemetery where the Pavlinkos lie buried, that the primary rule to be followed in the interpretation of a will is to ascertain the intention of the testator. Can anyone go to the graves of the Pavlinkos and say that we do not know what they meant? They said in English and in Carpathian that they wanted their property to go to Elias Martin.

We have also said time without number that the intent of the testator must be gathered from the four corners of his will. Whether it be from the four corners of the will signed by Vasil Pavlinko or whether from the eight corners of the wills signed by Vasil and Hellen Pavlinko, all set out before the court below, the net result is always the same, namely that the residue of the property of the last surviving member of the Pavlinko couple was to go to Elias Martin. In the face of all the pronouncements of the law as to the fidelity with which the intention of the testator must be followed, on what possible basis can we now ignore the intention expressed by the Pavlinkos so clearly, so conclusively, and so all-encompassingly?

The Majority says that there is nothing we can do to effectuate the expressed intention of Vasil Pavlinko. But, I respectfully submit, the Majority does not make a serious effort to effectuate that expressed intent. The Majority contents itself with saying that 'the facts are unusual and the result very unfortunate.' But the results do not need to be unfortunate. In re King's Will, 369 Pa. 523, 531, 87 A.2d 469, 474, we said that: 'What offends against an innate sense of justice, decency and fair play offends against good law.' Certainly the results being affirmed by this Court offend against an innate sense of justice. Elias Martin is being turned out of Court when there is no need for such a peremptory eviction. The Majority authorizes the eviction on the basis of a decision rendered by this Court in 1878 in the case of Alter's Appeal, 67 Pa. 341. There, wife and husband, also signed wrong papers and the Court in that post-Civil War period, held nothing could be done to correct the error. But even if we say that the Alter decision makes impossible the transferring of the signature of Vasil Pavlinko to the will written in his name, I still do not see how it prevents this Court from enforcing the provision in the will which *was* signed by Vasil Pavlinko. In the Alter case an attempt was made to reform the will 'by striking off the signature 'Catherine Alter,' and causing the name 'George A. Alter' to be signed thereto' so that the paper so signed could be 'admitted to probate as the will of George A. Alter.' But in our case here, no such substitution is being sought. What Elias Martin seeks is admission to probate of a testamentary writing *actually signed by the testator Vasil Pavlinko.*

Moreover, in the Alter case, as distinguished from the Pavlinko will, George A. Alter left everything to himself. Even if we accept the Majority's conclusion, based on the Alter case, that all provisions in the Pavlinko will, which refer to himself, must be regarded as nullities, not correctable by parol evidence because they evince no latent ambiguities, it does not follow that the residuary clause must perish. The fact that some of the provisions in the Pavlinko will cannot be executed does not strike down the residuary clause, which is meaningful and stands on its own two feet. * * * We know that one of the very purposes of a residuary clause is to provide a catch-all for undisposed-of or ineffectually disposed-of property.

> 'A residuary gift carries with it, and is presumed to have been so intended, not only all the estate which remains not specifically disposed of at the time the will is executed, *but all that, for any reason, which is illy disposed of, or fails as to the legatees originally intended.* In re Wood's Estate, 209 Pa. 16, (57 A. 1103).' (In re Jull's Estate, 370 Pa. 434, 442, 88 A.2d 753, 756.) (Emphasis supplied.)

And the Wills Act itself specifically provides:

> 'A devise or bequest not being part of the residuary estate which shall fail or be void because the beneficiary fails to survive the testator or because it is contrary to law *or otherwise incapable of taking effect* or which has been

revoked by the testator or is undisposed of or is released or disclaimed by the beneficiary, if it shall not pass to the issue of the beneficiary under the provisions * * * provided for by law, shall be included in the residuary devise or bequest, if any, contained in the will.' (Emphasis supplied.) 20 P.S. § 180.14(9).

The Majority also relies on In re Bryen's Estate, 218 Pa. 122, 195 A. 17, 20, but in that case the testator failed to sign the prepared will at the end. He affixed his signature to a page which was 'in effect nothing more than a detached and independent paper not sequentially integrated with the others to form with them a testamentary instrument.' But here, I repeat, there was a complete testamentary instrument signed by Vasil Pavlinko at the end thereof and with testamentary intent.

The Majority calls upon In re Churchill's Estate, 260 Pa. 94, 103 A. 533, as further substantiation of its position, but the testator in that case failed to sign the testamentary writing at the end.

And, so far as In re Gray's Will, 365 Pa. 411, 76 A.2d 169, additionally cited by the Majority, is concerned, it clearly is not applicable to the facts in the case at bar because, there, the mark of the testator was not made in accordance with the provisions of the Wills Act.

I see no insuperable obstacle to probating the will signed by Vasil Pavlinko. Even though it was originally prepared as the will of his wife, Hellen, he did adopt its testamentary provisions as his own. Some of its provisions are not effective but their ineffectuality in no way bars the legality and validity of the residuary clause which is complete in itself. I would, therefore, probate the paper signed by Vasil Pavlinko. Here, indeed, is a situation where we could, if we wished, consistent with authority and precedent, and without endangering the integrity of the Wills Act, put in to effect the time-honored proverb that 'where there's a will, there's a way.'

In fact, we have here two wills, with signposts unerringly pointing to the just and proper destination, but the Court still cannot find the way.

* * *

Estate of Gibbs
Supreme Court of Wisconsin, 1961
14 Wis. 2d 490, 111 N.W.2d 413

FAIRCHILD, Justice.

* * * The evidence leads irresistibly to the conclusion that Mr. and Mrs. Gibbs intended legacies to respondent, and that the use of the middle initial 'J.' and the address of North 46th street resulted from some sort of mistake.

Respondent testified that he met Mr. Gibbs about 1928. From 1930 to 1949 he was employed as superintendent of a steel warehouse where Mr. Gibbs was his superior. They worked in close contact. Until 1945 the business belonged to the Gibbs Steel Company. In that year the business was sold, but Mr. Gibbs stayed on for four years in a supervisory capacity. Respondent remained with the new company until 1960. After 1949 Mr. Gibbs occasionally visited the plant and saw the respondent when there. From 1935 to 1955 respondent took men occasionally to the Gibbs home to do necessary work about the place. He also visited there socially several times a year and saw both Mr. and Mrs. Gibbs. Mrs. Gibbs had made a few visits at the plant before 1949 and respondent had seen her there. Mr. Gibbs did not visit respondent's home, although on a few occasions had telephoned him at home. Mr. Gibbs always called respondent 'Bob.'

Miss Krueger, who had been the Gibbs' housekeeper for 24 years up to 1958 and was a legatee under both wills, corroborated much of respondent's testimony. She also testified that Mr. Gibbs had told her he made a will remembering various people including 'the boys at the shop,' referring to them as 'Mike, Ed and Bob.'

Miss Pacius, a legatee under both wills, who had been Mr. Gibbs' private secretary for many years while he was in business, testified to Mr. Gibbs' expressions of high regard for respondent. Another former employee also testified to a similar effect.

Of the individuals named in the wills as legatees, all except two were shown to be relatives of Mr. or Mrs. Gibbs, former employees, neighbors, friends, or children of friends. The two exceptions were named near the end of the will and proof as to them may have been inadvertently omitted. 'Mike,' named in the will, was a warehouse employee under the supervision of respondent.

The attorney who drew several wills for Mr. and Mrs. Gibbs produced copies of most of them. They were similar in outline to the wills admitted to probate except that Mr. Gibbs' wills executed before Mrs. Gibb's death bequeathed his property to her, if she survived. The first ones were drawn in 1953 and each contained a bequest to 'Robert Krause, of Milwaukee, Wisconsin, if he survives me, one per cent (1%).' There was testimony that Mrs. Gibbs' will, executed in August, 1955, contained the same language. In the 1957 wills the same bequest was made to 'Robert Krause, now of 4708 North 46th Street, Milwaukee, Wisconsin.' In several other instances street addresses of legatees were given for the first time in 1957. In the 1958 wills the same bequest was made to 'Robert J. Krause, now of 4708 North 46th Street, Milwaukee, Wisconsin.' The scrivener also produced a hand-written memorandum given to him by Mr. Gibbs for the purpose of preparing Mr. Gibbs' 1958 will, and the reference on that memorandum corresponding to the Krause bequest is 'Bob, 1%.' Four bequests (to Gruener, Krause, Preuschl and Owen) appear in the same order in each of the wills and are reflected in the memorandum referred to as 'Fred Gruener, Bob, Mike, and Ed.' Gruener, Preuschl and Owen were former employees of Gibbs Steel Company, as was respondent. Owen's residence is given as Jefferson, Wisconsin, in all the wills. In the 1953 wills, the residence of Gruener, Krause and Preuschl was given only as Milwaukee, Wisconsin. A street address was inserted for the first time in each case in the 1957 wills, and repeated in the later ones.

Prior to 1950 respondent had lived at several different locations. From 1950 until April, 1960, he lived at 2325 North Sherman boulevard. We take judicial notice that this address and 4708 North 46th street are in the same general section of the city of Milwaukee, and that both are a number of miles distant from the Gibbs' home. We also take judicial notice that the telephone directory for Milwaukee and vicinity listed 14 subscribers by the name of Robert Krause with varying initials in October, 1958, and 15 in October of 1959. The listing for appellant gives his middle initial J. as well as his street address.

The only evidence which suggests even a possibility that Mr. or Mrs. Gibbs may have known of appellant may be summarized as follows:

For a time, appellant had a second job as a part time taxi driver, and he recalled an elderly lady who was his passenger on a lengthy taxi trip in June, 1955. He did not recall where he picked her up. He had driven her across the city, waiting for her while she visited in a hospital, and then driven her back across the city. The place where he let her out, however, was not her home. He did not recall that she had given him her name, but she had inquired as to his. They had conversed about the illness of appellant's wife and his working at an extra job in order to make ends meet. She had expressed sympathy and approval of his efforts. Presumably when he was notified that his name appeared in the Gibbs' wills as legatee, he endeavored to find an explanation of his good fortune and concluded that the lady in question must have been Mrs. Gibbs. The 1955 taxi ride, however, could not explain the gift to Robert Krause in the 1953 wills, and it is clear that the same legatee was intended in the Krause bequests in all the wills. Moreover, appellant's description of his taxi passenger differed in several particulars from the description of Mrs. Gibbs given by other witnesses.

* * * As stated above, the county court could reach no other conclusion upon consideration of the extrinsic evidence than that Mr. and Mrs. Gibbs intended to designate respondent as their legatee. The difficult question is whether the court could properly consider such evidence in determining testamentary intent.

Under rules as to construction of a will, unless there is ambiguity in the text of the will read in the light of surrounding circumstances, extrinsic evidence is inadmissible for the purpose of determining intent. * * *

A latent ambiguity exists where the language of the will, though clear on its face, is susceptible of more than one meaning, when applied to the extrinsic facts to which it refers. * * *

There are two classes of latent ambiguity. One, where there are two or more persons or things exactly measuring up to the description in the will; * * * the other where no person or thing exactly answers the declarations and descriptions of the will, but two or more persons or things answer the description imperfectly. Extrinsic evidence must be resorted to under these circumstances to identify which of the parties, unspecified with particularity in the will, was intended by the testator. * * *

Had the probated wills used the language of the 1953 wills 'To Robert Krause of Milwaukee,' such terms would have described both appellant and respondent, as well as a number of other people. Upon such ambiguity of the first type above mentioned becoming apparent, extrinsic evidence would be admissible in order to determine which Robert Krause Mr. and Mrs. Gibbs had in mind as their legatee.

Had the will said 'To my former employee, Robert J. Krause of 4708 North 46th Street,' neither appellant nor respondent would have exactly fulfilled the terms. Latent ambiguity of the second type would thus have appeared, and again extrinsic evidence would be admissible to determine what individual testators had in mind.

The wills containing, as they do, similar bequests to a long list of individuals, each bearing some relationship of blood, friendship, or former employment to Mr. or Mrs. Gibbs, come close to implying that every legatee named has some such relationship. Nevertheless the wills do not refer to Krause as standing in any particular relationship.

The terms of the bequest exactly fit appellant and no one else. There is no ambiguity.

> 'An ambiguity is not that which may be made doubtful by extrinsic proof tending to show an intention different from that manifested in the will, but it must grow out of the difficulty of identifying the person whose name and description correspond with the terms of the will.' * * *

Under the circumstances before us, can a court properly consider evidence showing that some of the words were used by mistake and should be stricken or disregarded? It is traditional doctrine that wills must not be reformed even in the case of demonstrable mistake. * * * This doctrine doubtless rests upon policy reasons. The courts deem it wise to avoid entertaining claims of disappointed persons who may be able to make very plausible claims of mistake after the testator is no longer able to refute them.

Although the courts subscribe to an inflexible rule against reformation of a will, it seems that they have often strained a point in matters of identification of property or beneficiaries in order to reach a desired result by way of construction. In Will of Stack, [214 Wis. 98, 251 N.W. 470 (1934)], * * * where the will devised 'Block 64,' the court included part of block 175 in the provision to conform to the unexpressed intent of the testator. In Will of Boeck, * * * [160 Wis. 577, 152 N.W. 155 (1915)], * * * where the will devised the 'northeast quarter of the northwest quarter' of a section, which was not owned by the testator, the court held such provision passed the southeast quarter of the northwest quarter, to conform to the misexpressed intent of the testator. In Moseley v. Goodman, [138 Tenn. 10, 195 S.W. 590 (1917)], * * * where testator bequeathed property to 'Mrs. Moseley,' the court denied the claim of Mrs. Lenoir Moseley to the gift and held that Mrs. Trimble had been intended by the testator. Mrs. Trimble was known to the testator by the nickname 'Mrs. Moseley.'

In Miller's Estate, [26 Pa. Super. 443 (1904)], * * * testator left property to 'William Wilson's children.' Relying on evidence that testator frequently confused William Wilson with his brother Seth, the court held the gift should go to the children of Seth Wilson, who had been intended by the testator. In Groves v. Culph, [132

Ind. 186, 31 N.E. 569 (1892)], * * * testator devised a remainder interest in part of lot 15 to his daughter. The court, to conform to testator's true intent, included part of lot 16 in this devise. In Castell v. Togg [163 Eng.Rep. 102 (1836)], * * * and Geer v. Winds, [4 S.C.Eq., 4 Desaus 85 (1810)], * * * the testator omitted a child from his will by mistake. The court inserted in the will the gift which had been intended for the child by the parent. In Beaumont v. Feld, [24 Eng.Rep. 673 (1723)], * * * a bequest to 'Catharine Earnley' was proven to have been intended for Gertrude Yardley, and was given to the latter, and in Masters v. Masters, [24 Eng.Rep. 454 (1718)], * * * a gift to 'Mrs. Sawyer' was given to Mrs. Swopper, because testator knew no one by the former name. In the two cases last mentioned, no one with the name given in the will claimed the gift.

We are also aware of the rule which allows a court in probating a will to deny probate to a provision in the document which was included by mistake. British courts will deny probate to a single word, or part of a sentence, thereby completely altering the provided dispositions. * * *

We conclude that details of identification, particularly such matters as middle initials, street addresses, and the like, which are highly susceptible to mistake, particularly in metropolitan areas, should not be accorded such sanctity as to frustrate an otherwise clearly demonstrable intent. Where such details of identification are involved, courts should receive evidence tending to show that a mistake has been made and should disregard the details when the proof establishes to the highest degree of certainty that a mistake was, in fact, made.

We therefore consider that the county court properly disregarded the middle initial and street address, and determined that respondent was the Robert Krause whom testators had in mind.

Orders affirmed.

BROADFOOT and BROWN, JJ., dissenting.

Erickson v. Erickson

Supreme Court of Connecticut, 1998
246 Conn. 359, 716 A.2d 92

BORDEN, Associate Justice.

The dispositive issue in this appeal is whether, pursuant to General Statutes (Rev. to 1995) § 45a-257 (a), the trial court should have admitted extrinsic evidence regarding the decedent's intent that his will would not be revoked automatically by his subsequent marriage.[2] The named plaintiff, Alicia Erickson, * * * who is the

---

2. General Statutes (Rev. to 1995) § 45a-257 (a) provides: "If, after the making of a will, the testator marries or is divorced or his marriage is annulled or dissolved or a child is born to the testator or a minor child is legally adopted by him, or a child is born as a result of A.I.D. as defined in section 45a-771, to which the testator has consented in accordance with subsection (a) of

daughter of the decedent, Ronald K. Erickson, appeals * * * from the judgment of the trial court in favor of the defendant, Dorothy Erickson, [formerly Dorothy A. Mehring] * * * the executrix of the estate of the decedent, dismissing the plaintiff's appeal from the decree of the Probate Court for the district of Madison. The Probate Court had admitted the will of the decedent to probate. The trial court ruled that the decedent's will, which had been executed shortly before his marriage to the defendant, provided for the contingency of marriage.

The plaintiff claims on her appeal that the trial court improperly concluded that the decedent's will provided for the contingency of marriage. * * * The defendant claims on her cross appeal that the trial court improperly excluded certain extrinsic evidence regarding the decedent's intent. We conclude that the trial court should have permitted the defendant to introduce extrinsic evidence of the decedent's intent. Accordingly, we reverse the judgment of the trial court and order a new trial.

Certain facts in this appeal are undisputed. On September 1, 1988, the decedent executed a will. At that time, he had three daughters and was unmarried. Two days later, on September 3, 1988, he married the defendant. He died on February 22, 1996.

The six articles of his will provide as follows.[7] The first article provides for the payment of funeral expenses and debts by the estate. The second article states that

---

section 45a-772, and no provision has been made in such will for such contingency, such marriage, divorce, annulment, dissolution, birth or adoption of a minor child shall operate as a revocation of such will * * *."

Section 45a-257 (a) was repealed by 1996 Public Acts, No. 96-95, and, to the extent that §45a-257 (a) dealt with the effect of marriage on a will, it has been replaced by General Statutes §45a-257a, which provides: Failure of testator to provide for surviving spouse who married testator after execution of will. Determination of share of estate. (a) If a testator fails to provide by will for the testator's surviving spouse who married the testator after the execution of the will, the surviving spouse shall receive the same share of the estate the surviving spouse would have received if the decedent left no will unless: (1) It appears from the will that the omission was intentional; or (2) the testator provided for the spouse by transfer outside the will and the intent that the transfer be in lieu of a testamentary provision is shown by the testator's statements, or is reasonably inferred from the amount of the transfer or other evidence.

'(b) In satisfying a share provided in subsection (a) of this section, devises and legacies made by the will abate in accordance with section 45a-426.'

The effective date of §45a-257a was January 1, 1997. Therefore, that statute does not apply to this case because the will in question was executed in 1988. At that time, the applicable statute was General Statutes §45-162, which was transferred to §45a-257 in 1991. Because that statute remained unchanged until Public Act 96-95, hereafter references to §45a-257 are to the 1995 revision of the statute.

7. The decedent's will provides in relevant part:

"Article I: I order and direct that my funeral expenses and my just debts, if any, except such as are barred by the Statute of Limitations or otherwise outlawed, be paid as soon as may be practicable; provided, however, that if any such debts are secured by mortgages, my Executrix or Executor, as the case may be, shall pay such debts so secured only if, in her or his discretion, such payment shall appear to be for the benefit of my estate; and provided further that all legacy, succession, inheritance, transfer and estate taxes which

the residue of the estate will pass to the defendant. The third article provides that if the defendant predeceases the decedent, one half of the residuary estate will pass in equal parts to the decedent's three daughters, Laura Erickson Kusy, Ellen Erickson Cates and Alicia Erickson, and one half of the residuary estate will pass in equal parts to Thomas Mehring, Christopher Mehring, Maureen Mehring and Kathleen Mehring, the children of the defendant. The fourth article appoints the defendant as the executrix of the will, with Attorney Robert O'Brien as the contingent executor in the event that the defendant is unable to or refuses to serve as executrix. The fifth article gives the executrix or executor the power to dispose of property of the estate as necessary. The sixth article appoints the defendant as the guardian of any of the decedent's children who have not reached the age of eighteen at the time of his death.

The Probate Court admitted the decedent's will to probate. The plaintiff appealed from the Probate Court's judgment. Prior to trial, the plaintiff filed a motion in limine to exclude extrinsic evidence of the decedent's intent. The plaintiff argued that "[§] 45a-257 makes the Court's inquiry very simple: to determine whether the

---

may become payable by reason of my death, whether or not levied on property or estate passing by this, my Last Will and Testament, shall be paid by my Executrix or Executor out of my residuary estate in the same manner as an expense of administration, and shall not be pro rated or apportioned among or charged against the respective devisees, legatees, beneficiaries, transferees or other recipients, nor charged against any property passing or which may have passed to any of them, and that my Executrix or Executor shall not be entitled to reimbursement for any portion of any such tax from any person.

"Article II: All the rest, residue and remainder of my estate and property (hereinafter called my residuary estate) of every nature, character and description, whether real, personal or mixed, and wheresoever situate, of which I may die seized or possessed, or in or to which I may in any wise be interested or entitled at the time of my death, or under or with respect to which I shall have any power of disposition or appointment at the time of my death, I give, devise and bequeath to DOROTHY A. MEHRING, of Madison, Connecticut, provided she survives me.

"Article III: If said DOROTHY A. MEHRING predeceases me, I give, devise and bequeath my said residuary estate as follows:

"A. ONE-HALF (1/2), in equal parts, to my daughters, LAURA ERICKSON, ELLEN ERICKSON and ALICIA ERICKSON, all of Madison, Connecticut, or to the survivors or survivor of them.

"B. ONE-HALF (1/2), in equal parts, to THOMAS MEHRING and CHRISTOPHER MEHRING, both of Madison, Connecticut, and MAUREEN MEHRING and KATHLEEN MEHRING, both of Guilford, Connecticut, or to the survivors or survivor of them.

"Article IV: I hereby nominate, constitute, designate and appoint said DOROTHY A. MEHRING to be the Executrix of this, my Last Will and Testament, or in the event of her inability or refusal to act, I hereby nominate, constitute, designate and appoint ATTORNEY ROBERT J. O'BRIEN, of West Hartford, Connecticut, to be the Executor of this, my Last Will and Testament, and I order and direct that in no event shall my Executrix or Executor, as the case may be, be required to give any bond, undertaking or other security for the faithful performance of her or his duties as Executrix or Executor."

* * *

will was revoked, the Court need examine only [the decedent's] will, his marriage certificate to [the defendant], and his death certificate. Extrinsic evidence regarding [the decedent's] intentions is inadmissible because the language of [the decedent's] will is unambiguous, and therefore under . . . [§] 45a-257 the operation of the marriage to revoke the will is automatic and mandatory." The defendant, in opposition to the plaintiff's motion, made a detailed offer of proof to show the contrary intent of the decedent.[8]

The admission of certain evidence was undisputed, namely, the will, the marriage certificate of the decedent and the defendant, and the decedent's death certificate. The trial court denied the plaintiff's motion in limine with respect to the evidence that Thomas Mehring, Christopher Mehring, Maureen Mehring and Kathleen Mehring, who were named beneficiaries in the will, are the children of the

---

8. The defendant's offer of proof provided: "May it please the court, if [O'Brien and the defendant] were permitted to testify they would testify as follows. [O'Brien] would testify that he is an attorney before the Hartford [bar], that he was for many years prior to the marriage in 1988 the attorney for [the decedent].

In addition to being his attorney on a variety of business and personal matters, he was also a close friend of [the decedent]. He was aware that [the decedent] was courting [the defendant] who became [his wife] and he was invited to their wedding which was scheduled for September 3, 1988.

About one week prior to that time he received a call from [the decedent] saying he and [the defendant] immediately after the wedding were going to go to New York and then take a Concorde flight to Ireland and they wanted to arrange, as many of us do prior to events like that, for their wills to be drafted prior to the marriage ceremony.

He gave him instructions that the wills would be identical, that is, that all of his estate was to go to [the defendant]. If [the defendant] should predecease him it should go to, half should go to his children, half to [the defendant's] children. That [the defendant] should be the administratrix of the will, the executrix, excuse me, the executrix of the will and that she would be appointed guardian of his children, and that [her] will be exactly the same.

On Thursday, September 1, two days before the wedding, the two of them went to Hartford and executed the wills. I would offer [the defendant's] will as a piece of evidence. And I represent to the court that it is a mirror image of [the decedent's] will that you have admitted as an exhibit. She, like [the decedent], leaves everything to him. If he should predecease her half of her estate goes to his children, half to her children. He appoints her guardian of his children and appoints [her] executor of his estate.

During the course of the execution of the wills there was no conversation whatsoever about the fact that the Saturday marriage would revoke the will that had been drafted on Thursday. The wedding to take place two days later would revoke the will that had been drafted on Thursday, although there was considerable discussion about the marriage itself and the festivities and the guests and things like that.

[O'Brien] would testify that the reason that he did not place in the will any specific mention of the marriage or talk about it at all with [the defendant] or [the decedent] was because in his view when a man executes a will two days before his marriage in which he leaves everything to the woman that he's about to marry, makes her guardian of his children, makes her administrator of the, executor, executrix of the estate, and if she should predecease him, leaves half of his estate to her kids.

Clearly makes provision in the will for not just a contingency, but the imminent [inevitability] of the marriage that's going to take place two days later. So he didn't think there was any necessary that he had to put in words when it was so clear that it was making—"

* * *

defendant. The court granted the motion in limine, however, with respect to any other evidence regarding the decedent's intent.

With respect to the other issue at trial, namely, whether the decedent's will provided for the contingency of his marriage to the defendant, the trial court, in a de novo proceeding, concluded that the Probate Court properly had admitted the will to probate because the will provided for the contingency of marriage. The trial court reasoned that "[the decedent's] will bequeathed all of his estate to the woman he was licensed to marry and did marry two days later. In his will, he named her executrix and designated her the guardian of his daughters, whose mother had previously died. The nature of these provisions, coupled with the extreme closeness in time of the marriage constitutes clear and convincing evidence of provision for the contingency of marriage. It would be preposterous to assume that [the decedent] was instead executing a will to make provisions that were to be revoked two days later." Accordingly, the trial court rendered judgment affirming the Probate Court's judgment admitting the will, and denied the plaintiff's appeal. This appeal followed.

The plaintiff claims that because the will did not expressly provide for the contingency of marriage, the trial court improperly concluded that the decedent's will provided for the contingency of marriage and, therefore, that his subsequent marriage did not automatically revoke his will under §45a-257 (a). The plaintiff argues that in determining whether a will provides for contingency of a subsequent marriage, the court may consider only the language of the will, and that the will in question in this case does not include any language referring to the contingency of marriage, such as "the words 'if I marry,' 'when I marry,' 'my future wife' or even 'my fiancee.' In fact the words 'wife,' 'spouse' and 'marry' do not appear within the four corners of the will."

In contrast, the defendant claims that the trial court improperly excluded extrinsic evidence of the decedent's intent establishing that his subsequent marriage to her would not result in the revocation of his will. * * * In the alternative, the defendant argues that there is sufficient language within the will itself, without resort to extrinsic evidence, to indicate that the decedent did not intend for his will to be revoked upon his marriage to her.

We conclude that the will, in and of itself, did not provide for the contingency of the subsequent marriage of the decedent and, therefore, under existing case law, properly would have been revoked by that marriage pursuant to §45a-257 (a). We also conclude, however, that under the circumstances of this case, the trial court improperly excluded evidence of a mistake by the scrivener that, if believed, would permit a finding that the will provided for the contingency of marriage. We therefore reverse the judgment of the trial court and order a new trial in which such evidence may be considered by the trial court.

On the basis of existing case law, the question of whether a will provides for the contingency of a subsequent marriage must be determined: (1) from the language

of the will itself; and (2) without resort to extrinsic evidence of the testator's intent.
* * * Fulton Trust Co. v. Trowbridge, 126 Conn. 369, 372, 11 A.2d 393 (1940) (execution of will followed by adoption of child; no language in will providing for such contingency); Strong v. Strong, 106 Conn. 76, 79–80, 137 A. 17 (1927) (execution of will followed by birth of child; no language in will providing for such contingency); cf. Czepiel v. Czepiel, 146 Conn. 439, 442, 151 A.2d 878 (1959) (language in will provided for possible subsequent marriage); Blake v. Union & New Haven Trust Co., 95 Conn. 194, 196–97, 110 A. 833 (1920) (language in will provided for subsequent birth of child). Applying this standard, we conclude that the trial court should not have admitted the will because, notwithstanding the inferences that the trial court drew from the dates of the marriage license and the will, and from the identity of certain of the named beneficiaries in the will, there was *no language in the will* providing for the contingency of the subsequent marriage of the decedent. Thus, this will fell on that side of the dividing line encompassing those wills that do not, in and of themselves, provide for such a contingency; see Fulton Trust Co. v. Trowbridge, *supra*, at 372, 11 A.2d 393; Strong v. Strong, *supra*, at 80, 137 A. 17; and beyond that side of the line encompassing those wills that do provide for such a contingency. See Czepiel v. Czepiel, *supra*, at 440, 151 A.2d 878; Blake v. Union & New Haven Trust Co., *supra*, at 196, 110 A. 833.

This conclusion does not, however, end our inquiry in this case. In Connecticut Junior Republic v. Sharon Hospital, 188 Conn. 1, 2, 448 A.2d 190 (1982), this court considered the issue of "whether extrinsic evidence of a mistake by a scrivener of a testamentary instrument is admissible in a proceeding to determine the validity of the testamentary instrument." In a three to two decision, this court held that such evidence is not admissible. *Id.*, at 9, 448 A.2d 190. Upon further consideration, we now conclude that the reasons given by the dissent in that case are persuasive and apply to the facts of the present case. We, therefore, overrule *Connecticut Junior Republic,* and hold that if a scrivener's error has misled the testator into executing a will on the belief that it will be valid notwithstanding the testator's subsequent marriage, extrinsic evidence of that error is admissible to establish the intent of the testator that his or her will be valid notwithstanding the subsequent marriage. Furthermore, if those two facts, namely, the scrivener's error and its effect on the testator's intent, are established by clear and convincing evidence, they will be sufficient to establish that "provision has been made in such will for such contingency," within the meaning of § 45a-257 (a).

In Connecticut Junior Republic v. Sharon Hospital, *supra*, 188 Conn. at 9, 448 A.2d 190, this court reasserted the familiar rule that, although extrinsic evidence is not admissible to prove an intention not expressed in the will itself or to prove a devise or bequest not contained in the will, such evidence is admissible to identify a named devisee or legatee, to identify property described in the will, to clarify ambiguous language in the will, and to prove fraud, incapacity or undue influence. In rejecting the claim that extrinsic evidence should also be admissible to prove a scrivener's error, the majority relied principally on our existing case law and on the risk of subverting the policy of the statute of wills. *Id.*, at 23, 448 A.2d 190 (Peters, J., dissenting). The majority acknowledged, however, that, as with any rule of law, time and experience could persuade to the contrary. "[P]rinciples of law which serve one generation well may, by reason of changing conditions, disserve a later one. . . . Experience can and often does demonstrate that a rule, once believed sound, needs modification to serve justice better." (Citations omitted; internal quotation marks omitted.) *Id.*, at 17–18, 448 A.2d 190. We are now persuaded to the contrary.

The dissent in that case by Justice Peters and joined by Justice Shea, concluded that it "would permit extrinsic evidence of a scrivener's error to be introduced in litigation concerned with the admissibility of a disputed will to probate." *Id.*, at 22, 448 A.2d 190. The dissent gave three principal reasons for its conclusion, each of which we consider to be persuasive and each of which applies to this case. See *id.*, at 22–26, 448 A.2d 190.

First, given that extrinsic evidence is admissible to prove that a will was executed by the testator "in reliance on erroneous beliefs induced by fraud, duress, or undue influence"; *id.*, at 22, 448 A.2d 190; there is no discernible policy difference between that case and a case in which "a will is executed in reliance on erroneous beliefs induced by the innocent error, by the innocent misrepresentation, of the scrivener of a will." *Id.*, at 23, 448 A.2d 190. In each instance, "the testamentary process is distorted by the interference of a third person who misleads the testator into making a testamentary disposition that would not otherwise have occurred." *Id.*, at 22–23, 448 A.2d 190. "In each instance, extrinsic evidence is required to demonstrate that a will, despite its formally proper execution, substantially misrepresents the true intent of the testator." *Id.*, at 23, 448 A.2d 190.

Similarly, in the present case, there is no discernible policy difference between extrinsic evidence offered to show fraud, duress or undue influence, and extrinsic evidence offered to show that a scrivener's error induced the decedent to execute a will that he believed would survive his subsequent marriage. In both instances, the testamentary process was distorted by the interference of a third person who misled the testator into executing a will that would not otherwise have been executed—in the present case, a will that would be revoked upon his marriage because it did not contain language providing for the contingency of marriage. Thus, as in the case of fraud, duress or undue influence, extrinsic evidence is required to demonstrate that the will that the testator executed did not substantially state his true intention. * * *

Second, the dissent recognized that, based on the policy of the statute of wills, the "risk of subversion of the intent of a testator, who cannot personally defend his testamentary bequest, is without doubt a serious concern." *Id.*, at 24, 448 A.2d 190. The dissent, however, persuasively underscored the counterbalancing "risk of blindly enforcing a testamentary disposition that substantially misstates the testator's true intent." *Id.* Again drawing on the analogy to the case of fraud, duress or undue influence, the dissent stated that "[h]ad the decedent's lawyer deliberately and fraudulently altered the second codicil, the relevant extrinsic evidence would unquestionably have been admitted." *Id.*, at 25, 448 A.2d 190. The dissent contended that "innocent misrepresentation is treated as generally equivalent to fraud in terms of its legal consequences." *Id.* Therefore, the dissent asserted, the "[s]tatute of [w]ills does not compel enforcement of testamentary dispositions that a testator never intended to make." *Id.*

Similarly, in the present case, had the decedent's attorney deliberately and fraudulently, rather than innocently but mistakenly, misrepresented to the decedent that his will would be valid despite his subsequent marriage, it is at least arguable that the beneficiaries of that fraudulent conduct, namely, the heirs-at-law of the decedent who would inherit in the event of his intestacy, would not be permitted to take advantage of that fraud, and that a court of equity could impress a constructive trust on their inheritance. We conclude that, analogously, in this case, the extrinsic evidence should be admissible to establish the decedent's true intent.

Third, the dissent examined and rejected the two main objections to the admission of extrinsic evidence of a scrivener's error. One objection was "that whatever error the scrivener may have made was validated and ratified by the testator's act in signing his will." *Id.*, at 26, 448 A.2d 190. The dissent responded, correctly in our view, that, although "signing [a] will creates a strong presumption that the will accurately represents the intentions of the testator, that presumption is a rebuttable one." *Id.* Similarly, in the present case, although the fact that the decedent signed the will may create a rebuttable presumption that he did not intend it to survive his subsequent marriage, that presumption should be rebuttable by persuasive extrinsic evidence to the contrary.

The other objection was "that allowing extrinsic evidence of mistake will give rise to a proliferation of groundless will contests." *Id.* The dissent presented a two part response, with which we also agree. First, it noted that, "[i]n the law of contracts, where the parol evidence rule has undergone considerable erosion, this risk has not been found to have been unmanageable. In the law of wills, the risk is limited by the narrowness of the exception that this case would warrant . . . [namely, to] permit the opponent of a will to introduce extrinsic evidence of the error of a scrivener, and [to] require proof of such an extrinsic error to be established by clear and convincing evidence." *Id.*, at 26–27, 448 A.2d 190

Similarly, in the present case, the admissibility of such extrinsic evidence, in our view, will not prove to be any less manageable than in cases of parol evidence in contract disputes. Furthermore, we would impose the same elevated burden of proof on the proponent of the will in a case such as this. The proponent would have to establish the scrivener's error by clear and convincing evidence.

We recognize that the dissent's position in *Connecticut Junior Republic* would have resulted in the consideration of extrinsic evidence of a scrivener's error offered for the purpose of *preventing* admission of a testamentary document to probate, rather than for the purpose of *procuring* such admission, as in the present case.

Regardless of that distinction, however, the mistake doctrine advocated by the dissent in *Connecticut Junior Republic* applies equally to the present case. The dissent in *Connecticut Junior Republic* phrased the issue in that case as follows: "Must the true intent of the testator be thwarted when, because of the mistake of a scrivener, he has formally subscribed to a written bequest that substantially misstates his testamentary intention?" *Id.*, at 22, 448 A.2d 190. That is precisely the issue in the present case. The dissent in *Connecticut Junior Republic* answered that question in the negative, recognizing that evidence of a scrivener's mistake should be admissible where offered to establish that a written bequest *should not be admitted* to probate because its execution was the product of a mistake of the scrivener and, therefore, did not embody the disposition intended by the testator. *Id.*, at 22–23, 448 A.2d 190. Likewise, in the present case, evidence of a scrivener's mistake should be admissible to establish that a written bequest *should be admitted* to probate because the disposition provided by the bequest would have obtained, in accordance with the decedent's intent, but for the scrivener's mistake.

Finally, we address one other consideration that was not present in *Connecticut Junior Republic,* which might be perceived to be present in this case. That is the potential for past reliance by testators on our prior case law. We do not believe that this is a persuasive consideration. It is very unlikely that, in reliance on such case law, any testators executed wills and deliberately omitted language providing for the contingency of marriage in order to be sure that their wills would be revoked by a subsequent marriage. Moreover, it is very unlikely that any testators, having married after executing such wills, deliberately did not make new testamentary dispositions in reliance on the proposition that their prior wills had been revoked by that subsequent marriage.

Applying these principles to the facts of the present case, we conclude that the extrinsic evidence offered, if believed, could prove clearly and convincingly that there was a scrivener's error that induced the decedent to execute a will that he intended to be valid despite his subsequent marriage. The offer of proof indicates that the evidence would be susceptible to an inference by the fact finder that there had been an implied assertion by the scrivener that the will would be valid despite the decedent's subsequent marriage. This inference could have been bolstered, moreover, by the evidence of the conversations between the decedent and the scrivener shortly before the decedent's death.

The judgment is reversed and the case is remanded for a new trial.

In this opinion KATZ, PALMER and PETERS, JJ., concurred.

BERDON, Associate Justice, concurring.

Although I have some reservation with identifying the error on the part of the attorney as a "scrivener's error" in this case, I concur in the result reached by the majority. More specifically, I agree that Connecticut Junior Republic v. Sharon Hospital, 188 Conn. 1, 448 A.2d 190 (1982) should be overruled. Justice Peters' dissent in *Connecticut Junior Republic,* as joined by Justice Shea, points out that the opponent of a will should be allowed "to introduce extrinsic evidence of the error of a scrivener, and [that] . . . proof of such an extrinsic error [must] be established by clear and convincing evidence." *Id.*, at 26, 448 A.2d 190. Although "antiquity does not automatically disqualify common law precedents"; *id.*, at 23, 448 A.2d 190 (Peters, J., dissenting); our law should serve modern needs.

Restatement (Third) of Property: Wills and Other Donative Transfers (2019)

§ 12.1 Reforming Donative Documents to Correct Mistakes.

A donative document, though unambiguous, may be reformed to conform the text to the donor's intention if it is established by clear and convincing evidence (1) that a mistake of fact or law, whether in expression or inducement, affected specific terms of the document; and (2) what the donor's intention was. In determining whether these elements have been established by clear and convincing evidence, direct evidence of intention contradicting the plain meaning of the text as well as other evidence of intention may be considered.

Uniform Probate Code (2019)

§ 2-503. Harmless Error.

Although a document or writing added upon a document was not executed in compliance with Section 2-502, the document or writing is treated as if it had been executed in compliance with that section if the proponent of the document or writing establishes by clear and convincing evidence that the decedent intended the document or writing to constitute:

> (1) the decedent's will,
>
> (2) a partial or complete revocation of the will,
>
> (3) an addition to or an alteration of the will, or
>
> (4) a partial or complete revival of his [or her] formerly revoked will or of a formerly revoked portion of the will.

Uniform Trust Code (2019)

§ 415. Reformation to Correct Mistakes.

The court may reform the terms of a trust, even if unambiguous, to conform the terms to the settlor's intention if it is proved by clear and convincing evidence that both the settlor's intent and the terms of the trust were affected by a mistake of fact or law, whether in expression or inducement.

Notes

The remedy for mistake is different from the remedy for failure to complete the necessary formalities. Formality deficiency is addressed through Professor Langbein's doctrine of substantial compliance, *see* John H. Langbein, *Substantial*

Compliance With the Wills Act, 88 Harv. L. Rev. 489 (1975), or is incorporated into the Uniform Probate Code, *see* Unif. Prob. Code § 2-503 (2014) (Harmless Error), or in the *Restatement (Third) of Property (Wills & Don. Trans.)* § 3.3 (1999) ("A harmless error in executing a will may be excused if the proponent establishes by clear and convincing evidence that the decedent adopted the document as his or her will."). A mistake in the will—particularly if the mistake is of the plain meaning variety—is more like a deficiency in an intentionality and may be addressed by courts, as was done in cases like *Estate of Gibbs,* or through the *Restatement (Third) of Property (Wills & Don. Trans.)* § 12.1 (2003) (Reforming Donative Documents to Correct Mistakes), which allows for clear and convincing evidence to correct the mistake. In addition, New Jersey uses a doctrine of probable intent to fill gaps in wills. *See* Engle v. Seigel, 74 N.J. 287, 377 A.2d 892 (1977). But other courts retain a strict approach to the introduction of extrinsic evidence to resolve any inconsistencies. *See, e.g.,* Knupp v. District of Columbia, 578 A.2d 702 (1990). For some analysis of the approaches, see Pamela R. Champine, *My Will Be Done: Accommodating the Erring and the Atypical Testator,* 80 Neb. L. Rev. 387 (2001).

Similar to the issue raised in *Erickson,* in Langston v. Langston, 371 Ark. 404, 266 S.W.3d 716 (2006), the Supreme Court of Arkansas held that a holographic will, written by a man when he was in the process of seeking a divorce from his wife, was revoked by operation of law when the couple's final decree of divorce was entered. The court relied upon the lack of any language to the contrary in the holograph and applied the strict sequence of when the will was written and when the divorce occurred to hold that any extrinsic evidence of any intent contrary to the application of the statute was irrelevant. For a commentary on the *Langston* case, see Michael T. Flannery, *Revoking a Valid Will, Even When the Revocation Frustrates the Clearly-Established Intent of the Testator: Langston v. Langston (Ark.),* LexisNexis Expert Commentary, 2008 Emerging Issues 2061 (Apr. 2008) (available at Lexis, Emerging Issues, Combined Area of Law library).

V. Contracts and Wills

Competent adults may enter into contracts that affect the terms of a will or inheritance in general. But in examining these contracts, it is important to understand that there are two distinct claims at issue: contractual remedies and will remedies. Thus, if an adult enters into a contract to make or revoke a will or to appoint under a power of appointment, or agrees not to contest a will, what is at issue is merely the validity of the contract, itself, and not the validity of the will or the power of appointment, or the contest of the will. The two issues are distinct, and claims may be based on either contract law or the law of wills. *See generally* Kent Greenawalt, *A Pluralist Approach to Interpretation: Wills and Contracts*, 42 S.D. L. Rev. 533 (2005). What follows are examples of an integrated state statute addressing the interaction between contracts and wills, and the most common forms of contracts affecting Last Wills and Testaments—prenuptial agreements.

A. Contrasting Claims

Markey v. Estate of Markey
Supreme Court of Indiana, 2015
38 N.E.3d 1003

MASSA, Justice. . . .

Betty Markey passed away in August of 1998, survived by her husband, John, and their only child, David. That same month, John married Frances; the two had been seeing each other for several years while Betty lived in a nursing home. Shortly after reciting their vows, John and Frances contracted to make mutual wills. Consistent with that contract, the wills provided that upon the death of whoever died later, the couple's estate would be divided equally between David and Frances's grand-daughter, Gillian. The contract further mandated the wills would not be revoked, specifying the beneficiaries could bring suit:

> Each of the parties agrees never to revoke or alter in any way, for any rea-son, his or her Will executed pursuant to this Agreement. Should any Will required by this Agreement be revoked, either party, any beneficiary . . . , or the personal representative of any of them may bring an action in law for monetary damages, or an action in equity for specific performance or other appropriate equitable relief, including the imposition of a constructive trust on the property of any estate in the hands of a personal representative or of any beneficiaries.

[Citation to Record omitted]. David received a copy of the contract and the mutual wills.

About a decade later, John died, and all of his assets passed to Frances, including over half a million dollars in Exxon stock that David's mother inherited from her parents. Although David and Frances maintained a relationship for some time, they eventually had a falling out and stopped communicating. In 2010, unbeknownst to David, Frances executed a subsequent will, revoking the mutual will with John. In this subsequent will, Frances devised all of her property equally between her own two children, Madonna Reda and Stephen Routson, and she appointed Stephen per-sonal representative. . . . Frances died on July 29, 2012. Stephen admitted her will to probate on August 22 and published notice of its administration in the Western Wayne News on September 5 and 12. Although Stephen had David's father's ashes, he made no effort to contact David following Frances's death. David did not learn about her death or the subsequent will until April 25, 2013. Four days later, and nine months after Frances's death, David sued Frances's estate, Stephen, and Madonna to enforce the contract.

The parties agree that Frances's actions were contrary to the valid contract between her and David's father. They disagree, however, about the time frame in which David could seek to enforce it: Madonna moved for summary judgment, arguing David's complaint was time-barred because it was filed more than three months after Frances's will was admitted to probate. In opposition, David maintained he timely filed because he did so within nine months of Frances's death. He reasoned (or, perhaps, conceded) that his claim to enforce the contract constituted a "claim" falling under the Probate Code, but further argued he was a reasonably ascertainable creditor of the estate entitled to actual notice, and since he did not receive that notice, he had nine months to file under Indiana Code section 29–1–7–7(e) (Supp.2014). The trial court, however, relied on *Keenan v. Butler's* holding that a breach of contract regarding mutual wills is neither a claim in probate nor a will contest. 869 N.E.2d 1284, 1289 (Ind.Ct.App.2007), *trans. not sought*. And it found persuasive a footnote in that case concerning the time to file such a breach of contract action:

> We have not been asked to decide whether there is a time limit within which an action for breach of contract to make a will must be filed. However, statutes of repose, here limiting the time to file to three months, govern both claims and will contests. For timely administration of an estate, a breach of contract to make a will action should similarly be limited. Where the action is challenging the distribution pursuant to a probated will, the petition must be filed within three months of the order admitting the will to probate.

Id. at 1290 n. 6 (internal citations omitted). Because David filed more than three months after Frances's will was admitted, the trial court granted summary judgment for Madonna.... David appealed, arguing the trial court erred in relying upon *Keenan* because that case considered the question of subject-matter jurisdiction, not time to file, and it should not be extended beyond its unique facts. He also contended that a three-month limitation period would violate his right to due process. But a unanimous panel of our Court of Appeals disagreed, affirming the outcome below. *Markey v. Estate of Markey*, 13 N.E.3d 453, 460 (Ind.Ct.App.2014). It held David's action for breach of contract was not a "claim" under the Probate Code, so—regardless of whether or not he was a reasonably ascertainable creditor—"his action was not eligible for the nine-month limitation period for filing." *Id.* at 458. Instead, the panel found his suit barred by the three-month limitation period suggested in *Keenan. Id.* It also saw no due process violation since Stephen published notice and the evidence did not show David was entitled to actual notice. *Id.* at 459.... David sought transfer, pointing to—among other things—both lower courts' improper reliance on the common law definition of "claim" rather than the more recent statutory definition enacted by our legislature in the Probate Code. We granted David's petition to transfer, thereby vacating the opinion below. *Markey v. Estate of Markey*, 21 N.E.3d 838 (Ind.2014) (table); Ind. Appellate Rule 58(A)....

[David] argues his claim for breach of contract to make and not revoke mutual wills constitutes a "claim" as defined by our Probate Code. We agree.... In 1953, based upon the work of the Indiana Probate Code Study Commission and guided by the American Bar Association's Model Probate Code, our General Assembly enacted our state's modern Probate Code, "the first major modification of Indiana law relating to the administration of decedents' estates in more than half a century." *Possession and Control of Estate Property During Administration: Indiana Probate Code Section 1301*, 29 Ind. L.J. 251, 252 (1954). Up until that time, much of our law on the subject came from Chapter 9 of the Acts of 1881. *Id.* at n. 3. The revisions were substantial; thus, "care must be taken in evaluating court decisions before 1954 in the probate field because of the extent to which they may have been influenced by principles of law repudiated or varied by the Probate Code." 1A John S. Grimes, *Henry's Probate Law and Practice of the State of Indiana* § 5 at 22 (7th ed. 1978).

Under our current statutory scheme, although claims may be brought against an estate, they must be brought rather swiftly. Indeed, one of the basic tenets underlying the procedural provisions in our Probate Code is "the uniform and expeditious distribution of property of a decedent." *Inlow v. Henderson, Daily, Withrow & DeVoe*, 787 N.E.2d 385, 395 (Ind.Ct.App.2003) (quoting *Kuzma v. Peoples Trust & Sav. Bank, Boonville*, 132 Ind.App. 176, 183, 176 N.E.2d 134, 138 (1961)). For this reason, the Non-claim Statute provides that, in general, claims must be filed within three months of publication about the estate's administration:

> Except as provided in IC 29-1-7-7, all claims against a decedent's estate . . . whether due or to become due, absolute or contingent, liquidated or unliquidated, founded on contract or otherwise, shall be forever barred against the estate, the personal representative, the heirs, devisees, and legatees of the decedent, unless filed with the court in which such estate is being administered within: (1) three (3) months after the date of the first published notice to creditors[.]

Ind.Code § 29–1–14–1(a) (2004).

There is an exception to this three-month limit, however, stemming from the personal representative's obligation to serve actual notice on a "creditor of the decedent . . . who is known or reasonably ascertainable."[1] Ind.Code § 29-1-7-7(d) (Supp.2014). If the personal representative fails to serve actual notice within one month of the first published notice, the reasonably ascertainable creditor gets an additional two months to file, once he finally receives actual notice. Ind.Code § 29-1-7-7(e). But, no matter the notice date, all claims are barred nine months after the decedent's death. *Id.* . . . So here, for David's suit to be eligible for filing up until the nine-month bar, he must (1) have a "claim" and (2) be a reasonably

---

1. Although reasonably ascertainable creditor is not explicitly defined, the Code does provide some useful context: "A personal representative shall exercise reasonable diligence to discover the reasonably ascertainable creditors of the decedent. . . ." Ind.Code § 29–1–7–7.5(a) (2004). That responsibility includes (1) reviewing reasonably available financial records, and (2) making reasonable inquiries of individuals who are likely to know about the decedent's debts. Ind.Code § 29–1–7–7.5(b). If the personal representative complies with the two requirements, creditors who are not discovered are presumed not to be reasonably ascertainable. Ind.Code § 29–1–7–7.5(d).

ascertainable creditor.[2] . . . Conveniently, "claims" is defined in the first chapter of the Probate Code, and it "includes liabilities of a decedent which survive, *whether arising in contract or in tort or otherwise*, funeral expenses, the expense of a tombstone, expenses of administration, and all taxes imposed by reason of the person's death." Ind.Code § 29-1-1-3(a)(2) (Supp.2014) (emphasis added). That definition "appl[ies] throughout this article, unless otherwise apparent from the context." Ind.Code § 29-1-1-3(a). Turning to the Non-claim Statute at issue here, neither its language nor context give any indication that the broad definition penned by the enacting legislature should not apply. Indeed, quite the opposite is true; the Non-claim Statute uses similarly broad language in setting forth the general limit for "all claims . . . *whether founded in contract or otherwise*." Ind.Code § 29-1-14-1(a) (emphasis added). Relying on this broad definition makes sense: given the goal of swift administration, all causes of action against an estate should be subjected to shortened filing limitations laid out in the Code rather than, for instance, the ten-year statute of limitations for traditional breach of contract claims. *See* Ind.Code § 34-11-2-11 (2014). . . . Although the lower courts needed not wait on us, *see S. Ry. Co. v. Howerton*, 182 Ind. 208, 220, 105 N.E. 1025, 1029 (1914) ("[T]he common law is not continued in force where the same subject is covered by a statute."), we hold the statutory definition of claims supersedes the common law definition we set out 75 years ago. *See Dague v. Piper Aircraft Corp.*, 275 Ind. 520, 529, 418 N.E.2d 207, 213 (1981) ("[O]ne of the acknowledged functions of legislation is to change the common law to reflect change of time and circumstances"). Under the plain language of that definition, David Markey's claim for breach of contract to make and not revoke mutual wills is a claim governed by the Probate Code. It is a liability that survives Frances's death and sounds in contract.

Of course, David's having a claim in probate does not answer the question of whether that claim was timely filed. The general limit for such claims is three months, and he concedes he filed outside of that window. For his claim to survive, David must not only be a claimant but also a "creditor" who is "known or reasonably ascertainable." Ind.Code § 29–1–7–7(e). This issue, however, was not fully adjudicated below: because the trial court found David's claim untimely under *Keenan*—which applied the wrong definition of "claims"—it did not reach the question of whether David fits the exception to the Non-claim Statute under Indiana Code section 29–1–7–7. . . . [footnote omitted]. And we find the record on appeal inadequate for us to reach a resolution today, as the parties have not fully briefed whether David is a creditor of the estate . . . [footnote omitted] or whether he was reasonably ascertainable. . . . [footnote omitted]. Moreover, answering this question may very well require that the parties engage in further discovery, which the trial court had initially limited based on its review of *Keenan* that we reject. . . .

2. It is undisputed that Stephen, as personal representative, did not notify David of Frances's death or of the administration of her estate.

[footnote omitted]. We thus remand to the trial court to determine whether David's claim in probate should proceed as timely filed. . . .

RUSH, C.J., and DICKSON, RUCKER, and DAVID, JJ., concur.

Uniform Probate Code (2019)

§ 2-514. Contracts Concerning Succession.

A contract to make a will or devise, or not to revoke a will or devise, or to die intestate, if executed after the effective date of this Article, may be established only by (i) provisions of a will stating material provisions of the contract, (ii) an express reference in a will to a contract and extrinsic evidence proving the terms of the contract, or (iii) a writing signed by the decedent evidencing the contract. The execution of a joint will or mutual wills does not create a presumption of a contract not to revoke the will or wills.

California Probate Code (2019)

§ 21700. Contract to make will or devise; establishment; effect of execution of joint will or mutual wills; applicable law.

(a) A contract to make a will or devise or other instrument, or not to revoke a will or devise or other instrument, or to die intestate, if made after the effective date of this statute, can be established only by one of the following:

(1) Provisions of a will or other instrument stating the material provisions of the contract.

(2) An expressed reference in a will or other instrument to a contract and extrinsic evidence proving the terms of the contract.

(3) A writing signed by the decedent evidencing the contract.

(4) Clear and convincing evidence of an agreement between the decedent and the claimant or a promise by the decedent to the claimant that is enforceable in equity.

(5) Clear and convincing evidence of an agreement between the decedent and another person for the benefit of the claimant or a promise by the decedent to another person for the benefit of the claimant that is enforceable in equity.

(b) The execution of a joint will or mutual wills does not create a presumption of a contract not to revoke the will or wills.

(c) A contract to make a will or devise or other instrument, or not to revoke a will or devise or other instrument, or to die intestate, if made prior to the effective date of this section, shall be construed under the law applicable to the contract prior to the effective date of this section.

B. Disclaimers by Spouses

Once the validity of spousal status has been established, a spouse may: (1) take an intestate share, no matter what the length of the marriage; (2) have standing to contest any Last Will and Testament if the will provides less than what would otherwise be received; (3) elect to take a spouse's elective share; (4) take the family maintenance amounts available to the surviving spouse; (5) take under any ERISA pension device as a surviving spouse; and (6), take as an omitted spouse if circumstances, as dictated by statute, indicate that he or she was forgotten by the testator. And, as is pertinent to this section, the spouse may disclaim—release and renounce—any of these opportunities.

In re Estate of Davis

Court of Appeals of Tennessee, 2006
213 S.W.3d 288

D. MICHAEL SWINEY, J. * * *

The appeal involves the validity of an antenuptial agreement entered into thirty years before Wife's death. In May of 1969, Husband and Wife were married after an eight week courtship. Two days before the wedding, Husband was told that he needed to sign an antenuptial agreement (the "Agreement"). The Agreement was signed by Husband the next day at the office of Wife's attorney. Husband was not represented by an attorney. Husband and Wife remained married for approximately thirty years and were still married when Wife passed away in 1999.

The Agreement provides, in relevant part, as follows[1]:

WHEREAS, the parties hereto contemplate a marriage with each other at an early date and are desirous of entering into this contract and agreement for the purpose of insuring harmony in their relations and freedom of action, one from another, in the management of their business after said marriage; and

WHEREAS, each of said parties are seized and possessed of valuable property, real and/or personal, and have individual rights and each have an earning capacity and each of said parties is desirous of retaining absolute and full control of their said property, including any additions thereto, during the term of their marriage and of relinquishing all rights of every kind or character whether marital or by virtue of the statutes of descent and distribution or whether by dower or curtesy in the properties of the other; and

WHEREAS, the parties have attached hereto a general statement of their respective financial conditions and assets which do not purport to be all inclusive, the values set forth on which do not purport to be necessarily accurate but rather are estimates, and, whereas, the parties would have entered into this agreement whether the said statements accurately reflect all assets or properly reflect the true value of the assets and each

---

1. The Agreement refers to Wife as the "Party of the First Part," and Husband as the "Party of the Second Part."

party recognizes that there may be other assets or other property values but would have entered into this agreement regardless of the same. * * *

Even though the Agreement indicates that each of the parties to that Agreement was attaching a "general statement of their respective financial conditions," apparently no one was able to locate such an attachment of Wife's assets. The Agreement was introduced as an exhibit at trial, but there were no lists attached to it.

Wife's first husband was the famed country music singer Jim Reeves, who tragically died in an airplane crash in 1964. When Jim Reeves died, Wife inherited various business ventures and real property from Jim Reeves' estate. Just prior to Wife's marriage five years later to Husband, Wife's assets were worth roughly four million dollars, and Wife's annual income from investments and businesses, etc., was approximately $300,000 to $400,000.[2] When Wife died after approximately thirty years of marriage to Husband, she left Husband $100,000 in her will. Wife's will was prepared in 1976.

After Wife's will was admitted to probate, Husband filed a "Petition for Elective Share, Year's Support, Homestead and Exempt Property." Certain other heirs under the will as well as the Administrator of the Estate responded to the petition, claiming the Agreement barred Husband from electing to take against the will. The issues surrounding the validity of the Agreement were severed from all other estate and probate issues, and in October of 2001 the Trial Court conducted a hearing pertaining solely to whether the Agreement was enforceable. * * *

Husband testified that he signed the Agreement on May 23, which was the day before the wedding. Although Wife was represented by the attorney who drafted the Agreement, Husband was not represented by an attorney. Husband learned one day before he signed the Agreement that Wife wanted such an agreement signed. Husband stated that he wrote out a list of his assets when he was at Wife's attorney's office. Husband identified the handwritten list which he prepared and which was admitted as an exhibit at trial. Husband stated that to his knowledge, his list never was typed. Husband testified that when he entered into the Agreement, his assets were valued at between $25,000 and $30,000. Husband stated that a list of Wife's assets was not prepared in his presence.[3]

Husband testified that he did not know the value or liabilities associated with Wife's house, an office building which Wife owned, the value of her car, or the value of Jim Reeves Enterprises when he signed the Agreement. Husband further stated that he did not know the liabilities associated with Jim Reeves Enterprises or the amount of annual income generated by that business. * * *

2. These figures represent Husband's assessment offered at trial as to Wife's net worth and income. This was the only proof presented at trial as to the value of Wife's holdings and income.

3. When Husband testified that he never saw a list of assets before signing the Agreement, the Trial Court sustained an objection to that testimony based on the parol evidence rule. The Trial Court also sustained the same objection when Husband was asked if he was advised by anyone as to the value of Wife's assets.

Husband candidly acknowledged that he knew prior to the marriage that Wife had substantially more assets than he did, but he added that he did not know the extent of her wealth. After they were married, Husband learned that Wife had annual income of $100,000 from the publishing companies and another $100,000 from the contract with RCA. Husband further stated that when including other royalties as well as income from Jim Reeves Enterprises, Wife's annual income was close to $300,000 to $400,000. Husband added that he did know the value of two lots Wife owned in the Bahamas, and that value was $52,000. * * *

Accordingly, the Trial Court entered an order stating that the Agreement was enforceable, thereby prohibiting Husband from electing against the provisions of the will which provided that Husband would receive $100,000. The Trial Court certified its judgment as a final judgment pursuant to Tenn. R. Civ P. 54.02, and this appeal followed. Husband claims the Trial Court erred when it determined that it had been proven by a preponderance of the evidence that he received a full and fair disclosure of Wife's assets prior to entering into the Agreement. Husband's second issue is his claim that the Trial Court erred when it ruled that the parol evidence rule barred Husband from testifying that Wife never attached a list of her assets to the Agreement, and that he never saw such a list.

* * *

The Agreement was entered into in 1969, more than a decade before the Tennessee Legislature enacted the statute governing enforcement of antenuptial agreements which is now codified at Tenn.Code Ann. § 36–3–501. This statute provides:

> Enforcement of antenuptial agreements.—Notwithstanding any other provision of law to the contrary, except as provided in § 36–3–502, any antenuptial or prenuptial agreement entered into by spouses concerning property owned by either spouse before the marriage that is the subject of such agreement shall be binding upon any court having jurisdiction over such spouses and/or such agreement if such agreement is determined, in the discretion of such court, to have been entered into by such spouses freely, knowledgeably and in good faith and without exertion of duress or undue influence upon either spouse. The terms of such agreement shall be enforceable by all remedies available for enforcement of contract terms.

* * *

The question is whether Wife made a full and fair disclosure of the nature, extent, and value of her holdings. Assuming that Wife did make a list of her holdings, the Agreement unequivocally states that such a list did "not purport to be all inclusive, the values set forth on which do not purport to be necessarily accurate but rather are estimates." Since Wife's list cannot be located, assuming there was a list, we are unable to determine if that missing list actually was sufficiently detailed such that there was a full and fair disclosure to Husband of Wife's holdings. Nor do we think that the language in the Agreement itself can be interpreted as sufficient proof that the list was a full and fair disclosure when the Agreement specifically states that the list may not be all inclusive and any values set forth may not be accurate. In short, even if we agree with the Trial Court that a list was created, we do not believe the language in the Agreement is in any way sufficient to reasonably conclude that the list contained a full and fair disclosure of Wife's assets when the Agreement states that all assets may not be included and for those assets that are included, their values may not be accurate. * * *

The next issue is whether Husband had full knowledge of Wife's holdings even without such a disclosure directly being made. There are some of Wife's assets which Husband probably could be charged with having a reasonable knowledge of their value, such as Wife's house and car and perhaps even some of her jewelry. However, the bulk of Wife's assets were of a type that a person cannot simply look at and get a reasonable understanding of its value. For example, while Husband had been to the offices of Jim Reeves Enterprises, there is nothing in the record to indicate that simply being present at the business office could in any way give Husband a means by which to reasonably ascertain its value. This is even more apparent when considering that there were three recording companies being operated by Jim Reeves Enterprises. The same can be said about the RCA contract. Simply because Husband knew it existed does not mean he had any knowledge as to what the contract reasonably was worth. We cannot simply impute this knowledge to Husband, especially when there is no evidence that Wife ever discussed the value of her holdings with Husband at any time before they were married. In addition, Husband testified that he was not even aware of some real property and other assets that were owned by Wife. It is important to note that with regard to Husband's *298 testimony, the Trial Court made a specific credibility determination when stating it found Husband to be credible and that he was not being dishonest.

The burden of proof was on the heirs and the Administrator of the Estate who were asserting the validity of antenuptial agreement. They were required to prove by a preponderance of the evidence that the Agreement was valid because Husband signed the Agreement after being fully and fairly informed of the nature, extent, and value of Wife's holdings. We conclude that the preponderance of the evidence weighs against the Trial Court's finding that this burden was met. We, therefore, reverse the judgment of the Trial Court which found the Agreement valid and enforceable. * * *

The judgment of the Trial Court is reversed, and this cause is remanded to the Trial Court for further proceedings consistent with this Opinion and for collection of the costs below. Costs on appeal are taxed to the Appellees Vergie Reeves Thomas, Louis Reeves McNeese, Joe Lynn Reeves, and Linda Reeves Elliott, and Ames Davis, Administrator C.T.A. of the Estate of Mary Reeves Davis.

Notes

During the 1970s and 1980s, states embraced the right of couples, prior to marriage and during marriage, to execute agreements that affected property rights at divorce or at death. By 1983, the Uniform Premarital Agreement Act was promulgated and was eventually adopted by more than half of the states. Additional acts were promulgated. *See, e.g.,* Unif. Prob. Code § 2-213 (Waiver of Right to Elect and of Other Rights); Restatement (Third) of Property, § 9.4 (2003); Model Marital Property Act, § 10 (1983); Internal Revenue Code, §§ 401, 417. The most recent attempt at uniformity is the Uniform Premarital and Marital Agreement Act (UPMAA), enacted to instill greater due process and substantive fairness. Specifically, under Section 9(f) of the Act, a state may refuse enforcement of an agreement if enforcement would result in substantial hardship at the time of enforcement. Likewise, the UPMAA applies the same set of principles to both premarital and marital agreements. *See generally* Barbara A. Atwood, *Marital Contracts and the Meaning of Marriage,* 54 Ariz. L. Rev. 11 (2012); J. Thomas Oldham, *With All My Worldly Goods I Thee Endow, or Maybe Not: A Reevaluation of the Uniform Premarital Agreement Act After Three Decades,* 19 Duke J. Gender L. & Pol'y 83 (2011).

The *Davis* decision illustrates the necessity of full and fair disclosure of all assets owned by either party to the agreement. Section 9(a) of the UPMAA lists the elements required for adequate disclosure, and they are more extensive than in previous code provisions: (1) freedom from duress; (2) access to independent legal representation; (3) if no legal representation, then the parties had a written notice of waiver of rights; and (4) the terms were unconscionable at the time of signing the agreement, or in those states adopting this, when the agreement was to be enforced. Several decisions illustrate what conduct may be deemed unconscionable. *See, e.g.,* Fetters v. Fetters, 26 N.E.3d 1016 (Ind. Ct. App. 2015) (holding that agreement between 16-year-old pregnant woman and man twice her age should not be enforced when couple divorced after sixteen years of marriage because agreement was unconscionable at time of execution); Owen v. Owen, 759 S.E.2d 468 (W. Va. 2014) (holding agreement unenforceable because wife did not have independent counsel, and there was no specific explanation of rights wife was waiving, especially those associated with property acquired during course of marriage that would be deemed marital property, subject to equitable distribution); Sanderson v. Sanderson, No. 2012-CA-01153-SCT, 2014 WL 7085870 (Miss. Dec. 11, 2014), *as modified on denial of reh'g* (Aug. 13, 2015) (holding that agreement was not unconscionable because financial statements were attached to prenuptial agreement, wife had advice of independent counsel that agreement was one-sided but chose to proceed, and, although agreement was signed in close proximity to wedding, informal nature and scope of wedding, combined with presence of independent counsel and attachment of financial disclosures, did not indicate level of coercion or surprise that would make wife's entry into agreement involuntary); McLeod v. McLeod, 145 So. 3d 1246 (Miss. Ct. App. 2014) (holding that agreement was not unconscionable because prenuptial agreement was fair, as would support its enforceability, even though wife was not represented by attorney, wife had opportunity to retain attorney, wife communicated with husband's attorney over course of few weeks about agreement prior to execution, husband and wife signed prenuptial agreement, and, while signing agreement, wife asserted that she understood agreement's terms).

Uniform Premarital and Marital Agreements Act (2012)

§ 6. Formation Requirements.

A premarital agreement or marital agreement must be in a record and signed by both parties. The agreement is enforceable without consideration.

§ 7. When Agreement Effective.

A premarital agreement is effective on marriage. A marital agreement is effective on signing by both parties.

§ 9. Enforcement.

(a) A premarital agreement or marital agreement is unenforceable if a party against whom enforcement is sought proves:

(1) the party's consent to the agreement was involuntary or the result of duress;

(2) the party did not have access to independent legal representation under subsection (b);

(3) unless the party had independent legal representation at the time the agreement was signed, the agreement did not include a notice of waiver of rights under subsection (c) or an explanation in plain language of the marital rights or obligations being modified or waived by the agreement; or

(4) before signing the agreement, the party did not receive adequate financial disclosure under subsection (d).

(b) A party has access to independent legal representation if:

(1) before signing a premarital or marital agreement, the party has a reasonable time to:

(A) decide whether to retain a lawyer to provide independent legal representation; and

(B) locate a lawyer to provide independent legal representation, obtain the lawyer's advice, and consider the advice provided; and

(2) the other party is represented by a lawyer and the party has the financial ability to retain a lawyer or the other party agrees to pay the reasonable fees and expenses of independent legal representation.

(c) A notice of waiver of rights under this section requires language, conspicuously displayed, substantially similar to the following, as applicable to the premarital agreement or marital agreement:

"If you sign this agreement, you may be:

Giving up your right to be supported by the person you are marrying or to whom you are married.

Giving up your right to ownership or control of money and property.

Agreeing to pay bills and debts of the person you are marrying or to whom you are married.

Giving up your right to money and property if your marriage ends or the person to whom you are married dies.

Giving up your right to have your legal fees paid."

(d) A party has adequate financial disclosure under this section if the party:

(1) receives a reasonably accurate description and good-faith estimate of value of the property, liabilities, and income of the other party;

(2) expressly waives, in a separate signed record, the right to financial disclosure beyond the disclosure provided; or

(3) has adequate knowledge or a reasonable basis for having adequate knowledge of the information described in paragraph (1).

(e) If a premarital agreement or marital agreement modifies or eliminates spousal support and the modification or elimination causes a party to the agreement to be eligible for support under a program of public assistance at the time of separation or marital dissolution, a court, on request of that party, may require the other party to provide support to the extent necessary to avoid that eligibility.

(f) A court may refuse to enforce a term of a premarital agreement or marital agreement if, in the context of the agreement taken as a whole[:]

[(1)] the term was unconscionable at the time of signing[; or

(2) enforcement of the term would result in substantial hardship for a party because of a material change in circumstances arising after the agreement was signed].

(g) The court shall decide a question of unconscionability [or substantial hardship] under subsection (f) as a matter of law.

VI. Ademption and Exoneration

Property may be classified as one of four types: (1) *Residuary*—when the property is identified as that which remains after everything else has been distributed. Residuary property benefits least from the intent of the testator or settlor. An illustration of residuary property would be: "All of the rest, residue, and remainder . . ."; (2) *General*—when the property given to another comes from the general assets of the estate, without regard to source. For example: "One thousand dollars to my niece . . ."; (3) *Demonstrative*—when the property given is to come from a particular source, such as when the testator provides: "One thousand dollars to my niece, from my account with Bank of America . . ."; and (4) *Specific*—when the testator or settlor transfers all of something—or a unique item—to another, thereby exhibiting the highest degree of intent that this special item—this specific thing—should go to another. For example: "My wristwatch engraved with my initials and dated '1-18-44,' is to go to. . . ." Classification of the property will be very important for ademption by extinction and exoneration, but not for ademption by satisfaction. All of these doctrines have ancient roots, but the Uniform Probate Code has made substantial changes. Therefore, be attentive to the Code provisions and ask how the Code would have affected the outcome of the cases if it had been enacted in the state.

A. Ademption by Extinction

McGee v. McGee

Supreme Court of Rhode Island, 1980
122 R.I. 837, 413 A.2d 72

WEISBERGER, Justice.

This is a complaint for declaratory judgment, in which the plaintiff administrator, Richard J. McGee (Richard), sought directions from the Superior Court in respect to the construction of certain provisions of the will of his mother, Claire E. McGee, and instructions relating to payment of debts and distribution of assets from the testatrix's estate. The sole issue presented by this appeal concerns the question of the ademption of an allegedly specific legacy to the grandchildren of the decedent and the consequent effect of such ademption upon payment of a bequest in the amount of $20,000 to Fedelma Hurd (Hurd), a friend of the testatrix. The provisions of the will pertinent to this appeal read as follows:

> "CLAUSE ELEVENTH:
>
> I give and bequeath to my good and faithful friend FEDELMA HURD, the sum of Twenty Thousand ($20,000.00) Dollars, as an expression to her of my appreciation for her many kindnesses.
>
> "CLAUSE TWELFTH:
>
> I give and bequeath all of my shares of stock in the Texaco Company, and any and all monies standing in my name on deposit in any banking institution as follows:
>
>> (a) My Executor shall divide the shares of stock, or the proceeds thereof from a sale of same, *with all of my monies, standing on deposit in my name, in any bank*, into three (3) equal parts and shall pay 1/3 over to the living children of my beloved son, PHILIP; 1/3 to the living children of my beloved son, RICHARD and 1/3 over to the living children of my beloved son, JOSEPH. Each of my grandchildren shall share equally the 1/3 portion given to them." (Emphasis added.)

At the time of the execution of the will and up until a short time before the death of the testatrix, a substantial sum of money was on deposit in her name at the People's Savings Bank in Providence. About five weeks prior to his mother's death, Richard, proceeding pursuant to a written power of attorney as modified by an addendum executed the following month, withdrew approximately $50,000 from these savings accounts. Of this amount, he applied nearly $30,000 towards the purchase of four United States Treasury bonds, commonly denominated as "flower bonds," from the Federal Trust Company in Waterville, Maine (Richard then resided in that state). His objective in executing this transaction was to effect an advantageous method of satisfying potential federal estate tax liability. * * * The bonds, however, did not serve the intended purpose since at the time of Mrs. McGee's death her gross estate was such that apparently no federal estate tax liability was incurred. The remainder of the monies withdrawn from the savings accounts were deposited in Claire McGee's checking account to pay current bills and in a savings account in Richard's name to be transferred to his mother's account as the need might arise for the payment of her debts and future obligations. The sole sum that is now the subject of this appeal is the approximately $30,000 held in the form of United States Treasury bonds.

The complaint for declaratory judgment sought instructions concerning whether the administrator should first satisfy the specific legacy to the grandchildren from the proceeds of the sale of the flower bonds or whether he should first pay the $20,000 bequest to Fedelma Hurd, since the estate lacked assets sufficient to satisfy both bequests.

After hearing evidence and considering legal memoranda filed by the parties, the trial justice found that the bequest to the grandchildren contained in the twelfth clause of the will constituted a specific legacy. He held further, however, that Rhode Island regarded the concept of ademption with disfavor and he sought, therefore, to effectuate the intent of the testatrix. He proceeded to determine that since there is an assumption that one intends to leave his property to those who are the natural objects of his bounty, rather than to strangers, the administrator "should trace the funds used to purchase the Flower Bonds and should satisfy the specific legacy to the grandchildren" under the twelfth clause of the will. Consequently, the trial justice held that the legacy to Fedelma Hurd under the eleventh clause of the will must fail. This appeal ensued.

The McGee grandchildren suggest that the principal design of the testatrix's estate plan, ascertainable from a contemplation of the testamentary disposition of her property, was to benefit her family rather than "outsiders." They urge us to consider her intentions which they assure us were concerned, in part, with protecting the family interests from an anticipated reduction of the estate's value by taxes in determining whether the transfer of the funds in her accounts did in fact work an ademption. In addition, Richard points out that the decedent did not herself purchase these bonds. On the contrary, Richard acquired them in order to help discharge anticipated tax obligations of the estate and informed his mother of them only subsequently to the purchase. He argues, furthermore, not only that the funds with which he purchased the flower bonds originated in his mother's accounts, but also that since these bonds "are as liquid as cash" they are indeed monies standing in the decedent's name on deposit in a banking institution. He suggests that this description conforms in every respect to the formula drafted into the twelfth clause of her will. Merely the form of the legacy has changed, according to Richard, not its essential character, quality, or substance.

In response, appellant asserts that an ademption occurred by the voluntary act of the testatrix during her lifetime, since her son withdrew the funds as an authorized agent operating under a lawful power of attorney. There is evidence, moreover, that the testatrix subsequently ratified the purchase of the bonds when Richard afterwards told her of his actions and their intended effect upon estate taxes. * * * As a consequence, Hurd asserts that there was no longer any money standing on deposit in the name of the testatrix in any bank with which to discharge the specific legacy to the grandchildren. These transactions resulted in an extinction of the subject matter of the legacy. Hurd argues, in addition, that the intention of the testatrix, even if discernible, is irrelevant to the question of the ademption of the bequest. She therefore contends that her general legacy should be payable from the proceeds of the sale of the flower bonds.

At the outset, we recognize that the instant case concerns specifically the concept of ademption by extinction, a legal consequence that may attend a variety of circumstances occasioned either by operation of law or by the actions of a testator himself or through his guardian, conservator, or agent. Gardner v. McNeal, 117 Md. 27, 82 A. 988 (1911); In re Wright, 7 N.Y.2d 365, 165 N.E.2d 561, 197 N.Y.S.2d 711 (1960). In particular, a testamentary gift of specific real or personal property may be adeemed—fail completely to pass as prescribed in the testator's will—when the particular article devised or bequeathed no longer exists as part of the testator's estate at the moment of his death because of its prior consumption, loss, destruction, substantial change, sale, or other alienation subsequent to the execution of the will. In consequence, neither the gift, its proceeds, nor similar substitute passes to the beneficiary, and this claim to the legacy is thereby barred. Atkinson, Handbook of the Law of Wills § 134 at 741, 743–44 (2d ed. 1953); 6 Bowe & Parker, Page on the Law of Wills § 54.1 at 242, § 54.9 at 256–57 (1962); Note, Wills: Ademption of Specific Legacies and Devises, 43 Cal.L.Rev. 151 (1955).

The principle of ademption by extinction has reference only to specific devises and bequests and is thus inapplicable to demonstrative or general testamentary gifts. 6 Page, *supra* § 54.3 at 245, § 54.5 at 248. In Haslam v. de Alvarez, 70 R.I. 212, 38 A.2d 158 (1944), we prescribed the criteria for determining the character of a legacy, relying on the earlier case of Dean v. Rounds, 18 R.I. 436, 27 A. 515 (1893), wherein we held that "(a) specific legacy, as the term imports, is a gift or bequest of some definite specific thing, something which is capable of being designated and identified." *Id.* When the testator intends that the legatee shall receive the exact property bequeathed rather than its corresponding quantitative or *ad valorem* equivalent, the gift is a specific one, and when "the main intention is that the legacy be paid by the delivery of the identical thing, and that thing only, and in the event that at the time of the testator's death such thing is no longer in existence, the legacy will not be paid out of his general assets." Hanley v. Fernell, 54 R.I. 84, 86, 170 A.

88, 89 (1934). In particular, the designation and identification of the specific legacy in a testator's will describe the gift in a manner that serves to distinguish it from all other articles of the same general nature and prevents its distribution from the general assets of the testator's estate. 6 Page, *supra* § 48.3 at 11–12.

In the case at bar, the trial justice construed the twelfth clause of Mrs. McGee's will as bequeathing a specific legacy to her grandchildren. While it is true that the party who contends the legacy is a specific one must bear the burden of proof on this issue, DiCristofaro v. Beaudry, 113 R.I. 313, 320 A.2d 597 (1974), and appellant, in her brief, characterized the twelfth clause as a bequest of a particular residuary gift, the trial justice apparently found that petitioner's contentions met the burden and that the testatrix clearly considered the bequest a specific one.

Without a doubt, the trial justice properly interpreted the McGee grandchildren's bequest, primarily because of the tone of the other provisions, the tenor of the entire instrument, see Hanley v. Fernell, 54 R.I. at 86, 170 A. at 89; Gardner v. Viall, 36 R.I. 436, 90 A. 760 (1914), and the specificity with which the testatrix described that portion of the twelfth clause relative to the Texaco stock. Additionally, money payable out of a fund rather than out of the estate generally described with sufficient accuracy and satisfiable only out of the payment of such fund, Haslam v. de Alvarez, or a bequest of money deposited in a specific bank, Hanley v. Fernell, is, as a rule, a specific legacy. When a will bequeaths "the money owned by one which is on deposit" in a designated bank, although the amount remains unspecified, the gift is nevertheless identifiable and definite, apart from all other funds or property in the testator's estate; and the legacy is specific. Willis v. Barrow, 218 Ala. 549, 552, 119 So. 678, 680 (1929); Prendergast v. Walsh, 58 N.J.Eq. 149, 42 A. 1049 (Ch.1899). Despite the fact that Mrs. McGee did not name any particular bank in the twelfth clause of her will, she bequeathed all the money in her name "in any bank." In view of the fact that she expected all of her money remaining at her death to go to her grandchildren and, further, the money to be payable from a particular source that is, accounts in her name in banking institutions we conclude that the legacy was sufficiently susceptible of identification to render it a specific one.

Accordingly, since the bequest to the grandchildren is specific, we must now determine whether or not it was adeemed by the purchase of the bonds. Note, Ademption and the Testator's Intent, 74 Harv.L.Rev. 741 (1961). In connection with the early theory of ademption, the courts looked to the intention of the testator as the basis of their decisions. 6 Page, *supra* § 54.14 at 265. But ever since the landmark case of Ashburner v. MacGuire, 2 Bro.C.C. 108, 29 Eng.Rep. 62 (Ch.1786), wherein Lord Thurlow enunciated the "modern theory," courts have utilized the identity doctrine or "in specie" test. This test focuses on two questions only: (1) whether the gift is a specific legacy and, if it is, (2) whether it is found in the estate at the time of the testator's death. Atkinson, *supra* § 134 at 742; Note, 74 Harv.L.Rev. at 742; Comment, Ademption in Iowa—A Closer Look at the Testator's Intent, 57 Iowa L. Rev. 1211 (1972). The extinction of the property bequeathed works an ademption regardless of the testator's intent. In re Tillinghast, 23 R.I. 121, 123–24, 49 A. 634, 635 (1901); Humphreys v. Humphreys, 2 Cox Ch. 184, 30 Eng.Rep. 85 (Ch.1789); 6 Page, *supra* § 54.15 at 266.

The legatees of the twelfth clause argue that the subject matter of the specific bequest, although apparently now unidentifiable in its previous form, actually does exist in the estate of their grandmother but in another form as the result of an exchange or transfer of the original property. But there is a recognized distinction between a bequest of a particular item and a gift of its proceeds, see generally Annot., 45 A.L.R.3d 10 (1972); and the testatrix, in the instant case, did recognize the distinction in the twelfth clause of her will by bequeathing the Texaco stock "or the proceeds thereof from a sale of same" but omitting to include similar provisions regarding proceeds in connection with the language immediately following which described the bank-money legacy. It appears that the testatrix's intention, manifest on the face of her will, was that her grandchildren receive only the money in her bank accounts and not the money's proceeds or the investments that represent the conversion of that money into other holdings. Atkinson, *supra* § 134 at 743–44; 6 Page, *supra* § 54.9 at 256–57, § 54.16 at 268–70; see Gardner v. McNeal, 117 Md. 27, 82 A. 988 (1911).

In accordance with the generally accepted "form and substance rule," a substantial change in the nature or character of the subject matter of a bequest will operate as an ademption; but a merely nominal or formal change will not. In re Peirce, 25 R.I. 34, 54 A. 588 (1903) (no ademption since transfer of stock after consolidation of banks without formal liquidation was exchange and not sale); Willis v. Barrow, 218 Ala. 549, 119 So. 678 (1929) (no ademption by transfer of money from named bank to another since place of deposit was merely descriptive); In re Hall, 60 N.J.Super. 597, 160 A.2d 49 (1960) (no ademption by transfer of the money from banks designated in will to another one since location was formal description only and did not affect substance of testamentary gift).

Since the money previously on deposit in Mrs. McGee's bank accounts no longer exists at the time of her death, the question arises whether the change was one of form only, rather than substance. We have determined that the change effected by Richard was not merely formal but was substantial. There is no language in the will that can be construed as reflecting an intention of the testatrix to bequeath a gift of bond investments to her grandchildren. The plain and explicit direction of the twelfth clause of the will is that they should receive whatever remained in her bank accounts at the time of her death. Since no sums of money were then on deposit, the specific legacy was adeemed. Clearly, this case is dissimilar to those in which the fund, at all times kept intact, is transferred to a different location, as in *Willis* and *Prendergast*, where the money merely "changed hands," not character. See also In re Tillinghast, 23 R.I. 121, 49 A. 634 (1901) (no ademption by mere act of transferring mortgages to own name since they were in specie at the time of testatrix's death). The fact that Mrs. McGee did not herself purchase the bonds is not significant. Disposal or distribution of the subject matter of a bequest by an agent of the testator or with the testator's authorization or ratification similarly operates to adeem the legacy. Gardner v. McNeal, 117 Md. 27, 82 A. 988 (1911); In re Wright, 7 N.Y.2d 365, 165 N.E.2d 561, 197 N.Y.S.2d 711 (1960); Glasscock v. Layle, 21 Ky.Law.Rep. 860, 53 S.W. 270 (Ky.1899). * * *

Accordingly, we hold that the trial justice erred in allowing the admission of extrinsic evidence regarding Mrs. McGee's intent. We further hold that the specific legacy in the twelfth clause of the testatrix's will is adeemed and the legatees' claim to this bequest is thereby barred. We direct the trial justice to order the petitioner to satisfy the general pecuniary legacy bequeathed in the eleventh clause of the will from the sale of the flower bonds, with the excess to pass under the residuary (fourteenth) clause of the will.

The respondent's appeal is sustained, the judgment below is reversed, and the cause is remanded to the Superior Court for proceedings consistent with this opinion.

Wasserman v. Cohen

Supreme Judicial Court of Massachusetts, 1993
414 Mass. 172, 606 N.E.2d 901

LYNCH, Justice.

This appeal raises the question whether the doctrine of ademption by extinction applies to a specific gift of real estate contained in a revocable *inter vivos* trust. The plaintiff, Elaine Wasserman, brought an action for declaratory judgment in the Middlesex Division of the Probate and Family Court against the defendant, David E. Cohen (trustee), as he is the surviving trustee of a trust established by Frieda M. Drapkin (Drapkin). In her complaint the plaintiff requested that the trustee be ordered to pay her the proceeds of the sale of an apartment building which, under the trust, would have been conveyed to the plaintiff had it not been sold by Drapkin prior to her death. Pursuant to the trustee's motion to dismiss under Mass.R.Civ.P. 12(b)(6), 365 Mass. 754 (1974), the probate judge dismissed the action. The plaintiff appealed. We granted the plaintiff's application for direct appellate review and now affirm.

1. We summarize the relevant facts. Frieda Drapkin created the Joseph and Frieda Drapkin Memorial Trust (trust) in December, 1982, naming herself both settlor and trustee. She funded the trust with "certain property" delivered on the date of execution, and retained the right to add property by *inter vivos* transfer and by will. Drapkin also reserved the right to receive and to direct the payment of income or principal during her lifetime, to amend or to revoke the trust, and to withdraw property from the trust. On her death, the trustee was directed to distribute the property as set out in the trust. The trustee was ordered to convey to the plaintiff "12-14 Newton Street, Waltham, Massachusetts, Apartment Building, (consisting of approximately 11,296 square feet)."

When she executed the trust, Drapkin held record title to the property at 12-14 Newton Street in Waltham, as trustee of Z.P.Q. Realty Trust. However, she sold the property on September 29, 1988, for $575,000, and had never conveyed her interest in the property to the trust. * * *

Drapkin died on March 28, 1989. Her will, dated December 26, 1982, devised all property in her residuary estate to the trust to be disposed of in accordance with the trust's provisions.

2. The plaintiff first contends that the probate judge erred in failing to consider Drapkin's intent in regard to the gift when she sold the property. We disagree.

We have long adhered to the rule that, when a testator disposes, during his lifetime, of the subject of a specific legacy or devise in his will, that legacy or devise is held to be adeemed, "whatever may have been the intent or motive of the testator in doing so." Walsh v. Gillespie, 338 Mass. 278, 280, 154 N.E.2d 906 (1959), quoting Richards v. Humphreys, 15 Pick. 133, 135 (1833). Baybank Harvard Trust Co. v. Grant, 23 Mass. App.Ct. 653, 655, 504 N.E.2d 1072 (1987). The focus is on the actual existence or nonexistence of the bequeathed property, and not on the intent of the testator with respect to it. Bostwick v. Hurstel, 364 Mass. 282, 295, 304 N.E.2d 186 (1973). To be effective, a specific legacy or devise must be in existence and owned by the testator at the time of his death. Moffatt v. Heon, 242 Mass. 201, 203–204, 136 N.E. 123 (1922). Baybank Harvard Trust Co. v. Grant, *supra*.

The plaintiff asks us to abandon the doctrine of ademption. She contends that, because the doctrine ignores the testator's intent, it produces harsh and inequitable results and thus fosters litigation that the rule was intended to preclude. See Note, Ademption and the Testator's Intent, 74 Harv.L.Rev. 741 (1961). This rule has been followed in this Commonwealth for nearly 160 years. See Richards v. Humphreys, *supra*. Whatever else may be said about it, it is easily understood and applied by draftsmen, testators, and fiduciaries. The doctrine seeks to give effect to a testator's probable intent by presuming he intended to extinguish a specific gift of property when he disposed of that property prior to his death. As with any rule, exceptions have emerged.[3] These limited exceptions do not lead us to the abandonment of the rule. Its so-called harsh results can be easily avoided by careful draftsmanship and its existence must be recognized by any competent practitioner. When we consider the myriad of instruments drafted in reliance on its application, we conclude that stability in the field of trusts and estates requires that we continue the doctrine.

---

3. This court has created two exceptions to the "identity" theory. In Walsh v. Gillespie, 338 Mass. 278, 154 N.E.2d 906 (1959), a conservator appointed for the testatrix five years after her will was executed sold shares of stock that were the subject of a specific legacy. The court held that the sale did not operate as an ademption as to the unexpended balance remaining in the hands of the conservator at the death of the testatrix. *Id.* at 284, 154 N.E.2d 906. In Bostwick v. Hurstel, 364 Mass. 282, 304 N.E.2d 186 (1973), a conservator had sold, then repurchased, stock that was the subject of a specific legacy and that had been split twice, before the death of the testatrix. The court held that the bequest of stock was not adeemed but emphasized, "we do not violate our rule that 'identity' and not 'intent' governs ademption cases." *Id.* at 296, 304 N.E.2d 186. See Baybank Harvard Trust Co. v. Grant, 23 Mass.App.Ct. 653, 655, 504 N.E.2d 1072 (1987).

3. The plaintiff also argues that deciding ademption questions based on a determination that a devise is general or specific is overly formalistic and fails to serve the testator's likely intent. She maintains that the court in Bostwick v. Hurstel, *supra,* moved away from making such classifications. In *Bostwick,* the court held that a gift of stock was not adeemed where the stock had been sold and repurchased prior to the death of the testatrix, and where it had been subject to two stock splits. However, the court confined the holding specifically to its facts. * * * See Bostwick v. Hurstel, *supra* at 294–295, 304 N.E.2d 186. In addition, the court stated: "Our holding does not indicate that we have abandoned the classification of bequests as general or specific for all purposes. We have no occasion at this time to express any opinion on the continuing validity of such distinctions in those cases where abatement or ademption of the legacy is at issue. . . ." *Id.* at 292, 304 N.E.2d 186. * * * We now have such an occasion, and we hold that, at least in regard to the conveyance of real estate at issue here, the practice of determining whether a devise is general or specific is the proper first step in deciding questions of ademption.

4. We have held that a trust, particularly when executed as part of a comprehensive estate plan, should be construed according to the same rules traditionally applied to wills. See Second Bank-State St. Trust Co. v. Pinion, 341 Mass. 366, 371, 170 N.E.2d 350 (1960) (doctrine of independent legal significance applied to pour-over trusts); Clymer v. Mayo, 393 Mass. 754, 473 N.E.2d 1084 (1985) (G.L. c. 191, § 9, which revokes dispositions made in will to former spouses on divorce or annulment, applied to trust executed along with will as part of comprehensive estate plan). In Clymer v. Mayo, *supra* at 766, 473 N.E.2d 1084, we reasoned that "[t]reating the components of the decedent's estate plan separately, and not as parts of an interrelated whole, brings about inconsistent results." We also quoted one commentator who wrote, "The subsidiary rules [of wills] are the product of centuries of legal experience in attempting to discern transferors' wishes and suppress litigation. These rules should be treated presumptively correct for will substitutes as well as for wills." *Id.* at 768, 473 N.E.2d 1084, quoting Langbien, The Nonprobate Revolution and the Future of the Law of Succession, 97 Harv.L.Rev. 1108, 1136–1137 (1984). We agree with this reasoning. As discussed above, the doctrine of ademption has a "long established recognition" in Massachusetts. See Second Bank-State St. Trust Co. v. Pinion, *supra,* 341 Mass. at 371, 170 N.E.2d 350. Furthermore, Drapkin created the trust along with her will as part of a comprehensive estate plan. Under the residuary clause of her will, Drapkin gave the majority of her estate to the trustee, who was then to dispose of the property on her death according to the terms of the trust. We see no reason to apply a different rule because she conveyed the property under the terms of the trust, rather than her will. Thus, we conclude that the doctrine of ademption, as traditionally applied to wills, should also apply to the trust in the instant case.

5. *Conclusion.* Since the plaintiff does not contest that the devise of 12-14 Newton Street was a specific devise, * * * it follows that the devise was adeemed by the act of Drapkin.

So ordered.

Uniform Probate Code (2019)

§ 2-606. Nonademption of Specific Devises; Unpaid Proceeds of Sale, Condemnation, or Insurance; Sale by Conservator or Agent.

(a) A specific devisee has a right to specifically devised property in the testator's estate at the testator's death and to:

(1) any balance of the purchase price, together with any security agreement, owed by a purchaser at the testator's death by reason of sale of the property;

(2) any amount of a condemnation award for the taking of the property unpaid at death;

(3) any proceeds unpaid at death on fire or casualty insurance on or other recovery for injury to the property;

(4) any property owned by the testator at death and acquired as a result of foreclosure, or obtained in lieu of foreclosure, of the security interest for a specifically devised obligation;

(5) any real property or tangible personal property owned by the testator at death which the testator acquired as a replacement for specifically devised real property or tangible personal property; and

(6) if not covered by paragraphs (1) through (5), a pecuniary devise equal to the value as of its date of disposition of other specifically devised property disposed of during the testator's lifetime but only to the extent it is established that ademption would be inconsistent with the testator's manifested plan of distribution or that at the time the will was made, the date of disposition or otherwise, the testator did not intend ademption of the devise.

(b) If specifically devised property is sold or mortgaged by a conservator or by an agent acting within the authority of a durable power of attorney for an incapacitated principal, or a condemnation award, insurance proceeds, or recovery for injury to the property is paid to a conservator or to an agent acting within the authority of a durable power of attorney for an incapacitated principal, the specific devisee has the right to a general pecuniary devise equal to the net sale price, the amount of the unpaid loan, the condemnation award, the insurance proceeds, or the recovery.

(c) The right of a specific devisee under subsection (b) is reduced by any right the devisee has under subsection (a).

(d) For the purposes of the references in subsection (b) to a conservator, subsection (b) does not apply if, after the sale, mortgage, condemnation, casualty, or recovery, it was adjudicated that the testator's incapacity ceased and the testator survived the adjudication for at least one year.

(e) For the purposes of the references in subsection (b) to an agent acting within the authority of a durable power of attorney for an incapacitated principal, (i) "incapacitated principal" means a principal who is an incapacitated person, (ii) no adjudication of incapacity before death is necessary, and (iii) the acts of an agent within the authority of a durable power of attorney are presumed to be for an incapacitated principal.

§ 2-605. Increase in Securities; Accessions.

(a) If a testator executes a will that devises securities and the testator then owned securities that meet the description in the will, the devise includes additional securities owned by the testator at death to the extent the additional securities were acquired by the testator after the will was executed as a result of the testator's ownership of the described securities and are securities of any of the following types:

    (1) securities of the same organization acquired by reason of action initiated by the organization or any successor, related, or acquiring organization, excluding any acquired by exercise of purchase options;

    (2) securities of another organization acquired as a result of a merger, consolidation, reorganization, or other distribution by the organization or any successor, related, or acquiring organization; or

    (3) securities of the same organization acquired as a result of a plan of reinvestment.

(b) Distributions in cash before death with respect to a described security are not part of the devise.

Problem

Decedent executed a valid Last Will and Testament on September 14, 1992. This will contained the following bequest: "I hereby give, devise, and bequeath any recovery or settlement which I may receive as a result of a railroad injury to be divided equally between my wife and my son." Nonetheless, on September 9, 1993, the decedent received a railroad settlement of $650,000 for personal injuries he had suffered. After attorney's fees and costs were satisfied, the decedent received the remaining $459,307.14, which the decedent invested in real estate, automobiles, and gifts for his friends. Then, on April 1, 1994, the decedent died of injuries sustained in a car accident.

On April 27, 1994, the personal representative for the estate filed a petition for probate of will and issuance of letters. Decedent's wife argued that the railroad settlement was adeemed by extinction and that, therefore, the division between her and the decedent's son was void. The son argues that there was no ademption and that the court can easily trace the money received into the assets subsequently purchased by the decedent. Was the settlement adeemed by extinction? *See In re* Estate of Warman, 682 N.E.2d 557 (Ind. Ct. App. 1997).

B. Ademption by Satisfaction

Uniform Probate Code (2019)

§ 2-609. Ademption by Satisfaction.

(a) Property a testator gave in his [or her] lifetime to a person is treated as a satisfaction of a devise in whole or in part, only if (i) the will provides for deduction of the gift, (ii) the testator declared in a contemporaneous writing that the gift is in satisfaction of the devise or that its value is to be deducted from the value of the devise, or (iii) the devisee acknowledged in writing that the gift is in satisfaction of the devise or that its value is to be deducted from the value of the devise.

(b) For purposes of partial satisfaction, property given during lifetime is valued as of the time the devisee came into possession or enjoyment of the property or at the testator's death, whichever occurs first.

(c) If the devisee fails to survive the testator, the gift is treated as a full or partial satisfaction of the devise, as appropriate, in applying Sections 2-603 and 2-604, unless the testator's contemporaneous writing provides otherwise.

Tax Considerations: Bequests and devises made within a valid Last Will and Testament or intestate succession (the probate estate) exclude assets passing through will substitutes (non-probate transfers). Thus, excluded are items such as joint tenancies, *inter vivos* powers of appointment, life insurance, and other payable on death contracts. Nonetheless, because these items are property owned at death, even though not passing through a Last Will and Testament, they are includable within the decedent's gross estate for federal estate tax purposes. *See* I.R.C. §§ 2031–2046. On the other hand, the tax ramifications of making an irrevocable transfer during lifetime involve gift taxes, which are described as part of the larger transfer tax scheme at Internal Revenue Code § 2001. Presently, there is a $14,000 annual exclusion for gifts to each donee. *See* Rev. Proc. 2009-50, 2009-45 I.R.B. 617. To qualify for the annual exclusion, the gift must be a gift of a present interest in the property transferred, which generally is defined as an "unrestricted right to the immediate use, possession, or enjoyment of property or the income from property." *See* 26 C.F.R. § 25.2503-3(b) (2010). The $14,000 annual exclusion per donee is doubled if the gift is made by two spouses. *See* 26 C.F.R. § 25.2513–1 (2016).

C. Exoneration of Debts

Uniform Probate Code (2019)

§ 2-607. Nonexoneration.

A specific devise passes subject to any mortgage interest existing at the date of death, without right of exoneration, regardless of a general directive in the will to pay debts.

Tax Considerations: In the event that exoneration applies, and, indeed, any time the estate is called upon to pay taxes or other expenses associated with probate, such as the spouse's elective share, the liability for these expenses should be apportioned among the estate's beneficiaries. Not to apportion the expenses will exhaust the residuary estate, defeat the intent of the testator, and burden estate administration. Integration of the probate and non-probate (will substitute) transfers is the difficult dilemma. The following decision is illustrative.

In re Valma M. Hanson Revocable Trust

Indiana Court of Appeals, 2002
779 N.E.2d 1218

KIRSCH, Judge.

Barry C. Bergstrom, Trustee of the Valma M. Hanson Revocable Trust ("Trust"), brings this interlocutory appeal of the trial court's order denying his motion to dismiss the action filed by Elizabeth Hanson and Bonnie Kuczkowski ("Petitioners") wherein they allege that Bergstrom had violated the terms of the Trust in his administration thereof. The issue Bergstrom presents upon appeal is whether the trial court erred in denying his motion to dismiss for failure to state a claim upon which relief can be granted.

We affirm.

* * *

On December 2, 1983, in Illinois, Valma Hanson executed an instrument that established the Trust. Hanson named herself as the original Trustee, but later she named Bergstrom as Trustee by amendment in 1992. Article Five of the Trust instrument directed the Trustee to pay the various taxes payable upon her death. Article Eight created a separate "Trust B" and directed that after her death, Trust B of the "Trust as then constituted" was to be divided and distributed pursuant to the provisions of "Schedule 'C'" of the Trust. Appellant's Appendix at 24. Schedule C, as amended in 1992, stated that the "Trust Estate as provided in Article Eight shall be divided and distributed" upon her death "as follows: 1. SPECIFIC DEVISE OF REAL ESTATE " then held in the Trust Estate was bequeathed to Bergstrom, and "2. . . . the balance of the assets included in the Trust Estate as constituted" was to be divided according to specified percentages among nine individuals[1] and one church. Appellant's Appendix at 47. The Trust instrument also specified that the "Trust Agreement and the trusts created hereby shall be construed, regulated and governed by and in accordance with the laws of the State of Illinois." Appellant's Appendix at 33.

On March 31, 1992, Hanson executed a last will and testament. In Article I of her will, she bequeathed all of her personal property to Bergstrom. In Article II, she exercised her testamentary power of appointment over the principal assets that were held in Trust A from her late husband's revocable trust to appoint Bergstrom and bequeath those assets to him. In Article III, the will provided the "GIFT OF RESIDUE TO TRUST," whereby "all the residue of [her] estate" was "give[n] and devise[d]" to Trust B of her Trust. Appellant's Appendix at 85. The will named Bergstrom as executor thereof. Also, the will stated that Hanson was "a resident of

---

1. One of the individuals named as a residuary beneficiary was Bergstrom with a 25% share indicated.

Lake County, Indiana," and the will was to be "construed and interpreted under the laws of the State of which I am now a resident." Appellant's Appendix at 85, 88.

Hanson died on December 1, 1998. Indiana inheritance tax and Federal estate tax returns were filed, and the taxes and expenses were paid from the residuary assets of Trust B. Bergstrom allocated the payment of the taxes and expenses exclusively to the non-real estate assets in Schedule C and did not assess a contribution against the balance of the assets in Trust B, which included the devise of realty to Bergstrom. After Bergstrom had distributed to himself the real estate held by Hanson at the time of her death and paid the taxes and expenses, no property was available for those identified to receive the specified percentage shares of "the balance of the assets" in Trust B. Appellant's Appendix at 47.

On behalf of the residuary beneficiaries other than Bergstrom, the instant petition was filed, asserting that as Trustee, Bergstrom had violated the terms of the Trust by failing to apportion the federal estate tax and Indiana inheritance tax against all the property in Trust B.[2] Petitioners asked that the Trust be docketed concerning "all issues with respect to the accounting and distribution of assets within the Trust," Appellant's Appendix at 16, while also seeking the removal of Bergstrom and payment of attorney's fees.

Bergstrom filed a motion to dismiss, arguing that the petition failed to state a claim upon which relief could be granted. Specifically, Bergstrom contended that (1) the terms of the Trust authorized the payment of death taxes to be made at his discretion as Trustee, and (2) Indiana's statute on the apportionment of federal estate taxes was "inapplicable . . . because the trust agreement specifies the application of Illinois law, which has no similar rule on apportionment." Appellant's Appendix at 72. The trial court denied Bergstrom's motion to dismiss, finding that the petition "states a claim on which relief can be granted because the Trust Agreement, as amended, should not be interpreted to permit payment of all death taxes from the residuary of the Trust." Appellant's Appendix at 7–8.

* * *

Bergstrom argues that the motion to dismiss should have been granted because the Trust instrument itself authorized his discretion in the payment of estate and inheritance taxes. The provision he relies upon is Article Five of the Trust, which as amended, reads as follows:

DISCRETIONARY PROVISIONS FOR TRUSTEE TO DEAL WITH SETTLOR'S ESTATE AND MAKE PAYMENTS OF DEBTS AND TAXES

After the Settlor's death, the Trustee, if in its discretion it deems it advisable, may pay all or any part of the Settlor's funeral expenses, legally enforceable

---

2. In their appellate brief, Petitioners assert that they "also raised issues which are related to the accuracy and completeness of the accounting of Bergstrom." Appellee's Brief at 9. However, they do not direct us to any such assertions in their petition, and we find only the assertion that he failed to apportion taxes.

claims against the Settlor or her estate, reasonable expenses of administration of her estate, any allowances by court order to those dependent upon the Settlor, *any estate, inheritance, succession, death or similar taxes payable by reason of the Settlor's death*, together with any interest thereon or other additions thereto, without reimbursement from the Settlor's executor or administrator, from any beneficiary of insurance upon the Settlor's life, or from any other person. *All such payments*, except of interest, *shall be charged generally against the principal of the Trust Estate includable in the Settlor's estate for Federal estate tax purposes* and any interest so paid shall be charged generally against the income thereof, provided, however, *any such payments of estate, inheritance, succession, death or similar taxes shall be charged against the principal constituting Trust B* and any interest so paid shall be charged against the income thereof. . . .

Appellant's Appendix at 39–40 (emphasis added).

Petitioners argue that because this Trust provision specifically directs that taxes are payable *generally* from the principal of Trust B, and the real estate distributed to Bergstrom was a part of the principal of the Trust, that real estate must not be excluded from being subject to the payment of a share of the estate taxes.[3] Petitioners further assert that "[t]he intent of Hanson in her Trust is clear on its face" and requires apportionment across all of the assets in Trust B. Appellees' Brief at 8. We agree.

Petitioners note that "both Indiana and Illinois law recognize the legal proposition that in construing a trust, the prime goal is to determine the settlor's intent by first looking at the plain language of the document." Appellant's Brief at 10. If the settlor's intent is clear from the plain language of instrument, and not against public policy, then we must honor the settlor's intent. Appellant's Brief at 10. Indeed, we have said that the primary objective "in interpreting a trust is to determine the intent of the settlor," which is an "age-old proposition." Matter of Fitton, 605 N.E.2d 1164, 1169 (Ind.Ct.App.1992). We must ascertain the settlor's intent and "give effect to" that intent. Ind. Dep't of State Revenue v. Nichols, 659 N.E.2d 694, 699 (Ind. Tax 1995). We examine the trust document as a whole to determine "the plain and unambiguous purpose of the settlor" as that intent appears "within the 'four corners' of the trust document." *Id.* (citations omitted). When interpreting a trust, we "must look to the language used in the instrument." Stowers v. Norwest Bank Indiana, 624 N.E.2d 485, 489 (Ind.Ct.App.1993), trans. denied (1995). Our determination of the settlor's intent based upon unambiguous trust document terms is a question of law. *Id.* Indiana's Trust Code provides that its rules of law are to "be interpreted and applied to the terms of the trust so as to implement the intent of the settlor and the purposes of the trust." IC 30-4-1-3. "If the rules of law and the terms

---

3. In their brief to the trial court opposing the motion to dismiss and in their appellate brief, Petitioners asserted that the expenses of administration should also have been so apportioned. However, no such assertion was presented to the trial court in Petitioners' amended petition for docketing of the Trust. See Appellant's Appendix at 12–16.

of the trust conflict, the terms of the trust shall control unless the rules of law clearly prohibit or restrict the article which the terms of the trust purport to authorize." *Id.*

The trust language authorizes the Trustee, in its discretion, to pay the various taxes due upon the settlor's death by charging them *generally* against the principal of the Trust Estate that was included in the settlor's estate for Federal estate tax purposes. "Principal" is defined as "the corpus or main body of an estate . . . distinguished from income." WEBSTER'S THIRD INT'L DICTIONARY 1802 (1976). Hence, the "balance of the assets," which the Trust directed to be distributed by percentage to the Petitioners, was part of the principal of the Trust Estate. Here, the principal of Trust B as shown on the federal estate tax return filed by Bergstrom consists of a Trust value of $1,027,351.00 and includes real estate valued at $388,046.00, which Bergstom passed to himself without any contribution for payment of taxes and expenses. Bergstrom paid taxes, including federal estate tax and Indiana inheritance tax, in the amount of $228,412.31 without assessing a proportionate share against each beneficiary's distribution. He specifically failed to allocate payment of the taxes to the balance of the assets in Trust B, which included the real estate.

As the primary beneficiary, Bergstrom inherited over three-quarters of a million dollars after taxes, while the other named beneficiaries received nothing. We are left with the sense that Bergstrom had an irreconcilable conflict of interest and that paying the taxes from the assets set aside for the other beneficiaries thwarted Hanson's testamentary intent that they share in her estate.[4] The Trust specified a number of gifts to nine individuals and a church and if Hanson had intended Bergstrom to be the sole beneficiary (the net effect of non-apportionment), she could easily have stated this in the instrument. She made her intent clear by specifically stating that the taxes be charged *generally* against the principal of the Trust included in her estate. The principal included the real estate, and taxes paid from the trust were to be charged against it as is the case with the non-real property assets.

Bergstrom argues that we should be guided by Illinois law because Hanson specified the application of Illinois law in her Trust. Illinois has not adopted an apportionment rule. In Estate of Maierhofer, 328 Ill.App.3d 987, 989, 263 Ill.Dec. 124, 767 N.E.2d 850, 852 (2002), the Appellate Court of Illinois most recently affirmed that Illinois does not follow "the principle of equitable apportionment"[5] *when the instrument is silent as to the source of probate tax payment.* Rather, "the burden on the residue rule" — that "taxes, debts and expenses of administration attributable to probate assets are borne by the residuary estate *in the absence of a contrary indication in the [instrument]"* — is the rule for "estate tax liability in Illinois." *Id.* at 990,

---

4. Most egregious is the fact that the share set aside for the United Methodist Church was utilized to pay death taxes notwithstanding the fact that it is a charitable donation exempt from such taxes and that it appears Bergstrom took a deduction on the federal estate tax return for the gift.

5. The Illinois court explained that equitable apportionment "is a term used to describe the process of distributing the burden of estate expenses among beneficiaries in the same proportion they cause such expenses to be incurred." 328 Ill.App.3d at 990, 263 Ill.Dec. 124, 767 N.E.2d at 852.

263 Ill.Dec. 124, 767 N.E.2d at 853. The Illinois court noted that "courts of this state have consistently applied the burden on the residue rule," a rule that "Illinois lawyers have long relied on," with countless instruments "drafted on this assumption." *Id.* at 990, 263 Ill.Dec. 124, 767 N.E.2d at 852 (citations omitted).

Contrary to Bergstrom's argument, because the intent of the settlor is clear from the language of the trust instrument, we conclude that apportioning the payment of taxes across all of the assets in Trust B, not just those going to the remaining beneficiaries, is consistent with Illinois law that payment should be from the residuary estate "in the absence of a contrary indication." *Id.* at 989, 263 Ill.Dec. 124, 767 N.E.2d at 852. Bergstrom's argument must fail because it ignores the plain language used by Hanson herself concerning payment of the taxes.

Based upon the language of the Trust instrument, we find that Petitioners have stated a set of facts and circumstances that can support the relief they requested. Consequently, the trial court did not err in denying Bergstrom's motion to dismiss.

Affirmed.

BROOK, C.J., concurs.

DARDEN, J., dissents with separate opinion.

DARDEN, Judge, dissenting.

I must respectfully disagree with the majority's conclusion that the trust instrument expressed the clear intent that the payment of taxes be apportioned "across all of the assets in Trust B." Slip Op. at 9. In my opinion, the trust instrument expressed Hanson's clear intent that it be entirely a matter of the Trustee's discretion as to what assets constituting the principal of her estate would be utilized to pay taxes. Although I am more than willing to acknowledge that the result of the Trustee's exercise of that discretion can be seen as inequitable when the Petitioners had been named as potential residuary beneficiaries, I cannot turn a blind eye to the unambiguous language of the trust instrument written by Hanson.[6]

As the majority notes, the trust instrument authorizes the Trustee, in its discretion, to pay the various taxes owing upon the settlor's death from the principal of the Trust Estate that was included in the settlor's estate for Federal estate tax purposes. However, in my opinion, that is exactly what happened. "Principal" is defined as "the corpus or main body of an estate ... distinguished from income." WEBSTER'S THIRD INT'L DICTIONARY (1976) p. 1802. Hence, the "balance of the assets," which (after the specific devise of real estate to Bergstrom) the Trust directed to be distributed by percentage to the Petitioners, was part of the principal of the Trust Estate.

---

6. It is worth noting that there is no assertion that undue influence or fraud induced Hanson in her drafting of the trust instrument; nor do Petitioners claim a lack of capacity on the part of Hanson. I am also mindful of the effect of time — from when Hanson drafted the trust instrument until her death — on the total assets remaining at the time of her death, both as to her need to use resources for her own maintenance and the fluctuation of the value of equities in her estate based on market forces.

If Hanson had desired that the Trustee pay the taxes by assessing a proportionate share against each beneficiary's distribution—the real estate specifically devised to Bergstrom as well as the Petitioners' shares—she could have written the trust instrument to so state. For example, the Trust could have provided that the tax payments by the Trustee should be "charged generally, in shares proportionate to the respective beneficiaries' distributions, against the principal of the Trust Estate. . . ." However, by the clear language she used in the trust instrument, Hanson did not direct the Trustee to apportion among the beneficiaries the tax burden owing upon her death.

Absent such a specific direction upon the part of Hanson, I would next consider the fact that Hanson specified the application of Illinois law. As the majority notes, Indiana's Trust Code provides that its rules of law are to "be interpreted and applied to the terms of the trust so as to implement the intent of the settlor and the purposes of the trust." See Ind.Code § 30-4-1-3. "If the rules of law and the terms of the trust conflict, the terms of the trust shall control unless the rules of law clearly prohibit or restrict the article which the terms of the trust purport to authorize." *Id.* Petitioners direct us to no authority that would prohibit Hanson, as settlor, from specifying the application of Illinois law in the administration of her trust. Consequently, because it was her intent that Illinois law apply, I would turn to the law of that state and its application to the terms of the Trust.

In Estate of Maierhofer, 328 Ill.App.3d 987, 989, 263 Ill.Dec. 124, 767 N.E.2d 850, 852 (2002), the Appellate Court of Illinois most recently affirmed that Illinois does not follow "the principle of equitable apportionment" when the instrument is silent as to source of probate tax payment. Rather, "the burden on the residue rule" is the rule for "estate tax liability in Illinois." 328 Ill.App.3d at 989, 990, 767 N.E.2d at 852, 853. The Illinois court noted that its courts "have consistently applied the burden on the residue rule," a rule that "Illinois lawyers have long relied on," with countless instruments "drafted on this assumption." 328 Ill.App.3d at 990, 767 N.E.2d at 852 (citations omitted). Therefore, the fact that as Trustee, Bergstrom used the discretion given to him to pay the death taxes from the residuary estate[7] is not only consistent with the terms of the Trust, but it is consistent with Illinois law that payment should be from the residuary estate "in the absence of a contrary indication." 328 Ill.App.3d at 989, 767 N.E.2d at 852.

The Petitioners also argued to the trial court that Indiana law should apply because Hanson executed her will in Indiana, her real and personal property were located in Indiana, and she was a resident of Indiana at the time of her death. However, I would also find this argument to fail because it ignores the plain language used in the will by Hanson concerning payment of the taxes.

Indiana law provides that federal estate taxes "shall be" apportioned "among all" of the estate's beneficiaries "unless" the decedent has "otherwise" directed in the

---

7. BLACK's defines "residuary estate" as "[t]he part of a decedent's estate remaining after all debts, expenses, taxes, and specific bequests and devises have been satisfied." BLACK's LAW DICTIONARY 569 (7th ed. 1999).

will. Ind.Code § 29-2-12-2. Hanson's will directed that taxes "payable by reason of [her] death" be paid "out of the principal of [her] residuary estate." (App. 86). Under Hanson's will, the principal of her "residuary estate" can be read to be either (1) all of Trust B or (2) the "balance of the assets" to be distributed to Petitioners after the specific devise of real estate to Bergstrom. Under either interpretation, the payment of taxes by Bergstrom does comport with the specific direction of Hanson's will that taxes be paid from the residuary estate, and the statute does not dictate a contrary result.[8] Consistent with the statute, I would find that the Trust directed the Trustee to make the tax payment from the principal — and, as previously noted, that is what I find Bergstrom to have done.

Based upon the language of the Trust instrument and of Hanson's will, it appears to me that the Petitioners have stated a set of facts and circumstances that cannot support the relief they requested; therefore, I believe Bergstrom's motion to dismiss should have been granted.

VII. Lapse

Ademption by extinction concerns an item of *property* lost or transferred between the execution of the Last Will and Testament and the effective date of the will, at the death of the testator; lapse has another focus. The doctrine of lapse concerns a *human person* who dies prior to the effective date of the will, and that person leaves descendants surviving. Thus, if a valid will is executed in the year 2000 and contains the phrase: "One million dollars to my sister, Sadie," and Sadie dies in 2002 with the will being probated at the death of the testator in 2005, the bequest to Sadie could be said to "lapse" because you cannot give property to a dead person. If it does lapse, then the bequest may pass to an alternate legatee, the residuary estate, or the decedent's intestate estate. Is this what was intended by the testator? Or should the state make some allowance for any perceived lack of clarity on the part of the testator and provide a substitution for the testator's intent? This entire chapter has provided examples of substitutions for testators' intent. The following case illustrates how a state anti-lapse statute substitutes for testators' intent, and the sections that follow explore attendant issues.

Estate of Kehler

Supreme Court of Pennsylvania, 1980
488 Pa. 165, 411 A.2d 748

ROBERTS, Justice.

Testator, Emerson Kehler, died in April of 1975. By paragraph THIRD of his will, he disposed of the residue of his estate:

---

8. The statute specifies that for apportionment purposes, the term "will" includes a trust. I.C. § 29-2-12-1.5.

> All the rest, residue and remainder of my estate, real, personal and mixed, of whatsoever nature and wheresoever situated, I give, devise and bequeath unto my brother, RALPH KEHLER, of Reading, Pennsylvania, and my sisters, VIOLA WELKER, of Lavelle, Pennsylvania, ADA SHARTEL, of Reading, Pennsylvania, and GERTRUDE KRAPF, of Stroudsburg, Pennsylvania, and to the survivor or survivors of them, equally, share and share alike, to have and to hold unto themselves, their heirs and assigns forever.

Ralph Kehler predeceased testator, but Ralph Kehler's daughter, appellant Ethel Chupp, survived testator.

At issue on this appeal is whether appellant may take the share of the residue her father Ralph Kehler would have received had he survived testator. Appellant takes the position that testator's intent concerning the disposition of the bequest to a predeceased sibling is ambiguous. She maintains, therefore, that the relevant "anti-lapse" statute, 20 Pa.C.S. § 2514(9), applies. Section 2514(9) provides:

Rules of interpretation

In the absence of a contrary intent appearing therein, wills shall be construed as to real and personal estate in accordance with the following rules:

* * *

(9) Lapsed and void devises and legacies; substitution of issue. A devise or bequest to a child or other issue of the testator or to his brother or sister or to a child of his brother or sister whether designated by name or as one of a class shall not lapse if the beneficiary shall fail to survive the testator and shall leave issue surviving the testator but shall pass to such surviving issue who shall take per stirpes the share which their deceased ancestor would have taken had he survived the testator: Provided, That such a devise or bequest to a brother or sister or to the child of a brother or sister shall lapse to the extent to which it will pass to the testator's spouse or issue as a part of the residuary estate or under the intestate laws. * * *

The Orphans' Court Division of the Court of Common Pleas of Northumberland County disagreed. It concluded that the language of testator's will, particularly "and to the survivor or survivors of them," manifests testator's "contrary intent" within the meaning of section 2514 to limit takers to those named siblings who are living at testator's death, thus precluding operation of subsection (9). We agree with appellant that the orphans' court misinterpreted testator's will.

This Court has not yet held that a testator must expressly provide for a possible lapse to manifest "contrary intent" overcoming operation of the anti-lapse statute. See Corbett Estate, 430 Pa. 54, 61 n.7, 241 A.2d 524, 527 n.7 (1968). Surely, however, a "contrary intent" must appear with reasonable certainty. See *id.* at 62–63, 241 A.2d at 527–28. Accord, Sykes Estate, 477 Pa. 254, 257, 383 A.2d 920, 921 (1978).

Testator's will here permits no such certainty. In paragraph THIRD of his will, Testator fails to make an express statement concerning his intended disposition of residue in the event a named beneficiary predeceases him. Instead, he merely states his desire to leave the residue to his named siblings "and to the survivor or survivors of them." By contrast, in other paragraphs of his will, testator expressly provides for the possibility of lapse. In paragraph FIRST, in which testator gives his nephew Emerson Asher Shoemaker a monetary gift, testator provides:

> I give and bequeath the sum of One Thousand ($1,000.00) Dollars, unto my nephew, EMERSON ASHER SHOEMAKER, of Reading, Pennsylvania, should he survive me, but if he predeceases me, then this paragraph of my Will shall be null and void and of no effect.

In Paragraph SECOND, testator employs the identical language manifesting an intent to provide a lapse in another bequest of $1,000 to another nephew, Larry Welker. There, testator again stated "if he predeceases me, then this paragraph of my Will shall be null and void and of no effect."

Testator's careful use of express language directing a lapse of these bequests in his will raises considerable doubt that he intended a lapse in paragraph THIRD, where no such language is used. It cannot now be said with the requisite reasonable certainty that testator intended a lapse of residuary bequests under paragraph THIRD. In accordance with the Legislature's directive contained in 20 Pa.C.S. § 2514(9), it must be presumed that testator did not intend his bequest to Ralph Kehler to lapse. By way of the same statute, appellant may share in the residuary estate.

Decree vacated and case remanded for proceedings consistent with this opinion. Each party pays own costs.

NIX, J., did not participate in the consideration or decision of this case.

LARSEN, J., filed a dissenting opinion, in which EAGEN, C. J., joins.

LARSEN, Justice, dissenting.

I dissent. I believe the testator clearly expressed his intention in Paragraph Third to distribute the residue of his estate to the survivor or survivors of the four named siblings. It is not surprising that testator used different language in the first and second paragraphs as those paragraphs mentioned only one individual each paragraph was a specific monetary legacy to a specific individual.

The majority observes the testator "merely states his desire to leave the residue to his named siblings 'and to the survivor or survivors of them.'" I agree with this observation, but contrary to the majority, I would affirm the Orphans' Court because of this "merely stated" expression of intent, and would affirm the distribution of the estate in accordance with his intent.

EAGEN, C. J., joins in this dissenting opinion.

* * *

Problem

Decedent died with a valid Last Will and Testament that contained a residuary clause that bequeathed one-half of his residuary estate to his stepdaughter "if she survives me." Sadly, the stepdaughter predeceased the decedent by seventeen days, survived by her own adult child. This child petitioned the court to take her deceased mother's share under the state's anti-lapse statute. That statute provides: "When a devisee or legatee, being a child, stepchild, grandchild, brother or sister of the testator, dies before him, and no provision has been made in the will for such contingency, the issue of such devisee or legatee shall take the estate so devised or bequeathed." The child argues that the statute directs that the share going to her mother comes to her because there is no provision made to the contrary in the will, in accordance with the mandate of the statute. The residuary legatees argue, to the contrary, that the state's anti-lapse provision should not apply. As probate judge, how would you distribute the portion that would have gone to the stepchild? *See* Ruotolo v. Tietjen, 93 Conn. App. 432, 890 A.2d 166 (2006).

A. Intent of the Testator

An anti-lapse statute is a default statute; it is effective only when the intent of the testator has not been clearly stated. Thus, if the testator were to state clearly that the anti-lapse statute should not apply, then the wishes of the testator would be given effect. Perhaps the testator would include a clause that simply stated: "Any statute that seeks to prevent lapse shall not apply." Such explicitness is most often lacking. Instead, the testator is more likely to write into the instrument: "One million dollars to Sadie if she survives me." While these words of survivorship may be sufficient to overcome the applicability of the state's anti-lapse statute, there are circumstances under which they may not. For example, in 1990, the Uniform Probate Code introduced a revised version of the anti-lapse statute—a revision that also is incorporated into the 2008 Code revision. Under the Code's anti-lapse provision, "words of survivorship, such as in a devise to an individual 'if he survives me,' or in a devise to 'my surviving children,' are not, in the absence of additional evidence, a sufficient indication of an intent contrary to application of [the anti-lapse statute's provisions]." UNIF. PROB. CODE § 2-603(b)(3). "Additional evidence" could be a provision for an alternate taker if the lapsed individual died, or a statement that the anti-lapse provision does not apply. Few states have adopted the revised Code language just recited (*see* Alaska, Colorado, Hawaii, Michigan, Montana, New Mexico, and North Dakota). Support for the provision is found in the *Restatement (Third) of Property*, § 5.5 h (1999), and from its major proponents, *see* Edward C. Halbach, Jr. & Lawrence W. Waggoner, *The UPC's New Survivorship and Antilapse Provision*, 55 ALB. L. REV. 1091 (1992). The essential point to remember is that attorneys need to exercise careful drafting. *See* John L. Garvey, *Drafting Wills and Trusts: Anticipating the Birth and Death of Possible Beneficiaries*, 71 OR. L. REV. 47 (1992). Careful drafting also will minimize malpractice suits. *See* Danaya C. Wright, *Commentary on Reid Kress Weisbord and David Horton, Boilerplate and Default Rules in Wills Law: An Empirical Analysis*, 102 IOWA L. REV. ONLINE 123 (2018).

B. Simultaneous Death

To prevent inheritance by those who die simultaneously with the decedent, states have enacted simultaneous death statutes similar to that contained in Uniform Probate Code § 2-702(a), which provides that "an individual who is not established to have survived an event . . . by 120 hours is deemed to have predeceased the [testator's death]." This time requirement, rather than mere survivorship, also has been adopted by the Uniform Simultaneous Death Act, § 4 (1993). Thus, even though, technically, a beneficiary under a will may survive the testator, if the survivorship is not by at least 120 hours, the beneficiary will be treated as if he or she predeceased the testator, and the anti-lapse statute will apply.

In addition to the general survivorship requirements of the Uniform Probate Code § 2-702, which is applicable to wills and other governing instruments, the Code has adopted a 2008 revised Uniform Probate Code § 2-104, which is applicable to persons taking under intestate succession and to persons in gestation. The provision requires that it be established by clear and convincing evidence that a person born prior to the death of the decedent survived the death of the decedent by at least 120 hours. Unif. Prob. Code § 2-104(a)(1). And when an individual is in gestation at the decedent's death, for that person-in-gestation to take, there must be clear and convincing evidence that the child lived for 120 hours after birth. Unif. Prob. Code § 2-104(a)(2).

C. Relatives

Legislators seek to protect families, and, thus, anti-lapse statutes almost always apply to predeceasing relatives of the testator. Thus, if a testator dies with a valid will in existence, devising or bequeathing property to a named relative, that relative is protected under the statute. These relatives tend to be by consanguinity rather than affinity, thus a testator's grandparents and their descendants would be covered by the statute, but a spouse and the spouse's relatives would not. There are some exceptions. For example, the Unif. Prob. Code § 2-603(b) (2019) (Substitute Gift) includes a stepchild of the decedent as protected. Some states make the statute applicable to all. *See, e.g.,* N.H. Rev. Stat. Ann. § 551:12 (2019) ("The heirs in the descending line of a legatee or devisee, deceased before the testator, shall take the estate bequeathed or devised, in the same manner the legatee or devisee would have taken it if he had survived.") Establishing a relationship between the testator and the predeceasing legatee is the first step. Afterwards, there is the necessity that this relative have issue (descendants) who survive the testator to take by representation. Georgia does not require that the predeceasing legatee be a relative of the decedent. Anyone who fits the class of persons to take, who leaves surviving descendants, qualifies under the state's statute. *See* Ga. Code Ann. § 53-4-64 (2019).

D. Time Applicability

At common law, if a bequest or devise were made to a legatee or devisee who was dead at the time of the execution of the will, the gift was void; if made to a legatee or devisee who died between the time of the execution of the will and the death of the decedent, the bequest or devise lapsed. Thus, there was a distinction and it most often arose in the context of a bequest such as "to the children of my sister, Sadie." If Sadie had children die before execution of the will, and children who died after execution of the will but before the death of the testator, and each predeceasing child was survived by issue, the question arose as to the applicability of any anti-lapse statute. Some statutes allow for the anti-lapse provision to apply to all predeceasing relatives, regardless of whether they die prior to execution of the will or between execution and the date of death of the decedent. *See, e.g.*, VA. CODE ANN. § 64.2–414 (2019). Some states still retain the common law distinction and prohibit applicability of the anti-lapse statute to relatives predeceasing execution of the will. *See, e.g.*, N.Y. EST., POWERS & TRUSTS L. § 3-3.3 (McKinney 2019); TEX. ESTS. CODE ANN. § 255.153 (West 2019).

E. Class Gifts

If a testator provided: "One million dollars to the children of my daughter, Sadie," and Sadie had three children survive the testator by more than 120 hours, but one died prior to the testator, survived by one child of her own, should the anti-lapse statute apply to the predeceasing child of Sadie? Or should the surviving members of the class we call "Sadie's children" take all of the money to the exclusion of the other? This is the dilemma of whether anti-lapse should apply to class gifts, since it is arguable that, when the testator used class (children) language, the testator intended to prevent the application of any anti-lapse statute and allow the survivor to take all. Consider the approaches in the following cases:

Dawson v. Yucus

Illinois Appellate Court, 1968
97 Ill. App. 2d 101, 239 N.E.2d 305

CHARLES E. JONES, Justice.

In this will construction case plaintiffs seek a decree finding Clause Two of the will of Nelle G. Stewart, deceased, is a devise to a class. Plaintiffs appeal a trial court decree rendered for defendants.

Nelle G. Stewart, of Girard, Illinois, died on May 29, 1965, leaving a duly executed will dated March 3, 1959, and containing ten dispositive clauses. The first clause directed payment of debts and funeral expenses. The second clause, the interpretation of which is the sole issue in this case, provided:

'Through the Will of my late husband, Dr. Frank A. Stewart, I received an undivided one-fifth (1/5) interest in two hundred sixty-one and thirty-eight hundredths (261.38) acres of farm lands located in Sections Twenty-eight (28), Twenty-nine (29), Thirty-two (32) and Thirty-three (33) in Township Fourteen (14) North, Range Four (4) West of the Third Principal Meridian in Sangamon County, Illinois, and believing as I do that those farm lands should go back to my late husband's side of the house, I therefore give; devise and bequeath my one-fifth (1/5) interest in said farm lands as follows: One-half (1/2) of my interest therein to Stewart Wilson, a nephew, now living in Birmingham, Michigan and One-half (1/2) of my interest to Gene Burtle, a nephew, now living in Mission, Kansas.'

Clauses three and four made bequests of personalty to Ina Mae Yucus, Lola Eades, Hazel Degelow and Ella Hickey. Clauses five, six and seven made bequests of cash to charities. Clause eight provided for the payment of reasonable allowance to Ina Mae Yucus or Hazel Degelow should illness make it necessary for the testatrix to live in either of their homes. Clause nine directed the executrix to convert all 'the rest, residue and remainder of my property * * * of whatever kind and character and wheresoever situate, including void or lapsed legacies * * * into cash * * * and the proceeds divided equally between Ina Mae Yucus and Hazel Degelow, or to the survivor or survivors of them, should any of said named persons predecease me.' Clause ten appoints Ina Mae Yucus executrix and waives bond.

After the will was admitted to probate, Stewart Wilson filed suit to construe the will alleging that the devise in clause two was a class gift, that Gene Burtle, one of the devisees in clause two, died after the date of execution of the will but before the testatrix and that plaintiff, as the survivor of the class, was entitled to the entire one-fifth interest in the farm. After the complaint was filed, Stewart Wilson conveyed the interest he allegedly received as survivor of the class to the two children of the deceased Gene Burtle and they were substituted as plaintiffs. The defendants, the executrix and the beneficiaries named in the residuary clause of the will, filed answer denying that clause two was a gift to a class, asserting that it was a devise to two specific individuals and that upon the death of Gene Burtle prior to that of the testatrix, the gift to him lapsed and passed into the residuary clause of the will.

At the trial the court found that the death of Gene Burtle prior to that of the testatrix created a latent ambiguity and admitted extrinsic evidence relating to testatrix' intentions. There is no serious dispute over the facts shown by the evidence presented by plaintiffs. Nelle G. Stewart was the widow of Dr. Frank A. Stewart and received as a devisee in his will a one-fifth interest in a 261 acre farm in Sangamon County. Nelle G. Stewart and Dr. Frank A. Stewart had no children. At the death of Dr. Stewart his surviving blood relatives were Gene Burtle, Stewart Wilson, William C. Stewart and Robert T. Stewart, his nephews and Patti S. Lusby, his niece. Nelle G. Stewart knew all of these relatives of Dr. Stewart. Of these relatives of Dr. Stewart, only Gene Burtle and Stewart Wilson had a close personal relationship with the testatrix. Gene Burtle died on May 15, 1963, and the testatrix knew of his death but made no changes in her previously executed will. There was evidence from four witnesses that in conversations had with testatrix she stated she wanted the one-fifth interest in the farm to go either to her husband's side of the house, or to Gene Burtle and Stewart Wilson because she felt especially close to them and none other of Dr. Stewart's relatives had any contact with her.

The trial court held, we think correctly, that clause two of testatrix' will did not create a class gift and that the gift in that clause to Gene Burtle lapsed and, pursuant to the Illinois Lapse Statute, Chapt. 3, Sec. 49, I. R.S.1965, passed into the residue of her estate.

The definition of class gifts and pertinent rules of construction as followed by Illinois courts are set forth in the case of Strohm v. McMullen, 404 Ill. 453, 89 N.E.2d 383:

> 'The definition of a class gift adopted by this court, as laid down by Mr. Jarman in his work on Wills, Vol. 1, p. 534, 5th Am.Ed., is: 'A gift to a class is defined * * * as a gift of an aggregate sum to a body of persons uncertain in number at the time of the gift, to be ascertained at a future time, and who are all to take in equal or in some other definite proportions, the share of each being dependent for its amount upon the ultimate number of persons.' Volunteers of America v. Peirce, 267 Ill. 406, 108 N.E. 318; Blackstone v. Althouse, 278 Ill. 481, 116 N.E. 154, L.R.A.1918B, 230; Henry v. Henry, 378 Ill. 581, 39 N.E.2d 18.
>
> A class, in its ordinary acceptation, is a number or body of persons with common characteristics or in like circumstances, or having some common attribute, and, as applied to a devise, it is generally understood to mean a number of persons who stand in the same relation to each other or to the testator.' Blackstone v. Althouse, 278 Ill. 481, 116 N.E. 154, 157, L.R.A.1918B, 230. And it has been definitely decided in this State that in determining whether a devise is to a class or to individuals depends upon the language of the will. If from such language it appears that the amounts of their shares are uncertain until the devise or bequest takes effect, the beneficiaries will generally be held to take as a class; but where at the time of making the gifts the number of beneficiaries is certain, and the share each is to receive is also certain, and in no way dependent for its amount upon the number who shall survive, it is not a gift to a class, but to the individuals. Volunteers of America v. Peirce, 267 Ill. 406, 108 N.E. 318; Blackstone v. Althouse, 278 Ill. 481, 116 N.E. 154, L.R.A.1918B, 230; Strauss v. Strauss, 363 Ill. 442, 2 N.E.2d 699, 105 A.L.R. 1386; Henry v. Henry, 378 Ill. 581, 39 N.E.2d 18; Peadro v. Peadro, 400 Ill. 482, 81 N.E.2d 192.
>
> 'There is an exception to the rule that naming the individual prevents the gift from becoming a class gift, stated in Strauss v. Strauss, 363 Ill. 442, 2 N.E.2d 699, 105 A.L.R. 1386, holding that the mere fact that the testator mentions by name the individuals who make up the class is not conclusive, and that if the intention to give a right of *survivorship* is collected from the remaining provisions of the will, as applied to the existing facts, such an

intention must prevail. This is in accord with the general rule applying to construction of wills, that the intention of the testator, if clearly manifested from the whole will, must prevail over rules of construction. This rule was recognized in the late case of Peadro v. Peadro, 400 Ill. 482, 81 N.E.2d 192, 194, where the gift after a life estate was devised as follows: 'shall be equally divided, share and share alike, between Earl D. Peadro, Berniece F. Peadro, Roy F. Peadro and Irtys A. Peadro, or the survivor of them to be their sole and absolute property.' In that case we held there was no class gift, saying: 'This court recognizes the rule that a gift to persons named is a gift to them individually and not as a class, and will treat the gift as one to individuals, unless reasons are found in the language and structure of the will for deciding that the intent of the testator, which is, of course, paramount to the rule, would be best subserved by disregarding the rule and treating the gift as one to a class.'

Also, see Restatement of Property, Future Interests, Sections 279, 280 and 281.

Admittedly the gift in clause two is not made with the usual generic class description such as 'children', 'brothers', 'nephews', 'cousins', 'issues', 'decedents', or 'family' but is in fact to two named individuals, conditions which militate against construction of the clause as a class gift. However, plaintiffs argue that because of the death of Gene Burtle prior to that of the testatrix a latent ambiguity exists and extrinsic evidence was properly received to show the true intention of the testatrix in clause two of her will, and that the phrase in clause two, 'and believing as I do that these farm lands should go back to my husband's side of the house,' together with the extrinsic evidence, clearly requires class gift construction. * * *

In this case the testatrix named the individuals, Stewart Wilson and Gene Burtle, and gave them each a one-half portion of her interest in the farm, thus making certain the number of beneficiaries and the share each is to receive. The shares in no way depend upon the number who shall survive the death of the testatrix. There is nothing in the language of the will that indicates the testatrix intended to create a class or survivorship gift. The only other provision of the will, also contained in clause two, that has any bearing on the question is the statement, '* * * believing as I do that those farm lands should go back to my late husband's side of the house * * *.' While it is true that this language recites testatrix' desire that the one-fifth interest in the farm go back to her husband's side of the house, it does not indicate a survivorship gift was intended. Her intention to return the farm to her husband's side of the house was fulfilled when she named Stewart Wilson and Gene Burtle as the donees of the interest. And we are not persuaded that the extrinsic evidence offered by plaintiffs is sufficient to require a finding that the testatrix intended a class or survivorship gift as in the *Strauss* and *Krog* cases. There is no evidence which requires, or, in view of the *Strohm* and *O'Connell* cases, would even permit, construing this specific devise of equal one-half portions to two named individuals as a class gift.

Further emphasis for the result we have reached is supplied by other factors found in the will and extrinsic evidence. First, the testatrix created a survivorship gift of the residue of her estate in the ninth clause of her will, thus indicating she knew how to manifest an intent to create a class or survivorship gift; hence, the language of clause two, phrased differently, was intended to create a gift to individuals distributively. Restatement of Property, Future Interests, Sec. 280, Comment g., No. 1. Paragraph No. 2 of the same Restatement citation provides, 'The specification * * * of an exact proportion in the subject matter of the conveyance, which is to be received by each of the named and described persons, is strongly indicative of an intent to make a gift to individuals distributively whenever the * * * proportions so specified equals the entire subject matter given by the limitation in question.' Secondly, the common characteristic of the alleged class described by plaintiffs is that of relation to Dr. Stewart, or, in the words of clause two, the class is of 'my late husband's side of the house.' However, this characteristic is also shared by three other heirs of Dr. Stewart of the same degree of relationship to him as Stewart Wilson and Gene Burtle. It thus appears that Gene Burtle and Stewart Wilson do not constitute the alleged class but are individuals named from the class.

The factors that distinguish the *Strauss* case from this case were furnished by the Supreme Court in Strohm v. McMullen, *supra*, where they analyzed the *Strauss* case and found that the 'mentioning of the names of the children (in the *Strauss* case) was only one of four different ways in which the residuary legatees were designated, the others in themselves being sufficient to bring the donees within a class.' Nor do we feel that the *Krog* case is 'on all fours' with this one. In that case the language found to create a class gift was much different than that used in the instant will, and the testatrix enjoyed a much closer relationship with the Hafkas than that between Mrs. Stewart and Gene Burtle and Stewart Wilson. Extrinsic evidence shows that the 'close personal relationship' consisted of friendly visits by the Burtles and Wilsons about every summer when they came from their homes in Michigan and Kansas to visit in Springfield and Girard. In *Krog,* the testatrix received many years of personal services from the Hafkas and stated upon several occasions that she did not want any of her heirs to have any of her property. Further, few of the controlling factors enumerated by the court in deciding that case are present here. For instance, the always present presumption that the testatrix intended not to die intestate as to any of her property was relied upon in the *Krog* case, but here no partial intestacy will result from the non-class construction. Here there is a general testamentary scheme favoring the beneficiaries of the residue of Mrs. Stewart's estate; namely, Ina Mae Yucus and Hazel Degelow—persons with whom she was obviously on an intimate and friendly basis as shown by the fact that she left them the residue of her estate and, per clause eight of her will, contemplated living in either of their homes.

The devise in clause two was not to persons who come within the designation of a class but was to individuals distributively. It was not so made or limited to prevent the operation of the Illinois Lapse Statute which must be given its intended effect. The court below correctly held that upon the death of Gene Burtle prior to that of the testatrix the devise to him lapsed and passed under the residuary clause of the will. The Decree will be affirmed.

Affirmed.

CRAVEN, Acting P.J., and TRAPP, J., concur.

* * *

In re Moss

Court of Appeal, England, 1899
[1899] 2 Ch. 314, aff'd [1901] A.C. 187 (H.L.)

WALTER Moss by his will dated in 1876, after appointing his wife Elizabeth Moss and his niece Elizabeth Jane Fowler his executrixes, and making sundry devises and bequests, gave all his share or interest in the Daily Telegraph newspaper unto the said E. Moss and E. J. Fowler "upon trust to pay the income thereof to my said wife for her life, and after her decease, upon trust for the said E. J. Fowler and the child or children of my sister Emily Walter who shall attain the age of twenty-one years equally to be divided between them as tenants in common." And he gave the residue of his estate and effects to his wife. And he empowered his trustees with the consent of his wife * * *.

The testator died in 1893, and his will was proved by his widow, Elizabeth Moss, alone. At the date of his will there were living his niece Elizabeth Jane Fowler, who was then slightly under twenty-one, his sister Emily Walter, and five children of Emily Walter.

Elizabeth Jane Fowler died in 1891, in the testator's lifetime, a spinster. Emily Walter and her five children survived the testator.

The testator's widow, Elizabeth Moss, the tenant for life of his Daily Telegraph share and his residuary legatee, died in 1897, having by her will given her residuary estate, including any share or portion of a share in the Daily Telegraph newspaper which might belong to her at her death, to her trustees in trust for sale and to stand possessed of the proceeds, after payment of her funeral and testamentary expenses, debts, and legacies, in trust for William George Kingsbury absolutely; and she appointed him and another her trustees and executors.

At her death all the five children of Emily Walter were living and had attained twenty-one.

The question was whether, in consequence of the death of Elizabeth Jane Fowler in the lifetime of her uncle, the testator, the share bequeathed to her in his Daily Telegraph share had lapsed and fallen into his residuary estate, or whether the entirety passed to Emily Walter's five children: in other words, whether the gift by the testator of his Daily Telegraph share was a gift to a class, so that these five children, as the survivors of the class, took the whole.

To have this question decided, an originating summons was taken out by W. G. Kingsbury and his co-trustee and co-executor of the testator's widow, Elizabeth Moss, W. G. Kingsbury being also her residuary legatee, against Emily Walter's five children and also against Emily Walter as the present trustee of the Daily Telegraph share, to have it declared that the bequest of the testator's share in the Daily Telegraph newspaper upon trust, after the death of his wife, for Elizabeth Jane Fowler and the child or children of Emily Walter who should attain twenty-one equally, was not a gift to a class, but that the share bequeathed to Elizabeth Jane Fowler had lapsed by her death in the testator's lifetime and thus fell into the residue of the estate.

The summons was heard on December 14, 1898, by North J., who, after saying the cases upon the point were so irreconcilable that he should act independently of them, held that, as he could find nothing in the will to shew that Elizabeth Jane Fowler was included in the class, the share given to her lapsed by reason of her death in the testator's lifetime, and so passed to the plaintiffs.

The defendants, the five children of Emily Walter, appealed.

LINDLEY M.R.

It is very difficult to construe this will by the light of the authorities. I entirely agree with North J. that the authorities do not help one much, because they are in inextricable confusion. I do not think there is any case which can be cited by either side which cannot be matched by a case on the other side more or less difficult to distinguish from it. The practical question which we have to decide on this will is, Who are the persons now entitled to the share of the testator in the *Daily Telegraph* newspaper? There are several rival views. One view is, and that is the one adopted by the learned judge below, that the share which Elizabeth Jane Fowler would have taken if she were alive—that is, one-sixth, as I understand it—has lapsed and has fallen into the residuary estate, so that, according to that view, one-sixth of that share has gone to persons who were certainly never intended to take it. That is obvious. That may be the legal result of the gift, but it is obvious it was never dreamt of by the testator. What he intended was that his share should go amongst the persons he has named and to no one else.

Now the difficulty lies in this. We hear about classes, and gifts to classes, and definitions of classes. You may define a class in a thousand ways: anybody may make any number of things or persons a class by setting out an attribute more or less common to them all and making that the definition of the class. We have been referred, and not improperly at all, to Mr. Jarman's definition of a class for the purpose for which lawyers want it—that is, in construing a will—and I think Mr. Swinfen Eady is right in saying that, looking at that definition, this case does come within it. But after all, whether you call this a class or whether you call it a number of persons who are treated by the testator as if they were the class, appears to me to be merely a matter of language. One is very reluctant to frame definitions unless one can make a law to accord with the definitions, which judges cannot do. Now what is to be done with the share of this lady who has died? The testator says it is to be equally divided between her and the children of Emily Walter, to be equally divided between them all. If some of them are dead, are the shares of those who are dead to go to those who survive, or are they to go to someone else? That is the practical question; and whether you call the persons a class or "in effect" a class—as Mr. Theobald does in a passage of his work on wills, where he says (4th ed. p. 645), "it is clear that a gift to A., and the children of B., may in effect be a gift to a class, if the testator treats the legatees as a class" — or whether you call them a number of persons who are to be treated as a class, is quite immaterial. The guiding question here is, What is to be done with this *Daily Telegraph* share which is to be divided amongst these legatees? It seems to me that it is to go to such of them as shall be living. That is the obvious intention. The alternative view takes the share away where it was never intended to go, and upon that ground it appears to me that we ought to differ from the learned judge. I confess, and I say so frankly, that if this case had come before me in the first instance I should have decided it as North J. did, but my brother Romer has convinced me that is not right.

SIR F. H. JEUNE.

I agree. I do not propose to add anything that may tend to make the decisions which are already contradictory and complicated still more so.

ROMER L.J.

In the absence of any context negativing this view, I think that, when a testator gives property X. to A. and a class of persons — say the children of B. — in equal shares, he intends that the whole of X. shall pass by his gift if any one of the children of B. survive him, even although A. does not. Clearly, if A. survived and none of the children of B. survived so as to share, then A. would take the whole, for A. would either have to take the whole or nothing, unless indeed it could be said that you are to look at the number of children of B. living at the date of the will and say there is an intestacy as to the share of each child dying between the date of the will and the testator's death; but that to my mind is clearly an untenable proposition. If then the testator intended that A. should take the whole if none of the children of B. survived him to share, I think also he intended the children of B. to take the whole if A. did not survive so as to share. There is no satisfactory distinction, to my mind, between those two cases. I think that, in such a gift as I have mentioned, what the testator really means is that the property is to be shared equally by a body constituted of such of the following as should be existing at the date of the testator's death, that is to say, A. and the children of B. And generally, when the testator — there being nothing to negative the view in the rest of the will — gives property to be shared at a particular period equally between a class properly so called and an individual or individuals, I think that what the testator prima facie must be taken to mean is that you are to see which part of that aggregated body is to share in that property at the time it comes for distribution, and that such a gift is really a gift to a class: and though I am perfectly well aware of the danger there is in attempting to lay down general propositions — and few judges would more shrink from doing so than I, knowing as I do how a general proposition laid down often hampers judges in dealing with succeeding cases — yet I do think in the present case I may venture to make the following statement, especially as the cases are so complicated and there is no express decision of the Court of Appeal or of the House of Lords upon the point. In my opinion it is correct to say that a gift by will to a class properly so called and a named individual such as A. equally, so that the testator contemplates

A. taking the same share that each member of the class will take, is prima facie a gift to a class.

For those reasons, applying those principles to the case before us, I have no hesitation in saying that, in my opinion, the gift here was a gift to a class, and that Elizabeth Jane Fowler was only intended to share as one of a class; and that inasmuch as she did not survive so as to share, the rest of the class takes the whole of the property.

* * *

F. Non-Probate Transfers

The extensive anti-lapse provisions contained in Uniform Probate Code § 2-603 are applicable to persons taking under a valid Last Will and Testament. "It does not apply to beneficiary designations in life insurance policies, retirements plans, or transfer-on-death accounts, nor does it apply to *inter vivos* trusts, whether revocable or irrevocable." Unif. Prob. Code § 2-603 cmt. (2019). Nonetheless, Uniform Probate Code § 2-706 applies anti-lapse provisions to "beneficiary designations" arising because of "an insurance or annuity policy, of an account with POD designation, of a security registered in beneficiary form (TOD), or of a pension, profit-sharing, retirement, or similar benefit plan, or other nonprobate transfer at death." Unif. Prob. Code § 2-706 cmt. (2019). As we will discuss, *infra*, the anti-lapse provision also will apply to future interests under Uniform Probate Code § 2-707. For now, note the similarities between § 2-603, which is applicable to wills, and § 2-706, below, which is applicable to non-probate transfers.

Uniform Probate Code (2019)

§ 2-706. Life Insurance; Retirement Plan; Account With POD Designation; Transfer-on-Death Registration; Deceased Beneficiary.

* * *

(b) [**Substitute Gift.**] If a beneficiary fails to survive the decedent and is a grandparent, a descendant of a grandparent, or a stepchild of the decedent, the following apply:

(1) Except as provided in paragraph (4), if the beneficiary designation is not in the form of a class gift and the deceased beneficiary leaves surviving descendants, a substitute gift is created in the beneficiary's surviving descendants. They take by representation the property to which the beneficiary would have been entitled had the beneficiary survived the decedent.

(2) Except as provided in paragraph (4), if the beneficiary designation is in the form of a class gift, other than a beneficiary designation to "issue," "descendants," "heirs of the body," "heirs," "next of kin," "relatives," or "family," or a class described by language of similar import, a substitute gift is created in the surviving descendants of any deceased beneficiary. The property to which the beneficiaries would have been entitled had all

of them survived the decedent passes to the surviving beneficiaries and the surviving descendants of the deceased beneficiaries. Each surviving beneficiary takes the share to which he [or she] would have been entitled had the deceased beneficiaries survived the decedent. Each deceased beneficiary's surviving descendants who are substituted for the deceased beneficiary take by representation the share to which the deceased beneficiary would have been entitled had the deceased beneficiary survived the decedent. For the purposes of this paragraph, "deceased beneficiary" means a class member who failed to survive the decedent and left one or more surviving descendants.

(3) For the purposes of Section 2-701, words of survivorship, such as in a beneficiary designation to an individual "if he survives me," or in a beneficiary designation to "my surviving children," are not, in the absence of additional evidence, a sufficient indication of an intent contrary to the application of this section.

(4) If a governing instrument creates an alternative beneficiary designation with respect to a beneficiary designation for which a substitute gift is created by paragraph (1) or (2), the substitute gift is superseded by the alternative beneficiary designation only if an expressly designated beneficiary of the alternative beneficiary designation is entitled to take.

G. Powers of Appointment

In a power of appointment, assets are transferred to a trustee, who will administer the trust for the benefit of a named beneficiary for life. If the beneficiary may "appoint" these assets at his or her death, the legal description is that this is a general testamentary power of appointment. For example, if a trust were declared by which someone were to transfer one million dollars in trust for the support of Sadie for her life, and then, as she appoints the remainder, to whomever Sadie designates in her will, Sadie would have a life estate in a support trust. But Sadie would also have what we will later refer to as a general testamentary power of appointment. That means that she may appoint to (bequeath to) anyone she wishes in her valid will. If, in that will, she appoints to someone who predeceases her, may the anti-lapse apply even though the trust was created by someone other than Sadie? The short answer is, "Yes," if the applicable issues we have identified so far apply to allow it. The Uniform Probate Code specifically applies the anti-lapse statute to powers of appointment: "'Devise' includes an alternate devise, a devise in the form of a class gift, and an exercise of a power of appointment." UNIF. PROB. CODE § 2-603(a)(3) (2019). "'Testator' includes the donee of a power of appointment if the power is exercised in the testator's will." *Id.* at (a)(7). Furthermore, the predeceasing devisee may be a relative of either the testator or the person exercising the power of appointment. *See id.* at (b) (Substitute Gift). We will examine powers of appointment in greater depth *infra*.

Uniform Probate Code (2019)

§ 2-603. Antilapse; Deceased Devisee; Class Gifts.

(a) [**Definitions.**] In this section: * * *

> (3) "Descendant of a grandparent," as used in subsection (b), means an individual who qualifies as a descendant of a grandparent of the testator or of the donor of a power of appointment under the (i) rules of construction applicable to a class gift created in the testator's will if the devise or exercise of the power is in the form of a class gift or (ii) rules for intestate succession if the devise or exercise of the power is not in the form of a class gift. * * *

> (6) "Devisee" includes (i) a class member if the devise is in the form of a class gift, (ii) an individual or class member who was deceased at the time the testator executed his [or her] will as well as an individual or class member who was then living but who failed to survive the testator, and (iii) an appointee under a power of appointment exercised by the testator's will.

> (7) "Stepchild" means a child of the surviving, deceased, or former spouse of the testator or of the donor of a power of appointment, and not of the testator or donor. * * *

> (9) "Testator" includes the donee of a power of appointment if the power is exercised in the testator's will.

(b) [**Substitute Gift.**] If a devisee fails to survive the testator and is a grandparent, a descendant of a grandparent, or a stepchild of either the testator or the donor of a power of appointment exercised by the testator's will, the following apply: * * *

> (5) Unless the language creating a power of appointment expressly excludes the substitution of the descendants of an appointee for the appointee, a surviving descendant of a deceased appointee of a power of appointment can be substituted for the appointee under this section, whether or not the descendant is an object of the power.

Chapter 5

Restraints on Transfer of Wealth

Tool Bar

Any person with standing has a right to contest the formalities and intentionalities of a Last Will and Testament. Chapter Three explores these possibilities. But states have developed procedures by which they may object to decisions made by a decedent at death which, if made during lifetime, the decision would have greater probability of success. For example, an elderly widow may be able to demolish her memory-laden home during her lifetime if she is afraid her children may vandalize it. But if she directs her personal representative to do the demolishing after her death, her wishes will most likely be thwarted by general public policy concerns. *See* Eyerman v. Mercantile Trust Co., 524 S.W.2d 210 (Mo. App. 1975). And nearly everyone would agree that a person should not inherit under probate or non-probate transfer if the inheritance only came about because of an intentional homicide by the heir, but what if the potential heir perpetrated domestic violence, elder abuse, or abandoned the decedent during life? There are other issues, like to what extent should the state be responsible for protecting the economic rights of a surviving spouse or minor and adult children? What is the responsibility of the state to provide citizens an efficient and cost-effective means of transferring property at death? These are the issues raised in this chapter. As an attorney, you will be directly involved in the administration of the probate system and, thus, you should consider this chapter in the context of striving for efficiency and fairness.

I. General Public Policy

A. Common Law Restraints

Clark v. Office of Personnel Management

U.S. Court of Appeals for the Federal Circuit, 2001
256 F.3d 1360

MICHEL, Circuit Judge.

Phillip Clark ("Clark") petitions for review of the final decision of the Merit Systems Protection Board ("Board"), made final on March 13, 2000, when the full Board declined to review the initial decision of the Administrative Judge ("AJ"). The AJ had affirmed the Office of Personnel Management's ("OPM") denial of Clark's application for the Basic Employee Death Benefit ("BEDB"), to which the surviving spouse of a federal employee is entitled if the employee worked for at least 18 months under the Federal Employees Retirement System ("FERS"). Clark v. Office of Pers. Mgmt., No. AT-0843-99-683-I-1 (M.S.P.B. Oct. 14, 1999). As executor of the estate of Michael Clark ("Michael"), Clark filed a timely petition for review with this court under 5 U.S.C. §7703 (1994), and we have jurisdiction pursuant to 28 U.S.C. §1295(a)(9) (1994). Because the federal statute regarding the BEDB, 5 U.S.C. §8442(b) (1994), is silent as to whether a killer or his or her estate may receive federal death benefits earned by his or her victim, and because OPM concluded, based on the Alabama state authorities' substantial evidence, that Michael killed Melonie Clark ("Melonie"), OPM was thus correct in following the principle of Alabama law to prevent Michael's estate from collecting the BEDB earned by his victim. Accordingly, we affirm.

* * *

Melonie, a Department of Defense ("DOD") civilian employee at Fort McClellan, Alabama, was married to Michael. The couple had two children together. On August 19, 1994, allegedly in the midst of a child custody dispute, Michael traveled to the home of Melonie's parents, where Melonie and the children were temporarily staying. While the details of what occurred that day are not entirely clear, there was an exchange of gunfire that left Michael, Melonie and both of Melonie's parents dead.

The two children, ages three and seven, apparently witnessed the events. One of the children allegedly told investigators that his father had killed himself. An investigation by the Talladega County Sheriff's Office revealed that Michael intentionally caused the death of Melonie by shooting her, and that he then committed suicide. A postmortem examination found that Michael had been shot once in the abdomen and once in the hand before he committed suicide. The examination further revealed that the bullets which wounded Michael had been fired from a different gun than that which Michael used to commit suicide. Melonie's death certificate states that her death was a "homicide" caused by a "gunshot to face," and lists her time of death as 5:10 p.m., August 19, 1994. Michael's death certificate states that his death was a "suicide" caused by a "gunshot to head," and lists his time of death as 5:14 p.m., August 19, 1994.

Pursuant to 5 U.S.C §8442(b) and its implementing regulation, 5 C.F.R. §843.309(a) (1994), if a federal employee dies after completing at least 18 months of civilian service, that employee's spouse is entitled to receive the BEDB, as a result of that employee's participation in FERS.[1] Clark, Michael's brother, is the executor and conservator of Michael's estate, as well as the guardian of the two children. As executor of Michael's estate, Clark submitted an application to OPM in order to obtain the BEDB to which he claims Michael was entitled as a result of Melonie's participation in FERS.

In a letter dated August 10, 1998, which formalized an initial decision dated June 19, 1998, and subsequently in a final reconsideration decision dated June 16, 1999, OPM denied Clark's application, citing the principle that one who kills his spouse cannot inherit from that spouse. OPM noted in its final decision that "because it is against public policy to permit an individual to profit from his or her own wrongdoing, Mr. Clark's estate's claim for FERS basic employee death benefit as the estate of the widower of Mrs. Melonie G. Clark was disallowed. OPM follows the common law concept that you cannot profit from a crime." Letter from OPM to Clark of 6/16/99, at 2.

Clark appealed OPM's decision to the Board. In an initial decision dated October 14, 1999, the AJ held that pursuant to the Code of Alabama §43-8-253 (1994) ("Slayer Statute"), one who kills his or her spouse is deemed to have predeceased the decedent. The Slayer Statute provides in relevant part that "[a] final judgment of conviction of felonious and intentional killing is conclusive for purposes of this section. In the absence of a conviction of felonious and intentional killing the court may determine by a preponderance of the evidence whether the killing was felonious and intentional for purposes of this section."

The AJ reasoned that Michael, being deemed to have "died before" Melonie, was never considered a "surviving spouse" and consequently neither he nor his estate is entitled to the BEDB. In response to Clark's argument that the Slayer Statute does not apply to a determination of eligibility for *federal* benefits, the AJ held that state law is used to determine relevant familial relationships, in particular to determine

1. Section 8442(b), chapter 5, of the U.S.C., entitled "Rights of a widow or widower," states that, "[i]f an employee or Member dies after completing at least 18 months of civilian service creditable under section 8411 and is survived by a widow or widower, the widow or widower is entitled to ... [a survivor benefit]." Section 843.309(a), chapter 5 of the C.F.R., entitled "Federal Employees Retirement System—Death Benefits and Employee Refunds—Current and Former Spouse Benefits," similarly states that "if an employee or Member dies after completing at least 18 months of civilian service creditable under Subpart C of Part 842 of this chapter and is survived by a current spouse who meets the requirements of §843.303, the current spouse is entitled to the basic employee death benefit ..."

who may be deemed "the surviving spouse" for purposes of distributing survivor benefits: "Although the death benefit is provided for by statute, questions involving the relationships of individuals such as Michael and Melonie are determined by state law and not Federal law." *Clark,* slip op. at 3.

On March 13, 2000, the full Board denied Clark's petition for review, making the AJ's decision the final decision of the Board. Subsequently, Clark filed a timely petition for review with this court.

* * *

The scope of judicial review of decisions of the Board is narrowly limited by statute. Specifically, this court must affirm the Board's decision unless we find it to be arbitrary, capricious, an abuse of discretion, or otherwise not in accordance with law; obtained without procedures required by law, rule or regulation having been followed; or unsupported by substantial evidence. 5 U.S.C. §7703(c) (1994); Kewley v. Dep't of Health & Human Servs., 153 F.3d 1357, 1361 (Fed.Cir.1998).

OPM is a federal agency charged with the distribution of the BEDB, pursuant to 5 U.S.C. §8442(b) and 5 C.F.R. §843.309(a). The statute and its implementing regulation provide in relevant part that if an employee dies after completing at least 18 months of civilian service and is survived by a spouse, that spouse will receive a benefit. However, neither the statute nor its implementing regulation explicitly addresses whether a survivor benefit should be given to one who has become a widow or widower by intentionally killing his or her spouse. OPM and the Board thus relied on state law principles to determine whether Michael was deemed to be a "surviving spouse," and hence whether Clark, as the executor of Michael's estate, was entitled to receive the BEDB.

As noted by the Board, we have previously affirmed reliance on state law principles to determine eligibility for federal benefits. See *Clark,* slip op. at 3, citing Rogers v. Office of Pers. Mgmt., 87 F.3d 471, 473 (Fed.Cir.1996) (relying in part on the presumption of validity under Texas *state law* in favor of the latest marriage to determine which of two "wives" was married to the deceased federal employee at the time of his death and thus which "wife" was entitled to his survivor annuity) (emphasis added); Money v. Office of Pers. Mgmt., 811 F.2d 1474, 1479 (Fed.Cir.1987) (affirming the Board's determination that eligibility for federal benefits should be decided based upon which one of two marriages would be recognized as valid by California *state* courts) (emphasis added).

OPM determined that Alabama state law prohibits killers from profiting from their crimes. In Weaver v. Hollis, 247 Ala. 57, 22 So.2d 525 (1945), a case cited by OPM, Letter from OPM to Clark of 6/16/99, at 2, the Supreme Court of Alabama held that, "[t]he basic reasons behind the denial of the right of the husband to inherit from the wife whom he has feloniously killed is so compelling, we now declare that in this jurisdiction he cannot do so." *Weaver,* 22 So.2d at 529. We note that *Weaver* in fact predates by decades the Slayer Statute, which was not passed by the Alabama Legislature until 1982.

Alabama's intent to preclude killers from profiting from their crimes is further evidenced through the Slayer Statute. In enacting the Slayer Statute, the Alabama Legislature decided that one who "feloniously and intentionally" kills his or her spouse is deemed to have predeceased the decedent and is thus ineligible to receive "surviving spouse" benefits. See Ala.Code § 43-8-253(a). In the opinion affirming OPM's denial of Clark's BEDB application, the Board reasoned that, "the FERS death benefit [BEDB] is a benefit that accrues only to a surviving spouse . . . [a]nd since the Alabama law provides that Michael should be deemed to have predeceased Melonie, then his estate is not entitled to the benefit." *Clark,* slip op. at 2–3.

However, before applying the principle of Alabama law to deny Clark's BEDB application, OPM first examined the evidence before it to determine whether Michael had intentionally and feloniously caused the death of his wife. OPM reviewed the death certificates from the Deputy Coroner, which stated that Melonie's death had been deemed a "homicide" and Michael's death a "suicide." OPM also submitted a written request to the Talladega County Sheriff's Office to obtain further information regarding the case. In response to its request, OPM received and considered a letter from the County Sheriff's Office, dated June 14, 1999, which detailed the conclusions of the Chief Investigator: "[T]he investigation did reveal that Michael H. Clark did intentionally cause the death of his wife, Melonie Gentry Clark, by shooting her with a firearm, along with other members of her family, and then committed suicide prior to the arrival of law enforcement on the scene." Letter from the Talladega County Sheriff's Office to OPM of 6/14/99.

Based on this evidence from appropriate state authorities, OPM in its final decision concluded that it should follow the principle of Alabama law in the instant case, and that therefore Michael's intentional killing of Melonie prevented his estate from obtaining the BEDB: "We have a report from the Talladega County Sheriff's Office indicating that Mr. Clark intentionally caused the death of Mrs. Clark by shooting her with a firearm. Based on this information, we found that Mr. Clark and subsequently his estate were not entitled to a basic employee death benefit." Letter from OPM to Clark of 6/16/99, at 1. While neither OPM nor the Board was bound by the conclusions of the state authorities, both reasonably concluded, based on the content of the documents before them, that the principle of Alabama law should be followed to deny Clark's BEDB application. Their conclusions were supported by substantial evidence and were in accordance with law.

We additionally note that this principle of Alabama law is long-standing and widespread. As stated above, the policy that a killer may not profit from his or her crime precedes by decades the Slayer Statute, which was not passed by the Alabama Legislature until 1982. In fact, the Supreme Court recently noted in dictum that the principles underlying state slayer statutes are "well established in the law and ha[ve] a long historical pedigree." Egelhoff v. Egelhoff, 532 U.S. 141, —, 121 S.Ct. 1322, 1330, 149 L.Ed.2d 264 (2001) (citing Riggs v. Palmer, 115 N.Y. 506, 22 N.E. 188 (1889)). Similarly, in this court, we have upheld the propriety of this principle in order to prevent one who has intentionally killed a spouse from benefitting from the crime. In Lofton v. West, 198 F.3d 846 (Fed.Cir.1999), we stated that the Department of Veterans Affairs ("DVA"), in light of the universality of this principle, acted reasonably in promulgating a regulation which adopted the rule that a "slayer" may not obtain benefits as a result of "intentionally and wrongfully" causing the death of his or her spouse. *Id.* at 850. We reasoned in *Lofton* that "Congress legislates against a common law background, and [the relevant regulation] simply codifies a long-standing common law principle known as the 'slayer's rule,' which bars wrongdoers from obtaining insurance and other benefits as a direct consequence of their wrongful acts." *Id.*

Clark argues to this court that he is entitled to the BEDB because, in the absence of a conviction, the Slayer Statute requires a finding by an Alabama probate court that Michael intentionally killed Melonie. Clark asserts that absent such a finding, the Slayer Statute is inapplicable and consequently he is entitled to the BEDB from OPM. On the other hand, OPM argues that Clark is not entitled to the BEDB because the Code of Alabama does not limit the term "court" in the Slayer Statute to only include an Alabama probate court, and that therefore OPM and the Board can constitute "courts" for purposes of the statute.

We disagree with both contentions. The plain language of the Code of Alabama clearly contemplates that, absent a conviction, determinations of intentional killings for purposes of the Slayer Statute will be made by an Alabama "court." See Ala.Code § 43-8-253(e). However, merely because the Slayer Statute is technically inapplicable to the instant case does not preclude OPM, nor the Board, from relying on the state law principle behind the statute. As stated above, the Slayer Statute codified a long-standing Alabama state principle, which is also found in virtually all other states, see *Egelhoff*, 532 U.S. at — —, 121 S.Ct. at 1330, as well as in federal common law. See *Lofton*, 198 F.3d at 850. If there had been a conviction or an Alabama court finding, OPM would have been required to apply the Slayer Statute. However, the absence of a conviction and of a probate court finding did not necessarily preclude OPM from lawfully relying on the Slayer Statute's underlying principles.

We certainly do not hold that it is always appropriate for OPM to rely on state law to deny an individual federal benefits. In some instances, the federal statute might contain an explicit provision which contradicts a state principle, in which case OPM would not be able to rely on such principle. Nor do we hold that OPM was required to accept the state authorities' conclusions that Michael had intentionally killed his wife. Rather, we hold only that because the federal statute in question was silent on the subject of killers obtaining the BEDB earned by their victims, OPM was entitled to look to Alabama state law to determine that the estate of a "slayer" may not obtain "surviving spouse" benefits. Furthermore, because there was substantial evidence that Michael did indeed intentionally cause the death of his wife, we hold that OPM lawfully concluded that the principle of Alabama's "slayer's rule" applied to the instant case, and consequently OPM correctly denied Clark's BEDB application.

Furthermore, we note that in regard to the instant case, federal common law is in accordance with the state law principle. See *Lofton*, 198 F.3d at 850; Mutual Life Insurance Co. v. Armstrong, 117 U.S. 591, 6 S.Ct. 877, 881, 29 L.Ed. 997 (1886). Thus, Clark would still not be entitled to the BEDB even had the Board relied on federal common law. Consequently, we do not reach the hypothetical, and unlikely, question of whether, if a state court should rule in the future that slayers may obtain benefits from their victims, OPM may rely on such a state law principle that contradicts federal common law. See *Egelhoff*, 532 U.S. at — —, 121 S.Ct. at 1330 (stating in dictum that "the principles underlying the [slayer] statutes . . . have been adopted by nearly every State").

* * *

Based on substantial evidence from Alabama state authorities that Michael intentionally killed Melonie, OPM reasonably relied on the principle of Alabama law in order to deny Clark's BEDB application. Thus, the Board's approval of OPM's reliance on Alabama law, and its decision affirming OPM's ruling, was based on substantial evidence and was in accordance with law. Accordingly, the Board's decision is

AFFIRMED.

Notes

The case demonstrates the effect of a state slayer statute, but also the court's willingness to utilize the "statute's underlying principles" to bar inheritance where it may reasonably be concluded that an heir intentionally killed the person from whom he or she was to inherit. The court allows title to pass to the "slayer," but because no one should be able to profit from his or her own wrongdoing, the court applies the equitable device of a constructive trust to then transfer title to persons other than the slayer. *See, e.g., In re* Estate of Mahoney, 126 Vt. 31, 220 A.2d 475 (1966). Because equity is involved, courts may fashion a constructive trust remedy that not only deprives the slayer but also deprives heirs of the slayer from inheriting too. This would make certain that the slayer does not eventually inherit from them and, thus, gain by his or her own wrongdoing. *See, e.g., In re* Estate of Mueller, 275 Ill. App. 3d 128, 655 N.E.2d 1040, *rev. denied*, 660 N.E.2d 1269 (1995). *See generally* John MacLeod & Reinhard Zimmermann, *Unworthiness to Inherit, Public Policy, Forfeiture: The Scottish Story*, 87 Tul L. Rev. 741 (2013); Carla Spivack, *Killers Shouldn't Inherit from Their Victims—Or Should They?*, 48 Ga. L. Rev. 145 (2013); Nili Cohen, *The Slayer Rule*, 92 B.U. L. Rev. 793 (2012).

A Wisconsin court held that a decedent's wife and daughter were not barred from inheriting from the decedent's intestate estate even though they assisted him in committing suicide. Since they did not intentionally kill him, there was no public policy restraint. *See In re* Estate of Schunk, 314 Wis.2d 483, 760 N.W.2d 446 (2008). Additional judicial decisions involve the impact of a state's slayer statute. *See, e.g.,* Fiel v. Hoffman, No. 4D14-1048, 2015 WL 4549604 (Fla. Dist. Ct. App. July 29, 2015) (holding that state slayer statute does not prohibit children of slayer from inheriting); Willingham v. Matthews, 163 So. 3d 1016 (Ala. 2014) (holding that when slayer statute provides that slayer is treated as having predeceased victim, effect is not to allow victim to inherit from slayer as having survived the slayer); Addison v. Metro. Life Ins. Co., 5 F. Supp. 2d 392 (W.D. Va. 1998) (holding that, as matter of federal common law, beneficiary who murdered spouse was not entitled to ERISA benefits). And Veterans Affairs regulations prevent the payout of life insurance benefits pursuant to a "slayer" type of scheme. *See* 38 C.F.R. § 9.5(e)(1)-(2) (2015).

Applicability of any slayer statute may be had through a civil determination under a "preponderance of the evidence" test, or through a criminal determination under a "beyond a reasonable doubt" test. *See Restatement (Third) of Property; Wills and Other Donative Transfers*, § 8.4 (2003) (Homicide—The Slayer Rule). In California, if one spouse is convicted of attempted murder, the injured spouse is entitled to 100 percent of the community interest in the retirement and pension benefits of the injuring spouse. *See* CAL. FAM. CODE § 782.5 (West 2015).

Uniform Probate Code (2019)

§ 2-803. **Effect of Homicide on Intestate Succession, Wills, Trusts, Joint Assets, Life Insurance, and Beneficiary Designations.** * * *

(b) [**Forfeiture of Statutory Benefits.**] An individual who feloniously and intentionally kills the decedent forfeits all benefits under this Article with respect to the decedent's estate, including an intestate share, an elective share, an omitted spouse's or child's share, a homestead allowance, exempt property, and a family allowance. If the decedent died intestate, the decedent's intestate estate passes as if the killer disclaimed his [or her] intestate share.

(c) [**Revocation of Benefits Under Governing Instruments.**] The felonious and intentional killing of the decedent:

> (1) revokes any revocable (i) disposition or appointment of property made by the decedent to the killer in a governing instrument, (ii) provision in a governing instrument conferring a general or nongeneral power of appointment on the killer, and (iii) nomination of the killer in a governing instrument, nominating or appointing the killer to serve in any fiduciary or representative capacity, including a personal representative, executor, trustee, or agent; and

> (2) severs the interests of the decedent and killer in property held by them at the time of the killing as joint tenants with the right of survivorship [or as community property with the right of survivorship], transforming the interests of the decedent and killer into equal tenancies in common. * * *

(g) [**Felonious and Intentional Killing; How Determined.**] After all right to appeal has been exhausted, a judgment of conviction establishing criminal accountability for the felonious and intentional killing of the decedent conclusively establishes the convicted individual as the decedent's killer for purposes of this section. In the absence of a conviction, the court, upon the petition of an interested person, must determine whether, under the preponderance of evidence standard, the individual would be found criminally accountable for the felonious and intentional killing of the decedent. If the court determines that, under that standard, the individual would be found criminally accountable for the felonious and intentional killing of the decedent, the determination conclusively establishes that individual as the decedent's killer for purposes of this section.

Shapira v. Union National Bank

Ohio Court of Common Pleas, Mahoning County, 1974
39 Ohio Misc. 28, 315 N.E.2d 825

HENDERSON, Judge.

This is an action for a declaratory judgment and the construction of the will of David Shapira, M.D., who died April 13, 1973, a resident of this county. By agreement of the parties, the case has been submitted upon the pleadings and the exhibit.

The portions of the will in controversy are as follows:

> 'Item VIII. All the rest, residue and remainder of my estate, real and personal, of every kind and description and wheresoever situated, which I may own or have the right to dispose of at the time of my decease, I give, devise and bequeath to my three (3) beloved children, to wit: Ruth Shapira Aharoni, of Tel Aviv, Israel, or wherever she may reside at the time of my death; to my son Daniel Jacob Shapira, and to my son Mark Benjamin Simon Shapira in equal shares, with the following qualifications: * * *

> '(b) My son Daniel Jacob Shapira should receive his share of the bequest only, if he is married at the time of my death to a Jewish girl whose both parents were Jewish. In the event that at the time of my death he is not married to a Jewish girl whose both parents were Jewish, then his share of this bequest should be kept by my executor for a period of not longer than seven (7) years and if my said son Daniel Jacob gets married within the seven year period to a Jewish girl whose both parents were Jewish, my executor is hereby instructed to turn over his share of my bequest to him. In the event, however, that my said son Daniel Jacob is unmarried within the seven (7) years after my death to a Jewish girl whose both parents were Jewish, or if he is married to a non Jewish girl, then his share of my estate, as provided in item 8 above should go to The State of Israel, absolutely.'

The provision for the testator's other son Mark, is conditioned substantially similarly. Daniel Jacob Shapira, the plaintiff, alleges that the condition upon his inheritance is unconstitutional, contrary to public policy and unenforceable because of its unreasonableness, and that he should be given his bequest free of the restriction. Daniel is 21 years of age, unmarried and a student at Youngstown State University.

The provision in controversy is an executory devise or legacy, under which vesting of the estate of Daniel Jacob Shapira or the State of Israel is not intended to take place necessarily at the death of the testator, but rather conditionally, at a time not later than seven years after the testator's death. The executory aspect of the provision, though rather unusual, does not render it invalid. Heath v. City of Cleveland (1926), 114 Ohio St. 535, 151 N.E. 649.

* * *

Plaintiff's argument that the condition in question violates constitutional safeguards is based upon the premise that the right to marry is protected by the Fourteenth Amendment to the Constitution of the United States. Meyer v. Nebraska (1923), 262 U.S. 390, 43 S.Ct. 625, 67 L.Ed. 1042; Skinner v. Oklahoma (1942), 316 U.S. 535, 62 S.Ct. 1110, 86 L.Ed. 1655; Loving v. Virginia (1967), 388 U.S. 1, 87 S.Ct. 1817, 18 L.Ed.2d 1010. In Meyer v. Nebraska, holding unconstitutional a state statute prohibiting the teaching of languages other than English, the court stated that the Fourteenth Amendment denotes the right to marry among other basic rights. In Skinner v. Oklahoma, holding unconstitutional a state statute providing for the sterilization of certain habitual criminals, the court stated that marriage and procreation are fundamental to the very existence and survival of the race. In Loving v. Virginia, the court held unconstitutional as violative of the Equal Protection and Due Process Clauses of the Fourteenth Amendment an antimiscegenation statute under which a black person and a white person were convicted for marrying. In its opinion the United States Supreme Court made the following statements, 388 U.S. at page 12, 87 S.Ct. at page 1823:

'There can be no doubt that restricting the freedom to marry solely because of racial classifications violates the central meaning of the Equal Protection Clause.

'* * * The freedom to marry has long been recognized as one of the vital personal rights essential to the orderly pursuit of happiness by free men.

'Marriage is one of the 'basic civil rights of man,' fundamental to our very existence and survival. * * * The Fourteenth Amendment requires that the freedom of choice to marry not be restricted by invidious racial discriminations. Under our Constitution, the freedom to marry, or not marry, a person of another race resides with the individual and cannot be infringed by the State.'

From the foregoing, it appears clear, as plaintiff contends, that the right to marry is constitutionally protected from restrictive state legislative action. Plaintiff submits, then, that under the doctrine of Shelley v. Kraemer (1948), 334 U.S. 1, 68 S.Ct. 836, 92 L.Ed. 1161, the constitutional protection of the Fourteenth Amendment is extended from direct state legislative action to the enforcement by state judicial proceedings of private provisions restricting the right to marry. Plaintiff contends that a judgment of this court upholding the condition restricting marriage would, under

Shelley v. Kraemer, constitute state action prohibited by the Fourteenth Amendment as much as a state statute.

In Shelley v. Kraemer the United States Supreme Court held that the action of the states to which the Fourteenth Amendment has reference includes action of state courts and state judicial officials. Prior to this decision the court had invalidated city ordinances which denied blacks the right to live in white neighborhoods. In Shelley v. Kraemer owners of neighboring properties sought to enjoin blacks from occupying properties which they had bought, but which were subjected to privately executed restrictions against use or occupation by any persons except those of the Caucasian race. Chief Justice Vinson noted, in the course of his opinion at page 13, 68 S.Ct. at page 842: 'These are cases in which the purposes of the agreements were secured only by judicial enforcement by state courts of the restrictive terms of the agreements.'

In the case at bar, this court is not being asked to enforce any restriction upon Daniel Jacob Shapira's constitutional right to marry. Rather, this court is being asked to enforce the testator's restriction upon his son's inheritance. If the facts and circumstances of this case were such that the aid of this court were sought to enjoin Daniel's marrying a non-Jewish girl, then the doctrine of Shelley v. Kraemer would be applicable, but not, it is believed, upon the facts as they are.

Counsel for plaintiff asserts, however, that his position with respect to the applicability of Shelley v. Kraemer to this case is fortified by two later decisions of the United States Supreme Court: Evans v. Newton (1966), 382 U.S. 296, 86 S.Ct. 486, 15 L.Ed.2d 373 and Pennsylvania v. Board of Directors of City Trusts of the City of Philadelphia (1957), 353 U.S. 230, 77 S.Ct. 806, 1 L.Ed.2d 792.

Evans v. Newton involved land willed in trust to the mayor and city council of Macon, Georgia, as a park for white people only, and to be controlled by a white board of managers. To avoid the city's having to enforce racial segregation in the park, the city officials resigned as trustees and private individuals were installed. The court held that such successor trustees, even though private individuals, became agencies or instrumentalities of the state and subject to the Fourteenth Amendment by reason of their exercising powers or carrying on functions governmental in nature. The following comment of Justice Douglas seems revealing: 'If a testator wanted to leave a school or center for the use of one race only and in no way implicated the State in the supervision, control, or management of that facility, we assume arguendo that no constitutional difficulty would be encountered.' 382 U.S. 300, 86 S.Ct. 489.

The case of Pennsylvania v. Board, as the full title, above, suggests, is a case in which money was left by will to the city of Philadelphia in trust for a college to admit poor white male orphans. The court held that the board which operated the college was an agency of the state of Pennsylvania, and that, therefore, its refusal to admit the plaintiffs because they were negroes was discrimination by the state forbidden by the Fourteenth Amendment.

So, in neither Evans v. Newton nor Pennsylvania v. Board was the doctrine of the earlier Shelley v. Kraemer applied or extended. Both of them involved restrictive actions by state governing agencies, in one case with respect to a park, in the other case with respect to a college. Although both the park and the college were founded upon testamentary gifts, the state action struck down by the court was not the judicial completion of the gifts, but rather the subsequent enforcement of the racial restrictions by the public management.

Basically, the right to receive property by will is a creature of the law, and is not a natural right or one guaranteed or protected by either the Ohio or the United States constitution. Patton v. Patton (1883), 39 Ohio St. 590; Hagerty v. State (1897), 55 Ohio St. 613, 45 N.E. 1046; State, ex rel. Taylor v. Guilbert (1904), 70 Ohio St. 229, 71 N.E. 636; Magoun v. Illinois Trust and Savings Bank (1898), 170 U.S. 283, 18 S. Ct. 594, 42 L.Ed. 1037; 55 Ohio Jurisprudence 2d 535, Wills, Section 64; 57 American Jurisprudence 138, Wills, Section 153. It is a fundamental rule of law in Ohio that a testator may legally entirely disinherit his children. 56 Ohio Jurisprudence 2d 252, Wills, Section 742; 55 Ohio Jurisprudence 2d 564, Wills, Section 101; Wilson v. Behr (C.A. Hamilton (1936)), 57 Ohio App. 117, 121, 12 N.E.2d 300, 5 O.O. 424. This would seem to demonstrate that, from a constitutional standpoint, a testator may restrict a child's inheritance. The court concludes, therefore, that the upholding and enforcement of the provisions of Dr. Shapira's will conditioning the bequests to his sons upon their marrying Jewish girls does not offend the Constitution of Ohio or of the United States. United States National Bank of Portland v. Snodgrass (1954), 202 Or. 530, 275 P.2d 860, 50 A.L.R.2d 725; Gordon v. Gordon (1955), 332 Mass. 197, 124 N.E.2d 228; 54 Mich.L.Rev. 297 (1955); cf. 39 Minn.L.Rev. 809 (1955).

* * *

The condition that Daniel's share should be 'turned over to him if he should marry a Jewish girl whose both parents were Jewish' constitutes a partial restraint upon marriage. If the condition were that the beneficiary not marry anyone, the restraint would be general or total, and, at least in the case of a first marriage, would be held to be contrary to public policy and void. A partial restraint of marriage which imposes only reasonable restrictions is valid, and not contrary to public policy: 5 Bowe-Parker: Page on Wills 460, Section 44.25; 56 Ohio Jurisprudence 2d 243, Wills, Section 729; 52 American Jurisprudence 2d 1023, Marriage, Section 181. The great weight of authority in the United States is that gifts conditioned upon the beneficiary's marrying within a particular religious class or faith are reasonable. 5 Bowe-Parker; Page on Wills 461, Section 44.25; 52 American Jurisprudence 2d 1025, Marriage, Section 183; 56 Ohio Jurisprudence 2d 245, Wills, Section 731; 1 Prentice-Hall, Estate Planning, Law of Wills, 373, Paragraph 375.20; 1 Restatement of the Law, Trusts 2d, 166, Section 62(h); National Bank v. Snodgrass (*supra*), annotation, 50 A.L.R.2d 740; Gordon v. Gordon, *supra*; In re Harris (1955), 143 N.Y.2d 746; Matter of Seaman (1916), 218 N.Y. 77, 112 N.E. 576; Matter of Liberman (1939), 279 N.Y. 458, 18 N.E.2d 658; In re Silverstein's Will (1956), 155 N.Y.S.2d 598; In re Clayton's Estate (Phila.Co.Pa.1930), 13 Pa.D. & C. 413; Pacholder v. Rosenheim (1916), 129 Md. 455, 99 A. 672.

Plaintiff contends, however, that in Ohio a condition such as the one in this case is void as against the public policy of this state. In Ohio, as elsewhere, a testator may not attach a condition to a gift which is in violation of public policy. 56 Ohio Jurisprudence 2d 238, Wills, Section 722; Neidler v. Donaldson (P.C. Seneca 1966), 9 Ohio Misc. 208, 224 N.E.2d 404, 38 O.O.2d 360. There can be no question about the soundness of plaintiff's position that the public policy of Ohio favors freedom of religion and that it is guaranteed by Section 7, Article I of the Ohio Constitution, providing that 'all men have a natural and indefeasible right to worship Almighty God according to the dictates of their own conscience.' Plaintiff's position that the free choice of religious practice cannot be circumscribed or controlled by contract is substantiated by Hackett v. Hackett (C.A. Lucas 1958), 78 Ohio Law Abs. 485, 150 N.E.2d 431. This case held that a covenant in a separation agreement, incorporated in a divorce decree, that the mother would rear a daughter in the Roman Catholic faith was unenforceable. However, the controversial condition in the case at bar is a partial restraint upon marriage and not a covenant to restrain the freedom of religious practice; and, of course, this court is not being asked to hold the plaintiff in contempt for failing to marry a Jewish girl of Jewish parentage.

Counsel contends that if 'Dr. David Shapira, during his life, had tried to impose upon his son those restrictions set out in his Will he would have violated the public policy of Ohio as shown in Hackett v. Hackett. The public policy is equally violated by the restrictions Dr. Shapira has placed on his son by his Will.' This would be true, by analogy, if Dr. Shapira, in his lifetime, had tried to force his son to marry a Jewish girl as the condition of a completed gift. But it is not true that if Dr. Shapira had agreed to make his son an *inter vivos* gift if he married a Jewish girl within seven years, that his son could have forced him to make the gift free of the condition.

It is noted, furthermore, in this connection, that the courts of Pennsylvania distinguish between testamentary gifts conditioned upon the religious faith of the beneficiary and those conditioned upon marriage to persons of a particular religious faith. In In re Clayton's Estate, *supra* (13 Pa.D. & C. 413), the court upheld a gift of a life estate conditioned upon the beneficiary's not marrying a woman of the Catholic faith. In its opinion the court distinguishes the earlier case of Drace v. Klinedinst (1922), 275 Pa. 266, 118 A. 907, in which a life estate willed to grandchildren, provided they remained faithful to a particular religion, was held to violate the public policy of Pennsylvania. In Clayton's Estate, the court said that the condition concerning marriage did not affect the faith of the beneficiary, and that the condition, operating only on the choice of a wife, was too remote to be regarded as coercive of religious faith.

But counsel relies upon an Ohio case much more nearly in point, that of Moses v. Zook (C.A. Wayne 1934), 18 Ohio Law Abs. 373. This case involves a will in which the testatrix gave the income of her residual estate in trust to her niece and nephews for two years and then the remainder to them. Item twelve provides as follows: 'If any of my nieces or nephews should marry outside of the Protestant Faith, then they shall not receive any part of my estate devised or bequeathed to them.' The will contained no gift over upon violation of the marriage condition. The holding of the trial court was that item twelve was null and void as being against public policy and the seven other items of the will should be administered as specified in detail by the court. There is nothing in the reported opinion to show to what extent, if at all, the question of public policy was in issue or contested in the trial court; only one of the several other unrelated holdings of the trial court (not including the public policy holding) was assigned as error; and although the Court of Appeals adopted the unexcepted—to holdings of the trial court, there is no citation of authorities or discussion concerning the public policy question itself. The case was apparently not appealed to the Supreme Court, and no other cases in Ohio have been cited or found. Moses v. Zook differs in its facts in not containing a gift over upon breach of the condition, and appears not to have been a sufficiently litigated or reasoned establishment of the public policy of Ohio which this court should be obliged to follow.

The only cases cited by plaintiff's counsel in accord with the holding in Moses v. Zook are some English cases and one American decision. In England the courts have held that partial restrictions upon marriage to persons not of the Jewish faith, or of Jewish parentage, were not contrary to public policy or invalid. Hodgson v. Halford (1879 Eng.) L.R. 11 Ch.Div. 959, 50 A.L.R.2d 742. Other cases in England, however, have invalidated forfeitures of similarly conditioned provisions for children upon the basis of uncertainty or indefiniteness. Re Blaiberg (1940), Ch. 385 (1940), 1 All. Eng. 632, 50 A.L.R.2d 746; Clayton v. Ramsden (1943), A.C. 320 (1943), 1 All.Eng. 16–H.L., 50 A.L.R.2d 746; Re Donn (1944), Ch. 8 (1943), 2 All.Eng. 564, 50 A.L.R.2d 746; Re Moss' Trusts (1945), 1 All.Eng. 207, 61 Times L. 147, 50 A.L.R.2d 747. Since the foregoing decisions, a later English case has upheld a condition precedent that a granddaughter-beneficiary marry a person of Jewish faith and the child of Jewish parents. The court distinguished the cases cited above as not applicable to a condition precedent under which the legatee must qualify for the gift by marrying as specified, and there was found to be no difficulty with indefiniteness where the legatee married unquestionably outside the Jewish faith. Re Wolffe (1953), 1 Week L.R. 1211 (1953), 2 All.Eng. 697, 50 A.L.R.2d 747.

The American case cited by plaintiff is that of Maddox v. Maddox (1854), 52 Va. (11 Grattain's) 804. The testator in this case willed a remainder to his niece if she remain a member of the Society of Friends. When the niece arrived at a marriageable age there were but five or six unmarried men of the society in the neighborhood in which she lived. She married a non-member and thus lost her own membership. The court held the condition to be an unreasonable restraint upon marriage and void, and that there being no gift over upon breach of the condition, the condition was in terrorem, and did not avoid the bequest. It can be seen that while the court considered the testamentary condition to be a restraint upon marriage, it was primarily one in restraint of religious faith. The court said that with the small number of eligible bachelors in the area the condition would have operated as a virtual prohibition of the niece's marrying, and that she could not be expected to 'go abroad' in search of a helpmate or to be subjected to the chance of being sought after by a stranger. The court distinguished the facts of its case from those in England upholding conditions upon marriage by observing that England was 'already overstocked with inhabitants' while this country had 'an unbounded extent of territory, a large portion of which is yet unsettled, and in which increase of population is one of the main elements of national prosperity.' The other ground upon which the Virginia court rested its decision, that the condition was in terrorem because of the absence of a gift over, is clearly not applicable to the case at bar, even if it were in accord with Ohio law, because of the gift over to the State of Israel contained in the Shapira will.

In arguing for the applicability of the Maddox v. Maddox test of reasonableness to the case at bar, counsel for the plaintiff asserts that the number of eligible Jewish females in this county would be an extremely small minority of the total population especially as compared with the comparatively much greater number in New York, whence have come many of the cases comprising the weight of authority upholding the validity of such clauses. There are no census figures in evidence. While this court could probably take judicial notice of the fact that the Jewish community is a minor, though important segment of our total local population, nevertheless the court is by no means justified in judicial knowledge that there is an insufficient number of eligible young ladies of Jewish parentage in this area from which Daniel would have a reasonable latitude of choice. And of course, Daniel is not at all confined in his choice to residents of this county, which is a very different circumstance in this day of travel by plane and freeway and communication by telephone, from the horse and buggy days of the 1854 Maddox v. Maddox decision. Consequently, the decision does not appear to be an appropriate yardstick of reasonableness under modern living conditions.

Plaintiff's counsel contends that the Shapira will falls within the principle of Fineman v. Central National Bank (1961), 87 Ohio Law Abs. 236, 175 N.E.2d 837, 18 O.O.2d 33, holding that the public policy of Ohio does not countenance a bequest or device conditioned on the beneficiary's obtaining a separation or divorce from his wife. Counsel argues that the Shapira condition would encourage the beneficiary to marry a qualified girl just to receive the bequest, and then to divorce her afterward. This possibility seems too remote to be a pertinent application of the policy against bequests conditioned upon divorce. Most other authorities agree with Fineman v. Bank that as a general proposition, a testamentary gift effective only on condition that the recipient divorce or separate from his or her spouse is against public policy and invalid. 14 A.L.R.3d 1222. But no authorities have been found extending the principle to support plaintiff's position. Indeed, in measuring the reasonableness of the condition in question, both the father and the court should be able to assume that the son's motive would be proper. And surely the son should not gain the advantage of the avoidance of the condition by the possibility of his own impropriety.

Finally, counsel urges that the Shapira condition tends to pressure Daniel, by the reward of money, to marry within seven years without opportunity for mature reflection, and jeopardizes his college education. It seems to the court, on the contrary, that the seven year time limit would be a most reasonable grace period, and one which would give the son ample opportunity for exhaustive reflection and fulfillment of the condition without constraint or oppression. Daniel is no more being 'blackmailed into a marriage by immediate financial gain,' as suggested by counsel, than would be the beneficiary of a living gift or conveyance upon consideration of a future marriage—an arrangement which has long been sanctioned by the courts of this state. Thompson v. Thompson (1867), 17 Ohio St. 649.

In the opinion of this court, the provision made by the testator for the benefit of the State of Israel upon breach or failure of the condition is most significant for two reasons. First, it distinguishes this case from the bare forfeitures in Moses v. Zook, and in Maddox v. Maddox (including the technical in terrorem objection), and, in a way, from the vagueness and indefiniteness doctrine of some of the English cases. Second, and of greater importance, it demonstrates the depth of the testator's conviction. His purpose was not merely a negative one designed to punish his son for not carrying out his wishes. His unmistakable testamentary plan was that his possessions be used to encourage the preservation of the Jewish faith and blood, hopefully through his sons, but, if not, then through the State of Israel. Whether this judgment was wise is not for this court to determine. But it is the duty of this court to honor the testator's intention within the limitations of law and of public policy. The prerogative granted to a testator by the laws of this state to dispose of his estate according to his conscience is entitled to as much judicial protection and enforcement as the prerogative of a beneficiary to receive an inheritance.

It is the conclusion of this court that public policy should not, and does not preclude the fulfillment of Dr. Shapira's purpose, and that in accordance with the weight of authority in this country, the conditions contained in his will are reasonable restrictions upon marriage, and valid.

Notes

The reasonableness of the testator's restriction was instrumental in the result reached by the *Shapira* court, but other courts have looked to whether the restriction would produce so much harm as to be a violation of the public interest. *See, e.g., In re* Estate of Feinberg, 235 Ill. 2d 256, 919 N.E.2d 888 (2009) (testamentary trust created by grandfather that revoked trust assets from going to any grandchild who married a non-Jew was valid since grandchildren did not have vested interest in trust corpus and were not grandfather's heirs at law, and the provision did not violate public policy). In *Feinberg*, the state's trial court and appellate court found the grandfather's restriction a violation of public policy since it caused family strife, interfered with the fundamental right to marry, and was capable of exerting a continuing disruptive influence upon marriages in the future. But the state's supreme court disagreed and sustained the right of the grandfather to restrict the trust assets in accordance with his religious beliefs.

Restatement (Third) of Property (Wills & Don. Trans.) (2015)

§ 10.1 Donor's Intention Determines The Meaning Of A Donative Document and Is Given Effect to the Maximum Extent Allowed by Law.

The controlling consideration in determining the meaning of a donative document is the donor's intention. The donor's intention is given effect to the maximum extent allowed by law.

B. Statutory Restraints

McKinney v. Richitelli

North Carolina Supreme Court, 2003
357 N.C. 483, 586 S.E.2d 258

EDMUNDS, Justice.

Plaintiff Karen McKinney, acting individually and as the personal representative of the estate of her deceased son, Michael Edward McKinney * * * (Michael), brought this declaratory action against Michael's father, James Everett Richitelli (defendant), to determine the rights of the parties with respect to any proceeds of Michael's estate and to any proceeds of a wrongful death action brought on Michael's behalf. The Court of Appeals reversed the trial court's entry of summary judgment in favor of plaintiff. For the reasons discussed herein, we reverse the decision of the Court of Appeals.

Taken in the light most favorable to defendant, the evidence shows that plaintiff and defendant were married in 1976 and that their son, Michael, was born on 30 July 1977. Plaintiff and defendant were divorced in 1981. The district court entered a custody order awarding primary custody of Michael to plaintiff, while providing defendant visitation rights. Although the custody order required defendant to pay child support of $240.00 per month beginning on 1 October 1980, he failed to make any payments from 1 January 1981 through Michael's eighteenth birthday, 30 July 1995. Defendant admits that he had no contact or communication with Michael during this period, but explains that for most of these years, he was either incarcerated for theft and robbery convictions or suffering from drug and alcohol abuse.

Defendant's first contact with Michael after 1981 came when he wrote Michael in March 1997. At this time, Michael was nineteen years old, had been diagnosed with cancer, and would later file a medical malpractice action in which he alleged that a radiologist caused his illness. By defendant's accounts, after their initial contact, he and Michael visited with each other on at least three occasions and spoke regularly by telephone before Michael's death. Between October 1997 and December 1998, defendant sent Michael six checks totaling $3,150.

Michael's medical malpractice suit was filed on 13 May 1998, and he died intestate on 21 February 1999. After plaintiff was appointed as the personal representative of Michael's estate on 19 March 1999, she amended Michael's suit to include a wrongful death claim. While the wrongful death claim was pending, plaintiff on 6 July 2000 filed a declaratory judgment complaint against defendant, seeking a judicial determination of defendant's rights to any potential award resulting from the wrongful death suit. Defendant answered and moved to dismiss the declaratory judgment action pursuant to N.C. R. Civ. P. 12(b)(6). Following discovery, plaintiff filed a motion for summary judgment claiming she was entitled to judgment as a matter of law because defendant's behavior "during the period of 1981 through July 30, 1995 constituted a willful abandonment resulting in the loss of his right to intestate succession in any part of [Michael's] estate including wrongful death proceeds."

The motions were heard in the Superior Court, Wake County, on 31 January 2001. The key issue was the interpretation of N.C.G.S. § 31A-2, "Acts barring rights of parents," which provides as follows:

Any parent who has wil[l]fully abandoned the care and maintenance of his or her child shall lose all right to intestate succession in any part of the child's estate and all right to administer the estate of the child, except—

(1) Where the abandoning parent resumed its care and maintenance at least one year prior to the death of the child and continued the same until its death; or

(2) Where a parent has been deprived of the custody of his or her child under an order of a court of competent jurisdiction and the parent has substantially complied with all orders of the court requiring contribution to the support of the child.

N.C.G.S. § 31A-2 (2001). On 14 March 2001, the trial court denied defendant's motion to dismiss and granted plaintiff's motion for summary judgment by an order declaring "that pursuant to N.C.G.S. § 31A-2 defendant . . . has lost all right to intestate succession in any part of [Michael's] estate, including, but not limited to, the proceeds of any wrongful death claim because of his willful abandonment of the care and maintenance of [Michael] during his minority."

Defendant appealed, and in an unpublished opinion, the Court of Appeals reversed the trial court's judgment. McKinney v. Richitelli, 149 N.C.App. 973, 563 S.E.2d 100 (2002). The Court of Appeals noted that "our case law remains unclear whether a parent can resume a relationship with a child after the child reaches the age of majority and therefore fall within the first exception to N.C.G.S. § 31A-2," but concluded that a genuine issue of material fact existed as to whether defendant had resumed a relationship with Michael sufficient to invoke the exception set out in N.C.G.S. § 31A-2(1). The Court of Appeals' opinion and the briefs to this Court relied heavily on our order vacating In re Estate of Lunsford, 143 N.C.App. 646, 547 S.E.2d 483 (2001), a case similar to the one at issue, and remanding the case only for additional findings of fact by the trial court. In re Estate of Lunsford, 354 N.C. 571, 556 S.E.2d 292 (2001). However, in that order, we made no determinations as to questions of law. Because the record in the case at bar is sufficiently developed to allow us to reach the underlying issues, we do not consider arguments based on our order in Lunsford to be applicable.

Summary judgment may be granted in a declaratory judgment action "where 'the pleadings, depositions, answers to interrogatories, and admissions on file, together with the affidavits, if any, show that there is no genuine issue as to any material fact and that any party is entitled to a judgment as a matter of law.'" Williams v. Blue Cross Blue Shield of N.C., 357 N.C. 170, 178, 581 S.E.2d 415, 422 (2003) (quoting N.C.G.S. § 1A-1, Rule 56(c) (2001)). Plaintiff argues that the Court of Appeals erred in determining that a genuine issue of material fact existed as to whether defendant had resumed statutorily adequate care and maintenance of Michael.

In deciding whether summary judgment was proper in this case, we must undertake a three-fold inquiry. First, we must determine whether N.C.G.S. § 31A-2 applies after a child has reached his or her majority to prevent an abandoning parent from recovering through an offspring that was abandoned while a minor.[2] If so, we must next consider whether defendant abandoned Michael such that N.C.G.S. § 31A-2 precludes defendant from taking under intestate succession. Finally, if we find that defendant abandoned Michael, we must determine whether a parent who has abandoned his or her minor child may thereafter resume a parent-child relationship with the now-adult child and, by so doing, come under the exception set out in N.C.G.S. § 31A-2(1). See Heyward D. Armstrong, In re Estate of Lunsford and Statutory Ambiguity: Trying to Reconcile Child Abandonment and the Intestate Succession Act, 81 N.C. L.Rev. 1149 (2003).

We observe at the outset that N.C.G.S § 31A-2 is ambiguous because nowhere in chapter 31A of the General Statutes is the term "child" defined, nor is the meaning of the term clear from its context. Thus "child" here could reasonably mean either a minor offspring or an offspring of any age. Although defendant contends that the word "child" as used in the body of the statute logically refers to a "minor child," he argues that the word "child" as used in the exception set out in N.C.G.S. § 31A-2(1) refers to a child regardless of age. Under defendant's interpretation, a parent may reconcile with his or her offspring after the child has reached majority and thereafter take if the adult child dies intestate. In contrast, plaintiff argues that under N.C.G.S. § 31A-2 the continuous abandonment of a minor child by a parent permanently terminates that parent's right to participate in the intestate share when the child reaches his or her majority. Under plaintiff's interpretation, the exception set out in N.C.G.S. § 31A-2(1) can take effect only if the reconciliation occurs while the child is still a minor.

---

2. Logically, N.C.G.S. § 31A-2 must apply to an abandonment that initially occurs while the child is a minor. After all, a parent cannot abandon an emancipated or adult child when the parent has no further responsibility for the child.

In interpreting such a statutory ambiguity, we adhere to the following rules of construction:

> Where the language of a statute is clear and unambiguous, there is no room for judicial construction and the courts must construe the statute using its plain meaning. Utilities Comm. v. Edmisten, Atty. General, 291 N.C. 451, 232 S.E.2d 184 (1977). But where a statute is ambiguous, judicial construction must be used to ascertain the legislative will. Young v. Whitehall Co., 229 N.C. 360, 49 S.E.2d 797 (1948). The primary rule of construction of a statute is to ascertain the intent of the legislature and to carry out such intention to the fullest extent. Buck v. Guaranty Co., 265 N.C. 285, 144 S.E.2d 34 (1965). This intent "must be found from the language of the act, its legislative history and the circumstances surrounding its adoption which throw light upon the evil sought to be remedied." Milk Commission v. Food Stores, 270 N.C. 323, 332, 154 S.E.2d 548, 555 (1967).

Burgess v. Your House of Raleigh, Inc., 326 N.C. 205, 209, 388 S.E.2d 134, 136–37 (1990).

Our analysis begins with Avery v. Brantley, 191 N.C. 396, 131 S.E. 721 (1926). In Avery, the father abandoned his daughter, and the issue before us was the father's ability to recover in the negligence suit brought when his intestate daughter was killed in an accident. We considered two statutes then in effect. One statute, 1 N.C. Cons.Stat. § 189 (1920), terminated the rights of a natural parent to the care, custody, and services of a child once the parent gave up the child for adoption. The other statute, 1 N.C. Cons.Stat. 137(6) (Supp.1924), provided that a parent would inherit if a child died intestate. This second statute did not contain a provision limiting its operation when a parent had abandoned the child. Because the child in Avery had not been adopted, we held that the statutes could not be interpreted in pari materia and that the statute allowing the parents to inherit from their intestate daughter controlled. *Id.* at 400, 131 S.E. at 722. Accordingly, we concluded that the mother and father shared in the proceeds of the child's estate, even though the father had abandoned the child. *Id.* Thereafter, the General Assembly amended 137(6) to provide,

> [i]f, in the lifetime of its father and mother, a child dies intestate, without leaving husband, wife or child, or the issue of a child, its estate shall be equally divided between the father and mother. If one of the parents is dead at the time of the death of the child, the surviving parent shall be entitled to the whole of the estate. . . . Provided, that a parent, or parents, who has willfully abandoned the care, custody, nurture and maintenance of such child to its kindred, relatives or other person, shall forfeit all and every right to participate in any part of said child's estate under the provisions of this section.

Act of Mar. 9, 1927, ch. 231, 1927 N.C. Sess. Laws 591 (amending 1 N.C. Cons.Stat. § 137(6), later recodified as N.C.G.S. § 28-149(6) (1943)).

With the adoption in 1960 of a new Intestate Succession Act, N.C.G.S. ch. 29, N.C.G.S. § 28-149(6) was abolished. The General Statutes Commission, "cognizant of the inadequate statutory law relating to the inheritance of property by unworthy heirs," thereupon created a special committee to draft new legislation addressing the topic. Report of Drafting Committee to the General Statutes Commission, Special Report of the General Statutes Commission on an Act to Be Entitled "Acts Barring Property Rights," at 1 (Feb. 8, 1961). The committee responded by drafting a bill (enacted by the General Assembly and now codified as N.C.G.S. § 31A-2) that, among other provisions, prohibited abandoning parents from recovering through their intestate children. The committee stated that the purpose of this section was to "revise, broaden, and reintroduce" abolished N.C.G.S. § 28-149(6). *Id.* at 4. The committee reasoned that "[i]t seems very inequitable to allow a parent who has abandoned his child to inherit from such child when the child dies intestate." *Id.* However, the committee also provided two exceptions that allowed an abandoning parent to share in the intestate's estate. *Id.* The first of these exceptions encouraged an abandoning parent to resume his or her duties of care and maintenance of the child in an effort to renew the parent-child relationship. See N.C.G.S. § 31A-2(1).

It is apparent from this history that the legislative intent behind N.C.G.S. § 31A-2 was both to discourage parents from shirking their responsibility of support to their children and to prevent an abandoning parent from reaping an undeserved bonanza. Were we to hold that section 31A-2 has no application once a child reaches majority, a parent who has abandoned his or her child would nevertheless automatically inherit if the still-abandoned child died intestate after reaching the age of eighteen. Such an interpretation would frustrate the statute's purpose and effectively forgive the abandoning parent's dereliction. Therefore, we hold that N.C.G.S. § 31A-2 applies to any abandoned child dying intestate regardless of the child's age at death.

We next consider whether defendant abandoned Michael. While we have observed the difficulty of formulating a uniform definition of the term, we have explained "abandonment" of a child as "wil[l]ful or intentional conduct on the part of the parent which evinces a settled purpose to forego all parental duties and relinquish all parental claims to the child." Pratt v. Bishop, 257 N.C. 486, 501, 126 S.E.2d 597, 608 (1962); see also In re Young, 346 N.C. 244, 251, 485 S.E.2d 612, 617 (1997).

> Abandonment has also been defined as wil[l]ful neglect and refusal to perform the natural and legal obligations of parental care and support. It has been held that if a parent withholds his presence, his love, his care, the opportunity to display filial affection, and wil[l]fully neglects to lend support and maintenance, such parent relinquishes all parental claims and abandons the child.

Pratt v. Bishop, 257 N.C. at 501, 126 S.E.2d at 608; see also Lessard v. Lessard, 77 N.C.App. 97, 100–01, 334 S.E.2d 475, 477 (1985) (utilizing the Pratt definitions of abandonment in the context of N.C.G.S. § 31A-2), aff'd per curiam, 316 N.C. 546, 342 S.E.2d 522 (1986). "Maintenance" or support refers to a parent's financial obligation to provide support during the child's minority. See generally Wells v. Wells, 227 N.C. 614, 44 S.E.2d 31 (1947).

Applying these precepts to this case, the evidence, even viewed in the light most favorable to defendant, demonstrates that defendant abandoned Michael. From the time Michael was four until after his eighteenth birthday, defendant violated the court's order by failing to make any child support payments. Both in her brief and at oral argument, plaintiff claimed defendant owed approximately $42,000 in arrearages accrued during Michael's minority. Although defendant states that for a significant amount of that time he was either unemployed or in prison, at no point during this period did defendant attempt to modify the child support order. Even though defendant was entitled under the support order to visit Michael on alternate weekends, holidays, and two weeks in the summer, he did not see his son even once in fifteen years. Defendant admits that he had no communication with Michael at all during this period even though he was allowed to write letters from prison during his periods of incarceration. These findings demonstrate "wil[l]ful or intentional conduct on the part of the parent which evinces a settled purpose to forego all parental duties and relinquish all parental claims to the child." Pratt v. Bishop, 257 N.C. at 501, 126 S.E.2d at 608. Thus, we hold that defendant abandoned Michael as contemplated by N.C.G.S. § 31A-2.

Finally, we must determine whether defendant is entitled to the benefit of the exception provided in N.C.G.S. § 31A-2(1). Defendant argues that this exception applies to any abandoned child, whether or not that child has reached majority. He reasons that although the duty of maintenance or financial support ends at majority, the duty of care applies to a child of any age. Because he provided sufficient evidence to establish that he resumed the care and maintenance of Michael at least one year before Michael's death, defendant argues that his conduct in the final two years of Michael's life restored defendant's right to inheritance. We find defendant's arguments unpersuasive.

The critical inquiry as to N.C.G.S. § 31A-2(1) is not whether a parent can resume a relationship with a child, but whether a parent "resumed its care and maintenance at least one year prior to the death of the child and continued the same until its death." N.C.G.S. § 31A-2(1). The exception requires that the parent resume both the "care *and* maintenance" of the child. *Id.* (emphasis added). These requirements may not be read in the disjunctive. As stated above, while "care" pertains to love and concern for the child, "maintenance" refers to the financial support of a child during minority. See generally Wells v. Wells, 227 N.C. 614, 44 S.E.2d 31. Our jurisprudence establishes that "[t]he authority of the court to require support for a normal child ceases when the legal obligation to support no longer exists. The parents' duty to support . . . cease[s] upon emancipation." Shoaf v. Shoaf, 282 N.C. 287, 290, 192 S.E.2d 299, 302 (1972). "The age of emancipation is precisely fixed— eighteen." *Id.* at 291, 192 S.E.2d at 303. Although a parent may have a duty of support of an older child who is still in school, N.C.G.S. § 50-13.4(c)(2) (2001), there is no evidence to indicate this provision applies here. In the case at bar, defendant did not reestablish contact with Michael until he was almost twenty years old. Even assuming that defendant presented sufficient evidence that he resumed the care of Michael, defendant cannot resume the maintenance of Michael because his legal obligation to do so ceased at eighteen.

We held above that N.C.G.S. §31A-2 pertains to the estate of a child of any age. Under the logic of that analysis—that a parent who abandons a child should benefit from the death of the child only if the parent has resumed a parental relationship with the child—an abandoning parent who seeks to come under the exception in N.C.G.S. §31A-2(1) must renew both the care and the maintenance of the child during the child's minority, when care and maintenance are most valuable. See Williford v. Williford, 288 N.C. 506, 510, 219 S.E.2d 220, 223 (1975) (although issue not squarely presented, we held that "the plaintiff father, having abandoned the deceased *when the latter was a minor child,* may not now share in the proceeds of the settlement of the claim for wrongful death now in the hands of the administratrix") (emphasis added). Under the terms of the statute, the care and maintenance must continue for a year before the child's death. Therefore, we hold that, in order to benefit from this provision, a parent must renew such care and maintenance at least one year before the child reaches the age of eighteen.

This holding not only follows from the preceding historical and textual analysis, it is also consistent with our understanding of the General Assembly's overall intent. When an adult or emancipated child discerns that a parent who had previously abandoned him or her now sincerely seeks reconciliation, the child is free to execute a will making provisions for the no-longer-wayward parent. Although we acknowledge that this argument is of limited application to the facts before us because any recovery for Michael's wrongful death would pass under the laws of intestate succession even if he had written a will, see N.C.G.S. §28A-18-2(a) (2001), the larger principle that the abandoned child has the power to prevent a reconciled parent from being excluded from the child's estate informs our analysis. We believe that the General Assembly has adequately demonstrated an unwillingness to allow an abandoning parent to take from an abandoned adult child as the result of a mechanical application of the rules of intestate succession.

We hold that summary judgment in favor of plaintiff was proper in this case. Accordingly, we reverse the decision of the Court of Appeals.

REVERSED.

Notes

The statute in the *McKinney* decision was instrumental in barring the father from taking from the intestate son. But not all statutes are the same. For example, in Keybank National Association v. Hanns, No. 22692, 2009 WL 1111255 (Ohio Ct. App. Apr. 24, 2009), the Ohio Court of Appeals relied upon the state statute—Ohio Rev. Code §2105.10—to permit a noncustodial father to inherit from his disabled daughter's intestate estate. The father had not communicated with the daughter for a long time, but the statute only barred an intestate heir for abandonment if, without justifiable cause, the prospective heir of the minor had failed to communicate with, care for, and support the minor. This must occur for at least one year prior to the death of the minor. The court interpreted the statute as providing that if the parent performed *any of these three functions* within the year, then the parent had not abandoned the minor. Here, since the father's child support was less than one year in arrears, he had not abandoned the child for purposes of the statute. Nonetheless, the amount that he owed in past support was deducted from his share of the child's estate. In the absence of a statute, the court seems powerless to prevent intestate inheritance due to abandonment. *See, e.g., In re* Estate of Shellenbarger, 169 Cal. App. 4th 894, 86 Cal. Rptr. 3d 862 (2008) (failure to provide support not sufficient reason to deny father inheritance rights under state's intestate statutes, where man abandoned pregnant wife in 1962, divorced her, paid very little child support, and had not met child in 42 years, because statutes contained no prohibition from inheriting). However, in *In re* R.W., 398 N.J. Super. 266, 942 A.2d 1 (2008), where a mother had abused, neglected, and then abandoned her minor children, the mother was prohibited from inheriting her deceased child's estate, despite the lack of any exception that would prevent the mother from inheriting as an intestate heir under the applicable intestacy laws. For a commentary on the case, see Michael T. Flannery, *Let No Bad Deed Go Rewarded: The Case of In re R.W.*, LexisNexis Expert Commentary, 2009 EMERGING ISSUES 3556 (April 2009) (available at Lexis, Estates, Gifts and Trusts Emerging Issues library).

Statutory restraints may also bar an abandoning spouse from intestate succession from the other spouse. In the case of Estate of Joyner v. Joyner, 753 S.E.2d 192 (N.C. Ct. App. 2014), a husband and wife had been married for 26 years and continuously lived in the same house. The wife died intestate in January 2011, with the husband the only heir; the husband died one month later, also intestate. The wife's estate sought to bar the surviving husband's estate from inheriting due to the husband's abandonment, specifying that he: (1) refused to take his wife to the doctor without being paid for his time and gas; (2) refused to engage in intimacy with his wife; (3) moved into a separate bedroom; and (4) refused to provide food or financial support to his wife for the most recent six years of their marriage. But the court held that this conduct did not constitute abandonment sufficient under the North Carolina statute, N.C. Gen. Stat. §31A-1, which provides that a spouse "who willfully and without just cause abandons and refuses to live with the other spouse and is not living with the other spouse at the time of the spouse's death" loses intestate succession rights. Because the husband remained in the marital home, albeit in a separate bedroom, he did not abandon his spouse so as to lose intestacy rights.

Problem

Mother and father never married but had one child together, a daughter. Soon after the daughter's birth, the couple separated. The mother went to court to collect child support from the father, and he was ordered to pay, which he did in a random fashion until the daughter turned 18 years old. When the daughter was 20 years old, she was killed in an automobile accident and died intestate. Her mother then petitioned the court to prevent the father from inheriting a portion of the daughter's intestate estate. Under the state's statute, the mother argued that the father "willfully abandoned his duty to provide reasonable and adequate support" because the father only paid what was ordered by the court, never exceeding that minimal amount to meet the child's needs. The father admitted to being negligent in payment of support often, but consistently paid what was ordered by the court and always paid any arrears he owed. The mother argued that the small amount was not sufficient to raise the daughter and, hence, he abandoned his daughter and should be denied any share in her estate. As probate judge, how would you rule on the mother's petition? *See* Shearin v. Reid, 812 S.E.2d 381 (N.C. Ct. App. 2018).

II. Protection of Issue

In re Estate of Laura

Supreme Court of New Hampshire, 1997
141 N.H. 628, 690 A.2d 1011

THAYER, Justice.

The testator, Edward R. Laura, Sr., died on August 23, 1990. The petitioners, two generations of the testator's heirs who were excluded from his will, appeal a decision of the Rockingham County Probate Court (Maher, J.), approving the order of the Master (Gerald Taube, Esq.), that barred them from inheriting any portion of the testator's estate. On appeal, the petitioners argue that the probate court erred in: (1) ruling that the testator did not revoke his will when he drafted an unexecuted codicil in 1990; (2) ruling that the testator's great-grandchildren were not pretermitted heirs under RSA 551:10 (1974); and (3) refusing to segregate certain assets from the testator's estate. We affirm in part, vacate in part, and remand.

The record reveals the following facts. The testator had three children. Two children, Edward R. Laura, Jr. and Shirley Chicoine, survived him. Shirley and Edward each have three children. The testator's third child, Jo Ann Laura, died in 1974. She was survived by two children, Richard Chicoine and Neil F. Chicoine, Jr. Neil died in 1988 and is survived by two children, Cecilia Chicoine and Neil F. Chicoine, III, the testator's great-grandchildren. Richard, acting on behalf of himself and the testator's great-grandchildren, and Edward are the petitioners here.

Sometime prior to September 17, 1984, the testator hired an attorney to draft his will. The will was executed on September 26, 1984. It provided that the testator's estate would pass to his daughter, Shirley, who was also designated as the executrix of his estate. In addition, the will named the testator's deceased daughter, Jo Ann, and explicitly named his son, Edward, and his grandchildren, Richard and Neil, in a paragraph designed to disinherit them. Paragraph seven of the will provided:

> I have intentionally omitted to provide in this Will for any heirs at law, next
> of kin, or relatives of mine, by blood, marriage or adoption, specifically but
> not limited to my son, Edward and my grandchildren, Richard and Neil,
> except as aforesaid, and such omissions are not occasioned by accident or
> mistake.

The will did not mention the testator's two great-grandchildren. Cecilia Chicoine
was born one day before the will was executed; Neil F. Chicoine, III was not born
until two years after the will was executed.

In 1990, the testator attempted to execute a codicil to his will. The codicil would
have altered the disposition of his estate, giving three equal shares to Edward, Shirley, and Richard, and equal shares to Shirley's and Edward's respective children. The
parties agree, however, that the codicil was not properly witnessed and therefore did
not become effective. Although the petitioners presented testimony regarding the
drafting of the codicil, the codicil was not produced for probate.

Following the testator's death, his 1984 will was presented to the probate court.
The will was proved and allowed, and Shirley was appointed executrix on September 30, 1990. In 1991, Richard, on behalf of himself and the testator's great-
grandchildren, and Edward petitioned the probate court to reexamine the 1984
will. They challenged the will on several grounds: (1) the testator revoked his will
when he attempted to execute the ineffective codicil in 1990; (2) the testator's great-
grandchildren were entitled to an intestate share of his estate because they qualified
as pretermitted heirs under RSA 551:10; and (3) the testator's estate included assets
belonging to his deceased daughter, Jo Ann, that should be segregated and turned
over to Jo Ann's heirs.

* * *

The * * * issue on appeal is whether the probate court erred in ruling that the
testator's great-grandchildren were not entitled to an intestate share of his estate
under RSA 551:10.

RSA 551:10 protects a testator's heirs against unintentional omission from the
testator's will. See 7 DeGrandpre, *supra* § 11.02, at 99. It provides:

> Every child born after the decease of the testator, and every child or issue of
> a child of the deceased not named or referred to in his will, and who is not
> a devisee or legatee, shall be entitled to the same portion of the estate, real
> and personal, as he would be if the deceased were intestate.

RSA 551:10. The statute creates a rule of law that the omission of a child or issue of
a child from a will is accidental "unless there is evidence in the will itself that the
omission was intentional." In re Estate of MacKay, 121 N.H. 682, 684, 433 A.2d 1289,
1290 (1981) (quotation and emphasis omitted). "[T]he statute . . . is not a limitation
on the power to make testamentary dispositions but rather is an attempt to effectuate a testator's presumed intent. It prevents forgetfulness, not disinheritance." Royce
v. Estate of Denby, 117 N.H. 893, 896, 379 A.2d 1256, 1258 (1977).

Relying on the statute, the petitioners argue that the testator's great-grandchildren were not named or referred to in the testator's will and therefore are entitled to an intestate share of his estate. They contend that the testator's decision to specifically name Neil F. Chicoine, Jr., the father of the petitioning great-grandchildren, in paragraph seven of the will was irrelevant in determining whether they are pretermitted heirs under RSA 551:10. According to the petitioners, testators must name or refer to their children (or in this case, grandchildren) as well as the issue of their children (or in this case, great-grandchildren) in their wills; otherwise any issue not named or referred to is pretermitted. We disagree.

We hold that a testator who specifically names one heir in an effort to disinherit him has "referred to" the issue of that heir for purposes of the statute. Accord Towne v. Cottrell, 236 Or. 151, 387 P.2d 576, 578 (1963); see In re Barter's Estate, 86 Cal. 441, 25 P. 15, 16 (1890); Matter of Estate of Kane, 828 P.2d 997, 999 (Okla.Ct.App.1992). If a testator has a predeceased child who is neither named, referred to, nor a devisee or legatee under the testator's will, then the naming of the next degree of issue in the line of descent will successfully preclude issue more removed from the testator from invoking the statute. On the other hand, where an issue of a child is named, referred to, or a devisee or legatee, but the testator's child is neither named, referred to, nor a devisee or legatee, then the testator's child is pretermitted, provided the child has not predeceased the testator. See Gage v. Gage, 29 N.H. 533, 543 (1854). Our holding is supported by our case law, in which we have acknowledged that a testator's reference to an heir "need not be direct" to exclude the heir under RSA 551:10. See In re Estate of Osgood, 122 N.H. 961, 964, 453 A.2d 838, 840 (1982); cf. Gage, 29 N.H. at 543 (naming of an heir's issue is not sufficient reference to the heir to preclude application of RSA 551:10).

Here, the testator specifically named Neil Chicoine, Jr., the father of the great-grandchildren, in paragraph seven of his will. As a result, the testator "referred to" the descendant great-grandchildren for purposes of the pretermitted heir statute.

Furthermore, the testator named his daughter, Jo Ann—the grandmother of petitioners Cecilia and Neil—in his will. When a testator's child has been named, referred to, or is a devisee or legatee under the will, the child's issue cannot invoke the statute even if the issue are neither named, referred to, nor devisees or legatees under the will. Accordingly, the testator's great-grandchildren were not pretermitted heirs under RSA 551:10 and were not entitled to collect an intestate share of his estate.

* * *

Affirmed in part; vacated in part; remanded.

All concurred.

Notes

The New Hampshire statute is unique in that it applies to children and issue, and it includes children and issue born before or after execution of the Last Will and Testament. Any child or issue thereby "forgotten" would be able to take what he or she would take under the applicable intestate statute, unless there was evidence in the will, itself, that the omission was intentional. Most children or issue are provided for as members of a class within the language of the will. For example, "Whenever I refer to child or children, I refer to all of my children, issue of my body, or adopted by me." All children, no matter when born, would take as members of a class of children when the will speaks of children.

In its 1990 revision, the Uniform Probate Code significantly changed the manner in which it provided protection for an omitted child. These changes were further modified in the 2008 revision. Today's statute remains committed to providing a share of the decedent's estate for a child born or adopted after execution of the will, when the will makes no provision for the child. Unlike the New Hampshire statute in *Laura*, the Uniform Probate Code makes no provision for descendants of children; it only provides for children. A few states, called "Missouri" states, do not permit the introduction of extrinsic evidence to address the intent of the decedent testator. But other states, called "Massachusetts" states, allow extrinsic evidence to address whether the testator intended to disinherit the child. *See* B. Glenn, *Admissibility of Extrinsic Evidence to Show Testator's Intention As to Omission of Provision for Child*, 88 A.L.R.2d 616 (2008).

The most significant feature of the Uniform Probate Code is its attempt to treat children equally. Thus, if the testator has a child living when the will is executed, and the testator's will makes a provision for that child, then any omitted children "participate[] on a pro rata basis in the property devised, under trust or not, to the then-living children." UNIF. PROB. CODE § 2-302 cmt. (2009). This section is modeled, in part, on N.Y. Est. Powers & Trusts Law § 5-3.2. An example of this process, enacted by the Uniform Probate Code, is provided in its Comment:

> When G executed her will, she had two living children, A and B. Her will devised $7,500 to each child. After G executed her will, she had another child, C.
>
> C is entitled to $5,000. $2,500 (1/3 of $7,500) of C's entitlement comes from A's $7,500 devise (reducing it to $5,000); and $2,500 (1/3 of $7,500) comes from B's $7,500 devise (reducing it to $5,000).

UNIF. PROB. CODE § 2-302 cmt. (2019).

Not all states have adopted the approach of the Uniform Probate Code. For example, in Virginia, if a testator has a child in existence when the will is executed, and that child is provided for in the will, the omitted child, subsequently born or adopted, is given the *lesser of* the following:

> (i) such portion of the testator's estate as the afterborn or after-adopted child would have been entitled to if the testator had died intestate or (ii) the equivalent in amount to any bequests and devises to any child named in the will, and if there are bequests or devises to more than one child, then to the largest aggregate bequest or devise to any child.

VA. CODE ANN. §64.2-420(A) (2019) (emphasis added).

Whether a state statute providing for an omitted child should be applicable to *inter vivos* trusts was the issue confronted by the court in Kidwell v. Rhew, 371 Ark. 490, 268 S.W.3d 309 (2007). In *Kidwell*, during her life, a settlor created a valid trust, into which she had transferred real and personal property. Subsequently, the settlor died intestate, leaving the court to decide if Arkansas Code §28-39-407(b) should provide for an omitted child in the context of an *inter vivos* trust. Since the words of the statute specifically refer to the execution of a *will* and not to the creation of a *trust*, the court held that the statute was inapplicable to an *inter vivos* trust. There is scant authority for applying the omitted heir statutes to trusts, but there are recommendations for this in the future. *See, e.g., Restatement (Third) of Trusts* §25, cmt. E (2003); Alan Newman, *Revocable Trusts and the Law of Wills: An Imperfect Fit*, 43 REAL PROP., TRUST & EST. L.J. 523 (2008).

Uniform Probate Code (2019)

§2-302. Omitted Children.

(a) Except as provided in subsection (b), if a testator fails to provide in his [or her] will for any of his [or her] children born or adopted after the execution of the will, the omitted after-born or after-adopted child receives a share in the estate as follows:

(1) If the testator had no child living when he [or she] executed the will, an omitted after-born or after-adopted child receives a share in the estate equal in value to that which the child would have received had the testator died intestate, unless the will devised all or substantially all of the estate to the other parent of the omitted child and that other parent survives the testator and is entitled to take under the will.

(2) If the testator had one or more children living when he [or she] executed the will, and the will devised property or an interest in property to one or more of the then-living children, an omitted after-born or after-adopted child is entitled to share in the testator's estate as follows:

(A) The portion of the testator's estate in which the omitted after-born or after-adopted child is entitled to share is limited to devises made to the testator's then-living children under the will.

(B) The omitted after-born or after-adopted child is entitled to receive the share of the testator's estate, as limited in subparagraph (i), that the child would have received had the testator included all omitted after-born and after-adopted children with the children to whom devises were made under the will and had given an equal share of the estate to each child.

(C) To the extent feasible, the interest granted and omitted after-born or after-adopted child under this section must be of the same character, whether equitable or legal, present or future, as that devised to the testator's then-living children under the will.

(D) In satisfying a share provided by this paragraph, devises to the testator's children who were living when the will was executed abate ratably. In abating the devises of the then-living children, the court shall preserve to the maximum extent possible the character of the testamentary plan adopted by the testator.

(b) Neither subsection (a)(1) nor subsection (a)(2) applies if:

(1) it appears from the will that the omission was intentional; or

(2) the testator provided for the omitted after-born or after-adopted child by transfer outside the will and the intent that the transfer be in lieu of a testamentary provision is shown by the testator's statements or is reasonably inferred from the amount of the transfer or other evidence.

(c) If at the time of execution of the will the testator fails to provide in his [or her] will for a living child solely because he [or she] believes the child to be dead, the child is entitled to share in the estate as if the child were an omitted after-born or after-adopted child.

(d) In satisfying a share provided by subsection (a)(1), devises made by the will abate under Section 3-902.

Herbert E. Nass
Father Does Not Always Know Best
147 Trusts & Ests. 62 (May 2008)

The shock of actor Heath Ledger's untimely death has passed, but questions still linger. Although only 28 when he died, Ledger had a will. Yet, the multi-millionaire left his only child with a mere $145,000. . . .

Ledger executed his Australian will in Claremont, Western Australia on April 12, 2003. The document is a simple three pages, essentially stating that one-half of his estate is to be divided between his parents, Kim Francis Ledger and Sally Anne Bell, and the other half is to be divided equally among his sisters, Kathrine Anne Ledger, Ashleigh Kristen Bell and Olivia Jane Ledger, with the share of any sister to be held in trust until she reaches 18-years-old. There's no mention of Ledger's daughter Matilda Rose in the will because she was not born until two years later.

Id.

Karen Donovan
Michael Crichton's Posthumous Child
148 Trusts & Ests. 58 (Apr. 2009)

Michael Crichton, the author of . . . science fiction thrillers . . . left behind the makings of another kind of movie when he died on Nov. 4, 2008 at age 66.

In this drama, a famous, wealthy man dies and, four and [a] half months later, his fifth wife gives birth to a son [John]. But this [son] isn't mentioned in dad's will. So the child's mother gears up to battle a host of beneficiaries to secure the posthumous son's inheritance. . . .

All of Crichton's assets were left in trust. The probate petition cites a long list of trust beneficiaries. Among them is Taylor Anne Crichton, Crichton's daughter from another marriage, who turned 20 on Jan. 26, 2009. About two dozen other individuals, family and friends, as well as the John Michael Crichton Family Foundation Inc., also received notice [of litigation]. . . .

The only mention made of a child in Crichton's will is this: He states, "I have one (1) child." That's Taylor, a daughter from his marriage to Anne-Marie Martin, Crichton's fourth wife, an actress who co-wrote the screenplay for the 1996 film "Twister" with him, and with whom he reached a divorce settlement in 2003.

In a provision under the heading, "incontestability," the will states: "I have intentionally made no provision in this Will for any of my heirs or relatives who are not herein mentioned or designated, and I hereby generally and specifically disinherit every person claiming to be or who may be determined to be my heir-at-law, except as otherwise mentioned in this Will.". . . .

Ironically, had Adam Streisand, [the widow's] lawyer, drafted Crichton's will, young John's [Crichton's son's] hopes might have been dashed. In a November 2007 article for *The Hollywood Reporter*, called "Nine things entertainment lawyers should know about probate," Streisand observed: "Celebrities tend to be prolific in all things, including having children out of wedlock." To avoid heirs claiming their share as omitted children, Streisand wrote, a will or trust should "very specifically" indicate a "clear intention" not to provide for any child not named, "no matter when that child may be born (before or after the execution of the document.)"

Id. at 58–59.

Problem

Decedent adopted a baby girl in 1974. In 1990, the decedent wrote a valid holographic Last Will and Testament that stated:

I Paul Randall Mowry Jr. declare this to be my last will and testament, revoking all former wills and codicils. I hereby give all my estate real and personal to my brother, Joe Allen Mowry. I hereby appoint my brother Joe Allen Mowry to be the executor of my estate. No bond shall be required of my executor.

When decedent died in 2000, he was survived by his brother, sister, and adopted daughter. The daughter immediately filed a petition seeking to take a portion of the decedent's estate based on the fact that she and the decedent enjoyed a close family relationship and that he must have forgotten to include her in his will. The brother objects, relying upon the terms of the holographic will. If you were the attorney for the daughter, how would you best obtain for her a portion of the decedent's estate? *See* Estate of Mowry, 107 Cal. App. 4th 338, 131 Cal. Rptr.2d 855 (2003).

III. Protection of Spousal Persons

A. Who Is a Spouse?

On June 26, 2015, the Supreme Court of the United States held that the Fourteenth Amendment requires states to license a marriage between two people of the same sex and to recognize a marriage between two people of the same sex when their marriage was lawfully licensed and performed out-of-state. *See* Oberge-fell v. Hodges, 135 S. Ct. 2584 (2015). This decision permits same sex couples who meet other criteria imposed by state statute to acquire the status of spouse and all of the benefits arising from that status. Prior to the *Obergefell* decision, many states had enacted status arrangements that provided spousal status, without defining the status as marriage. Among these were "reciprocal beneficiary," "domestic partner-ship," and "civil union." Each permitted a person qualifying under the status to obtain all of the rights and benefits afforded to spouses within that state. Likewise, federal benefits became available when the United States Supreme Court held that the liberty protected by the Fifth Amendment's Due Process Clause contains within it the prohibition against denying to any person the equal protection of the laws. *See* United States v. Windsor, 133 S. Ct. 2675 (2013). It is likely that persons presently within alternative status arrangements will continue to be treated as spouses for state benefits, but uncertainty will persist for some time concerning property rights and taxation. *See, e.g.,* George D. Karibjanian, Obergefell: *The Final Word (But Not Really) on Same-Sex Marriage*, 154 TRUSTS & ESTS. 34 (Aug. 2015); Joshua S. Rubenstein & Jason J. Smith, *Ding Dong, Is DOMA Dead?*, 152 TRUSTS & ESTS. 40 (Jan. 2014).

In addition to statutory marriage, available in every state, fewer than eleven states permit common law marriage. If two adults, otherwise able to marry, hold them-selves out as husband and wife in a state that permits common law marriage, they are married, even though they did not obtain a license or have an officiant. *See, e.g., In re* Marriage of Winegard, 257 N.W.2d 609 (Iowa 1977). If the common law mar-riage is validly created, then it will be recognized in other states unless it violates strong state public policy. Only a decree of divorce may terminate a valid common law marriage and the spousal status conferred on the two parties.

B. Spousal Taxation at Death

The Internal Revenue Code provides extensive benefits to the distribution of assets to spouses. For example: first, spouses may utilize the unlimited gift tax marital deduction, *see* I.R.C. § 2523, as long as the gift is not disqualified under the nondeductible terminable interest rule, *see* I.R.C. § 2523(b). Second, only one-half of any marital joint tenancy is included in the gross estate of the first spouse to die. *See* I.R.C. § 2040(b). Third, there is an unlimited deduction allowed against the decedent's gross estate for all assets passing to the surviving spouse, *see* I.R.C. § 2056; the only exception to this broad policy benefit is if, "on the lapse of time, on the occurrence of an event or contingency, or on the failure of an event or contingency to occur, an interest passing to the surviving spouse will terminate or fail, no deduction will be allowed." I.R.C. § 2056(b)(1). No terminable interest applies if the decedent requires the spouse to survive by a period of six months or less, or if the decedent requires the spouse to survive a common disaster. *See* I.R.C. § 2056(b)(3). This is an important consideration in light of the rules on simultaneous death.

In spite of the restriction against devising a terminable interest, the law allows many restrictions to be placed upon the surviving spouse by the decedent, and still allows for the unlimited marital deduction. For example, in a valid Last Will and Testament, the decedent may provide the spouse with the right to income from the property for life, payable at least annually, *see* I.R.C. § 2056(b)(7); the Personal Representative may have discretion in providing for the property for the marital deduction, *see* Reg. § 20.2056(b)(7). And many trusts provide a surviving spouse with a life estate and a general power of appointment. *See* I.R.C. § 2056(b)(5). Estates seeking to take advantage of the marital deduction are likely to do so through what is called a QTIP trust—a Qualified Terminable Interest Property trust. The requirements are as follows:

(1) The spouse is entitled to all of the income for life, payable at least annually.

(2) No person, including the spouse, has the power to appoint any of the property to someone other than the spouse during the spouse's lifetime.

(3) The Personal Representative has made an election that the property passing to the surviving spouse should qualify for the marital deduction.

The restraint upon the surviving spouse is formidable, especially when compared to what the (surviving) spouse would have taken under most states' divorce process, whereby either the marital or community property is distributed, depending on whether the state follows a common law or a community property perspective. *See generally* Walter Wadlington, Raymond C. O'Brien & Robin Fretwell Wilson, Family Law In Perspective 1-5-132 (4th ed. 2018). At divorce, recognizing the economic partnership of marriage, it is very unlikely that the court would restrict the assets by imposing life estates on either divorcing party. Yet, under the QTIP arrangement, such restrictions are allowed in furtherance of tax policy and with prejudice to the surviving spouse's established economic interests.

Of course, the surviving spouse may statutorily elect against a Last Will and Testament, and this will be explored in the casebook material discussing augmented estate, *infra*. Nonetheless, for many married couples, the marital deduction trust is an important estate planning tool. The following decision illustrates the nature of a QTIP trust, the history of the marital deduction, and the attendant need to be precise in formulation.

Shelfer v. Commissioner

United States Court of Appeals, Eleventh Circuit, 1996
86 F.3d 1045

KRAVITCH, Circuit Judge:

The Commissioner of the Internal Revenue Service ("Commissioner") appeals the Tax Court's decision in favor of the estate of Lucille Shelfer. The court held that Lucille's estate was not liable for a tax deficiency assessed on the value of a trust from which she had received income during her lifetime. The estate of Lucille Shelfer's husband, Elbert, previously had taken a marital deduction for these trust assets, claiming that the trust met the definition of a qualified terminable interest property trust ("QTIP") pursuant to 26 U.S.C. § 2056(b)(7).

This case presents an issue of first impression for this circuit: whether a QTIP trust is established when, under the terms of the trust, the surviving spouse is neither entitled to, nor given the power of appointment over, the trust income accumulating between the date of the last distribution and her death, otherwise known as the "stub income." The Commissioner interprets the QTIP statutory provisions to allow such trusts to qualify for the marital deduction in the decedent's estate; accordingly, the value of the trust assets must be included in the surviving spouse's estate. We agree with the Commissioner and REVERSE the Tax Court.

* * *

Elbert Shelfer died on September 13, 1986 and was survived by his wife, Lucille. Elbert's will provided that his estate was to be divided into two shares, that were to be held in separate trusts. The income from each trust was to be paid to Lucille in quarterly installments during her lifetime. The first trust was a standard marital deduction trust consisting of one-third of the estate. It is not at issue in this case. The second trust, comprising the remaining two-thirds of the estate, terminated upon Lucille's death. The principal and all undistributed income was payable to Elbert's niece, Betty Ann Shelfer.

Elbert's will designated Quincy State Bank as the personal representative for his estate, and on June 16, 1987, the bank filed a tax return on behalf of the estate. The bank elected to claim a deduction for approximately half of the assets of the second trust under the QTIP trust provisions of 26 U.S.C. § 2056(b)(7). The IRS examined the return, allowed the QTIP deduction, and issued Quincy Bank a closing letter on May 10, 1989. The statute of limitations for an assessment of deficiency with respect to Elbert's return expired on June 16, 1990.

On January 18, 1989, Lucille died; Quincy State Bank served as personal representative for her estate. The bank filed an estate tax return on October 18, 1989 and did not include the value of the assets in the trust, even though the assets previously had been deducted on her husband's estate tax return. The IRS audited the return and assessed a tax deficiency for the trust assets on the ground that the trust was a QTIP trust subject to taxation. Quincy State Bank commenced a proceeding in tax court on behalf of Lucille's estate, claiming that the trust did not meet the definition of a QTIP trust because Lucille did not control the stub income; therefore, the Bank argued, the estate was not liable for tax on the trust assets under 26 U.S.C. §2044. The Tax Court agreed. The Commissioner appeals this decision.

* * *

The proper construction of a statutory provision is a purely legal issue; thus, we apply a *de novo* standard of review to the Tax Court's decision. Kirchman v. Commissioner, 862 F.2d 1486, 1490 (11th Cir.1989). As in any case involving the meaning of a statute, we begin our analysis with the language at issue.

26 U.S.C. §2056(b)(7)(B) provides, in relevant part:

(i) In general.—The term "qualified terminable income interest property" means property—

(I) which passes from the decedent,

(II) in which the surviving spouse has a qualifying income interest for life, and

(III) to which an election under this paragraph applies.

(ii) Qualifying income interest for life.—The surviving spouse has a qualifying income interest for life if—

(I) *the surviving spouse is entitled to all the income from the property, payable annually or at more frequent intervals,* or has a usufruct interest for life in the property, and

(II) no person has a power to appoint any part of the property to any person other than the surviving spouse. Subclause (II) shall not apply to a power exercisable only at or after the death of the surviving spouse.[1]

Lucille's estate contends, and the Tax Court held, that the phrase "all of the income" includes income that has accrued between the last distribution and the date of the spouse's death, or the stub income. They argue that "all" refers to every type of income. Stub income is a kind of income, and thus the surviving spouse must be entitled to stub income in order for the trust to qualify as a QTIP trust. They conclude that because Elbert's will did not grant Lucille control over the stub income, the QTIP election fails.

In contrast, the Commissioner and amicus * * * argue that the statute is satisfied if the surviving spouse controls "all of the income" that has been distributed. They contend that the requirement that income be, "payable annually or at more frequent

---

1. This section of the code is complemented by §2044, which provides for the inclusion of the QTIP assets in the estate tax return of the surviving spouse. It states that "[t]he value of the gross estate shall include the value of any property to which this section applies in which the decedent had a qualifying income interest for life." The statute does not further define "qualifying income interest for life," so we refer back to the definition given in §2056 above. (Emphasis added).

intervals," limits "all of the income" to distributed income, namely those payments that have been made to the surviving spouse during her life. See Estate of Howard v. Commissioner, 910 F.2d 633, 635 (9th Cir.1990) (concluding that "if [the surviving spouse] has been entitled to regular distributions at least annually, she has had an income interest for life").

The estate replies that the phrase "payable annually or at more frequent intervals" is separated from the preceding clause by commas, and thus is a parenthetical clause. Because parenthetical clauses are non-restrictive, it contends that the clause is merely a description of the distribution process and does not in any way limit the preceding requirement that the spouse must be entitled to "all of the income."

Both parties insist that their reading of the statute is "plain." We do not agree. Although the use of commas around the clause "payable annually or at more frequent intervals" does indicate a parenthetical clause, we refuse to place inordinate weight on punctuation and ignore the remainder of the sentence. It is equally plausible that the next clause is designed to provide a context from which to define "all of the income." * * * Cf. Smiley v. Citibank, 517 U.S. 735,—, 116 S.Ct. 1730, 1736, 135 L.Ed.2d 25 (1996) ("A word often takes on a more narrow connotation when it is expressly opposed to another word: 'car,' for example, has a broader meaning by itself than it does in a passage speaking of 'cars and taxis.'"). Nothing in this statutory provision on its face allows us to choose between these interpretations. Accordingly, we must look to other sources for guidance. * * *

Accordingly, we must look beyond the "plain language" of the statute for guidance. When faced with a similarly ambiguous tax code provision, the Supreme Court thoroughly examined the history and purpose of the tax provision at issue, past practices, and the practical implications of its ruling. Commissioner v. Engle, 464 U.S. 206, 104 S.Ct. 597, 78 L.Ed.2d 420 (1984). * * * We follow suit, beginning with the history and purpose of the marital deduction.

* * *

The marital deduction for estate taxes first appeared in §812(e) of the Internal Revenue Code of 1939, which was enacted by the Revenue Code of 1948. * * * The marital deduction provisions served the dual purposes of equalizing the tax treatment between persons in common-law and community property states * * * and "codify[ing] the long-standing notion that marital property belongs to the unitary estate of both spouses. . . ." Shelfer, 103 T.C. at 25 (Beghe, J., dissenting).

An essential goal of the marital deduction statutory scheme "from its very beginning, however, was that any property of the first spouse to die that passed untaxed to the surviving spouse should be taxed in the estate of the surviving spouse." Estate of Clayton v. Commissioner, 976 F.2d 1486, 1491 (5th Cir.1992). * * * In accordance with this intent, the statute proscribed deductions for terminable property interests. Terminable property interests are those interests that will terminate upon the occurrence of an event, the failure of an event to take place, or after a certain time period. * * * Because these interests could terminate prior to the death of the surviving spouse, they posed a risk that the assets would escape taxation in the spouse's estate tax return.

The original statute allowed three exceptions to the terminable property rule for interests that would not escape taxation in the spouse's estate. Property interests would qualify for the marital deduction under any of the following conditions: 1) the interest of the spouse was conditional on survival for a limited period and the spouse survived that period; 2) the spouse had a life estate in the property with the power of appointment over the corpus; or 3) the spouse received all life insurance or annuity payments during her lifetime with the power to appoint all payments under the contract. * * * To take advantage of these exceptions, however, the decedent had to relinquish all control over the marital property to the surviving spouse. * * *

Following the logic of the regulations, the person with the power to appoint the property in the trust corpus should be permitted to have the power to appoint the stub income; the stub income will then be subject to taxation along with the corpus property. Under the QTIP provisions, that person is the decedent. The trust corpus and the stub income would be taxable pursuant to §2044, which requires the spouse to include all previously deducted property in which she has a qualifying interest for life.[20] This comprehensive scheme, like that of the power of appointment trust, allows an initial deduction and later taxation of the property.[21]

Our conclusion that the trust income and the stub income can be treated the same for taxation purposes is consistent with the flush language of §2056(b)(7), which provides that any property can be appointed to someone other than the surviving spouse at or after the spouse's death. See Shelfer, 103 T.C. at 21–23 (Wells,

---

20. We acknowledge that §2044 does not expressly apply to stub income because it provides that the surviving spouse's estate must include all property over which the spouse had a qualifying income interest for life. Although we have already shown that the trust property can be a qualifying income interest for life even if the surviving spouse is not given control of the stub income, we have not determined whether the stub income can be part of the qualifying income interest for life. The Commissioner's regulation, now finalized at 26 C.F.R. §2044(b)(2), clarifies the issue by specifically including the stub income in the spouse's gross estate. We note that although the regulation was not finalized at the time of this action, it is the most consistent interpretation of the statute for the same reason that the regulations for the power of appointment trust are reasonable. Both regulations ensure that previously deducted property is taxed at the death of the surviving spouse. Moreover, both regulations are faithful to the statutory scheme. In the power of appointment regulations, the stub income is rendered subject to the power of appointment and becomes taxable. In the QTIP provisions, the stub income is included in the spouse's estate along with the trust corpus, both of which are not controlled by the spouse.

21. Our reading of the regulation does not disqualify a trust instrument that provides for the surviving spouse to have the power of appointment over the stub income or to receive the stub income as part of her estate. Under those circumstances, congressional goals will be served because the stub income will clearly be taxable and the couple will be considered one economic unit. We merely hold that the estate planning document at issue here also qualifies for the deduction because Congress provided a statutory scheme which will require taxation of the stub income if it reverts to the trust remainderman.

J., dissenting). Thus, under the terms of the statute, the trust corpus and the stub income can both be appointed to someone other than the surviving spouse after her death without disqualifying the trust from a marital deduction.

Examining the legislative history of the 1981 Act, we conclude that Congress intended to liberalize the marital deduction, to treat a husband and wife as one economic unit, and to allow the stub income to be treated in the same manner as the trust corpus for taxation purposes. These goals favor a broad interpretation of the statute that would allow the QTIP election in this case. Having assessed the legislative history and purpose of the statute, we turn to the practical implications of this interpretation. * * *

* * *

Our construction of the statute has several practical advantages over the Tax Court's position. First, it would assure certainty in estate planning. See Jacques T. Schlenger, et al., Failure to Pay Stub Income to Estate Defeats QTIP Election, 21 Est. Plan. 368 (1994) (noting that the Tax Court's decision in *Shelfer* leaves the "stub income" issue unsettled). * * * The status of trust instruments that were set up in accordance with the Commissioner's advice will not be in question and the validity of the Commissioner's final regulation on this matter will be affirmed. * * *

Second, our result comports with standard trust practices. Under the Tax Court's approach, a trust fund that made daily payments to the surviving spouse would qualify for the deduction because there would be no undistributed income; in contrast, one that made quarterly payments would be ineligible. In *Howard*, the Ninth Circuit noted that "no trust pays its beneficiaries on a daily basis. The statute did not impose such an unrealistic requirement for a trust to become a QTIP." *Howard*, 910 F.2d at 635. * * * Our reading of the statute gives meaning to the statutory terms requiring annual or more frequent distribution, not daily disbursements. See Tramel v. Schrader, 505 F.2d 1310, 1314 (5th Cir.1975) (citing cardinal rule that a statute should be construed such that no clause shall be superfluous). * * *

Finally, a broad reading of the marital deduction provisions benefits the federal Treasury and furthers Congressional intent to ensure taxation of all previously deducted property. In the instant case, for example, the corpus of $2,829,610 would be subject to taxation, for a gain of over $1,000,000 in tax deficiencies. The Tax Court's opinion would grant similar estates a substantial windfall, encouraging other executors of wills to disclaim the previously taken deduction. * * *

For all of these reasons, we conclude that our interpretation of the statute will better serve the practical realities of trust administration and estate taxation.

* * *

After determining that the statutory language is ambiguous, we looked beyond the statute to additional sources of information, such as the legislative history. Careful consideration of these documents leads us to discern two purposes for the 1981 Act: treating the married couple as one economic unit, and expanding the deduction to include arrangements that divest the surviving spouse of control over property. These congressional goals are best served by allowing the deduction in the decedent's estate and requiring subsequent inclusion in the surviving spouse's estate when trust documents do not grant control over the stub income to the surviving spouse. Accordingly, we REVERSE the Tax Court.

C. Pretermitted Spouse

In re Estate of Shannon

California Court of Appeal, Fourth District, 1990
224 Cal. App. 3d 1148, 274 Cal. Rptr. 338

HUFFMAN, Acting Presiding Justice.

Gilbert A. Brown, executor of the will of Lila Demos Shannon (also known as Lila King Demos), appeals on behalf of Lila's estate from an order of the probate court denying her petition for determination of heirship as an omitted spouse under Probate Code * * * section 6560 in the estate of Russell Donovan Shannon. We reverse.

* * *

On January 25, 1974, Russell, an unmarried widower, executed his last will and testament, naming his daughter, Beatrice Marie Saleski, executrix and sole beneficiary. The will also provided his grandson, Donald Saleski, would inherit his estate in the event Beatrice did not survive him for "thirty (30) days" and contained a disinheritance clause which provided as follows:

> SEVENTH: I have intentionally omitted all other living persons and relatives. If any devises, legatee, beneficiary under this Will, or any legal heir of mine, person or persons claiming under any of them, or other person or persons shall contest this Will or attack or seek to impair or invalidate any of its provisions or conspire with or voluntarily assist anyone attempting to do any of those things mentioned, in that event, I specifically disinherit such person or persons. [¶] If any Court finds that such person or persons are lawful heirs and entitled to participate in my estate, then in that event I bequeath each of them the sum of one ($1.00) dollar and no more.

On April 27, 1986, Russell married Lila. On February 22, 1988, Russell died. He did not make any changes in his will after his marriage to Lila and before his death. His 1974 will was admitted to probate May 9, 1988, and Beatrice was named executrix of his estate.

On September 27, 1988, Lila filed a petition for family allowance (§ 6540), to set apart probate homestead (§ 6520) and for determination of entitlement to estate distribution as an omitted surviving spouse (§§ 1080, 6560). The court denied the petition for family allowance and Lila withdrew her petition to set apart probate homestead. The remaining issue of Lila's entitlement to share in Russell's estate was heard December 14, 1988, and taken under submission.

On March 24, 1989, the probate court issued its order denying Lila's petition to determine heirship. She timely appealed only from this latter order. * * *

During the pendency of this appeal, Lila died and her son Brown was named executor of her estate and substituted in her place as appellant. * * * He has objected to the distribution of Russell's estate until after this appeal is decided.

* * *

On appeal, Lila contends she was a pretermitted spouse within the meaning of section 6560 and does not fall under any of the exceptions under section 6561 which would preclude her from sharing in Russell's estate as an omitted spouse. We agree and reverse.

Section 6560, added to the Probate Code in 1983, amended in 1984 and applicable to estates of decedents who died on or after January 1, 1985 (Stats.1983, ch. 842, § 55; Stats.1984, ch. 892, § 45), states:

> Except as provided in Section 6561, if a testator fails to provide by will for his or her surviving spouse who married the testator after the execution of the will, the omitted spouse shall receive a share in the estate consisting of the following property in the estate: [¶] (a) The one-half of the community property that belongs to the testator. ... [¶] (b) The one-half of the quasi-community property that belongs to the testator. ... [¶] (c) A share of the separate property of the testator equal in value to that which the spouse would have received if the testator had died intestate, but in no event is the share to be more than one-half the value of the separate property in the estate.

Section 6561 states:

> The spouse does not receive a share of the estate under Section 6560 if any of the following is established: [¶] (a) The testator's failure to provide for the spouse in the will was intentional and that intention appears from the will. [¶] (b) The testator provided for the spouse by transfer outside the will and the intention that the transfer be in lieu of a testamentary provision is shown by statements of the testator or from the amount of the transfer or by other evidence. [¶] (c) The spouse made a valid agreement waiving the right to share in the testator's estate.

Section 6560 supersedes that portion of former section 70 which had the effect of revoking the will as to the omitted spouse and giving that spouse the same share as the spouse would have taken if the testator had died intestate. (See Cal.Law Revision Com. com., 54A, (West's Ann.Prob.Code (1990 supp.) § 6560, p. 295.) Section 6561 supersedes the portion of former section 70 which stated, "unless provision has been made for the spouse by marriage contract, or unless the spouse is provided for in the will, or in such way mentioned therein as to show an intention not to make such provision; and no other evidence to rebut the presumption of revocation can be received." (Stats.1931, ch. 281, p. 590, §70.) These latter two provisions are continued in section 6561 in subdivision (a) and, in addition, section 6561 now recognizes an omitted spouse may waive the right to take property of the other spouse by testate or intestate succession (§6561(c)) and does not receive a share if the testator provided for the omitted spouse by a "transfer outside the will" that was intended to be in lieu of a testimentary provision (§6561(b)). See Cal.Law Revision Com. com., 54A West's Ann.Prob.Code, *supra*, §6561, p. 297.)

It is well established section 6560 reflects a strong statutory presumption of revocation of the will as to the omitted spouse based upon public policy. (Estate of Duke (1953) 41 Cal.2d 509, 261 P.2d 235.) Such presumption is rebutted only if circumstances are such as to fall within the literal terms of one of the exceptions listed in section 6561. (See Estate of Sheldon (1977) 75 Cal.App.3d 364, 142 Cal.Rptr. 119.) The burden of proving the presumption is rebutted is on the proponents of the will. (See Estate of Paul (1972) 29 Cal.App.3d 690, 697, 105 Cal.Rptr. 742.)

Here, Russell failed to provide for Lila in his will. Under the language of section 6560, she is thus an omitted spouse and the crucial inquiry becomes whether Beatrice met the burden of rebutting this presumption. Specifically, the issues are whether the will shows a specific intent to exclude Lila pursuant to section 6561(a) and whether Beatrice presented sufficient evidence to show Russell had intended to otherwise provide for Lila outside of his will in lieu of her taking under it pursuant to section 6561(b), or to show Lila waived her rights to share in his estate under section 6561(c).

The will on its face does not evidence an intent on Russell's part to disinherit Lila. As the presumption under section 6560 is only rebutted by a clear manifestation of such intent on the face of the will, "regardless of what may have been the wishes of the [decedent]" (Estate of Basore (1971) 19 Cal.App.3d 623, 627–628, 96 Cal.Rptr. 874; see also *Estate of Duke, supra,* 41 Cal.2d 509, 261 P.2d 235 and *Estate of Paul, supra,* 29 Cal.App.3d 690, 105 Cal.Rptr. 742), the section 6561(a) exception has not been established.

Contrary to Beatrice's reliance on Estate of Kurtz (1922) 190 Cal. 146, 210 P. 959 to argue the language "any legal heir of mine" in the disinheritance clause contained in Russell's will somehow shows his intent to disinherit Lila, whom he married 12 years after executing the will, that case has been effectively overruled by subsequent case law. (See Estate of Axcelrod (1944) 23 Cal.2d 761, 769–770, 147 P.2d 1 (conc. opn. of Carter, J.).) *Estate of Axcelrod, supra,* 23 Cal.2d at pp. 765–769, 147 P.2d 1 distinguished the *Kurtz* case and held a general provision in a will that the testator "intentionally omitted all of my heirs who are not specifically mentioned herein, intending thereby to disinherit them", may not be construed as mentioning a subsequently acquired spouse in such a way as to show an intention not to make provision for the spouse, where the testator at the time the will was executed had no spouse who could become "an heir." (Id. at p. 767, 147 P.2d 1.)

Case law has also held exclusionary clauses in wills which fail to indicate the testator contemplated the possibility of a future marriage are insufficient to avoid the statutory presumption. (Estate of Poisl (1955) 44 Cal.2d 147, 149–150, 280 P.2d 789; *Estate of Paul, supra,* 29 Cal.App.3d 690, 105 Cal.Rptr. 742.) Even testamentary clauses specifically disinheriting a named individual whom the testator planned to marry and a clause stating "any other person not specifically mentioned in this Will, whether related by marriage or not" have been held insufficient to disclose the explicit intention of a testator to omit provision for another woman the testator married after executing the will either as a member of the designated disinherited class or as a contemplated spouse. (Estate of Green (1981) 120 Cal.App.3d 589, 593, 174 Cal.Rptr. 654.) As there is no mention of Lila or the fact of a future marriage in the disinheritance clause of the will, it does not manifest Russell's intent to specifically disinherit Lila as his surviving spouse.

Nor have the circumstances of section 6561(b) or (c) been established. Beatrice asserts a retired California Highway Patrolmen Widow's and Orphan's Fund from which $2,000 was paid to Lila as Russell's beneficiary, coupled with a declaration of Russell's attorney "[t]hat in the twelve months immediately preceding [Russell's death, he] informed this declarant that he had remarried and that his wife was independently wealthy and that she had more than he had and that he wanted his daughter to have his estate upon his death . . .", evidence Russell's intent to provide for Lila outside the will in lieu of a testamentary provision and satisfy the requirements of section 6561(b). In support of this argument she cites a New Mexico case, Matter of Taggart (1980) 95 N.M. 117, 619 P.2d 562, which held the omission of an after-acquired spouse in a will can be shown to be intentional by a transfer outside the will such as life insurance or other joint arrangement based on evidence of the testator's statements, the amount of the transaction, or other evidence. She claims Russell's intent she take his entire estate is paramount and the presumption under section 6560 must yield to that intent. (See Estate of Smith (1985) 167 Cal.App.3d 208, 212, 212 Cal.Rptr. 923.)

However, as Lila notes, the evidence of the widow's and orphan's trust fund benefits and Beatrice's attorney's declaration were excluded from evidence at the court hearing on the probate heirship matter making it impossible for the court to base its determination on such claimed transfer.

Even assuming the evidence were properly before the probate court at the time of the hearing, such was insufficient to rebut the presumption of section 6560 because it does not show Russell provided the trust fund benefits for Lila in lieu of sharing in his estate.

Moreover, the facts presented at the probate hearing that Russell and Lila kept their property separate during the course of their marriage is not sufficient to show "a valid agreement waiving the right to share" in each other's estate pursuant to section 6561(c). (See Estate of Butler (1988) 205 Cal.App.3d 311, 318, 252 Cal.Rptr. 210.)

Beatrice has simply not met her burden of proving Russell's intent to disinherit Lila and rebut the presumption of revocation under section 6560. The probate court therefore erred in denying Lila's petition to determine heirship.

*   *   *

The order denying Lila's petition for heirship is reversed and remanded for further proceedings consistent with this opinion.

NARES and LIM * * * JJ., concur.

Notes

Of course, as with a pretermitted child, the testator may specifically include a clause in the will that states that a surviving spouse is not to be considered a pretermitted spouse as defined in the *Shannon* decision. A lack of specificity could result in the disappointed spouse receiving an intestate portion, the revocation of the entire will under operation of law, or litigation about what the testator actually intended, as was demonstrated in *Shannon*. The Uniform Probate Code differs from the California pretermitted spouse provision, favoring issue descended from a previous relationship taking under the will. How would the following Uniform Probate Code provision affect the *Shannon* decision? Note the process of abatement to satisfy the pretermitted spouse in the California code.

Uniform Probate Code (2019)

§ 2-301. Entitlement of Spouse; Premarital Will.

(a) If a testator's surviving spouse married the testator after the testator executed his [or her] will, the surviving spouse is entitled to receive, as an intestate share, no less than the value of the share of the estate he [or she] would have received if the testator had died intestate as to that portion of the testator's estate, if any, that neither is devised to a child of the testator who was born before the testator married the surviving spouse and who is not a child of the surviving spouse nor is devised to a descendant of such a child or passes under Sections 2-603 or 2-604 to such a child or to a descendant of such a child, unless:

(1) it appears from the will or other evidence that the will was made in contemplation of the testator's marriage to the surviving spouse;

(2) the will expresses the intention that it is to be effective notwithstanding any subsequent marriage; or

(3) the testator provided for the spouse by transfer outside the will and the intent that the transfer be in lieu of a testamentary provision is shown by the testator's statements or is reasonably inferred from the amount of the transfer or other evidence.

(b) In satisfying the share provided by this section, devises made by the will to the testator's surviving spouse, if any, are applied first, and other devises, other than a devise to a child of the testator who was born before the testator married the surviving spouse and who is not a child of the surviving spouse or a devise or substitute gift under Sections 2-603 or 2-604 to a descendant of such a child, abate as provided in Section 3-902.

California Probate Code (2019)

§ 21612. Manner of satisfying share of omitted spouse; intention of decedent.

(a) Except as provided in subdivision (b), in satisfying a share provided by this chapter:

> (1) The share will first be taken from the decedent's estate not disposed of by will or trust, if any.

> (2) If that is not sufficient, so much as may be necessary to satisfy the share shall be taken from all beneficiaries of decedent's testamentary instruments in proportion to the value they may respectively receive. The proportion of each beneficiary's share that may be taken pursuant to this subdivision shall be determined based on values as of the date of the decedent's death.

(b) If the obvious intention of the decedent in relation to some specific gift or devise or other provision of a testamentary instrument would be defeated by the application of subdivision (a), the specific devise or gift or provision may be exempted from the apportionment under subdivision (a), and a different apportionment, consistent with the intention of the decedent, may be adopted.

Problem

Decedent executed his Last Will and Testament in 2000, after which his spouse died. He later married again and was married to his current spouse for ten months before he died with only the 2000 will in existence. His current wife was not mentioned in the will, however, the decedent left her $4,000,000 from a life insurance policy, $52,000 in joint accounts, and $410,806 from retirement plans. The Last Will and Testament, which predated the decedent's marriage, left his estate to his children from a prior marriage, friends, and charity. Within the statute of limitations, the decedent's widow filed a petition seeking an intestate portion of the decedent's estate, claiming to be a pretermitted spouse. Based on the Uniform Probate Code or the California Probate Code, how would you rule on her petition? *See In re* Estate of King, 444 P.3d 863 (Colo. Ct. App. 2019).

D. Statutory Entitlements

Raymond C. O'Brien

*Integrating Marital Property
into a Spouse's Elective Share*

59 Cath. Univ. L. Rev. 617 (2010)

Prior to the last three decades of the twentieth century, when a woman married, she often surrendered her financial autonomy to her husband. Thus, under a common law that originated in England, a woman's personal property that she brought into a marriage, her services and earnings during marriage, and all dominion over the transfer of her husband's wealth were considered to be the property of her husband throughout the marriage. * * * A wife lost her legal identity when she married; her interests were subsumed within those of her husband, and as a result she lost her ability to contract with third parties. * * * Her husband, however, was obligated to provide for her necessities as long as they were reasonable. During the middle of the nineteenth century, a trend toward greater economic independence for married women emerged in some states. A few states enacted statutes that provided some rights to a married woman, particularly the right to her own earnings, to contract with third parties, and to buy and sell property without her husband's consent. Many states codified these and other advances by adopting various versions of the Married Women's Property Act. * * * Such newly adopted state legislation allowed a wife to assert a financial identity, but still required a husband to support his wife; in return, he remained head of the household.

Id. at 620–21.

Today, through legislative initiatives and constitutional prodding by the United States Supreme Court, married persons share an economic partnership during marriage and, in the event of divorce, they divide marital property according to a scheme premised on economic partnership. This scheme disregards the exclusivity of title and apportions ownership in accordance with community-property principles (or equitable principles, as they are labeled in separate-property states). This framework of equitable property division occurs at divorce. The task of the revised 2008 UPC's elective-share provision is to rework the division of marital property at death. Is it possible to divide marital property at death in a manner that is similar to the way property is held by spouses during life and divided by spouses in the event of divorce?

Id. at 624.

Traditionally, common-law dower and curtesy protected the surviving spouse from disinheritance. Eventually, states enacted statutory allowances, complementing any applicable federal benefits attached to survivorship of a spouse, such as Social Security and pension rights. * * * Although these spousal allowances have progressed, they still provide little benefit to the surviving spouse; they do not compensate for an equitable division of the economic partnership theory of marriage. Instead, these allowances reflect a duty of support — that is, the surviving spouse is entitled to support from a decedent spouse while the decedent, the person in whom title resides, is still the owner of the property and, as such, has the right to distribute the property itself. * * * There is a consistent clash between support rights *from* the marital property and ownership rights *in* the marital property.

Id. at 631.

1. Social Security

Because Social Security is a federal benefit, any state statutes that distribute social security property at death are inapplicable because they are preempted by Congress. *See* Boggs v. Boggs, 520 U.S. 833, 117 S. Ct. 1754 (1997) (formerly providing a unique community property right, the ability of a spouse to transfer his or her share of the community by Last Will and Testament without surviving the other spouse, but now preempted by federal law). Upon the death of a spouse, the surviving spouse is entitled to the greater of benefits based on their own earnings or an amount equal to one-hundred percent of the spouse's benefits. If the surviving spouse receives a government pension, and two-thirds of that pension is more than the benefit that the survivor would receive under Social Security, the Social Security benefit is eliminated. There are other exceptions to receiving benefits. *See* Social Security Administration, *Social Security Handbook*, https://www.socialsecurity.gov /OP_Home/handbook/handbook-toc.html (accessed Aug. 6, 2019). For offset provisions, see Social Security Administration, *Government Pension Offset* (Publication No. 05-10007), https://www.so cialsecurity.gov/pubs/EN-05-10007.pdf (accessed Aug. 6, 2019). Social Security requires recipients to notify the Administration if changes affecting benefits occur. *See Social Security Handbook* § 133.2.

2. Employee Retirement Security Act of 1974

The Employee Retirement Security Act of 1974 is a federal statute governing most pension plans and prohibits the assignment or alienation of pension benefits, with few exceptions. Thus, simply by being a surviving spouse under a covered pension plan, the spouse takes the benefits even though the decedent may have named another person as beneficiary. *See, e.g., In re* Lefkowitz, 767 F. Supp. 501 (S.D.N.Y. 1991). A spouse may waive his or her rights to an annuity, *see* 29 U.S.C. § 1055(c) (2) (2015), but any waiver of a pension must be witnessed by a notary or a plan representative, *see id.* at § 1055(c)(2)(A). Spouses are entitled to ERISA benefits if it is established that the recipient spouse abandoned the participant, but this abandonment must be established during the lifetime of the participant. *See, e.g.,* Igoe v. 1199 SEIU Health Care Employees Pension Fund, No. 12 Civ. 6308 (DLC), 2013 WL 3467028 (S.D.N.Y. July 10, 2013). At least one state court permitted a surviving spouse to obtain a portion of a former spouse's retirement benefits through the use of a constructive trust, even though the former spouse was married to another person at the time of his death. *See* Robinette v. Hunsecker, 96 A.3d 94 (Md. 2014). The ERISA plan designation is not affected by divorce, even if the participant did not want his or her spouse to receive the benefits of the plan following a final decree of divorce. *See* Raymond C. O'Brien, *Equitable Relief for ERISA Benefit Plan Designation Mistakes*, 67 CATH. U. L. REV. 433 (2018).

3. Homestead

To protect the surviving spouse and, perhaps, minor children from hardship, all states have homestead laws crafted to secure the family domicile, or something comparable, for at least the duration of a life estate of the surviving spouse. To apply, the decedent must have been domiciled in the state providing the homestead allowance. The Uniform Probate Code ignores the necessity of an actual home and, instead, provides a monetary amount of $22,500 for the surviving spouse, or to be divided among the surviving minor children. *See* UNIF. PROB. CODE § 2-402 (2019). But Florida, for example, allows up to one-half of an acre in a municipality or 160 acres elsewhere. *See* FLA. CONST. ART. 10, § 4(a)(1) (2018). But several cases have found that Florida's Homestead law is preempted by federal law. *See, e.g., In re* Osejo, 447 B.R. 352 (Bankr. S.D. Fla. 2011); *In re* Garcia, No. 09-33208-LMI, Ch. 7, 2010 Bankr. LEXIS 2194 (Bankr. S.D. Fla. July 6, 2010); *In re* John Richards Homes Bldg. Co. L.L.C., 298 B.R. 591 (Bankr. E.D. Mich. 2003). For a decision involving a marital domicile and how it is exempt from distribution under intestate succession and remains property of the surviving spouse, see *In re* Estate of Felhofer, 843 N.W.2d 57 (Wis. Ct. App. 2013).

4. Family Maintenance

Similar to spousal maintenance at separation and divorce, support from the estate is provided to the surviving spouse and minor children during the administration. While the Uniform Probate Code provides for a "reasonable allowance in money," *see* UNIF. PROB. CODE § 2-404(a) (2016), the court may take into account other resources available to the family and the current living standard in computing a figure. The allowance may be "suited to the condition in life of the surviving spouse and to the condition of the estate . . . ." 755 ILL. COMP. STAT. § 5/15-1(a) (2019). The allowance takes precedence in the administration of the estate and "is not chargeable against any benefit or share passing to the surviving spouse or children by the will of the decedent, unless otherwise provided, by intestate succession, or by elective share." UNIF. PROB. CODE § 2-404(b) (2019). Finally, note that the British courts are given vast discretion to distribute a decedent's estate among specified persons so as to make a reasonable financial provision. *See* (UNITED KINGDOM) INHERITANCE (PROVISION FOR FAMILY AND DEPENDENTS) ACT OF 1975, § 1(e) (as amended by the INHERITANCE AND TRUSTEES' POWERS ACT 2014).

5. Exempt Property

Regardless of any need of the surviving spouse, states often allow for a set portion of personal property to be exempt from the claims of creditors. If there is no surviving spouse, then decedent's children are entitled to the exemption. Uniform Probate Code § 2-403 provides a $15,000 exemption and is in addition to anything taken under the will, intestate succession, or election. California Probate Code § 141 allows a surviving spouse to waive, in whole or in part, the right to any exempt property being set aside.

6. Dower or Curtesy

Dower is a feudal entitlement for a surviving widow of one-third of the husband's land owned during marriage. Curtesy is a similar entitlement of a life estate for a surviving widower in all of the lands owned by the wife during marriage, as long as issue were born of the marriage. *See generally* ROGER W. ANDERSON, UNDERSTANDING TRUSTS AND ESTATES 146 (1994); 2 FREDERICK POLLOCK & FREDERIC W. MAITLAND, HISTORY OF ENGLISH LAW (2d ed., 1898). However, because gender distinctions are unconstitutional, and because the protection afforded in dower and curtesy involved only land, dower and curtesy were not responsive to today's needs, thus, states were prompted to abolish both. The Uniform Probate Code replaces them with an elective share available to either spouse, equally. *See* UNIF. PROB. CODE § 2-112 (2019). This will be discussed *infra*.

7. Universal Succession

European administration of estates allows for "universal succession" of any estate to the heirs without the appointment of a personal representative and the other steps necessary to administer an estate. The heirs will be responsible for payment of debts or taxes, each heir taking as a tenant in common, and none of them taking a fee for administration. California allows for universal succession between spouses only. *See* CAL. PROB. CODE §§ 13500–13660 (2019). But the Uniform Probate Code more resembles the European system by allowing "the heirs of an intestate or the residuary devisees under a will, excluding minors and incapacitated, protected, or unascertained persons," to become universal successors. *See* UNIF. PROB. CODE § 3-312 (2019). The procedure is described in Unif. Prob. Code §§ 3-313 to 3–322 (2019).

E. The Right to Elect

At the death of a decedent, a surviving spouse is confronted with personal loss, but there are also attendant economic issues confronting him or her. The decedent may have left a valid will devising property acquired during his or her marriage to someone other than the spouse. Or the decedent may have a will devising all property to the surviving spouse, but there may be non-probate transfers naming someone other than the surviving spouse as beneficiary, and these transfers may make up the bulk of the estate. Or the decedent may die intestate with only a small portion of the wealth accumulated during marriage passing through the intestate statutes to the surviving spouse and the bulk of the wealth passing through non-probate transfers to other beneficiaries. Should the surviving spouse "elect" against the will or seek to "augment" the probate estate with the non-probate transfers? What if the beneficiaries named in the will or the non-probate transfers are issue of the decedent and the surviving spouse? Eventually, these issue will inherit from the surviving spouse, so why not make it sooner rather than later? For a comprehensive discussion, see Michael T. Flannery, *Equating Marital and Probate Interests Through the Elective Share*, LexisNexis Expert Commentary, 2009 EMERGING ISSUES 4191 (Aug. 2009) (available at Lexis, Estates, Gifts and Trusts Emerging Issues library).

1. Support or Ownership

When confronted with the spouse's right to elect, states are divided on whether the right to elect against the estate of the decedent spouse should be a result of, first, the decedent's obligation to support the surviving spouse, or second, a partnership theory, by which the surviving spouse has an earned right to a portion of the marital property accumulated. The distinction between the two theories is described by Professor Lawrence W. Waggoner:

> Applied to the elective share, the partnership theory suggests that if the surviving spouse so elects, the survivor is entitled to force a transfer of the decedent's assets sufficient to equalize the marital assets. The support theory suggests that the surviving spouse is entitled to force a sufficient transfer of the decedent's assets to bring the survivor's assets up to a predetermined amount deemed to be at least minimally sufficient for support, should the value of the survivor's assets be below that amount at the decedent's death.

Lawrence W. Waggoner, *The Uniform Probate Code's Elective Share: Time for a Reassessment*, 37 MICH. U. J.L. REFORM 1, 4 (2003); *see also*, Lawrence W. Waggoner, *Spousal Rights in Our Multiple-Marriage Society: The Revised Uniform Probate Code*, 26 REAL PROP., PROB. & TRUST J. 683, 742–46 (1992).

2. Time for Election

There is a time limit on the right to elect. The Uniform Probate Code provides that:

> Except as provided in subsection (b), the election must be made by filing in the court and mailing or delivering to the personal representative, if any, a petition for the elective share within nine months after the date of the decedent's death, or within six months after probate of the decedent's will, whichever limitation later expires.

UNIF. PROB. CODE § 2-211(a) (2019).

3. Who May Elect

Unless a spouse waives his or her right to election through a valid prenuptial or postnuptial agreement, election may occur in the state in which the decedent was domiciled at the time of death. *See* UNIF. PROB. CODE § 2-202(d) (2019). *But see* Estate of Pericles, 266 Ill. App.3d 1096, 641 N.E.2d 10 (1994) (holding that situs of real property controls right to election). The right to elect is personal to the surviving spouse, but if the surviving spouse is incapacitated, an election may be made on behalf of the then-living incapacitated spouse by the spouse's conservator, guardian, or agent, under the authority of a durable power of attorney. UNIF.

Prob. Code § 2-212(a) (2019). Furthermore, the 1990 and 2008 Uniform Probate Codes create a custodial account trust whenever an election is made on behalf of an incapacitated spouse. This is to guarantee that the election amounts are used for the benefit of the spouse and not the spouse's heirs. Throughout the term of the trust, any money generated through the election may only be used for the "benefit of the beneficiary and individuals who were supported by the beneficiary when the beneficiary became incapacitated, or who are legally entitled to support by the beneficiary." *Id.* at § 2-212(c)(2). The trust remains in existence as long as the spouse is incapacitated; if the spouse should recuperate, the spouse may terminate the trust. Upon the death of the spouse, any unused funds shall be paid to the residuary clause of the Last Will and Testament of the spouse against whom the election was made, or to that spouse's heirs. *Id.* at § 2-212(c)(3). Some commentators point out that the custodial trust device is further illustration of the fact that the surviving spouse has no ownership interest in the election process; it is merely a support device, thereby negating any ownership rights in the surviving spouse. *See, e.g.*, Robert H. Sitkoff & Jesse Dukeminier, Wills, Trusts, and Estates, 522-25 (10th ed. 2017); Wilson v. Wilson, 224 Or. App. 360, 197 P.3d 1141 (2008) (holding that death of surviving spouse extinguishes need for support or election).

4. Community Property States

A minority of states are community property states, but these states also entitle a surviving spouse to a right of election. The practice of election in these states derives from a system in which

> Community Property states have always embraced the partnership theory of marriage: all property acquired by either spouse during the marriage is assumed to be the product of the joint efforts of the husband and wife. As a result, husband and wife each enjoy a one-half share in the community property. Each spouse, therefore, has a right to dispose by will of one-half of the community property; the other half automatically belongs to the surviving spouse.

Steward E. Sterk & Melanie B. Leslie, Estates and Trusts: Cases and Materials 497 (6th ed. 2019). Thus, property acquired during marriage is presumed to be community property, without regard to the manner in which title is held. This is a distinctive feature of community property—title is irrelevant—and it allows for an elective share to be identified more easily than what will occur in a common law state, where title does matter. Wisconsin is a state that has adopted the community property system through statute; it has done so through the Model Marital Property Act. The Act, illustrative of community property states, allows for the surviving spouse to elect an amount equal to no more than 50 percent of the augmented, deferred marital property estate, defined as the " total value of the deferred marital property of the spouses, irrespective of where the property was acquired, where the property was located at the time of a relevant transfer, or where the property is currently located, including real property located in another jurisdiction."

Wis. Stat. § 861.02(2)(b) (2019). In a community property state, it is possible for a pre-deceasing spouse to die with a valid will, leaving all of his or her property to someone other than the surviving spouse, thereby necessitating an election by the survivor. The subsequent right of the surviving spouse to one-half of the community may be summarized as follows:

> The testator is presumed to have made his will with the knowledge that his power of testamentary disposition did not extend to the surviving wife's interest in the community property. The presumption is further that he did not intend to devise or bequeath the one-half of the community property which, upon his death, would vest in his widow irrespective of any attempt that he might make to dispose of it by will. In the absence of anything in the instrument to indicate a contrary intent, the testamentary dispositions must accordingly be understood as intended to cover only the property which the testator had the right to devise or bequeath, i.e., his separate property and an undivided half of the community property.

GRACE GANZ BLUMBERG, COMMUNITY PROPERTY IN CALIFORNIA 548 (4th ed. 2003) (quoting Estate of Prager, 166 Cal. 450, 453–54, 137 P. 37, 38–39 (1913)). Suggestions have been made that common law (separate) property states should adopt the community property model of election at death. *See, e.g.,* Alan Newman, *Incorporating the Partnership Theory of Marriage Into Elective-Share Law: The Approximation System of the Uniform Probate Code and the Deferred-Community-Property Alternative,* 49 EMORY L.J. 487, 488 (2000); Charles H. Whitehead, *The Uniform Probate Code's Nod to the Partnership Theory of Marriage: The 1990 Elective Share Revisions,* 11 PROB. L.J. 125, 142 (1992). Some commentaries offer insights into the distinct contribution of community property. *See, e.g.,* Terry L. Turnipseed, *Community Property v. the Elective Share,* 72 LA. L. REV. 161 (2011); Raymond C. O'Brien, *Integrating Marital Property into a Spouse's Elective Share,* 59 CATH. U. L. REV. 617, 687 (2010).

5. *Common Law (Separate) Property States*

The vast majority of states are common law (separate property) states. The distinctive feature in these states is that, when acquired by a spouse, property may be titled in the name of that spouse, individually. Unlike community property states, title denotes ownership of the property even if acquired during marriage. The process in a common law state is further complicated by the fact that modern wealth most often transfers at death through non-probate transfers, rather than through a will or by intestate succession. For example, living trusts, annuities, life insurance, joint accounts, joint tenancies, payable-on-death accounts, and additional accounts all pass outside of the Last Will and Testament or intestate succession, in accordance with what has been termed the non-probate revolution. *See* John H. Langbein, *The Twentieth-Century Revolution in Family Wealth Transmission,* 86 MICH. L. REV. 722 (1988); John H. Langbein, *The Nonprobate Revolution and the Future of the Law of Succession,* 97 HARV. L. REV. 1108 (1984). In the wake of the vast proliferation of non-probate transfers, the issues raised in common law states pertaining to the rights of a surviving spouse are these:

(A) How to provide the surviving spouse with a share of the marital assets when title is in the name of the decedent and the decedent transferred the property to a third person through a non-probate device?

(B) Most of the state responses allow the surviving spouse to take from the probate estate—the will and/or intestate succession—but not from non-probate transfers. Thus, how is it possible to augment the probate estate with non-probate transfers?

(C) Should it make a difference if the non-probate transfer was revocable or irrevocable?

(D) Should there be a distinction between property acquired during the marriage (marital property) and property acquired separately or brought separately (separate property) into the marriage?

(E) Should the length of the marriage make a difference when the surviving spouse seeks to take a share of the decedent's assets at death?

(F) Should there be some similarity between what a surviving spouse receives at death and what that spouse would receive if there had been a divorce?

6. Distribution of Property at Divorce and at Death

The status of marriage has evolved. Today, each of the married partners is able to contract independently, to choose marital domicile, to be responsible for the necessities of the other, and to be sued by, and to sue, the other spouse in tort. The National Conference of Commissioners on Uniform State Laws observed in its 2008 revisions to the Uniform Probate Code that community property and common law states have melded the marital couple into an economic partnership of equals. As such, even though one party may remain at home and raise the children or maintain the household, both spouses share equal ownership in the marital or community property earned during the marriage. This ownership also extends to marital debt, services, and prerogatives. Stated succinctly, "[M]arriage is, among other things, an economic partnership to which both parties contribute as spouse, parent, wage earner, and homemaker." O'Brien v. O'Brien, 66 N.Y.2d 576, 489 N.E.2d 712 (1985). Increasingly, state courts have come to recognize this concept of economic partnership in distributing property at divorce. Today, there are few instances of long-term support for a divorcing spouse. Instead, marital property is assessed and divided equally in community property states, or equitably in common law states. Then, if unfairness may result, courts allow for either reimbursement or rehabilitation, but all with a goal of dividing assets quickly and efficiently, then allowing the divorcing couple to bid one another a fond fiscal farewell.

Sadly, courts and legislatures have been reticent to apply to death the economic lessons learned at divorce. "Family law implements both the partnership and support theories—the partnership theory *upon divorce* through the equitable distribution regimes and the support theory through the duty of support *during the marriage* and the right to alimony upon divorce. Traditional elective share law [at death] is the odd one out." Lawrence W. Waggoner, *The Uniform Probate Code's Elective Share: Time for a Reassessment*, 37 U. Mich. J.L. Reform 1, 4 (2003); Angela M. Vallario, *Spousal Election: Suggested Equitable Reform for the Division of Property at Death*, 52 Cath. U. L. Rev. 519 (2003).

Under common law, state elective share statutes, even when confronted with facts demonstrating that significant portions of marital property pass outside the reach of the surviving spouse because of title held in the decedent's name, there has been little legislative remedy. Instead, for the most part, the issue at death is this: Whether the surviving spouse's elective share includes marital property that has been irrevocably transferred during life, or whether the elective share should include property over which a modicum of dominion was retained by the decedent spouse through some form of joint ownership or method of revocation. States vary in the approach to this issue. Some states allow the surviving spouse a percentage of the *probate estate* only. This does not encompass the wealth that passes outside of probate at the death of the decedent through *non-probate transfers*. *See, e.g., In re* Estate of Myers, 825 N.W.2d 1 (Iowa 2012) (holding that payable-on-death certificates, which are non-probate assets, were not available for spouse's elective share under the state's statute).

Some states provide only a support amount to the surviving spouse, then, after a period of time, the property that provided the support reverts to the decedent's estate. Still other states ignore the length of the marriage in awarding the surviving spouse a share of the marital property, permitting a distribution of marital property far in excess of what is warranted under economic partnership. Thus, distribution of property at the death of one of the spouses is actually a haphazard process. In community property states, because of the traditional means of assessing community property, the process is simpler—a surviving spouse elects one-half of the community property, traditionally defined, and keeps all of his or her separate property. But in a common law (separate property) state, the reality of title, plus the extensive wealth often passing outside of probate, complicates the process. A few examples will illustrate the inequities that may result.

7. Common Law Illustrations of Spousal Elective Rights

MASSACHUSETTS: Mass. Gen Laws ch. 191, § 15 (2019):

Within six months after probate of a Last Will and Testament, a surviving spouse may elect to take the following: (1) if a decedent left issue, then one-third of the personal and real property; or (2) if the decedent left kindred but no issue, then $25,000 and one-half of the real and personal property; but (3) if the personal or real property value is greater than $25,000, then the surviving spouse only gets a life estate in the personal and real property shares; and (4) if the decedent left no issue and no kindred, the surviving spouse takes $25,000 and one-half of the real and personal property, absolutely.

GEORGIA: Ga. Code Ann. §§ 53-3-1; 53-3-2; 53-3-5; 53-3-6; 53-3-7 (2019):

Within two years after the death of the decedent spouse, a single surviving spouse may petition a court for a year's support and maintenance from a testate or intestate estate of the decedent. The year's support should be sufficient to maintain the standard of living the spouse enjoyed during life and should take into consideration the surviving spouse's separate property, earning capacity, and any other factors that the court thinks equitable and proper.

RHODE ISLAND: R.I. Gen. Laws § 33-25-2 (2019):

The surviving spouse is entitled to an elective share equivalent to a life estate in any real property in which the decedent spouse has not recorded the land transfer prior to the spouse's death. The fact that the decedent may have retained an interest in the real property, such as a life estate, does not make the land available to the elective share as long as the title has been recorded prior to the decedent's death. *See* Barrett v. Barrett, 894 A.2d 891, 898 (R.I. 2006).

MARYLAND: Md. Code Ann., Ests. and Trusts § 3-203 (as amended by 2019 Maryland Laws Ch. 197 (S.B. 398) (effective Oct. 1, 2019):

"Instead of property left to the surviving spouse by will, the surviving spouse may elect to take: (1) A one-third share of the net estate if there is also a surviving issue; or (2) A one-half share of the net estate if there is no surviving issue." *Id.*

The term used in the statute—net estate—includes property passing under "testate succession," which means only property passing according to the decedent's Last Will and Testament. Thus, all of the non-probate assets are excluded from election by the surviving spouse. These non-probate assets would include joint accounts, payable-on-death contracts, such as life insurance and annuities, *inter vivos* trusts, and joint tenancies. *But see* Karsenty v. Schoukroun, 406 Md. 469, 959 A.2d 1147 (2008) (offering cumbersome equitable means by which to expand scope of spouse's elective share).

F. Judicial Models for Reform

1. Testamentary Disposition

The task for any elective statute or judicial approach seeking to "augment" or enhance the property against which the surviving spouse may elect at the death of the decedent is to incorporate the vast array of non-probate transfers or *inter vivos* irrevocable gifts passing outside of the traditional probate estate. One method by which these non-probate transfers may be incorporated is to find that they lacked the characteristics to effectively establish themselves as non-probate transfers during the lifetime of the decedent. Unless the decedent effectively makes a transfer during lifetime, any property remaining at death must pass according to the requirements of a valid will. Such property would be classified as "Testamentary." Not being valid, non-probate transfers, testamentary property would be included in the augmented estate for election.

2. Illusory Transfer

As a method of enhancing the property against which the surviving spouse may elect, some courts have applied a test, asking whether the transfer was "illusory." This approach rejects motive or intent and, instead, asks if the decedent, at the time of the transfer, "in good faith divested himself of ownership of his property or has made an illusory transfer." *See* Newman v. Dore, 275 N.Y. 371, 379, 9 N.E.2d 966, 969 (1937). In *Newman*, the testator husband created a valid *inter vivos* trust three days before his death, transferring all of his property to that trust. When the surviving wife sought to take a portion of his assets through election, the state statute restricted her election to all real and personal property in the decedent's estate at the time of his death. But there was no property in his estate against which the wife could elect because everything had been transferred to an *inter vivos* trust. Judging by the substance of the trust and not its form, the court then held that the husband's intent to create a valid trust was insufficient when characterized by the ability to receive income, power to revoke, and power to control the trustee. It made illusory the elective share of his surviving spouse. Therefore, the trust was invalid, and the property passed through the estate and was subject to the elective share state statute.

The court in *Newman* makes an important distinction. The basis for calling the trust illusory is not in reference to the validity of the *inter vivos* trust; this trust is perfectly valid and will serve as a non-probate transfer. Instead, any *inter vivos* arrangement is illusory because it is illusory in reference to the surviving spouse's claim against it. The court makes this distinction when it opines: "We assume, without deciding, that except for the provisions of [the statute granting the spouse an elective share,] the trust would be valid. . . . That is enough to render it an unlawful invasion of the expectant interest of the wife." *Id.* at 380–81, 9 N.E.2d at 969. The value of the decision is that it initiated the dialogue about how to integrate non-probate property into the elective share of the surviving spouse. This process includes the following:

(a) that the spouses have a valid marriage;

(b) that the surviving spouse did not sign a valid prenuptial or postnuptial agreement;

(c) that title evidences ownership in a separate property jurisdiction;

(d) that the decedent spouse utilized ownership in a valid transfer of title through a non-probate device to someone other than the surviving spouse, without the consent of the surviving spouse;

(e) that the decedent spouse retains dominion over the property until death, or surrenders it within a specified period of time, prior to death;

(f) that the remaining assets passing to the surviving spouse are inadequate to satisfy the claims of the surviving spouse; and

(g) that the surviving spouse, personally or through a guardian, commences the statutory election process within the permissible period of time.

3. Intent to Defraud

Fraud is difficult to prove. Courts have sought to establish it on the part of the decedent in making a transfer by focusing on either the subjective intent of the decedent or any objective evidence, such as the length of time between establishing the non-probate transfer and the date of decedent's death. *See, e.g.,* Mo. Ann. Stat. § 474.150(1) (2015) (subjective intent); Hanke v. Hanke, 123 N.H. 175, 459 A.2d 246 (1983) (objective factors). If established, the property may be brought within the purview of the elective share.

4. Objective Factors

The exact parameters of what constitutes an illusory transfer under *Newman* proved elusive, so courts sought more objectivity. The Supreme Judicial Court of Massachusetts provided objective standards to apply in its 1984 *Sullivan* decision, *infra*. The objective is the same—to bring non-probate transfers within the scope of the state's elective share statute.

Sullivan v. Burkin

Supreme Judicial Court of Massachusetts, 1984
390 Mass. 864, 460 N.E.2d 572

WILKINS, Justice.

Mary A. Sullivan, the widow of Ernest G. Sullivan, has exercised her right, under G.L. c. 191, § 15, to take a share of her husband's estate. By this action, she seeks a determination that assets held in an *inter vivos* trust created by her husband during the marriage should be considered as part of the estate in determining that share. A judge of the Probate Court for the county of Suffolk rejected the widow's claim and entered judgment dismissing the complaint. The widow appealed, and, on July 12, 1983, a panel of the Appeals Court reported the case to this court. * * *

In September, 1973, Ernest G. Sullivan executed a deed of trust under which he transferred real estate to himself as sole trustee. The net income of the trust was payable to him during his life and the trustee was instructed to pay to him all or such part of the principal of the trust estate as he might request in writing from time to time. He retained the right to revoke the trust at any time. On his death, the successor trustee is directed to pay the principal and any undistributed income equally to the defendants, George F. Cronin, Sr., and Harold J. Cronin, if they should survive him, which they did. There were no witnesses to the execution of the deed of trust, but the husband acknowledged his signatures before a notary public, separately, as donor and as trustee.

The husband died on April 27, 1981, while still trustee of the *inter vivos* trust. He left a will in which he stated that he "intentionally neglected to make any provision for my wife, Mary A. Sullivan and my grandson, Mark Sullivan." He directed that, after the payment of debts, expenses, and all estate taxes levied by reason of his death, the residue of his estate should be paid over to the trustee of the *inter vivos* trust. The defendants George F. Cronin, Sr., and Harold J. Cronin were named coexecutors of the will. The defendant Burkin is successor trustee of the *inter vivos* trust. On October 21, 1981, the wife filed a claim, pursuant to G.L. c. 191, § 15, for a portion of the estate. * * * ["Election."]

Although it does not appear in the record, the parties state in their briefs that Ernest G. Sullivan and Mary A. Sullivan had been separated for many years. We do know that in 1962 the wife obtained a court order providing for her temporary support. No final action was taken in that proceeding. The record provides no information about the value of any property owned by the husband at his death or about the value of any assets held in the *inter vivos* trust. At oral argument, we were advised that the husband owned personal property worth approximately $15,000 at his death and that the only asset in the trust was a house in Boston which was sold after the husband's death for approximately $85,000.

As presented in the complaint, and perhaps as presented to the motion judge, the wife's claim was simply that the *inter vivos* trust was an invalid testamentary disposition and that the trust assets "constitute assets of the estate" of Ernest G. Sullivan. There is no suggestion that the wife argued initially that, even if the trust were not testamentary, she had a special claim as a widow asserting her rights under G.L. c. 191, § 15. If the wife is correct that the trust was an ineffective testamentary disposition, the trust assets would be part of the husband's probate estate. In that event, we would not have to consider any special consequences of the wife's election under G.L. c. 191, § 15, or, in the words of the Appeals Court, "the present vitality" of Kerwin v. Donaghy, 317 Mass. 559, 572, 59 N.E.2d 299 (1945).

We conclude, however, that the trust was not testamentary in character and that the husband effectively created a valid *inter vivos* trust. Thus, whether the issue was initially involved in this case, we are now presented with the question (which the executors will have to resolve ultimately, in any event) whether the assets of the *inter vivos* trust are to be considered in determining the "portion of the estate of the deceased" (G.L. c. 191, § 15) in which Mary A. Sullivan has rights. We conclude that, in this case, we should adhere to the principles expressed in Kerwin v. Donaghy, *supra*, that deny the surviving spouse any claim against the assets of a valid *inter vivos* trust created by the deceased spouse, even where the deceased spouse alone retained substantial rights and powers under the trust instrument. For the future, however, as to any *inter vivos* trust created or amended after the date of this opinion, we announce that the estate of a decedent, for the purposes of G.L. c. 191, § 15, shall include the value of assets held in an *inter vivos* trust created by the deceased spouse as to which the deceased spouse alone retained the power during his or her life to direct the disposition of those trust assets for his or her benefit, as, for example, by the exercise of a power of appointment or by revocation of the trust. Such a power would be a general power of appointment for Federal estate tax purposes (I.R.C. § 2041(b)(1) [1983]) and a "general power" as defined in the Restatement (Second) of Property § 11.4(1) (Tent. Draft No. 5, 1982).

We consider first whether the *inter vivos* trust was invalid because it was testamentary. A trust with remainder interests given to others on the settlor's death is not invalid as a testamentary disposition simply because the settlor retained a broad power to modify or revoke the trust, the right to receive income, and the right to invade principal during his life. Ascher v. Cohen, 333 Mass. 397, 400, 131 N.E.2d 198 (1956); Leahy v. Old Colony Trust Co., 326 Mass. 49, 51, 93 N.E.2d 238 (1950); Kerwin v. Donaghy, 317 Mass. 559, 567, 59 N.E.2d 299 (1945); National Shawmut Bank v. Joy, 315 Mass. 457, 473–475, 53 N.E.2d 113 (1944); Kelley v. Snow, 185 Mass. 288, 298–299, 70 N.E. 89 (1904). The fact that the settlor of such a trust is the sole trustee does not make the trust testamentary. In National Shawmut Bank v. Joy, *supra* 315 Mass. at 476–477, 53 N.E.2d 113, we held that a settlor's reservation of the power to control investments did not impair the validity of a trust and noted that "[i]n Greeley v. Flynn, 310 Mass. 23, 36 N.E.2d 394 [1941], the settlor was herself the trustee and had every power of control, including the right to withdraw principal for her own use. Yet the gift over at her death was held valid and not testamentary." We did, however, leave open the question whether such a trust would be testamentary "had the trustees been reduced to passive impotence, or something near it." *Id.* 315 Mass. at 476, 53 N.E.2d 113. We have held an *inter vivos* trust valid where a settlor, having broad powers to revoke the trust and to demand trust principal, was a cotrustee with a friend (Ascher v. Cohen, *supra* 333 Mass. at 400, 131 N.E.2d 198) or with a bank whose tenure as trustee was at the whim of the settlor (Leahy v. Old Colony Trust Co., *supra* 326 Mass. at 51, 93 N.E.2d 238). In Theodore v. Theodore, 356 Mass. 297, 249 N.E.2d 3 (1969), the settlor was the sole trustee of two trusts and had the power to revoke the trusts and to withdraw principal. The court assumed that the trusts were not testamentary simply because of this arrangement. The *Theodore* case involved trust assets transferred to the trust only by third persons. For the purposes of determining whether a trust is testamentary, however, the origin of the assets, totally at the disposal of the settlor once received, should make no difference. See Gordon v. Feldman, 359 Mass. 25, 267 N.E.2d 895 (1971), in which the court and the parties implicitly accepted as valid an *inter vivos* trust in which A conveyed to himself as sole trustee with the power in A to withdraw income and principal. We believe that the law of the Commonwealth is correctly represented by the statement in Restatement (Second) of Trusts § 57, comment h (1959), that a trust is "not testamentary and invalid for failure to comply with the requirements of the Statute of Wills merely because the settlor-trustee reserves a beneficial life interest and power to revoke and modify the trust. The fact that as trustee he controls the administration of the trust does not invalidate it."

We come then to the question whether, even if the trust was not testamentary on general principles, the widow has special interests which should be recognized. Courts in this country have differed considerably in their reasoning and in their conclusions in passing on this question. See 1 A. Scott, Trusts § 57.5 at 509–511 (3d ed. 1967 & 1983 Supp.); Restatement (Second) of Property—Donative Transfers, Supplement to Tent. Draft No. 5, reporter's note to § 13.7 (1982); Annot., 39 A.L.R.3d 14

(1971), Validity of Inter Vivos Trust Established by One Spouse Which Impairs the Other Spouse's Distributive Share or Other Statutory Rights in Property. In considering this issue at the May, 1982, annual meeting of the American Law Institute the members divided almost evenly on whether a settlor's surviving spouse should have rights, apart from specific statutory rights, with respect to the assets of an *inter vivos* trust over which the settlor retained a general power of appointment. See Proceedings of the American Law Institute, May, 1982, pp. 59–117; Restatement (Second) of Property—Donative Transfers, Supplement to Tent. Draft No. 5 at 28 (1982). * * *

The rule of Kerwin v. Donaghy, *supra* 317 Mass. at 571, 59 N.E.2d 299, is that "[t]he right of a wife to waive her husband's will, and take, with certain limitations, 'the same portion of the property of the deceased, real and personal, that . . . she would have taken if the deceased had died intestate' (G.L. [Ter.Ed.] c. 191, § 15), does not extend to personal property that has been conveyed by the husband in his lifetime and does not form part of his estate at his death. Fiske v. Fiske, 173 Mass. 413, 419, 53 N.E. 916 [1899]. Shelton v. Sears, 187 Mass. 455, 73 N.E. 666 [1905]. In this Commonwealth a husband has an absolute right to dispose of any or all of his personal property in his lifetime, without the knowledge or consent of his wife, with the result that it will not form part of his estate for her to share under the statute of distributions (G.L. [Ter.Ed.] c. 190, §§ 1, 2), under his will, or by virtue of a waiver of his will. That is true even though his sole purpose was to disinherit her." In the *Kerwin* case, we applied the rule to deny a surviving spouse the right to reach assets the deceased spouse had placed in an *inter vivos* trust of which the settlor's daughter by a previous marriage was trustee and over whose assets he had a general power of appointment. The rule of Kerwin v. Donaghy has been adhered to in this Commonwealth for almost forty years and was adumbrated even earlier. * * * The bar has been entitled reasonably to rely on that rule in advising clients. In the area of property law, the retroactive invalidation of an established principle is to be undertaken with great caution. See Boston Safe Deposit & Trust Co. v. Fleming, 361 Mass. 172, 181–182, 279 N.E.2d 342, appeal dismissed, 409 U.S. 813, 93 S.Ct. 46, 34 L.Ed.2d 69 (1972); Fiduciary Trust Co. v. Mishou, 321 Mass. 615, 636, 75 N.E.2d 3 (1947). Cf. Johnson Controls, Inc. v. Bowes, 381 Mass. 278, 282–283, 409 N.E.2d 185 (1980) (insurance contracts); Whitinsville Plaza, Inc. v. Kotseas, 378 Mass. 85, 97–98, 390 N.E.2d 243 (1979) (covenants not to compete made in deeds and leases); Rosenberg v. Lipnick, 377 Mass. 666, 667, 389 N.E.2d 385 (1979) (antenuptial agreements); Tucker v. Badoian, 376 Mass. 907, 918–919, 384 N.E.2d 1195 (1978) (Kaplan, J., concurring) (relative rights as to the flow of surface water). Contrast as to tort law, Payton v. Abbott Labs, 386 Mass. 540, 565–570, 437 N.E.2d 171 (1982). We conclude that, whether or not Ernest G. Sullivan established the *inter vivos* trust in order to defeat his wife's right to take her statutory share in the assets placed in the trust and even though he had a general power of appointment over the trust assets, Mary A. Sullivan obtained no right to share in the assets of that trust when she made her election under G.L. c. 191, § 15.

We announce for the future that, as to any *inter vivos* trust created or amended after the date of this opinion, we shall no longer follow the rule announced in Kerwin v. Donaghy. There have been significant changes since 1945 in public policy considerations bearing on the right of one spouse to treat his or her property as he or she wishes during marriage. The interests of one spouse in the property of the other have been substantially increased upon the dissolution of a marriage by divorce.[6] We believe that, when a marriage is terminated by the death of one spouse, the rights of the surviving spouse should not be so restricted as they are by the rule in Kerwin v. Donaghy. It is neither equitable nor logical to extend to a divorced spouse greater rights in the assets of an *inter vivos* trust created and controlled by the other spouse than are extended to a spouse who remains married until the death of his or her spouse.

The rule we now favor would treat as part of "the estate of the deceased" for the purposes of G.L. c. 191, § 15, assets of an *inter vivos* trust created during the marriage by the deceased spouse over which he or she alone had a general power of appointment, exercisable by deed or by will. This objective test would involve no consideration of the motive or intention of the spouse in creating the trust. We would not need to engage in a determination of "whether the [spouse] has in good faith divested himself [or herself] of ownership of his [or her] property or has made an illusory transfer" (Newman v. Dore, 275 N.Y. 371, 379, 9 N.E.2d 966 [1937]) or with the factual question whether the spouse "intended to surrender complete dominion over the property" (Staples v. King, 433 A.2d 407, 411 [Me.1981]). Nor would we have to participate in the rather unsatisfactory process of determining whether the *inter vivos* trust was, on some standard, "colorable," "fraudulent," or "illusory."

What we have announced as a rule for the future hardly resolves all the problems that may arise. There may be a different rule if some or all of the trust assets were conveyed to such a trust by a third person. Cf. Theodore v. Theodore, 356 Mass. 297, 249 N.E.2d 3 (1969). We have not, of course, dealt with a case in which the power of appointment is held jointly with another person. If the surviving spouse

---

6. At the time of a divorce or at any subsequent time, "the court may assign to either husband or wife all or any part of the estate of the other," on consideration of various factors, such as the length of the marriage, the conduct of the parties during the marriage, their ages, their employability, their liabilities and needs, and opportunity for future acquisition of capital assets and income. G.L. c. 208, § 34, as amended by St.1982, c. 642, § 1. The power to dispose completely of the property of the divorced litigants comes from a 1974 amendment to G.L. c. 208, § 34. See St.1974, c. 565. It made a significant change in the respective rights of the husband and wife and in the power of Probate Court judges. See Bianco v. Bianco, 371 Mass. 420, 422–423, 358 N.E.2d 243 (1976). We have held that the "estate" subject to disposition on divorce includes not only property acquired during the marriage from the efforts of the husband and wife, but also all property of a spouse "whenever and however acquired." Rice v. Rice, 372 Mass. 398, 400, 361 N.E.2d 1305 (1977). Without suggesting the outer limits of the meaning of the word "estate" under G.L. c. 208, § 34, as applied to trust assets over which a spouse has a general power of appointment at the time of a divorce, after this decision there should be no doubt that the "estate" of such a spouse would include trust assets held in a trust created by the other spouse and having provisions such as the trust in the case before us.

assented to the creation of the *inter vivos* trust, perhaps the rule we announce would not apply. We have not discussed which assets should be used to satisfy a surviving spouse's claim. We have not discussed the question whether a surviving spouse's interest in the intestate estate of a deceased spouse should reflect the value of assets held in an *inter vivos* trust created by the intestate spouse over which he or she had a general power of appointment. That situation and the one before us, however, do not seem readily distinguishable. See Schnakenberg v. Schnakenberg, 262 A.D. 234, 236–237, 28 N.Y.S.2d 841 (N.Y.1941). A general power of appointment over assets in a trust created by a third person is said to present a different situation. Restatement (Second) of Property—Donative Transfers, Supplement to Tent. Draft No. 5, reporter's note to § 13.7 at 29 (1982). Nor have we dealt with other assets not passing by will, such as a trust created before the marriage or insurance policies over which a deceased spouse had control. *Id.* at 30, 38.

The question of the rights of a surviving spouse in the estate of a deceased spouse, using the word "estate" in its broad sense, is one that can best be handled by legislation. See Uniform Probate Code, §§ 2-201, 2-202, 8 U.L.A. 74–75 (1983). See also Uniform Marital Property Act, § 18 (Nat'l Conference of Comm'rs on Uniform State Laws, July, 1983), which adopts the concept of community property as to "marital property." But, until it is, the answers to these problems will "be determined in the usual way through the decisional process." Tucker v. Badoian, 376 Mass. 907, 918–919, 384 N.E.2d 1195 (1978) (Kaplan, J., concurring).

We affirm the judgment of the Probate Court dismissing the plaintiff's complaint.

So ordered.

Notes

The facts in *Sullivan* are eerily familiar to those of *Newman*, fifty years earlier. The difference in *Sullivan* is that the court provided objective criteria as to when the non-probate transfer made the elective share of the surviving spouse illusory. Note that these objective factors include: (a) the *inter vivos* trust was created by the decedent; and (b) the decedent spouse, alone, retained the power to dispose of the trust assets. Not every court agreed with the objective criteria provided by *Sullivan. See, e.g.,* Hanke v. Hanke, 123 N.H. 175, 459 A.2d 246 (1983) (holding that the *Sullivan* test was difficult to apply).

G. Statutory Models for Reform

1. The 1965 New York Elective Share Statute

In 1965, the New York legislature enacted the first statutory approach to elective share—a codification that remains today and one that precipitated other states to take similar legislative action. *See, e.g.,* Me. Rev. Stat. Ann. § 2-201(a) (2019). The structure of the New York statute, which includes within its elective share process probate transfers, non-probate transfers, and absolute gifts made within a specified period of time, influenced the National Conference of Commissioners on Uniform State Laws to adopt the concept of "augmented estate" in its 1969 Uniform Probate Code approach to elective share. Successive revisions of the Code included the concept of "augmented estate," however. in its 2008 version, the Commissioners referred to augmented estate as the "marital estate" to better approximate a spouse's right to property at death with what a spouse would receive at divorce. *See* Raymond C. O'Brien, *Integrating Marital Property into a Spouse's Elective Share*, 59 CATH. U. L. REV. 617, 683-95, 702–14 (2010).

Although the Uniform Probate Code initially used the term "augmented estate" in 1969, the New York statute continues to use the term "net estate" as the concept encompassing probate, non-probate, and absolute gifts within the spouse's elective share. *See* N.Y. EST. POWERS & TRUSTS LAW § 5-1.1-A (McKinney 2019). The contribution of the New York approach is its manner of including all assets acquired during marriage within the elective share of a surviving spouse. The New York statute provides for the following:

Jurisdiction: A spouse may elect only if the decedent spouse was domiciled in the state at the time of death or if the decent chose the laws of the state to govern the disposition of his or her property situated in the state. *Id.* at § 5-1.1-A (c)(6)(3). The estate of the decedent includes all property owned by the decedent wherever situated. *Id.* at § 5-1.1-A (c)(7).

Eligibility: Only a person eligible to be a surviving spouse may elect against a predeceasing spouse's estate. Additionally, this spouse must survive within the requisite period of time under the state's simultaneous death statute. If the spouse is incapacitated, then an election may be made by a guardian or conservator on behalf of the spouse. *Id.* at § 5-1.1-A (b)(3). An election must be made within six months from the date of issuance of Letters Testamentary but not later than two years after the decedent's death. *Id.* at § 5-1.1-A (d)(1).

Net Estate: The net estate shall consist of the following:

(1) Probate estate: This includes property passing under the state's intestate laws or the decedent's Last Will and Testament.

(2) Non-probate estate: This includes property over which the decedent had an ownership interest at death, but the property passed other than through intestacy or a valid will. These include gifts causa mortis, joint accounts, payable on death contracts, joint tenancies, *inter vivos* trusts whereby the decedent retained a right to income or possession, any retirement plan not governed by federal supremacy under ERISA, and any general power of appointment. *Id.* at § 5-1.1-A (b)(1).

(3) Absolute *inter vivos* gifts: These include gifts made within one year of the death of the decedent, to the extent that the decedent did not receive full and adequate consideration, there was no consent made by the surviving spouse, and the gift was in excess, in aggregate, of $15,000 (as of 2019). *Id.* at § 5-1.1-A (b)(1)(A).

Elective Share Amount: The surviving spouse's elective share is the pecuniary amount equal to the greater of: (1) $50,000 or, if the capital value of the net estate is less than $50,000; then (2) one-third of the net estate. In computing the net estate, debts, administration expenses, and reasonable funeral expenses shall be deducted, but all estate taxes shall be disregarded. *Id.* at § 5-1.1-A (a)(2). Except as otherwise expressly provided in the will or other instrument making a transfer, a ratable contribution to the elective share shall be made by the beneficiaries and distributees. The contribution may be made in cash or in the specific property received from the decedent. *Id.* at § 5-1.1-A (c)(2).

Reductions: The elective share amount to which the surviving spouse is entitled is reduced by the capital value of any interest that passes absolutely from the decedent to the electing spouse under intestacy, a valid will, or a non-probate transfer, or to which the electing spouse has made an effective release or waiver. *Id.* at §§ 5-1.1-A (a)(4); 5-1.1-A (e).

2. The Uniform Probate Code: 1969 through 1993

As modern wealth has become progressively more complex, fluid, and global, the need to establish uniformity and predictability in the management and transfer of wealth has intensified. Uncertainty as to what a decedent may transfer without regard to spousal election is heightened by the fact that there are multiple approaches to the elective share rights of a spouse. *See* Jeffrey A. Schoenblum, Multistate Guide to Trusts and Trust Administration (2012); Colby T. Roe, *Arkansas Marriage: A Partnership Between A Husband and Wife, or a Safety Net for Support?*, 61 Ark. L. Rev. 735 (2009); Angela M. Vallario, *Spousal Election: Suggested Equitable Reform for the Division of Property At Death*, 52 Cath. U. L. Rev. 519 (2003); Ronald R. Volkmer, *The Complicated World of the Elective Spouse: In Re Estate of Myers and Recent Statutory Developments*, 33 Creighton L. Rev. 121 (1999); Susan N. Gary, *Marital Partnership Theory and the Elective Share*, 49 U. Miami L. Rev. 567 (1995). The objective of the Uniform Probate Code was to offer an opportunity for uniformity throughout the states—a goal that was thought to benefit estate planning and overall equity between the married partners. To better accomplish its goals, the Code has evolved over time.

a. The 1969 UPC

The first version of the Uniform Probate Code, promulgated by the National Commissioners on Uniform State Laws in 1969, was modeled on the New York statute, described *supra*. The Code provided a list of probate and non-probate transfers that were included in what came to be called the augmented estate, as compared to the net estate in the New York statute. The surviving spouse was given an elective share, or *one-third* of the augmented estate, which included many of the items on the list of items and powers contained within the New York statute. Commentators argued that the 1969 Code provision was defective in that it did not take into account the length of the marriage, and that the one-third share was similar to a spouse's dower rights and, hence, too much like a support mechanism, rather than a share of the marital property rightfully earned. For an incompetent spouse, election could be made on his or her behalf, but only if it could be proven that election was necessary to provide for the spouse's support. Also, only transfers made during the marriage were included, and life insurance payable to someone other than the surviving spouse was excluded. For further comment on the 1969 Code, see Charles H. Whitehead, *The Uniform Probate Code's Nod to the Partnership Theory of Marriage: The 1990 Elective Share Revisions*, 11 PROB. L.J. 125, 133 (1992). Many states still retain the one-third elective share. *See, e.g.*, ALASKA STAT. § 13.12.202(a) (2019) ("one third of the augmented estate"); N.J. STAT. ANN. § 3B:8-1 (West 2019) ("one-third of the augmented estate").

b. The 1990 UPC

The revised version of the elective share provision of the Code retained the augmented estate concept, but there were significant revisions. Most of these revisions were incorporated into the 2008 Code, but in 1990, they were a significant departure from the 1969 Code and the 1965 New York statute. Here is a list of features:

First, the revised 1990 Code provided a minimum support amount of $50,000, which was available if the married couple was married for a short period of time. This support amount was satisfied from any elective share amount to which the surviving spouse was entitled after computing the augmented estate. Hence, it was more of a division of marital property than an actual support award.

Second, in amassing the augmented estate, the Code embraced a marital partnership model. Gone is the designated amount of one-third of the augmented estate. It has been replaced with a share of the marital property. Thus, the 1990 Code incorporated *all property* within the marriage: "Property earned during the marriage need not be segregated from property acquired prior to the marriage or acquired during the marriage by gift or inheritance." Lawrence W. Waggoner, *Spousal Rights in Our Multiple-Marriage Society: The Revised Uniform Probate Code*, 26 REAL PROP., PROB. & TRUST J. 683, 734 (1992). Heretofore, separate property was distinguished from marital property, with the assumption being that the surviving spouse had no claim upon property that had not been the result of the marital union. But the 1990 Code, as well as the 2008 revision, introduced this radical shift, thus eliminating the litigation surrounding distinguishing separate property from marital property. The failure to distinguish is justified by complementing this feature with a method of apportionment based on an accrual time scale, calculated to correspond with the length of the marriage. Hence, the longer a couple is married, the greater percentage of the property is available to the elective share amount.

Third, the augmented estate includes the following:

(i) All of the decedent's net estate;

(ii) *Inter vivos* transfers to persons other than the surviving spouse, when the decedent: had a power of revocation; was given a general power of appointment by himself or herself, or by another person; had a joint interest in the property, or had the power to make a payable-on-death designation; as well as proceeds of insurance on the decedent's life, owned by the decedent, payable to any person other than the surviving spouse.

(iii) Property transferred by the decedent during marriage, over which he had control similar to that identified in (ii), or property irrevocably transferred to someone other than the surviving spouse if it exceeds ($10,000) and occurs in the last two years.

(iv) The value of decedent's *inter vivos* transfers to the surviving spouse; the value of the surviving spouse's property; and the surviving spouse's *inter vivos* transfers to others that would have been included in his or her augmented estate had he or she been the decedent.

Fourth, the 1990 Code first considered the surviving spouse's own assets when meeting the amount owed under election. The Code specified that the decedent's estate is liable to meet the needs of the surviving spouse's elective share "only if the elective share amount is not fully satisfied" by the sum of the surviving spouse's assets. UNIF. PROB. CODE § 2-207 (1990). Such a procedure is meant to prevent the surviving spouse from experiencing a windfall through the elective share.

Illustration: Ben and Elaine were married when they were in their twenties; they never divorced. Ben died at the age of sixty-two and is survived by Elaine; they enjoyed a long-term marriage that lasted for forty years. Ben leaves a valid Last Will and Testament, which completely disinherits Elaine from the assets that the couple had accumulated during their marriage, which was $600,000. Under the 1990 Code, because Ben and Elaine were married for more than fifteen years, they have achieved the maximum rate allowed—50%. The 1990 Code also considers all of the property of the couple, without regard to who holds title. Thus, under the 1990 Code, if Ben had title to all of the $600,000 of the marital assets, Elaine's claim would be $300,000 (fifty percent). If Ben had title to $500,000 of the marital assets, and Elaine had title to $100,000, Elaine's claim against Ben's estate would be $200,000, which is the amount needed to bring Elaine's assets up to the $300,000 necessary to meet her percentage under the 1990 accrual system for a marriage of more than fifteen years. In the second example, Elaine had assets titled in her name, thus, we can see how the new Code prevents a windfall by using her assets to contribute to her share of the elective share portion. If $300,000 were titled in her name, and $300,000 were titled in Ben's name, Elaine would have no claim against Ben's estate. Elaine's title-based ownership rights have already been recognized and met. *See* Lawrence W. Waggoner, *Spousal Rights in Our Multiple-Marriage Society: The Revised Uniform Probate Code*, 26 REAL PROP., PROB. & TRUST J. 683, 721 (1992).

3. The 2008 Uniform Probate Code

Primarily, the 2008 Code revision was intended to better represent the economic partnership theory of marriage. But the revision built upon what had been introduced in the 1990 Code. Already in place was the augmented estate model, which was necessary to include the various permeations of property that had developed with the globalization of wealth. Also, already present was the approximation schedule—the accrual system—based on the length of the marriage. But the 2008 revision incorporates specific changes: (1) it replaces the term augmented estate with marital estate; (2) it increases the supplemental support amount to $75,000; (3) it replaces the percentages of the augmented estate based on the length of the marriage, with the acknowledgment that the elective share is always fifty percent; and (4), it moves the accrual percentage system of the 1990 Code, ranging from 0% to 50%, to a new section, and doubles the percentages. Thus, the marital estate in a marriage that has lasted fifteen years or more is one-hundred percent of the sum of the four components described—the decedent's net probate estate, the decedent's non-probate transfers to others, the decedent's non-probate transfers to the surviving spouse, and the surviving spouse's net worth. *See* Lawrence W. Waggoner, *The Uniform Probate Code's Elective Share: Time for a Reassessment*, 37 U. Mich. J.L. Reform 1, 9 (2003).

If the decedent and spouse were married to each other:	The percentage is:
Less than 1 year	3%
1 year but less than 2 years	6%
2 years but less than 3 years	12%
3 years but less than 4 years	18%
4 years but less than 5 years	24%
5 years but less than 6 years	30%
6 years but less than 7 years	36%
7 years but less than 8 years	42%
8 years but less than 9 years	48%
9 years but less than 10 years	54%
10 years but less than 11 years	60%
11 years but less than 12 years	68%
12 years but less than 13 years	76%
13 years but less than 14 years	84%
14 years but less than 15 years	92%
15 years or more	100%

Unif. Prob. Code § 2-203 (2019).

a. Computation of the Elective Share

Illustration: Consider a couple married for more than five, but less than six, years. Each spouse is over the age of seventy years and, when the husband dies, his net estate is $300,000. He has created a revocable *inter vivos* trust worth $100,000, from which he derived income during his lifetime. At his death, the remainder—the corpus of the trust—went to his children from a prior marriage. The husband has made no transfers to his wife and, at the date of his death, she had net assets worth

$200,000; she had made no transfers to her husband. Under the 2008 Code revision, the process of arriving at the spouse's elective share would be the following:

First, the *elective share percentage* is fifty-percent of the marital estate, regardless of the length of the marriage;

Second, arrive at the *marital estate* by first combining the husband's net probate estate ($300,000), the husband's non-probate *inter vivos* trust, of which his children are the remainder beneficiaries ($100,000), and the wife's net assets ($200,000), for a total of $600,000. Then multiply this amount by 30 %, which is based on the length of the marriage. Since the couple was married for more than five, but less than six, years, multiply the $600,000 by 30 % to arrive at $180,000. This amount — $180,000 — becomes the marital estate.

Third, calculate the *elective share amount* by multiplying the marital estate by 50 % to arrive at $90,000. This is the amount to which the surviving spouse is entitled. This amount corresponds to the marital partnership theory of marriage. But the process continues.

Fourth, in satisfying the *elective share amount*, apply any voluntary transfers to the spouse, and utilize the spouse's marital assets first. Since the husband made no voluntary transfers to the wife by probate or non-probate transfers, the marital portion of the wife's assets is $60,000 (thirty percent of the wife's $200,000). In other words, she already has $60,000 of marital property, so this amount should be excluded from whatever she takes under her elective share.

Fifth, *meeting the balance* owed to the surviving spouse is done by starting with the $90,000 that was her elective share amount. Once that amount is achieved, deduct the $60,000 because she already has this. But there is an unsatisfied balance of $30,000 owed to the wife to provide her with her share of the marital estate. To meet this balance, the wife is entitled to take from the husband's net probate estate ($300,000) in a ratable fashion. If the probate estate is insufficient, then the wife is entitled to take from the non-probate transfers to others ($100,000) to meet the amount due.

b. Custodial Trust Option

§ 2-212. Right of Election Personal to Surviving Spouse; Incapacitated Surviving Spouse.

(a) [**Surviving Spouse Must Be Living at Time of Election.**] The right of election may be exercised only by a surviving spouse who is living when the petition for the elective share is filed in the court under Section 2-211(a). If the election is not exercised by the surviving spouse personally, it may be exercised on the surviving spouse's behalf by his [or her] conservator, guardian, or agent under the authority of a power of attorney.

(b) [**Incapacitated Surviving Spouse.**] If the election is exercised on behalf of a surviving spouse who is an incapacitated person, that portion of the elective-share and supplemental elective-share amounts due from the decedent's probate estate and recipients of the decedent's nonprobate transfers to others under Section 2-209(c) and (d) must be placed in a custodial trust for the benefit of the surviving spouse under the provisions of the [Enacting state] Uniform Custodial Trust Act, except as modified below. For the purposes of this subsection, an election on behalf of a surviving spouse by an agent under a durable power of attorney is presumed to be on behalf of a surviving spouse who is an incapacitated person. For purposes of the custodial trust established by this subsection, (i) the electing guardian, conservator, or agent is the custodial trustee, (ii) the surviving spouse is the beneficiary, and (iii) the custodial trust is deemed to have been created by the decedent spouse by written transfer that takes effect at the decedent spouse's death and that directs the custodial trustee to administer the custodial trust as for an incapacitated beneficiary.

(c)[**Custodial Trust.**] For the purposes of subsection (b), the [Enacting state] Uniform Custodial Trust Act must be applied as if Section 6(b) thereof were repealed and Sections 2(e), 9(b), and 17(a) were amended to read as follows:

> (1) Neither an incapacitated beneficiary nor anyone acting on behalf of an incapacitated beneficiary has a power to terminate the custodial trust; but if the beneficiary regains capacity, the beneficiary then acquires the power to terminate the custodial trust by delivering to the custodial trustee a writing signed by the beneficiary declaring the termination. If not previously terminated, the custodial trust terminates on the death of the beneficiary.

> (2) If the beneficiary is incapacitated, the custodial trustee shall expend so much or all of the custodial trust property as the custodial trustee considers advisable for the use and benefit of the beneficiary and individuals who were supported by the beneficiary when the beneficiary became incapacitated, or who are legally entitled to support by the beneficiary. Expenditures may be made in the manner, when, and to the extent that the custodial trustee determines suitable and proper, without court order but with regard to other support, income, and property of the beneficiary [exclusive of] [and] benefits of medical or other forms of assistance from any state or federal government or governmental agency for which the beneficiary must qualify on the basis of need.

> (3) Upon the beneficiary's death, the custodial trustee shall transfer the unexpended custodial trust property in the following order: (i) under the residuary clause, if any, of the will of the beneficiary's predeceased spouse against whom the elective share was taken, as if that predeceased spouse died immediately after the beneficiary; or (ii) to that predeceased spouse's heirs under Section 2-711 of [this State's] Uniform Probate Code.

4. The Equitable Model

Implied within both the New York statutory model and the far more complicated Uniform Probate Code model of elective share is the goal of equalizing what a spouse would receive at death with what the spouse would receive at divorce. If the economic partnership theory of marriage is to be implemented, then a spouse should not receive more at divorce than he or she would receive at death. The community property states better equalize death and divorce than do the common law states. Hence, the question arises as to why not draft an election statute for use in common law states that would mirror the manner in which property is divided at divorce, taking into consideration decedent's property passing through probate and non-probate transfers, disregarding the strict confines of title? Professor Angela M. Vallario developed such a model—an election model based on the equitable distribution of property system used by common law states at divorce. *See* Angela M. Vallario, *Spousal Election: Suggested Equitable Reform for the Division of Property at Death*, 52 Cath. U. L. Rev. 519 (2003). Her proposed statute includes, for purposes of right of election by the surviving spouse, the decedent's real and personal property, movable and immovable, tangible and intangible, wherever situated. *Id.* at 562. Specifically, this includes non-probate transfers "owned in substance" by the decedent immediately before death, *id.* at 563, any transfer made within a one-year period preceding the decedent's death, *id.* at 564, and any probate or non-probate property owned by the surviving spouse, *id.* at 565. The surviving spouse is to take one-half of this amount, *id.* at 562 , and if the award is "insufficient," on application by the surviving spouse, the court may award an additional amount, after taking into consideration the following: (1) support available to the surviving spouse from other sources and the spouse's earning capacity; and (2) such other relevant criteria as the court deems equitable and proper. *Id.* The burden of proof is upon the surviving spouse to show by a preponderance of the evidence that the elective share, alone, is insufficient. *Id.* The equitable factor of what the "court deems equitable and proper," is reflected in many state statutes providing for marital property distribution at divorce. *See, e.g.,* N.Y. Dom. Rel. L. § 236 (McKinney 2019).

The equitable basis of the proposed statute resonates with a clause for making "reasonable financial provision" for, among others, a surviving spouse, in the (United Kingdom) Inheritance (Provision for Family and Dependents) Act 1975, § 1(e) (as amended by the Inheritance and Trustees' Powers Act 2014). It also eliminates the need for the fixed $75,000 supplemental support award. *See* Unif. Prob. Code § 2-202(b) (2019). Also, by making the focus the "property acquired during marriage," the proposal adopts the sliding scale of the elective share, allowing for length of marriage to determine the amount of property coming under the purview of the election. This also will exclude separate property from being considered under election. Most of all, the statute provides for flexibility in approach to each marriage's dissolution at death, as is done at divorce.

IV. Administration

A. Limitations: Probate Versus Non-Probate Transfers

Probate technically means establishing the validity of the Last Will and Testament, but the term is often used to refer to the entire process by which all assets of the decedent, passing by testate or intestate succession, are identified and then distributed to heirs or intended legatees or devisees, and expenses are paid. A more accurate term for this process would be administration of the decedent's estate. Recall that one of the benefits of non-probate transfers is that no administration is necessary; items such as payable-on-death accounts, revocable trusts, or joint tenancies pass immediately upon the death of the decedent to named beneficiaries, without the necessity of administration. This is what makes them so popular and so private; they are fast and allow clients to by-pass the public process by which a will is established by probate as a public document and conduit of wealth transfer. But estate taxes on non-probate transfers may still be due, and sometimes title to real estate must be cleared. With probate, real and personal property, passing as it does through administration,

> devolves to the persons to whom it is devised by [a decedent's] last will or to those indicated as substitutes for them in cases involving lapse, renunciation, or other circumstances affecting the devolution of testate estate, or in the absence of testamentary disposition, to [his or her] heirs, or to those indicated as substitutes for them in cases involving renunciation or other circumstances affecting devolution of intestate estates, subject to homestead allowance, exempt property and family allowance, to rights of creditors, elective share of the surviving spouse, and to administration.

Unif. Prob. Code § 3-101 (2019). Procedures associated with administration have evolved over generations and will vary among states, yet there is a process that, with variations, will apply whenever a decedent dies leaving a valid will or property that passes according to intestate succession. What follows is a sketch of that process.

B. Administrative Process

1. Venue

Upon the death of a decedent, the proper question to ask is where to begin the process of administration. For example, "[i]f the decedent was domiciled in this state at the time of death, the proper county for proceedings concerning administration of the decedent's estate is the county in which the decedent was domiciled, regardless of where the decedent died." Cal. Prob. Code § 7051 (West 2019). Thus, domicile of the decedent governs the devolution of all personal property, wherever located, and any real property located in that state. If real property is located in another state, then there must be ancillary administration in that state, meaning that the will must be probated there to clear title to the real estate, *see* Unif. Prob. Code § 4-205 (2019), pay all debts, and collect all assets. *See* Unif. Prob. Code §§ 4-201 to 203 (2019). The same would be true if the decedent died intestate and owned personal and real property in more than one state.

2. Personal Representative

The Uniform Probate Code often refers to the executor (testate) or the administrator (intestate) by use of the ubiquitous term "personal representative"; the term eliminates any distinction between the two titles. To qualify as such, a person "must be appointed by order of the Registrar, qualify and be issued letters. Administration of an estate is commenced by the issuance of letters." *See* Unif. Prob. Code § 3-103 (2019). Any valid will may designate a Personal Representative, but if there is no will, or if it fails to appoint a Personal Representative, there is a prioritized list of possible appointees established by statute. *See, e.g., id.* at § 3-203. Once appointed by the court, the Personal Representative has specified duties to perform, the powers relating "back in time to give acts by the person appointed which are beneficial to the estate occurring prior to appointment the same effect as those occurring thereafter." *Id.* at § 3-701. For example, one of the first duties is probate of the will—establishing the validity of its formalities and intentionalities—but making no determination as to the substantive terms contained therein. Once the court accepts the administration of the estate, the Personal Representative is entitled to reasonable compensation unless other provisions are established in the will. *See id.* at § 3-719; Cal. Prob. Code §§ 10800–10805 (West 2019). An emerging power of the personal representative is access to digital accounts. *See* Gerry W. Beyer & Naomi Cahn, *When You Pass On, Don't Leave the Passwords Behind*, 26 Prob. & Prop. 40 (Jan./Feb. 2012). For a commentary on the burden of the decedent to clearly express his or her intent as to the appointment of an administrator, see Michael T. Flannery, The *Appointment of Probate Administrators and Estate of Garrett*, LexisNexis Expert Commentary, 2009 Emerging Issues 3561 (Apr. 2009) (available at Lexis, Estates, Gifts and Trusts Emerging Issues library).

3. Statute of Limitations

There are varying times as to the statute of limitations for submitting a will for probate. The Uniform Probate Code provides a three year period following the death of the decedent, with some exceptions. *See* Unif. Prob. Code § 3-108 (2019). Differing from submitting a will for probate, a proceeding to contest an informally probated will may be commenced within twelve months after such informal probate, or three years after the decedent's death, whichever is later. *Id.* In the case of small estates involving only personal property, there is a provision for minimal administration, but the process still must be commenced by the Personal Representative. *See, e.g., id.* at §§ 3-1201 to 1204; Cal. Prob. Code §§ 7660–66 (West 2019).

4. Informal and Formal Probate

As the name implies, informal probate means that the will lacks contest by any party and allows for a speedier distribution of the probate estate. *See* Unif. Prob. Code §§ 3-301 to 311 (2019). "Informal probate is conclusive as to all persons until superseded by an order in a formal intestacy proceeding." *Id.* at § 3-302.

> A formal testacy proceeding is litigation to determine whether a decedent left a valid will. A formal testacy proceeding may be commenced by an interested person filing a petition [Section 3-402(a)] in which [he or she]

requests that the Court, after notice and hearing, enter an order probating a will, or a petition to set aside an informal probate of a will or to prevent informal probate of a will which is the subject of a pending application, or a petition in accordance with Section 3-402(b) for an order that the decedent died intestate.

Id. at § 3-401. As the more juridical procedure, the Uniform Probate Code formal procedure establishes the parameters of notice, proof, testimony, finality, and effect of the order. *See id.* at §§ 3-402 to 414. Efforts and commentary continue supporting the reform of the probate process because of its cost and delay. *See, e.g.,* Jay A. Soled & Mitchell M. Gans, *Asset Preservation and the Evolving Role of Trusts in the Twenty-First Century,* 72 WASH. & LEE L. REV. 257 (2015); John H. Martin, *Non-Judicial Estate Settlement,* 45 U. MICH. J.L. REFORM 965 (2012); Iris J. Goodwin, *How the Rich Stay Rich: Using a Family Trust Company to Secure a Family Fortune,* 40 SETON HALL L. REV. 467 (2010); Karen J. Sneddon, *Beyond the Personal Representative: The Potential of Succession Without Administration,* 50 S. TEX. L. REV. 449 (2009).

5. Information

A Personal Representative is a fiduciary who shall observe the standards of care applicable to trustees. *Id.* at § 3-703(a). *See also* UNIF. PROB. CODE § 3-712 (2019) (Improper Exercise of Power; Breach of Fiduciary Duty); CAL. PROB. CODE §§ 9600–9606 (West 2019). As such, he or she has a strict duty of care, and one of the responsibilities is that, no later than thirty days after appointment, the Personal Representative must give information to the heirs and devisees, by ordinary mail, telling them of the appointment and that they are entitled to information from the Personal Representative regarding the administration. The Representative must also inform the heirs and devisees that they have the right to petition the court in any matter relating to the estate, including distribution of assets and expenses of administration. UNIF. PROB. CODE § 3-705 (2019). For a commentary on the use of "will registries" and the professional responsibility of attorneys leaving the practice of law but who retain estate planning documents for clients who cannot be located, see Michael T. Flannery, *State Bar of California Standing Committee on Professional Responsibility and Conduct, Formal Opinion No. 2007-173,* LexisNexis Expert Commentary, 2008 EMERGING ISSUES 2061 (May 2008) (available at Lexis, Emerging Issues, Combined Area of Law library).

6. Inventory and Appraisement

Within three months of appointment, a Personal Representative must prepare and file or mail an inventory of property owned by the decedent at the time of his or her death, listing items with reasonable detail, fair market value, and any debts against the property. The filing must be with the court, but a copy shall be sent to any interested person who requests it. UNIF. PROB. CODE § 3-706 (2019). The Personal Representative has a duty to modify the inventory as needed, *see id.* at § 3-708, and must pay taxes on, and take all steps necessary for management, protection and preservation of, the assets, *id.* at § 3-709.

7. Administration Powers of Personal Representative

Unless restricted by a valid will of the decedent, the Personal Representative is given an extensive array of powers to do such duties as selling assets, employing persons, voting stocks of other securities, *see id.* at § 3-715, or even running decedent's business, *see, e.g.,* Cal. Prob. Code § 9760 (West 2019). Employment of any person and the compensation paid to that person is subject to review by the court. *See* Unif. Prob. Code § 3-721 (2019). *See, e.g.,* Cal. Prob. Code §§ 10810–10814 (2019) (compensation paid to an attorney). If, for any reason, the original Personal Representative is unable to complete the estate administration, a successor "has the same power and duty as the original personal representative to complete the administration and distribution of the estate, as expeditiously as possible, but [he or she] shall not exercise any power expressly made personal to the [personal representative] named in the will." Unif. Prob. Code § 3-716 (2019).

8. Notice to Creditors

The Personal Representative must publish a notice to creditors once a week for three successive weeks, in a newspaper of general circulation in the decedent's domicile county, announcing his or her appointment, address, and notice that they must present claims within four months of the date of the first publication of the notice or be barred forever. *See id.* at § 3-801(a). California is more precise, providing that the first publication date of the notice shall be at least 15 days before the hearing. Three publications in a newspaper published once a week, or more often, with at least five days intervening between the first and last publication dates, not counting the publication dates, are sufficient. *See* Cal. Prob. Code § 8121(a) (West 2019). The Supreme Court of the United States has ruled that because the probate court is intimately involved throughout probate process, there is sufficient state action to warrant due process protection for any actual creditors, prior to extinguishing their claims. Thus, the Due Process Clause requires any creditor that is known or reasonably ascertainable to be given actual notice; general publication is insufficient. *See* Tulsa Professional Collection Services, Inc. v. Pope, 485 U.S. 478 (1988), *supra*.

9. Payment of Claims

The Personal Representative is empowered to pay claims against the decedent's estate, waive defenses, and, if assets are insufficient to pay all claims in full, make payment in the following order: (a) costs and expenses of administration; (b) reasonable funeral expenses; (c) debts and taxes, with preference under federal law; (d) reasonable and necessary medical and hospital expenses of the last illness of the decedent, including compensation of persons attending him or her; (e) debts and taxes, with preference under other laws of the state; (f) all other claims. Unif. Prob. Code § 3-805 (2019). There are a number of special provisions relating to abatement of assets, *id.* at § 3-902, distribution in kind, *id.* at § 3-907, and liability of a distributee when there has been an improper distribution of an asset, *id.* at § 3-909. In contracting in his fiduciary capacity, a Personal Representative is not individually liable unless he or she fails to reveal his representative capacity and identify the estate in his contracting. *Id.* at § 3-808.

10. Closing the Estate

After one year, the Personal Representative, or any interested person, may petition the court for an order of complete settlement of the estate. *See id.* at §§ 3-1001 to 3-1002. Most states require the Personal Representative to file a final accounting to the court, *see, e.g.,* Cal. Prob. Code § 10900 (West 2015), but the Uniform Probate Code does not do this, providing, instead, an optional sworn statement of the Personal Representative. *See* Unif. Prob. Code § 3-1003 (2019). The Uniform Probate Code provides that, no earlier than six months of his or her original appointment, the Personal Representative may file with the court a verified statement that he or she has determined that the time limit for the creditors' presentation of claims has expired, that all claims have been paid, and a copy of the statement has been sent to all distributees, creditors, and any other claimants. *Id.* Successors and creditors have six months after the filing of the closing statement to bring suit against the Personal Representative for any negligence in the performance of his or her duties. *Id.* at § 3-1005. But the Personal Representative could bring an inter partes proceeding, in which all the interested parties are joined for the purpose of obtaining a court order settling the account. This has the effect of discharging the Personal Representative from further liability and furthering the goal of finality. *See id.* at §§ 3-1001 to 3-1002.

11. Tax Considerations

The Personal Representative is responsible for the payment of taxes associated with the decedent's estate. *See* I.R.C. § 2002. With few exceptions, the estate tax is due nine months from the decedent's death. *See* I.R.C. § 6075. Generally, an estate will be allowed an automatic six month extension of time beyond the nine month due date to file the estate tax return, so long as Form 4768 is filed on or before the original due date. *See* Treasury Reg. § 20.6081-1 of the Procedure and Administration Regulations. The taxable estate equals the value of the gross estate less the deductions allowed under I.R.C. §§ 2053 to 2058. With respect to the value of the gross estate, the Personal Representative may elect to utilize an alternate valuation date if the value of the gross estate and the amount of the estate tax due will decrease. *See* I.R.C. § 2032. The alternate valuation date may be six months after the date of death of the decedent, and once the election is made, it is irrevocable.

C. Professional Responsibility

Hotz v. Minyard

Supreme Court of South Carolina, 1991
304 S.C. 225, 403 S.E.2d 634

GREGORY, Chief Justice.

This appeal is from an order granting respondents summary judgment on several causes of action. We reverse in part and affirm in part.

Respondent Minyard (Tommy) and appellant (Judy) are brother and sister. Their father, Mr. Minyard, owns two automobile dealerships, Judson T. Minyard, Inc. (Greenville Dealership), and Minyard-Waidner, Inc. (Anderson Dealership). Tommy has been the dealer in charge of the Greenville Dealership since 1977. Judy worked for her father at the Anderson Dealership beginning in 1983; she was also a vice-president and minority shareholder. In 1985, Mr. Minyard signed a contract with General Motors designating Judy the successor dealer of the Anderson Dealership.

Respondent Dobson is a South Carolina lawyer practicing in Greenville and a member of respondent Dobson & Dobson, P.A. (Law Firm). Dobson is also a certified public accountant, although he no longer practices as one. In 1985, Dobson sold the tax return preparation practice of Law Firm to respondent Dobson, Lewis & Saad, P.A. (Accounting Firm). Although his name is included in Accounting Firm's name, Dobson is merely a shareholder and director and does not receive remuneration as an employee.

Dobson did legal work for the Minyard family and its various businesses for many years. On October 24, 1984, Mr. Minyard came to Law Firm's office to execute a will with his wife, his secretary, and Tommy in attendance. At this meeting he signed a will which left Tommy the Greenville Dealership, gave other family members bequests totalling $250,000.00, and divided the remainder of his estate equally between Tommy and a trust for Judy after his wife's death. All present at the meeting were given copies of this will. Later that afternoon, however, Mr. Minyard returned to Dobson's office and signed a second will containing the same provisions as the first except that it gave the real estate upon which the Greenville dealership was located to Tommy outright. Mr. Minyard instructed Dobson not to disclose the existence of the second will. He specifically directed that Judy not be told about it.

In January 1985, Judy called Dobson requesting a copy of the will her father had signed at the morning meeting on October 24, 1984. At Mr. Minyard's direction, or at least with his express permission, Dobson showed Judy the first will and discussed it with her in detail.

Judy testified she had the impression from her discussion with Dobson that under her father's will she would receive the Anderson Dealership and would share equally with her brother in her father's estate. According to Dobson, however, he merely explained Mr. Minyard's intent to provide for Judy as he had for Tommy when and if she became capable of handling a dealership. Dobson made a notation to this effect on the copy of the will he discussed with Judy. Judy claimed she was led to believe the handwritten notes were part of her father's will.

In any event, Judy claims Dobson told her the will she was shown was in actuality her father's last will and testament. Although Dobson denies ever making this express statement, he admits he never told her the will he discussed with her had been revoked.

In January 1986, Mr. Minyard was admitted to the hospital for various health problems. In April 1986, he suffered a massive stroke. Although the date of the onset of his mental incompetence is disputed, it is uncontested he is now mentally incompetent.

Judy and Tommy agreed that while their father was ill, Judy would attend to his daily care and Tommy would temporarily run the Anderson Dealership until Judy returned. During this time, Tommy began making changes at the Anderson Dealership. Under his direction, the Anderson Dealership bought out another dealership owned by Mr. Minyard, Judson Lincoln-Mercury, Inc., which was operating at a loss. Tommy also formed a holding company which assumed ownership of Mr. Minyard's real estate leased to the Anderson Dealership. Consequently, rent paid by the dealership was greatly increased.

Judy questioned the wisdom of her brother's financial dealings. When she sought to return to the Anderson Dealership as successor dealer, Tommy refused to relinquish control. Eventually, in August 1986, he terminated Judy from the dealership's payroll.

Judy consulted an Anderson law firm concerning her problems with her brother's operation of the Anderson Dealership. As a result, on November 15, 1986, Mr. Minyard executed a codicil removing Judy and her children as beneficiaries under his will. Judy was immediately advised of this development by letter.

In March 1987, Judy met with Tommy, her mother, and Dobson at Law Firm's office. She was told if she discharged her attorneys and dropped her plans for a lawsuit, she would be restored under her father's will and could work at the Greenville Dealership with significant fringe benefits. Judy testified she understood restoration under the will meant she would inherit the Anderson Dealership and receive half her father's estate, including the real estate, as she understood from her 1985 meeting with Dobson. Judy discharged her attorneys and moved to Greenville. Eventually, however, Tommy terminated her position at the Greenville Dealership.

As a result of the above actions by Tommy and Dobson, Judy commenced this suit alleging various causes of action. The causes of action against Tommy for tortious interference with contract, a shareholder derivative suit for wrongful diversion of corporate profits, and fraud survived summary judgment and are not at issue here. Judy appeals the trial judge's order granting summary judgment on the remaining causes of action against Tommy, Dobson, and the professional associations. We address only the trial judge's ruling on the cause of action against Dobson for breach of fiduciary duty. Judy also appeals the dismissal of Minyard-Waidner, Inc. as a party defendant.

* * *

Judy's complaint alleges Dobson breached his fiduciary duty to her by misrepresenting her father's will in January 1985. As a result, in March 1987 she believed she would regain the Anderson Dealership if she refrained from pursuing her claim against her brother. This delay gave Tommy additional time in control of the Anderson Dealership during which he depleted its assets. Law Firm and Accounting Firm are charged with vicarious liability for Dobson's acts.

The trial judge granted Dobson, Law Firm, and Accounting Firm summary judgment on the ground Dobson owed Judy no fiduciary duty because he was acting as Mr. Minyard's attorney and not as Judy's attorney in connection with her father's will. We disagree.

We find the evidence indicates a factual issue whether Dobson breached a fiduciary duty to Judy when she went to his office seeking legal advice about the effect of her father's will. Law Firm had prepared Judy's tax returns for approximately twenty years until September 1985 and had prepared a will for her she signed only one week earlier. Judy testified she consulted Dobson personally in 1984 or 1985 about a suspected misappropriation of funds at one of the dealerships and as late as 1986 regarding her problems with her brother. She claimed she trusted Dobson because of her dealings with him over the years as her lawyer and accountant.

A fiduciary relationship exists when one has a special confidence in another so that the latter, in equity and good conscience, is bound to act in good faith. Island Car Wash, Inc. v. Norris, 292 S.C. 595, 599, 358 S.E.2d 150, 152 (Ct.App.1987). An attorney/client relationship is by nature a fiduciary one. In re: Green, 291 S.C. 523, 354 S.E.2d 557 (1987). Although Dobson represented Mr. Minyard and not Judy regarding her father's will, Dobson did have an ongoing attorney/client relationship with Judy and there is evidence she had "a special confidence" in him. While Dobson had no duty to disclose the existence of the second will against his client's (Mr. Minyard's) wishes, he owed Judy the duty to deal with her in good faith and not actively misrepresent the first will. We find there is a factual issue presented whether Dobson breached a fiduciary duty to Judy. We conclude summary judgment was improperly granted Dobson on this cause of action. See Standard Fire Ins. Co. v. Marine Contracting and Towing Co., 301 S.C. 418, 392 S.E.2d 460 (1990) (summary judgment).

Similarly, we find evidence to present a jury issue whether Law Firm should be held vicariously liable for Dobson's conduct since Dobson was acting in his capacity as a lawyer when he met with Judy to discuss the will in January 1985. There is no evidence, however, that Dobson was acting in his capacity as an accountant on that occasion since he was giving legal advice and not rendering accounting services. We find no basis for vicarious liability against Accounting Firm. Accordingly, we reverse the granting of summary judgment on this cause of action as to Dobson and Law Firm and affirm as to Accounting Firm.

Finally, the trial judge dismissed Minyard-Waidner, Inc., the Anderson Dealership, as a party defendant on the ground the complaint contains no allegation of wrongdoing by the corporate entity. Judy claims the corporation is the real party in interest in her shareholder's derivative action and should not be dismissed from the action.

Under former S.C.Code Ann. § 15-5-40 (1976), it was required that parties united in interest be joined as plaintiffs or defendants. A party whose consent could not be obtained could be named as a defendant. This Court never construed § 15-5-40 in the context of a shareholder derivative suit and it has now been superseded by the South Carolina Rules of Civil Procedure. Rule 23(b), SCRCP, governing derivative suits makes no mention of the need to name the corporation as a party defendant. Other jurisdictions have held that a shareholder derivative suit must be dismissed if the corporation is not named as a party defendant where the corporation is not defunct. See, *e.g.*, Wagner v. Bisco, 190 Ga. 474, 9 S.E.2d 650 (1940). The reasoning for such a rule is that the court must have all interested parties before it to fix their respective rights. Further, because a stockholder has no power to bind the corporation, the corporation must be named as a defendant if it has not brought the action in its own right. *Id.* While we decline at this time to adopt such a requirement, we hold a corporate defendant may be named in a shareholder's derivative suit as a party defendant even where no wrongdoing by the corporate entity is alleged.

Pursuant to Supreme Court Rule 23, we affirm the trial judge's order granting summary judgment on the remaining causes of action. The judgment of the circuit court is

REVERSED IN PART; AFFIRMED IN PART.

HARWELL, CHANDLER, FINNEY and TOAL, JJ., concur.

Chapter 6

Utilizing Future Interests

Tool Bar

I. Interests Held by the Settlor

Decedents' estates consists of property either given outright to others or held until some agreed upon time in the future and then given to others. Because property—wealth—is involved, it is treated with importance, and important things generate language, terms, and phrases, and a life of their own. Some of these terms and phrases originated at the time of the Norman Conquest of England in 1066. Forces were then set in motion, evolving incrementally into lists of terms, denoting statutes, presumptions, rules, and doctrines. FREDERICK POLLOCK & FREDERICK W. MAITLAND, THE HISTORY OF ENGLISH LAW BEFORE THE TIME OF EDWARD I 231 (2d ed. 1898).

By the signing of the Magna Carta in 1215, English courts promoted equity through its chancery courts, but equity always presupposed common law, thereby necessitating common law courts. The English Court of Chancery, responsible for equity, "deferred to common law outcomes unless [the Chancellor] saw good reason not to." John H. Langbein, Renee Lettow Lerner & Bruce P. Smith, History of the Common Law 287 (2009). Gradually trusts evolved.

Until the nineteenth century trust property consisted of real estate, even in the United States — the inheritor of the English system. Wealth evolved into what it is today — stocks, derivatives, mutual fund shares, and untold wealth contained in pension and contract accounts. These became the subject of terms and phrases from a bygone era. Gradually, as trust property evolved, trust management companies took responsibility for investment management, regulation, fiduciary administration, and transfer of assets from one beneficiary to the next. Thus, even though today's future interests involve companies and assets far removed from the past centuries that spawned the terms and phrases, the language still has pertinence and relevance. In reviewing the following material, maintain a sense of historical precedent but also recognize the current importance of terms and phrases.

First National Bank of Bar Harbor v. Anthony

Supreme Judicial Court of Maine, 1989
557 A.2d 957

ROBERTS, Justice.

The children of John M. Anthony, Deborah Alley and Christopher Anthony Perasco, appeal from a summary judgment of the Superior Court, Hancock County (*Smith, J.*), that denied their claim to a remainder interest in an *inter vivos* trust created by their now deceased grandfather, J. Franklin Anthony. The court determined that the gift to John M. Anthony, a child of the settlor, of the remainder interest lapsed as a result of John M. Anthony's death prior to the death of the settlor. Because we hold that the remainder interest of John M. Anthony was a present, vested interest at the time of the creation of the *inter vivos* trust, we vacate the judgment.

* * *

On May 14, 1975, J. Franklin Anthony, of Bar Harbor, established a revocable *inter vivos* trust with the First National Bank of Bar Harbor. The income was payable to the settlor for life, then to his widow, Ethel L. Anthony, should she survive him. Upon the death of both J. Franklin and Ethel L. Anthony, the corpus would be divided "in equal shares to [the settlor's] children, John M. Anthony, Peter B. Anthony and Dencie S. Tripp [now Fenno] free and clear of any trust."

Ethel Anthony predeceased her husband on November 22, 1982. On September 9, 1983, John M. Anthony died unmarried, leaving three children: Deborah Alley, Christopher Anthony Perasco and Paul Anthony.

J. Franklin Anthony died on April 2, 1984. On April 10, 1984, his will was admitted to Probate by the Hancock County Probate Court. The will left two-thirds of his estate to Peter B. Anthony and one-third to Dencie S. Fenno; the heirs of John M. Anthony were expressly omitted from the will.

* * *

The First National Bank of Bar Harbor, in its capacity as trustee, filed a complaint in the Superior Court requesting construction of the Anthony Trust. The children of John M. Anthony, grandchildren of the settlor, filed a motion for summary judgment. The grandchildren asserted that John M. Anthony's interest in the trust was vested, not contingent, at the time of its creation. John M.'s heirs, therefore, were entitled to his one-third interest in the trust.

The motion was opposed by Dencie S. Fenno and Peter B. Anthony, at that time arguing that the terms of the trust were ambiguous and that extrinsic evidence should be permitted to determine the intent of the settlor. Their memorandum was accompanied by two affidavits stating that affiant's understanding that the deceased settlor wished the children of John M. Anthony to receive nothing from the settlor's estate. In granting summary judgment against the movants, the court (1) declined to consider extrinsic evidence on the ground that the language of the trust was unambiguous, (2) determined that the gift of the remainder to named individuals "in equal shares" was a gift to the individuals and not to a class, (3) held that the gift to John M. Anthony lapsed because his interest did not vest until the death of the survivor of the settlor and his wife, and (4) declined to apply the Anti-Lapse Statute, 18-A M.R.S.A. § 2-605 (Supp. 1988), because the statute applies only to testamentary gifts. The court therefore directed the trustee to pay over the lapsed gift to John M. Anthony to the personal representative of the deceased settlor. This appeal followed.

* * *

Before us all parties now agree that the terms of the trust are unambiguous and that a summary judgment is appropriate. Moreover, all parties agree that the gift of the remainder interest "in equal shares" to the named children of the settlor was a gift to the individuals and not to a class. As a result, we need address only the court's holding that the gift to John M. Anthony lapsed upon his death prior to the death of the settlor.

The parties rely almost exclusively on our prior cases dealing with testamentary dispositions. These cases are of little assistance on the issue before us. Because a will is not operative until the death of the testator, an interest in a testamentary trust cannot vest prior to that event. On the other hand, an *inter vivos* trust is operative from the date of its creation. We must determine the settlor's intent as expressed in the trust instrument by examining the settlor's overall plan of disposition.

We note the following: (1) the settlor explicitly retained the right to change his beneficiaries if he wanted to alter the trust's disposition; (2) the settlor imposed no restrictions on what his children could do with their respective shares; (3) aside from his power to revoke or amend the trust, the settlor specifically limited his own benefit to income during his lifetime and payment of certain expenses associated with his death; (4) the settlor made survival an explicit condition of any benefit to his wife, but did not include such language in the case of his children. The unexercised right to make a change in beneficiaries, the absence of any control over how the children might dispose of their shares, and the overall assignment of economic benefits lead us to conclude that this plan of disposition effectively eliminated any further interest of the settlor in the trust principal unless he affirmatively chose to intervene. His failure to change the plan coupled with the omission of a survival requirement in the case of the children's shares, suggests a disposition to a predeceased child's estate rather than a reversion to the settlor's estate. As a result of this construction of the instrument, it may be said that the children's interests were vested, subject to defeasance or divestment if the settlor chose to amend or revoke the trust or change his beneficiaries.

We next address the question whether the settlor's reservation of the power of amendment or revocation should alter our conclusion that the children's interests vested. Substantial case law from other jurisdictions persuades us that it should not. A leading case decided by the Ohio Supreme Court holds that an *inter vivos* trust reserving to the settlor the income for life plus the power to revoke, with a remainder over at the death of the settlor, creates a vested interest in the remainderman subject to defeasance by the exercise of the power of revocation. First National Bank v. Tenney, 165 Ohio St. 513, 138 N.E.2d 15 (1956).

Similarly, an Illinois appellate court, reversing the trial court, held that a delay in enjoyment of possession does not imply a requirement of survival by the remainderman before the remainder is vested. First Galesburg National Bank & Trust Co. v. Robinson, 149 Ill.App.3d 584, 102 Ill.Dec. 894, 500 N.E.2d 995 (1986). The court concluded that the words "at the death of" do not refer to the time when the remainder vested, but rather to the time when the remainderman was entitled to possession. *Id.* 102 Ill.Dec. at 895, 500 N.E.2d at 996. The sons of the settlors, therefore, took a present right to the remainder upon execution of the trust instrument, although enjoyment was postponed until the termination of the life estates. *Id.* 102 Ill.Dec. at 895–96, 500 N.E.2d at 996–97.

Even when the settlor said "on [the settlor's] death the remainder shall vest," the *inter vivos* trust has been held to create a present interest subject to divestment by amendment or revocation. Randall v. Bank of America N.T. & S.A., 48 Cal. App.2d 249, 119 P.2d 754 (1941). An Indiana court has stated that the language of Restatement (Second) of Trusts § 112(f) that a person dying prior to the creation of a trust cannot be a beneficiary of that trust is inapplicable to persons living at the time of the creation of an *inter vivos* trust. Hinds v. McNair, 413 N.E.2d 586 (Ind. App.1980). . . . [additional citations omitted].

The trust instrument before us contains no requirement that the remainder beneficiaries survive the life tenants and we see no reason to imply a requirement of survival. Only the settlor's subsequent revocation or substitution would divest the remainder interest. Evidence presented by affidavit of the settlor's desire to revoke the contingent remainder and disinherit his son and son's heirs is simply not relevant. Although the settlor's intention is critical in interpreting the terms of a trust, that intention must be ascertained by analyzing the trust instrument. Mooney v. Northeast Bank & Trust Co., 377 A.2d 120, 122 (Me.1977). Only when the instrument is ambiguous can a court consider extrinsic evidence. *Id.* at 122.

Because John M. Anthony's interest vested at the time of the creation of the trust, we do not consider whether Maine's anti-lapse statute, 18-A M.R.S.A. § 2-605, could apply to an *inter vivos* trust.

The entry is:

Judgment vacated.

Remanded for determination of the appropriate instruction to the Trustee in accordance with the opinion herein.

Costs to be taxed against the trust estate.

All concurring.

Notes

(1) The first question to ask is whether the instrument created by the settlor was valid. The court held that it was valid and that it was a revocable *inter vivos* trust. The settlor's intent and the validity of that intent are always crucial as the settlor creates all interests in the corpus and income.

(2) Second, ask if the settlor retained any future control over the income or the corpus of the trust. The settlor did retain control over the future income of the trust, specifying that it would be payable to him and his wife for the remainder of their lives. They had life estates. Future control over the corpus specified that it would be paid in equal shares to his children at the termination of the life estates. The children had remainders.

(3) Third, ask if the remainders possessed by the children were vested, contingent, or vested subject to defeasance. These are the only three possibilities. If the remainder is vested, the children own it immediately, but it will only become possessory at the termination of the life estates. If the interest is contingent, the children will own it only when the condition is met at some point in the future, which is designated by the settlor and is most likely when it becomes possessory. Third, the children could have an interest described as vested subject to defeasance. What does this mean? The court notes that, because the settlor retained the right to revoke the trust, it is arguable that the children had a vested interest subject to defeasance through the settlor revoking the trust. In other words, the corpus belongs to the children now, but could be "defeased" by the settlor revoking the trust and taking it away. Perhaps a better example might be to pose a hypothetical, such as if the settlor's trust were to read: "Income to myself for life, and then corpus to my spouse, should she survive me, but if not, then to my children." Note that, here, the children have no

initial condition to meet—the interest is theirs immediately. However, they could be defeased by the spouse living longer than the settlor. The spouse has a condition to meet, but not the children, and if the spouse meets that condition, something adverse could affect the children's interest. Under the terms of the trust and the given hypothetical, the children do not have to meet any condition, hence they are vested. But they could be "defeased" by another party—the spouse—performing an act that would deprive them of their interest. Hence, the children have a vested interest subject to defeasance.

(4) If the children have a completely vested interest, they need not meet any conditions; it is theirs immediately, even though not possessory. Please note the distinction between vested and possessory. Thus, the children do not need to survive the settlor's death to have their estates take possession when the settlor dies, because the settlor did not specify survivorship as a condition to be met; it was vested in the children when the trust was established by the settlor. When the life estates end—i.e., when the settlor and his spouse die—the living children take possession, AND the estates of those children who predeceased will take on behalf of the predeceasing children. Thus, if, as was the case in this decision, a child predeceases the settlor, either the child's Last Will and Testament or the child's statutory intestate estate will pass the child's share of the corpus. This means that the surviving children will take less of the estate, and part of the settlor's corpus may go to strangers, who take under the predeceasing child's Last Will and Testament. But the language of the settlor should control, and the case demonstrates the three possibilities available to the settlor: vested, contingent, and vested subject to defeasance.

(5) Finally, it is important to note that the settlor created these interests through an *inter vivos* trust—a non-probate device and very popular among estate planners. These trusts have become the subject of statutory and judicial reform efforts. For example, while the issue of vesting is the issue presented in this decision, there is another legal doctrine mentioned in the final paragraph of the decision—anti-lapse, *see* Chapter Four: Section VII, Lapse. Traditionally, anti-lapse applies only to Last Wills and Testaments, but some states have begun utilizing it with non-probate transfers, such as the *inter vivos* trust used in the decision here. Lapse and vesting may result in different beneficiaries taking the corpus, so it is important to compare the two doctrines as you progress through the material.

If a settlor gives away an interest completely and presently, with no conditions, vesting, or vesting subject to defeasance, the settlor may be said to have given the interest in fee simple. In medieval law, there were only three possibilities: fee simple, fee tail, and life estates. This means that the interest is both possessory and indefeasible, vested in another right now. Similarly, if the settlor gives an interest to A for life and then to B, A has a life estate, and B has a vested remainder (note the absence of any condition that B survive A) that is a remainder in fee simple, too, since it belongs to B now, subject only to when B's interest becomes possessory at the death of A. The settlor no longer has any rights to the property. While this may sound convoluted, the consequences are real. B's interest is subject to taxation and attachment by creditors, and B can even sell that which he has—a vested remainder. The law simply seeks to provide an apparatus through the language of future interests that provides for recognizable rights.

If the settlor does not convey a fee simple interest, the settlor is seeking to control the property in such a manner that will allow for it to come back to the settlor or the settlor's estate. Modern trust law provides extensive rules regarding the settlor's ability to revoke trusts, particularly in reference to ability, method, withdrawal, contest, and liability of the trustee. *See, e.g.,* Unif. Trust Code §§ 601 to 604 (2014). Most often, because of taxation considerations, estate planners prefer the irrevocability of trusts, by which the settlor surrenders all rights over the property. But under the common law rules of future interests, the settlor may retain future rights in property while conveying less than the owned fee simple. This may be accomplished through one of the following:

A. Reversion

The easiest example of a reversion is the following: "settlor gives a life estate to A," but provides nothing further. Obviously, the settlor retains the vested fee simple interest, and possession will revert to the settlor at the death of A. Note that this is different from a remainder, whereby, at the death of A, the interest would go to a person *other than the* settlor.

B. Possibility of Reverter

A reversion is similar to a possibility of reverter in that this classification also keeps open the possibility that the property may return to the settlor. The difference is one of wording, as is often the case with future interests. For example, if the settlor conveys property to "A and his heirs for so long as A does well in school," the clause "for so long as A does well in school" is an added distinction that does not appear in a reversion. With the possibility of a reverter, here is added the special limitation that goes beyond a simple life estate and reversion to the settlor. Here, doing well in school makes this a "possibility" of reverter. In the realm of future interests, there is also the concern as to whether this possibility of reverter would be a determinable one. Because of the use of the words "for so long as," this is a determinable fee, since the event will occur as a result of consequences brought on by A. For our estate planning purposes, such distinctions are beyond the scope of inquiry, but there are historical distinctions to be made.

C. Right of Reentry

This power of reentry is most often classified as a right of termination by the settlor of what was given initially by the settlor. That is, if the settlor gives to A the right to live on a parcel of land in return for rent, the payment of the rent is a condition subsequent, and non-payment will result in termination of the tenancy by the settlor. Obviously, the use of words is important here so that it is possible to enforce the condition for termination of the estate originally given by the settlor. Once the condition has been met, however, the settlor has the right to terminate the estate and regain the property.

II. Interests in Persons Other Than the Settlor

A. Remainders

In First National Bank of Bar Harbor v. Anthony, discussed *supra*, the court was asked to distinguish among three types of remainders: vested, contingent, and vested subject to defeasance. Recall that the decision involved a trust with a life estate for the settlor and the settlor's spouse, and then the remainder to the named children at the death of the two life tenants. Nothing was to return to the settlor, so reversion, reverter, and right of reentry were not possibilities. The court ruled that the settlor had given the named children a vested remainder at the creation of the interest and future possession. What the court did not discuss was the effect that a "class" of remainder persons would have upon the interest conveyed.

Because the settlor named the children, there was no class designation involved. Classes include phrases such as "my children," or "my nephews and nieces," and the like. For further discussion of decreasing class members, *see* Chapter Four: Section VII, E. These are class designations, and when a settlor gives a remainder interest to a class, capable of increasing and decreasing according to future events, the law of remainders provides that the remainder is vested as to the present class members, but subject to partial divestment whenever any additional class member is born. Thus, if there are three class members at the execution of the Last Will and Testament, but five when the testator actually dies and the will speaks, then five class members will share in the bequest, not just three. Often the settlor will provide for life estates and then the remainder to my children, issue of my body, or adopted by me. This is a class designation. If the settlor provides for this class within an *inter vivos* trust — a common non-probate device — and has two children at the effective date of the conveyance, the two children have a vested remainder. But since additional children may be born to the settlor and, thus, also may take as remainder persons, a part of the original children's remainder is defeased upon the increase of class. An exception to this is when a settlor provides "a life estate for my life and then the remainder to my heirs at law." Since a living person has no heirs, the remainder class cannot be ascertained until the death of the settlor, thereby eliminating any concern over increase or decrease of class. Those persons designated as heirs at law at the death of the settlor take under the trust. *See* Chapter Seven: Section V.

B. Executory Interests

Unlike remainders, an executory interest is never vested until a point in the future, when a condition established by the settlor takes place. At that point in time, when the condition occurs, an executory interest divests the settlor of the interest, thereby causing the vested interest to "spring" from the settlor to the person or persons completing the condition. If an event in the future causes the interest to "shift" vesting from one person to the other, neither of whom is the settlor, this is called a "shifting" executory interest. These interests have historical validity because of the Statute of Uses and the Wills Act; the former of these creates a legal interest arising from executory interests, rather than equitable interests.

III. Analytical Principle

Between the time when a testator executes a valid Last Will and Testament and the date of death of the testator, significant changes could occur in reference to property and persons. *See* Chapter Four: Section VI (ademption—changes in property); Chapter Four: Section VII (lapse—changes in persons). Likewise, in the event that the testator creates a testamentary trust in a valid Last Will and Testament, with possession to occur at a point in the future, long after the death of the testator, further changes could occur in reference to property and persons. And if we depart from wills, if a settlor creates an *inter vivos* trust in named persons and makes possession of the corpus dependent upon an event to occur in the future, significant changes could occur in reference to property and persons between the time the settlor funds the trust and the occasion of the event in the future.

In both testamentary and *inter vivos* (non-probate) transactions, changes in property and persons are affected by different legal doctrines. For example, when a relative of the testator dies prior to the testator, survived by the relative's issue, every state and the Uniform Probate Code apply the doctrine of anti-lapse, which distributes the share the deceased relative would have received to the surviving issue of the relative in a manner resembling intestacy. *See* Chapter Four: Section VII. The modern Uniform Probate Code applies this doctrine of anti-lapse to non-probate, payable-on-death devices too. *See* UNIF. PROB. CODE § 2-706(b) (2019). However, if a testator dies with a valid Last Will and Testament that creates a testamentary trust payable at a point in the future, such as when the beneficiary turns thirty, anti-lapse does not apply. The doctrine governing disposition of the trust property, when the beneficiary dies prior to the occurrence of the event signaling possession, is vesting, whether the interest created by the testator is vested, contingent, or vested subject to defeasance.

The shifting patterns of interests and the different doctrines applicable to each can be daunting. There are testamentary and *inter vivos* transactions, plus different effective dates and issues dependent upon revocability or irrevocability. Thus, as a means of spatially diagraming the changes in persons and property, the corresponding legal issues, and the possible results, consider using the following chart, which delineates time frames and events to identify the issue presented and the applicable legal doctrine that should apply. The chart is called the Analytical Principle and it is described in more extensive detail at Raymond C. O'Brien, *Analytical Principle: A Guide for Lapse, Survivorship, Death Without Issue, and the Rule,* 10 Geo. Mason L. Rev. 383 (1988).

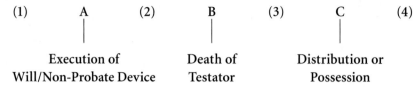

(1)	A	(2)	B	(3)	C	(4)

| | Execution of | | Death of | | Distribution or | |
| | Will/Non-Probate Device | | Testator | | Possession | |

The chart moves from left to right in time progression and has three major events that may occur. The A point in time is most often the execution of the Last Will and Testament, but it could also be the execution of a non-probate POD (payable on death) device, such as an insurance policy or an *inter vivos* trust. Applicable to this point will be the concern over the formalities and intentionalities of the will, *see* Chapter Three: Sections II and III, or the necessary ingredients of a valid trust, *see* Chapter Seven: Section I. Assuming the will or the non-probate device is valid, the next significant date is the date of the death of the testator or the settlor, in the case of a non-probate transfer. This is the B point. There are few instances when the death of the settlor of a non-probate transfer will be of particular significance in the application of legal doctrines; taxation and the Rule Against Perpetuities are two such instances. But in reference to a valid Last Will and Testament, the death of the testator is a significant event because, at that point, the will speaks and the provisions set in place at the A point in time are to be performed; vesting occurs, heirs are determined, and property is distributed.

Please note that, between the A point in time and the B point in time, significant changes in property and persons may have taken place. For example, testator may have bequeathed one hundred shares of Starbucks at the A point in time, but between then and the B point, there have been seven stock splits. Does the legatee who is to inherit the one hundred shares get all of the stock that resulted from the splits, or only one hundred shares, at the B point? Likewise, testator could have bequeathed one million dollars to "my children," and even though there were only two children at the A point, now there are five children at the B point. How many children take? And what if one of the children died between the A point and the B point, survived by issue? Would an anti-lapse statute apply to save the child's share for his or her issue?

The C point occurs when the testator has created a testamentary trust at the B point, or created a non-probate device at the A point—an *inter vivos* trust, for example—and, under the terms of either process, there is a point in time in the future when distribution must be made. The C point is that specific point in time. For example, in a valid Last Will and Testament, testator bequeaths one million dollars to Sadie, to be paid when she turns thirty. The C point would be when Sadie turns thirty. Or another example: Settlor executes a life insurance policy on settlor's life (A point), payable to Sadie upon settlor's death. The C point would be the death of the settlor, which happens to coincide with the B point.

The three points in the time chart are separated by time frames, when there is likely to be changes in persons and property. Time frame (1) has few events to precipitate the application of legal doctrines, but one would be class gifts and, often, the application of the anti-lapse statute. Examples of this will be provided *infra*. But Time frame (2) includes anti-lapse in each and every state statute, as well as class gift issues to accommodate increasing and decreasing class members. Changes in property may be reflected in this Time frame (2) as well. Time frame (3) is the time between the death of the testator and the occurrence of the event precipitating distribution of the corpus. In the case of a Last Will and Testament, this is the arena of vesting, contingency, and vesting subject to defeasance. Finally, Time frame (4) provides an opportunity to analyze powers of appointment. *See* Chapter Seven: Section VI. All three points in the chart (A-B-C) and all four time frames ((1)-(2)-(3)-(4)) provide us with a spatial method through which we can identify the legal issue involved and then apply the appropriate legal doctrine. Let us look at some examples:

A. Anti-Lapse

In a valid Last Will and Testament, testator bequeaths to her sister Sadie, one million dollars. The will is executed in 2000 (Point A) and, at that time, Sadie is in perfect health and has two children. Nonetheless, in 2003, Sadie dies in a tragic accident. By 2005, the testator dies with the same Last Will and Testament in effect (Point B). Sadie's legacy of one million dollars is still a part of the will, but the plaintiff, the residuary legatee of the will, argues that Sadie's bequest has lapsed because of her death prior to the testator in Time frame (2). Sadie's children, her surviving issue and the defendants in the case, argue that they should take the legacy under the state's anti-lapse statute and divide it among themselves. Who wins? First, note that the will is valid; this is always the first and foremost question. Then note that there is the death of Sadie in Time frame (2). This signals that anti-lapse is an issue, inviting consideration of the tool bar associated with anti-lapse. *See* Chapter Four: Section VII. Could vesting—a different doctrine—apply to someone dying in Time frame (2)? Yes, but only if no will were involved, for example, when the settlor executes a valid non-probate trust at Point A, with possession to be at Point C. With the exception of the most modern Uniform Probate Code § 2-706, anti-lapse only applies when we consider wills, not non-probate transfers.

B. Vesting

How would vesting be identified and analyzed using the chart? Of course, vesting may never be a consideration if property is to pass under a Last Will and Testament and the testator has not died. It is a maxim in law that a will speaks at death.

Therefore, vesting may never apply to Time frame (2) if we are discussing a Last Will and Testament. However, if, in a valid Last Will and Testament, the testator provides one million dollars to Sadie, with income from this to be paid to her each year until she turns thirty, and Sadie dies at age 28, survived by two children, with her own Last Will and Testament bequeathing all her property to National Geographic, what happens to the one million dollars? Using the Analytical Principle chart, we know that Sadie has died in Time frame (3), between Points B and C. She had a trust established for her by the testator but never reached the age for distribution. Was her interest in the corpus vested at the death of the testator? Yes, the corpus was vested in Sadie, to be paid when she turned thirty. There was no condition for her to meet to accomplish vesting. So, how should the property be distributed? If Sadie had died in Time frame (2), anti-lapse would apply, but since she died in Time frame (3), the applicable doctrine is vesting, not anti-lapse. Vesting would give the one million dollars to her estate, passing it to the National Geographic. The only recourse Sadie's children would have would be to challenge the validity of Sadie's will, thereby allowing the property to go to them via intestacy. This did not occur. Thus, note the difference between what happens in Time frame (2) and Time frame (3). Because of the anti-lapse statute that would pass the property only to issue of Sadie, not the National Geographic, there is a distinctive difference between the applicable legal doctrines, as well as the results between death in Time frames (2) and (3).

To review the rules as to vesting, contingent, or vested subject to defeasance, consider the following, ancient decision:

Clobberie's Case
Court of Chancery, England, 1677
2 Chan. Ca. 155, 2 Vent. 342, 86 Eng. Rep. 476

In one Clobberie's Case it was held, that where one bequeathed a sum of money to a woman, at her age of twenty-one years, or day of marriage, to be paid unto her with interest, and she died before either, that the money should go to her executor; and was so decreed by my Lord Chancellor Finch.

But he said, if money were bequeathed to one at his age of twenty-one years, if he dies before that age, the money is lost.

On the other side, if money be given to one to be paid at the age of twenty-one years; there, if the party dies before, it shall go to the executors.

C. Class Gifts

Recall that a class gift results when a testator or a settlor uses a term that is capable of increase and decrease; common terms are "children," "nephews," and "nieces." *See* Chapter Seven: Section V. Obviously, the testator or the settlor is seeking fluidity by using a term that will incorporate an expanding or contracting group of persons. For example, testator drafts a Last Will and Testament (Point A) and writes: "One million dollars to be divided among my children." At Point A, testator has two children, but at Point B, testator has four children. How many children take? Obviously, all four children will take because all four children were members of the class when the will speaks. But recall that if one of the children had died during Time frame (2), survived by issue, then the anti-lapse statute would apply since anti-lapse is applicable during Time frame (2). Now, the testator drafts a will that provides: "One million dollars to be divided among my children when the youngest of them reaches the age of thirty." At the time of testator's death, one child is twenty-one and, thus, the condition is not met, so a testamentary trust is put into place while waiting for the youngest child to reach thirty so the money may be dispersed. Before the youngest child reaches thirty, but after the death of the testator, a child of the testator dies. Does the estate of the deceased child have any claim to the one million dollars when the youngest child reaches thirty? Yes, because of vesting. Vesting applies in Time frame (3). Since there was no condition that the child live until the youngest reached thirty, each child had a vested interest at the death of the testator. Since the deceased child had a vested interest, the estate of the child will take the child's portion when the youngest child reaches thirty, and possession for all occurs. Please note that the estate of the child takes, and not the issue of the child, as was the case with anti-lapse.

One final example, utilizing Time frames (1), (2) and (3), will further demonstrate the utility of the chart. Testator drafts a valid Last Will and Testament and writes: "One million dollars to be divided among my children when the youngest of them reaches thirty." When testator writes this at Point A, one child has already died with surviving issue, prior to the execution of the will. Testator will have another child die with surviving issue after Point A and before Point B (Time frame (2)). Finally, another child will die with surviving issue after the death of testator and before the youngest child reaches the age of thirty (Time frame (3)), between Point B and Point C. When the youngest child reaches the age of thirty (Point C), three actual children survive. How should the one million dollar bequest be divided? The chart will allow us to spatially track the deaths of each child and suggest the legal doctrine to apply. Thus, since there was no condition of survivorship for children to live until the youngest reached thirty, the court may apply both anti-lapse and vesting doctrines.

When we look at the chart, we see that one child of the testator died in Time frame (1), survived by issue. Does anti-lapse apply to relatives of testator who die prior to the execution of the Last Will and Testament (Point A)? Yes, according to the Uniform Probate Code and many other state statutes. Second, should anti-lapse apply to children who die after execution of the Last Will and Testament, but prior to the death of the testator (Time frame (2))? Yes. Since both of these children had issue surviving the testator, the issue would take a share from the predeceasing parent under anti-lapse doctrines. Please note that anti-lapse does not provide any benefits to the estate of the deceased child; only the issue may take according to the statute, and, if there are no issue, the legacy lapses and is shared by the surviving class members. Then note that one child died with issue between the death of the testator (Point B) and when the youngest child turned thirty (Point C). Since this is Time frame (3), vesting applies, and the share of that child will go to the child's estate, not to issue, as was the case with anti-lapse. Finally, three children survived Point C, when the youngest of them reached the age of thirty. Into how many shares will the one million dollars be divided? The one million dollars will be divided into six shares:

One share will go to the issue of the child who died in Time frame (1), survived by issue.

One share will go to the issue of the child who died in Time frame (2), survived by issue.

One share will go to the estate—because of vesting—of the child who died in Time frame (3).

Three shares, one each, will go to the three children who survived Point C.

D. Powers of Appointment

When using the chart to understand powers of appointment, it is first necessary to review the language of powers because there are terms and phrases particular to that area of the law. *See* Chapter Seven: Section VI. Once the terms are mastered, it is necessary to understand that a power of appointment is a device attached to a trust. For example, a testator executes a valid Last Will and Testament, and then, at the death of the testator, that will provides: "One million dollars to Sadie, income for life, and then, at her death, as she shall appoint in her Last Will and Testament." Sadie has an income trust with a general, testamentary power of appointment. Of course, there are many legal issues that could apply to the testator's trust, and these may be reviewed at the materials associated with trusts in this casebook. But for now, please note that the testator (she wrote a will!) is also a settlor of a testamentary trust (she established a trust!) and a donor of a power of appointment. Sadie is a legatee under the will, a beneficiary under the trust, and a donee under the terms of the power of appointment. How may this be viewed spatially on the chart?

The base chart is the Last Will and Testament of the testator, settlor, donor. When the testator dies at Point B, Sadie survives and is able to begin to receive life income. Sadie's death is the condition that will bring about distribution, so Sadie's death is Point C. Up to this point, our only concerns are the validity of the Last Will and Testament of the testator, the validity of the trust, and the validity of the power of appointment. Assuming that all of these are valid, that they do not violate the Rule Against Perpetuities, and that Sadie effectively exercises her power of appointment, we then turn our attention to Sadie, the legatee, beneficiary, donee.

Since Sadie must exercise her power of appointment in a valid Last Will and Testament, we are going to create another chart for Sadie's exercise and place it on top of the base chart we created for the testator. But at which point? Since Point C is the point at which Sadie must exercise the power, that will be the point to which we attach Sadie's chart. Thus, since Sadie exercises with a Last Will and Testament at death, this is Sadie's Point B, and we are going to place it atop of the testator's Point C. Our objective is to place in spatial context the reality of the fact that the power of appointment being exercised by Sadie derives from the trust created by the original testator, settlor, donor.

Why is it necessary to combine the two legal devices, creation and exercise? One reason is the fact that if Sadie does not exercise the power of appointment, the corpus (appointment) will result back to the original testator, settlor, donor. Plus, the Rule Against Perpetuities will be applied from creation of the power by the donor. Another reason is to demonstrate that if Sadie does exercise the power of appointment but does so in favor of a person or group of persons who predecease her, then all of the rules of anti-lapse apply. Please recall that the anti-lapse statute will save a bequest made to a relative of the testator who predeceases the testator and is survived by issue; the issue take in place of the predeceasing relative. The most modern version of the Uniform Probate Code provides that anti-lapse will apply if the predeceasing appointee is a relative of the donee *or* the donor of the power of appointment, thus enlarging the scope of anti-lapse. *See* Unif. Prob. Code § 2-603 (2019). Another benefit of combining the base chart of the testator with the exercise by the donee of the power of appointment is the ability we have to estimate whether there is a violation of the Rule Against Perpetuities, and possibilities to correct the violations through various savings devices.

E. Rule Against Perpetuities

The dominance of the "Rule" has diminished significantly with the ascending adoption by states of the Uniform Statutory Rule Against Perpetuities (USRAP), now adopted into the Uniform Probate Code § 2-901 (2019). Some states have abolished the Rule, *see, e.g.,* N.J. Stat. § 46:2F-9 (2019). Other states have significantly weakened the impact of the Rule through adoption of statutes such as the Uniform Statutory Rule Against Perpetuities—a ninety year wait and see device. And still others allow for lengthy dynasty trusts, such as one thousand years in Alaska. *See generally* Lawrence W. Waggoner, *From Here to Eternity: The Folly of Perpetual Trusts,* Univ. Mich. L. Sch. Pub. L. & Leg. Theory Res. Paper No. 259 (2012). *See also* Eric Kades, *Of Piketty and Perpetuities: Dynastic Wealth in the Twenty-First Century (And Beyond),* 60 B.C. L. Rev. 145 (2019); Grayson M.P. McCouch, *Who Killed the Rule Against Perpetuities?,* 40 Pepp. L. Rev. 1291 (2013); Scott Andrew Shepard, *Which the Deader Hand? A Counter to the American Law Institute's Proposed Revival of Dying Perpetuities Rules,* 86 Tul. L. Rev. 559 (2012); John V. Orth, *Allowing Perpetuities in North Carolina,* 31 Campbell L. Rev. 399 (2009); William J. Turnier & Jeffrey L. Harrison, *A Malthusian Analysis of the So-Called Dynasty Trust,* 28 Va. Tax Rev. 779 (2009); Martha W. Jordan, *Requiem for Pennsylvania's Rule*

Against Perpetuities? 46 Duq. L. Rev. 555 (2008). We will discuss the Rule Against Perpetuities further in Chapter Seven, *infra*. Before using the chart to better understand the Rule, you should review the terms and variations associated with the Rule. *See* Chapter Seven: Section VII.

There are many ways in which the Rule may be stated, *see* Chapter Seven: Section VII, but perhaps this is most appropriate for our purposes:

> Standing at the creation of the interest, is there any possibility that any interest may not vest within a life in being plus twenty-one years?

A great deal of law is capsulized in that one sentence! Using it, we now revisit the example given in the preceding material on powers of appointment. That is, the testator executed a valid Last Will and Testament and, when the testator died, it became valid, providing for one million dollars to Sadie, income for life, then, at her death, as she shall appoint by her Last Will and Testament. Please recall that Sadie has a life estate in trust, coupled with a general, testamentary power of appointment. Because the testator's Last Will and Testament is linked to Sadie's trust and exercise of the power of appointment, we have linked the chart of the testator with the chart of Sadie's exercise of the power of appointment. Thus, the testator's Point C and Sadie's Point B are one and the same; Sadie's valid exercise of the power of appointment is the point of distribution of the corpus (Point B) of the testator's Last Will and Testament (Point C). The two instruments are linked for purposes of anti-lapse and powers of appointment. But they are also linked for purposes of the Rule Against Perpetuities. Why?

The Rule Against Perpetuities provides that all interests must vest within a life in being plus twenty-one years. The life must be in being at the creation of the interest, but when we look at Sadie's power of appointment, when is the interest created? You cannot say it is created when Sadie exercises the power of appointment (Point C for the testator, Point B for Sadie), because she is simply exercising a power given to her by the donor of the power, the testator. Thus, creation for purposes of the Rule is when the testator created the power in the Last Will and Testament, the testator's Point B. We need to use the "relation back" doctrine to return to the creation by the testator to determine if there is a Rule violation when Sadie exercises the power. And since we know that Sadie was a "life in being" at the creation of the power (testator's Point B), and we know that Sadie exercises the power in her Last Will and Testament (Sadie's Point B, testator's Point C), we know that all interests become vested at that point, and there is no Rule violation. Please note that we need to use the "relation back" doctrine because the testator/donor gave to Sadie, the beneficiary/donee, a general testamentary power of appointment. The same relation back would have occurred if the donor had given Sadie a special power of appointment. In any power other than a general *inter vivos* power, most states require creation to be when the donor creates the power, not when the donee exercises the power. *See, e.g.,* Unif. Prob. Code § 2-902 (2010). This is one major reason why the two charts must be seen in tandem.

But let us utilize the chart in a manner that will demonstrate a violation of the Rule. We continue with the same example as before: Testator executes a valid Last

Will and Testament and, when it speaks (Point B), the testator gives Sadie one million dollars, income for life, and then as she shall appoint in her Last Will and Testament (Point C for the testator and Point B for Sadie). When Sadie exercises her power of appointment in her valid Last Will and Testament (Point B for Sadie), she exercises the power by creating a trust for her children for life and then for her grandchildren surviving. If no grandchild survives, then to National Geographic. Now return to the chart and note the following conclusions:

(1) Creation under the relation back doctrine remains the creation by the testator in the testator's Last Will and Testament (testator's Point B).

(2) When we look at the exercise by Sadie, we know that all of the interests created by Sadie do not become vested until we determine if a grandchild survives at least one of Sadie's children at Sadie's Point C. Please note that the grandchildren have a contingent interest, and National Geographic has a vested interest subject to defeasance.

(3) The death of the last of Sadie's children brings about indefeasible vesting in either the grandchildren or National Geographic, therefore, the children are the measuring lives.

(4) Are all of the measuring lives also lives in being? To be in being, they must all be there at the creation of the power, when the testator dies. The answer is, "no," unless it was completely impossible for Sadie to have any more children (measuring lives) after testator's Point B, when creation occurred. If there is any *possibility* of having an additional measuring life who would not be a life in being at the creation of the interest (testator's Point B), then the Rule is violated, no matter what *actually* happens when the appointment of the trust becomes completely vested at Sadie's Point C.

The chart allows for a spatial examination of all of the interests involved. Furthermore, it can be of additional assistance when we examine, in more detail, reformation devises (savings clauses) to correct the violation of the Rule in the example just given. Reformation could consist of cy pres, second look, and even the doctrine of capture. All of these are discussed in reference to the Rule Against Perpetuities in Chapter Seven: Section VII.

IV. Survival

Often courts are confronted with the issue of whether the settlor's trust of future interests was meant to require survivorship in any beneficiary. The issue is important in considering vesting versus contingent interests, anti-lapse, the Rule Against Perpetuities, and class gifts, to name but a few circumstances. Secondly, to what point did the settlor intend to require survivorship? Usually, the debate over the point of survivorship is between the death of the settlor or the death of a life tenant. There are significant consequences to these two determinations. Consider the following decision and the Uniform Probate Code that follows.

Security Trust Co. v. Irvine

Delaware Court of Chancery, 1953
33 Del. Ch. 375, 93 A.2d 528

BRAMHALL, Vice Chancellor.

In this case this court is asked to determine two issues: (1) whether or not the residuary estate left to brothers and sisters of the testator vested as of the date of his death or at the time of the death of the last life tenant; (2) if it should be decided that the residuary estate vested as of the time of the death of the testator, do the life tenants take as members of the class of brothers and sisters receiving the residuary estate?

Plaintiff is trustee under the last will and testament of James Wilson, deceased, who died on July 29, 1918, leaving a last will and testament dated October 25, 1915. After providing for certain specific bequests, testator gave and devised all his 'real and mixed estate' to the Security Trust and Safe Deposit Company,—now the Security Trust Company,—to two sisters, Martha B. Wilson and Mary E. Wilson, during their joint lives and during the lifetime of the survivor of them. Testator further provided that in the event that his sister, Margaret W. Irvine, should be left a widow, she should share equally with the two sisters above named in the benefits of the trust so provided. As to the remainder, testator provided as follows:

> 'Upon the death of two sisters, Martha B. Wilson and Mary E. Wilson, and the survivor of them, then it is my will that all of my real and mixed estate and any proceeds that may have arisen from the sale of any part thereof, together with any unexpended income there may be, shall be equally divided among my brothers and sisters, share and share alike, their heirs and assigns forever, the issue of any deceased brother or sister to take his or her parent's share.'

Testator was survived by his five brothers and sisters: Samuel H. Wilson, Margaret W. Irvine, Martha B. Wilson, Mary E. Wilson, and Henry Wilson. At the time of the execution of the will the ages of the brothers and sisters ranged from 39 to 52 years. Martha B. Wilson and Mary E. Wilson, the two life tenants, died respectively on June 9, 1928, and August 18, 1951, unmarried and without issue, the trust therefore terminating on the latter date. The other devisees all predeceased Mary E. Wilson, the surviving life tenant. Samuel H. Wilson died on October 26, 1926, leaving to survive him three children, Frazer Wilson, Jeannette A. Wilson, and Samuel H. Wilson, Jr., and Grace Wilson Gearhart, daughter of a deceased son, Francis Paul Wilson. Samuel H. Wilson, Jr. died in 1924, unmarried and without issue.

Samuel Irvine, one of the defendants, is the sole residuary legatee under the will of Margaret W. Irvine, deceased. Martha B. Wilson died testate on June 9, 1928, leaving her residuary estate to her two nieces, Margaret Gregg Wilson, now Margaret W. Hanby, and Mary Hope Wilson, each an undivided one-half interest therein.

Mary E. Wilson died testate on August 18, 1951, leaving her entire residuary estate to Margaret W. Hanby, after providing for the payment of her debts and a legacy to Mary Hope Wilson in the sum of $100.

The estate of Martha B. Wilson has been closed, the final account having been passed on February 9, 1935; the estate of Mary E. Wilson has also been closed, the final account in that estate having been passed on September 15, 1952.

I must first determine whether or not the remainder interest of the testator became vested at the time of his death or at the time of the death of the last life tenant, Mary E. Wilson, on August 18, 1951. In order to resolve this question the intention of the testator at the time of the drafting of the will must first be ascertained. If it should be clear that testator intended this provision of the will to take effect at some future date, then the intention of the testator, so far as it may be legally carried out, will prevail. However, in reaching my conclusion, I must accept certain well recognized rules of construction.

The law favors the early vesting of devised estates and will presume that words of survivorship relate to the death of the testator, if fairly capable of that construction. In the absence of a clear and unambiguous indication of an intention to the contrary, the heirs will be determined as of the date of the death of the testator and not at some future date. When the language employed by the testator annexes futurity, clearly indicating his intention to limit his estate to take effect upon a dubious and uncertain event, the vesting is suspended until the time of the occurrence of the event. See Delaware Trust Company v. Delaware Trust Company, Del.Ch., 91 A.2d 44, and cases therein cited.

The assertion that it is indicated in the will that the testator intended the residuary estate to be vested as of the date of the death of the last life tenant is based upon the contentions: (1) the fact that testator left a life estate to two of his sisters and then gave the residuary estate to his brothers and sisters indicates that testator did not intend the two sisters to share in his residuary estate and therefore the residuary estate did not vest until the date of the death of the last life tenant; (2) the use of the words 'upon the death of two sisters' and the provision in the will of testator that his estate 'should be equally divided among my brothers and sisters' indicates an intention that testator intended a future vesting of his residuary estate

Whatever may be the law in other states it is well settled in this state that the fact that a life tenant is a member of a class, in the absence of any clear indication in the will to the contrary, does not prevent the life tenant from participating in the remainder of testator's estate as a part of the class. Wright v. Gooden, 6 Houst. 397. The opinion of this court in the case of Delaware Trust Company v. Delaware Trust Company, *supra*, is not in conflict. In the Delaware Trust Company case the testatrix, after creating several life estates, the last of which was to her only son, provided that the residue and remainder of her estate should go to her heirs-at-law. In her trust *inter vivos* executed at the same time, she provided that the remainder, consisting of the proceeds of the sale of some Pennsylvania real estate, should go to the heirs-at-law of her husband. In that case the only son was the only heir-at-law of both the testatrix and her husband. This court decided that the intention of the testatrix as manifested by the general scheme or purpose as found in her will and in her trust agreement, was to create an estate to take effect as of the date of the death of the last life tenant. It was there stated that the use of the words 'my heirs-at-law' and 'heirs-at-law of my husband', where the son was the sole heir-at-law of both, along with other circumstances therein mentioned, demonstrated the intention of the testatrix to provide for future vesting. Here the testator in his will showed only an intention to postpone the enjoyment of the remainder until after the death of the life tenants. Where the will merely postpones the time of vesting the residuary estate would vest as of the time of the death of testator. The fact that the life tenants were also members of the class to whom the remainder of testator's estate was devised, would not prevent an early vesting of the remainder estate.

As to the use of the word 'upon', it is equally clear under the decisions in this state and elsewhere, that this word and other words of this nature refer only to the time of payment and not to the substance of the devise. Cann v. Van Sant, 24 Del.Ch. 300, 11 A.2d 388; In re Nelson's Estate, 9 Del.Ch. 1, 74 A. 851. Other Delaware cases are to the same effect. In any event, the use of this word, and the provision for dividing its remainder, under the circumstances of this case would not alone be sufficient to overcome the presumption of immediate vesting.

It is contended on behalf of certain defendants that even though it should be determined that the gift to the brothers and sisters vested as of the date of the death of testator, the life tenants should be excluded from membership in the class of brothers and sisters. They base their contention upon the fact that testator in another item of his will gave them a life interest in his residuary estate.

In endeavoring to ascertain the intention of testator, it is uniformly held that such a provision is not of itself sufficient to prevent the life tenant from participating in the remainder as part of the class. See cases cited in 13 A.L.R. 620. It is not sufficient to show the absence of an intention to include the life tenants; there must be some indication of a clear and unambiguous nature to exclude them. Dillman v. Dillman, 409 Ill. 494, 499, 100 N.E.2d 567; Carver v. Wright, 119 Me. 185, 109 A. 896. I can find no incongruity in the mere fact that testator provided a life estate for his two sisters and later gave the remainder to his brothers and sisters, of which the two sisters were part of the class. They were unmarried. They were no longer young. It seems to be clear from the several provisions in the will of the testator that it was his purpose to provide for them. Such provision does not indicate to me that testator did not intend that they should participate further in his estate. Certainly there is no legal inconsistency in life tenants participating in the remainder. The theory that the testator particularly desired to see that his sisters were provided for is at least as strong as the supposition that he intended to exclude them from participating in the remainder.

I conclude that the life tenants should participate in the remainder devised by testator to his brothers and sisters.

Having determined that the life tenants should participate in the provision for the brothers and sisters, I must next consider the effect of the provision that the 'issue of any deceased brothers or sisters to take his or her parent's share'.

As to the brothers and sisters who died leaving issue, it was specifically provided that such issue should take the interest of such brother or sister leaving issue. Their interest was thereby divested, their issue being substituted in their place. In such case, the brother or sister dying leaving issue would have no power of disposition of his or her interest in the estate. In re Nelson's Estate, *supra*.

The will of testator is silent as to any provision relative to any of the brothers and sisters dying without leaving issue. Martha B. Wilson, Mary E. Wilson and Margaret W. Irvine, three sisters of testator, left no issue at the time of their death. Was their interest divested by their death, even though they left no issue, or did their estates receive an absolute interest, free and clear of any conditions subsequent?

Under the will of testator, the death of the life tenants leaving issue caused their interest to be divested. I have determined that the brothers and sisters received an absolute estate, subject to the provision that the interest of any brother or sister dying prior to the death of the life tenant should go by substitution to the issue of such brother or sister. However, this provision of the will does not apply where there is no issue, since there would then be no limitation upon their estate. The decisions in this state are silent as to what would happen under such circumstances. However, the weight of authority in other states is to the effect that in the event of the death of the devisees leaving no issue, the interest of such devisees is not divested by their death. McArthur v. Scott, 113 U.S. 340, 5 S.Ct. 652, 28 L.Ed. 1015; Plitt v. Plitt, 167 Md. 252, 173 A. 35, 109 A.L.R. 1; Jacobs v. Whitney, 205 Mass. 477, 91 N.E. 1009; Rutledge v. Fishburne, 66 S.C. 155, 44 S.E. 564; Gardner v. Vanlandingham, 334 Mo. 1054, 69 S.W.2d 947. Since the estates created were absolute except for the condition subsequent, and since the subsequent condition has been removed, the estates of the sisters dying without issue would have an absolute interest unrestricted by any condition.

I believe that such a determination would be in accord with the plain intention of the testator. He apparently desired to provide for his own brothers and sisters and their issue. If he had desired to provide that the interest of any brother or sister dying without issue should go to the surviving brothers or sisters or had intended to make some other similar provision, it would have been easy for him to do so. The fact that he did not, indicates that he had no such intention. I concluded that the interests of Martha B. Wilson, Mary E. Wilson and Margaret W. Irvine, were not divested by their death without issue and that their interests in the estate of the testator under the residuary clause of the will should go to their respective estates.

The estates of Martha B. Wilson and Mary E. Wilson have been closed. In accordance with the opinion of this court in Cooling v. Security Trust Co., 29 Del.Ch. 286, 76 A.2d 1, their shares may be distributed by the trustee directly to the persons entitled to receive the same, the trustees first seeing that any taxes which may be due or any costs which may be incurred by reason thereof are paid.

An order will be signed on notice in accordance with this opinion.

Notes

The holding in *Irvine* represents the traditional method of interpretation of future interests, which allows for remainders to be vested, subject to divestment, only if the remainderman is survived by issue. Note how the court is adamant in its adherence to recognized rules of construction that favor early vesting, and survivorship as relating to the death of the testator. Unless clearly evidenced by the testator, vesting occurs at the death of the testator, not at the death of the life tenant or some other event. When the court adopted these rules into its holding, what was the result? Who received the estate under the Last Will and Testament of James Wilson?

Now compare that result to what would happen if the following Uniform Probate Code provision had been in existence and applicable at the time of the decision. Particularly, compare Unif. Prob. Code § 2-707(b): "A future interest under the terms of a trust is contingent on the beneficiary's surviving the distribution date. . . ." with what happens if the beneficiary does not survive. Who would take the estate of James Wilson under this provision? As you compare, ask if there are advantages to the Uniform Probate Code provision and if they outweigh the more traditional approach. Then ask if there is a similarity between §§ 2-707 and 2-603 (anti-lapse), and how they work in practice.

Problem

Decedent executed a valid Last Will and Testament in 1998 and died eleven days later, survived by her four children. Each child received specific items of property, and the residue of the decedent's estate was to be divided among her four children, whom she named individually. One clause in the will specifically directed that her home be sold and the proceeds divided among her surviving children

> five (5) years after my son, Wesley Ray Bolton, has returned from prison and in the meantime I direct that the premises may be occupied by my two daughters provided that they pay all of the costs associated with the property. The property may be sold at an earlier date if all of the parties agree.

Prior to the event specified, five years after the return of Wesley Ray Bolton, another of decedent's sons died, survived by a spouse and five children. All of the parties subsequently agreed to sell the property and divide the proceeds from the sale of the home. The surviving spouse, and the children of the son who died between the death of his mother and the sale of the home, seek to share in the proceeds, but the three surviving children object. How would you rule on the petition of the surviving spouse and children to share in the proceeds of the sale? *See In re* Will of Bolton, 2008WL2775648 (N.J. Super. Ct. 2008).

A. Substitute Takers

Uniform Probate Code (2019)

§ 2-707. Survivorship With Respect to Future Interests Under Terms of Trust; Substitute Takers. * * *

(b) [Survivorship Required; Substitute Gift.] A future interest under the terms of a trust is contingent on the beneficiary's surviving the distribution date. If a beneficiary of a future interest under the terms of a trust fails to survive the distribution date, the following apply:

(1) Except as provided in paragraph (4), if the future interest is not in the form of a class gift and the deceased beneficiary leaves surviving descendants, a substitute gift is created in the beneficiary's surviving descendants. They take by representation the property to which the beneficiary would have been entitled had the beneficiary survived the distribution date.

(2) Except as provided in paragraph (4), if the future interest is in the form of a class gift, other than a future interest to "issue," "descendants," "heirs of the body," "heirs," "next of kin," "relatives," or "family," or a class described by language of similar import, a substitute gift is created in the surviving descendants of any deceased beneficiary. The property to which the beneficiaries would have been entitled had all of them survived the distribution date passes to the surviving beneficiaries and the surviving descendants of the deceased beneficiaries. Each surviving beneficiary takes the share to which he [or she] would have been entitled had the deceased beneficiaries survived the distribution date. Each deceased beneficiary's surviving descendants who are substituted for the deceased beneficiary take by representation the share to which the deceased beneficiary would have been entitled had the deceased beneficiary survived the distribution date. For the purposes of this paragraph, "deceased beneficiary" means a class member who failed to survive the distribution date and left one or more surviving descendants.

(3) For the purposes of Section 2-701, words of survivorship attached to a future interest are not, in the absence of additional evidence, a sufficient indication of an intent contrary to the application of this section. Words of survivorship include words of survivorship that relate to the distribution date or to an earlier or an unspecified time, whether those words of survivorship are expressed in condition-precedent, condition-subsequent, or any other form.

(4) If the governing instrument creates an alternative future interest with respect to a future interest for which a substitute gift is created by paragraph (1) or (2), the substitute gift is superseded by the alternative future interest if:

(A) the alternative future interest is in the form of a class gift and one or more members of the class is entitled to take in possession or enjoyment; or

(B) the alternative future interest is not in the form of a class gift and the expressly designated beneficiary of the alternative future interest is entitled to take in possession or enjoyment. * * *

(e) [If No Other Takers and If Future Interest Created by Exercise of Power of Appointment.] If, after the application of subsections (b) and (c), there is no surviving taker and if the future interest was created by the exercise of a power of appointment:

(1) the property passes under the donor's gift-in-default clause, if any, which clause is treated as creating a future interest under the terms of a trust; and

(2) if no taker is produced by the application of paragraph (1), the property passes as provided in subsection (d). For purposes of subsection (d), "transferor" means the donor if the power was a nongeneral power and means the donee if the power was a general power.

B. Anti-Lapse

Uniform Probate Code (2019)

§ 2-603. Antilapse; Deceased Devisee; Class Gifts.

* * *

(b) * * * If a devisee fails to survive the testator and is a grandparent, a descendant of a grandparent, or a stepchild of either the testator or the donor of a power of appointment exercised by the testator's will, the following apply:

* * *

(3) For the purposes of Section 2-601, words of survivorship, such as in a devise to an individual "if he survives me," or in a devise to "my surviving children," are not, in the absence of additional evidence, a sufficient indication of an intent contrary to the application of this section.

* * *

Notes

There are few cases addressing the statutory provision of UPC § 2-707 or its similarity to the anti-lapse provision of § 2-603. In one unpublished opinion, the Michigan Court of Appeals held that an intervivos trust sufficiently indicated an intent on the part of the settlor to avoid the application of § 2-707, which would have created a substitute gift. The court mentioned the similarity between substitute takers and anti-lapse. *See In re* Esther Wiggins Bertling Trust, No. 250555, 2004 WL 2365047 (Mich. Ct. App. Oct. 21, 2004). And in a decision from the Wisconsin Court of Appeals, a descendant of a beneficiary who did not survive until the date of distribution argued that the state's anti-lapse statute should apply, but the court held that the testator's intent was clear that survivorship was required and that any statutory formulation is only a default when there is no expressed intent discernable. *See In re* Estate of Smith, 591 N.W.2d 898 (Wis. Ct. App. 1999). For some assistance in discussing the meaning of survivorship, the intent of the settlor, and the role of the courts, see JOHN A. BORRON, JR., SIMES AND SMITH—THE LAW OF FUTURE INTERESTS, § 575 (3d ed. 2018); Melanie B. Leslie & Stewart E. Sterk, *Revisiting the Revolution: Reintegrating the Wealth Transmission System*, 56 B.C. L. REV. 61, 73-74 (2015); Reid K. Weisbord, *Federalizing Principles of Donative Intent and Unanticipated Circumstances,* 67 VAND. L. REV. 1931 (2014); Lawrence W. Waggoner, *The Uniform Probate Code Extends Anti-Lapse-Type Protection to Poorly Drafted Trusts,* 94 MICH. L. REV. 2309 (1996); Jesse Dukeminier, *The Uniform Probate Code Upends the Law of Remainders,* 94 MICH. L. REV. 148 (1995).

V. Heirs, Descendants, Issue

Estate of Woodworth

California Court of Appeal, Fifth District, 1993
18 Cal. App. 4th 936, 22 Cal. Rptr. 2d 676

DIBIASO, Acting P. J.

The Regents of the University of California (Regents) appeal from an order of the probate court which rejected their claim to the remainder of a testamentary trust. We will reverse. We will apply the common law preference for early vesting and hold that, absent evidence of the testator's intent to the contrary, the identity of "heirs" entitled to trust assets must be determined at the date of death of the named ancestor who predeceased the life tenant, not at the date of death of the life tenant.

* * *

Harold Evans Woodworth died testate in 1971. His will was there-after admitted to probate; in 1974 a decree of distribution was entered. * * * According to this decree,[1] a portion of the estate was distributed outright to the testator's surviving spouse, Mamie Barlow Woodworth. The balance of the estate was distributed to Mamie Barlow Woodworth and the Bank of America, to be held, administered and distributed in accord with the terms of a testamentary trust established by the will of Harold Evans Woodworth. The life tenant of the trust was Mamie Barlow Woodworth. Among the trust provisions was the following:

'This trust shall terminate upon the death of MAMIE BARLOW WOODWORTH. Upon the termination of this trust, my trustee shall pay, deliver and convey

---

1. The decedent's will was not introduced in the probate court proceedings. A decree of distribution is a conclusive determination of the terms of a testamentary trust and the rights of all parties claiming any interest under it. (Estate of Easter (1944) 24 Cal.2d 191, 194 [148 P.2d 601].)

all of the trust estate then remaining, including all accrued and/or undistributed income thereunto appertaining, to MRS. RAY B. PLASS, also known as Elizabeth Woodworth Plass, [Elizabeth Plass] whose present address is 90 Woodland Way, Piedmont, California, if she then survives, and if not then to her heirs at law.'

Elizabeth Plass was the testator's sister; he also had two brothers who predeceased him. One died without issue. The other was survived by two children, Elizabeth Woodworth Holden, a natural daughter, and James V. Woodworth, an adopted son.

Elizabeth Plass died in 1980; she was survived by her husband, Raymond Plass. Raymond Plass died testate in 1988. In relevant part, he left the residue of his estate to the Regents for use on the university's Berkeley campus.

Mamie Woodworth, the life tenant, died in 1991. Thereafter, Wells Fargo Bank, as successor trustee of the Woodworth trust, petitioned the probate court pursuant to Probate Code section 17200 to determine those persons entitled to distribution of the trust estate. The petition alleged that "The petitioner [was] uncertain as to whether Elizabeth Plass's 'heirs at law' under [the decree] should be determined as of February 14, 1980, the date of her death, or August 13, 1991, the date of Mamie [Barlow] Woodworth's death."

It is undisputed that (1) as of February 14, 1980, Elizabeth Plass's heirs at law were her husband, Raymond Plass; her niece, Elizabeth Woodworth Holden; and her nephew, James V. Woodworth; and (2) as of August 13, 1991, Elizabeth Plass's heirs at law were Elizabeth Woodworth Holden and James V. Woodworth (the Woodworth heirs).

At the hearing in the probate court, the Woodworth heirs offered extrinsic evidence, in the form of their own declarations, concerning the purported intent of the testator. However, relying only on the language of the decree of distribution,[2] the probate court concluded that the identity of the heirs entitled to the trust assets must be determined as of the date of death of the life tenant. The probate court therefore ordered the trustee to deliver the remaining trust assets in equal shares to the Woodworth heirs.

* * *

The decree of distribution constitutes a final and conclusive adjudication of the testamentary disposition which the deceased made of his property. (Estate of Miner (1963) 214 Cal.App.2d 533, 538 [29 Cal.Rptr. 601].) Thus, the outcome of this appeal turns on the proper construction to be given to the provision in the decree which directs the distribution of the trust assets upon termination. (Estate of Easter, *supra*, 24 Cal.2d 191, 194–195.) Because the probate court's ruling was based entirely upon the language of the decree, we are not bound by the probate court's conclusion.

---

2. There is nothing in the record before us which suggests the trial court's ruling was founded, in whole or part, upon any extrinsic evidence.

(Estate of Dodge (1971) 6 Cal.3d 311, 318 [98 Cal.Rptr. 801, 491 P.2d 385].) Instead, we must make an independent determination of the meaning of the decree. (Parsons v. Bristol Development Co. (1965) 62 Cal.2d 861, 865–866 [44 Cal.Rptr. 767, 402 P.2d 839].) In addition, since the probate court did not rely upon any purported evidence of intent, any reference we may make to the "record" in this case will not include such evidence; we review the propriety of the probate court order as if the extrinsic evidence did not exist.

* * *

The Regents contend the probate court erroneously failed to apply the general rule of construction which requires that the identity of "heirs" entitled to take a remainder interest be determined as of the date of death of the denominated ancestor, in the absence of any contrary intent expressed by the testator. (See Estate of Stanford (1957) 49 Cal.2d 120, 124 [315 P.2d 681]; Estate of Liddle (1958) 162 Cal. App.2d 7 [328 P.2d 35]; and Estate of Newman (1924) 68 Cal.App. 420, 424 [229 P. 898].) Had the probate court construed the decree in accord with this principle, the Regents would have been entitled to share in the trust assets as a residuary legatee of Raymond Plass, an heir at law of Elizabeth Plass at the time of her death in 1980.

The Woodworth heirs respond by asserting the probate court's decision is consistent with an exception to the general rule which requires that the determination be made at the date of death of the life tenant. (See Wells Fargo Bank v. Title Ins. & Trust Co. (1971) 22 Cal.App.3d 295, 300 [99 Cal.Rptr. 464]; and Estate of McKenzie (1966) 246 Cal.App.2d 740 [54 Cal.Rptr. 888].) (4)(See fn. 3.), (3b) Under this principle, the Regents have no interest in the trust assets, because Raymond Plass predeceased Mamie Barlow Woodworth.[3]

* * *

Estate of Liddle, *supra*, 162 Cal.App.2d 7, reflects the common law preference for vested rather than contingent remainders.[4] Thus, unless a particular instrument disclosed a different intent on the part of the testator, a remainder to a class of persons, such as children, became vested in the class when one or more of its members came into existence and could be ascertained, even though the class was subject to

---

3. It is undisputed that had the testator in this case died on or after January 1, 1985, the Regents would have no claim to the trust assets. Under Probate Code sections 6150 and 6151, which have been in effect since 1985 (see Prob. Code, § 6103), a devise of a future interest to a class, such as heirs, includes only those who fit the class description at the time the legacy is to take effect in enjoyment.

4. The bias for early vesting was also evident in several now repealed provisions of the Probate Code. For example, former section 28 provided: "Testamentary dispositions, including devises and bequests to a person on attaining majority, are presumed to vest at the testators's death."

Former section 123 read in part: "A testamentary disposition to a class includes every person answering the description at the testator's death; but when the possession is postponed to a future period, it includes also all persons coming within the description before the time to which possession is postponed."

open for future additional members. (Estate of Stanford, *supra*, 49 Cal.2d at p. 125.) Furthermore, the fact that takers of a postponed gift were described by a class designation did not, under the common law rule, give rise to any implied condition of survival. (Id. at p. 126.)

The circumstances involved in *Liddle* are substantially indistinguishable from those of the present case. In *Liddle*, the remainder of a testamentary trust was to be distributed to the testatrix's attorney or, in the event of his death, the attorney's heirs at law. Although the attorney survived the testatrix, he predeceased the life tenant. The attorney's only heir, his wife, died intestate several years before the death of the life tenant. (*Liddle*, *supra*, 162 Cal.App.2d at pp. 9–10.) The wife's heirs and the administrator of her estate clashed with certain remote cousins of the attorney over the ownership of the trust assets.

The appellate court ruled in favor of the wife's estate. (162 Cal.App.2d at pp. 20–21.) Relying upon statutes, treatises, and case law expressing common law notions, including Estate of Stanford, *supra*, 49 Cal.2d 120, the court construed the phrase "heirs at law" according to its technical meaning, that is, the person or persons who are entitled to succeed to the property of an intestate decedent. (*Liddle*, *supra*, 162 Cal.App.2d at pp. 14–15.) The *Liddle* court then held the members of this class must be determined as of the death of the named ancestor. The rule was summarized as follows:

> 'Normally, when a gift has been made to the "heirs" or "next of kin" of a named individual, the donor has said in effect that he wants the property distributed as the law would distribute it if the named person died intestate. Accordingly, the normal time for applying the statute of descent or distribution is at the death of the named individual. This is, however, merely a rule of construction, and if the testator or grantor manifests an intention that the statute be applied either at an earlier or a later time, such intention will be given effect.' (*Liddle*, *supra*, 162 Cal.App.2d at p. 19, 328 P.2d 35.)

The designated ancestor in *Liddle* was the attorney. Because his wife was his intestate heir at the time he died, the court found she was the proper recipient of the trust estate.

* * *

On the other hand, *Wells Fargo Bank*, *supra*, 22 Cal.App.3d 295, 300, reflects the application of an exception to the early vesting principle. In *Wells Fargo Bank*, a woman had conveyed, by a grant deed, a life estate in certain real property to her daughter, with remainders to the grantor's two other children. If the life tenant died without issue and the two other children died without issue before the grantor's death, the instrument provided that the remainder interest in the property would belong to the grantor's "heirs." (*Wells Fargo Bank*, *supra*, 22 Cal.App.3d 295, 297–298.) The trial court determined the heirs should be ascertained as of the date of the grantor's death.

The Court of Appeal reversed. Because the remainder to the other children or their issue was contingent upon their surviving the life tenant, the court held the substitutional gift to the heirs was also contingent, thereby requiring the identification of the class members as of the death of the life tenant:

'In this type of case . . . the class of heirs is determined upon termination of the trust because the question whether the testator's heirs would take at all having been postponed until the resolution of contingency, the question of the identity of the heirs has likewise been deemed to have been postponed by the testator. [Citations.]' (*Wells Fargo Bank, supra*, 22 Cal.App.3d 295, 300, 99 Cal.Rptr. 464.)

This concept was also recognized in *Estate of McKenzie, supra*, 246 Cal.App.2d 740, a case cited in *Wells Fargo Bank*:

'There is another class of cases in which the word 'heirs' has been held to refer to persons other than those who were heirs at the time of the testator's death. . . . In this type of case, the class of heirs is determined upon termination of the trust, because the gift to heirs was a substituted one, the primary gift being contingent. (Simes & Smith, The Law of Future Interests (2d ed.) §735, p. 210.) The question whether the testator's heirs would take at all having been postponed until the resolution of the contingency, the question of the identity of the heirs in such cases has likewise been deemed to have been postponed by the testator. (See In Re Sayre's Will [1956] 1 App. Div.2d 475 [151 N.Y.S.2d 506, 509–512].)' (Estate of McKenzie, at p. 745.) The *McKenzie* court did not apply this exception, however, because the trust language before it did not create a contingent, substitutional gift. (*Estate of McKenzie, supra*, 246 Cal.App.2d at p. 745, 54 Cal.Rptr. 888.)

The *Liddle* court also considered but rejected the exception:

'The fact that the gift to the described group is substitutional does not cause the postponement of the application of the statute to a period subsequent to the death of the designated ancestor.' (*Liddle, supra*, 162 Cal.App.2d at p. 19, 328 P.2d 35.)

The court reasoned:

'[i]f it were held at bar that [the attorney's wife] took a contingent estate at the death of [the testatrix], that fact did not alter the further one that the contingency was fulfilled when she survived her husband, and what was previously a contingent remainder (if it was one) became vested in her as his sole heir at law.' (*Liddle, supra*, 162 Cal.App.2d at p. 17, 328 P.2d 35.)

* * *

The will of Harold Evans Woodworth created a contingent remainder in Elizabeth Plass, with a substitutional gift to her heirs at law. Although it appears we are therefore free to choose between *Liddle* and *Wells Fargo Bank*, in reality this is not so; the contingent, substitutional gift exception to the rule of early vesting applies only to grants of remainder interests which differ materially from the one now before us.

An authority relied upon in *McKenzie*, and by implication in *Wells Fargo Bank*, for the exception is Simes & Smith, The Law of Future Interests (2d ed.) §735, page 210. (*Estate of McKenzie, supra*, 246 Cal.App.2d at p. 745.) However, under consideration at the cited portion of this treatise is the situation where "a testator devises a life estate or defeasible fee to *a person who is one of his heirs*, followed by a remainder or executory interest to the testator's heirs." (Simes & Smith, *supra*, §735, p. 206, italics added.) As Simes and Smith point out, in such circumstances, some courts have rejected the general rule that the members of the class are to be determined at the death of the ancestor (i.e., the testator), and instead have applied an exception which identifies the heirs who will take the remainder as those in being upon the death of the holder of the life estate or defeasible fee. (Id., at pp. 206–210.) The rationale for these decisions is an assumption the testator did not intend to give both a present and a future interest to the same person. (See Simes & Smith, *supra*, §735, at pp. 206–210.)

Wells Fargo Bank involved a bequest of the same type as that which is the subject of section 735 of the Simes and Smith treatise. In *Wells Fargo Bank*, the estate of the life tenant would have been entitled to receive a portion of the remainder if the identity of the grantor's heirs was determined at the time of the grantor's death rather than at the date of the life tenant's death. (*Wells Fargo Bank, supra*, 22 Cal. App.3d at p. 298.) The *Wells Fargo Bank* court essentially adopted the analysis in section 735 of Simes and Smith that:

> '[I]f the general rule is applied, an incongruous result would be reached by taking the property away from [the holder of the possessory interest] because he died without issue and giving it back to him because of the same reason.' (*Wells Fargo Bank, supra*, 22 Cal.App.3d at p. 300, 99 Cal.Rptr. 464.)

The *Wells Fargo Bank* court relied on three New York appellate decisions: In re Pelham's Will (1970) 63 Misc.2d 377 [312 N.Y.S.2d 285]; In re Patterson's Estate (1965) 45 Misc.2d 797 [257 N.Y.S.2d 742]; and In re Sayre's Will (1956) 1 A.D.2d 475 [151 N.Y.S.2d 506].[5] In each of these cases, there existed at least the possibility that the estate of an interim beneficiary who did not survive the termination of a preceding interest, and therefore did not or would not receive an outright interest in the testator's property, would nonetheless be entitled to share in the remainder. In In re Pelham's Will, *supra*, 312 N.Y.S.2d at page 288, the two heirs determined at the testator's death were "the same persons who would take as intestate distributees had the testator made no alternative gift of the remainder." In In re Patterson's Estate, *supra*, 257 N.Y.S.2d at page 745, identifying the testator's heirs at his death could have "result[ed] in a distribution of trust remainders through the estates of

---

5. This opinion was also cited in *Estate of McKenzie, supra*, 246 Cal.App.2d at page 745, as additional authority for the existence of the exception.

the same persons who were the income beneficiaries and contingent remaindermen of the trusts." In *In re Sayre's Will, supra,* 151 N.Y.S.2d at page 511, ". . . although the specific remainder to [an interim beneficiary] failed when she predeceased the life tenant, still she could qualify for a share as an heir."

By contrast, in the instant case we do not have a contingent, substituted gift to a class of recipients which includes the deceased interim beneficiary. As in *Liddle,* the class of contingent, substituted heirs does not encompass any prior contingent interim beneficiary. The named remainderman, Elizabeth Plass, did not lose her interest because she died without issue. She lost her interest because she died before the death of the life tenant. According to the record, neither Mamie Barlow Woodworth nor — of course — Elizabeth Plass is an heir at law of Elizabeth Plass.

Thus, we believe the exception to the general rule of early vesting, as implemented in *Wells Fargo Bank,* should not be applied to the remainder interest contained in the decree of distribution here.

* * *

For the reasons which follow, we find no other justification for departing from *Liddle.* First, there is nothing in the language of the other provisions of the decree of distribution before us which reveals the testator's intent or desire. Since the record does not include Harold Evans Woodworth's will, we cannot resort to it to attempt to divine his wishes. (See *Estate of Stanford, supra,* 49 Cal.2d at pp. 130–134.)

Second, the fact that the university, an entity, is not a relative of Elizabeth Plass or one of her heirs at law is not material. (See *Wells Fargo Bank, supra,* 22 Cal.App.3d at p. 301.) Unlike the *Wells Fargo Bank* court, we are unwilling to say that application of the general rule "would result in thwarting the expressed intention of the Grantor by distributing the corpus of the trust to persons or entities other than [Elizabeth Plass's] heirs." (*Wells Fargo Bank, supra,* 22 Cal.App.3d at p. 301.) Had the instrument in *Wells Fargo Bank* satisfactorily disclosed the grantor's intentions regarding the distribution of the remainder interest in the property, there would have been no need for the court to have even considered the competing rules of construction in order to decide the case. (See *Estate of Stanford, supra,* 49 Cal.2d at p. 127.)

It would be pure speculation for us to conclude that Harold Evans Woodworth would not have wanted Raymond Plass to inherit a portion of the trust assets. It appears from the record that Raymond Plass and Elizabeth Plass were married at the time the testator executed his will. It has long been the law in California that a husband is an heir of his deceased wife. (*Estate of Liddle, supra,* 162 Cal.App.2d at p. 16.) Nothing in the decree forecloses the possibility the testator took into account the fact that Elizabeth Plass might predecease, and Raymond Plass might outlive, Mamie Barlow Woodworth, resulting in Raymond Plass's succession to a portion of the trust remainder.

Third, the rule of construction which favors descent according to blood in cases of ambiguity in testamentary dispositions (see *Wells Fargo Bank, supra,* 22 Cal. App.3d at p. 302; Estate of Boyd (1938) 24 Cal.App.2d 287, 289 [74 P.2d 1049]) should likewise not determine the result in this case. The general rule favoring early vesting was well established long before the testator died. We do not think it should be abandoned in order to carry out some purportedly perceived, but entirely speculative, notion about the intent of the testator based upon events which occurred well after the testator's death. (See *Estate of McKenzie, supra*, 246 Cal.App.2d at p. 748.) As we noted earlier, it is perfectly conceivable that Harold Evans Woodworth took into account in making his will the possibility that his property would pass to Raymond Plass and thereafter be transferred to strangers to the Woodworth line.

In this connection, the *Wells Fargo Bank* court in part rationalized its decision with the observation that:

> 'by allowing such beneficiary to take as an heir regardless of his failure to survive might well end in an unacceptable result, namely that the remainder would not vest in the heirs of the grantor, but in the beneficiary's heirs or his residuary legatees who, in turn, need not be the heirs or relatives of the grantor at all (*In re Sayre's Will, supra*, [151 N.Y.S.2d at] pp. 510–511).' (*Wells Fargo Bank, supra*, 22 Cal.App.3d at p. 300, 99 Cal.Rptr. 464.)

Such an outcome is unacceptable, however, only if it is contrary to the testator's clear intent. (6), (5b) In the absence of any firm indication of testamentary intent, the rules of construction must be implemented in order to ensure uniformity and predictability in the law, rather than disregarded in order to carry out a court's ad hoc sense of what is, with perfect hindsight, acceptable in a particular set of circumstances. (See *Estate of McKenzie, supra*, 246 Cal.App.2d at pp. 748–749.)

Former Probate Code section 122 (repealed 1985), relied upon by the Woodworth heirs as an additional reason to uphold the probate court order, is not relevant. The section read:

> 'Words in a will referring to death or survivorship, simply, relate to the time of the testator's death, unless possession is actually postponed, when they must be referred to the time of possession.'

The crucial question in this case is whether the decree's language imposes a survivorship condition to membership in the class of Elizabeth Plass's heirs. Since we have determined it does not, former section 122 has no effect. In substance, the Woodworth heirs argue that because possession of the remainder of the trust assets in this case was postponed, the statute requires that a condition of survivorship be imposed upon the recipients of the remainder. This is an unwarranted reading of the section, and one which turns its language upside down.

Last, none of the other exceptions identified in *Wells Fargo Bank* to the early vesting rule applies under the circumstances of this case. This is not a situation where the "... life tenant is the sole heir, but the will devises the remainder to the testator's 'heirs.'" (*Wells Fargo Bank, supra*, 22 Cal.App.3d at p. 300; *Estate of Wilson* (1920) 184 Cal. 63 [193 P. 581].)

In addition, the language of the decree does not contain any "expression of futurity in the description of the ancestor's heirs" (*Wells Fargo Bank, supra*, 22 Cal. App.3d at p. 300), such as "my then living heirs-at-law" (Estate of Layton (1933) 217 Cal. 451, 454 [19 P.2d 793, 91 A.L.R. 480]; see also *Estate of McKenzie, supra*, 246 Cal.App.2d at p. 744). When, as here, "'the gift is in terms "then to the heirs" of a designated person, the word "then" merely indicates the time of enjoyment and has no significance in relation to the rule [of early vesting].'" (*Estate of Miner, supra*, 214 Cal.App.2d at p. 542.) The use of the word "then" in the instant decree did nothing more than create a contingent remainder in Elizabeth Plass. Whatever reliance the trial court placed upon the term was therefore erroneous.[6]

Further, the rule in *Estate of Easter, supra*, 24 Cal.2d 191, does not apply because the decree in the present case does not use the word "vest." In *Easter*, the California Supreme Court considered a decree of distribution which provided: "'Upon the death of the [life tenant/widow of the testator] the trust . . . shall terminate and all of the property . . . *shall go to and vest in* the heirs at law of the [testator].'" (Id., at p. 195, italics in original.) Certain claimants argued the remainder was determinable at the time of the testator's death, in the absence of a clearly expressed contrary intent. The Supreme Court disagreed, finding no uncertainty in the decree. By providing that two things should occur upon the death of the life tenant, i.e., (1) the trust shall terminate and (2) the property shall go to and vest in the testator's heirs at law, the decree clearly indicated an intent that the interests of the heirs should vest at the time of the termination of the trust. "Any other construction would ignore the normal and usual meaning of the words 'shall go to and vest in the heirs at law.'" (*Estate of Easter, supra*, 24 Cal.2d at p. 195.) Later, in *Estate of Stanford, supra*, 49 Cal.2d at page 130, the Supreme Court made it clear that the rule of early vesting was not applied in *Easter* because of the presence in the decree of the technical word "vest." (See also *McKenzie, supra*, 246 Cal.App.2d at p. 745; and *Wells Fargo Bank, supra*, 22 Cal.App.3d at p. 300.)

Finally, and contrary to the contention of the Woodworth heirs, we do not find the words "pay to" contained in the instant decree to be equivalent to the word "vest" or otherwise constitute an "expression of futurity" for purposes of determining the identity of the relevant heirs. (*Wells Fargo Bank, supra*, at p. 300.) Rather, the instruction pertains to the time when the recipients of the assets are entitled to have them. (*Estate of Miner, supra*, 214 Cal.App.2d at p. 542.)

* * *

Accordingly, we must reverse the probate court's ruling that the Regents have no claim to the assets of the testamentary trust. Because the trial court did not

---

6. The trial court's written decision included the following statement:
"It was the intent of the decedent in using the word 'then' in relation to the disposition to Elizabeth Woodworth Plass that the determination of the identity of the heirs be made as of the time of the death of the life tenant and the termination of the trust."

consider the extrinsic evidence presented by the parties, we take no position with respect to it or its effect. It may be evaluated by the probate court on remand.

The judgment (order) appealed from is reversed.

Thaxter, J., and Brown, J., . . . concur.

Notes

The Doctrine of Worthier Title applies in some states and, as such, provides that when a settlor transfers property in trust, retaining a life estate in the settlor or in another, and then provides that the remainder should go to the settlor's heirs, it is presumed that the settlor intended to retain a reversion in the settlor's estate and did not intend to create a remainder in the settlor's heirs. While the rule may be rebutted with evidence of a different intent, many states have abolished the rule completely. *See, e.g.,* Unif. Prob. Code § 2-710 (2019) (Worthier-Title Doctrine Abolished). Likewise, the Rule in Shelley's Case provides that, when land is conveyed to a donee for life, then to the donee's heirs, there is no contingent remainder in the donee's heirs; the donee retains the remainder. Likewise, state statutes have abolished the rule's application. *See, e.g., Restatement (Second) of Property, Don. Trans.* § 30.1 (2019).

Uniform Probate Code (2019)

§ 2-711. Future Interests in "Heirs" and Like.

If an applicable statute or a governing instrument calls for a present or future distribution to or creates a present or future interest in a designated individual's "heirs," "heirs at law," "next of kin," "relatives," or "family," or language of similar import, the property passes to those persons, including the state, and in such shares as would succeed to the designated individual's intestate estate under the intestate succession law of the designated individual's domicile if the designated individual died when the disposition is to take effect in possession or enjoyment. If the designated individual's surviving spouse is living but is remarried at the time the disposition is to take effect in possession or enjoyment, the surviving spouse is not an heir of the designated individual.

§ 2-708. Class Gifts to "Descendants," "Issue," or "Heirs of the Body"; Form of Distribution if None Specified.

If a class gift in favor of "descendants," "issue," or "heirs of the body" does not specify the manner in which the property is to be distributed among the class members, the property is distributed among the class members who are living when the interest is to take effect in possession or enjoyment, in such shares as they would receive, under the applicable law of intestate succession, if the designated ancestor had then died intestate owning the subject matter of the class gift.

Chapter 7

Creation, Classification, and Utilization of Trusts

Tool Bar

I. Elements of a Valid Trust

The evolution of the equitable device that would eventually be known as a trust originated during medieval times but has since evolved into an estate planning tool used today to avoid probate, shelter the assets of many dependent persons, and reduce or eliminate tax liability. With the gradual erosion of the Rule Against Perpetuities, trusts may now span multiple generations, providing a legacy to the persons creating them, income to multiple trustees, and benefit to countless beneficiaries. Statutes have replaced the shadowy interplay of law and equity from which the earliest forms of trusts originated, so that today, American trust law is dominated by the enactment of the Uniform Trust Code (2000), the Uniform Custodial Trust Act (1987), the Uniform Prudent Investor Act (1994), and the Uniform Principal and Income Act (1997). *See generally* David Horton, *Tomorrow's Inheritance: The Frontiers of Estate Planning Formalism*, 58 B.C. L. Rev. 539 (2017); John Morley, *The Common Law Corporation: The Power of the Trust in Anglo-American Business History*, 116 Colum. L. Rev. 245 (2016); Ruiqiao Zhang, *A Comparative Study of the Introduction of Trusts into Civil Law and Its Ownership of Trust Property*, 21 Trusts & Trustees 902 (2015). Federal law governs trillions of dollars held for pensions under trust management, all managed by the Employee Retirement Income Security Act of 1974 (ERISA).

While many trusts benefit charitable enterprises, such as the Pew Foundation, and some benefit cemeteries and pets (often called honorary trusts), the majority of trusts benefit private individuals. Typically, a private trust will be created by a person seeking to provide for her or his spouse, then to their children for their lives, and then the remainder to their grandchildren. The trust may be created during lifetime (*inter vivos*) or at death, through a valid Last Will and Testament (testamentary). The person creating the trust (settlor) must transfer legal title over the trust property (Res/Corpus) to a person or group of persons (Trustee(s)), with specific instructions as to what to do (Trust Purpose) for the persons who benefit from the income or corpus of the trust (Beneficiaries). With modern estate planning, which allows for creative ways to manage assets and achieve personal objectives, the possibilities are endless.

But the law of trusts contains pitfalls for the unwary, as there are significant differences between wills and trusts. Termination or revocation of a trust is different from the law applicable to a Last Will and Testament, compensation for beneficiaries has changed as wealth is defined differently, *see, e.g.,* Unif. Principal and Income Act (1997), and transfers to minors may be made through the Unif. Transfers to Minors Act (1986). Taxation of trusts is perhaps the most significant issue facing the estate planner, but there are many examples of successful avoidance of state and federal tax liability with proper planning. And, of course, the burden upon a trustee is significant: the Trustee must be prudent and administer the trust with impartiality and loyalty, and the Trustee must be properly compensated, *see, e.g.,* Unif. Trust Code (2014). All of these elements will be explored as this chapter describes the creation, classification, and utilization of trusts. We begin with the elements of a successful trust.

A. Settlor

Uniform Trust Code (2019)

§ 103. Definitions (as amended 2004).

* * *

(15) "Settlor" means a person, including a testator, who creates, or contributes property to, a trust. If more than one person creates or contributes property to a trust, each person is a settlor of the portion of the trust property attributable to that person's contribution except to the extent another person has the power to revoke or withdraw that portion.

§ 402. Requirements for Creation.

(a) A trust is only created if:

    (1) the settlor has the capacity to create a trust;

    (2) the settlor indicates an intention to create the trust. * * *

§ 602. Revocation or Amendment of Revocable Trust.

(a) Unless the terms of a trust expressly provide that the trust is irrevocable, the settlor may revoke or amend the trust.

§ 603. Settlor's Powers; Powers of Withdrawal.

(a) While a trust is revocable and the settlor has capacity to revoke the trust, rights of the beneficiaries are subject to the control of, and the duties of the trustee are owed exclusively to, the settlor.

(b) During the period the power may be exercised, the holder of a power of withdrawal has the rights of a settlor of a revocable trust under this section to the extent of the property subject to the power.

Notes

The settlor of the trust, as the creator, establishes the parameters of the trust. Any statute that applies to trusts serves only as a default mechanism. *See* Jeffrey A. Cooper, *Empty Promises: Settlor's Intent, the Uniform Trust Code, and the Future of Trust Investment Law,* 88 B.U. L. Rev. 1165 (2008); *Restatement (Third) of Property* § 10.1 (2015) ("The controlling consideration in determining the meaning of a donative document is the donor's intent."); Unif. Prud. Inv. Act § 1(b) (1994) ("The prudent investor rule, a default rule, may be expanded, restricted, eliminated, or otherwise altered by the provisions of a trust."). But often the intentions of the settlor are vague, permitting statutes or independent trustees to act in accordance with statutory guidelines or the trustee's obligation to act with prudence and "solely in the interests of the beneficiaries." Unif. Prud. Inv. Act § 5 (1994). There are significant cases in which the courts have had to decide if the settlor's intention was vague enough to allow for the trustee to act within the parameters of the trust, or whether emergencies not anticipated by the settlor could justify a departure from the settlor's intent, thereby allowing the trustee to act independently. The following decision offers an example.

In re Pulitzer's Estate

Surrogate's Court, New York County, New York, 1931
139 Misc. Rep. 575, 249 N.Y.S. 87

FOLEY, S.

This is a proceeding for the judicial settlement of the accounts of the trustees of a certain trust under the will of Joseph Pulitzer. The trustees also seek a construction of the will and codicils and particularly of a certain article of a codicil which relates to that trust. They request the advice and direction of the surrogate. They also seek the instructions and determination of the court as to the propriety, price, manner, and time of sale of a substantial portion of the assets of the Press Publishing Company, the stock of which constitutes a material part of the assets of the trust here involved. They request the approval of the contract for such sale dated January 31, 1931, and a supplemental contract dated February 14, 1931. A serious and imperative emergency is claimed to exist, whereby, if such a sale is not made, a valuable asset of the trust estate may be in great part or wholly lost to the trust, the life tenants, and remaindermen.

At the very outset, the functions and duties of the surrogate in this situation should be made clear. There are four questions to be determined by me, as follows:

(a) Regardless of any prohibition or limitation contained in the will and codicils, have the trustees, in the present exigency, power and authority to sell the assets of a company, the stock of which is included in the trust?

(b) If a prohibition is contained in the will, has the Surrogate's Court, under its equitable jurisdiction, the power to modify the terms of the trust and authorize the sale of such assets by the trustees?

(c) Do the proofs submitted to the surrogate justify the exercise of that power in the emergency?

(d) A fourth question is presented, which will be considered in the secondary part of this decision: Has the surrogate the legal power to approve the contract and supplemental contract and the specific terms of the proposed sale of the assets by the Press Publishing Company?

In answer to the first three questions, I hold that the trustees, as the representatives of the estate, have the power and general authority to participate as corporate officers and holders of the estate stock in the sale of the property of the company, and that the equitable powers of the Surrogate's Court should be invoked to generally authorize them to make such a sale. I hold further that there is an implied power of sale in the will, which, in the present crisis, may be exercised by the trustees. I hold further that the proofs presented to me as to the financial condition of the Press Publishing Company, its diminishing assets and increasing loss of revenue in its business operations, create a duty in the trustees to act for the protection of the beneficiaries of the trust.

As to the fourth question, I am firmly of the opinion and hold that the Surrogate's Court entirely lacks the power to approve the specific terms of the contract, submitted here, for the sale of the assets by the Press Publishing Company to the Consolidated Newspaper Corporation, because this court has no jurisdiction over the internal affairs of a corporation, the stock of which is owned in part by an estate and in part by stockholders in their individual right or title. In other words, general authority will be granted to the trustees and power is found to exist for them to exercise such authority. But the responsibility for the selection of the purchaser, the details of the transaction, the selling price, the terms of payment, and the credit of the purchaser rest upon the officers and directors of the corporation.

Joseph Pulitzer died in the year 1911. He left a will and four codicils which were admitted to probate by this court on November 29, 1911. The provisions directly pertinent to the issues here are contained in the first codicil, which is dated March 23, 1909. By its terms he gave the shares of the capital stock of the Press Publishing Company, which were owned by him, and his shares of the Pulitzer Publishing Company, of St. Louis, in trust for the life of each of the two youngest of his sons, Joseph Pulitzer, Jr., and Herbert Pulitzer. The period of the two lives mentioned was defined by him as the 'trust term.' There were directions to pay the income in certain fractional shares to his three sons and to certain other persons. Further provisions were made for payment to the male descendants of the sons in case of the death of any of the sons during the 'trust term.' Upon the expiration of the 'trust term' there was a direction to divide the said stock under varying conditions. If one of the sons survives, he is to take 'the shares of stock of said Companies' held for his benefit, and the remainder is to be divided among the male descendants of his sons and daughters. Certain other provisions for the vesting of the remainders and for gifts over are contained, which are not important here.

To distinguish it from the residuary trust, the particular trust here has been called the 'Newspaper Trust.' Its trustees are the testator's three sons, Ralph Pulitzer, Herbert Pulitzer, and Joseph Pulitzer, Jr. The Pulitzer Publishing Company publishes the St. Louis Post Dispatch. The Press Publishing Company publishes the New York World, the Sunday World, and the Evening World. The trustees of the so-called 'Newspaper Trust' hold within the trust a very large majority of shares of the Press Publishing Company. The remaining shares are owned by the trustees individually. The paragraph particularly sought to be construed here, which deals with the powers of the trustees and the limitations thereon, is contained in article seventh of the codicil of March 23, 1909, and reads as follows: 'I further authorize and empower my Executors and Trustees to whom I have hereinbefore bequeathed my stock in the Pulitzer Publishing Company of St. Louis, at any time, and from time to time, to sell and dispose of said stock, or any part thereof, at public or private sale, at such prices and on such terms as they may think best, and to hold the proceeds of any stock sold in trust for the beneficiaries for whom such shares were held in lieu thereof, and upon the same trusts. This power of sale is not to be construed as in any respect mandatory, but purely discretionary. This power of sale, however, is limited to the said stock of the Pulitzer Publishing Company of St. Louis, and shall not be taken to authorize or empower the sale or disposition under any circumstances whatever, by the Trustees of any stock of the Press Publishing Company, publisher of 'The World' newspaper. I particularly enjoin upon my sons and my descendants the duty of preserving, perfecting and perpetuating 'The World' newspaper (to the maintenance and upbuilding of which I have sacrificed my health and strength) in the same spirit in which I have striven to create and conduct it as a public institution, from motives higher than mere gain, it having been my desire that it should be at all times conducted in a spirit of independence and with a view to inculcating high standards and public spirit among the people and their official representatives, and it is my earnest wish that said newspaper shall hereafter be conducted upon the same principles.'

There are fifteen remaindermen in existence. One of them is an adult; the other fourteen are infants. Because of a possible adversity of interest they are represented here by two separate special guardians. The adult life tenants and remainderman join in requesting the relief sought by the trustees.

Counsel for the trustees contend that the express denial of a power of sale contained in the paragraph was modified and cut down, as a matter of testamentary intent, by Mr. Pulitzer in its subsequent language, wherein he expressed his desire and his earnest wish as to the perpetuation of the paper and the standards and ideals for its management by his sons and their descendants. They contend further that the instructions to 'my sons and my descendants' indicated a definite differentiation of Mr. Pulitzer's purpose to guide them in their individual capacity rather than in their duties as trustees. They also contend that the prohibition was against disposal of the stock and not of the assets of the company. There is some support to be found in the provisions of the will for these contentions. Indication of an intent to authorize a sale in certain emergencies is thus found in article VI of the codicil dated May 11, 1910.

But I prefer to place my determination here upon broader grounds and upon the power of a court of equity, in emergencies, to protect the beneficiaries of a trust from serious loss, or a total destruction of a substantial asset of the corpus. The law, in the case of necessity, reads into the will an implied power of sale. The law also assumes that a testator had sufficient foresight to realize that securities bequeathed to a trustee may become so unproductive or so diminished in value as to authorize their sale where extraordinary circumstances develop, or crisis occurs. Such was the law in this state prior to the making of Mr. Pulitzer's Will. He is charged with knowledge of it. It was laid down in the leading case of Toronto Gen. Trusts Co. v. Chicago, B. & Q. R. Co., 64 Hun, 1, 8, 18 N. Y. S. 593, 596, affirmed on opinion below, 138 N. Y. 657, 34 N. E. 514. It was against applied by Chief Judge Cardozo in Mertz v. Guaranty Trust Co., 247 N. Y. 137, 144, 159 N. E. 888, 890, 57 A. L. R. 1114. 'A trustee finds upon his hands an investment, mandatory in its origin, but so charged as to be no longer mandatory, even if permitted. A power of sale attaches in such circumstances by implication of law.' * * *

Courts of equity in other jurisdictions have found power to relieve against the provisions of the instrument by granting the authority to dispose of perishable property or wasting assets, despite the express command or wishes contained in the will. Thus in Weld v. Weld, 23 R. I. 311, 50 A. 490, the prohibition of the will was against the sale of securities unless par was obtained for them, and the estate was required to be kept together until the death of every individual who was named as an annuitant. Authority to sell was found to exist. In Stout v. Stout, 192 Ky. 504, 233 S. W. 1057, the principal asset of the estate consisted of a business which the trustees were directed to continue. The court authorized the trustees to sell the business which had become unprofitable by reason of the advent of national prohibition. In Johns v. Montgomery, 265 Ill. 21, 26, 106 N. E. 497, 499, L. R. A. 1916B, 1073, Ann. Cas. 1916A, 996, where the trust deed required the retention of the land and its operation for agricultural purposes, the court recognized its duty and that of the trustee to protect the estate. The opinion recites: "Exigencies often arise not contemplated by the party creating the trust, and which, had they been anticipated, would undoubtedly have been provided for, where the aid of the court of chancery must be invoked to grant relief imperatively required, and in such cases the court must, as far as may be, occupy the place of the party creating the trust, and do with the fund what he would have dictated, had he anticipated the emergency.' [From Curtis v. Brown, 29 Ill. 201]. * * * The facts here present the alternative of modifying the trust agreement or else losing the entire trust estate. * * * In our opinion the facts present a case calling for the interposition of a court of equity in order to preserve a trust estate which would otherwise ultimately be lost to its owners.' See also Packard v. Illinois Trust & Savings Bank, 261 Ill. 450, 104 N. E. 257; Curtis v. Brown, 29 Ill. 201; Denegre v. Walker, 214 Ill. 113, 73 N. E. 409, 105 Am. St. Rep. 98, 2 Ann. Cas. 787; Re Mercer Home for Disabled Clergymen of the Presbyterian Faith, 162 Pa. 232, 29 A. 731; N. J. Nat. Bank & Trust Co. v. Lincoln Mortgage & Title Guaranty Co., 105 N. J. Eq. 557, 148 A. 713. * * *

The extreme circumstances in the pending case surely justify the alternative of disregarding the directions of the testator, if mandatory, and reading into the will a power of sale. Briefly summarized, the proofs submitted to me show that the losses in the business operations of the three newspapers owner by the Press Publishing Company for the five years from 1926 to 1930 averaged $811,822.10 per year. In 1929 the loss was $1,062,749.80. In 1930 the loss was $1,975,604.77. In 1930 the loss grew, despite economies effected that year, aggregating $1,250,000. The advertising lineage of the three newspapers has greatly declined in recent years. The total circulation of the three newspapers has likewise declined in the last three years. The reserves of the corporation have diminished to the extent of $3,025,000 in the past five years. The present reserves, it is stated, would not permit continued publication of the newspapers for more than three months. The testimony showed that the decline in revenue was not due to the business depression caused by the panic of 1929, but antedated it by at least two years. The trustees have attempted to correct the deterioration which has occurred, by employing specialists and experts in the advertising and circulation fields. The loss for the year 1931, it is estimated, will be $2,500,000. The Press Publishing Company has certain other income (aside from newspaper operation), from syndicate participation and investment activities. Despite the profits and income derived from these sources, the loss of the Press Publishing Company from all its operations has averaged, during the past five years, $427,000 per year. The loss for 1930 was $1,677,625.80.

It is interesting to note that a somewhat similar situation existed in the sale of the New York Times in 1893. George Jones was one of the largest stock owners in the enterprise—the New York Times Association. He left the stock in trust. His will provided: 'Whereas I am the owner of forty-six shares of the capital stock of the association 'The New York Times,' I direct that my executors shall not sell, or otherwise dispose of the same, or any of them, during the said trust. I give to my executors full power to sell any and all other property, real or personal, constituting the said trust estate, and direct them to invest the proceeds as they shall consider safe and proper.' There, as here, the newspaper was conducted by the trustees. The newspaper became financially unproductive. An equity receivership resulted. Involved in the action there came in question the sale of the assets of the association and the right of the executors of George Jones to sell the stock in contravention of the terms of the trust. Despite the command of the testator, the executors were authorized by the court of equity to liquidate the shares held by the estate. The decree approving that direction and authorizing the sale of the New York Times was made by Justice, afterwards Presiding Justice, Morgan J. O'Brien, upon August 8, 1893, and the newspaper was sold pursuant to its direction.

The trustees here find themselves in a crisis where there is no self-help available to them. A judicial declaration is necessary, not only as to their general authority, but as to the effect of the words of Mr. Pulitzer contained in his will. The widest equity powers exist in the Surrogate's Court of this statute by the grant of legislative authority contained in section 40 of the Surrogate's Court Act. Matter of Raymond v. Davis' Estate, 248 N. Y. 67, 71, 161 N. E. 421.

I accordingly hold, in this phase of the decision, that the terms of the will and codicils do not prohibit the trustees from disposing of any assets of the Press Publishing Company, that the trustees have general power and authority to act in the conveyance of the assets proposed to be sold, and that this court, in the exercise of its equitable jurisdiction, should authorize them by an appropriate direction in the decree to exercise such general authority.

The secondary relief sought in this application is the approval by the surrogate of the proposed contracts for the sale of the New York World, the Sunday World, and the Evening World, and other intangibles by the Press Publishing Company.

When analyzed and stripped of the extraneous issues, the question here is a simple one. A contract has been made by a corporation, the Press Publishing Company, for the sale of certain of its assets to another corporation—the Consolidated Newspaper Corporation. The trustees of this estate are not parties to that contract in their fiduciary capacity as such trustees. Their signatures in that capacity do not appear on the contract. The estate does not own all the stock of the Press Publishing Company. There are six directors including the trustees. Three of the directors have no personal interest in this estate. I am asked as surrogate to approve a private contract between these two corporations. In other words, the corporate activities of all the officers and directors and stockholders of the Press Publishing Company are attempted to be directly brought within the jurisdiction of the Surrogate's Court, and their actions sought to be approved. Upon and since the argument of the questions involved in this proceeding, other offers have been made for the purchase of the corporation assets involved in the contracts between the two corporations. One of these offers comes from a group of veteran employees of the newspapers. In view of my conclusion that I have no power to entertain any offer, the details of such bids should be submitted to the Press Publishing Company.

In this general situation, consideration must be given primarily to the jurisdiction of this court to act. The Surrogate's Court has no legal power to set itself up as a regulatory body over corporate action. It is not authorized to determine disputes between stockholders of a corporation, where any of such stockholders may hold their shares by individual title and ownership. It has no right to pass on conflicting offers of purchase of corporate assets. With the exceptions which I have made later in this decision, the fact that an estate may own part of the stock affords not even a pretense of power in the court over corporate conduct. Nor can any unwarranted use of judicial power justify the conversion of the court into an auction room for bidders for property owned by such a corporation. The argument for such power in the court not only ignores the law, but becomes ridiculous when the rights of other stockholders, holding by individual ownership, are considered. Their interest in the corporation cannot be jeopardized by any such extra-judicial acts.

The basic jurisdiction of this court is to administer justice in matters relating to the estates of decedents. The limitations upon that jurisdiction are found in the statutes, and particularly in the Surrogate's Court Act, and the decisions construing such laws. I am unable to find any decision which authorizes the surrogate to interfere in a case like the pending proceeding, either as a matter of statutory authority, or within the equitable powers vested in this court. Exceptional cases may arise where the executor or trustee may be committing waste of the assets by virtue of the voting power given to him over the estate stock. But control or prevention in such cases may be exercised not over the corporation but only by direct action of the court against the fiduciary. That distinction is clear. Ample control over corporations in appropriate cases has been given to the Supreme Court.

In this question of our jurisdiction, it matters not whether the interest of the estate in the corporation be large or small, whether the percentage of ownership of the stock be 90 per cent. or 10 per cent. In no event is the Surrogate's Court permitted to intervene in its internal affairs. A different situation might arise and different responsibilities accrue where the entire stock of the corporation was owned by the estate. In cases of that character, the court, in its equitable powers, might disregard the corporate entity.

The pernicious effects of a policy of intermeddling must be obvious. If the surrogate may reach in by order or decree to authorize the specific sale of the assets of a corporation, irreparable damage might be done to the rights of other stockholders, and particularly minority stockholders. The rights of creditors may likewise by prejudiced. Neither of these groups of interested persons can be brought in as parties before the surrogate, and his decree in its legal effect upon them, would be futile and void. Further effects of that pernicious policy can be plainly visualized. Administrators, executors, and trustees could importune this court for authority to determine internal corporate action, the disposal of corporate assets, the increase of capital stock, questions of mergers, and all the other innumerable forms of corporate activities. These questions would be thrust upon a court in the midst of its other and proper business, and appeals made to a judicial officer, who could not and should not be asked to become acquainted with the intimate busienss details of the problem, or the wisdom or desirability of the action sought to be approved.

Inevitably, the motives of many of the fiduciaries would be to secure a form of judicial sanction of transactions for the purpose of influencing the opinions or conduct of other stockholders. A method would thereby develope by which the responsibility of the officers and directors of a corporation could be evaded by them and the burden cast upon the surrogate. Such a proposal is contrary to common sense, logic, and the law itself. We are dealing here, not with the assets owned by the estate. We are asked to go a long step further and to deal with the assets of a corporation, part of the stock of which is owned by the estate. The provisions of section 215 of the Surrogate's Court Act apply to the sale of personal property only where it is directly owned by the estate. It has no application to a case where a corporate entity intervenes. The powers of the surrogate under section 215, Surrogate's Court Act, to advise the representative, or to instruct him as to the sale of securities owned by the estate, has been sparingly exercised by the Surrogates' Courts and only in exceptional cases. That policy has been founded upon the responsibility of the executor or trustee selected by the decedent himself to discharge the duty placed upon him by law or the terms of the will. My distinguished predecessor, Mr. Surrogate Fowler, clearly enunciated this rule of guidance in Schleif's Estate (Sur.) 169 N. Y. S. 814. See, also, Matter of Quinby's Will (Wingate, S.) 134 Misc. Rep. 296, 303, 235 N. Y. S. 308; Matter of Goldfarb's Estate, 93 Misc. Rep. 401, 157 N. Y. S. 137; Matter of Ximenez, 107 Misc. Rep. 460, 176 N. Y. S. 694.

In the treatment of the relation of the executor or trustee to the internal corporate management, distinction should be drawn between the situation here, where judicial approval of a specific corporate contract is sought, and, on the other hand, the responsibility to the estate of the fiduciary for bad faith, fraud, or embezzlement as an officer or director of the corporation. In the latter case the law finds a method of surcharging the representative for his faithless conduct. For the violation of the trust in the misappropriation of the assets of the corporation, the representative or his surety has been held liable. Matter of Auditore's Will, 249 N. Y. 335, 164 N. E. 242.

The mere fact that the estate may own some of the stock does not justify a trespass into a field beyond our jurisdiction. General authority in the trustees has been found by me. Specific authority to make the particular contract or to approve its terms is lacking. The surrogate cannot examine, therefore, into the advisability of the terms of the proposed sale or give any judicial recognition to the consummation of the specific contracts of the corporation submitted here.

My determination that I have no jurisdiction to approve the particular corporate contracts, or their specific terms, or the manner of the sale, is not to be construed to indicate either approval or disapproval of the specific terms of the transaction. The responsibility of consummation rests squarely upon the officers and directors of the Press Publishing Company. They have the duty to weigh the advantages of the proposed sale or any other offers submitted to them. A separate responsibility rests upon them because of their separate status as trustees of this estate. They hold dual trust positions. Their duties as trustees of the estate and the measure of the loyalty to the beneficiaries, and particularly the infants, have been repeatedly stated in the authorities. Costello v. Costello, 209 N. Y. 252, 261, 103 N. E. 148, 152.

The three directors, in their separate capacity as trustees of this estate, are required to exercise their discretion, diligence, judgment, and prudence under the rules laid down for observance by trustees. They are 'bound, in the management of the matters of the trust, to act in good faith and employ such vigilance, sagacity, diligence, and prudence as in general prudent men of discretion and intelligence in like matters employ in their own affairs.' Costello v. Costello, *supra*.

The trustees should act in the exercise of the power and general authority found to be vested in them by the surrogate, in accordance with the legal obligations and standards of duty required of them as such trustees.

Submit decree on notice settling the account, construing the will, and containing appropriate provisions in accordance with the foregoing conclusions. The decree may contain a provision reserving for determination by supplemental decree the question of the construction of subdivision 6 of article VI of the codicil of March 23, 1909, or any subsequent modification thereof. The disposition of that question is not directly involved in the issues determined by this decision.

Notes

As we will discuss *infra*, modern trustees may be able to employ means other than equity to modify unambiguous mandates created by a settlor. For example, the trustee may be able to decant, which is

> the act of distributing the assets of an old trust to a new one with more desirable terms. It provides an easy method for correcting errors or ambiguities, adapting a trust to changes in a settlor's objectives or changes in a

beneficiary's circumstances, taking advantage of new planning opportunities or adding flexibility to a trust.

Peter J. Melcher, Robert S. Keebler & Steven J. Oshins, *A Guide to Trust Decanting*, 154 Trusts & Ests. 15 (May 2015) (citing judicial examples of Phipps v. Palm Beach Trust Co., 196 So. 299 (Fla. 1940) (holding trustee with power to distribute principal to beneficiaries has common law power to create another trust), and statutory approaches, *see, e.g.*, Del. Code Ann., tit. 12, §3528; Va. Code Ann. §64.2-778.1). Today, more than half of all states have decanting statutes. New York was the first state to adopt a decanting statute in 1992. *See* Stewart E. Sterk, *Trust Decanting: A Critical Perspective*, 38 Cardozo L. Rev. 1993 (2017). In 2015, the National Conference of Commissioners on Uniform State Laws promulgated the Uniform Trust Decanting Act, which borrows from existing state statutes but contains some innovations. Decanting will be discussed, *infra*.

B. Trustees

1. Private and Corporate Trustees

Uniform Trust Code (2019)

§801. Duty to Administer Trust.

Upon acceptance of a trusteeship, the trustee shall administer the trust in good faith, in accordance with its terms and purposes and the interests of the beneficiaries, and in accordance with this [Code].

§806. Trustee's Skills.

A trustee who has special skills or expertise, or is named trustee in reliance upon the trustee's representation that the trustee has special skills or expertise, shall use those special skills or expertise.

§815. General Powers of Trustee.

(a) A trustee, without authorization by the court, may exercise:

   (1) powers conferred by the terms of the trust; and

   (2) except as limited by the terms of the trust:

      (A) all powers over the trust property which an unmarried competent owner has over individually owned property;

      (B) any other powers appropriate to achieve the proper investment, management, and distribution of the trust property; and

      (C) any other powers conferred by this [Code].

(b) The exercise of a power is subject to the fiduciary duties prescribed by this [article].

§1006. Reliance on Trust Instrument.

A trustee who acts in reasonable reliance on the terms of the trust as expressed in the trust instrument is not liable to a beneficiary for a breach of trust to the extent the breach resulted from the reliance.

§ 1013. Certification of Trust.

(a) Instead of furnishing a copy of the trust instrument to a person other than a beneficiary, the trustee may furnish to the person a certification of trust containing the following information:

> (1) that the trust exists and the date the trust instrument was executed;

> (2) the identity of the settlor;

> (3) the identity and address of the currently acting trustee;

> (4) the powers of the trustee;

> (5) the revocability or irrevocability of the trust and the identity of any person holding a power to revoke the trust;

> (6) the authority of cotrustees to sign or otherwise authenticate and whether all or less than all are required in order to exercise powers of the trustee;

> (7) the trust's taxpayer identification number;

> (8) the manner of taking title to trust property.

§ 708. Compensation of Trustee.

(a) If the terms of the trust do not specify the trustee's compensation, a trustee is entitled to compensation that is reasonable under the circumstances.

(b) If the terms of a trust specify the trustee's compensation, the trustee is entitled to be compensated as specified, but the court may allow more or less compensation if:

> (1) the duties of the trustee are substantially different from those contemplated when the trust was created; or

> (2) the compensation specified by the terms of the trust would be unreasonably low or high.

§ 705. Resignation of Trustee.

(a) A trustee may resign:

> (1) upon at least 30 days' notice to the qualified beneficiaries, the settlor, if living, and all cotrustees; or

> (2) with the approval of the court.

(b) In approving a resignation, the court may issue orders and impose conditions reasonably necessary for the protection of the trust property.

(c) Any liability of a resigning trustee or of any sureties on the trustee's bond for acts or omissions of the trustee is not discharged or affected by the trustee's resignation.

Notes

A trustee may be a private individual, a group of individuals, or, as is often the case, a private corporate body, such as the United States Trust Company. In all cases, the trustee is the one who holds legal title to the trust property once it has been transferred by the settlor. The beneficiaries hold equitable title, allowing for them to enforce their interests upon the trustee. To qualify as a trustee, the state may require posting a bond or a formal appointment by the court. The corporation may also have requirements under its corporate charter before commencing duties as a corporate trustee, and in all cases, there may be prohibitions for some. For example, the federal Employee Retirement Income Security Act of 1974 (ERISA) prohibits any person from serving as a fiduciary if the person has been convicted of a crime involving moral turpitude. *See* 29 U.S.C. § 1111 (2015).

Unless the settlor specifies otherwise, no trust will fail for want of a trustee; the court is able to appoint another should no trustee qualify. But once nominated, accepted, and appointed as trustee, the trustee may resign only under the terms of the trust instrument or with the approval of the court. More than likely, the reasons given for the trustee's resignation must include a good faith explanation involving a poor relationship with the beneficiaries or personal family necessities. In some cases, the trustee may also be the settlor of the trust, and this invites an added consideration — merger. Each trust must have a separation of legal and equitable interests. Thus, if the settlor, the trustee, and the beneficiary are all the same person, then the trust has been terminated, and the trustee's duties are at an end. If, however, there are multiple persons, all of whom are settlors, trustees, and beneficiaries, then the trust is still viable, as there is more than one person, and one may enforce duties against the other. *See, e.g.,* First Alabama Bank v. Webb, 373 So. 2d 631 (Ala. 1979).

Charles A. Redd
The Most Disrespected Decision in Estate Planning
153 Trusts & Ests. 13 (July 2014)

[The author considers the following to be appropriate characteristics of a trustee: (1) Does the individual under consideration as trustee possess sufficient expertise and the necessary experience to do the job? (2) Is the proposed trustee independent, or does the proposed trustee have an inherent conflict of interest? (3) Does the trustee have an appropriate fiduciary demeanor? (4) Will the trustee being considered be around long enough to see the job done? (5) Where is the proposed trustee located? (6) Will the trustee expect to be paid? And (7) Is the trustee accountable?]

Lawrence M. Friedman
The Dynastic Trust
73 Yale L.J. 547 (1964)

Trust companies, in rudimentary forms, were known before the Civil War, but their great growth took place toward the end of the century. Outside of Boston, the trust company played the role of the Boston trustee — it provided a rational, institutional base for legal and business experience in drafting, forming, managing and perpetuating long-term trusts.... Ultimately, too, the trust companies provided for the first time a strong interest group which could exert pressure on legislatures for general liberalization of trust investment rules. . . . Caretaker trusts were more likely to be silent or ambiguous on the investment power; for these trusts, the existing rules were perhaps tolerable. Moreover, the early trust business of corporate fiduciaries was not strictly comparable to modern trust management. Trust funds were simply deposited with the companies; the company guaranteed a fixed return, much like a savings bank or an insurance company handling the proceeds of a policy under a settlement option. . . . Investment policy, therefore, meant general bank investment policy—the same policy applicable to savings deposits and the bank's own capital.

Id. at 564–65.

John H. Langbein
The Uniform Prudent Investor Act and the Future of Trust Investing
81 Iowa L. Rev. 641 (1996)

Why have the professional investment managers performed so poorly? Modern Portfolio Theory supplies a crisp answer to that question. In a nutshell, the insight is that the professional portfolio managers are *not* incompetent bunglers, indeed, just the opposite. They are so good at what they do that they effectively cancel each other out.

Id. at 657.

To outperform the market—that is, consistently to identify undervalued or overvalued securities in advance of other investors—an investor must predict future earnings with superior speed and accuracy. . . . New information about individual companies is disseminated rapidly as a result of modern communications systems. The securities laws have largely choked off inside information as a source of advantage in trading. Economic developments, technological innovation, foreign affairs, political events, social changes—all profoundly affect the prices of securities, yet these phenomena are notoriously difficult to foresee.

Id.

Trusteeship entails three relatively distinct functions: investment, administration, and distribution. *Investment* includes not only the initial selection of securities or other assets, but also the tasks of monitoring the investments for continuing suitability, investing new funds, and voting the shares. *Administration* includes the range of accounting, reporting, and tax filing. The responsibility for taking custody of securities is another branch of trust administration. Unusual trust assets may require other administrative work—maintaining and leasing real estate, insuring and safekeeping the Picasso and the diamond tiara, and so forth. *Distribution* is sometimes mechanical, but trust instruments often bestow upon the trustee the discretion to spray, sprinkle, invade, accumulate, terminate, and so forth. Distribution, therefore, requires interpreting and applying the sometimes complex language of the trust instrument; and it commonly involves contact with the current beneficiaries, in order to keep abreast of their needs and circumstances.

Id. at 665.

John H. Langbein
The Contractarian Basis of the Law of Trusts
105 Yale L.J. 625 (1995)

Private trustees still abound, but the prototypical modern trustee is the fee-paid professional, whose business is to enter into and carry out trust agreements. These entities thrive on their expertise in investment management, trust accounting, taxation, regulation, and fiduciary administration. In the United States . . . these institutional trustees are commonly corporate fiduciaries, . . . that is, profit-seeking enterprises, often listed on the New York Stock Exchange and called something like the Wells Fargo Bank or the Northen Trust Company.

Id. at 638–39.

Another indication that professional conduct in important trust functions has become the benchmark of American trust law is the growing pressure on amateur trustees to yield to professionals. The *Restatement (Third) of Trusts: Prudent Investor Rule* reverses the old rule that forbade trustees to delegate important trust functions. It imposes a duty on trustees to assess their own competence, in order to decide "whether, to whom and in what manner to delegate fiduciary authority in the administration of a trust." . . . The Uniform Prudent Investor Act of 1994 strongly accords. . . .

Id. at 640.

2. Directed Trusts: Trust Protectors

Uniform Trust Code (2019)

§ 808. Powers to Direct.

* * *

(b) If the terms of a trust confer upon a person other than the settlor of a revocable trust power to direct certain actions of the trustee, the trustee shall act in accordance with an exercise of the power unless the attempted exercise is manifestly contrary to the terms of the trust or the trustee knows the attempted exercise would constitute a serious breach of a fiduciary duty that the person holding the power owes to the beneficiaries of the trust.

* * *

(d) A person, other than a beneficiary, who holds a power to direct is presumptively a fiduciary who, as such, is required to act in good faith with regard to the purposes of the trust and the interests of the beneficiaries. The holder of a power to direct is liable for any loss that results from breach of a fiduciary duty.

Minassian v. Rachins

District Court of Appeal of Florida, Fourth District, 2014
152 So. 3d 719

WARNER, J.

In the midst of litigation in which the trustee of a family trust was being sued for accountings and breach of fiduciary duty, the trustee appointed a "trust protector," as allowed by the terms of the trust, to modify the trust's provisions. These modifications were unfavorable to the litigation position of the beneficiaries, and they filed a supplemental complaint to declare the trust protector's modifications invalid. The trial court found that, because the trust was unambiguous, the trust protector had no authority to change the terms of the trust. We conclude, however, that the trust provisions were ambiguous, that the settlor allowed for the trust protector to act to effectuate his intent, and that the amendment was not invalid. We therefore reverse.[1]

Zaven Minassian ("husband") executed a statement of trust in 1999 and executed a re-statement of trust in 2008. The restatement created a revocable trust, which became irrevocable upon his death. He named himself and his wife as the sole trustees. After his death in 2010, his children filed a complaint against his wife alleging that she was improperly administering the trust. They claimed she had breached her fiduciary duties, sought a surcharge against her, and demanded an accounting of the trust. . . .

The husband established the trust for the primary purpose of taking care of himself and his wife. Both he and his wife remained trustees of the trust during the life of the husband, the settlor. Article 8 of the restatement of trust provides that, if the wife survived the husband, the trustee should divide the trust property into two separate trusts: the Marital Trust and the Family Trust. However, if the federal estate tax was not in effect at the time of the husband's death, the trust directed creation of only the Family Trust. The parties agree the latter circumstance occurred, and only the Family Trust was created.

Article 10, which created the Family Trust, empowers the trustee to distribute net income and principal of the Family Trust to the wife "as my Trustee, in its sole and absolute discretion, shall consider advisable for my spouse's health, education, and maintenance." The trustee is directed to "be mindful that my primary concern

---

1. We conclude that we have jurisdiction pursuant to Florida Rule of Appellate Procedure 9.110(k), as the issue regarding the amendment of the trust by the trust protector is separate from the initial issues in the case and arose after the filing of the original complaint. This is the only issue for which this court has jurisdiction at this time.

and objective is to provide for the health, education, and maintenance of my spouse, and that the preservation of principal is not as important as the accomplishment of these objectives." One of the provisions regarding investments empowers the trustee to purchase life insurance on the wife's life "as an investment for the Family Trust." . . . Article 10 also provides that "The Family Trust shall *terminate* at the death of my spouse. The remainder of the Family Trust, including any accrued and undistributed net income, shall be administered as provided in the Articles that follow." (Emphasis added). Article 11, which immediately follows, provides:

> *It is not my desire to create a Common Trust for the benefit of my beneficiaries.* Upon the death of my spouse, or if my spouse predeceases me, all of the trust property which has not been distributed under prior provisions of this agreement shall be divided, administered, and distributed under the provisions of the Articles that follow.

The provisions for administration after the death of the settlor's wife are contained in Article 12, which is entitled "The Distribution of My Trust Property." Section 1 is entitled, "Creation of Separate Shares," and provides: "All trust property not previously distributed under the terms of my trust shall be divided into a separate *trust share* for each of" the children. (Emphasis added). It directs the trustee to "create a *trust share* for each beneficiary. . . ." (Emphasis added). Article 15 names "Comerica Bank and Trust, National Association" as "Trustee for any trust share created under Article Twelve . . . or any other trust share created after the deaths of both me and my spouse. . . ." . . .

The wife moved to dismiss the children's complaint against her, arguing they lacked standing because they were not beneficiaries of the trust. She pointed to the trust provisions in Articles 10–12, indicating that the Family Trust would terminate upon her death, and thus argued the children could not be beneficiaries of this trust. Instead, she argued, new trusts were to be created upon her death, of which the children would be the beneficiaries. The children claimed they had standing because the trust provisions did not create a new trust, but instead created separate shares in the existing Family Trust for each child upon the wife's death. . . . After reviewing the trust, the court denied the motion to dismiss, finding that Article 12's use of the word "shares," to describe the interest the children would receive after the death of the wife, prevented the court from concluding that new trusts were created. The court found "the wording simply [was not] clear" and decided it "would be inappropriate on the standing grounds to deny a forum for [the children] to seek relief."

After the trial court denied the motion, the wife appointed a "trust protector" pursuant to Article 16, Section 18 of the trust. This section authorizes the wife, after the husband's death, to appoint a trust protector "to protect . . . the interests of the beneficiaries as the Trust Protector deems, in its sole and absolute discretion, to be in accordance with my intentions. . . ." The trust protector is empowered to modify or amend the trust provisions to, *inter alia*: (1) "correct ambiguities that might otherwise require court construction"; or (2) "correct a drafting error that defeats my intent, as determined by the Trust Protector in its sole and absolute discretion, following the guidelines provided in this Agreement[.]" The trust protector can act without court authorization under certain circumstances. The trust directs the trust protector, prior to amending the trust, to "determine my intent and consider the interests of current and future beneficiaries as a whole," and to amend "only if the amendment will either benefit the beneficiaries as a group (even though particular beneficiaries may thereby be disadvantaged), or further my probable wishes in an appropriate way." The trust provided that "any exercise . . . of the powers and discretions granted to the Trust Protector shall be in the sole and absolute discretion of the Trust Protector, and shall be binding and conclusive on all persons."

The wife filed an affidavit from her appointed trust protector stating he had "amend[ed], clarif[ied], and correct[ed] ambiguities to the Trust" to effectuate the settlor's intent. He purported to amend Article 12 to clarify that it was meant to create a new trust after the wife's death, and grant the children shares in the new trust. The new Article 12 was entitled, "The Distribution of the Remaining, if any, Trust Property Upon the Death of [the Wife]," and Section 1 was entitled, "Creation of a Trust With Separate Shares." The new Section 1 provided, "Upon the death of [the wife] and the termination of the Family Trust as provided in Article Ten, Section 7, if there is any property remaining, it shall be disbursed to a *new* trust to be created upon the death of [the wife] with a separate share for each of" the children. (Emphasis added). . . . The children filed a supplemental complaint challenging the validity of the provisions amended by the trust protector. Both parties then moved for summary judgment as to the validity of the trust protector amendments.

The court entered an order granting the children's motion for partial summary judgment and denying the wife's motion. The court found the trust protector's amendment was improper because it did not benefit the beneficiaries as a group or further the settlor's probable wishes, as required under the trust. The court found the amendment did not benefit all the beneficiaries because it would leave the children without the ability to challenge the actions of the wife as trustee, leaving her "to do as she wishes without having to annually account to the children. . . ." The court found the trust protector's amendment also did not further the settlor's probable wishes in an appropriate way because the settlor "clearly intended to provide for his children from the Family Trust at the time of his wife's death[.] The children were to share in whatever remained." . . . The court did not rely on the testimony of the trust protector in determining the husband's intent, instead finding that, "by examining the four corners of the document, and also examining the plain language he used, the meaning of the document is clear." The court relied on the original Article 12's reference to "trust shares." The court also noted that, in the provisions regarding the trust protector, the trust restatement referred to "my spouse and beneficiaries." The court found this indicated "the entire trust was intended not only to benefit his wife, but also his children," because it "shows that when he speaks of his 'beneficiaries' he is referring to individuals other than his wife."

The court relied on several provisions it saw as establishing "[t]he continuity of the trust beyond the life or remarriage of the wife[.]" It cited the trustee's authority to purchase life insurance on the settlor's wife "as an investment for the Family Trust," reasoning, "[t]here would be no need for such an investment if the Family Trust ceased to exist upon the wife's death." The court rejected the literal language of Article 10, Section 7—which provides the Family Trust terminates on the death of the wife and the remainder shall be administered as provided in the articles following Article 10—because "there would be no 'remainder' if the trust actually terminated, and the '[a]rticles that follow' create 'separate trust shares' not trusts." . . . As further proof that Article 12 did not create a new trust for the children upon the wife's death, the court relied on Article 12, Section 2, which noted that the trust shares of the husband's children, if passed down by inheritance, would be "administered as a separate trust[.]" The court reasoned that this "shows [the husband] knew how to create new trusts, and only does so after his children die[.]" The court concluded, "If the Trust Protector wished to amend a drafting error to effectuate the settlor's intent or benefit all the beneficiaries, he should have amended Article 10, Section 7, which speaks of termination of the trust[.]" . . . The court entered partial summary judgment for the children, invalidating the amended provisions, and the wife timely appealed. . . .

We first address the validity of the trust protector provision in the trust, because if it is invalid under Florida law, then any amendments created by the trust protector would likewise be invalid. On the other hand, if those provisions are valid, then the trust provides that the trust protector can exercise his powers in his sole and absolute discretion, and his actions are binding and conclusive on all persons.

The Florida Trust Code provides: "The terms of a trust may confer on a trustee *or other person a power to direct the modification or termination of the trust.*" § 736.0808(3), Fla. Stat. (2008) (emphasis added). This section was adopted from the Uniform Trust Code, which contains identical language in section 808(c). See Unif. Trust Code § 808 (2000). The commentary to this section states:

> Subsections (b)–(d) ratify the use of *trust protectors* and advisers. . . . Subsection (c) is similar to Restatement (Third) of Trusts Section 64(2) (Tentative Draft No. 3, approved 2001). . . . "Trust protector," a term largely associated with offshore trust practice, is more recent and usually connotes the grant of greater powers, sometimes including the power to amend or terminate the trust. Subsection (c) [as enacted in section 736.0808(3), Florida Statutes] ratifies the recent trend to grant third persons such broader powers. . . .

> The provisions of this section may be altered in the terms of the trust. *See* Section 105. A settlor can provide that the trustee must accept the decision of the power holder without question. Or a settler could provide that the holder of the power is not to be held to the standards of a fiduciary. . . .

Id. at Editors' Notes (emphasis supplied). *See generally* Peter B. Tiernan, *Evaluate and Draft Helpful Trust Protector Provisions*, 38 Estate Planning 24 (July 2011).

The children make two arguments as to the inapplicability of section 736.0808(3). First, they contend that this provision conflicts with "the black letter common law rule . . . that a trustee may not delegate discretionary powers to another." Second, they argue that sections 736.0410–736.04115 and 736.0412, Florida Statutes, provide the exclusive means of modifying a trust under the Florida Trust Code. We reject both arguments. . . . As to the conflict with the common law, which precludes non-delegation of a trustee's discretionary powers, this argument fails for two reasons. First, it is not the trustee that is delegating a duty in this case, but the settlor of the trust, who delegates his power to modify to a third person for specific reasons. Second, "The common law of trusts and principles of equity supplement [the Florida Trust Code], *except to the extent modified by this code* or another law of this state." §736.0106, Fla. Stat. (2008) (emphasis added); *see also* Abraham Mora, et al., 12 Fla. Prac., Estate Planning §6:1 (2013–14 ed.) ("The common law of trusts supplements the Florida Trust Code unless it contradicts the Florida Trust Code or any other Florida law."). Thus, section 736.0808, Florida Statutes, supplements common law, and to the extent the common law conflicts with it, it overrides common law principles. . . . Sections 736.0410–736.04115 and 736.0412, Florida Statutes, provide means of modifying a trust under the Florida Trust Code. The children argue the terms of the trust cannot prevail over these provisions, so as to add a method of modification via trust protector, because section 736.0105 provides, "The terms of a trust prevail over any provision of this code except . . . [t]he ability to modify a trust under s. 736.0412, except as provided in s. 736.0412(4)(b)." §736.0105(2)(k), Fla. Stat. (2008). Yet section 736.0808(3), Florida Statutes, expressly allows a trust to confer the power to direct modification of the trust on persons other than trustees. "[A] court must consider the plain language of the statute, give effect to all statutory provisions, and construe related provisions in harmony with one another." *Hechtman v. Nations Title Ins. of New York*, 840 So.2d 993, 996 (Fla.2003). These provisions of Chapter 736 can be harmonized by concluding that the sections on modifying trusts do not provide the exclusive means to do so, at least insofar as a trust document grants a trust protector the power to do so. Otherwise, section 736.0808(3) would have no effect. Therefore, we conclude that the Florida Statutes do permit the appointment of a trust protector to modify the terms of the trust.

The trial court found that the trust protector acted outside his powers, because he amended a trust instrument that the trial court found to be unambiguous. Thus, the trial court concluded, the trust protector's amendment was contrary to the husband's intent, as expressed in the unambiguous trust document. We, however, conclude that the instrument was indeed ambiguous. . . .

The provisions of the trust at issue here are conflicting. Article 10 provides that on the death of the trustee, the trust shall terminate. Article 11 states that it is not the intent of the settlor to create a common trust for his wife and other beneficiaries. However, Article 12 then directs that upon the death of the wife the trust assets shall be distributed into separate trust "shares" for the beneficiaries. The term "share" makes these trust provisions ambiguous, as it is unclear whether the term share constitutes a new trust. . . . Other provisions in the trust document support the interpretation, contrary to the trial court's one-trust interpretation, that the husband intended to create separate trusts for the wife and children. Article 11 contains his specific admonition that he did not intend to create a common trust. In the trust protector provisions, the document several times refers to the creation of multiple trusts: a trust protector "may be appointed for *any* trust created in this agreement"; "*All trusts* created under this instrument need not have or continue to have the same Trust Protector"; and "the Trust Protector may, with respect to *any* trust as to which the Trust Protector is acting. . . ." (Emphasis added). Article 15 of the trust also includes provisions for appointing a trustee for "My Beneficiaries' Separate Trusts," i.e., "any trust share created under Article Twelve . . . or any other trust share created after the deaths of both me and my spouse. . . ." Article 15, Section 3(f) provides that a beneficiary who attains the age of 35 shall serve as the trustee of his or her respective trust share. These are but some of the provisions which refer to both trusts and trust shares, even though the overall structure of the trust contemplates something separate and apart from the Family Trust.

Moreover, the provisions relied upon by the trial court in determining that there was only one trust (the Family Trust) do not unambiguously support its conclusion. First, the court believed that the reference to multiple " 'beneficiaries' in the plural" showed that the Family Trust was to benefit the children, but that language is also consistent with the existence of multiple trusts. . . . Second, the court pointed to Article 10, Section 7 — that the wife shall not receive any benefits from the trust should she remarry, but could again receive benefits under the Family Trust if her re-marriage ends — as indicating the continuity of the trust beyond the life or remarriage of the wife. This, however, does not defeat the argument that the Family Trust terminates on her death, because Article 10, Section 7 covers only her remarriage. Thus, the family trust would continue until her death, but the wife could not draw from it after remarriage. This is not at all inconsistent with termination at the death of the wife. . . . Third, while the court thought that the ability to purchase life insurance on the wife showed that only one trust was intended, that provision was simply an investment provision and the trustee could not use trust income for such purchase. The trustee might wish to purchase life insurance on the settlor's wife as an investment for the Family Trust or to pay last expenses for the wife, even if the Family Trust terminates on her death, because the remaining property in the trust will be used to fund the children's trusts. . . .

In sum, the single-trust interpretation reached by the trial court does not appear to be unambiguously supported by the trust document. We therefore reject the trial court's conclusion that the trust is unambiguous. In fact, we find that it is patently ambiguous on the issue of whether a new trust is created, where the language in the trust instrument dictates that the Family Trust terminates on the death of the wife. . . . Although the trial court did not consider it, there was uncontradicted evidence in the record as to the husband's intent, including an affidavit and deposition from the trust protector, who was the original drafter of the trust instrument. "Where as here . . . there is a patent ambiguity as to the testator's intent, the court below was free to consider extrinsic evidence on the subject." *First Union Nat'l Bank of Fla., N.A. v. Frumkin*, 659 So.2d 463, 464 (Fla. 3d DCA 1995). . . . The trust protector testified in a deposition that he met with the husband twice, first in person to discuss his estate planning desires, and second over the phone to discuss and execute the documents he had drafted. During the husband's life, the husband and wife's "lives revolved around horse racing and legal gambling," and, in the trust, the husband wanted "to provide for [the wife] in the way they had lived in the past. . . ." The plan was "to create a separate Trust for the benefit of his children" which "would be created only if the Family Trust described in Article 10 . . . was not exhausted during [the wife's] lifetime[.]" The purpose of Article 10, Section 7 and Article 11 was "to assure that the Family Trust was not in any way associated to a new Trust that might be created for his children." The trust protector also stated, "This challenge by the children is exactly what [the husband] expected." The trust protector noted that the husband referred to his daughter in derogatory terms, and that the daughter had not seen her father in years. . . . From the trust protector's affidavit, it appears that the husband settled on the multiple-trust scheme for the very purpose of preventing the children from challenging the manner in which the wife spent the money in the Family Trust during her lifetime. The trust protector also testified that his law firm always recommends this split-trust approach, rather than what he referred to as a "pot trust . . . where everything goes into the pot for the beneficiaries." He testified, "We have never done it the other way you're talking about, about keeping the same trust." On that basis, he prepared the amendments to the trust to reflect this intent of the testator.

Based upon our conclusion that the trust agreement was ambiguous and the trust protector's amendments were made to effectuate the settlor's intent, the amendments that he made to the trust are within his powers. The amendments may have disadvantaged the children, but the trust protector was authorized the correct ambiguities with the limitation that he act either to benefit a group of beneficiaries or to further the husband's probable wishes. He acted to correct ambiguities in a way to further the husband's probable wishes. As the drafting agent, he was privy to what the husband intended. . . . It was the settlor's intent that, where his trust was ambiguous or imperfectly drafted, the use of a trust protector would be his preferred method of resolving those issues. Removing that authority from the trust protector and assigning it to a court violates the intent of the settlor.

We therefore reverse the partial final judgment of the trial court and remand with directions that the trust protector's amendments are valid. We reject all other arguments made by the children against the validity of these provisions, although not ruling on any matters beyond that issue.

CONNER and KLINGENSMITH, JJ., concur.

Notes

The leading decision on directed trusts and trust protectors remains Shelton v. Tamposi, 62 A.3d 741 (N.H. 2013). *See* Michael Kendall & Victoria Thavaseelan,

Divided Duties, 152 TRUSTS & ESTS. 30 (Mar. 2013) (discussing the legal implications of the *Shelton* decision—a pivotal case illustrating decanting). In the *Minassian* decision, the court describes the role of the trust protector and relies upon the provision in Florida law based on Section 808 of the Uniform Trust Code. Discussion of the role of the trust protector continues. *See, e.g.*, Alan Newman, *Trust Law in the Twenty-Frist Century: Challenges to Fiduciary Accountability*, 29 QUINNIPIAC PROB. L.J. 261 (2016); Lawrence A. Frolik, *Trust Protectors: Why They Have Become "The Next Big Thing,"* 50 REAL PROP. TRUSTS & ESTS. L.J. 267 (2015); Alexander A. Bove, Jr., *Should a Special Needs or Medicaid Trust Have a Protector?*, 153 TRUSTS & ESTS. 23 (Nov. 2014); Michael L. Van Cise & Kathryn Baldwin Hecker, *Removal and Replacement of Trustees*, 152 TRUSTS & ESTS. 24 (Dec. 2013); Alexander A. Bove, Jr., *Exposing the Trust Protector*, 151 TRUSTS & ESTS. 48 (May 2012).

In 2017, the National Conference of Commissioners on Uniform State Laws promulgated the Uniform Directed Trust Act (UDTA) in an effort to address complications arising when a "directed trustee" works in tandem with a "trust director." Specifically, the Act provides that a *trust director* has the same default and mandatory fiduciary duties as a trustee in a like position and under similar circumstances. *See* UDTA § 8. As a result, a trust beneficiary now has recourse for misconduct by a trust director for any breach of the director's fiduciary duty to the beneficiary. The beneficiary also has recourse against the directed trustee, but only to the extent of the trustee's willful misconduct. *See id.* at *Pref. Note.* The Act seeks to absorb the fiduciary law of each enacting state, including a trustee's default and mandatory fiduciary duties, such as the duty to diversify and provide information to the beneficiaries. *See id.* at § 8, cmt.

Charles E. Rounds, Jr.
The Uniform Directed Trust Act
156 TRUSTS & ESTS. 24 (Dec. 2017)

The public policy that the UDTA would implement is that a trust director should be a fiduciary with an affirmative duty to act. A breach of the trust director's fiduciary duty should be a breach of trust. A beneficiary's primary recourse for misconduct by a trust director should be an action against the director for breach of the director's fiduciary duty to the beneficiary. The directed trustee incurs secondary liability only to the extent of his own willful misconduct.

Id. at 25-26.

Alexander A. Bove, Jr.
Selecting a Trust Protector
152 TRUSTS & ESTS. 13 (Feb. 2013)

There is no question of the value of a protector, when one is needed. For instance, many of us are aware of the substantial expense, time and publicity associated with a petition for reformation of a trust or removal of a trustee when a drafting error surfaces, circumstances change or the beneficiaries simply want a different trustee. If instead, a protector had the power to amend the trust or remove and replace the trustee, the matter becomes incredibly simple and straightforward, except in unusual cases. The role of the protector can be vital to a trust and, therefore, the selection of the protector is equally vital.

C. Beneficiaries

Trusts may have as beneficiaries three categories—private, charitable, and honorary. These categories most often define the scope of the trust and any particular responsibilities. (1) Private beneficiaries are the most common beneficiaries, including family members and friends. (2) Charitable beneficiaries are defined as such through state and federal statutes, as well as common law usage, based mostly on purposes associated with the Statute of Charitable Uses, 43 Eliz. I, c.4 (1601). (3) Honorary beneficiaries may include those beneficiaries similar to both private and charitable enterprise, such as pets and human cemeteries. If the beneficiaries of a trust qualify as charitable, there will be immunity from any Rule Against Perpetuities restraint, and additional tax benefits will likely result. Trusts involving pets invoke deep emotions, but often run afoul of the Rule Against Perpetuities and surviving relatives. The Uniform Trust Code seeks to make some delineation among the three categories.

1. Private Trusts
Uniform Trust Code (2019)
§ 103. Definitions.* * *

(3) "Beneficiary" means a person that:

(A) has a present or future beneficial interest in a trust, vested or contingent; or

(B) in a capacity other than a trustee, holds a power of appointment over trust property.

Clark v. Campbell

Supreme Court of New Hampshire, 1926
82 N.H. 281, 133 A. 166

SNOW, J.

The ninth clause of the will of deceased reads:

My estate will comprise so many and such a variety of articles of personal property such as books, photographic albums, pictures, statuary, bronzes, bric-a-brac, hunting and fishing equipment, antiques, rugs, scrap books, canes and masonic jewels, that probably I shall not distribute all, and perhaps no great part thereof during my life by gift among my friends. Each of my trustees is competent by reason of familiarity with the property, my wishes and friendships, to wisely distribute some portion at least of said property. I therefore give and bequeath to my trustees all my property embraced within the classification aforesaid in trust to make disposal by the way of a memento from myself, of such articles to such of my friends as they, my trustees, shall select. All of said property, not so disposed of by them, my trustees are directed to sell and the proceeds of such sale or sales to become and be disposed of as a part of the residue of my estate.

The question here reserved is whether or not the enumeration of chattels in this clause was intended to be restrictive or merely indicative of the variety of the personal property bequeathed. The question is immaterial, if the bequest for the benefit of the testator's "friends" must fail for the want of certainty of the beneficiaries.

By the common law there cannot be a valid bequest to an indefinite person. There must be a beneficiary or a class of beneficiaries indicated in the will capable of coming into court and claiming the benefit of the bequest. Adye v. Smith, 44 Conn. 60, 26 Am. Rep. 424, 425. This principle applies to private but not to public trusts and charities. Harrington v. Pier, 105 Wis. 485, 82 N. W. 345 . . . [citations omitted]. * * *

We must therefore conclude that this clause presents the case of an attempt to create a private trust, and clearly falls within the principle of well-considered authorities. Nichols v. Allen, 130 Mass. 211, 212, 39 Am. Rep. 445; Blunt v. Taylor, 119 N. E. 954, 230 Mass. 303, 305. In so far as the cases cited by the petitioners upon this phase of the case are not readily distinguishable from the case at bar, they are in conflict with the great weight of authority. The question presented, therefore, is whether or not the ninth clause provides for definite and ascertainable beneficiaries, so that the bequest therein can be sustained as a private trust.

In this state the identity of a beneficiary is a question of fact to be found from the language of the will, construed in the light of all the competent evidence rather than by the application of arbitrary rules of law. It is believed that in no other jurisdiction is there greater liberality shown in seeking the intention of the testator in this, as in other particulars. Trustees of South Newmarket Methodist Seminary v. Peaslee, 15 N. H. 317; Goodhue v. Clark, 37 N. H. 525, 532; Goodale v. Mooney, *supra*; Harriman v. Harriman, 59 N. H. 135; Galloway v. Babb, 77 N. H. 259, 260, 90 A. 968; Remick v. Merrill, 80 N. H. 225, 227, 116 A. 344; Adams v. Hospital, 132 A. 525, 81 N. H. ___. We find, however, no case in which our courts have sustained a gift where the testator has attempted to delegate to a trustee the arbitrary selection of the beneficiaries of his bounty through means of a private trust.

Like the direct legatees in a will, the beneficiaries under a trust may be designated by class. But in such case the class must be capable of delimitation, as "brothers and sisters," "children," "issue," "nephews and nieces." A bequest giving the executor authority to distribute his property "among his relatives and for benevolent objects in such sums as in their judgment shall be for the best" was sustained upon evidence within the will that by "relatives" the testator intended such of his relatives within the statute of distributions as were needy, and thus brought the bequest within the line of charitable gifts, and excluded all others as individuals. Goodale v. Mooney, 60 N. H. 528, 536, 49 Am. Rep. 334. See Portsmouth v. Shackford, 46 N. H. 423, 425; Gafney v. Kenison, 64 N. H. 354, 356, 10 A. 706. Where a testator bequeathed his stocks to be apportioned to his "relations" according to the discretion of the trustee, to be enjoyed by them after his decease, it was held to be a power to appoint amongst his relations who were next of kin under the statute of distribution. Varrell v. Wendell, 20 N. H. 431, 436. Likewise where a devise over after a particular estate was to the testator's "next of kin" simpliciter. Pinkham v. Blair, 57 N. H. 226, 243. See Snow v. Durgin, 70 N. H. 121, 122, 47 A. 89. Unless the will discloses a plain purpose to the contrary, the words "relatives" or "relations," to prevent gifts from being void for uncertainty, are commonly construed to mean those who would take under statutes of distribution or descent. 2 Schouler on Wills, § 1008; Thompson on Wills, 181; Thompson v. Thornton, 197 Mass. 273, 83 N. E. 880; Drew v. Wakefield, 54 Me. 291, 298.

In the case now under consideration the cestuis que trust are designated as the "friends" of the testator. The word "friends," unlike "relations," has no accepted statutory or other controlling limitations, and in fact has no precise sense at all. Friendship is a word of broad and varied application. It is commonly used to describe the undefinable relationships which exist, not only between those connected by ties of kinship or marriage, but as well between strangers in blood, and which vary in degree from the greatest intimacy to an acquaintance more or less casual. "Friend" is sometimes used in contradistinction to "enemy." "A friendless man is an outlaw." Cowell, Bouvier. Although the word was formerly sometimes used as synonymous with relatives (5 Com. Dig. 336; Sugden on Powers [1823] 519), there is no evidence that it was so used here. The inference is to the contrary. The testator in the will refers to eight different persons, some of them already deceased, by the title of "friends." He never uses the appellation concurrently with "nephew" or "niece," which words occur several times in describing legatees. Nor is there anything to indicate that the word "friends" in the ninth clause was intended to apply only to those who had been thus referred to in the will. See Hall v. Wiggin, 67 N. H. 89, 90, 29 A. 671. There is no express evidence that the word is used in any restricted sense. The only implied limitation of the class is that fixed by the boundaries of the familiarity of the testator's trustees with his friendships. If such familiarity could be held to constitute such a line of demarcation as to define an ascertainable group, it is to be noted that the gift is not to such group as a class, the members of which are to take in some definite proportion (1 Jarman on Wills, 534; 2 Schouler, § 1011), or according to their needs, but the disposition is to "such of my friends as they, my trustees may select." No sufficient criterion is furnished to govern the selection of the individuals from the class. The assertion of the testator's confidence in the competency of his trustees "to wisely distribute some portion" of the enumerated articles "by reason of familiarity with the property, my wishes and friendships" does not furnish such a criterion.

Where, after expressing confidence in the discretion of his executors and trustees, the testator gave the remainder of his estate to them "for certain purposes which I have made known to them," and authorized them to "make such distribution and division of my estate as I have indicated to them, and as they shall deem proper for the fulfillment of my wishes so well known to them," it was held that the trust created was not sufficiently definite for execution. Blunt v. Taylor, 230 Mass, 303, 305, 119 N. E. 954. A bequest to executors "particularly for the purpose of giving to any relatives of mine who without apparent reason I may have overlooked, such sum as may seem to them or him, under all the circumstances, fitting, suitable and proper," was held void for indefiniteness, notwithstanding the aid of the statute of distributions. Minot v. Parker, 189 Mass. 176, 75 N. E. 149. A limitation over, after the death of the testatrix's son without heirs, "to whoever has been his best friend," was held to be "too indefinite for any one to determine who was intended as the object of the testatrix's bounty." Early v. Arnold, 119 Va. 500, 89 S. E. 900. Where an executor was given direction to distribute in a manner calculated to carry out "wishes which I have expressed to him or may express to him," and such wishes had been orally communicated to the executor by the testator, the devise could not be given effect as against the next of kin. Olliffe v. Wells, 130 Mass. 221, 224, 225. Much less can effect be given to the uncommunicated wishes of the testator here.

* * *

Where a gift is impressed with a trust, ineffectively declared, and incapable of taking effect because of the indefiniteness of the cestui que trust, the donee will hold the property in trust for the next taker under the will, or for the next of kin by way of a resulting trust. Varrell v. Wendell, 20 N. H. 431, 438; Lyford v. Laconia, 75 N. H. 220, 223, 72 A. 1085, 22 L. R. A. (N. S.) 1062, 139 Am. St. Rep. 680; Sheedy v. Roach, 124 Mass. 472, 476, 26 Am. Rep. 680; Nichols v. Allen, 130 Mass. 211, 212, 39 Am. Rep. 445; Blunt v. Taylor, *supra*; Drew v. Wakefield, 54 Me. 291, 295. The trustees therefore hold title to the property enumerated in the paragraph under consideration to be disposed of as a part of the residue, and the trustees are so advised. This conclusion makes it unnecessary to answer the question reserved * * * .

* * *

Case discharged.

All concurred.

2. Charitable Trusts

Uniform Trust Code (2019)

§405. Charitable Purposes; Enforcement.

(a) A charitable trust may be created for the relief of poverty, the advancement of education or religion, the promotion of health, governmental or municipal purposes, or other purposes the achievement of which is beneficial to the community.

(b) If the terms of a charitable trust do not indicate a particular charitable purpose or beneficiary, the court may select one or more charitable purposes or beneficiaries. The selection must be consistent with a settlor's intention to the extent it can be ascertained.

(c) The settlor of a charitable trust, among others, may maintain a proceeding to enforce the trust.

§ 413. Cy Pres.

(a) Except as otherwise provided . . . if a particular charitable purpose becomes unlawful, impossible to achieve, or wasteful:

> (1) the trust does not fail, in whole or in part;

> (2) the trust property does not revert to the settlor or the settlor's successors in interest; and

> (3) the court may apply cy pres to modify or terminate the trust by directing that the trust property be applied or distributed, in whole of in part, in a manner consistent with the settlor's charitable purposes.

Register of Wills for Baltimore City v. Cook

Court of Appeals of Maryland, 1966
241 Md. 264, 216 A.2d 542

OPPENHEIMER, Judge.

* * *

Jessie Marjorie Cook died December 29, 1960, a resident of Baltimore City, and her will was probated in the Orphans' Court of Baltimore City. The provisions involved read as follows:

> 'TWENTY-SECOND: I give and bequeath unto Helen Elizabeth Brown and Rose S. Zetzer, attorneys at law, the sum of $10,000.00 to be held in Trust for the following purposes: to pay unto the Maryland Branch of the National Woman's Party, One Hundred ($100.) Dollars per year for a period of ten years, if said organization remains in existence and is active for that length of time; the rest and residue of said bequest in trust shall be used to help further the passage of and enactment into law of the EQUAL RIGHTS AMENDMENT to the Constitution of the United States; the said Trustees or their successors, if any, shall have absolute control of said sum of money and use the same as in their joint judgment may seem best to carry out the purposes for which this bequest is intended.

> 'TWENTY-THIRD: I give and bequeath unto Helen Elizabeth Brown and Rose S. Zetzer, attorneys at law, in Trust and to their successors, in trust, the sum of $25,000.00 for the purpose of aiding and assisting any woman who may be in distress or suffer any injury to herself or her property as a result of any inequalities in the laws of the State of Maryland or of any of

the United States; said Trustees or their successors in trust shall have absolute control of said trust fund and shall use the same as in their best judgment jointly may be deemed advisable to carry out the purposes for which said bequest is intended and their decision shall be final.

'In the event, however, that said Trustees shall be unable to agree, each Trustee shall select one competent person who shall consider the matter and file their opinion. If these two arbitrators fail to agree, then these two shall mutually select a competent third person and the decision of any two of the three persons thus selected shall be conclusive and be accepted as final.

'TWENTY-EIGHTH: All the rest and residue of my estate, whether real, personal or mixed and wheresoever situate, which I now own, possess or to which I may be entitled to at the time of my death, or at any time thereafter, I give, devise and bequeath in Trust to my Trustees above named; viz: Helen Elizabeth Brown and Rose S. Zetzer, to be used to further the cause of equality for women in civil and economic rights and to carry on the work for women in accordance with the objectives as outlined in paragraphs Nos. 'Twenty-second' and 'Twenty-third' herein.'

* * *

In the hearing before the Maryland Tax Court, the two trustees named in the will, Helen Elizabeth Brown and Rose S. Zetzer, both testified. In addition, various documents were offered in evidence. One exhibit was a statement of the purposes and functions of the Maryland Branch of the National Woman's Party, of which Miss Brown is a past president. The statement reads in part as follows:

'The Maryland Branch of the National Woman's Party has for its fundamental objective to secure for women complete equality under the law with respect to their property, personal, social economic and civil rights and privileges, and to that end to inform, detail and specify what rights and privileges women possess presently, and to what extent these rights and privileges are curtailed or limited. These rights and limitations of rights are brought to focus by way of public discussion and education. Furthermore, to accomplish these purposes, the National Woman's Party, Maryland Branch, whose membership consists of businesswomen, homemakers, lawyers, and civic minded women, arrange, through public meetings and discussion groups, to further the cause of equality of opportunity under the law for women in business, professions and public offices and encourage the enlightened representatives and leaders in our community to remove every vestige of discrimination which is rampant in many of our antiquated customs * * *.'

The testimony shows that the Maryland organization works for the passage of the Equal Rights Amendment, and to remove discriminations in the laws against women throughout the United States. It is a branch of the National Woman's Party, which is incorporated. At the time Miss Cook's will was probated, the Maryland Branch may not have been incorporated.

Another exhibit put into evidence was the report of the President's Commission on the Status of Women made in 1963. This report includes the following statements: 'Eight out of ten women are in paid employment outside of the home at some time during their lives * * *' 'In the face of these amendments, however [the Fifth and Fourteenth Amendments to the Federal Constitution] there remain, especially in certain State laws and official practices, distinctions based on sex which discriminate against women.' 'Lower pay rates for women doing the same work as men are not uncommon.' While in 1963 the Federal Fair Labor Standards Act of 1938 was amended to require equal pay for equal work, 'State laws should establish the principle of equal pay for comparable work.' 'In many specific areas of State law, the disabilities of married women are considerable.'

The testatrix was deeply interested in women's rights. Her trustees conceive their duties as 'educational primarily and charitable.' Miss Zetzer testified that a major legal 'discrimination' in Maryland is the wife's obligation to accept a suitable domicile selected by her husband. The trustees believe, however, that there is greater and more serious legal discrimination in other states. There was also testimony that, in Maryland, discriminations have been found in certain employment practices and that women still do not have equal pay for equal work. * * *

The case, in our view, involves two questions. First, is the general nature of the bequest charitable under the Maryland law?; and, second, if the first question is answered in the affirmative, are the trusts exclusively for charitable purposes, in view of the right of the trustees to employ the funds to support candidates for political office who favor women's rights, to contribute to the Maryland Branch of the National Woman's Party, and to work for the passage of the Equal Rights Amendment? Counsel agree that, if the trusts are not charitable, the bequests are taxable.

* * *

The bequest to the trustees in the Twenty-Second paragraph of the will is for two purposes: Payments to the Maryland Branch of the National Woman's Party and to help further the passage of the Equal Rights Amendment to the Constitution of the United States, which is designed to prohibit discrimination against women by reason of their sex. The bequest to the trustees in the Twenty-Third paragraph is for the purpose of aiding and assisting any woman who may be in distress or suffer any injury to herself or her property as a result of any inequalities in the laws of Maryland or of the United States. The residuary bequest to the trustees in the Twenty-Eighth paragraph is to further the cause of equality of women in civil and economic rights and to carry on the work for women in accordance with the objectives outlined in the Twenty-Second and Twenty-Third paragraphs.

The primary purposes of all the trusts, in our view, are the elimination of discriminations against women and to give relief to women injured by such discriminations. The passage of the Equal Rights Amendment is one of the methods set forth by the testatrix to endeavor to accomplish these objectives, both directly and by contributions to the Maryland Branch of the National Woman's Party.

Trusts to eliminate discriminations and to provide relief for the persons discriminated against have been generally upheld as charitable. Collier v. Lindley, 203 Cal. 641, 266 P. 526 (1928), and Edgeter v. Kemper, Ohio Prob., 136 N.E.2d 630 (1955) (trust to eliminate discriminations against Indians and to provide for their relief); Lewis's Estate, 152 Pa. 477, 25 A. 878 (1893) (trust to eliminate discrimination against Negroes); In re Murphey's Estate, 7 Cal.2d 712, 62 P.2d 374 (1936) (trust to eliminate discriminations against Jews).

> 'If the general purposes for which a trust is created are such as may be reasonably thought to promote the social interest of the community, the mere fact that a majority of the people and the members of the court believe that the particular purpose of the settlor is unwise or not adapted to the accomplishment of the general purposes, does not prevent the trust from being charitable * * *
>
> 'The Courts do not take sides or attempt to decide which of two conflicting views of promoting the social interest of the community is the better adapted to the purpose, even though the views are opposed to each other * * *' Restatement, Trusts 2d (1959) § 374 comment 1.

By the great weight of authority, if a trust is essentially charitable in nature, it is still charitable even though one of its purposes is to endeavor to effectuate a change of existing law. George v. Braddock, 45 N.J.Eq. 757, 18 A. 881, 6 L.R.A. 511 (1889); Garrison v. Little, 75 Ill.App. 402 (1897); Taylor v. Hoag, 273 Pa. 194, 116 A. 826, 21 A.L.R. 946 (1922); Collier v. Lindley, *supra*. See also Haines v. Allen, 78 Ind. 100 (1881).

Restatement, Trusts 2d (1959) § 374 comment j reads as follows:

> '*Change in existing law.* A trust may be charitable although the accomplishment of the purpose for which the trust is created involves a change in the existing law. If the purpose of the trust is to bring about changes in the law by illegal means, such as by revolution, bribery, illegal lobbying or bringing improper pressure to bear upon members of the legislature, the purpose is illegal. See § 377. The mere fact, however, that the purpose is to bring about a change in the law, whether indirectly through the education of the electors so as to bring about a public sentiment in favor of the change, or through proper influences brought to bear upon the legislators, does not prevent the purpose from being legal and charitable.'

Bogert and Scott take the same view.

> 'Many American decisions and, it is submitted, the better reasoned cases, declare that trusts which seek to bring about better government by changing laws or constitutional provisions are charitable, so long as the settlor

directed that the reforms should be accomplished peaceably, by the established constitutional means, and not by war, riot, or revolution.' Bogert, Trusts & Trustees (2d ed.1964); § 378, 'Changes in the Law.'

'In the United States the notion that a trust for a purpose otherwise charitable is not charitable if the accomplishment of its purposes involves a change in existing laws has been pretty thoroughly rejected. Many reforms can be accomplished only by a change in the law, and there seems to be no good reason why the mere fact that they can be accomplished only through legislation should prevent them from being valid charitable purposes.' 4 Scott, Trusts (2d ed.1956) § 374.4 at 2677.

* * *

The provisions of the testatrix's will make it evident to us that her primary objective was to provide funds for the elimination of discriminations against women and that support of the passage of the Equal Rights Amendment and other national or state legislation to this end was merely an incidental means to the accomplishment of the general purpose. All the provisions of the will look only to legal means to effectuate the objective. The bequests do not provide in any way for contributions to a political party as such. Whatever may be the views of individuals, laymen or judges, as to the need or desirability of the passage of the Equal Rights Amendment or similar legislation, our system of government is not opposed to attempts to secure legislative changes by legal means. Indeed, the channelling [sic] of efforts to effect social or political changes to the public discussions involved in proposed constitutional amendments or legislation, rather than by possible violence or subversion, is fundamental to our democracy.

Realistically, a charitable purpose such as that of the testatrix, can often only be effectuated by legislative change. Recognition of that fact by the testatrix does not alter what we have found to be the essentially charitable nature of the bequests here involved.

* * *

Even though the bequests are charitable in nature, the exemption clause of the statute provides in effect that they are taxable unless they are exclusively for religious, charitable or similar purposes. The National Woman's Party and its Maryland Branch are non-profit organizations. In the sense that the bequests here involved do not provide for or permit personal benefit of any private shareholder or individual, except members of the designated class of beneficiaries of the fund, they are exclusively for a charitable purpose. The question remains, however, as to whether the provisions which permit the use of the funds in an endeavor to charge existing laws make the charitable purpose non-exclusive.

The Maryland law contains no provision similar to that in the federal income and estate tax statutes, which specifically provide that the deduction is to be allowed only if no substantial part of the activities of the donee or legatee is carrying on propaganda or otherwise attempting to influence legislation.

If, as we have found the purposes of the trust here involved are charitable, they are no less charitable because of the means authorized to effectuate them, when, as here, those means are legal and not against public policy. Contributions to political parties are not involved. Although efforts to bring about changes in the law are envisioned and authorized, these are only ways to effectuate the purposes; they do not make the purposes themselves less charitable in nature or dilute their nature. Had the General Assembly wished to exclude bequests otherwise charitable from the exemption if a substantial part of a bequest is used in attempts to influence legislation, it could easily have done so by incorporating in the Maryland statute a clause similar to the provisions which the Congress has had in effect for several decades.

The appellant relies on federal cases construing the federal statutes in respect of charitable deductions. It is true that several earlier federal decisions take the same point of view as did the Massachusetts cases as to the effect of efforts to change the law upon the charitable nature of the organizations involved. In Slee v. Commissioner, *supra*, while the court found that the American Birth Control League was organized for charitable purposes, it held that the taxpayer could not deduct gifts to the League from his gross income because the League worked for the repeal of laws preventing birth control and was therefore not exclusively charitable under the Internal Revenue Act then in effect. Leubuscher v. Commissioner of Internal Revenue, 54 F.2d 998 (2d Cir. 1932) is to the same effect; in that case, a legacy to a club incorporated to advocate the single tax doctrine of Henry George was held not deductible under the estate tax law as a legacy for a corporation organized exclusively for educational purposes, because the organization had for its purposes the effectuation of a change in the existing system of taxation. Vanderbilt v. Commissioner of Internal Revenue, 93 F.2d 360 (1st Cir. 1937) involved the deductibility from the gross estate of a bequest to the National Woman's Party. The court held that although the corporation was not organized for profit and no part of its earnings enured to the benefit of any shareholder or individual, the efforts to enact and repeal laws were political activities and that, therefore, the bequest was not deductible as being exclusively educational.

These cases were decided before the Internal Revenue Code had been amended by the addition of the phrase 'and no substantial part of the activities of which is carrying on propaganda, or otherwise attempting, to influence legislation.' Girard Trust Co. v. Commissioner of Internal Revenue, 122 F.2d 108, 110, 138 A.L.R. 448 (3rd Cir. 1941) was decided after the amendment. In that case, the testatrix had left a bequest to the Board of Temperance, Prohibition and Public Morals of the Methodist Episcopal Church. The commissioner had disallowed the exemption and the Board of Tax Appeals confirmed his action. Part of the activity of the Board of Temperance was an attempt to influence legislation. The court reversed the Board of Tax Appeals and held that the bequest was deductible. Judge Goodrich, for the majority, said:

> '* * * [W]e had Sunday observance laws long before prohibition of alcohol became an important issue. The advocacy of such regulation before party committees and legislative bodies is a part of the achievement of the desired

result in a democracy. The safeguards against its undue extension lie in counter-pressures by groups who think differently and the constitutional protection, applied by courts, to check that which interferes with freedom of religion for any.

'Nor has the law sought to draw such a bright line between the exercise of private and public influence. Judge Hand has pointed out that the promoters of a charity are not unclassed when the charity seeks a special charter or when a society to prevent cruelty to children seeks positive support of law to accomplish its ends or when a university seeks legislation to provide its appropriations. Surely a church would not lose its exemption as a religious institution if, pending a proposal to repeal Sunday observance laws, the congregation held a meeting on church property and authorized a committee to appear before a legislative body to protest against the repeal. The majority of the charitable trust cases recognize the validity of a gift to prohibit or minimize manufacture and sale of intoxicating liquor. They are not directly controlling, of course. But they furnish a strong analogy.'

International Reform Federation v. District Unemployment Compensation Bd., 76 U.S.App.D.C. 282, 131 F.2d 337, 340 (D.C.Cir. 1942) involved an exemption, not under the Internal Revenue laws, but under the District of Columbia Unemployment Compensation Act. The question was whether the Federation was an employer within the meaning of the Act. The Act exempted any corporation or foundation organized exclusively for religious, charitable, scientific, educational, or other similar purposes from the requirement that every employer must make payments to the fund. The Federation had as some of its purposes the enactment of laws prohibiting the alcoholic liquor traffic and traffic in white slaves and narcotics. The Compensation Board contended that, even if the Federation should be classed as a corporation organized for charitable, religious or educational purposes, it was not organized and operated exclusively for those purposes. The court disagreed and held the Federation was not subject to the Act. Chief Judge Groner, for the majority of the court, said:

'It would seem to us to be going very far to say that these legislative activities accomplish a metamorphosis in appellant's character whereby it is changed from a charitable or educational to a political organization. Such activities have never been classified as lobbying in the sense in which that activity has been either prohibited or licensed. Hence we see no actual difference between the education of the individual—admittedly proper—and the education of the legislator, where both are directed to a common end, and that end, not the advancement, by political intrigue or otherwise, of the fortunes of a political party, but merely the accomplishment of national social improvement. There is nothing new in this position, and it has found support in many cases.'

* * *

Taken as a whole, the trend of the federal decisions indicates to us that efforts to change the law do not necessarily affect the exclusive charitable nature of an organization, despite the restriction contained in the Internal Revenue Code, which, as we have pointed out, is not a part of the Maryland law.

We find that the bequests here involved are exclusively charitable within the meaning of the Maryland statute and therefore are deductible.

Order affirmed; costs to be paid by the appellant.

Melanie Grayce West
Charitable Giving in U.S. Continues to Rise

WALL ST. J. (June 16, 2015) http://www.wsj.com/articles/charitable-giving-in-u-s
-continues-to-rise-1434427261

Mirroring growth in the domestic economy, charitable giving by Americans rose to a record $358.38 billion last year [2014], surpassing a previous high of $355.17 billion in 2007, according to a closely watched annual report. The study from the Giving USA Foundation, a Chicago-based nonprofit, uses data from the Internal Revenue Service and the Bureau of Economic Analysis among other sources, and looks at all donations—from individuals to corporations, to churches and museums. In inflation-adjusted dollars, total giving rose 5.4% over 2013, according to the report. As a percentage of gross domestic product—widely considered a factor in how much donors give to charity—giving was 2.1%.

National Philanthropic Trust
Charitable Giving Statistics

http://www.nptrust.org/philanthropic-resources/charitable-giving-statistics/

In 2014, the largest source of charitable giving came from individuals at $258.51 billion, or 72% of total giving; followed by foundations ($53.97 billion/15%), bequests ($28.13 billion/8%), and corporations ($17.77 billion/5%). [Citations omitted.]

In 2014, the majority of charitable dollars went to religion (32%), education (15%), human services and grantmaking foundations (12%), and health (8%). [Citations omitted.]

Arts, culture, and the humanities experienced the largest giving increase in 2014, receiving 9.2% more than the previous year. [Citations omitted.]

It is estimated that between $6.6 trillion and $27.4 trillion in charitable bequests will be made between 1998–2052. [Citations omitted.]

Robert F. Sharpe, Jr.
On the Upswing

154 TRUSTS & ESTS. 33 (Jan. 2015)

Studies reveal that older individuals make most of the large charitable gifts [http://philanthrophy.com/section/Philanthrophy-50/370]. A recent compilation of the largest 50 charitable gifts made in 2013 published by the Chronicle of Philanthropy revealed that 80 percent of the donors were age 65 or older [http://philanthropy.com/section/Outlook-2013/693/]. The oldest baby boomers will be age 69 in 2015, with millions passing age 69 each year. This demographic development may prove to be a driving force underlying growth in philanthropy—as important as economic and political changes. Advisors should be prepared to help greying baby boomers make what, in many cases, will be their 'gifts of a lifetime' in 2015 and beyond.

Id. at 35.

Al W. King III

Are Inventive Trusts Gaining Popularity?

156 TRUSTS & ESTS. 9 (Oct. 2017)

Baby Boomers are expected to transfer $30 trillion to their heirs (mainly Millennials) in the next 30 to 40 years. The Millennial generation is projected to be worth $24 trillion by 2020. One in three Baby Boomers would rather leave their money to charity than to their families, and 61 percent of wealthy parents aren't confident that their children are well prepared to handle financial inheritance

Id. at 10.

3. Honorary Trusts

Uniform Trust Code (2019)

§ 408. Trust for Care of Animal.

(a) A trust may be created to provide for the care of an animal alive during the settlor's lifetime. The trust terminates upon the death of the animal or, if the trust was created to provide for the care of more than one animal alive during the settlor's lifetime, upon the death of the last surviving animal.

(b) A trust authorized by this section may be enforced by a person appointed in the terms of the trust or, if no person is so appointed, by a person appointed by the court. A person having an interest in the welfare of the animal may request the court to appoint a person to enforce the trust or to remove a person appointed.

(c) Property of a trust authorized by this section may be applied only to its intended use, except to the extent the court determines that the value of the trust property exceeds the amount required for the intended use. Except as otherwise provided in the terms of the trust, property not required for the intended use must be distributed to the settlor, if then living, otherwise to the settlor's successors in interest.

Uniform Probate Code (2019)

§ 2-907(b). Honorary Trusts; Trusts for Pets.

(b) [**Trusts for Pets.**] Subject to this subsection and subsection (c), a trust for the care of a designated domestic or pet animal is valid. The trust terminates when no living animal is covered by the trust. A governing instrument must be liberally construed to bring the transfer within this subsection, to presume against the merely precatory or honorary nature of the disposition, and to carry out the general intent of the transferor. Extrinsic evidence is admissible in determining the transferor's intent.

In re Searight's Estate

Ohio Court of Appeals, Ninth District, 1950
87 Ohio App. 417, 95 N.E.2d 779

HUNSICKER, Judge.

George P. Searight, a resident of Wayne county, Ohio, died testate on November 27, 1948. Item 'third' of his will provided:

> 'I give and bequeath my dog, Trixie, to Florence Hand of Wooster, Ohio, and I direct my executor to deposit in the Peoples Federal Savings and Loan Association, Wooster, Ohio, the sum of $1000.00 to be used by him to pay Florence Hand at the rate of 75 cents per day for the keep and care of my dog as long as it shall live. If my dog shall die before the said $1000.00 and the interest accruing therefrom shall have been used up, I give and bequeath whatever remains of said $1000.00 to be divided equally among those of the following persons who are living at that time, to wit: Bessie Immler, Florence Hand, Reed Searight, Fern Olson and Willis Horn.'

At the time of his death, all of the persons, and his dog, Trixie, named in such item third, were living.

Florence Hand accepted the bequest of Trixie, and the executor paid to her from the $1000 fund, 75 cents a day for the keep and care of the dog. The value of Trixie was agreed to be $5.

The Probate Court made a determination of inheritance tax due from the estate of George P. Searight, deceased, the pertinent part of this judgment reading as follows:

> 'The court further finds that the value of the dog Trixie is taxable as a succession to Florence Hand; that the said dog inherits the sum of $1000.00 with power to consume both the interest and principal at a limited rate; that the state of Ohio, Sec. 5332, levying a tax on successions to property does not levy a tax upon the succession to any property passing to an animal; that the $1000.00 bequest to said dog is therefore not taxable; that the remainder of the $1000.00, if any, remaining after the death of said dog is taxable in the hands of the remaindermen; that there is no certain life expectancy of said dog, and that a tax should therefore be assessed upon the entire bequest to the contingent beneficiaries, subject to the right of refund as provided in Sec. 5343, Ohio General Code, upon final determination of the exact succession to each of the five remaindermen, or the survivor of

them, reserving all rights of refund to a prior deceased remainderman to the estate of such remainderman, and reserving likewise the rights of the state of Ohio to assess any excess to all remaindermen.

'Wherefore, it is ordered by the court that Florence Hand, as successor to the title of the said dog Trixie, be taxed at the rate prescribed by law on the value of said dog, to wit, $5.00; that Bessie Immler, Florence Hand, Reed Searight, Fern Olson and Willis Horn, as contingent beneficiaries and remaindermen of the said $1000.00, each be taxed on $200.00 at the rate prescribed by law, subject to refund or assessment of any excess as indicated in the findings herein * * *.'

The Department of Taxation of Ohio appeals to this court from such judgment, claiming the Probate Court erred: In holding that the bequest in item third to the extent it was paid to Florence Hand for the care of Trixie, is not a succession to property passing in trust or otherwise, to or for the use of a person; in not holding that the bequest of $1000 to the extent it was to be paid to Florence Hand for the care of Trixie was a bequest or succession to the said Florence Hand, subject to Ohio inheritance taxes; in holding that the bequest of $1000.00 was a bequest to a dog to the extent it is paid to Florence Hand for the care of Trixie; in holding that a bequest of $1000 to the extent it is paid to Florence Hand for the care of Trixie is not subject to Ohio inheritance taxes; in holding that a bequest for the care of Trixie is a valid bequest; in not holding that the sum of $1000 was a succession of property passing to the remaindermen named in item third; in not making a final order holding that the entire bequest of $1000 was subject to Ohio inheritance taxes on the amount of $200 due to each remainderman.

The questions presented by this appeal on questions of law are:

1. Is the testamentary bequest for the care of Trixie (a dog) valid in Ohio—

(a) as a proper subject of a so-called 'honorary trust'?

(b) as not being in violation of the rule against perpetuities?

2. Is the bequest set forth in item third of testator's will subject to the inheritance tax laws of Ohio?

1 (a). The creation of a trust for the benefit of specific animals has not been the subject of much litigation in the courts, and our research, and that of able counsel in this case, have failed to disclose any reported case on the subject in Ohio. The few reported cases in this country, in England and in Ireland have been the subject of considerable comment by the writers of text books and by the law reviews of leading law schools.

* * *

We do not have, in the instant case, the question of a trust established for the care of dogs in general or of an indefinite number of dogs, but we are here considering the validity of a testamentary bequest for the benefit of a specific dog. This is not a charitable trust, nor is it a gift of money to the Ohio Humane Society or a county humane society, which societies are vested with broad statutory authority, Section 10062, General Code, for the care of animals.

Text writers on the subject of trusts and many law professors designate a bequest for the care of a specific animal as an 'honorary trust'; that is, one binding the conscience of the trustee, since there is no beneficiary capable of enforcing the trust. * * *

The object and purpose sought to be accomplished by the testator in the instant case is not capricious or illegal. He sought to effect a worthy purpose—the care of his pet dog.

Whether we designate the gift in this case as an 'honorary trust' or a gift with a power which is valid when exercised is not important, for we do know that the one to whom the dog was given accepted the gift and indicated her willingness to care for such dog, and the executor proceeded to carry out the wishes of the testator.

'Where the owner of property transfers it upon an intended trust for a specific non-charitable purpose and there is no definite or definitely ascertainable beneficiary designated, no trust is created; but the transferee has power to apply the property to the designated purpose, unless he is authorized by the terms of the intended trust so to apply the property beyond the period of the rule against perpetuities, or the purpose is capricious.' I Restatement of the Law of Trusts, Section 124.

To call this bequest for the care of the dog, Trixie, a trust in the accepted sense in which that term is defined is, we know, an unjustified conclusion. The modern authorities, as shown by the cases cited earlier in this discussion, however, uphold the validity of a gift for the purpose designated in the instant case, where the person to whom the power is given is willing to carry out the testator's wishes. Whether called an 'honorary trust' or whatever terminology is used, we conclude that the bequest for the care of the dog, Trixie, is not in and of itself unlawful.

In Ohio, by statute, Section 10512-8, General Code, the rule against perpetuities is specifically defined, and such statute further says:

'It is the intention by the adoption of this section to make effective in Ohio what is generally known as the common law rule against perpetuities.'

It is to be noted, in every situation where the so-called 'honorary trust' is established for specific animals, that, unless the instrument creating such trust limits the duration of the trust—that is, the time during which the power is to be exercised—to human lives, we will have 'honorary trusts' established for animals of great longevity, such as crocodiles, elephants and sea turtles.

* * *

The lives, in being, which are the measure of the period set out in the rule against perpetuities, must be determined from the creating instrument.

If we then examine item third of testator's will, we discover that, although the bequest for his dog is for 'as long as it shall live,' the money given for this purpose is $1000 payable at the rate of 75¢ a day. By simple mathematical computation, this sum of money, expended at the rate determined by the testator, will be fully exhausted in three years and 238-1/3 days. If we assume that this $1000 is deposited in a bank so that interest at the high rate of 6% per annum were earned thereon, the time needed to consume both principal and interest thereon (based on semi-annual computation of such interest on the average unused balance during such six month period) would be four years, 57 1/2 days.

It is thus very apparent that the testator provided a time limit for the exercise of the power given his executor, and that such time limit is much less than the maximum period allowed under the rule against perpetuities.

We must indulge the presumption that the testator was cognizant of the rule against perpetuities and the construction placed upon it by the courts, and that he prepared his will possessed of such knowledge. Everhard et al., Trustees v. Brown, 75 Ohio App. 451, at page 459, 62 N.E.2d 901.

We therefore conclude that the bequest in the instant case for the care of the dog, Trixie, does not, by the terms of the creating instrument, violate the rule against perpetuities.

2. We next consider the problem of the inheritance tax, if any, to be levied on the bequest contained in item third of testator's will.

Section 5332, General Code, says, in part:

'A tax is hereby levied upon the succession to any property passing, in trust or otherwise, to or for the use of a person, institution or corporation, in the following cases:

'1. When the succession is by will or by the intestate laws of this state from a person who was a resident of this state at the time of his death.'* * *

'4. Whenever any person or corporation shall exercise a power of appointment derived from any disposition of property heretofore or hereafter made, such appointment when made shall be deemed a succession taxable under the provisions of this subdivision of this chapter in the same manner as if the property to which such appointment relates belonged absolutely to the donee of such power, and had been bequeathed or devised by said donee by will * * *.'

This statute determines that a tax shall be levied upon succession to all property passing to a person, institution or corporation. Certainly, a dog is neither an institution nor a corporation. Can it be successfully contended that a dog is a person? A 'person' is defined as '3. A human being.' Webster's New International Dictionary, Second Edition.

We have hereinabove indicated that the bequest for the dog, Trixie, comes within the designation of an 'honorary trust,' and, as such, is proper in the instant case. A tax based on the amount expended for the care of the dog cannot lawfully be levied against the monies so expended, since it is not property passing for the use of a 'person, institution or corporation.'

The executor herein had a power granted to him to use the funds for the support of the dog, which he proceeded to fulfill. Is it possible that such a power could be considered as a power of appointment within the terms of subsection 4 of Section 5332, General Code, and, hence, subject to taxation thereunder?

On this point, we need look for no other authority than that contained in 3 Restatement of the Law of Property (Future Interests), Section 318(2), which states the rule as follows:

> '(2) The term power of appointment does not include a power of sale, a power of attorney, a power or revocation, a power to cause a gift of income to be augmented out of principal, a power to designate charities, a charitable trust, a discretionary trust, or an honorary trust.'

Thus, an intended trust (honorary trust) for the support of a specific animal does not create a power of appointment, as such term is used in the inheritance tax statute. Section 5332, General Code.

We therefore conclude that no succession tax may be levied against such funds as are expended by the executor in carrying out the power granted to him by item third of testator's will.

The judgment of the Probate Court is affirmed.

Judgment affirmed.

STEVENS, P. J., and DOYLE, J., concur.

Notes

One of the more notable trusts for pets was created by Leona Helmsley's Last Will and Testament, whereby Ms. Helmsley bequeathed $12 million to her dog named "Trouble." After her death, a New York court held that the amount was excessive and reduced it to $2 million, in light of the dog's expenses. Ms. Helmsley also bequeathed $3 million for the maintenance of the Helmsley mausoleum where she and her husband are buried. Ms. Helmsley died in 2007, and her dog, Trouble, died on December 13, 2010, at the age of 12. The facts concerning both honorary trusts — for her pet and her cemetery mausoleum — are described in the following excerpt.

RAYMOND C. O'BRIEN & MICHAEL T. FLANNERY
THE PRUDENT INVESTING OF TRUSTS
(2009)

> Probably the most famous trust provision for a pet . . . was the one created by real estate mogul and hotelier Leona Helmsley, who died in August 2007, at the age of 87, as the 247th richest person in the world, according to Forbes magazine. . . . Helmsley left $12 million of her estimated $8 billion estate for the care of her 8-year-old Maltese Terrier, "Trouble," while entirely

disinheriting two grandchildren and igniting a firestorm of criticism over the exorbitant provision for the dog.... Helmsley's generous bequest to Trouble was a continuation of how she treated the dog in life. The pampered pup was known to wear expensive outfits adorned with diamond collars, and to eat food prepared by Helmsley's personal chef, which servants would scoop out of porcelain bowls and feed to the dog with their fingers....

The dichotomy of Helmsley's sentiments toward people and animals is evident in the terms of her Last Will and Testament, which provides, in part:

> F. I leave the sum of Twelve Million Dollars ($12,000,000) to the Trustees of the LEONA HELMSLEY 2005 TRUST, established under an instrument dated on or about the date of this Will, to be disposed of in accordance with the provisions of that Trust agreement. I leave my dog, Trouble, if she survives me, to my brother, ALVIN ROSENTHAL, if he survives me, or if he does not survive me, to my grandson DAVID PANZIRER. I direct that when my dog, Trouble, dies, her remains shall be buried next to my remains in the Helmsley Mausoleum at Woodlawn Cemetary, Bronx, New York, or in such other mausoleum as I may be interred pursuant to this will.

> G. I have not made any provisions in this Will for my grandson CRAIG PANZIRER or my granddaughter MEEGAN PANZIRER for reasons which are known to them.

Last Will and Testament of Leona M. Helmsley, http://www.nytimes.com/packages/pdf/nyregion/city_room/20070829_helmsleywill.pdf [hereinafter "Helmsley Will"]. It is believed that Helmsley disinherited two of her only son's children because they did not name any of their children after her late husband.... Helmsley also entrusted $10 million (plus $5 million in cash) to benefit her brother, Alvin Rosenthal, and $5 million to each of her grandsons, David and Walter Panzirer (plus another $5 million in cash to each), as well as $100,000 to her chauffeur, Nicholas Celea.... However, the awards to the grandsons were contingent on them visiting the grave of their father, Jay Panzirer (Helmsley's only child from her first marriage), every year and signing a registration book that would be placed in the mausoleum to prove that they had been present....

Although the $12 million trust for Trouble was just a fraction of one percent of Helmsley's estimated $8 billion estate, it was the largest bequest in her will, and many found the gift to be Helmsley's final snub to humanity. The bulk of Helmsley's $8 billion estate consists of the Leona M. and Harry B. Helmsley Charitable Trust—ranked seventh on the list of the nation's most valuable foundations. Jose Martinez, *Queen of Philanthropy*, Daily News (N.Y.), Sept. 2, 2007, at 10 (#1: The Bill and Melinda Gates Foundation (33 billion); #2: The Ford Foundation ($11.6 billion); #3: The J. Paul Getty Trust (9.6 billion); #4: The Robert Wood Johnson Foundation (9.3

billion); #5: The William and Flora Hewlett Foundation (8.5 billion); #6: Lilly Endowment, Inc. (8.3 billion)). In 2003, Helmsley drafted a two-page "mission statement" that provided two purposes for the trust: (1) to help indigent people, and (2) to provide "for the care and welfare of dogs." . . . In 2004, Helmsley deleted the first purpose regarding the indigent, thereby leaving the entire trust for the care of dogs. . . . The mission statement was never incorporated into the will or the trust document, however, and as public ire over her final wishes grew, the executors scrambled to figure out how to dispose of an $8 billion trust for the care of animals and $12 million on a single, spoiled dog.

Unfortunately, neither Alvin Rosenthal nor David Panzirer wanted to care for the cantankerous Trouble. When they refused, the dog spent several months at Helmsley's 28-room Connecticut mansion, Dunnellen Hall, being cared for by housekeepers. . . . It was not long, however, before Trouble received more than two dozen death threats, and in October 2007, Trouble was flown on a private jet to Helmsley's Sandcastle Hotel in Florida, to be cared for by the general manager, Carl Lekic. . . . Trouble maintains a full time security team at a cost of $100,000 per year, plus $60,000 for a guardian, $8,000 for grooming, $3,000 for miscellaneous expenses, $1,200 for food, and up to $18,000 for medical care. . . .

In 2008, Helmsley's grandchildren contested Helsmley's will, claiming that Helsmley had been mentally incompetent and did not possess the mental capacity to be able to execute a valid will. . . . Their claim was supported by reports that Helmsley believed that her late Husband, Harry, spoke to her through the dog and told her that he did not approve of the mausoleum in which he was buried. . . . In fact, in 2007, Helmsley's $12 million gift to Trouble ranked third on the list of the "101 Dumbest Moments in Business." . . . Evidently, Manhattan Surrogate Judge Renee Roth agreed when, in April 2008, she reduced Trouble's trust fund from $12 million to $2 million, with the reduced $10 million to go to Helmsley's charitable foundation. . . . New York law allows a court to reduce such gifts if they are deemed to be excessive. . . . The court and the State Attorney General further approved of an agreement for the Helmsley estate to pay $6 million to Helmsley's disinherited grandchildren ($4 million, tax-free, to Craig Panzirer, and $2 million, tax-free, to Meegan Wesolko), who agreed to withdraw their claims regarding Helmsley's mental capacity. . . . The agreement also reduced the gifts to Helmsley's other grandchildren, Walter and David Panzirer, from $10 million to $9.5 million, and the gift to her brother, Alvin Rosenthal, from $15 million to $14 million. . . .

Despite her reputation, Helmsley had demonstrated enormous philanthropic tendencies in her final years, having donated more than $35 million to charity in the last decade of her life. . . . She gave $5 million to help families of New York City firefighters after September 11, 2001, and $25 million to New York-Presbyterian Hospital. . . . She also gifted $3 million in 2004, including $1 million for the Helen Keller National Center for Deaf-Blind Youths and Adults, $500,000 for the colon rectal surgery program at New York-Presbyterian Hospital, and $1,000 for the Alzheimer's Association. . . . At $8 billion, Helmsley's Charitable Trust holds more than ten times the total assets of all 7,381 animal-related nonprofit groups that report to the Internal Revenue Service. . . . Under New York Law, non-profit foundations are required to spend 5 percent of the charity (in Helsmley's case — $400 million) each year. . . . This leaves Helmsley's executors [Alvin Rosenthal (her brother), David and Walter Panzirer (her grandsons), Sandor Frankel (her lawyer), and John Codey (the friend who gave her "Trouble")] and the public debating the most prudent way to administer the trust.

Id. at 356–59.

In addition to the $12 million trust created by Leona Helmsley for her dog, Trouble, . . . Helmsley's Last Will and Testament also provided for her own interment and the maintenance of her burial site. Her Last Will and Testament provided, in part:

> I direct that I be interred wearing my gold wedding band (which is never to be removed from my finger) and that my remains be interred next to my beloved husband, HARRY B. HELMSLEY, and next to my beloved son, JAY PANZIRER, at the Helmsley mausoleum at Woodlawn Cemetery, Bronx, New York. If the remains of my husband HARRY B. HELMSLEY, and my son JAY PANZIRER are relocated to another mausoleum in another cemetery, then I direct that my remains be interred next to them in any such other mausoleum in such other cemetery. I further direct that permission be granted as the need arises for the interment in the Helmsley mausoleum of the remains of my brother, ALVIN ROSENTHAL, if he wishes, and my brother's wife, SUSAN ROSEN-THAL, if she wishes, but for no other person. I also direct that anything bearing the HELMSLEY name must be maintained in "mint" condition and in the manner that it has been accustomed to, maintaining the outstanding Helmsley reputation.

Helmsley Will, *supra*. Helmsley also directed that:

> when my dog, Trouble, dies, her remains shall be buried next to my remains in the Helmsley mausoleum at Woodlawn cemetery, Bronx, New York, or in such other mausoleum as I may be interred pursuant to this will.

Id. The will also provided $3 million for "The Helmsley Perpetual Care Trust," which is described in Helmsley's will as follows:

> (1) The Trust shall provide for the perpetual care and maintenance of
> (i) the Helmsley Mausoleum at Woodlawn Cemetery, Bronx, New York,

containing the remains of my husband, Harry B. Helmsley and my son, Jay Panzirer, and my remains, or such other final resting place as may be designated * * *, (ii) the Brakmann Mausoleum at Woodlawn Cemetery, Bronx, New York, and (iii) the Rosenthal/Roman burial lots located at the Mt. Hebron cemetery, Flushing, New York, containing the remains of my mother, Ida Rosenthal, my father, Morris Rosenthal, my sister, Sylvia Roman, and my brother-in-law, Irving Roman (collectively (i), (ii) and (iii) shall be referred to as the "Final Resting Places").

(2) My Trustees shall distribute any part of the trust income and principal, at any time or times, as my Trustees shall determine in their sole discretion is advisable (i) for the care, cleaning, maintenance, repair and preservation of the interior and exterior of the Final Resting Places, and (ii) for the care, planting and cultivation of the lawn, trees, shrubs, flowers, plants or hedges located on the cemetery plots on which the Final Resting Places are located. I direct that my Trustees arrange for the Mausoleums to be acid washed or steam cleaned at least once a year. Any undistributed net income shall be added to principal at intervals determined by my Trustees. I direct my Trustees to maintain the Final Resting Places in excellent condition, and to arrange for inspection of the Final resting Places as often as may be necessary (but not less often than quarterly) to ensure their proper care and maintenance.

(3) The duration of this trust shall be perpetual, it being my intention to create a trust for cemetery purposes pursuant to Section 8-1.5 of the New York estates, Powers and trusts Law ("EPTL"), and I direct that all of the provisions of this Article shall be construed accordingly. If any of the Final Resting Places are in cemeteries which are razed or otherwise cease to function as cemeteries, I direct that such Final resting Places be moved to another cemetery and the provisions of this paragraph C continue to apply to said new Final Resting Place or Places.

(4) Any funds which a court determines are no longer needed to carry out the purposes of this trust for cemetery purposes shall be paid over to The Leona M. And Harry B. Helmsley Charitable Trust created by a Trust Agreement dated April 23, 1999, of which I am the Settlor and initially the sole Trustee, as such Trust Agreement may be amended and restated from time to time in accordance with its provisions ("THE LEONA M. AND HARRY B. HELMSLEY CHARITABLE TRUST"), and I direct the Trustees of THE LEONA M. AND HARRY B. HELMSLEY CHARITABLE TRUST to add the same to the principal of THE LEONA M. AND HARRY B. HELMSLEY CHARITABLE TRUST and dispose of the same for charitable purposes in accordance with the provisions thereof.

Id. . . .

In true Helmsley style, of course, these provisions created much conflict. In July 2004, Helmsley filed a $150 million law suit against Woodlawn Cemetery because of a disagreement about construction of a community mausoleum in the field next to her private mausoleum that she claimed ruined the "open view, serenity and tranquillity." . . . In the first law suit of its kind, she likened the Helmsley tomb, which cost $350,000 when built and has the capacity to hold 10,000 bodies, to that built in 353 B.C. for King Mausolus, which is known as one of the seven wonders of the world. . . . Others describe her section of the cemetery as somewhat of an eyesore. . . .

As a result, Helmsley moved the remains of her husband and son to a new, $1.4 million family mausoleum at Sleepy Hollow Cemetery, in Westchester County, New York, which is where Leona Helmsley was buried when she died. . . . The new 1,300 square foot tomb is the biggest building in the cemetery and features 12 granite columns and three stained-glass windows that display the New York City skyline. . . . Although even this construction had its road blocks and resulted in hefty fines for various permit violations, "[Helmsley] made various donations to offset some of the things that were done." . . . Unfortunately, Helmsley's dog, Trouble, will never enjoy the peace and tranquility of being interred next to Helmsley in Sleepy Hollow Cemetery. New York law prohibits animals from being interred in human cemeteries, and officials at Sleepy Hollow cemetery have stated that they have no intention of honoring Helmsley's final request for the dog to be buried with her. . . . For this to occur, all of the bodies would have to be exhumed and re-buried on private property, or all of the bodies could be buried in a pet cemetery, which New York law would allow, provided all of the bodies were cremated. . . .

Id. at 361–63.

D. Property: Ascertainable and Contractual

Uniform Trust Code (2019)

§ 103. Definitions. * * *

(12) "Property" means anything that may be the subject of ownership, whether real or personal, real or equitable, or any interest therein.

Brainard v. Commissioner of Internal Revenue

United States Circuit Court of Appeals, Seventh Circuit, 1937
91 F.2d 880

SPARKS, Circuit Judge.

This petition for review involves income taxes for the year 1928. The question presented is whether under the circumstances set forth in the findings of the Board of Tax Appeals, the taxpayer created a valid trust, the income of which was taxable to the beneficiaries under section 162 of the Revenue Act of 1928. * * *

The facts as found by the Board of Tax Appeals are substantially as follows: In December, 1927, the taxpayer, having decided that conditions were favorable, contemplated trading in the stock market during 1928. He consulted a lawyer and was advised that it was possible for him to trade in trust for his children and other members of his family. Taxpayer thereupon discussed the matter with his wife and mother, and stated to them that he declared a trust of his stock trading during 1928 for the benefit of his family upon certain terms and conditions. Taxpayer agreed to assume personally any losses resulting from the venture, and to distribute the profits, if any, in equal shares to his wife, mother, and two minor children after deducting a reasonable compensation for his services. During 1928 taxpayer carried on the trading operations contemplated and at the end of the year determined his compensation at slightly less than $10,000, which he reported in his income tax return for that year. The profits remaining were then divided in approximately equal shares among the members of his family, and the amounts were reported in their respective tax returns for 1928. The amounts allocated to the beneficiaries were credited to them on taxpayer's books, but they did not receive the cash, except taxpayer's mother, to a small extent.

In addition to these findings the record discloses that taxpayer's two children were one and three years of age. Upon these facts the Board held that the income in controversy was taxable to the petitioner as a part of his gross income for 1928, and decided that there was a deficiency. It is here sought to review that decision.

In the determination of the questions here raised it is necessary to consider the nature of the trust, if any, that is said to have been created by the circumstances hereinbefore recited. It is clear that the taxpayer, at the time of his declaration, had no property interest in 'profits in stock trading in 1928, if any,' because there were none in existence at that time. Indeed it is not disclosed that the declarer at that time owned any stock. It is obvious, therefore, that the taxpayer based his declaration of trust upon an interest which at that time had not come into existence and in which no one had a present interest. In the Restatement of the Law of Trusts, vol. 1, Sec. 75, it is said that an interest which has not come into existence or which has ceased to exist can not be held in trust. It is there further said: "A person can, it is true, make a contract binding himself to create a trust of an interest if he should thereafter acquire it; but such an agreement is not binding as a contract unless the requirements of the law of Contracts are complied with * * *

"Thus, if a person gratuitously declares himself trustee of such shares as he may thereafter acquire in a corporation not yet organized, no trust is created. The result is the same where instead of declaring himself trustee, he purports to transfer to another as trustee such shares as he may thereafter acquire in a corporation not yet organized. In such a case there is at most a gratuitous undertaking to create a trust in the future, and such an undertaking is not binding as a contract for lack of consideration * * *

If a person purports to declare himself trustee of an interest not in existence, or if he purports to transfer such an interest to another in trust, he is liable as upon a contract to create a trust if, but only if, the requirements of the law of Contracts are complied with. See, also, Restatement, Sec. 30b; Bogert, Trusts and Trustees, vol. 1, Sec. 112. In 42 Harvard Law Review 561, it is said: 'With logical consistency, the courts have uniformly held that an expectancy cannot be the subject matter of a trust and that an attempted creation, being merely a promise to transfer property in the future, is invalid unless supported by consideration.' Citing Lehigh Valley R. R. Co. v. Woodring, 116 Pa. 513, 9 A. 58. Hence, it is obvious under the facts here presented that taxpayer's declaration amounted to nothing more than a promise to create a trust in the future, and its binding force must be determined by the requirements of the law of contracts.

It is elementary that an executory contract, in order to be enforceable, must be based upon a valuable consideration. Here there was none. The declaration was gratuitous. If we assume that it was based on love and affection that would add nothing to its enforceability, for love and affection, though a sufficient consideration for an executed conveyance, is not a sufficient consideration for a promise. Sullivan v. Sullivan, 122 Ky. 707, 92 S.W. 966, 7 L.R.A. (N.S.) 156, 13 Ann.Cas. 163 * * * [citations omitted].

What has been said, however, does not mean that the taxpayer had no right to carry out his declaration after the subject matter had come into existence, even though there were no consideration. This he did and the trust thereby became effective, after which it was enforceable by the beneficiaries.

The questions with which we are concerned are at what times did the respective earnings which constitute the trust fund come into existence, and at what times did the trust attach to them. It is obvious that the respective profits came into existence when and if such stocks were sold at a profit in 1928. Did they come into existence impressed with the trust, or was there any period of time intervening between the time they came into existence and the time the trust attached? If there were such intervening time, then during that time the taxpayer must be considered as the sole owner of the profits and they were properly taxed to him as a part of his income.

It is said in the Restatement of the Law of Trusts, Sec. 75c: 'If a person purports to declare himself trustee of an interest not in existence or if he purports to transfer such an interest to another in trust, no trust arises even when the interest comes into existence in the absence of a manifestation of intention at that time.' This we think is especially applicable where, as here, there was no consideration for the declaration. It is further stated, however, in the Restatement, Sec. 26k: "If a person manifests an intention to become trustee at a subsequent time, his conduct at that subsequent time considered in connection with his original manifestation *may be* a sufficient manifestation of intention at that subsequent time to create a trust. * * * the act of acquiring the property coupled with the earlier declaration of trust may be a sufficient manifestation of an intention to create a trust at the time of the acquisition of the property. (Our italics, here and hereafter.) In subsection 1 it is said ' * * * Mere silence, however, ordinarily will not be such a manifestation. Whether silence is or is not such a manifestation is a question of interpretation.' In such interpretation, subsection m is quite pertinent and controlling: A promise to create a trust in the future is *enforceable*, if * * * the requirements for an enforceable contract are complied with. Whether a promise to transfer property in trust or to become trustee creates in the promisee a right to recover damages for breach of the promise, and whether such a promise is specifically enforceable, are determined by the law governing contracts. Thus, if the owner of property transfers the property in trust and agrees to pay a sum of money to the trustee to be held upon the same trust, he is not liable for failing to pay the money if the promise was made gratuitously * * * but if the promise was made for consideration * * * the promisor is liable thereon. So also, a promise to create a trust of property if thereafter acquired by the promisor imposes no liability upon the promisor if the promise was gratuitous. * * *"

* * *

From what has been said we are convinced that appellant's profits in question were not impressed with a trust when they first came into existence. The Board was obviously of the impression that the trust first attached when appellant credited them to the beneficiaries on his books of account. This act, it seems to us, constituted his first subsequent expression of intention to become a trustee of the fund referred to in his original and gratuitous declaration. Prior to that time we think it is clear that the declaration could not have been enforced against him, and that his mere silence with respect thereto should not be considered as an expression of his intention to establish the trust at a time earlier than the credits. * * *

It is no doubt true that the proffered decree is binding upon the parties to that suit, and it will not be appealed from, because all parties thereto are satisfied with it; but we think it can not be binding on the government, which was not a party, and which of course has no right of appeal.

The order of the Board is affirmed.

Notes

May trust property cease to exist through commingling? A modern decision concerning the viability of a trust corpus is State *ex. rel.* Ins. Com'r of West Virginia v. Blue Cross Blue Shield of West Virginia, 219 W. Va. 541, 638 S.E.2d 144 (2006). The facts involved a petition by the United Mine Workers of America, seeking the return of money given to Blue Cross, arguing that the money was trust property and not part of what had become the bankruptcy estate of Blue Cross. The Union had established an emergency health care program for its members, with Blue Cross Blue Shield, and had given the company $1 million, obligating Blue Cross to invest the money until the program ended. The program was extended three times, and Blue Cross was depositing money into a "sinking fund" to pay off the $1 million, but filed for bankruptcy protection before the money was returned. The issue was whether the money was the corpus of a trust initiated by the Union, or whether it had become part of the general assets of Blue Cross, thereby losing its distinctiveness. The court held that a trust had come into existence through an agreement between the Union and Blue Cross, and the fact that the trust property had been commingled with general assets of Blue Cross did not dissipate the identity of the property; it retained its character as trust property. Now, upon bankruptcy, when all of the assets of Blue Cross enter into receivership, the equitable remedy of tracing may be used to locate and separate the trust assets belonging to the Union and to return them to the Union/settlor because the trust may no longer be performed. The property does not have to be specifically identified among the assets. Once the trust proceeds can be traced to any fund, the entire fund is available for repayment of the trust corpus.

Unthank v. Rippstein

Supreme Court of Texas, 1964
386 S.W.2d 134

STEAKLEY, Justice.

Three days before his death C. P. Craft penned a lengthy personal letter to Mrs. Iva Rippstein. The letter was not written in terms of his anticipated early death; in fact, Craft spoke in the letter of his plans to go to the Mayo Clinic at a later date. The portion of the letter at issue reads as follows:

> Used most of yesterday and day before to 'round up' my financial affairs, and to be sure I knew just where I stood before I made the statement that I would send you $200.00 cash the first week of each month for the next 5 years, also to send you $200.00 cash for Sept. 1960 and thereafter send that amount in cash the first week of the following months of 1960, October, November and December.'; opposite which in the margin there was written:

> I have stricken out the words 'provided I live that long' and hereby and herewith bind my estate to make the $200.00 monthly payments provided for on this Page One of this letter of 9-17-60.

Mrs. Rippstein, Respondent here, first sought, unsuccessfully, to probate the writing as a codicil to the will of Craft. The Court of Civil Appeals * * * held that the writing was not a testamentary instrument which was subject to probate. We refused the application of Mrs. Rippstein for writ of error with the notation 'no reversible error.' See Rule 483, Texas Rules of Civil Procedure.

The present suit was filed by Mrs. Rippstein against the executors of the estate of Craft, Petitioners here, for judgment in the amount of the monthly installments which had matured, and for declaratory judgment adjudicating the liability of the executors to pay future installments as they mature. The trial court granted the motion of the executors for summary judgment. The Court of Civil Appeals reversed and rendered judgment for Mrs. Rippstein * * * , holding that the writing in question established a voluntary trust under which Craft bound his property to the extent of the promised payments; and that upon his death his legal heirs held the legal title for the benefit of Mrs. Rippstein to that portion of the estate required to make the promised monthly payments.

In her reply to the application for writ of error Mrs. Rippstein states that the sole question before us is whether the marginal notation constitutes 'a declaration of trust whereby (Craft) agrees to thenceforth hold his estate in trust for the explicit purpose of making the payments.' She argues that Craft imposed the obligation for the payment of the monies upon all of his property as if he had said 'I henceforth hold my estate in trust for (such) purpose.' She recognizes that under her position Craft became subject to the Texas Trust Act in the management of his property. Collaterally, however, Mrs. Rippstein takes the position that it being determinable by mathematical computation that less than ten per cent of the property owned by Craft at the time he wrote the letter would be required to discharge the monthly payments, the 'remaining ninety per cent remained in Mr. Craft to do with as he would.' Her theory is that that portion of Craft's property not exhausted in meeting his declared purpose would revert to him by way of a resulting trust eo instante with the legal and equitable title to such surplus merging in him.

These arguments in behalf of Mrs. Rippstein are indeed ingenious and resourceful, but in our opinion there is not sufficient certainty in the language of the marginal notation upon the basis of which a court of equity can declare a trust to exist which is subject to enforcement in such manner. The uncertainties with respect to the intention of Craft and with respect to the subject of the trust are apparent. The language of the notation cannot be expanded to show an intention on the part of Craft to place his property in trust with the result that his exercise of further dominion thereover would be wrongful except in a fiduciary capacity as trustee, and under which Craft would be subject to suit for conversion at the hands of Mrs. Rippstein if he spent or disposed of his property in a manner which would defeat his statement in the notation that a monthly payment of $200.00 in cash would be sent her the first week of each month. It is manifest that Craft did not expressly declare that all of his property, or any specific portion of the assets which he owned at such time, would constitute the corpus or res of a trust for the benefit of Mrs. Rippstein; and inferences may not be drawn from the language used sufficient for a holding to such effect to rest in implication. The conclusion is compelled that the most that Craft did was to express an intention to make monthly gifts to Mrs. Rippstein accompanied by an ineffectual attempt to bind his estate in futuro; the writing was no more than a promise to make similar gifts in the future and as such is unenforceable. The promise to give cannot be tortured into a trust declaration under which Craft while living, and as trustee, and his estate after his death, were under a legally enforceable obligation to pay Mrs. Rippstein the sum of $200.00 monthly for the five-year period.

The controlling tests were stated by this Court in McMurray v. Stanley, 69 Tex. 227, 6 S.W. 412 (1887):

> It has been often said that, in cases of this kind, three things must be shown before a court of equity will declare a trust to exist, and enforce it: First, that the words of the testator ought to be construed as imperative, and hence

imposing on the trustee an obligation; secondly, that the subject to which the obligation relates must be certain; thirdly, that the person intended to be the beneficiary under the trust be also certain.

* * *

Mrs. Rippstein relies principally on three decisions in support of her theory that the ten per cent of Craft's property required to discharge the monthly payments can be carved out and made to constitute the subject of the trust: McMurray v. Stanley, *supra*; Estes v. Estes, 267 S.W. 709 (Tex.Com.App.1924); and Monday v. Vance, 92 Tex. 428, 49 S.W. 516 (1899). In Monday v. Vance the husband and wife deeded property in trust for the permanent support of the wife and the children, and for the education of the children. The deed did not prescribe how the property should devolve after the trust was executed, but there was no uncertainty, regarding the establishment of the trust itself. It was held that the effect of the deed was merely to carve out of the estate in the property the usufructuary interest for the support of the wife and the maintenance and education of the children, and to leave what remained unaffected by the conveyance. Estes v. Estes considered a will which created a life estate in B. T. Estes with a vested remainder in fee simple in Bennie Estes; and which also impressed the income from the property in the hands of B. T. Estes with an active trust in favor of Bennie. As relevant here, the court cited what it termed the 'universal rule that, in the absence of express terms defining the estate conferred upon the trustee, the trustee takes exactly that quantity of interest which the purposes of the trust requires, and no more.' But there was no uncertainty regarding the intention of the testatrix. In McMurray v. Stanley this court considered a will under which the testatrix gave all of her property to her husband with full power of disposition, but directed that 'at his death, should he have any of said property still remaining in his possession not disposed of or used by him, that the same shall be given by him' to her nieces. It was held that the intention to create a trust was manifested by the whole instrument, and that the property remaining in the possession of the husband at the time of his death could be shown with as much certainty as any other fact. Here, again, the court was enforcing clear intention, and in so doing it was held that the subject to which the trust attached was sufficiently certain.

We also note that Mrs. Rippstein presented the alternative point in the Court of Civil Appeals (which that court did not reach) that the marginal notation was an instrument in writing which imports consideration; and that she was entitled to summary judgment against the estate of Craft for the monthly payments since the executors of the estate wholly failed to meet their burden of proving a want of consideration. This alternative position was also asserted by counsel for Mrs. Rippstein in oral argument before this Court.

The common law rule was stated by this Court in Jones v. Holliday, 11 Tex. 412 (1854):

> A consideration is essential to the validity of a simple contract, whether it be verbal or in writing. This rule applies to all contracts not under seal, with the

exception of bills of exchange and negotiable notes, after they had been negotiated and passed into the hands of an innocent indorsee. * * * In contracts
under seal a consideration is implied, in the solemnity of the instrument.

In 1858 the Legislature enacted what became Article 7093 of the 1911 codification
providing as follows: '*Every contract in writing** * * [all italics are added] hereafter made shall be held to import a consideration in the same manner and as fully
as sealed instruments have heretofore done.' It was said by this Court in Harris v.
Cato, 26 Tex. 338 (1862), that 'The object of this law was to dispense with a mere
formality in the execution of a certain class of contracts. And as by the common law
these instruments when under seal imported a consideration, it was provided, by the
clause of the sentence under consideration, that the same effect should be given *to
them* when subsequently executed without a scroll or seal.'

Article 7093 of the 1911 codification was omitted in the 1925 codification. Article
27 of the 1925 codification, however read, and still reads, in part, as follows: 'No
private seal or scroll shall be required in this State on any written instrument except
such as are made by corporations.' In an opinion adopted by this Court in Wright
v. Robert & St. John Motor Co., 127 Tex. 278, 58 S.W.2d 67 (1933), it was stated that
Article 27 of the 1925 codification included the substance of Articles 7092 and 7093
of the 1911 codification. It was further held that:

> If the seal was required under the common law on simple contracts such
> as this to import a consideration, and the statute now provides that no seal
> shall be required, it follows that the only effect the statute can possibly have
> on such a contract is to dispense with the common-law rule requiring the
> seal in order to import a consideration.

It is apparent that Article 27 cannot be held to provide that all written instruments import a consideration, regardless of the kind or type of writing the instrument may purport to be. The marginal notation under consideration here does not
purport to be a contract, or to embody a bilateral agreement between Craft and
Mrs. Rippstein, or to be the result of a meeting of their minds, or to possess the element of mutuality of obligation. A contractual obligation to pay the monthly payments cannot be imposed against the estate of Craft on the theory that the executors
thereof were under the burden in this proceeding, which they did not discharge, of
alleging and proving a want of consideration.

The judgment of the Court of Civil Appeals is reversed and that of the trial court
is affirmed.

Speelman v. Pascal

Court of Appeals of New York, 1961
10 N.Y.2d 313, 178 N.E.2d 723

DESMOND, Chief Judge.

Gabriel Pascal, defendant's intestate who died in 1954, had been for many
years a theatrical producer. In 1952 an English corporation named Gabriel Pascal

Enterprises, Ltd., of whose 100 shares Gabriel Pascal owned 98, made an agreement with the English Public Trustee who represented the estate of George Bernard Shaw. This agreement granted to Gabriel Pascal Enterprises, Ltd., the exclusive world rights to prepare and produce a musical play to be based on Shaw's play 'Pygmalion' and a motion picture version of the musical play. The agreement recited, as was the fact, that the licensee owned a film scenario written by Pascal and based on 'Pygmalion'. In fact Pascal had, some time previously, produced a nonmusical movie version of 'Pygmalion' under rights obtained by Pascal from George Bernard Shaw during the latter's lifetime. The 1952 agreement required the licensee corporation to pay the Shaw estate an initial advance and thereafter to pay the Shaw estate 3% of the gross receipts of the musical play and musical movie with a provision that the license was to terminate if within certain fixed periods the licensee did not arrange with Lerner and Loewe or other similarly well-known composers to write the musical play and arrange to produce it. Before Pascal's death in July, 1954, he had made a number of unsuccessful efforts to get the musical written and produced and it was not until after his death that arrangements were made, through a New York bank as temporary administrator of his estate, for the writing and production of the highly successful 'My Fair Lady'. Meanwhile, on February 22, 1954, at a time when the license from the Shaw estate still had two years to run, Gabriel Pascal, who died four and a half months later, wrote, signed and delivered to plaintiff a document as follows:

Dear Miss Kingman

'This is to confirm to you our understanding that I give you from my shares of profits of the Pygmalion Musical stage version five per cent (5%) in England, and two per cent (2%) of my shares of profits in the United States. From the film version, five per cent (5%) from my profit shares all over the world.

As soon as the contracts are signed, I will send a copy of this letter to my lawyer, Edwin Davies, in London, and he will confirm to you this arrangement in a legal form.

This participation in my shares of profits is a present to you, in recognition for your loyal work for me as my Executive Secretary.

Very sincerely yours,
Gabriel Pascal.

The question in this lawsuit is: Did the delivery of this paper constitute a valid, complete, present gift to plaintiff by way of assignment of a share in future royalties when and if collected from the exhibition of the musical stage version and film version of 'Pygmalion'? A consideration was, of course, unnecessary (Personal Property Law, Consol.Laws, c. 41, § 33, subd. 4).

In pertinent parts the judgment appealed from declares that plaintiff is entitled to receive the percentages set out in the 1954 agreement, requires defendant to render plaintiff accountings from time to time of all moneys received from the musical play and the firm version, and orders defendant to make the payments required by the agreement. The basic grant from the Shaw estate was to Gabriel Pascal Enterprises, Ltd., a corporation, whereas the document on which plaintiff sues is signed by Gabriel Pascal individually and defendant makes much of this, arguing that Gabriel Pascal, as distinguished from his corporation, owned no rights when he delivered the 1954 document to plaintiff. However, no such point was made in the courts below and no mention of it is made in the motion papers, affidavits, etc., on which plaintiff was granted summary judgment. It is apparent that all concerned in these transactions disregarded any distinction between Pascal's corporation in which he owned practically all the stock, and Pascal individually, as is demonstrated by the agreement between Lerner-Loewe-Levin, writers and producers of 'My Fair Lady', and Gabriel Pascal's estate. Actually, all this makes little difference since what Pascal assigned to plaintiff was a percentage from Pascal's 'shares of profits' and this would cover direct collections or collections through his corporation.

Defendant emphasizes also the use of the word 'profits' in the February, 1954 letter from Pascal to plaintiff, and suggests that this means that plaintiff was not to get a percentage of Pascal's gross royalties but a percentage of some 'profits' remaining after deduction of expenses. Again, the answer is that no such point was made in the proceedings below or in this record and everyone apparently assumed, at least until the case reached this court, that what the defendant Pascal estate will get from the musical play and movie is royalties collectible in full under the agreements pursuant to which 'My Fair Lady' has been and will be produced. In this same connection defendant talks of possible creditors of the Pascal corporation and inquires as to what provision would be made for them if plaintiff were to get her percentages of the full royalties. This, too, is an afterthought and no such matter was litigated below.

The only real question is as to whether the 1954 letter above quoted operated to transfer to plaintiff an enforcable right to the described percentages of the royalties to accrue to Pascal on the production of a stage or film version of a musical play based on 'Pygmalion'. We see no reason why this letter does not have that effect. It is true that at the time of the delivery of the letter there was no musical stage or film play in existence but Pascal, who owned and was conducting negotiations to realize on the stage and film rights, could grant to another a share of the moneys to accrue from the use of those rights by others. There are many instances of courts enforcing assignments of rights to sums which were expected thereafter to become due to the assignor. A typical case is Field v. Mayor of City of New York, 6 N.Y. 179. One Bell, who had done much printing and similar work for the City of New York but had no present contract to do any more such work, gave an assignment in the amount of $1,500 of any moneys that might thereafter become due to Bell for such work. Bell did obtain such contracts or orders from the city and money became due to him therefor. This court held that while there was not at the time of the assignment any presently enforcable or even existing chose in action but merely a possibility that there would be such a chose in action, nevertheless there was a possibility of such which the parties expected to ripen into reality and which did afterwards ripen into reality and that, therefore, the assignment created an equitable title which the courts would enforce. A case similar to the present one in general outline is Central Trust Co. of New York v. West India Improvement Co., 169 N.Y. 314, 62 N.E. 387, where the assignor had a right or concession from the Colony of Jamaica to build a railroad on that island and the courts upheld a mortgage given by the concession owner on any property that would be acquired by the concession owner in consideration of building the railroad if and when the railroad should be built. The Court of Appeals pointed out in Central Trust Co., at page 323, 62 N.E. at page 389 that the property as to which the mortgage was given had not yet come into existence at the time of the giving of the mortgage but that there was an expectation that such property, consisting of securities, would come into existence and accrue to the concession holder when and if the latter performed the underlying contract. This court held that the assignment would be recognized and enforced in equity. The cases cited by appellant (Young v. Young, 80 N.Y. 422; Vincent v. Rix, 248 N.Y. 76, 161 N.E. 425; Farmers' Loan & Trust Co. v. Winthrop, 207 App.Div. 356, 202 N.Y.S. 456, mod. 238 N.Y. 477, 144 N.E. 686) are not to the contrary. In each of those instances the attempted gifts failed because there had not been such a completed and irrevocable delivery of the subject matter of the gift as to put the gift beyond cancellation by the donor. In every such case the question must be as to whether there was a completed delivery of a kind appropriate to the subject property. Ordinarily, if the property consists of existing stock certificates or corporate bonds, as in the Young and Vincent cases (*supra*), there must be a completed physical transfer of the stock certificates or bonds. In Farmers' Loan & Trust Co. v. Winthrop (*supra*) the dispute was as to the effect of a power of attorney but the maker of the power had used language which could not be construed as effectuating a present gift of the property which the donor expected to receive in the future from another estate. The Farmers' Loan & Trust Co. case does not hold that property to be the subject of a valid gift must be in present physical existence and in the possession of the donor but it does hold that the language used in the particular document was not sufficient to show an irrevocable present intention to turn over to the donee securities which would come to the donor on the settlement of another estate. At page 485 of 238 N.Y., at page 687 of 144 N.E. this court held that all that need be established is 'an intention that the title of the donor shall be presently divested and presently transferred' but that in the particular document under scrutiny in the Farmers' Loan & Trust Co. case there was lacking any language to show an irrevocable intent of a gift to become operative at once. In our present case there was nothing left for Pascal to do in order to make an irrevocable transfer to plaintiff of part of Pascal's right to receive royalties from the productions.

* * *

The judgment should be affirmed, with costs.

DYE, FULD, FROESSEL, VAN VOORHIS, BURKE and FOSTER, JJ., concur.

Judgment affirmed.

E. Intent: Precatory and Purpose

The words of a settlor are often ambiguous, thereby creating various possibilities when the settlor transfers property to another: Was the transfer intended to be a gift, a loan, a life estate, or a trust? What is the test by which we differentiate one from the other? The result will be important in the eventual distribution of the property. If the property was a gift, there is no further need of court intervention; if the property was a loan, the loan should be repaid upon the death of the "settlor"; if the property was a life estate, the property reverts to the "settlor" or successors in interest at the death of the life tenant. If a "trust accountability" will be required of the trustee, and the beneficiary is required to accomplish the purpose of the trust, what, then, is the test by which a trust, rather than a gift or loan, is established? For commentary on the use of words in the new digital age, see David A. Hoffman, *Relational Contracts of Adhesion*, 85 U. Chi. L. Rev. 1395 (2018).

Uniform Trust Code (2019)

§ 103. Definitions. * * *

(18) "Terms of a trust" means the manifestation of the settlor's intent regarding a trust's provisions as expressed in the trust instrument or as may be established by other evidence that would be admissible in a judicial proceeding.

§ 810. Recordkeeping and Identification of Trust Property.

(a) A trustee shall keep adequate records of the administration of the trust.

(b) A trustee shall keep trust property separate from the trustee's own property.

(c) Except as otherwise provided in subsection (d), a trustee shall cause the trust property to be designated so that the interest of the trust, to the extent feasible, appears in the records maintained by a party other than a trustee or a beneficiary.

(d) If the trustee maintains records clearly indicating the respective interests, a trustee may invest as a whole the property of two or more separate trusts.

Jimenez v. Lee

Supreme Court of Oregon, 1976
274 Or. 457, 547 P.2d 126

O'CONNELL, Chief Justice.

This is a suit brought by plaintiff against her father to compel him to account for assets which she alleges were held by defendant as trustee for her. Plaintiff appeals from a decree dismissing her complaint.

Plaintiff's claim against her father is based upon the theory that a trust arose in her favor when two separate gifts were made for her benefit. The first of these gifts was made in 1945, shortly after plaintiff's birth, when her paternal grandmother purchased a $1,000 face value U.S. Savings Bond which was registered in the names of defendant 'and/or' plaintiff 'and/or' Dorothy Lee, plaintiff's mother.

It is uncontradicted that the bond was purchased to provide funds to be used for plaintiff's educational needs. A second gift in the amount of $500 was made in 1956 by Mrs. Adolph Diercks, one of defendant's clients. At the same time Mrs. Diercks made identical gifts for the benefit of defendant's two other children. The $1,500 was deposited by the donor in a savings account in the names of defendant and his three children.

In 1960 defendant cashed the savings bond and invested the proceeds in common stock of the Commercial Bank of Salem, Oregon. Ownership of the shares was registered as 'Jason Lee, Custodian under the Laws of Oregon for Betsy Lee (plaintiff).' At the same time, the joint savings account containing the client's gifts to defendant's children was closed and $1,000 of the proceeds invested in Commercial Bank stock.[1] Defendant also took title to this stock as 'custodian' for his children.

The trial court found that defendant did not hold either the savings bond or the savings account in trust for the benefit of plaintiff and that defendant held the shares of the Commercial Bank stock as custodian for plaintiff under the Uniform Gift to Minors Act (ORS 126.805–126.880). Plaintiff contends that the gifts for her educational needs created trusts in each instance and that the trusts survived defendant's investment of the trust assets in the Commercial Bank stock.

It is undisputed that the gifts were made for the educational needs of plaintiff. The respective donors did not expressly direct defendant to hold the subject matter of the gift 'in trust' but this is not essential to create a trust relationship. * * * It is enough if the transfer of the property is made with the intent to vest the beneficial ownership in a third person. That was clearly shown in the present case. Even defendant's own testimony establishes such intent. When he was asked whether there was a stated purpose for the gift, he replied:

> * * * Mother said that she felt that the children should all be treated equally and that she was going to supply a bond to help with Elizabeth's educational needs and that she was naming me and Dorothy, the ex-wife and mother of Elizabeth, to use the funds as may be most conducive to the educational needs of Elizabeth.

Defendant also admitted that the gift from Mrs. Diercks was 'for the educational needs of the children.' There was nothing about either of the gifts which would suggest that the beneficial ownership of the subject matter of the gift was to vest in defendant to use as he pleased with an obligation only to pay out of his own funds a similar amount for plaintiff's educational needs. * * *

---

1. The specific disposition of the balance of this account is not revealed in the record. Defendant testified that the portion of the gift not invested in the stock 'was used for other unusual needs of the children.' Defendant could not recall exactly how the money was used but thought some of it was spent for family vacations to Victoria, British Columbia and to satisfy his children's expensive taste in clothing.

Defendant himself demonstrated that he knew that the savings bond was held by him in trust. In a letter to his mother, the donor, he wrote: 'Dave and Bitsie (plaintiff) & Dorothy are aware of the fact that I hold $1,000 each for Dave & Bitsie in trust for them on account of your E-Bond gifts.' It is fair to indulge in the presumption that defendant, as a lawyer, used the word 'trust' in the ordinary legal sense of that term.

Defendant further contends that even if the respective donors intended to create trusts, the doctrine of merger defeated that intent because plaintiff acquired both legal and equitable title when the savings bond was registered in her name along with her parents names and when Mrs. Diercks' gift was deposited in the savings account in the name of plaintiff and her father, brother and sister. The answer to this contention is found in II Scott on Trusts § 99.4, p. 811 (3d ed 1967):

> A trust may be created in which the trustees are A and B and the sole beneficiary is A. In such a case it might be argued that there is automatically a partial extinguishment of the trust, and that A holds an undivided half interest as joint tenant free of trust, although B holds a similar interest in trust for A. The better view is, however, that there is no such partial merger, and that A and B will hold the property as joint tenants in trust for A. * * *

Having decided that a trust was created for the benefit of plaintiff, it follows that defendant's purchase of the Commercial Bank stock as 'custodian' for plaintiff under the Uniform Gift to Minors Act was ineffectual to expand defendant's powers over the trust property from that of trustee to that of custodian.[4]

Defendant's attempt to broaden his powers over the trust estate by investing the trust funds as custodian violated his duty to the beneficiary 'to administer the trust solely in the interest of the beneficiary.' Restatement (Second) of Trusts § 170, p. 364 (1959).

The money from the savings bond and savings account are clearly traceable into the bank stock. Therefore, plaintiff was entitled to impose a constructive trust or an equitable lien upon the stock so acquired. * * * Plaintiff is also entitled to be credited for any dividends or increment in the value of that part of the stock representing plaintiff's proportional interest. Whether or not the assets of plaintiff's trust are traceable into a product, defendant is personally liable for that amount which would have accrued to plaintiff had there been no breach of trust. * * * Defendant is, of

---

4. If defendant were 'custodian' of the gifts, he would have the power under the Uniform Gift to Minors Act (ORS 126.820) to use the property 'as he may deem advisable for the support, maintenance, education and general use and benefit of the minor, in such manner, at such time or times, and to such extent as the custodian in his absolute discretion may deem advisable and proper, without court order or without regard to the duty of any person to support the minor, and without regard to any other funds which may be applicable or available for the purpose.' As custodian defendant would not be required to account for his stewardship of the funds unless a petition for accounting were filed in circuit court no later than two years after the end of plaintiff's minority. ORS 126.875. As the trustee of an educational trust, however, defendant has the power to use the trust funds for educational purposes only and has the duty to render clear and accurate accounts showing the funds have been used for trust purposes. See ORS 128.010; Restatement (Second) of Trusts § 172 (1959).

course, entitled to deduct the amount which he expended out of the trust estate for plaintiff's educational needs. However, before he is entitled to be credited for such expenditures, he has the duty as trustee to identify them specifically and prove that they were made for trust purposes. A trustee's duty to maintain and render accurate accounts is a strict one. This strict standard is described in Bogert on Trusts and Trustees § 962, pp. 10–13 (2d ed 1962):

> It is the duty of the trustees to keep full, accurate and orderly records of the status of the trust administration and of all acts thereunder. * * * 'The general rule of law applicable to a trustee burdens him with the duty of showing that the account which he renders and the expenditures which he claims to have been made were correct, just and necessary. * * * He is bound to keep clear and accurate accounts, and if he does not the presumptions are all against him, obscurities and doubts being resolved adversely to him.' (Quoting from White v. Rankin, 46 NYS 228, 18 AppDiv 293, 294, affirmed without opinion 162 NY 622, 57 NE 1128 (1897).) * * * He has the burden of showing on the accounting how much principal and income he has received and from whom, how much disbursed and to whom, and what is on hand at the time. * * *

Defendant did not keep separate records of trust income and trust expenditures. He introduced into evidence a summary of various expenditures which he claimed were made for the benefit of plaintiff. It appears that the summary was prepared for the most part from cancelled checks gathered together for the purpose of defending the present suit. This obviously did not meet the requirement that a trustee 'maintain records of his transactions so complete and accurate that he can show by them his faithfulness to his trust.' * * *

In an even more general way defendant purported to account for the trust assets in a letter dated February 9, 1966, written to plaintiff shortly after her 21st birthday when she was in Europe where she had been receiving instruction and training in ballet. In that letter defendant revealed to plaintiff, apparently for the first time, that her grandmother had made a gift to her of a savings bond and that the proceeds of the bond had been invested in stock. Without revealing the name of the stock, defendant represented that it had doubled in value of the bond from $750 to $1,500. The letter went on to suggest that plaintiff allocate $1,000 to defray the cost of additional ballet classes and that the remaining $500 be held in reserve to defray expenses in returning to the United States and in getting settled in a college or in a ballet company.

Defendant's letter was in no sense a trust accounting. In the first place, it was incomplete; it made no mention of Mrs. Diercks' gift. Moreover, it was inaccurate since it failed to reveal the true value attributable to the Commercial Bank stock. There was evidence which would put the value of plaintiff's interest in the stock at considerably more than $1,500.[9]

---

9. It appears that with the accumulation of cash and stock dividends the total value of plaintiff's interest at the time she received defendant's letter would amount to as much as $2,135. This figure is an approximation derived from the incomplete stock price information before us. It is

Defendant contends that even if a trust is found to exist and that the value of the trust assets is the amount claimed by plaintiff there is sufficient evidence to prove that the trust estate was exhausted by expenditures for legitimate trust purposes. Considering the character of the evidence presented by defendant, it is difficult to understand how such a result could be reached. As we noted above, the trust was for the educational needs of plaintiff. Some of the expenditures made by defendant would seem to fall clearly within the purposes of the trust. These would include the cost of ballet lessons, the cost of subscribing to a ballet magazine, and other items of expenditure related to plaintiff's education.[10] But many of the items defendant lists as trust expenditures are either questionable or clearly outside the purpose of an educational trust. For instance, defendant seeks credit against the trust for tickets to ballet performances on three different occasions while plaintiff was in high school. The cost of plaintiff's ticket to a ballet performance might be regarded as a part of plaintiff's educational program in learning the art of ballet, but defendant claims credit for expenditures made to purchase ballet tickets for himself and other members of the family, disbursements clearly beyond the purposes of the trust.

Other expenditures claimed by defendant in his 'accounting' are clearly not in furtherance of the purposes of the trust. Included in the cancelled checks introduced into evidence in support of defendant's claimed offset against the trust assets were: (1) checks made by defendant in payment of numerous medical bills dating from the time plaintiff was 15 years old (these were obligations which a parent owes to his minor children); (2) checks containing the notation 'Happy Birthday' which plaintiff received from her parents on her 17th, 18th and 22nd birthdays; (3) a 1963 check with a notation 'Honor Roll, Congratulations, Mom and Dad'; (4) defendant's check to a clothier which contains the notation 'Betsy's Slacks and Sweater, Pat's Sweater, Dot's Sweater' (defendant attempted to charge the entire amount against the trust); (5) defendant's check to a Canadian Rotary Club for a meeting attended when he joined plaintiff in Banff after a summer ballet program; (6) $60 sent to plaintiff to enable her to travel from France, where she was studying ballet, to Austria to help care for her sister's newborn babies. There were also other items improperly claimed as expenditures for plaintiff's educational benefit, either because the purpose of the outlay could not be identified or because defendant claimed a double credit.[11]

---

important only to demonstrate that defendant did not render an adequate accounting. Our calculation does not include the value of plaintiff's interest in stock purchased with the proceeds of Mrs. Diercks' gift.

10. Defendant's failure to keep proper records makes it difficult, if not impossible, to determine whether some of these expenditures were made from the trust estate or from defendant' own funds. Moreover, it is unclear in some instances whether the expenditure was for educational purposes or simply for recreation. Thus defendant charges plaintiff with expenses incurred in connection with a European tour taken by plaintiff. It is not disclosed as to whether this was to provide an educational experience for plaintiff or for some other purpose.

11. The double counting occurs where defendant claims credit for cashier's checks sent to plaintiff while she was staying in Europe and at the same time also claims credit for his personal checks used to purchase the cashier's checks.

It is apparent from the foregoing description of defendant's evidence that the trial court erred in finding that 'Plaintiff in these proceedings has received the accounting which she sought and * * * is entitled to no further accounting.' The trial court also erred in finding that 'Defendant did not hold in trust for the benefit of Plaintiff' the product traceable to the two gifts.

The case must, therefore, be remanded for an accounting to be predicated upon a trustee's duty to account, and the trustee's burden to prove that the expenditures were made for trust purposes. There is a moral obligation and in proper cases a legal obligation for a parent to furnish his child with higher education. * * * Where a parent is a trustee of an educational trust, as in the present case, and he makes expenditures out of his own funds, his intent on one hand may be to discharge his moral or legal obligation to educate his child or on the other hand to follow the directions of the trust. * * * It is a question of fact in each case as to which of these two purposes the parent-trustee had in mind at the time of making the expenditures. * * * In determining whether defendant has met this strict burden of proof, the trial court must adhere to the rule that all doubts are resolved against a trustee who maintains an inadequate accounting system.

The decree of the trial court is reversed and the cause is remanded for further proceedings consistent with this opinion.

The Hebrew University Association v. Nye

Supreme Court of Connecticut, 1961
148 Conn. 223, 169 A.2d 641

KING, Associate Justice.

The plaintiff obtained a judgment declaring that it is the rightful owner of the library of Abraham S. Yahuda, a distinguished Hebrew scholar who died in 1951. The library included rare books and manuscripts, mostly relating to the Bible, which Professor Yahuda, with the assistance of his wife, Ethel S. Yahuda, had collected during his lifetime. Some of the library was inventoried in Professor Yahuda's estate and was purchased from the estate by his wife. There is no dispute that all of the library had become the property of Ethel before 1953 and was her property when she died on March 6, 1955, unless by her dealings with the plaintiff between January, 1953, and the time of her death she transferred ownership to the plaintiff. While the defendants in this action are the executors under the will of Ethel, the controversy as to ownership of the library is, in effect, a contest between two Hebrew charitable institutions, the plaintiff and a charitable trust or foundation to which, as hereinafter appears, Ethel bequeathed the bulk of her estate.

The pertinent facts recited in the finding may be summarized as follows: Before his death, Professor Yahuda forwarded certain of the books in his library to a warehouse in New Haven with instructions that they be packed for overseas shipment. The books remained in his name, no consignee was ever specified, and no shipment was made. Although it is not entirely clear, these books were apparently the ones which Ethel purchased from her husband's estate. Professor Yahuda and his wife had indicated to their friends their interest in creating a scholarship research center in Israel which would serve as a memorial to them. In January, 1953, Ethel went to Israel and had several talks with officers of the plaintiff, a university in Jerusalem. One of the departments of the plaintiff is an Institute of Oriental Studies, of outstanding reputation. The library would be very useful to the plaintiff, especially in connection with the work of this institute. On January 28, 1953, a large luncheon was given by the plaintiff in Ethel's honor and was attended by many notables, including officials of the plaintiff and the president of Israel. At this luncheon, Ethel described the library and announced its gift to the plaintiff. The next day, the plaintiff submitted to Ethel a proposed newspaper release which indicated that she had made a gift of the library to the plaintiff. Ethel signed the release as approved by her. From time to time thereafter she stated orally, and in letters to the plaintiff and friends, that she 'had given' the library to the plaintiff. She refused offers of purchase and explained to others that she could not sell the library because it did not belong to her but to the plaintiff. On one occasion, when it was suggested that she give a certain item in the library to a friend, she stated that she could not, since it did not belong to her but to the plaintiff.

Early in 1954, Ethel began the task of arranging and cataloguing the material in the library for crating and shipment to Israel. These activities continued until about the time of her death. She sent some items, which she had finished cataloguing, to a warehouse for crating for overseas shipment. No consignee was named, and they remained in her name until her death. In October, 1954, when she was at the office of the American Friends of the Hebrew University, a fund raising arm of the plaintiff in New York, she stated that she had crated most of the miscellaneous items, was continuously working on cataloguing the balance, and hoped to have the entire library in Israel before the end of the year. Until almost the time of her death, she corresponded with the plaintiff about making delivery to it of the library. In September, 1954, she wrote the president of the plaintiff that she had decided to ship the library and collection, but that it was not to be unpacked unless she was present, so that her husband's ex libris could be affixed to the books, and that she hoped 'to adjust' the matter of her Beth Yahuda and her relations to the plaintiff. A 'beth' is a building or portion of a building dedicated to a particular purpose.

The complaint alleged that the plaintiff was the rightful owner of the library and was entitled to possession. It contained no clue, however, to the theory on which ownership was claimed. The prayers for relief sought a declaratory judgment determining which one of the parties owned the library and an injunction restraining the defendants from disposing of it. The answer amounted to a general denial. The only real issues raised in the pleadings were the ownership and the right to possession of the library. As to these issues, the plaintiff had the burden of proof. Kriedel v. Krampitz, 137 Conn. 532, 534, 79 A.2d 181; Holt v. Wissinger, 145 Conn. 106, 109, 139 A.2d 353. The judgment found the 'issues' for the plaintiff, and further recited that 'a trust [in relation to the library] was created by a declaration of trust made by Ethel S. Yahuda, indicating her intention to create such a trust, made public by her.' We construe this language, in the light of the finding, as a determination, that, at the luncheon in Jerusalem, Ethel orally constituted herself a trustee of the library for future delivery to the plaintiff. The difficulty with the trust theory adopted in the judgment is that the finding contains no facts even intimating that Ethel ever regarded herself as trustee of any trust whatsoever, or as having assumed any enforceable duties with respect to the property. The facts in the finding, in so far as they tend to support the judgment for the plaintiff at all, indicate that Ethel intended to make, and perhaps attempted to make, not a mere promise to give, but an executed, present, legal gift *inter vivos* of the library to the plaintiff without any delivery whatsoever.

Obviously, if an intended or attempted legal gift *inter vivos* of personal property fails as such because there was neither actual nor constructive delivery, and the intent to give can nevertheless be carried into effect in equity under the fiction that the donor is presumed to have intended to constitute himself a trustee to make the necessary delivery, then as a practical matter the requirement of delivery is abrogated in any and all cases of intended *inter vivos* gifts. Of course this is not the law. A gift which is imperfect for lack of a delivery will not be turned into a declaration of trust for no better reason than that it is imperfect for lack of a delivery. Courts do not supply conveyances where there are none. Cullen v. Chappell, 2 Cir., 116 F.2d 1017, 1018. This is true, even though the intended donee is a charity. Organized Charities Ass'n v. Mansfield, 82 Conn. 504, 510, 74 A. 781. The cases on this point are collected in an annotation in 96 A.L.R. 383, which is supplemented by a later annotation in 123 A.L.R. 1335. The rule is approved in 1 Scott, Trusts § 31.

It is true that one can orally constitute himself a trustee of personal property for the benefit of another and thereby create a trust enforceable in equity, even though without consideration and without delivery. 1 Scott, op. cit. § 28; § 32.2, p. 251. But he must in effect constitute himself a trustee. There must be an express trust, even though oral. It is not sufficient that he declare himself a donor. 1 Scott, op. cit. § 31, p. 239; 4 *id.* § 462.1. While he need not use the term 'trustee,' nor even manifest an understanding of its technical meaning or the technical meaning of the term 'trust,' he must manifest an intention to impose upon himself enforceable duties of a trust nature. Cullen v. Chappell, *supra*; Restatement (Second), 1 Trusts §§ 23, 25; 1 Scott, op. cit., pp. 180, 181. There are no subordinate facts in the finding to indicate that Ethel ever intended to, or did, impose upon herself any enforceable duties of a trust nature with respect to this library. The most that could be said is that the subordinate facts in the finding might perhaps have supported a conclusion that at the luncheon she had the requisite donative intent so that, had she subsequently made a delivery of the property while that intent persisted, there would have been a valid, legal gift *inter vivos*. See cases such as Bachmann v. Reardon, 138 Conn. 665, 667, 88 A.2d 391; Hammond v. Lummis, 106 Conn. 276, 280, 137 A. 767, and Burbank v. Stevens, 104 Conn. 17, 23, 131 A. 742. The judgment, however, is not based on the theory of a legal gift *inter vivos* but on that of a declaration of trust. Since the subordinate facts give no support for a judgment on that basis, it cannot stand.

While this is dispositive of the appeal adversely to the plaintiff, it may assist in the retrial if certain other matters are briefly mentioned.

By her will, which was executed on November 19, 1953, Ethel provided for the establishment of a foundation in Israel to perpetuate her name and that of her husband, if, as proved to be the case, she failed to establish the foundation during her lifetime. The will also named special trustees, in Israel, to carry out the project in case none were appointed by her before she died. By the second clause of her will, she gave 'all * * * [her] real and the remainder of * * * [her] personal estate' to two named trustees, residing in New Haven, in trust to liquidate and, from the proceeds, to pay debts, funeral and testamentary expenses, death taxes, and legacies. By the third clause, she directed the New Haven trustees to transfer the balance of the proceeds to the trustees of the foundation in Israel. The only other dispositive provision in the will was one in the eighth clause bequeathing to her sister most of the furniture, silver and jewelry. In its memorandum of decision, the trial court seized upon the distinction drawn in the second clause between real estate and personal estate, and the use of the word 'remainder' in connection with the personal estate, as constituting a recognition by Ethel that she had already disposed of the library. Also, in the finding it is stated that the word 'remainder' as used in the second clause meant the personal property other than the library. There is no justification for that finding or for the statement in the memorandum of decision. The word 'remainder' must have been used, not in the technical sense of an estate limited to take effect in possession at the expiration of a prior estate created by the same instrument, but in the loose sense of 'rest' or 'balance.' As such, it would naturally refer to the rest or balance of the personal property owned by the testatrix and not otherwise given by the will, that is, the balance over and above that disposed of in the eighth clause. It could hardly refer to the balance exclusive of the library, because if Ethel did not own the library it would not be affected by her will and there would be no need of excluding it from the operation of the will. A trust res is no part of the trustee's personal estate.

The finding, besides reciting the conclusion of the court that Ethel constituted herself the trustee of an express oral trust for the benefit of the plaintiff, contained the conclusion that she intended 'to give' the library to the plaintiff and 'took all the steps for delivery of possession * * * to the plaintiff which the circumstances afforded'. If the court meant by the quoted language to indicate that a legal *inter vivos* gift was effected, there would be a material inconsistency within the finding and between the judgment and the finding. This would be so because there is a well-recognized distinction between a gift *inter vivos* and a declaration of trust; a single transaction cannot be both. 38 C.J.S. Gifts §8, p. 785. A similar inconsistency within the finding is indicated, if not established, by the conclusion that the plaintiff acted to its detriment in reliance upon 'the declaration of gift and trust.' Furthermore, while the doctrine of reliance might constitute a reason for the imposition of a constructive trust; 1 Scott, Trusts §§ 31.3, 31.4; note, 12 A.L.R.2d 961, 963; 1 Corbin, Contracts §§ 200–206, 209; Restatement, 1 Contracts § 90; it could play no part in a decision predicated, as the judgment showed the present one was, on an express oral trust, since such a trust needs no consideration for its validity.

To support a factual conclusion of an executed *inter vivos* gift, there would have to be a donative intention and at least a constructive delivery. See cases such as Candee v. Connecticut Savings Bank, 81 Conn. 372, 374, 71 A. 551, 22 L.R.A.,N.S., 568; McMahon v. Newtown Savings Bank, 67 Conn. 78, 80, 34 A. 709. It is true that the donative intention need not be expressed, nor the delivery made, in any particular form or mode. Fasano v. Meliso, 146 Conn. 496, 502, 152 A.2d 512, and cases cited. Here, there was no actual delivery of the library; nor was there any constructive delivery. Candee v. Connecticut Savings Bank, *supra*; Prendergast v. Drew, 103 Conn. 88, 91, 130 A. 75; 24 Am.Jur. 745, § 28; 1 Scott, op. cit., p. 230. No manual delivery of the library could have been made at the time of the expression of the donative intention in Jerusalem, since the library was then in the United States. But there is nothing in the finding to show that constructive delivery was attempted in Jerusalem or that any delivery of any kind was attempted after Ethel's return to the United States. Ethel did not, for instance, make any delivery either of the library or of a document of title purporting to represent the ownership of the library. See McMahon v. Newtown Savings Bank, *supra*; notes, 63 A.L.R. 537, 550, 48 A.L.R.2d 1405, 1413. For a constructive delivery, the donor must do that which, under the circumstances, will in reason be equivalent to an actual delivery. It must be as nearly perfect and complete as the nature of the property and the circumstances will permit. 24 Am.Jur. 744, § 27. Just what, if any, form of constructive delivery would have been adequate, under the circumstances of this case, when Ethel was in Jerusalem, or what form of actual or constructive delivery would have been adequate after her return to the United States, we have no occasion to determine, since the finding discloses no delivery whatsoever.

The judgment declaring that the plaintiff is the owner of the library is without support in the finding and cannot stand. We cannot, however, as the defendants urge, remand the case for the entry of judgment in their favor, since, as previously pointed out, the finding within itself contains inconsistencies, is at variance with the recitals in the judgment, and is based upon an erroneous view of the controlling law. What finding would have been made had these errors not crept in we have no means of knowing. The case must therefore be remanded for a new trial. See cases such as Thomas F. Rogers, Inc. v. Hochberg, 143 Conn. 22, 25, 118 A.2d 910.

There is error, the judgment is set aside and a new trial is ordered.

In this opinion the other judges concurred.

Notes

The *Hebrew University* case was eventually resolved with a subsequent decision, which held that the delivery of the memorandum, coupled with the decedent's acts and declarations, constituted a *gift* and, thus, Hebrew University was able to obtain the books from the decedent's estate. *See* The Hebrew University Association v. Nye,

26 Conn. Supp. 342, 223 A.2d 397 (1966). Recall that transfer is necessary to make a gift, see *Restatement (Third) of Trusts* § 16(2) (2019). How was that accomplished in the instant decision? If the "settlor" transfers a legal life estate to a named donee, there is a distinction to be made: The legal life tenant has sole ownership and control over the property, but when there is a trust involved, a trustee has control over the property and is responsible to the court for such things as prudence and management. Finally, note that the intent of the settlor may not be unlawful: "A trust may be created only to the extent its purposes are lawful, not contrary to public policy, and possible to achieve." Unif. Trust Code § 404 (2019).

II. Classification of Trusts

Even though there are three main categories of trusts—private, charitable, and honorary—there are a number of classifications that have arisen, almost all within modern estate planning parameters. These following few classifications are identified to give the student a better understanding of the usage and variety of trust features available today.

A. Mandatory Trusts

As the word mandatory implies, the settlor of a mandatory trust mandates specific acts to be performed by the Trustee. For example: "One million dollars in trust for Sadie, her tuition to be paid each year in any course of legal studies at an accredited law school leading to a juris doctor degree." Even though the tuition will fluctuate, the duties of the Trustee are express and mandatory. Compare this to the following type of trust.

B. Discretionary Trusts

Marsman v. Nasca

Massachusetts Appeals Court, 1991
30 Mass. App. 789, 573 N.E.2d 1025

DREBEN, Justice.

This appeal raises the following questions: Does a trustee, holding a discretionary power to pay principal for the "comfortable support and maintenance" of a beneficiary, have a duty to inquire into the financial resources of that beneficiary so as to recognize his needs? If so, what is the remedy for such failure? A Probate Court judge held that the will involved in this case imposed a duty of inquiry upon the trustee. We agree with this conclusion but disagree with the remedy imposed and accordingly vacate the judgment and remand for further proceedings.

* * *

Sara Wirt Marsman died in September, 1971, survived by her second husband, T. Frederik Marsman (Cappy), and her daughter by her first marriage, Sally Marsman Marlette. Mr. James F. Farr, her lawyer for many years, drew her will and was the trustee thereunder. * * *

Article IIA of Sara's will provided in relevant part:

> It is my desire that my husband, T. Fred Marsman, be provided with *reasonable maintenance, comfort and support* after my death. Accordingly, if my said husband is living at the time of my death, I give to my trustees, who shall set the same aside as a separate trust fund, one-third (1/3) of the rest, residue and remainder of my estate . . . ; they shall pay the net income therefrom to my said husband at least quarterly during his life; and *after having considered the various available sources of support for him*, my trustees shall, if they deem it necessary or desirable from time to time, in their sole and uncontrolled discretion, pay over to him, or use, apply and/or expend for his direct or indirect benefit such amount or amounts of the principal thereof as they shall deem advisable for his *comfortable support and maintenance*. (Emphasis supplied).

Article IIB provided:

> Whatever remains of said separate trust fund, including any accumulated income thereon on the death of my husband, shall be added to the trust fund established under Article IIC. . . .

Article IIC established a trust for the benefit of Sally and her family. Sally was given the right to withdraw principal and, on her death, the trust was to continue for the benefit of her issue and surviving husband.

The will also contained the following exculpatory clause:

> No trustee hereunder shall ever be liable except for his own willful neglect or default.

> During their marriage, Sara and Cappy lived well and entertained frequently. Cappy's main interest in life centered around horses. An expert horseman, he was riding director and instructor at the Dana Hall School in Wellesley until he was retired due to age in 1972. Sally, who was also a skilled rider, viewed Cappy as her mentor, and each had great affection for the other. Sara, wealthy from her prior marriage, managed the couple's financial affairs. She treated Cappy as "Lord of the Manor" and gave him money for his personal expenses, including an extensive wardrobe from one of the finest men's stores in Wellesley.

In 1956, Sara and Cappy purchased, as tenants by the entirety, the property in Wellesley which is the subject of this litigation. Although title to the property passed to Cappy by operation of law on Sara's death, Sara's will also indicated an intent to convey her interest in the property to Cappy. In the will, Cappy was also given a life estate in the household furnishings with remainder to Sally.

After Sara's death in 1971, Farr met with Cappy and Sally and held what he termed his "usual family conference" going over the provisions of the will. At the time of Sara's death, the Wellesley property was appraised at $29,000, and the principal of Cappy's trust was about $65,600.

Cappy continued to live in the Wellesley house but was forced by Sara's death and his loss of employment in 1972 to reduce his standard of living substantially. He married Margaret in March, 1972, and, shortly before their marriage, asked her to read Sara's will, but they never discussed it. In 1972, Cappy took out a mortgage for $4,000, the proceeds of which were used to pay bills. Farr was aware of the transaction, as he replied to an inquiry of the mortgagee bank concerning the appraised value of the Wellesley property and the income Cappy expected to receive from Sara's trust.

In 1973, Cappy retained Farr in connection with a new will. The latter drew what he described as a simple will which left most of Cappy's property, including the house, to Margaret. The will was executed on November 7, 1973.

In February, 1974, Cappy informed the trustee that business was at a standstill and that he really needed some funds, if possible. Farr replied in a letter in which he set forth the relevant portion of the will and wrote that he thought the language was "broad enough to permit a distribution of principal." Farr enclosed a check of $300. He asked Cappy to explain in writing the need for some support and why the need had arisen.[5] The judge found that Farr, by his actions, discouraged Cappy from making any requests for principal.

Indeed, Cappy did not reduce his request to writing and never again requested principal. Farr made no investigation whatsoever of Cappy's needs or his "available sources of support" from the date of Sara's death until Cappy's admission to a nursing home in 1983 and, other than the $300 payment, made no additional distributions of principal until Cappy entered the nursing home.

By the fall of 1974, Cappy's difficulty in meeting expenses intensified.[6] Several of his checks were returned for insufficient funds, and in October, 1974, in order that he might remain in the house, Sally and he agreed that she would take over the

---

5. He also suggested, despite the will's direction that Cappy's trust be set aside as a separate trust, that when principal was paid to Cappy, a proportionate distribution (i.e., twice the sum given to Cappy) be made to Sally. Farr indicated that he was sending a copy of the letter to Sally and hoped "to hear from her." The judge read the letter to imply that Sally should be consulted when and if Cappy requested principal. We need not consider whether this reading is warranted.

6. After Sara's death, Cappy's income was limited, particularly considering the station he had enjoyed while married to Sara. In 1973, including the income from Sara's trust of $2,116, his income was $3,441; in 1974 it was $3,549, including trust income of $2,254; in 1975, $6,624, including trust income of $2,490 and social security income of $2,576. Margaret's income was also minimal; $499 in 1974, $4,084 in 1975, including social security income of $1,686. Cappy's income in 1976 was $8,464; in 1977, $8,955; in 1978, $9,681; in 1979, $10,851; in 1980, $11,261; in 1981, $12,651; in 1982, $13,870; in 1983, $12,711; in 1984, $12,500; in 1985, $12,567; in 1986, $12,558. The largest portion from 1975 on came from social security benefits.

mortgage payments, the real estate taxes, insurance, and major repairs. In return, she would get the house upon Cappy's death.

Cappy and Sally went to Farr to draw up a deed. Farr was the only lawyer involved, and he billed Sally for the work. He wrote to Sally, stating his understanding of the proposed transaction, and asking, among other things, whether Margaret would have a right to live in the house if Cappy should predecease her. The answer was no. No copy of the letter to Sally was sent to Cappy. A deed was executed by Cappy on November 7, 1974, transferring the property to Sally and her husband Richard T. Marlette (Marlette) as tenants by the entirety, reserving a life estate to Cappy. No writing set forth Sally's obligations to Cappy.

The judge found that there was no indication that Cappy did not understand the transaction, although, in response to a request for certain papers by Farr, Cappy sent a collection of irrelevant documents. The judge also found that Cappy clearly understood that he was preserving no rights for Margaret, and that neither Sally nor Richard nor Farr ever made any representation to Margaret that she would be able to stay in the house after Cappy's death.

Although Farr had read Sara's will to Cappy and had written to him that the will was "broad enough to permit a distribution of principal," the judge found that Farr failed to advise Cappy that the principal of his trust could be used for the expenses of the Wellesley home. The parsimonious distribution of $300 and Farr's knowledge that the purpose of the conveyance to Sally was to enable Cappy to remain in the house, provide support for this finding. After executing the deed, Cappy expressed to Farr that he was pleased and most appreciative. Margaret testified that Cappy thought Farr was "great" and that he considered him his lawyer.[7]

Sally and Marlette complied with their obligations under the agreement. Sally died in 1983, and Marlette became the sole owner of the property subject to Cappy's life estate. Although Margaret knew before Cappy's death that she did not have any interest in the Wellesley property, she believed that Sally would have allowed her to live in the house because of their friendship. After Cappy's death in 1987, Marlette inquired as to Margaret's plans, and, subsequently, through Farr, sent Margaret a notice to vacate the premises. Margaret brought this action in the Probate Court.

After a two-day trial, the judge held that the trustee was in breach of his duty to Cappy when he neglected to inquire as to the latter's finances. She concluded that, had Farr fulfilled his fiduciary duties, Cappy would not have conveyed the residence owned by him to Sally and Marlette. The judge ordered Marlette to convey the house to Margaret and also ordered Farr to reimburse Marlette from the remaining portion of Cappy's trust for the expenses paid by him and Sally for the upkeep of the property. If Cappy's trust proved insufficient to make such payments, Farr was

---

7. The judge noted that Farr, in response to an interrogatory filed by the plaintiff, stated that he rendered legal services to Sara from approximately 1948–1971; to Cappy from approximately 1951–1987; to Sally from 1974 until prior to her death; and to Marlette since 1983.

to be personally liable for such expenses. Both Farr and Marlette appealed from the judgment, from the denial of their motions to amend the findings, and from their motions for a new trial. Margaret appealed from the denial of her motion for attorney's fees. As indicated earlier, we agree with the judge that Sara's will imposed a duty of inquiry on the trustee, but we disagree with the remedy and, therefore, remand for further proceedings.

2. *Breach of trust by the trustee.* Contrary to Farr's contention that it was not incumbent upon him to become familiar with Cappy's finances, Article IIA of Sara's will clearly placed such a duty upon him. In his brief, Farr claims that the will gave Cappy the right to request principal "in extraordinary circumstances" and that the trustee, "was charged by Sara to be wary should Cappy request money beyond that which he quarterly received." Nothing in the will or the record supports this narrow construction. To the contrary, the direction to the trustees was to pay Cappy such amounts "as they shall deem advisable for his comfortable support and mainte-nance." This language has been interpreted to set an ascertainable standard, namely to maintain the life beneficiary "in accordance with the standard of living which was normal for him before he became a beneficiary of the trust." Woodberry v. Bunker, 359 Mass 239, 243, 268 N.E.2d 841 (1971). Dana v. Gring, 374 Mass. 109, 117, 371 N.E.2d 755 (1977). See Blodget v. Delaney, 201 F.2d 589, 593 (1st Cir.1953).

Even where the only direction to the trustee is that he shall "in his discretion" pay such portion of the principal as he shall "deem advisable," the discretion is not absolute. "Prudence and reasonableness, not caprice or careless good nature, much less a desire on the part of the trustee to be relieved from trouble . . . furnish the standard of conduct." Boyden v. Stevens, 285 Mass. 176, 179, 188 N.E. 741 (1934), quoting from Corkery v. Dorsey, 223 Mass. 97, 101, 111 N.E. 795 (1916). Holyoke Natl. Bank v. Wilson, 350 Mass. 223, 227, 214 N.E.2d 42 (1966).

That there is a duty of inquiry into the needs of the beneficiary follows from the requirement that the trustee's power "must be exercised with that soundness of judgment which follows from a due appreciation of trust responsibility." Boyden v. Stevens, 285 Mass. at 179, 188 N.E. 741. Woodberry v. Bunker, 359 Mass. at 241, 268 N.E.2d 841. In Old Colony Trust Co. v. Rodd, 356 Mass. 584, 586, 254 N.E.2d 886 (1970), the trustee sent a questionnaire to each potential beneficiary to deter-mine which of them required assistance but failed to make further inquiry in cases where the answers were incomplete. The court agreed with the trial judge that the method employed by the trustee in determining the amount of assistance required in each case to attain "comfortable support and maintenance" was inadequate. There, as here, the trustee attempted to argue that it was appropriate to save for the beneficiaries' future medical needs. The court held that the "prospect of illness in old age does not warrant a persistent policy of niggardliness toward individu-als for whose comfortable support in life the trust has been established. The pay-ments made to the respondent and several other beneficiaries, viewed in light of their assets and needs, when measured against the assets of the trust show that little consideration has been given to the 'comfortable support' of the beneficiaries." *Id.* at

589–590, 254 N.E.2d 886. See 3 Scott, Trusts § 187.3 (Fratcher 4th ed. 1988) (action of trustee is "arbitrary" where he "is authorized to make payments to a beneficiary if in his judgment he deems it wise and he refuses to inquire into the circumstances of the beneficiary"). See also Kolodney v. Kolodney, 6 Conn.App. 118, 123, 503 A.2d 625 (1986).

Farr, in our view, did not meet his responsibilities either of inquiry or of distribution under the trust. The conclusion of the trial judge that, had he exercised "sound judgment," he would have made such payments to Cappy "as to allow him to continue to live in the home he had occupied for many years with the settlor" was warranted.

3. *Remedy against Marlette.* The judge, concluding that, had Farr not been in breach of trust, "[C]appy would have died owning the house and thus able to devise it to his widow, the plaintiff," ordered Marlette to convey the house to Margaret. This was an inappropriate remedy in view of the judge's findings. She found that, although the relationship between Cappy and Sally was "close and loving," there was "no fiduciary relation between them" and that Sally and Marlette "were not unjustly enriched by the conveyance." She also found that "Sally and Richard Marlette expended significant monies over a long period of time in maintaining their agreement with [C]appy."

Because the conveyance was supported by sufficient consideration (the agreement to pay the house expenses) and because Sally and Marlette had no notice of a breach of trust and were not themselves guilty of a breach of fiduciary duty, they cannot be charged as constructive trustees of the property. Jones v. Jones, 297 Mass. 198, 207, 7 N.E.2d 1015 (1937). That portion of the judgment which orders Marlette to convey the property is vacated.

4. *Remainder of Cappy's trust.* The amounts that should have been expended for Cappy's benefit are, however, in a different category. More than $80,000 remained in the trust for Cappy at the time of his death. As we have indicated, the trial judge properly concluded that payments of principal should have been made to Cappy from that fund in sufficient amount to enable him to keep the Wellesley property. There is no reason for the beneficiaries of the trust under Article IIC to obtain funds which they would not have received had Farr followed the testatrix's direction. The remedy in such circumstances is to impress a constructive trust on the amounts which should have been distributed to Cappy but were not because of the error of the trustee. Even in cases where beneficiaries have already been paid funds by mistake, the amounts may be collected from them unless the recipients were bona fide purchasers or unless they, without notice of the improper payments, had so changed their position that it would be inequitable to make them repay. 5 Scott, Trusts § 465, at 341 (Fratcher 4th ed.1989). Allen v. Stewart, 214 Mass. 109, 113, 100 N.E. 1092 (1913). Welch v. Flory, 294 Mass. 138, 144, 200 N.E. 900 (1936). See National Academy of Sciences v. Cambridge Trust Co., 370 Mass. 303, 307, 346 N.E.2d 879 (1976). Here, the remainder of Cappy's trust has not yet been distributed, and there is no reason to depart from the usual rule of impressing a constructive trust in favor of

Cappy's estate on the amounts wrongfully withheld. There is also no problem as to the statute of limitations. The period of limitations with respect to those we hold to be constructive trustees (the beneficiaries of the trust under Article IIC) has not run as, at the earliest, their entitlement to funds occurred at Cappy's death in 1987.

That Cappy assented to the accounts is also no bar to recovery by his estate. The judge found that he was in the dark as to his rights to receive principal for the upkeep of the home. An assent may be withdrawn by a judge "if it is deemed improvident or not conducive to justice." Swift v. Hiscock, 344 Mass. 691, 693, 183 N.E.2d 875 (1962). See Akin v. Warner, 318 Mass. 669, 675, 63 N.E.2d 566 (1945). The accounts were not allowed, and we need not consider the effect of G.L. c. 206, § 24, * * * which permits the impeachment of an account after a final decree has been entered only for "fraud or manifest error." See Holyoke Natl. Bank v. Wilson, 350 Mass. at 228, 214 N.E.2d 42; National Academy of Sciences v. Cambridge Trust Co., 370 Mass. at 309, 346 N.E.2d 879.

The amounts to be paid to Cappy's estate have not been determined. * * * On remand, the Probate Court judge is to hold such hearings as are necessary to determine the amounts which should have been paid to Cappy to enable him to retain possession of the house.

5. *Personal liability of the trustee.* Farr raises a number of defenses against the imposition of personal liability, including the statute of limitations, the exculpatory clause in the will, and the fact that Cappy assented to the accounts of the trustee. The judge found that Farr's breach of his fiduciary duty to inquire as to Cappy's needs and his other actions in response to Cappy's request for principal, including the involvement of Sally in distributions of principal despite Sara's provision that Cappy's trust be administered separately, led Cappy to be unaware of his right to receive principal for house expenses. The breach may also be viewed as a continuing one. In these circumstances we do not consider Cappy's assent, see Swift v. Hiscock, 344 Mass. at 693, 183 N.E.2d 875, or the statute of limitations to be a bar. See Greenfield Sav. Bank v. Abercrombie, 211 Mass. 252, 259, 97 N.E. 897 (1912); Allen v. Stewart, 214 Mass. at 113, 100 N.E. 1092; Akin v. Warner, 318 Mass. at 675–676, 63 N.E.2d 566. The judge also found that Margaret learned of Cappy's right to principal for house expenses only when she sought other counsel after his death.

The more difficult question is the effect of the exculpatory clause. As indicated in part 3 of this opinion, we consider the order to Marlette to reconvey the property an inappropriate remedy. In view of the judge's finding that, but for the trustee's breach, Cappy would have retained ownership of the house, the liability of the trustee could be considerable.

Although exculpatory clauses are not looked upon with favor and are strictly construed, such "provisions inserted in the trust instrument without any overreaching or abuse by the trustee of any fiduciary or confidential relationship to the settlor are generally held effective except as to breaches of trust 'committed in bad faith or intentionally or with reckless indifference to the interest of the beneficiary.'" New

England Trust Co. v. Paine, 317 Mass. 542, 550, 59 N.E.2d 263 (1945), S.C., 320 Mass. 482, 485, 70 N.E.2d 6 (1946). See Dill v. Boston Safe Deposit & Trust Co., 343 Mass. 97, 100–102, 175 N.E.2d 911 (1961); Boston Safe Deposit & Trust Co. v. Boone, 21 Mass.App.Ct. 637, 644, 489 N.E.2d 209 (1986). The actions of Farr were not of this ilk and also do not fall within the meaning of the term used in the will, "willful neglect or default."

Farr testified that he discussed the exculpatory clause with Sara and that she wanted it included. Nevertheless, the judge, without finding that there was an over-reaching or abuse of Farr's fiduciary relation with Sara, held the clause ineffective. Relying on the fact that Farr was Sara's attorney, she stated: "One cannot know at this point in time whether or not Farr specifically called this provision to Sara's attention. Given the total failure of Farr to use his judgment as to [C]appy's needs, it would be unjust and unreasonable to hold him harmless by reason of the exculpatory provisions he himself drafted and inserted in this instrument."

Assuming that the judge disbelieved Farr's testimony that he and Sara discussed the clause, although such disbelief on her part is by no means clear, the conclusion that it "would be unjust and unreasonable to hold [Farr] harmless" is not sufficient to find the overreaching or abuse of a fiduciary relation which is required to hold the provision ineffective. See Restatement (Second) of Trusts § 222, comment d (1959).[10] We note that the judge found that Sara managed all the finances of the couple, and from all that appears, was competent in financial matters.

There was no evidence about the preparation and execution of Sara's will except for the questions concerning the exculpatory clause addressed to Farr by his own counsel. No claim was made that the clause was the result of an abuse of confidence. See Boston Safe Deposit & Trust Co. v. Boone, 21 Mass.App.Ct. at 644, 489 N.E.2d 209.

The fact that the trustee drew the instrument and suggested the insertion of the exculpatory clause does not necessarily make the provision ineffective. Restatement (Second) of Trusts § 222, comment d. No rule of law requires that an exculpatory clause drawn by a prospective trustee be held ineffective unless the client is advised independently. Cf. Barnum v. Fay, 320 Mass. 177, 181, 69 N.E.2d 470 (1946).

---

10. The Restatement lists six factors which may be considered in determining whether a provision relieving the trustee from liability is ineffective on the ground that it was inserted in the trust instrument as a result of an abuse of a fiduciary relationship at the time of the trust's creation. The six factors are:

> (1) whether the trustee prior to the creation of the trust had been in a fiduciary relationship to the settlor, as where the trustee had been guardian of the settlor; (2) whether the trust instrument was drawn by the trustee or by a person acting wholly or partially on his behalf; (3) whether the settlor has taken independent advice as to the provisions of the trust instrument; (4) whether the settlor is a person of experience and judgment or is a person who is unfamiliar with business affairs or is not a person of much judgment or understanding; (5) whether the insertion of the provision was due to undue influence or other improper conduct on the part of the trustee; (6) the extent and reasonableness of the provision.

The judge used an incorrect legal standard in invalidating the clause. While recognizing the sensitivity of such clauses, we hold that, since there was no evidence that the insertion of the clause was an abuse of Farr's fiduciary relationship with Sara at the time of the drawing of her will, the clause is effective.

Except as provided herein, the motions of the defendants for a new trial and amended findings are denied. The plaintiff's claim of error as to legal fees fails to recognize that fees under G.L. c. 215, § 45, are a matter within the discretion of the trial judge. We find no abuse of discretion in the denial of fees.

The judgment is vacated, and the matter is remanded to the Probate Court for further proceedings to determine the amounts which, if paid, would have enabled Cappy to retain ownership of the residence. Such amounts shall be paid to Cappy's estate from the trust for his benefit prior to distributing the balance thereof to the trust under Article IIC of Sara's will. * * *

So ordered.

Uniform Trust Code (2019)

§ 814. Discretionary Powers; Tax Savings.

(a) Notwithstanding the breadth of discretion granted to a trustee in the terms of the trust, including the use of such terms as "absolute," "sole," or "uncontrolled," the trustee shall exercise a discretionary power in good faith and in accordance with the terms and purposes of the trust and the interests of the beneficiaries.

§ 1008. Exculpation of Trustee.

(a) A term of a trust relieving a trustee of liability for breach of trust is unenforceable to the extent that it:

(1) relieves the trustee of liability for breach of trust committed in bad faith or with reckless indifference to the purposes of the trust or the interests of the beneficiaries; or

(2) was inserted as the result of an abuse by the trustee of a fiduciary or confidential relationship to the settlor.

(b) An exculpatory term drafted or caused to be drafted by the trustee is invalid as an abuse of a fiduciary or confidential relationship unless the trustee proves that the exculpatory term is fair under the circumstances and that its existence and contents were adequately communicated to the settlor.

§ 1009. Beneficiary's Consent, Release, or Ratification.

A trustee is not liable to a beneficiary for breach of trust if the beneficiary consented to the conduct constituting the breach, released the trustee from liability for the breach, or ratified the transaction constituting the breach, unless:

(1) the consent, release, or ratification of the beneficiary was induced by improper conduct of the trustee; or

(2) at the time of the consent, release, or ratification, the beneficiary did not know of the beneficiary's rights or of the material facts relating to the breach.

Kim Kamin
Ethical Considerations in Thorny Trusteeships
154 Trusts & Ests. 52 (May 2015)

[Exculpation] provisions seek to exonerate trustees from liability for certain acts and omissions. But, courts will strictly construe such clauses, and those clauses won't apply to breaches of fiduciary duties falling outside the clauses' scope. [Citation omitted.] Exculpation clauses won't relieve a trustee of liability for breaches of trust committed intentionally, in bad faith, with reckless indifference to the beneficiary's interests or for profits the trustee derived from the breach. [Citation omitted.] In determining whether an exculpatory clause was inserted into the trust instrument as a result of an abuse of a fiduciary or confidential relationship, factors to consider include the extent and reasonableness of the provision, as well as whether: (1) a fiduciary relationship existed prior to the creation of the trust; (2) the settlor received independent advice; (3) the settlor is a person of experience and judgement; and (4) the provision was inserted due to undue influence or other improper conduct. [Citation omitted.]

Id. at 52–53.

Alexander A. Bove, Jr.
The Death of the Trust
153 Trusts & Ests. 51 (Feb. 2014)

A disturbing trend is afoot regarding fiduciary liability: States are passing laws that exculpate fiduciaries from virtually all liability other than outright fraud or criminal acts. This approach, together with the option of totally exculpating the trust advisor, is seriously undermining our centuries-old respect of the trust relationship. The logical and, unfortunately, likely outcome of this trend is the death of the trust as we know it.

* * *

The issue is that we appear to be headed towards practical abandonment of liability for losses caused by the negligence of parties to whom our clients have entrusted their assets. Should we not take it upon ourselves to reject this trend, reject blanket exculpation provisions for trustees and trust advisors, give our clients' interests the higher priority and let those with the responsibility bear the responsibility?

Id. at 55.

C. Grantor/Crummey Trusts

Often a settlor will create a trust of assets to favor a certain class of beneficiaries and to achieve certain tax benefits. For example, in the *Brainard* decision, discussed *supra*, the settlor declared himself Trustee of undetermined assets for the benefit of his mother, spouse, and children. One incentive for doing so may have been to place whatever income was generated into their income brackets, rather than his own. The settlor was probably responsible for their support and he was providing it with his after-tax dollars from his tax bracket. Why not assist his dependents in meeting their own needs with dollars earned in their lower tax brackets? The settlor was attempting to create a grantor trust, often called a Clifford trust.

Congress and the Internal Revenue Service have made grantor trusts extremely difficult to create, lessening the incentive to save taxes by shifting income. I.R.C. §§ 671 to 677 govern the taxation of grantor trusts. *See also* Robert T. Danforth, *The Use of Grantor Trusts in Estate Planning*, TAX MGMT. ESTS., GIFTS & TRUST J. 103 (Mar/Apr. 2006). As a general rule, if the settlor or the settlor's spouse retains control over the property, then the settlor remains the owner of the property and is entitled to the income, and the deductions associated with it. Thus, Family Estate Trusts will not avoid income taxes for the settlor, *see* I.R.C. § 212 (2015), with minor exceptions, income from the trust will be taxed to the settlor if the trust corpus will revert to the settlor or the settlor's spouse, *see id.* at § 673, and the settlor is taxed on the income if the settlor or the settlor's spouse retains administrative powers allowing for financial benefits that would not be available in an arms-length transaction, *see id.* at § 675. The point is that a grantor trust is a complicated endeavor and should be employed only with expert legal assistance.

Tax Considerations: The taxation of grantor trusts needs to be addressed in more detail for those persons seeking a better understanding of their popularity and utilization. The issue arises in the context of a parent seeking to generate income in lower tax bracket dependents, rather than themselves. Obviously, the point is to pay less income taxes on the money earned, yet meet the needs of family members. When Congress passed legislation taxing a portion of the unearned income of children under the age of 14 at the parents' marginal tax rate if the parents' marginal tax rate is higher than the child's, the ability to shift income was drastically curtailed. *See* I.R.C. § 1(g)(2); Melanie McCoskey, Joanie Sompayrac & Paul Streer, *Kiddie Tax Raises Costs, Complexity, and Need for Tax Planning*, PRACTICAL TAX STRATEGIES, May 2002, at 279. Indeed, the curtailment of income-shifting—the Kiddie Tax—was an element identified in the Tax Reconciliation Act of 1986 and the Revenue Reconciliation Act of 1990. Parents—grantors—are left with few options if they wish to reduce income or estate taxes, take advantage of the annual gift tax exclusion, provide for a separate estate for minors, or create a tax-deferred fund to pay for college education. The rules are complicated and require expert assistance. *See, e.g.,* Brenda J. Rediess-Hoosein, *Methods of Transferring Assets to Minors Affected by Recent Tax Changes*, 18 EST. PLAN., March/April 1991, at 86. For further commentary on the use of Grantor Trusts, see, *e.g.,* David L. Case, *Conversion from Non-Grantor to Grantor Trust: Tax Issues*, 46 EST. PLAN. 11 (2019); Evan H. Farr, *Asset Protection Planning for Veterans' Benefits Eligibility*, 46 EST. PLAN. 26 (2019); Adam Hofri-Winogradow, *The Demand for Fiduciary Services: Evidence from the Market in Private Donative Trusts*, 68 HASTINGS L.J. 931 (2017).

Internal Revenue Code Sections §§ 671 to 677 provide labyrinthine income tax rules that determine whether a grantor will be treated as the owner of an *inter vivos* trust. Many of these rules focus on a retained power exercisable by a grantor, or a non-adverse party, or both. Internal Revenue Code § 676 provides that the grantor will be treated as the owner of a trust (including income and capital gains earned by the trust) where, at the time, the grantor (or a non-adverse party or both) retains the right to revoke the trust. Internal Revenue Code § 677(a) provides that a grantor is treated as the owner of any portion of a trust, the income from which is, or may be, distributed to the grantor or the grantor's spouse or held or accumulated for future distribution to the grantor or the grantor's spouse. These are only some of the rules.

Less complicated than grantor trusts, but often used in conjunction with issue (children), are Internal Revenue Code § 2503(c) trusts. These devices address the issue raised in I.R.C. § 2503(b), which requires that the donee of a gift have a present interest in the property transferred to qualify for the annual exclusion amount for each donee child. There is an exception to this rule in I.R.C. § 2503(c), which allows estate planners to create a trust, the transfers to which qualify for the annual exclusion under § 2503(b), and at the same time permits the parents to maintain control over the assets given to the trust for the child's benefit. The trust must meet the requirements of I.R.C. § 2503(c), which allows the trustee to have discretionary authority to distribute or accumulate the trust's income or principal to the child before he or she reaches 21. The trustee's discretionary payments may include items such as support, health, and education. However, when the child turns 21, the principal and interest must be paid to the child, or if the child dies prior to attaining age 21, the principal and income must be paid to the child's estate, or such persons as the child appoints pursuant to a general testamentary power of appointment. *See* I.RC. § 2041. The trust may provide specific takers in default if the power is not exercised by the child. Through the trustee, the parent has control over the funds throughout the child's minority, and then at death, if the child does not exercise the power of appointment, the parent has established a control mechanism through takers in default. Powers of appointment will be discussed in greater detail, *infra,* but they play a role in these § 2503(c) trusts, and in one other similar arrangement — Crummey Trusts.

A Crummey Trust allows a parent to give to the child, for example, assets, in trust, covered by a general power of appointment, and, in so doing, to appoint the asset to himself or herself for a limited period of time. This is the crucial feature. At the end of a limited time period, the power lapses if it is not exercised by the donee (the child) of the power, and the property remains in the trust. Because the donee had the power to appoint to himself or herself for a period of time, the donee had a present interest in the assets and, thus, qualifies for the annual gift tax exclusion in I.R.C. § 2503(b), even though the reality is that the parent is still in control of the asset through the trustee. The term "Crummey Trust" derives its name from Crummey v. Commissioner, 397 F.2d 82 (9th Cir. 1968).

Finally, of particular interest to students, tuition paid by someone other than the student on behalf of the student, if paid directly to an educational institution, is not a gift subject to taxation. Also, payments made for medical care are not considered gifts. *See* I.R.C. § 2503(e)(2).

D. Oral Trusts

Uniform Trust Code (2019)

§ 407. Evidence of Oral Trust.

Except as required by a statute other than this [Code], a trust need not be evidenced by a trust instrument, but the creation of an oral trust and its terms may be established only by clear and convincing evidence.

New York Estates, Powers & Trusts Law (2019)

§ 7-1.17. Execution, amendment and revocation of lifetime trusts

(a) Every lifetime trust shall be in writing and shall be executed and acknowledged by the initial creator and, unless such creator is the sole trustee, by at least one trustee thereof, in the manner required by the laws of this state for the recording of a conveyance of real property or, in lieu thereof, executed in the presence of two witnesses who shall affix their signatures to the trust instrument.

(b) Any amendment or revocation authorized by the trust shall be in writing and executed by the person authorized to amend or revoke the trust, and except as otherwise provided in the governing instrument, shall be acknowledged or witnessed in the manner required by paragraph (a) of this section, and shall take effect as of the date of such execution. Written notice of such amendment or revocation shall be delivered to at least one other trustee within a reasonable time if the person executing such amendment or revocation is not the sole trustee, but failure to give such notice shall not affect the validity of the amendment or revocation or the date upon which same shall take effect. No trustee shall be liable for any act reasonably taken in reliance on an existing trust instrument prior to actual receipt of notice of amendment or revocation thereof.

Goodman v. Goodman

Supreme Court of Washington, 1995
128 Wash. 2d 366, 907 P.2d 290

JOHNSON, Justice.

This case involves a family dispute between Clive Goodman's mother, Gladys Goodman, and his children over property he transferred to Gladys before his death in 1983. A jury found Gladys held Clive's property in trust for his children and wrongfully withheld the property. The trial judge granted judgment notwithstanding the verdict (JNOV),[1] having found the children commenced the action after the

---

1. Under CR 50, as amended, a JNOV is now a judgment as a matter of law.

limitations period had run. At issue is whether the trial court erred by granting JNOV because Gladys did not propose jury instructions on the statute of limitations defense, and whether there were disputed facts regarding the limitations period such that it could not be decided as a matter of law. Because in this case the issue of when the statute of limitations began to run was susceptible to more than one reasonable interpretation, it presented a question of fact that could not be decided on a motion for a JNOV. We reverse.

Clive Goodman died in November 1983 after a three-year struggle with a liver disease. His illness required frequent hospitalizations and complicated medical procedures. About five years before his death, Clive gave Gladys general power of attorney. About one year before his death, he transferred his major asset, Ozzie's East Tavern, to Gladys. Gladys sold the tavern on an installment contract in 1982 for $70,000; she deposited the proceeds of the sale in her bank account.

Clive was survived by four children: Scott, Craig, Michelle, and his stepdaughter Tamara. When Clive died in 1983, Scott was seventeen, Craig was sixteen, Michelle was thirteen, and Tamara was twenty-one. He was also survived by Shirley Golden, his first wife and mother of all the children. Shirley and Clive had divorced in 1972, but remained close friends until his death.

Some eight years after Clive's death, when Scott was 25 years old, he asked Gladys for the first time for money from the sale of Ozzie's East and Clive's other assets. When Scott asked Gladys for the money, she reportedly told him she had taken care of Clive and felt she deserved it.

Scott then hired an attorney and was appointed personal representative of Clive's estate. He sued Gladys in that capacity in 1991, alleging that Clive intended Gladys to hold Clive's property for the benefit of his children until they were the age of majority or were able to receive and manage the property on their own. Gladys pleaded laches as an affirmative defense and counterclaimed for offset of money she had loaned to Clive or had paid on his behalf.

At trial, Shirley testified Clive had a will, had transferred all of his property to Gladys, and intended his children to have his property when they were old enough to responsibly manage it. She testified that shortly after the funeral, Gladys told her there was no will but she would give the children Clive's money when they were old enough to be responsible. Shirley relayed this information to the children. The children did not have a problem with Gladys holding Clive's property in trust. Shirley thought about hiring an attorney at this time but could not afford one. She stated:

> I wasn't concerned at all about the moneys. I felt very confident that there wouldn't be a problem with it. She [Gladys] told me the same things Dee [Clive] had told me.

Report of Proceedings, vol. I at 68. Shirley first became concerned when Scott asked Gladys about the property in 1991.

Clive's stepdaughter Tamara testified she had seen Clive's will in 1977 and briefly discussed it with him. Based on that conversation, she believed Clive's property would be divided among the children. About one year after Clive's death, Tamara heard from relatives that all of Clive's property was in Gladys' name, and the children were not entitled to anything. She believed she discussed this with her siblings and Shirley around Christmas 1983. Shirley does not recall discussing this with Tamara.

Gladys testified she never had a conversation with Shirley regarding Clive's property or a will. She also testified Clive gave her the money to repay numerous loans and out of love and appreciation.

At the close of Scott's case, Gladys moved for a directed verdict on the grounds the limitations period had run. The trial court reserved ruling on this motion.

At the close of testimony, the trial court instructed the jury to decide whether Clive transferred his property to Gladys as a gift or to hold in trust for the benefit of the children. It defined a trust as:

> A trust can be defined as a right of property, real or personal, held by one party for the benefit of another. It is a confidence placed in one person, who is termed a trustee, for the benefit of another, respecting property which is held by the trustee for the benefit of another. A trust need not be in writing. A trust can arise or be implied from circumstances as a result of the presumed intention of the parties as gathered from the nature of the transaction between them.

Clerk's Papers at 28. Gladys did not offer a jury instruction on the statute of limitations defense, nor did she except to the trial court's failure to give one.

The jury found Gladys held the property in trust for the benefit of Clive's children, and the children incurred damages of $60,000 as a result of Gladys' wrongful retention of the trust property. They also found Gladys was entitled to an offset of $11,000.

Following the verdict, the trial court granted Gladys' motion for a JNOV, finding that the children should have discovered the cause of action more than three years before Scott commenced the action. The Court of Appeals agreed. It found the statute of limitations issue presented a factual question, but affirmed the trial court because the facts were susceptible of only one reasonable interpretation: the children were put on notice of facts, which with the exercise of due diligence would have led to discovery of the wrongdoing as each of them turned eighteen and received nothing. Because the youngest child turned eighteen more than three years before the commencement of the action, the suit was time barred. Goodman v. Goodman, No. 13005-3-III, slip op. at 7 (Mar. 28, 1995).

In reviewing a JNOV, this court applies the same standard as the trial court. Peterson v. Littlejohn, 56 Wash.App. 1, 8, 781 P.2d 1329 (1989). A JNOV is proper only when the court can find, "as a matter of law, that there is neither evidence nor reasonable inference therefrom sufficient to sustain the verdict." Brashear v. Puget

Sound Power & Light Co., 100 Wash.2d 204, 208–09, 667 P.2d 78 (1983) (quoting Hojem v. Kelly, 93 Wash.2d 143, 145, 606 P.2d 275 (1980)). A motion for a JNOV admits the truth of the opponent's evidence and all inferences that can be reasonably drawn therefrom, and requires the evidence be interpreted most strongly against the moving party and in the light most favorable to the opponent. No element of discretion is involved. Davis v. Early Constr. Co., 63 Wash.2d 252, 254–55, 386 P.2d 958 (1963). Viewing the evidence in the light most favorable to the non-moving party, we hold the statute of limitations defense presented a question of fact that could not be decided as a matter of law.

The parties and the courts below have referred to the trust as a constructive trust. A constructive trust is an equitable remedy imposed by courts when someone should not in fairness be allowed to retain property. Farrell v. Mentzer, 102 Wash. 629, 174 P. 482 (1918); see generally George T. Bogert, Trusts § 77 (6th ed. 1987). An express trust, on the other hand, arises because of expressed intent and involves a fiduciary relationship in which the trustee holds property for the benefit of a third party. In re Lutz, 74 Wash.App. 356, 365, 873 P.2d 566 (1994).

Scott's theory in this case, consistent with the jury instructions, was that Clive intended Gladys to hold his personal property in trust until the children reached majority or were mature enough to handle it. In support of this theory, Shirley testified:

A. The only thing[ ] that was said, was the day of the funeral. . . . [Gladys] said that she was not giving them [the children] any money until they got older. Because she didn't want them blowing it.

Q. Did you relay that to the children?

A. Yes.

Q. Did she indicate how much older they would have to get?

A. Until they were responsible. See, we have had a few problems with Scott. And—just took him a little longer than it does other people to grow up.

Report of Proceedings, vol. I at 19–20.

Q. Well, did you ever explain to them what you perceived to be Mrs. Goodman's role in holding onto the property?

A. Well, they just knew that their grandmother was going to—give them the money after they reached a certain age. I didn't know what the certain age was. One child could be—responsible at this age. Another one won't. So I didn't know what she was waiting for. Or—I never questioned it because Dee had told me that they were going to be taken care of, they weren't going to get their money until they were—older.

Report of Proceedings, vol. I at 24.

Consistent with this and other testimony, the jury found Clive intended Gladys to hold his property in trust for the children. This being the case, the trust at issue is properly characterized as an express trust.

An action based on an express (or constructive trust) is subject to the three-year statute of limitations contained in RCW 4.16.080. Viewcrest Coop. Ass'n v. Deer, 70 Wash.2d 290, 294–95, 422 P.2d 832 (1967); Arneman v. Arneman, 43 Wash.2d 787, 800, 264 P.2d 256, 45 A.L.R.2d 370 (1953). The statute of limitations on an express trust action begins to run when the beneficiary of the trust discovers or should have discovered the trust has been terminated or repudiated by the trustee.[2] Rogich v. Dressel, 45 Wash.2d 829, 841, 278 P.2d 367 (1954). A repudiation occurs when the trustee by words or other conduct denies there is a trust and claim the trust property as his or her own. The repudiation must be plain, strong, and unequivocal. O'Steen v. Estate of Wineberg, 30 Wash.App. 923, 932, 640 P.2d 28, review denied, 97 Wash.2d 1016 (1982). Whether the statute of limitations bars a suit is a legal question, but the jury must decide the underlying factual questions unless the facts are susceptible of but one reasonable interpretation. Washburn v. Beatt Equip. Co., 120 Wash.2d 246, 263, 840 P.2d 860 (1992); Richardson v. Denend, 59 Wash.App. 92, 95, 795 P.2d 1192 (1990), review denied, 116 Wash.2d 1005, 803 P.2d 1309 (1991).

Thus, the trial court could only grant a JNOV on this issue as a matter of law if no triable issue of fact existed as to when Gladys repudiated or terminated the trust. See Haslund v. City of Seattle, 86 Wash.2d 607, 621, 547 P.2d 1221 (1976). The jury found Gladys held Clive's property in trust for the children. Although no findings were made concerning the terms of the trust, the trial testimony supports Scott's view that Clive intended Gladys to hold the property until the children reached majority or were mature enough to handle it. Had the evidence only been that Clive intended Gladys to hold his property until the children reached majority, the repudiation would have occurred when each child turned eighteen and received nothing as the trial court found. But given the jury's verdict and the evidence that Clive intended the children to have his property when they were mature enough to handle it, it can hardly be said as a matter of law that the repudiation occurred when each child turned eighteen. A reasonable interpretation of the evidence is the repudiation occurred in 1991 when Gladys told Scott for the first time she deserved Clive's money and would not give him anything. Under these circumstances, when Gladys repudiated the trust is susceptible to more than one reasonable interpretation, and the trial court erred.

Having decided the trial erred by granting JNOV, it is unnecessary to resolve the second issue—whether a trial court may grant a JNOV on the grounds the action is barred by the statute of limitations when the jury is not instructed on the statute of limitations, but the moving party earlier asks for a directed verdict on this issue. We note, however, that the "take out" rule in Browne v. Cassidy, 46 Wash.App. 267, 728 P.2d 1388 (1986) is not implicated because Gladys moved for a directed verdict on the limitations issue.

---

2. The statute of limitations begins to run on a constructive trust when the beneficiary discovers or should have discovered the wrongful act which gave rise to the constructive trust. *Arneman*, 43 Wash.2d at 800, 264 P.2d 256.

Both parties requested attorney's fees in their briefs to the Court of Appeals under RAP 18.1 and RCW 11.96.140. We will not review the Court of Appeals decision denying attorney's fees because Scott's petition for review does not identify attorney's fees as an issue for review. RAP 13.4; RAP 13.7(b).

DURHAM, C.J., DOLLIVER, SMITH, MADSEN, ALEXANDER and TALMADGE, JJ., and PEKELIS, Judge Pro Tem., concur.

SANDERS, J., did not participate.

Notes

Although they should not be, oral trusts are quite common: "I am giving you this now, and this is what I want you to do with it." Or perhaps, "In my Last Will and Testament, I am leaving you the farm, and I expect you to take care of Sadie with its proceeds." In each instance, the deed or will omitted any reference to the oral arrangement. Oral trusts are dangerous devices because of the havoc they play upon written instruments, valid deeds, and wills. The Statute of Frauds (1677) was an excellent bar to the enforcement of oral trusts but often allowed fraud to be perpetrated. The only recourse was to petition the court to enforce the oral trust on the basis of a constructive trust—an equitable remedy that seeks to right a wrong (unjust enrichment). But before arguing a constructive trust, if there is some writing that can be incorporated into a will, or allows for the proof of an oral *inter vivos* arrangement, then the level of proof is often met to sustain the oral arrangement. Please note the Uniform Trust Code § 407 and N.Y. Ests., Powers & Trusts L. § 7-1.17, provided *supra*, and ask how these statutes treat oral trusts.

E. Resulting and Constructive Trusts

A resulting trust arises through operation of law whenever the settlor has created a trust and it fails for any reason whatsoever. Perhaps the purpose has been accomplished, and trust property remains; perhaps the beneficiary dies with property remaining; or the settlor may have specified a named trustee, and that trustee dies or is no longer able to perform. Under these circumstances and more, the trust property will revert, through operation of law, back to the settlor or to the settlor's estate. Likewise, a constructive trust seeks to remedy bad acts, and it, too, arises by operation of law. Its purpose is to prevent unjust enrichment. It may arise whenever a person should not profit from his or her wrongdoing, such as murder, unfulfilled promises by someone in a confidential relationship, and domestic abuse.

Hieble v. Hieble

Supreme Court of Connecticut, 1972
164 Conn. 56, 316 A.2d 777

SHAPIRO, Associate Justice.

In this action the plaintiff sought a reconveyance of real property in the town of Killingworth which she had transferred to the defendant, claiming that he had agreed to reconvey the same to her, upon request, if she recovered from an illness. The trial court rendered judgment for the plaintiff and the defendant has appealed.

The trial court's finding of facts, which is not attacked, discloses that on May 9, 1959, the plaintiff, without consideration, transferred the title of her real estate by survivorship deed to her son, the defendant, and to her daughter. The plaintiff, who had that year undergone surgery for malignant cancer, feared a recurrence but believed that she would be out of danger if the cancer did not reappear within five years. She and the grantees orally agreed that the transfer would be a temporary arrangement; that she would remain in control of the property and pay all expenses and taxes; that once the danger of recrudescence had passed, the defendant and his sister would reconvey the property to the plaintiff on request. After the transfer, the plaintiff continued to reside on the property with her aged mother, whom she supported, her daughter and the defendant. In 1960, after the plaintiff expressed displeasure over the daughter's marriage, the daughter agreed to relinquish her interest in the property. A deed was prepared and the daughter and son, through a strawman, transferred title to the land to the plaintiff and her son in survivorship. In 1964, five years after the original conveyance, the plaintiff requested that the defendant reconvey his legal title to her, since she considered herself out of risk of a recurrence of cancer.

The plaintiff at that time needed money to make improvements on the land, particularly, to install running water and indoor plumbing facilities as a convenience for her aged mother. The defendant procrastinated, feigning concern about the boundaries of an adjacent forty-acre parcel which the plaintiff had given him in 1956. Although the defendant refused to convey his interest in the jointly-owned premises, some friends of the plaintiff ultimately prevailed on him to sign a mortgage for an improvement loan in 1965. Thereafter, the defendant assured the plaintiff that he would never marry but would continue to live with her. These were his reasons for refusing reconveyance until his marriage plans were disclosed. Although the plaintiff proposed that her son could keep the property if he remained single, he did marry in 1967 and moved out of the house. After her attempts to obtain his voluntary reconveyance failed, the plaintiff brought suit in 1969. Throughout the entire period of time material to this litigation, the plaintiff has borne all expenses and costs of improvement to the property.

From these facts the trial court concluded that a constructive trust * * * should be decreed on the basis of the oral agreement, the confidential relationship of the parties and their conduct with respect to the property. The defendant's appeal raises primarily the claim that the elements necessary to establish a confidential relationship, as the basis for a constructive trust, are lacking.

It hardly needs reciting that under our Statute of Frauds, General Statutes §52-550, oral agreements concerning interests in land are unenforceable. See Hanney v. Clark, 124 Conn. 140, 144–145, 198 A. 577. In this jurisdiction, however, the law is established that the Statute of Frauds does not apply to trusts arising by operation of law. Reynolds v. Reynolds, 121 Conn. 153, 158, 183 A. 394; Ward v. Ward, 59 Conn. 188, 196, 22 A. 149.

The case before us presents one of the most vexatious problems facing a court of equity in the area of constructive trusts, namely, whether equity should impose a constructive trust where a donee who by deed has received realty under an oral promise to hold and reconvey to the grantor has refused to perform his promise. See 3 Bogert, Trusts and Trustees (2d Ed.) §495; Costigan, 'Trusts Based on Oral Promises,' 12 Mich.L.Rev. 423, 515. Our task here, however, is considerably alleviated, since the defendant has not attacked the court's finding that the alleged agreement was in fact made, nor does he contest the receipt of parol evidence as having violated the Statute of Frauds. See, for example, Brown v. Brown, 66 Conn. 493, 34 A. 490; Todd v. Munson, 53 Conn. 579, 589, 4 A. 99; Dean v. Dean, 6 Conn. 284, 287–289. Although the deed recited that consideration was given for the 1959 transfer, the defendant does not attack the finding that there was no consideration for the conveyance. Indeed, in his brief the defendant abandons the claim that a recital of consideration suffices to rebut an allegation of a trust. See Andrews v. New Britain National Bank, 113 Conn. 467, 470, 155 A. 838. In addition, the complications typically involved in constructive trusts—for example, the claims of third parties or the testimony of deceased persons—are not present here. See the discussion in Hanney v. Clark, *supra*, 124 Conn. 144–146, 198 A. 577. In this case the plaintiff was both settlor and beneficiary of the trust.

Since the finding of facts is not challenged, the conclusion of the court that the parties stood in a confidential relationship must stand unless it is unreasonably drawn or unless it involves an erroneous application of law. Johnson v. Zoning Board of Appeals, 156 Conn. 622, 624, 238 A.2d 413; Davis v. Margolis, 107 Conn. 417, 422, 140 A. 823. The defendant's attack on this conclusion is without merit. He argues that because the plaintiff initiated the transfer and was a woman of mature years, and because he was an inexperienced young man, a court of equity should not recognize a relationship of confidentiality between them. We grant that the bond between parent and child is not per se a fiduciary one; it does generate, however, a natural inclination to repose great confidence and trust. See Suchy v. Hajicek, 364 Ill. 502, 509, 510, 4 N.E.2d 836; Wood v. Rabe, 96 N.Y. 414, 426. Coupled with the plaintiff's condition of weakness, her recent surgery, her anticipation of terminal illness, and the defendant's implicit reassurances of his faithfulness, this relationship becomes a classic example of the confidentiality to which equity will fasten consequences. See Restatement (Second), 1 Trusts §44, pp. 115–16; 3 Bogert, *supra*, §482. * * *

The defendant's next contention questions the sufficiency of the evidence to justify the imposition of a constructive trust. Since he does not attack the finding that there was an underlying oral agreement, he cannot question the sufficiency of evidence to support that finding. Brockett v. Jensen, 154 Conn. 328, 331, 225 A.2d 190; Davis v. Margolis, 107 Conn. 417, 422, 140 A. 823. Presumably, the defendant objects to the sufficiency of this 1959 oral agreement, standing by itself, to create a constructive trust. Here, three points are in order. First, the trial court reached its conclusion not only on the basis of that agreement but also on the conduct of the parties and the circumstances surrounding the conveyance, seen as a whole. As we have already noted, the defendant has failed to sustain his attack on the court's conclusion that a confidential relationship existed. Second, where a confidential relationship has been established, there is substantial authority that the burden of proof rests on the party denying the existence of a trust—and then, by clear and convincing evidence to negate such a trust. See Suchy v. Hajicek, *supra*, 364 Ill. 510, 4 N.E.2d 836; 89 C.J.S. Trusts § 155.[2] Our decision in Wilson v. Warner, 84 Conn. 560, 80 A. 718, is not contrary. There, in regard to an alleged resulting trust in decedent's estate, the court said (pp. 564, 565, 80 A. p. 719): 'But in all cases where the claimed trust title to land is disputed, the facts from which such trust may be implied should be clearly and satisfactorily established.' Third, as this court held in Dowd v. Tucker, 41 Conn. 197, 205, cited in Fisk's Appeal, *supra*, 81 Conn. 440, 71 A. 559, it is unnecessary to find fraudulent intent for the imposition of a constructive trust. Whether there be fraud at the inception or a repudiation afterward, the whole significance of such cases lies in the unjust enrichment of the grantee through his unconscionable retention of the trust res. See Dodson v. Culp, 217 Ga. 299, 122 S.E.2d 109; Kent v. Klein, 352 Mich. 652, 91 N.W.2d 11; Costigan, 'Trusts Based on Oral Promises,' 12 Mich.L.Rev. 536.

The defendant's argument that the reconveyances in 1960 extinguished his obligation has no support in the finding. Rather, the court's finding of facts concerning his conduct subsequent to the 1960 transfers undermines his position. The court found that the defendant countered the plaintiff's request with delay, pretending concern about the boundaries of his adjacent forty-acre parcel; that he gave, as a reason for refusing to reconvey, assurances that he would never marry and that he would continue to reside with his mother. Of more weight to a court of equity, however, is the fact that the 1960 transfers effected no essential legal or equitable change in the defendant's initial undertaking. The finding reveals that his interest remained that of a joint tenant with right of survivorship upon the sister's surrender of her title to the plaintiff. Not only has the defendant failed to substantiate his contention, but his claim that the plaintiff's case must fail for lack of a concomitant renewal of the oral agreement in 1960 misconceives the nature of a constructive trust. See the discussion in Moses v. Moses, 140 N.J.Eq. 575, 580–581, 53 A.2d 805. Indeed, the defendant's assertion could amount to no more than a unilateral attempt to extinguish the original oral agreement. In short, the absence of an express renewal of the defendant's promise does not impair the soundness of the court's conclusion. * * *

Finally, the defendant makes the claim that the plaintiff has unclean hands. There is nothing in the record to suggest that the 1959 transfer was an attempt to defraud

---

2. The same allocation of the burden of proof and a similar standard of proof have been imposed where a claimed gift of realty is contested between persons in confidential relationship. See McCutcheon v. Brownfield, 2 Wash.App. 348, 356, 467 P.2d 868; 38 Am.Jur.2d, Gifts, § 106.

creditors or to secrete assets from government agencies. Granted that the plaintiff offered to let her son keep the property in order to dissuade him from taking a wife, it cannot be said, as a matter of law, that her hands are tainted with an attempt to tamper with marriage, especially in view of the defendant's earlier assurances that he would never get married.

In light of the unattacked finding of the court that the defendant in fact had agreed to reconvey the property to the plaintiff upon request and the conclusion of the court, amply supported by the finding of fact, that a confidential relationship existed between the plaintiff and the defendant, the case comes squarely within the provisions of § 44 of the Restatement (Second) of Trusts: 'Where the owner of an interest in land transfers it *inter vivos* to another in trust for the transferor, but no memorandum properly evidencing the intention to create a trust is signed, as required by the Statute of Frauds, and the transferee refuses to perform the trust, the transferee holds the interest upon a constructive trust for the transferor, if . . . (b) the transferee at the time of the transfer was in a confidential relation to the transferor.'

There is no error.

In this opinion the other judges concurred.

Restatement (Third) of Trusts (2019)

§ 24. Result of Noncompliance With Statute of Frauds, cmts. h–j.

h(1). Burden of proof. In a proceeding to impose a constructive trust under this Comment *h*, where the transfer to the alleged trustee was accomplished by an instrument of transfer that does not disclose the existence of an intention to create a trust, the proof of that intent must be by clear and convincing evidence. A preponderance of the evidence is then sufficient to establish the intended interests of the beneficiaries.

i. Other cases: transfer "in trust." Where the owner of property transfers it *inter vivos* to another by a deed that states that the transfer is made "in trust" or to the transferee "as trustee," but the trust is unenforceable under a statute of frauds because the instrument does not provide the necessary terms of a trust, the transferee who refuses to perform the trust will not be permitted to retain the property free of trust.

On the face of the instrument of transfer it appears that the transferee takes only the legal title, and therefore holds upon resulting trust for the transferor unless the intended express trust is voluntarily performed (Comment *b*) or can be enforced on the basis of part performance (Comment *c*), or unless the rule of Subsection (2) applies. Ordinarily, the apparent resulting trust will be recognized and the transferee will be required to hold for the transferor by implication of law. See §§ 7 and 8. There is no need of a constructive trust to prevent a transferee's unjust enrichment.

A constructive trust may nevertheless be required in some situations, upon the same circumstances and rationale that support constructive trusts for intended beneficiaries of oral trusts in Comment *h*. That is, the transferee will hold upon such a constructive trust for the intended beneficiaries and purposes when necessary to avoid unjust enrichment of some or all of the transferor's successors in interest.

Notes

The court in *Heible* did not impute "unclean hands" to the mother's transfer of the real estate to her children. If it had, a constructive trust would have been unavailable to her as a remedy for the son's unjust enrichment. But other decisions have viewed similar conduct differently. *See, e.g,* Pappas v. Pappas, 320 A.2d 809 (Conn. 1973) (holding that a constructive trust was unavailable because of fraud perpetrated by the transferor). While the *Pappas* decision involved an attempt to conceal assets from a divorcing spouse, the *Heible* decision involved a person's attempt to qualify for Medicaid assistance provided for a person with very limited resources. For an explanation of Medicaid eligibility, see Raymond C. O'Brien & Michael T. Flannery, The Fundamentals of Elder Law 361–82 (2015); Raymond C. O'Brien, *Selective Issues on Effective Medicaid Estate Recovery Statutes*, 65 Cath. U. L. Rev. 27, 67–74 (2015).

F. Spendthrift Trusts

1. Traditional Spendthrift Trusts

Uniform Trust Code (2019)

§ 502. Spendthrift Provision.

(a) A spendthrift provision is valid only if it restrains both voluntary and involuntary transfer of a beneficiary's interest.

(b) A term of a trust providing that the interest of a beneficiary is held subject to a "spendthrift trust," or words of similar import, is sufficient to restrain both voluntary and involuntary transfer of the beneficiary's interest.

(c) A beneficiary may not transfer an interest in a trust in violation of a valid spendthrift provision and, except as otherwise provided in this [article], a creditor or assignee of the beneficiary may not reach the interest or a distribution by the trustee before its receipt by the beneficiary.

§ 503. Exceptions to Spendthrift Provision.

(a) In this section, "child" includes any person for whom an order or judgment for child support has been entered in this or another State.

(b) Even if a trust contains a spendthrift provision, a beneficiary's child, spouse, or former spouse who has a judgement or court order against the beneficiary for support or maintenance, or a judgment creditor who has provided services for the protection of a beneficiary's interest in the trust, may obtain from a court an order attaching present or future distributions to or for the benefit of the beneficiary.

(c) A spendthrift provision is unenforceable against a claim of this State or the United States to the extent a statute of this State or federal law so provides.

§ 504. Discretionary Trusts; Effect of Standard.

* * *

(b) Except as otherwise provided in subsection (c), whether or not a trust contains a spendthrift provision, a creditor of a beneficiary may not compel a distribution that is subject to the trustee's discretion, even if:

> (1) the discretion is expressed in the form of a standard of distribution; or

> (2) the trustee has abused the discretion.

(c) To the extent a trustee has not complied with a standard of distribution or has abused a discretion:

> (1) a distribution may be ordered by the court to satisfy a judgement or court order against the beneficiary for support or maintenance of the beneficiary's child, spouse, or former spouse; and

> (2) the court shall direct the trustee to pay to the child, spouse, or former spouse such amount as is equitable under the circumstances but not more than the amount the trustee would have been required to distribute to or for the benefit of the beneficiary had the trustee complied with the standard or not abused the discretion.

Bacardi v. White

Supreme Court of Florida, 1985
463 So. 2d 218

ALDERMAN, Justice.

Adriana Bacardi seeks review of the decision of the District Court of Appeal, Third District, in White v. Bacardi, 446 So.2d 150 (Fla. 3d DCA 1984), which expressly and directly conflicts with Gilbert v. Gilbert, 447 So.2d 299 (Fla. 2d DCA 1984).[1]

---

1. The facts in *Gilbert*, as stated by the Second District Court, are as follows:
In the judgment of dissolution, the court ordered the husband to pay permanent periodic alimony of $2,500 per month and lump sum alimony in the amount of $35,000 payable in six-month installments of $3,500. The court also required that he be responsible for reasonable and necessary medical expenses of the wife attributable to her multiple sclerosis and that he pay her attorney's fees of $24,750. The husband never paid the attorney's fees and later stopped paying alimony and the wife's medical expenses. The court entered a writ of ne exeat and held him in contempt, but these actions proved futile because he fled the jurisdiction. He is now thought to be living in England. The husband also removed his assets from the state, thereby thwarting the wife's efforts to collect the arrearages.
In her efforts to enforce the dissolution judgment, the wife sought to garnish the husband's interest in a trust established by Emily H. Gilbert for the benefit of various beneficiaries and administered by Southeast Bank as trustee. The trust contained the following paragraph:
5.2—Spendthrift Provision; the interest of each beneficiary in the income or principal of each trust hereunder shall be free from the control or interference of any creditor of a

The issue presented is whether disbursements from spendthrift trusts can be garnished to satisfy court ordered alimony and attorney's fee payments before such disbursements reach the debtor-beneficiary. The Third District in Bacardi held that a former wife of a spendthrift trust beneficiary may not reach the income of that trust for alimony before it reaches the beneficiary unless she can show by competent and substantial evidence that it was the settlor's intent that she participate as a beneficiary. We quash the decision of the district court and hold that disbursements from spendthrift trusts, in certain limited circumstances, may be garnished to enforce court orders or judgments for alimony before such disbursements reach the debtor-beneficiary.[2] We also hold that an order or judgment for attorney's fees awarded incident to the divorce or the enforcement proceedings may be collected in the same manner.

The facts relevant to this holding are as follows. Luis and Adriana Bacardi were married for approximately two years and had no children. When the marriage ended in divorce, they entered into an agreement whereby Mr. Bacardi agreed to pay Mrs. Bacardi alimony of $2,000 per month until the death of either of them or until she remarried. The final judgment dissolving their marriage incorporated this agreement.

Shortly thereafter Mr. Bacardi ceased paying alimony. Mrs. Bacardi subsequently obtained two judgments for the unpaid alimony, with execution authorized, in the total amount of $14,000. She also obtained a third judgment for attorney's fees in the amount of $1,000 awarded incident to the divorce. In aid of execution on the three judgments, she served a writ of garnishment on Robert White as a trustee of a spendthrift trust created by Mr. Bacardi's father for the benefit of his son Luis. Additionally, she obtained a continuing writ of garnishment against the trust income for future alimony payments as they became due.

The trust instrument contained a spendthrift provision which stated:

No part of the interest of any beneficiary of this trust shall be subject in any event to sale, alienation, hypothecation, pledge, transfer or subject to any

---

beneficiary or of any spouse of a married beneficiary and shall not be subject to attachment or susceptible of anticipation or alienation.

Notwithstanding this provision, the court entered judgment in garnishment against the bank as trustee for $50,500 arrearages in alimony and medical expenses and $18,000 in attorney's fees. The court also entered a continuing writ of garnishment directing the bank to pay to the wife out of the trust the periodic and lump sum alimony as it becomes due. *Id.* at 300–01.

The *Gilbert* court held:

In light of our strong public policy toward requiring persons to support their dependents, we hold that spendthrift trusts can be garnished for the collection of arrearages in alimony. We also believe that a claim for attorney's fees awarded incident to the divorce is collectible in the same manner. *Id.* at 302.

2. Although this case involves a garnishment to enforce court orders or judgments for alimony, the rationale of our holding would also apply to child support cases.

debt of said beneficiary or any judgment against said beneficiary or process in aid of execution of said judgment.

Both Luis Bacardi and Mr. White appealed the trial court's garnishment order. They asserted that under this spendthrift provision, the trust could not be garnished for the collection of alimony and incident attorney's fees. The district court agreed, reversed the trial court's order, and remanded the case for further proceedings.

The district court noted that this state has long recognized the validity of spendthrift trust provisions, Waterbury v. Munn, 159 Fla. 754, 32 So.2d 603 (1947), and further that Florida has no statutory law limiting or qualifying spendthrift provisions where alimony payments are involved. In deciding this case, the district court aligned itself with what it believed to be both the modern trend and the best reasoned view. It stated that its holding squares with the public policy of this state as expressed in Waterbury v. Munn. It concluded that the legislature, rather than the courts, should resolve the question whether that public policy should yield to the competing public policy of enforcing support.

Respondents urge that we approve the district court's decision and hold that the settlor's intent prevails over any public policy arguments which would allow the alienation of disbursements from the trust. They contend that an ex-wife's debt is no different than any ordinary debt even though it represents unpaid alimony and related attorney's fees and that, therefore, her claim should be treated the same as the claim of any other creditor. They assert that it is clear from reading the spendthrift provision that the settlor did not intend Adriana Bacardi to participate as a beneficiary and that this intent precludes garnishment.

This case involves competing public policies. On the one hand, there is the long held policy of this state that recognizes the validity of spendthrift trusts. On the other hand, there is the even longer held policy of this state that requires a former spouse or a parent to pay alimony or child support in accordance with court orders. When these competing policies collide, in the absence of an expression of legislative intent, this Court must decide which policy will be accorded the greater weight.

We recognize that spendthrift trusts serve many useful purposes such as protecting beneficiaries from their own improvidence, protecting parties from their financial inabilities, and providing a fund for support, all of which continue to have merit. We acknowledge that one of the basic tenets for the construction of trusts is to ascertain the intent of the settlor and to give effect to this intent. See West Coast Hospital Association v. Florida National Bank, 100 So.2d 807 (Fla.1958). We are also aware that some courts of other jurisdictions have refused to invade spendthrift income for alimony and support solely on the basis that the settlor's intent controls. For example, in Erickson v. Erickson, 197 Minn. 71, 266 N.W. 161 (1936), the Minnesota Supreme Court held that the ex-wife of a spendthrift trust beneficiary could not reach his interest for alimony and support and stated:

> When unrestrained by statute it is the intent of the donor, not the character of the donee's obligation, which controls the availability and disposition of his

gift. The donee's obligation to pay alimony or support money, paramount though it may be, should not, in our opinion, transcend the right of the donor to do as he pleases with his own property and to choose the object of his bounty. Our conclusion does not arise out of any anxiety for the protection of the beneficiary. In the absence of statute and within the limits as to perpetuities, a donor may dispose of his property as he fees fit, and this includes corpus or principal as well as income.

Id. at 78, 266 N.W. at 164 (emphasis supplied). Accord Bucknam v. Bucknam, 294 Mass. 214, 200 N.E. 918 (1936); Dinwiddie v. Baumberger, 18 Ill.App.3d 933, 310 N.E.2d 841 (1974).

Other jurisdictions have permitted an ex-spouse to reach the income of a spendthrift trust for alimony and child support on public policy grounds finding that the legal obligation of support is more compelling than enforcing the settlor's intent. See Safe Deposit & Trust Co. v. Robertson, 192 Md. 653, 65 A.2d 292 (1949) (spendthrift trust provisions should not be extended to alimony claims because the ex-spouse is a favored suitor and the claim is based upon the strongest public policy grounds); Lucas v. Lucas, 365 S.W.2d 372 (Tex.Civ.App.1962) (public policy will not allow a spendthrift trust beneficiary to be well taken care of when those who he has a legal duty to support must do without such support); Dillon v. Dillon, 244 Wis. 122, 11 N.W.2d 628 (1943) (public policy will not prohibit spendthrift trust funds from being reached by a beneficiary's wife). See also Restatement (Second) of Trusts § 157 (1959).

This state has always had a strong public policy favoring the enforcement of both alimony and child support orders. For example, in Brackin v. Brackin, 182 So.2d 1 (Fla.1966), we held that the basis of an order awarding alimony or support money is the obligation imposed by law that a spouse do what in equity and good conscience he or she ought to do under the circumstances. We said: "Unlike judgments and decrees for money or property growing out of other actions, alimony and support money may have no foundation other than the *public policy* which requires the husband to pay what he ought to pay. . . ." *Id.* at 6 (emphasis supplied). In City of Jacksonville v. Jones, 213 So.2d 259 (Fla. 1st DCA 1968), the district court stated "*[t]he public policy* of this state requires that judicial orders providing for payment of child support be enforceable." *Id.* at 259.

We have weighed the competing public policies and, although we reaffirm the validity of spendthrift trusts, we conclude that in these types of cases the restraint of spendthrift trusts should not be an absolute bar to the enforcement of alimony orders or judgments. Florida's interest in the enforcement of these awards under certain limited circumstances is paramount to the declared intention of the settlor and the restraint of a spendthrift trust.

In not every case where someone is attempting to enforce alimony orders or judgment, however, will garnishment of a spendthrift trust be appropriate. This enforcement alternative should be allowed only as a last resort. If the debtor himself or his property is within the jurisdiction of this state's courts, the traditional methods of enforcing alimony arrearages may be sufficient. In this event, there would be no overriding reason to defeat the intent of the settlor. Florida courts have a variety of methods available to enforce alimony and child support. When these traditional remedies are not effective, it would be unjust and inequitable to allow the debtor to enjoy the benefits of wealth without being subject to the responsibility to support those whom he has a legal obligation to support.

We further limit this right of garnishment to disbursements that are due to be made or which are actually made from the trust. If, under the terms of the trust, a disbursement of corpus or income is due to the debtor-beneficiary, such disbursement may be subject to garnishment. If disbursements are wholly within the trustee's discretion, the court may not order the trustee to make such disbursements. However, if the trustee exercises its discretion and makes a disbursement, that disbursement may be subject to the writ of garnishment.

This case raises another issue. The trial court ordered a continuing garnishment against the Bacardi trust for future payments of alimony as the sums became due. This order was challenged on appeal by the trustee and the debtor-beneficiary. In light of its holding that the trust was not subject to garnishment, the district court did not consider this issue. Since we quash the district court's holding, it is appropriate that we consider and resolve this issue.

The same point was presented and decided by the Second District in Gilbert v. Gilbert. In that case, the husband objected to a continuing writ of garnishment for future alimony against his spendthrift trust. He argued that section 61.12(2), Florida Statutes (1981), which authorized continuing writs of garnishment to enforce orders for alimony and child support, is applicable only to the garnishment of an employer. The Second District, in responding to this argument, held that the same result could be obtained under the provisions of section 61.11, Florida Statutes (1981), which reads as follows:

> 61.11 *Effect of judgment of alimony.* — A judgment of alimony granted under s. 61.08 or s. 61.09 releases the party receiving the alimony from the control of the other party, and the party receiving the alimony may use his alimony and acquire, use, and dispose of other property uncontrolled by the other party. When either party is about to remove himself or his property out of the state, or fraudulently convey or conceal it, the court may award a ne exeat or injunction against him or his property and make such orders as will secure alimony to the party who should receive it.

The *Gilbert* court said:

> The remedy is drastic but appropriate to cope with the husband's misconduct. We, therefore, sustain the continuing aspect of the order in lieu of ne exeat as necessary to secure payment of alimony. The bank may continue to administer the trust according to its provisions, but to protect itself it will need to withhold all payments due to the husband in excess of alimony then due and owing in order to secure the future alimony payments. The bank

is entitled to seek the court's instructions, and the order is always subject to modification upon a proper showing by any interested party. *Id.* at 302–03.

We agree that the continuing aspect of such orders may be sustained in lieu of ne exeat as necessary to secure payment of alimony. It should be remembered, however, that a continuing garnishment against a spendthrift trust in lieu of ne exeat is also a "last resort" remedy that is available only when the traditional methods of enforcing alimony arrearages are not effective. We also note that where a continuing garnishment is appropriate, the trustee, if it wishes to make payments to the debtor-beneficiary in excess of alimony then due, should seek court approval before it makes such payments. The court may then authorize such payments if sufficient assets remain in the trust or if other provisions are made to secure the payment of alimony to the person who should receive it.

We also hold that an order awarding attorney's fees or a judgment for such fees which result from the divorce or enforcement proceedings are collectible in the same manner. Such awards represent an integral part of the dissolution process and are subject to the same equitable considerations. If the ex-spouse must pay attorney's fees out of the support awards, it only reduces the amount of support available to the needy party. This is especially true where post-decretal services are required by an attorney to enforce such awards.

Accordingly, we quash the decision of the district court and remand this case for further proceedings consistent with our opinion.

It is so ordered.

ADKINS, OVERTON, McDONALD, EHRLICH and SHAW, JJ., concur.

BOYD, C.J., dissents.

Notes

Absent a spendthrift clause, creditors may ordinarily attach any interest generated by the trust as though the trust property were property of the beneficiary. But some states may limit the amount a creditor may take. *See, e.g.,* Cal. Prob. Code § 15306.5 (2019) (limited to 25 percent of payment otherwise made to beneficiary); Okla. Stat. tit. 60, § 175.25 (2015) ("all income due or to accrue in the future to the beneficiary in excess of Twenty-five Thousand Dollars ($25,000.00) per calendar year shall be subject to garnishment by creditors of the beneficiary and shall be fully alienable by the beneficiary."). Most professional trusts contain language establishing their spendthrift character, but some states automatically make a trust a spendthrift one, even in the absence of an express intent by the settlor that the trust is a spendthrift trust. *See, e.g.,* N.Y. Est. Powers & Trusts L. § 7-1.5 (2008).

Restatement (Third) of Trusts (2019)

§ 57. Forfeiture For Voluntary Or Involuntary Alienation.

Except with respect to an interest retained by the settlor, the terms of a trust may validly provide that an interest shall terminate or become discretionary upon an attempt by the beneficiary to transfer it or by the beneficiary's creditors to reach it, or upon the bankruptcy of the beneficiary.

Problem

In 1964, grandparents created an *inter vivos* trust to benefit their three grand-children, the only beneficiaries of the trust. The father of the three beneficiaries was named as trustee and he served as such until his death, when the trust terminated. The settlors inserted a spendthrift clause into the trust that prohibited the voluntary and involuntary transfer of a beneficiary's interest in the trust. In 2000, one of the benefi-ciary's assigned his interest in the trust to his two siblings, who also were beneficiaries, directing that his share be held in trust for their children. The trustee performed the assignment for the transferor and, in return, awarded $75,000 from the trust to the transferor. In 2010, the trustee died and the trust terminated, but in connection with the final accounting, the transferor argued that the assignment of his interest was invalid because the provision of the trust prohibited the assignment. The transferor then requested a return of his interest in the trust, together with a surcharge.

The two siblings, who were the recipients of the transferor's largesse, argued that the spendthrift clause must be viewed within the broad discretionary powers of the trustee and that the trustee acted within his authority when he allowed the assign-ment. Furthermore, they argued that the spendthrift clause is moot, since it cannot invalidate the transfer made more than twelve years earlier. If you were the probate judge asked to resolve this family dispute and rule upon the trustee's ability to make the transfer, explain how you would proceed. *See In re* Indenture of Trust Dated January 13, 1964, 235 Ariz. 40, 326 P.3d 307 (2014).

2. Self-Settled Asset Protection Trusts

In re Mortensen

United States Bankruptcy Court (D. Alaska)
2011 WL 5025249

DONALD MacDONALD IV, Bankruptcy Judge. . . .

Thomas Mortensen, the debtor and one of the defendants herein, is a self-employed project manager. He has a master's degree in geology but has not worked in that field for 20 years. He manages the environmental aspects of construction projects. Mortensen has contracted with major oil companies for work in the past. . . . In 1994, Mortensen and his former wife purchased 1.25 acres of remote, unimproved real property located near Seldovia, Alaska.[1] They paid $50,000.00 cash for the purchase. The parties divorced in 1998. Mortensen received his former wife's interest in the property. Subsequently, improvements were made to the property. A small shed was placed on the parcel in 2000 and some other small structures were

---

1. Mortensen testified that he accesses the property by taking a boat from Homer to Seldovia, then driving about 7 miles down an old logging road out of Seldovia and, finally, switching to a narrower footpath or ATV trail to reach the parcel.

built on it from 2001 through 2004. There is power to the property along with a well and septic system. The debtor transferred the property to a self-settled trust on February 1, 2005. The transfer of this property is the focal point of the current dispute.

Mortensen's divorce was a contested proceeding. In 1998, when the court divided the parties' assets and liabilities, Mortensen argued that the Seldovia property had been purchased with an inheritance and was to remain his sole and separate property. The court rejected his argument. It found that Mortensen wasn't credible on the issue, . . . [footnote omitted] and that the property was joint marital property. . . . [footnote omitted]. Nonetheless, Mortensen received the Seldovia property. He also received $61,581.00 from his wife's SBS account, another $24,000.00 in cash from the refinance of the couple's home and other miscellaneous personal property. In total, Mortensen received assets of $164,402.00 in the divorce. . . . [footnote omitted]. Mortensen was not liable for any debt arising out of the marital estate. His ex-wife received the family home. She assumed an encumbrance against the home and was obligated to remove Mortensen's name from a $78,000 obligation encumbering the home. . . . [footnote omitted]. There was no credit card debt described in the courts findings and conclusions and no credit card debt was to be assumed by either party to the divorce. . . . [footnote omitted].

In June of 2004, Mortensen filed a motion to impose child support against his ex-wife. . . . [footnote omitted]. Despite a joint custody arrangement, he asked for an increase in child support due to a decrease in his income. After the superior court granted his uncontested request, Mortensen's former spouse filed a Rule 60(b) motion. He filed an opposition to the motion on July 30, 2004. In his opposition, Mortensen stated:

> The property settlement and other expenses of the divorce drove me deeply into debt. After the divorce my debt continued to increase due to the ongoing legal expenses and the time required from profitable work in order to respond to two more years of repeated motions from the defendant. The defendant continued with motion practice for two years after the divorce ended. The defendant did not cease the motion practice until Judge Shortell told her in 2000 that he would consider awarding me attorney's fees if she persisted in filing frivolous motions. Saddled with debt and with increasing competition in my shrinking business market I have not recovered from the financial carnage of the divorce. . . . [footnote omitted].

Mortensen's income fluctuated substantially from year to year after the divorce. His 1999 income tax return was not placed into evidence. At a hearing held in state court on December 22, 2004, Mortensen revealed his annual income from 2000 through 2004. His net income in 2000 was $32,822.00. . . . [footnote omitted]. He also cashed out an annuity for $102,023.18 that year. In 2001, Mortensen had net income of $16,985.00. . . . [footnote omitted]. In 2002, his annual income dipped to $3,236.00. . . . [footnote omitted]. 2003 yielded income of $13,185.00. . . . [footnote omitted]. Mortensen's 2004 income was "about the same" as 2003. . . . [footnote omitted]. Prior to the divorce, Mortensen had averaged $50,000.00 to $60,000.00

a year in net income. . . . [footnote omitted]. . . . Mortensen didn't reveal his interest in establishing an asset protection trust at the hearing in December of 2004. Mortensen had heard about Alaska's asset protection trust scheme in casual conversation. He researched the topic and, using a template he had found, drafted a document called the "Mortensen Seldovia Trust (An Alaska Asset Preservation Trust)." Mortensen then had the trust document reviewed by an attorney. He said only minor changes were suggested by the attorney. . . . The express purpose of the trust was "to maximize the protection of the trust estate or estates from creditors' claims of the Grantor or any beneficiary and to minimize all wealth transfer taxes." . . . [footnote omitted]. The trust beneficiaries were Mortensen and his descendants. Mortensen had three children at the time the trust was created. . . . Mortensen designated two individuals, his brother and a personal friend, to serve as trustees. His mother was named as a "trust protector," and had the power to remove and appoint successor trustees and designate a successor trust protector. She could not designate herself as a trustee, however. The trustees and Mortensen's mother are named defendants in this adversary proceeding.

The trust was registered on February 1, 2005. . . . [footnote omitted]. As required by AS 34.40.110(j), Mortensen also submitted an affidavit which stated that: 1) he was the owner of the property being placed into the trust, 2) he was financially solvent, 3) he had no intent to defraud creditors by creating the trust, 4) no court actions or administrative proceedings were pending or threatened against him, 5) he was not required to pay child support and was not in default on any child support obligation, 6) he was not contemplating filing for bankruptcy relief, and 7) the trust property was not derived from unlawful activities. . . . [footnote omitted]. . . . On February 1, 2005, Mortensen quitclaimed the Seldovia property to the trust, as contemplated in the trust document. . . . [footnote omitted]. Per the trust, this realty was "considered by the Grantor and the Grantor's children to be a special family place that should not be sold and should remain in the family." . . . [footnote omitted]. . . . To facilitate this purpose, the trustees of the trust were requested, but not directed, to maintain and improve the Seldovia property "in the trust for the benefit, use and enjoyment of the Grantor's descendants and beneficiaries." . . . [footnote omitted]. . . . The Seldovia property was worth roughly $60,000.00 when it was transferred to the trust in 2005. Mortensen's mother sent him checks totaling $100,000.00 after the transfer. Mortensen claims this was part of the deal in his creation of the trust; his mother was paying him to transfer the property to the trust because she wanted to preserve it for her grandchildren. This desire is corroborated by notes his mother included with the two $50,000.00 checks she sent to him. The first check, No. 1013, was dated February 22, 2005, and referenced the Seldovia Trust, which had been registered just three weeks earlier. . . . [footnote omitted]. A short, handwritten note from Mortensen's mother, bearing the same date stated:

> Enclosed is my check # 1013 in the amount of fifty thousand dollars, as we have discussed, to pay you for the Seldovia property that you have put into the trust for my three special "Grands"!

In the next few weeks there will be a second check mailed to you in the amount of fifty thousand dollars, making a total of $100,000.00.

What a lot of fun memories have been made there! . . . [footnote omitted].

Mortensen's mother wrote him a second check on April 8, 2005. . . . [footnote omitted]. This check also referenced the Seldovia Trust. It was accompanied by a typewritten note which said, "Here we go with the second and final check for the Seldovia property in the amount of fifty thousand dollars, totaling in all $100,000.00, as we have been talking about." . . . [footnote omitted]. . . . Mortensen says he used the money his mother sent him to pay some existing debts and also put about $80,000.00 of the funds into the trust's brokerage account as "seed money" to get the trust going and to pay trust-related expenses, such as income and property taxes. There was no promissory note for the money he lent to the trust. Mortensen said these funds were invested, some profits were made, and he was repaid "pretty much" all of the loan within about a year's time. . . . Mortensen says the Seldovia property is recreational property. It was used primarily by him and his three children, but other family members also used it. Before the trust was created, Mortensen had lived on the property the majority of the time, and he says he could have exempted it from creditors' claims as an Alaska homestead if he had retained it rather than placing it in the trust. In support of this contention, he has provided copies of his 2004 Alaska voter registration application, . . . [footnote omitted] his 2003 fishing certificate, . . . [footnote omitted] his 2004 Alaska PFD application (filed in 2005), . . . [footnote omitted] a January, 2005, jury summons, . . . [footnote omitted] and his Alaska driver's license, . . . [footnote omitted] which all indicate that he resided in Seldovia when the trust was created. . . . Mortensen's financial condition has deteriorated since the establishment of the trust. His income has been sporadic. . . . [footnote omitted]. He used the cash he received from his mother and his credit cards to make speculative investments in the stock market and to pay living expenses. His credit card debt ballooned after the trust was created. In 2005, total credit card debt ranged from $50,000.00 to $85,000.00. . . . [footnote omitted]. When he filed his petition in August of 2009, Mortensen had over $250,000.00 in credit card debt. The $100,000.00 he received from his mother has been lost.

Mortensen claims that he was always able to make at least the minimum monthly payment on his credit card debts until he became ill in April of 2009. He needed immediate surgery and was hospitalized for almost two weeks. His illness required a long period of convalescence. Mortensen says he tried to return to work but was on pain medication which made him "fuzzy." He lost several work contracts while he was recovering. He first considered filing bankruptcy in early August, 2009. . . . Mortensen filed his chapter 7 petition on August 18, 2009. He owned no real property at the time of filing, but his Schedule B itemized personal property with a value of $26,421.00. He scheduled no secured or priority claims. General unsecured claims totaled $259,450.01, consisting of $8,140.84 in medical debt and $251,309.16 in credit card debt on 12 separate credit cards. His interest in the Seldovia Trust was not scheduled, but Mortensen disclosed the creation of the trust on his statement of financial affairs. His monthly income was listed as $4,221.00, consisting of $321.00 in child support and the balance as income from the operation of his business as a geologist and permits consultant. Mortensen indicates that he expected his income to decrease due to his ongoing health issues and the increasingly unfavorable market conditions for his profession. His itemized monthly expenses totaled $5,792.00, which exceeded his income by more than $1,500.00. Expenses included $1,350.00 for rent, $600.00 for "income and FICA tax obligations, not withheld," and $1,650.00 for expenses from the operation of his business. . . .

The trustee alleges that Mortensen failed to establish a valid asset protection trust under Alaska's governing statutes because Mortensen was insolvent when the trust was created on February 1, 2005. Under A.S. 34.40.110(j)(2), the settlor of an Alaskan asset protection trust must file an affidavit stating that "the transfer of the assets to the trust will not render the settlor insolvent." . . . [footnote omitted]. "Insolvent" is not defined in Alaska's asset protection trust statute or in any cases arising thereafter. The trustee applies the Bankruptcy Code's definition of insolvency found in 11 U.S.C. § 101(32), which provides that the term "insolvent" means:

> (A) with reference to an entity other than a partnership and a municipality, financial condition such that the sum of such entity's debts is greater than all of such entity's property, at a fair evaluation, exclusive of—
>
> > (i) property transferred, concealed, or removed with intent to hinder, delay, or defraud such entity's creditors; and
> >
> > (ii) property that may be exempted from property of the estate under section 522 of this title; . . . [footnote omitted]

While there is no indication that Alaska would adopt a similar definition in the trust statute, other states have adopted a similar approach.[34] I conclude that insolvency is established for purposes of Alaska's asset protection trust law if the debtor's liabilities exceed its assets, excluding the value of fraudulent conveyances and exemptions. Here, the applicable exemptions will be determined under state rather than federal law, because this court is applying Alaska law to determine if the trust was correctly established. The federal exemption statutes have no role in making that determination.

The trustee contends that the $100,000.00 received from Mortensen's mother was a gift and cannot be considered as an asset in making a determination of solvency. I respectfully disagree. Mortensen and his mother had an oral agreement for the creation of a trust for the benefit of Ms. Mortensen-Belound's grandchildren. Mortensen was to place the Seldovia property in trust and in return, his mother promised to pay him $100,000.00. Mortensen performed his end of the bargain.

---

34. *See* 37 Am.Jur.2d *Fraudulent Conveyances and Transfers* §§ 20, 21 (1964).

Based on his mother's promise, he transferred the Seldovia property to an irrevocable trust on February 1, 2005. . . . [footnote omitted]. His partial performance took the agreement outside the statute of frauds. . . . [footnote omitted]. As noted in § 90(1) of the *Restatement (Second) of Contracts*:

> (1) A promise which the promisor should reasonably expect to induce action or forbearance on the part of the promisee or a third person and which does induce such action or forbearance is binding if injustice can be avoided only by enforcement of the promise. The remedy granted for breach may be limited as justice requires.[37]

Ms. Mortensen-Belound's promise of payment should reasonably have been expected to induce action on the part of Mortensen and it did induce such action. The promise was binding on Ms. Mortensen-Belound and the proper remedy for a breach would have been payment of $100,000.00. Justice could have been avoided only by enforcement of the promise because Mortensen's creation of the trust was irrevocable. Justice would not require limitation of a remedy for breach because the damages are clearly liquidated. It is proper to include the $100,000.00 in Mortensen's balance sheet to determine solvency as a contract right existing as of February 1, 2005.

Mortensen prepared a balance sheet on March 8, 2010, which reconstructs his financial status as of February 1, 2005. . . . [footnote omitted]. This balance sheet shows that Mortensen had $153,020.00 in assets as of February 1, 2005. Some of those assets may have been exempt. He had a brokerage account designated as "ML SEP" for $3,606.00. This may be a form of pension plan that is exempt under AS 09.38.017. His other liquid assets may be exempt in the sum of $1,750.00 under A.S. 09.38.020 as it existed in 2005. The only other exemption for Mortensen would have been for an automobile in the amount of $3,750.00. After deductions for exemptions, Mortensen had assets totaling $143,914.00. . . . Mr. Mortensen's balance sheet lists liabilities totaling $49,711.00 as of February 1, 2005. . . . [footnote omitted]. This sum may be low. At his § 341 creditors' meeting held on September 24, 2009, Mortensen testified that he owed roughly $85,000.00 on credit cards at the time the trust was created. . . . [footnote omitted]. Using either figure, however, Mortensen was solvent at the time he created the trust. The trust was created in accordance with Alaska law. . . . Battley seeks judgment against Mortensen under 11 U.S.C. § 548(e), which contains a ten-year limitation period for setting aside a fraudulent transfer. Section 548(e) provides:

> (e)(1) In addition to any transfer that the trustee may otherwise avoid, the trustee may avoid any transfer of an interest of the debtor in property that was made on or within 10 years before the date of the filing of the petition, if—
>
> (A) such transfer was made to a self-settled trust or similar device;
>
> (B) such transfer was by the debtor;

---

37. *Restatement (Second) of Contracts* § 90 (1981).

(C) the debtor is a beneficiary of such trust or similar device; and

(D) the debtor made such transfer with actual intent to hinder, delay, or defraud any entity to which the debtor was or became, on or after the date that such transfer was made, indebted. . . . [footnote omitted].

Section 548(e) was added to the Bankruptcy Code in 2005, as part of the Bankruptcy Abuse Prevention and Consumer Protection Act. . . . [footnote omitted]. Section 548(e) "closes the self-settled trusts loophole" and was directed at the five states that permitted such trusts, including Alaska.[43] Its main function "is to provide the estate representative with an extended reachback period for certain types of transfers."[44] However, the "actual intent" requirement found in §548(e)(1)(D) is identical to the standard found in §548(a)(1)(A) for setting aside other fraudulent transfers and obligations.[45] . . . Mortensen's trust, established under AS 34.40.110, satisfies the first three subsections of §548(e) — the Seldovia property was transferred to a self-settled trust, Mortensen made the transfer, and he is a beneficiary of the trust. The determinative issue here is whether Mortensen transferred the Seldovia property to the trust "with actual intent to hinder, delay, or defraud" his creditors.[46] . . . Mortensen says he did not have this intent when he created the trust and that he simply wanted to preserve the property for his children. Battley counters that Mortensen's intent is clear from the trust language itself. The trust's stated purpose was "to maximize the protection of the trust estate or estates from creditors' claims of the Grantor or any beneficiary and to minimize all wealth transfer taxes." . . . [footnote omitted]. Mortensen argues that the trust language cannot be used to determine intent because Alaska law expressly prohibits it. Under Alaska law, "a settlor's expressed intention to protect trust assets from a beneficiary's potential future creditors is not evidence of an intent to defraud."[48] But is this state statutory provision determinative when applying §548(e)(1)(D) of the Bankruptcy Code?

Ordinarily, it is state law, rather than the Bankruptcy Code, which creates and defines a debtor's interest in property.[49]

Unless some federal interest requires a different result, there is no reason why such interests should be analyzed differently simply because an interested party is involved in a bankruptcy proceeding.[50]

---

43. 5 COLLIER ON BANKRUPTCY ¶ 548.10[1], [3][a] n. 6 (N. Alan Resnick & Henry J. Sommer eds., 16th ed.).

44. *Id.*, ¶ 548.10[2].

45. 11 U.S.C. §548(a)(1)(A), (e)(1)(D), *see also* 5 COLLIER ON BANKRUPTCY ¶ 548.10[3][d].

46. 11 U.S.C. §548(e)(1)(D).

48. AS 34.40.110(b)(1).

49. *Butner v. United States*, 440 U.S. 48, 55 (1979).

50. *Id.*

Here, Congress has codified a federal interest which requires a different result. Only five states allow their citizens to establish self-settled trusts.[51] Section 548(e) was enacted to close this "self-settled trust loophole."[52] As noted by Collier:

> [T]he addition of section 548(e) is a reaction to state legislation overturning the common law rule that self-settled spendthrift trusts may be reached by creditors (and thus also by the bankruptcy trustee.)[53]

It would be a very odd result for a court interpreting a federal statute aimed at closing a loophole to apply the state law that permits it. I conclude that a settlor's expressed intention to protect assets placed into a self-settled trust from a beneficiary's potential future creditors can be evidence of an intent to defraud. In this bankruptcy proceeding, AS 34.40.110(b)(1) cannot compel a different conclusion.

To establish an avoidable transfer under § 548(e), the trustee must show that the debtor made the transfer with the actual intent to hinder, delay and defraud present or future creditors by a preponderance of the evidence.[54] Here, the trust's express purpose was to hinder, delay and defraud present and future creditors. However, there is additional evidence which demonstrates that Mortensen's transfer of the Seldovia property to the trust was made with the intent to hinder, delay and defraud present and future creditors. . . . First, Mortensen was coming off some very lean years at the time he created the trust in 2005. His earnings over the preceding four years averaged just $11,644.00 annually. . . . [footnote omitted]. He had burned through a $100,000.00 annuity which he had cashed out in 2000. He had also accumulated credit card debt of between $49,711.00 to $85,000.00 at the time the trust was created. He was experiencing "financial carnage" from his divorce. Comparing his low income to his estimated overhead of $5,000.00 per month (or $60,000.00 per year), Mortensen was well "under water" when he sought to put the Seldovia property out of reach of his creditors by placing it in the trust. . . . Further, when Mortensen received the $100,000.00 from his mother he didn't pay off his credit cards. Rather, he transferred $80,000.00 into the trust after paying a few bills and began speculating in the stock market. He had a substantial credit card debt due to AT & T, approximately $15,200.00, . . . [footnote omitted] which was not paid in 2005. This debt had increased to $19,096.00 by the time he filed his bankruptcy petition. . . . [footnote omitted]. In 2005, Mortensen also owed Capital 1 approximately $6,350.00 in credit card debt. . . . [footnote omitted]. This debt had bumped up to $7,525.00 when he filed for bankruptcy. . . . [footnote omitted]. He had a Discover card with a balance of $12,588.00 as of Feb. 1, 2005. . . . [footnote omitted]. He owed Discover $11,905.00 when he filed bankruptcy. . . . [footnote omitted].

---

51. In addition to Alaska, Delaware, Nevada, Rhode Island and Utah permit the creation of self-settled trusts.

52. 5 COLLIER ON BANKRUPTCY ¶ 548.10[1], *citing* H.R.Rep. No. 109–31, 109th Cong., 1st Sess. 449 (2005) (statement of Rep. Cannon).

53. 5 COLLIER ON BANKRUPTCY ¶ 548.10[3][a] (footnotes omitted).

54. *Consolidated Partners Inv. Co. v. Lake*, 152 B.R. 485, 488 (Bankr.N.D.Ohio 1993).

Mortensen claims he paid these accounts off on a number of occasions and then re-borrowed against them. I can find no evidence of such pay-offs in the documentary evidence and I don't believe Mortensen. Nor do I believe that the trust repaid Mortensen the $80,000 in 2006. If that had been the case, Mortensen wouldn't have needed to borrow another $29,000.00 on his credit cards. . . . [footnote omitted]. I conclude that Mortensen's transfer of the Seldovia property and the placement of $80,000.00 into the trust constitutes persuasive evidence of an intent to hinder, delay and defraud present and future creditors. . . . Mortensen alleged that the purpose of the trust was to preserve the Seldovia property for his children. Yet he used the trust as a vehicle for making stock market investments. In 2005, the trust had capital gains of nearly $7,000.00. . . . [footnote omitted]. In 2006, the trust had capital gains of over $26,000.00. . . . [footnote omitted]. In 2007, the trust had capital gains of $6,448.00. . . . [footnote omitted]. In 2008 and 2009 the trust had either no capital gain income or experienced losses. . . . [footnote omitted]. The trust also made a car loan to one of Mortensen's acquaintances. These activities had no relationship to the trust's alleged purpose. . . . The bottom line for Mr. Mortensen is that he attempted a clever but fundamentally flawed scheme to avoid exposure to his creditors. When he created the trust in 2005, he failed to recognize the danger posed by the Bankruptcy Abuse Protection and Consumer Protection Act, which was enacted later that year. Mortensen will now pay the price for his actions. His transfer of the Seldovia property to the Mortensen Seldovia Trust will be avoided. . . .

Alaska Statute (2016)

§ 34.40.110. Restricting transfers of trust interests.

(a) A person who in writing transfers property in trust may provide that the interest of a beneficiary of the trust, including a beneficiary who is the settlor of the trust, may not be either voluntarily or involuntarily transferred before payment or delivery of the interest to the beneficiary by the trustee. Payment or delivery of the interest to the beneficiary does not include a beneficiary's use or occupancy of real property or tangible personal property owned by the trust if the use or occupancy is in accordance with the trustee's discretionary authority under the trust instrument. A provision in a trust instrument that provides the restrictions described in this subsection is considered to be a restriction that is a restriction on the transfer of the transferor's beneficial interest in the trust and that is enforceable under applicable nonbankruptcy law within the meaning of 11 U.S.C. 541(c)(2) (Bankruptcy Code), as that paragraph reads on September 15, 2004, or as it may be amended in the future. In this subsection,

> (1) "property" includes real property, personal property, and interests in real or personal property;

> (2) "transfer" means any form of transfer, including deed, conveyance, or assignment.

(b) If a trust contains a transfer restriction allowed under (a) of this section, the transfer restriction prevents a creditor existing when the trust is created or a person who subsequently becomes a creditor from satisfying a claim out of the beneficiary's interest in the trust, unless the creditor is a creditor of the settlor and

(1) the creditor establishes by clear and convincing evidence that the settlor's transfer of property in trust was made with the intent to defraud that creditor, and a cause of action or claim for relief with respect to the fraudulent transfer complies with the requirements of (d) of this section; however, a settlor's expressed intention to protect trust assets from a beneficiary's potential future creditors is not evidence of an intent to defraud;

(2) the trust, except for an eligible individual retirement account trust, provides that the settlor may revoke or terminate all or part of the trust without the consent of a person who has a substantial beneficial interest in the trust and the interest would be adversely affected by the exercise of the power held by the settlor to revoke or terminate all or part of the trust; in this paragraph, "revoke or terminate" does not include a power to veto a distribution from the trust, a testamentary or lifetime nongeneral power of appointment or similar power, or a right to receive a distribution of income or principal under (3)(A), (B), (C), or (D) of this subsection;

(3) the trust, except for an eligible individual retirement account trust, requires that all or a part of the trust's income or principal, or both, must be distributed to the settlor; however, this paragraph does not apply to a settlor's right to receive the following types of distributions, which remain subject to the restriction provided by (a) of this section until the distributions occur:

(A) income or principal from a charitable remainder annuity trust or charitable remainder unitrust; in this subparagraph, "charitable remainder annuity trust" and "charitable remainder unitrust" have the meanings given in 26 U.S.C. 664 (Internal Revenue Code) and as it may be amended;

(B) a percentage of the value of the trust each year as determined from time to time under the trust instrument, but not exceeding the amount that may be defined as income under AS 13.38 or under 26 U.S.C. 643(b) (Internal Revenue Code) and as it may be amended;

(C) the transferor's potential or actual use of real property held under a qualified personal residence trust within the meaning of 26 U.S.C. 2702(c) (Internal Revenue Code) or as it may be amended in the future; or

(D) income or principal from a grantor retained annuity trust or grantor retained unitrust that is allowed under 26 U.S.C. 2702 (Internal Revenue Code) or as it may be amended in the future; or

(4) at the time of the transfer, the settlor is in default by 30 or more days of making a payment due under a child support judgment or order.

Notes

Traditionally, spendthrift trusts could not be used by a settlor to isolate himself or herself from his or her own creditors. *See, e.g.,* Unif. Trust Code § 505 (2000); *Restatement (Second) of Trusts* § 156 (1959). Nonetheless, wealthy settlors were able to deposit assets in "offshore accounts" to which their own creditors would have no access, thereby safeguarding their own assets from the claims of their own creditors. *See* Stewart E. Sterk, *Asset Protection Trusts: Trust Law's Race to the Bottom?*, 85 Cornell L. Rev. 1035, 1048 (2000).Anxious to attract capital growth, American states enacted their own laws to permit what would become known as domestic asset protection trusts. The Alaska statute, *supra*, is one such statute. Today, more than a third of the states permit settlors to avoid their own creditors through the use of these asset protection trusts. Because these domestic asset protections trusts are relatively recent, the impact of other laws related to fraudulent transfers has yet to be fully explored. *See, e.g.,* Uniform Voidable Transactions Act (UVTA), at https://www.uniformlaws .org/HigherLogic/System/DownloadDocumentFile.ashx?DocumentFileKey =1a5715f1-679d-1a43-e82c-c2aaa2238f86&forceDialog=0 (accessed Aug. 6, 2019).

For commentary on the issues raised by asset protection trusts, see Mark Merric, Daniel G. Worthington, Paul MacArthur & John E. Sullivan III, *Best Situs for DAPTs in 2019*, 158 Trusts & Ests. 60 (2019) (ranking three different asset protection features of states with DAPT statutes); Gideon Rothschild & Daniel S. Rubin, *Minimize Creditor Challenges to Self-Settled Spendthrift Trusts*, 157 Trusts & Ests. 14 (Nov. 2018) (suggesting ways in which a client can avoid a determination that the transfer was fraudulent); Mark Merric & Daniel G. Worthington, *Find the Best Situs for Domestic Asset Protection Trusts*, 154 Trusts & Ests. 45 (Jan. 2015) (listing the top states as Alaska, Delaware, Ohio, Nevada, South Dakota, and Tennessee); Jay A. Soled & Mitchell M. Gans, *Asset Preservation and the Evolving Role of Trusts in the Twenty-First Century*, 72 Wash. & Lee L. Rev. 257 (2015). *See also* Toni 1 Trust v. Wacker, 413 P.3d 1199 (Alaska 2018) (holding that the Alaska DAPT statute cannot control the jurisdictional question involved in any case).

Edward D. Brown & Hudson Mead
Divorce and the Self-Settled Trust

153 Trusts & Ests. 34 (Feb. 2014)

If a client creates a self-settled trust in a DAPT state, but doesn't reside in that state, there's a risk the non-DAPT state law might prevail in refusing to recognize the DAPT state's protections. Many commentators have raised the issue regarding whose law the forum court (where the divorce takes place) will apply. If the non-DAPT forum court law applies, will the trust assets be insulated from the court's rulings?

Id. at 36

> Regardless of state law, if a trust is funded at a time when the settlor has any claims pending, threatened or expected, the trust assets won't be protected. Those transfers are referred to as 'fraudulent transfers' or 'fraudulent conveyances.'

Id. at 37.

> If a future creditor is unknown and unexpected, then this isn't, generally, the type of creditor that can make a successful claim of fraudulent transfer (for example, a person injured in a car accident subsequent to funding the trust). However, in the divorce context, if a trust is created at a time when the settlor is contemplating or anticipating that a divorce could be on the horizon, the transfers to that trust can be unwound, forcing the trust assets to be accessible to the other spouse. Also, if the transfers to the trust leave the settlor virtually insolvent, those transfers can be undone. It's critical that any funding of the trust be accomplished at a time and in a manner that doesn't fall within a fraudulent transfer scenario.

Id.

G. Charitable Trusts

1. Administration of Charities

Estate of Wilson

New York Court of Appeals, 1983
59 N.Y.2d 461, 452 N.E.2d 1228, 465 N.Y.S.2d 900

Chief Judge Cooke.

These appeals present the question whether the equal protection clause of the Fourteenth Amendment is violated when a court permits the administration of private charitable trusts according to the testators' intent to finance the education of male students and not female students. When a court applies trust law that neither encourages, nor affirmatively promotes, nor compels private discrimination but allows parties to engage in private selection in the devise or bequest of their property, that choice will not be attributable to the State and subjected to the Fourteenth Amendment's strictures.

* * *

The factual patterns in each of these matters are different, but the underlying legal issues are the same. In each there is imposed a decedent's intention to create a testamentary trust under which the class of beneficiaries are members of one sex.

In Matter of Wilson, article ELEVENTH of Clark W. Wilson's will provided that the residuary of his estate be held in trust (Wilson Trust) and that the income "be applied to defraying the education and other expenses of the first year at college of five (5) young men who shall have graduated from the Canastota High School, three (3) of whom shall have attained the highest grades in the study of science and two (2) of whom shall have attained the highest grades in the study of chemistry, as may be certified to by the then Superintendent of Schools for the Canastota Central School District." Wilson died in June, 1969 and for the next 11 years the Wilson Trust was administered according to its terms.

In early 1981, the Civil Rights Office of the United States Department of Education received a complaint alleging that the superintendent's acts in connection with the Wilson Trust violated title IX of the Education Amendments of 1972 (US Code, tit 20, § 1681 et. seq.), which prohibits gender discrimination in Federally financed education programs. The Department of Education informed the Canastota Central School District that the complaint would be investigated. Before the investigation was completed, the school district agreed to refrain from again providing names of students to the trustee. The trustee, Key Bank of Central New York, initiated this proceeding for a determination of the effect and validity of the trust provision of the will.

The Surrogate's Court held that the school superintendent's co-operation with the trustee violated no Federal statute or regulation prohibiting sexual discrimination, nor did it implicate the equal protection clause of the Fourteenth Amendment. The court ordered the trustee to continue administering the trust.

A unanimous Appellate Division, Third Department, modified the Surrogate's decree. The court affirmed the Surrogate's finding that the testator intended the trust to benefit male students only and, noting that the school was under no legal obligation to provide the names of qualified male candidates, found "administration of the trust according to its literal terms is impossible." (87 AD2d, p 101.) The court then exercised its cy pres power to reform the trust by striking the clause in the will providing for the school superintendent's certification of the names of qualified candidates for the scholarships. The candidates were permitted to apply directly to the trustee.

Matter of Johnson also involves a call for judicial construction of a testamentary trust created for the exclusive benefit of male students. By a will dated December 13, 1975, Edwin Irving Johnson left his residuary estate in trust (Johnson Trust). Article SIXTH of the will provided that the income of the trust was to "be used and applied, each year to the extent available, for scholarships or grants for bright and deserving young men who have graduated from the High School of [the Croton-Harmon Union Free] School District, and whose parents are financially unable to send them to college, and who shall be selected by the Board of Education of such School District with the assistance of the Principal of such High School."

Johnson died in 1978. In accordance with the terms of the trust, the board of education, acting as trustee, announced that applications from male students would be accepted on or before May 1, 1979. Before any scholarships were awarded, however, the National Organization for Women, filed a complaint with the Civil Rights

Office of the United States Department of Education. This complaint alleged that the school district's involvement in the Johnson Trust constituted illegal gender-based discrimination.

During the pendency of the Department of Education's investigation, a stipulation was entered into between the executrix of the will, the president of the board of education, and the Attorney-General. The parties sought "to avoid administering the educational bequest set forth in Article Sixth in a manner which is in conflict with the law and public policy prohibiting discrimination based on sex". The stipulation provided that "all interested parties agree to the deletion of the word 'men' in Article Sixth of the Will and the insertion of the word 'persons' in its place." The Attorney-General then brought this proceeding by petition to the Surrogate's Court to construe article SIXTH of the will.

The Surrogate found that the trustee's unwillingness to administer the trust according to its terms rendered administration of the trust impossible. The court, however, declined to reform the trust by giving effect to the stipulation. Rather, it reasoned that the testator's primary intent to benefit "deserving young men" would be most closely effected by replacing the school district with a private trustee.

A divided Appellate Division, Second Department, reversed, holding that under the equal protection clause of the Fourteenth Amendment, a court cannot reform a trust that, by its own terms, would deny equal protection of law. The court reasoned that inasmuch as an agent of the State had been appointed trustee, the trust, if administered, would violate the equal protection clause. Judicial reformation of the trust by substituting trustees would, in that court's view, itself constitute State action in violation of the Fourteenth Amendment. The court determined that administration of the trust was impossible and, in an exercise of its cy pres power, reformed the trust by eliminating the gender restriction.

* * *

The court, of course, cannot invoke its cy pres power without first determining that the testator's specific charitable purpose is no longer capable of being performed by the trust (see, *e.g.*, Matter of Scott, *supra*; Matter of Swan, 237 App Div 454, affd sub nom. Matter of St. Johns Church of Mt. Morris, 263 NY 638; Matter of Fairchild, 15 Misc 2d 272). In establishing these trusts, the testators expressly and unequivocally intended that they provide for the educational expenses of male students. It cannot be said that the accomplishment of the testators' specific expression of charitable intent is "impossible or impracticable." So long as the subject high schools graduate boys with the requisite qualifications, the testators' specific charitable intent can be fulfilled.

Nor are the trusts' particular limitation of beneficiaries by gender invalid and incapable of being accomplished as violative of public policy. It is true that the eradication in this State of gender-based discrimination is an important public policy. Indeed, the Legislature has barred gender-based discrimination in education (see Education Law, § 3201-a), employment (see Labor Law, §§ 194. 197. 220-e; General

Business Law, § 187), housing, credit, and many other areas (see Executive Law, § 296). As a result, women, once viewed as able to assume only restricted roles in our society (see Bradwell v State, 16 Wall [83 US] 130, 141), now project significant numbers "in business, in the professions, in government and, indeed, in all walks of life where education is a desirable, if not always a necessary, antecedent" (Stanton v Stanton, 421 US 7, 15). The restrictions in these trusts run contrary to this policy favoring equal opportunity and treatment of men and women. A provision in a charitable trust, however, that is central to the testator's or settlor's charitable purpose, and is not illegal, should not be invalidated on public policy grounds unless that provision, if given effect, would substantially mitigate the general charitable effect of the gift (see 4 Scott, Trusts [3d ed], § 399.4).

Proscribing the enforcement of gender restrictions in private charitable trusts would operate with equal force towards trusts whose benefits are bestowed exclusively on women. "Reduction of the disparity in economic condition between men and women caused by the long history of discrimination against women has been recognized as * * * an important governmental objective" (Califano v Webster, 430 US 313, 317). There can be little doubt that important efforts in effecting this type of social change can be and are performed through private philanthropy (see, generally, Commission on Private Philanthropy and Public Needs, Giving in America: Toward a Stronger Voluntary Section [1975]). And, the private funding of programs for the advancement of women is substantial and growing (see Bernstein, Funding for Women's Higher Education: Looking Backward and Ahead, Grant Magazine, vol 4, No. 4, pp. 225–229; Ford Foundation, Financial Support of Women's Programs in the 1970's [1979]; Yarrow, Feminist Philanthropy Comes Into Its Own, NY Times, May 21, 1983, p 7, col 2). Indeed, one compilation of financial assistance offered primarily or exclusively to women lists 854 sources of funding (see Schlacter, Directory of Financial Aids for Women [2d ed, 1981]; see, also, Note, Sex Restricted Scholarships and the Charitable Trust, 59 Iowa L Rev 1000, 1000–1001, & nn 10, 11). Current thinking in private philanthropic institutions advocates that funding offered by such institutions and the opportunities within the institutions themselves be directly responsive to the needs of particular groups (see Ford Foundation, op cit , at pp 41–44; Fleming, Foundations and Affirmative Action, 4 Foundation News No. 4, at pp 14–17; Griffen, Funding for Women's Programs, 6 Grantsmanship Center News, No. 2, at pp 34–45). It is evident, therefore, that the focusing of private philanthropy on certain classes within society may be consistent with public policy. Consequently, that the restrictions in the trusts before this court may run contrary to public efforts promoting equality of opportunity for women does not justify imposing a per se rule that gender restrictions in private charitable trusts violate public policy.

Finally, this is not an instance in which the restriction of the trusts serves to frustrate a paramount charitable purpose. In Howard Sav. Inst. v Peep (34 NJ 494), for example, the testator made a charitable bequest to Amherst College to be placed in trust and to provide scholarships for "deserving American born, Protestant, Gentile boys of good moral repute, not given to gambling, smoking, drinking or similar acts." Due to the religious restrictions, the college declined to accept the bequest as contrary to its charter. The court found that the college was the principal beneficiary of the trust, so that removing the religious restriction and thereby allowing the college to accept the gift would permit administration of the trust in a manner most closely effectuating the testator's intent (see, also, Matter of Hawley, 32 Misc 2d 624; Coffee v Rice Univ., 408 SW2d 269 [Tex]).

In contrast, the trusts subject to these appeals were not intended to directly benefit the school districts. Although the testators sought the school districts' participation, this was incidental to their primary intent of financing part of the college education of boys who attended the schools. Consequently, severance of the school districts' role in the trusts' administration will not frustrate any part of the testators' charitable purposes. Inasmuch as the specific charitable intent of the testators is not inherently "impossible or impracticable" of being achieved by the trusts, there is no occasion to exercise cy pres power.

Although not inherently so, these trusts are currently incapable of being administered as originally intended because of the school districts' unwillingness to cooperate. These impediments, however, may be remedied by an exercise of a court's general equitable power over all trusts to permit a deviation from the administrative terms of a trust and to appoint a successor trustee.

A testamentary trust will not fail for want of a trustee (see EPTL 8-1.1; see, also, Matter of Thomas, 254 NY 292) and, in the event a trustee is unwilling or unable to act, a court may replace the trustee with another (see EPTL 7-2.6; SCPA 1502; see, also, Matter of Andrews, 233 App Div 547; 2 Scott, Trusts [3d ed], § 108.1). Accordingly, the proper means of continuing the Johnson Trust would be to replace the school district with someone able and willing to administer the trust according to its terms.

* * *

It is argued before this court that the judicial facilitation of the continued administration of gender-restrictive charitable trusts violates the equal protection clause of the Fourteenth Amendment (see US Const, 14th Amdt, § 1). The strictures of the equal protection clause are invoked when the State engages in invidious discrimination (see Moose Lodge No. 107 v Irvis, 407 US 163, 173, 176–177; Burton v Wilmington Parking Auth., 365 US 715, 721; Civil Rights Cases, 109 US 3). Indeed, the State itself cannot, consistent with the Fourteenth Amendment, award scholarships that are gender restrictive (see Mississippi Univ. for Women v Hogan, 458 US 718; Kirchberg v Feenstra, 450 US 455; Stanton v Stanton, 421 US 7, *supra*).

The Fourteenth Amendment, however, "erects no shield against merely private conduct, however discriminatory or wrongful." * * * [citations omitted]. Private discrimination may violate equal protection of the law when accompanied by State participation in, facilitation of, and, in some cases, acquiescence in the discrimination * * * [citations omitted]. Although there is no conclusive test to determine when State involvement in private discrimination will violate the Fourteenth Amendment (see Reitman v Mulkey, *supra*, at p 378), the general standard that has evolved is whether "the conduct allegedly causing the deprivation of a federal right [is] fairly attributable to the state" (Lugar v Edmondson Oil Co., 457 US 922, 937). Therefore, it is a question of "state responsibility" and "[o]nly by sifting facts and weighing circumstances can the * * * involvement of the State in private conduct be attributed its true significance" (Burton v Wilmington Parking Auth., 365 US 715, 722, *supra*).

The Supreme Court has identified various situations in which the State may be deemed responsible for discriminatory conduct with private origins. For example, one such instance appears when the State delegates one of its inherent functions to private parties and those parties engage in discrimination (see Lloyd Corp. v Tanner, 407 US 551; Food Employees v Logan Plaza, 391 US 308; Evans v Newton, 382 US 296; Terry v Adams, 345 US 461; Marsh v Alabama, 326 US 501). Another arises when the State does not directly enforce or abet the private discrimination, but substantially facilitates and profits from it (Burton v Wilmington Parking Auth., 365 US 715, *supra*).

"The Court has never held, of course, that discrimination by an otherwise private entity would be violative of the Equal Protection Clause if the private entity receives any sort of benefit of service at all from the State, or if it is subject to State regulation in any degree whatever" (Moose Lodge No. 107 v Irvis, 407 US 163, 173, *supra*). Rather, "the State must have 'significantly involved itself with invidious discriminations' * * * in order for the discriminatory action to fall within the ambit of the constitutional prohibition" (id.; see, also, Rendell-Baker v Kohn, 457 US 830; Gilmore v City of Montgomery, 417 US 556).

The State generally may not be held responsible for private discrimination solely on the basis that it permits the discrimination to occur (see Flagg Bros. v Brooks, 436 US 149, 164; Jackson v Metropolitan Edison Co., 419 US 345, 357, *supra*; Moose Lodge No. 107 v Irvis, 407 US 163, 176, *supra*; Evans v Abney, 396 US 435, *supra*). Nor is the State under an affirmative obligation to prevent purely private discrimination (see Reitman v Mulkey, 387 US 369, 376, 377, *supra*). Therefore, when the State regulates private dealings it may be responsible for private discrimination occurring in the regulated field only when enforcement of its regulation has the effect of compelling the private discrimination (see Flagg Bros. v Brooks, *supra*; Moose Lodge No. 107 v Irvis, *supra*; Shelley v Kraemer, 334 US 1, *supra*; cf. Adickes v Kress & Co., 398 US 144, 170).

In Shelley v Kraemer (*supra*), for example, the Supreme Court held that the equal protection clause was violated by judicial enforcement of a private covenant that prohibited the sale of affected properties to "people of Negro or Mongolian Race." When one of the properties was sold to a black family, the other property owners sought to enforce the covenant in State court and the family was ordered to move from the property. The Supreme Court noted "that the restrictive agreements standing alone cannot be regarded as violative of any rights guaranteed to petitioners by the Fourteenth Amendment. So long as the purposes of those agreements are effectuated by voluntary adherence to their terms, it would appear clear that there has been no action by the State and the provisions of the Amendment have not been violated" (334 US, at p 13). The court held, however, that it did have before it cases "in which the States have merely abstained from action leaving private individuals free to impose such discriminations as they see fit. Rather, these are cases in which the States have made available to such individuals the full coercive power of the government to deny petitioners, on the grounds of race or color, the enjoyment of property rights" (id., at p 19). It was not the neutral regulation of contracts permitting parties to enter discriminatory agreements that caused the discrimination to be attributable to the State. Instead, it was that the State court's exercise of its judicial power directly effected a discriminatory act.

In Barrows v Jackson, (346 US 249, *supra*), the court applied the same reasoning when it held that a court's awarding damages against a party who has breached a racially restrictive covenant also violates the equal protection clause. The court reiterated that "voluntary adherence [to the covenant] would constitute individual action only" (id., at p 253). But, "[t]o compel respondent to respond in damages would be for the State to punish her for failure to perform her covenant to continue to discriminate against non-Caucasians in the use of her property * * * Thus, it becomes not respondent's voluntary choice but the State's choice that she observe her covenant or suffer damages" (id., at p 254).

More recently, the Supreme Court considered whether a State's regulation of private clubs licensed to serve liquor caused a club's restrictive membership policy to be attributable to the State (see Moose Lodge No. 107 v Irvis, 407 US 163, *supra*). The court held that although the State extensively regulated these private clubs, it was not responsible for the private discrimination simply because the regulation permitted the discrimination to occur. The court stated that "[h]owever detailed this type of regulation may be in some particulars, it cannot be said to in any way foster or encourage * * * discrimination" (407 US, at pp 176–177). The court distinguished the regulatory scheme's general neutral effect on the discrimination from a situation in which that scheme could be used to compel discrimination. One of the regulations provided that "'[e]very club licensee shall adhere to all of the provisions of its Constitution and By-Laws'" (id., at pp 177). The court acknowledged that if this regulation were used (at p 178) "to place state sanctions behind [the licensee's] discriminatory membership rules," the Fourteenth Amendment would be implicated. Accordingly, the court enjoined enforcement of the regulation.

A court's application of its equitable power to permit the continued administration of the trusts involved in these appeals falls outside the ambit of the Fourteenth Amendment. Although the field of trusts is regulated by the State, the Legislature's failure to forbid private discriminatory trusts does not cause such trusts, when they arise, to be attributable to the State (see Flagg Bros. v Brooks, 436 US 149, 165, *supra*; see, also, Evans v Abney, 396 US 435, 458 [Brennan, J., dissenting], *supra*).

It naturally follows that, when a court applies this trust law and determines that it permits the continued existence of private discriminatory trusts, the Fourteenth Amendment is not implicated.

In the present appeals, the coercive power of the State has never been enlisted to enforce private discrimination. Upon finding that requisite formalities of creating a trust had been met, the courts below determined the testator's intent, and applied the relevant law permitting those intentions to be privately carried out. The court's power compelled no discrimination. That discrimination had been sealed in the private execution of the wills. Recourse to the courts was had here only for the purpose of facilitating the administration of the trusts, not for enforcement of their discriminatory dispositive provisions.

This is not to say that a court's exercise of its power over trusts can never invoke the scrutiny of the Fourteenth Amendment. This court holds only that a trust's discriminatory terms are not fairly attributable to the State when a court applies trust principles that permit private discrimination but do not encourage, affirmatively promote, or compel it.

The testators' intention to involve the State in the administration of these trusts does not alter this result, notwithstanding that the effect of the courts' action respecting the trusts was to eliminate this involvement. The courts' power to replace a trustee who is unwilling to act as in Johnson or to permit a deviation from an incidental administrative term in the trust as in Wilson is a part of the law permitting this private conduct and extends to all trusts regardless of their purposes. It compels no discrimination. Moreover, the minimal State participation in the trusts' administration prior to the time that they reached the courts for the constructions under review did not cause the trusts to take on an indelible public character (see Evans v Newton, 382 US 296, 301; Commonwealth of Pennsylvania v Brown, 392 F2d 120).

In sum, the Fourteenth Amendment does not require the State to exercise the full extent of its power to eradicate private discrimination. It is only when the State itself discriminates, compels another to discriminate, or allows another to assume one of its functions and discriminate that such discrimination will implicate the amendment.

Accordingly, in Matter of Wilson, the order of the Appellate Division should be affirmed, with costs payable out of the estate to all parties appearing separately and filing separate briefs.

In Matter of Johnson, the order of the Appellate Division should be reversed, with costs payable out of the estate to all parties appearing separately and filing separate briefs and the decree of the Surrogate's Court, Westchester County, reinstated.

Meyer, J. (concurring in Matter of Wilson and dissenting in Matter of Johnson).

I would affirm in both cases. Although the Constitution does not proscribe private bias, it does proscribe affirmative State action in furtherance of bias.

In Matter of Wilson the trust is private and the only involvement of a public official (the superintendent of schools) is his certification of a student's class standing, information which is, in any event, available to any student applying to the trustee for a scholarship. There is, therefore, no State action.

In Matter of Johnson, however, the trustee is the board of education, a public body. The establishment of a public trust for a discriminatory purpose is constitutionally improper, as Presiding Justice Mollen has fully spelled out in his opinion. For the State to legitimize that impropriety by replacement of the trustee is unconstitutional State action. The only permissible corrective court action is, as the Appellate Division held, excision of the discriminatory limitation.

In *Matter of Wilson*:

JASEN, JONES, WACHTLER, MEYER and SIMONS, JJ., concur with COOKE, C.J..

MEYER, J., concurs in a memorandum.

Order affirmed, etc.

In *Matter of Johnson*:

JASEN, JONES, WACHTLER and SIMONS, JJ., concur with COOKE, C.J.

MEYER, J., dissents and votes to affirm in a memorandum.

Order reversed, etc.

Notes

Definitions of Charity: The Uniform Trust Code defines charitable trusts along well-established categories, *see* UNIF. TRUST CODE § 405(a) (2019), and allows for a similar purpose to be chosen by a court if the original charitable purpose envisioned by the settlor is no longer a possibility, *id.* at § 405(b). But case law and statutes have made clear that a charitable purpose does not include invidious discrimination, violation of strong public policy, or the promotion of private — as compared to public — aspirations. For example, gifts to aid political parties have been held to be charitable, *see* Liapis' Estate, 88 Pa. D. & C. 303 (1954); George Bernard Shaw's bequest to develop a new English alphabet did not provide a sufficient public benefit to be charitable, *see* Public Trustee v. Day (*In re* Shaw), 1 W.L.R. 729 (1957); and it is questionable if racial or gender restrictions would survive present day scrutiny of valid trust purposes, *see, e.g.*, Estate of Wilson, 59 N.Y.2d 461, 452 N.E.2d 1228, 465 N.Y.S.2d 900 (1983) (gender restriction); Podberesky v. Kirwan, 38 F.3d 147 (4th Cir. 1994), *cert. denied*, 514 U.S. 1120 (1995) (race restriction). *See generally* Mary Kay Lundwall, *Inconsistency and Uncertainty in the Charitable Purposes Doctrine*, 41 WAYNE L. REV. 1341 (1995). If gender or racial classifications make the trust invalid, courts have been willing to reform the trust under the doctrine of cy pres and prevent the corpus from reverting to the settlor. *See, e.g., In re* Certain Scholarship Funds, 133 N.H. 227, 575 A.2d 1325 (1990).

Brie Williams
The Next Chapter in Giving
156 Trusts & Ests. 62 (Oct. 2017)

Women already own more than half of the investable assets in the United States and control decision making for $11 trillion dollars. Many are using their influence to direct philanthropic investments to socially conscious vehicles, such as investing in women moving out of poverty, solving to provide future generations with both roots and wings.

Baby Boomer women gave 89 percent more to charity than Baby Boomer men, and women in the top 25 percent of permanent income gave 156 percent more than men in that same category.

Id. at 64–65.

Susan Colpitts & Wistar Morris
The Prudent Philanthropist
151 Trusts & Ests. 33 (June 2012)

In 2010, Warren Buffett and Bill and Melinda Gates made news with the The Giving Pledge, an effort to encourage the very wealthy to commit a minimum of 50 percent of their wealth to charity. The challenge has certainly resonated with the ultra-wealthy; over 80 of America's richest families have publically made the pledge. The effort has also created a conversation among many affluent families and their advisors about the desirability of such a plan, the assets required for such a pledge to be realistic and how to implement so bold an initiative. We find that first generation wealth creators are often quite conservative in the amounts of wealth they want their children to inherit—for fear that too much dampens the entrepreneurial spirit that has provided so much excitement for the first generation. Also, many express gratitude and some humility about their success, which seem to create a tie to philanthropy. These notions arise not just in the hearts and minds of billionaires, but also for those families with just $10 million, $20 million or $30 million in net worth. For this bracket of wealth, the 'how' and 'when' of making such significant gifts are critical to the preservation of a family's financial security and the maximization of tax and other benefits.

Robert F. Sharpe, Jr.
The Philanthropic Age Divide
154 Trusts & Ests. 10 (May 2015)

[I]n 2014, over 40 percent of individuals who made the largest gifts were at least age 80, roughly 60 percent were at least age 70 and almost 75 percent were age 60 and older.

2. Monitoring of Charities

In re Milton Hershey School Trust
Commonwealth Court of Pennsylvania, 2005
867 A.2d 674

OPINION BY Judge PELLEGRINI. * * *

The Milton Hershey School Alumni Association (Association) appeals an order of the Court of Common Pleas of Dauphin County (trial court) dismissing for lack of standing the Association's challenge to the rescission of an agreement between the Office of Attorney General (OAG), the Milton Hershey School (School) and the Hershey Trust Company (Trust Company) that prohibited conflicts of interests and other actions by the trust managers that were deemed inimical to the interests of the orphan beneficiaries. * * *

Because standing is largely determined by the type of interest a party is asserting, it is necessary to determine the sufficiency of the interest and to set forth in some detail what the object of that interest is—in this case, the School and the Trust Company. In 1909, Milton and Catherine Hershey (the Hersheys) established the Milton Hershey School, a charitable institution funded by the Milton Hershey School Trust (Trust). The School provides residential care for dependent and at-risk children, or "orphan" children as the term was then used. The Hersheys originally contributed 12,000 acres of land to the corpus of the trust and bequeathed virtually their entire fortune for the purpose of saving orphan children.

The deed of trust is the original agreement between the Hersheys, the Hershey Trust Company as Trustee of the Trust, and the Managers of the Trust (originally, Milton Hershey, W.H. Lebkichner and John E. Snyder). The original deed was amended in 1976 and provides that the School is to be administered by the Trust Company and the Board of Managers. It states that the School was organized to "receive and admit to the School as many poor, healthy children as may from time to time be determined by the Managers, to the extent, capacity, and income of the School will provide for and shall be adequate to maintain." (Reproduced Record at 23a).

As directed by the deed of trust, the members of the School's Board of Managers are also members of the Board of Directors of the Trust Company. The deed endows the Board of Managers and the Trust Company with decision-making responsibility for all aspects of running the School and for management and administration of Trust assets. Together, they are charged with making all decisions about the use of trust funds, land development and sales, admissions and education under the standards set forth in the deed of trust. For instance, the sale of land owned by the Trust is administered as follows: "[T]he Trustee may from time to time, but only with the approval of the Managers, sell and convey in fee simple any part or portion of the lands conveyed by this deed, or which may have been brought or otherwise acquired, which in the judgment of the Managers is not necessary to be kept for the purposes of the School[.]" (*Id.* at 21a).

The deed of trust provides that the beneficiaries of the Trust are the orphan children attending the School. Children cared for by the Trust within the orphan parameters established by the Hersheys have a high degree of social and financial need and would otherwise require residential care in other facilities, such as foster care. Once enrolled, these children have all of their educational, physical, spiritual and other needs met by the Trust in a setting commonly referred to as the children's home. Those within the care of the Trust establish familial bonds with each other, viewing the School as a home and viewing other children at the School as a type of surrogate family. These bonds cross generational lines, and adults who had been within the care of the School have shown a devotion and commitment to the welfare of children later entering the School's care.

At the direction of Milton Hershey, the Association was created 74 years ago and is comprised entirely of orphan graduates of the School. It is a tax-exempt organization under Section 501(c)(3) of the Internal Revenue Code, 26 U.S.C. § 501(c)(3), incorporated under the laws of Pennsylvania. One of its functions is to directly serve orphan beneficiaries and to continue the bonds that form in orphanhood while under the care of the School. Pursuant to the Association's Articles of Incorporation, its purpose includes:

> the promoting in every proper way of the interests of Milton Hershey School, including . . . the establishment and maintenance of supplemental educational programs and activities for students . . . that encourage habits of thrift, industry, leadership, scholarly achievement, and other attributes of good citizenship; and to foster among its graduates an attachment to their Alma Mater.

(Brief for Appellant, Attachment 4). From its office on the School's property (owned by the Trust), the Association provides student-related functions and young graduate assistance programs, including programs directed at mentoring, job shadowing, transitioning, general graduate assistance and graduate crisis services. Orphan children that graduate from the School often become members of the Association.

The Association is not a division of the School or of the Trust Company. It was not named in the deed of trust and is not an intended beneficiary of the Trust. As the deed states, "[a]ll children shall leave the institution and cease to be the recipients of its benefits upon the completion of the full course of secondary education being offered at the School." (Reproduced Record at 25a). The Managers of the Trust may, in their discretion, contribute to the higher education of a graduate of the School, in which case graduates would continue to be beneficiaries of the Trust, but generally, once orphans graduate from the School, they are no longer Trust beneficiaries.

Though the Association is not a division of the School, a division of the Trust, or a beneficiary of the Trust, it has participated in many efforts aimed at protecting the charitable intent of the Trust, i.e., to assure that Trust assets are used to promote the child-saving mission of the Hersheys. It has made efforts in the past to prevent Trust resources from being diverted to non-child purposes and has lobbied the OAG and the Trust Company for assistance in this regard.

Another participant in the affairs of the Trust is the OAG. The OAG is charged with enforcing the duties of charitable trustees and protecting the public. In addition to overseeing the Trust administration, the OAG also holds the position that in exercising that duty, it is seeking to protect the community and general public in addition to the orphan beneficiaries designated as such under the terms of the deed of trust.

From 1970 to 2003, Trust assets grew from $200 million to $5.5 billion (at the time this action was filed with the trial court).[1] It is currently the largest residential childcare charity in the world, dwarfing any comparable facility in asset size. Other entities owned by, controlled by or affiliated with the Trust, such as Hershey Entertainment & Resort Company (HERCO) and the Hershey Medical Center (HMC), also enjoyed tremendous growth during this period. * * *

While Trust assets grew during this period, the number of children served by the Trust decreased, as did the amount of land appropriated to house the orphaned children (from approximately 10,000 acres to 2,000 acres). To illustrate, some of the land formerly designated for the School use was closed, sold, abandoned or transferred to HERCO, thereby reducing the amount of homes that could house roughly 310 orphans. Another example dates back to 1963, where the OAG and the Trust Company successfully sought removal of 500 acres of land and $50 million in cash from the Trust to build HMC for Penn State University.

Beginning in 1990, the Association began observing what it believed were Trust activities that diverted from the Trust's charitable intent to help orphan children. As alleged in its petition before the trial court, the Association noticed that School enrollment policies were altered to disfavor or turn away children requiring year-round residential care. In addition, it observed that education, housing and other policies were similarly altered to reflect the differing needs of the enrolled children who increasingly did not require substantially year-round residential care. It also observed that the childcare facilities at the School reached crisis levels in 2001 because of overcrowding, safety concerns and incidents of physical or sexual abuse resulting in a one-year moratorium on enrollment.

The Association became actively involved in efforts to quell what it believed were gross deviations from the charitable intent of the Trust. For instance, the Association reacted to an attempt by the Trust to end entirely the vocational education program mandated by the deed of trust, a program that targets non-college bound students. The Association's efforts resulted in an agreement signed by the OAG and the Trust compelling the Trust to preserve some form of vocational education at

---

1. The Association asserts in its brief that the total could be up to $6.3 billion. For our purposes, we will use the $5.5 billion figure.

the School. The Association also participated as *amicus curiae* in a proceeding initiated by the Trust Company to create the Catherine Hershey Institute of Learning and Development (CHILD) and to divert land to public use that was ultimately rejected by the trial court because it found that CHILD would have violated the Trust's charitable intent.

With the Association's concerns elevating, it alerted the OAG to what the Association believed were serious improprieties associated with the administration of the Trust. The Association alleged that conflicts of interest among the Trust Managers mired their ability to properly administer the Trust to carry out its charitable intent of saving orphan children. It also alleged that there were improper enrollment policies, improper and unsafe residential policies, and improper utilization of Trust assets to serve only orphan children and as many of them as possible. The Association believed that these actions taken as a whole constituted a perversion of the Trust's charitable intent.

Responding to the concerns raised by the Association, the OAG initiated and conducted an exhaustive 12-month investigation into the administration of the Trust. * * * On December 5, 2001, the OAG determined that the Trust Company was diverting from the Trust's charitable intent and called for broad reforms. The OAG made clear that conflicts of interest burdened the Trust Company's decisions and emphasized that personnel changes would be inadequate to address the failures of the Trust, requiring instead structural reforms to obtain lasting improvements to Trust administration. The OAG threatened legal action if necessary to obtain the reforms. As a result, the parties (the OAG, the School and the Trust Company) participated in negotiations. The Association participated in an advisory role and contributed millions of dollars to the process. Though it was not a party to the ultimate agreement, the Association acted to protect its own central purpose of preserving bonds formed in orphanhood and furthering the child-saving mission of the Trust.

On July 31, 2002, the parties reached an agreement (July 2002 Reform Agreement) outlining the reforms that the parties negotiated. The Reform Agreement purported to (1) end all conflicts of interests; * * * (2) ensure the admission of needy children; * * * (3) mandate a foster care program; * * * (4) restrict land transfers and land uses that focused on anything but childcare; * * * (5) reform academic standards for admissions and expulsions; * * * and (6) require biannual status reports to the OAG. * * *

After the Reform Agreement was executed, the highly publicized litigation over the controversial sale of a controlling interest in Hershey Foods Corporation (HFC) took place. See In re Milton Hershey School Trust, 807 A.2d 324 (Pa.Cmwlth.2002). Though, ultimately, there was no sale of HFC, there was a significant reorganization of leadership within the Trust Managers shortly after the attempted sale. As a result of the reorganization of leadership within the Trust Company and the Board of Managers of the School, the OAG, the School and the Trust Company determined that the Reform Agreement should be modified.

On June 27, 2003, the OAG, the School and the Trust executed an agreement (June 2003 Agreement) modifying the July 2002 Reform Agreement. The background statement included within that agreement indicated that because personnel changes in the Trust Company resulting from the attempted sale of HFC obviated the need for the reforms as they were presented in the original July 2002 Reform Agreement, the parties needed to modify that agreement. By comparison, the June 2003 Agreement (1) modified the provisions relating to conflicts of interest; (2) deleted the income and poverty level guidelines set forth in the July 2002 Agreement aimed at assuring the admission of truly needy children; (3) deleted the foster care program; (4) modified the restriction on land transfers to "sales" and exempting the notice requirement for the sale of land that is already commercially used; (5) modified the academic standards; and (6) changed the status report requirement from biannual, face-to-face meetings to annual written reports.

On September 4, 2003, the Association filed the petition for rule to show cause at issue in this case, seeking rescission of the June 2003 Agreement, reinstatement of the July 2002 Reform Agreement, appointment of a guardian, and appointment of a trustee *ad litem*. The School and the Trust Company filed preliminary objections to the petition, alleging that the Association lacked standing to challenge the rescission of the July 2002 Agreement.

The trial court granted the preliminary objections of the School and the Trust. In finding that the Association lacked standing, the trial court rejected the Association's contention that it was bringing suit on behalf of current and potential students because the Association's composition was limited to past members of the School. It also rejected the Association's contention that it was the only party that could protect current and potential students because it argued that the OAG's interest in the Trust was to benefit the public at large, not just the students at the School. Noting that the Association was not part of the original deed of trust, was not a party to any of the agreements, and was merely an advisor during the negotiations that led to the July 2002 Reform Agreement, the trial court refused to confer standing upon the Association because there was no evidence of a complete perversion of the charitable purpose of the Trust and no evidence that the OAG would fail in its purpose of supervising the Trust.

The Association has appealed that determination to this Court. The sole issue on appeal is whether the Association has standing to bring an action to rescind the July 2003 Agreement and reinstate the June 2002 Reform Agreement. * * *

Fundamentally, the standing requirement in Pennsylvania "is to protect against improper plaintiffs." Application of Biester, 487 Pa. 438, 442, 409 A.2d 848, 851 (1979). Juxtaposed against the federal standards,[15] the test for standing in Pennsyl-

---

15. Lujan v. Defenders of Wildlife 504 U.S. 555, 112 S.Ct. 2130, 119 L.Ed.2d 351 (1992). The federal test is a three part inquiry: (1) Has the party bringing the action alleged an "injury in fact"? (2) Is there a causal connection between the alleged wrongdoing and the injury suffered? (3) Will a favorable ruling by the court likely redress the alleged injury? *Id.* at 560, 112 S.Ct. 2130. The injury

vania is a flexible rule of law, perhaps because the lack of standing in Pennsylvania does not necessarily deprive the court of jurisdiction, whereas a lack of standing in the federal arena is directly correlated to the ability of the court to maintain jurisdiction over the action. Compare Jones Memorial Baptist Church v. Brackeen, 416 Pa. 599, 207 A.2d 861 (1965) with Raines v. Byrd, 521 U.S. 811, 117 S.Ct. 2312, 138 L.Ed.2d 849 (1997). Thus, Pennsylvania courts are much more expansive in finding standing than their federal counterparts.

In William Penn Parking Garage, Inc. v. City of Pittsburgh, 464 Pa. 168, 346 A.2d 269 (1975), our Supreme Court held that a party has standing to sue if he or she has a "substantial, direct, and immediate interest" in the subject matter of the litigation.[16] Id. at 192, 346 A.2d at 281. In William Penn, residents, taxpayers and operators of parking lots were affected by a tax ordinance that imposed a tax on patrons of non-residential parking places. The plaintiffs challenged the ordinance and were held to have standing because they were aggrieved by the ordinance. In other words, those challenging the taxing ordinances in that case were parking lot taxpayers and were able to bring their action for that reason because they showed a substantial, direct and immediate interest in the imposition of the tax.

Guided by much of our Supreme Court's discussion in William Penn, cases that followed elaborated on the substantial-direct-immediate test. The elements have been defined as follows:

> A "substantial" interest is an interest in the outcome of the litigation which surpasses the common interest of all citizens in procuring obedience to the law. . . . A "direct" interest requires a showing that the matter complained of caused harm to the party's interest. . . . An "immediate" interest involves the nature of the causal connection between the action complained of and the injury to the party challenging it, . . . and is shown where the interest the party seeks to protect is within the zone of interests sought to be protected by the statute or constitutional guarantee in question.

---

must be concrete and particularized to the plaintiff; the causation must be fairly traceable to the defendant before the court, and the relief sought must actually be obtainable from the court. Id. Notably, federal standing rules limit access to the courts because Article III of the United States Constitution, U.S. Const. art. III, limits the judiciary's power to decide only "cases or controversies," and the United States Supreme Court has developed additional "prudential" limitations on the judiciary's ability to decide cases. As a result, a plaintiff must first pass the constitutional standard under Lujan and also convince the court that there are no prudential limitations on the court's ability to hear the case. Thus, Lujan arguably returns the constitutional component of federal standing jurisprudence to one of true judicial restraint, thereby limiting the types of plaintiffs that the courts would otherwise tolerate. See Cass R. Sunstein, What's Standing After Lujan? Of Citizen Suits, "Injuries," and Article III, 91 MICH. L. REV. 163 (1992).

16. Initially, there was a "pecuniary" component to the standing requirement, but as acknowledge by the William Penn Court and other courts that followed, there is no requirement that the plaintiff suffer any pecuniary harm. William Penn, 464 Pa. at 193, 346 A.2d at 281; In re McCune, 705 A.2d 861, 865 (Pa.Super.Ct.1997) (noting that standing does not require a "direct economic interest").

South Whitehall Township Police Service v. South Whitehall Township, 521 Pa. 82, 86–87, 555 A.2d 793, 795 (1989) (internal citations omitted).

Although the substantial-direct-immediate test is the general rule for determining the standing of a party before the court, there have been a number of cases following *William Penn* that have granted standing to parties who otherwise failed to meet this test. These so-called "taxpayer standing" cases are best described as relaxations of the general standing rule where the party asserting the action can show that (1) government action will otherwise go unchallenged unless standing is granted; (2) those most directly affected by government action would benefit and would not challenge the action; (3) judicial relief is appropriate; (4) alternative remedies are not available; and (5) no one other than the party asserting the action is better suited to demonstrate an injury distinct from that of an ordinary taxpayer. See Consumer Party of Pennsylvania v. Commonwealth, 510 Pa. 158, 507 A.2d 323 (1986) (citing Biester) (granting standing to a taxpayer challenging the constitutionality of a legislative pay raise).

This exception has been utilized by our courts to grant standing to taxpayers challenging a variety of governmental actions. For example, the courts have granted standing to taxpayers challenging judicial elections on the grounds that those elections were scheduled in a year contrary to that prescribed by Pennsylvania's Constitution; * * * to the state bar association, Pennsylvania attorneys, taxpayers and electors challenging the placement of a proposed state constitutional amendment on the ballot; * * * and to a state senator challenging the governor's failure to submit nominations to the state senate within the constitutional period. * * * The theory underlying these cases is that public policy considerations favor a relaxed application of the substantial-direct-immediate test, particularly the "direct" element that requires the party bringing the action to have an interest that surpasses that of the common people. *Consumer Party.*

Finally, certain public officials have standing to represent the interest of the public both under their authority as representatives of the public interest and under the doctrine of *parens patriae*. The doctrine of "*parens patriae*" refers to the "ancient powers of guardianship over persons under disability and of protectorship of the public interest which were originally held by the Crown of England as 'father of the country,' and which as part of the common law devolved upon the states and federal government." In re Milton Hershey School Trust, 807 A.2d 324, 326 n. 1 (Pa. Cmwlth.2002) (quoting In re Pruner's Estate, 390 Pa. 529, 532, 136 A.2d 107, 109 (1957)) (citations omitted). Under parens patriae standing, the attorney general is asserting and protecting the interest of another, not that of the Commonwealth. For example, public officials have an interest as *parens patriae* in the life of an unemancipated minor. Commonwealth v. Nixon, 563 Pa. 425, 761 A.2d 1151 (2000). * * *

All of that leads us to the question before us: who has an interest in challenging the actions of the board of directors of a charitable trust? As mentioned above, because charitable trusts benefit a class of the public and not specific individuals, a guardian of the public interest is ordinarily charged with supervising and overseeing the administration of a charitable trust. In Pennsylvania, and all other states, for that matter, the attorney general under its *parens patriae* authority is the watch dog that supervises the administration of charitable trusts to ensure that the object of the trust remains charitable and to ensure that the charitable purpose of the trust is carried out. *Pruner's Estate.* The attorney general has the power and duty to oversee the administration of the trust and, consequently, has standing in any case involving a charity. See David Villar Patton, *The Queen, The Attorney General, and the Modern Charitable Fiduciary: A Historical Perspective on Charitable Enforcement Reform,* 11 U. Fl. J.L. & Pub. Pol'y 131, 159–61 (2000) (outlining the historical development of charitable trust enforcement by the attorney general from 13th Century England through the American Revolution). In fact, no trust can declare itself charitable without submitting to the supervision and inspection of the attorney general, Commonwealth v. Barnes Foundation, 398 Pa. 458, 159 A.2d 500 (1960), and the attorney general may intervene in any action involving charitable bequests and trusts under Section 204(c) of the Commonwealth Attorneys Act. * * *

Unlike other states, however, the OAG takes the position that it has the power to oppose that which may be in the best interests of the trust and examine the effects that the actions of the trust have on the larger community. *In re Hershey School Trust.* In its petition opposing the Trust's proposed sale of its controlling interest in HFC, the OAG acknowledged that the sale would likely diversify and increase the assets of the Trust, but nonetheless objected to the sale because any sale would have profound negative consequences for the Hershey community and surrounding areas, including but not limited to the closing and/or withdrawal of HFC from the local community, together with a dramatic loss of the region's employment opportunities, related businesses and tax base. Agreeing with that view, the trial court, in that case, held that the OAG could take those views into consideration and ordered that those concerns were sufficient to stop any efforts by the Trust to sell its interest in HFC. *Id.* As defined by the OAG, its role, in certain circumstances, is to protect the interests of both the beneficiaries of the Trust and the surrounding community and, where necessary, to balance those interests.[21]

While an attorney general is the only person that has automatic standing in the enforcement of charitable trusts, Pennsylvania and other states have expanded the class of plaintiffs who can intervene and challenge the actions of a charity so long as the potential plaintiff shows a "special interest" in the proceeding. Previously, it

---

21. Pennsylvania's version of the Uniform Prudent Investor Rule, 20 Pa.C.S. §§ 7201–7214, was amended at the behest of the OAG to require that fiduciaries (including the Trust's Board of Managers) consider:

> (6) an asset's special relationship or special value, if any, to the purposes of the trust or to one or more of the beneficiaries, including, in the case of a charitable trust, the special relationship of the asset and its economic impact as a principal business enterprise on the community in which the beneficiary of the trust is located and the special value of the integration of the beneficiary's activities with the community where that asset is located[.]20 Pa.C.S. § 7203(c)(6).

was thought that the attorney general should have the exclusive power to enforce charitable trusts (1) to protect trustees from frequent, unreasonable and vexatious litigation by parties who have no stake in the charity at all; (2) to prevent harassment; and (3) to safeguard the assets of the charity from loss due to needless litigation. In re Nevil's Estate, 414 Pa. 122, 199 A.2d 419 (1964); Mary Grace Blasko et al., *Standing to Sue in the Charitable Sector*, 28 U.S.F. L. Rev. 37, 41 (1993) (hereafter "Blasko"). However, criticisms of exclusive attorney general enforcement power * * * gave rise to the need for courts to give third parties the ability to bring enforcement actions against charitable organizations. As Section 391 of the Second Restatement of Trusts states:

> A suit can be maintained for the enforcement of a charitable trust by the Attorney General or other public officer, or by a co-trustee, *or by a person who has a special interest in the enforcement of the charitable trust, but not by persons who have no special interest* or by the settlor or his heirs, personal representatives or next of kin.

Restatement (Second) Trusts § 391 (1959) (emphasis added).

The special interest concept has been part of Pennsylvania law since the early 1950s. See Wiegand v. Barnes Foundation, 374 Pa. 149, 97 A.2d 81 (1953) (citing Restatement (Second) Trusts § 391). * * * In Valley Forge Historical Society v. Washington Memorial Chapel, 493 Pa. 491, 426 A.2d 1123 (1981), our Supreme Court elaborated on the circumstances contemplated under the special interest doctrine that allows parties other than the attorney general to enforce a charitable trust. In that case, the Historical Society sought to restrain the trustees of the Memorial Chapel from evicting the Society from its quarters in the Chapel. The Society and the Chapel had a common settlor. Under the deed of trust, the Chapel acquired the land upon which the Society also maintained its quarters, and the land was donated to be used to advance "religious and patriotic purposes," thereby creating a charitable trust. Responding to the Society's request for equitable relief, the Chapel argued that the Society lacked standing to enforce the charitable trust because the attorney general did not participate, and he alone was the only party with standing to enforce the trust.

Noting that only the attorney general, a member of the charitable organization (i.e., a member of the Chapel), or one with a "special interest" in the trust could enforce its provisions, and noting that the Society was neither the attorney general nor a member of the charitable organization, the Court held that the Society had a special interest in the trust and had standing to petition the court for equitable relief. The Court reasoned as follows: (1) the Society and the Chapel had a close, cordial relationship, both having occupied the same building for many years; (2) the common founder of both organizations intended for both to "aid in the development of patriotism" in a religious and educational manner; (3) the Society made significant monetary contributions to the Chapel; (4) the Society, by its origins, its link to the Chapel and its professed purpose, distinguished it from any other historical society; and (5) there was no risk of vexatious and unreasonable litigation by the Society.

Based on a review of other jurisdictions that have reached this issue, a multi-factor approach, an approach that was presaged by our Supreme Court in *Valley Forge*, is used by courts to determine whether a party has a "special interest" in the enforcement of a charitable trust:

> It is clear that courts often use the "special interest" doctrine to ensure that charities are subject to some form of effective scrutiny, especially on important issues. This mechanism will increase in fairness and predictability, and consequently in value, if courts adhere to a specific formulation of the doctrine. The multi-factor test used so far by only a few courts seems to be an effective approach. It is flexible and can readily accommodate factual variations such as the level of activity of the relevant attorney general or the crucial quality of the complained-of actions. Certain factors should always play important roles. In particular, the presence of sincere allegations of managerial bad faith, and a request for a limited remedy should favor a grant of standing to private parties. A claim that the complained-of acts will have an extraordinary impact on the charity should be especially persuasive in the plaintiffs' favor. On the other hand, the authors hope that the influence of subjective social factors will wither away. *The nature of the relationship between the charity and the plaintiffs probably will remain a less easily measured factor, but the existence of a well-defined and limited group of plaintiffs who have a clear interest in the operation of the charity should favor a grant of standing.* If courts allow suits by larger groups of plaintiffs with more vague interests, they should understand that this could substantially expand the range of potential plaintiffs in charitable abuse cases.

> In short, we recommend that courts explicitly adopt the multi-factor approach used in the Escondido (San Diego Boy Scouts)[24] and Alco Gravure cases.[25] This method would allow courts to grant standing to private

24. In San Diego County Council, Boy Scouts of America v. City of Escondido, 14 Cal.App.3d 189, 92 Cal.Rptr. 186 (1971), the County Council of the Boy Scouts and several individual scouts brought suit to enjoin the city's proposed sale of a piece of property held in trust for the scouts' benefit. The attorney general did not participate. Using a multi-factor approach to determine whether the Council had standing to enforce the trust, the court emphasized the relationship between the plaintiffs and the charity, noting that "the administration of charitable trusts stands only to benefit if in addition to the Attorney General other suitable means of enforcement are available." *Id.* at 190. The court stated that the Council of Boy Scouts was charged by its articles of incorporation and bylaws with protecting and representing its district and the scouts within, and the court stated that it could "think of no more responsive or responsible party to represent the boy scouts of the Palomar District in such litigation." *Id.* at 190.

25. In Alco Gravure, Inc. v. Knapp Foundation, 64 N.Y.2d 458, 490 N.Y.S.2d 116, 479 N.E.2d 752 (1985), potential beneficiaries of a charitable trust sued to prevent a non-profit corporation from transferring its assets to another charity with a similar, but not identical, purpose. The court first noted that both the attorney general and a trial judge approved the transfer of assets and implied that it would deny standing to a private plaintiff challenging the administration of a charity. However, it recognized that the individual plaintiffs' status as preferred beneficiaries would be eliminated had the transfer occurred. Using a multi-factor approach, the court held that because

plaintiffs needed to keep charities accountable on important matters while avoiding excessive and undesirable litigation burdens on those charities, all with greater consistency and predictive value than is currently the case.

Blasko et al., *supra*, at 83–84 (internal footnotes omitted) (emphasis added).

Blasko's article concludes that the following five factors "consistently influence a court's willingness to allow a private party to sue for the enforcement of charitable obligations": (1) the extraordinary nature of the acts complained of and the remedy sought; (2) the presence of fraud or misconduct on the part of the charity or its directors; (3) the attorney general's availability or effectiveness; (4) the nature of the benefited class and its relationship to the charity; and (5) subjective, case-specific circumstances. Blasko et al., *supra*, at 61–78 (adopted with modification by Robert Schalkenbach Foundation v. Lincoln Foundation, Inc., 91 P.3d 1019, 208 Ariz. 176 (Ct.App.2004) ("[W]e give special emphasis to . . . the nature of the benefited class and its relationship to the trust, the nature of the remedy requested, and the effectiveness of attorney general enforcement of the trust.")).

Guided by the reasoning in *Valley Forge*, we will utilize this multi-factor test to determine whether the Association has standing under the special interest doctrine. This approach is consistent with the concern in *Valley Forge* of preventing unnecessary litigation involving charities and the concern of assuring that the philanthropic purpose of any given charity is carried out, notwithstanding the extent of the involvement by the attorney general. This approach also assures judicial scrutiny in situations where important charitable issues are at stake and where the attorney general's involvement is otherwise lacking, ineffective or conflicted. Finally, this approach is consistent with the general purpose of standing law—to protect against improper plaintiffs—by specifically emphasizing the special relationship between the plaintiff seeking enforcement of the trust and the trust itself. *Valley Forge.* * * *

The Association argues that it has met the special interest test for challenging the modification of the July 2002 Reform Agreement.[26] The Association points out that it was instrumental in bringing to the OAG's attention the substantial

---

the remedy sought was to preserve the existence of the charity itself, because the benefited class was small and identifiable, and because beneficiaries would be directly harmed by the transfer of the assets, the plaintiffs had a special interest sufficient to challenge the transfer.

26. The Association also contends that it meets the general direct-immediate-substantial test for standing because (1) its vast efforts to secure the July 2002 Reform Agreement at the OAG's request and the subsequent rescission resulted in direct harm to the Association; and (2) and its unique dual purpose of assuring the bonds developed in orphanhood and assuring that the purpose of the Trust is carried out is essential to the existence of the Association. The Association alternatively argues that it meets the taxpayer exception to the general direct-immediate-substantial test because (1) rescission of the July 2002 Reform Agreement will go unchallenged were we to refuse standing; (2) judicial relief is appropriate; (3) other relief is not available; and (4) the Association is in the best position to seek reinstatement. We need not reach these issues in light of the manner in which we resolve standing in this case.

growth in Trust assets (exceeding $5 or $6 billion) concomitantly with a decrease in the number of orphan children served. In addition, the Association also raised concerns about potential conflicts of interest amongst the Trust directors and potential mismanagement of trust funds that led to a decline in serving orphan children at the School. The Association was instrumental in having the OAG seek the July 2002 Reform Agreement that sought to remedy these problems, problems that were acknowledged by the OAG, by eliminating conflicts of interest, by reworking admissions and academic standards, by restricting land transfers and sales, and by requiring status reports to the OAG. Given the nature of these events, given the enormous amount of money at stake, and given that the Association merely seeks to determine whether the July 2002 Reform Agreement will better serve the charitable purpose of the Trust instead of the June 2003 Agreement struck by the OAG, the School, and the Trust, the Association has pled a special interest in this matter.

The Association also has a special interest because of its relationship with the benefited class and the charity itself. Similar to the Historical Society in *Valley Forge*, the Association has historically maintained a close, cordial relationship with the Trust for over 70 years, and it has made monetary contributions to the School on a number of occasions. The members of the Association are all successful participants of the School, and the Association has its office on Trust lands where it conducts student-related activities and graduate assistance programs for students at the School. The Association was created by Mr. Hershey, settlor of the Trust, and the Association's articles of incorporation and bylaws require that it maintain the common bonds formed during orphanhood and preserve the charitable, child-saving purpose of the Trust. In addition, the Association is particularly well-suited to evaluate the performance of this Trust because of its intimate knowledge of orphanhood, poverty and other alternative foster care facilities. At bottom, the Association, whose membership consists exclusively of past beneficiaries of the Hershey Trust, is the only other party with a sufficient relationship to the Trust that would have any interest in assuring that its charitable purpose was achieved.

Furthermore, the risk of vexatious or unreasonable litigation by the Association is virtually non-existent in this case. This is not a situation where a mere potential beneficiary with a speculative interest in the charity is seeking to interfere with the administration of the Trust or where a member of the general public is disagreeing with the administration of the Trust. This is also not a situation where the Association wishes to drain Trust assets by litigating each and every decision made by trust managers. The Association only seeks the reasons why the July 2002 Reform Agreement was replaced by the June 2003 Agreement when the Reform Agreement was the result of an extensive investigation funded in part by the Association to aid the OAG, which concluded that potential conflicts of interests amongst trust managers and potential asset mismanagement interfered with the Trust's charitable mission. That inquiry is neither vexatious nor unreasonable. Given the nature of this Trust, its status as the largest residential childcare charity in the world, and the fact that the OAG agreed to modify the July 2002 Reform Agreement, this scrutiny will serve the public interest in assuring that the Trust is operating efficiently and effectively to serve its beneficiaries. * * *

Accordingly, because the Association has a "special interest" in this proceeding, it should have been allowed to challenge the modification of the July 2002 Reform Agreement, and for the foregoing reasons, the order of the trial court is reversed and the matter is remanded for hearings on the Association's petition. * * *

AND NOW, this 31st day of January, 2005, the order of the trial court in the above-captioned matter is reversed and the matter is remanded for hearings on the Association's petition. * * *

Dissenting Opinion by President Judge COLINS, joined by Judges COHN JUBE-LIRER and SIMPSON.

Dissenting Opinion by President Judge COLINS.

I must respectfully dissent from the majority opinion while, at the same time, comment that it is one of the finest pieces of legal scholarship that I have read in my 25 years on the bench.

The reasons for my dissent follow briefly.

As noted [in] the majority opinion:

As directed by the deed of trust, the members of the School's Board of Managers are also members of the Board of Directors of the Trust Company. The deed endows the Board of Managers and the Trust Company with decision-making responsibility for all aspects of running the School and for management and administration of Trust assets.

Further, the majority opinion * * * state[s]:

The Association is not a division of the School or of the Trust Company. It is not named in the deed of trust and is not an intended beneficiary of the Trust. As the deed states, "[a]ll children shall leave the institution and cease to be the recipients of its benefits upon the completion of the full course of secondary education being offered at the School." * * * The Managers of the Trust may, in their discretion, contribute to the higher education of a graduate of the School, in which case graduates would continue to be beneficiaries of the Trust, but generally, once orphans graduate from the School, they are no longer Trust beneficiaries.

Unfortunately, this is where this Court's inquiry must end. It is clear from the historical background of this saga that the Settlors in no way intended to give the Alumni Association standing in the administration of the Trust. The Settlor, Milton Hershey, was also the creator of the Alumni Association. To now give the Association legal rights that were expressly excluded by the Settlor of the Trust is a dangerous expansion of standing not supported by over 300 years of case law within the Commonwealth.

The Attorney General of the Commonwealth, pursuant to well-accepted principles of "*parens patriae*," as noted by the majority:

> is the watch dog that supervises the administration of charitable trusts to ensure that the object of the trust remains charitable and to ensure that the charitable purpose of the trust is carried out. * * * The attorney general has the power to oversee the administration of the trust and, consequently, has standing in any case involving charity. See David Villar Patton, *The Queen, The Attorney General, and the Modern Charitable Fiduciary: A Historical Perspective on Charitable Enforcement Reform*, 11 U. Fl. J.L. & Pub. Pol'y 131, 159–61 (2000) (outlining the historical development of charitable trust enforcement by the attorney general from 13th Century England through the American Revolution).

To allow the Alumni Association standing, no matter how eleemosynary its purpose may be, interferes with the efficient performance of the Attorney General's statutorily-mandated duties, as well as being violative of the wishes of the Settlor of the Trust and founder of the Alumni Association.

Such a quantum leap away from historical concepts of standing, based upon public policy considerations, and a judicially-created "special interest," may only be undertaken by the Supreme Court of the Commonwealth.

Judge COHN JUBELIRER and Judge SIMPSON join in this dissent.

Notes

The Milton Hershey School, a charitable institution with more than $12 billion in assets under management, was supported by the Hershey Trust Company, funded in large part with Hershey stock. The Company was designated by the trust instrument to administer the trust. The Milton Hershey School Alumni Association was founded to promote the interests of the school, and the standing it seeks, to challenge the administration of the trust, seems consistent with its mission. The Commonwealth Court of Pennsylvania explains in the *Hershey* decision all of the reasons why the Association has standing to challenge the administration of the trust. Thus, the case addresses this issue: Who has an interest in challenging the actions of the board of directors of a charitable trust? The court acknowledges that the state attorney general has automatic standing, but the court expands standing to persons with a "special interest" in the enforcement of a charitable trust. Eventually, this special interest exception to enforcement supervision was rejected by the Supreme Court of Pennsylvania. *See In re* Milton Hershey School, 590 Pa. 35, 911 A.2d 1258 (2006). The state's highest court held that the Association had no special interest in the trust; nothing in the settlor's trust, nor any gain or loss to the Association, justified giving to it a special interest for enforcement. Holding in a similar fashion, the Connecticut Superior Court ruled that because a

> donor cannot confer standing upon the plaintiff by simply stating that citizens of New Britain have standing to sue to enforce the provisions of the

deed, the only issue before the court is whether the provision in the deed creates a specific interest in the gift for the plaintiff. The plain language in the provision does not create such a special interest, as the plaintiff has a legal interest that is shared by all members of the community.

Lechowicz v. Costco Wholesale Corp., No. CV146026620, 2014 WL 5286577 (Conn. Super. Ct. Sept. 11, 2014). Joseph Mead & Michael Pollack, *Courts, Constituencies, and the Enforcement of Fiduciary Duties in the Nonprofit Sector*, 7 U. PITT. L. REV. 281 (2016); Susan N. Gary, *The Problems with Donor Intent: Interpretation, Enforcement, and Doing the Right Thing*, 85 CHI.-KENT L. REV. 977 (2010).

Enforcement of Charity: The Uniform Trust Code allows for a settlor, among others, to enforce a charitable trust, thereby providing for a mechanism for enforcement at present and into the future. *See* UNIF. TRUST CODE § 405(c) (2014). The state attorney general, who is the other person responsible for enforcement of the charitable purposes, often requires reporting by the trustee, *see, e.g.,* N.Y. EST., POWERS & TRUSTS L. § 8-1.4 (McKinney 2015), thereby furthering the requirements of the Uniform Trust Code, *see* UNIF. TRUST CODE § 813 (2016) (Duty to Inform and Report). Matters for supervision by the attorney general would include prudent investing by the trustee. *See, e.g., Restatement (Second) of Trusts* § 389 (1959); UNIF. PRUDENT INVESTOR ACT (1994). Yet, while the attorney general is responsible for enforcement, the courts remain the final arbiters in matters such as cy pres. *See, e.g.,* Town of Brookline v. Barnes, 327 Mass. 201, 97 N.E.2d 651 (1951). Some would argue that the attorney general is a poor choice for enforcement of charitable trusts. *See, e.g.,* Kenneth L. Karst, *The Efficiency of the Charitable Dollar: An Unfulfilled State Responsibility*, 73 HARV. L. REV. 433 (1960). There are few federal or state penalties. The federal Internal Revenue Code imposes tax penalties on private charitable foundations that do not distribute annually at least five percent of the value of the endowment. *See* I.R.C. § 4942 (2004). Failure to do so will result in a 15 % excise tax of any undistributed income. Repeated failure to distribute funds will entail stiffer penalties. *See id.* at § 6684.

3. Taxation and Charities

A contribution made to what may be termed a charity is only deductible as such if made to, or for the use of, the following organizations: (1) The United States, a state, local government, the District of Columbia, or a United States Possession. And the gift must be exclusively for public, rather than private, purposes. (2) A corporation, trust, community chest, fund, or foundation, created in the United States and organized exclusively for religious, charitable, scientific, literary or educational purposes, or for national or international sports competitions, or for the prevention of cruelty to children or to animals. No part of the charity's earnings may go to benefit any private person, and the charity must not be disqualified for tax exemption under I.R.C. § 501(c)(3) by attempting to influence legislation. (3) A cemetery not operated for profit or for the benefit of any private shareholder or individual. (4) A post or organization of war veterans, or its auxiliary society or unit, organized in the

United States or its possessions, if no part of the net earnings inures to the benefit of any private shareholder or individual. (5) For individual donors only, a domestic fraternal society, or association, operating under the lodge system, if the contributions are used exclusively for religious, charitable, scientific, literary, or educational purposes, or for the prevention of cruelty to children or animals. I.R.C. § 170(c).

Estates and trusts are allowed unlimited income tax charitable deduction for amounts that are paid to recognized charities out of gross income earned during the tax year. *See id.* at § 642(c). And if an individual makes a charitable gift during lifetime, he or she is entitled to a gift tax charitable deduction. *See id.* at § 2522. If a decedent makes a charitable gift at death through a valid Last Will and Testament, his or her estate is entitled to the estate tax charitable deduction for the property transferred to charity. *See id.* at § 2055.

Sometimes an individual may make a gift or trust that benefits both the individual and a charity. This type of arrangement is generally referred to as a "split-interest" trust because both an individual and a charity have an interest in the trust. If the transfer is in the form of a trust whereby a charity receives the remainder interest after a life interest is paid to an individual, no charitable deduction is permitted. However, if the trust qualifies as a charitable remainder annuity trust (CRAT) or a charitable remainder unitrust trust (CRUT), the individual will receive a charitable deduction for the value of the remainder interest that will pass to charity under the terms of the trust.

The annuity trust allows for a specified amount not less than five percent, nor more than fifty percent, of the initial net fair market value of all of the property placed in the trust to be paid to the individual. And the annuity amount must be paid at least annually to the income beneficiary, and the value of the remainder interest must be at least ten percent of the initial net fair market value of all the property in the trust. Furthermore, the trust must prohibit additional future contributions, and the term of the trust may be the individual's life or a term of years that does not exceed 20 years. After the death of the individual or the end of the term, the corpus of the trust passes to charity. *See id.* at § 664(d)(1). The advantage of the annuity trust is that the amount that the non-charitable beneficiary — the individual — receives is fixed.

A unitrust (CRUT) must pay the income beneficiary, annually, an amount based on a fixed percentage of the net fair market value of the trust's assets, which must be valued annually. The fixed percentage cannot be less than five percent, nor more than fifty percent, of the net fair market value of the trust assets. At the death of the beneficiary or after a term of years not to exceed 20, the assets pass to the charity. *See id.* at § 664(d)(2). Unlike the CRAT, additional contributions may be made to the CRUT. There are alternatives to the CRUT described above. First, the unitrust may provide that the non-charitable beneficiary receives the fixed percentage amount of the net fair market value of the assets or the amount of the trust income, whichever is lower (a NICRUT). *See id.* at § 664(d)(3)(A). If the trust earns no income, the trust does not pay the income beneficiary. Second, the trust may provide that the non-charitable beneficiary receive the lower of the fixed percentage amount of the net fair market value of the assets or the trust income, whichever is lower, and, in years in which the income is lower than the required fixed percentage amount, the trust can distribute amounts of income to the extent that the previous year's income exceeded the amount required to be distributed (a NIMCRUT). *See id.* at § 664(d)(3)(B). Third, a trust can start out as a NIMCRUT and, upon a certain event, convert to a standard CRUT (a FlipCRUT). *See id.* at § 664(f). Drafting charitable annuity trusts or unitrusts is difficult and requires precision. The following decisions is illustrative.

Putnam v. Putnam

Supreme Judicial Court of Massachusetts, 1997
425 Mass. 770, 682 N.E.2d 1351

WILKINS, Chief Justice.

Here on direct appellate review is a reservation and report of an action seeking the reformation of the Stanton W. Putnam charitable remainder unitrust (unitrust). The plaintiff settlor of the unitrust (Putnam) contends that the trust instrument, drafted by a lawyer now deceased, provides for annual distributions to Putnam or to a named successor (King) that (a) are inconsistent with his intent to benefit the charities that have remainder interests in the unitrust and (b) greatly reduce the tax benefits that he intended to flow from the unitrust's creation.

All named defendants have assented to the reformation of the unitrust. The judge reported the case on the facts stated in the complaint and did so on the assumption that the Internal Revenue Service, which is not a party, would be bound only by a decision of this court, a point on which we express no view. The record has been supplemented on appeal by additional facts.

Putnam created the unitrust on December 29, 1989. The trust owns real estate in Truro which has an estimated value of less than $400,000. The property, which is for sale, has produced no income to the trust. Putnam expected to receive no distribution from the trust and did not review the terms of the trust when he executed it. In fact, the trust instrument directs the trustee annually to distribute "first from the net income, and to the extent that such net income is insufficient, from the principal of the trust, an amount (the 'unitrust amount') equal to ten percent of the net fair market value of the trust assets." The distributions are to be made quarterly to Putnam during his life and then to King, if he survives Putnam, for life but for no more than twenty years from Putnam's death. Then the trust assets are to be distributed in equal shares to the named charities.[2]

---

2. The trust instrument grants the trustee the power to amend the terms of the trust for the purpose of complying with the requirements of a qualified charitable remainder unitrust under the Internal Revenue Code.

A charitable remainder trust provides for a specified distribution, at least annually, to one or more beneficiaries, at least one of which is not a charity, for life or for a term of years, with an irrevocable remainder interest in one or more charities. I.R.C. § 664 (1994); Treas. Reg. § 1.664-1(a) (1997). The plaintiff's unitrust qualifies as a "charitable remainder unitrust" under § 664(d)(2) of the I.R.C. Each year, subject to an exception we shall discuss later, a charitable remainder unitrust must distribute a fixed percentage (which may not be less than five per cent) of the net fair market value of the assets valued each year, to one or more noncharitable beneficiaries (also called "income beneficiaries") for a certain term. I.R.C. § 664(d)(2)(A). At the end of the term, the trust assets pass to, or for the use of, one or more qualified charities. I.R.C. § 664(d)(2)(C). The unitrust conforms to these requirements, but its mandate that ten per cent of the value of the trust assets be distributed annually reduces substantially the prospective value of the charitable remainders.

An exception to the fixed percentage distribution requirements just discussed permits distribution of only net income to a noncharitable beneficiary. I.R.C. § 664(d)(3). This method obviously protects the trust principal from intrusion. Putnam relies on this provision in seeking to reform the unitrust instrument to conform to what he intended when he created the unitrust.

We have allowed the reformation of an ambiguous trust instrument based on extrinsic evidence of the settlor's intent and provisions in the instrument that showed that the lawyer who drafted it failed to carry out the settlor's intent. Berman v. Sandler, 379 Mass. 506, 510–511, 399 N.E.2d 17 (1980). We have also allowed reformation of trust instruments that were not ambiguous but which produced results that were proved to be clearly inconsistent with the settlor's estate tax objectives. See Pond v. Pond, 424 Mass. 894, 898–899, 678 N.E.2d 1321 (1997); Simches v. Simches, 423 Mass. 683, 687–688, 671 N.E.2d 1226 (1996); Loeser v. Talbot, 412 Mass. 361, 365, 589 N.E.2d 301 (1992). See Restatement of Property (Donative Transfers) § 12.2 (Tent. Draft No. 1 1995). In deciding trust reformation issues, we have made no distinction based on whether the settlor was living when the case was presented for decision. See Berman v. Sandler, *supra* at 510, 399 N.E.2d 17. Indeed, the crucial evidence of intent and mistake may well be available from the lawyer who drafted (or misdrafted) the instrument rather than from the settlor. Nor have we made any distinction based on whether a trust instrument was or was not ambiguous.[3]

---

3. We have disallowed extrinsic evidence to "explain" the terms of an unambiguous will. See Putnam v. Putnam, 366 Mass. 261, 266, 316 N.E.2d 729 (1974), and cases cited. The circumstances known to the testator at the time of the will's execution have been admissible, however, in aid of interpreting a will to ascertain the testator's intent. *Id.* at 266–267, 316 N.E.2d 729.

For reasons that may no longer be meaningful, we have been less willing to recognize the possibility of proof of mistake in the drafting of a will (as opposed to an *inter vivos* trust) that is unambiguous on its face. The case may be hard to make, however, for denying reformation of a will where, in substantively similar circumstances, we would allow reformation of a trust instrument. See Restatement of Property (Donative Transfers) § 12.1 comment c (Tent. Draft No. 1 1995).

The existence of a mistake in the drafting of a trust instrument must be established by "full, clear, and decisive proof." Berman v. Sandler, *supra* at 509, 399 N.E.2d 17, quoting Coolidge v. Loring, 235 Mass. 220, 224, 126 N.E. 276 (1920), quoting Richardson v. Adams, 171 Mass. 447, 449, 50 N.E. 941 (1898). That standard is similar to proof by "clear and convincing evidence." See Restatement of Property Donative Transfers) § 12.1 (Tent. Draft No. 1 1995). The point is not, however, so much that the burden of proof is heightened as it is that the judge who considers the reformation claim must make thorough and reasoned findings that deal with all relevant facts and must demonstrate a conviction that the proof of mistake was clear and well-founded.

The unitrust with which we are concerned in this case is not ambiguous. One might create such a trust, although in practical terms the trust might generate limited benefits for the charity or charities and thus limited tax benefits for the settlor. In this case, however, it seems clear that the settlor was not interested in receiving significant distributions of principal from the trust. The trust assets, real estate in Truro, had not been sold and had produced no income. The charitable gifts, with the related tax benefits, appear to have been the settlor's goal in creating the unitrust. The provision for distribution of ten per cent of the fair market value of the trust assets each year, made up first from income and then from principal to the extent needed, would considerably deplete the amounts likely to be available for the charities. A reformation of the trust to limit distributions to noncharitable beneficiaries to the income of the trust, as I.R.C. § 664(d)(3) permits, is appropriate in the circumstances.

The request for an award of attorney's fees and costs payable from the assets of the unitrust is denied. The lawyer who made the drafting error was a member of the firm that appears for the plaintiff to correct the error. A judgment shall be entered in the Probate and Family Court allowing the amendment of the unitrust in the form set forth in the first request for relief of the complaint.[4]

So ordered.

Evidence of intention, perhaps inadmissible for the purpose of interpretation of a trust instrument, may be relevant and admissible on the issue of mistake, that is, to support the reformation of the instrument.

4. The record in this case is unnecessarily scant. We have not been furnished with calculations showing the difference in the value of the charitable gifts under the trust (a) as drafted and (b) as reformed. We have not even been given the ages of the noncharitable income beneficiaries, facts that are crucial in calculating the date on which the charities will likely be paid. We do not know whether Putnam ever received income from the real estate now in the trust. Nor do we have an affidavit from Putnam (and perhaps others) stating his intention in creating the trust. Although on the facts of this case the charitable giving and tax objectives are sufficiently apparent to permit reformation of the trust instrument, the requirement of clear and decisive proof in such cases counsels that a full factual record supporting reformation be made.

Notes

Subsequent courts have been willing to modify mistaken trust terms to qualify for the tax benefits of charitable remainder trusts and effectuate the intent of the settlor. *See, e.g.,* Bank of America, N.A. v. Sweeney, 876 N.E.2d 840 (Mass. 2007) (granting a petition to reform the terms of decedent's will so as to create a charitable remainder trust); *but see* Pellegrini v. Breitenbach, 926 N.E.2d 544 (Mass. 2010) (holding that decedent's will could not be reformed because there was insufficient proof that decedent intended a trust, let alone a charitable remainder trust). The Uniform Trust Code permits reformation of trust terms, but only to conform the terms of the settlor's intention, proven by clear and convincing evidence, that both the settlor's intent and the terms of the trust were affected by a mistake of fact or law. Unif. Trust Code § 415.

Charitable remainder trusts have proliferated with the expanding number of older persons seeking to avoid capital gains taxes, further charitable causes, and retain a bit of income. Commentary abounds on what precautions to take in creating these trusts. *See, e.g.,* Conrad Teitell, Daniel G. Johnson & Katherine A. McAllister, *Diversifying Charitable Remainder Trust Investments,* 156 Trusts & Ests. 39 (Oct. 2017) (identifying each of the different types of CRT investments and precautions to take); Robert F. Sharpe, Jr., *The Charitable Planning Balancing Act,* 154 Trusts & Ests. 7, 8 (July 2015); Michael J. Jones, *The 5 Percent Solution,* 153 Trusts & Ests. 38 (June 2014) (describing the best uses of CRUTs and CRATs); Paul S. Lee & Stephen S. Schilling, *CRTs Are Back (In Four Delicious Flavors),* 153 Trusts & Ests. 31 (Oct. 2014) (discussing how different assets may prompt different types of charitable remainder trusts); Conrad Teitell, Heather J. Rhoades & Margaret E. St. John, *Termination of Charitable Remainder Trusts,* 153 Trusts & Ests. 57 (Oct. 2014) (cautioning donors to be aware of penalties and the variety of charitable remainder trusts available).

H. Pour Over Trusts

Modern estate planning integrates retirement programs (payable-on-death accounts), insurance policies (including long-term care insurance), and *inter vivos* trusts, all of which may coalesce in a valid Last Will and Testament. Needless to say, federal and state taxation policies play a role, and, increasingly, international wealth must be factored. For example, an estate planning attorney may recommend to a client that he or she name as beneficiary on any Keogh, IRA, or life insurance policy the testamentary trust established in a valid Last Will and Testament. Conversely, the Last Will and Testament may name as legatee of "all of my property, both real and personal," an *inter vivos* trust executed during the lifetime of the settlor. This interaction between *inter vivos* and testamentary transactions is often referred to as pour over. If a will bequeaths property to a trust, it is a pour over will; if an *inter vivos* trust names as beneficiary the Last Will and Testament, it is a pour over trust. Traditionally, the *inter vivos* trust was considered a fact of independent significance, and a valid will was permitted to name it as a legatee, even though it was unfunded.

Pour over practice is evidenced in Uniform Probate Code § 2-512, which follows *infra*. But there was often concern as to whether the pour over was legal if no trust property existed prior to the death of the testator, when the will actually pours property into the trust. How could you pour over into something that had no independent significance? To remedy this dilemma, states enacted Uniform Probate Code § 2-511. If the state adopts the provisions of § 2-511, there is no necessity to fund the *inter vivos* trust during the lifetime of the settlor. Compare the two following provisions to identify the distinction, remembering that pour over trusts are most often revocable *inter vivos* trusts, which is the next type of trust to be considered and a valuable estate planning tool.

Uniform Probate Code (2019)

§ 2-512. Events of Independent Significance.

A will may dispose of property by reference to acts and events that have significance apart from their effect upon the dispositions made by the will, whether they occur before or after the execution of the will or before or after the testator's death. The execution or revocation of another individual's will is such an event.

§ 2-511. Uniform Testamentary Additions to Trusts Act (1991).

(a) A will may validly devise property to the trustee of a trust established or to be established (i) during the testator's lifetime by the testator, by the testator and some other person, or by some other person, including a funded or unfunded life insurance trust, although the settlor has reserved any or all rights of ownership of the insurance contracts, or (ii) at the testator's death by the testator's devise to the trustee, if the trust is identified in the testator's will and its terms are set forth in a written instrument, other than a will, executed before, concurrently with, or after the execution of the testator's will or in another individual's will if that other individual has predeceased the testator, regardless of the existence, size, or character of the corpus of the trust. The devise is not invalid because the trust is amendable or revocable, or because the trust was amended after the execution of the will or the testator's death.

(b) Unless the testator's will provides otherwise, property devised to a trust described in subsection (a) is not held under a testamentary trust of the testator, but it becomes a part of the trust to which it is devised, and must be administered and disposed of in accordance with the provisions of the governing instrument setting forth the terms of the trust, including any amendments thereto made before or after the testator's death.

(c) Unless the testator's will provides otherwise, a revocation or termination of the trust before the testator's death causes the devise to lapse.

I. Revocable *Inter Vivos* Trusts

Clymer v. Mayo

Supreme Court of Massachusetts, 1985
393 Mass. 754, 473 N.E.2d 1084

HENNESSEY, Chief Justice.

This consolidated appeal arises out of the administration of the estate of Clara A. Mayo (decedent). We summarize the findings of the judge of the Probate and Family Court incorporating the parties' agreed statement of uncontested facts.

At the time of her death in November, 1981, the decedent, then fifty years of age, was employed by Boston University as a professor of psychology. She was married to James P. Mayo, Jr. (Mayo), from 1953 to 1978. The couple had no children. The decedent was an only child and her sole heirs at law are her parents, Joseph A. and Maria Weiss.

In 1963, the decedent executed a will designating Mayo as principal beneficiary. In 1964, she named Mayo as the beneficiary of her group annuity contract with John Hancock Mutual Life Insurance Company; and in 1965, made him the beneficiary of her Boston University retirement annuity contracts with Teachers Insurance and Annuity Association (TIAA) and College Retirement Equities Fund (CREF). As a consequence of a $300,000 gift to the couple from the Weisses in 1971, the decedent and Mayo executed new wills and indentures of trust on February 2, 1973, wherein each spouse was made the other's principal beneficiary. Under the terms of the decedent's will, Mayo was to receive her personal property. The residue of her estate was to "pour over" into the *inter vivos* trust she created that same day.

The decedent's trust instrument named herself and John P. Hill as trustees. As the donor, the decedent retained the right to amend or revoke the trust at any time by written instrument delivered to the trustees. In the event that Mayo survived the decedent, the trust estate was to be divided into two parts. Trust A, the marital deduction trust, was to be funded with an amount "equal to fifty (50%) per cent of the value of the Donor's 'adjusted gross estate,' . . . for the purpose of the United States Tax Law, less an amount equal to the value of all interest in property, if any, allowable as 'marital deductions' for the purposes of such law. . . ." Mayo was the income beneficiary of Trust A and was entitled to reach the principal at his request or in the trustee's discretion. The trust instrument also gave Mayo a general power of appointment over the assets in Trust A.

The balance of the decedent's estate, excluding personal property passing to Mayo by will, or the entire estate if Mayo did not survive her, composed Trust B. Trust B provided for the payment of five initial specific bequests totalling [sic] $45,000. After those gifts were satisfied, the remaining trust assets were to be held for the benefit of Mayo for life. Upon Mayo's death, the assets in Trust B were to be held for "the benefit of the nephews and nieces of the Donor" living at the time of her death. The trustee was given discretion to spend so much of the income and principal as necessary for their comfort, support, and education. When all of these nephews and nieces reached the age of thirty, the trust was to terminate and its remaining assets were to be divided equally between Clark University and Boston University to assist in graduate education of women.

On the same day she established her trust, the decedent changed the beneficiary of her Boston University group life insurance policy from Mayo to the trustees. One month later, in March, 1973, she also executed a change in her retirement annuity contracts to designate the trustees as beneficiaries. At the time of its creation in 1973, the trust was not funded. Its future assets were to consist solely of the proceeds of these policies and the property which would pour over under the will's residuary clause. The judge found that the remaining trustee has never received any property or held any funds subsequent to the execution of the trust nor has he paid any trust taxes or filed any trust tax returns.

Mayo moved out of the marital home in 1975. In June, 1977, the decedent changed the designation of beneficiary on her Boston University life insurance policy for a second time, substituting Marianne LaFrance for the trustees.[2] LaFrance had lived with the Mayos since 1972, and shared a close friendship with the decedent up until her death. Mayo filed for divorce on September 9, 1977, in New Hampshire. The divorce was decreed on January 3, 1978, and the court incorporated into the decree a permanent stipulation of the parties' property settlement. Under the terms of that settlement, Mayo waived any "right, title or interest" in the decedent's "securities, savings accounts, savings certificates, and retirement fund," as well as her "furniture, furnishings and art." Mayo remarried on August 28, 1978, and later executed a new will in favor of his new wife. The decedent died on November 21, 1981. Her will was allowed on November 18, 1982, and the court appointed John H. Clymer as administrator with the will annexed.

What is primarily at issue in these actions is the effect of the Mayos' divorce upon dispositions provided in the decedent's will and indenture of trust. In the first action, the court-appointed administrator of the decedent's estate petitioned for instructions with respect to the impact of the divorce on the estate's administration. Named as defendants were Mayo, the decedent's parents (the Weisses), and the trustee under the indenture of trust (John P. Hill).

The second case involved a complaint for declaratory and equitable relief filed by the Weisses. Named as defendants were Hill, Mayo, Clymer, the beneficiaries named in Trust B (Hill, Michael Z. Fleming, Renee N. Watkins, LaFrance, Mary Ann Mayo, Boston University, and Clark University), James Mayo's nephews and niece (John Chamberlain, Allan Chamberlain, and Mira Hinman), and the administrators of the Boston University Retirement Plan (TIAA/CREF). The Weisses sought a declaration that the divorce revoked all gifts to Mayo set forth in the will and indenture of trust, including the power of appointment conferred upon Mayo

---

2. Upon the decedent's death the benefits under said policy were paid to LaFrance.

under the trust. The Weisses also alleged that the trust was unfunded, not lawfully created, or alternatively was revoked, and therefore any purported gift to the trust had lapsed. The Weisses asked the court to set aside the trust on the grounds that Mayo and his father allegedly had engaged in fraud, deceit, undue influence, and abuse of a fiduciary relationship in its creation. Additionally, the court was asked to construe the phrase "nephews and nieces" in connection with the trust, and to order that the terms of the Mayos' divorce stipulation precluded Mayo from receiving funds from the decedent's retirement plan. Finally, the plaintiffs sought to have Hill removed as trustee.

In the third action, the Weisses petitioned the court for removal of Clymer as administrator on the ground that he had failed to exercise impartiality in his fiduciary duties.

* * *

For the reasons to follow we affirm the judge's conclusions that: (1) the decedent established a valid trust under G.L. c. 203, § 3B; (2) Mayo's interest in Trust A was terminated as a result of the divorce; (3) the Chamberlains and Hinman are entitled to take as intended beneficiaries under Trust B, with the remainder interest to be divided equally between Clark University and Boston University; and (4) the Weisses lack standing to petition for removal of the estate's administrator. However, we reverse the judge's ruling that Mayo is to take under Trust B, and we remand the question of attorneys' fees for reconsideration.

* * *

The Weisses claim that the judge erred in ruling that the decedent's trust was validly created despite the fact that it was not funded until her death. They rely on the common law rule that a trust can be created only when a trust res exists. New England Trust Co. v. Sanger, 337 Mass. 342, 348, 149 N.E.2d 598 (1958). Arguing that the trust never came into existence, the Weisses claim they are entitled to the decedent's entire estate as her sole heirs at law.

In upholding the validity of the decedent's pour-over trust, the judge cited the relevant provisions of G.L. c. 203, § 3B, inserted by St.1963, c. 418, § 1, the Commonwealth's version of the Uniform Testamentary Additions to Trusts Act. "A devise or bequest, the validity of which is determinable by the laws of the commonwealth, may be made to the trustee or trustees of a trust established or to be established by the testator . . . including a funded or unfunded life insurance trust, although the trustor has reserved any or all rights of ownership of the insurance contracts, if the trust is identified in the will and the terms of the trust are set forth in a written instrument executed before or concurrently with the execution of the testator's will . . . *regardless of the existence, size or character of the corpus of the trust*" (emphasis added). The decedent's trust instrument, which was executed in Massachusetts and states that it is to be governed by the laws of the Commonwealth, satisfies these statutory conditions. The trust is identified in the residuary clause of her will and the terms of the trust are set out in a written instrument executed contemporaneously with the will. However, the Weisses claim that G.L. c. 203, § 3B, was not intended to change the common law with respect to the necessity for a trust corpus despite the clear language validating pour-over trusts, "regardless of the existence, size or character of the corpus." The Weisses make no showing of legislative intent that would contradict the plain meaning of these words. It is well established that "the statutory language is the principal source of insight into legislative purpose." Bronstein v. Prudential Ins. Co. of America, 390 Mass. 701, 704, 459 N.E.2d 772 (1984). Moreover, the development of the common law of this Commonwealth with regard to pour-over trusts demonstrates that G.L. c. 203, § 3B, takes on practical meaning only if the Legislature meant exactly what the statute says concerning the need for a trust corpus.

This court was one of the first courts to validate pour-over devises to a living trust. In Second Bank-State St. Trust Co. v. Pinion, 341 Mass. 366, 371, 170 N.E.2d 350 (1960), decided prior to the adoption of G.L. c. 203, § 3B, we upheld a testamentary gift to a revocable and amendable *inter vivos* trust established by the testator before the execution of his will and which he amended after the will's execution. Recognizing the importance of the pour-over devise in modern estate planning, we explained that such transfers do not violate the statute of wills despite the testator's ability to amend the trust and thereby change the disposition of property at his death without complying with the statute's formalities. "We agree with modern legal thought that a subsequent amendment is effective because of the applicability of the established equitable doctrine that subsequent acts of independent significance do not require attestation under the statute of wills." *Id.* at 369, 170 N.E.2d 350.

At that time we noted that "[t]he long established recognition in Massachusetts of the doctrine of independent significance makes unnecessary statutory affirmance of its application to pour-over trusts." *Id.* at 371, 170 N.E.2d 350. It is evident from Pinion that there was no need for the Legislature to enact G.L. c. 203, § 3B, simply to validate pour-over devises from wills to funded revocable trusts.

However, in Pinion, we were not presented with an unfunded pour-over trust. Nor, prior to G.L. c. 203, § 3B, did other authority exist in this Commonwealth for recognizing testamentary transfers to unfunded trusts. The doctrine of independent significance, upon which we relied in Pinion, assumes that "property was included in the purported *inter vivos* trust, prior to the testator's death." Restatement (Second) of Trusts § 54, comment f (1959). That is why commentators have recognized that G.L. c. 203, § 3B, "[m]akes some . . . modification of the Pinion doctrine. The act does not require that the trust res be more than nominal or even existent." E. Slizewski, Legislation: Uniform Testamentary Additions to Trusts Act, 10 Ann.Surv. of Mass.Law § 2.7, 39 (1963). See Osgood, Pour Over Will: Appraisal of Uniform Testamentary Additions to Trusts Act, 104 Trusts 768, 769 (1965) ("The Act . . . eliminates the necessity that there be a trust corpus").

By denying that the statute effected such a change in the existing law, the Weisses render its enactment meaningless. "An intention to enact a barren and ineffective provision is not lightly to be imputed to the Legislature." Insurance Rating Bd. v.

Commissioner of Ins., 356 Mass. 184, 189, 248 N.E.2d 500 (1969). By analogy, in Trosch v. Maryland Nat'l Bank, 32 Md.App. 249, 252, 359 N.E.2d 564 (1976), the court construed Maryland's Testamentary Additions to Trusts Act as "conditionally abrogating the common law rule . . . that a trust must have a corpus to be in existence." Despite minor differences in the relevant language of Maryland's Estates and Trusts Act, § 4-411,[3] and our G.L. c. 203, § 3B, we agree with the court's conclusion that "the statute is not conditioned upon the existence of a trust but upon the existence of a trust instrument" (emphasis in original). *Id.* at 253, 359 N.E.2d 564. The Weisses urge us to follow Hageman v. Cleveland Trust Co., 41 Ohio App.2d 160, 324 N.E.2d 594 (1974), rev'd on other grounds, 45 Ohio St.2d 178, 182, 343 N.E.2d 121 (1976), where the court held that an *inter vivos* trust had to be funded during the settlor's life to receive pour-over assets from a will. However, in reaching this conclusion the court relied on a statute differing from G.L. c. 203, § 3B, in its omission of the critical phrase: "regardless of the existence, size or character of the corpus of the trust." See Ohio Rev.Code Ann. § 2107.63 (Baldwin 1978).

For the foregoing reasons we conclude, in accordance with G.L. c. 203, § 3B, that the decedent established a valid *inter vivos* trust in 1973 and that its trustee may properly receive the residue of her estate. We affirm the judge's ruling on this issue.

* * *

The judge terminated Trust A upon finding that its purpose — to qualify the trust for an estate tax marital deduction — became impossible to achieve after the Mayos' divorce. Mayo appeals this ruling. It is well established that the Probate Courts are empowered to terminate or reform a trust in whole or in part where its purposes have become impossible to achieve and the settlor did not contemplate continuation of the trust under the new circumstances. Gordon v. Gordon, 332 Mass. 193, 197, 124 N.E.2d 226 (1955). Ames v. Hall, 313 Mass. 33, 37, 46 N.E.2d 403 (1943).

The language the decedent employed in her indenture of trust makes it clear that by setting off Trusts A and B she intended to reduce estate tax liability in compliance with then existing provisions of the Internal Revenue Code. Therefore we have no disagreement with the judge's reasoning. See Putnam v. Putnam, 366 Mass. 261, 267, 316 N.E.2d 729 (1974). However, we add that our reasoning below — that by operation of G.L. c. 191, § 9, Mayo has no beneficial interest in the trust — clearly disposes of Mayo's claim to Trust A.

* * *

---

3. Maryland Estates and Trusts Code Ann. § 4-411 (1974), reads:

A legacy may be made in form or in substance to the trustee in accordance with the terms of a written *inter vivos* trust, including an unfunded life insurance trust although the settlor has reserved all rights of ownership in the insurance contracts, if the trust instrument has been executed and is in existence prior to or contemporaneously with the execution of the will and is identified in the will, without regard to the size or character of the corpus of the trust or whether the settlor is the testator or a third person.

The judge's decision to uphold Mayo's beneficial interest in Trust B was appealed by the Weisses, as well as by Boston University and Clark University. The judge reasoned that the decedent intended to create a life interest in Mayo when she established Trust B and failed either to revoke or to amend the trust after the couple's divorce. The appellants argue that we should extend the reach of G.L. c. 191, §9, to revoke all Mayo's interests under the trust.[4] General Laws c. 191, §9, as amended through St.1977, c. 76, §2, provides in relevant part:

> If, after executing a will, the testator shall be divorced or his marriage shall be annulled, the divorce or annulment shall revoke any disposition or appointment of property made by the will to the former spouse, any provision conferring a general or special power of appointment on the former spouse, and any nomination of the former spouse, as executor, trustee, conservator or guardian, unless the will shall expressly provide otherwise. Property prevented from passing to a former spouse because of revocation by divorce shall pass as if a former spouse had failed to survive the decedent, and other provisions conferring a power of office on the former spouse shall be interpreted as if the spouse had failed to survive the decedent.

The judge ruled that Mayo's interest in Trust B is unaffected by G.L. c. 191, §9, because his interest in that trust is not derived from a "disposition . . . made by the will" but rather from the execution of an *inter vivos* trust with independent legal significance. We disagree, but in fairness we add that the judge here confronted a question of first impression in this Commonwealth.

General Laws c. 191, §9, was amended by the Legislature in 1976 to provide in the event of divorce for the revocation of testamentary dispositions which benefit the testator's former spouse. St.1976, c. 515, §6. The statute automatically causes such revocations unless the testator expresses a contrary intent. In this case we must determine what effect, if any, G.L. c. 191, §9, has on the former spouse's interest in the testator's pour-over trust.

While, by virtue of G.L. c. 203, §3B, the decedent's trust bore independent significance at the time of its creation in 1973, the trust had no practical significance until her death in 1981. The decedent executed both her will and indenture of trust on February 2, 1973. She transferred no property or funds to the trust at that time. The trust was to receive its funding at the decedent's death, in part through her life insurance policy and retirement benefits, and in part through a pour-over from the will's residuary clause. Mayo, the proposed executor and sole legatee under the will, was also made the primary beneficiary of the trust with power, as to Trust A only, to reach both income and principal.

During her lifetime, the decedent retained power to amend or revoke the trust. Since the trust was unfunded, her co-trustee was subject to no duties or obligations

---

4. None of the parties contests the judge's ruling that G.L. c. 191, §9, revokes those provisions in the decedent's will which benefitted Mayo.

until her death. Similarly, it was only as a result of the decedent's death that Mayo could claim any right to the trust assets. It is evident from the time and manner in which the trust was created and funded, that the decedent's will and trust were integrally related components of a single testamentary scheme. For all practical purposes the trust, like the will, "spoke" only at the decedent's death. For this reason Mayo's interest in the trust was revoked by operation of G.L. c. 191, § 9, at the same time his interest under the decedent's will was revoked.

It has reasonably been contended that in enacting G.L. c. 191, § 9, the Legislature "intended to bring the law into line with the expectations of most people. . . . Divorce usually represents a stormy parting, where the last thing one of the parties wishes is to have an earlier will carried out giving everything to the former spouse." Young, Probate Reform, 18 Boston B.J. 7, 11 (1974). To carry out the testator's implied intent, the law revokes "any disposition or appointment of property made by the will to the former spouse." It is indisputable that if the decedent's trust was either testamentary or incorporated by reference into her will, Mayo's beneficial interest in the trust would be revoked by operation of the statute. However, the judge stopped short of mandating the same result in this case because here the trust had "independent significance" by virtue of c. 203, § 3B. While correct, this characterization of the trust does not end our analysis. For example, in Sullivan v. Burkin, 390 Mass. 864, 867, 460 N.E.2d 572 (1984), we ruled prospectively that the assets of a revocable trust will be considered part of the "estate of the decedent" in determining the surviving spouse's statutory share.

Treating the components of the decedent's estate plan separately, and not as parts of an interrelated whole, brings about inconsistent results. Applying c. 191, § 9, the judge correctly revoked the will provisions benefiting Mayo. As a result, the decedent's personal property—originally left to Mayo—fell into the will's residuary clause and passed to the trust. The judge then appropriately terminated Trust A for impossibility of purpose thereby denying Mayo his beneficial interest under Trust A. Yet, by upholding Mayo's interest under Trust B, the judge returned to Mayo a life interest in the same assets that composed the corpus of Trust A—both property passing by way of the decedent's will and the proceeds of her TIAA/CREF annuity contracts. * * *

Restricting our holding to the particular facts of this case—specifically the existence of a revocable pour-over trust funded entirely at the time of the decedent's death—we conclude that G.L. c. 191, § 9, revokes Mayo's interest under Trust B.[7]

* * *

---

7. As an alternative ground the appellants argue that the terms of the Mayos' divorce settlement, in which Mayo waived "any right, title or interest" in the assets that later funded the decedent's trust, amount to a disclaimer of his trust interest. We decline to base our holding on such reasoning because a disclaimer of rights "must be clear and unequivocal." Second Bank-State St. Trust Co. v. Yale Univ. Alumni Fund, 338 Mass. 520, 524, 156 N.E.2d 57 (1959), and we find no such disclaimer in the Mayos' divorce agreement.

According to the terms of G.L. c. 191, §9, "[p]roperty prevented from passing to a former spouse because of revocation by divorce shall pass as if a former spouse had failed to survive the decedent. . . ." In this case, the decedent's indenture of trust provides that if Mayo failed to survive her, "the balance of 'Trust B' shall be held . . . for the benefit of the nephews and nieces of the Donor living at the time of the death of the Donor." The trustee is directed to expend as much of the net income and principal as he deems "advisable for [their] reasonable comfort, support and education" until all living nephews and nieces have attained the age of thirty. At that time, the trust is to terminate and Boston University and Clark University are each to receive fifty per cent of the trust property to assist women students in their graduate programs.

The decedent had no siblings and therefore no nephews and nieces who were blood relations. * * * However, when she executed her trust in 1973, her husband, James P. Mayo, Jr., had two nephews and one niece — John and Allan Chamberlain and Mira Hinman. Before her divorce, the decedent maintained friendly relations with these young people and, along with her former husband, contributed toward their educational expenses. The three have survived the decedent.

The Weisses, Boston University, and Clark University appeal the decision of the judge upholding the decedent's gift to these three individuals. They argue that at the time the decedent created her trust she had no "nephews and nieces" by blood and that, at her death, her marital ties to Mayo's nephews and niece had been severed by divorce. Therefore, they contend that the class gift to the donor's "nephews and nieces" lapses for lack of identifiable beneficiaries.

The judge concluded that the trust language created an ambiguity, and thus he considered extrinsic evidence of the decedent's meaning and intent. Based upon that evidence, he decided that the decedent intended to provide for her nieces and nephews by marriage when she created the trust. Because the decedent never revoked this gift, he found that the Chamberlains and Hinman are entitled to their beneficial interests under the trust. We agree.

The appellants claim that no ambiguity is presented by the decedent's gift to her "nephews and nieces" and therefore the judge erred in considering extrinsic evidence of the meaning of this phrase. It is axiomatic that "[t]he intent of the testator governs the interpretation of his will." Sullivan v. Roman Catholic Archbishop of Boston, 368 Mass. 253, 257, 331 N.E.2d 57 (1975). See G.L. c. 191, §1A. It is equally well established that we "ascertain the intention of the testator from the whole instrument, attributing due weight to all its language, considered in the light of the circumstances known to him at the time of its execution and to give effect to that intent unless some positive rule of law forbids." Fitts v. Powell, 307 Mass. 449, 454, 30 N.E.2d 377 (1940). Gustafson v. Svenson, 373 Mass. 273, 275, 366 N.E.2d 761 (1977). Where "a reading of the whole will produces a conviction that the testator must necessarily have intended an interest to be given which is not bequeathed or devised by express or formal words, the court must supply the defect by implication and so mould the language of the testator as to carry into effect as far as possible the intention which it is of opinion that he has sufficiently declared." Fitts, *supra.*

The judge was thus well within his discretion in considering the facts and circumstances known to the decedent at the time she executed her indenture of trust. The purpose of his inquiry was not to alter but to explain the language of the trust. Extrinsic evidence is admissible for this purpose even where no ambiguity is presented. Smith, The Admissibility of Extrinsic Evidence in Will Interpretation Cases, 64 Mass.L.Rev. 123 (1979). In fact, however, the decedent's bequest created a latent ambiguity. The gift to the "nephews and nieces of the Donor" posed problems in the identification of the intended donees. See Putnam v. Putnam, 366 Mass. 261, 266, 316 N.E.2d 729 (1974); Hardy v. Smith, 136 Mass. 328 (1884); Dane v. Walker, 109 Mass. 179 (1872). The relevant evidence included the decedent's lack of siblings, her relationship to Mayo's nephews and niece, and her contributions to their education. Combining these facts with the language used by the decedent, it is clear that the Chamberlains and Hinman were her intended beneficiaries.

* * *

The appellants reject these authorities on the ground that the Mayos' divorce left the decedent without any nephews and nieces—by blood or marriage—at the time of her death. They argue that even if the decedent had intended to provide for the Chamberlains and Hinman when she executed her indenture of trust, we should rule that the Mayos' divorce somehow "revoked" this gift. According to Boston University, since the beneficiaries are identified by their relationship to the decedent through her marriage and not by name, we should presume that the decedent no longer intended to benefit her former relatives once her marriage ended. General Laws c. 191, § 9, does not provide the authority for revoking gifts to the blood relatives of a former spouse. The law implies an intent to revoke testamentary gifts between the divorcing parties because of the profound emotional and financial changes divorce normally engenders. There is no indication in the statutory language that the Legislature presumed to know how these changes affect a testator's relations with more distant family members. We therefore conclude that the Chamberlains and Hinman are entitled to take as the decedent's "nephews and nieces" under Trust B.

* * *

In sum, we conclude that the decedent established a valid trust under G.L. c. 203, § 3B; Mayo's beneficial interest in Trust A and Trust B is revoked by operation of G.L. c. 191, § 9; the Chamberlains and Hinman are entitled to take the interest given to the decedent's "nephews and nieces" under Trust B, leaving the remainder to Clark University and Boston University; the Weisses lack standing to remove the estate administrator; and the judge's award of attorneys' fees is vacated and remanded for reconsideration.

So ordered.

Notes

The case is fascinating because it invites consideration of a modern estate plan, the validity of pour over devices and the challenges they have faced, and the comparison of revocability of *inter vivos* and testamentary devices. Indeed, the case also considers remedies for mistake and a few of the consequences of divorce, *see* UNIF. PROB. CODE § 2-804 (2019) (revocation of probate and non-probate transfers by divorce). As a result of legislation, the traditional doctrines of incorporation by reference or facts of independent significance are no longer needed to validate pour over from a Last Will and Testament into an unfunded *inter vivos* revocable trust.

Today the revocable *inter vivos* trust is a familiar tool to estate planning attorneys because: (1) it provides the ability to avoid probate, thereby guaranteeing a significant savings in costs, since any assets already placed in the *inter vivos* trust do not pass according to a Last Will and Testament; (2) property passes quickly, since there is no administration; (3) there is no necessity for publication and disclosure of who got what, and how, since the *inter vivos* trust does not have to pass through the probate procedure; (4) the law of another jurisdiction may be applied—community property rather than common law, for example—and there is no possibility of a change in applicable law, even if the jurisdiction should change; (5) there are far fewer contests because no Last Will and Testament is being probated; (6) ancillary probate is avoided; and (7) more than one party—perhaps two spouses—can create the revocable trust to accommodate their own lifestyles and to provide in a specific way for surviving beneficiaries. The revocable *inter vivos* trust has few advantages when it comes to the right of the surviving spouse and elective share, *see* UNIF. PROB. CODE § 2-205 (2019), creditors, *see* State Street Bank & Trust Co. v. Reiser, *infra*, or estate tax laws, *see* I.R.C. §§ 2036, 2038 (2019).

Because of its advantages, revocable *inter vivos* trusts have become prolific, *see* *Restatement (Third) of Trusts* § 25 (2019), far surpassing the nascent origin prophesied by Norman F. Dacey's HOW TO AVOID PROBATE, which was first published in 1965. *See also* John H. Langbein, *The Nonprobate Revolution and the Future of the Law of Succession*, 97 HARV. L. REV. 1125 (1984). But with the popularity of revocable *inter vivos* trusts have come professional responsibility issues and concern over the unauthorized practice of law by non-attorneys. These concerns have prompted legislation. *See, e.g.*, 815 Ill. COMP. STAT. ANN. § 505/2BB (West 2015) (Assembly, drafting, execution and funding of living trust documents by corporations or non-lawyers). Consider the following decisions.

Committee on Professional Ethics v. Baker

Supreme Court of Iowa, 1992
492 N.W.2d 695

LAVORATO, Justice.

Before us is a report of the Grievance Commission recommending that attorney William D. Baker be reprimanded.

The commission found that Baker acted unethically in the following ways: aiding the unauthorized practice of law; permitting others to influence his professional judgment in providing legal services to clients referred to him, resulting in conflicts of interest; and accepting improper referrals.

Baker is a sole practitioner and has practiced law in Des Moines since 1967. He focuses primarily on real estate, probate, estate planning, and trusts.

Rex Voegtlin is a certified financial planner and sole shareholder of Diversified Resource Management, Inc., located in West Des Moines. During 1989 and 1990 Voegtlin was presenting seminars in which he touted living trusts as an estate planning device. (Living or loving trusts have been promoted as a way of avoiding probate.) One of Voegtlin's advertisements concerning these seminars is in evidence. The ad urges people to attend and learn "how to avoid probate and minimize estate taxes with an estate plan that includes a living trust." In a newsletter—also in evidence—Voegtlin condemns probate as too expensive and time consuming.

In 1989 James Miller, a lawyer, was a trust officer for Hawkeye Bank and Trust of Des Moines, a former client of Baker's. In the summer of that year Miller attended one of Voegtlin's seminars and met him for the first time. Sometime after that meeting the two agreed to work jointly in putting on Voegtlin's seminars. Miller's reason for doing so was to attract new business for his bank. The two conducted about eight to ten of these joint seminars from October 1989 to May or June 1990, when Miller quit. About 90 to 100 people attended the first three or four of these seminars. From that point on attendance fell to about 50 or 60.

Shortly before Miller agreed to these joint seminars, he and Voegtlin met with Baker in August 1989. Miller knew Baker because Baker had previously done work for the bank. Miller and Voegtlin asked Baker if he would accept referrals from them. Baker said he was interested but wanted to have several questions answered. Partly for that reason, Miller and Baker attended a seminar in Colorado to see how a living trust seminar might work.

Thereafter, Miller, on behalf of the bank, and Voegtlin agreed to cosponsor seminars on living trusts. Baker told the two he would accept referrals from them for the preparation of living trusts and related documents, and he began doing so in the fall of 1989.

After Baker agreed to accept referrals from Voegtlin and Miller, he attended one seminar the two put on in October 1989. The seminar dealt generally with estate planning and more specifically with the use of a living trust as a way to avoid probate.

Over time the seminars and referrals developed this way. Voegtlin would advertise a free seminar in which the benefits of a living trust would be explained. Voegtlin and Miller would divide up the time during which each would speak. Voegtlin would close the seminar by offering free individual consultations. Usually about half of those attending would seek individual consultations. They did so by filling out a form giving their names, addresses, phone numbers, and their desire for the consultation. The forms were left with Voegtlin who would then follow up and arrange the consultations.

Before the consultations, these "clients"—as Voegtlin described them—would complete a general information planning form in which they would list their names, addresses, family members, and assets. At the consultations, which were held in Voegtlin's office, the clients would present the form at which point Voegtlin and Miller would review it as well as the clients' goals. The primary goal was, of course, to avoid probate.

Voegtlin and Miller would then talk about the various estate planning options the clients had. They would discuss the living trust in a general way—what it can do and what it cannot do. Voegtlin would diagram on a blackboard how a living trust works. The use of marital trusts, family trusts, and generation-skipping trusts was explained—how they worked and how they fit into an estate plan. The diagram would be individualized to include the clients' beneficiaries by name and the names of the trustees.

Voegtlin would also diagram how a will works so the clients could understand the difference between a living trust and a will. Voegtlin would then take a Polaroid picture of the diagrams and give it to the clients. Miller would talk about the duties of a bank trustee and what a bank does on a day-to-day basis when acting as a trustee.

Eventually during the consultations, Voegtlin, Miller, and the clients would reach a consensus as to which estate plan was best for the clients. By this time Voegtlin and Miller had made a determination as to which documents would be necessary to carry out the estate plan.

At this point Voegtlin and Miller would tell the clients that the clients needed to employ a licensed attorney to prepare the documents. If the clients had an attorney, the two would suggest that the clients' attorney be employed. If the clients had no attorney, the two would give the clients a list of attorneys to consider. Baker was among those attorneys listed. The two told the clients that most clients chose Baker because he was a competent attorney, his fees were reasonable, and he was prompt. The evidence shows that from October 1989 through October 1991, Baker accepted about 100 of these referrals. Fewer than ten were received by other attorneys.

Frequently Voegtlin would telephone Baker during the consultations. Voegtlin would tell him that the clients who were there wanted to proceed with the living trust and wanted him to do the legal work. Voegtlin would use a speaker phone so that the clients could also talk to Baker. Voegtlin would remain and listen to the conversation.

Sometimes Voegtlin would not follow this procedure. Instead Voegtlin or Miller would bring the materials discussed at the consultations to Baker and ask if he would accept the referral. A few times clients themselves would go to Baker's office with the materials. The materials would include (1) a copy of the financial form,

(2) a general outline of the terms to be included in the clients' living trust, and (3) a description of other necessary documents.

Baker would then call the clients to go over their materials and discuss any questions that either he or they might have. Baker would ask if they were still interested. Some were; others were not. If the clients expressed an interest in proceeding, Baker would tell them that he would prepare a draft of what they wanted and send the draft to them for their review. If the clients did not proceed, Baker would not charge them for any work he might have done for them.

If the clients wanted to proceed, Baker would tell them to bring the trust documents to a meeting at Voegtlin's office. At the meeting Baker would go through the documents and explain them to the clients. Voegtlin was often, but not always, at these meetings. The clients executed the documents at these meetings unless corrections were necessary. If corrections were necessary, the corrections were made and the documents were either executed then or later.

There were times when the clients met Baker at his office. Those times occurred when the clients did not want to involve Voegtlin or the bank.

Not surprisingly, the documents frequently named Voegtlin or Diversified as the person to fund the trust. Voegtlin's wife—also a certified financial planner—usually performed this task. Funding the trust simply means having the clients sign whatever forms or documents that are necessary to transfer personal property from the clients' names to the living trust. Voegtlin's fee for funding the trust and financial advice related to this task was $1000. The advice, for example, might include recommending exchanging a low-interest producing asset for a higher-interest producing one.

In May 1990 Voegtlin asked Baker to furnish him with a sample living trust and accompanying documents that Baker was using for the clients Voegtlin and Miller were referring to him. Voegtlin told Baker he wanted sample documents to show clients who were interested in seeing what Baker's trust looked like. Voegtlin apparently used these documents in his seminars.

The sample living trust and the accompanying documents are in evidence. The accompanying documents included a "Declaration of Trust Ownership," a "Power of Attorney," a "Special Power of Attorney," an "Anatomical Gift," a "Declaration Relating to [the] Use of Life-Sustaining Procedures," a "Petition for Appointment of Guardian (Standby)," a "Declaration of Gift Memorandum," and a "Supplemental Financial Planning Letter." Miller's bank is named in the power of attorney form. The special power of attorney form designates Voegtlin as the attorney-in-fact. The supplemental financial planning letter contains, among other provisions, the following:

> *Financial Planner: This document and related instruments were recommended by Mr. Rex Voegtlin, Certified Financial Planner and Registered Investment Adviser.* He was instrumental in developing a financial and investment framework for my living will as well as death estate. Since Mr. Voegtlin is

familiar with my financial planning goals, it is my wish that you notify him upon my demise to help coordinate a smooth financial transition of my invested estate. His address is 1415 28th Street, Suite 110, West Des Moines, Iowa 50265.

(Emphasis added.)

On December 8, 1989, two members of the Commission on the Unauthorized Practice of Law (UPC), a commission established by this court, met with Miller, several bank officials, and Baker. The purpose of the meeting was to determine who actually prepared the living trust documents and to discuss certain misleading statements about Iowa probate fees made in the brochure distributed at the seminars. Miller assured the two UPC members that Baker prepared the living trust documents. Baker concurred. Miller also assured them that the attendees at the seminar who were interested in living trusts were urged to use their attorneys. If they had none they were encouraged to use Baker. Finally, Miller assured the two UPC members that he would continue to urge all attendees to use attorneys to review or prepare all legal instruments. Miller agreed to quit distributing the misleading brochures at the seminars.

Several weeks later one of the two UPC members wrote Miller a letter summarizing what Miller had said. The letter also informed Miller that "[i]n light of our discussion the [UPC] anticipates no further formal action at this time."

In July 1990 the Committee on Professional Ethics and Conduct of the Iowa State Bar Association published interpreting opinions 90-1 and 90-2. Formal opinion 90-32 was published in November 1990. The subject of each opinion was the marketing of living trusts. Opinion 90-32 stated that it was improper for Iowa lawyers to participate in living trust programs like those conducted by Diversified. After publication of opinions 90-1 and 90-2, Baker was the only attorney who continued accepting referrals from Voegtlin.

In February 1991 two members of the UPC met with Baker concerning its investigation of Voegtlin and Diversified. At Baker's disciplinary hearing, one of the two investigating UPC members testified this way:

Q. According to Mr. Baker, would he attend the first meeting between the client and Mr. Voegtlin? A. The way I understood the process is Mr. Voegtlin would get the client initially interested at the seminars. Mr. Voegtlin would then meet with the individual without Mr. Baker, another attorney present, and discuss what the client needed, what legal documents would be prepared, whether they need a will, a living trust, guardianship, standby guardianship, a trust. And then Mr. Baker would be called in to draw up the documents, but he was not usually in attendance at that first meeting.

Q. So it was your understanding from Mr. Baker that Mr. Voegtlin would discuss at the initial meeting with the client what types of instruments would be needed? A. Yes, and advise the client what the standard package was and what were the varieties of changes they might need for their particular situation.

* * *

Q. Would it be fair to say, based on the information that Mr. Baker gave you, that Mr. Voegtlin would tell Mr. Baker specific documents that would be needed in a given situation? A. That was my understanding, that they had sort of a standard package of documents that Mr. Baker indicated were developed early on that he got from Hawkeye Bank when Hawkeye Bank was involved in doing these trusts, that he had modified them in some respects but the basic package of documents Mr. Baker had and then at Mr. Voegtlin's direction would decide we need will A or will B or trust A or trust B or whatever type was needed.

* * *

Q. . . . When does it say Voegtlin's doing this? A. My understanding was that Mr. Voegtlin, when he called Mr. Baker, would tell him that "We need pour-over will A," or, "We need pour-over will B," or, "We need just A or B," and described the client's specific situation and that Voegtlin was giving the legal advice and directing him as to what documents to prepare.

* * *

Q. When you talked with Mr. Baker about what he might recommend to clients, did he tell you that he merely explained the pros and cons of living trusts to the clients and let them make up their own mind, or did he say that he recommended living trusts to his clients? . . . A. My understanding is by the time that the people got to Mr. Baker that it was a done deal, in that the decisions had already been discussed with Mr. Voegtlin about what they needed, that they needed the living trust, and that he basically then prepared the documents for their signature.

* * *

Q. Was there any discussion with Mr. Baker as to whether when he got a referral from Mr. Voegtlin he ever recommended anything to them other than the living trust? A. That was one thing I was curious about, is whether as an attorney he was exercising some independent judgment on these clients, and I asked him about that, and he had indicated that he had about 50 to 60 referrals from Mr. Voegtlin over what I understood to be some time period from about 1989, and he indicated he had never suggested to the client that the living trust was not appropriate for their situation.

Baker also told the two UPC investigating members he was worried that he might be aiding in the unauthorized practice of law and might be accepting improper referrals. The two urged Baker to seek an opinion about his concerns from the Committee on Professional Ethics and Conduct.

In March 1991 Baker did write to this committee raising his concerns about opinion 90-32. Baker requested guidance on variations of the scenarios discussed and published in that opinion. Of course, these variations concerned his business referral relationship with Voegtlin.

In May 1991 Baker heard back from the committee. The committee wrote Baker a letter in which it refused to provide him an advisory opinion about his inquiry. This refusal was premised on the rules of the committee, which permit advisory opinions only in "proposed actions of members of the bar." The letter informed Baker that his request was confined to past and/or continuing actions, effectively foreclosing an advisory opinion from that body. The committee, however, did advise Baker that what he described might "involve impropriety and should be reviewed." The committee closed by asking for more information. Baker responded shortly thereafter, providing greater details about Voegtlin's referrals to him.

In April 1991 two members of the UPC met with Voegtlin and his attorney about procedures Voegtlin used in recommending living trusts and referring legal matters. The UPC did not make a determination that Voegtlin was involved in the unauthorized practice of law. Apparently, the UPC is delaying its determination because of this disciplinary proceeding against Baker. The UPC has, however, referred the matter to the attorney general's office for investigation of consumer fraud.

The Committee on Professional Ethics and Conduct filed a complaint against Baker in October 1991. The complaint alleges that Baker's involvement with Voegtlin in the living trust marketing scheme violated several disciplinary rules and ethical considerations of the Iowa Code of Professional Responsibility for Lawyers and formal opinion 90-32.

The record made in the hearing before the commission included the complaint, the committee's requests for admission, witness testimony, and exhibits. Baker responded affirmatively to the majority of both requests for admission and testified in his own behalf.

After finding that the allegations of the complaint were true, the commission recommended that Baker be publicly reprimanded for (1) aiding in the unauthorized practice of law; (2) permitting others to influence his professional judgment in providing legal services to clients referred to him, resulting in a conflict of interest; and (3) accepting improper referrals.

The committee must prove the allegations of the complaint by a convincing preponderance of the evidence. Committee on Professional Ethics & Conduct v. Lawler, 342 N.W.2d 486, 487 (Iowa 1984). Although Baker did not appeal, we still review de novo the record made before the commission. Iowa Sup.Ct.R. 118.10. We independently decide the matter and take appropriate action on it. *Id.* In our review we consider the findings of fact made by the commission but are not bound by them. Committee on Professional Ethics & Conduct v. Conzett, 476 N.W.2d 43, 44 (Iowa 1991).

* * *

We first turn our attention to the commission's finding that Baker aided Voegtlin in the unauthorized practice of law. Whether we agree with this finding requires a two step analysis. First, did Voegtlin's actions constitute the unauthorized practice of law? If so, did Baker aid those actions?

A. *Voegtlin's actions.* This court has refrained from attempting an all-inclusive definition of the practice of law. Rather it decides each case in this area largely on its own particular facts. Bump v. Barnett, 235 Iowa 308, 315, 16 N.W.2d 579, 583 (1944). EC 3-5 of the Iowa Code of Professional Responsibility for Lawyers takes the same tack: "It is neither necessary nor desirable to attempt the formulation of a single, specific definition of what constitutes the practice of law." EC 3-5.

However, EC 3-5 goes on to tell us what the practice of law includes:

> *However, the practice of law includes,* but is not limited to, representing another before the courts; giving of legal advice and counsel to others relating to their rights and obligations under the law; and preparation or *approval of the use of legal instruments by which legal rights of others are either obtained, secured or transferred* even if such matters never become the subject of a court proceeding. Functionally, the practice of law relates to the rendition of services for others that call for the professional judgment of a lawyer. The essence of the professional judgment of the lawyer is his educated ability to relate the general body and philosophy of law to a specific legal problem of a client; and thus, the public interest will be better served if only lawyers are permitted to act in matters involving professional judgment. Where this professional judgment is not involved, nonlawyers, such as court clerks, police officers, abstracters, and many governmental employees, may engage in occupations that require a special knowledge of law in certain areas. But the services of a lawyer are essential in the public interest whenever the exercise of professional legal judgment is required.

(Emphasis added.)

In short, the practice of law includes the obvious: representing another before the court. But the practice of law includes out-of-court services as well. For example, one who gives legal advice about a person's rights and obligations under the law is practicing law. Or one who prepares legal instruments affecting the rights of others is practicing law. Or one who approves the use of legal instruments affecting the rights of others is practicing law.

Practically speaking, professional judgment lies at the core of the practice of law. When lawyers use their educated ability to apply an area of the law to solve a specific problem of a client, they are exercising professional judgment. The phrase "educated ability" in EC 3-5 refers to the system of analysis lawyers learn in law school. They learn to recognize issues first and then how to solve those issues in an ethical manner, using their knowledge of the law. See EC 3-2 ("Competent professional judgment is the product of a trained familiarity with law and legal processes, a disciplined, analytical approach to legal problems, and a firm ethical commitment."). The practice of law is no different: lawyers determine what the issues are and use their knowledge of the law to solve them in an ethical way. This is the art of exercising professional judgment.

In contrast, nonlawyers who use their knowledge of the law for informational purposes alone are not exercising a lawyer's professional judgment. For example, an abstracter must have knowledge of what constitutes a lien on real estate. An abstracter uses this knowledge, which is legal in nature, when the abstracter shows the lien in the abstract of title. In doing so, the abstracter is simply furnishing the title examiner—a lawyer—information that the lawyer needs in advising the client on the marketability of title. In this scenario, the abstracter is simply furnishing information; the title examiner is exercising professional judgment on a legal question. The abstracter is not practicing law; the title examiner is.

From the evidence in this case, it is clear that Voegtlin's actions met one of the practicing law tests articulated in EC 3-5: "approval of the use of legal instruments by which legal rights of others are either obtained, secured or transferred." Voegtlin met with the clients. He advised them about what they needed in the way of estate planning. He advised them in particular about what documents they would need and how those documents would need to be tailored to meet their particular situation. In the words of one UPC investigator, by the time the clients got to Baker "it was a done deal." Baker was merely a scrivener. Voegtlin had already made the major decisions; he, rather than Baker, was exercising professional judgment. The "smoking gun" on this point is found in the supplemental financial planning letter. This document acknowledges that the financial planning letter and related instruments were recommended by Voegtlin.

Voegtlin's actions fit neatly into what one court considered to be the unauthorized practice of law:

> Giving legal advice, directly or indirectly to individuals or groups concerning the application, preparation, advisability or quality of any legal instrument or document or forms thereof in connection with the disposition of property *inter vivos* or upon death, including *inter vivos* trusts and wills.

In re the Florida Bar, 215 So.2d 613, 613–14 (Fla.1968) (per curiam) (petition by state bar and securities broker to determine whether certain activities of securities broker constituted the unauthorized practice of law). We adopt this test as a supplement to EC 3-5 and as an expanded definition of the practice of law.

For all of these reasons, we agree with the commission that Voegtlin was engaged in the unauthorized practice of law.

B. *Baker's actions.* DR 3-101(A) prohibits a lawyer from aiding a nonlawyer in the unauthorized practice of law. EC 3-1 exhorts the legal profession to actively discourage the unauthorized practice of law. EC 3-3 reminds lawyers that the disciplinary rules prohibit a lawyer from submitting to the control of others in the exercise of the lawyer's judgment. EC 3-4 also reminds lawyers that "[p]roper protection of members of the public demands that no person be permitted to act in the confidential and demanding capacity of a lawyer unless he is subject to the regulations of the legal profession."

We agree with the commission that in one way or another Baker violated DR 3-101(A), EC 3-1, EC 3-3, and EC 3-4. From our review of the record, we see Voegtlin's seminars, his newsletters, and his referrals to Baker as nothing more than a scheme on Voegtlin's part to reap substantial fees. Indeed, he targeted clients having estates in excess of $600,000. The scheme worked because Voegtlin preached through his seminars and newsletters that clients should use a living trust because our probate system "takes too long and is too expensive." Voegtlin controlled the whole process from the initial interview to the final meeting when the clients executed the documents in his office. He did so by recommending the living trust, the necessary tailored documents to effectuate it, and a lawyer who he believed would not counsel against his advice. In fact, when Voegtlin sold clients on a living trust, Baker never once counseled against using it.

Instead of discouraging Voegtlin from these actions, Baker actually encouraged them in a number of ways. First, Baker allowed Voegtlin to exercise the professional judgment Baker should have exercised. Second, Baker allowed Voegtlin to act in a confidential capacity with the clients who were referred to Baker. Third, Baker furnished Voegtlin with forms to be used at his seminar. Fourth, Baker accepted approximately 100 referrals from Voegtlin. Last, Baker gave Voegtlin advice on his newsletters.

Our experience with "living trusts" teaches us that they may be a very poor substitute for probate. Unlike probate fees, the fees charged by nonlawyers like Voegtlin who tout living trusts are not subject to court scrutiny. Lack of court scrutiny can easily lead to unnecessary and excessive fees.[1] The point is whether a living trust is appropriate in a given case calls for the exercise of independent professional judgment by a lawyer.

* * *

The commission found that Baker permitted Voegtlin to influence his professional judgment in providing legal services to clients referred to Baker, resulting in a conflict of interest.

This finding is predicated on alleged violations of DR 5-107(B) and EC 5-1.

---

1. Recent action taken by the Illinois attorney general has focused on these potentials for abuse. He has sued a group selling living trusts kits to elderly people in Illinois. He alleges that the group has engaged in the unauthorized practice of law and has violated the state's consumer fraud law. Among other things, he alleges that the group is charging as much as $2999 for services which could be obtained at a much lower cost. He has characterized the group's actions as "using a 'one-size-fits-all' approach, [selling] living trusts to individuals for whom the documents [are] neither appropriate nor necessary." David N. Anderson, AG Joins ISBA's 'Living Trust' Battle, Ill.St.B.Ass'n B.News, October 15, 1992, at 1.

DR 5-107(B) provides:

> *A lawyer shall not permit a person who recommends, employs, or pays him to render legal services for another to direct or regulate his professional judgment in rendering such legal services.*

(Emphasis added.)

EC 5-1 provides:

> The professional judgment of a lawyer should be exercised, within the bounds of the law, solely for the benefit of his client and free of compromising influences and loyalties. Neither his personal interests, the interests of other clients, *nor the desires of third persons should be permitted to dilute his loyalty to his client.*

(Emphasis added.)

The commission found sufficient evidence to establish a violation of DR 5-107(B) and EC 5-1. We agree.

We have already found that Voegtlin, not Baker, exercised professional judgment as to the appropriateness of a living trust and the particular documents necessary to effectuate it. We have also referred to the reasons why Voegtlin promoted living trusts. All of this is another way of saying that Baker permitted Voegtlin to "direct or regulate his professional judgment" in rendering legal services to the referred clients. DR 5-107(B).

All of this is also another way of saying that Baker permitted Voegtlin's desires to "dilute [Baker's] loyalty to his client[s]." EC 5-1. Like the commission, we find that the prospect of receiving additional referrals constituted the "compromising influences" mentioned in EC 5-1. The number of referrals was many—approximately 100 in all. And the fees generated by them were substantial—approximately $40,000 in total. It is significant to us that Baker came to eventually realize that he was the only lawyer receiving these referrals, and that fact bothered him.

* * *

The commission found that Baker accepted improper referrals in violation of formal opinion 90-32. As we said earlier in division I(B) of this opinion, the referrals were one way Baker aided Voegtlin in the unauthorized practice of law. We offer no opinion on the validity of formal opinion 90-32. We think it would be inappropriate to peg an ethical violation on this opinion for several reasons. First, the opinion is based in part on a disciplinary rule that we hesitate to say has any application to this case. Second, although we express no opinion one way or the other, we hesitate to approve the practice of charging an attorney with the violation of a formal opinion. Last, the referrals were inextricably intertwined with the unauthorized practice of law issue. Any discipline resulting from accepting improper referrals should therefore be limited to the allegations of aiding in the unauthorized practice of law.

* * *

Until this court speaks, generally it is not clear what constitutes the practice of law in a particular set of circumstances. We agree with one writer's assessment of this problem:

> Because of the marked lack of precision in the definition of unauthorized practice, it would be intolerable to hold a lawyer to a prophet's standard of clairvoyance about unclear areas of practice in a jurisdiction.

C.W. Wolfram, Modern Legal Ethics 846 (1986). What is implicated here is a potential issue of fair notice. Our rules on the unauthorized practice of law resolve this problem of fair notice by authorizing the UPC to seek an injunction if it believes a person is engaged in the unauthorized practice of law. See Unauthorized Practice of Law Commission Rule 118A.1. Such a person will then be on notice of what specific conduct is prohibited before that person is punished. These reasons, in part, convince us that any discipline here in excess of a reprimand would not be appropriate.

Four additional facts enter our decision on discipline here. First, Baker has for many years enjoyed an excellent reputation as an active practicing lawyer. Second, Baker fully cooperated with all investigations related to the complaint. Third, no client referred by Voegtlin (1) complained about any living trust or other documents Baker prepared or (2) suffered any financial loss based upon these documents. Last, Baker sought clarification from the committee before the complaint was filed and received no satisfaction. Instead, the committee filed the complaint.

We do not condone Baker's behavior in this matter. He was ill-advised to continue accepting referrals from Voegtlin when it became apparent that such conduct might be improper. What he should have done is to follow the old ethics adage, "if you have doubt, don't do it." Baker did the opposite. We view his past professional judgment as misguided, and we expect him to guard against even the appearance of impropriety in his future professional relationships.

We reprimand Baker for aiding Voegtlin in the unauthorized practice of law and for allowing Voegtlin to direct or regulate Baker's professional judgment in rendering legal services to Baker's clients.

Costs are assessed to Baker under Iowa Supreme Court Rule 118.22.

ATTORNEY REPRIMANDED.

State Street Bank & Trust Co. v. Reiser

Massachusetts Appeals Court, 1979
7 Mass. App. Ct. 633, 389 N.E.2d 768

KASS, Justice.

State Street Bank and Trust Company (the bank) seeks to reach the assets of an *inter vivos* trust in order to pay a debt to the bank owed by the estate of the settlor of the trust. We conclude that the bank can do so.

* * *

Wilfred A. Dunnebier created an *inter vivos* trust on September 30, 1971, with power to amend or revoke the trust and the right during his lifetime to direct the disposition of principal and income. He conveyed to the trust the capital stock of five closely held corporations. Immediately following execution of this trust, Dunnebier executed a will under which he left his residuary estate to the trust he had established.

About thirteen months later Dunnebier applied to the bank for a $75,000 working capital loan. A bank officer met with Dunnebier, examined a financial statement furnished by him and visited several single family home subdivisions which Dunnebier, or corporations he controlled, had built or were in the process of building. During their conversations, Dunnebier told the bank officer that he had controlling interests in the corporations which owned the most significant assets appearing on the financial statement. On the basis of what he saw of Dunnebier's work, recommendations from another bank, Dunnebier's borrowing history with the bank, and the general cut of Dunnebier's jib, the bank officer decided to make an unsecured loan to Dunnebier for the $75,000 he had asked for. To evidence this loan, Dunnebier, on November 1, 1972, signed a personal demand note to the order of the bank. The probate judge found that Dunnebier did not intend to defraud the bank or misrepresent his financial position by failing to call attention to the fact that he had placed the stock of his corporations in the trust.

Approximately four months after he borrowed this money Dunnebier died in an accident. His estate has insufficient assets to pay the entire indebtedness due the bank.

Under Article Fourteen of his *inter vivos* trust, Dunnebier's trustees " . . . may in their sole discretion pay from the principal and income of this Trust Estate any and all debts and expenses of administration of the Settlor's estate." The bank urges that, since the *inter vivos* trust was part of an estate plan in which the simultaneously executed will was an integrated document, the instruction in Dunnebier's will that his executor pay his debts * * * should be read into the trust instrument. This must have been Dunnebier's intent, goes the argument.

Leaving to one side whether the precatory language in the will could be read as mandatory, and whether the language of that separate, albeit related, instrument, constitutes a surrounding circumstance (see Hull v. Adams, 286 Mass. 329, 333, 190 N.E. 510 (1934); Dumaine v. Dumaine, 301 Mass. 214, 218, 16 N.E.2d 625 (1938)) which could guide us in interpreting the trust, * * * we find the trust agreement manifests no such intent by Dunnebier. Article Fourteen speaks of the sole discretion of the trustees. Subparagraphs A and B of Article Five, by contrast, direct the trustees unconditionally to pay two $15,000 legacies provided for in Dunnebier's will if his estate has insufficient funds to do so. It is apparent that when Dunnebier wanted his trustees unqualifiedly to discharge his estate's obligations, he knew how to direct them. As to those matters which Dunnebier, as settlor, left to the sole discretion of his trustees, we are not free to substitute our judgment for theirs as to what is wise or most to our taste. The court will substitute its discretion only on those relatively rare occasions when it is necessary to prevent an abuse of discretion. Sylvester v. Newton, 321 Mass. 416, 421–422, 73 N.E.2d 585 (1947); Nexon v. Boston Safe Deposit and Trust Co., 5 Mass.App.—,— — —* * *, 364 N.E.2d 1077 (1977). Restatement (Second) of Trusts § 187 (1959) (see particularly comment (j), which says that where such adjectives as "absolute" or "unlimited" or "uncontrolled" modify the word "discretion" the trustees may act unreasonably, so long as not dishonestly or from a motive other than the accomplishment of the purposes of the trust). Here, the trustees could have considered preservation of the trust corpus for the benefit of the beneficiaries as most consistent with the trust purpose.

During the lifetime of the settlor, to be sure, the bank would have had access to the assets of the trust. When a person creates for his own benefit a trust for support or a discretionary trust, his creditors can reach the maximum amount which the trustee, under the terms of the trust, could pay to him or apply for his benefit. Ware v. Gulda, 331 Mass. 68, 70, 117 N.E.2d 137 (1954). Restatement (Second) of Trusts § 156(2) (1959). This is so even if the trust contains spendthrift provisions. Pacific Natl. Bank v. Windram, 133 Mass. 175, 176–177 (1882). Merchants Natl. Bank v. Morrissey, 329 Mass. 601, 605, 109 N.E.2d 821 (1953). Restatement (Second) of Trusts § 156(1) (1959). Under the terms of Dunnebier's trust, all the income and principal were at his disposal while he lived.

We then face the question whether Dunnebier's death broke the vital chain. His powers to amend or revoke the trust, or to direct payments from it, obviously died with him, and the remainder interests of the beneficiaries of the trust became vested. The contingencies which might defeat those remainder interests could no longer occur. Greenwich Trust Co. v. Tyson, 129 Conn. 211, 225, 27 A.2d 166 (1942). In one jurisdiction, at least, it has been held that when the settlor of a revocable living trust dies, the property is no longer subject to his debts. Schofield v. Cleveland Trust Co., 135 Ohio St. 328, 334, 21 N.E.2d 119 (1939). See generally McGovern, The Payable on Death Account and Other Will Substitutes, 67 N.W.L.Rev. 7, 26–29 (1972). Cf. Griswold, Spendthrift Trusts § 475 (2d ed. 1947).

Traditionally the courts of this Commonwealth have always given full effect to *inter vivos* trusts, notwithstanding retention of powers to amend and revoke during life, even though this resulted in disinheritance of a spouse or children and nullified the policy which allows a spouse to waive the will and claim a statutory share, G.L. c. 191, § 15. See National Shawmut Bank of Boston v. Joy, 315 Mass. 457, 474–475, 53 N.E.2d 113 (1944); Kerwin v. Donaghy, 317 Mass. 559, 567, 59 N.E.2d 299 (1945); Ascher v. Cohen, 333 Mass. 397, 400, 131 N.E.2d 198 (1956). It might then be argued that a creditor ought to stand in no better position where, as here, the trust device was not employed in fraud of creditors.

There has developed, however, another thread of decisions which takes cognizance of, and gives effect to, the power which a person exercises in life over property. When a person has a general power of appointment, exercisable by will or by deed, and exercises that power, any property so appointed is, in equity, considered part of his assets and becomes available to his creditors in preference to the claims of his voluntary appointees or legatees. Clapp v. Ingraham, 126 Mass. 200, 202 (1879); Shattuck v. Burrage, 229 Mass. 448, 452, 118 N.E. 889 (1918); State Street Trust Co. v. Kissel, 302 Mass. 328, 333, 19 N.E.2d 25 (1939). Compare Prescott v. Wordell, 319 Mass. 118, 120, 65 N.E.2d 19 (1946). These decisions rest on the theory that as to property which a person could appoint to himself or his executors, the property could have been devoted to the payment of debts and, therefore, creditors have an equitable right to reach that property. It taxes the imagination to invent reasons why the same analysis and policy should not apply to trust property over which the settlor retains dominion at least as great as a power of appointment. The Restatement of Property has, in fact, translated the doctrine applicable to powers of appointment to trusts: "When a person transfers property in trust for himself for life and reserves a general power to appoint the remainder and creates no other beneficial interests which he cannot destroy by exercising the power, the property, though the power is unexercised, can be subjected to the payment of the claims of creditors of such person and claims against his estate to whatever extent other available property is insufficient for that purpose." Restatement of Property, § 328 (1940). See also, for the assimilation of a power to revoke to a general power of appointment, concurring opinion of Goodman, J., in Massachusetts Co. v. Berger, 1 Mass.App. 624, 628 n.3, 305 N.E.2d 123 (1973).

As an estate planning vehicle, the *inter vivos* trust has become common currency. See Second Bank State St. Trust Co. v. Pinion, 341 Mass. 366, 371, 170 N.E.2d 350 (1960). Frequently, as Dunnebier did in the instant case, the settlor retains all the substantial incidents of ownership because access to the trust property is necessary or desirable as a matter of sound financial planning. Psychologically, the settlor thinks of the trust property as "his", as Dunnebier did when he took the bank's officer to visit the real estate owned by the corporation whose stock he had put in trust. See Fiduciary Trust Co. v. First Natl. Bank, 344 Mass. 1, 9, 181 N.E.2d 6 (1962). In other circumstances, persons place property in trust in order to obtain expert management of their assets, while retaining the power to invade principal and to amend and revoke the trust. It is excessive obeisance to the form in which property is held to prevent creditors from reaching property placed in trust under such terms. See Restatement of Property, § 328, Comment a (1940).

This view was adopted in United States v. Ritter, 558 F.2d 1165, 1167 (4th Cir. 1977). In a concurring opinion in that case Judge Widener observed that it violates public policy for an individual to have an estate to live on, but not an estate to pay his debts with. *Id.* at 1168. The Internal Revenue Code institutionalizes the concept that a settlor of a trust who retains administrative powers, power to revoke or power to control beneficial enjoyment "owns" that trust property and provides that it shall be included in the settlor's personal estate. I.R.C. §§ 2038 and 2041.

We hold, therefore, that where a person places property in trust and reserves the right to amend and revoke, or to direct disposition of principal and income, the settlor's creditors may, following the death of the settlor, reach in satisfaction of the settlor's debts to them, to the extent not satisfied by the settlor's estate, those assets owned by the trust over which the settlor had such control at the time of his death as would have enabled the settlor to use the trust assets for his own benefit. Assets which pour over into such a trust as a consequence of the settlor's death or after the settlor's death, over which the settlor did not have control during his life, are not subject to the reach of creditors since, as to those assets, the equitable principles do not apply which place assets subject to creditors' disposal.

The judgment is reversed, and a new judgment is to enter declaring that the assets owned by the trust (Wilfred A. Dunnebier Trust, I) up to the time of Dunnebier's death can be reached and applied in satisfaction of a judgment entered in favor of the plaintiff against the estate of Dunnebier, to the extent assets of the estate are insufficient to satisfy such a judgment.

So ordered.

Notes

The *State Street Bank & Trust Co.* decision, which held that a decedent's non-probate assets are available to pay debts and expenses after the probate estate is exhausted, is but one facet in the interaction between probate and non-probate transfers. Note that in meeting the claims of the spouse's elective share under augmented estate, the Uniform Probate Code made nearly all non-probate assets available to the surviving spouse. *See* Unif. Prob. Code § 2-205 (2019). However, here, too, the elective share must be satisfied from the probate estate before the non-probate estate may be used to satisfy the unsatisfied balance. *See id.* at § 2-209. For a discussion of some of these issues, see generally Raymond C. O'Brien, *Integrating Marital Property Into a Spouse's Elective Share*, 59 Cath. U. L. Rev. 617 (2010); Michael T. Flannery, *Equating Marital and Probate Interests Through the Elective Share*, LexisNexis Expert Commentary, 2009 Emerging Issues 4191 (Aug. 2009) (available at Lexis, Estates, Gifts and Trusts Emerging Issues library). The Uniform Probate Code, *infra*, clarifies what the beneficiary of a non-probate transfer is expected to contribute to satisfy a creditor's claim.

Uniform Probate Code (2019)

§ 6-102. Liability of Nonprobate Transferees for Creditor Claims and Statutory Allowances.

(a) In this section, "nonprobate transfer" means a valid transfer effective at death, other than a transfer of a survivorship interest in a joint tenancy of real estate, by a transferor whose last domicile was in this state to the extent that the transferor immediately before death had power, acting alone, to prevent the transfer by revocation or withdrawal and instead to use the property for the benefit of the transferor or apply it to discharge claims against the transferor's probate estate.

(b) Except as otherwise provided by statute, a transferee of a nonprobate transfer is subject to liability to any probate estate of the decedent for allowed claims against decedent's probate estate and statutory allowances to the decedent's spouse and children to the extent the estate is insufficient to satisfy those claims and allowances. The liability of a nonprobate transferee may not exceed the value of nonprobate transfers received or controlled by that transferee.

(c) Nonprobate transferees are liable for the insufficiency described in subsection (b) in the following order of priority:

(1) a transferee designated in the decedent's will or any other governing instrument, as provided in the instrument;

(2) the trustee of a trust serving as the principal nonprobate instrument in the decedent's estate plan as shown by its designation as devisee of the decedent's residuary estate or by other facts or circumstances, to the extent of the value of the nonprobate transfer received or controlled;

(3) other nonprobate transferees, in proportion to the values received.

(d) Unless otherwise provided by the trust instrument, interests of beneficiaries in all trusts incurring liabilities under this section abate as necessary to satisfy the liability, as if all of the trust instruments were a single will and the interests were devises under it.

(e) A provision made in one instrument may direct the apportionment of the liability among the nonprobate transferees taking under that or any other governing instrument. If a provision in one instrument conflicts with a provision in another, the later one prevails.

(f) Upon due notice to a nonprobate transferee, the liability imposed by this section is enforceable in proceedings in this state, whether or not the transferee is located in this state.

(g) A proceeding under this section may not be commenced unless the personal representative of the decedent's estate has received a written demand for the proceeding from the surviving spouse or a child, to the extent that statutory allowances are affected, or a creditor. If the personal representative declines or fails to commence a proceeding after demand, a person making demand may commence the proceeding in the name of the decedent's estate, at the expense of the person making the demand and not of the estate. A personal representative who declines in good faith to commence a requested proceeding incurs no personal liability for declining.

(h) A proceeding under this section must be commenced within one year after the decedent's death, but a proceeding on behalf of a creditor whose claim was allowed after proceedings challenging disallowance of the claim may be commenced within 60 days after final allowance of the claim.

(i) Unless a written notice asserting that a decedent's probate estate is nonexistent or insufficient to pay allowed claims and statutory allowances has been received from the decedent's personal representative, the following rules apply:

(1) Payment or delivery of assets by a financial institution, registrar, or other obligor, to a nonprobate transferee in accordance with the terms of

the governing instrument controlling the transfer releases the obligor from all claims for amounts paid or assets delivered.

(2) A trustee receiving or controlling a nonprobate transfer is released from liability under this section with respect to any assets distributed to the trust's beneficiaries. Each beneficiary to the extent of the distribution received becomes liable for the amount of the trustee's liability attributable to assets received by the beneficiary.

J. Dynasty Trusts

Rhode Island General Laws (2019)

§ 34-11-38. Rule against perpetuities reform.

The common law rule against perpetuities shall no longer be deemed to be in force and/or of any effect in this state, provided, the provisions of this section shall not be construed to invalidate or modify the terms of any interest which would have been valid prior to the effective date of this act, and, provided further, that the provisions of this section shall apply to both legal and equitable interests.

In re Estate of Feinberg

Supreme Court of Illinois, 2009
235 Ill. 2d 256, 335 Ill. Dec. 863, 919 N.E.2d 888

[When Max Feinberg died in 1986 he was survived by his wife, Erla and their adult children, Michael and Leila, and five grandchildren. Prior to his death he executed a valid Last Will and Testament that contained a testamentary trust. The terms of the trust specified that all of his assets were used for the benefit of his wife for the duration of her life. Then, upon her death, the assets were to be distributed to Max's descendants in accordance with what was called the "beneficiary restriction clause." "This clause directed that 50% of the assets be held in trust for the benefit of the then-living descendants of Michael and Leila during their lifetimes. The division was to be on a per stirpes basis, with Michael's two children as lifetime beneficiaries of one quarter of the trust and Leila's three children as lifetime beneficiaries of the other one quarter of the trust. However, any such descendant who married outside the Jewish faith or whose non-Jewish spouse did not convert to Judaism within one year of marriage would be 'deemed deceased for all purposes of this instrument as of the date of such marriage' and that descendant's share of the trust would revert to Michael; and Leila." *Id*. at 891.

In addition, the trust instrument gave Erla a special exclusive testamentary power of appointment over the distribution of the assets of both trusts and a limited special intervivos power of appointment over some of the trust assets. Under this provision, Erla was allowed to exercise her power of appointment only in favor of Max's descendants. Thus, she would not name as remaindermen individuals who were not Max's descendants or appoint to a charity. Erla did in fact exercise this special exclusive intervivos power of appointment in 1997, directing that, upon her death, each of her two children and any of her grandchildren who were not deemed deceased under Max's beneficiary restriction clause receive $250,000. In keeping with Max's original plan, if any grandchild was deemed deceased under the beneficiary restriction clause, Erla directed that his or her share be paid to Michael or Leila.

"All five grandchildren married between 1990 and 2001. By the time of Erla's death in 2003, all five grandchildren had been married for more than one year. Only Leila's son, Jon, met the conditions of the beneficiary restriction clause and was entitled to receive $250,000 of the trust assets as directed by Erla." *Id.* at 892.

The beneficiary restriction clause was challenged by descendants of Max as violating public policy because the settlor "used a religious description to define a class or category of descendants he wished to benefit, rather than mention them by name." *Id.* at 892. The state trial court invalidated the beneficiary restriction clause on public policy grounds. A divided appellate court affirmed, holding that under Illinois law and under the Restatement (Third) of Trusts, the provision in the case before us is invalid because it seriously interferes with and limits the right of individuals to marry a person of their own choosing. In reaching this conclusion, the appellate court relied on decisions of dating back as far as 1898 and, as noted, on the Restatement (Third) of Trusts. Nonetheless, the Supreme Court of Illinois reversed, holding that the "public policy of the state of Illinois as expressed in the Probate Act is, thus, one of broad testamentary freedom, constrained only by the rights granted to a surviving spouse and the need to expressly disinherit a child born after execution of the will if that is the testator's desire." *Id.* at 895. "The record, via the testimony of Michael and Leila, reveals that Max's intent in restricting the distribution of his estate was to benefit those descendants who opted to honor and further his commitment to Judaism by marrying within the faith. Max had expressed his concern about potential extinction of the Jewish people, not only by Holocaust, but by gradual dilution as a result of intermarriage with non-Jews. While he was willing to share his bounty with a grandchild whose spouse converted to Judaism, this was apparently as far as he was willing to go." *Id.* at 896. "While the beneficiary restriction clause, when given effect via Erla's distribution provision, has resulted in family strife, it is not 'so capable of producing harm that its enforcement would be contrary to the public interest.'" *Id.* at 903 (quoting *Kleinwort Benson North America, Inc. v. Quantum Financial Services, Inc.*, 181 Ill. 2d 214, 229 Ill. Dec. 496, 692 N.E.2d 269 (1998).]

Notes

The *Feinberg* decision involves the validity of a restraint on marriage, which has been discussed previously in Chapter Five, *supra*. But the facts also illustrate the fundamentals of a dynasty trust. The settlor sought to restrict his wealth to his lineal descendants, permitting his wife to select beneficiaries only among those of his descendants who met the conditions he imposed. The vehicle by which she could benefit—or appoint—his descendants was a special exclusive power of appointment, something to be discussed later in this chapter, *infra*. In a more typical dynasty trust, a member of succeeding generations of beneficiaries or an institutional representative could exercise the power and benefit descendants until the dynasty is exhausted, conceivably long into the future. Released by the abolition of the Rule Against Perpetuities, the availability of advantageous trust situs locations, and the increasing federal estate tax exemption, dynasty trusts have increased in popularity. The following commentary illustrate the dynamics of dynasty trusts.

Lawrence W. Waggoner
From Here to Eternity: The Folly of Perpetual Trusts
Univ. Mich. L. Sch. Pub. L. & Leg. Theory Res. Paper No. 259 (2012)

The perpetual trusts that are now in existence are only in their first or second decade, so experience with them as they continue past the boundary set by traditional perpetuity law is lacking. Nevertheless, some projections can be made, since the prototypical perpetual trust is a discretionary trust for the benefit of the settlor's descendants from time to time living forever (or for several centuries).

* * *

As the settlor's genetic relationship with the beneficiaries diminishes, the number of descendant-beneficiaries will proliferate geometrically. One hundred and fifty years after creation, a perpetual trust could have about 450 living beneficiaries; after 250 years, more than 7,000 living beneficiaries; after 350 years, about 114,500 living beneficiaries.

* * *

Will those documents be looked upon as modern, sophisticated, and up-to-date centuries from now? Consider the devices used centuries ago by English landowners to control family estates through subsequent generations. Such devices, which were then considered modern, sophisticated, and up-to-date, first took the form of the unbarrable entail and, after the entail became barrable, the strict settlement. These devices and the terminology associated with them became obsolete long ago. If the past is any guide to the future, an early 21st century perpetual-trust document will seem as obsolete to those in distant centuries as a 17th century document appears to us today.

* * *

Jesse Dukeminier & James E. Krier
The Rise of the Perpetual Trust
50 UCLA L. Rev. 1303 (2003)

One New York City lawyer guesses, based on his own experience, that the number of perpetual trusts created nationwide now runs into the thousands per year; his firm "alone probably does 100 or more annually." His brother works for an Alaska trust company that has done "700 or so I would guess. South Dakota and Delaware institutions probably have more." . . .

Id. at 1316 (quoting letter from Jonathan G. Blattmachr to Jesse Dukeminier (July 9, 2002)).

The longer trusts endure, the more troublesome they become, thanks largely to uncertainty. . . .

After some years pass, events never anticipated by trust settlors and their lawyers are likely to occur—for example, changes in the number, needs, and abilities of beneficiaries; changes in tax law and trust doctrine; changes in investment opportunities, in the rate of inflation and the value of the dollar; changes in trustees and the quality of their performance. The welfare of beneficiaries might be reduced in consequence, or economic waste might result.

Id. at 1327.

Todd A. Flubacher
How to Deal With Repeal
156 Trusts & Ests. 16 (Mar. 2017)

There are many important non-tax motivations for creating trusts irrespective of estate tax planning. Trusts are the only estate-planning tool that can provide liberal use, enjoyment and disposition of assets while avoiding taxes, creditors, divorce settlements and spendthrift heirs that cause dissolution of wealth in future generations. . . . Clients rarely want all of their wealth to pass immediately into the hands of their heirs, particularly if an untimely death would cause assets to fall into the hands of heirs who are unprepared to handle it. Clients with special assets, such as privately held businesses and real estate, often prefer such assets to be held in trust, instead of passing outright to descendants. Perhaps one of the strongest motivations for trust planning will be the desire to protect assets from dreaded son-in-laws and daughter-in-laws.

Id. at 19.

Notes

More than two-thirds of the states currently permit dynasty, or perpetual, trusts. Despite their popularity, however, there are those who argue that the trust terms and conditions will soon become obsolete. *See* Lawrence W. Waggoner, *From Here to Eternity: The Folly of Perpetual Trusts*, U. Mich. L. Sch. Pub. L. & Leg. Theory Res. Paper No. 259 (2012). Also, there are those who argue that the dynasty trust income growth cannot keep pace with the increasing number of trust beneficiaries, and this shortcoming may result in trust termination. *See* Lucy M. Marsh, *The Demise of Dynasty Trusts: Returning the Wealth to the Family*, 5 Est. Plan & Community Prop.

L.J. 23 (2012). For continuing commentary on the relative merits of dynasty trusts, see, *e.g.*, Thomas E. Simmons, *Innovative Strategy for Creating a Quasi-Dynastic Trust*, 46 Est. Plan. 03 (2019); Jay A. Soled, *Reimagining the Estate Tax in the Automation Age*, 9 UC Irvine L. Rev. 787 (2019) (arguing for reinstatement of a meaningful estate tax to combat dynastic wealth); Kristine S. Knaplund, *"Adoptions Shall Not Be Recognized": The Unintended Consequences for Dynasty Trusts*, 7 UC Irvine L. Rev. 545 (2017) (discussing how to determine heirs in an age of ART).

K. Non-Probate Contracts

While a revocable *inter vivos* trust is a popular means of avoiding probate and speedily passing property to another, there are other devices commonly used that involve concerns similar to trusts. For example, recipients of all nonprobate transfers can be required to contribute to creditors of the decedent, including statutory allowances, if the probate estate is insufficient. The Uniform Probate Code provides statutory means of assigning liability for decedents' debts. The list following that provision, although not exhaustive, provides other commonly used methods of avoiding probate while retaining liability.

1. Payable-on-Death Contracts

Estate of Hillowitz

Court of Appeals of New York, 1968
22 N.Y.2d 107, 238 N.E.2d 723, 291 N.Y.S.2d 325

Chief Judge Fuld.

This appeal stems from a discovery proceeding brought in the Surrogate's Court by the executors of the estate of Abraham Hillowitz against his widow, the appellant herein. The husband had been a partner in an "investment club" and, after his death, the club, pursuant to a provision of the partnership agreement, paid the widow the sum of $2,800, representing his interest in the partnership. "In the event of the death of any partner," the agreement recited, "his share will be transferred to his wife, with no termination of the partnership." The executors contend in their petition that the above provision was an invalid attempt to make a testamentary disposition of property and that the proceeds should pass under the decedent's will as an asset of his estate. The widow maintains that it was a valid and enforceable contract. Although the Surrogate agreed with her, the Appellate Division held that the agreement was invalid as "an attempted testamentary disposition" (24 A D 2d 891). * * *

A partnership agreement which provides that, upon the death of one partner, his interest shall pass to the surviving partner or partners, resting as it does in contract, is unquestionably valid and may not be defeated by labeling it a testamentary disposition. * * * [citations omitted]. We are unable to perceive a difference in principle between an agreement of this character and one, such as that before us, providing for a deceased partner's widow, rather than a surviving partner, to succeed to the decedent's interest in the partnership. * * * [citations omitted].

These partnership undertakings are, in effect, nothing more or less than third-party beneficiary contracts, performable at death. Like many similar instruments, contractual in nature, which provide for the disposition of property after death, they need not conform to the requirements of the statute of wills. (See, *e.g.*, Matter of Fairbairn, 265 App. Div. 431, 433, mot. for lv. to app. den. 291 N. Y. 828.) Examples of such instruments include (1) a contract to make a will (see, *e.g.*, Ga Nun v. Palmer, 216 N. Y. 603, 610; Phalen v. United States Trust Co., 186 N. Y. 178, 184; Gilman v. McArdle, 99 N. Y. 451, 461); (2) an *inter vivos* trust in which the settlor reserves a life estate (see, *e.g.*, Matter of Ford, 304 N. Y. 598; City Bank Farmers Trust Co. v. Cannon, 291 N. Y. 125; City Bank Farmers Trust Co. v. Charity Organization Soc., 264 N. Y. 441; and (3) an insurance policy. (See, *e.g.*, Hutchings v. Miner, 46 N. Y. 456, 460–461; Johnston v. Scott, 76 Misc. 641, 648; Ambrose v. United States, 15 F. 2d 52; see, also, Ward v. New York Life Ins. Co., 225 N. Y. 314; Note, 53 A L R 2d 1112.)

In short, members of a partnership may provide, without fear of running afoul of our statute of wills, that, upon the death of a partner, his widow shall be entitled to his interest in the firm. This type of third-party beneficiary contract is not invalid as an attempted testamentary disposition.

The executors may derive little satisfaction from McCarthy v. Pieret (281 N. Y. 407), upon which they heavily rely. In the first place, it is our considered judgment that the decision should be limited to its facts. And, in the second place, the case is clearly distinguishable from the one now before us in that the court expressly noted that the "facts . . . indicate a mere intention on the part of the mortgagee to make a testamentary disposition of the property and not an intention to convey an immediate interest" and, in addition, that the named beneficiaries "knew nothing of the provisions of the extension agreement" (p. 413).

The order of the Appellate Division should be reversed, with costs in this court and in the Appellate Division, and the order of the Surrogate's Court reinstated.

Judges Burke, Scileppi, Bergan, Breitel and Jasen concur with Chief Judge Fuld; * * *

Order reversed, etc.

Notes

To avoid courts treating arrangements like the one in *Estate of Hillowitz* as testamentary, the Uniform Probate Code § 6-101 (2019) specifically provides that this and similar transfers at death are nontestamentary. A question then arises as to the revocability of these transfers through such events as divorce, whether statutory anti-lapse should apply if the beneficiary of the payable-on-death arrangement predeceases the decedent survived by issue, and finally, whether there should be a requirement of survivorship by 120 hours. The answer is "yes" to all three questions. *See* Unif. Prob. Code §§ 2-702(c) (survivorship), 2-706 (anti-lapse), and 2-804(b) (revocation) (2019). As to whether the beneficiary of a payable-on-death contract may be changed with a provision in a valid Last Will and Testament, the following decision is illustrative. Please compare the decision with Uniform Probate Code § 6-213(b), which provides that a right of survivorship arising from a contract of deposit between a depositor and a financial institution (checking account, savings account, certificate of deposit) or a payable-on-death designation may not be altered by a Last Will and Testament.

Cook v. Equitable Life Assurance Society

Indiana Court of Appeals, First District, 1981
428 N.E.2d 110

RATLIFF, Judge.

Margaret A. Cook, Administratrix C.T.A. of the Estate of Douglas D. Cook (Douglas); Margaret A. Cook; and Daniel J. Cook (Margaret and Daniel) appeal from an entry of summary judgment granted by the trial court in favor of Doris J. Cook Combs (Doris) in an interpleader action brought by The Equitable Life Assurance Society of the United States (Equitable). We affirm.

* * *

Douglas purchased a whole life insurance policy on March 13, 1953, from Equitable, naming his wife at that time, Doris, as the beneficiary. On March 5, 1965, Douglas and Doris were divorced. The divorce decree made no provision regarding the insurance policy, but did state the following: "It is further understood and agreed between the parties hereto that the provisions of this agreement shall be in full satisfaction of all claims by either of said parties against the other, including alimony, support and maintenance money." Record at 85–86.

After the divorce Douglas ceased paying the premiums on his life insurance policy, and Equitable notified him on July 2, 1965, that because the premium due on March 9, 1965, had not been paid, his whole life policy was automatically converted to a paid-up term policy with an expiration date of June 12, 1986. The policy contained the following provision with respect to beneficiaries:

> BENEFICIARY. The Owner may change the beneficiary from time to time prior to the death of the Insured, by written notice to the Society, but any such change shall be effective only if it is endorsed on this policy by the Society, and, if there is a written assignment of this policy in force and on file with the Society (other than an assignment to the Society as security for an advance), such a change may be made only with the written consent of the assignee. The interest of a beneficiary shall be subject to the rights of any assignee of record with the Society.

> Upon endorsement of a change of beneficiary upon this policy by the Society, such change shall take effect as of the date the written notice thereof was signed, whether or not the Insured is living at the time of endorsement,

but without further liability on the part of the Society with respect to any proceeds paid by the Society or applied under any option in this policy prior to such endorsement.

If the executors or administrators of the Insured be not expressly designated as beneficiary, any part of the proceeds of this policy with respect to which there is no designated beneficiary living at the death of the Insured and no assignee entitled thereto, will be payable in a single sum to the children of the Insured who survive the Insured, in equal shares, or should none survive, then to the Insured's executors or administrators.

Record at 2 and 59.

On December 24, 1965, Douglas married Margaret, and a son, Daniel, was born to them. On June 7, 1976, Douglas made a holographic will in which he bequeathed his insurance policy with Equitable Life to his wife and son, Margaret and Daniel:

Last Will & Testimint [sic]

I Douglas D. Cook

Being of sound mind do Hereby leave all my Worldly posessions to my Wife and son, Margaret A. Cook & Daniel Joseph Cook. being my Bank Accounts at Irwin Union Bank & trust to their Welfair my Insurance policys with Common Welth of Ky. and Equitable Life. all my machinecal tools to be left to my son if He is Interested in Working with them If not to be sold and money used for their welfair all my Gun Collection Kept as long as they, my Wife & Son and then sold and money used for their welfair

> I sighn this
> June 7-1976
> at Barth Conty
> Hospital Room
> 1114 Bed 2
> /s/ Douglas D. Cook
> /s/ 6-7-76 Margaret A. Cook wife
> /s/ Chas. W. Winkler
> /s/ Mary A. Winkler"

This will was admitted to probate in Bartholomew Superior Court after Douglas's death on June 9, 1979. On August 24, 1979, Margaret filed a claim with Equitable for the proceeds of Douglas's policy, but Equitable deposited the proceeds, along with its complaint in interpleader, with the Bartholomew Circuit Court on March 14, 1980. Discovery was made; interrogatories and affidavits were filed; and all parties moved for summary judgment. The trial court found that there was no genuine issue as to any material fact respecting Doris's claim to the proceeds of the policy and entered judgment in her favor as to the amount of the proceeds plus interest, a total of $3,154.09. Margaret and Daniel appeal from this award.

* * *

Doris agrees that less than strict compliance with policy change requirements may be adequate to change a beneficiary where circumstances show the insured has done everything within his power to effect the change. Nevertheless, Doris asserts that Indiana adheres to the majority rule finding an attempt to change the beneficiary of a life insurance policy by will, without more, to be ineffectual. We agree with Doris. * * *

Indiana courts have recognized exceptions to the general rule that strict compliance with policy requirements is necessary to effect a change of beneficiary. Three exceptions were noted by this court in Modern Brotherhood v. Matkovitch, (1914) 56 Ind.App. 8, 14, 104 N.E. 795, and reiterated in Heinzman v. Whiteman, (1923) 81 Ind.App. 29, 36, 139 N.E. 329, trans. denied:

> '1. If the society has waived a strict compliance with its own rules, and in pursuance of a request of the insured to change the beneficiary, has issued a new certificate to him, the original beneficiary will not be heard to complain that the course indicated by the regulations was not pursued. 2. If it be beyond the power of the insured to comply literally with the regulations, a court of equity will treat the change as having been legally made. 3. If the insured has pursued the course pointed out by the laws of the association, and has done all in his power to change the beneficiary; but before the new certificate is actually issued, he dies, a court of equity will decree that to be done which ought to be done, and act as though the certificate had been issued.'

In Modern Brotherhood the insured had attempted to change the beneficiary of a mutual benefit insurance certificate in accordance with the terms of the certificate, but was thwarted in her attempts to do so by wrongful acts of the original beneficiary. It was impossible, therefore, for the insured to comply literally with the bylaws and regulations of the society for changing beneficiaries even though she notified the society of her desires to change the beneficiary on her certificate and also indicated those desires in her will. The court on appeal held that the trial court had erred in sustaining a demurrer to paragraph three of the complaint which stated facts sufficient to constitute an action upon equitable principles, but had properly sustained a demurrer to paragraph four of the complaint which merely stated that the insured had changed the beneficiaries of her certificate by will. The court repeated the rule of Holland at 56 Ind.App. 16, 104 N.E. 795: "Our courts have indicated that the rule in this State is, that without some other fact or facts, in aid of the change the insured cannot change the beneficiary by the execution of a will."

The public policy considerations undergirding this rule and its limited exceptions involve protection of the rights of all the parties concerned and should not be viewed, as appellants advocate, for the exclusive protection of the insurer. Indiana, in fact, has specifically rejected this position. In Stover v. Stover, (1965) 137 Ind. App. 578, 204 N.E.2d 374, 380, on rehearing 205 N.E.2d 178, trans. denied, the court recognized an insured's right to rely on the provisions of the policy in regard to change of beneficiary:

> We must reject appellant's contention that the provisions set forth in the certificate, as mentioned above, are for the exclusive benefit of the insurance company and may be waived at will. The deceased insured himself is entitled to rely upon such provisions that he may at all times know to whom the proceeds of the insurance shall be payable.

In Holland the court also recognized that the beneficiary had a right in the executed contract which was subject to defeat only by a change of beneficiary which had been executed in accord with the terms of the insurance contract: "In that contract Anna Laura, the beneficiary, had such an interest as that she had, and has, the right to insist that in order to cut her out, the change of beneficiary should be made in the manner provided in the contract." 111 Ind. 127, 12 N.E. 116. And in Borgman v. Borgman, (1981) Ind.App., 420 N.E.2d 1261, trans. denied, this court held that an interpleader action by a life insurance company does not affect the parties' rights.

Clearly it is in the interest of insurance companies to require and to follow certain specified procedures in the change of beneficiaries of its policies so that they may pay over benefits to persons properly entitled to them without subjection to claims by others of whose rights they had no notice or knowledge. Certainly it is also in the interest of beneficiaries themselves to be entitled to prompt payment of benefits by insurance companies which do not withhold payment until the will has been probated in the fear of later litigation which might result from having paid the wrong party. The legislature reflects this concern with certainty in the area of insurance beneficiaries in Ind.Code 27-1-12-14 by permitting changes of beneficiaries in insurance policies upon written notice to the insurance company when accompanied by the policy. Finally, society's interest in the conservation of judicial energy and expense will be served where the rule and its limited exceptions are clearly stated and rigorously applied.

* * *

We may be sympathetic to the cause of the decedent's widow and son, and it might seem that a departure from the general rule in an attempt to do equity under these facts would be noble. Nevertheless, such a course is fraught with the dangers of eroding a solidly paved pathway of the law and leaving in its stead only a gaping hole of uncertainty. Public policy requires that the insurer, insured, and beneficiary alike should be able to rely on the certainty that policy provisions pertaining to the naming and changing of beneficiaries will control except in extreme situations. We, therefore, invoke a maxim equally as venerable as the one upon which appellants rely in the determination of this cause: Equity aids the vigilant, not those who slumber on their rights.

Judgment affirmed.

NEAL, P. J., and ROBERTSON, J., concur.

2. Multiple Party Bank Accounts

Franklin v. Anna National Bank of Anna

Illinois Appellate Court, Fifth District, 1986
140 Ill. App. 3d 533, 488 N.E.2d 1117

WELCH, Justice:

Plaintiff Enola Stevens Franklin, as executor of the Estate of Frank A. Whitehead, deceased, commenced this action in the circuit court of Union County against defendant Anna National Bank, alleging that the funds in a joint savings account were the property of the estate. The bank interpleaded Cora Goddard, who asserted her right to the money as the surviving joint owner. After a bench trial, the circuit court entered judgment for Mrs. Goddard. Mrs. Franklin appeals. We reverse.

* * *

Decedent died December 22, 1980. His wife Muriel Whitehead died in 1974. Mrs. Goddard was Muriel's sister. Decedent had eye surgery in May of 1978, and according to Mrs. Goddard was losing his eyesight in 1978. In April of 1978 Mrs. Goddard moved to Union County to help decedent and live with him. On April 17, 1978, Mrs. Goddard and decedent went to the bank, according to Mrs. Goddard to have his money put in both their names so she could get money when they needed it, "and he wanted me to have this money if I outlived him."

A bank employee prepared a signature card for savings account number 3816 and Mrs. Goddard signed it. A copy of this card was in evidence at trial. The signatures of decedent and Mrs. Goddard appear on both sides of the card. It appears that Muriel Whitehead's signature was "whited out" and Mrs. Goddard's signature added. The front of the card states that one signature is required for withdrawals. The back of the card states that all funds deposited are owned by the signatories as joint tenants with right of survivorship.

Mrs. Goddard testified that she did not deposit any of the money in savings account 3816. She made no withdrawals, though she once took decedent to the bank so he could make a withdrawal. According to Mrs. Goddard, on the day she signed the signature card decedent "asked me if I needed my money because they had bought cemetery lots from me, and I told him, not at this time, that I didn't need it. He wanted to know if I needed any more money at that time and I said, no, and I said, just leave it in here and I will get it out whenever I need it." According to Mrs. Goddard, decedent promised to pay her a thousand dollars for the lots; she was never paid. Asked whether she ever had the passbook for savings account 3816 in her possession, Mrs. Goddard answered, "Only while I was at Frank's. It was there."

Later in 1978, Mrs. Franklin began to care for decedent. In January, 1979, decedent telephoned the bank, then sent Mrs. Franklin to the bank to deliver a letter to Mrs. Kedron Boyer, a bank employee. The handwritten letter, dated January 13, 1979, and signed by decedent, stated: "I Frank Whitehead wish by Bank accounts be changed to Enola Stevens joint intendency [sic]. Nobody go in my lock box but me." According to Mrs. Franklin, Mrs. Boyer told her to tell decedent he would have to specify what type of account he was referring to. Decedent gave Mrs. Franklin a second letter which Mrs. Franklin delivered to Mrs. Carol Williams at the bank (Mrs. Boyer was absent). This handwritten letter, dated January 13, 1979, stated: "I Frank Whitehead want Enola Stevens and me only go in my lock box. Account type Saving and Checking. In case I can't see she is to take care of my bill or sick." According to Mrs. Franklin, Mrs. Williams said she would take care of it and give the letter to Mrs. Boyer. Mrs. Franklin testified that she signed the savings passbook in the presence of decedent and Mrs. Boyer. Mrs. Franklin took her present last name on May 8, 1979.

Mrs. Boyer, Mrs. Williams, and bank president Delano Mowery all testified at trial. These witnesses explained the usual procedures for account changes. None remembered much of the circumstances surrounding the bank's receipt of the January 13, 1979, letters. According to Mr. Mowery, the bank would not remove a signature from a signature card based on a letter; the most recent signature card the bank had for savings account 3816 was signed by decedent and Mrs. Goddard.

Mrs. Goddard's attorney's assertion at trial that there were no monthly statements on savings account 3816 was uncontradicted.

The trial court found that Mrs. Goddard was the sole owner of the funds in savings account 3816 by right of survivorship as surviving joint tenant, and that no part of the funds became part of decedent's estate.

Mrs. Franklin argues that decedent did not intend to make a gift of savings account 3816 to Mrs. Goddard.

The instrument creating a joint tenancy account presumably speaks the whole truth. In order to go behind the terms of the agreement, the one claiming adversely thereto has the burden of establishing by clear and convincing evidence that a gift was not intended. (Murgic v. Granite City Trust & Savings Bank (1964), 31 Ill.2d 587, 590, 202 N.E.2d 470, 472.) Each case involving a joint tenancy account must be evaluated on its own facts and circumstances. (In re Estate of Hayes (1971), 131 Ill. App.2d 563, 568, 268 N.E.2d 501, 505.) The form of the agreement is not conclusive regarding the intention of the depositors between themselves. (In re Estate of Schneider (1955), 6 Ill.2d 180, 186, 127 N.E.2d 445, 449.) Evidence of lack of donative intent must relate back to the time of creation of the joint tenancy. (In re Estate of Stang (1966), 71 Ill.App.2d 314, 317, 218 N.E.2d 854, 856.) The decision of the donor, made subsequent to the creation of the joint tenancy, that he did not want the proceeds to pass to the survivor, would not, in itself, be sufficient to sever the tenancy. (Estate of Zengerle (1971), 2 Ill.App.3d 98, 101, 276 N.E.2d 128, 130.) However, it is proper to consider events occurring after creation of the joint account in determining whether the donor actually intended to transfer his interest in the account at his death to the surviving joint tenant. Matter of Estate of Guzak (1979), 69 Ill.App.3d 552, 555, 26 Ill.Dec. 716, 718, 388 N.E.2d 431, 433.

We examine the instant facts in light of the above principles: There appears no serious doubt that in January of 1979, just nine months after adding Mrs. Goddard's name to savings account 3816, decedent attempted to remove Mrs. Goddard's name and substitute Mrs. Franklin's. The second of decedent's handwritten letters to the bank in January of 1979 indicates decedent's concern that he might lose his sight and be unable to transact his own banking business. These facts show that decedent made Mrs. Goddard (and later Mrs. Franklin) a signatory for his own convenience, in case he could not get his money, and not with intent to effect a present gift. (See Dixon Nat'l Bank v. Morris (1965), 33 Ill.2d 156, 159, 210 N.E.2d 505, 506; Estate of Guzak.) It does not appear that Mrs. Goddard ever exercised any authority or control over the joint account. (See Estate of Guzak.) While decedent's statement that he wanted Mrs. Goddard to have the money in the account if she outlived him suggests decedent's donative intent, taken literally decedent's statement is inconsistent with intent to donate any interest during decedent's lifetime. (See Lipe v. Farmers State Bank of Alto Pass (1970), 131 Ill.App.2d 1024, 1026, 265 N.E.2d 204, 205.) Mrs. Goddard does not argue that there was a valid testamentary disposition in her favor, nor could we so find on the instant facts.

Of the many cases cited by the parties for comparison with the case at bar, the most persuasive is In re Estate of Schneider (1955), 6 Ill.2d 180, 127 N.E.2d 445. In Estate of Schneider the decedent's executor filed a petition alleging the funds in joint bank accounts belonged to the estate and not to Ralston, the surviving joint tenant. Ralston testified that all of the money in the account was deposited by the decedent, that the decedent at no time told Ralston he wanted Ralston to have any of the money, and that when Ralston's name was added to the accounts the decedent said, "I want your name on these bank accounts so that in case I am sick you can go and get the money for me." The trial court concluded that the decedent intended to retain actual ownership of the money. Our supreme court agreed. We reach the same conclusion here. In the case at bar, decedent's attempts to change the account show his consistent view of the account as his own. The surrounding circumstances show decedent's concern for his health and his relatively brief use of Mrs. Goddard (and later Mrs. Franklin) to assure his access to his funds. The money in account 3816 should have been found to be the property of the estate.

For the foregoing reasons, the judgment of the circuit court of Union County is reversed, and this cause is remanded for entry of judgment in favor of plaintiff.

REVERSED.

KARNS and HARRISON, JJ., concur.

Notes

Because a joint account may be created through multiple types of forms, as was demonstrated in the *Franklin* decision, the issue is how to determine the true intent of the depositor. While some courts apply a presumption of a gift when a deposit is made, the Uniform Probate Code provides that joint accounts belong to the respective parties in proportion to what each deposited, unless there is clear and convincing evidence to the contrary. *See, e.g.*, Robinson v. Delfino, 710 A.2d 154 (R.I. 1998); Unif. Prob. Code §6-211(b), *infra*. Note, too, that joint accounts, such as the one in the *Franklin* decision, require survivorship for a depositor to take possession; anti-lapse is inapplicable. But the Uniform Probate Code applies anti-lapse protection to other payable-on-death contracts, such as life insurance and retirement accounts. *See* Unif. Prob. Code § 2-706 (2019).

Recognizing the multiplicity of multiple-person accounts, the Uniform Probate Code provides extensive suggested codification to address each of the issues that have arisen. *See* Unif. Prob. Code §§ 2-6-201 through 6-227. Compare the following two sections of the Code with the holding in the *Franklin* decision, *supra*.

Uniform Probate Code (2019)

§6-211. Ownership During Lifetime.

(a) In this section, "net contribution" of a party means the sum of all deposits to an account made by or for the party, less all payments from the account made to or for the party which have not been paid to or applied to the use of another party and a proportionate share of any charges deducted from the account, plus a proportionate share of any interest or dividends earned, whether or not included in the current balance. The term includes deposit life insurance proceeds added to the account by reason of death of the party whose net contribution is in question.

(b) During the lifetime of all parties, an account belongs to the parties in proportion to the net contribution of each to the sums on deposit, unless there is clear and convincing evidence of a different intent. As between parties married to each other, in the absence of proof otherwise, the net contribution of each is presumed to be an equal amount.

(c) A beneficiary in an account having a P.O.D designation has no right to sums on deposit during the lifetime of any party.

(d) An agent in an account with an agency designation has no beneficial right to sums on deposit.

§6-212. Rights at Death.

(a) Except as otherwise provided in this part, on death of a party sums on deposit in a multiple-party account belong to the surviving party or parties. If two or more parties survive and one is the surviving spouse of the decedent, the amount to which the decedent, immediately before death, was beneficially entitled under Section 6-211 belongs to the surviving spouse. If two or more parties survive and none is the surviving spouse of the decedent, the amount to which the decedent, immediately before death, was beneficially entitled under Section 6-211 belongs to the surviving parties in equal shares, and augments the proportion to which each survivor, immediately before the decedent's death, was beneficially entitled under Section 6-211, and the right of survivorship continues between the surviving parties.

(b) In an account with a P.O.D designation:

(1) On death of one of two or more parties, the rights in sums on deposit are governed by subsection (a).

(2) On death of the sole party or the last survivor of two or more parties, sums on deposit belong to the surviving beneficiary or beneficiaries. If two or more beneficiaries survive, sums on deposit belong to them in equal and undivided shares, and there is no right of survivorship in the event of death of a beneficiary thereafter. If no beneficiary survives, sums on deposit belong to the estate of the last surviving party.

(c) Sums on deposit in a single-party account without a P.O.D designation, or in a multiple-party account that, by the terms of the account, is without right of survivorship, are not affected by death of a party, but the amount to which the decedent, immediately before death, was beneficially entitled under Section 6-211 is transferred as part of the decedent's estate. A P.O.D designation in a multiple-party account without right of survivorship is ineffective. For purposes of this section, designation of an account as a tenancy in common establishes that the account is without right of survivorship.

(d) The ownership right of a surviving party or beneficiary, or of the decedent's estate, in sums on deposit is subject to requests for payment made by a party before the party's death, whether paid by the financial institution before or after death, or unpaid. The surviving party or beneficiary, or the decedent's estate, is liable to the payee of an unpaid request for payment. The liability is limited to a proportionate share of the amount transferred under this section, to the extent necessary to discharge the request for payment.

3. Totten Trusts

Green v. Green

Supreme Court of Rhode Island, 1989
559 A.2d 1047

FAY, Chief Justice.

This case comes before the Supreme Court on the plaintiff's appeal from a Superior Court judgment denying her petition to recover assets distributed to the defendants upon the death of her husband. The trial justice held that the defendants were entitled to the funds of numerous trusts created by the decedent during his lifetime. We affirm that decision. * * *

George L. Green (Green) died intestate on March 7, 1985, and was survived by his wife, Hilda A. Green, plaintiff, and three children from a prior marriage, George L. Green, Jr., Elizabeth A. Swope, and James D. Green, defendants. The plaintiff also has one daughter from a prior marriage.

Green and plaintiff were married in 1949. During the marriage both husband and wife worked to contribute financially to the marriage and also to the upkeep of various properties. The Greens owned some property jointly, and other property was recorded in Green's name alone. Green owned eight cottages on Cape Cod, which he rented to tourists. The plaintiff assisted Green by cleaning and preparing the cottages for the arrival of new guests. Green also owned a condominium in Florida, which was used by Green and plaintiff as a residential unit.

Green assumed responsibility for a majority of the couple's finances, including the purchase and sale of their real estate holdings. Whereas Green paid for the rent, heat, and food, plaintiff was responsible for the telephone bill, laundry bill, and various other miscellaneous bills. The plaintiff kept her own checking account, which she funded with money earned from employment outside the home. The funds in this account were used to buy goods for her daughter and herself.

Throughout the Greens' marriage Green maintained a strong relationship with his three children. Green's daughter, Elizabeth Swope (Swope), was exceptionally close to her father. Green enlisted Swope's aid in filing his tax returns, divulged the contents of his financial record book to Swope, which listed his holdings of stock and trust accounts, and told her of his specific intention to avoid a will and probate. Green also informed Swope that the funds in each of his eight bank accounts were left in trust to be distributed upon his death to the named beneficiaries.

Upon Green's death, his Rhode Island estate-tax return revealed a gross estate of $258,125: $218,574 in eight separate bank accounts, $38,651 in securities, and $900 in personal property. Green had contributed all the money in each of the eight bank accounts, and each account was held in trust for one of his heirs. Green was named as trustee on all eight accounts, and he retained physical possession of the bankbooks throughout his life. Most of his stocks were also held jointly with one of the heirs. Because these assets were held either jointly or in trust, it was unnecessary for them to pass through probate as the remainder of the estate did.

The plaintiff's share of her late husband's estate comprised personal property (stocks) totaling $2,432 and, as the named beneficiary, the contents of two bank accounts totaling $25,000. The funds in the remaining bank accounts were distributed to the other named beneficiaries following Green's death, and the accounts were subsequently closed by each bank.

Thereafter, plaintiff filed a petition with the Pawtucket Probate Court. She requested a widow's allowance and also the recovery of all funds distributed to Green's three children pursuant to the trust accounts. The petition was denied, and plaintiff filed two appeals in the Superior Court, pursuant to G.L.1956 (1984 Reenactment) § 33-23-1. The plaintiff sought the overturn of the denial of a widow's allowance and a determination that the bank accounts were not valid trust accounts, thereby causing the estate to recover all funds formerly distributed.

The two appeals were consolidated and subsequently tried without a jury. The trial justice found that plaintiff was entitled to a widow's allowance totaling $10,000, provided the estate had ample funds. This portion of the decision was not appealed.

Focusing on the trust accounts, the trial justice further noted that throughout the years activity on the trust accounts had been minimal. Although Green had made one withdrawal of approximately $2,000 and also reported all interest earned from said accounts on his tax returns, the trial justice determined that Green fully intended that upon his death the accounts were to be distributed to the named beneficiaries, including plaintiff. Furthermore, the trial justice noted that Green had told his daughter of his specific intent to avoid probate. The trial justice held that the trust accounts were valid totten trusts and as such the funds were properly distributed to each of the named beneficiaries. The plaintiff now appeals this portion of the trial justice's decision.

An initial examination of the law regarding totten trusts will be helpful to our analysis. A totten trust is defined as a deposit in trust by the settlor of his own money for the benefit of another. Black's Law Dictionary 1356 (West 5th ed.1979). The creation of a valid totten trust requires retention of the subject matter of the trust by the settlor or the trustee for the benefit of the named beneficiary. Petition of Atkinson, 16 R.I. 413, 415–16, 16 A. 712, 713 (1889). The settlor may be the named trustee, but this is not necessary to the validity of the trust.[1] Black's Law Dictionary 1356. During the settlor's lifetime the trust is revocable, and the settlor may use the funds for his own benefit. Id. Upon the settlor's death, however, the trust becomes irrevocable and is the exclusive property of the beneficiary. Peoples Savings Bank v. Webb, 21 R.I. 218, 42 A. 874 (1899).

For over one hundred years we have recognized that a totten trust is a valid tool for transferring assets upon the settlor's death. See Slepkow v. McSoley, 54 R.I. 210, 172 A. 328 (1934); Petition of Atkinson, 16 R.I. 413, 16 A. 712 (1889); Ray v. Simmons, 11 R.I. 266 (1875). In our line of cases interpreting totten trusts, we have distinguished a totten trust from a gift. See Slepkow, 54 R.I. at 213, 172 A. at 329; Peoples Savings Bank, 21 R.I. at 220, 42 A. at 874; Atkinson, 16 R.I. at 415, 16 A. at 713. The validity of a totten trust, unlike a gift, does not require delivery of the subject matter to the beneficiary. Slepkow, 54 R.I. at 213, 172 A. at 329; Peoples Savings Bank, 21 R.I. at 220, 42 A. at 874; Atkinson, 16 R.I. at 415, 16 A. at 713.

Because of the distinction between a trust and a gift, the settlor's intention is critical to the validity of a totten trust. The intention to create a trust must be shown by the settlor through a clear act and/or declaration and must be made during his lifetime. Malley v. Malley, 69 R.I. 407, 412, 34 A.2d 761, 763 (1943). The settlor is not required to use any particular form of words to create a trust but must convey the property to another in trust or unequivocally declare that he holds it in praesenti in trust or as trustee for another. Ray, 11 R.I. at 268. * * *

---

1. Although the settlor is not required to serve as trustee, in this case the decedent, Green, acted as both the settlor and the trustee.

Turning to the instant case, the principal issue is whether defendants are beneficially entitled to the sums of money in each account, which were placed on deposit by their father, Green. It is uncontradicted that all eight accounts were in the name of Green as trustee for each named beneficiary. We believe that Green specifically intended to dispose of his property through totten trusts. Therefore, the beneficiaries are entitled to the full amount of these trusts.

The trial justice ruled that the funds in the trust accounts are properly the funds of the beneficiaries named on each of the accounts. The trial justice stated that Green's intent—as shown by the form of the accounts as trusts, by the testimony that Green wanted to avoid probate, by the statements to Swope, and by the knowledge of all the beneficiaries that they were to inherit from said accounts—was to form totten trusts. Relying upon this evidence, the trial justice determined that at the time of the creation of said accounts Green had established perfectly valid in praesenti trusts and the full effect of the trusts was to take place at the time of his death.

It is clear from Swope's testimony and Green's acts during his lifetime that he fully intended to dispose of his property through bank accounts naming his heirs as beneficiaries. After carefully reviewing the testimony and evidence entered below, we are of the opinion that the trial justice's findings regarding Green's intention and the validity of the totten trusts were not clearly wrong.

The form of the accounts at Green's death created a prima facie case that the accounts were totten trusts. The plaintiff argued that the presumption in favor of a valid trust disappears when any evidence is presented contrary to the prima facie case. The plaintiff presented as contradictory evidence testimony that all the beneficiaries did not know of the existence of the accounts during Green's lifetime, that at all times Green maintained control of the passbooks, and that he withdrew funds from one of the accounts. Although Green retained control of the passbooks, paid taxes on all interest accumulated, and withdrew approximately $2,000 from one of the accounts, his retention of control created valid revocable trusts during his lifetime. We are of the opinion that Green's control, disposition, and appropriation of the funds in the accounts does not invalidate the trusts or render them testamentary. Therefore, we find that plaintiff's evidence is insufficient to rebut the prima facie existence and validity of the accounts as totten trusts.

We also believe that the trial justice's findings of fact are supported by substantial evidence. In making these findings, the trial justice did not misconceive or overlook material evidence. Consequently we find that the trial justice did not err in determining that Green fully intended to create valid totten trust bank accounts during his lifetime. Furthermore, on the basis of this review, we hold that the funds in each account were properly distributed to the named beneficiary and should not revert back to the estate for distribution pursuant to our intestacy laws.

For the reasons stated, the plaintiff's appeal is hereby denied and dismissed. The judgment appealed from is affirmed, and the papers in this case are remanded to the Superior Court with our decision endorsed thereon.

Notes

To keep some control over property, settlors often deposit money with a financial institution simply "in trust" for another, without specifying specific duties, retaining the right to revoke, or changing the name of the beneficiary. The case of *In re* Totten, 179 N.Y. 112, 71 N.E. 748 (1904), was the first to sustain these trusts against claims that they were invalid testamentary transfers. The absence of specified duties make these Totten Trusts more like payable-on-death accounts, therefore, the Uniform Probate Code abolishes the concept of a Totten Trust and simply calls them P.O.D. accounts. *See* Unif. Prob. Code § 6-201(8) (2019). States and commentators often refer to these trusts as "tentative trusts" or "saving account trusts," but the nature of the arrangement is the same. *See Restatement (Third) of Trusts* § 26 (2019).

4. Joint Tenancy

In common law states, many, if not most, married couples own the homes in which they are living under tenancy by the entirety. This form of ownership is reserved to marriage and exists only in common law jurisdictions. Thus, upon death, the decedent's interest in the property ceases to exist and the surviving spouse owns the real property absolutely, without the necessity of probate. Hence, this is a non-probate device and is very advantageous because of speed. Likewise, if two or more unmarried persons in a common law state or a community property state wish to achieve the same non-probate result, the two parties may hold title as joint tenants. The essential difference between tenancy by the entirety and joint tenancy, and tenants in common is that, in the former two, survivorship is implied in the title; a Last Will and Testament has no effect upon the joint tenancy. Whereas, with tenants in common, one party may devise his or her interest to another; there is a lack of non-probate survivorship.

Joint tenancy prompts a few caveats:

First, property held as joint tenants will be available to the creditors of the decedent contributor in accordance with the rules previously discussed in connection with the *Reiser* decision;

Second, the surviving spouse of the decedent contributor will likely be able to include these assets within any elective share computed under augmented estate; *see* Unif. Prob. Code §§ 2-202 to 2-210;

Third, the survivorship requirement imposed by statutes such as Uniform Probate Code § 2-104 (survival by 120 hours) is applicable;

Fourth, joint tenants may be transformed into tenants in common if they were married, but their marriage ends in divorce or annulment, *see id.* at § 2-804(b); *but see* Life Insurance Co. of North America v. Ortiz, 535 F.3d 990 (9th Cir. 2008) (in absence of revocation statute, when man designated wife as beneficiary of life insurance policy and divorced her six years later but did not change policy, former spouse was still entitled to take proceeds of policy since neither divorce decree nor language of insurance contract revoked POD designation); and

Fifth, the provisions of anti-lapse, by which an issue is substituted for a prede-ceasing taker, is inapplicable; survivorship is required, *see* Unif. Prob. Code § 2-706 (2019).

Uniform Probate Code (2019)

§ 6-212. Rights at Death.

(a) Except as otherwise provided in this part, on death of a party sums on deposit in a multiple-party account belong to the surviving party or parties. If two or more parties survive and one is the surviving spouse of the decedent, the amount to which the decedent, immediately before death, was beneficially entitled under Section 6-211 belongs to the surviving spouse. If two or more parties survive and none is the surviving spouse of the decedent, the amount to which the decedent, immediately before death, was beneficially entitled under Section 6-211 belongs to the surviving parties in equal shares, and augments the proportion to which each survivor, immediately before the decedent's death, was beneficially entitled under Section 6-211, and the right of survivorship continues between the surviving parties. * * *

5. Security Accounts

While bank deposits first come to mind when thinking of multiple party accounts, *see, e.g.*, Franklin v. Anna National Bank of Anna, *supra*, much of today's wealth is held in mutual funds and investor brokerage accounts. To address the concerns generated by these accounts, the Uniform Probate Code §§ 6-301 to 6-311 provides a procedure similar to payable-on-death provisions (here called transfer-on-death or "TOD"). Specifically, Uniform Probate Code § 6-306 provides that:

> [t]he designation of a TOD beneficiary on a registration in beneficiary form has no effect on ownership until the owner's death. A registration of a security in beneficiary form may be canceled or changed at any time by the sole owner or all then surviving owners with the consent of the beneficiary.

Uniform Probate Code (2019)

§ 6-307. Ownership on Death of Owner.

On death of a sole owner or the last to die of all multiple owners, ownership of securities registered in beneficiary form passes to the beneficiary or beneficiaries who survive all owners. On proof of death of all owners and compliance with any applicable requirements of the registering entity, a security registered in beneficiary form may be reregistered in the name of the beneficiary or beneficiaries who survived the death of all owners. Until division of the security after the death of all owners, multiple beneficiaries surviving the death of all owners hold their interests as tenants in common. If no beneficiary survives the death of all owners, the security belongs to the estate of the deceased sole owner or the estate of the last to die of all multiple owners.

III. Modification and Termination

Once a trust has been created by a competent settlor, the traditional argument is that the settlor's Trustee now has the legal ownership of the property but is responsible to the settlor for the terms and conditions of the trust purpose. "The founder of [the] trust was the absolute owner of [the] property . . . [with] the entire right to dispose of it, either by an absolute gift . . . or by a gift with such restrictions or limitations, not repugnant to law, as [the settlor] saw fit to impose." Broadway National Bank v. Adams, 133 Mass. 170 (1882). But should the settlor be able to have a change of heart and terminate (revoke) the trust or modify its purposes? And should the beneficiaries be able to do the same? Finally, under what terms and conditions may the Trustee modify or terminate the trust? Consider the following circumstances.

A. Settlor

Connecticut General Life Insurance Co. v. First National Bank of Minneapolis

Supreme Court of Minnesota, 1977
262 N.W.2d 403

YETKA, Justice.

Appeal from judgment and order denying appellant's motion for amended findings of fact, conclusions of law, and order for judgment. The plaintiff, Connecticut General Life Insurance Co., filed a complaint in interpleader on September 9, 1974. After answers and counterclaims were filed, plaintiff deposited disputed life insurance proceeds with the court and was dismissed from the proceedings. After a trial without a jury, the District Court in Hennepin County determined that the disputed insurance proceeds were to be paid to the First National Bank of Minneapolis, as trustee of the John W. Aughenbaugh Trust. * * * Mrs. Marilyn Aughenbaugh appeals from that determination. We affirm.

On February 2, 1965, Connecticut General Life Insurance Co. (Connecticut General) issued John W. Aughenbaugh a life insurance policy. At that time there was in existence a Last Will and Testament of John W. Aughenbaugh, executed on or about March 16, 1964, which left his estate to Elizabeth Ann Aughenbaugh. On May 4, 1967, John W. Aughenbaugh executed a new will. On the same date he executed an instrument creating the John W. Aughenbaugh Revocable Insurance Trust (the trust). First National Bank of Minneapolis (respondent) was named as trustee. Part of the funding for the trust was to be provided by the Connecticut General policy. The trust was not funded in any respect except by the insurance policies listed. The respondent, First National Bank of Minneapolis, was made beneficiary of the Connecticut General Insurance policy; the trust beneficiaries were Elizabeth Ann Aughenbaugh and three Aughenbaugh children. There were other trusts created in the instrument but they are not in issue in the present case.

In February 1972 the last premium was paid. At that time John W. Aughenbaugh and Elizabeth Ann Aughenbaugh were married and living in Minneapolis. On November 10, 1972, they were divorced, and on February 14, 1973, John W. Aughenbaugh and Marilyn L. Melaas (appellant) were married in Nevada.

In April 1973 Aughenbaugh and his second spouse moved to Arizona. On or about October 16, 1973, John W. Aughenbaugh executed a document entitled "Will." The will purported to "supercede and cancel any previous wills or trusts established by me." It was entrusted by John Aughenbaugh to his wife Marilyn after it was executed. He died on October 21, 1973. The will was probated in Arizona. After several exchanges of documents between Connecticut General and appellant, the present action was instituted raising the issue as to whether the will executed by John W. Aughenbaugh on October 16, 1973, operated to revoke the John W. Aughenbaugh Revocable Insurance Trust, created May 4, 1967. The trial court held in the negative.

Appellant appears to raise five points in her brief, but three of those issues depend primarily upon whether the trust is *inter vivos* or testamentary in nature. The remaining two issues involve interpretation of the trust agreement itself.

* * *

Unless the trust can be characterized as testamentary, appellant's contentions that it can be revoked without notice and that it was impliedly revoked by the settlor's subsequent divorce and remarriage must fail. Appellant cites no authority for the proposition that a revocable life insurance trust is testamentary, even when the trust instrument is executed contemporaneously with a will. Thus, if the trust was *inter vivos*, much of the force of appellant's argument is lost.

In Minnesota, as in the overwhelming majority of jurisdictions, * * * a revocable life insurance trust is not testamentary, even though the settlor reserves the right to revoke or otherwise change it. In re Estate of Soper, 196 Minn. 60, 65, 264 N.W. 427, 430 (1935).

The only argument which appellant raises is that the trust would have no funds and would thus not operate or take effect until the death of the testator and is thus similar to other testamentary dispositions. She does not address the authorities or case law and advances no reasons for this court to change well settled trust law. Further, the appellant notes that Minn.St. 525.223, the Uniform Testamentary Additions to Trusts Act, appears to treat such trusts as non-testamentary. This statute allows the creation of "pour over" trusts and allows certain estate assets to be put into trusts which might otherwise fail because of lack of testamentary formalities. Thus, the trust was in force and there was a trustee appointed and acting at the time the new will of Mr. Aughenbaugh was executed in October, 1973.

* * *

It is the general rule that where a settlor reserves the power to revoke a trust by a transaction *inter vivos*, as for example by notice to the trustee, he cannot revoke the trust by his will. Restatement, Trusts (2d) § 330, comment j; Bogert, Trusts and Trustees, § 1001 (2 ed.); IV Scott on Trusts, § 330.8 (3 ed.). * * * The trust involved in the present case includes the following clause:

> 3.1) *Reservations Affecting the Trust.* Donor reserves the right to amend this agreement from time to time in any and all respects; to revoke the trust hereby created, in whole or in part; and to change the identity or number (or both) of the trustee or trustees hereunder, *by written instrument executed by Donor and delivered to any trustee* (or to Donor's wife if no trustee is acting at a particular time) *during Donor's lifetime*; provided, however, that the duties and responsibilities of the Trustee shall not be substantially increased by any such amendment without its written consent. (Italics supplied.)

The trial court interpreted this clause to mean that the trust could only be revoked by written instrument as set forth above. We agree.

Although the clause is not a model of good drafting, appellant concedes that the obvious intent of the section and the requirement of written notice is to protect the trustee. But once this purpose is conceded, any claimed ambiguity in this section of the trust disappears. Maximum protection for the trustee is provided by requiring all major changes to be made by notice to the trustee. * * *

This position, taken by the trial court, appears reasonable because the trustee would wish to know of any major change in its duties; revocation or amendment of the trust would constitute as major a change as an increase or decrease in the number of trustees. The sense of the clause, taken as a whole, is that changes which do not substantially increase the duties and responsibilities of the trustee may be made unilaterally by giving written notice, but that the trustee must concur in substantial increases in its duties.

Affirmed.

TODD, J., took no part in the consideration or decision of this case.

Notes

The preceding decision involves the right of a settlor to modify or terminate a trust. Because the settlor creates the trust, power over the trust begins with the terms of creation. If the settlor establishes a method of revocation or modification, then those terms will suffice. Nonetheless, increasingly, when the trust is silent as to revocation, the courts will presume the power to revoke. *See, e.g.,* UNIF. TRUST CODE § 602(a): "Unless the terms of a trust expressly provide that the trust is irrevocable, the settlor may revoke or amend the trust." This is a reversal of what traditionally occurred, but Professor Langbein thinks the point is moot since any competent drafter of any trust instrument will always include a reference to revocability or irrevocability.

One method of revoking an irrevocable trust may be to "decant" the trust. *See, e.g.,* Morse v. Kraft, 992 N.E.2d 1021 (Mass. 2013) (permitting trustees to decant trust assets). This involves permitting the trustee "to exercise distribution authority to modify the terms and conditions upon which trust property is held for its beneficiaries, including limiting or changing trust beneficiaries." Rashad Wareh & Eric Dorsch, *Decanting: A Statutory Cornucopia*, 151 TRUSTS & ESTS. 22 (Mar. 2012). *See also*, Kristin T. Abati & Renat V. Lumpau, *Decanting Without a Statute*, 153 TRUSTS & ESTS. 20 (Feb. 2014). Some states permit a trustee to decant through legislation. *See, e.g.*, N.Y. ESTS., POWERS AND TRUSTS L. § 10-6.6 (2019). Far more states permit modification or termination of an irrevocable trust only when authorized by provisions of the Uniform Trust Code. With the exception of Article 6, which permits settlors with capacity to revoke or modify revocable trusts, Article 4 addresses the termination or modification of irrevocable trusts. Please note the following:

(1) Consent of Settlor and all Beneficiaries: Section 411(a) permits modification or termination of an irrevocable trust if the settlor and all of the beneficiaries agree, even if the modification or termination is inconsistent with a material purpose of the trust.

(2) Consent of all Beneficiaries: Section 411(b) permits modification or termination of an irrevocable trust if the material purpose of the trust has been accomplished. "Material purposes are not readily to be inferred. A finding of such a purpose generally requires some showing of a particular concern or objective on the part of the settlor, such as concern with regard to the beneficiary's management skills, judgment, or level of maturity." RESTATEMENT (THIRD) OF TRUSTS § 65 cmt. d (Tentative Draft No. 3, approved 2001).

(3) Unanticipated Circumstances: Section 412 permits modification or termination because of circumstances not anticipated by the settlor and when modification or termination will further the purposes of the trust. "To the extent practicable, the modification must be made in accordance with the settlor's probable intention." The section suggests modification if the existing trust would be impractical, wasteful, or impair the trust's administration.

(4) Cy Pres: Section 413 specifies that if a trust is charitable—defined under Section 405(a)—a court may modify the trust under a court's cy pres power if the charitable purpose becomes unlawful, impracticable, impossible to achieve, or wasteful. A court's cy pres power is available unless there is an alternate provision in the trust specifying that the trust property is to revert to the settlor and the settlor is still living, or if fewer than 21 years have elapsed since the date of the trust's creation.

(5) Uneconomic Trust: Section 414 specifies that, upon notifying the qualified beneficiaries, a trustee may terminate a trust whenever the trust property has a total value of less than $50,000 and the trustee concludes that the value of the trust property is insufficient to justify the cost of administration. Upon termination of the trust, the trustee shall distribute the trust property in a manner consistent with the purposes of the trust.

(6) Correcting Mistakes: Section 415 permits a trustee to reform the terms of a trust, even if unambiguous, to conform to the settlor's true intention, if this intention may be established by clear and convincing evidence.

(7) Taxation Objectives: Section 416 permits a court to modify the terms of a trust in a manner that is not contrary to the settlor's probably intent, to encompass modifications having a retroactive effect.

B. Beneficiaries

Adams v. Link

Supreme Court of Errors of Connecticut, 1958
145 Conn. 634, 145 A.2d 753

KING, Associate Justice.

The defendants Link and the United States Trust Company of New York are the executors and trustees under the will and codicil of Mildred A. Kingsmill, late of Darien. Mrs. Kingsmill left, as her sole heirs at law, two brothers, Orson Adams, Jr., and Alvin P. Adams, and a sister, Ethel A. Martin. This action grows out of, although it is distinct from, an appeal by Orson Adams, Jr., and Alvin P. Adams, two of the three heirs at law, from the admission of the will and codicil to probate.

In the view which we take of the case, only the right to terminate the trust created in paragraph sixth of the will need be considered. This paragraph disposed of the residue by a trust. It provided for the payment of the net income for life, in monthly or quarterly instalments at their written election, to Joan K. Pringle and Mayes M. Foeppel, neither of whom was an heir at law. At the death of the survivor, the trust was to terminate and distribution of the corpus was to be made to the New York Association for the Blind. In fact, Joan K. Pringle, predeceased the testatrix, leaving Mayes M. Foeppel as the sole income beneficiary and entitled, under the terms of the trust, to the entire net income for life.

During the pendency of the appeal from probate, a so-called compromise agreement was entered into between Mayes M. Foeppel, party of the first part, the New York Association for the Blind, party of the second part, and the three heirs at law of the testatrix, parties of the third part. The agreement in effect provided that (1) the appeal from the admission of the will and codicil to probate would be withdrawn; (2) 15 per cent of the residuary estate, i.e. the trust corpus, would be paid outright to the three heirs at law in equal shares; (3) 37 per cent would be paid outright to the New York Association for the Blind; and (4) 48 per cent would be paid outright to Mayes M. Foeppel less a deduction of $15,000 which would be used to establish a new trust, the precise terms of which are not material. Basically, it was for the education of a son of Alvin P. Adams, and upon completion of his education the trust would terminate and any unused corpus and interest would be returned to Mayes M. Foeppel. The compromise agreement was by its express terms made subject to the approval of the Superior Court. The defendant executors and trustees refused to participate in the agreement or to carry it out. The present action, the plaintiffs in which include all parties to the agreement except the New York Association for the Blind, which was made a party defendant, seeks in effect (a) the approval of the agreement by the Superior Court, and (b) a decree compelling the defendant executors and trustees to carry it out. Since the provision for the New York Association for the Blind was a charitable gift, the attorney general was made a defendant to represent the public interest, under the provisions of § 212 of the General Statutes. The court refused to approve the agreement, and from this action the plaintiffs took this appeal.

While the parties have extensively argued and briefed a number of questions, one basic proposition is dispositive of, and fatal to, the position taken by the plaintiffs. No corrections of the finding which could benefit them in this view of the case can be made.

The fundamental effect of the compromise agreement, if approved by the court, would be to abolish the trust. Our rule as to the right of the beneficiaries of a testamentary trust to have it terminated has been set forth in a number of cases, including Ackerman v. Union & New Haven Trust Co., 90 Conn. 63, 71, 96 A. 149; De Ladson v. Crawford, 93 Conn. 402, 411, 106 A. 326, and Hills v. Travelers Bank & Trust Co., 125 Conn. 640, 648, 7 A.2d 652, 173 A.L.R. 1419. The rule has also in effect been applied to the right of the beneficiaries to terminate an inter-vivos trust. Gaess v. Gaess, 132 Conn. 96, 101, 42 A.2d 796, 160 A.L.R. 432. Here a testatrix, in her will, established a trust in admittedly clear and unambiguous language; she has now died; and the trust beneficiaries and the heirs at law have joined in a plan to set aside the trust and substitute a distribution of the testatrix' estate more to their liking. Such a testamentary trust may be terminated only by a decree of a court of equity, regardless of any stipulation by all parties in interest. Peiter v. Degenring, 136 Conn. 331, 336, 71 A.2d 87. Our rule as set forth in Hills v. Travelers Bank & Trust Co., *supra*, is: Conditions precedent which should concur in order to warrant termination of a testamentary trust by judicial decree are (1) that all the parties in interest unite in seeking the termination, (2) that every reasonable ultimate purpose of the trust's creation and existence has been accomplished, and (3) that no fair and lawful restriction imposed by the testator will be nullified or disturbed by such a result. 'The function of the court [of equity] with reference to trusts is not to remake the trust instrument, reduce or increase the size of the gifts made therein or accord the beneficiary more advantage than the donor directed that he should enjoy, but rather to ascertain what the donor directed that the donee should receive and to secure to him the enjoyment of that interest only.' Hills v. Travelers Bank & Trust Co., *supra* [125 Conn. 640, 7 A.2d 655]; Peiter v. Degenring, *supra*. The underlying rationale of our rule is the protection, if reasonably possible, of any reasonable, properly expressed, testamentary desire of a decedent. 3 Scott, Trusts (2d Ed.) § 337.

It appears that all the interested beneficiaries have joined in the agreement under consideration. For the purposes of this case only, we will assume, without in any way deciding, that the plaintiffs are correct in their claim that the defendant executors and trustees have no standing to attack the compromise. This assumption is permissible because the compromise was in terms made contingent upon court approval, and this approval could not be compelled by any agreement of the trust beneficiaries among themselves. Peiter v. Degenring, *supra*. This we may assume, without deciding, that he first condition precedent under our rule is satisfied. But see Loring, A Trustee's Handbook (5th Ed.) § 122 p. 316, § 123 p. 318. The second and third conditions precedent have not, however, been satisfied. The obvious objectives of the testatrix were to provide (a) an assured income for life for Mayes M. Foeppel, and (b) at her death an intact corpus for the New York Association for the Blind. In carrying out these objectives, the testatrix took two important steps. In the first place, the management of the trust corpus was committed to trustees selected by her and in whose financial judgment she is presumed to have had confidence. Secondly, expenditure of any principal by the life beneficiary was precluded. Taken together, these two steps would tend to achieve, and in all reasonable probability would achieve, the testatrix' two basic objectives. To abolish the trust and turn over a fraction of the corpus outright to the life beneficiary would be to enable her in a moment to lose the protection of the practically assured life income provided by the testatrix. The two basic objectives of the trust's creation and existence were reasonable and commendable and cannot be fully accomplished prior to the death of the life beneficiary. Peiter v. Degenring, *supra*, 136 Conn. 337, 71 A.2d 90; 3 Scott, op. cit., § 337.1, p. 2454. Obviously, had the testatrix intended to entrust the life beneficiary with the handling of any part of the corpus, she would have so provided by a simple, outright gift.

The plaintiffs attempt to avoid the impact of our rule by two main claims. The first is that since the protection accorded the life beneficiary could be lost by her voluntary alienation of the income or by its involuntary alienation through attachment or seizure under an order in equity, the testatrix could not have intended to protect the beneficiary. This amounts in effect to a claim that only a spendthrift trust is protected from termination by agreement of all interested beneficiaries. The case against termination under our rule is of course even stronger where a spendthrift trust is involved, as in Mason v. Rhode Island Hospital Trust Co., 78 Conn. 81, 84, 61 A. 57. 3 Scott, op. cit., § 337.2. But the operation of our rule is not restricted to such trusts. The mere fact that the testatrix failed to provide the maximum possible protection for the life beneficiary by creating a spendthrift trust under the terms of what is now § 3195d of the 1955 Cumulative Supplement[1] does not warrant a conclusion that she intended no protection at all, so that we can consider that the trust no longer has any purpose. *Id.*, p. 2454.

---

1. Sec. 3195d provides a procedure for the attachment of such an unrestricted life estate as was here created, but further provides:

> When any such trust shall have been expressly provided to be for the support of the beneficiary or his family, a court of equity having jurisdiction may make such order regarding the surplus, if any, not required for the support of the beneficiary or his family, as justice and equity may require.

There is no merit in the plaintiffs' claim that in Peiter v. Degenring, *supra*, there was a change in, or a relaxation of, our rule. The facts in that case were peculiar. The testator's brother was seventy-eight years old and under a conservator. The testator created a trust for the payment to the brother or his conservator of 'so much of the income and principal of my estate as may be necessary for his support and comfort, using the income first.' In other words, the beneficiary was given neither principal nor income except as necessary for his support and comfort. The parties stipulated that the brother owned personal estate the annual income of which was greatly in excess of his needs for comfort and support, that he had not been entitled to receive and had not received any money from the trust, and that there was no possibility that he would be entitled to received any money from it at any time. The proposal of all interested parties was that the trust be terminated upon the payment to the brother of $10,000, which of course would be under the management of the conservator. We held that a decree terminating the trust could not be granted on any stipulation of the parties but only, if at all, upon the basis of facts found by testimony offered before the court, and that the trust should not be terminated 'unless those facts clearly establish that no purpose it was designed to serve would be defeated or jeopardized.' *Id.*, 136 Conn. 340, 71 A.2d 91. There is nothing in the decision inconsistent with our rule as set forth in the other cases cited by us. The Peiter case does hold that evidence may be offered of facts, not apparent from the provisions of the trust instrument itself, which, if proved, would warrant a conclusion that the trust does not serve a legal and useful purpose and should be terminated. *Ibid.* We also held in the Peiter case that if satisfactory proof was made of the peculiar facts therein, it might warrant a conclusion by the court that in all reasonable probability the trust would remain inactive during the beneficiary's life and, if so, a termination might be ordered, as in the case of any useless trust. The Peiter case in nowise helps the plaintiffs here. * * *

Here the provisions of the will itself are being drastically changed so as to abolish a trust contrary to our rule. This cannot be done. It follows that the court below was not in error in denying approval of the agreement. Indeed, it was the only decision which could properly have been made. This conclusion makes unnecessary the consideration of the other grounds of appeal.

There is no error.

In this opinion the other judges concurred.

Notes

Because the settlor was unavailable to provide consent to the modification of the terms of the trust, the court was required to enforce the terms as mandated by the settlor. The result was harsh—mandated by the rules of the times, the material purpose rule of the court in Claflin v. Claflin, 149 Mass. 19, 20 N.E. 454 (1889). But with the advent of the Uniform Trust Code, many states have relaxed their stringent reliance on the *Claflin* doctrine and now allow for modification, even if the settlor is not available to consent to the modification. Thus, under the facts of the *Adams* decision, today, the court would likely have allowed modification based on a change in "circumstances not anticipated by the settlor," and the fact that the change will "further the purposes of the trust." Unif. Trust Code § 412(a). Likewise, and more in accord with the theory of *Claflin*, all of the beneficiaries of the trust may modify or terminate a trust if "the court concludes that continuance of the trust is not necessary to achieve any material purpose of the trust." *Id.* at § 411(b). While a spendthrift clause is not a material purpose for purposes of termination, *id.* at § 411(c), the question of what is material to the trust is still a subject of litigation and a significant hurdle to overcome. *See Restatement (Third) of Trusts* § 65(2) (2019) (using the term "material purpose," but allowing for reasons to outweigh it).

Problem

In her Last Will and Testament, the decedent created a testamentary trust giving a life estate, first, to her oldest child, and then continuing throughout each of the lives of her remaining children. Following the death of her last child, the life estates would then progress through the lives of her grandchildren. The corpus of the trust consisted of two parcels of land and was to terminate at the death of her last grandchild, when the property was to be distributed to her great-grandchildren. The trust was performed for a number of years but then the last remaining child of the decedent petitioned the court to terminate the trust and have the property transferred to him. He argues that the decedent's intent was primarily to benefit her children and, since he is the last survivor, he should be the beneficiary. He concludes that the decedent would have intended the property to pass to the person with whom she enjoyed the closets relationship—her only surviving child.

The grandchildren and the great-grandchildren agree that the trust should be terminated because of expenses and unwarranted maintenance, but they seek to have the property transferred to the great-grandchildren. Their petition to terminate is based on their assertion that the decedent's purpose can no longer be fulfilled because the corpus is expensive to maintain and the costs far exceed any income produced. Therefore, the probate court is confronted with whether the trust should be terminated in accordance with statutory law and, if so, to whom the corpus should be distributed. How would you rule? *See In re* Testamentary Trust Established by Last Will and Testament of Northcraft, 2017 WL 943248 (Pa. Super. Ct. 2017).

C. Trustee

McNeil v. McNeil

Supreme Court of Delaware, 2002
798 A.2d 503

WALSH, Justice.

This is an appeal from a decision of the Court of Chancery which determined that the trustees of a large *inter vivos* trust had breached their fiduciary duties by ignoring the interests of a beneficiary. By way of a remedy, the court ordered a make-up distribution to the petitioner, surcharged the trustees, and removed certain of the trustees. The court rejected the beneficiary's request to further divide the trust and prevent the adoption of a unitrust formula. Upon full review of the record, we conclude that the Vice Chancellor properly exercised his discretion under applicable trust law in granting relief to the beneficiary, except with respect to the replacement of a trustee. As to that latter ruling, we conclude that the trust instrument, in the first instance, controlled the process for replacement. Accordingly, we affirm in part and reverse in part. * * *

The decision of the Court of Chancery is contained in a seventy-four page opinion detailing the court's factual findings and legal conclusions following a six day trial. * * * Because the parties do not dispute the factual findings of the Vice Chancellor, we recite only those facts necessary for an understanding of the contentions of the parties.

The trust in dispute was one of five trusts established by Henry Slack McNeil, Sr. ("McNeil, Sr.") in 1959 from the proceeds of the sale of a pharmaceutical company owned by him to Johnson and Johnson. Four of the trusts, referred to as the "Sibling Trusts," were designated for the benefit of McNeil, Sr.'s four children: Henry, Jr. ("Hank"), Barbara, Marjorie, and Robert. The fifth trust, established by McNeil, Sr. for his wife, Lois, came to be known as the Lois Trust. Each of the separate children's trusts was intended to accommodate the needs of the respective beneficiary with authorization to the trustees to afford each the means to live an affluent lifestyle. The children were quite young at the time of the creation of the trusts, ranging in age from eight to fifteen. It was not until some years later that the trustees of the Sibling Trusts were called upon to provide the children an independent source of income.

Although the children were under the impression, an impression apparently fostered by their father, that their interests in the Lois Trust were that of remaindermen, the terms of the trust provided otherwise. The trust instrument gave its trustees considerable discretion to "distribute any part or all of the income and principal of the trust to or among my lineal descendants and their spouses, and Lois." Thus, all of McNeil, Sr.'s children, and their descendants, were not remaindermen but current beneficiaries. It was the lack of such knowledge and its unequal dissemination that is at the root of the litigation between Hank and the trustees, with Hank's siblings ("The Other Siblings") also joined as defendants.

The original trustees of the Lois Trust included three individuals, George Brodhead, Robert C. Fernley, and Henry W. Gadsden, as general trustees, and Wilmington Trust Company as the administrative trustee. Later, Gadsden and Fernley were replaced by Charles E. Mather, III, a close friend of McNeil, Sr., and Provident National Bank ("PNC"). There is little question that Brodhead, a close friend and attorney for McNeil, Sr., was the dominant trustee, to whom the other trustees, and all the siblings, deferred. There is also no doubt, however, that all trustees, including the administrative trustees, were aware that the McNeil siblings enjoyed the status of current beneficiaries of the Lois Trust.

At some point, Hank became estranged from his parents and his siblings. A direct result of this estrangement was that Hank received nothing under his father's will and, upon the later death of his mother, only two million dollars, a paltry sum in comparison to that received by his siblings. Hank was not without substantial wealth, however, since his own trust responded to many, but not all, of his requests for distribution. Eventually, Hank sued the trustees of his trust, who were essentially the same as the trustees of the Lois Trust, seeking a greater distribution. The trustees requested Hank's own children, Cameron and Justin, take a position on Hank's petition because, under a mirror image provision of the Lois Trust, Hank's children were also current beneficiaries. Thus, it could be argued that Hank's request for additional distributions was adverse to all of his living descendants. Prior to the trustees' notification, Cameron and Justin had been unaware of their status. The question of Hank's right to distribution under his trust, *vis-a-vis* the entitlement of his children to share a current distribution, ultimately resulted in separate litigation in the Court of Chancery. * * *

Claiming to have been misled, if not deceived, by the trustees of the Lois Trust concerning his current beneficiary status, Hank filed a complaint in the Court of Chancery seeking, *inter alia*, a make-up distribution from the trust, removal of and a surcharge against the trustees, and a restructuring of the trust operation. In addition to the trustees, other interested parties joined, or were joined, in the litigation, including Hank's siblings, Cameron and Justin, and a guardian *ad litem* representing the unborn beneficiaries of the Lois Trust. * * *

The Vice Chancellor ultimately concluded that Hank's "outsider" status, which began during his father's lifetime, was continued by the trustees of the Lois Trust. By contrast, however, The Other Siblings not only benefitted directly from their parents' estates, but were made privy to many aspects of the operation of all five trusts and, through their participation in a family holding company, Claneil Industries, were never "outside the loop." The Vice Chancellor further concluded that not only did the trustees rebuff Hank's efforts to learn the specifics of the Lois Trust, they acquiesced in Lois' wish, expressed strongly during her lifetime, not to invade principal. That principal consisted primarily of Johnson and Johnson stock and had appreciated substantially in value over the life of the trust. * * * The Other Siblings were content with Lois' direction to permit principal to grow but the matter came to a head upon Lois' death in 1998, when the trustees proposed to make distribution of the Lois Trust in four equal divisions. The trustees also sought to adopt a "unitrust" approach for distribution under which the beneficiaries would receive a percentage of the total value of the trust, both principal and income, each year.

After trial, the Vice Chancellor determined that the trustees had breached their fiduciary duties by failing to inform Hank of his current beneficiary status in a timely fashion, showing partiality to the other siblings, and allowing the trust to operate "on autopilot." Since the trustees had considerable distribution discretion, the court recognized that it was somewhat "speculative" to fashion a remedy for the failure of the trustees to respond to requests never made, particularly given Lois' strongly expressed desire to maintain the trust corpus. Nevertheless, the court concluded that any uncertainty with respect to the appropriateness of the remedy should be resolved against the trustees, who failed to fulfill their obligation to consider the interests of different generations of the McNeil Family. A make-up distribution equal to 7.5 percent of the value of Hank's resulting trust was ordered to be shared by Hank with Cameron and Justin under the unitrust formula.

The Vice Chancellor also determined that the trustees' failure to discharge their fiduciary duties warranted some penalty. In particular, he faulted the institutional trustees, PNC and Wilmington Trust, who "failed to bring their professional expertise to bear in assisting lay trustees." PNC was removed as a trustee and all Lois Trustees were surcharged one-fifth of commissions received for the years 1987 to 1996. The Vice Chancellor declined to remove certain other individual trustees but appointed Edward L. Bishop, one of Hank's trustees, as a replacement trustee for PNC for the resulting trusts. * * *

The individual and corporate trustees of the Lois Trust, John C. Bennett, Jr., Charles E. Mather, III, PNC Bank, N.A. and Wilmington Trust Company (the "Lois Trustees") have appealed from that portion of the Vice Chancellor's decision imposing a surcharge on their trustees' commission and removing PNC as a trustee. While accepting the Vice Chancellor's factual findings, they nonetheless argue that those findings do not permit the conclusion that any breach of fiduciary duty owed to Hank occurred. They point to the language of the trust instrument, which confers on the trustees extraordinarily broad authority to manage the trusts, as indicative of McNeil, Sr.'s intention to protect the trustees from personal liability and "judicial second-guessing." The conduct of the Lois Trustees, it is contended, must be reviewed over the span of forty years, during which time they deferred to the wishes of McNeil, Sr. and his wife, and, as a consequence, the trust prospered and all beneficiaries, including Hank, ultimately benefitted. * * *

The Lois Trustees rely upon the express terms of the trust instrument as defining their duties. Three provisions of the Lois Trust appear to bear on this issue. Article II(a) gives the trustees wide discretion to distribute income or principal to any, all, or none of the beneficiaries as they see fit. Statements of this type are generally viewed as a definition of the trustees' powers, not as exculpatory of the liability of a trustee. See George Gleason Bogert, The Law of Trusts and Trustees, § 542 (1993) ("The grant of absolute or uncontrolled discretion to the trustee in the administration of the trust, without an exculpatory clause, may not relieve the trustee of liability for imprudent exercises of his powers . . ."). Further, Article III(e) of the Lois Trust specifies, "Decisions by the committee [of trustees] . . . [are] not subject to review by any court." Courts, however, flatly refuse to enforce provisions relieving a trustee of all liability. Id. (noting that exculpatory clauses that "provide[ ] that the trustee is not to be accountable to anyone . . . [are] not upheld"). A trust in which there is no legally binding obligation on a trustee is a trust in name only and more in the nature of an absolute estate or fee simple grant of property.

Finally, Article IV(c) states, "Any action taken by the trustees in good faith shall be proper, and I relieve the trustees of all personal liability except for gross negligence or willful wrongdoing." Generally, a trustee must act as the reasonable and prudent person in managing the trust. * * * Courts often permit the settlor of a trust to exculpate a trustee for failure to exercise due care, however, so long as such conduct does not rise to the level of gross negligence. * * *

A reasonable construction of these provisions, read together, is that the Lois Trustees were exculpated for ordinary negligence, but not the duty to (i) inform beneficiaries or (ii) treat them impartially. The duties to furnish information and to act impartially are not subspecies of the duty of care, but separate duties. See Restatement (Second) of Trusts §§ 173, 174, and 183 (1959) (devoting separate sections to a trustee's duty of care, duty to furnish information, and duty to act impartially). Whatever may have been McNeil, Sr.'s intention in this regard, he did not expressly relieve the trustees of the duties which formed the basis for Hank's petition in the Court of Chancery.

There is ample record support for the Vice Chancellor's conclusion that the Lois Trustees violated their duty to provide information. It may be the case that McNeil, Sr. and Lois did not favor treating their offspring as current beneficiaries of the Lois Trust, and that it was defensible for some of the trustees who served later on to assume that notification had already been accomplished. Nevertheless, both PNC and Wilmington Trust, institutional trustees with policies of notification, should have known better. Moreover, Henry's repeated attempts to get information should have put the trustees on notice that he did not know he was a current beneficiary. A trustee has a duty to furnish information to a beneficiary upon reasonable request. Furthermore, even in the absence of a request for information, a trustee must communicate essential facts, such as the existence of the basic terms of the trust. That a person is a current beneficiary of a trust is indeed an essential fact.

The Lois Trustees, and Brodhead in particular, denied important information to Hank even after he made a reasonable request for information. PNC's representative rebuffed a similar request, and Wilmington Trust's representative even misled Henry by telling him he was a remainderman in the Lois Trust. The trustees each had a vested interest in the way they had been doing business, and giving Hank information would have forced them to re-examine that method. Although Brodhead obviously dominated the trustees and controlled their approach to Hank, each trustee was charged with an independent fiduciary obligation which did not permit them to defer to Brodhead's exclusionary views.

At the same time they were excluding Hank from knowledge of the terms of the trust and its operating results, the Lois Trustees shared that information with The Other Siblings, albeit in an indirect fashion through their participation in Claneil. This partiality precluded Hank from making distribution demands under circumstances not shared by his siblings. The trustees' claim that they distributed tens of millions of dollars to Hank from his own trust is no defense to their blatant failure to inform him of his current beneficiary status in the Lois Trust. As the Vice Chancellor noted, Hank "was at an obvious informational disadvantage to his Siblings with regard to the Lois Trust." The record amply supports the Vice Chancellor's conclusion that the Lois Trustees failed to discharge the fiduciary duties owed to all beneficiaries of the trust. Accordingly, we affirm that ruling. * * *

In sum, we affirm all rulings of the Court of Chancery which are the subject of the appeals and cross-appeals in this matter save one: the replacement of PNC with Bishop. As to that ruling, we reverse and remand to the Court of Chancery for further proceedings consistent with this opinion.

Notes

Any trustee holds legal title to the trust corpus and is obligated to "administer the trust in good faith, in accordance with its terms and purposes and the interests of the beneficiaries." UNIF. TRUST CODE § 801. Absent express terms of the trust or authorization by the court, the ability of a trustee to modify or terminate a trust is limited to fiduciary duties, specifically proper investment, management, and distribution of the trust property. *Id.* at § 815.

The *McNeil* decision illustrates how a trustee may breach its fiduciary obligations to report, be impartial among all of the beneficiaries, and distribute trust property in accordance with trust terms. The decision illustrates the limitations upon a trustee—that it cannot modify or terminate the written terms of the trust instrument without court authorization or in furtherance of fiduciary duty. However, note that the trustees had wide discretion to distribute income or principal to any, all, or none of the beneficiaries. This discretion must be exercised impartially and with a duty of loyalty to the beneficiaries. Loyalty is defined as the obligation of the trustee not to place his or her own interests over those of the beneficiaries. *Restatement (Second) of Trusts* § 170(1) (1959); UNIF. TRUST CODE § 802(a).

Whenever a trustee is given discretionary power to distribute the trust corpus, if the state permits, the trustee has an option to decant the trust corpus to a new trust, presumptively with terms more conducive to what the trustee considers to be the settlor's intent. There are limitations placed upon the trustee, specifically that in "exercising the decanting power, an authorized fiduciary shall act in accordance with its fiduciary duties, including the duty to act in accordance with the purposes of the first trust." UNIF. TRUST DECANTING ACT § 4. *See generally* Stephanie Vara, *Two Cheers for Decanting: A Partial Defense of Decanting Statutes as a Tool for Implementing Freedom of Disposition*, 32 QUINNIPIAC PROB. L.J. 23 (2018) (analyzing various decanting statutes). As to the ability of a beneficiary to remove a trustee, see the following provisions from the Uniform Trust Code and the Restatement.

Uniform Trust Code (2019)

§ 706. Removal of Trustee.

(a) The settlor, a cotrustee, or a beneficiary may request the court to remove a trustee, or a trustee may be removed by the court on its own initiative.

(b) The court may remove a trustee if:

    (1) the trustee has committed a serious breach of trust;

    (2) lack of cooperation among cotrustees substantially impairs the administration of the trust;

(3) because of unfitness, unwillingness, or persistent failure of the trustee to administer the trust effectively, the court determines that removal of the trustee best serves the interests of the beneficiaries; or

(4) there has been a substantial change of circumstances or removal is requested by all of the qualified beneficiaries, the court finds that removal of the trustee best serves the interests of all of the beneficiaries and is not inconsistent with a material purpose of the trust, and a suitable cotrustee or successor trustee is available.

(c) Pending a final decision on a request to remove a trustee, or in lieu of or in addition to removing a trustee, the court may order such appropriate relief under Section 1001(b) as may be necessary to protect the trust property or the interests of the beneficiaries.

§ 603. Settlor's Powers; Powers of Withdrawal.

(a) While a trust is revocable and the settlor has capacity to revoke the trust, rights of the beneficiaries are subject to the control of, and the duties of the trustee are owed exclusively to, the settlor.

(b) During the period the power may be exercised, the holder of a power of withdrawal has the rights of a settlor of a revocable trust under this section to the extent of the property subject to the power.

Restatement (Third) of Trusts (2019)

§ 37. cmt e(1) [Removal Of Trustee].

Friction between trustee and beneficiaries. Friction between the trustee and some of the beneficiaries is not a sufficient ground for removing the trustee unless it interferes with the proper administration of the trust. Beneficiaries may be resentful when property they expected to inherit is placed in trust, or of reasonable exercise of a trustee's discretion with regard to matters of administration or the alleged underperformance of the trustee's investment program. Such resentment ordinarily does not warrant removal of the trustee; but a serious breakdown in communications between beneficiaries and a trustee may justify removal, particularly if the trustee is responsible for the breakdown or it appears to be incurable.

Serious friction between co-trustees may also warrant removal of one or both of them.

§ 37. cmt f [Removal Of Trustee].

Trustee named by settlor. The court will less readily remove a trustee named by the settlor than one appointed by a court. Courts may also show some but a lesser degree of deference with regard to a trustee appointed by beneficiaries or others pursuant to the terms of a trust. Such deference, however, may no longer be justified if, after being designated, a corporate trustee undergoes a significant structural change, such as by merger, or any trustee significantly reduces the level or quality of service to the trust or its beneficiaries.

If the trustee named by the settlor is unfit to act as trustee—for example, is under an incapacity, or is shown to be dishonest or entirely lacking the qualifications necessary for proper administration of the trust—a court will remove or refuse to confirm the trustee. Compare § 29, Comment m.

Ordinarily, a court will not remove a trustee named by the settlor upon a ground that was known to the settlor at the time the trustee was designated, even though a court would not itself have appointed that person as trustee. In cases of unfitness to serve (*supra*), however, a court may remove a trustee even upon a ground known to the settlor at the time of designation.

Problem

When decedent died in 1998, he left a valid last Will and Testament that contained a valid trust for the support and education of his nieces, and then, at their death, the corpus was to be distributed to their heirs in equal shares. The decedent named a bank as trustee, but the beneficiaries grew dissatisfied with the income generated from the trust and the desire of the beneficiaries to terminate the trust. Eventually, the beneficiaries petitioned the court for the removal of the trustee and for the husband of one of the beneficiaries to be appointed as a replacement. The beneficiaries alleged that the removal of the Bank served the interests of all the beneficiaries, that it was not inconsistent with a material purpose of the trust, and that a suitable successor trustee was available. In addition, they asserted that they had completed their educational goals that the trust administration fees had exceeded trust income in recent years, and that their suggested replacement was available to serve as successor trustee free of charge. The bank/trustee refused to resign voluntarily, arguing that to replace it as trustee would violate the state statutes that are identical to the Uniform Trust Code and the Restatement. If you were the probate judge, how would you rule on the petition submitted by the beneficiaries? *See In re* Trust Created for Fenske, 303 Neb. 430, 930 N.W.2d 43 (2019).

IV. Prudent Administration of Trusts

A. Defining Prudence

In re Estate of Janes

Court of Appeals of New York, 1997
90 N.Y.2d 41, 681 N.E.2d 332, 659 N.Y.S.2d 165

LEVINE, Judge.

Former State Senator and businessman Rodney B. Janes (testator) died on May 26, 1973, survived solely by his wife, Cynthia W. Janes, who was then 72 years of age. Testator's $3,500,000 estate consisted of a $2,500,000 stock portfolio, approximately 71% of which consisted of 13,232 shares of common stock of the Eastman Kodak

Company. The Kodak stock had a date-of-death value of $1,786,733, or approximately $135 per share.

Testator's 1963 will and a 1969 codicil bequeathed most of his estate to three trusts. First, the testator created a marital deduction trust consisting of approximately 50% of the estate's assets, the income of which was to be paid to Mrs. Janes for her life. In addition, it contained a generous provision for invasion of the principal for Mrs. Janes's benefit and gave her testamentary power of appointment over the remaining principal. The testator also established a charitable trust of approximately 25% of the estate's assets which directed annual distributions to selected charities. A third trust comprised the balance of the estate's assets and directed that the income therefrom be paid to Mrs. Janes for her life, with the remainder pouring over into the charitable trust upon her death.

On June 6, 1973, the testator's will and codicil were admitted to probate. Letters testamentary issued to petitioner's predecessor, Lincoln Rochester Trust Company, and Mrs. Janes, as coexecutors, on July 3, 1973. Letters of trusteeship issued to petitioner alone. By early August 1973, petitioner's trust and estate officers, Ellison Patterson and Richard Young had ascertained the estate's assets and the amount of cash needed for taxes, commissions, attorneys' fees, and specific bequests.

In an August 9, 1973 memorandum, Patterson recommended raising the necessary cash for the foregoing administrative expenses by selling certain assets, including 800 shares of Kodak stock, and holding "the remaining issues * * * until the [t]rusts [were] funded." The memorandum did not otherwise address investment strategy in light of the evident primary objective of the testator to provide for his widow during her lifetime. In a September 5, 1973 meeting with Patterson and Young, Mrs. Janes, who had a high school education, no business training or experience, and who had never been employed, consented to the sale of some 1,200 additional shares of Kodak stock. Although Mrs. Janes was informed at the meeting that petitioner intended to retain the balance of the Kodak shares, none of the factors that would lead to an informed investment decision was discussed. At that time, the Kodak stock traded for about $139 per share; thus, the estate's 13,232 shares of the stock were worth almost $1,840,000. The September 5 meeting was the only occasion where retention of the Kodak stock or any other investment issues were taken up with Mrs. Janes.

By the end of 1973, the price of Kodak stock had fallen to about $109 per share. One year later, it had fallen to about $63 per share and, by the end of 1977, to about $51 per share. In March 1978, the price had dropped even further, to about $40 per share. When petitioner filed its initial accounting in February 1980, the remaining 11,320 shares were worth approximately $530,000, or about $47 per share. Most of the shares were used to fund the trusts in 1986 and 1987.

In addition to its initial accounting in 1980, petitioner filed a series of supplemental accountings that together covered the period from July 1973 through June 1994. In August 1981, petitioner sought judicial settlement of its account. Objections to the accounts were originally filed by Mrs. Janes in 1982, and subsequently by the

Attorney-General on behalf of the charitable beneficiaries (collectively, "object-ants"). In seeking to surcharge petitioner for losses incurred by the estate due to petitioner's imprudent retention of a high concentration of Kodak stock in the estate from July 1973 to February 1980, during which time the value of the stock had dropped to about one third of its date-of-death value, objectants asserted that peti-tioner's conduct violated EPTL 11-2.2(a)(1), the so-called "prudent person rule" of investment. When Mrs. Janes died in 1986, the personal representative of her estate was substituted as an objectant.

Following a trial on the objections, the Surrogate found that petitioner, under the circumstances, had acted imprudently and should have divested the estate of the high concentration of Kodak stock by August 9, 1973. The court imposed a $6,080,269 surcharge against petitioner and ordered petitioner to forfeit its com-missions and attorneys' fees. In calculating the amount of the surcharge, the court adopted a "lost profits" or "market index" measure of damages espoused by object-ants' expert—what the proceeds of the Kodak stock would have yielded, up to the time of trial, had they been invested in petitioner's own diversified equity fund on August 9, 1973. * * *

No precise formula exists for determining whether the prudent person standard has been violated in a particular situation; rather, the determination depends on an examination of the facts and circumstances of each case (see, Purdy v. Lynch, 145 N.Y. 462, 475, 40 N.E. 232; see also, Matter of Hahn, 62 N.Y.2d 821, 824, 477 N.Y.S.2d 604, 466 N.E.2d 144). In undertaking this inquiry, the court should engage in " 'a balanced and perceptive analysis of [the fiduciary's] consideration and action in light of the history of each individual investment, viewed at the time of its action or its omission to act'" (Matter of Donner, 82 N.Y.2d 574, 585, 606 N.Y.S.2d 137, 626 N.E.2d 922 [quoting Matter of Bank of N.Y., 35 N.Y.2d 512, 519, 364 N.Y.S.2d 164, 323 N.E.2d 700]). And, while a court should not view each act or omission aided or enlightened by hindsight (see, Matter of Bank of N.Y., *supra*, at 519, 364 N.Y.S.2d 164, 323 N.E.2d 700; see also, Matter of Clark, 257 N.Y. 132, 136, 177 N.E. 397; Purdy v. Lynch, *supra*, at 475–476, 40 N.E. 232), a court may, nevertheless, examine the fiduciary's conduct over *the entire course of the invest-ment* in determining whether it has acted prudently (see, Matter of Donner, *supra*, at 585–586, 606 N.Y.S.2d 137, 626 N.E.2d 922). Generally, whether a fiduciary has acted prudently is a factual determination to be made by the trial court (see, *id.*; see also, Matter of Rothko, 43 N.Y.2d 305, 318, 401 N.Y.S.2d 449, 372 N.E.2d 291; Matter of Hubbell, 302 N.Y. 246, 258, 97 N.E.2d 888).

As the foregoing demonstrates, the very nature of the prudent person standard dictates against any absolute rule that a fiduciary's failure to diversify, in and of itself, constitutes imprudence, as well as against a rule invariably immunizing a fiduciary from its failure to diversify in the absence of some selective list of elements of hazard, such as those identified by petitioner. Indeed, in various cases, courts have deter-mined that a fiduciary's retention of a high concentration of one asset in a trust or estate was imprudent without reference to those elements of hazard (see, Matter of

Donner, *supra*, at 585–586, 606 N.Y.S.2d 137, 626 N.E.2d 922; see also, Matter of Curtiss, 261 App.Div. 964, 25 N.Y.S.2d 819, affd. without opn. 286 N.Y. 716, 37 N.E.2d 452; Cobb v. Gramatan Natl. Bank & Trust Co., 261 App.Div. 1086, 26 N.Y.S.2d 917). The inquiry is simply whether, under all the facts and circumstances of the particular case, the fiduciary violated the prudent person standard in maintaining a concentration of a particular stock in the estate's portfolio of investments.

Moreover, no court has stated that the limited elements of hazard outlined by petitioner are the only factors that may be considered in determining whether a fiduciary has acted prudently in maintaining a concentrated portfolio. Again, as commentators have noted, one of the primary virtues of the prudent person rule "*lies in its lack of specificity,* as this permits the propriety of the trustee's investment decisions to be measured in light of the business and economic circumstances existing at the time they were made" (Laurino, Investment Responsibility of Professional Trustees, 51 St John's L Rev 717, 723 [1977] [emphasis supplied]).

Petitioner's restrictive list of hazards omits such additional factors to be considered under the prudent person rule by a trustee in weighing the propriety of any investment decision, as: "the amount of the trust estate, the situation of the beneficiaries, the trend of prices and of the cost of living, the prospect of inflation and of deflation" (Restatement [Second] of Trusts § 227, comment e). Other pertinent factors are the marketability of the investment and possible tax consequences (id., comment o). The trustee must weigh all of these investment factors as they affect the principal objects of the testator's or settlor's bounty, as between income beneficiaries and remainder persons, including decisions regarding "whether to apportion the investments between high-yield or high-growth securities" (Turano and Radigan, New York Estate Administration ch. 14, § P, at 409 [1986]).

Moreover, and especially relevant to the instant case, the various factors affecting the prudence of any particular investment must be considered in the light of the "circumstances of the trust itself rather than [merely] the integrity of the particular investment" (9C Rohan, N.Y. Civ. Prac-EPTL ¶ 11-2.2 [5], at 11-513, n. 106 [1996]). As stated in a leading treatise:

> [t]he trustee should take into consideration the circumstances of the particular trust that he is administering, both as to the size of the trust estate and the requirements of the beneficiaries. He should consider each investment *not as an isolated transaction but in its relation to the whole of the trust estate* (3 Scott, Trusts § 227.12, at 477 [4th ed]).

* * *

Likewise, contrary to petitioner's alternative attack on the decisions below, neither the Surrogate nor the Appellate Division based their respective rulings holding petitioner liable on any absolute duty of a fiduciary to diversify. Rather, those courts determined that a surcharge was appropriate because maintaining a concentration in Kodak stock, under the circumstances presented, violated certain critical obligations of a fiduciary in making investment decisions under the prudent person rule. First, petitioner failed to consider the investment in Kodak stock in relation to the entire portfolio of the estate (see, Matter of Bank of N.Y., *supra*, at 517; 3, 364 N.Y.S.2d 164, 323 N.E.2d 700 Scott, op. cit.), i.e., whether the Kodak concentration itself created or added to investment risk. The objectants' experts testified that even high quality growth stocks, such as Kodak, possess some degree of volatility because their market value is tied so closely to earnings projections (cf., Turano and Radigan, op. cit., at 409). They further opined that the investment risk arising from that volatility is significantly exacerbated when a portfolio is heavily concentrated in one such growth stock.

Second, the evidence revealed that, in maintaining an investment portfolio in which Kodak represented 71% of the estate's stock holdings, and the balance was largely in other growth stocks, petitioner paid insufficient attention to the needs and interests of the testator's 72-year-old widow, the life beneficiary of three quarters of his estate, for whose comfort, support and anticipated increased medical expenses the testamentary trusts were evidently created. Testimony by petitioner's investment manager, and by the objectants' experts, disclosed that the annual yield on Kodak stock in 1973 was approximately 1.06%, and that the aggregate annual income from all estate stockholdings was $43,961, a scant 1.7% of the $2.5 million estate securities portfolio. Thus, retention of a high concentration of Kodak jeopardized the interests of the primary income beneficiary of the estate and led to the eventual need to substantially invade the principal of the marital testamentary trust.

Lastly, there was evidence in the record to support the findings below that, in managing the estate's investments, petitioner failed to exercise due care and the skill it held itself out as possessing as a corporate fiduciary (see, Matter of Donner, 82 N.Y.2d, at 578, 606 N.Y.S.2d 137, 626 N.E.2d 922, *supra*; Restatement [Second] of Trusts § 227, Comment on Clause [a]). Notably, there was proof that petitioner (1) failed initially to undertake a formal analysis of the estate and establish an investment plan consistent with the testator's primary objectives; (2) failed to follow petitioner's own internal trustee review protocol during the administration of the estate, which advised special caution and attention in cases of portfolio concentration of as little as 20%; and (3) failed to conduct more than routine reviews of the Kodak holdings in this estate, without considering alternative investment choices, over a seven-year period of steady decline in the value of the stock.

Since, thus, there was evidence in the record to support the foregoing affirmed findings of imprudence on the part of petitioner, the determination of liability must be affirmed (Matter of Donner, 82 N.Y.2d, at 584, 606 N.Y.S.2d 137, 626 N.E.2d 922, *supra*). * * *

As we have noted, in determining whether a fiduciary has acted prudently, a court may examine a fiduciary's conduct throughout the entire period during which the investment at issue was held (see, Matter of Donner, 82 N.Y.2d, at 585–586, 606 N.Y.S.2d 137, 626 N.E.2d 922, *supra*). The court may then determine, within that period, the "reasonable time" within which divesture of the imprudently held investment should have occurred (see, Matter of Weston, 91 N.Y. 502, 510–511). What constitutes a reasonable time will vary from case to case and is not fixed or arbitrary (see, *id.*, at 510–511). The test remains "the diligence and prudence of prudent and intelligent [persons] in the management of their own affairs" (id., at 511 [citations omitted]). Thus, in *Donner*, we upheld both the Surrogate's examination of the fiduciary's conduct throughout the entire period during which the investment at issue was retained in finding liability, and the Surrogate's selection of the date of the testator's death as the time when the trustee should have divested the estate of its substantial holdings in high-risk securities (82 N.Y.2d, at 585–586, 606 N.Y.S.2d 137, 626 N.E.2d 922, *supra*).

Again, there is evidentiary support in the record for the trial court's finding, affirmed by the Appellate Division, that a prudent fiduciary would have divested the estate's stock portfolio of its high concentration of Kodak stock by August 9, 1973, thereby exhausting our review powers on this issue. Petitioner's own internal documents and correspondence, as well as the testimony of Patterson, Young, and objectants' experts, establish that by that date, petitioner had all the information a prudent investor would have needed to conclude that the percentage of Kodak stock in the estate's stock portfolio was excessive and should have been reduced significantly, particularly in light of the estate's over-all investment portfolio and the financial requirements of Mrs. Janes and the charitable beneficiaries. * * *

In imposing liability upon a fiduciary on the basis of the capital lost, the court should determine the value of the stock on the date it should have been sold, and subtract from that figure the proceeds from the sale of the stock or, if the stock is still retained by the estate, the value of the stock at the time of the accounting (see, Matter of Garvin, *supra*, at 521, 177 N.E. 24; Matter of Frame, 245 App.Div. 675, 686, 284 N.Y.S. 153 6 Warren's Heaton, Surrogates' Courts § 100.01[4][b][i] [misnumbered in original as § 101.01[4][b][i2], at 100-9 [6th ed. rev. 1997]). Whether interest is awarded, and at what rate, is a matter within the discretion of the trial court (see, Woerz v. Schumacher, 161 N.Y. 530, 538, 56 N.E. 72, rearg. denied 163 N.Y. 610, 57 N.E. 1128; King v. Talbot, 40 N.Y., at 95, *supra*; CPLR 5001[a]; SCPA 2211[1]; 6 Warren's Heaton, op. cit.; 3 Scott, op. cit., § 207, at 255–256). Dividends and other income attributable to the retained assets should offset any interest awarded (see, Matter of Garvin, *supra*, at 521, 177 N.E. 24). * * *

Accordingly, the order of the Appellate Division should be affirmed, without costs.

KAYE, C.J., and TITONE, BELLACOSA, SMITH, CIPARICK and WESLEY, JJ., concur.

Order affirmed, without costs.

Notes

The definition of what constitutes prudence has evolved. *Janes* was decided in 1997 under the Prudent Person Rule, but eventually New York adopted another definition of prudence more in accord with the Uniform Prudent Investor Act. *See In re* HSBC Bank USA, N.A., 98 A.D.3d 300, 308, 947 N.Y.S.2d 292, 299 (2012). For a discussion of what constitutes prudence in modern investment accounts, see Ian Ayers &

Edward Fox, *Alpha Duties: The Search of Excess Returns and Appropriate Fiduciary Duties*, 97 Tex. L. Rev. 445 (2019) (suggesting that failure to diversify can be justified by sufficient expectations that the portfolio with generate above market returns). For a case where the court held that the trustee was not in breach of fiduciary duty because of a failure to diversify, see *In re* JP Morgan Chase Bank, N.A., 133 A.D.3d 1292, 20 N.Y.S.3d 499 (2015) (holding that income, taxation, and value may rebut the presumption of diversification). For a more complete discussion of all of the elements of prudence in the administration of modern trusts, see RAYMOND C. O'BRIEN & MICHAEL T. FLANNERY, THE PRUDENT INVESTING OF TRUSTS (2009). For additional analysis, see Charles A. Reed, *When Diversification By a Trustee May Not Be Necessary*, 158 TRUSTS & ESTS., 13 (May 2019); Jay A. Soled & Mitchell M. Gans, *Asset Preservation and the Evolving Role of Trusts in the Twenty-First Century*, 72 WASH. & LEE L. REV. 257 (2015); Paul S. Lee, Anne K. Bucciarelli & Stephanie Shen Torosian, *Managing Trusts in a Mad, Mad, Mad, Mad World*, 153 TRUSTS & ESTS. 12 (Feb. 2014).

Uniform Prudent Investor Act (2019)

§ 2. Standard of Care; Portfolio Strategy; Risk and Return Objectives.

(a) A trustee shall invest and manage trust assets as a prudent investor would, by considering the purposes, terms, distribution requirements, and other circumstances of the trust. In satisfying this standard, the trustee shall exercise reasonable care, skill, and caution.

(b) A trustee's investment and management decisions respecting individual assets must be evaluated not in isolation but in the context of the trust portfolio as a whole and as a part of an overall investment strategy having risk and return objectives reasonably suited to the trust.

(c) Among circumstances that a trustee shall consider in investing and managing trust assets are such of the following as are relevant to the trust or its beneficiaries:

(1) general economic conditions;

(2) the possible effect of inflation or deflation;

(3) the expected tax consequences of investment decisions or strategies;

(4) the role that each investment or course of action plays within the overall trust portfolio, which may include financial assets, interests in closely held enterprises, tangible and intangible personal property, and real property;

(5) the expected total return from income and the appreciation of capital;

(6) other resources of the beneficiaries;

(7) needs for liquidity, regularity of income, and preservation or appreciation of capital; and

(8) an asset's special relationship or special value, if any, to the purposes of the trust or to one or more of the beneficiaries.

(d) A trustee shall make a reasonable effort to verify facts relevant to the investment and management of trust assets.

(e) A trustee may invest in any kind of property or type of investment consistent with the standards of this [Act].

(f) A trustee who has special skills or expertise, or is named trustee in reliance upon the trustee's representation that the trustee has special skills or expertise, has a duty to use those special skills or expertise.

§ 3. Diversification

A trustee shall diversify the investments of the trust unless the trustee reasonably determines that, because of special circumstances, the purposes of the trust are better served without diversifying.

John H. Langbein
Uniform Prudent Investor Act and the Future of Trust Investing
81 Iowa L. Rev. 641 (1996)

In giving context to the prudence label, the Act makes three great changes in the law. All three were presaged in the 1992 Restatement [Second]. First, the Act articulates a greatly augmented duty to diversify trust investments. . . . Next, in place of the old preoccupation with avoiding speculation, the Act substitutes a requirement of sensitivity to the risk tolerance of the particular trust, directing the trustee to invest for "risk and return objectives reasonably suited to the trust." . . . Finally, the Act reverses the much criticized nondelegation rule of former law and actually encourages trustees to delegate investment responsibilities to professionals.

Id. at 645–46.

Andrew M. Parker
Visible and Hidden Risks
152 Trusts & Ests. 60 (Sept. 2013)

Holding a diversified portfolio of assets has become a well-respected technique for reducing overall portfolio risk. Modern portfolio theory is founded on this notion of finding an 'optimal mix' of uncorrelated assets to maximize portfolio return 'per unit of risk.' This concept lost some credibility in 2008, when markets witnessed a global investor 'flight to safety;' nonetheless, the mathematical concept remains true.

The issue is understanding what factors impact asset prices and correlation. Each market environment holds its own unique features, and the key is to recognize them. In most periods, the price of stocks, emerging market currencies and REITs would be unrelated. But, the combination of historically low interest rates, along with a heightened investor demand for a defined yield, has tied these asset prices together. In short, this is essentially a hidden risk that may surprise investors.

Over time, this short-term market behavior will fade and underlying market fundamentals will reassert themselves as the driver of asset pricing. For investors with an appropriate long-term horizon, the recent price moves will also fade away as noise. However, those investors who sought higher yields in portfolios supporting short-term goals and objectives, the recent correlated price declines may have indeed been a nasty shock.

Id. at 63.

Problem

In 2000, a mother created a revocable *inter vivos* trust, naming herself as trustee and a bank as successor trustee in the event of her incapacity or death. In 2004, she became incapacitated, and the successor trustee assumed duties as trustee. Seven years later, she died, and the trust became irrevocable. At the time the trust was created in 2000, the corpus of the trust consisted of stock in three separate banks and a local piece of real estate. At the time of the decedent's death, the value of the assets totaled $2.5 million. There also was an additional $27,000 in personal property.

Immediately after the decedent's death, one of her two children sued the trustee, alleging breach of trust, breach of fiduciary duty, mismanagement, negligence, and breach of the duty to diversify. Specifically, the son argued that for the four years prior to his mother's death—a period in which she was incapacitate—the trustee failed to diversify the assets of the trust. This petition was prompted by the fact that immediately after the death of the decedent, the shares of all three banks plummeted, resulting in a loss for the decedent's two children. In response, the trustee argues, first, that the trust provided the trustee with the option of retaining the securities. Second, he argues that, upon the death of his mother, the trustee sent the son/petitioner a letter offering either to sell the securities and give the son the value or to hold the securities, but advising the son that this option would entail market risks. The response of the son at that time was that he would prefer to receive the securities themselves. Third, he argues that the stock had a low basis and would generate excessive taxes if the stocks were sold, and that the special circumstances of large dividends and acknowledgement of risks by the son negated the duty to diversify. Based on the *Janes* decision and the relevant statutes and excerpts, how would you rule on the petition by the son? *See* Glass v. SunTrust Bank, 523 S.W.3d 61 (Tenn. Ct. App. 2016).

Americans for the Arts v. Ruth Lilly Charitable Remainder Annuity Trust
Court of Appeals of Indiana, 2006
855 N.E.2d 592

BAKER, Judge.

The primary question presented by this appeal is whether National City Bank of Indiana (National City), as trustee of two charitable trusts created by Ruth Lilly's (Ruth) estate plan, was required to diversify the trust assets. Although as a general rule, trustees have a duty to diversify, the trust instrument may modify that duty by permitting the trustee to retain certain—or all—trust assets. Concluding that the relevant documents at issue herein sufficiently relieved National City of the duty to diversify the trust assets, we affirm the judgment of the trial court. * * *

Ruth is the sole surviving great-grandchild of Eli Lilly, the founder of Eli Lilly & Company (Lilly). In 1981, the Marion County Probate Court appointed National City to be conservator of Ruth's estate. In 2001, the probate court directed the bank to draft a new estate plan for Ruth, and on November 27, 2001, National City petitioned the probate court to implement certain changes in the estate plan pursuant to a statute permitting a court to authorize a conservator to:

> [m]ake gifts, outright or in trust, on behalf of the protected person to or for the benefit of prospective legatees, devisees or heirs, including any person serving as the protected person's guardian, or to other individuals or charities, to whom or in which it is shown that the protected person had an interest. . . .

Ind.Code § 29-3-9-4(a). In its petition, National City asserted two primary reasons for the creation of Ruth's new estate plan: (1) Ruth, while subject to conservatorship protection but without court involvement, had executed twenty-two testamentary documents disposing in excess of $1 billion that likely would have generated years of costly and burdensome litigation upon her death; and (2) Ruth's existing plan generated significant, unnecessary taxes. National City, therefore, hoped to simplify, streamline, and improve the financial efficiency of the estate plan.

On November 28 and 29, 2001, National City sent notice to all interested parties, including the appellants, enclosing the petition and proposed estate plan and giving notice of a hearing on the petition on December 17, 2001. The interested parties, including the appellants and Ruth, took part in the process and were represented by sophisticated legal counsel. Indeed, the reputable firms representing the appellants included Cravath, Swaine & Moore LLP, Ice Miller LLP, Duane Morris LLP, and Bose McKinney & Evans LLP. For their efforts in this matter, the attorneys were paid nearly $250,000 in legal fees from Ruth's estate. The attorneys collectively spent well over 400 hours reviewing the proposed estate plan, proposing a number of changes, and raising extensive objections to the proposed plan. But none of the appellants objected to paragraph 10(b) of the trust documents, which is at issue on appeal and described more fully below. The probate court addressed all objections and ultimately approved National City's estate plan (the Estate Plan) on December 21, 2001. No party appealed from the probate court's approval of the Estate Plan.

Part of the Estate Plan created two charitable remainder annuity trusts (CRATs). CRAT # 1 provides Ruth with a lifetime annuity and CRAT # 2 gives money to six of her nieces and nephews for five years. Both CRATs name the same three charities as remainder beneficiaries-appellant-respondent The Poetry Foundation (Poetry), which is to receive 35% of the remaining assets of the CRATs, appellant-respondent Lilly Endowment, Inc. (Lilly Endowment), which will also receive 35% of the remaining assets, and appellant-respondent Americans for the Arts (AFTA), which will receive 30% of the remaining assets. National City is the trustee of, and has sole investment discretion for, both trusts.

The language of the trust documents that is at issue in this case is contained in paragraph 10 of the CRATs and is the same in both documents. In pertinent part, paragraph 10(b) provides that, in its capacity as trustee of the CRATs, National City:

> shall have the following powers and rights and all others granted by law

> * * *

> (b) *To retain indefinitely any property received by the trustee* and invest and reinvest the trust property in stocks, bonds, mortgages, notes, shares of stock of regulated investment companies or other property of any kind, real or personal, including interests in partnerships, limited liability companies, joint ventures, land trusts or other title-holding trusts, investment trusts or other business organizations as a limited or general partner, shareholder, creditor or otherwise, and *any investment made or retained by the trustee in good faith shall be proper despite any resulting risk or lack of diversification or marketability and although not of a kind considered by law suitable for trust investments.*

Appellant's App. p. 189–90, 202 (emphases added).

On January 18, 2002, the CRATs were funded as planned—entirely with Lilly stock—3,155,404 shares in CRAT # 1 and 657,376 shares in CRAT # 2. On that date, Lilly stock was selling at approximately $75 per share, giving the CRATs a combined initial value of approximately $286 million. By March 2002, National City had formulated a draft Investment Policy Statement for the CRATs, the purpose of which was "to identify and present the investment objectives, investment guidelines and performance measurement standards" for the CRATs' assets. Appellants' App. p. 2507-14. National City sold significant portions of the Lilly stock held by the CRATs by July 2002, and by October 2002, most of the Lilly stock—the value of which had declined significantly since January 2002—had been sold and the CRATs were fully diversified.

In November 2002, National City petitioned the probate court to approve of "its formulation and implementation of the diversification of the investment in Eli Lilly and Company stock held by the [CRATs]." *Id.* p. 183. Poetry and AFTA objected and counterclaimed, alleging that the bank's delay in diversifying was negligent, a breach of fiduciary duty, and a violation of the Indiana Uniform Prudent Investor Act (PIA), * * * and seeking to surcharge the bank for the alleged resulting loss to the CRATs. * * *

On June 1, 2005, National City filed a motion for summary judgment, arguing that its actions with respect to the CRATs were permitted by paragraph 10(b) of the CRATs, which gave National City the power "to retain indefinitely any property" it received as trustee and provided that "any investment made or retained by the trustee in good faith shall be proper despite any resulting risk or lack of diversification." *Id.* p. 189–90, 202. National City argued that the first clause eliminated its duty to comply with the PIA and that the latter clause exculpated it from any liability for failing to timely diversify the assets of the CRATs. Poetry and AFTA responded that: (1) National City was not excused from complying with the PIA, (2) the exculpatory clause is invalid because the bank, as trustee, put it in the trusts to protect itself, and (3) Indiana Code section 30-4-3-32(b) prohibits trustees from being exculpated against liability for "reckless indifference to the interest of the beneficiaries." * * *

Before addressing the substance of the appellants' arguments, we have concluded that it is incumbent upon us to consider the appellants' silence prior to their responses to the underlying pleading filed by National City. In particular, at no point did the appellants object to the clauses at issue in paragraph 10(b) of the CRATs, which they now argue are inherently unenforceable, or to National City's alleged conflict of interest stemming from the three proverbial hats—Ruth's conservator, drafter of the documents, and trustee—that it has worn throughout the parties' relationship.

Initially, we again emphasize that National City, acting as Ruth's conservator, voluntarily stepped in to overhaul her extraordinarily—and unnecessarily—complicated estate plan that was sure to result in protracted litigation and astronomical tax bills. After it had created a proposed estate plan, the bank notified all interested parties, including the appellants, provided them with a copy of the proposal, and afforded them time to read, digest, comment upon, and, if necessary, object to the document. The interested parties, including the appellants and Ruth, through her counsel, took extensive part in the process and were represented by sophisticated legal counsel. Indeed, the appellants' attorneys proposed a number of changes and raised numerous objections to the proposed plan. But Ruth, the appellants, and their respective attorneys were silent with respect to paragraph 10(b) and National City's relationship to the parties and the process. * * *

We are not determining whether the appellants were required to object to an action or a proposed action taken by National City, namely, its failure to diversify. Rather, we are determining whether the appellants were required to object to a provision in the proposed estate plan just as they objected to and proposed changes to other provisions in the proposed plan. At the time the parties were negotiating the terms of the CRATs, National City had neither taken nor contemplated taking an action that would constitute a breach of trust. That is simply not the issue. National City and the probate court afforded the appellants and their attorneys every opportunity to question or object to every facet of the proposed estate plan. The appellants chose not to quarrel with any portion of paragraph 10(b), and they are not now entitled to turn back the clock and claim that, in hindsight, the clauses are problematic and unenforceable.

The appellants next contend that that National City should have called paragraph 10(b) to their attention or to the attention of Ruth, her family members, or the probate court. They observe that National City's employee who was placed in charge of the CRATs characterized the trusts as "very complicated" and noted that two months after the Estate Plan was approved by the probate court, he and the rest of the bank's professionals were "still trying to understand the impact of the plan. . . ." Appellants' App. p. 2466. Thus, according to the appellants, National City "buried" the Exculpatory Clause in a complicated document at the end of one of seventeen clauses labeled "Trustee's Powers." Poetry Br. p. 23.

At the risk of being redundant, we again emphasize that the appellants were all represented by numerous sophisticated attorneys who are experienced in the area of trusts and estate planning. The attorneys spent well over 400 hours and amassed nearly $250,000 in legal fees poring over the documents, formulating objections and proposed changes, and presenting their objections and suggestions to the probate court. No party was naïve, unrepresented, or taken advantage of in this situation. Moreover, paragraph 10(b) is neither buried nor misleadingly labeled. Indeed, it takes up one-half of one page in a ten-page document. The language is signaled with a double-spaced lead-in indicating that the provisions to follow encompass all of the powers and rights of the trustee in administering the document. Under these circumstances, we do not conclude that National City was required to call paragraph 10(b) to the attention of any involved parties.

Finally, the appellants contend that "the trustee must establish the substantive fairness of the clause regardless of the notice—or lack thereof—to those at risk." Poetry Br. p. 23 (emphasis in original). Thus, even though the appellants raised no objection to paragraph 10(b), National City must still establish its substantive fairness. The probate court did not require the bank to make this showing, and the appellants contend that there is no way that National City could have done so because the clause provides no benefit to anyone other than the bank itself.

After reviewing the cases relied upon by the appellants for their argument regarding the obligation to establish the substantive fairness of the clause at issue, we conclude that these cases are distinguishable inasmuch as they involve self-dealing fiduciaries who exerted undue influence over a subordinate party to take advantage of a position of trust. See Matter of Good, 632 N.E.2d 719, 721 (Ind.1994) (attorney drafted will for client and was then convicted of 11 counts of theft based on transactions he made in client's name; court noted that transactions between attorney and client are presumed fraudulent and attorney has burden of establishing the transaction's fairness); Hudson v. Davis, 797 N.E.2d 277, 285 (Ind.Ct.App.2003) (fiduciary of elderly man entered into "exceptionally favorable" contract with him for purchase of property); Clarkson v. Whitaker, 657 N.E.2d 139, 144 (Ind.Ct.App.1995) (attorney drafted will under which he became beneficiary); Givens v. Rose, 178 Ind.App. 590, 598–99, 383 N.E.2d 448, 454 (1978) (fiduciary of disabled woman removed money from bank account after her death); Teegarden v. Ristine, 57 Ind.App. 158, 106 N.E. 641, 643 (1914) (attorney acting as widow's real estate agent induced her to execute deed to attorney's wife, selling property for less than one-third of its valued amount).

Under those circumstances, the burden deservedly shifts to the fiduciary to prove that the transaction was fair. Here, on the other hand, the bank owed no duty to the appellants at the time of the drafting of the CRATs, the appellants participated in the drafting, there is no evidence of self-dealing by National City, and the probate court approved the CRAT documents. Thus, the bank has no obligation to prove the substantive fairness of the Exculpatory Clause.

The appellants insist that they have alleged—and raised a material issue of fact with respect to—self-dealing on the part of National City. In particular, they note that there is no dispute that the bank, acting as conservator of Ruth's estate, drafted the Estate Plan and the CRATs. Additionally, they contend that no parties benefited from paragraph 10(b) other than National City itself.

We observe, however, that there is no evidence that National City "benefited" from the insertion of paragraph 10(b). Its failure to diversify the assets of the CRATs did not result in a windfall or a profit of any kind to the bank. Unlike the cases in which a trustee is found to have engaged in self-dealing, here, National City did not receive a profit or benefit at the expense of the beneficiaries of the CRATs. Thus, even if we were to conclude that the bank is required to establish the substantive fairness of the clauses at issue, we see nothing in the record tending to suggest that it would be unable to make such a showing. * * *

Dovetailing with their argument regarding alleged self-dealing on the part of the bank, the appellants next contend as a general matter that by inserting the clauses at issue into paragraph 10(b), National City committed an inherent breach of trust and/or fiduciary duty. Before addressing the merits of this claim, we must again observe that at no point prior to the underlying litigation did the appellants object to the fact that National City was acting as Ruth's conservator, drafting the documents, and preparing to become the trustee of the CRATs. Moreover, although the appellants became concerned about National City's failure to diversify the assets of the CRATs and even filed counterclaims against the bank for its handling of the trusts, they have never—to this day—sought to have National City removed as trustee.

The appellants' failure to object to the bank's status and actions notwithstanding, we note briefly that there is no evidence in the record to support a conclusion that by including the clauses at issue, the bank in any way breached a fiduciary duty to or abused a confidential relationship with Ruth. Indeed, we note that neither Ruth nor Lilly Endowment has ever complained about the bank's conduct with respect to the CRATs. Ruth and the appellants were represented by experienced and sophisticated legal counsel who undertook an exhaustive review of the proposed estate plan and were afforded an opportunity to raise objections and suggest revisions. The probate court oversaw the entire process. There is simply no evidence in the record that the bank exerted undue influence over Ruth or that it in any way acted improperly in drafting and negotiating the terms of the CRATs.

The above discussion notwithstanding, we will address the substance of the appellants' arguments. * * * The appellants contend that the clause in the trust documents providing general authorization for National City to retain investments (the

Retention Clause) does not override or nullify the statutory provision of the prudent investor rule requiring the trustee to diversify the trust assets. The Retention Clause, which is found at the beginning of paragraph 10(b) in the CRATs, provides that National City is empowered to "retain indefinitely any property received by the trustee...." Appellants' App. p. 189–90, 202.

The PIA provides generally that a trustee "shall invest and manage trust assets as a prudent investor would...." Ind.Code § 30-4-3.5-2(a). The Act goes on to mandate that a trustee " shall diversify the investments of the trust unless the trustee reasonably determines that, because of special circumstances, the purposes of the trust are better served without diversifying." *Id.* § -3 (emphasis added). The PIA, however, also provides that the prudent investor rule "may be expanded, restricted, eliminated, or otherwise altered by the provisions of a trust. A trustee is not liable to a beneficiary to the extent that the trustee acted in reasonable reliance on the provision of the trust." *Id.* § -1(b).

The appellants concede that the prudent investor rule, including the duty to diversify, may be altered by the trust document. They insist, however, that in this case, the general power contained within the Retention Clause is insufficient to override the duty to diversify. They look first to the Restatement (Third) of Trusts, which provides as follows:

> A general authorization in an applicable statute or in the terms of the trust to retain investments received as part of a trust estate does not ordinarily abrogate the trustee's duty with respect to diversification or the trustee's general duty to act with prudence in investment matters.

Restatement (Third) of Trusts § 229 cmt. d. First, we observe that the Restatement is "not a statute whose precise wording is entitled to deference as an act of an equal branch of government." PSI Energy, Inc. v. Roberts, 829 N.E.2d 943, 958 (Ind.2005). Furthermore, we observe that comment (d) goes on to provide that the terms of a trust "may permit the trustee to retain all of the investments made by the settlor, or a larger proportion of them than would otherwise be permitted." Thus, the Restatement (Third) of Trusts leaves open a comfortable window enabling the settlor to lessen the trustee's duty to diversify by including a clause to that effect in the trust instrument. * * *

The record herein reveals no relationship between National City and the Lilly stock that was retained as an asset of the CRATs for a period of time. Furthermore, there is no allegation that National City acted in bad faith and no evidence supporting a conclusion that it engaged in self-dealing. Under these circumstances, we conclude that the general Retention Clause in the CRATs combined with the clause explicitly lessening the trustee's duty to diversify is sufficient to except National City from the default duty to diversify trust assets. * * *

Finally, the appellants argue that whether diversification was properly and timely accomplished is an issue of fact not appropriate for summary judgment adjudication. Estate of Janes, 90 N.Y.2d 41, 659 N.Y.S.2d 165, 681 N.E.2d 332, 336 (1997) (holding that whether divestiture of an imprudently-held investment occurred within a reasonable time is a factual determination to be made by the trial court). As a general rule, that statement may be true, but the Exculpatory Clause modifies that rule by including an explicit standard with which to judge the actions of the trustee. Specifically, the Exculpatory Clause provides that so long as National City acted in good faith, any investment it retained is proper even if there was a resulting lack of diversification. Thus, because of the language included in paragraph 10(b) of the CRATs, all we need to determine is whether National City acted in good faith. Inasmuch as the appellants have never argued that the bank acted in bad faith, the trial court properly determined as a matter of law that National City acted in good faith in its administration of the CRATs and that the bank should not be held liable for its failure to diversify the assets of the CRATs.

The judgment of the trial court is affirmed.

SULLIVAN, J., and MAY, J., concur.

Notes

Unless equity demands otherwise, *see In re* Pulitzer's Estate, *supra*, the expressed intention of the settlor of the trust controls as to whether diversification is required of any prudent trustee. *See, e.g., In re* Trust of Post, 2018WL3862756 (N.J. App. 2018). For further discussion of diversification in the context of prudence, see Stewart E. Sterk, *Rethinking Trust Law Reform: How Prudent is Modern Prudent Investor Doctrine?*, 95 CORNELL L. REV. 851 (2010). For whether diversification affected the financial collapse of 2008, see, *e.g.*, John Hilsenrath & Mark Magnier, *Signals from U.S., China Show How Much Global Economy Has Shifted Since Crisis* (Mar. 8, 2015, at http://www.wsj.com/articles/signals-from-u-s-china-show-how-much-global-economy-has-shifted-since-crisis-1425835340 (comparing the current economic paces of different regions of the world to 2008); Binyamin Appelbaum, *Fed Misread Crisis in 2008, Records Show*, N.Y. TIMES, Feb. 21, 2014, at http://www.nytimes.com/2014/02/22/business/federal-reserve-2008-transcripts.html (discussing analytical missteps by the federal reserve just after the beginning of the financial crisis, according to newly released meeting transcripts).

B. Sole Interest: Loyalty, Earmarking, and Commingling

Uniform Trust Code (2019)

§ 802(b)(4). [Duty of Loyalty].

* * *

(b) Subject to the rights of persons dealing with or assisting the trustee as provided in Section 1012, a sale, encumbrance, or other transaction involving the investment or management of trust property entered into by the trustee for the trustee's own personal account or which is otherwise affected by a conflict between the trustee's fiduciary and personal interests is voidable by a beneficiary affected by the transaction unless: * * *

(4) the beneficiary consented to the trustee's conduct, ratified the transaction, or released the trustee in compliance with Section 1009 * * *

§ 1009. Beneficiary's Consent, Release, or Ratification.

A trustee is not liable to a beneficiary for breach of trust if the beneficiary consented to the conduct constituting the breach, released the trustee from liability for the breach, or ratified the transaction constituting the breach, unless:

(1) the consent, release, or ratification of the beneficiary was induced by improper conduct of the trustee; or

(2) at the time of the consent, release, or ratification, the beneficiary did not know of the beneficiary's rights or of the material facts relating to the breach.

In re Estate of Hines

District of Columbia Court of Appeals, 1998
715 A.2d 116

TERRY, Associate Judge:

This case arises out of the administration of a decedent's estate. Appellant, the court-appointed personal representative, sold the real property of the estate to herself and her brother without court permission and without the knowledge or written consent of the other heirs of the decedent. Two of those heirs, claiming that appellant had acted improperly, brought suit seeking her removal as personal representative, appointment of a successor personal representative, and nullification of the sale of the property. Ruling that appellant had breached her fiduciary duty to the estate and had acted in contravention of statute and court order, the trial court granted appellees' motion for summary judgment. We affirm. * * *

Charles H. Hines died on February 25, 1981. He devised a life estate in the family home on Florida Avenue, N.W., to his wife Ruth, with the remainder to their three children, William Hines, Marjorie Burke, and Sallie Archie, in equal shares, as tenants in common. Mr. Hines' will designated William Hines as the personal representative of the estate, but William * * * never submitted the will to probate. William predeceased his mother and left his one-third interest in the property to his children, Caryn and Gary Hines, in equal shares. Some time thereafter Marjorie assigned one-tenth of her interest to her daughter, Tanya Hall.

On December 30, 1992, following the death of Ruth Hines, Caryn petitioned the court to appoint her as the personal representative of the estate of Charles Hines. The court issued an Abbreviated Probate Order appointing her as personal representative and requiring her to post a general bond in the amount of $1,000. The order also stated that she must file an additional bond, in an amount to be fixed by the court, before accepting assets in excess of that amount. Caryn posted a general bond in the amount of $1,000, which was never increased.

On January 29, 1993, Marjorie, Tanya, Sallie, Caryn, and Gary met at the office of Caryn's attorney to discuss what should be done with the Florida Avenue house.

They agreed to retain an appraiser to determine both the fair market value and fair rental value of the property. In addition, they agreed (1) that Marjorie's daughter, Linda Johnson, could live in the house temporarily, on condition that she pay rent and not interfere with efforts to sell the property; * * * (2) that the property would be listed for sale with a Realtor; and (3) that the net proceeds of the sale would be distributed according to the terms of Charles Hines' will.

A few weeks later, on February 20, the property was appraised at a fair market value of $75,000. The appraiser reported, however, that the property was in need of repair after an extended period of deferred maintenance. When a further inspection revealed more than 100 housing code violations, a contractor was hired to repair and refurbish the property at a cost of about $10,000.

In May 1993 Marjorie told Caryn that she wanted to purchase the house for herself. Accordingly, on May 8 Marjorie and Caryn executed a sales contract which provided, among other things, that the sales price would be $70,000, that the property would be sold "as is," that the seller (the estate) would pay $3,000 toward the closing costs, that the seller could declare the contract null and void if the purchaser (Marjorie) failed to obtain financing within fifteen days, and that settlement was to occur within sixty days after the date of the contract.

By June 1994, Marjorie had not settled on the property, * * * and Caryn had received only one other offer to purchase the property. * * * On June 14 Caryn and her brother Gary executed a contract to purchase the property for themselves. The contract provided, among other things, that the sale price would be $70,000 and the seller (the estate) would pay $3,000 towards closing costs. Caryn signed the contract both as seller (on behalf of the estate) and as purchaser. The contract was silent as to who would pay for repairs to the house, nor did it expressly disclaim any warranties. Caryn admittedly concealed the transaction from Marjorie, * * * failed to obtain court approval for the purchase, and did not obtain consent for the transaction from either Marjorie or Sallie, the other two principal heirs.

On July 1, 1994, following the completion of most of the repairs, the property was reappraised at a fair market value of $84,000. Linda Johnson received a letter from the Realtor on August 22 stating that the property was about to be sold and that she would have to vacate the premises; the letter, however, did not disclose the identity of the purchasers. On September 7 Caryn and Gary closed on the purchase of the property. Some time later, in her Second and Final Account as personal representative, Caryn reported to the court that the estate had received $60,481.15 from the sale of the property to herself and her brother Gary.

Marjorie thereupon filed a complaint seeking Caryn's removal as personal representative and asking the court to set aside the sale of the property; her daughter Tanya later joined as a co-plaintiff. In her answer to the complaint, Caryn admitted that she had sold the house to herself and her brother without the knowledge and consent of either Marjorie or Sallie, each of whom held a one-third interest. She also admitted that she had paid only $70,000, which was $14,000 less than the appraised value of the property at the time of the sale. Along with her answer, Caryn filed a motion seeking *nunc pro tunc* authorization of the sale. The parties then filed cross-motions for summary judgment, and the court granted Marjorie and Tanya's motion in a fourteen-page order reciting the facts as we have summarized them here. Caryn noted this appeal, contending that the trial court erred in setting aside the sale of the property. * * *

The general rule applicable to this case was stated by the Supreme Court more than 150 years ago:

> [T]he law ... prohibits a party from purchasing on his own account that which his duty or trust requires him to sell on account of another, and from purchasing on account of another that which he sells on his own account. In effect, he is not allowed to unite the two opposite characters of buyer and seller, because his interests, when he is the seller or buyer on his own account, are directly conflicting with those of the person on whose account he buys or sells.

Michoud v. Girod, 45 U.S. (4 How.) 503, 555, 11 L.Ed. 1076 (1846). "Confidence in the loyalty and impartiality of a fiduciary is not maintained by one who is at once the seller and the buyer of the subject of sale." Harlan v. Lee, 174 Md. 579, 592, 199 A. 862, 869 (1938). Thus it has long been settled in the District of Columbia that a fiduciary may not purchase property which he holds in a fiduciary capacity "for his own benefit or on his own behalf, directly or indirectly," and that the person or persons to whom the fiduciary duty is owed—in this case, the other heirs—may seek to have any such sale voided or nullified. Holman v. Ryon, 61 App. D.C. 10, 13, 56 F.2d 307, 310 (1932) (citations omitted); see Goldman v. Rubin, 292 Md. 693, 704, 441 A.2d 713, 720 (1982); Uniform Probate Code (U.L.A.) §3-713 (1983). A personal representative owes a fiduciary duty to the estate and its beneficiaries. D.C. Code §20-701(a) (1989). This duty is breached when the personal representative's exercise of power over the estate is contrary to law or in violation of a court order. See D.C.Code §20-743 (1989). Moreover, a fiduciary breaches her duty when she fails to disclose material information to the beneficiaries. See Vicki Bagley Realty, Inc. v. Laufer, 482 A.2d 359, 365 (D.C.1984) (fiduciary duty "encompasses an obligation to inform the principal of every development affecting his interest" (citing cases)); Eddy v. Colonial Life Insurance Co., 287 U.S.App. D.C. 76, 79, 919 F.2d 747, 750 (1990).

Superior Court Probate Rule 112(b) stated, at all times relevant to this case, that "[u]nless the will authorizes the sale or exchange of real estate and excuses the filing of a bond, or unless all interested persons have waived the filing of a bond ... sales of real property in the District of Columbia shall be made in accordance with D.C.Code §20-742(b)." * * * Section 20-742(b), in turn, provided that in order to sell real property of an estate, the personal representative must obtain a court order authorizing the sale. "The Court shall give this order upon certification by the personal representative that the penalty amount of the bond has been expanded by an amount equal to the fair market value of the real estate. . . ." D.C.Code §20-742(b)

(1989). * * * The Abbreviated Probate Order issued in this case also required Caryn, as personal representative, to increase her bond before accepting assets in excess of $1,000. She never did so.

Given the applicable substantive law, the only material facts in this case are (1) Caryn's failure to obtain court approval prior to the sale of the real property, (2) Caryn's failure to increase the amount of her bond before accepting the property as an asset of the estate, and (3) Caryn's failure to inform the other heirs of her sale of the property to herself and her brother. By Caryn's own admissions and deposition testimony, those facts are undisputed.

Appellant argues nevertheless that summary judgment was improper because there is a genuine issue as to whether she and her brother purchased the property for less than its fair market value. We disagree. Although this may be a disputed issue of fact, it is not material because it does not affect the outcome of the case. See Anderson v. Liberty Lobby, 477 U.S. at 248, 106 S.Ct. 2505. The law does not differentiate between an unauthorized sale at fair market value and an unauthorized sale below fair market value; both are prohibited. Moreover:

> It is a wholesome doctrine, based upon reasons of public policy, that a [fiduciary] may not purchase or deal in [the] property [of the estate] for his own benefit or on his own behalf. . . ." So jealous is the law of dealings of this character by persons holding confidential relations to each other that the [beneficiary] may avoid the transaction, even though the sale was without fraud, the property sold for its full value, and no actual injury to his interests be proven. . . . ."

Holman v. Ryon, *supra*, 61 App. D.C. at 13, 56 F.2d at 310 (citations omitted); cf. Mosser v. Darrow, 341 U.S. 267, 272–273, 71 S.Ct. 680, 95 L.Ed. 927 (1951). Therefore, "[i]t is wholly immaterial whether the property brings its full value." Bassett v. Shoemaker, 46 N.J.Eq. 538, 542, 20 A. 52, 53 (1890); accord, Potter v. Smith, 36 Ind. 231, 239 (1871) ("however innocent the purchase may be in a given case, it is poisonous in its consequences"), quoted in In re Estate of Garwood, 272 Ind. 519, 528, 400 N.E.2d 758, 763 (1980). Thus any factual dispute as to the fair market value of the property does not preclude the entry of summary judgment.

Finally, appellant maintains that she is at least entitled "to obtain reimbursement for the substantial monies paid and/or invested in the property after her purchase." The record, however, is inadequate to support this claim, for it contains no information about the amount or extent of any such "monies paid and/or invested in the property." We therefore reject this argument for lack of record support, under well-established principles of appellate review. See Cobb v. Standard Drug Co., 453 A.2d 110, 111 (D.C.1982).

In summary, when a personal representative directly or indirectly purchases on her own account an asset of the estate at a sale which was not authorized by the court or the beneficiaries, the sale is voidable at the behest of any beneficiary. See, *e.g.*, Michoud v. Girod, *supra*, 45 U.S. (4 How.) at 555–558; Strates v. Dimotsis,

110 F.2d 374, 376 (5th Cir.), cert. denied, 311 U.S. 666, 61 S.Ct. 24, 85 L.Ed. 427 (1940); In re Estate of Garwood, *supra*, 272 Ind. at 528, 400 N.E.2d at 764; Smith v. Withey, 309 Mich. 364, 365, 15 N.W.2d 671, 672 (1944); Alburger v. Crane, 5 N.J. 573, 576, 76 A.2d 812, 814 (1950). In this case it is undisputed that appellant purchased real property belonging to the estate without the necessary authorization. Her conflict of interest was obvious and flagrant. We therefore hold that the trial court, after appellees raised an objection to the sale, acted properly in declaring the transaction void. That judgment is accordingly

Affirmed.[9]

Notes

For commentary on the duty of loyalty, see, *e.g.*, Daniel Harris, *Loyalty Loses Ground to Market Freedom in the U.S. Supreme Court*, 10 Wm. & Mary Bus. L. Rev. 615 (2019); Stephen R. Galoob & Ethan J. Leib, *Fiduciary Loyalty, Inside and Out*, 92 S. Cal. L. Rev. 69 (2018); Tamar Frankel, *Fiduciary Law in the Twenty-First Century*, 91 B.U. L. Rev. 1289 (2011); George G. Bogert & George T. Bogert, The Law of Trusts and Trustees § 543 (Rev. 2d ed. 1993). For additional case law on a trustee's duty of loyalty, see, *e.g.*, *In re* Estate of Moncur, 812 N.W.2d 485 (S.D. 2012) (holding that the beneficiary is entitled to a hearing on whether the trustee acted in good faith); Reinhardt Univ. v. Castleberry, 734 S.E.2d 117 (Ga. App. 2012) (discussing the use of a constructive trust to remedy a breach of loyalty by a trustee); Mendoza v. Gonzales, 204 P.3d 995 (Wyo. 2009) (beneficiaries' consent to trustee to transfer trust property to himself was not obtained by improper means and, thus, their consent was not void).

Restatement (Third) of Trusts (2019)

§ 78 cmt. [Duty Of Loyalty].

Undivided loyalty: prohibitions and rationale. * * * The rationale [of loyalty] begins with a recognition that it may be difficult for a trustee to resist temptation when personal interests conflict with fiduciary duty. * * * [T]he policy of the trust law is * * * to remove altogether the occasions of temptation rather than to monitor fiduciary behavior and attempt to uncover and punish abuses when a trustee has actually succumbed to temptation. This policy of strict prohibition also provides a reasonable circumstantial assurance (except as waived by the settlor or an affected

---

9. On December 28, 1994, the Council of the District of Columbia enacted the Probate Reform Act of 1994, D.C. Act 10-386, 42 D.C. Register 63 (1994), renumbered as D.C. Law 10-241, 42 D.C. Register 1640 (1995). Section 4 of that Act, 42 D.C. Register at 84, as amended by section 2 of D.C. Law 11-54, 42 D.C. Register 5854 (1995), provides that it shall be applicable only to estates of decedents who died on or after July 1, 1995. Since Charles Hines died in 1981, the 1994 Act does not affect this case.

Nevertheless, it is worth observing that the 1994 Act is consistent with our holding today. The 1994 Act provides, among other things, that "[a]ny sale . . . to the personal representative . . . or any other transaction which is affected by a substantial conflict of interest on the part of the personal representative, may be set aside by the court in proceedings initiated by any interested person. . . ." D.C.Code § 20-743.1 (1997).

beneficiary) that beneficiaries will not be deprived of a trustee's disinterested and objective judgment.

Restatement (Second) of Trusts (1959)

§ 170(1) cmt. t [Duty of Loyalty].

Terms of the trust. By the terms of the trust the trustee may be permitted to sell trust property to himself individually, or as trustee to purchase property from himself individually, or to lend to himself money held by him in trust, or otherwise to deal with the trust property on his own account. The trustee violates his duty to the beneficiary, however, if he acts in bad faith, no matter how broad may be the provisions of the terms of the trust in conferring power upon him to deal with the trust property on his own account.

John H. Langbein
*Questioning the Trust Law Duty of Loyalty:
Sole Interest or Best Interest?*
114 Yale L.J. 929 (2005)

Because the trust relationship places the beneficiary's property under the control of the trustee, the danger inheres that the trustee will misappropriate the property for personal advantage. The duty of loyalty, which forbids that behavior, is an essential principle of trust fiduciary law.

Id. at 987.

[T]he law should allow inquiry into the merits of a trustee's defense that the conduct in question served the best interest of the beneficiary.

Id. at 988.

The reform urged . . . is to allow a conflicted trustee to defend on the ground that the particular transaction was prudently undertaken in the best interest of the beneficiaries. Permitting this defense would effectively turn the sole interest rule into a best interest rule. . . . [T]he way to implement the change is to reduce the presumption of wrongdoing that now attaches to a conflict-tinged transaction from conclusive to rebuttable, allowing the trustee to show that the conflict was harmless or beneficial.

Id. at 989.

[The] Article takes the view that a transaction prudently undertaken to advance the best interest of the beneficiaries best serves the purpose of the duty of loyalty, even if the trustee also does or might derive some benefit. A transaction in which there has been conflict or overlap of interest should be sustained if the trustee can prove that the transaction was prudently undertaken in the best interest of the beneficiaries. In such a case, inquiry into the merits is better than "no further inquiry."

Id. at 932.

Problem

Mother and father created an *inter vivos* trust in 2004, naming themselves as initial trustees and then their three children as co-trustees, but there was nothing in the trust instrument specifying if the trustees must act unanimously or by a majority vote. The corpus of the trust consisted mostly of real estate, including the marital home. The beneficiaries were the two parents, and the remainder beneficiaries were the three children, who were the co-trustees. By 2015, the three siblings began their duties as co-trustees, but by 2016, discord spread among them. One of the co-trustees wanted to buy a portion of the trust property as an individual, and the sale was contingent on court approval. To gain this approval, another of the co-trustees supported the sale of the trust property to the other co-trustee. However, the third co-trustee objected, claiming that such a sale violated the trustee's fiduciary duty, and petitioned the court for removal of the potential, purchasing co-trustee and the other, supportive trustee for breach of the duty of loyalty. These two co-trustees argue that a majority of co-trustees may approve a sale under the state's statute and that the transaction was a fair one. If you were the probate court asked to approve the sale of the property to one of the co-trustees, with the approval of the second, how would you rule based on the *Hines* decision and the material following? *See* Matter of GNB III Trust, 2019 Ark. App. 171, 574 S.W.3d 159.

C. Impartiality

1. Power to Allocate

Citizens & Southern National Bank v. Haskins

Supreme Court of Georgia, 1985
254 Ga. 131, 327 S.E.2d 192

CLARKE, Justice.

These appeals arise from a suit filed by Louis and Harry Haskins as individual co-trustees and as beneficiaries along with their sister, Ester Friedman (hereinafter "plaintiffs"), against a corporate co-trustee, Citizens and Southern National Bank ("CSNB"); Sidney Haskins, the other individual co-trustee and those who held remainder interests in the trust were also named as defendants. The trust at issue was established in the will of Arthur Haskins, who died in 1959, and named three of his sons and CSNB as co-trustees; the trust was funded in 1974.

Arthur Haskins was survived by five children and twelve grandchildren. The trust provides that income be paid equally to his five children during their lifetimes and to descendants of a deceased child per stirpes. The trust terminates upon the death of the last surviving child or grandchild who was in life at the time of Arthur Haskins' death. At termination, the corpus is to be distributed to the lineal descendants per stirpes.

The will directs that the trust pay income equally to each child "during their lifetime at least annually or at such more frequent intervals as the trustees may agree upon." The will also sets forth an allocation clause for the trust; because the use of this allocation clause is in contention in the litigation we now set it out here in full:

> * * * My executors and trustees shall have discretion to determine whether items should be charged or credited to income or corpus or allocated between income and corpus in such manner as they may deem equitable and fair under all the circumstances, including the power to amortize or fail to amortize any part or all of any premium or discount, to treat any part or all of the profit resulting from the maturity or sale of any asset, whether purchased at a premium or at a discount, as income or corpus or apportion the same between income and corpus, to apportion the sales price of any asset between income and corpus, to treat any dividend or other distribution on any investment as income or corpus or apportion the same between income and corpus, and, except as provided in paragraph (j) above, charge any expense against income or corpus or apportion the same and to provide or fail to provide a reasonable reserve against depreciation or obsolescence on any asset subject to depreciation or obsolescence, as they may reasonably deem equitable and just under all the circumstances.

When the trust was funded in 1974, the co-trustees were CSNB, David Haskins, Louis Haskins and Sidney Haskins. David Haskins died in 1979 and was replaced by Harry Haskins under the terms of the will.

This action was filed by Louis, Harry and their sister Ester Friedman; she is an income beneficiary along with the other children but not a co-trustee. Co-trustee Sidney was named as a party defendant. The plaintiffs contended that the corporate trustee, CSNB, had been negligent in its management of the trust, violated its fiduciary duties, breached its contractual duties, made unauthorized investments and misrepresented the status of the trust properties to the co-trustees. They sought actual damages, punitive damages and expenses of litigation. Plaintiffs also contended that the corporate trustee, CSNB, had breached the trust by failing to properly exercise its discretion as required by the allocation clause and sought removal of CSNB as co-trustee. The complaint also asked for an interpretation of the allocation and for the court to order an allocation of capital to income. The issue of damages was tried before a jury with the issues of the allocation clause, removal of trustee and trustee fees being reserved for the court. The plaintiffs were seeking actual damages of approximately $400,000 based upon allegations of bonds purchased negligently and without authority and which had either been sold at a loss or were still in the trust, failure to communicate recommendations to sell certain stock and negligence in either selling or failing to sell other stocks.

After a lengthy trial the jury found CSNB, as co-trustee, to be responsible for losses in value of the Haskins trust. By way of a special verdict form they awarded $28,167 as loss on bonds purchased and still held by the trust. The jury awarded no damages for stocks sold at a loss or bonds sold at a loss. The jury declined to award punitive damages but did award attorney fees in the amount of $10,000 finding the bank had been stubbornly litigious or had caused plaintiffs unnecessary trouble and expense.

The trial court disposed of the remaining issues without a jury. He made findings on the plaintiffs' request for allocation and CSNB's request on guidelines for future allocations. The court found that the corpus of the trust was valued at approximately $907,000 when funded in 1974 and approximately $1,456,695 at the time of trial. An allocation under the terms of the trust from corpus to income had not been made since December of 1974. The court did not remove any trustees, ordered that an allocation from corpus to income of $250,000 be made immediately and paid to the income beneficiaries and ordered that no further allocation be made until two years after the death of the last surviving child of Arthur Haskins. He ordered trustee fees due to CSNB under a contract with Arthur Haskins to be paid from corpus and declined to award further attorney fees to either the plaintiff or to CSNB.

The trust assets as originally composed were almost entirely common stocks. At a February, 1975 meeting of the co-trustees, it was agreed to leave around 60% in common stock, place 35% in income yielding corporate bonds of short or intermediate maturity dates and 5% in short term government obligations. The security and stocks were put in nominee status in the name of Bibbco, a corporation owned by CSNB. After disagreements arose, co-trustee Sidney Haskins requested in writing to the bank that the securities be returned to the names of the individual co-trustees in May of 1978.

Disagreements over the allocation clause began in June of 1975. In the beginning of 1976, a new account officer took over the Haskins trust for the bank and later in 1976, the relationship between the co-trustees further deteriorated.

There were no meetings between the individual co-trustees and the bank from March of 1976 to August of 1978. Plaintiffs contended below that the bank officials refused to deal with them personally and that the trust portfolio was not reviewed or monitored during that time, all in violation of the bank's duty to the trust. The minutes of the bank's trust committees and notes of the portfolio manager reflect no activity for extended periods. When a trustees meeting was held in August of 1978, another controversy came to the surface when objections were made by David Haskins to a fee contract submitted by the bank. At this point the bank threatened to resign as co-trustee. * * * The trial court tried without a jury the issues of plaintiffs' entitlement to allocation, the removal of CSNB as corporate trustee, removal of the plaintiff co-trustees or excluding them from allocation decisions, trustee fees for CSNB and the requests from each side for attorney fees.

The court ordered that a $250,000 allocation to income beneficiaries be made immediately. It was ruled that CSNB was entitled to trustee fees of $21,664.96 for services between 1976 and 1983 and that the individual trustees be paid no fees for that period but would receive future fees as they came due under the fee contract. The fee to CSNB was ordered paid from corpus. The court ruled that all parties would bear their own attorney fees except for the guardian ad litem appointed by the court to represent the remaindermen; the trustees were ordered to pay him $5,000 from the corpus of the trust.

In the CSNB appeal it is contended the judge abused his discretion in allocating $250,000 to income and in depriving the trustees of allocation powers, erred in not removing Louis and Harry Haskins as co-trustees, erred in awarding its trustee fees from corpus and not awarding interest and erred in failing to award attorney fees to CSNB for defending the suit. In the cross-appeal the plaintiffs contend it was error to fail to remove CSNB as co-trustee, error to fail to allow reimbursement of their expenses from corpus, and to remove all allocation discretion from co-trustees. The appeal of the guardian ad litem representing the remaindermen takes issue with the $250,000 allocation to income beneficiaries and the award of trustee fees to CSNB from corpus.

The award of $250,000 was based upon several factors. No allocation had been made since 1974 and there was evidence that CSNB views any allocation to income beneficiaries as not being in the best interest of the remaindermen and therefore improper at any time. During this period when CSNB refused to negotiate on allocation, the corpus of the trust increased approximately $550,000. The court also considered the intentions of Arthur Haskins in funding the trust which provides for payments to his children *at least* annually and provides for allocation to income (as set forth in the beginning of this opinion). The court found the $250,000 was reasonable in light of the failure of the co-trustees to agree to any allocation for 9 years, the present ages of the children of Arthur Haskins, 73, 71, 68 and 63, and because of the court's decision that no further allocation which would benefit these children be made.

As to future allocations benefitting the grandchildren of Arthur Haskins per stirpes, he ruled that no allocation to income be made until two years after the death of the last surviving child. If the corporate trustee again decided allocation to be inappropriate at that time the question will again be considered by the court upon a petition by the income beneficiaries. This prohibition extends only to allocation; the court ordered that regular income continue to be distributed according to the terms of the trust. The court concluded there was sufficient evidence before it to remove CSNB as co-trustee and to remove Louis and Harry as co-trustees, thereby leaving Sidney and another court-appointed corporate trustee to manage the trust. The court instead chose the course of removing their allocation discretion, leaving the day-to-day management as Arthur Haskins desired, with his sons and CSNB.

In trusts like the present one with successive beneficiaries, that is income to a beneficiary for life and the principal later to other beneficiaries, "the interests of the two beneficiaries are to a certain extent antagonistic, and the trustee is under a duty so to administer the trust as to preserve a fair balance between them." Scott, [The Law of Trusts], § 232 [(3rd ed.)]. Scott also recognizes in this section that it is "not uncommon" for a settlor to provide that principal be applied to income for a life beneficiary.

While there are rules for categorizing items as income or principal, the settlor may authorize the trustee to allocate interests to income which would otherwise be principal and vice versa. Scott, *supra*, § 236.15; Bogert, [The Law of Trusts and Trustees], § 816 [(Rev. 2d ed.)]. When exercising this power the trustee must "act impartially as between income and principal beneficiaries . . . [the trustee] should take into consideration the purposes of the settlor as shown by the language of the instrument, his relations with the beneficiaries when the trust was drawn, and the financial and other conditions surrounding the beneficiaries at the beginning of the trust and at the time for the allocation of the receipt." Bogert, *supra*, § 816 at 363. See also 27 ALR2d 1313. Discretion given in instruments to trustees to allocate must be examined in light of the intentions of the testator or settlor. In re Heard's Estate, 107 Cal.App.2d 225, 236 P.2d 810 (1951).

All of the parties before the court in this case were asking the court to intervene on the issue of allocation. CSNB's complaint in regard to the allocation is that it is too high and not justified under the facts of this case. The appeal of the guardian ad litem representing the remaindermen joins in this complaint. The question on appeal is not whether the court abused its discretion in ordering an allocation from principal to income but whether the allocation ordered is excessive. The court decision was not only based upon the increase in value and intent of the testator, but also on the failure of CSNB to exercise its allocation discretion, the court's refusal to remove any co-trustees, and its mandate that no further allocation be made to the children of Arthur Haskins. Thus the propriety of amount of the allocation is dependent upon the court's conclusion that no trustees would be removed, even though he found the facts before him would authorize removal of plaintiff-co-trustee and CSNB.

A trustee may be removed by the court "if his continuing to act as a trustee would be detrimental to the interests of the beneficiary. The matter is one for the exercise of a reasonable discretion by the court." Restatement [of Trusts 2d], * * * § 107 [(1959)] (comment a). This discretion of the court in deciding removal issues is generally not interfered with by appellate courts absent an abuse of discretion. Bogert, *supra*, § 527. Griffith v. First National Bank etc., 249 Ga. 143, 287 S.E.2d 526 (1982). A trustee appointed by the settlor is less readily removed by the court. Restatement, *supra*, § 107 (comment f); Bogert, *supra*, § 527; Scott, *supra*, § 107.1. "The court will not ordinarily remove a trustee named by the settlor upon a ground existing at the time of his appointment and known to the settlor and in spite of which the settlor appointed him, although the court would not have appointed him trustee." Restatement, *supra*, § 107 (comment f). See also Lovett v. Peavy, 253 Ga. 79, 316 S.E.2d 754 (1984), on conflict of interest known to settlor.

Grounds for removal include failure to act, unreasonable failure to cooperate with co-trustees, commission of a serious breach of trust, crimes and dishonesty. See Restatement, *supra*; Bogert, *supra*; Scott, *supra*. It has also been said that a finding of negligence does not automatically require removal and that hostility or friction is not enough in and of itself; in these instances the court must decide if their existence will cause future problems, and/or impede the performance of the trust by making the performance of duties of a trustee impossible. Bogert, *supra*, § 527; Scott, *supra*, § 107; Restatement, *supra*, § 107.

A court may control the discretionary acts of a trustee when the trustee fails to act; "if the trustee is authorized in his judgment to make certain payments to a beneficiary in the discretion of the trustee, and instead of exercising any judgment in the matter he arbitrarily declines to make any payment, the court may interpose." Scott, *supra*, § 187.3. The court may also interpose its judgment when a trustee is acting from improper motives in exercising discretion. Scott, *supra*, § 187.5. The question of motives and conflict of interest arises when the trust gives discretionary powers to make payments to a trustee who is also the beneficiary of such payments. Scott, *supra*, § 187.6. In Armington v. Meyer, 103 R.I. 211, 236 A.2d 450 (1967), the court held that because of a conflict of interest in exercising discretion over payments, the beneficiary-trustees must petition the court to intercede and take over their duties on that issue. The court also stated that if there existed other co-trustees who could exercise this power without conflict the decision could be left to those remaining trustees. Rather than remove a trustee it has been held proper for a court to choose the alternative measure of substituting its judgment for the trustee's. Rogers v. Rogers, 111 N.Y. 228, 18 N.E. 636 (1888).

In *Griffith*, *supra*, relied on by CSNB we stated that in discretionary matters "the trial court could have properly substituted its judgment for that of the trustee only if the trustee had exhibited some abuse of discretion such as bad faith or fraud or if the conduct of the trustee is infected with some other abuse of discretion." 249 Ga. *supra* 143, 146, 287 S.E.2d 526. This court has held that where discretion is not exercised or not exercised properly a court may interpose itself and exercise the power for the benefit of the beneficiaries, in conformance with the intent of the testator/settlor. Ansley v. Pace etc., 68 Ga. 402 (1882); Collins v. Collins, 157 Ga. 85, 121 S.E. 218 (1924); Prince v. Barrow, 120 Ga. 810, 48 S.E. 412 (1904). "A court will interfere whenever the exercise of discretion by the trustee is infected with fraud or bad faith, misbehavior, or misconduct, arbitrariness, abuse of authority or perversion of the trust, oppression of the beneficiary, or want of ordinary skill or judgment." Citizens & Southern National Bank v. Orkin, 223 Ga. 385, 388, 156 S.E.2d 86 (1967). * * *

We must now determine if the decree of the court in this case meets this standard. Arthur Haskins named his sons as co-trustees and gave them discretion to allocate income to themselves; as stated earlier, it is presumed he knew of the conflict of interest in this situation and courts are reluctant to remove such trustees. See Peavy, *supra*. As a balance, he named CSNB as a co-trustee who would participate in this discretionary decision. However, the trial court, after listening to the two weeks of testimony before the jury and refusing to overturn its finding of mismanagement and breach of trust also found in the non-jury action that CSNB would never view an allocation as proper. This was viewed as a failure to act or failure to exercise the discretion necessary in order for the trust to operate according to the intent and wishes of Arthur Haskins.

An alternative would have been for the trial court to remove the beneficiary/ co-trustees or to remove them from allocation decisions, this latter classification could involve Sidney Haskins as well as plaintiffs, and to remove CSNB because of its failure to cooperate and consider the best interests of all beneficiaries, both income and remaindermen, and its refusal to consider allocation. The court could appoint a new corporate co-trustee and order that any allocation have court approval. This would remove the necessity for the court's restriction on future allocations. We do not find this or other alternatives to be required because the court may take into account the expense and administrative difficulties attendant to that course of action. Such problems may well negatively impact on the best interest of the parties and thereby outweigh any disadvantage of the exercise of judicial direction in the administration of the trust estate. We therefore find no abuse of discretion in the court's order relative to the allocation. * * *

Judgment affirmed.

All the Justices concur.

Notes

Often the trustee must exercise a fiduciary responsibility to income beneficiaries and, at the same time, to remainder beneficiaries. Inherently, their interests conflict because the income beneficiaries are likely to benefit more from income-producing investments (*e.g.*, bonds and annuities), while the remainder beneficiaries seek long-term gain investments (*e.g.*, stocks). To protect the trustee and accommodate both types of beneficiaries, the Uniform Principal and Income Act (1997) "helps the trustee who has made a prudent, modern portfolio-based investment decision that has the initial effect of skewing return from all the assets under management, viewed as a portfolio, as between income and principal beneficiaries. The Act gives the trustee a power to reallocate the portfolio return suitably." Unif. Principal and Income Act (1997), Prefatory Note. Sections 103 and 104 should be read in tandem. The paramount consideration in Applying Section 104(a) is the requirement in Section 103(b) that a fiduciary "shall administer a trust or estate impartially, based on what is fair and reasonable to all of the beneficiaries, except to the extent that the terms of the trust or the will clearly manifest an intention that the fiduciary shall or may favor one or more of the beneficiaries." *Id.* at § 103 cmt.

For commentary on a trustee's duty to manage a portfolio, see, *e.g.*, Paul S. Lee, Anne K. Bucciarelli & Stephanie Shen Torosian, *Managing Trusts in a Mad, Mad, Mad, Mad World*, 153 Trusts & Ests. 12 (Feb. 2013); Akane R. Suzuki, Tomoko Nakada, Shigehisa Miyake & Hidehito Ogaki, *Navigating United States-Japan Estate Planning*, 152 Trusts & Ests. 65 (Nov. 2013); Michael T. Flannery, *Special Accounting Issues for All Living Trusts under the Uniform Principal and Income Act*, Lexis-Nexis Expert Commentary, 2009 Emerging Issues 4336 (Sept. 2009); John H. Langbein, *The Uniform Prudent Investor Act and the Future of Trust Investing*, 81 Iowa L. Rev. 641 (1996). The *Haskins* decision, *supra*, illustrates the trustee's allocation power, and the following provisions from the Uniform Principal and Income

Act provide the basis for the trustee's allocation authority. Pertinent to this decision is Section 105, which establishes judicial control over the trustee's allocation duties and the theme that trustees are not expected to achieve perfection; they are, however, required to make conscious decisions in good faith and with proper motives.

Uniform Principal and Income Act (2019)

§ 103. Fiduciary Duties; General Principles.

(a) In allocating receipts and disbursements to or between principal and income, and with respect to any matter within the scope of [Articles] 2 and 3, a fiduciary:

> (1) shall administer a trust or estate in accordance with the terms of the trust or the will, even if there is a different provision in this [Act];
>
> (2) may administer a trust or estate by the exercise of a discretionary power of administration given to the fiduciary by the terms of the trust or the will, even if the exercise of the power produces a result different from a result required or permitted by this [Act];
>
> (3) shall administer a trust or estate in accordance with this [Act] if the terms of the trust or the will do not contain a different provision or do not give the fiduciary a discretionary power of administration; and
>
> (4) shall add a receipt or charge a disbursement to principal to the extent that the terms of the trust and this [Act] do not provide a rule for allocating the receipt or disbursement to or between principal and income.

(b) In exercising the power to adjust under Section 104(a) or a discretionary power of administration regarding a matter within the scope of this [Act], whether granted by the terms of a trust, a will, or this [Act], a fiduciary shall administer a trust or estate impartially, based on what is fair and reasonable to all of the beneficiaries, except to the extent that the terms of the trust or the will clearly manifest an intention that the fiduciary shall or may favor one or more of the beneficiaries. A determination in accordance with this [Act] is presumed to be fair and reasonable to all of the beneficiaries.

§ 105. Judicial Control of Discretionary Power.

(a) The court may not order a fiduciary to change a decision to exercise or not to exercise a discretionary power conferred by this [Act] unless it determines that the decision was an abuse of the fiduciary's discretion. A fiduciary's decision is not an abuse of discretion merely because the court would have exercised the power in a different manner or would not have exercised the power.

* * *

Uniform Fiduciary Income and Principal Act (2019)

§ 203. Fiduciary's Power to Adjust.

(a) Except as otherwise provided in the terms of a trust or this section, a fiduciary, in a record, without court approval, may adjust between income and principal if the fiduciary determines the exercise of the power to adjust will assist the fiduciary to administer the trust or estate impartially.

(b) This section does not create a duty to exercise or consider the power to adjust under subsection (a) or to inform a beneficiary about the applicability of this section.

(c) A fiduciary that in good faith exercises or fails to exercise the power to adjust under subsection (a) is not liable to a person affected by the exercise or failure to exercise.

(d) In deciding whether and to what extent to exercise the power to adjust under subsection (a), a fiduciary shall consider all factors the fiduciary considers relevant, including relevant factors in Section 201(e) and the application of Sections 401(i), 408, and 413.

(e) A fiduciary may not exercise the power under subsection (a) to make an adjustment or under Section 408 to make a determination that an allocation is insubstantial if:

(1) the adjustment or determination would reduce the amount payable to a current income beneficiary from a trust that qualifies for a special tax benefit, except to the extent the adjustment is made to provide for a reasonable apportionment of the total return of the trust between the current income beneficiary and successor beneficiaries;

(2) the adjustment or determination would change the amount payable to a beneficiary, as a fixed annuity or a fixed fraction of the value of the trust assets, under the terms of the trust;

(3) the adjustment or determination would reduce an amount that is permanently set aside for a charitable purpose under the terms of the trust, unless both income and principal are set aside for the charitable purpose;

(4) possessing or exercising the power would cause a person to be treated as the owner of all or part of the trust for federal income tax purposes;

(5) possessing or exercising the power would cause all or part of the value of the trust assets to be included in the gross estate of an individual for federal estate tax purposes;

(6) possessing or exercising the power would cause an individual to be treated as making a gift for federal gift tax purposes;

(7) the fiduciary is not an independent person;

(8) the trust is irrevocable and provides for income to be paid to the settlor and possessing or exercising the power would cause the adjusted principal or income to be considered an available resource or available income under a public-benefit program; or

(9) the trust is a unitrust under [Article] 3.

(f) If subsection (e)(4), (5), (6), or (7) applies to a fiduciary:

(1) a co-fiduciary to which subsection (e)(4) through (7) does not apply may exercise the power to adjust, unless the exercise of the power by the remaining co-fiduciary or co-fiduciaries is not permitted by the terms of the trust or law other than this [act]; or

(2) if there is no co-fiduciary to which subsection (e)(4) through (7) does not apply, the fiduciary may appoint a co-fiduciary to which subsection (e)(4) through (7) does not apply, which may be a special fiduciary with limited powers, and the appointed co-fiduciary may exercise the power to adjust under subsection (a), unless the appointment of a co-fiduciary or the exercise of the power by a co-fiduciary is not permitted by the terms of the trust or law other than this [act].

(g) A fiduciary may release or delegate to a co-fiduciary the power to adjust under subsection (a) if the fiduciary determines that the fiduciary's possession or exercise of the power will or may:

(1) cause a result described in subsection (e)(1) through (6) or (8); or

(2) deprive the trust of a tax benefit or impose a tax burden not described in subsection (e)(1) through (6).

(h) A fiduciary's release or delegation to a co-fiduciary under subsection (g) of the power to adjust under subsection (a):

(1) must be in a record;

(2) applies to the entire power, unless the release or delegation provides a limitation, which may be a limitation to the power to adjust:

(A) from income to principal;

(B) from principal to income;

(C) for specified property; or

(D) in specified circumstances;

(3) for a delegation, may be modified by a re-delegation under this subsection by the co-fiduciary to which the delegation is made; and

(4) subject to paragraph (3), is permanent, unless the release or delegation provides a specified period, including a period measured by the life of an individual or the lives of more than one individual.

(i) Terms of a trust which deny or limit the power to adjust between income and principal do not affect the application of this section, unless the terms of the trust expressly deny or limit the power to adjust under subsection (a).

(j) The exercise of the power to adjust under subsection (a) in any accounting period may apply to the current period, the immediately preceding period, and one or more subsequent periods.

(k) A description of the exercise of the power to adjust under subsection (a) must be:

(1) included in a report, if any, sent to beneficiaries under [Uniform Trust Code Section 813(c)]; or

(2) communicated at least annually to [the qualified beneficiaries determined under [Uniform Trust Code Section 103(13)], other than [the Attorney General]][all beneficiaries that receive or are entitled to receive income from the trust or would be entitled to receive a distribution of principal if the trust were terminated at the time the notice is sent, assuming no power of appointment is exercised].

2. Unitrust Option

In re Heller

Court of Appeals of New York, 2006
6 N.Y.3d 649, 849 N.E.2d 262, 816 N.Y.S.2d 403

ROSENBLATT, J.

In September 2001, New York enacted legislation that transformed the definition and treatment of trust accounting income. The Uniform Principal and Income Act (EPTL art. 11-A) and related statutes (L. 2001, ch. 243), including the optional unitrust provision (EPTL 11-2.4), are designed to facilitate investment for total return on a portfolio. The appeal before us centers on the optional unitrust provision, which permits trustees to elect a regime in which income is calculated according to a fixed formula and based on the net fair market value of the trust assets. We hold that a trustee's status as a remainder beneficiary does not in itself invalidate a unitrust election made by that trustee, and that a trustee may elect unitrust status retroactively to January 1, 2002, the effective date of EPTL 11-2.4. * * *

In his will, after making certain other gifts of personal property and money, Jacob Heller created a trust to benefit his wife Bertha Heller (should she survive him) and his children. Heller provided that his entire residuary estate be held in trust during Bertha's life. He appointed his brother Frank Heller as trustee and designated his sons Herbert and Alan Heller as trustees on Frank's death. Every year Bertha was to receive the greater of $40,000 or the total income of the trust. Heller named his daughters (Suzanne Heller and Faith Willinger, each with a 30% share) and his sons and prospective trustees (Herbert and Alan Heller, each with a 20% share) as remainder beneficiaries.

Jacob Heller died in 1986, and his wife Bertha survives him. When Heller's brother Frank died in 1997, Herbert and Alan Heller became trustees. From that year until 2001, Bertha Heller received an average annual income from the trust of approximately $190,000. In March 2003, the trustees elected to have the unitrust provision apply, pursuant to EPTL 11-2.4(e)(1)(B)(I). As required by EPTL 11-2.4(e)(1)(B)(III), they notified trust beneficiaries Bertha Heller, Suzanne Heller and Faith

Willinger. The trustees sought to have unitrust treatment applied retroactively to January 1, 2002, the effective date of EPTL 11-2.4. As a result of that election, Bertha Heller's annual income was reduced to approximately $70,000.

Appellant Sandra Davis commenced this proceeding, as attorney-in-fact for her mother Bertha Heller, and on August 1, 2003 moved for summary judgment, seeking, among other things, an order annulling the unitrust election and revoking the letters of trusteeship issued to Herbert and Alan Heller. She also sought a determination that the election could not be made retroactive to January 1, 2002. Surrogate's Court granted the branch of her summary judgment motion that sought to void the trustees' retroactive application of the unitrust election, but denied the branches of her motion seeking annulment of the unitrust election itself and other relief.

Davis appealed Surrogate's Court's order, and Herbert and Alan Heller cross-appealed. The Appellate Division affirmed the order to the extent that it denied Davis's summary judgment motion and reversed so much of the order as annulled the retroactive application of the unitrust election. It also granted leave to appeal and certified the following question to us: "Was the opinion and order of [the Appellate Division] dated August 15, 2005, properly made?" We conclude that it was and now affirm. * * *

The 2001 legislation that forms the subject of this appeal was designed to make it easier for trustees to comply with the demands of the Prudent Investor Act of 1994. * * * In addition to enacting EPTL article 11-A (Uniform Principal and Income Act), the Legislature both added EPTL 11-2.3(b)(5) to the Prudent Investor Act and included the optional unitrust provision, EPTL 11-2.4.

Under the former Principal and Income Act (EPTL 11-2.1), * * * a trustee was required to balance the interests of the income beneficiary against those of the remainder beneficiary (see EPTL 11-2.1[a][1]), and was constrained in making investments by the act's narrow definitions of income and principal (see EPTL 11-2.1[b]). A trustee who invested in nonappreciating assets would ensure reasonable income for any income beneficiary, but would sacrifice growth opportunities for the trust funds, as inflation eroded their value; if the trustee invested for growth, remainder beneficiaries would enjoy an increase in the value of the trust at the expense of income beneficiaries. * * * Moreover, the need to invest so as to produce what the former Principal and Income Act defined as income led to investment returns that failed to represent the benefits envisaged as appropriate by settlors. * * *

The Prudent Investor Act encourages investing for total return on a portfolio. Unless the governing instrument expressly provides otherwise, the act requires that trustees "pursue an *overall* investment strategy to enable the trustee to make appropriate present and future distributions to or for the benefit of the beneficiaries under the governing instrument, in accordance with risk and return objectives reasonably suited to the *entire* portfolio" (EPTL 11-2.3[b][3][A] [emphasis added]).

The 2001 legislation allows trustees to pursue this strategy uninhibited by a constrained concept of trust accounting income. First, the Prudent Investor Act now authorizes trustees

> "to adjust between principal and income to the extent the trustee considers advisable to enable the trustee to make appropriate present and future distributions in accordance with clause (b)(3)(A) if the trustee determines, after applying the rules in article 11-A, that such an adjustment would be fair and reasonable to all of the beneficiaries, so that current beneficiaries may be given such use of the trust property as is consistent with preservation of its value" (EPTL 11-2.3[b][5] [A]).

A trustee investing for a portfolio's total return under the Prudent Investor Act may now adjust principal and income to compensate for the effects of the investment decisions on distribution to income beneficiaries (see 14 Warren's Heaton, Surrogates' Courts, at App 5-25-5-27). Alternatively, the optional unitrust provision lets trustees elect unitrust status for a trust (EPTL 11-2.4), by which income is calculated according to a fixed formula.

In a unitrust pursuant to EPTL 11-2.4, an income beneficiary receives an annual income distribution of "four percent of the net fair market values of the assets held in the trust on the first business day of the current valuation year" (EPTL 11-2.4[b][1]), for the first three years of unitrust treatment. This is true regardless of the actual income earned by the trust. Starting in the fourth year, the value of the trust assets is determined by calculating the average of three figures: the net fair market value on the first business day of the current valuation year and the net fair market values on the first business days of the prior two valuation years (see EPTL 11-2.4 [b][2]). Income generated in excess of this amount is applied to principal.

Under the 2001 legislation, then, a trustee may invest in assets, such as equities, that outperform other types of investment in the long term but produce relatively low dividend yields for an income beneficiary, and still achieve impartial treatment of income and remainder beneficiaries. The trustee may accomplish this either by adjusting as between principal and income (see 14 Warren's Heaton, Surrogates' Courts, at App. 5-25–5-27) or by electing unitrust status with the result that the income increases in proportion to the value of the principal (id. at App. 5-14). If a trust's assets are primarily interests in nonappreciating investments producing high yields for income beneficiaries, a unitrust election may initially result in a substantial decrease in the distribution to any income beneficiary, at least until the portfolio is diversified. This case presents such a scenario. * * *

Davis argues that the trustees are barred as a matter of law from electing unitrust status because they are themselves remainder beneficiaries, and that, in any case, they may not elect unitrust status retroactively to January 1, 2002. The Appellate Division held that the legislation does not impede unitrust election by an interested trustee, that such an election is not inconsistent, per se, with common-law limitations on the conduct of fiduciaries and that the statute permits trustees to select retroactive application. We agree.

EPTL 11-2.3(b)(5), the 2001 statute that gives trustees the power to adjust between principal and income, expressly prohibits a trustee from exercising this power if "the trustee is a current beneficiary or a presumptive remainderman of the trust" (EPTL 11-2.3[b][5] [C][vii]) or if "the adjustment would benefit the trustee directly or indirectly" (EPTL 11-2.3[b] [5][C] [viii]). Tellingly, the Legislature included no such prohibition in the simultaneously enacted optional unitrust provision, EPTL 11-2.4. Moreover, in giving a list of factors to be considered by the courts in determining whether unitrust treatment should apply to a trust, the Legislature mentioned no absolute prohibitions (see EPTL 11-2.4[e][5][A]), and created a presumption in favor of unitrust application (EPTL 11-2.4[e][5][B]). We conclude that the Legislature did not mean to prohibit trustees who have a beneficial interest from electing unitrust treatment.

It is certainly true that the common law in New York contains an absolute prohibition against self-dealing, in that "a fiduciary owes a duty of undivided and undiluted loyalty to those whose interests the fiduciary is to protect" (Birnbaum v. Birnbaum, 73 N.Y.2d 461, 466, 541 N.Y.S.2d 746, 539 N.E.2d 574 [1989]). "The trustee is under a duty to the beneficiary to administer the trust solely in the interest of the beneficiary" (Restatement [Second] of Trusts § 170[1]). In this case, however, the trustees owe fiduciary obligations not only to the trust's income beneficiary, Bertha Heller, but also to the other remainder beneficiaries, Suzanne Heller and Faith Willinger. That these beneficiaries' interests happen to align with the trustees' does not relieve the trustees of their duties to them. Here, we cannot conclude that the trustees are prohibited from electing unitrust treatment as a matter of common-law principle.

That the trustees are remainder beneficiaries does not, by itself, invalidate a unitrust election. Nevertheless, a unitrust election from which a trustee benefits will be scrutinized by the courts with special care. In determining whether application of the optional unitrust provision is appropriate, it remains for the Surrogate to review the process and assure the fairness of the trustees' election, by applying relevant factors including those enumerated in EPTL 11-2.4(e)(5)(A). Application of these factors here presents questions of fact precluding summary judgment. * * *

Davis seeks to reinstate Surrogate's Court's determination that the unitrust election could not be made retroactive to January 1, 2002. In our view, however, the Legislature structured EPTL 11-2.4 so that it could be applied retroactively. EPTL 11-2.4(d) (1) provides that a trustee who elects unitrust status may specify the date on which the interest of a beneficiary begins. Thus, the statute vests trustees with authority to determine the effective date of unitrust elections.

Moreover, EPTL 11-2.4(b)(6) instructs a trustee who elects unitrust treatment to "determine the unitrust amount properly payable for any preceding and current valuation year of the trust" (emphasis added), unless the election is "expressly made effective prospectively as permitted under clause (e)(4)(a)." The trustee is then required to pay to, or recover from, the current beneficiary the difference between the unitrust amount and any amount actually paid for any completed valuation year. (EPTL 11-2.4[b][6].) This provision envisages retroactive application of a unitrust regime. The required recomputation of preceding years' beneficial interests would serve no purpose if retroactive application were barred.

EPTL 11-2.4(e)(4)(A), on which Surrogate's Court relied, is not to the contrary. This section provides that the optional unitrust provision

> "shall apply to a trust . . . as of the first year of the trust in which assets first become subject to the trust, unless the governing instrument or the court in its decision provides otherwise, or unless the election in accordance with clause (e)(1)(B) is expressly made effective as of the first day of the first year of the trust commencing after the election is made."

On the most plausible interpretation of this less than lucid provision, EPTL 11-2.4(e)(4)(A) actually contemplates retroactivity, insofar as it provides the initial funding of the trust as a default starting point for unitrust treatment of a trust created on or after January 1, 2002. Certainly, EPTL 11-2.4(e)(4) (A) should not be read as taking away from trustees the authority given them by EPTL 11-2.4(d)(1) to specify the effective date of a unitrust election.

We therefore hold that a trustee may elect unitrust status for a trust retroactively to January 1, 2002, the effective date of EPTL 11-2.4. Appellant's remaining contentions lack merit.

Accordingly, the order of the Appellate Division should be affirmed, with costs, and the certified question answered in the affirmative.

Chief Judge KAYE and Judges G.B. SMITH, CIPARICK, GRAFFEO, READ and R.S. SMITH concur.

Order affirmed, etc.

Notes

Unitrusts paying a percentage of the asset to a named beneficiary were discussed previously in the context of charities, *see* Charitable Trusts. Through the use of charitable remainder trusts (CRTs), charitable remainder unitrusts (CRUTs), and charitable remainder annuity trusts (CRATs), donors may maximize tax savings and accomplish charitable purposes. *See generally* Michael J. Jones, *The 5 Percent Solution*, 153 TRUSTS & ESTS. 38 (June 2014). The concept of a unitrust may be used to meet a trustee's duty to be impartial towards income and remainder beneficiaries, as is illustrated in the *Heller* decision, *supra*. For a discussion of the use of unitrusts, see, *e.g.*, Benjamin S. Candland, Stephen W. Murphy, and Abbey L. Farnsworth, *Intricacies of the Uniform Principal and Income Act—Part 3*, 45 EST. PLAN. 3 (2017); Richard W. Nenno, *The Power to Adjust and Total-Return Unitrust Statutes: State Developments and Tax Considerations*, 42 REAL PROP. PROB. & TR. J. 657 (2008); Ronald R. Volkmer, *Nebraska's "Total Return Trust" Statute: Unitrust Conversion and the Challenges of Managing a Trust and Drafting a Trust*, 40 CREIGHTON L. REV. 135 (2006).

D. Delegation

Shriners Hospital for Crippled Children v. Gardiner

Supreme Court of Arizona, 1987
152 Ariz. 527, 733 P.2d 1110

HAYS, Justice (Retired).

Laurabel Gardiner established a trust to provide income to her daughter, Mary Jane Gardiner; her two grandchildren, Charles Gardiner and Robert Gardiner; and a now-deceased daughter-in-law, Jean Gardiner. The remainder of the estate passes to Shriners Hospitals for Crippled Children (Shriners) upon the death of the life income beneficiaries. In re Estate of Gardiner, 5 Ariz.App. 239, 240, 425 P.2d 427, 428 (1967). Laurabel appointed Mary Jane as trustee, Charles as first alternate trustee, and Robert as second alternate trustee. Mary Jane was not an experienced investor, and she placed the trust assets with Dean Witter Reynolds, a brokerage house. Charles, an investment counselor and stockbroker, made all investment decisions concerning the trust assets. At some point in time, Charles embezzled $317,234.36 from the trust. Shriners brought a petition to surcharge Mary Jane for the full $317,234.36. The trial court denied the petition, but a divided court of appeals reversed. Shriners Hospitals for Crippled Children v. Gardiner, 152 Ariz. 519, 733 P.2d 1102, (Ct.App.1986).

We granted review on three issues:

1) Whether Mary Jane's delegation of investment power to Charles was a breach of Mary Jane's fiduciary duty.

2) Whether Mary Jane's delegation to Charles of investment power was the proximate cause of the loss of $317,234.36.

3) Whether Robert can properly continue to act as successor trustee and as guardian and conservator for the predecessor trustee Mary Jane. * * *

In Arizona, a trustee has the duty to "observe the standard in dealing with the trust assets that would be observed by a prudent man dealing with the property of another." A.R.S. § 14-7302. If the trustee breaches that responsibility, he is personally liable for any resulting loss to the trust assets. Restatement (Second) of Trusts §§ 201, 205(a). A trustee breaches the prudent man standard when he delegates responsibilities that he reasonably can be expected personally to perform. Restatement (Second) of Trusts § 171.

We believe that Mary Jane breached the prudent man standard when she transferred investment power to Charles. Mary Jane argues, and we agree, that a trustee lacking investment experience must seek out expert advice. Although a trustee must seek out expert advice, "he is not ordinarily justified in relying on such advice, but must exercise his own judgment." Restatement (Second) of Trusts § 227. In re Will of Newhoff, 107 Misc.2d 589, 595, 435 N.Y.S.2d 632, 637 (1980) (a trustee must not only obtain information concerning investment possibilities but also is "under a duty to use a reasonable degree of skill in selecting an investment"). Mary Jane, though, did not evaluate Charles' advice and then make her own decisions. Charles managed the trust fund, not Mary Jane. A prudent investor would certainly participate, to some degree, in investment decisions.

The dissent in the court of appeals stated that "there is nothing to indicate the trustee 'gave up her trusteeship' or 'delegated' the 'complete management' of trust assets to Charles." Shriners Hospitals for Crippled Children, 152 Ariz. at 525, 733 P.2d at 1108, (Froeb, C.J., dissenting). While we agree that the record on appeal is meager, Mary Jane unquestionably transferred trustee discretion to Charles.

Mary Jane's second accounting of the Gardiner trust states:

> From time to time the Trustee made investments ("investments") in the money market and also in the purchase and sale of shares of stock listed on the New York Stock Exchange, the American Stock Exchange and the Over-the-Counter Markets.... *All of said investments were made on behalf of the Trust Estate by a person qualified in that business, [Charles] who was selected by and in whom the Trustee justifiably had the utmost trust and confidence.*

(emphasis added)

Most damning, however, are the admissions of Mary Jane's own attorney.

> Now, we can show, if the Court pleases, by way of evidence if counsel will not accept my avowal, we can show that Charles Gardiner for the past many years, including several years prior to and since these assets were placed in his hands for investment, was in the business of a consultant and in the business of investing and selecting investments in the stock market, and this he did. And it was only natural that Mary Jane would turn to him to make that selection, to invest those funds and to account in an appropriate proceeding if, as and when required. So the prudent man rule has been adhered to here. She got a man who is capable and fortunately he was a man who was designated as an alternate trustee *and for all practical purposes really served as trustee.*

(emphasis added)

Together, the accounting and admissions establish that Charles was functioning as a surrogate trustee. Mary Jane was not exercising any control over the selection of investments. She clearly breached her duties to act prudently and to personally perform her duties as a trustee. In re Kohler's Estate, 348 Pa. 55, 33 A.2d 920 (1943) (fiduciary may not delegate to another the performance of a duty involving discretion and judgment).

Even on appeal, Mary Jane does not argue that she, in fact, exercised any discretionary investment power. Instead, she argues that her lack of investment experience made it prudent for her to delegate her investment power. She relies on the Restatement (Second) of Torts § 171 * * * [duty not to delegate]:

> The trustee is under a duty to the beneficiary not to delegate to others the doing of acts which the trustee can reasonably be required personally to perform.

Mary Jane asserts that her lack of investment experience prevented her from personally exercising investment power and consequently permitted delegation of that power. The standard of care required, however, is measured objectively. In re Mild's Estate, 25 N.J. 467, 480–81, 136 A.2d 875, 882 (1957) (the standard of care required of a trustee does not take into account the "differing degrees of education or intellect possessed by a fiduciary"). The trustee must be *reasonable* in her delegation. A delegation of investment authority is unreasonable and therefore Mary Jane's delegation is a breach of trust. See Estate of Baldwin, 442 A.2d 529 (Me.1982) (bank trustee liable for losses incurred when it failed to monitor management of grocery store despite bank's lack of expertise in grocery store management).

It is of no import that Charles was named as alternate trustee. A trustee is not permitted to delegate his responsibilities to a co-trustee. Restatement (Second) of Trusts § 224(2)(b); see also *id.*, comment a (improper for co-trustee A to direct co-trustee B to invest trust funds without consulting A). Certainly, then, a trustee is subject to liability when she improperly delegates her investment responsibility to an alternate trustee. Bumbaugh v. Burns, 635 S.W.2d 518, 521 (Tenn.App.1982) (impermissible for trustee to delegate discretion as to investment of funds to co-trustee).

Mary Jane also argues that broad language in the trust document permitted her to delegate her investment authority to Charles. A trust document may allow a trustee to delegate powers ordinarily nondelegable. The Gardiner Trust permits the trustee "to employ and compensate attorneys, accountants, agents and brokers." This language does not bear on Mary Jane's delegation of investment authority. Mary Jane did not simply employ Charles; she allowed him to serve as surrogate trustee. We view this language as merely an express recognition of the trustee's obligation to obtain expert advice, not as a license to remove herself from her role as a trustee. * * *

Mary Jane next argues that there is no causal connection between her breach and the loss suffered by the trust. The court of appeals rejected this argument in a summary fashion, stating that "the trustee offers no evidence to meet this burden of showing that the loss would have occurred anyway." Shriners Hospitals for Crippled Children, 152 Ariz. at 523, 733 P.2d at 1106. We disagree.

The very nature of the loss indicates that the breach was not causally connected to the loss. The accounting indicates that Charles embezzled the funds.

> Without the knowledge or consent of the Trustee, said person received from said investments, and diverted to his own use, a total believed by the Trustee to aggregate $317,234.36 ($116,695.55 on January 16, 1981 and $200,537.81 on March 4, 1981). The trustee did not learn of said diversions

until long after they occurred. No part of the amount so diverted had been returned or paid to the Trustee or the Trust Estate. . . .

If the trust had suffered because poor investments were made, the delegation of investment authority would unquestionably be the cause of the loss. Otherwise, a causal connection between Charles' diversion of funds and Mary Jane's breach is absent unless the delegation of investment authority gave Charles control and dominion over the trust fund that permitted the defalcation.

A causal connection does not exist simply because "but for" Mary Jane's opening of the account at Dean Witter Reynolds, no loss would have occurred. A trustee is not personally liable for losses not resulting from a breach of trust. Restatement (Second) of Trusts § 204; Citizens & Southern Nat'l Bank v. Haskins, 254 Ga. 131, 134, 327 S.E.2d 192, 197 (1985). Mary Jane did not breach her duty by establishing an account at Dean Witter Reynolds, a major brokerage house. Charles was not only the type of person Mary Jane was obliged to seek out for investment advice, but he was a person whom Laurabel Gardiner indicated was trustworthy by naming him as second alternate trustee. Furthermore, the Dean Witter Reynolds account was apparently in Mary Jane's name. If Dean Witter Reynolds wrongfully allowed Charles access to the fund, Mary Jane is not personally liable. Restatement (Second) of Trusts § 225 (trustee not generally liable for wrongful acts of agents employed in administration of estate).

Unfortunately, the record does not reveal the nature of the diversion. The relative culpability of Charles, Mary Jane and Dean Witter Reynolds is unclear. The trial court found that Mary Jane was without fault and, therefore, did not consider the causal connection between Mary Jane's breach and Charles's defalcation. The inadequacy of the record demands a remand for a determination of the relationship between Mary Jane's delegation of investment authority and Charles' diversion of funds. * * *

If, after remand, the trial court determines that Mary Jane is personally liable for the diversion of funds, Robert must be removed as trustee.[1] A trustee is liable to a beneficiary if he fails to "redress a breach of trust committed by the predecessor [trustee]." Restatement (Second) of Trusts § 223(2). Robert would, therefore, have a duty to enforce the surcharge against his aunt and ward, Mary Jane. The conflict between personal responsibilities and trust obligations is obvious and great. Estate of Rothko, 43 N.Y.2d 305, 319, 401 N.Y.S.2d 449, 454, 372 N.E.2d 291, 296 (1977) (while a trustee is administering the trust he must refrain from placing himself in position where his personal interest does or may conflict with interest of beneficiaries). Another trustee, without such conflicts, would have to be appointed.

The decision of the court of appeals is vacated, and the case is remanded for further proceedings consistent with this opinion.

GORDON, C.J., and FELDMAN, V.C.J., and HOLOHAN, J., concur. * * *

---

1. Robert Gardiner is currently serving as trustee because Mary Jane is an invalid and Charles is untrustworthy. Robert is also Mary Jane's guardian-conservator.

Notes

Delegation of trust duties was not permitted under the Second Restatement if the trustee could reasonably have been expected to perform the function. *Restatement (Second) of Trusts* § 171 (1959). Likewise, a trustee could not delegate to another the duty to select investments. *Id.* at § 171 cmt. H. (1959). This non-delegation rule was criticized as not in keeping with modern portfolio practice, and, today, delegation is allowed and flourishing. The following provisions demonstrate the extent and scope of delegation.

Restatement (Third) of Trusts: Prudent Investor Rule (2019)

§ 90 [1992 § 277] cmt. j. [General Standard Of Prudent Investment].

Duty with respect to delegation. In administering the trust's investment activities, the trustee has power, and may sometimes have a duty, to delegate such functions and in such manner as a prudent investor would delegate under the circumstances. * * *

Many factors affect the nature and extent of prudent and therefore permissible delegation. These factors include the almost infinite variety that exists in * * * investment objectives and techniques and in the types, circumstances, and goals of trusts.

§ 90 [1992 § 227] cmt. d. [General Standard Of Prudent Investment].

To the extent necessary or appropriate to the making of informed investment judgments by the particular trustee, care also involves securing and considering the advice of others on a reasonable basis. It is ordinarily satisfactory that this information and advice be obtained from sources on which prudent investors in the community customarily rely.

Uniform Prudent Investor Act (2019)

§ 9. Delegation of Investment and Management Functions.

(a) A trustee may delegate investment and management functions that a prudent trustee of comparable skills could properly delegate under the circumstances. The trustee shall exercise reasonable care, skill, and caution in:

> (1) selecting an agent;
>
> (2) establishing the scope and terms of the delegation, consistent with the purposes and terms of the trust; and
>
> (3) periodically reviewing the agent's actions in order to monitor the agent's performance and compliance with the terms of the delegation.

Uniform Trust Code (2019)

§ 807(a). [Delegation by Trustee].

(a) A trustee may delegate duties and powers that a prudent trustee of comparable skills could properly delegate under the circumstances. The trustee shall exercise reasonable care, skill, and caution in:

(1) selecting an agent;

(2) establishing the scope and terms of the delegation, consistent with the purposes and terms of the trust; and

(3) periodically reviewing the agent's actions in order to monitor the agent's performance and compliance with the terms of the delegation.

§ 703(e). [Cotrustees].

(e) A trustee may not delegate to a cotrustee the performance of a function the settlor reasonably expected the trustees to perform jointly. Unless a delegation was irrevocable, a trustee may revoke a delegation previously made.

E. Disclosure

Merrill Lynch, Pierce, Fenner & Smith, Inc. v. Cheng

United States Court of Appeals, District of Columbia Circuit, 1990
901 F.2d 1124, 284 U.S. App. D.C. 72

TIMBERS, Senior Circuit Judge:

Appellants Merrill Lynch, Pierce, Fenner & Smith, Inc. ("Merrill Lynch") and William J. Grace, Jr. appeal from an order entered June 19, 1989, in the District Court for the District of Columbia, Royce C. Lamberth, *District Judge*, which directed a verdict in favor of appellees Rolando and Anita Ong Cheng (hereinafter, "the Chengs", "Dr. Cheng" or "Cheng") on their counterclaim and third-party complaint alleging breach of fiduciary duty.

This diversity action was commenced by Merrill Lynch to recover monies allegedly owed by the Chengs as a result of certain securities transactions in the Chengs' options account with Merrill Lynch. The Chengs responded by filing a counterclaim against Merrill Lynch and a third-party complaint against their broker Grace, an employee of Merrill Lynch, for breach of fiduciary duty, negligence and fraud.

After being informed that the jury was hung, the district court, upon reconsideration, granted the Chengs' motion for a directed verdict on the breach of fiduciary duty count, and entered judgment against appellants in the amount of $96,264. It held, as a matter of law, that appellants breached their fiduciary duty by purchasing options on the Chengs' behalf without authorization and that the Chengs did not ratify the unauthorized transactions. For the same reasons, the court denied Merrill Lynch's motion for a directed verdict and dismissed its complaint.

On appeal, appellants assert that: (1) the district court erred in holding that they owed fiduciary duties to the Chengs; (2) the issue whether they breached fiduciary duties should have been submitted to the jury; (3) the issue whether the Chengs ratified the unauthorized transactions should have been submitted to the jury; and (4) the court improperly denied their motion for a directed verdict.

For the reasons which follow, we affirm the order of the district court in all respects. * * *

We shall summarize only those facts and prior proceedings believed necessary to an understanding of the issues raised on appeal.

This diversity action arises from purchases of IBM options in May 1986 by Rolando and Anita Ong Cheng through their stockbroker, William J. Grace, Jr., an employee of Merrill Lynch. In May 1985, Dr. Rolando Cheng, an orthopedic surgeon residing in Ashland, Kentucky, had called Grace and indicated that he was interested in opening an account with him. Shortly thereafter, Grace opened an account for the Chengs at the Merrill Lynch office in Washington, D.C. During the one year period between May 1985 and April 1986, the Chengs' portfolio grew from $34,000 to approximately $300,000.

On March 16, 1986, the Chengs signed a Merrill Lynch options agreement. Between April 1986 and May 1986, Dr. Cheng engaged in several IBM options transactions. The dispute here involved arose out of transactions entered into on May 5, 1986. That morning, Dr. Cheng called Grace to discuss the possibility of buying more IBM options. He explicitly instructed Grace to purchase additional options, but "only if his account could afford it." Due to a computer malfunction, Grace received incorrect information as to whether the Chengs' account could afford additional purchases. He overbought the account by about $119,000.

Upon reaching Dr. Cheng the evening of May 6, Grace advised him that Merrill Lynch had made a mistake and had overbought the options for his account "per his instructions that previous morning." Instead of informing Dr. Cheng, however, that he had the right to reject the unauthorized transactions, Grace told him:

> "Look, we still like IBM. We still think IBM is going to do well. There are two things we can do. We can sell out of these things or you can go ahead and keep the positions and send more money in."

In other words, Dr. Cheng was given two choices: either sell the options at a loss since the price of the options had gone down since the purchase date or send in money to cover the $119,000 debit and hope the price would go up. In addition, Grace informed Dr. Cheng that, if he did not meet the margin call, Merrill Lynch would have to liquidate his positions.

According to Grace, Dr. Cheng instructed him to sell off the remaining stocks in the account to reduce the debit and indicated that he would send additional funds. Dr. Cheng sent $40,000, which was received by Merrill Lynch on May 12, 1986. Upon receiving no additional funds from Dr. Cheng, Merrill Lynch eventually closed out his remaining positions.

As a result of these transactions, Merrill Lynch claimed that the Chengs owed the firm $28,614.06 plus interest and, in September 1986, commenced an action against the Chengs. The Chengs responded by filing a counterclaim against Merrill Lynch and a third-party complaint against Grace, for breach of fiduciary duty, negligence and fraud. The district court denied appellants' pretrial motions for summary judgment on the Chengs' counterclaim and third-party complaint, but granted their motions to dismiss a securities fraud count. * * *

Appellants contend that they did not owe a fiduciary duty to the Chengs because their account with Merrill Lynch was "non-discretionary". While admitting that Grace, as a stockbroker, breached a duty to transact business only with prior authorization, appellants claim that such duty is not a fiduciary one. That duty, they assert, is based merely on "a general standard of care in the industry". Moreover, although they do not dispute that the Chengs had the right to reject the unauthorized transactions, they claim that Grace did not have a duty to inform the Chengs of such right, since it is a matter of common knowledge that a customer may reject trades he does not order. We disagree. We hold that basic principles of agency law control here and that those principles required Grace to inform the Chengs of their right to reject the unauthorized options.

The district court found that the Chengs' account with Merrill Lynch was "non-discretionary". With respect to a non-discretionary account, the customer must give prior approval for all transactions. Hotmar v. Lowell H. Listrom & Co., 808 F.2d 1384, 1385 (10th Cir.1987); Leib v. Merrill Lynch, Pierce, Fenner & Smith, Inc., 461 F. Supp. 951, 952 (E.D.Mich.1978). A broker handling such an account has certain duties, including "the duty not to misrepresent any fact material to the transaction" and "the duty to transact business only after receiving prior authorization from the customer". *Id.* at 953 (listing broker's duties with respect to a non-discretionary account).

A "discretionary" account, on the other hand, is one in which the broker determines which investments to make and carries out such transactions without prior authorization. Hotmar, *supra*, 808 F.2d at 1385; Leib, *supra*, 461 F.Supp. at 953. We are mindful that other courts have held that, while a broker handling a discretionary account has a fiduciary duty to his customer, there is no such duty with respect to a non-discretionary account. *E.g.*, Commodity Futures Trading Comm'n v. Heritage Capital Advisory Services, Ltd., 823 F.2d 171, 173 (7th Cir.1987); Caravan Mobile Home Sales v. Lehman Bros. Kuhn Loeb, 769 F.2d 561, 567 (9th Cir.1985); Leboce, S.A. v. Merrill Lynch, Pierce, Fenner & Smith, Inc., 709 F.2d 605, 607 (9th Cir.1983); Shearson Hayden Stone, Inc. v. Leach, 583 F.2d 367, 371–72 (7th Cir.1978); Leib, *supra*, 461 F.Supp. at 953; but see Moholt v. Dean Witter Reynolds, Inc., 478 F.Supp. 451, 453 (D.D.C.1979) (brokers are quasifiduciaries "held to a high degree of trustworthiness and fair dealing"). * * *

In the instant case, Grace purchased the IBM options here involved in direct violation of Dr. Cheng's explicit instructions. Under District of Columbia law, Grace had the duty fully to disclose all material facts regarding the unauthorized transactions. Whether or not that duty be characterized as a fiduciary one, Grace was obligated to advise Dr. Cheng of all reasonable courses of action and not just those that inured to Grace's benefit. While that duty may be difficult to categorize, reasonable persons would agree, as a simple matter of fairness, that there is such a duty. See Restatement, *supra*, § 13 comment a (agent has "duty to deal fairly with the principal in all transactions between them"); cf. Achilles v. New England Tree Export Co., 369 F.2d 72, 74 (2d Cir.1966) (Medina, J.) ("call this particular . . . judgment what one will, it does substantial justice and we will not disturb it").

The district court found that Grace breached this duty by failing to advise Dr. Cheng of his right to reject the unauthorized IBM options and by "affirmatively misle[ading]" him into believing that he had only two choices: sell the options (at a loss) or meet the margin call. Viewing the evidence in the light most favorable to appellants, we agree.

We hold that appellants breached their duty to inform the Chengs of their right to disavow the unauthorized trades and that the district court properly directed a verdict in favor of the Chengs. * * *

As a final matter, we reject appellants' contention that the evidence, viewed in the light most favorable to them, establishes that Dr. Cheng was a sophisticated investor who was aware of all of his choices and voluntarily chose to ratify the trades here involved. Ratification occurs only when the customer, with full knowledge of the facts, manifests his intention to adopt the unauthorized transaction. Lewis v. Washington Metropolitan Area Transit Authority, 463 A.2d 666, 671 (D.C.1983). Since the Chengs were not advised of their right to reject the unauthorized trades, we agree with the district court that, as a matter of law, there could not have been ratification. Restatement, *supra*, § 416 (ratification is not a defense when principal "is caused to ratify by the misrepresentation . . . of the agent"); see also Nye v. Blyth Eastman Dillon & Co., 588 F.2d 1189, 1197 (8th Cir.1978). * * *

We hold, as a matter of law, that appellants breached their duty to advise the Chengs of their right to disavow the unauthorized trades here involved. We also hold, as a matter of law, that the Chengs did not ratify those trades. Accordingly, we hold that the district court properly granted the Chengs' motion for a directed verdict and properly entered judgment in their favor.

Affirmed.

Notes

The *Cheng* decision involves what the court terms a non-discretionary account—one in which the broker possesses little discretion over an account, simply buying or selling at the direction of the customer. There is a continuing debate over whether there is a fiduciary duty with such an account, but the court's holding avoids this singular issue, holding that even in a non-discretionary account, there remains a duty to not misrepresent material facts to a client. For a discussion of the fiduciary duty of a broker and a trustee, see, *e.g.*, Peter D. Isakoff, *Agents of Change: The Fiduciary*

Duties of Forwarding Market Professionals, 61 DUKE L.J. (2012); Barbara Black, *How to Improve Retail Investor Protection After the Dodd-Frank Wall Street Reform and Consumer Protection Act*, 13 U. PA. J. BUS. L. 59 (2010); Thomas Lee Hazen, *Are Existing Stock Broker Standards Sufficient? Principles, Rules, and Fiduciary Duties*, 2010 COLUM. BUS. L. REV. 710.

Uniform Trust Code (2019)

§ 813. Duty to Inform and Report.

(a) A trustee shall keep the qualified beneficiaries of the trust reasonably informed about the administration of the trust and of the material facts necessary for them to protect their interests. Unless unreasonable under the circumstances, a trustee shall promptly respond to a beneficiary's request for information related to the administration of the trust.

(b) A trustee:

(1) upon request of a beneficiary, shall promptly furnish to the beneficiary a copy of the trust instrument;

(2) within 60 days after accepting a trusteeship, shall notify the qualified beneficiaries of the acceptance and of the trustee's name, address, and telephone number;

(3) within 60 days after the date the trustee acquires knowledge of the creation of an irrevocable trust, or the date the trustee acquires knowledge that a formerly revocable trust has become irrevocable, whether by the death of the settlor or otherwise, shall notify the qualified beneficiaries of the trust's existence, of the identity of the settlor or settlors, of the right to request a copy of the trust instrument, and of the right to a trustee's report as provided in subsection (c); and

(4) shall notify the qualified beneficiaries in advance of any change in the method or rate of the trustee's compensation.

§ 105. Default and Mandatory Rules.

* * *

(b) The terms of a trust prevail over any provisions of this [Code] except: * * *

(8) the duty under Section 813(b)(2) and (3) to notify qualified beneficiaries of an irrevocable trust who have attained 25 years of age of the existence of the trust, of the identity of the trustee, and of their right to request trustee's report;

(9) the duty under Section 813(a) to respond to the request of a [qualified] beneficiary of an irrevocable trust for trustee's reports and other information reasonably related to the administration of a trust.

F. Record Keeping

John H. Langbein
*Questioning the Trust Law Duty of Loyalty:
Sole Interest or Best Interest?*
114 YALE L.J. 929 (2005)

Regulatory authorities emphasize trust recordkeeping as part of their audit and examination standards, . . . and courts draw adverse inferences against trustees whose recordkeeping has been substandard. . . .

Id. at 948.

Stark v. United States Trust Co. of New York

United States District Court, S.D. New York, 1978
445 F. Supp. 670

EDWARD WEINFELD, District Judge.

On April 29, 1965, the late Henry Harwood Rousseau created four *inter vivos* trusts (the "Trusts") for the benefit of each of his four daughters and their descendants (the "beneficiaries"). Named as Trustee in each of the Trusts was the defendant, United States Trust Company of New York ("USTC" or the "Trustee"). Plaintiffs, the beneficiaries, brought this action to recover losses incurred in the Trusts, allegedly the result of defendant's lack of prudent management. [1] Their charges center about defendant's retention in the Trusts of shares of stock in Clorox Co. ("Clorox"), Evans Products Co. ("Evans") and Coleco Industries, Inc. ("Coleco"), and their basic contention is that at an undetermined and unspecified time [2] following the death of the settlor in February 1972, USTC should have sold these stocks. Resisting plaintiffs' charges, the Trustee contends that in retaining these holdings it acted in good faith, exercised its judgment in a reasonable manner and measured up to the standard of prudent conduct imposed upon fiduciaries.

During the course of a five-day trial, defendant moved to dismiss the claim at the close of plaintiffs' case and renewed the motion at the end of trial; decision was reserved in each instance. Upon a word-by-word reading of the trial transcript, a review of the Court's trial notes, appraisal of the trial witnesses particularly defendant's employees in charge of the trust accounts, whose testimony the Court finds

---

1. The complaint originally contained three counts. Counts I and III, dealing with claims against the defendant as executor and testamentary trustee under Rousseau's will and alleging improper distribution of estate assets, were dismissed on November 4, 1976. This Court has jurisdiction of the remaining claim by virtue of the diversity of citizenship of the parties.

2. At the close of trial, in response to the Court's question of when the three stocks should have been sold, plaintiff's counsel stated:

> I think to pin that point would be very difficult. I think that the question really is not an answerable one in this sense. I don't think there was any single day on which we would say they must have sold them. . . .

credible and a study of various exhibits, the Court concludes upon the totality of the entire record that the charge of fiduciary breach by the Trustee has not been sustained and accordingly judgment on the merits is granted in favor of the defendant. We reach this conclusion whether the standard of conduct applied is that of the "prudent man" * * * or, as the plaintiffs here urge, a higher and more rigorous standard to be applied to professional fiduciaries who advertise their special skill and qualifications. * * *

Under the terms of each Trust agreement, which for purposes relevant herein are identical, the daughter for whom it was created and her issue may receive income and/or principal in the "absolute discretion" of the Trustee during the Trust term. Upon termination, a Trust's property is to be distributed to the daughter's surviving issue, *per stirpes*, or if none, to other designated remaindermen. Each Trust runs until twenty-one (21) years after the death of the last surviving daughter.

Rousseau's apparent objective was long term capital appreciation for the Trusts' duration and the considerable discretion vested in the Trustee was presumably designed to accomplish this. Thus, in addition to the Trustee's discretion with respect to payment of income and principal, paragraph Third of each agreement, which outlines the Trustee's powers, specifically provides that the powers are to be construed in the "broadest possible manner." Subsection (1), relevant herein, in substance empowers the Trustee, in its absolute discretion, to retain in the Trust any property received from the settlor, regardless of whether the Trust is invested disproportionately in such securities and provides that the Trustee shall neither be liable nor subject to surcharge or criticism for loss of income or principal caused by such retention or on the ground that such retained securities constitute an excessive portion of the Trust.[5]

The three stocks in question, Clorox, Evans and Coleco, were included in the Trusts' portfolios by direct gift or upon Rousseau's initiative. It is clear that he regarded these as desirable investments for the Trusts' purposes as he had been

---

5. Subsection (1) provides that the Trustee has:

Power to retain for such period as it shall deem proper any property received in trust hereunder, be it at the creation of the trust or by way of addition at a later date. Without limiting the absolute discretion of the Trustee, it shall be authorized to retain for such period as it shall deem proper any stocks, bonds or other securities, including voting trust certificates, conversion or subscription rights, warrants and/or options received in trust hereunder at the execution of this indenture, or by way of addition at a later date, of Moore's Super Stores, Inc. or any successor corporation (later Evans), or of any other corporation, and to exercise any and all rights and privileges accorded to it as the holder thereof as it, in its absolute discretion, deems to be in the best interest of the trust, and to purchase by subscription, exercise of conversion or subscription rights, warrants and/ or options, or otherwise additional securities of any such corporation, even to the extent that the trust concerned may be invested largely or entirely in such securities. The trustee shall not be held liable for loss of principal or income caused by the retention of such securities nor shall it be subject to criticism or surcharge upon the ground that said securities constitute an excessive portion of the trust.

interested in the affairs of these companies and was familiar with the management of each. All were listed on the New York Stock Exchange. In addition to these securities, the Trustee purchased additional securities on its own initiative. During Rousseau's lifetime and up to the date of his death the estate appreciated substantially; some securities, including Evans, were sold by the Trustee over Rousseau's objections and considerable profits were realized. * * * When Rousseau died in February 1972, each Trust contained 1000 shares of Clorox common stock, 2,002 shares of Evans common stock and 2,211 shares of Coleco common stock, valued at approximately $940,000. By January 1975, the total value of the three stocks had dropped to $93,000. Essentially, defendant's administration of the Trusts during the period following Rousseau's death in 1972 is the focus of this dispute. * * *

Within defendant's investment division, which deals with *inter vivos* trusts such as those in question, a number of sub-groups perform various functions. The Investment Policy Committee ("IPC") predicts broad economic trends, evaluates the market environment and makes general recommendations on portfolio strategy.[7] The Stock Selection Committee ("SSC") follows a universe of approximately 300–500 stocks (of a total 2500 held in one or more of the Company's portfolios) and codes these stocks with symbols suggesting[8] to those dealing directly with the portfolios the SSC's judgment of that stock's prospects and an appropriate course to take with respect to its purchase, sale or retention.[9] Both the SSC and the IPC rely upon the Trustee's research department and analysts therein, which provide reports on both whole industries and a specific company within an industry if that company is coded by the SSC, and upon the research library, which contains files on approximately 1600 companies and is kept current.

The actual responsibility for the day-to-day handling of customer accounts, however, rests with the portfolio manager (the "PM"). The PM makes the actual decisions for purchase, retention or sale of any security in a portfolio and is charged with keeping abreast of developments in the stocks and industries represented in an account. External and internal sources provide the information: externally, the Wall Street Journal, other business periodicals, securities ratings services, company publications,

---

7. The IPC, made up of senior USTC officers, including the chief economist, the head of the investment division and senior group and department heads, meets regularly and publishes its opinions, known as Investment Policy Statements, at least monthly.

8. The code is intended solely as guidance and is in no way a directive.

9. The SSC is composed of senior research analysts, senior portfolio managers and members of the economics department. Among the possible codings given stocks were and are: (a) "P", standing for "purchase", indicating SSC judgment that the stock is approved for purchase in all accounts; (b) "HS", standing for "hold for sale," which applies where in the SSC's opinion long term prospects are such that the stock should not have a continuing place among long term holdings, but where circumstances including a price overly depressed relative to the perceived near term potential of the stock make prompt sale inadvisable; (c) "CS", standing for "consider switch," which is a recommendation for reduction or elimination of holdings in favor of stocks with superior prospects; and (d) "thin," which when added to any of the above codes indicates limited marketability of a particular stock and thus possible problems in executing orders concerning that stock.

quotrons and current tickertape are available. Internally, research department reports, the IPC's economic forecasts and, where available, the SSC's decisions provide guidance to a PM. When a stock is not carried in the coded universe of SSC stocks, a PM has the additional responsibility of staying current on each non-coded company carried in a portfolio handled; no internal analyses can be relied upon to help synthesize all the relevant information. However, using outside sources of information periodicals, outside research firms' analyses and publications of the followed company itself, all of which are in library files the PM reaches a decision. * * *

The Rousseau portfolio was reviewed more often than was required by USTC policy. Prior to each visit by a member of the Rousseau family, the account was examined and the holdings evaluated for continued suitability. Similarly, each time an event of significance took place in any of these investments, that company's securities were reevaluated. Moreover, USTC was also co-executor of Rousseau's estate which contained substantial investments in these three companies, and Loud and Leonard repeatedly met with the portfolio manager assigned to the Rousseau estate and the account would be reviewed prior to and during these discussions. In all, the Trusts were reviewed by Loud and/or Leonard on more than forty occasions from 1972–75.

Concededly, USTC's forecasts of the economic climate for the period of 1972 through 1975 were not 100% accurate; its predictions concerning the course of the economy and stock market were not fully realized. For example, in November 1972, the IPC predicted that economic expansion would continue through 1973 and into 1974 and there would be no recession, when in fact the economy underwent a dramatic slowdown at that time. In May and June of 1973, the IPC cautioned the portfolio managers that stocks should not be sold to raise cash "in periods of market weakness." Perhaps most importantly, despite the economic slump, the IPC was of the opinion that the market had overly discounted equity securities and continued to recommend investment therein, especially in "quality growth stocks" with "proven ability to generate and maintain above-average and consistent profitability and growth in earnings." However, the Trustee explains, a number of factors affecting the economy were unforeseen and for the most part unforeseeable: the Arab oil embargo, inflation, consistently high interest rates, decline in discretionary purchasing power and the effects of Watergate, to name a few. * * *

Plaintiffs, citing the sharp drop in market price and the extensive changes undergone by these companies, argue that the Trustee was negligent and failed to meet its fiduciary responsibilities. More specifically, plaintiffs argue that USTC was negligent with respect to Clorox in that: (a) no internal research or analysis of any sort was done by any USTC employee, Loud [the portfolio manager] included; (b) Clorox was not followed by the Research Department or coded by the SSC but was followed solely by Loud; and (c) although Loud testified to having read the library's Clorox file, the financial press coverage and other outside reports on Clorox, (i) there is no indication in the files such as a memorandum or note from Loud that in fact she read them; (ii) she never attended a Clorox shareholders meeting, an analysts meeting on Clorox or actually spoke with Clorox management or an outside analyst about Clorox; and (iii) even if in fact she did read the library files, there are no reports therein dated between March 1972 and April 1973 and therefore Loud was uninformed about Clorox at that time.

Plaintiffs find imprudence in the Trustee's retention of Evans in that: (a) Rousseau was a director of Evans and his death deprived USTC of an important source of information; * * * (b) Evans was coded HS for over three years in violation of USTC's own internal policy; and (c) the analyst following Evans had recommended a change of code to CS in March of 1974, which Loud knew about and which was rejected by the SSC, the latter recoding the stock in November of that year after the stock's price became still more depressed.

Finally, as for Coleco, plaintiffs charge that: (a) the company's acquisition policy did not manifest itself until after Rousseau's death, thus removing any influence his support of the company might have had on retention decisions; (b) the SSC recoding of Coleco in July, 1973, from P-thin to HS based on a "revision of [its] fundamental view of the company" should have been made earlier in view of the price decline; and (c) the Trustee improperly failed to sell Coleco, still coded HS, despite other negative analyses and evaluations of Coleco and the industries it was in. In short, plaintiffs charge that the defendant failed to follow Clorox at all, did no comprehensive or in depth study of Evans or Coleco, ignored warning signs in Evans and Coleco, and failed to closely follow fundamental changes in each company. Finally, plaintiffs charge that the Trustee failed to diversify the portfolio or employ the assets of the Trusts profitably.

The Trustee responds that the record discloses that each of the securities was closely and carefully followed by the designated PM; that the decision to retain or to sell at a given time was made in the exercise of a good faith and prudent judgment based upon existing and reasonably projected economic factors in sum, that plaintiffs are now applying a hindsight judgment rather than viewing its conduct as of the time of the occurrence of events and against the background of existing conditions. * * *

In the substantial body of New York law governing the duties and responsibilities of trustees and applicable herein, * * * a number of fundamental principles have evolved which are relevant to and determinative of the issues in this case. It is clear that a trustee is neither insurer nor guarantor of the value of a trust's assets. * * * A trustee's performance is not judged by success or failure i. e., right or wrong * * * and while negligence may result in liability, a mere error in judgment will not. * * * Neither prophecy nor prescience is expected of trustees * * * and their performance must be judged not by hindsight but by facts which existed at the time of the occurrence. * * * A distinction is made between the acts of a trustee with respect to securities received from the settlor of a trust and those purchased by the trustee. Retention of assets given by a settlor may be prudent where purchase of those assets might not, especially if a trust instrument specifically so provides. * * *

But of probably greatest relevance is the substantial body of case law uniformly rejecting the notion that the decline of a stock's market price forbids retention by a trustee of a trust's holding in that stock. * * * It is not inherently negligent for a trustee to retain stock in a period of declining market values, * * * nor is there any magic percentage of decline which, when reached, mandates sale. * * * Indeed, the market's fluctuations have expressly been rejected as a trustworthy indicia of a holding's value especially in times of general economic decline. * * * Similarly, the fact that a stock may not be desirable for long term investment does not mean that a trustee is under a duty to sell it at the first possible opportunity. * * *

Stripped to its bare essentials, the plaintiffs' argument is that the Trustee was negligent and imprudent in retaining these securities because of their sharp drop in market price and allegedly insufficient analysis. Case law is clear, however, that the former charge is irrelevant if the latter charge is unfounded. * * * Even putting aside for one moment the effect of the Trust instruments' authorization for retention of stocks Rousseau contributed and its exoneration of liability for so doing, under the facts of this case, the Court need not resolve the disputed issue of what standard should be applied to defendant's conduct.[33] For even if one applies the more

---

33. As established in King v. Talbot, 40 N.Y. 76, 85–86 (1869) and reiterated recently in Matter of Bank of New York, 35 N.Y.2d 512, 518–19, 364 N.Y.S.2d 164, 169, 323 N.E.2d 700, 704 (1974), a "trustee is [bound to employ] such diligence and such prudence in the care and management, as in general, prudent men of discretion and intelligence in such matters, employ in their own like affairs." Plaintiffs argue that any application of this standard herein must take into consideration the fact that the defendant is a professional fiduciary, and consequently, having held itself out as possessing greater knowledge and skill than the average person, must be judged by a higher standard. In support, they rely largely upon general authority and cases from other jurisdictions. E. g., Estate of Beach, 15 Cal.3d 632, 125 Cal.Rptr. 570, 542 P.2d 994 (1975); Liberty Title and Trust Co. v. Plews, 142 N.J.Eq. 493, 60 A.2d 630 (Ch. 1948), aff'd in part, rev'd in part, 6 N.J. 28, 77 A.2d 219 (1950); Estate of Killey, 457 Pa. 474, 326 A.2d 372 (1974); Restatement (Second) of Trusts s 174; 2 Scott on Trusts s 174 at 1410–13 (3d ed. 1967); Uniform Probate Code s 7-302.

The scant New York authority relied upon by plaintiffs does not directly support their contentions. Isham v. Post, 141 N.Y. 100, 104–05, 35 N.E. 1084 (1894), dealt with agency-principal relations and specifically not with the defendant's capacity therein as trustee. Matter of Clark, 136 Misc. 881, 242 N.Y.S. 210 (Sur.Ct. Westchester County 1930), aff'd, 232 App.Div. 781, 249 N.Y.S. 923 (2d Dep't), rev'd, 257 N.Y. 132, 177 N.E. 397 (1931), also cited by plaintiffs, provides them with slender support at best. The Surrogate in Clark held that a corporate trustee's conduct was measured by a standard more stringent than that applied to an individual, found a breach of that standard and assessed the corporate trustee with a surcharge. 242 N.Y.S. at 220–21. Although not referring specifically to this portion of the Surrogate's opinion, the Court of Appeals pointedly applied to the corporate trustee defendant the standard of King v. Talbot, *supra*, the same standard applied to individuals, 257 N.Y. at 136, 177 N.E. 397, found no breach and reversed. That this remains the standard seems implicit in the recent Court of Appeals ruling in Matter of Bank of New York, *supra*, where the King individual standard was again applied to a corporate trustee. 35 N.Y.2d at 518–19, 364 N.Y.S.2d at 169, 323 N.E.2d 700. Finally, two lower New York state courts have expressly rejected the argument put forward here. Matter of Flint, 240 App.Div. 217, 226, 269 N.Y.S. 470, 479 (2d Dep't 1934), aff'd, Central Hanover Bank & Trust Co., 266 N.Y. 607, 195 N.E. 221 (1935); Matter of Pate, 84 N.Y.S.2d 853, 858 (Sur.Ct. N.Y. County 1948), aff'd 276 App. Div. 1008, 95 N.Y.S.2d 903 (1st Dep't 1950). Thus, despite plaintiffs' argument to the contrary, the New York cases apparently do not distinguish between institutional and individual trustees in the standard applied to a trustee's conduct. As indicated above, however, this issue need not be determined in this case.

stringent standard suggested by plaintiffs modifying the traditional standard of a prudent person of discretion and intelligence * * * and holding the defendant as a professional trustee to a higher standard plaintiffs' claim of inadequate attention and insufficient analysis must be rejected. The Trustee's retention decisions were the result of careful and informed deliberation; the fact that in retrospect they may have been wrong or unwise is no ground for surcharge. * * *

In the first place, the IPC's economic forecasts must be taken into account. This, the USTC unit charged with guiding the investment division with broad economic analyses, admittedly erred and obviously could not have foreseen certain events. The IPC's prediction that there would be no recession in 1973 or 1974, for example, placed emphasis on purchase and retention of common stocks with growth potential. There was no way, to choose another example, that the Arab oil embargo or its effects on the economy could have been expected—nations, no less than individuals did not anticipate such actions. Indeed, daily we witness instances of public officials and financial experts, specialists in the fields of economics, fiscal and monetary affairs, whose forecasts of events fall far wide of eventualities. Given the breadth of information and analyses the IPC reports contain, their predictions certainly were not without a reasonable basis which is all that is required. And these forecasts guided the portfolio managers, Loud included.

The fact that Loud did not speak to an analyst, write a note to the Clorox file that she had read a report, do her own analysis or clip articles from the Wall Street Journal is irrelevant. She testified and in the Court's opinion truthfully that she read the analyses and articles. Information contained therein, most of it extremely favorable to Clorox, was sufficient to support her retention decisions. And although no outside analytical reports on Clorox from March 1972 to April 1973 are in the Clorox file, the file did contain two prospectuses concerning the issuance of securities, notice of the annual shareholders meeting and a proxy statement circulated during that period. In addition, the financial press covered all developments in Clorox's acquisition program, plus published its financial reports. Loud also testified that she might well have read other analysts' reports which came out at that time. She was aware of the changes in the company and the fact that her opinions of Clorox were shared by the majority of analysts suggests that her judgment was reasonable. Plaintiffs cite no legal authority for their novel proposition that a trustee, even a professional trustee, violates its fiduciary duty unless it acts solely upon its own analyses committed to writing, * * * and the Court refuses to so hold. The issue is whether an overall and knowledgeable judgment was brought to bear; whether the defendant's conduct under all the circumstances was prudent. The fact is that in this case, given the information available to Loud and her use of it, the defendant's conduct amply met that standard. The evidence fully sustains a finding that Loud was not only attentive to all matters pertaining to Clorox, but that she and her associate exercised a considered, informed, prudent and reasonable judgment in the discharge of their fiduciary duties.

Despite the fact that Evans was coded by the SSC and followed by an analyst, plaintiffs persistently allege that there was insufficient attention paid to the stock.

Loud read the reports, communicated with the analyst regularly, followed the company in the financial press and was aware of changes in the company. The SSC and analyst considered it on numerous occasions memoranda and other documentary evidence alone indicates more than twenty times in the three-year period. Loud reviewed the holding on an even greater number of occasions. The claim of inattention or negligence is simply unsupported. Plaintiffs' further attempt to support this allegation by observing that an HS code was repeatedly placed on Evans stock, noting that this code is by USTC policy "temporary" and thus concluding that it was imprudent to wait for projected price recovery for as long as the Trustee did, fails to account for the realities of the situation. True, the USTC coding procedures manual provides that "under no circumstances (should HS) be used as a haven for compromise." But the fact that a coding is designed to be temporary does not mean that on successive occasions, an informed and deliberate SSC could not reasonably conclude that the stock's price would in fact rise, especially when it was deemed underpriced in the market. As cogently explained at trial, in a number of coded stocks during 1973–74, HS was repeatedly retained based upon USTC's economic outlook and investment strategy it believed that the market in due course would recover and that large numbers of stocks were unduly depressed. Finally, the evidence clearly shows that the eventual recoding of Evans was prompted by a wholly unexpected announcement that earnings projections would not be met and that operations would only break even and the sale of the stock based largely on the resultant loss of Evans' dividend both clearly reasoned decisions.

As to Coleco, plaintiffs' allegations of inattention are similarly unfounded for the same reasons described above. Again, Loud followed the company in the financial press, discussed it with the research analyst regularly, attended a shareholders' meeting and met with management. The fact that there are negative statements about the company in the SSC and analysts' reports does not mean that they had to be acted upon immediately. Indeed, their presence confirms the fact that aware of all relevant factors and bearing in mind the IPC's forecast, the judgments to retain Coleco pending price appreciation were reasoned and informed.

In sum, as stated by the New York State Court of Appeals in Matter of Clark,[36] a case factually similar to this:

> With all the advices which the trustee received from those well versed in the . . . trade and in finance, and those experienced in the vagaries of the stock exchange, counseling delay, how can it be said that it was negligent in omitting to make prompt disposal of the stocks? Under the circumstances, we think that the trustee, as the event has proven, was guilty, at the very most, of an error of judgment, in not making sale of the stocks at an earlier date. It may have been deficient in prevision and prophesy; it was not lacking in the exercise of care.[37]

---

36. 257 N.Y. 132, 177 N.E. 397 (1931).
37. Id. at 139–40, 177 N.E. at 399.

No extended discussion is warranted by plaintiffs' charge that defendant was negligent in not diversifying the Trusts' portfolios which allegedly contained too many "speculative" securities. In the first place, the allegation is factually unfounded. Originally, the Trusts each contained four times as much Evans' stock as they did at Rousseau's death three quarters of the original Evans' holdings were sold in 1966–68 at the Trustee's insistence and over Rousseau's objections for the precise purpose of diversification. * * * Indeed, Rousseau's criticism of the handling of the account which lead to the brief hiatus in Loud's stewardship was that the portfolio was being managed too conservatively. And when Rousseau died in 1972, the portfolio was invested in such established concerns as Pepsico and IBM. Legally, the allegation is irrelevant. Under New York law, an investment must be found faulty for some reason other than the percentage of the trust it constitutes, * * * which as indicated above has not been shown.

Indeed, this analysis has thus far ignored the provisions of the Trust agreements and measured the Trustee's conduct by the standard urged by plaintiffs. However, the provisions of each agreement provide an equally cogent ground for rejecting plaintiffs' claims: they specifically authorize the Trustee in its absolute discretion to retain any property received in the Trusts regardless of whether it constitutes a disproportionate amount of a total Trust corpus and expressly provide that the Trustee will not be subject to criticism or surcharge for so doing. Similarly, each agreement provides that the "trustee shall not be held liable for loss of principal or income caused by the retention" of securities contributed by Rousseau, and that retention decisions are in the Trustee's absolute discretion. Although absolute discretion "does not mean . . . that it might be recklessly or willfully abused,"[40] exoneration provisions are recognized under New York law in *inter vivos* trusts such as these and protect a trustee from liability absent recklessness, fraud or intentional wrongdoing. * * * There is no allegation of fraud and plaintiffs have failed to prove either negligence or imprudence in this case; manifestly they have not shown recklessness or conscious wrongdoing. There is simply no factual basis which would justify a disregard of the settlor's express provisions.

In sum, with respect to each Trust, it has not been established that any losses resulted from imprudence or negligence. To the contrary, the evidence abundantly establishes that deliberate, informed and experienced attention and professional judgment were brought into play with respect to each decision that was made at the time of decision.

The foregoing shall constitute the Court's Findings of Fact and Conclusions of Law. Judgment is granted on the merits for the defendant and may be entered accordingly.

---

40. Carrier v. Carrier, 226 N.Y. 114, 125, 123 N.E. 135 (1919) (Cardozo, J.).

Notes

As demonstrated in the *Stark* decision, proper record keeping can both insulate a trustee from accusations of improper conduct and incriminate the negligent. Among the elements to be recorded are the following: (a) tax profiles; (b) liquidity needs; (c) investment strategy plan; (d) risk versus return strategy; (e) inflation and deflation analysis; (f) portfolio diversification analysis; (g) income and corpus distributions; (h) history of client communications; and (i) cotrustee approval. For discussion of modern practices, see, *e.g.*, John T. Stinson, *Digital-Age Record Retention Practices for Trusts*, 44 Est. Plan. 38 (2017). For an example of a state statute mandating recordkeeping and consequences for failing to do so, see 15 Wis. Practice, § 10:106 (9th ed. 2018). *Duty of the trustee to keep adequate records.*

> Unless the terms of the trust provide otherwise, a trustee is obligated to keep adequate records of the administration of the trust. This duty to keep adequate records is 'implicit in the duty to act with prudence and the duty to report to beneficiaries.' If the records are not clear and accurate, all presumptions are against the trustee, and the obscurities and doubts are to be taken adversely against the trustee.

Id.

G. Socially Responsible Investing

Uniform Prudent Investor Act (2019)

§ 5. cmt. [Loyalty].

No form of so-called "social investing" is consistent with the duty of loyalty if the investment activity entails sacrificing the interests of trust beneficiaries — for example, by accepting below-market returns — in favor of the interests of the persons supposedly benefitted by pursuing the particular social cause. * * * In 1994 the Department of Labor issued an Interpretive Bulletin reviewing its prior analysis of social investing questions and reiterating that pension trust fiduciaries may invest only in conformity with the prudence and loyalty standards of ERISA §§ 403–404. * * * The Bulletin reminds fiduciary investors that they are prohibited from "subordinat[ing] the interests of participants and beneficiaries in their retirement income to unrelated objectives."

Blankenship v. Boyle

United States District Court, District of Columbia, 1971
329 F. Supp. 1089

GESELL, District Judge.

This is a derivative class action brought on behalf of coal miners who have a present or future right to benefits as provided by the United Mine Workers of America

Welfare and Retirement Fund of 1950. Plaintiffs have qualified under Rule 23.2 of the Federal Rules of Civil Procedure. Jurisdiction is founded on diversity and on the general jurisdiction of this Court, 11 D.C.Code § 521, in effect at the time suit was filed. Defendants are the Fund and its present and certain past trustees; the United Mine Workers of America; and the National Bank of Washington and a former president of that Bank. * * *

Plaintiffs seek substantial equitable relief and compensatory and punitive damages for various alleged breaches of trust and conspiracy. Defendants oppose these claims on the merits and in addition interpose defenses of laches and the statute of limitations. The issues were specified at pretrial conferences, and after extensive discovery the case was tried to the Court without a jury. Following trial, the case was fully argued and detailed briefs were exchanged. This Opinion constitutes the Court's findings of fact and conclusions of law on the issues of liability and equitable relief. * * *

The Fund was created by the terms of the National Bituminous Coal Wage Agreement of 1950, executed at Washington, D.C., March 5, 1950, between the Union and numerous coal operators. It is an irrevocable trust established pursuant to Section 302(c) of the Labor-Management Relations Act of 1947, 29 U.S.C. § 186(c), and has been continuously in operation with only slight modifications since its creation.

The Fund is administered by three trustees: one designated by the Union, one designated by the coal operators, and the third a 'neutral party designated by the other two.' The Union representative is named Chairman of the Board of Trustees by the terms of the trust. Each trustee, once selected, serves for the term of the Agreement subject only to resignation, death, or an inability or unwillingness to serve. The original trustees named in the Agreement were Charles A. Owen for the Operators, now deceased; John L. Lewis for the Union, now deceased; and Miss Josephine Roche. The present trustees are W. A. (Tony) Boyle, representing the Union; C. W. Davis, representing the Operators; and Roche, who still serves.[2]

Each coal operator signatory to the Agreement (there are approximately fifty-five operator signatories) is required to pay a royalty (originally thirty cents, and now forty cents per ton of coal mined) into the Fund. These royalty payments represent in excess of ninety-seven percent of the total receipts of the Fund, the remainder being income from investments. In the year ending June 30, 1968, royalty receipts totalled $163.1 million and investment income totalled $4.7 million. Total benefit expenditures amounted to $152 million.

In general, the purpose of the Fund is to pay various benefits, 'from principal or income or both,' to employees of coal operators, their families and dependents. These benefits cover medical and hospital care, pensions, compensation for

---

2. Lewis and Boyle have been the only Union trustees. There has been a succession of Operator trustees. Owen served until 1957, followed in sequence by Henry Schmidt, George Judy, Guy Farmer and C. W. Davis.

workrelated injuries or illness, death or disability, wage losses, etc. The trustees have considerable discretion to determine the types and levels of benefits that will be recognized. While prior or present membership in the Union is not a prerequisite to receiving welfare payments, more than ninety-five percent of the beneficiaries were or are Union members.

The Fund has maintained a large staff based mainly in Washington, D.C., which carries out the day-to-day work under policies set by the trustees. Roche, the neutral trustee, is also Administrator of the Fund serving at an additional salary in this full-time position. Thomas Ryan, the Fund's Comptroller, is the senior staff member next in line.

The trustees hold irregular meetings, usually at the Fund's offices. Formal minutes are prepared and circulated for approval. In the past, a more detailed and revealing record of discussions among the trustees has been prepared and maintained in the files of the Fund by the Fund's counsel, who attended all meetings. The Fund is regularly audited, and a printed annual report summarizing the audit and other developments was published and widely disseminated to beneficiaries, Union representatives, and coal operators, as well as to interested persons in public life.

From the outset the trustees contemplated that the Fund would operate on a "pay-as-you-go" basis—that is, that the various benefits would be paid out largely from royalty receipts rather than solely from income earned on accumulated capital. Always extremely liquid, the Fund invested some of its growing funds in United States Government securities and purchased certificates of deposit. It also purchased a few public utility common stocks, and in very recent years invested some amounts in tax-free municipal securities. * * *

From its creation in 1950, the Fund has done all of its banking business with the National Bank of Washington. In fact, for more than twenty years it has been the Bank's largest customer. When this lawsuit was brought, the Fund had about $28 million in checking accounts and $50 million in time deposits in the Bank. The Bank was at all times owned and controlled by the Union which presently holds 74 percent of the voting stock. Several Union officials serve on the Board of Directors of the Bank, and the Union and many of its locals also carry substantial accounts there. Boyle, President of the Union, is also Chairman of the Board of Trustees of the Fund and until recently was a Director of the Bank. * * * Representatives of the Fund have also served as Directors of the Bank, including the Fund's house counsel and its Comptroller. The Fund occupies office space rented from the Union for a nominal amount, located in close proximity to the Union's offices. * * *

The precise duties and obligations of the trustees are not specified in any of the operative documents creating the Fund and are only suggested by the designation of the Fund as an 'irrevocable trust.' There appears to have been an initial recognition by the trustees of the implications of this term. Lewis, who was by far the dominant factor in the development and administration of the Fund, stated at Board meetings that neither the Union's nor the Operators' representative was responsible to any special interest except that of the beneficiaries. He declared that each trustee should act solely in the best interests of the Fund, that the day-to-day affairs of the Fund were to be kept confidential by the trustees, that minutes were not to be circulated outside the Fund, and that the Fund should be soundly and conservatively managed with the long-term best interests of the beneficiaries as the exclusive objective. While he ignored these strictures on a number of occasions, as will appear, his view is still accepted by counsel for the Fund in this action, who took the position at oral argument that the duties of the trustees are equivalent to the duties of a trustee under a testamentary trust. Counsel stated, 'You can't be just a little bit loyal. Once you are a trustee, you are a trustee, and you cannot consider what is good for the Union, what is good for the operators, what is good for the Bank, anybody but the trust.' (Tr. 2590). * * *

Before dealing in detail with the specific breaches of trust alleged, a general comment concerning the conduct of the trustees is appropriate to place the instances of alleged misfeasance into proper context. It has already been noted that the trustees did not hold regular meetings but only met subject to the call of the Chairman. There was, accordingly, no set pattern for deciding policy questions, and often matters of considerable import where resolved between meetings by Roche and Lewis without even consulting the Operator trustee.

The Fund's affairs were dominated by Lewis until his death in 1969. Roche never once disagreed with him. Over a period of years, primarily at Lewis' urging, the Fund became entangled with Union policies and practices in ways that undermined the independence of the trustees. This resulted in working arrangements between the Fund and the Union that served the Union to the disadvantage of the beneficiaries. Conflicts of interest were openly tolerated and their implications generally ignored. * * * Not only was all the money of the Fund placed in the Union's Bank without any consideration of alternative banking services and facilities that might be available, but Lewis felt no scruple in recommending that the Fund invest in securities in which the Union and Lewis, as trustee for the Union's investments, had an interest. Personnel of the Fund went on the Bank's board without hindrance, thus affiliating themselves with a Union business venture. In short, the Fund proceeded without any clear understanding of the trustees' exclusive duty to the beneficiaries, and its affairs were so loosely controlled that abuses, mistakes and inattention to detail occurred. * * *

Th[e] issue relates to the Fund's purchases of stock of certain electric utility companies, principally Cleveland Electric Illuminating Company and Kansas City Power & Light Company. While these stocks are on the list approved for trustees, the propriety of these investments is challenged on the ground that they were made primarily for the purpose of benefiting the Union and the operators, and assisting them in their efforts to force public utilities to burn Union-mined coal. The investments have declined in value and are said to have been in violation of the trustees' duty of undivided loyalty to the beneficiaries.

In the late 1950's and early 1960's, the Union was engaged in a vigorous campaign to force public utility companies to purchase Union-mined coal. Public relations and organizational campaigns to this end were pressed vigorously in several cities.

Lewis, then a trustee, worked closely with Cyrus S. Eaton, a Cleveland business-man. It is undisputed that between February and April 1955 the Fund purchased 30,000 shares of Cleveland Electric, and in March of that year the Union loaned Eaton money to enable him to buy an additional 20,000 shares. Eaton then went on the Board of Directors of Cleveland Electric. Similarly, between January and March 1955 the Fund purchased 55,000 shares of Kansas City Power & Light, and in June of the same year the Union loaned Eaton money to buy an additional 27,000 shares. In each of the years from 1956 to 1965 the Fund gave a general proxy for all of its shares in Cleveland Electric and Kansas City Power & Light to Eaton. The Union and Eaton were pressing the managements of each company to force them to buy Union-mined coal. The Fund purchased both Cleveland Electric and Kansas City Power & Light stock on the recommendation of Lewis, who was then fully familiar with the Union's activities affecting these companies and proxies were given to the Union by the Fund at Lewis' request.

Schmidt, who became a trustee of the Fund in 1958, was president of the principal coal operator standing to benefit from Cleveland Electric's additional purchases of Union-mined coal. He was acquainted with the activities of the Fund and of the Union with respect to Cleveland Electric, and actively encouraged them. When the Union's campaign to push Union-mined coal focused on Cleveland Electric in 1962 and 1963, the Fund purchased an additional 90,000 shares, with the hearty approval of Schmidt.

Further indication that these particular challenged stock purchases were made primarily for the collateral benefits they gave the Union is found in a general course of conduct. Lewis and Widman, the Union man spearheading the efforts to force utilities to buy Union-mined coal, discussed some seventeen utility companies on the Fund's investment list, looking toward the possibility of obtaining proxies from fifteen. Proxies were in fact given the Union by the Fund not only on Cleveland Electric and Kansas City Power & Light, but on the shares the Fund held in Union Electric, Ohio Edison, West Penn Electric, Southern Company and Consolidated Edison. The intimate relationship between the Union's financial and organizing activities and the utility investment activities of the trustees demonstrates that the Fund was acting primarily for the collateral benefit of the Union and the signatory operators in making most of its utility stock acquisitions. These activities present a clear case of self-dealing on the part of trustees Lewis and Schmidt, and constituted a breach of trust. Roche knowingly consented to the investments, and must also be held liable. The Union is likewise liable for conspiring to effectuate and benefit by this breach of trust. * * *

No considerations of equity intervene to bar prospective remedies for misman-agement of the Fund by its trustees. The Fund has been seriously compromised. It has failed to develop a coherent investment policy geared to immediate or long-term goals. It has collaborated with the Union contrary to the trustees' fiduciary duties, and has left excessive sums of money on deposit with the Union's Bank in order to assist the Union. In their day-to-day decisions, the trustees have overlooked their exclusive obligation to the beneficiaries by improperly aiding the Union to collect back dues and by cutting off certain beneficiaries unfairly.

Alongside these serious deficiencies must be placed the pioneer role of the Fund, which by constant effort has led in the development of a broad program of welfare benefits for a distressed segment of the working population. The many beneficial and well-motivated actions cannot, however, excuse the serious lapses which have resulted in obvious detriments to many beneficiaries. There is an urgent need for reformation of policies and practices which only changes in the composition of the Board of Trustees, an adjustment of its banking relationship, and other equitable relief can accomplish.

Further proceedings must be conducted on the measure of damages, but as the Court indicated before trial it is desirable at this stage to establish the nature of equitable relief which must be taken for the protection of the beneficiaries. Equitable relief shall take the following form.

Neither Boyle nor Roche shall continue to serve as a trustee. Each shall be replaced by June 30, 1971, under the following procedures. A new trustee must first be named by the Union. Consonant with the provisions of the Agreement, the new Union trustee and the existing trustee representing the Operators shall then select a new neutral trustee. The neutral trustee shall be designated on or before June 15, 1971, and the designation will then be submitted for approval by this Court before the new trustee takes office on June 30.

The newly constituted Board of Trustees selected as required by the decree shall then immediately determine whether or not Roche shall continue as Administrator of the Fund. No trustee shall serve as Administrator after June 30, 1971.

Upon the selection of a replacement for Boyle and the neutral trustee, the newly constituted Board of Trustees shall be required to obtain independent professional advice to assist them in developing an investment policy for creating maximum income consistent with the prudent investment of the Fund's assets, and such a program shall be promptly put into effect.

The Fund shall by June 30, 1971, cease maintaining banking accounts with or doing any further business of any kind with the National Bank of Washington. Following termination of this relationship, the Fund shall not have any account in a bank in which either the Union, any coal operator or any trustee has controlling or substantial stock interest. No employee, representative or trustee of the Fund shall have any official connection with the bank or banks used by the Fund after June 30, 1971. The Fund shall not maintain non-interest-bearing accounts in any bank or other depository which are in excess of the amount reasonably necessary to cover immediate administrative expenses and to pay required taxes and benefits on a current basis.

A general injunction shall be framed enjoining the trustees from the practices here found to be breaches of trust and generally prohibiting the trustees from operating the Fund in a manner designed in whole or in part to afford collateral advantages to the Union or the operators.

Counsel are directed to confer and prepare a proposed form of decree carrying out the equitable relief here specified. This proposed decree shall be presented to the Court and any disagreements as to form settled on May 13, 1971, at 4:00 p.m. On May 21, 1971, plaintiffs shall furnish the Court and defendants with a precise statement of the amounts of compensatory damages and attorneys' fees and expenses claimed in light of this Opinion, a statement of the method used to compute the claims, and a list of witnesses to be called at the damages phase of this proceeding. No punitive damages will be awarded. A hearing as to compensatory damages is set for June 21, 1971, at 9:30 a.m. * * *

Notes

As we have seen, good intentions on the part of a trustee are not sufficient to overcome the penalties for imprudence, and the *Blankenship* case offers an example. The case was decided prior to the standards provided by ERISA, but the court's holding is sound in that a trustee may not engage in self-dealing, and the long-term prudent investing of assets takes precedence over political benefit for the union or the coal miners. But what is ethical investing? Both in private wealth management and in the large portfolios held by pension funds, there is often a desire to invest ethically. How is this accomplished? For a survey of current thinking on socially responsible investing, see generally Daniel C. Esty & Quentin Karpilow, *Harnessing Investor Interest in Sustainability: The Next Frontier in Environmental Information Regulation*, 36 Yale J. on Reg. 625 (2019) (discussing the need for socially responsible investing); Tom C.W. Lin, *Incorporating Social Activism*, 98 B.U. L. Rev. 1535 (2018); John F. McCabe & Nina A. Farran, *Impact Investing for Trustees*, 154 Trusts & Ests. 23 (June 2015) (suggesting that times have changed and challenging John Langbein's and Richard Posner's view that social investing is contrary to prudence); William Sanders, *Resolving the Conflict Between Fiduciary Duties and Socially Responsible Investing*, 35 Pace L. Rev. 535–79 (2014); Edward J. Finley II & Andrew N. King, *Socially Responsible Investing,* 152 Trusts & Ests. 49 (Sept. 2013) (suggesting that socially responsible investing has become part of an acceptable fiduciary portfolio).

John F. McCabe & Nina A. Farran
Impact Investing for Trustees
154 Trusts & Ests. 23 (June 2015)

To the extent that an impact investment [socially responsible investing] program the trustee pursues is expected to generate competitive returns with adequate diversification (and subject to reasonable fees), aligning a portfolio with the beneficiaries' values seems consistent with the UPIA. Furthermore, a trustee who obtains the consent of all of the beneficiaries may certainly proceed with an impact investment program with minimal risk. In those situation in which the consent of the beneficiaries is unobtainable, the trustee must balance the interests of all of the beneficiaries (including future beneficiaries), though interesting questions would be raised by a legal standard that requires the trustee to make investments that are inconsistent with the values of one or more of the beneficiaries. [Citations omitted.] And, the settlor of the trust may override all of these considerations by drafting the trust agreement to explicitly allow the trustee to engage in (or direct the trustee to proceed with) an impact investment program.

Id. at 28.

Edward J. Finley II & Andrew N. King
Socially Responsible Investing
152 Trusts & Ests. 49 (Sept. 2013)

Perhaps one of the most notable examples of the impact of [an earlier form of socially responsible investing (SRI)] is the fall of apartheid in South Africa. In 1975, Rev. Leon H. Sullivan, then a member of the Board of Directors of General Motors Corporation, drafted an ethical framework for companies operating in South Africa, which was then still under apartheid law. This framework, which became known as the "Sullivan Principles," called for companies to maintain fair employment practices, regardless of race, and the active pursuit of improved living conditions for people of non-European descent. The grown anti-apartheid movement used the Sullivan Principles as a focal point, as it pressured American companies to pursue anti-apartheid practices. [Citations omitted.] ...

Id. at 49.

Later, in the 1980s, the movement led to a disinvestment campaign in which anti-apartheid activists lobbied for institutions, such as university endowments and public pension funds, to remove investments in companies that didn't adhere to the principles. ... Specifically, student protests caused the number of universities participating in the disinvestment campaign to rise from 53 in 1985 to 155 by August 1988. Overall, the Sullivan Principles and the accompanying disinvestment campaign contributed to a reduction of U.S. direct investment in South Africa from $2.28 billion in 1982 to $1.27 billion in 1988 and are considered to have played a meaningful role in ending the apartheid system. [Citations omitted.] ...

Id. at 49–50.

Studies ... have supported the emerging view among institutional investors and family offices alike that investors needn't sacrifice performance in pursuit of a portfolio that's aligned with their [SRI] views. And, the discipline and selection involved with [SRI] criteria often leads to outper-formance versus non-SRI investment strategies. . . . In fact, a survey of 195 fund managers by Mercer Investment Consulting in 2005 revealed not only that positive screens for [SRI] factors are a method used in SRI investing, but also that traditional investment managers are increasingly employing these screens to target companies whose strong [SRI] practices limit vari-ous risks and liabilities and can be expected to generate superior financial performance. [Citations omitted.]

Id. at 51.

V. Class Gifts

A class gift is created by a testator or a settlor, with the intention of creating a gift in favor of persons belonging to a group that is capable of increasing or decreasing on its own. For example, in a Last Will and Testament, the testator may write: "All of my property, both real and personal, I hereby give, devise, and bequeath to my children." At the time the testator executes the will, the testator has one child, but when the testator dies some years later and the will speaks, the testator has three children. How many children take? Obviously, the testator intended that all of the children should take because all are members of a "class," and none has been excluded through specific language. Likewise, if, in a valid *inter vivos* trust, a settlor, writes: "Income to myself for life, and then the remainder to my children, to be paid when the youngest turns twenty-one," and the settlor has one child when the trust is created but three children when the settlor dies, and the youngest child turns twenty-one, how many children should take? Once again, since a class designation was used, all of the children meeting the description should take when the corpus of the trust becomes available. Class gifts are intended to be fluid and flexible, and these two examples provide illustrations of class members increasing until distribu-tion occurs.

But there also can be decreasing members of a class, and this raises different issues. For example, if, as in the previous example, the testator writes: "All of my property, both real and personal, I hereby give, devise, and bequeath to my children," what happens if one of these children dies before the testator, and the child has descen-dants who survive the testator? If the state's anti-lapse statute applies to class gifts, then the descendants of the pre-deceasing child will take the portion that his or her deceased parent would have taken as a member of a class, if the parent had survived. Because the child was a relative of the testator, anti-lapse is free to apply (you may review the material concerning anti-lapse at Chapter Four, Section VII, *supra*). But there may be a decrease in the members of a class in an *inter vivos* trust — some-thing to which anti-lapse will not apply. Return to the previous example of a settlor who creates an *inter vivos* trust and writes: "To myself for life, and then the remain-der to my children, to be paid when the youngest turns twenty-one." If the settlor has a child who dies after the settlor creates the trust but before the death of the settlor *and* when the youngest child turns twenty-one, and that predeceasing child leaves descendants and an estate, should a portion of the trust go to the descendants or to the estate? The answer is, "yes," but the portion that would have gone to the child, had the child survived as a member of the class, now goes to the estate of the deceased child, when the settlor dies and the youngest child turns twenty-one. The descendants do not take as they would have done under the anti-lapse statute. The reason the estate takes is due to vesting.

To explain vesting, we know that when the settlor established the trust during the settlor's lifetime, the settlor provided that the corpus would be distributed to the children whenever the settlor died and the youngest child then, or in the future, turned twenty-one. But note that the settlor did not create a condition that the child survive until the later of these two events. Instead, the settlor provided that the corpus would be paid at that point. *See* Clobberie's Case, 2 Vent. 342, 86 Eng. Rep. 476 (1677). Vesting occurred first; possession or payment occurred in the future. Thus, a child has a vested interest in the remainder simply by being alive or born during the trust period. And at the point of distribution—the death of the settlor and the youngest child turning twenty-one—the child or the estate takes possession or payment.

There are other issues concerning class gifts, but the issues surrounding increase and decrease abound. Careful drafting and a knowledge of construction issues will prevent a multitude of litigation.

A. Increase of Class

In re Evans' Estate
Supreme Court of Wisconsin, 1957
274 Wis. 459, 80 N.W.2d 408

FAIRCHILD, Chief Justice.

Before taking up the question of whether or not the judgment entered April 17, 1942 is *res judicata* as to grandchildren born after the date of death of the testator, it seems well to pass upon the nature and inclusiveness of the bequest. If the gift grant in Article Third is to a class, and that class is so fixed by the terms of the bequest that there may be an interval of time during which the class may increase, then the gift is one which vests in the existing number of the class and such other persons as thereafter become members of the class. That interval continues to the point of time or event which is specified and certain. The gift we are considering is to 'my grandchildren,' and because of the absence of an alternative gift over or reversion in favor of the testator's heirs, it bespeaks an intention of a vested gift. The grandchildren living at the death of the testator are members of the class, but the class is subject to a change by addition of after-born grandchildren who came into being before the coming of the event which closes forever the membership in the class.

The time fixed for closing the class is set in the bequest: 'After each grandchild reaches the age of thirty years, he is to be paid his full share of the principal sum of this bequest together with the interest which has accumulated thereon.' This controls the increase in membership in the class. The time of the distribution of the *corpus* settles the question of maximum membership. In the absence of words in the will indicating a contrary intent, a testator would naturally desire to include all grandchildren born at the time of the distribution of the *corpus*. In Simes, The Law of Future Interests, we find the following recognition of rules of construction:

> 'The maximum membership in the class is determined when the time for distribution has arrived. The class may increase until that time, and persons born thereafter are excluded.' Sec. 634, p. 69.

> 'The time for distribution arrived when the first member of the class attained the designated age.' Sec. 644, p. 89.

> In 5 American Law of Property, the following rules are recognized:

> When a class gift is postponed until the occurrence of some * * * event, such as the attainment of age twenty-one * * *. the class does not normally close until the first member of the class attains the designated age. Sec. 22.44, p. 372.

> 'It must be kept in mind that the probable desire of the average transferor, when he describes his transferees by a group designation, is to benefit as many persons who comply with the description as he can, without at the same time causing too much inconvenience.' Sec. 22.43, p. 364.

The gift may be so made that the class may either increase or decrease after the death of the testator until the arrival of the fixed point of time or the happening of the specified event. It may be so worded that there may be an interval of time during which the class may increase but during which it cannot decrease. The most common example of this kind of gift is one which vests in the existing members of a class and in such other persons as thereafter become members of the class up to the point of time or event which is specified. Page on Wills, sec. 1052. It is considered that the three grandchildren born after the death of the testator and before the distribution of the *corpus* are members of the class and inherit as such.

The question of *res adjudicata* we conclude to be without merit. In his will the deceased made a gift to a class, to wit, his grandchildren. As previously construed herein, such class might increase in membership after his death until the arrival of a fixed point of time to be determined as of the date when the first grandchild reaches the age of thirty. The bequest vested in the existing members of the class and in such other persons as thereafter became members, up until such a point of time when the first distribution of the *corpus* was directed to be made. At the time the will was admitted to probate, there were then in existence six grandchildren who were members of the class, with the possibility of an increase in the membership before the point of distribution would be reached.

The appellant contends that the final decree entered in the estate construed the bequest as not permitting the opening up of the class after the death of the testator to admit after-born grandchildren, and that such determination is *res adjudicata* as to the rights of all after-born grandchildren. The petition propounding the will for probate was made January 27, 1940. In those proceedings it was ordered that notice of hearing be published in the Weekly Home News, a newspaper published in Spring Green, Wisconsin. The publication was made. Prior to the admission of the will to probate, the court appointed a guardian *ad litem*, reciting that the six grandchildren were minors interested in said estate, and included therein the words 'guardian *ad litem* for said minors and all unknown minors and incompetents, for the sole purpose of appearing for them and taking care of their interests in the proceedings in said matter.' On February 7, the will was admitted to probate. On March 17, the letters testamentary were issued, and the inventory properly filed. The final account and petition for settlement were dated August 2, 1941; and on August 6 of that year the court directed that the hearing be held on the final account, and that notice thereof be given by publication in the Weekly Home News. In the order determining the inheritance tax, one-sixth of the $50,000 trust estate was taxed to each of the grandchildren who survived the decedent. On April 17, 1942, final judgment was entered, and in that judgment the court found that the deceased was survived by the widow and his children and by the six grandchildren. The First National Bank of Madison was appointed trustee. The trust estate created by the bequest, and referred to in the final judgment, was assigned in such final decree as follows:

> 'To Maxine A. Perry, Barbara A. Perry, Evan F. Evans, Thomas E. Evans, Keith A. Pope and Wayne E. Pope, grandchildren, the sum of Fifty Thousand ($50,000.00) less such amounts as have heretofore been paid by said executor for inheritance tax upon the distributive shares of each such grandchild * * * the same to be held in trust by the First National Bank of Madison, Wisconsin, subject to the terms and conditions as set forth in the will of said deceased as follows:
>
> 'That the income shall be allowed to accumulate until said grandchildren shall respectively become of legal age.
>
> 'That when each such grandchild becomes of legal age he shall receive his proportionate share of such accumulated income, and thereafter all income on his proportionate share shall be paid to him annually until he reaches the age of thirty years.
>
> 'That when each such grandchild becomes thirty years of age he shall be paid his full share of the principal of said trust, together with all interest accumulated thereon.'

Thereafter, commencing as of the date that the first grandchild became of age, the trustee has paid interest to the grandchild as provided in the judgment; and on March 26, 1955, when Maxine A. Perry (Tesia), the oldest of such grandchildren, attained the age of thirty years, the trustee paid to her one-sixth of the corpus of the trust and was discharged as trustee to her.

Three children have been born to Alice Pope Draper, one of the children of the deceased, since the death of the deceased: to wit: Walter Draper, born on November 1, 1945; Margaret Anne Draper, born on February 13, 1951; and Susan K. Draper, born on June 30, 1953.

On August 9, 1955, the trustee having been advised of the birth of such subsequent-born grandchildren, and being concerned as to whether they might possibly have an interest in such trust, petitioned the court to construe the judgment and the will of the deceased to so determine. The appellant trustee urges that the judgment entered in 1942 is *res adjudicata* as to all persons, including those born after the death of the decedent. The guardian ad litem, appearing for the after-born grandchildren, urges that they have never had their day in court, that from the time for petition of the probate of the will of John C. Evans, on January 27, 1940, and through the entire proceedings in the county court there has never been any one or some one representing these after-born children, who are plainly members of the class to which the $50,000 was bequeathed. Their interests had never been given consideration until the appointment of a guardian for them on August 15, 1955, which occurred in the instant proceedings.

* * *

Inasmuch as and because the trial court erroneously held that membership in the class opened up each time a new grandchild is born, until such time as the entire trust *corpus* was distributed the order must be modified to correct this error.

We do not continue a discussion of other questions not necessary for a determination of the material issues.

Order modified so as to provide that membership in the class permanently closed when the oldest grandchild arrived at the age of thirty years, and as so modified it is affirmed. Cause remanded for further proceedings according to law.

Notes

Administrative Convenience Closing. The intention of the testator controls as to when the class closes. Under the Rule of Administrative Convenience, this means that the class will close whenever a member may demand his or her share of the corpus. Remember that this is a rule of convenience and it will result in great inconvenience for the class member born after the first point of distribution. The careful drafter will plan ahead for all contingencies. *See generally* John L. Garvey, *Drafting Wills and Trusts: Anticipating the Birth and Death of Possible Beneficiaries,* 71 Or. L. Rev. 47 (1992).

As with many things in life, there are exceptions to the Rule of Administrative Convenience. The first exception is found in the common law and provides that, if, when the interest was to become possessory (a class member could demand a share) and there was no member of the class then in existence to demand a share, then the rule of administrative convenience will not apply; the common law provides that we wait until the class membership has been exhausted. *See Restatement (Second) of Property, Donative Transfers* § 26.1(2) (2019). For example, in the case of a settlor who creates a trust for himself for life, and then the remainder to his grandchildren, at the settlor's death, no grandchild has yet been born, but there are child-bearing children of the settlor in existence, so there is no one to demand a share, nor is there an estate to which we may give a share. Thus, the common law holds that, rather than waiting until the first grandchild is born and could demand a share, we wait until there is no longer any possibility of any grandchild being born. Only at the death of all of the children of the settlor or similar event—when there is no longer the possibility of any additional grandchild being born—do we distribute the trust corpus to any of the grandchildren in existence and the estates of any who have predeceased the event. The common law rule leaves the class open for a significant period of time and benefits more class members, but it certainly lessens the share of the first grandchild to be born, who would have taken all under the rule of administrative convenience.

The second exception states that if a specific sum is given to each member of a class, the class closes at the death of the settlor, regardless of whether any members of the class are then alive. This is really an extension of the rule of administrative convenience, since it would be very inconvenient to guess how many class members might be able to take each of the specific shares. Rather than guess, the class is closed immediately, and if no member of the class is in existence to take, then the trust fails and results back to the estate from which it was generated.

Membership. Who is included in the class is an issue as well. The Uniform Probate Code provides that adopted individuals, non-marital individuals, and the descendants of both are included as class members. Likewise, within the terms "brothers and sisters" and "nephews and nieces" are included relationships of the half blood. *See* UNIF. PROB. CODE § 2-705(a) (2019). "Terms of relationship that do not differentiate relationships by blood from those of affinity, such as 'uncles,' 'aunts,' 'nieces,' or 'nephews', are construed to exclude relatives by affinity." *Id.*

Distribution. If the class gift refers to issue or descendants—rather than the more exclusive class term of children—how should the class gift be distributed if some members of the "issue" or "descendants" have predeceased and some have survived? The most obvious answer is to look to the intestate statute, *see* Chapter Two, Section IV, C, *supra*, and determine if the state statute used: (1) the old Uniform Probate Code system of complete per stirpes; (2) the new Uniform Probate Code system of complete per capita; (3) a next of kin approach; or (4) the strict method. The Restatement (Second) of Property, Donative Transfers § 28.2 does not utilize the state intestate statute to determine class meaning of issue and descendants but, instead, adopts the old Uniform Probate Code system of per capita and per stirpes at each generation.

The revised Uniform Probate Code makes a distinction for whenever the words "issue per stirpes" are used. Whenever "issue per stirpes" is used, the new Uniform Probate Code utilizes the old Uniform Probate Code system of per stirpes at each generation. Whenever that term is not used, per capita at each generation, in accordance with the New Uniform Probate Code, is used. *See* UNIF. PROB. CODE §§ 2-708 & 2-709(c) (2010). Sometimes the operative instrument may direct that, upon the occurrence of an event, the property be distributed to "my heirs." Like issue and descendants, this is a class designation, and the question becomes one of determining when the class of heirs should close. Observe the following decision and the Uniform Probate Code section that follows.

Harris Trust and Savings Bank v. Beach

Supreme Court of Illinois, 1987
118 Ill. 2d 1, 513 N.E.2d 833

Justice SIMON delivered the opinion of the court:

In construing either a trust or a will the challenge is to find the settlor's or testator's intent and, provided that the intention is not against public policy, to give it effect. (See Hull v. Adams (1948), 399 Ill. 347, 352, 77 N.E.2d 706.) Courts search for intent by analyzing both the words used in the instrument and the circumstances under which they were drafted, including: "the state of the testator's property, his family, and the like." (Armstrong v. Barber (1909), 239 Ill. 389, 404, 88 N.E.2d 246.) When, however, the instrument fails to make the settlor's or testator's intention clear, courts often resort to rules of construction to determine the meaning of the terms used in the document. (Hull v. Adams (1948), 399 Ill. 347, 352, 77 N.E.2d 706.) Rules of construction, which are applied in the same manner to both wills and trusts, are court created presumptions of what the ordinary settlor or testator would have intended the ambiguous terms to mean; they are merely the court's own assessments of what the person probably meant when the provision was drafted. (Harris Trust & Savings Bank v. Jackson (1952), 412 Ill. 261, 266–67, 106 N.E.2d 188.) Such rules should not be allowed to defeat what the ordinary settlor would have intended. When a rule of construction tends to subvert intentions, the rule is no longer legitimate and must be discarded. H. Carey and D. Schuyler, Illinois Law of Future Interests 190–93 (Cum. Pocket Part 1954).

In this case Harris Trust and Savings Bank, Robert Hixon Glore and William Gray III, trustees of two trusts, sought instructions from the circuit court of Cook County regarding to whom and in what manner the trusts should be distributed. The central controversy is over the proper construction of the remainder over to the heirs following the death of a life tenant: specifically, the question is whether the settlor intended that his heirs be ascertained at his death, or whether he desired that they be determined after the death of his wife, who was the life tenant.

The pertinent facts in this case are as follows: Frank P. Hixon and Alice Green entered into an antenuptial agreement dated March 30, 1921, and following that, they were married. The agreement created a trust consisting of 200 shares of preferred stock of Pioneer Investment Company, a Hixon family holding company. The trust provided that Alice was to receive the net income of the trust for life and that she could "dispose of Fifty Thousand ($50,000) Dollars of said fund in such a manner as she" deemed fit and proper. In exchange for the provisions made for her in the trust, Alice surrendered any interest, including dower, which she might have had in Hixon's estate. If Hixon survived Alice, the trust property was to be reconveyed to him. If Alice survived Hixon, the trust provided that on her death "the balance of said trust fund shall be divided among the heirs of the party of the first part [Hixon], share and share alike."

On May 31, 1926, Hixon created a second trust to provide for Alice. The principal of this trust consisted of 300 shares of stock of Pioneer Investment Company. This trust provided that Alice was to receive the income from the principal for life and upon her death "this trust shall terminate, and the trust fund shall be distributed equally among my [Hixon's] heirs."

In 1930, Hixon executed his will, which was interpreted by our appellate court and is not at issue in this case (Harris Trust & Savings Bank v. Beach (1985), 145 Ill.App.3d 682, 99 Ill.Dec. 438, 495 N.E.2d 1173), leaving gifts to specific individuals and charities. He divided the residue of his estate equally among his daughters, Ellen Glore and Dorothy Clark and in trust for Alice. Hixon died in 1931, when he was 69 years old. He was survived by Alice, who was then 49, by Dorothy and Ellen, who were then 38 and 36, respectively, and by his grandchildren, Frances Glore Beach, Charles F. Glore, Jr., and Robert Hixon Glore, who were then minors.

Alice lived for 51 more years. Both the 1921 and the 1926 trusts continued for her benefit until she died in February 1982. At that time, Hixon's then living descendants were his grandchildren, Frances Glore Beach and Robert Hixon Glore (the grandchildren), and the children of his deceased grandchild, Charles F. Glore, Jr.—Charles F. Glore III, Sallie Glore Farlow, and Edward R. Glore (the great-grandchildren). The parties agree that both the 1921 and the 1926 trust should be distributed in the same manner.

If Hixon's heirs are those surviving at his death, the trust estates will pass under the wills of his two daughters, Ellen H. Glore and Dorothy H. Clark, who both died in 1973. Ellen had three children. One child, as noted above—Charles F. Glore, Jr.—is deceased and survived by three children, Hixon's great-grandchildren. Ellen's other two children—the grandchildren Robert and Frances—are living and are parties to this suit. Dorothy had no children. The devisees under her will are defendants California Institute of Technology, Santa Barbara Foundation, Santa Barbara Cottage Hospital and the Kansas Endowment Association (collectively the charities), and her husband Alfred. Alfred is deceased and his portion of the assets would be distributed to his devisees, Frederick Acker, as special trustee under the will of Charles F. Glore, Jr., and Robert Hixon Glore. On the other hand, if the heirs are determined at the time of Alice's death, the trust estates will be divided among Hixon's now-living descendants — the two grandchildren and three great-grandchildren.

The four charities assert that the heirs should be those heirs alive at Hixon's death; this determination would include them since they were devisees under Dorothy's will. The grandchildren and the great-grandchildren argue that the heirs should be those who were surviving at Alice's death, but they disagree over whether the trust should be divided *per stirpes* (by each share) or *per capita* (by each head).

All parties seeking distribution in their favor filed motions for summary judgment, and the circuit court granted the motion in favor of the charities. That court held that the class of heirs should be ascertained at Hixon's death. The court concluded that the heirs would be only Hixon's two daughters, since Alice was excluded under the terms of the antenuptial agreement. * * *

The word "heirs" refers to "those persons appointed by the law to inherit an estate in case of intestacy." (Le Sourd v. Leinweber (1952), 412 Ill. 100, 105, 105 N.E.2d 722.) When used in its technical sense, the testator's or settlor's heirs are, of course, determined at the time of his or her death. (Hull v. Adams (1948), 399 Ill. 347, 352, 77 N.E.2d 706.) This court, however, has never adopted the technical meaning of the word "heirs" as a rule of law. We have observed that "'heirs' when used in a will does not necessarily have a fixed meaning. It may mean children or, where there are no children, it may mean some other class of heirs * * * if the context of the entire will *plainly shows* such to have been the intention of the testator." (Emphasis added.) (Stites v. Gray (1955), 4 Ill.2d 510, 513, 123 N.E.2d 483.) A determination of the class of heirs, therefore, is governed by the settlor's or testator's intention rather than by a fixed rule of law. The rule in Illinois, however, has been that, unless the settlor's intention to the contrary is "plainly shown" in the trust document, courts will rely upon the technical meaning of the term "heirs" by applying it as a rule of construction. (Harris Trust & Savings Bank v. Jackson (1952), 412 Ill. 261, 266, 106 N.E.2d 188.) The charities are, therefore, correct in their observation that presently our rule of construction requires us to determine heirs at the settlor's death unless the trust or will provides clear evidence to the contrary. (See, *e.g.,* Stites v. Gray (1955), 4 Ill.2d 510, 513, 123 N.E.2d 483; Le Sourd v. Leinweber (1952), 412 Ill. 100, 105, 105 N.E.2d 722; Hull v. Adams (1948), 399 Ill. 347, 352, 77 N.E.2d 706.) The initial question we must address is whether we should continue to adhere to this standard of proof.

The charities contend that this high degree of proof is necessary to rebut the rule of construction because of the policy favoring early vesting of remainders. They refer to one leading commentator's views on implied survivorship and its detrimental effects on early vesting (see Halbach, Future Interests: Express and Implied Conditions of Survival, 49 Cal.L.Rev. 297, 304–07 (1961)), as well as to Evans v. Giles (1980), 83 Ill.2d 448, 47 Ill.Dec. 349, 415 N.E.2d 354, and to Dyslin v. Wolf (1950), 407 Ill. 532, 96 N.E.2d 485, which are factually distinguishable from this case, to bolster their position. However, they overlook that two eminent scholars in the field of Illinois future interest law revised their views regarding the policy in favor of early vesting. In the supplement to their treatise entitled the Illinois Law of Future Interests, Carey and Schuyler observe that "it was the rule regarding the destructibility of contingent remainders that caused courts to favor the early vesting of estates. * * * But now, in this state and in many others, there is no rule of destructibility. If the original reason for favoring early vesting is gone, why continue to favor it?" H. Carey and D. Schuyler, Illinois Law of Future Interests 190 (Cum. Pocket Part 1954); Ill.Rev.Stat.1985, ch. 30, par. 40.

Briefly stated, the destruction of contingent remainders was an archaic device which frequently frustrated grantors' intentions by prematurely defeating an interest subject to a condition. By vesting remainders as quickly as possible the drastic effects of destructibility "could be contained by a rule of construction which resulted in declaring that future interests were vested and hence indestructible." (H. Carey and D. Schuyler, Illinois Law of Future Interests 190 (Cum. Pocket Part 1954)). Our legislature abolished destructibility when it passed "An Act concerning future interests" in 1921 (Ill.Rev.Stat.1985, ch. 30, par. 40). However, despite the passage of this statute, vesting remainders as quickly as possible was such an imbedded rule of construction that in many cases courts continued to adhere to it without question and regardless of the consequences.

Early vesting frequently frustrates intentions by casting property to strangers. (H. Carey and D. Schuyler, Illinois Law of Future Interests 193 (Cum. Pocket Part 1954); see also DeKowin v. First National Bank of Chicago (N.D.Ill.1949), 84 F.Supp. 918, rev'd on other grounds (C.A.Ill.1949), 179 F.2d 347 (property goes to second wife of son-in-law); Peadro v. Peadro (1948), 81 N.E.2d 192, 400 Ill. 482 (property falls into the hands of the second wife of the testator's niece's widower).) Carey and Schuyler observe that if interests following life estates "are said to be contingent on survivorship, * * * children of the life tenant will take all the property, which seems to accord more with what the testator wanted." H. Carey and D. Schuyler, Illinois Law of Future Interests 192 (Cum. Pocket Part 1954).

In their 1954 supplement to their treatise on future interests, Professors Carey and Schuyler re-examined their earlier view that early vesting is axiomatic. (See H. Carey and D. Schuyler, Illinois Law of Future Interests 399 (1941); H. Carey and D. Schuyler, Illinois Law of Future Interests 190–93 (Cum. Pocket Part 1954). They state:

> One does not readily differ from men so learned as Professor Gray and Professor Kales, both of whom seemed satisfied with the axiom that 'the law favors the early vesting of estates.' Accordingly, at the time the principal text was written, and even in 1947, when the first supplement to this was published, the authors were much inclined unquestioningly to accent this ancient dogma. But subsequent further reflection causes one to wonder if the maxim has lost much, if not most of its utility. (H. Carey and D. Schuyler, Illinois Law of Future Interests 190 (Cum. Pocket Part 1954).)

They conclude that "the desirability of retaining the rule of early vesting as a rule of construction * * * warrant[s] a microscopic scrutiny of it by those charged with the administration of justice." (H. Carey and D. Schuyler, Illinois Law of Future Interest 193 (Cum. Pocket Part (1954).) In the instant case, we have an interest following a life estate. If we follow both the circuit and appellate court's decision and vest the heirs' interest as quickly as possible, a large portion of the estate will fall into the hands of strangers. If we reduce the burden of proving that a grantor intended to use "heirs" in a nontechnical sense and if that vests the gift at the termination of the life estate, obviously only those heirs surviving the life tenant will share in the remainder.

Whether survivorship ought to be implied is not a case of first impression before this court. A rule of construction regarding implied survivorship was set forth in Drury v. Drury (1915), 271 Ill. 336, 111 N.E. 140, where this court held that when a gift to a class was "postponed pending the termination of the life estate * * * *only those* took who were in existence at the termination of the life estate." (Emphasis added.) (271 Ill. 336, 341, 111 N.E. 140.) The effect of Drury was to delay the vesting of the gift by adding or implying survivorship for the class of remaindermen to share in the estate.

Hofing v. Willis (1964), 31 Ill.2d 365, 373, 201 N.E.2d 852, clarified Drury by stating that implied survivorship was not a mandatory rule of construction. Rather, according to the court in Hofing, the grantor's intent regarding this issue should remain paramount. While a later case, Evans v. Giles (1980), 83 Ill.2d 448, 456, 47 Ill.Dec. 349, 415 N.E.2d 354, also criticized the Drury rule, the rationale in that case was that implied survivorship defeated the policy against early vesting. In neither Hofing nor Evans did this court hold that it was inappropriate to imply survivorship when there was evidence that the grantor intended to do so. Further, Hofing, Evans and Dyslin are distinguishable in an important respect: the gift was not to a class of heirs—a term which is vague and imports futurity—but rather in Hofing to a group of sisters, in Giles to a specific individual, and in Dyslin to the grandchildren.

We agree with Professors Carey and Schuyler that early vesting of remainders should no longer be followed in this State without question. Early vesting is an axiom which must not get in the way when a contrary intent is demonstrated by a preponderance of the evidence. Requiring *clear and convincing* evidence or a *plain showing* to rebut the presumption in favor of the technical meaning of the term "heirs" (see Stites v. Gray (1955), 4 Ill.2d 510, 513, 123 N.E.2d 483; Le Sourd v. Leinweber (1952), 412 Ill. 100, 105, 105 N.E.2d 722; Hull v. Adams (1948), 399 Ill. 347, 352, 77 N.E.2d 706), has its roots in the maxim favoring early vesting of remainders. Frequently this policy, as is the case here, frustrates what the ordinary settlor would have intended. We hold that because the primary reason for early vesting is no longer as important as it formerly was, proof by the preponderance of the evidence that the settlor, testator, or donor intended to use the term "heirs" in its nontechnical sense is sufficient to delay the vesting of a gift to a time other than at the grantor's death.

The result of delaying a gift to the heirs is not dramatic. The fear that a contingent remainder could be prematurely destroyed no longer exists. Further, should a predeceased member of the class be excluded from the gift, the result is not drastic.

If the predeceased "heir" leaves issue, as is the case here, the settlor's own blood still enjoys the gift. If, on the other hand, a predeceased member fails to leave issue, as also occurred here, the gift is prevented from falling into the hands of strangers. In sum, by altering the degree of proof necessary to delay the vesting of a gift to the heirs, we do no harm. Instead, we further the ordinary grantor's intent, which is exactly what a proper rule of construction ought to do. Consequently, in this case we must determine which parties have offered the preponderant proof as to Hixon's intent — the charities or the grandchildren and great-grandchildren.

Hixon's trusts, as the charities stress, do not explicitly state the point at which his heirs should be determined. The 1921 trust provides that the "balance of said trust fund shall be divided among the heirs," and the 1926 trust states that "the trust shall be distributed equally among my [Hixon's] heirs." When the trusts are considered as a whole, however, it becomes apparent that the documents revolve totally around Alice's life and death; Hixon's life and death play only secondary roles. As the grandchildren and great-grandchildren note, the trusts were created for Alice's benefit in exchange for her rights to dower or any other portion of Hixon's estate. The trusts were intended to last throughout her life, and depending upon when she died, the trust principal would either revert to Hixon or be distributed to his heirs. Alice's central role in the trust is indicative of Hixon's intent to make her and not himself the point of reference for determining the heirs. Under similar circumstances, our appellate court found the testator's frequent reference to the life tenant's death to be evidence of his intent to look towards the future and to ascertain the heirs at the life tenant's death rather than at his own. (See Handy v. Shearer (1967), 81 Ill.App.2d 461, 464, 225 N.E.2d 414.) In that case the court stated that the frequent references to the life tenant's death suggested "that it was an event and a point of time that weighed heavily in the testator's plan and in his thinking. * * * By using the date of the widow's remarriage or death as a date for the determination of 'my legal heirs,' testator's plan is complete." 81 Ill.App.2d 461, 464, 225 N.E.2d 414.

The circumstances under which Hixon created the trust provide additional evidence of his intent to vest the gift at Alice's death. Hixon was 20 years older than Alice and he would consequently have expected her trusts to last for a considerable time after his own death. During this time, changes in the family through births and deaths would certainly occur. Rather than leave the remainder of the principal to his daughters, as he left the residue of his estate in his will, his use of an indefinite term such as "heirs" covered the inevitable changes in family circumstances that might occur.

Alice's power of appointment over $50,000 of the trust principal is also evidence of Hixon's intent to ascertain the heirs at her death. The grandchildren and great-grandchildren observe that this power might prevent the heirs from ever enjoying the trust principal; the trust could be worth $50,000 or less when Alice exercised her power of appointment and thus there would be no trust principal left to distribute. The grandchildren's and great-grandchildren's claim that it would be senseless to vest the gift upon Hixon's death when one could not be certain until Alice exercised her power of appointment whether or not there were any assets left for the heirs to possess and enjoy, certainly has merit. * * *

Pottgieser is the only decision in this State that the charities refer to which set forth this particular exception, and a case decided a half century later never mentions Pottgieser. In Hull v. Adams (1948), 399 Ill. 347, 77 N.E.2d 706, this court concluded that the rule is applicable whenever it is unclear whether the gift to a class is a contingent or vested remainder. This court stated in Hull:

> It is a general rule that where the donees of a testamentary gift constitute a class, and the only words importing the gift are found in the direction to divide, distribute or pay or to sell the property and distribute or pay over the proceeds in the future, the gift will not vest until the time arrives to pay, divide or distribute, and the members of the class who are to take are to be ascertained at that time and not at the death of the testator. It [the rule] is invoked by the courts to aid in determining the vested or contingent character of future interests. (399 Ill. 347, 357, 77 N.E.2d 706.)

In the present case, the gift to the heirs in the 1921 trust was contingent when it was executed because it was conditioned upon Alice surviving Hixon; if she failed to do so the trust would revert and the heirs' interest would be defeated. Whether the gift to the heirs continues to be contingent on the heirs surviving Alice or whether their gift vests at Hixon's death is precisely the issue we are confronted with in this case. Consequently, the divide and pay over rule appears to operate and, in view of the ambiguity confronting us, gives us an additional clue as to Hixon's intent.

The provision in the 1921 trust creating a reversion in Hixon should Alice predecease him also advances the grandchildren's and great-grandchildren's argument that Hixon's intention was that the heirs be determined at Alice's death. The reversionary clause conditioned the duration of the trust on Alice's survival. If Alice failed to survive Hixon, the trust would terminate and Hixon's reversion would operate. On the other hand, if Alice survived Hixon, the reversion would not take effect and the principal would be distributed to the heirs. The grandchildren and great-grandchildren persuasively stress that considering the heirs at Hixon's death would lead to nearly the same result as if the reversion had occurred. In both instances the bulk of the principal would pass through the estates of Hixon's two daughters. Hixon's intention that the result was to be different should Alice survive and the reversion fail is an indication that Hixon must have intended that his heirs be determined at Alice's death. Viewing all of these indications with respect to Hixon's intent together, we conclude that the preponderant proof favors the position of the grandchildren and great-grandchildren and Hixon's heirs should therefore be determined at Alice's death.

* * *

The final question is whether the gift to the grandchildren and great-grandchildren should be distributed *per stirpes* or *per capita*. The great-grandchildren contend that because Hixon used the words "share and share alike" and instructed the trustees to distribute the gift "equally," the gift must be divided on a *per capita* basis. The great-grandchildren accurately observe that, "When the words 'equally,' 'equal among,' 'share and share alike,' or other similar words, are used to indicate an equal division among a class, the persons among whom the division is to be made are usually held to take *per capita* unless a contrary intention is discoverable from the will." (Dollander v. Dhaemers (1921), 297 Ill. 274, 278, 130 N.E. 705.) However, "'it is worthy of remark that the leading cases which sustain a distribution *per capita* intimate that a very small indication of intent to the contrary would change the rule.'" (297 Ill. 274, 280, 130 N.E. 705, quoting Eyer v. Beck (1888), 70 Mich. 179, 181, 38 N.W. 20.) When a testator leaves his estate to his or her heirs, courts generally conclude that the testator intended the gift to be distributed in accordance with laws of descent and distribution which provide for a *per stirpes* distribution. (Carlin v. Helm (1928), 331 Ill. 213, 221–22, 162 N.E. 873; see also Ill.Rev.Stat.1985, ch. 110 1/2 , par. 2-1.) Under these circumstances we have stated that "a gift to issue 'equally' and 'share and share alike' does not require that each of such issue shall have an equal share with the other; that the mandate is satisfied if the issue of equal degree taking per stirpes share equally." Condee v. Trout (1942), 379 Ill. 89, 93, 39 N.E.2d 350.

In the present case, Hixon left the remainder in the trust principal to his heirs. That he provided for his heirs to share equally in that gift fails to rebut the presumption in favor of a *per stirpes* distribution; the gift to the class of heirs is a sufficient indication that Hixon intended the remainder to be divided in accordance with the laws of descent and distribution. This conclusion is bolstered by the wording of the statute, in effect both at Hixon's death and when he executed the trusts, which used the terms "equally among" and in "equal parts" in describing the *per stirpes* distribution of estates. That Hixon employed the words "equally" and "share and share alike" in his instructions to the trustees regarding the division of his estate is therefore not inconsistent with an intention that the heirs share equally under a *per stirpes* distribution. See Ill.Rev. Stat.1937, ch. 39, sec. 1.

The cases cited by the great-grandchildren in which the court provided for a *per capita* distribution are distinguishable. In Carlin v. Helm (1928), 331 Ill. 213, 222, 162 N.E. 873, not only was the gift made to *named individuals* and not to a class, but also the court stated that had the gift been devised to the class of heirs, it would have divided the remainder differently. In Northern Trust Co. v. Wheeler (1931), 345 Ill. 182, 177 N.E. 884, another case cited by the great-grandchildren, the language explicitly stated that the remainder be divided *per capita*.

We conclude that the remainder in the heirs should be distributed *per stirpes* with the three great-grandchildren each taking one-ninth of the estate and the two grandchildren each taking one-third. The judgments of both the circuit and appellate courts are reversed and the case is remanded for a distribution of the trust principal in a manner consistent with this opinion.

Judgments reversed; cause remanded.

GOLDENHERSH, J., took no part in the consideration or decision of this case.

Uniform Probate Code (2019)

§ 2-711. Future Interests in "Heirs" and the Like.

If an applicable statute or governing instrument calls for a present or future distribution to or creates a present or future interest in a designated individual's "heirs," "heirs at law," "next of kin," "relatives," or "family," or language of similar import, the property passes to those persons, including the state, and in such shares as would succeed to the designated individual's intestate estate under the intestate succession law of the designated individual's domicile if the designated individual died when the disposition is to take effect in possession or enjoyment. If the designated individual's surviving spouse is living but is remarried at the time the disposition is to take effect in possession or enjoyment, the surviving spouse is not an heir of the designated individual.

Notes

The issue of who should be included in class membership continues to be the subject of litigation. *See, e.g.,* Frederic S. Schwartz, *Misconceptions of the Will as Linguistic Behavior and Misperception of the Testator's Intention: The Class Gift Doctrine,* 86 Det. Mercy L. Rev. 443 (2009); Frederic S. Schwartz, *The New Restatement of Property and Class Gifts: Losing Sight of the Testator's Intention,* 22 Quinnipiac Prob. L.J. 221 (2009). The issue is simpler if the settlor names takers or even creates a class of persons that may be made distinguishable through the introduction of extrinsic evidence. But the issue becomes more complicated when a third party settlor creates a trust to benefit persons not genetically linked or unknown, for example: "my daughter's children" or "my nieces and nephews." Obviously, careful drafting on the part of the scrivener could rectify any confusion, but such precision is most often lacking; otherwise we would not be in court. And making the matter even more complicated is the arrival of advances in medical technology, which may result in an increasing class through assisted reproductive technology, such as posthumous conception. *See, e.g., In re* Martin B., 17 Misc. 3d 198, 841 N.Y.S.2d 207 (2007) (allowing posthumously conceived grandchildren to take under grandfather's trust benefitting "issue and descendants"). The Uniform Probate Code's most recent revision, *supra,* sought to address these and other issues.

Raymond C. O'Brien
The Momentum of Posthumous Conception: A Model Act
25 J. Contemp. Health L. & Pol'y 332 (2009)

This Article addresses the scenario of when, through advanced medical technology, a procedure is performed resulting in the birth of a child more than three hundred days—a time suggested by some statutes—after the death of the gamete provider. The embryo may result from in vitro fertilization or from a woman being artificially inseminated with the sperm of a deceased male gamete provider. And of course the woman could have predeceased too and left a viable ova, that was then fertilized with the sperm of a living or a deceased male to create an embryo, which was then placed into a surrogate, a gestational carrier. The essential element is that the act, which results in a future birth, occurs after the death of one or both of the gamete providers. This is the essence of posthumous conception. That is, once the egg and sperm are brought together through assisted reproductive technology to form an embryo, both or either of the persons who donated the sperm and egg or embryo are dead, perhaps for a long time. If this is the point of conception, then the issue arises as to whether the resulting posthumously conceived infant should qualify under the law for paternity, inheritance and benefits. How long should the law wait for conception before terminating status? The law strives for certainty and medical technology has made certainty an elusive prey.

Id. at 335–36.

B. Decrease of Class

Any decrease in class membership involves the anti-lapse statute, vesting of interests, or both. For example, a testator provides in a valid Last Will and Testament that, "at death, one million dollars is to be held in trust for any children, income for them for life, and then, at the death of the last child, to be divided among the grandchildren." At the death of the last child of the testator—the moment when the remainder interest is to be divided among the class of grandchildren—there are three grandchildren then living. Nonetheless, one grandchild dies prior to the testator, survived by issue, and another grandchild dies after the testator but before the death of the last child. Into how many shares should the trust corpus be divided? The answer is "five." The three surviving class members take each of their respective shares, the issue of the grandchild who died prior to the testator take under the state's anti-lapse statute. The grandchild who survived the testator but did not survive the last child has a vested interest, and a share will go to his or her estate. If the testator had directed that the grandchildren must survive the children, then the results could be different. Compare the following decision with the often-criticized Uniform Probate Code provision that follows.

Usry v. Farr

Supreme Court of Georgia, 2001
274 Ga. 438, 553 S.E.2d 789

FLETCHER, Chief Justice.

At issue in this appeal is when title to the remainder interest under the will of Watson Usry vested. On summary judgment, the trial court held that the remainder vested at the time of Usry's death and not at the death of the life tenant. Because Usry's will expressed the intention of providing for those who survive him and all five grandchildren survived him, we affirm.

Watson Usry died in 1967. The relevant clause of Usry's will provided successive life estates in his lands, first to his wife Lucille and then to their children, with the remainder to his grandchildren. Usry had three children, the last of whom died in 2000. There are five appellants: the four children of Usry's son Jack, and Jack's widow, Evelyn. Usry's fifth grandson, Hoyt, died in 1970 leaving three young children, all of whom were alive at the time of Usry's death. * * * Hoyt's three children are the appellees. Appellants claim that the remainder vested upon the death of the last life tenant and not upon the death of Usry. Therefore, because they are the only grandchildren who survived the life tenants, they take all lands under the will. Appellees contend that the remainder vested upon Usry's death, and that Hoyt, who survived Usry, had a vested interest under the will, and therefore his children stand in his shoes and take under the will along with appellants.

* * * The construction of a will is a question of law for the court. * * * The cardinal rule for construing wills is to ascertain and give effect to the testator's intent. * * * Item Three of the will provided,

> I will, bequeath and devise all of the land, with improvements thereon, which I may own at my death to my Wife, LUCILLE, to be hers for and during her lifetime, and at her death same is to go to my children who may survive my wife, and to my grandchildren with restrictions as follows: Any of my children taking land under this Item shall have a life interest therein, share and share alike, with any grandchildren who take hereunder taking the part which their father or mother would have taken. Upon the death of my last surviving child title in fee simple to said lands shall vest in my grand-children, per stirpes and not per capita.

The first sentence of Item Three establishes a life estate first in Usry's wife Lucille and then in the children who survive Lucille. This sentence imposes a requirement that the children survive Lucille before taking under Item three. In contrast, no requirement that the grandchildren survive the life tenants is imposed. Therefore, at Usry's death, fee simple title vested in his five grandchildren, who were all alive at that time. The possessory interest vested when Usry's son Ned, the last life tenant, died in April 2000. At that time, the grandchildren were entitled to take possession, with the appellees taking the share that had vested in Hoyt.

The testator's intention that the only survivorship requirement apply to his life appears expressly in Item Eight of the will. In that provision, Usry declared that "my entire plan of disposition is the result of a conscientious effort to provide for the welfare of my loved ones who survive me, and to fairly divide and distribute the worldly goods for which I have worked so hard." Because we must construe the will as a whole, we must consider this clause in construing the remainder of the will. * * * Usry's stated intention of providing for those who survive him is fatal to the claim of appellants who would defer vesting well beyond the death of Usry until the conclusion of the life estates.

The dissent's concern that this construction provides an anomalous result is not well-founded. The testator himself decided to leave successive life estates to his widow and children. Obviously, if his children were to enjoy a life estate that followed their mother's life estate, the children had to survive their mother. Because the testator decided that his children were to enjoy only a life estate, there is nothing unusual about his further providing for title to vest in his loved ones who survive him.

* * * Usry's express intention with regard to a survivorship requirement is consistent with the statutory rule in Georgia favoring vesting of title as of the time of the testator's death. * * * Appellants contend that the last sentence of Item Three demonstrates an intention that the remainder vest, not at the testator's death, but at the conclusion of the life estates. However, this Court has repeatedly held that virtually identical language is not sufficient to divest the remainder share from one who survives the testator but predeceases the life tenant. * * * In view of the strong preference in Georgia for early vesting, the language required to render a remainder contingent upon surviving the life tenant must be clear and unambiguous. * * * The last sentence of Item Three fails to meet this standard when considered along with Item Eight. To the extent that this sentence would permit a construction favoring a contingent remainder, it must give way to the construction favoring a vested remainder, where both constructions are possible. * * *

We construe the final sentence of Item Three, and similar language in Item Five,[9] to refer to the time the grandchildren take possession in the land and become entitled to enjoy the title to the remainder, which had vested at Usry's death. This construction is consistent with our case law that recognizes that a vested remainder will have both a vesting of title and a vesting of possession. * * *

* * * Appellants also rely on a deed of assent executed by Usry's widow as executrix in 1968. That deed refers to property devised in Usry's will as being left to "the living grandchildren of Watson Usry." The deed of assent, prepared after the testator's death, is irrelevant to determining the testator's intent.

Judgment affirmed.

All the Justices concur, except THOMPSON, J., who concurs in the judgment only, and BENHAM, CARLEY and HINES, JJ., who dissent.

* * *

CARLEY, Justice, dissenting.

The law of Georgia favors the early vesting of remainders "in all cases of doubt," but not where "a manifest intention to the contrary shall appear." OCGA § 44-6-66. "[T]his preference for vested interests is only a presumption and will give way to a clear intent to make the interest subject to a contingency." Verner F. Chaffin, Studies

9. "If my daughter-in-law, EVELYN, has not married again by the time the title to my land vests in my grand-children, as per Item Three of this Will, then I desire that she take a child's part. . . ."

in the Georgia Law of Decedents' Estates and Future Interests, p. 332 (1978). Because the controlling terms of Watson Usry's will leave no doubt of his clear intent that his grandchildren must survive their parents to inherit, their remainders are contingent and the preference for early vesting does not apply in this case. Therefore, I dissent to the majority's affirmance of the trial court's erroneous ruling.

Item Three of Mr. Usry's will creates a life estate in his widow and then in those of their children who survived her. Thus, he clearly intended that his children's interests not vest at his death, but at the death of his wife. With regard to the grandchildren, Item 3 provides: "Upon the death of my last surviving child *title in fee simple to said lands shall vest* in my grand-children, per stirpes and not per capita." (Emphasis supplied.) A "fee simple" estate "'is the entire and absolute property in the land; no person can have a greater estate or interest.' [Cit.]" Houston v. Coram, 215 Ga. 101, 102(1), 109 S.E.2d 41 (1959). Thus, Item 3 clearly expresses the testator's intent that his grandchildren would have *no* interest in the property until such time as the entire and absolute estate passed to them at the death of the last life tenant.

Despite this clear expression of Mr. Usry's intent, the majority concludes that what he really meant was for title to pass to his grandchildren at his death and that only possession be postponed until the death of his last surviving child. This is patently erroneous, as *title* cannot vest both at the time of the testator's death and then again at the death of the last life tenant. As the majority correctly notes, "there are two vestings of a *vested remainder*," a vesting of title and a vesting of possession. (Emphasis supplied.) Crawley v. Kendrick, 122 Ga. 183, 184(1), 50 S.E. 41 (1905). However, the issue here is whether the grandchildren's remainders are vested or contingent. OCGA § 44-6-61. The will does not specify that their interests vest at the testator's death with possession delayed until the last life tenant dies. The instrument unambiguously provides that the grandchildren take no "title" until that time. One can hold title without possession or possession without title. However, fee simple title in the grandchildren vests either at the time of Mr. Usry's death or when his last child dies. The will expressly indicates that his children must survive his widow to take a life estate and, by postponing the vesting of *title* in his grandchildren, implicitly requires that they survive the life tenants. See Ruth v. First Nat. Bank of Atlanta, 230 Ga. 490, 493, 197 S.E.2d 699 (1973).

> The importance of *Ruth* is that the court did look to the will as a whole rather than focusing on the particular words used in the bequest, and determined that the testator's intention, even though he used the word "absolutely," was that the bequest was not to vest until the death of the testator or the life tenant, whichever last occurred.

Chaffin, *supra* at p. 355 (1978). See also Fourth Nat. Bank of Columbus v. Brannon, 227 Ga. 191, 192(1), 179 S.E.2d 232 (1971).

The error in the majority's analysis is that it equates the absence of an *express* requirement for survivorship as conclusive evidence of the testator's intent to create vested, rather than contingent, remainders. However, the law favors the early vesting of remainders only in cases of doubt, and no doubt arises simply because the testator did not specifically provide that the remaindermen must survive to take. A postponement of the vesting of title can be the functional equivalent of a survivorship requirement. See Wells v. Ellis, 184 Ga. 645, 646(1), 192 S.E. 380 (1937). The applicable rule of construction is to ascertain the testator's intent based upon a consideration of the entire will and the circumstances surrounding its execution. Timberlake v. Munford, 267 Ga. 631, 632, 481 S.E.2d 217 (1997). Contrary to the majority opinion, the testator's will did not provide "for title to vest in his loved ones who survive him." In Item 8 of Mr. Usry's will, he expressed only the general intent "to provide for the welfare of my loved ones who survive me. . . ." However, the relevant inquiry is the construction of the specific provisions of the instrument so as to determine how he intended to provide for them. There is a distinction between the expression of a general testamentary intent to provide for survivors, as in Item 8, and a specific provision for the vesting of title in those who survive, as in Item 3. In Item 3, Mr. Usry created life estates for his widow and children, and provided that his grandchildren would not take title until the death of the last surviving child. Thus, he obviously did not intend to provide for the welfare of all of his survivors, since only those children who outlived his widow were to take life estates. Under the majority's anomalous construction, the remainder to a grandchild who survived Mr. Usry and died before his or her own parent would be vested, but the parent of that grandchild would have no interest unless he or she outlived Mrs. Usry. Based upon the will as a whole, the more reasonable interpretation is that the testator intended all remainders to be contingent upon survival until the time of vesting. Mr. Usry accomplished that intent by expressly providing that his children survive his widow and by specifically providing that title would not pass to his grandchildren until the death of the last life tenant. * * *

The trial court erred in misapplying the preference for early vesting so as to violate the testator's manifest intent to create contingent remainders for his children and grandchildren. Because the majority endorses, rather than corrects that error, I dissent.

I am authorized to state that Justice BENHAM and Justice HINES join in this dissent.

Uniform Probate Code (2019)

§ 2-707. Survivorship With Respect to Future Interests Under Terms of Trust; Substitute Takers.

* * *

(b) [**Survivorship Required; Substitute Gift.**] A future interest under the terms of a trust is contingent on the beneficiary's surviving the distribution date. If a beneficiary of a future interest under the terms of a trust fails to survive the distribution date, the following apply:

(1) Except as provided in paragraph (4), if the future interest is not in the form of a class gift and the deceased beneficiary leaves surviving descendants, a

substitute gift is created in the beneficiary's surviving descendants. They take by representation the property to which the beneficiary would have been entitled had the beneficiary survived the distribution date.

(2) Except as provided in paragraph (4), if the future interest is in the form of a class gift, other than a future interest to "issue," "descendants," "heirs of the body," "heirs," "next of kin," "relatives," or "family," or a class described by language of similar import, a substitute gift is created in the surviving descendants of any deceased beneficiary. The property to which the beneficiaries would have been entitled had all of them survived the distribution date passes to the surviving beneficiaries and the surviving descendants of the deceased beneficiaries. Each surviving beneficiary takes the share to which he [or she] would have been entitled had the deceased beneficiaries survived the distribution date. Each deceased beneficiary's surviving descendants who are substituted for the deceased beneficiary take by representation the share to which the deceased beneficiary would have been entitled had the deceased beneficiary survived the distribution date. For the purposes of this paragraph, "deceased beneficiary" means a class member who failed to survive the distribution date and left one or more surviving descendants.

(3) For the purposes of Section 2-701, words of survivorship attached to a future interest are not, in the absence of additional evidence, a sufficient indication of an intent contrary to the application of this section. Words of survivorship include words of survivorship that relate to the distribution date or to an earlier or an unspecified time, whether those words of survivorship are expressed in condition-precedent, condition-subsequent, or any other form.

(4) If the governing instrument creates an alternative future interest with respect to a future interest for which a substitute gift is created by paragraph (1) or (2), the substitute gift is superseded by the alternative future interest if:

(A) the alternative future interest is in the form of a class gift and one or more members of the class is entitled to take in possession or enjoyment; or

(B) the alternative future interest is not in the form of a class gift and the expressly designated beneficiary of the alternative future interest is entitled to take in possession or enjoyment.

Notes

More than a third of the states have enacted the substitute gift provision of UPC § 2-707. *See* ROBERT H. SITKOFF & JESSE DUKEMINIER, WILLS, TRUSTS, AND ESTATES 886 (10th ed. 2017) (Alaska, Arizona, Colorado, Florida, Hawaii, Illinois, Iowa, Massachusetts, Michigan, Montana, New Mexico, North Dakota, Ohio, Pennsylvania,

South Dakota, Tennessee, and Utah). The provision has been criticized by many commentators. *See, e.g.,* David M. Becker, *Eroding the Common Law Paradigm for Creation of Property Interests and the Hidden Costs of Law Reform,* 83 WASH. U. L. Q. 773 (2005); Laura E. Cunningham, *The Hazards of Tinkering with the Common Law of Future Interests: The California Experience,* 48 HASTINGS L. J. 667 (1997); Jesse Dukeminier, *The Uniform Probate Code Upends the Law of Remainders,* 94 MICH. L. REV. 148 (1995). But other commentators have attempted to place substituted gift within the context of anti-lapse and emerging trends in the law. *See, e.g.,* Lawrence W. Waggoner, *Class Gifts Under the Restatement (Third) of Property,* 22 OHIO N. U. L. REV. 993 (2007); Mary Louise Fellows & Gregory S. Alexander, *Forty Years of Codification of Estates and Trusts Law; Lessons for the Next Generation,* 40 GA. L. REV. 1049 (2006); Lawrence C. Waggoner, *The Uniform Probate Code Extends Antilapse-Type Protection to Poorly Drafted Trusts,* 94 MICH. L. REV. 2309 (1996).

VI. Powers of Appointment

If, in a valid Last Will and Testament, or in an *inter vivos* trust, a settlor were to give to Sadie one million dollars, income for life, then the remainder to Sadie's issue, Sadie would have a life income trust, and her issue would have a vested remainder. But if the settlor were to give to Sadie one million dollars, income for life, then as she shall appoint in her Last Will and Testament, Sadie would be the beneficiary of a life income trust, but Sadie would also be what is called a donee of a general testamentary power of appointment. Please note the difference between the two procedures. In both of the procedures, a Trustee is involved, and there is a distribution of life income to Sadie, but in the latter of the two, the Trustee is to distribute the remainder at Sadie's death to those persons named to take in Sadie's Last Will and Testament. Thus, Sadie has a power of appointment. If Sadie dies without a Last Will and Testament and, thus, does not appoint, the trust corpus will result back to the settlor. The scope of the power of appointment, the effectiveness of Sadie's exercise, and the mechanisms by which a court seeks to determine the settlor's intent, are all part of the realm of powers of appointment. Substantive doctrines regarding mistake, the Rule Against Perpetuities, and even fraud, all play a role in powers of appointment. As in most areas of the law, there is a distinctive language that is applicable that must be learned to understand the focus and operation of the concept. Consider the following.

A. Elements of a Valid Power

1. The **definition** of a power of appointment is found in the Uniform Powers of Appointment Act § 101(13) (2019): "'Power of appointment' means a power that enables a powerholder acting in a nonfiduciary capacity to designate a recipient of an ownership interest in or another power of appointment over the appointive property. The term does not include a power of attorney." This power is what separates a power of appointment from a life estate; a power provides flexibility by giving the settlor/donor the eyes of the donee of the power, long into the future. It is an indispensable tool of estate planning.

2. The **donor** of a power of appointment is the person who creates the power. This person is likely a settlor of the trust, through which the power of appointment operates, or a testator, if the power is created in a Last Will and Testament. The intention of the donor is significant: the more restrictive the power of appointment, the more the intention of the donor will matter.

3. The **donee** of a power of appointment is the one who exercises the power of appointment. Although rare, the donee could also be the donor. The donee could also possess a life estate in the corpus, thereby being a beneficiary also. And there could be more than one donee. The validity of the donee's exercise, and the manner in which that exercise will prompt analysis under the Rule Against Perpetuities, will be significant.

4. Appointees of a power of appointment are those persons to whom the donee may appoint. Sometimes they are referred to as the object of the power. Obviously, an appointee may be an institution, and there may be one or more appointees. Issues of class gift, anti-lapse, and vesting will be significant issues when discussing appointees.

5. Takers in default are those persons named by the donor to take if the donee does not exercise the power of appointment conferred, or, in the case of special powers, those who are eligible to take the appointment if the donee exercises ineffectively.

6. Testamentary/*Inter vivos* Power of appointment regards the time when the donee may exercise the power of appointment, not when the donor creates the power. Thus, if the donor gives to the donee a life estate, and then the donee may appoint, the power is testamentary, since the donee may only exercise at the end of a life estate. Obviously, a valid Last Will and Testament will be necessary for the donee to have a valid exercise.

7. General power of appointment refers to the scope of the permissible appointees from whom the donee may choose. The Uniform Powers of Appointment Act § 101(6) (2019) defines it as follows: "General power of appointment means a power of appointment exercisable in favor of the powerholder, the powerholder's estate, a creditor of the powerholder, or a creditor of the powerholder's estate." This language results from the Internal Revenue Code § 2041(b), signaling that any general power will be includable in the gross taxable estate of any donee possessing one, and it is subject to the elective share of any surviving spouse, or bona fide creditor. Please note that, for a power to be general, the power given to the donee does not require the donee to be able to exercise in favor of all three of these groups, but any one of them would be sufficient to make the power general. For example: "One million dollars to Sadie, income for life, and then as she shall appoint to her estate or among her siblings." The ability to appoint among her siblings would not make this a general power, but the ability to appoint to her estate *would* make this a general power.

8. Special power of appointment occurs whenever a donee is prohibited from appointing to one of the three groups mentioned in the Restatement as creating a general power. Hence, if the settlor provides: "One million dollars to Sadie, income for life, and then as she shall appoint among her siblings," the power is a special one. Because a special power limits the choices of the donee, the donor retains greater control, thereby prompting the question as to whether the donor wanted the donee to "exclude" some members that could be included within the special power, or was the donee so restricted as to be prohibited from excluding, hence possessing a non-exclusive power? *See Uniform Powers of Appointment Act* § 101(10) (2019). If the power is interpreted as being non-exclusive, it creates very little, if any, discretion in the donee, thus defeating the purposes of powers of appointment. Thus, the Restatement takes the position that, absent a contrary intent, special powers of appointment are presumptively exclusive. *See Restatement (Second) of Property, Donative Transfers*, § 21.1 (1986). The donor must be very explicit in defining the power as non-exclusive — "to give to all equally" — before the court is likely to define the power as non-exclusive. Please note that the classification of a power as exclusive or non-exclusive may only be accomplished within the scope of a special power. Since a donee may appoint to anyone in a general power, the ability to exclude is automatic.

No particular form of words is necessary to create a power of appointment; the court will simply look to a modicum of discretion given to the putative donee. Thus, it is important to be able to identify a power of appointment and to classify its attributes. Being able to do so will lessen the possibility of error when considering what is to follow: release of the power, effective exercise, mistaken exercise, applicability of anti-lapse, fraud upon the power, and the application of the Rule Against Perpetuities and the Relation Back Doctrine. So, before going any further, make certain that you can identify the features of the following trust.

> **Case:** During her lifetime, the settlor created a valid *inter vivos* trust of one million dollars, to pay the income to her daughter, Sadie, for life, then at Sadie's death, United States Trust Company was to pay the corpus to those of her issue that Sadie designated in her Last Will and Testament. In the event that Sadie were to die without a Last Will and Testament, duly probated, or she were to die without issue, then United States Trust Company was to pay the remainder to the National Geographic Society.

Even though the words "power of appointment" were never used, Sadie had discretion to pick and choose among her issue at the time of her death, thereby a power was created in Sadie, the donee. Sadie, of course, had a life estate, but at her death, she could appoint what was a special exclusive testamentary power of appointment, with the National Geographic Society being a taker in default. The power was special because Sadie could not appoint to herself, her creditors, or her estate — her issue do not constitute her estate. Since there was no restriction on the ability of Sadie to "exclude" issue, the power is exclusive. And because the power may be exercised only at her death, the power is testamentary. The fact that the donor created the power during her lifetime does not make the power an *inter vivos* one. If you have mastered this, then ask the following questions: (1) What if Sadie wanted to release the power? — how would she do this? (2) What does Sadie have to say in her Last Will and Testament to exercise the power? Does she have to mention it specifically? (3) What should the court do if Sadie exercises the power in favor of her spouse, and not a named appointee? (4) What if Sadie appoints to a particular issue in her Last Will and Testament, but that issue predeceases her, survived by issue? Should we apply anti-lapse? (5) If Sadie exercises the power of appointment by creating yet another trust in favor of one child, and then, at the death of that child, to that child's issue, how should the Rule Against Perpetuities be utilized? We shall discuss these questions in the material that follows.

Tax Considerations: Classifications of powers of appointment as general or special, *inter vivos* or testamentary, and whether they have been exercised or released, are all very important to the treatment that powers of appointment receive under the Internal Revenue Code. For example, if the donee has the ability to appoint to the donee himself or herself, or to the donee's estate or creditors, the donee has a general power of appointment. If the donee exercises the power or releases the power during the donee's lifetime, the donee has made a transfer and is responsible for the gift tax. *See* I.R.C. § 2514. A gift tax is also imposed if there is a lapse of the power at any time during the life of the donee, so long as the appointment is greater than $5,000 or 5% of the aggregate value, at the time of the lapse, of the assets out of which the exercise of the lapsed powers could have been satisfied. *See id.* at § 2041(b)(2).

If the decedent possesses a general power of appointment over property at death, the value of the property to which the power applies is included in his or her estate, even if the power is not exercised. *See id.* at § 2041. If the donee had only a special power of appointment, the value of the property subject to the appointment is not subject to the estate tax. *See* Treasury Reg. § 20.2041-1(c)(1).

There are two exceptions to the rule that includes property over which the donee had a general power of appointment within either the gift tax or the estate tax. One is that if the donee is given a power by the donor that could be included within the donee's taxable estate or gift tax, but the donee is "limited by an ascertainable standard relating to health, education, support, or maintenance" of the donee, *see* I.R.C. § 2041(b)(1), the power is not considered as general and hence not includable in the gift and estate tax calculations for the donee. And second, if the donee is given no more than $5,000 or 5% of the aggregate value and the donee had the power to consume or invade that amount, then the maximum amount includable within the donee's estate is $5,000 or 5% of the corpus. *See id.* at § 2041(b)(2). The rules regarding the taxation of powers of appointment are not as complicated as other areas, but, obviously, a careful drafting is required. *See, e.g.,* W. Brian Dowis & Ted D. Englebrecht, *Qualified Disclaimers: An Analysis,* 46 Real Est. Tax'n 29 (2018) (explaining proper forms of disclaimers); Wendy C. Gerzog, *Toward a Reality-Based Estate Tax,* 57 B.C. L. Rev. 1037 (2016) (proposing changes to the estate tax); Wendy C. Gerzog,

The New Super-Charged PAT (Power of Appointment Trust), 48 Hous. L. Rev. 507 (2011) (suggesting how to draft a QTIP trust).

Estate of Vissering v. Commissioner

United States Court of Appeals, Tenth Circuit, 1993
990 F.2d 578

LOGAN, Circuit Judge.

The estate of decedent Norman H. Vissering appeals from a judgment of the Tax Court determining that he held at his death a general power of appointment as defined by I.R.C. § 2041, and requiring that the assets of a trust of which he was cotrustee be included in his gross estate for federal estate tax purposes. The appeal turns on whether decedent held powers permitting him to invade the principal of the trust for his own benefit unrestrained by an ascertainable standard relating to health, education, support, or maintenance. The trust was created by decedent's mother in Florida and specifies that Florida law controls in the interpretation and administration of its provisions.

The estate argues that decedent was not a trustee at the time of his death because a New Mexico court's adjudication that he was incapacitated two months before his death divested him of those powers. Decedent was not formally removed as trustee; if he ceased to serve it was by operation of Florida law. However, we assume for purposes of this opinion that decedent continued as trustee until his death and that his powers are to be adjudged as if he were fully competent to exercise them at the time of his death. * * *

The trust at issue was created by decedent's mother, and became irrevocable on her death in 1965. Decedent and a bank served as cotrustees. Under the dispositive provisions decedent received all the income from the trust after his mother's death. On decedent's death (his wife, a contingent beneficiary, predeceased him), remaining trust assets were to be divided into equal parts and passed to decedent's two children or were held for their benefit. Decedent developed Alzheimer's disease and entered into a nursing home in 1984, but he tendered no resignation as trustee, nor did his guardian or conservator do so on his behalf after he was found to be incapacitated.

The Tax Court's decision, based entirely upon stipulated facts, resolved only questions of law, and consequently our review is de novo. First Nat'l Bank v. Commissioner, 921 F.2d 1081, 1086 (10th Cir.1990).

Under I.R.C. § 2041 a decedent has a general power of appointment includable in his estate if he possesses at the time of his death a power over assets that permits him to benefit himself, his estate, his creditors, or creditors of his estate. A power vested in a trustee, even with a cotrustee who has no interest adverse to the exercise of the power, to invade principal of the trust for his own benefit is sufficient to find the decedent trustee to have a general power of appointment, unless the power to invade is limited by an ascertainable standard relating to health, education, support, or maintenance. Treas.Reg. §20.2041-1(c), -3(c)(2). See, *e.g.*, Estate of Sowell v. Commissioner, 708 F.2d 1564, 1568 (10th Cir.1983) (invasion of trust corpus in case of emergency or illness is an ascertainable standard under §2041(b)(1)(A)); Gaskill v. United States, 561 F.Supp. 73, 78 (D.Kan.1983) (life estate with power of disposition but not to consume the proceeds did not create general power of appointment under §2041(b)(1)(A)), aff'd mem., 787 F.2d 1446 (10th Cir.1986); see also Merchants Nat'l Bank v. Commissioner, 320 U.S. 256, 261, 64 S.Ct. 108, 111, 88 L.Ed. 35 (1943) (invasion of trust corpus for "the comfort, support, maintenance and/or happiness of my wife" is not a fixed standard for purposes of charitable deductions); Ithaca Trust Co. v. United States, 279 U.S. 151, 154, 49 S.Ct. 291, 291, 73 L.Ed. 647 (1929) (invasion of trust corpus for any amount "that may be necessary to suitably maintain [decedent's wife] in as much comfort as she now enjoys" is a fixed standard for purposes of charitable deduction).

The relevant provisions of the instant trust agreement are as follows:

During the term of [this trust], the Trustees shall further be authorized to pay over or to use or expend for the direct or indirect benefit of any of the aforesaid beneficiaries, whatever amount or amounts of the principal of this Trust as may, in the discretion of the Trustees, be required for the continued comfort, support, maintenance, or education of said beneficiary.

Tax Ct. ex. 3-C at 5–6. The Internal Revenue Service (IRS) and the Tax Court focused on portions of the invasion provision providing that the trust principal could be expended for the "comfort" of decedent, declaring that this statement rendered the power of invasion incapable of limitation by the courts.

We look to state law (here Florida's) to determine the legal interests and rights created by a trust instrument, but federal law determines the tax consequences of those interests and rights. Morgan v. Commissioner, 309 U.S. 78, 80, 60 S.Ct. 424, 425–26, 84 L.Ed. 585 (1940); Maytag v. United States, 493 F.2d 995, 998 (10th Cir.1974). The absence of clear and controlling state precedent regarding the use of the term "comfort" in trust documents for purposes of determining a general power of appointment under federal estate tax law has prompted the estate and amici to request that we certify this question to the Supreme Court of Florida. Because recent changes in Florida trust law significantly curtail the number of trusts that might be affected by such a certification, * * * and because the language of each trust document in any event requires individualized attention, we deny the motion to certify to the Florida Supreme Court.

Despite the decision in Barritt v. Tomlinson, 129 F.Supp. 642 (S.D.Fla.1955), which involved a power of invasion broader than the one before us, we believe the Florida Supreme Court would hold that a trust document permitting invasion of principal for "comfort," without further qualifying language, creates a general power of appointment. Treas.Reg. §20.2041-1(c). See First Virginia Bank v. United States, 490 F.2d 532, 533 (4th Cir.1974) (under Virginia law, right of invasion for beneficiary's "comfort and care as she may see fit" not limited by an ascertainable standard); Lehman v. United States, 448 F.2d 1318, 1320 (5th Cir.1971) (under Texas law, power to invade corpus for "support, maintenance, comfort, and welfare" not limited by ascertainable standard); Miller v. United States, 387 F.2d 866, 869 (3d Cir.1968) (under Pennsylvania law, power to make disbursements from principal in amounts "necessary or expedient for [beneficiary's] proper maintenance, support, medical care, hospitalization, or other expenses incidental to her comfort and well-being" not limited by ascertainable standard); Estate of Schlotterer v. United States, 421 F.Supp. 85, 91 (W.D.Pa.1976) (power of consumption "to the extent deemed by [beneficiary] to be desirable not only for her support and maintenance but also for her comfort and pleasure" not limited by ascertainable standard); Doyle v. United States, 358 F.Supp. 300, 309–10 (E.D.Pa.1973) (under Pennsylvania law, trustees' "uncontrolled discretion" to pay beneficiary "such part or parts of the principal of said trust fund as may be necessary for her comfort, maintenance and support" not limited by ascertainable standard); Stafford v. United States, 236 F.Supp. 132, 134 (E.D.Wisc.1964) (under Wisconsin law, trust permitting husband "for his use, benefit and enjoyment during his lifetime," unlimited power of disposition thereof "without permission of any court, and with the right to use and enjoy the principal, as well as the income, if he shall have need thereof for his care, comfort or enjoyment" not limited by ascertainable standard).

However, there is modifying language in the trust before us that we believe would lead the Florida courts to hold that "comfort," in context, does not permit an unlimited power of invasion. The instant language states that invasion of principal is permitted to the extent "*required* for the *continued* comfort" of the decedent, and is part of a clause referencing the support, maintenance and education of the beneficiary. Invasion of the corpus is not permitted to the extent "determined" or "desired" for the beneficiary's comfort but only to the extent that it is "required." Furthermore, the invasion must be for the beneficiary's "continued" comfort, implying, we believe, more than the minimum necessary for survival, but neverthe-less reasonably necessary to maintain the beneficiary in his accustomed manner of living. These words in context state a standard essentially no different from the examples in the Treasury Regulation, in which phrases such as "support in reason-able comfort," "maintenance in health and reasonable comfort," and "support in his accustomed manner of living" are deemed to be limited by an ascertainable stan-dard. Treas.Reg. §20.2041-1(c)(2). See, *e.g.*, United States v. Powell, 307 F.2d 821, 828 (10th Cir.1962) (under Kansas law, invasion of the corpus if "it is necessary or advisable . . . for the maintenance, welfare, comfort or happiness" of beneficiaries, and only if the need justifies the reduction in principal, is subject to ascertainable standard); Hunter v. United States, 597 F.Supp. 1293, 1295 (W.D.Pa.1984) (power to invade for "comfortable support and maintenance" of beneficiaries is subject to ascertainable standard).

We believe that had decedent, during his life, sought to use the assets of the trust to increase significantly his standard of living beyond that which he had previ-ously enjoyed, his cotrustee would have been obligated to refuse to consent, and the remainder beneficiaries of the trust could have successfully petitioned the court to disallow such expenditures as inconsistent with the intent of the trust instrument. The Tax Court erred in ruling that this power was a general power of appointment includable in decedent's estate.

REVERSED and REMANDED.

B. Exercise of a Power

Beals v. State Street Bank & Trust Co.

Supreme Judicial Court of Massachusetts, 1975
367 Mass. 318, 326 N.E.2d 896

WILKINS, Justice.

The trustees under the will of Arthur Hunnewell filed this petition for instructions, seeking a determination of the proper distribution to be made of a portion of the trust created under the residuary clause of his will. A judge of the Probate Court reserved decision and reported the case to the Appeals Court on the pleadings and a stipulation of facts. We transferred the case here.

Arthur Hunnewell died, a resident of Wellesley, in 1904, leaving his wife and four daughters. His will placed the residue of his property in a trust, the income of which was to be paid to his wife during her life. At the death of his wife the trust was to be divided in portions, one for each then surviving daughter and one for the then surviving issue of any deceased daughter. Mrs. Hunnewell died in 1930. One of the four daughters predeceased her mother, leaving no issue. The trust was divided, therefore, in three portions at the death of Mrs. Hunnewell. The will directed that the income of each portion held for a surviving daughter should be paid to her during her life and on her death the principal of such portion should 'be paid and disposed of as she may direct and appoint by her last Will and Testament duly probated.' In default of appointment, the will directed that a daughter's share should be distributed to 'the persons who would be entitled to such estate under the laws then governing the distribution of intestate estates.'

This petition concerns the distribution of the trust portion held for the testator's daughter Isabella H. Hunnewell, later Isabella H. Dexter (Isabella). Following the death of her mother, Isabella requested the trustees to exercise their discretionary power to make principal payments by transferring substantially all of her trust share 'to the Dexter family office in Boston, there to be managed in the first instance by her husband, Mr. Gordon Dexter.' This request was granted, and cash and securities were transferred to her account at the Dexter office. The Hunnewell trustees, however, retained in Isabella's share a relatively small cash balance, an undivided one-third interest in a mortgage and undivided one-third interest in various parcels of real estate in the Commonwealth, which Isabella did not want in kind and which the trustees could not sell at a reasonable price at the time. Thereafter, the trustees received payments on the mortgage and proceeds from occasional sales of portions of the real estate. From her one-third share of these receipts, the trustees made further distributions to her of $1,900 in 1937, $22,000 in 1952, and $5,000 in 1953.

In February, 1944, Isabella, who was then a resident of New York, executed and caused to be filed in the Registry of Probate for Norfolk County an instrument which partially released her general power of appointment under the will of her father. See G.L. c. 204, §§ 27–36, inserted by St.1943, c. 152. Isabella released her power of appointment 'to the extent that such power empowers me to appoint to any one other than one or more of the . . . descendants me surviving of Arthur Hunnewell.'

On December 14, 1968, Isabella, who survived her husband, died without issue, still a resident of New York, leaving a will dated May 21, 1965. Her share in the trust under her father's will then consisted of an interest in a contract to sell real estate, cash, notes and a certificate of deposit, and was valued at approximately $88,000. Isabella did not expressly exercise her power of appointment under her father's will. The residuary clause of her will provided in effect for the distribution of all 'the rest, residue and remainder of my property' to the issue per stirpes of her sister Margaret Blake, who had predeceased Isabella.[1] The Blake issue would take one-half of Isabella's trust share, as takers in default of appointment, in all events. If, however, Isabella's will should be treated as effectively exercising her power of appointment under her father's will, the Blake issue would take the entire trust share, and the executors of the will of Isabella's sister Jane (who survived Isabella and has since died) would not receive that one-half of the trust share which would go to Jane in default of appointment.[2]

In support of their argument that Isabella's will did not exercise the power of appointment under her father's will, the executors of Jane's estate contend that (1) Massachusetts substantive law governs all questions relating to the power of appointment, including the interpretation of Isabella's will; (2) the power should be treated as a special power of appointment because of its partial release by Isabella; and (3) because Isabella's will neither expresses nor implies any intention to exercise the power, the applicable rule of construction in this Commonwealth is that a general residuary clause does not exercise a special power of appointment. The

---

1. The significant portion of the residuary clause reads as follows: 'All the rest, residue and remainder of my property of whatever kind and wherever situated (including any property not effectively disposed of by the preceding provisions of this my will and all property over which I have or may have the power of appointment under or by virtue of the last will and testament dated November 27, 1933 and codicils thereto dated January 7, 1935 and January 8, 1935 of my husband, the late Gordon Dexter) . . . I give, devise, bequeath and appoint in equal shares to such of my said nephew GEORGE BATY BLAKE and my said nieces MARGARET CABOT and JULIA O. BEALS as shall survive me and the issue who shall survive me of any of my said nephew or nieces who may predecease me, such issue to take per stirpes.'

2. The parties agree that in these circumstances the intestate recipients, and the proportion due to each, are the same under the laws governing the distribution of intestate estates in Massachusetts and New York.

Blake issue, in support of their argument that the power was exercised, contend that (1) Isabella's will manifests an intention to exercise the power and that no rule of construction need be applied; (2) the law of New York should govern the question whether Isabella's will exercised the power and, if it does, by statute New York has adopted a rule that a special power of appointment is exercised by a testamentary disposition of all of the donee's property; and (3) if Massachusetts law does apply, and the will is silent on the subject of the exercise of the power, the principles underlying our rule of construction that a residuary clause exercises a general power of appointment are applicable in these circumstances.

* * * We turn first to a consideration of the question whether Isabella's will should be construed according to the law of this Commonwealth or the law of New York.[3] There are strong, logical reasons for turning to the law of the donee's domicil at the time of death to determine whether a donee's will has exercised a testamentary power of appointment over movables. See Restatement 2d: Conflict of Laws, § 275, comment c (1971); Scott, Trusts, § 642, p. 4065 (3d ed. 1967); Scoles, Goodrich's Conflict of Laws, §§ 175–177, p. 346 (4th ed. 1964). Most courts in this country which have considered the question, however, interpret the donee's will under the law governing the administration of the trust, which is usually the law of the donor's domicil. * * * [Citations omitted]. This has long been the rule in Massachusetts. * * * [Citations omitted]. Indeed, the rule is so well established that parties have conceded the point from time to time. * * * [Citations omitted].[4]

If the question were before us now for the first time, we might well adopt a choice of law rule which would turn to the substantive law of the donee's domicil, for the purpose of determining whether the donee's will exercised a power of appointment. However, in a field where much depends on certainty and consistency as to the applicable rules of law, we think that we should adhere to our well established rule.

---

3. The applicable rules of construction where a donee's intention is not clear from his will differ between the two States. In the absence of a requirement by the donor that the donee refer to the power in order to exercise it, New York provides by statute that a residuary clause in a will exercises not only a general power of appointment but also a special power of appointment, unless the will expressly or by necessary implication shows the contrary. 17B McKinney's Consol.Laws of N.Y.Anno., EPTL, c. 17-b, § 10-6.1 (1967). See Matter of Hopkins, 46 Misc.2d 273, 276, 259 N.Y.S.2d 565 (1964). "Necessary implication" exists only where the will permits no other construction. Matter of Deane, 4 N.Y.2d 326, 330, 175 N.Y.S.2d 21, 151 N.E.2d 184 (1958). In Massachusetts, unless the donor has provided that the donee of the power can exercise it only by explicit reference to the power, a general residuary clause in a will exercises a general power of appointment unless there is a clear indication of a contrary intent. Boston Safe Deposit & Trust Co. v. Painter, 322 Mass. 362, 366–367, 77 N.E.2d 409 (1948); Second Bank-State St. Trust Co. v. Yale Univ. Alumni Fund, 338 Mass. 520, 524, 156 N.E.2d 57 (1959). However, in Fiduciary Trust Co. v. First Natl. Bank, 344 Mass. 1, 6–10, 181 N.E.2d 6 (1962), we held that a general residuary clause did not exercise a special testamentary power of appointment in the circumstances of that case.

4. Of course, the law of the donee's domicil would be applied if the donor expressed such an intention. See Walker v. Treasurer & Recr. Gen., 221 Mass. 600, 603, 109 N.E. 647 (1915); Greenough v. Osgood, 235 Mass. 235, 237–238, 126 N.E. 461 (1920); Amerige v. Attorney Gen., 324 Mass. 648, 657–658, 88 N.E.2d 126 (1949).

Thus, in interpreting the will of a donee to determine whether a power of appointment was exercised, we apply the substantive law of the jurisdiction whose law governs the administration of the trust.

* * * Considering the arguments of the parties, we conclude that there is no indication in Isabella's will of an intention to exercise or not to exercise the power of appointment given to her under her father's will. A detailed analysis of the various competing contentions would not add to our jurisprudence.[5] In the absence of an intention disclosed by her will construed in light of circumstances known to her when she executed it, we must adopt some Massachusetts rule of construction to resolve the issue before us. The question is what rule of construction. We are unaware of any decided case which, in this context, has dealt with a testamentary general power, reduced to a special power by action of the donee.[6]

* * * We conclude that the residuary clause of Isabella's will should be presumed to have exercised the power of appointment. We reach this result by a consideration of the reasons underlying the canons of construction applicable to general and special testamentary powers of appointment. Considered in this way, we believe that a presumption of exercise is more appropriate in the circumstances of this case than a presumption of nonexercise.

When this court first decided not to extend to a special power of appointment the rule of construction that a general residuary clause executes a general testamentary power (unless a contrary intent is shown by the will), we noted significant distinctions between a general power and a special power. Fiduciary Trust Co. v. First Natl. Bank, *supra*, 344 Mass. at 6–10, 181 N.E.2d 6. A general power was said to be a close approximation to a property interest, a 'virtually unlimited power of disposition' * * *, while a special power of appointment lacked this quality * * *. We observed that a layman having a general testamentary power over property might not be expected to distinguish between the appointive property and that which he owns outright, and thus 'he can reasonably be presumed to regard this appointive property as his own' * * *. On the other hand, the donee of a special power would not reasonably regard such appointive property as his own: '[h]e would more likely consider himself to be, as the donor of the power intended, merely the person

---

5. Isabella's residuary clause disposed of her 'property.' Because the trustees had agreed to distribute her trust portion to her and had largely done so and because, in a sense, she had exercised dominion over the trust assets by executing the partial release, a reasonable argument might be made that she regarded the assets in her portion of the trust as her 'property.' However, a conclusion that she intended by implication to include assets over which she had a special power of appointment within the word 'property' is not justifiable because her residuary clause refers expressly to other property over which she had a special power of appointment under the will of her husband.

6. Clearly Isabella had only a special power of appointment after she partially released the general power given to her under her father's will. See Jeffers Estate, 394 Pa. 393, 398–399, 147 A.2d 402 (1959); Mearkle Estate, 23 Pa.D. & C.2d 661, 665 (1960). And, of course, if she had totally released the power of appointment, her will could have had no effect on the devolution of 'her' portion of the trust under her father's will.

chosen by the donor to decide who of the possible appointees should share in the property (if the power is exclusive), and the respective shares of the appointees' * * *.

Considering the power of appointment given to Isabella and her treatment of that power during her life, the rationale for the canon of construction applicable to general powers of appointment should be applied in this case. This power was a general testamentary power at its inception. During her life, as a result of her request, Isabella had the use and enjoyment of the major portion of the property initially placed in her trust share. Prior use and enjoyment of the appointive property is a factor properly considered as weighing in favor of the exercise of a power of appointment by a will. Fiduciary Trust Co. v. First Natl. Bank, *supra*, at 10, 181 N.E.2d 6. Isabella voluntarily limited the power by selecting the possible appointees. In thus relinquishing the right to add the trust assets to her estate, she was treating the property as her own. Moreover, the gift under her residuary clause was consistent with the terms of the reduced power which she retained. In these circumstances, the partial release of a general power does not obviate the application of that rule of construction which presumes that a general residuary clause exercises a general power of appointment.

* * * A decree shall be entered determining that Isabella H. Dexter did exercise the power of appointment, partially released by an instrument dated February 25, 1944, given to her by art. Fourth of the will of Arthur Hunnewell and directing that the trustees under the will of Arthur Hunnewell pay over the portion of the trust held under art. Fourth of his will for the benefit of Isabella H. Dexter, as follows: one-third each to George Baty Blake and Julia O. Beals; and one-sixth each to Margaret B. Elwell and to the estate of George B. Cabot. The parties shall be allowed their costs and counsel fees in the discretion of the probate court.

So ordered.

QUIRICO, Justice (with whom TAURO, Chief Justice, joins), concurring in the result.

I concur in the court's conclusion that the general residuary clause in the will of Isabella H. Dexter exercised the power of appointment given to her by art. Fourth of the will of Arthur Hunnewell. However, I would reach that result without regard to whether the power of appointment was, either when it was created or when it was exercised, a general power of appointment or a special power of appointment, and without perpetuating the distinction made between the two types of powers in our decision in Fiduciary Trust Co. v. First Natl. Bank, 344 Mass. 1, 6–10, 181 N.E.2d 6–8 (1962). I would hold that the 'settled canon of construction that a general residuary clause will operate as an execution of a general testamentary power unless a contrary intent is shown by the will' (Fiduciary Trust Co. case, 5, 181 N.E.2d), quoting from Second Bank-State St. Trust Co. v. Yale Univ. Alumni Fund, 338 Mass. 520, 524, 156 N.E.2d 57 (1959), which has been a part of the case law of this Commonwealth at least since our decision in Amory v. Meredith, 7 Allen 397 (1863), applies equally to the execution of a special power of appointment, provided, of course, that (a) the residuary clause includes any beneficiary within the scope of the special power of appointment, (b) the instrument creating the special power does not prohibit its exercise by a general residuary clause, and (c) the residuary clause includes no disclaimer of intent to exercise the special power.

It is with reluctance that I advocate a departure from the holding in the Fiduciary Trust Co. case which was decided in 1962 by a quorum of distinguished Justices of this court, but I am persuaded to do so by the policy considerations discussed below. The Fiduciary Trust Co. case itself represented a departure from views expressed, by way of dicta, in several cases which preceded it. In Stone v. Forbes, 189 Mass. 163, 169, 75 N.E. 141, 143 (1905), we said: 'If it were necessary to determine the question we should hesitate to follow the . . . [distinction drawn in the English cases between the exercise of general and special powers by a residuary clause]. There is certainly less reason for doing so since Amory v. Meredith than before. There would seem to be no good reason why the question whether a special power of appointment had been exercised should not be determined by the same rules that are applied in other cases to the construction or interpretation of wills.' In several other cases the opportunity to rule that a general residuary clause does not ordinarily exercise a special power of appointment was also declined. Worcester Bank & Trust Co. v. Sibley, 287 Mass. 594, 598, 192 N.E. 31 (1934); Pitman v. Pitman, 314 Mass. 465, 475, 50 N.E.2d 69 (1943). Frye v. Loring, 330 Mass. 389, 394–395, 113 N.E.2d 595 (1953). In the last cited case we referred to Am.Law of Property, §23.40(a) (1952). That source provides: 'The reasoning supporting the Massachusetts presumption that a residuary clause was intended to exercise powers of appointment applies with equal force whether the power in question is general or special.'

The basic judicial objective in this and similar cases is to ascertain the testamentary intent of the donee of the power. I am unable to accept the proposition that a testator who subscribes to a will which includes a residuary clause in substantially the common form, broadly covering 'all the rest, residue and remainder of my property' does not thereby express quite clearly an intention to dispose of all of the property and estate which can be the subject of testamentary disposition by him. Neither am I able to accept the proposition that such language, reasonably construed, permits any inference that the testator intended, by the use of such broad language, to exercise a general power of appointment but not a special one.

In its decision in the Amory case, *supra*, from which there evolved the 'settled canon of construction that a general residuary clause will operate as an execution of a general testamentary power unless a contrary intent is shown by the will,' this court first reviewed the development of the law of England on this subject. It cited several English cases which had held that a will would not operate to execute a power of appointment unless it referred expressly to the power or to the subject of the power, and that 'a mere residuary clause gave no sufficient indication of intention to execute a power' (399). This court then noted criticism of the English rule, particularly because of its emphasis on the distinction between 'power' and 'property,' stating that 'the refinements and subtleties to which this distinction leads are great and perplexing' (398). It then noted that the rule was changed by a statute (St. 7 Will. IV and 1 Vict. c. 26, § 27), declaring 'that a general devise of real or personal estate, in wills thereafter made, should operate as an execution of a power of the testator over the same, unless a contrary intention should appear on the will'; and then quoted the comment of Judge Story (1 Story R. 458, note), to the effect that as a result of the statute, '[t]he doctrine, therefore, has at last settled down in that country [England] to what would seem to be the dictate of common sense, unaffected by technical niceties' (400). For further discussions and citations of cases on the development of the law on this subject in England and in this country, see Restatement: Property, § 343(1), comment d (1940); Am.Law of Property, § 23.40 (1952); 104 Trusts and Estates 814 (1965); 51 Cornell L.Q. 1, 9–10 (1965); 16 A.L.R.3d 911, 920–924 (1967); 62 Am.Jur.2d, Powers, §§ 51–52 (1972).

It is apparent that in the case of Fiduciary Trust Co. v. First Natl. Bank, 344 Mass. 1, 181 N.E.2d 6 (1962), the court distinguished general powers and special powers in part on the basis of the distinction between powers and property.[1] The latter is the same distinction of which this court said in the Amory case, *supra*: '[T]he refinements and subtleties to which this distinction leads are great and perplexing' (7 Allen 398). Indeed, the case now before us represents one of the perplexities resulting from a rule based on such a distinction. These unnecessary 'refinements and subtleties' inevitably breed litigation initiated either by competing claimants or by a fiduciary, often a professional fiduciary, seeking to avoid or minimize the risk of liability to himself by obtaining the protection of a judicial declaration, usually at considerable expense to the intended beneficiaries. We should, if possible, develop and apply rules of law which will eliminate the occasion for such litigation. One stop in that direction would be to hold that a general residuary clause in a will is equally competent to execute a special power of appointment as it is to exercise a general power. See Bostwick & Hurstel, ___ Mass. ___, ___ 304 N.E.2d 186 (1973).

Notes

Whenever a donee neglects to refer to the donor's power of appointment, we may say that the donee's instrument is "open-ended." An open-ended residuary clause in the will of a donee makes no reference to the power of appointment. To address the issue of whether the donee intended to exercise the power, states have adopted many rules to best accommodate the donor's intent. The following are illustrative.

First, if the donor is truly concerned about inadvertent exercise of the power of appointment by an unwitting donee, the donor may provide in the instrument

---

1. The court said, 344 Mass. at 9, 181 N.E.2d at 11: 'We think that, unlike a general power, a special power is not 'a close approximation to a property interest . . .'. It is our opinion that the traditional common law distinction between 'property' and 'powers' . . . which with regard to general powers has in effect been overridden in cases cited above, persists with undiminished validity in the case of special powers and would alone serve as a sufficiently sound rationale for the nonapplicability of the canon in question to special powers.'

creating the power that the donee must *specifically mention* the power of appointment to exercise it. *See, e.g.,* UNIF. PROB. CODE § 2-704 (2019). Any competent drafter should consider addressing this issue when creating a power of appointment in a donee.

Second, the vast majority of states and code references provide that an open-ended residuary clause (no reference made to power of appointment) *does not* exercise any power of appointment. *See, e.g., Restatement (Third) of Property: Donative Transfers* § 25.3 (Prelim. Draft No. 4, 1995). Often, these same states allow for extrinsic evidence to be admitted to demonstrate that the open-ended clause does, in fact, exercise the power, thus creating a presumption against exercise, which may be rebutted through extrinsic proof. *See Restatement (Second) of Property, Donative Transfers* § 17.3 (1986).

Third, a minority of states make a distinction between a general power and a special power, and hold that, barring a necessity of specific reference imposed by a donor, an open-ended residuary clause *does* exercise a general power of appointment and will exercise a special power if the appointees are proper objects of the special power of appointment. The Uniform Probate Code § 2-608 provides that, in the absence of the donor's requirement of a specific reference, an open-ended residuary clause in a Last Will and Testament does exercise a general power of appointment, as long as the donor has not provided for a taker in default. The Uniform Powers of Appointment Act (2017) resembles the Uniform Probate Code in that an open-ended residuary clause may only exercise a general power, and only if the donor did not provide for a taker in default. *Id.* at § 302(2).

The *Beals* decision illustrates the traditional rule that the donor's domicile controls the effectiveness of the power of appointment and the exercise of that power. More modern statutes provide that the "exercise, release, or disclaimer of the power, or the revocation or amendment of the exercise, release or disclaimer of the power, is governed by the law of the powerholder's domicile at the relevant time." UNIF. POWERS OF APPOINTMENT ACT § 103(2) (2019). But note that modern statutes permit an open-ended residuary clause to exercise the power of appointment under the doctrine of substantial compliance. *See id.* at § 304. The donee must intend to exercise the power, and the exercise may not impair a material purpose of the donor.

Problem

When the decedent died, he left a valid Last Will and Testament that contained the following clause:

> The marital trust shall terminate upon the death of the Donor's said wife, whereupon the Trustee shall transfer and pay over to said wife's estate all accrued and accumulated income and shall transfer and pay over the principal then remaining, of said trust as the Donor's said wife shall have appointed by will executed after the Donor's death, making specific reference to the power hereby created, with the right in her discretion to appoint

to her estate or any other person or persons without limitation, upon any terms, condition, limitations and trusts, including the right to create new powers of appointment, and in default of such appointment or to the extent that said remaining principal is not effectively appointed, the Trustee shall add said remaining principal to the principal of the family trust established pursuant to the provisions of Article FIFTH of this instrument.

Upon the death of the decedent's wife, she left a valid Last Will and Testament and a codicil to that will. The codicil referenced the "marital trust left me by my late husband" and then made individual bequests to a series of beneficiaries. The husband's will provided for takers in default in the event that his wife did not exercise the power or appointment. These takers claim that the wife failed to exercise the power and that they now take the appointment. If you were the probate judge, how would you rule on their petition? *See* Guarino v. Fish, 1988 WL 1052314 (Va. Cir. Ct. 1988).

C. Scope of a Power

In re Carroll's Will

Court of Appeals of New York, 1937
274 N.Y. 288, 8 N.E.2d 864

HUBBS, Judge.

In 1910 William Carroll died leaving a will by the fourth paragraph of which he devised and bequeathed the residue of his estate to his executors in trust to pay the income to his wife during her life. By the fifth paragraph he directed that upon the death of the wife the residuary trust be divided into two equal shares, the proceeds of one to be for the use and benefit of his daughter, Elsa, during her life, and the proceeds of the other share for the use and benefit of his son, Ralph, during his life. In the fifth paragraph he gave his daughter power by her last will and testament to dispose of the property so set aside for her use 'to and among her children or any other kindred who shall survive her and in such shares and manner as she shall think proper.' A similar power of appointment was given to Ralph to dispose of his share 'to and among his kindred or wife.' With respect to the share set aside for the use of the daughter, Elsa, the will provided that, in the absence of any valid disposition of the corpus by her, it should pass 'to her then surviving child or children, descendant or descendants' and, should there be no surviving child or descendant of the daughter, then the share on her decease should pass to the donor's 'surviving heirs or next-of-kin, according to the nature of the estate.'

Elsa died on June 26, 1933, without leaving any child or descendant her surviving. The mother, Grace Carroll, survived her and was living at the time of the trial, as was also the brother, Ralph. Elsa left a will by which she left $5,000 to her brother, and $250,000 to one Paul Curtis, a cousin, such bequest to go to his son if he predeceased her. The remainder of her share of the estate of her father she gave to her executors in trust.

When Elsa's will was drawn, the petitioning executor, Content, as her attorney, prepared the will and attended to its execution and also prepared a letter directed to Elsa by the legatee Paul Curtis, which letter read as follows: 'I am informed that by your last will and testament you have given and bequeathed to me the sum of Two Hundred and Fifty Thousand Dollars ($250,000). In the event that you should predecease me and I should receive the bequest before mentioned, I hereby promise and agree, in consideration of the said bequest, that I will pay to your husband, Foster Milliken, Jr., the sum of One Hundred Thousand Dollars ($100,000) out of the said bequest which you have given to me by your said will.'

It is not contended by any of the parties to this proceeding that Foster Milliken, Jr., husband of Elsa, was of her kindred, and, therefore, a proper object of the power granted to his wife in her father's will. The question here involved is as to the effect of the attempted provision for her husband upon the bequest to Paul Curtis.

Content testified that he had advised Elsa that she could not lawfully make her husband a beneficiary of any part of her father's estate; that she had drawn a previous will in which she had given the residue of the estate of her father to her brother, Ralph, with a request that he pay to her husband the sum of $10,000 per annum; that he advised her that that provision could not be enforced; that on October 6, 1931, she told him that she was not satisfied; that she was growing away from her brother and that she wanted to increase the bequest to her cousin Paul Curtis; that she had given Curtis $50,000 in a prior will; that she wanted to leave him $250,000 and that he prepared the will with the prior will before him and on October 13 she and Mrs. Elliott came to his office where she executed the will; that after the will was executed she told him: 'Paul would like to do something for Foster. He would like to leave him some of this money I am leaving to him, and Paul is perfectly willing to put this in writing to show his good faith.' He then talked with Paul, dictated the letter, and had it signed. He was not sure whether the letter was delivered to Elsa or whether he kept it for her. Curtis testified that several days before the will was executed Elsa told him she was going to make a new will; that she knew if her brother, Ralph, heard about it he would probably start a row with her mother; that she had previously left Curtis $50,000 and his son $50,000, and that she was going to leave him $150,000 and add to it $100,000 which she would like him to give to Mr. Milliken; that he told her if she wanted him to do so, he would sign a paper to that effect; that she said she did not know whether it would be necessary but if she wanted him to she would make a date for him to go down to Mr. Content's office; that she called him upon the day the will was executed and asked him to meet her there; that he was not present when the will was executed but that he went in afterwards and heard the letter dictated and signed it.

The surrogate determined that the promise made by Curtis so vitiated and permeated the bequest to him that the appointment constituted a fraud upon the power and made the bequest to him void.

The Appellate Division, two justices dissenting, decided that the only reasonable interpretation to be placed upon the transaction is that Elsa desired to appoint

$150,000 to her cousin and an additional $100,000 to her husband; accordingly, that the lawful appointment of $150,000 to Curtis is separable from the unlawful appointment of $100,000 to him for the benefit of the husband.

It seems to us that the conclusion is inescapable that the testimony of Content, the attorney who drew the instruments, and of Curtis, who was the legatee, do not affect the true intent and purpose of the letter. Stress is laid upon the fact as testified to by Content that the testatrix, Elsa, did not tell him of the understanding with Curtis until after the will had been executed. Nevertheless, it appears from the testimony of Curtis that she had an understanding with him prior to the execution of the will and the writing constituted only a record of the actual prior agreement. The surrogate had the benefit of hearing the witnesses testify and of observing their conduct. He found nothing in their testimony to detract from the force of the letter signed by Curtis. Concededly, the attempted bequest for the benefit of the husband was not valid. Curtis alone testified that he was to receive $150,000 and the husband $100,000. Content testified that she told him she wanted to leave Curtis $250,000, and that he did not know until after the will was drawn of the understanding between Curtis and the testatrix. The letter says that the agreement to pay the husband $100,000 is in consideration of a bequest of $250,000. No one can say whether she would have left Curtis $100,000, $150,000, or a lesser or greater sum had it not been for the agreement to take care of her husband. Only by speculation can it be said that she would have left him $150,000 had it not been for that agreement. Had it not been for her continued possession either personally or by her attorney of the promise on the part of Curtis, no one can say but what she might have changed the will. Curtis was a party to the attempted fraud on the power. If the bequest to him be sustained to the extent of $150,000 on his own testimony, he suffers no penalty. It seems to us that on the facts, the conclusion of the surrogate was correct; that the entire bequest is involved in the intent to defeat the power and that it is impossible to separate and sustain the bequest to Curtis to the extent of $150,000.

* * *

In the case at bar we have written evidence which is corroborative of a prior agreement. It seems to us that the surrogate was quite correct in concluding that it is impossible to separate the valid from the invalid disposition. To say that it clearly appears that the donee would have given $150,000 to Curtis had the bargain not been made is not justified. It clearly appears than an object of the appointment to Curtis was to secure a benefit to the husband of the donee who was excluded by the donor of the power from being an appointee or benefiting from the exercise of the power. The purpose of the donee was to accomplish by an agreement with Curtis an end entirely foreign to the intent of the donor of the power. Her act constituted a fraud on the power in which Curtis actively participated. There was a bargain between the donee and Curtis by which, in consideration of the appointment, he agreed to dispose of a part of the legacy in favor of a person who was not an object of the power. That bargain resulted in vitiating not only the provision for donee's husband but also the bequest to Curtis within the meaning of the authorities heretofore cited.

The wording of the letter which he signed was 'in consideration of the said bequest' he would pay to donee's husband $100,000 'out of the said bequest' of $250,000. It is hard to see how those plain words can be construed otherwise than a bargain to share his bequest of $250,000 with another not an object of the power. Such a bargain under all the authorities makes the entire bequest void. Cf. 46 Yale Law Journal, 344; 49 C.J. 1298.

The appellant Ralph C. Carroll contends that, in permitting the donee to appoint to any of her kindred, the donor used the word 'kindred' in a narrow sense and intended to limit the possible beneficiaries of the power to her next of kin. If correct in that contention, since the donee died without children, the result would be that she could appoint only to her brother, the appellant Ralph Carroll. There is no inconsistency or ambiguity in the will of William Carroll evidenced by the fact that he gave to his daughter a power of appointment to her children or any other of her kindred. Kindred has a well-established meaning, 'blood relatives,' as distinguished from that limited number of blood relatives embraced under the term 'next of kin.' William Carroll in his will used the words next of kin where it is apparent that it was his intention that the property was to pass as in the case of intestacy. The surrogate has determined that kindred was used in the generally accepted meaning of the word. That determination has been affirmed by the Appellate Division and there appears no reason for according to it a limited application.

∗ ∗ ∗

The order of the Appellate Division should be modified in accordance with this opinion and, as so modified, affirmed, without costs.

CRANE, C. J., and O'BRIEN, LOUGHRAN, FINCH, and RIPPEY, JJ., concur.

LEHMAN, J., dissents and votes to affirm.

Judgment accordingly.

Notes

Any donee must exercise within the parameters of the power given. For example, if a donee is given a testamentary power, it cannot be exercised during the donee's lifetime, and vice versa. *See, e.g.,* Seidel v. Werner, *infra.* The donee of a testamentary power may contract to exercise or not exercise the power if the donee is also the donor of the power and the donor has reserved the power to revoke in a revocable trust. UNIF. POWER OF APPOINTMENT ACT § 406 (2019).

The donee of a special power may exercise by creating another power of appointment in a permissible appointee, or by creating another trust in that permissible appointee. *Id.* at § 305 (c). As the *Carroll* decision illustrates, an "exercise of a power of appointment in favor of a permissible appointee is ineffective to the extent the appointment is a fraud on the power." *Id.* at § 307 (b).

D. Ineffective Exercise

If the donee has sufficiently exercised the power of appointment, thereby avoiding the open-ended residuary clause issue, the next issue that may occur is ineffective exercise by the donee. For example, the donee of a *general* testamentary power of appointment exercises by creating another trust that violates the Rule Against Perpetuities, results in a lapsed bequest, or violates a condition of the appointment. Or the donee of a *special* exclusive testamentary power of appointment exercises in favor of a non-permissible appointee. One solution would be to simply result the appointment back to the donor's estate, which is what would occur if there were no exercise at all by the donee of a general power. But when there has been an attempted exercise by the donee, the law proceeds in a different fashion. Consider the following three situations.

1. Allocation of Assets. If the donee of a special power of appointment properly exercises the power in a valid Last Will and Testament's residuary clause, it is possible that the donee could inadvertently blend the donee's personal assets with the donor's appointment, and, worse, the donee could appoint to an impermissible appointee and a permissible appointee. May a court "allocate" the estate of the donee to provide for both appointees? *See* Unif. Powers of Appointment Act § 308 (2019): "If a powerholder exercises a power of appointment in a disposition that also disposes of property the powerholder owns, the owned property and the appointive property must be allocated in the permissible manner that best carries out the powerholder's intention."

2. General Powers: Capture. Whenever there has been an attempted exercise of the general power by the donee, courts will apply the doctrine of capture to keep the appointment in the estate of the donee, rather than have it revert to the estate of the donor. Allowing the appointment to be "captured" in the donee reflects "an intent [by the donee] to assume control of the appointive property for all purposes and not merely for the limited purpose of giving effect to the expressed appointment." *Restatement (Second) of Property, Donative Transfers*, § 23.2 (1986).

The Unif. Powers of Appointment Act § 309 specifies, unlike the Restatement, that if there is an ineffective exercise of the general power, the gift in default clause controls, not an automatic capture by the donee. But if there is no gift in default clause, then the appointment passes first to the donee, and if none, then the appointment reverts to the donor's estate. Permitting the appointment to go first to the gift in default is a distinct difference from what is the traditional rule. Under that rule, any ineffective exercise almost always resulted in "capture" by the donee, regardless of any gift in default provision. The modern approach results from a trend towards better drafting and, hence, more importance given to gift in default clauses. *See id.* at § 309 cmt. Of course, if the donee of the general power fails to make any attempt to exercise, then the appointment goes to the gift in default clause. If this is impossible, then it reverts to the estate of the donor. *Id.* at § 310. The fact that a donor may have included a taker-in-default will not defeat capture; the taker-in-default provision is applicable only if the donee attempts no exercise at all, or the donor has expressed an intent that capture not apply.

3. Special Powers: Implied Gift. Whenever a donor has created a special power, the donor has delegated far less discretion to the donee. Thus, capturing the appointment in the estate of the donee when there is an ineffective exercise is not an option. Courts are willing to create an implied gift in the permissible appointees if the donee: (1) ineffectively exercises, or (2) does not exercise at all. *See id.* at § 311. Please contrast this with general powers and capture, where there must be an attempted exercise and takers-in-default do not matter. California does not refer to implied gifts but, instead, uses "imperative powers," providing that: "A power is 'imperative' where the creating instrument manifests an intent that the permissible appointees be benefitted even if the donee fails to exercise the power." CAL. PROB. CODE §§ 613, 671 (West 2019). How, then, would implied gifts be utilized? Please consider the following decision.

Loring v. Marshall

Supreme Judicial Court of Massachusetts, 1985
396 Mass. 166, 484 N.E.2d 1315

WILKINS, Justice.

This complaint, here on a reservation and report by a single justice of this court, seeks instructions as to the disposition of the remainder of a trust created under the will of Marian Hovey. * * * In Massachusetts Inst. of Technology v. Loring, 327 Mass. 553, 99 N.E.2d 854 (1951), this court held that the President and Fellows of Harvard College, the Boston Museum of Fine Arts, and Massachusetts Institute of Technology (the charities) would not be entitled to the remainder of the trust on its termination. The court, however, did not decide, as we now must, what ultimate disposition should be made of the trust principal.

Marian Hovey died in 1898, survived by a brother, Henry S. Hovey, a sister, Fanny H. Morse, and two nephews, John Torrey Morse, Third, and Cabot Jackson Morse. By her will, Marian Hovey left the residue of her estate in trust, the income payable in equal shares to her brother and sister during their lives. Upon her brother's death in 1900, his share of the income passed to her sister, and, upon her sister's death in 1922, the income was paid in equal shares to her two nephews. John Torrey Morse, Third, died in 1928, unmarried and without issue. His share of the income then passed to his brother, Cabot Jackson Morse, who remained the sole income beneficiary until his death in 1946.

At that point, the death of the last surviving income beneficiary, Marian Hovey's will provided for the treatment of the trust assets in the following language:

> At the death of the last survivor of my said brother and sister and my two said nephews, or at my death, if none of them be then living, the trustees shall divide the trust fund in their hands into two equal parts, and shall transfer and pay over one of such parts to the use of the wife and issue of

each of my said nephews as he may by will have appointed; provided, that if his wife was living at my death he shall appoint to her no larger interest in the property possessed by me than a right to the income during her life, and if she was living at the death of my father, he shall appoint to her no larger interest in the property over which I have a power of disposition under the will of my father than a right to the income during her life; and the same limitations shall apply to the appointment of income as aforesaid. If either of my said nephews shall leave no such appointees then living, the whole of the trust fund shall be paid to the appointees of his said brother as afore-said. If neither of my said nephews leave such appointees then living the whole trust fund shall be paid over and transferred in in [sic] equal shares to the Boston Museum of Fine Arts, the Massachusetts Institute of Tech-nology, and the President and Fellows of Harvard College for the benefit of the Medical School; provided, that if the said Medical School shall not then admit women to instruction on an equal footing with men, the said President and Fellows shall not receive any part of the trust property, but it shall be divided equally between the Boston Museum of Fine Arts and the Massachusetts Institute of Technology.[4]

The will thus gave Cabot Jackson Morse, the surviving nephew, a special power to appoint the trust principal to his "wife and issue" with the limitation that only income could be appointed to a widow who was living at Marian Hovey's death.[5] Cabot Jackson Morse was survived by his wife, Anna Braden Morse, who was living at Marian Hovey's death, and by his only child, Cabot Jackson Morse, Jr., a child of an earlier marriage, who died in 1948, two years after his father. Cabot Jackson Morse left a will which contained the following provisions:

Second: I give to my son, Cabot Jackson Morse, Jr., the sum of one dollar ($1.00), as he is otherwise amply provided for.

Third: The power of appointment which I have under the wills of my aunt, Marian Hovey, and my uncle, Henry S. Hovey, both late of Gloucester, Mas-sachusetts, I exercise as follows: I appoint to my wife, Anna Braden Morse, the right to the income during her lifetime of all of the property to which my power of appointment applies under the will of Marian Hovey, and I appoint to my wife the right during her widowhood to the income to which I would be entitled under the will of Henry S. Hovey if I were living.

---

4. The parties have stipulated that at the relevant time the Harvard Medical School admitted women to instruction on an equal footing with men.

5. We are concerned here only with "property possessed" by the testatrix at her death and not property over which she had "a power of disposition under the will of [her] father." That property was given outright to his widow under the residuary clause of the will of Cabot Jackson Morse. See Frye v. Loring, 330 Mass. at 396, 113 N.E.2d 595. See also Loring v. Morse, 332 Mass. at 64, 123 N.E.2d 360.

Fourth: All the rest, residue and remainder of my estate, wherever situated, real or personal, in trust or otherwise, I leave outright and in fee simple to my wife, Anna Braden Morse.

In Welch v. Morse, 323 Mass. 233, 81 N.E.2d 361 (1948), we held that the appointment of a life interest to Anna Braden Morse was valid, notwithstanding Cabot Jackson Morse's failure fully to exercise the power by appointing the trust principal. Consequently, the trust income following Cabot Jackson Morse's death was paid to Anna Braden Morse until her death in 1983, when the principal became distributable. The trustees thereupon brought this complaint for instructions.

The complaint alleges that the trustees "are uncertain as to who is entitled to the remainder of the Marian Hovey Trust now that the trust is distributable and specifically whether the trust principal should be paid in any one of the following manners: (a) to the estate of Cabot Jackson Morse, Jr. as the only permissible appointee of the remainder of the trust living at the death of Cabot Jackson Morse; (b) in equal shares to the estates of Cabot Jackson Morse, Jr. and Anna Braden Morse as the only permissible appointees living at the death of Cabot Jackson Morse; (c) to the estate of Anna Braden Morse as the only actual appointee living at the death of Cabot Jackson Morse; (d) to the intestate takers of Marian Hovey's estate on the basis that Marian Hovey failed to make a complete disposition of her property by her will; (e) to Massachusetts Institute of Technology, Museum of Fine Arts and the President and Fellows of Harvard College in equal shares as remaindermen of the trust; or (f) some other disposition." Before us each named potential taker claims to be entitled to trust principal.

In our 1951 opinion, *Massachusetts Inst. of Technology v. Loring*, 327 Mass. at 555–556, 99 N.E.2d 854, we explained why in the circumstances the charities had no interest in the trust: "The rights of the petitioning charities as remaindermen depend upon the proposition that Cabot J. Morse, Senior, did not leave an 'appointee' although he appointed his wife Anna Braden Morse to receive the income during her life. The time when, if at all, the 'whole trust fund' was to be paid over and transferred to the petitioning charities is the time of the death of Cabot J. Morse, Senior. At that time the whole trust fund could not be paid over and transferred to the petitioning charities, because Anna Braden Morse still retained the income for her life. We think that the phrase no 'such appointees then living' is not the equivalent of an express gift in default of appointment, a phrase used by the testatrix in the preceding paragraph." In *Frye v. Loring*, 330 Mass. 389, 393, 113 N.E.2d 595 (1953), the court reiterated that the charities had no interest in the trust fund.

It is apparent that Marian Hovey knew how to refer to a disposition in default of appointment from her use of the terms elsewhere in her will. She did not use those words in describing the potential gift to the charities. A fair reading of the will's crucial language may rightly be that the charities were not to take the principal unless no class member who could receive principal was then living (i.e., if no possible appointee of principal was living at the death of the surviving donee). Regardless of how the words "no such appointees then living" are construed, the express circumstances under which the charities were to take did not occur. The question is what disposition should be made of the principal in the absence of any explicit direction in the will.

Although in its 1951 opinion this court disavowed making a determination of the "ultimate destination of the trust fund," the opinion cited the Restatement of Property § 367(2) (1940), and 1 A. Scott, Trusts § 27.1 (1st ed.1939) * * * to the effect that, when a special power of appointment is not exercised and absent specific language indicating an express gift in default of appointment, the property not appointed goes in equal shares to the members of the class to whom the property could have been appointed. For more recent authority, see 5 American Law of Property § 23.63, at 645 (A.J. Casner ed.1952 & Supp.1962) ("The fact that the donee has failed to apportion the property within the class should not defeat the donor's intent to benefit the class"); Restatement (Second) of Property § 24.2 (Tent. Draft No. 7, 1984). * * *

Applying this rule of law, we find no specific language in the will which indicates a gift in default of appointment in the event Cabot Jackson Morse should fail to appoint the principal. The charities argue that the will's reference to them suggests that in default of appointment Marian Hovey intended them to take. On the other hand, in Welch v. Morse, 323 Mass. at 238, 81 N.E.2d 361, we commented that Marian Hovey's "will discloses an intent to keep her property in the family." The interests Marian Hovey gave to her sister and brother were life interests, as were the interests given to her nephews. The share of any nephew who died unmarried and without issue, as did one, was added to the share of the other nephew. Each nephew was limited to exercising his power of appointment only in favor of his issue and his widow. * * * We think the apparent intent to keep the assets within the family is sufficiently strong to overcome any claim that Marian Hovey's will "expressly" or "in specific language" provides for a gift to the charities in default of appointment. * * *

If we were to depart from the view taken thirty-four years ago in Massachusetts Inst. of Technology v. Loring, 327 Mass. 553, 99 N.E.2d 854 (1951), and now were to conclude that under the terms of Marian Hovey's will the charities were to receive the trust principal, we would face the problem that, under normal principles of res judicata, our earlier decision against the charities is binding on them. Any suggestion that our 1951 decision did not bind the charities because the Attorney General was not a party to that proceeding is not supported by authority. The charities themselves brought the earlier action and chose not to name the Attorney General as a party. That action preceded the enactment of G.L. c. 12, § 8G, inserted by St.1954, c. 529, § 1, which made the Attorney General a necessary party to the proceedings concerning the application of funds to public charities. Moreover, our 1951 opinion did not concern a compromise settlement between a charity and its adversaries, a situation in which the Attorney General's involvement would then have been required. See Springfield Safe Deposit & Trust Co. v. Stoop, 326 Mass. 363, 95 N.E.2d 161 (1950). To conclude now that the Attorney General's involvement was indispensable to a valid determination in the 1951 action would cast a shadow over hundreds of pre-1954 decisions concerning charitable interests under wills and trusts. See Eustace v. Dickey, 240 Mass. 55, 86, 132 N.E. 852 (1921). * * *

The same arguments made by the charities and the Attorney General in this case were considered and rejected in 1951. Surely in a case such as this, at least in the absence of a statute to the contrary, the public interest in protecting the charities' rights was fully accommodated by the Justices of this court in its prior decision. The Attorney General does not suggest in his answer that, if the named charities could not take, other charities should take in their stead by application of the doctrine of cy-pres.

What we have said disposes of the claim that the trust principal should pass to Marian Hovey's heirs as intestate property, a result generally disfavored in the interpretation of testamentary dispositions. See Fiduciary Trust Co. v. State St. Bank & Trust Co., 360 Mass. 652, 656, 277 N.E.2d 120 (1971); New England Merchants Nat'l Bank v. Frost, 357 Mass. 158, 163, 257 N.E.2d 439 (1970); Loring v. Clapp, 337 Mass. 53, 59, 147 N.E.2d 836 (1958). The claim of the executors of the estate of Anna Braden Morse that her estate should take as the class, or at least as a member of the class, must fail because Marian Hovey's will specifically limits such a widow's potential stake to a life interest.

A judgment shall be entered instructing the trustees under the will of Marian Hovey to distribute the trust principal to the executors of the estate of Cabot Jackson Morse, Jr. The allowance of counsel fees, costs, and expenses from the principal of the trust is to be in the discretion of the single justice.

So ordered. . . .

E. Release of a Power

Seidel v. Werner

Supreme Court, New York County, 1975
81 Misc. 2d 220, 364 N.Y.S.2d 963 *aff'd on opinion below*, 50 A.D.2d 743,
376 N.Y.S.2d 139

Samuel J. Silverman, J. . . .

* * *

Plaintiffs, trustees of a trust established in 1919 by Abraham L. Werner, sue for a declaratory judgment to determine who is entitled to one half of the principal of the trust fund—the share in which Steven L. Werner, decedent (hereinafter "Steven"), was the life beneficiary and over which he had a testamentary power of appointment. The dispute concerns the manner in which Steven exercised his power of appointment and is between Steven's second wife, Harriet G. Werner (hereinafter "Harriet"), along with their children, Anna G. and Frank S. Werner (hereinafter "Anna" and "Frank") and Steven's third wife, Edith Fisch Werner (hereinafter "Edith").

Anna and Frank claim Steven's entire share of the trust remainder on the basis of a Mexican consent judgment of divorce, obtained by Steven against Harriet on

December 9, 1963, which incorporated by reference and approved a separation agreement, entered into between Steven and Harriet on December 1, 1963. That agreement included the following provision:

> 10. The Husband shall make, and hereby promises not to revoke, a will in which he shall exercise his testamentary power of appointment over his share in a trust known as 'Abraham L. Werner Trust No. 1' by establishing with respect to said share a trust for the benefit of the aforesaid Children, for the same purposes and under the same terms and conditions, as the trust provided for in Paragraph '9' of this Agreement, insofar as said terms and conditions are applicable thereto.

> Paragraph 9 in relevant part provides for the wife to receive the income of the trust, upon the death of the husband, for the support and maintenance of the children, until they reach 21 years of age, at which time they are to receive the principal in equal shares.

On March 20, 1964, less than four months after entry of the divorce judgment, Steven executed a will in which, instead of exercising his testamentary power of appointment in favor of Anna and Frank, he left everything to his third wife, Edith:

> First, I give, devise and bequeath all of my property . . . including . . . all property over which I have a power of testamentary disposition, to my wife, EDITH FISCH WERNER.

Steven died in April, 1971 and his will was admitted to probate by the Surrogate's Court of New York County on July 11, 1973.

* * * Paragraph 10 of the separation agreement is a contract to exercise a testamentary power of appointment not presently exercisable (EPTL 10-3.3) and as such is invalid under EPTL 10-5.3, which provides as follows:

> (a) The donee of a power of appointment which is not presently exercisable, or of a postponed power which has not become exercisable, cannot contract to make an appointment. Such a contract, if made cannot be the basis of an action for specific performance or damages, but the promisee can obtain restitution of the value given by him for the promise unless the donee has exercised the power pursuant to the contract.

This is a testamentary power of appointment. The original trust instrument provided in relevant part that:

> "Upon the death of such child [Steven] the principal of such share shall be disposed of as such child shall by its last will direct, and in default of such testamentary disposition then the same shall go to the issue of such child then surviving per stirpes."

It is not disputed that New York law is determinative of the validity of paragraph 10 of the separation agreement; the separation agreement itself provides that New York law shall govern.

The reasoning underlying the refusal to enforce a contract to exercise a testamentary power was stated by Judge Cardozo in the case of Farmers' Loan and Trust Co. v Mortimer (219 NY 290, 293–294):

> The exercise of the power was to represent the final judgment, the last will, of the donee. Up to the last moment of his life he was to have the power to deal with the share as he thought best . . . To permit him to bargain that right away would be to defeat the purpose of the donor. Her command was that her property should go to her son's issue unless at the end of his life it remained his will that it go elsewhere. It has not remained his will that it go elsewhere; and his earlier contract cannot nullify the expression of his final purpose. 'It is not, I apprehend, to be doubted,' says Rolt, L. J., in Cooper v Martin (LR [3 Ch App] 47, 58) 'that equity . . . will never uphold an act which will defeat what the person creating the power has declared, by expression or necessary implication, to be a material part of his intention.' (See also, Matter of Brown, 33 NY2d 211.)

* * * [Court's discussion of res judicata and comity omitted].

* * * As indicated, the statute makes a promise to exercise a testamentary power in a particular way unenforceable. However, EPTL 10-5.3 (subd [b]) permits a donee of a power to release the power, and that release, if in conformity with EPTL 10-9.2, prevents the donee from then exercising the power thereafter.

Under the terms of the trust instrument, if Steven fails to exercise his power of appointment, Anna and Frank (along with the children of Steven's first marriage) take the remainder, i.e., the property which is the subject of Steven's power of appointment. Therefore, Harriet, Anna and Frank argue that at a minimum Steven's agreement should be construed as a release of his power of appointment, and that Anna and Frank should be permitted to take as on default of appointment.

There is respectable authority—by no means unanimous authority, and none binding on this court—to the effect that a promise to appoint a given sum to persons who would take in default of appointment should, to that extent, be deemed a release of the power of appointment. (See Restatement, Property, § 336 [1940]; Simes and Smith, Law of Future Interests, § 1016 [1956].)

This argument has the appeal that it seems to be consistent with the exception that the release statute EPTL 10-5.3 (subd [b]) carves out of EPTL 10-5.3 (subd [a]); and is also consistent with the intentions and reasonable expectations of the parties at the time they entered into the agreement to appoint, here in the separation agreement; and that therefore perhaps in these circumstances the difference between what the parties agreed to and a release of the power of appointment is merely one of form. Whatever may be the possible validity or applicability of this argument to other circumstances and situations, I think it is inapplicable to this situation because:

(a) It is clear that the parties did not intend a release of the power of appointment. (Cf. Matter of Haskell, 59 Misc 2d 797.) Indeed, the agreement—unlike a release of a power of appointment—expressly contemplates that something will be done by the donee of the power in the future, and that that something will be an exercise of the power of appointment. Thus, the agreement, in the very language said to be a release of the power of appointment, says (par 10, *supra*):

> "The Husband *shall* make . . . a will in which he *shall* exercise his testamentary power of appointment." (Emphasis added.)

(b) Nor is the substantial effect of the promised exercise of the power the same as would follow from release of, or failure to exercise the power.

(i) Under the separation agreement, the power is to be exercised so that the entire appointive property shall be for the benefit of Anna and Frank; under the trust instrument, on default of exercise of the power, the property goes to all of Steven's children (Anna, Frank and the two children of Steven's first marriage). Thus the agreement provides for appointment of a greater principal to Anna and Frank than they would get in default of appointment.

(ii) Under the trust instrument, on default of exercise of the power, the property goes to the four children absolutely and in fee. The separation agreement provides that Steven shall create a trust, with income payable to Harriet as trustee, for the support of Anna and Frank until they both reach the age of 21, at which time the principal shall be paid to them or the survivor; and if both fail to attain the age of 21, then the principal shall revert to Steven's estate. Thus, Anna and Frank's interest in the principal would be a defeasible interest if they did not live to be 21; and indeed at Steven's death they were both still under 21 so that their interest was defeasible.

(iii) Finally, under the separation agreement, as just noted, if Anna and Frank failed to qualify to take the principal, either because they both died before Steven or before reaching the age of 21, then the principal would go to Steven's estate. Under the trust instrument, on the other hand, on default of appointment and an inability of Anna and Frank to take, Steven's share of the principal would not go to Steven's estate, but to his other children, if living, and if not, to the settlor's next of kin.

In these circumstances, I think it is too strained and tortuous to construe the separation agreement provision as the equivalent of a release of the power of appointment. If this is a release then the exception of EPTL 10-5.3 (subd [b]) has swallowed and destroyed the principal rule of EPTL 10-5.3 (subd [a]).

I note that in Wood v American Security and Trust Co. (253 F Supp 592, 594), the principal case relied upon by Harriet, Anna and Frank on this point, the court said:

> "The Court finds that it is significant that the disposition resulting from the agreement is in accordance with the wishes of the testator in the event the power should not be exercised."

Furthermore, the language of the instrument in that case was much more consistent with the nonexercise of the powers of appointment than in the case at bar.

Accordingly, I hold that the separation agreement is not the equivalent of a total or partial release of the power of appointment.

* * * Anna and Frank also seek restitution out of the trust fund of the value given by them in exchange for Steven's unfulfilled promise. EPTL 10-5.3 (subd [a]) provides that although the contract to make an appointment cannot be the basis for an action for specific performance or damages, "the promisee can obtain restitution of the value given by him for the promise unless the donee has exercised the power pursuant to contract."

Anna and Frank's remedy is limited, however, to the claim for restitution that they have (and apparently have asserted) against Steven's estate. They may not seek restitution out of the trust fund, even if their allegation that the estate lacks sufficient assets to meet this claim were factually supported, because the trust fund was not the property of Steven, except to the extent of his life estate, so as to be subject to the equitable remedy of restitution, but was the property of the donor of the power of appointment until it vested in someone else. (Farmers' Loan & Trust Co. v Mortimer, 219 NY 290, 295, *supra*; see Matter of Rosenthal, 283 App Div 316, 319; see, also, EPTL 10-7.1 and 10-7.4.)

* * *

Accordingly, on the motions for summary judgment I direct judgment declaring that defendant Edith Fisch Werner is entitled to the one-half share of Steven C. Werner in the principal of the Abraham L. Werner trust; to the extent that the counterclaims and cross claims asserted by Harriet, Anna and Frank seek relief other than a declaratory judgment, they are dismissed.

Uniform Powers of Appointment Act (2019)

§ 401. Disclaimer. As provided by [cite state law on disclaimer or the Uniform Disclaimer of Property Interests Act]:

(1) A powerholder may disclaim all or part of a power of appointment.

(2) A permissible appointee, appointee, or taker in default of appointment may disclaim all or a part of an interest in appointive property.

§ 403. Method of Release. * * *

(b) A powerholder of a releasable power of appointment may release the power in whole or in part:

(1) by substantial compliance with a method provided in the terms of the instrument creating the power; or

(2) if the terms of the instrument creating the power do not provide a method or the method provided in the terms of the instrument is not expressly made exclusive, by a record manifesting the powerholder's intent by clear and convincing evidence.

F. Rights of Creditors

Irwin Union Bank & Trust Co. v. Long

Indiana Court of Appeals, 1974
160 Ind. App. 509, 312 N.E.2d 908

LOWDERMILK, Judge.

On February 3, 1957, Victoria Long, appellee herein, obtained a judgment in the amount of $15,000 against Philip W. Long, which judgment emanated from a divorce decree. This action is the result of the filing by appellee of a petition in proceedings supplemental to execution on the prior judgment. Appellee sought satisfaction of that judgment by pursuing funds allegedly owed to Philip W. Long as a result of a trust set up by Laura Long, his mother.

Appellee alleged that the Irwin Union Bank and Trust Company (Union Bank) was indebted to Philip W. Long as the result of its position as trustee of the trust created by Laura Long. On April 24, 1969, the trial court ordered that any income, property, or profits, which were owed to Philip Long and not exempt from execution should be applied to the divorce judgment. Thereafter, on February 13, 1973, the trial court ordered that four percent (4%) of the trust corpus of the trust created by Laura Long which benefited Philip Long was not exempt from execution and could be levied upon by appellee and ordered a writ of execution. Union Bank, as trustee, filed its motion to set aside the writ of execution. Said motion was overruled by the trial court, whereupon Union Bank filed its motion to correct errors, which was by the court overruled.

The pertinent portion of the trust created by Laura Long is as follows, to-wit:

* * *

Withdrawal of Principal.

When Philip W. Long, Jr. has attained the age of twenty-one (21) years and is not a full-time student at an educational institution as a candidate for a Bachelor of Arts or Bachelor of Sciences degree, Philip W. Long shall have the right to withdraw from principal once in any calendar year upon thirty (30) days written notice to the Trustee up to four percent (4%) of the market value of the entire trust principal on the date of such notice, which right shall not be cumulative; provided, however, that the amount distributable hereunder shall not be in excess of the market value of the assets of the trust on the date of such notice other than interests in real estate.

The primary issue raised on this appeal is whether the trial court erred in allowing execution on the 4% of the trust corpus.

Appellant contends that Philip Long's right to withdraw 4% of the trust corpus is, in fact, a general power of appointment. Union Bank further contends that since Philip Long has never exercised his right of withdrawal, pursuant to the provisions of the trust instrument, no creditors of Philip Long can reach the trust corpus.

Appellant points out that if the power of appointment is unexercised, the creditors cannot force the exercise of said power and cannot reach the trust corpus in this case.

Appellee posits that the condition precedent to Philip Long's right of withdrawal has been met and therefore Philip Long has an absolute right to the present enjoyment of 4% of the trust corpus simply by making a written request to the trustee. Appellee contends that this is a vested right and is consistent with the intentions of the donor, Laura Long. Appellee further contends in her brief that the right of withdrawal is not a power of appointment, but is, rather, a power of augmentation and relies upon the Restatement of the Law of Property, § 318, which reads as follows, to-wit:

Definition — Power of Appointment.

(1) Except as stated in Subsection (2), a power of appointment, as the term is used in this Restatement, is a power created or reserved by a person (the donor) having property subject to his disposition enabling the donee of the power to designate, within such limits as the donor may prescribe, the transferees of the property or the shares in which it shall be received.

(2) The term power of appointment does not include a power of sale, a power of attorney, a power of revocation, a power to cause a gift of income to be augmented out of principal, a power to designate charities, a charitable trust, a discretionary trust, or an honorary trust.'

However, in oral argument, appellee stated that the label that is put on the provision of the trust instrument is immaterial.

It is the position of appellee that if the right of withdrawal is not a power of appointment under § 318, *supra*, then the cases and authorities relied upon by appellant which relate to powers of appointment will not be in point.

Appellee also argues that Philip has absolute control and use of the 4% of the corpus and that the bank does not have control over that portion of the corpus if Philip decides to exercise his right of withdrawal. Appellee argues that the intention of Laura Long was to give Philip not only an income interest in the trust but a fixed amount of corpus which he could use as he saw fit. Thus, Philip Long would have a right to the present enjoyment of 4% of the trust corpus. A summation of appellee's argument, as stated in her brief, is as follows: 'So it is with Philip — he can get it if he desires it, so why cannot Victoria get it even if Philip does not desire it?' * * *

It is elementary that courts will seek to ascertain the intention of the testator by giving a full consideration to the entire will. See 29 I.L.E. Wills, § 174. The trust created in the will of Laura Long, in our opinion, has the legal effect of creating a power of appointment in Philip Long under Item V C of the trust.

Philip Long has never exercised his power of appointment under the trust. Such a situation is discussed in II Scott on Trusts, § 147.3 as follows:

* * * Where the power is a special power, a power to appoint only among a group of persons, the power is not beneficial to the donee and cannot, of

course, be reached by his creditors. Where the power is a general power, that is, a power to appoint to anyone including the donee himself or his estate, the power is beneficial to the donee. If the donee exercises the power by appointing to a volunteer, the property appointed can be reached by his creditors if his other assets are insufficient for the payment of his debts. But where the donee of a general power created by some person other than himself fails to exercise the power, his creditors cannot acquire the power or compel its exercise, nor can they reach the property covered by the power, unless it is otherwise provided by statute. . . .

Indiana has no statute which would authorize a creditor to reach property covered by a power of appointment which is unexercised.

In Gilman v. Bell, *supra*, the court analyzed the situation where a general power of appointment was unexercised and discussed the position of creditors of the donee of the power as follows:

But it is insisted, that, conceding it to be a mere naked power of appointment in favor of himself, in favor of creditors he should be compelled by a court of equity to so appoint, or be treated as the owner, and the property subjected to the payment of his debts. The doctrine has been long established in the English courts, that the courts of equity will not aid creditors in case there is a non-execution of the power. . . .

The creditors' rights against an unexercised power of appointment was also discussed in 62 Am.Jur.2d, Powers, § 107, as follows:

It is established by the great weight of authority, and may be regarded as settled, that an unexercised general power of appointment does not render the property subject thereto equitable assets of the donee, nor make it liable for his debts or the debts of his estate, although his own property is insufficient to pay them. . . .

See, also, Quinn v. Tuttle (1962), 104 N.H. 1, 177 A.2d 391.

Appellee concedes that if we find that Philip Long had merely an unexercised power of appointment then creditors are in no position to either force the exercise of the power or to reach the trust corpus. Thus, it is clear that the trial court erred when it overruled appellant's motion to set aside the writ of execution.

Having found reversible error on the primary issue, it is unnecessary for this court to discuss other issues raised in this appeal.

Reversed and remanded.

ROBERTSON, P. J., and LYBROOK, J., concur.

Notes

As the original owner of the appointment, the donor is responsible to any and all creditors of the donor only. The issue for consideration concerns the donee's responsibility to the donee's creditors, and whether the appointment may be used to satisfy those responsibilities. The liability of the donee to his or her creditors will depend on the power given by the donor. Obviously, the more power given to the donee, the more likely will the creditors of the donee be able to reach the appointment. Consider the following possibilities.

1. General *inter vivos* power of appointment. Other than if the donor gave to the donee outright, with no power attached at all, this is an extensive delegation of power over the appointment, and the creditors of the donee should always be able to reach the appointment after the personal property of the donee has been exhausted. *See, e.g.,* Cal. Prob. Code § 682 (West 2019); Unif. Powers of Appointment Act § 502(a) (2019). In addition, any general *inter vivos* power is included in the bankruptcy estate of the donee during the donee's lifetime. *See* 11 U.S.C. § 541(b)(1) (effective Apr. 1, 2019).

2. General testamentary power of appointment. The creditors of a donee of a general testamentary power of appointment should not be able to reach the appointment assets, at least not until the death of the donee. *See* Unif. Powers of Appointment Act § 504 (2019). *See generally* Ira Mark Bloom, *Powers of Appointment Under the Restatement (Third) of Property*, 33 Ohio N.U. L. Rev. 755, 779–90 (2007). Nonetheless, if the donor and the donee are the same person, creditors may reach the appointment. *See Restatement (Third) of Property: Donative Transfers*, § 21.3, (Prelim. Draft No. 4, 1995).

3. Special powers, *inter vivos* and testamentary. Because very little delegation has been given by the donor to the donee, creditors of the donee may not reach the appointment. *See, e.g.,* Cal. Prob. Code § 681 (West 2019).

4. Spouses. A spouse's claim for support is treated as if it were a creditor's claim. *See, e.g., id.* at § 684. Nonetheless, if a donee possesses a general testamentary power of appointment, the power is available for inclusion within the augmented estate of the decedent.

VII. The Rule Against Perpetuities

A. Public Policy

The late Jesse Dukeminier, a renowned professor of both property law and decedents' estates, introduced his casebook material on the Rule Against Perpetuities with an evolution of historical English statutes, commencing with the Statute de Donis (1285), through the decision of the Duke of Norfolk's Case (1682), and the classic law review article by Professor W. Barton Leach, *Perpetuities in a Nutshell*, 51 Harv. L. Rev. 638 (1938). Professor Dukeminier included in his discussion photographs of the Sixth Duke of Norfolk and the First Earl of Nottingham, and, as was his trademark, a few bons mots to capture the background of a duke's beheading and the lament over dead-hand control of property. *See* Jesse Dukeminier, Stanley M. Johanson, James Lindgren & Robert H. Sitkoff, Wills, Trusts, and

ESTATES 673 (7th ed. 2005). Any student of decedents' estates soon realized that what was to follow was not a legal bump in the road, but rather a doctrine with lengthy roots in the law's attempt to limit perpetuities, entails, dead hand control, restrictions on land, and family advantage. Modern students might even have seen in the Rule Against Perpetuities an egalitarian tool to foster marketability of property at each generation and a curative device to refashion trust purposes to accommodate present changed circumstances. *See generally* Jesse Dukeminier, *A Modern Guide to Perpetuities,* 74 CAL. L. REV.1867 (1986); *Restatement (Second) of Property, Donative Transfers,* Pt. 1, Introductory Note (1983); JESSE DUKEMINIER & JAMES E. KRIER, PROPERTY 291 (4th ed. 1998).

At its core, the Rule Against Perpetuities is a rule of public policy limiting the ability of persons to control both real and personal property so as to accommodate private purposes. For example, a settlor may not prohibit in perpetuity the family home from being sold; a parent may not prohibit in perpetuity alienation of a private trust income and corpus; a private company may not be controlled dynastically throughout successive generations. The law sought to make certain that, within a reasonable time, some person would own a fee simple interest in property not burdened by any trust and, thus, be able to sell, encumber, or re-trust the property in accordance with current objectives. To accomplish this, the law crafted a device to confine all contingent remainders and executory interests created in transferees to a human life in being, plus twenty-one years. If there is any possibility that a contingency may occur to allow vesting to occur in anyone not a life in being, now or within twenty-one years, the entire trust will fail.

Often the Rule resulted in the inadvertent termination of trusts because of poor drafting by attorneys, *see, e.g.,* Lucas v. Hamm, 56 Cal.2d 583, 364 P.2d 685 (1961), judicial wizardry, as courts sought to salvage a settlor's intent, *see, e.g.,* Second National Bank of New Haven v. Harris Trust & Savings Bank, 29 Conn. Supp. 275, 283 A.2d 226 (Sup. Ct. 1971) (decrying "exaltation of verbalism over substance"), or, more recently, judicial and legislative reform devices, *see, e.g.,* 20 PA. STAT. ANN. § 6104 (2019) (wait and see doctrine). More than half of the states have adopted the Uniform Statutory Rule Against Perpetuities (1990), now adopted as Part 9 of the Uniform Probate Code (2019). And in a remarkable break with the past, some states have abolished the Rule completely, often with the avowed goal of providing a mechanism to create dynasty trusts. *See* Reid Kress Weisbord, *Trust Term Extension,* 67 FLA. L. REV. 73, 108 n.161 (2015) (listing options states currently apply to Rule Against Perpetuities); Scott Andrew Shepard, *A Uniform Perpetuities Reform Act,* 16 N.Y.U. J. LEGIS. & PUB. POL'Y 89 (2013); Scott Andrew Shepard, *Which the Deader Hand? A Counter to the American Law Institute's Proposed Revival of Dying Perpetuities Rules,* 86 TUL. L. REV. 559 (2012).

The evolution of the Rule places a burden on the practitioner of estate planning and administration who seeks to provide competent representation amidst shifting legal parameters. But even greater stakes are involved. The Rule is a public policy formulation providing a limit on private trusts. In the early twenty-first century, in their eagerness to abolish the rule, states also abolished the public policy that spawned it. Permeating the following material is an important question: What will occur if the Rule is abolished?

B. Statement of the Rule

The classic statement of the Rule, culled from the accumulations of centuries, was formulated by John Chipman Gray: "No interest is good unless it must vest, if at all, not later than twenty-one years after some life in being at the creation of the interest." JOHN C. GRAY. THE RULE AGAINST PERPETUITIES 191 (4th ed. 1942). Since the Rule applies to all future interests created within testamentary trusts and *inter vivos* trusts, it is assumed that the trust and the instrument in which it is written are valid under the proper rules applicable to formalities and intentionalities. If so, we progress to the elements of the Rule itself. First, please note the phrase "life in being," used in Professor Chipman's formulation. A life in being must be a human life, hence the concern over honorary trusts and vesting to occur upon the death of a pet — a non-human life. *See* UNIF. PROB. CODE § 2-907 (2019). The life in being may also be a life in gestation, not yet born but able to postpone vesting through the future interest created because, simply by being conceived, the life is treated as being in existence at the creation of the interest. Second, these lives in being may also be what are called "measuring lives." A measuring life is that person or persons, upon whose death, or the occurrence of an event, vesting will occur. For example, settlor creates a testamentary trust and writes: "One million dollars to my grand-children, to be paid only if she or he turns twenty-one." The settlor has created a contingent interest — the grandchild takes only if the grandchild turns twenty-one. If no grandchild turns twenty-one, the corpus of the trust reverts to the settlor's estate. Note that the grandchild is a measuring life because, when the grandchild turns twenty-one, there is an occurrence of an event that brings about vesting. *See generally* David M. Becker, *A Methodology for Solving Perpetuities Problems Under the Common Law Rule: A Step-by-Step Process That Carefully Identifies All Testing Lives in Being,* 67 WASH. U. L. REV. 949 (1989); Jesse Dukeminier, *Perpetuities: The Measuring Lives,* 85 COLUM. L. REV. 1648, 1665–74 (1985). Professor Dukeminier suggested that the statement of the Rule should be re-formulated to require vesting after the death of all persons in being when the interest is created who can affect the vesting of the interest. *Id.* at 1713. It is important to be able to identify both of these terms and then apply them in the following question: Standing at the creation of the instrument, is there any possibility that any interest will not vest within a life in being plus twenty-one years? If the answer is "Yes," the Rule is violated.

1. Standing at the Creation of the Instrument

Creation is when the instrument speaks. There are three possibilities: (1) a valid Last Will and Testament speaks at the death of the testator, not when the will is executed; (2) in a valid *inter vivos* trust that is revocable, nothing begins in perpetuity until the death of the settlor or whenever the settlor can no longer revoke the trust instrument. If the *inter vivos* trust is irrevocable (recall that most jurisdictions make all trusts irrevocable unless the trust expressly says otherwise), creation is when the trust is created by the settlor, not when the settlor dies or surrenders any power; (3) according to the rules applicable to powers of appointment, if a donor of a power of appointment creates any power other than a general *inter vivos* power in a donee, under the relation back doctrine, any exercise by the donee must be read back into the creation of the power by the donor. We will see examples of this relation back doctrine as we progress through the material. For the present, identify the issue in the following decision.

Cook v. Horn

Supreme Court of Georgia, 1958
214 Ga. 289, 104 S.E.2d 461

WYATT, Presiding Justice.

It is first contended that, under the provisions of the trust instrument, the petitioners take a fee-simple interest in the trust fund rather than a life interest, and that, being sui juris and not spendthrifts (it being conceded by all parties that Code, § 108-111.1 does not apply to this instrument), the trust is executed and the petitioners are entitled to have the corpus of the trust distributed to them. While there is language in certain paragraphs of the trust agreement which by themselves could be construed to enlarge the gift to these petitioners into a fee simple interest, a consideration of all the instrument discloses that this was not the settlor's intent. He provided that the trust should be divided into as many parts as he had children, and that each child was to receive the proceeds from his or her trust for and during his or her natural life. This, without more, would, under the law prior to the enactment of Code, § 108-111.1, amount to a gift of a fee-simple interest, the petitioners being sui juris and not spendthrifts. However, the settlor then provided remainders to the issue of his children upon the death of said children, and he set out in detail how the remainders were to be paid and administered. The language appearing in paragraphs F, G, and H of section V. considered in connection with the section V, considered in connection with the clearly apparent intention of the settlor as determined from the whole instrument. Accordingly, as is held above, the petitioners took a life interest in the corpus of the trust estate with remainders to their issue, and the trusts are executory since the remaindermen will not be determined until the petitioners die.

It is next contended that the instrument in question violates the rule against perpetuities, and that since the limitations beyond the petitioners are void, they are entitled to have the property delivered to them. In order to determine this question, it is necessary first to determine when this instrument took effect, whether at the time it was executed and delivered, or at the death of the settlor. This question is settled by the decision of this court in Wilson v. Fulton National Bank, 188 Ga. 691, 4 S.E.2d 660, where an instrument similar in all material respects to that here under consideration was held to create a valid trust, to convey a present interest, and not to be testamentary in character.

It is contended that, if the trust instrument is effective to convey a present interest at the time it was executed and delivered, as is held above, then the limitations beyond the petitioners are void as violative of the rule against perpetuities, because there was a possibility at that time that the settlor would have additional children born to him thereafter, by whose life the duration of the trust would be limited. This result does not necessarily follow. While there is a scarcity of authority on this question, and none that we have found in Georgia, the prevailing opinion by both the courts of other jurisdictions and recognized text writers is that, when a settlor has the power during his lifetime to revoke or destroy the trust estate for his own exclusive personal benefit, the question whether interests, or any of them, created by an instrument or deed of trust are void because in violation of the rule against perpetuities, is to be determined as of the date of the settlor's death and not as of the date the instrument is executed and delivered. * * * [Citations omitted].

While none of these authorities is binding upon this court, the conclusion reached by them is in accord with the aim of and reason for the rule against perpetuities, which is to prevent the tying up of property for an unreasonable length of time and to prohibit unreasonable restraint upon the alienation of property. So long as the settlor of an *inter vivos* trust has the absolute right to revoke or terminate the trust for his own exclusive personal benefit, there is no tying up of property and no restraint upon the alienability of the property in the trust fund, and thus no reason to include this time during which the trust is so destructible in determining whether a limitation is violative of the rule against perpetuities. Restatement, Property, sec. 373 states: 'The period of time during which an interest is destructible, pursuant to the uncontrolled volition, and for the exclusive personal benefit of the person having such a power of destruction is not included in determining whether the limitation is invalid under the rule against perpetuities.' We conclude that this rule is a sound one, which does no violence to the rule against perpetuities, but is in complete accord with its aim and purpose.

In the instant case, the settlor, during his lifetime, had an absolute right to revoke or terminate the trust, to change the beneficiaries in the policies, and to receive any and all benefits under the policies. Therefore, under the rulings above made, the time from which it will be determined whether any of the limitations in the trust agreement are void for remoteness is the date of the settlor's death. When so considered, it is apparent that none of the limitations in the instrument violate the rule against perpetuities, since all limitations under the instrument will end and all interests vest within twenty-one years after the death of the settlor's children plus the usual period of gestation, and, of course, no children can be born to the settlor after his death plus the usual period of gestation. It follows, the limitations over to the issue of the children of the settlor are valid, and the petitioners are not entitled to have the trust terminated for any reason alleged. The judgment of the court below dismissing the petition on general demurrer was therefore not error.

Judgment affirmed.

All the Justices concur.

2. Is There Any Possibility?

If there is any possibility that any interest will not vest within a life in being, plus twenty-one years, the Rule is violated. Remember that actuality is not what matters to the Rule; rather, possibility — logical possibility to be precise — is what matters. Thus, we are concerned with what might happen with the measuring lives if they are the persons upon whom the contingency depends. For example, if a testator were to provide in a valid Last Will and Testament the following: "One million dollars to my children if any one of them turns twenty-five." The date of creation is the death of the testator. In addition, let us say that there are three children, and that all three are over the age of four. Therefore, all are in existence; no one is in gestation. We know that the measuring lives are the children because one of them must turn twenty-five to meet the condition of vesting. And since the event of turning twenty-five must occur within the lives of the lives in being (the children), and the event must occur within twenty-one years, there is no violation of the Rule. But, on the other hand, if the interest were created in an irrevocable trust, and the settlor were still alive and able to have additional children, then the Rule would be violated. In that case, the date of creation would be the creation of the trust by the settlor. The *possibility* that the settlor could then have a child, who would be a measuring life (to turn 25) but is not a life in being, creates the possibility that the child will turn twenty-five more than twenty-one years after any life in being. If the settlor were unable to have children, then this would not be a possibility, and there would be no violation of the Rule. We can review possibilities in the following examples.

a. Afterborn Measuring Lives

Dickerson v. Union National Bank of Little Rock

Supreme Court of Arkansas, 1980
268 Ark. 292, 595 S.W.2d 677

GEORGE ROSE SMITH, Justice.

The principal question on this appeal is whether a trust created by the holographic will of Nina Martin Dickerson, who died on June 21, 1967, is void under the rule against perpetuities, because it is possible that the interest of the various beneficiaries may not vest within the period allowed by that rule. Cecil H. Dickerson, Jr., one of the testatrix's two sons, attacks the validity of the trust. The chancellor rejected Cecil's attack on two grounds: First, Cecil should have raised the question of the validity of the trust in the probate court in connection with the probate of the will and the administration of the estate. His failure to do so makes the issue res judicata. Second, on the merits, the trust does not violate the rule against perpetuities. We disagree with the chancellor on both grounds.

The facts are not in dispute. The testatrix was survived by her two children. Cecil, 50, was single, and Martin, 45, was married. At that time the two sons had a total of seven children, who of course were the testatrix's grandchildren.

The testatrix named the appellee bank as executor and directed that at the close of the administration proceedings the bank transfer to itself as trustee all the assets of the estate. The terms of the trust are quite long, but we may summarize them as follows:

The trust is to continue until the death of both sons and of Martin's widow, *who is not otherwise identified*. The income is to be divided equally between the two sons during their lives, except that Cecil's share is to be used in part to provide for a four-year college education for his two minor children, who are named, and for the support and education of any bodily heirs by a later marriage. When the two named minor children finish college, their share of the income is to revert to Cecil. Upon Martin's death his share of the income is to be paid monthly to his widow and children living in the home, but the share of each child terminates and passes to the widow when that child marries or becomes self-supporting. The trustee is given discretionary power to make advance payments of principal in certain cases of emergency or illness. If either son and his wife and all his bodily heirs die before the final distribution of the trust assets, that son's share in the estate and in the income passes to the other son and then to his bodily heirs.

As far as the rule against perpetuities is concerned, the important part of the will is paragraph VIII, from which we quote:

> VIII. This Trust shall continue until the death of both my sons and my son Martin's widow and until the youngest child of either son has reached the age of twenty-five years, then at that time, the Trust shall terminate and the Union National Bank Trustee shall distribute and pay over the entire balance of the Trust Fund in their hands to the bodily heirs of my son, Cecil H. Dickerson, and the bodily heirs of my son, William Martin Dickerson, in the same manner and in the same proportions as provided for by the general inheritance laws of Arkansas.

Upon the death of the testatrix in 1967, her will was presented to the Faulkner Probate Court by her son Cecil, who lived in Conway, Arkansas. (The other son, Martin, was living in Indiana.) The probate court entered a routine order reciting that the will had been properly executed, admitting the instrument to probate, and appointing the bank as executor, without bond. On May 31, 1968, the probate court entered another routine order approving the executor's first and final accounting, allowing fees to the executor and its attorneys, discharging the executor, and closing the administration of the estate. That order made no reference to the validity of the trust or to the manner in which the assets of the estate were to be distributed. * * *

[T]he trust is void because there is a possibility that the estate will not vest within a period measured by a life or lives in being at the testatrix's death, plus 21 years. A bare possibility is enough. "The interest must vest within the time allowed by the rule. If there is any possibility that the contingent event may happen beyond the limits of the rule, the transaction is void." Comstock v. Smith, 255 Ark. 564, 501 S.W.2d 617 (1973).

The terms of this trust present an instance of the "unborn widow," a pitfall that is familiar to every student of the rule against perpetuities. This trust is not to terminate until the deaths of Cecil, Martin, and Martin's widow, but the identity of Martin's widow cannot be known until his death. Martin might marry an 18-year-old woman twenty years after his mother's death, have additional children by her, and then die. Cecil also might die. Martin's young widow, however, might live for another 40 or 50 years, after which the interests would finally vest. But since Cecil and Martin would have been the last measuring lives in being at the death of the testatrix, the trust property would not vest until many years past the maximum time allowed by the rule. The rule was formulated to prevent just such a possibility uncertainty about the title to real or personal property for an unreasonably long time in the future.

The violation of the rule, except for the interposition of a trust, is actually so clear that the appellee does not argue the point. Instead, it insists that the property would vest in Cecil and Martin's bodily heirs at their deaths, with only the right of possession of the property being deferred until the termination of the trust.

This argument overlooks the fact that the words "bodily heirs" were used in the decisive paragraph VIII of the will not as words of limitation, to specify the duration of an estate granted to Cecil and Martin, but as words of purchase, to specify the persons who would take at the termination of the trust. Obviously the identity of those persons cannot be determined until the death of Martin's widow; so the ownership would not vest until that time.

A vested remainder, simply stated, is a present interest that cannot be defeated by any contingency. Such an interest can be transferred by deed, by will, or by inheritance, even though the right of possession may not accrue until some time in the future. The simplest example is a conveyance or devise to A for life, remainder to B. Since A must eventually die, B's remainder is a present vested interest which cannot be defeated by any contingency. As we said in Hurst v. Hilderbrandt, 178 Ark. 337, 10 S.W.2d 491 (1928), in describing a vested remainder: "[T]here is some person in esse known and ascertained, who, by the will or deed creating the estate, is to take and enjoy the estate, and whose right to such remainder no contingency can defeat." To the same effect see Steele v. Robinson, 221 Ark. 58, 251 S.W.2d 1001 (1952); National Bank of Commerce v. Ritter, 181 Ark. 439, 26 S.W.2d 113 (1930); Restatement of Property, § 157, Comment f (1936).

Here the testatrix directed that at the termination of the trust the property be distributed as provided by the general inheritance laws of Arkansas. At the time of the deaths of Cecil and Martin it would be utterly impossible to say who would take, in the case we have supposed, at the death of Martin's young widow 50 years later. Under our law the surviving descendants would then take per capita if they were related to Cecil and Martin in equal degree, but per stirpes if in unequal degree. Ark.Stat.Ann. §§ 61-134 and -135 (Repl.1971). If there were no surviving descendants of one brother, the entire property would go to the surviving descendants of the other. If there were no surviving descendants of either, the property would revert to the testatrix's estate and go to her collateral heirs. Thus it is really too plain for argument that the interest of every descendant (or "bodily heir") of Cecil or Martin would be contingent upon his surviving the death of Martin's widow, at which time and only at which time the title would finally vest.

A subordinate issue, that of estoppel is relied upon by the dissenting opinion. Cecil certainly did not represent that the trust, as distinguished from the will, was valid, nor did the bank nor anyone else rely to its detriment upon the supposed validity of the trust.

Reversed and remanded for further proceedings.

HICKMAN, J., dissent[ing] * * * [is omitted].

Notes

This case is often used to illustrate possibility. First, there is a possibility that Martin may have a widow (a status person not otherwise identified) who would not be a life in being when the testatrix died, but nonetheless would be a measuring life for purposes of the Rule. Second, there is the possibility that either son will have a "youngest child," who will be less than four when all of the lives in being die. If that child then turns twenty-five more than twenty-one years from that date, to bring about vesting, the Rule would be violated. The court focuses on the first possibility—the unborn widow of Martin—but both possibilities exist to cause havoc with the Rule. The lesson for any competent drafter is to avoid any reference to a "status person" when writing an instrument. For example, "When the pope becomes a Baptist," or, to use a more common occurrence, "For my surviving heirs whenever my estate is distributed." Since a "slothful personal representative"—potentially not a life in being when the testator dies—may not distribute the estate for more than twenty-one years, long after all of the lives in being are deceased, the event could occur beyond the Rule and, hence, violate the requirement of a life in being plus twenty-one years. NEW YORK EST., POWERS & TRUSTS L. § 9-1.3(c) (McKinney 2019) provides that, whenever a status term is used—spouse, executor, widow—"it shall be presumed that the reference is to a person in being on the effective date of the instrument." Likewise, with any contingency related to the estate or transfer tax, it is "presumed that the creator of such estate intended such contingency to occur, if at all, within twenty-one years from the effective date of the instrument creating such estate." *Id.* at § 9-1.3(d).

b. Fertile Octogenarians

English law was premised on biblical injunctions, among them that all things were possible to God. Hence, it is possible for God to do all things, including allowing a woman to conceive late in her life, even in her eighties. This is the premise of fertile octogenarian cases, made most famous in the English decision of Jee v. Audley, 1 Cox 324, 29 Eng. Rep. 1186 (1787). The decision concerned a testator, who created a life estate in his wife, and then to his niece and the issue of her body. But if there be no issue of her body, then to be equally divided among the daughters of testator's kinsman, John Lee, and his wife, Elizabeth Lee. The kinsman and his wife were in their seventies, but the court read the bequest as saying that, when choosing the daughters, we should choose only those daughters who were alive when the issue of the niece finally expired. This event could happen after any life in being if we could presume that John and Elizabeth could have a daughter who was not a life in being but, nonetheless, is a measuring life. The court held that it was possible for John and Elizabeth to have additional daughters and, hence, the event may not take place within a life in being plus twenty-one years.

Fertile octogenarians involve women and the ability to produce viable eggs; men are commonly thought of as being capable of producing sperm throughout their lives. To prevent the application of the possibility of after-born children adversely affecting trusts, states have enacted statutes presuming that a woman is incapable of bearing children after the age of fifty-five. *See, e.g.,* N.Y. Est., Powers & Trusts L. §§ 9-1.2 & 9-1.3 (McKinney 2019). Some courts take judicial notice of infertility due to such causes as a complete hysterectomy. *See, e.g., In re* Latouf's Will, 887 N.J. Super. 137, 208 A.2d 411 (1965). New York is also quick to legislate that it is presumed that a male cannot have a child before the male reaches the age of fourteen, and that a female may not have a child before the age of twelve. *See* N.Y. Est., Powers & Trusts L. § 9-1.3(e)(1) (2019). Please note the distinction between men and women and the presumption of fertility in the following decision.

Ward v. Van der Loeff

House of Lords, United Kingdom, 1924 [1924] A.C. 653

Testator, William John Dalzell Burnyeat, died in 1916. He was survived by his wife, Hildegard, by his mother and father [each being 67 years of age], and by two brothers and two sisters. Testator had no children. At the time of Testator's death, Testator's brothers and sisters each had children who were living.

In 1921, Testator's widow married Mr. Van der Loeff, who was not a natural-born British subject. After Testator's death and after the marriage of Hildegard and Van der Loeff, one of the testator's siblings had a child—Philip Ponsonby Burnyeat.

Testator executed a Will in 1915 and a codicil in 1916. In the Will, Testator left his estate in trust for his wife for life, with the remainder to his children. However, as provided in the Will, because Testator died without children, he gave his wife a power to appoint the trust fund among the children of Testator's brothers and sisters. In default of appointment, he gave the trust fund, in equal shares, to all of the children of his brothers and sisters.]

VISCOUNT HALDANE L.C:

* * *

About the validity of these trusts no question arises. But it is otherwise with the codicil made by the testator. It was in these terms:

> I declare that the life interest given to my said wife by my said will shall be terminable on her remarriage unless such remarriage shall be with a natural born British subject. I revoke the power of appointment among the children of my brothers and sisters given to my said wife by my said will. And I declare that after her death my trustees shall stand possessed of the residuary trust funds in trust for all or any the children or child of my brothers and sisters who shall be living at the death of my wife or born at any time afterwards before any one of such children for the time being in existence attains a vested interest and who being a son or sons attain the age of twenty-one, or being a daughter or daughters attain that age or marry if more than one, in equal shares.

On the construction of the will and codicil, two questions arise. The first is, whether the limitation in favour of children, contained in the concluding words of the codicil, is valid, having regard to the rule against perpetuities. The second is whether, if invalid, this new limitation and the wording of the codicil have been at all events efficacious as expressing a revocation of his bequest to children contained in the will. If the limitation to children in the codicil be invalid, and that in the will has not been revoked, then a further question arises, whether the gift in the will operated in favour of any children of the brothers and sisters who were not born until after the testator's death. Philip Ponsonby Burnyeat, who is one of the parties to these appeals, was a son of the testator's brother, Myles Fleming Burnyeat, but was not born until after the testator's death and the remarriage of his widow. It is argued against his claim that the life interest of the widow was effectively determined by the provision in the codicil and that the class of children to take was finally ascertained at that date as the time of distribution. If this be so, Philip Ponsonby Burnyeat is excluded.

P. O. Lawrence J. was the judge before whom this summons came in the first instance. He decided that the gift in the codicil in favour of the children of the testator's brothers and sisters was so framed as to be void for perpetuity. He held further, that the codicil operated to revoke the residuary gift in the will only so far as the substituted provision in the codicil was valid, and that the gift in the will in favour of these children, therefore, took effect, but merely in favour of such of the children as were born before the remarriage of the testator's widow. Philip Ponsonby Burnyeat was thus excluded. * * *

My Lords, the principle to be applied in construing instruments for the purpose of ascertaining whether the direction they contain infringes the rule against perpetuity is a well settled one. It was repeated with emphasis in this House in Pearks v. Moseley * * *, where it was laid down that in construing the words the effect of the rule must in the first instance be left out of sight, and then, having in this way defined the intention expressed, the Court had to test its validity by applying the rule to the meaning thus ascertained. It is only therefore if, as matter of construction, the words in the codicil, taken in the natural sense in which the testator used them, do not violate the rule that they can be regarded as giving a valid direction. Looking at the language of the testator here, I am wholly unable to read it as not postponing the ascertainment of possible members of the class beyond the period of a life in being and twenty-one years afterwards. No doubt if we were warranted in interpreting the testator as having referred only to the children of those of his brother and sisters who were alive at his death we might read his language in a way which would satisfy the law. But for so restricting the natural meaning of his words there is no justification in the language used in the context. He speaks of his brothers and sisters generally, and there is no expression which excludes the children of other possible brothers and sisters of the whole or half blood who might in contemplation of law be born. He has nowhere indicated an intention that his words are not to be construed in this, their natural meaning. I think, therefore, that the class to be benefited was not one all the members of which were, as a necessary result of the words used, to be ascertained within the period which the law prescribes, and that the gift in the codicil in favour of children of brothers and sisters is wholly void.

The next question is whether the codicil, although inoperative to this extent, was yet operative to revoke the gift to children of brothers and sisters contained in the will. After consideration, I have come to the conclusion that it was not so operative. There is indeed a revocation expressed in the codicil, but it is confined to the power of appointment given to the wife. It does not extend to what follows. That is, in terms, an attempt at a substantive and independent gift, and, as it is wholly void, I think, differing on this point from the Court of Appeal, that the provision in the will stands undisturbed. There is nothing else in the codicil which purports to affect it. It can make no difference that the class of children is a new and different class if the constitution of the new class is wholly inoperative in law. If it fails, then unless an independent and valid intention to revoke has been independently of it expressed, no revocation can take place. There is no such independent expression of intention here.

The only other point is at what period the class of children of brothers and sisters who took under the will is to be ascertained. I think that according to a well-known rule, the period is that of distribution; in other words, taking the valid alteration in the codicil into account, the remarriage of the widow with a foreign subject. Philip Ponsonby Burnyeat is thus excluded.

The result is that the judgment of P.O. Lawrence J. should be restored. * * *

[Opinion of VISCOUNT CAVE omitted].

* * *

LORD DUNEDIN:

My Lords, the main question in this case seems to me to be determined by what was said in this House by Lord Cairns in the two cases of Hill v. Crook * * * and Dorin v. Dorin. * * * In the former of these cases that noble and learned Lord laid down that when you wish to vary the meaning of a word denoting a class of relations from what the prima facie meaning of that word is — he actually said it of the words legitimate children, but the application is obviously wider — there are two classes of cases only where the primary signification can be departed from. The one is where it is impossible in the circumstances that any person indicated by the prima facie meaning can take under the bequest. That is not the case here because probably in law, though scarcely in fact, the idea of other brothers and sisters to the testator coming into existence could not be excluded, but in any case the half-brother or sister was a real possibility. The second class of cases is where you find something in the will itself, that is, in the expressions used in the will, to exclude the prima facie interpretation. That also seems to me absent. He has used the words "brother and sister" without explanation or glossary, and I am afraid he must take the consequences. * * * [other opinions omitted].

Notes

Advances in medical technology have increased the possibility of conception for both men and women. For example, surrogacy contracts allow for maternity to be established with someone other than the surrogate. *See, e.g., In re* Infant R., 922 N.E.2d 59 (Ind. Ct. App. 2010) (establishing maternity through clear and convincing evidence, rebutting presumption attached to surrogate). There is the added issue of posthumous conception. *See* Raymond C. O'Brien, *The Immediacy of Genome Editing and Mitochondrial Replacement*, 9 WAKE FOREST J. OF L. & POL'Y 419 (2019) (describing science's ability to edit human genomes resulting in babies with specific characteristics); Raymond C. O'Brien, *Assessing Assisted Reproductive Technology*, 27 CATH. U. J. OF L. & TECH. 1 (2018) (describing the increasing use of ART among the world's population); Lynda Wray Black, *The Birth of a Parent: Defining Parentage for Lenders of Genetic Material*, 92 NEB. L. REV. 799 (2014); Harvey L. Fiser & Paula K. Garrett, *Life Begins at Ejaculation: Legislating Sperm as the Potential to Create Life and the Effects on Contracts for Artificial Insemination*, 21 AM. U. J. GENDER SOC. POLICY & L. 39 (2012); Kristine S. Knaplund, *Children of Assisted Reproduction*, 45U. MICH. J.L. REFORM 899 (2012); Julie A. Nice, *The Descent of Responsible Procreation: A Genealogy of an Ideology*, 45 LOY. L.A. L. REV. 781 (2012); Raymond C. O'Brien, *The Momentum of Posthumous Conception: A Model Act*, 25 J. CONTEMP. L. & POL'Y 332 (2009); Kimberly E. Naguit, Note, *The Inadequacies of Missouri Intestacy Law: Addressing the Rights of Posthumously Conceived Children*, 74 Mo. L. REV. 889 (2009).

The newly revised Uniform Parentage Act (2019) includes an updated surrogacy provision to better establish parenthood among the increasing percentage of the population utilizing surrogacy. *See* UNIF. PARENTAGE ACT, Article 8 (2019). The revised Act permits greater access to children born as a result of assisted reproductive technology to identify information regarding their gamete providers. *Id.* at Article 9. The revisions to the Act were partly in response to the rapid changes in the establishment of parenthood.

c. Charitable Trusts

Brown v. Independent Baptist Church

Supreme Judicial Court of Massachusetts, 1950
325 Mass. 645, 91 N.E.2d 922

QUA, Chief Justice.

The object of this suit in equity, originally brought in this court, is to determine the ownership of a parcel of land in Woburn and the persons entitled to share in the proceeds of its sale by a receiver.

Sarah Converse died seised of the land on July 19, 1849, leaving a will in which she specifically devised it 'to the Independent Baptist Church of Woburn, to be holden and enjoyed by them so long as they shall maintain and promulgate their present religious belief and faith and shall continue a Church; and if the said Church shall be dissolved, or if its religious sentiments shall be changed or abandoned, then my will is that this real estate shall go to my legatees hereinafter named, to be divided in equal portions between them. And my will further is, that if my beloved husband, Jesse Converse, shall survive me, that then this devise to the aforesaid Independent Church of Woburn, shall not take effect till from and after his decease; and that so long as he shall live he may enjoy and use the said real estate, and take the rents and profits thereof to his own use.' Then followed ten money legacies in varying amounts to different named persons, after which there was a residuary clause in these words, 'The rest and residue of my estate I give and bequeath to my legatees above named, saving and except therefrom the Independent Baptist Church; this devise to take effect from and after the decease of my husband; I do hereby direct and will that he shall have the use and this rest and residue during his life.'

The husband of the testatrix died in 1864. The church named by the testatrix ceased to 'continue a church' on October 19, 1939.

The parties apparently are in agreement, and the single justice ruled, that the estate of the church in the land was a determinable fee. We concur. First Universalist Society of North Adams v. Boland, 155 Mass. 171, 174, 29 N.E. 524, 15 L.R.A. 231; Institution for Savings in Roxbury and its Vicinity v. Roxbury Home for Aged Women, 244 Mass. 583, 585–586, 139 N.E. 301; Dyer v. Siano, 298 Mass. 537, 540, 11 N.E.2d 451. The estate was a fee, since it might last forever, but it was not an absolute fee, since it might (and did) 'automatically expire upon the occurrence of a stated event.' Restatement: Property, § 44. It is also conceded, and was ruled, that the specific executory devise over to the persons 'hereinafter named' as legatees was void for remoteness. This conclusion seems to be required by Proprietors of Church in Brattle Square v. Grant, 3 Gray 142, 152, 155–156, 63 Am.Dec. 725; First Universalist Society of North Adams v. Boland, 155 Mass. 171, 173, 29 N.E. 524, 15 L.R.A. 231, and Institution for Savings in Roxbury and its Vicinity v. Roxbury Home for Aged Women, 244 Mass. 583, 587, 139 N.E. 301. See Restatement: Property, § 44, illustration 20. The reason is stated to be that the determinable fee might not come to an end until long after any life or lives in being and twenty-one years, and in theory at least might never come to an end, and for an indefinite period no clear title to the entire estate could be given.

Since the limitation over failed, it next becomes our duty to consider what became of the possibility of reverter which under our decisions remained after the failure of the limitation. First Universalist Society of North Adams v. Boland, 155 Mass. 171, 175, 29 N.E. 524, 15 L.R.A. 231; Institution for Savings in Roxbury and its Vicinity v. Roxbury Home for Aged Women, 244 Mass. 583, 587, 139 N.E. 301. Restatement: Property, § 228, illustration 2, and Appendix to Volume II, at pages 35–36, including note 2. A possibility of reverter seems, by the better authority, to be assignable *inter vivos* (Restatement: Property, § 159; Sims, Future Interests, § 715; see Tiffany, Real Property, 3d Ed., § 314, note 31), and must be at least as readily devisable as the other similar reversionary interest known as a right of entry for condition broken, which is devisable, though not assignable. * * * It follows that the possibility of reverter passed under the residuary clause of the will to the same persons designated in the invalid executory devise. It is of no consequence that the persons designated in the two provisions were the same. The same result must be reached as if they were different.

The single justice ruled that the residuary clause was void for remoteness, apparently for the same reason that rendered the executory devise void. With this we cannot agree, since we consider it settled that the rule against perpetuities does not apply to reversionary interests of this general type, including possibilities of reverter. Proprietors of the Church in Brattle Square v. Grant, 3 Gray, 142, 148, 63 Am.Dec. 725. French v. Old South Society in Boston, 106 Mass. 479, 488–489; Tobey v. Moore, 130 Mass. 448, 450. First Universalist Society of North Adams v. Boland, 155 Mass. 171, 175–176, 29 N.E. 524, 15 L.R.A. 231; Restatement: Property, § 372, Tiffany, Real Property, 3d Ed., § 404. See Gray, Rule Against Perpetuities, 4th Ed., §§ 41, 312, 313. For a full understanding of the situation here presented it is necessary to keep in mind the fundamental difference in character between the attempted executory devise to the legatees later named in the will and the residuary gift to the same persons. The executory devise was in form and substance an attempt to limit or create a new future interest which might not arise or vest in anyone until long after the permissible period. It was obviously not intended to pass such a residuum of the testatrix's existing estate as a possibility of reverter, and indeed if the executory devise had been valid according to its terms the whole estate would have passed from the testatrix and no possibility of reverter could have been left to her or her devisees. The residuary devise, on the other hand, was in terms and purpose exactly adapted to carry any interest which might otherwise remain in the testatrix, whether or not she had it in mind or knew it would exist. Thayer v. Wellington, 9 Allen 283, 295, 85 Am.Dec. 753; Wellman v. Carter, 286 Mass. 237, 249–250, 190 N.E. 493.

We cannot accept the contention made in behalf of Mrs. Converse's heirs that the words of the residuary clause 'saving and except therefrom the Independent Baptist Church' were meant to exclude from the operation of that clause any possible rights in the *land* previously given to the church. We construe these words as intended merely to render the will consistent by excluding the church which also had been 'above named' from the list of '*legatees*' who were to take the residue.

The interlocutory decree entered December 16, 1947, is reversed, and a new decree is to be entered providing that the land in question or the proceeds of any sale thereof by the receiver shall go to the persons named as legatees in the will, other than the Independent Baptist Church of Woburn, or their successors in interest. Further proceedings are to be in accord with the new decree. Costs and expenses are to be at the discretion of the single justice.

So ordered.

Notes

Traditionally, courts have been willing to reform charitable trusts under the doctrine of "cy pres" to accommodate a purpose "as near as" the original invalidated trust purpose as possible. Most often, the cy pres doctrine is used when a charitable beneficiary is no longer in existence. *See, e.g.,* Estate of Crawshaw, 249 Kan. 388, 819 P.2d 613 (1991). But the Uniform Trust Code § 413(a) makes the doctrine applicable whenever "a particular charitable purpose becomes unlawful, impracticable, [or] impossible to achieve. . . ." Unif. Trust Code § 413(a) (2019). In addition, if the settlor has provided for distribution of the trust property to a non-charitable beneficiary, this will apply, rather than cy pres, only if: "(1) the trust property is to revert to the settlor and the settlor is still living; or (2) fewer than 21 years have elapsed since the date of the trust's creation." *Id.* at § 413(b). Although the issue of failure of a charitable trust because of violation of the Rule Against Perpetuities is of concern, there is greater concern over discrimination by the charitable institution and violation of the Fourteenth Amendment. *See, e.g.,* Estate of Wilson, 59 N.Y.2d 461, 452 N.E.2d 1228, 465 N.Y.S.2d 900 (1983) (Fourteenth Amendment only bars state discrimination, not private discrimination). *But see* Bob Jones University v. United States, 461 U.S. 574, 103 S. Ct. 2017 (1983) (denial of federal tax exemption extended to "discriminating" charities, even though qualifying as charitable for state law).

For additional commentary on the doctrine of cy pres, see Allison Anna Tait, *Keeping Promises and Meeting Needs: Public Charities at a Crossroads*, 102 Minn. L. Rev. 1789 (2018); Susan N. Gary, *Restricted Charitable Gifts: Public Benefit, Public Voice*, 81 Alb. L. Rev. 565 (2017–2018); Melanie B. Leslie, *Time to Sever the Dead Hand: Fisk University and the Cost of the* Cy Pres *Doctrine*, 31 Cardozo Arts & Ent. L.J. 1 (2012); Alan L. Feld, *Who Are the Beneficiaries of Fisk University's Stieglitz Collection?*, 91 B.U. L. Rev. 873 (2011).

C. Application to Class Gifts

Much of what has been provided, *supra*, refers to class gifts. For example, if a settlor were to provide in a testamentary trust: "For my spouse for life, then to my children, issue of my body or adopted by me, for life, and then to my surviving issue per stirpes," we have multiple class designations. Between the time the settlor executes the Last Will and Testament and the settlor's death, there is the possibility of increase and decrease of class membership in children and issue. Yet, in neither of the classes is there a Rule violation. Using the analysis provided previously (standing at the creation of the instrument — the settlor's death — which is when the will speaks), it is impossible for the settlor to have a spouse who is not a life in being. In addition, the measuring lives at the settlor's death are the settlor's children. Since the Uniform Trust Code prohibits the possibility of afterborn children being conceived by using frozen sperm, there is no possibility of there being a measuring life that is not a life in being. Thus, the Rule will not prohibit a distribution of the trust assets to those issue surviving the death of the settlor's last child. But not all trusts are similarly situated. Traditionally, the Rule is violated if it is *possible* that *any* member of the class may receive a vested interest at a time beyond the lives in being, plus twenty-one years. The following case provides an example and a judicial solution.

American Security & Trust Co. v. Cramer

United States District Court, District of Columbia, 1959
175 F. Supp. 367

YOUNGDAHL, District Judge.

Six of the eleven * * * defendants before the Court have moved for summary judgment. A hearing has been held and memoranda of points and authorities have been submitted. Plaintiff, trustee of a testamentary trust, is a stakeholder in this controversy among competing heirs. Since all the material facts have been stipulated, * * * the Court is free to render summary judgment.

Abraham D. Hazen, a resident of the District of Columbia, died in the District on December 4, 1901. His will, executed on October 16, 1900, was admitted to probate on March 11, 1902.

Testator was survived by Hannah E. Duffey, who is referred to in his will as his 'adopted daughter'. At the time of the testator's death, Hannah had two children: Mary Hazen Duffey (now Cramer), born November 12, 1897, and Hugh Clarence Duffey, born July 11, * * * 1899. After the testator's death, Hannah gave birth to two more children: Depue Hazen Duffey, born October 9, 1903, and Horace Duffey, born July 8, 1908.

The will provided for the payment of debts and certain specific bequests and then provided that the residue of the estate be put in trust for the benefit of testator's wife for life. At her death, one-half of the corpus was to be, and has been, given to testator's sister and brothers;[4] the other half, composed of realty, remained in trust for Hannah for life. At Hannah's death, the income was to go to the children of

---

4. The testator left no mother or father surviving him, and he had no natural children. See files and records in Equity Action No. 52600 for July 22, 1935 (findings of fact by Luhring, J.).

Hannah 'then living or the issue of such of them as may then be dead leaving issue surviving' Hannah, and then 'upon the death of each the share of the one so dying shall go absolutely to the persons who shall then be her or his heirs at law according to the laws of descent now in force in the said District of Columbia'. * * * [footnote omitted].

Testator's widow died on October 31, 1916; Hannah died on May 21, 1915.

On October 5, 1917, the heirs of the testator brought an action in equity to have the provisions of the seventh paragraph of the will stricken as being in violation of the rule against perpetuities. The Supreme Court of the District of Columbia held that the interests of Hannah's children under the will were valid and the Court of Appeals affirmed. Hazen v. American Security & Trust Co., 1920, 49 App.D.C. 297, 265 F. 447. * * * [footnote omitted]. The validity of the remainders over, after the death of each child, was expressly not ruled upon as the life estates were not 'so intimately connected with the gift over as to require us now to determine the validity of such gifts.' * * *

Hugh, one of the four life tenants after the death of the widow and Hannah, died on December 19, 1928 and shortly thereafter the trustee brought a bill for instructions; this time the validity of the remainder over to Hugh's heirs was in issue. On January 2, 1930, Judge Bailey ruled that 'the remainder provided by the will after his (Hugh's) death to the persons who shall then be his heirs at law became vested within the period prescribed by law and is valid.' * * *

On December 13, 1954, Depue died and for the fourth time a suit concerning this trust was started in this court. The trustees desired instructions as to the disposition of Depue's one-sixth share. While this action was pending, on December 18, 1957, Horace died. A supplemental bill was then filed, asking for instructions as to the disposition of this one-sixth share as well. The remainder over after the death of the sole living life tenant, Mary, cannot yet take effect; however, due to the request of all the parties concerned, and in order to save both the time of this court and the needless expense it would otherwise cost the estate, the Court will also pass on the validity of this remainder.

The law that governs the questions here involved is the law in effect at the time of the testator's death: December 4, 1901. * * *

The common-law rule against perpetuities, as stated by Professor Gray, is as follows:

> No interest is good unless it must vest, if at all, not later than twenty-one years after some life in being at the creation of the interest. * * *

The effect of the rule is to invalidate ab initio certain future interests that might otherwise remain in existence for a period of time considered inimicable [sic] to society's interest in having reasonable limits to dead-hand control and in facilitating the marketability of property. The policy of the law is to permit a person to control the devolution of his property but only for a human lifetime plus twenty-one years and actual periods of gestation. With careful planning, this period could be as long as one hundred years—and this is long enough.

A gift to a class is a gift of an aggregate amount of property to persons who are collectively described and whose individual share will depend upon the number of persons ultimately constituting the class. Evans v. Ockershausen, 1938, 69 App.D.C. 285, 292, 100 F.2d 695, 702, 128 A.L.R. 177. The members of the class must be finally determined within a life or lives in being plus twenty-one years and actual periods of gestation, or the gift will fail. Put another way, the class must close within the period of the rule against perpetuities, if the class gift is to be valid. Unless a contrary intent is indicated by the testator, the class will close when any member of the class is entitled to immediate possession and enjoyment of his share of the class gift. Applying these basic principles to the trust here involved, it is seen that the life estates to Hannah's children had to vest, if at all, at the termination of the preceding life estates of the widow and Hannah. Since Hannah's children had to be born within Hannah's lifetime, and since Hannah was a life in being, the class (Hannah's children) physiologically had to close within the period of the rule.[11] This has already been so held. Hazen v. American Security & Trust Co., *supra*, at note 6. Furthermore, the remainder over at Hugh's death has been held valid. The Court now holds that the remainder limited to the heirs of Mary is valid. Both Hugh and Mary were lives in being at the testator's death; the remainders limited to their heirs had to vest, if at all, within the period of the rule. Horace and Depue were born after the testator died; the remainders over at their deaths are invalid.

In applying the rule against perpetuities, it does not help to show that the rule might be complied with or that, the way things turned out, it actually was complied with.[12] After the testator's death, Hannah might have had more children; one of these might have lived more than twenty-one years after the death of all the lives in being at the testator's death. The vesting of the remainder in this after-born's heirs would take place after the expiration of lives in being and twenty-one years, since the heirs could not be ascertained until the after-born's death and an interest cannot be vested until the interest holder is ascertained. Consequently, because of the

---

11. The fact that the will provided 'the said half shall be held for the use and benefit of the children of said adopted daughter then living or the issue of such of them as may then be dead leaving issue surviving my said adopted daughter * * *' (emphasis supplied) does not cast any doubt on the above. If one of Hannah's children predeceased Hannah and also failed to leave issue, the other children would have increased shares; but still, the class would be determined, i.e., close, within a life in being (Hannah's).

12. A few jurisdictions have adopted a 'wait and see' doctrine which has the effect of neutralizing the possible interest-invalidating events and taking into consideration only the actual events. Perhaps this is a desirable change, but the District of Columbia has not adopted this doctrine and to do so this Court is of the opinion a statute would be necessary. See discussion of the doctrine in Simes and Smith, *supra*, note 10 at §1230 and for an example of such a statute, see Mass.Acts (1954), c. 641, enacted as chapter 184A of Mass.Gen.Laws.

possibility that this could happen, even though, in fact, it did not,[13] the remainders limited to the heirs of Horace and Depue (both after-borns) are invalid as a violation of the rule against perpetuities.

Counsel have not argued the point of whether the invalidity of the remainders to the heirs of Horace and Depue serves to taint the otherwise valid remainders to the heirs of Mary and Hugh. Of course, the remainder after Hugh's life estate has already been distributed and is not properly in issue. Nevertheless, as shall be demonstrated, it (and the remainder to the heirs of Mary) are not affected by the two invalid remainders, since the four remainders are to subclasses and stand (or fall) separately. * * *

In the instant case, the language of the will compels the Court to read it as a devise of remainders to subclasses and within the rule of Catlin. The provision in issue reads, in part:

> * * * and *each* of the children of said adopted daughter shall take only for and during the terms of their *respective* lives and upon the death of *each* the share of the *one* so dying shall go absolutely to the persons who shall then be *her or his* heirs at law * * * (Emphasis supplied).

The Court deems it advisable to mention that it thoroughly explored the possible applicability here of the Rule in Shelley's Case. Prior to January 2, 1902, this ancient principle of law * * * was in force in the District of Columbia. * * * Noyes v. Parker, 1937, 68 App.D.C. 13, 92 F.2d 562. If it could be utilized in the case at hand, the remainders limited to the heirs of each of Hannah's children would be converted into a remainder in the child himself. This, for one thing, would save the two remainders found invalid and prevent their defaulting to the heirs of the testator.

Assuming, without deciding, that the remainders here are equitable (because the trust is active), nevertheless the rule does not apply because the remainders were not limited to 'heirs' but instead went to 'her or his heirs at law according to the laws of descent now in force in the said District of Columbia'. * * *

When a remainder in fee after a life estate fails, there is no enlargement or diminution of the life estate; rather there is then a reversion in the heirs of the testator. Hilton v. Kinsey, 1950, 88 U.S.App.D.C. 14, 17, 185 F.2d 885, 888, 23 A.L.R.2d 830; Simes and Smith, *supra*, at note 10 § 1263, and numerous cases cited. The two one-sixth shares held invalid shall pass to the successors in interest to the heirs of Abraham D. Hazen.

---

13. Mary, a life in being at testator's death, is still alive. Therefore, the heirs of Horace and Depue would *actually* be taking within the period of the rule, but in this area of imagination-run-wild, actualities do not count; what could happen is all that matters.

In this case, the above suppositions are not unreasonable since Hannah was in her middle thirties when the testator died. But cf. the cases of 'the fertile octogenarian', 'the unborn widow' and 'the magic gravel pit' in Professor Leach's classic article, 'Perpetuities in a Nutshell', 51 Harv.L.R. 638, 642–645 (1938).

Since it is undisputed that the late George E. Sullivan, an attorney, had a contingent fee contract, dated March 16, 1922, with the heirs of the testator, entitling him to twenty percent of whatever property was finally held to pass to the heirs of the testator by virtue of the failure of the remainders, and since this has now been brought to fruition, the estate of Edith B. Sullivan, the sole heir of George E. Sullivan, is entitled to a twenty percent share of the two one-sixth interests.

Counsel have stipulated that Hannah was referred to in testator's will as his 'adopted daughter'; there is no agreement as to whether she actually was legally adopted. No proof of a legal adoption has been offered. On the other hand, there is considerable reason to say that Hannah never was, in fact, legally adopted. In 1927 a full hearing was held on the matter and at that time Hannah's husband, mother and numerous friends were alive and testified; these persons have since passed away and the Court is of the opinion that nothing could be gained by ordering a further hearing at this time.

It is clear from the transcript of the hearing that Hannah was treated by the testator and his wife just as if she were their natural daughter. She lived with them, was always referred to as 'our daughter', and used their name. Her formal wedding invitation referred to her as the Hazens' daughter; the community believed she was the Hazens' natural daughter. While there is little testimony on the question of whether she was ever legally adopted, what there is, leads to the conclusion that she had not been. * * * Moreover, it would appear that it was impossible for her ever to have been legally adopted since the original adoption statute provided for the adoption of 'minor children' only. 28 Stat. 687, ch. 134 (passed February 26, 1895). * * * Hannah was at least twenty-six years of age in 1895. * * *

One matter remains. The Court has been urged to terminate the trust and order distribution of three-sixths of the original corpus to the life tenant, Mary. This life tenant is presently sixty-two years of age; she is a widow and has three adult children. These three children and their wives have signed an 'assignment' of their interests in the trust to Mary. Although the legal significance of this 'assignment', standing alone, is questionable, in light of the fact that the children are not their mother's heirs but only presumptive heirs until she dies, nevertheless, it is significant to show that the only persons likely to become remaindermen are willing to have the income beneficiary take the corpus. The intent of the testator is clear:

> I do direct that Mary Hazen Duffey, the daughter of my adopted daughter and the namesake of my wife and for whom my wife and I have the greatest affection, shall if living at the death of her mother take a share three times as large as the share of each of the other children of my said adopted daughter * * *.

It seems obvious that the testator had Mary's interest uppermost in his mind. Last year, Mary's share of the income from the trust amounted to $750.51 which was hardly sufficient for her subsistence; her needs would be amply provided for were she to receive the share of the corpus. If General Hazen were now alive, there would seem to be little doubt but that he would wish to join with Mary's children to have the trust terminated and the corpus distributed to the one for whom he had 'the greatest affection' and who was to receive 'a share three times as large as the share of each of the other children'. In light of the realities of the situation, the desire of all concerned to have the trust terminated, and the evident purpose of the will, the Court shall order the trust terminated and the corpus distributed to the life tenant. Cf. Wolcott's Petition, 1948, 95 N.H. 23, 56 A.2d 641, 1 A.L.R.2d 1323. This, however, is conditioned upon the furnishing of a bond to protect any unascertained remaindermen.

Defendant Blakelock's motion for summary judgment is granted. Defendant Mary Duffey Cramer's prayer for additional relief is granted to the extent of having her receive that portion of the corpus presently supplying the income to which she is entitled as a life tenant, conditioned on her furnishing a bond or undertaking with surety approved by the court.

Counsel will submit an appropriate order.

Notes

Additional courts have adopted approaches to save at least part of a settlor's trust that would otherwise be void under the Rule Against Perpetuities. For example, in Estates of Coates, 438 Pa. Super. 195, 652 A.2d 331 (1994), the court applied the doctrine of vertical separability to sustain income through great-grandchildren, thereby acknowledging that gifts to subclasses may be evaluated separately, as long as the number of shares is definitely fixed within the time required by the Rule. But the competent drafter should recognize the pitfalls of the "all or nothing" approach to class gifts and the Rule and should draft instruments accordingly. To properly draft an instrument, first review the materials regarding increase and decrease of class gifts, *supra*, and eliminate the possibility of any afterborn class members who may take an interest in the trust after the date or creation. *See generally* W. Barton Leach, *The Rule Against Perpetuities and Gifts to Classes*, 51 HARV. L. REV. 1329 (1938).

D. Application to Powers of Appointment

Recall that a power of appointment exists when a donor — a settlor of an *inter vivos* trust, or a testator of a valid Last Will and Testament — deposits an appointment — corpus — with a trustee, with the instruction to do whatever the donee says to do with the appointment at the appropriate time. Because a trust is involved, so too are future interests, and, thus, the Rule may void the trust. To properly evaluate the validity of any power of appointment under the Rule Against Perpetuities, first review the language used to establish the power and the options available to the donee, *supra*, then there are three distinct steps in any analysis:

(1) Is the power created by the donor valid? Thus, if the donor were to create a power of appointment using an instrument that was invalid because of a defect in intentionalities or formalities, then analysis ceases. Likewise, if any of the required elements of a trust is missing, analysis ceases. These are conditions explored in previous chapters and sections, but it is always necessary to remember that even the most complicated testamentary trust exists because of the validity of the testamentary instrument—the Last Will and Testament. But if a valid power exists, then:

(2) Has the donee exercised the power within the permissible period under the Rule? Recall that there are rules as to whether the donee's open-ended residuary clause exercises a power of appointment. If the donee has exercised the power correctly, then the question becomes whether the exercise is within the period of the Rule. Stated another way, we can ask if, standing at the creation of the power by the donor, there is any possibility that the donee may exercise the power beyond the period of the Rule, which is a life in being plus twenty-one years. For example, if a donor were to establish an irrevocable *inter vivos* trust to provide life income to his children, and then as his last child should appoint in a valid Last Will and Testament, this would be an invalid power. Invalidity results from the possibility that, standing at the creation of the power—during the life of the settlor, not at the death of the settlor—there is a possibility that the settlor could have an additional child who would not be a life in being at creation but may exercise the power more than twenty-one years after the death of the last life in being. If the donor/settlor had created a revocable trust and power of appointment, the power would be valid because the date of creation would be at the death of the donor/settlor. Likewise, the power would be valid if the power were created in the Last Will and Testament of the donor/settlor. If there is no possibility that the power may be exercised by the donee beyond the period of the Rule, we can then address the last issue.

(3) When the donee exercises the power created by the donor, has the donee created a subsequent trust that, when analyzed from the time of creation, but in light of the facts at the time of exercise, there is a possibility that all interests will not vest within a life in being plus twenty-one years? This final step in the analysis is premised on the "relation back" doctrine. Even if the power is validly created and validly exercised by the donee within the period of the Rule, it may still be invalid if, when the donee exercises, the exercise relates back to the donor's date of creation and, thereby, violates the Rule. The doctrine is logical because it recognizes that, in any power other than a general *inter vivos* power (presently exercisable), the donor has retained some control over the donee's selection. Hence, any exercise should be computed from creation of the power by the donor, not simply exercise by the donee. We will see this analysis demonstrated in the following cases, but also keep in mind that if there is a violation of the Rule Against Perpetuities in conjunction with a power of appointment, the court will apply the rules previously discussed regarding ineffective exercise, capture for general powers, and implied gifts for special powers.

Industrial National Bank of Rhode Island v. Barrett

Supreme Court of Rhode Island, 1966
101 R.I. 89, 220 A.2d 517

PAOLINO, Justice.

This is a bill in equity brought by the Industrial National Bank of Rhode Island, executor and trustee, and Aline C. Lathan, co-executor, under the will of Mary M. Tilley, deceased, for construction of the latter's will and for instructions to the executors and trustee thereunder. The adult respondents have filed an answer to the bill and all minor and contingent interests and those of persons unascertainable or not in being are represented by a guardian ad litem appointed for that purpose by the court. The guardian has filed an answer neither admitting nor denying the bill's allegations and submitting the interests of his respective wards to the court's care and protection.

* * *

It appears that Arthur H. Tilley, husband of the deceased, died January 28, 1959. Under the eighth clause of his will, admitted to probate February 5, 1959, he devised the property, which qualified for the full marital deduction, to the Industrial National Bank, in trust, with directions to pay the net income at least quarterly to his wife for life and such amounts of the corpus annually or at more frequent intervals as she should in writing request, for her comfort and support, and without being accountable to any court or remainderman therefor. He also conferred upon her a general testamentary power of appointment over the corpus remaining at her death.

Mary M. Tilley died October 28, 1963. Under the fourth clause of her will, admitted to probate November 7, 1963, she exercised her general testamentary power of appointment to the Industrial National Bank, in trust 'to pay over the net income thereof to and for the use and benefit of my granddaughters, Aline C. Lathan and Evelyn M. Barrett * * * equally for and during the term of their natural lives, and upon the death of either of them, to pay over said net income to her issue, *per stirpes* and not *per capita*.' The trustee was also given uncontrolled discretion to pay over to either of said grandchildren, or the issue of any deceased grandchild, for specific purposes, portions of the principal. Finally, the testatrix provided the trust would terminate 'twenty one (21) years after the death of the last survivor of the younger grandchild or issue of either grandchild of mine living at my death * * *.'

On the date of Arthur H. Tilley's death, Aline C. Lathan and Evelyn M. Barrett and one great-grandchild were in being. On the date of Mary M. Tilley's death the aforesaid respondents plus six additional great-grandchildren were in being. One great-grandchild was born subsequent to her death.

At various times within the three-year period preceding her death, Mrs. Tilley made gifts of stock to her respondent granddaughters which were included in her estate for federal estate tax purposes at a gross valuation of $92,995.50. The corpus of the marital trust created under clause eighth of Arthur H. Tilley's will was reported at a value of $65,610.51. The total valuation of her probate estate exclusive of the trust which she appointed was $25,666.18 and the total charges against her estate, including debts, administration expenses, state and federal inheritance and estate taxes total $28,188.44.

* * *

The complainants contend that Mrs. Tilley's exercise of the power of appointment created under her husband's will does not violate the rule against perpetuities on two alternative grounds.

First, they say, in clause eighth of his will, Arthur H. Tilley manifested a clear intent to bestow upon his wife an unlimited power to consume the trust principal giving her in effect a general power of appointment exercisable during her lifetime. In support of this contention, complainants point to the broad discretionary power bestowed on Mrs. Tilley to invade the principal for her comfort and support which, coupled with her general testamentary power of appointment, they argue, created an absolute interest although not actually designated as such. In this connection complainants cite cases which hold, in construing language similar to that in clause eighth, that actual 'need' of a beneficiary is not a measure of 'comfort' and 'support'—see In the Matter of Woollard's Will, 295 N.Y. 390, 68 N.E.2d 181; In re Walsh's Will, 193 Misc. 785, 85 N.Y.S.2d 207, and New Jersey Title Guarantee & Trust Co. v. Dailey, 123 N.J.Eq. 205, 196 A. 703—and distinguish those which require the beneficiary to show 'reasonableness,' 'good faith,' or that the beneficiary's other assets are factors to be considered as being premised solely on the principle that a life tenant owes other beneficiaries of the trust or other remaindermen, neither present here, a duty not to consume the principal unnecessarily. See 33 Am.Jur., Life Estates, Remainders, etc., §§ 242, 243, pp. 728, 729.

Consequently complainants urge the perpetuities period should be computed from the date of Mrs. Tilley's death when she exercised the power.

The cardinal principle in the construction of wills is that the intention of the testator if definitely ascertainable and lawful must govern. Rhode Island Hospital Trust Co. v. Bateman, 93 R.I. 116, 172 A.2d 84; Industrial Trust Co. v. Saunders, 71 R.I. 94, 42 A.2d 492.

Clause eighth directs the Industrial National Bank to hold certain property qualifying for the marital deduction:

> in trust, nevertheless, * * * to pay over the net income thereof, at least quarterly, to my wife, Mary M. Tilley, for and during her life, and I authorize and direct my said Trustee, annually or at more frequent intervals, whenever my said wife shall in writing so direct, to pay over to her, *for her own comfort and support*, such part of the principal as she shall direct, and without being accountable to any court or remainderman therefor. Upon the death of my said wife, I confer upon her the power by her Will to appoint the entire corpus of the trust remaining at her death, free of trust, which

power is exercisable in favor of the estate of my said wife, or in favor of such other distributees, and in such amounts and upon such terms, trusts, powers and limitations as she shall appoint in her Will. (Italics ours.)

The problem before us is to ascertain the extent of the gift the testator intended to bestow upon his wife. In cases such as these the extent and nature of a restriction depends upon the intent of the testator and accordingly, since different combinations of language and circumstances are endless, each will must be construed separately, rules of construction being guides only in a general sense.

We note first that instead of giving the property outright to his widow, the decedent chose to impress it with a trust. The provisions of that trust reflect his intent to make available to her something more than a life estate but something less than a fee. As we read clause eighth with reference to the provision for principal payments we find no language to indicate the trustee was invested with discretion to make them in consideration of the widow's actual needs or other assets, but rather that the discretion to determine the dollar amount payable rested solely in Mrs. Tilley.

Nevertheless the power must be read in reference to the matter for which it was given. In this context Mrs. Tilley did not have a general disposing power over the corpus because, in good-faith compliance with the settlor's plan of disposition, she could withdraw only those sums which she needed for her comfort and support.

However, complainants argue, since neither the beneficiary nor the trustee was accountable to any court or remainderman in regard to these payments, there was no review for her withdrawals, which, in reality, left her in complete control of the fund.

We do not agree. The pertinent language directs the trustee 'annually or at more frequent intervals, whenever my said wife shall in writing so direct, to pay over to her, for her own comfort and support, such part of the principal as she shall direct, *and without being accountable to any court or remainderman therefor.*' (Italics ours.) As we read this sentence the phrase 'and without being accountable to any court or remainderman therefor' applies to the trustee only, as it is used as a conjunctive thought to the first half of the sentence of which the trustee is the subject. While the discretion thus conferred on the trustee is broad, it is not so broad as to relieve it of the obligation to exercise the responsibility and in good faith. See Industrial National Bank v. Rhode Island Hospital, R.I., 207 A.2d 286, and cases cited on page 290. Moreover, and notwithstanding the discretion conferred on the trustee, Mrs. Tilley would have been accountable for withdrawals not made pursuant to the power bestowed on her. A power including one to direct payments of principal is special or limited if it may be exercised only for the use or support of a certain person, even though that person is the donee of the power. 5 Page on Wills (Bowe-Parker rev.) § 45.2, p. 498.

The complainants next contend that even if Mrs. Tilley had only a general testamentary power of appointment, the better-reasoned authorities hold the perpetuity period should be counted from the date of the power's exercise rather than its creation, which would make the gift here vest within the prescribed time.

Before reaching complainants' contention there is an initial problem we feel necessitates some discussion here. Clause fourth of Mrs. Tilley's will provides the trust created thereunder will terminate 'twenty one (21) years after the death of the last survivor of the younger grandchild or issue of either grandchild of mine living at my death * * *.' It is clear the testatrix set out the measuring lives alternatively as 'the last survivor of the younger grandchild' or the 'issue of either grandchild * * *.' Since both are modified by the phrase 'living at my death' the rule is satisfied on that point.

The difficulty arises in determining what person the testatrix designated when she used the word 'survivor.' After reading the clause as a whole we believe that this was but an inartistic reference by her draftsman to one of her grandchildren's issue. For a general discussion of this problem, see Perpetuities: A Standard Saving Clause To Avoid Violations Of The Rule, by W. Barton Leach and James K. Logan, 74 Harv.L.Rev. 1141 (1961).

Since this provision was manifestly intended as a savings clause to obviate any violation of the rule, we will give effect to the testatrix' obvious intent that this trust be created and will adopt the above interpretation, thereby removing any initial impediment to complainants' contention on this point. See Gray, The Rule Against Perpetuities (4th ed.) § 633, p. 601, where Gray said 'When the expression which a testator uses is really ambiguous, and is fairly capable of two constructions, one of which would produce a legal result, and the other a result that would be bad for remoteness, it is a fair presumption that the testator meant to create a legal rather than an illegal interest.' * * *

In the case of a general power of appointment by will, however, the weight of authority counts the perpetuity period from the date of creation on the ground that since the donee cannot freely alienate the property during his life, he is not the practical owner thereof. A minority view disagrees with this position on the theory that the concept of actual ownership clouds the substance of the matter, which is that if the person having the power without the ownership may appoint to whomsoever he pleases at the time he exercises it, he is in the same position *in respect to the perpetuity* as if he were actually the owner. Thorndike, General Powers and Perpetuities, 27 Harv.L.Rev., pp. 705, 717. Also see Northern Trust Co. v. Porter, 368 Ill. 256, 13 N.E.2d 487, for leading citations on both positions.

Since this is a case of first impression, we have read with interest the authorities supporting the above positions. See Gray, General Testamentary Powers And The Rule Against Perpetuities, 26 Harv.L.Rev., p. 720; Thorndike, General Powers And Perpetuities, *supra*; Annot., 1 A.L.R. 374; and Northern Trust Co. v. Porter, *supra*. From this reading it appears that the early English cases in counting the perpetuity period did not distinguish between a general power to appoint by deed and will and a general power to appoint by will only and we think the cases following this position are the more persuasive.

In essence the majority jurisdictions characterize a general power of appointment by will as being in the nature of a special power, and, as such, a part of the creating instrument of the donor. They reach this result solely on the ground that because the donor has tied up ownership of the property until the donee's death, the restraint on alienation is sufficient to count the perpetuity period from the power's creation.

We think that this position misapprehends the fundamental concepts involved here. The law does not prohibit an estate being tied up for the life of any one individual, but prohibits only restraint beyond lives in being plus twenty-one years. See Thorndike, *supra*. When the donee exercises his power, he is at that time the practical owner thereof, for the purposes of the rule, as he can appoint to anyone of his choice as well as his own estate. Furthermore when he exercises the power he can create, unlike the case of a special power, estates entirely independent from those created or controlled by the donor, and so, as to the donee, the power is a general one. See Perpetuities In Perspective: Ending The Rule's Reign Of Terror, by W. Barton Leach, 65 Harv.L.Rev. 721.

Consequently, we hold the trust created by clause fourth of Mrs. Tilley's will pursuant to her general testamentary power of appointment is valid. We arrive at this conclusion not only because logic favors its adoption but also because we believe it is in line with the trend to obviate the technical harshness of the rule against perpetuities and decide cases on the substance of things. 6 American Law of Property §24.45 (1952), p. 118; 3 Restatement, Property §343 (1940), p. 1913; Union & New Haven Trust Co. v. Taylor, 133 Conn. 221, 50 A.2d 168. For a learned discussion of this problem, see Perpetuities In A Nutshell, 51 Harv.L.Rev. 638, and Perpetuities: The Nutshell Revisited, 78 Harv.L.Rev. 973, both being articles by W. Barton Leach.

⋆ ⋆ ⋆

CONDON, C. J., and POWERS, J., not participating.

Notes

The case provides an example of the relation back doctrine, its rationale, and both sides of the controversy over point of creation. The most significant issue is whether a general testamentary power should be treated as any special power under the Rule Against Perpetuities. The court's conclusion is that it should not be treated as such. Some states have adopted this approach by statute. *See, e.g.,* Del. Code Ann. tit. 25, §501 (effective June 19, 2019) (exercise by the donee of *any* power is point of creation for the Rule); S.D. Codified Laws §43-5-5 (2019); Wis. Stat. Ann. §700.16(1) (c) (2019) (only special powers of appointment are computed from the time of creation by the donor). However, the Uniform Probate Code §2-902(a) adopts principles of general property law, thus accepting the Second Restatement of Property §1.2, comment d, which provides for computing testamentary and special powers from creation by the donor. The argument may be made that, by adopting the approach of *Barrett*—that the period of the Rule should commence with exercise by the donee of a general testamentary power (and any general *inter vivos* power)—the court is simply applying a policy that will result in a less stringent Rule Against Perpetuities. *See generally* Melanie B. Leslie, *The Case Against Applying the Relation-Back Doctrine to the Exercise of General* Powers *of Appointment*, 14 CARDOZO L. REV. 219 (1992); Robert L. Fletcher, *Perpetuities: Basic Clarity, Muddled Reform*, 63 WASH. L. REV. 791 (1988); Lawrence M. Jones, *The Rule Against Perpetuities and Powers of Appointment: An Old Controversy Revived*, 54 IOWA L. REV. 456 (1968). If there is a violation of the Rule, analysis must then shift to what to do. Of consequence will be the nature of the power (general or special), the presence of a taker in default (if the power is special), and the willingness of a court to fashion its own remedy. The following case is illustrative of these issues.

Second National Bank of New Haven v. Harris Trust & Savings Bank

Connecticut Superior Court, New Haven County, 1971
29 Conn. Super. 275, 283 A.2d 226

SHEA, Judge.

* * *

In New Haven on April 21, 1922, Caroline Haven Trowbridge, a resident of that city, created an *inter vivos* trust with the plaintiff as trustee. The income of the trust was given to the settlor's daughter, Margaret Trowbridge Marsh, and she was also given a general testamentary power of appointment over one-half of the corpus. The remaining one-half, as well as the half subject to the power in default of its exercise, would be distributed to Margaret's surviving children or issue per stirpes or, if there were none, to another daughter of the settlor, Mary Brewster Murray, or her surviving issue per stirpes. During the life of the settlor, a power was reserved to 'revoke, modify or alter' the terms of the trust 'respecting the payment of income.' The settlor, Caroline, died in New Haven on June 26, 1941, without having exercised this power.

Margaret, the life tenant and donee of the testamentary power, a resident of Winnetka, Illinois, died on April 13, 1969, leaving a will purporting to exercise the power by creating another trust, giving the income to her daughter, Mary Marsh Washburne, for a period of thirty years. At that time the trust estate would be distributed to Mary, if living, or, if not, to her surviving children or their descendants per stirpes, with outright distribution at age twenty-one. On April 4, 1949, before she executed her will, Margaret had partially released her power of appointment, converting it into a special testamentary power by limiting its exercise to the benefit of the class described in subsection (2)(A) of § 811(f) of the Internal Revenue Code of 1939, as amended, 56 Stat. 942, which included her descendants.

Mary, the named beneficiary of the power of appointment as exercised, was born on October 25, 1929. As one of the two surviving children of Margaret, she would share equally with her brother, Charles Allen Marsh, the half of the trust created by Caroline subject to the power, in default of its exercise. If Margaret's exercise of the power under her will is fully effective, the defendant Harris Trust and Savings Bank, as executor and trustee would receive this half of the trust to pay the income to Mary for thirty years following her mother's death, and ultimately to distribute the corpus to Mary. If she did not live that long, upon her death the defendant trustee would make distribution to Mary's surviving children or their surviving descendants.

It appears that all of the living persons having any interest in the trust have been made parties. A guardian ad litem has been appointed to represent any unborn or undetermined persons who may have an interest and also to represent the five children of Mary, all of whom are minors.

* * *

The first problem is whether the exercise of the testamentary power of appointment by Margaret's will is invalid because of a claimed violation of the rule against perpetuities.

It is well established that a donee of a power of appointment, in exercising the power, acts as a mere conduit of the donor's bounty. 'Whenever such a power is in fact exercised, the validity of the appointment is determined by precisely the same rule as if the original testator, who created the power, had made in his own will the same provision in favor of the same appointee.' Bartlett v. Sears, 81 Conn. 34, 42, 70 A. 33, 36. 'The appointment is 'read back' into the instrument creating the power, as if the donee were filling in blanks in the donor's instrument.' 6 American Law of Property § 24.34.

So far as perpetuities are concerned, the period of the rule is reckoned from the date of creation of the power, not from the date of its exercise. Gray, Rule against Perpetuities (4th Ed.) § 515, p. 499. Where the power has been created by a will, the period is measured from the time of the death of the testator. Gray, op. cit. § 520; Simes & Smith, Future Interests (2d Ed.) § 1226. Where a deed is the source of the power, the date of delivery would ordinarily start the running of the period. Gray, loc. cit.; Simes & Smith, loc. cit.

In the case of *inter vivos* instruments, there is an exception for revocable transfers, for the reason that the policy of the rule is not violated where the grantor may at will terminate any future interests by revoking the grant. Where such an unconditional power of revocation is reserved, the period of perpetuities is calculated from the time the power of revocation ceased, usually at the death of the grantor unless the power was released earlier. 6 American Law of Property § 24.59; Gray, op. cit. § 524.1.

In this case, the defendants who seek to uphold the validity of the exercise of the power by Margaret's will claim that Caroline did retain a power to revoke the trust. The provision upon which they rely is paragraph (i) of the trust instrument, which reads as follows: '* * * as a measure of protection against possible contingencies, I hereby expressly reserve to myself power to revoke, modify or alter the terms hereof respecting the payment of income during my own life, by an instrument in writing, signed, dated and acknowledged, and delivered to the trustee.' It seems clear that a power 'to revoke, modify or alter the terms * * * respecting the payment of income' would not include a power to revoke the provisions for disposition of the principal of the trust. Such a partial power of revocation could affect only the life tenant, Margaret, during the life of the settlor, Caroline. Such a power would not qualify for the exception applicable to a full and unconditional power of revocation, because the remoteness of the future interests created could not be affected by any exercise of the power. 6 American Law of Property § 24.59.

Since the demise of our Connecticut Statute on Perpetuities in 1895, the common-law rule has been followed that no future interest is good unless it must vest, if at all, not later than twenty-one years after some life in being at the creation of the interest. Wilbur v. Portland Trust Co., 121 Conn. 535, 537, 186 A. 499; Cleaveland, Hewitt & Clark, Probate Law and Practice, §§ 446. 447. As applied to this case, the rule would bar any future interest which might not vest within twenty-one years after the life of some person in being on April 21, 1922, the date the trust was established. Since Mary was not born until October 25, 1929, she was not in being at the creation of the trust and her life cannot be taken as a measuring life under the rule against perpetuities. The only relevant life mentioned in the trust is that of Margaret, and, therefore, any valid future interest must vest no later than twenty-one years after her death on April 13, 1969.

In exercising the power of appointment, Margaret in her will used the language of an absolute gift to Mary of the income for thirty years and then a distribution to her of the principal of the trust. The next sentence adds the provision that upon Mary's death within the thirty-year period (or prior to the death of the testatrix, Margaret) the principal of the trust would be distributed to Mary's children or descendants of deceased children surviving her. Such unconditional words of gift would ordinarily be construed as creating a vested interest subject to defeasance upon the occurrence of the condition subsequent contained in the later clause. Howard v. Batchelder, 143 Conn. 328, 336, 122 A.2d 307, 310. 'If the conditional element is incorporated into the description of, or into the gift to, the remainder-man, then the remainder is contingent; but if, after words giving a vested interest, a clause is added divesting it, the remainder is vested.' Gary, op. cit. § 108; Howard v. Batchelder, *supra*, 334, 122 A.2d 307. Such exaltation of verbalism over substance has been criticized, but it is rigidly adhered to in the legalistic sophistry which comprises much of the lore of future interests. As it was once remarked, 'I am quite aware that this is all largely (a) matter of words, but so is much of the law of property; and unless we treat such formal distinctions as real, that law will melt away and leave not a rack behind.' Commissioner of Internal Revenue v. City Bank Farmers' Trust Co., 2 Cir., 74 F.2d 242, 247.

'An interest is 'vested' for purposes of the Rule when the following conditions exist: a. any condition precedent attached to the interest is satisfied, and b. the taker is ascertained, and c. where the interest is included in a gift to a class, the exact amount or fraction to be taken is determined.' 6 American Law of Property § 24.18. The language creating the gift to Mary imposes no condition precedent, but rather a condition subsequent, i.e. her death within thirty years after Margaret's death. Since the gift is to a named person the identity of the taker is established. The third requirement (c) is not applicable to a gift to an individual.

The construction of the gift of the remainder to Mary as vested rather than contingent is reinforced by the intermediate gift of the income to her. 6 American Law of Property § 24.19. A gift in favor of a named individual has historically been treated as vested and not subject to the rule unless it is expressly subject to a condition precedent. Restatement, 4 Property § 370, comment g. The preference of the law for vested rather than contingent interests certainly dictates such a construction in this case, where even the grammatical form of a condition subsequent has been observed by the draftsman. That the use of a condition subsequent rather than precedent is often the touchstone of validity in perpetuities cases is demonstrated by the following textbook illustrations: 'Case 20. T bequeaths a fund in trust to pay the income to A for life and then to pay the principal to such of A's children as shall reach the age of twenty-five. Reaching the age of twenty-five is a condition precedent attached to the gift to the children. Assuming that A survives the testator and can have further children, an after-born child of A can reach twenty-five at a date later than twenty-one years after lives in being at T's death. Therefore the remainder to A's children is void. Case 21. T bequeaths a fund in trust to pay the income to A for life and then to pay the principal to A's children, but if all of A's children die under the age of twenty-five, then to pay the principal to B. Again the condition is too remote. But it is a condition subsequent. The remainder to the children is vested subject to divestment upon a remote condition; the divesting contingency is void; therefore the children have an indefeasibly vested remainder.' 6 American Law of Property § 24.19, p. 60. It is well recognized that the form of language used rather than the substance of the condition is determinative as to whether the condition is precedent or subsequent. 5 American Law of Property § 21.31, p. 177. 'Whether a remainder is vested or contingent depends upon the language employed.' Gray, op. cit. § 108.

In a case similar in many respects to this one, an appointment was made to a named great-grandnephew, a year old at the time of exercise of the power, by the will of the donee of a power created by an *inter vivos* transfer, of income until age twenty-five, and then of principal when he attained that age; in the event of his death prior thereto, the principal would be distributed to the boy's father, who was named. It was held, despite the use of some contingent language, that the remainder to the great-grandnephew was valid under the rule, because it might be construed as vested subject to defeasance upon death prior to age twenty-five. The gift over to the father was ruled invalid as in violation of the terms of the power. Dean v. First National Bank, 217 Or. 340, 341 P.2d 512.

The gift to Mary's children, following the same verbal formalism, is a contingent remainder, because it is expressly subject to the condition that they survive their

854 · CREATION, CLASSIFICATION, AND UTILIZATION OF TRUSTS

mother and that she not live until termination of the thirty-year trust. White v. Smith, 87 Conn. 663, 669–673, 89 A. 272. It is also contingent because, as a gift to a class (surviving children and surviving descendants of deceased children), the fractional interest of each member of the class cannot be ascertained until the contingency (Mary's death) happens. Gray, op. cit. §§ 369–375.

'It is well established that the rule against perpetuities does not affect vested interests, even though enjoyment may be postponed beyond the period of the rule.' Connecticut Trust & Safe Deposit Co. v. Hollister, 74 Conn. 228, 232, 50 A. 750; Restatement, 4 Property § 386, comment j. It would not operate therefore, to invalidate either the gift of the income to Mary for life or thirty years or the gift of the remainder after the thirty years. Colonial Trust Co. v. Brown, 105 Conn. 261, 272, 135 A. 555; Bartlett v. Sears, 81 Conn. 34, 44, 70 A. 33. Both of these gifts vested in interest at the death of Margaret within the period of the rule, and the postponement of enjoyment beyond the period of the rule would not invalidate them. Howard v. Batchelder, 143 Conn. 328, 336, 122 A.2d 307.

The permissible duration of a trust in not governed by the rule against perpetuities. Restatement, 4 Property § 378; Gray, op. cit. §§ 232–246. It is no objection, therefore, that Mary's life estate may last beyond the period of the rule. It is also of no significance that her remainder interest may be defeated by her death, which may occur after that time. A vested remainder is exempt from the rule even though it may be subject to complete defeasance. Restatement, 4 Property § 370. The rule does bar the contingent remainder to Mary's children because it may vest more than twenty-one years after the death of Margaret, whose life must be taken as the measuring life. This result, abhorrent to the rule, would occur if Mary should die more than twenty-one but less than thirty years after her mother.

It is argued that the court should apply the cy pres doctrine to save the remainder to Mary's children by reducing the period of the trust to a maximum of twenty-one years. In a similar case, the Supreme Court of Hawaii expressly applied this doctrine to revise the testator's will as suggested. In re Estate of Chun Quan Yee Hop, 469 P.2d 183 (Haw.). This judicial innovation has received favorable comment, but such a change in the established law of this state ought to be reserved for our Supreme Court. The earlier case of Edgerly v. Barker, 66 N.H. 434, 31 A. 900, in which the cy pres doctrine was first applied by any court in a perpetuities situation, is the subject of a lengthy condemnation by Professor Gray. Gray, op. cit. §§ 857–893.

It is also claimed that General Statutes § 45-95 is applicable. This statute embodies the so-called 'second look' doctrine, and reads as follows: 'In applying the rule against perpetuities to an interest in real or personal property limited to take effect at or after the termination of one or more life estates in, or lives of, persons in being when the period of said rule commences to run, the validity of the interest shall be determined on the basis of facts existing at the termination of such one or more life estates or lives. For the purpose of this section, an interest which must terminate not later than the death of one or more persons is a life estate although it may terminate at an earlier time.' This statute permits the validity of the interests created to be determined on the basis of the facts existing upon the death of Margaret, the measuring life under the rule against perpetuities. In fact, this has been the reference point for the court's consideration of the validity of the interests involved, because, apart from the statute, the actual exercise of the power of appointment, and not the possibility of its exercise in some other manner, is the criterion under the rule. Gray, op. cit. § 510. 'In the case of all powers of appointment * * * facts can be considered which exist at the time of the exercise of the power.' 6 American Law of Property § 24.24, p. 77. The conclusion that the remainder to Mary's children is invalid would not be changed unless the statute were construed to authorize a second look after Mary's life, an interpretation which its language does not support.

Another statute relied upon is General Statutes § 45-96, which reads as follows: 'If an interest in real or personal property would violate the rule against perpetuities as modified by section 45-95 because such interest is contingent upon any person attaining or failing to attain an age in excess of twenty-one, the age contingency shall be reduced to twenty-one as to all persons subject to the same age contingency.' It seems too clear for argument that the remainder to Mary's children is not 'contingent upon any person attaining or failing to attain an age in excess of twenty-one.' Section 45-96 is not applicable.

'If future interests created by any instrument are avoided by the Rule against Perpetuities, the prior interests become what they would have been had the limitation of the future estate been omitted from the instrument.' Gray, op. cit. § 247. Obviously, the consequences which follow upon the invalidity of a subsequent interest depend upon the intention of the donor. Restatement, 2 Property § 228; 5 American Law of Property § 21.48. 'A presumption is generally recognized that the precedent interest becomes indefeasible as a result of the ineffectiveness of the divesting interest * * *.' 5 American Law of Property § 21.48; Restatement, 2 Property § 229. 'But it will take clear language to show an intention to have the determining limitation taken separately from the remote gift. * * * If the prior estate be a fee simple the void conditional limitation cannot, it is submitted, thus operate as a contingent termination of the prior estate.' Gray, op. cit. § 250. 'Where a divesting interest is void, the interest which would otherwise have been divested becomes absolute.' 6 American Law of Property § 24.47, p. 124.

A gift of trust principal payable at an age beyond the period of the rule, subject to a limitation over in the event of nonattainment of that age, is a common occasion for the application of these principles to result in an indefeasibly vested remainder. *Id.*, p. 125 (Case 72); Restatement, 4 Property § 384, comment g. 'When a subsequent condition or limitation over is void, * * * the estate becomes vested in the first taker, discharged of the condition or limitation over, according to the terms in which it was granted or devised; if for life, it then takes effect as a life estate; if in fee, then as a fee simple absolute.' Howe v. Hodge, 152 Ill. 252, 279, 38 N.E. 1083, 1090; Safe Deposit & Trust Co. v. Sheehan, 169 Md. 93, 109, 179 A. 536.

Under these principles, the gift of the remainder to Mary becomes indefeasibly vested because of the invalidation of the contingent remainder to her children.

In summary, the court has concluded that Mary has a valid income interest, in the half of the trust subject to the power of appointment, for thirty years and is then entitled to receive the principal. If she dies before then, the principal would be distributed to her estate, because her remainder has become indefeasibly vested.

Accordingly, it is ordered that the plaintiff trustee turn over to the defendant Harris Trust and Savings Bank one-half of the trust, to be held by that defendant to pay the income (including accumulated income) to the defendant Mary Marsh Washburne until April 13, 1999, when the principal shall be distributed to her. In the event of her earlier death, the principal shall be distributed to her estate. The court's advice is not sought with respect to any question pertaining to the remaining half of the trust fund.

* * *

Judgment may enter accordingly.

Notes

The case distinguishes between irrevocability (corpus) and revocability (income) in reference to creation and the relation back doctrine. According to the Connecticut court, in either case, we must compute from creation by the donor, in light of the facts at exercise by the donee. Commentators have suggested that the doctrine of marshaling of assets could have saved the appointment, *see, e.g., Second Restatement (Second) of Property* §§ 22.1 & 22.2 (1986), and, of course, if the thirty years could have been reduced to twenty-one, there would have been a simpler solution, *see, e.g., In re* Estate of Kreuzer, 243 A.D.2d 207, 674 N.Y.S.2d 505 (1998). Of course, the best remedy is proper drafting by competent attorneys. But if in doubt, attorneys should utilize savings clauses as a remedy for all types of Rule violations.

E. Savings Clauses

Many publications offer drafting advice to attorneys preparing estate planning documents, to include trusts and wills. *See, e.g.,* Dwight F. Bickel & Michael T. Flannery, Living Trusts: Forms and Practice (Matthew Bender 2019–2020); L. Paul Hood, Jr., *How to Avoid Common Sources of Drafting Errors*, 45 Est. Plan. 32 (2018); Kathryn D. Betts & Kyle R. Jaep, *The Dawn of Fully Automated Contract Drafting: Machine Learning Breaths New Life into a Decades-Old Promise,* 15 Duke L. & Tech. Rev. 216 (2017). However, the temptation to be simple is easily forsaken, and, hence, the prudent drafter would be wise to include a savings clause in any estate plan containing a future interest. Such a clause becomes "operative only if some part of the disposition violates the [Rule and] directs the disposition of the offending interest in such a manner as to prevent such violation." Mark Reutlinger, Wills, Trusts, and Estates: Essential Terms and Concepts 206 (1993). One of the earliest and most often used of savings clauses may be found at W. Barton Leach & James K. Logan, *Perpetuities: A Standard Savings Clause to Avoid Violations of the Rule,* 74 Harv. L. Rev. 1141 (1961). For more recent suggestions, see

DAVID M. BECKER, PERPETUITIES AND ESTATE PLANNING 133–84 (1993). Professor Jesse Dukeminier offers an example of such a clause:

> Notwithstanding any other provision in this instrument, this trust shall terminate, if it has not previously terminated, 21 years after the death of the survivor of the beneficiaries of the trust living at the date this instrument becomes effective. In case of such termination the then remaining principal and undistributed income of the trust shall be distributed to the then income beneficiaries in the same proportions as they were, at the time of termination, entitled to receive the income. The term "beneficiaries" includes persons originally named as beneficiaries in this instrument as well as persons, living at the date this instrument becomes effective, subsequently named as beneficiaries by a donee of a power of appointment over the trust assets exercising such power.

ROBERT H. SITKOFF & JESSE DUKEMINIER, WILLS, TRUSTS, AND ESTATES 901 (10th ed. 2017).

F. Reformation Devices

The preceding material contains references to reform of the harsh consequences of the Rule, but they are piecemeal and often parochial. England, on the other hand, has been quick to reform the Rule. *See generally* Robert J. Lynn, *Perpetuities Reform: An Analysis of Developments in England and the United States*, 113 U. PA. L. REV. 508 (1965). Until very recently, domestic courts and legislatures were convinced that the Rule was a staple in American public policy, and, thus, every attempt should be made to alleviate any "mistakes" made by drafters of long-term trusts. Scholars and commentators offered multiple views as to how public policy may be served and, at the same time, how testamentary intent may be fostered. *See, e.g.*, Paul G. Haskell, *A Proposal for a Simple and Socially Effective Rule Against Perpetuities*, 66 N.C. L. REV. 545 (1988); Lawrence W. Waggoner, *Perpetuity Reform*, 81 MICH. L. REV. 1718 (1983); W. Barton Leach, *Perpetuities in Perspective: Ending the Rule's Reign of Terror*, 65 HARV. L. REV. 721 (1952). Yet, even amidst the reform movement, there was an appeal to drafters of legal documents to draft in conformity with the requirements of the orthodox Rule. *See, e.g.*, Robert J. Lynn, *Perpetuities Literacy for the 21st Century*, 50 OHIO ST. L.J. 219 (1989). What follows is a list of reformation devices to validate interests that otherwise violate the Rule.

1. Wait and See

Pennsylvania was the first state to adopt a statute allowing actual, rather than possible, events to measure the Rule. *See* ROBERT J. LYNN, THE MODERN RULE AGAINST PERPETUITIES 10(1966). However, additional states utilize actuality, either by statute or common law. *See* IOWA CODE ANN. § 558.68 (West 2019); 33 ME. REV. STAT. ANN. §§ 101–106 (2019); Murphy Exploration Prod. Co. v. Sun Operating Ltd. P'Ship, 747 So. 2d 260 (Miss. 1999) (for Mississippi); Great Bay Sch. & Training Ctr.,

559 A.2d 1329 (N.H. 1989) (for New Hampshire); Ohio Rev. Code Ann. § 2131.08 (West 2019); 20 Pa. Cons. Stat. Ann. § 6104 (West 2019); Vt. Stat. Ann. tit. 27, § 501 (2019).

The point of Wait and See is to allow for actual events to occur, even though, standing at the creation of the interest, there may well be a possibility of remote vesting that violates the Rule. If a settlor were to provide, in an *inter vivos* irrevocable trust, one million dollars for his children for life, and then to his grandchildren surviving, there could be a Rule violation. The violation would occur because the settlor could have additional children, whom the grandchildren survive, and one of the survivor's children could be born after the creation of the trust and live longer than twenty-one years after any life in being, bringing about the vesting in the surviving grandchildren. But under Wait and See, the courts allow actual events to be considered. Therefore, the trust commences as valid because we are allowed to wait and see what actually happens. According to one proponent of Wait and See, the court should use all of the lives in being and make them the measuring lives for the duration of the trust. If the trust actually vests within this period, then everyone is satisfied, even though, at the creation of the interest, there was the definite possibility of invalidity. Any continuance of the trust beyond this period is void. *See* Jesse Dukeminier, *Perpetuities: The Measuring Lives,* 85 Colum. L. Rev. 1648, 1656 (1985); 20 Pa. Cons. Stat. § 6104(b) (2019).

Like the Wait and See doctrine, Second Look lessens the possibility of a Rule violation by allowing for actual facts to be considered in approximating the Rule. But the Second Look doctrine involves powers of appointment, hence, in considering any violation of the Rule, we are allowed to use facts as they exist at the time of the exercise of the power by the donee. Thus, under this approach, we do not have to be bound by the creation of the power when the power is a general testamentary power or any special power; this is the case under the relation back doctrine. Instead, we can take into account the facts as they exist at the time of the exercise of the power. But note, there is still the possibility that the power could violate the Rule, even though we are looking at the actual facts as they existed at the time of the exercise. Unlike USRAP, there is no provision that allows us to use cy pres to fix the violation, unless there is an independent cy pres provision applicable within the state.

2. Cy Pres

By adopting a cy pres statute, a state allows the courts to give effect to the general intent of the settlor of a trust whenever that general intent may be discerned. For example, the Missouri statute provides, in part:

> When any limitation or provision violates the rule against perpetuities or a rule or policy corollary thereto and reformation would more closely approximate the primary purpose or scheme of the grantor, settlor or testator than total invalidity of the limitation or provision, upon the timely filing of a petition in a court of competent jurisdiction, by an party in interest,

all parties in interest having been served by process, the limitation or provision shall be reformed, if possible, to the extent necessary to avoid violation of the rule or policy and, as so reformed, shall be valid and effective.

Mo. Rev. Stat. Ann. § 442.555(2) (West 2015).

In addition to Missouri, Texas has adopted Cy Pres. *See* Tex. Prop. Code Ann. § 5.043 (2019). States like New York have adopted specific cy pres contingencies, such as ones that reduce offending age contingencies. *See, e.g., In re* Estate of Kreuzer, 243 A.D.2d 207, 674 N.Y.S.2d 505 (1998); N.Y. Est., Powers & Trusts L. §§ 9-1.2 & 9-1.3 (2019). Traditionally, states liked to combine Wait and See and Cy Pres to allow for modification at the end of the period of waiting for actual events to occur. *See* Jesse Dukeminier, *Kentucky Perpetuity Law Restated and Reformed,* 49 Ky. L.J. 3 (1960). Seeking more certainty, scholars crafted a better version of Wait and See, which is modeled on the English model of perpetuity reform. It is called the Uniform Statutory Rule Against Perpetuities (2003) (USRAP).

3. Uniform Statutory Rule Against Perpetuities (2003) (USRAP)

The Uniform Statutory Rule Against Perpetuities, now adopted as part of the Uniform Probate Code, § 9, is similar to Wait and See in that the statute does two things: (1) if all interests vest within a life in being plus twenty-one years (the common law rule), all is well; but (2) the statute allows for a fixed 90-year period in which all of the interests have an opportunity to vest, even though there may be a possibility, standing at the creation of the interest, that not all interests will vest within the Rule. At the end of the 90-year period, any interest that has not vested is reformed by the court to best comply with the intention of the settlor.

Drafters in states that retain the Rule Against Perpetuities modified by USRAP will still need to know the intricacies of the Rule for determining when the interest commences and when it vests. The advantage, however, is that no interest may violate the Rule since, if, at the end of the 90 year period, there can still be a violation, the trustee may use cy pres to modify the trust. For further explanation see, *e.g.,* Lynn Foster, *Fifty-One Flowers: Post-Perpetuities War Law and Arkansas's Adoption of USRAP,* 9 UALR L. Rev. 411 (2007); Mary Louise Fellows & Gregory S. Alexander, *Forty Years of Codification of Estates and Trusts Law: Lessons for the Next Generation,* 40 Ga. L. Rev. 1049 (2006).

Uniform Probate Code (2019)

§ 2-901. Statutory Rule Against Perpetuities.

(a) [**Validity of Nonvested Property Interest.**] A nonvested property interest is invalid unless:

(1) when the interest is created, it is certain to vest or terminate no later than 21 years after the death of an individual then alive; or

(2) the interest either vests or terminates within 90 years after its creation.

(b) [Validity of General Power of Appointment Subject to a Condition Precedent.] A general power of appointment not presently exercisable because of a condition precedent is invalid unless:

(1) when the power is created, the condition precedent is certain to be satisfied or becomes impossible to satisfy no later than 21 years after the death of an individual then alive; or

(2) the condition precedent either is satisfied or becomes impossible to satisfy within 90 years after its creation.

(c) [Validity of Nongeneral or Testamentary Power of Appointment.] A nongeneral power of appointment or a general testamentary power of appointment is invalid unless:

(1) when the power is created, it is certain to be irrevocably exercised or otherwise to terminate no later than 21 years after the death of an individual then alive; or

(2) the power is irrevocably exercised or otherwise terminates within 90 years after its creation.

(d) [Possibility of Post-death Child Disregarded.] In determining whether a nonvested property interest or a power of appointment is valid under subsection (a)(1), (b)(1), or (c)(1), the possibility that a child will be born to an individual after the individual's death is disregarded.

(e) [Effect of Certain "Later-of" Type Language.] If, in measuring a period from the creation of a trust or other property arrangement, language in a governing instrument (i) seeks to disallow the vesting or termination of any interest or trust beyond, (ii) seeks to postpone the vesting or termination of any interest or trust until, or (iii) seeks to operate in effect in any similar fashion upon, the later of (A) the expiration of a period of time not exceeding 21 years after the death of the survivor of specified lives in being at the creation of the trust or other property arrangement or (B) the expiration of a period of time that exceeds or might exceed 21 years after the death of the survivor of lives in being at the creation of the trust or other property arrangement, that language is inoperative to the extent it produces a period of time that exceeds 21 years after the death of the survivor of the specified lives.

§ 2-902. When Nonvested Property Interest or Power of Appointment Created.

(a) Except as provided in subsections (b) and (c) and in Section 2-905(a), the time of creation of a nonvested property interest or a power of appointment is determined under general principles of property law.

(b) For purposes of Subpart 1 of this Part, if there is a person who alone can exercise a power created by a governing instrument to become the unqualified beneficial owner of (i) a nonvested property interest or (ii) a property interest subject to a power of appointment described in Section 2-901(b) or (c), the nonvested property interest or power of appointment is created when the power to become the unqualified beneficial owner terminates. [For purposes of Subpart 1 of this Part, a joint power with respect to community property or to marital property under the Uniform Marital Property Act held by individuals married to each other is a power exercisable by one person alone.]

(c) For purposes of Subpart 1 of this Part, a nonvested property interest or a power of appointment arising from a transfer of property to a previously funded trust or other existing property arrangement is created when the nonvested property interest or power of appointment in the original contribution was created.

§ 2-903. Reformation.

Upon the petition of an interested person, a court shall reform a disposition in the manner that most closely approximates the transferor's manifested plan of distribution and is within the 90 years allowed by Section 2-901(a)(2), 2-901(b)(2), or 2-901(c)(2) if:

(1) a nonvested property interest or a power of appointment becomes invalid under Section 2-901 (statutory rule against perpetuities);

(2) a class gift is not but might become invalid under Section 2-901 (statutory rule against perpetuities) and the time has arrived when the share of any class member is to take effect in possession or enjoyment; or

(3) a nonvested property interest that is not validated by Section 2-901(a)(1) can vest but not within 90 years after its creation.

G. Abolition of the Rule

Delaware Code (2019)

Title 25, § 503. Rule against perpetuities.

(a) No interest created in real property held in trust shall be void by reason of the common-law rule against perpetuities or any common-law rule limiting the duration of noncharitable purpose trusts, and no interest created in personal property held in trust shall be void by reason of any rule, whether the common-law rule against perpetuities, any common-law rule limiting the duration of noncharitable purpose trusts, or otherwise.

(b) In this State, the rule against perpetuities for real property held in trust is that at the expiration of 110 years from the later of the date on which a parcel of real property or an interest in real property is added to or purchased by a trust or the date the trust became irrevocable, such parcel or interest, if still held in such trust, shall be distributed in accordance with the trust instrument regarding distribution of such property upon termination of the trust as though termination occurred at that time, or if no such provisions exist, to the persons then entitled to receive the income of the trust in proportion to the amount of the income so receivable by such beneficiaries, or in equal shares if specific proportions are not specified in the trust instrument. In the event that the trust instrument does not provide for distribution upon termination and there are no income beneficiaries of the trust, such parcel or interest shall be distributed to such then living persons who are then determined to be the trustor's or testator's distributees by the application of the intestacy laws of this State then in effect governing the distribution of intestate real property as though the trustor or testator had died at that particular time, intestate, a resident of this State, and owning the property so distributable.

This rule shall not apply to the following trusts, all of which may be perpetual:

(1) A trust for the benefit of 1 or more charitable organizations as described in §§ 170(c), 2055(a) and 2522(a) of the United States Internal Revenue Code of 1986 (Title 26 of the United States Code)[26 U.S.C. §§ 170(c), 2055(a) and 2522(a)], or under any similar statute;

(2) A trust created by an employer as part of a stock bonus plan, pension plan, disability or death benefit plan or profit sharing plan for the exclusive benefit of some or all of its employees, to which contributions are made by such employer or employees, or both, for the purpose of distributing to such employees the earnings or the principal, or both earnings and principal, of the fund held in trust;

(3) A statutory trust formed under Chapter 38 of Title 12 for which a certificate of statutory trust is on file in the office of the Secretary of State; or

(4) A trust of real or personal property created for the perpetual care of cemeteries pursuant to the provisions of subchapter IV of Chapter 35 of Title 12.

(c) For purposes of this rule against perpetuities, trusts created by the exercise of a power of appointment, whether nongeneral or general, and whether by will, deed or other instrument, shall be deemed to have become irrevocable by the trustor or testator on the date on which such exercise became irrevocable. Donors, not donees, of nongeneral powers of appointment and donees exercising, not donors of, general powers of appointment, shall be deemed the trustors or testators for purposes of distributions to the trustor's or testator's distributees pursuant to subsection (b) of this section. Notwithstanding the foregoing, in the case of a power of appointment described in § 504 of this title as a "first power," and subject to § 504(a) of this title, trusts created by the exercise of the power of appointment, whether by will, deed or other instrument, shall be deemed to have become irrevocable by the trustor or testator on the date on which the first power was created.

(d) The rule contained in this section is subject to §§ 501 and 502 of this title concerning powers of appointment.

* * *

Rhode Island General Laws (2019)

§ 34-11-38. Rule against perpetuities reform

The common law rule against perpetuities shall no longer be deemed to be in force and/or of any effect in this state, provided, the provisions of this section shall not be construed to invalidate or modify the terms of any interest which would have been valid prior to the effective date of this act, and, provided further, that the provisions of this section shall apply to both legal and equitable interests.

Notes

The earlier Rule reformation devices of Wait and See, and then Cy Pres, offered little challenge to the authority of the Rule Against Perpetuities in American law; they were simply corrective measures. But when the Uniform Statutory Rule Against Perpetuities was drafted and enacted in so many states, the prohibitions inherent in lives in being and measuring lives ceased. Drafters of wills and *inter vivos* trusts were able to rely upon the assurance that an interest crafted into a document would last at least ninety years, long after anyone could remember having a claim to the trust corpus. Professor Jesse Dukeminier was among the first to predict that, with the USRAP, the abolishment of the Rule Against Perpetuities was close at hand. *See* Jesse Dukeminier, *The Uniform Statutory Rule Against Perpetuities: Ninety Years in Limbo*, 34 UCLA L. Rev. 1023, 1025–27 (1987). Other commentators suggest that the Rule's demise results from the desire to avoid estate taxation. *See, e.g.*, Ira Mark Bloom, *The GST Tax Tail is Killing the Rule Against Perpetuities*, Tax Notes (Apr. 24, 2000); Joel C. Dobris, *The Death of the Rule Against Perpetuities, or the RAP Has No Friends*, 35 Real Prop., Prob. & Trust J. 601 (2000); Angela M. Vallario, *Death by a Thousand Cuts: The Rule Against Perpetuities*, 25 J. Legis. 141 (1999). For some states, the rationale for abolishment may be to provide a mechanism to foster "dynasty" trusts, which pay income to beneficiaries forever. *See* Joel C. Dobris, *Changes in the Role and the Form of the Trust at the New Millennium, or, We Don't Have to Think of England Anymore*, 62 Alb. L. Rev. 543 (1998). All of the beneficiaries and the settlor could remain in a state retaining the Rule, but if the trust is established within a state that has abolished the Rule, a proper dynasty trust may exist in perpetuity. *See* Stewart E. Sterk, *Asset Protection Trusts: Trust Law's Race to the Bottom?*, 85 Cornell L. Rev. 1035 (2000); Verner F. Chaffin, *Georgia's Proposed Dynasty Trust: Giving the Dead Too Much Control*, 35 Ga. L. Rev. 1 (2000).

The Rule arose from a public policy focused on providing each generation with the ability to gift property without the restraint of preceding generations. The Rule fostered marketability, taxation of large wealth accumulations, addressing present circumstances, and in all of these circumstances, limiting dead hand control. In wondering about the future of the Rule in American law, the late Professor Jesse Dukeminier liked to quote from a comment allegedly made by Alexis Tocqueville: "What is the most important for democracy is not that great fortunes should not exist, but that great fortunes should not remain in the same hands. In that way there are rich men, but they do not form a class." Melvin L. Oliver, Thomas M. Shapiro & Julie E. Press, *Them That's Got Shall Get: Inheritance and Achievement in Wealth Accumulation*, in The Politics of Wealth and Inequality 73–74 (Richard E. Ratcliff, Melvin L. Oliver & Thomas M. Shapiro eds., 1995).

Chapter 8

Planning for Incapacity

Tool Bar

The final chapter of this casebook returns to the Family Affair raised in the first chapter. Recall that an aging woman has just lost her husband of many years and her daughters are concerned that she has begun to exhibit indications of early dementia. One of the daughters raises the issue of bringing her mother to live with her, her husband, and their three children. Such a move would permit the daughter to manage her mother's safety and personal care, but it would have consequences for the daughter's family. Alternatives would include permitting the mother to remain in her home, perhaps with a caretaker, or moving the mother to an assisted living facility. However, the costs associated with assisted living can be very high, "from $55,000 to $75,000 a year and up to $180,000 annually for nursing care." Russell N. Adler, Peter J. Strauss & Regina Kiperman, *America's Long-Term Care Crisis*, 153 Trusts & Ests. 44, 44–45 (July 2013). Medicare does not pay for long term care and private payments can exceed $7,000 per month for home care, or $16,000 per month in a nursing home. Brian Andrew Tully, *Wealth or Health?*, 157 Trusts & Ests. 34 (2018). Few persons think to have long term care insurance, so what is a family to do?

The daughter's dilemma is associated with the aging of America: "78 percent of middle-aged adults believe that they'll be responsible for caring for an aging family member." Karen Clegler Hansen, *The Modern Family*, 152 TRUSTS & ESTS. 18 (Aug. 2013). Moreover, the Department of Health and Human Services notes: "The population age 65 and over has increased from 37.2 million in 2006 to 49.2 million in 2016 (a 33% increase) and is projected to almost double to 98 million in 2060. By 2040, there will be about 82.3 million older persons, over twice their number in 2000. Administration for Community Living, Administration on Aging, 2017 Profile of Older Americans, at 3 (Apr. 2018), at https://acl.gov/sites/default/files /Aging%20and%20Disability%20in%20America/2017OlderAmericansProfile.pdf (accessed Aug. 8, 2019). "[T]he population age 65 and over numbered 49.2 million in 2016 (the most recent year for which data are available). They represented 15.2% of the population, about one in every seven Americans." *Id.* at 2. And deaths related to dementia-related illnesses have increased 145% from 2007–2017. Letha Sgritta McDowell, *Signs Your Client has Dementia*, 158 TRUSTS & EST. 55 (July 2019).

In past generations, wills, trusts, and non-probate transfers permitted persons to transfer wealth to succeeding generations. While this remains true, the issues discussed in the preceding chapters must now be adapted to permit aging property owners to simultaneously plan for their own incapacity during the last decades of their ever-increasing lives. As human longevity has lengthened, the issue now is not so much how to dispense wealth to succeeding generations but, rather, how to preserve enough wealth to live comfortably, how to anticipate disruptions caused by dementia, and of course, eventually, how to provide for causes and family that will survive.

VIRGINIA MORRIS
HOW TO CARE FOR AGING PARENTS
2 (1996)

Although it can become too late quite suddenly, it is never too soon to talk to your parent about the future—her medical care, housing, finances and personal concerns. Obviously if your mother has been diagnosed with cancer or emphysema, these talks are urgent. But even if she is still relatively healthy and independent, discussing her future is vital. Many preparations, such as buying long-term care insurance or getting on a wait list for a nursing home, must be done well in advance. And you need to know how she wants things handled if she grows too sick or frail to handle them on her own.

Discussing the future also helps prepare your family emotionally for what may come. If your father is encouraged now to explore the possibility of moving out of his house, it will be easier for him to make the move if it becomes necessary. And these talks give your parent and family members a chance to air their worries and concerns, to reassure one another, and to learn the truth about any haunting questions. If your mother has been diagnosed with cancer, for example, she may be secretly terrified that she will be in constant pain or be left to die alone in a hospital room. When you create a context within which she can voice such concerns, you can help her learn about pain control and explore various in-home nursing services. And she can be reassured that you will be there for her throughout the time that remains.

Id.

I. Planning Options

A. Making Arrangements

In planning for arrangements upon death, it is important that relevant, personal information, including a list of assets, be available to guide family members and successor trustees in carrying out intentions. The following form serves as an example.[1]

Information for Heirs and Family

In the event of our deaths, or if at any time we should become incapacitated and unable to manage our own affairs, the following information is provided to assist our family (and whenever we refer to an asset as being "owned," it should be understood that we are including property held in a Living Trust established by us):

Notice:

Under each category shown in the form, you may wish to add additional entries as deemed appropriate.

NOTIFICATIONS

In the event of our deaths, please notify the following:

Name   Telephone/Email

_____   _____

_____   _____

_____   _____

_____   _____

_____   _____

LOCATION OF IMPORTANT PAPERS

Location of Last Will and Testament: _____

Location of Trust Agreement: _____

Location of Birth and/or Baptismal Certificates: _____

Location of Marriage Certificate: _____

Location of Military Service Records: _____

---

1. Dwight F. Bickel & Michael T. Flannery, Living Trusts: Forms and Practice, at § 7.07, 7-115 (Matthew Bender, 2019).

Location of Educational Records: _____

LocationofImportantFamilyHistoryInformation:_____

Location of Other Important Papers: _____

LIST OF PASSWORDS FOR ELECTRONIC ACCOUNTS

_____   _____

_____   _____

_____   _____

CHECKING AND SAVINGS ACCOUNTS (Identify Separate Property Accounts)

Bank Name: _____

Branch: _____

Account No(s): _____

Bank Name: _____

Branch: _____

Account No(s): _____

SAFE DEPOSIT BOXES

Bank Name: _____

Branch: _____

Box No(s): _____

Bank Name: _____

Branch: _____

Box No(s): _____

BROKER & MUTUAL FUNDS ACCOUNTS (Identify Separate Property Accounts)

Firm Name: _____

Address: _____

Acct. No(s): _____

Contact Person: _____

Firm Name: _____

Address: _____

Acct. No(s): _____

Contact Person: _____

STOCK & BOND CERTIFICATES

Company/Issuer: _____

Location Where Kept: _____

Company/Issuer: _____

Location Where Kept: _____

LIFE INSURANCE

Insurance Company: _____

Policy No. _____

Insured: _____

Face Amount of Policy: $_____

Place Policy is Kept: _____

Agent or Contact Person: _____

Insurance Company: _____

Policy No. _____

Insured: _____

Face Amount of Policy: $_____

Place Policy is Kept: _____

Agent or Contact Person: _____

ANNUITY CONTRACTS

Insurance Company: _____

Contract No. _____

Annuitant: _____

Face Amount: $_____

Place Contract is Kept: _____

Agent or Contact Person: _____

Insurance Company: _____

Contract No. _____

Annuitant: _____

Face Amount: $_____

Place Contract is Kept: _____

Agent or Contact Person: _____

OWNED REAL ESTATE (Identify Separate Property Parcels)

PERSONAL RESIDENCE

Property Location: _____

Mortgage Holder (if any): _____

Property Insurance Carried by: _____

Place Where Property Records are Kept: _____

OTHER REAL ESTATE

Property Location: _____

Mortgage Holder (if any): _____

Property Insurance Carried by: _____

Place Where Property Records are Kept: _____

RECEIVABLES (Identify Separate Property Assets)

REAL ESTATE CONTRACTS, MORTGAGES, AND DEEDS OF TRUST

Due From: _____

Type of Security Instrument: _____

Held for Collection at: _____

Escrow/Collection Acct. No. _____

Location of Personal Records: _____

Due From: _____

Type of Security Instrument: _____

Held for Collection at: _____

Escrow/Collection Acct. No. _____

Location of Personal Records: _____

UNSECURED NOTES RECEIVABLE

Due From: _____

Held for Collection at: _____

Escrow/Collection Acct. No. _____

Location of Original Note and Personal Records: _____

Due From: _____

Held for Collection at: _____

Escrow/Collection Acct. No. _____

Location of Original Note and Personal Records: _____

BUSINESS INTERESTS (Private Corporations, Partnerships, Proprietorships)

Name: _____

Location: _____

Type of Business: _____

Partners or Principal Associates: _____

OTHER INVESTMENTS

Description & Location: _____

Description & Location: _____

MOTOR VEHICLES AND MOBILE HOMES

Year _____ Make & Model: _____

Lienholder (if any): _____

Year _____ Make & Model: _____

Lienholder (if any): _____

OTHER IMPORTANT PROPERTY (Identify Separate Property Assets)

Description: _____

Location (if not at personal residence): _____

Description: _____

Location (if not at personal residence): _____

UNPAID DEBTS AND LOANS (Other than Ordinary Monthly Bills and Mortgage Loans)

Creditor: _____

Address: _____

Account/Loan No. _____

OTHER PERSONAL INFORMATION

Location of Income Tax Records: _____

Accountant or Tax Preparer: _____

Family Attorney: _____

Physicians: _____

Church Affiliation: _____

Contact Person: _____

Lodges or Associations Who Should be Notified of Death: _____

Contact Person: _____

FINAL INSTRUCTIONS

NOTICE:

Many states allow you to give legally binding instructions for disposition of your body, by signing a formal notarized document in a form prescribed by law. If you wish to provide such legally binding instructions, entering information on this page does NOT eliminate the need to prepare and sign such a formal notarized document.

The following information is provided to assist those who survive us in making necessary arrangements after our deaths:

[MALE GRANTOR]

Disposition of my remains:

_____ Cremation. Ashes to be _____

_____ Interment at _____

_____ Other instructions: _____

_____

Preferred Funeral Home: _____

Suggest a memorial in lieu of flowers?

_____ Yes _____ No. If "Yes," type of memorial: _____

Should an obituary be published? _____ Yes _____ No

Directions About Funeral Service: _____

[FEMALE GRANTOR]

Disposition of my remains:

_____ Cremation. Ashes to be _____

_____ Interment at _____

_____ Other instructions: _____

_____

Preferred Funeral Home: _____

Suggest a memorial in lieu of flowers?

_____ Yes _____ No. If "Yes," type of memorial: _____

Should an obituary be published? _____ Yes _____ No

Directions About Funeral Service: _____

B. Anatomical Gifts

Revised Uniform Anatomical Gift Act (2019)

§4. Who May Make Anatomical Gift Before Donor's Death.

Subject to Section 8, an anatomical gift of a donor's body or part may be made during the life of the donor for the purpose of transplantation, therapy, research, or education in the manner provided in Section 5 by:

(1) the donor, if the donor is an adult or if the donor is a minor and is:

(A) emancipated; or

(B) authorized under state law to apply for a driver's license because the donor is at least [insert the youngest age at which an individual may apply for any type of driver's license] years of age;

(2) an agent of the donor, unless the power of attorney for health care or other record prohibits the agent from making an anatomical gift;

(3) a parent of the donor, if the donor is an unemancipated minor; or

(4) the donor's guardian.

§ 5. Manner of Making Anatomical Gift Before Donor's Death.

(a) A donor may make an anatomical gift:

(1) by authorizing a statement or symbol indicating that the donor has made an anatomical gift to be imprinted on the donor's driver's license or identification card;

(2) in a will;

(3) during a terminal illness or injury of the donor, by any form of communication addressed to at least two adults, at least one of whom is a disinterested witness; or

(4) as provided in subsection (b).

(b) A donor or other person authorized to make an anatomical gift under Section 4 may make a gift by a donor card or other record signed by the donor or other person making the gift or by authorizing that a statement or symbol indicating that the donor has made an anatomical gift be included on a donor registry. If the donor or other person is physically unable to sign a record, the record may be signed by another individual at the direction of the donor or other person and must:

(1) be witnessed by at least two adults, at least one of whom is a disinterested witness, who have signed at the request of the donor or the other person; and

(2) state that it has been signed and witnessed as provided in paragraph (1).

(c) Revocation, suspension, expiration, or cancellation of a driver's license or identification card upon which an anatomical gift is indicated does not invalidate the gift.

(d) An anatomical gift made by will takes effect upon the donor's death whether or not the will is probated. Invalidation of the will after the donor's death does not invalidate the gift.

§ 9. Who May Make Anatomical Gift of Decedent's Body or Part.

(a) Subject to subsections (b) and (c) and unless barred by Section 7 or 8, an anatomical gift of a decedent's body or part for purpose of transplantation, therapy, research, or education may be made by any member of the following classes of persons who is reasonably available, in the order of priority listed:

(1) an agent of the decedent at the time of death who could have made an anatomical gift under Section 4(2) immediately before the decedent's death;

(2) the spouse of the decedent;

(3) adult children of the decedent;

(4) parents of the decedent;

(5) adult siblings of the decedent;

(6) adult grandchildren of the decedent;

(7) grandparents of the decedent;

(8) an adult who exhibited special care and concern for the decedent;

(9) the persons who were acting as the [guardians] of the person of the decedent at the time of death; and

(10) any other person having the authority to dispose of the decedent's body.

(b) If there is more than one member of a class listed in subsection (a)(1), (3), (4), (5), (6), (7), or (9) entitled to make an anatomical gift, an anatomical gift may be made by a member of the class unless that member or a person to which the gift may pass under Section 11 knows of an objection by another member of the class. If an objection is known, the gift may be made only by a majority of the members of the class who are reasonably available.

(c) A person may not make an anatomical gift if, at the time of the decedent's death, a person in a prior class under subsection (a) is reasonably available to make or to object to the making of an anatomical gift.

§ 16. Sale or Purchase of Parts Prohibited.

(a) Except as otherwise provided in subsection (b), a person that for valuable consideration, knowingly purchases or sells a part for transplantation or therapy if removal of a part from an individual is intended to occur after the individual's death commits a [[felony] and upon conviction is subject to a fine not exceeding [$50,000] or imprisonment not exceeding [five] years, or both] [class[ ] felony].

(b) A person may charge a reasonable amount for the removal, processing, preservation, quality control, storage, transportation, implantation, or disposal of a part.

§ 17. Other Prohibited Acts.

A person that, in order to obtain a financial gain, intentionally falsifies, forges, conceals, defaces, or obliterates a document of gift, an amendment or revocation of a document of gift, or a refusal commits a [[felony] and upon conviction is subject to a fine not exceeding [$50,000] or imprisonment not exceeding [five] years, or both] [class[ ] felony].

Notes

The Revised Uniform Anatomical Gift Act was enacted to address the increasing need for donations of human organs, eyes, and tissue. "As of January 2006 there were over 92,000 individuals on the waiting list for organ transplantations, and the list keeps growing." Unif. Ana. Gift Act (2019) (Prefatory Note). The first version of the Act was enacted in 1968; it was adopted by all of the states, but advances in technology, new federal regulations, and continuing amendments made by the individual states made successive revisions necessary.

> The most significant contribution of the 1968 Act was to create a *right* to donate organs, eyes, and tissue. This right was not clearly recognized at common law. By creating this right, individuals became empowered to donate their parts or their loved one's parts to save or improve the lives of others.

Unif. Ana. Gift Act (2006) (Prefatory Note) (emphasis added). The 1987 revision of the Act was adopted in only 26 jurisdictions and, of course, it did not incorporate changes made in federal law after 1987. Thus, the 2006 revision seeks to address these concerns and respond to the medical, technological advances that have been made since previous versions. Currently, 36 states, the District of Columbia, and the Virgin Islands have adopted the Act. *See* Uniform Law Commission, *Anatomical Gift Act* 2006, at https://www.uniformlaws.org/committees/community-home?communitykey=015e18ad-4806-4dff-b011-8e1ebc0d1d0f&tab=groupdetails (accessed Aug. 9, 2019). *See also*, Meredith M. Havekost, Note. *The Waiting Game: How States Can Solve the Organ-Donation Crisis*, 72 Vand. L. Rev. 691 (2019); Lelli Manfared & Lois Shepherd, *Organ Procurement Now: Does the United States Still "Opt in?"*, 2017 U. Ill. L. Rev. 1003; Reid Kress Weisbord, *Anatomical Intent*, 124 Yale L.J. Forum 117, 119 (2014) (noting that the Revised Uniform Anatomical Gift Act has been adopted in "some form . . . in forty-six states"); Daniel G. Orenstein & Layne M. Bettini, *Flipping the Light Switch: New Perspectives on Default to Donation for Organs and Tissues*, 23 Annals Health L. 141, 143 n.10 (2014) ("The Uniform Anatomical Gift Act . . . has been [adopted by] forty-six states and the District of Columbia, and has been proposed in Pennsylvania in 2014."). The more significant elements within the 2006 Act include the following:

First, there is no presumption of a gift of an organ. An individual or a designated person must "opt-in" to a donation to allow for it to occur. Plus, an individual can make arrangements so that another may never be able to make an organ donation on his or her behalf;

Second, the Act expands the list of persons who may make an organ donation on behalf of another person during that person's lifetime, to include health-care agents, parents, and guardians;

Third, the Act allows minors who are able to apply for a driver's license to be able to be a donor of an organ;

Fourth, the Act expands the list of persons able to consent to a donation of an organ after an individual has died;

Fifth, the Act permits members of a class of persons able to consent to an organ donation to make an organ donation from another person, individually, if there are no known objections by other members of the class;

Sixth, the Act encourages and establishes standards for donor registries;

Seventh, the Act enables procurement organizations to gain access to registries, medical records, and records of the state's motor vehicle department;

Eighth, the Act recognizes the validity of anatomical gifts made under the laws of other jurisdictions; and

Ninth, the Act clarifies default rules for the interpretation of a document, the interaction between a health care directive and an anatomical gift, and cooperation between procurement organizations and coroners; and it allows for electronic signatures.

The goals of the Act, as well as the increasing need for organ donations, have prompted many suggestions for reform. *See, e.g.,* Lois Sheperd, *The End of End-of-Life Law*, 92 N.C. L. Rev. 1693 (2014); Judy K. Davis & Karen Skinner, *Gerontology and the Law: A Selected Annotated Bibliography, 2009–2011 Update*, 86 S. Cal. L. Rev. 1389 (2013).

C. Durable Power of Attorney

Uniform Power of Attorney Act (2019)

§ 103. Applicability.

This [act] applies to all powers of attorney except:

(1) a power to the extent it is coupled with an interest in the subject of the power, including a power given to or for the benefit of a creditor in connection with a credit transaction;

(2) a power to make health-care decisions;

(3) a proxy or other delegation to exercise voting rights or management rights with respect to an entity; and

(4) a power created on a form prescribed by a government or governmental subdivision, agency, or instrumentality for a governmental purpose.

§ 104. Power of Attorney Is Durable.

A power of attorney created under this [act] is durable unless it expressly provides that it is terminated by the incapacity of the principal.

§ 105. Execution of Power of Attorney.

A power of attorney must be signed by the principal or in the principal's conscious presence by another individual directed by the principal to sign the principal's name on the power of attorney. A signature on a power of attorney is presumed to be genuine if the principal acknowledges the signature before a notary public or other individual authorized by law to take acknowledgments.

§ 106. Validity of Power of Attorney.

(a) A power of attorney executed in this state on or after [the effective date of this [act]] is valid if its execution complies with Section 105.

(b) A power of attorney executed in this state before [the effective date of this [act]] is valid if its execution complied with the law of this state as it existed at the time of execution.

(c) A power of attorney executed other than in this state is valid in this state if, when the power of attorney was executed, the execution complied with:

> (1) the law of the jurisdiction that determines the meaning and effect of the power of attorney pursuant to Section 107; or

> (2) the requirements for a military power of attorney pursuant to 10 U.S.C. Section 1044b [, as amended].

(d) Except as otherwise provided by statute other than this [act], a photocopy or electronically transmitted copy of an original power of attorney has the same effect as the original.

§ 108. Nomination of [Conservator or Guardian]; Relation of Agent to Court-Appointed Fiduciary.

(a) In a power of attorney, a principal may nominate a [conservator or guardian] of the principal's estate or [guardian] of the principal's person for consideration by the court if protective proceedings for the principal's estate or person are begun after the principal executes the power of attorney. [Except for good cause shown or disqualification, the court shall make its appointment in accordance with the principal's most recent nomination.]

(b) If, after a principal executes a power of attorney, a court appoints a [conservator or guardian] of the principal's estate or other fiduciary charged with the management of some or all of the principal's property, the agent is accountable to the fiduciary as well as to the principal. [The power of attorney is not terminated and the agent's authority continues unless limited, suspended, or terminated by the court.]

§ 109. When Power of Attorney Effective.

(a) A power of attorney is effective when executed unless the principal provides in the power of attorney that it becomes effective at a future date or upon the occurrence of a future event or contingency.

(b) If a power of attorney becomes effective upon the occurrence of a future event or contingency, the principal, in the power of attorney, may authorize one or more persons to determine in a writing or other record that the event or contingency has occurred.

(c) If a power of attorney becomes effective upon the principal's incapacity and the principal has not authorized a person to determine whether the principal is incapacitated, or the person authorized is unable or unwilling to make the determination, the power of attorney becomes effective upon a determination in a writing or other record by:

> (1) a physician [or licensed psychologist] that the principal is incapacitated within the meaning of Section 102(5)(A); or

(2) an attorney at law, a judge, or an appropriate governmental official that the principal is incapacitated within the meaning of Section 102(5)(B).

(d) A person authorized by the principal in the power of attorney to determine that the principal is incapacitated may act as the principal's personal representative pursuant to the Health Insurance Portability and Accountability Act, Sections 1171 through 1179 of the Social Security Act, 42 U.S.C. Section 1320d, [as amended,] and applicable regulations, to obtain access to the principal's health-care information and communicate with the principal's health-care provider.

§ 110. Termination of Power of Attorney or Agent's Authority.

(a) A power of attorney terminates when:

(1) the principal dies;

(2) the principal becomes incapacitated, if the power of attorney is not durable;

(3) the principal revokes the power of attorney;

(4) the power of attorney provides that it terminates;

(5) the purpose of the power of attorney is accomplished; or

(6) the principal revokes the agent's authority or the agent dies, becomes incapacitated, or resigns, and the power of attorney does not provide for another agent to act under the power of attorney.

(b) An agent's authority terminates when:

(1) the principal revokes the authority;

(2) the agent dies, becomes incapacitated, or resigns;

(3) an action is filed for the [dissolution] or annulment of the agent's marriage to the principal or their legal separation, unless the power of attorney otherwise provides; or

(4) the power of attorney terminates.

(c) Unless the power of attorney otherwise provides, an agent's authority is exercisable until the authority terminates under subsection (b), notwithstanding a lapse of time since the execution of the power of attorney.

(d) Termination of an agent's authority or of a power of attorney is not effective as to the agent or another person that, without actual knowledge of the termination, acts in good faith under the power of attorney. An act so performed, unless otherwise invalid or unenforceable, binds the principal and the principal's successors in interest.

(e) Incapacity of the principal of a power of attorney that is not durable does not revoke or terminate the power of attorney as to an agent or other person that, without actual knowledge of the incapacity, acts in good faith under the power of attorney. An act so performed, unless otherwise invalid or unenforceable, binds the principal and the principal's successors in interest.

(f) The execution of a power of attorney does not revoke a power of attorney previously executed by the principal unless the subsequent power of attorney provides that the previous power of attorney is revoked or that all other powers of attorney are revoked.

§ 114. Agent's Duties.

(a) Notwithstanding provisions in the power of attorney, an agent that has accepted appointment shall:

(1) act in accordance with the principal's reasonable expectations to the extent actually known by the agent and, otherwise, in the principal's best interest;

(2) act in good faith; and

(3) act only within the scope of authority granted in the power of attorney.

(b) Except as otherwise provided in the power of attorney, an agent that has accepted appointment shall:

(1) act loyally for the principal's benefit;

(2) act so as not to create a conflict of interest that impairs the agent's ability to act impartially in the principal's best interest;

(3) act with the care, competence, and diligence ordinarily exercised by agents in similar circumstances;

(4) keep a record of all receipts, disbursements, and transactions made on behalf of the principal;

(5) cooperate with a person that has authority to make health-care decisions for the principal to carry out the principal's reasonable expectations to the extent actually known by the agent and, otherwise, act in the principal's best interest; and

(6) attempt to preserve the principal's estate plan, to the extent actually known by the agent, if preserving the plan is consistent with the principal's best interest based on all relevant factors, including:

(A) the value and nature of the principal's property;

(B) the principal's foreseeable obligations and need for maintenance;

(C) minimization of taxes, including income, estate, inheritance, generation-skipping transfer, and gift taxes; and

(D) eligibility for a benefit, a program, or assistance under a statute or regulation.

(c) An agent that acts in good faith is not liable to any beneficiary of the principal's estate plan for failure to preserve the plan.

(d) An agent that acts with care, competence, and diligence for the best interest of the principal is not liable solely because the agent also benefits from the act or has an individual or conflicting interest in relation to the property or affairs of the principal.

(e) If an agent is selected by the principal because of special skills or expertise possessed by the agent or in reliance on the agent's representation that the agent has special skills or expertise, the special skills or expertise must be considered in determining whether the agent has acted with care, competence, and diligence under the circumstances.

(f) Absent a breach of duty to the principal, an agent is not liable if the value of the principal's property declines.

(g) An agent that exercises authority to delegate to another person the authority granted by the principal or that engages another person on behalf of the principal is not liable for an act, error of judgment, or default of that person if the agent exercises care, competence, and diligence in selecting and monitoring the person.

(h) Except as otherwise provided in the power of attorney, an agent is not required to disclose receipts, disbursements, or transactions conducted on behalf of the principal unless ordered by a court or requested by the principal, a guardian, a conservator, another fiduciary acting for the principal, a governmental agency having authority to protect the welfare of the principal, or, upon the death of the principal, by the personal representative or successor in interest of the principal's estate. If so requested, within 30 days the agent shall comply with the request or provide a writing or other record substantiating why additional time is needed and shall comply with the request within an additional 30 days.

§ 301. Statutory Form Power of Attorney.

A document substantially in the following form may be used to create a statutory form power of attorney that has the meaning and effect prescribed by this [act].

[INSERT NAME OF JURISDICTION] STATUTORY FORM POWER OF ATTORNEY IMPORTANT INFORMATION

This power of attorney authorizes another person (your agent) to make decisions concerning your property for you (the principal). Your agent will be able to make decisions and act with respect to your property (including your money) whether or not you are able to act for yourself. The meaning of authority over subjects listed on this form is explained in the Uniform Power of Attorney Act [insert citation].

This power of attorney does not authorize the agent to make health-care decisions for you.

You should select someone you trust to serve as your agent. Unless you specify otherwise, generally the agent's authority will continue until you die or revoke the power of attorney or the agent resigns or is unable to act for you.

Your agent is entitled to reasonable compensation unless you state otherwise in the Special Instructions.

This form provides for designation of one agent. If you wish to name more than one agent you may name a coagent in the Special Instructions. Coagents are not required to act together unless you include that requirement in the Special Instructions.

If your agent is unable or unwilling to act for you, your power of attorney will end unless you have named a successor agent. You may also name a second successor agent.

This power of attorney becomes effective immediately unless you state otherwise in the Special Instructions.

If you have questions about the power of attorney or the authority you are granting to your agent, you should seek legal advice before signing this form.

DESIGNATION OF AGENT

I _____ name the following

(Name of Principal)

Name of Agent:

_____

Agent's Address:

_____

Agent's Telephone Number:

_____

DESIGNATION OF SUCCESSOR AGENT(S) (OPTIONAL)

If my agent is unable or unwilling to act for me, I name as my successor agent:

Name of Successor Agent:

_____

Successor Agent's Address:

_____

Successor Agent's Telephone Number:

_____

If my successor agent is unable or unwilling to act for me, I name as my second successor agent:

Name of Second Successor Agent:

_____

Second Successor Agent's Address:

_____

Second Successor Agent's Telephone Number:

_____

GRANT OF GENERAL AUTHORITY

I grant my agent and any successor agent general authority to act for me with respect to the following subjects as defined in the Uniform Power of Attorney Act [insert citation]:

(INITIAL each subject you want to include in the agent's general authority. If you wish to grant general authority over all of the subjects you may initial "All Preceding Subjects" instead of initialing each subject.)

(___) Real Property
(___) Tangible Personal Property
(___) Stocks and Bonds
(___) Commodities and Options
(___) Banks and Other Financial Institutions
(___) Operation of Entity or Business
(___) Insurance and Annuities
(___) Estates, Trusts, and Other Beneficial Interests
(___) Claims and Litigation
(___) Personal and Family Maintenance
(___) Benefits from Governmental Programs or Civil or Military Service
(___) Retirement Plans
(___) Taxes
(___) All Preceding Subjects

GRANT OF SPECIFIC AUTHORITY (OPTIONAL)

My agent MAY NOT do any of the following specific acts for me UNLESS I have INITIALED the specific authority listed below:

(CAUTION: Granting any of the following will give your agent the authority to take actions that could significantly reduce your property or change how your property is distributed at your death. INITIAL ONLY the specific authority you WANT to give your agent.)

(___) Create, amend, revoke, or terminate an *inter vivos* trust
(___) Make a gift, subject to the limitations of the Uniform Power of Attorney Act [insert citation to Section 217 of the act] and any special instructions in this power of attorney
(___) Create or change rights of survivorship
(___) Create or change a beneficiary designation
(___) Authorize another person to exercise the authority granted under this power of attorney
(___) Waive the principal's right to be a beneficiary of a joint and survivor annuity, including a survivor benefit under a retirement plan
(___) Exercise fiduciary powers that the principal has authority to delegate
[(___) Disclaim or refuse an interest in property, including a power of appointment]

LIMITATION ON AGENT'S AUTHORITY

An agent that is not my ancestor, spouse, or descendant MAY NOT use my property to benefit the agent or a person to whom the agent owes an obligation of support unless I have included that authority in the Special Instructions.

SPECIAL INSTRUCTIONS (OPTIONAL)

You may give special instructions on the following lines:

_____

_____

_____

_____

_____

_____

_____

_____

EFFECTIVE DATE

This power of attorney is effective immediately unless I have stated otherwise in the Special Instructions.

NOMINATION OF [CONSERVATOR OR GUARDIAN] (OPTIONAL)

If it becomes necessary for a court to appoint a [conservator or guardian] of my estate or [guardian] of my person, I nominate the following person(s) for appointment:

Name of Nominee for [conservator or guardian] of my estate:

_____

Nominee's Address:

_____

Nominee's Telephone Number:

_____

Name of Nominee for [guardian] of my person:

_____

Nominee's Address:

_____

Nominee's Telephone Number:

_____

RELIANCE ON THIS POWER OF ATTORNEY

Any person, including my agent, may rely upon the validity of this power of attorney or a copy of it unless that person knows it has terminated or is invalid.

SIGNATURE AND ACKNOWLEDGMENT

_____

_____

Your Signature Date

_____

Your Name Printed

_____

_____

Your Address

_____

Your Telephone Number

State of _____

[County] of _____

This document was acknowledged before me on _____,

(Date)

by _____.

(Name of Principal)

_____ (Seal, if any)

Signature of Notary

My commission expires: _____

[This document prepared by:

_____

_____

IMPORTANT INFORMATION FOR AGENT

Agent's Duties

When you accept the authority granted under this power of attorney, a special legal relationship is created between you and the principal. This relationship imposes upon you legal duties that continue until you resign or the power of attorney is terminated or revoked. You must:

(1) do what you know the principal reasonably expects you to do with the principal's property or, if you do not know the principal's expectations, act in the principal's best interest;

(2) act in good faith;

(3) do nothing beyond the authority granted in this power of attorney; and

(4) disclose your identity as an agent whenever you act for the principal by writing or printing the name of the principal and signing your own name as "agent" in the following manner:

(Principal's Name) by(Your Signature) as Agent

Unless the Special Instructions in this power of attorney state otherwise, you must also:

(1) act loyally for the principal's benefit;

(2) avoid conflicts that would impair your ability to act in the principal's best interest;

(3) act with care, competence, and diligence;

(4) keep a record of all receipts, disbursements, and transactions made on behalf of the principal;

(5) cooperate with any person that has authority to make health-care decisions for the principal to do what you know the principal reasonably expects or, if you do not know the principal's expectations, to act in the principal's best interest; and

(6) attempt to preserve the principal's estate plan if you know the plan and preserving the plan is consistent with the principal's best interest.

Termination of Agent's Authority

You must stop acting on behalf of the principal if you learn of any event that terminates this power of attorney or your authority under this power of attorney. Events that terminate a power of attorney or your authority to act under a power of attorney include:

(1) death of the principal;

(2) the principal's revocation of the power of attorney or your authority;

(3) the occurrence of a termination event stated in the power of attorney;

(4) the purpose of the power of attorney is fully accomplished; or

(5) if you are married to the principal, a legal action is filed with a court to end your marriage, or for your legal separation, unless the Special Instructions in this power of attorney state that such an action will not terminate your authority.

Liability of Agent

The meaning of the authority granted to you is defined in the Uniform Power of Attorney Act [insert citation]. If you violate the Uniform Power of Attorney Act [insert citation] or act outside the authority granted, you may be liable for any damages caused by your violation.

If there is anything about this document or your duties that you do not understand, you should seek legal advice.

Notes

A power of attorney is a useful device by which an individual may confer upon an agent the power to make financial or property decisions. Under the common law, such a power is suspended during periods when the principal is incompetent or unable to act in his or her own behalf. But if the principal signs a durable power of attorney, including these specific words, the power will continue during incapacity. And of course, all powers cease upon the death of the principal, who is superseded by the administrator or personal representative of the estate. The 2006 version of the Uniform Power of Attorney Act contains some unique changes: (1) it is automatically a durable power unless stated otherwise; (2) there is a provision allowing for reciprocity with other jurisdictions; (3) the signature of the principal may be done by proxy or acknowledgment; (4) the agent appointed under the Act continues to have authority under the Act unless a court-appointed fiduciary has been given, by a court, specific authority to the contrary; (5) the powers become effective upon signing, but the principal may specify what must occur to trigger the powers, such as incapacity; (6) revocation of the authority of an agent occurs whenever the agent is a spouse of the principal and an action is commenced to dissolve the marriage; (7) exculpation of an agent is allowed, with the exception of dishonesty or reckless indifference; (8) there is a list of persons who may petition the court to review an agent's conduct; (9) the Act provides protection for those who accept an invalid power of attorney; and (10) the Act provides that other remedies at law are available to petitioners.

For additional commentary, see Nina A. Kohn, *For Love and Affection: Elder Care and the Law's Denial of Intra-Family Contracts*, 54 HARV. C.R.-C.L. L. REV. 211 (2019); Mikaela L. Louie, Comment. *Respecting the Right to Research: Proxy Consent and Subject Assent in Alzheimer's Disease Clinical Trials*, 94 WASH. L. REV. 887 (2019); Letha Sgritta McDowell, *Signs Your Client Has Dementia*, 159 TRUSTS & ESTS. 55 (July 2019) Martin M. Shenkman & Jonathan G. Blattmacher, *Powers of Attorney for Our Aging Client Base*, 154 TRUSTS & ESTS. 28 (July 2015); Alexander A. Boni-Saenz, *Personal Delegations*, 78 BROOK. L. REV. 1231 (2013); Nina A Kohn, Jeremy A. Blumenthal & Amy T. Campbell, *Supported Decision-Making: A Viable Alternative to Guardianship?*, 117 PENN ST. L. REV. 1111 (2013); Raymond C. O'Brien, *Attorney Responsibility and Client Incapacity*, 30 J. CONTEMP. HEALTH L. & POL'Y 59 (2013); Michael L. Perlin, *"Striking for the Guardians and Protectors of the Mind": The Convention on the Rights of Persons with Mental Disabilities and the Future of Guardianship Laws*, 117 PENN ST. L. REV. 1159 (2013).

Franzen v. Norwest Bank Colorado

Supreme Court of Colorado, 1998
955 P.2d 1018

Justice SCOTT delivered the Opinion of the Court.

This case arises out of a disagreement over the disposition of assets in a trust created for the benefit of Frances Franzen by her late husband, James Franzen. In Norwest Colorado v. Franzen, No. 95CA0386 (Colo.App. June 27, 1996) (not selected for publication), the court of appeals held that James O'Brien, Mrs. Franzen's brother, was authorized to dissolve the trust by virtue of a power of attorney executed by Mrs. Franzen. The court of appeals also held, moreover, that the trustee was not liable for litigation expenses associated with challenging O'Brien's authority to dissolve the trust. We affirm the judgment of the court of appeals in its entirety. * * *

* * *

On February 4, 1992, James Franzen, the settlor, executed an instrument creating a trust designed to provide for himself and his wife, Frances Franzen, in their old age. The corpus of the trust initially consisted of three bank accounts containing a total of $74,251.19, but it did not include certain other assets held by Mr. and Mrs. Franzen as joint tenants, such as the family home. Norwest Bank, then known as United Bank of Denver, * * * was named as the sole trustee in the trust agreement.

James Franzen was terminally ill when he created the trust, and he died four months later. Upon Mr. Franzen's death, a trust officer at the bank sent a letter to Frances Franzen, who was living in a nursing home, notifying her that she had "certain rights regarding the trust." A copy of the trust agreement was enclosed, and the letter referred to Article 5.1, which states:

> At ... [James'] death, if Frances survives ... [him], she may direct ... [the] trustee in writing to deliver the residuary trust estate to her within three months of [James'] death. If she does not so direct, this trust shall continue to be administered as provided in Article 3. If she so directs, the trust shall terminate on the date the trust estate is distributed to her.

The letter asked Mrs. Franzen for a decision in writing by August 1, 1992, "so that we have time to make arrangements for the transfer of assets if necessary." A handwritten note at the bottom of the letter, signed by Mrs. Franzen and dated July 14, 1992, says, "I wish to leave the trust intact for my lifetime."

The bank, concerned about the disposition of the vacant house and other assets not included in the trust, contacted Mrs. Franzen's nephews, who were named as remaindermen of the trust. The two nephews were reluctant to assume responsibility for Mrs. Franzen's affairs, though, and Mrs. Franzen's brother, James O'Brien, intervened. O'Brien moved Mrs. Franzen to a nursing home in Kentucky, where he lived, and asked the bank to turn over Mrs. Franzen's assets to him.

In the course of dealing with the bank, the nephews expressed concerns about O'Brien's motives. The bank declined to comply with O'Brien's request, and filed a Petition for Instruction and Advice in the Denver Probate Court (probate court). Before the hearing, O'Brien sent the bank a copy of a power of attorney purporting to authorize him to act in Mrs. Franzen's behalf and a letter attempting to revoke the trust and to remove the bank as trustee, citing Article 6.2 and Article 8 of the trust agreement.

Article 6.2 of the trust provides that after the death of James Franzen, Frances Franzen "may remove any trustee," and that "[a]ny removal under this ... [paragraph] may be made without cause and without notice of any reason and shall become effective immediately upon delivery of ... [written notice] to the trustee" unless Frances Franzen and the trustee agree otherwise.

Article 8 of the trust agreement gives James Franzen "the right to amend or revoke this trust in whole or in part ... by a writing delivered to ... [the] trustee. ... After my death, Frances may exercise these powers with respect to the entire trust estate."

The hearing was continued, and the bank filed a Petition for Appointment of a Conservator, asking the probate court to appoint someone to manage and protect Mrs. Franzen's assets. When the hearing on both petitions was held, the probate court ruled that the power of attorney had created a valid agency but that the trust had not been revoked and continued in existence. The probate court found that Mrs. Franzen needed protection, but a conservator was not available, so the Court appointed the bank as "special fiduciary" with responsibility for both trust and non-trust assets pursuant to sections 15-14-408 and 15-14-409, 5 C.R.S. (1997). The probate court ordered the bank to use the assets to make payments for Mrs. Franzen's benefit.

Franzen appealed the probate court rulings. On appeal, the court of appeals reversed, holding that the power of attorney authorized O'Brien to remove the bank as trustee and to revoke the trust. The court of appeals also held, however, that the bank was not liable for expenditures made in good faith after receiving the removal and revocation letter, including the legal fees incurred in the course of opposing O'Brien's efforts.

While the removal and revocation were effective immediately upon receipt of O'Brien's letter, the court of appeals held, the bank was entitled to disburse trust funds in good faith pending judicial resolution of O'Brien's claim that the trust had been dissolved. The court of appeals found that the probate court's award of administration and attorney fees to be paid by the trust estate to the bank were reasonable and appropriate compensation for the bank's duties as a fiduciary under the circumstances, and hence, declined to hold the bank liable.

* * *

A power of attorney is an instrument by which a principal confers express authority on an agent to perform certain acts or kinds of acts on the principal's behalf. See Willey v. Mayer, 876 P.2d 1260 (Colo.1994). In Colorado, the use and interpretation of such instruments is governed by statute. See §§ 15-14-601 to -610, 5 C.R.S. (1997). Under the power of attorney statute, the scope of an agent's authority to alter a trust is narrowly construed. "An agent may not revoke or amend a trust that is revocable or amendable by the principal without specific authority and specific reference to the trust in the agency instrument." § 15-14-608(2), 5 C.R.S. (1997).

Norwest notes that the power of attorney executed by Mrs. Franzen did not refer specifically to the Franzen trust. Thus, Norwest argues, O'Brien was not authorized to remove the trustee or revoke the trust. The statutory specificity requirement, however, did not take effect until January 1, 1995, almost two years after the power of attorney was executed by Mrs. Franzen.

General principles of statutory construction lead us to conclude that the power of attorney statute is inapplicable to any agency instrument executed prior to its effective date. See § 2-4-202, 1 C.R.S. (1997) (statutes are presumed prospective); see also People v. Munoz, 857 P.2d 546, 548 (Colo.App.1993) (applying the statute). In addition, the General Assembly expressly stated that the power of attorney statute does not "in any way invalidate any agency or power of attorney executed . . . prior to January 1, 1995," conclusively demonstrating that no retroactive effect was intended. See § 15-14-611, 5 C.R.S. (1997).

Norwest responds that the specificity requirement in section 15-14-608(2) merely restated the common law in effect prior to its adoption, so the same result should be reached even though the statute was not intended to be applied retroactively. The bank asserts that the common law would require the power of attorney to refer to the trust by name.

Unfortunately for Norwest, the cases it cites state no such common law rule. Instead, these cases stand for the unremarkable proposition that a power of attorney giving an agent broad authority to act on behalf of the principal should be construed in light of the surrounding circumstances. Where a broadly worded power of attorney arguably authorizes acts that may be inconsistent with the principal's interests or intent, the instrument should not be interpreted as allowing the agent to undertake such acts in the absence of specific authority.

For example, in Estate of Casey v. Commissioner of Internal Revenue, 948 F.2d 895 (4th Cir.1991), the Fourth Circuit applied Virginia law to hold that an agent acting under a power of attorney that conferred wide-ranging authority to act on the principal's behalf was not authorized to give away the principal's property. The court said, "[T]he failure to enumerate a specific power, particularly one with the dangerous implications of the power to make unrestricted gifts of the principal's assets, reflects deliberate intention." *Id.* at 898.

Similarly, in Bryant v. Bryant, 125 Wash.2d 113, 882 P.2d 169 (1994), the Supreme Court of Washington held that an agent acting under a broadly worded power of attorney was not authorized to make gifts of the principal's assets. The court noted the consensus view that "gift transfers or transfers without substantial consideration inuring to the benefit of the principal violate the scope of authority conferred by a general power of attorney to sell, exchange, transfer, or convey property for the benefit of the principal." *Id.* 882 P.2d at 172 (citation omitted). The other cases cited by Norwest are to the same general effect. See, *e.g.*, De Bueno v. Castro, 543 So.2d 393, 394–95 (Fla.App. 1989); Realty Growth Investors v. Council of Unit Owners, 453 A.2d 450, 454–55 (Dela.1982); Brown v. Laird, 134 Or. 150, 291 P. 352, 354–55 (1930)

The basic rule recognized in these cases logically might extend by analogy to situations where a power of attorney gives an agent wide authority to make decisions on behalf of the principal but makes no mention of the power to alter the principal's rights under any trust. We are willing to assume, for the sake of argument, that the scope of the agent's authority under the common law in such circumstances would not extend to revocation of a trust established to benefit the principal.

Even so, we are not persuaded that under the common law, an agency instrument must expressly refer to a particular trust by name in order to confer authority on the agent to revoke it. Under the reasoning of the cases previously cited, the terms of the power of attorney need only evince an intention to authorize the agent to make decisions concerning the principal's interests in trusts generally, not necessarily a particular trust.

Section 1(c) of the power of attorney executed by Mrs. Franzen expressly authorizes O'Brien to

> manage . . . and in any manner deal with any real or personal property, tangible or intangible, or any interest therein . . . in my name and for my benefit, upon such terms as . . . [O'Brien] shall deem proper, *including the funding, creation, and/or revocation of trusts* or other investments.

(Emphasis added.)

We have little trouble concluding that the quoted language expressly authorizes O'Brien to revoke the Franzen trust, even though it does not mention the trust specifically by name.

* * *

Mrs. Franzen contends that Norwest should be strictly liable for trustee and attorney fees spent after the removal and revocation letter was received from O'Brien. In essence, she argues that a trustee should be held liable for all expenses incurred after a trust it oversees is revoked, even if it incurs the expenses in reliance on a court ruling—later vacated on appeal—that the trust remains in effect.

Mrs. Franzen cites a host of authority in support of her contention that a trustee is liable for any act in excess of his or her authority, even if it was undertaken in good faith or in reliance on the advice of counsel. See, e.g., Morgan v. Indep. Drivers Ass'n Pension Plan, 975 F.2d 1467, 1470 (10th Cir.1992); Moore v. Adkins, 2 Kan. App.2d 139, 576 P.2d 245, 255 (1978).

She acknowledges that a trustee is entitled to indemnification for the expenses of prosecuting and defending actions on behalf of the trust, but notes that indemnification is available only if the need for litigation was not caused by the fault of the trustee. See In re Estate of McCart, 847 P.2d 184, 187–88 (Colo.App.1992); 3A William F. Fratcher, Scott on Trusts § 244 (4th ed.1988).

Nowhere in the authorities cited by Mrs. Franzen can we find support for the view that a trustee is liable for acts in excess of his or her authority when the acts are undertaken in reliance on a court order, even when the ruling underlying the order is overturned on appeal. Both Morgan and Moore involved actions taken by fiduciaries in reliance on mistaken professional advice, not a court order. In fact, the reason why good faith reliance on the advice of counsel is not a defense to liability for a breach of duty is that a trustee has the option of seeking instruction from a court rather than depending on the potentially erroneous advice of a lawyer. See Restatement (Second) Trusts § 226 cmt. b & § 201 cmt. b (1957).

As for the propriety of Norwest's commencement of litigation to determine its responsibilities as trustee, we see no legal or equitable basis for imposing liability on the bank. At the time O'Brien sent the removal and revocation letter, the bank's representatives had reason to suspect that Frances Franzen might be incompetent and hence lack the capacity to execute a valid power of attorney authorizing O'Brien to act in her behalf. In addition, the remaindermen of the trust and others had expressed concerns about whether O'Brien was acting in Mrs. Franzen's interests.[3]

---

3. We express no opinion concerning the motivations or credibility of Mrs. Franzen's friends and family members, some of whom claimed that O'Brien was attempting to gain control of the trust assets for personal benefit and was acting without Mrs. Franzen's knowledge or assent. The point is not whether O'Brien was in fact acting in Mrs. Franzen's best interests, but that the bank

If the bank had turned over the trust assets as requested and Mrs. Franzen were later demonstrated to have been incompetent to execute the power of attorney, or if O'Brien had absconded with the money, then the bank would have faced liability for breach of its duty of care as a fiduciary. The remaindermen would likely have pointed out that they warned the bank about the possibility of irregularity in O'Brien's request.

Of course, to the extent that the bank was entitled to compensation for administering the trust only as long as the trust remained in existence and it remained the trustee, the bank's interests were served by challenging O'Brien's authority under the power of attorney and the terms of the trust agreement. However, the bank's interest in maintaining the trust with itself as trustee does not, ipso facto, demonstrate that the litigation did not benefit the trust estate.

Under the circumstances, then, the bank's decision to obtain a judicial determination of its responsibilities under the trust agreement was not only reasonable, but it appears to have been fully consistent with the bank's duty to protect the interests of the trust and its beneficiaries. Thus, we conclude that the need for litigation did not arise due to any fault on the part of Norwest, and the bank is entitled to indemnification.

* * *

In conclusion, we hold that under the common law, a power of attorney that appears to give the agent sweeping powers to dispose of the principal's property is to be narrowly construed in light of the circumstances surrounding the execution of the agency instrument. However, the principal may confer authority to amend or revoke trusts on an agent without referring to the trusts by name in the power of attorney.

Moreover, a trustee is not liable for administration or related attorney fees incurred in reliance on an order of the probate court that is later vacated on appeal. Where the trustee acts in good faith to seek direction from a court concerning its responsibilities in relation to a trust it oversees, the trustee is entitled to indemnification for any associated legal expenses.

Accordingly, we affirm the judgment of the court of appeals in its entirety.

Problem

In 2015, a principal, who was about to enter into a long term care facility, executed a durable power of attorney naming his agent as his attorney in fact. Once empowered, the agent was given the option of signing an Alternative Dispute Resolution (ADR) agreement whereby any disputes between the principal and the facility would be resolved by arbitration. The facility made clear that admission to the

---

acted reasonably in light of the available information when it sought instructions from a neutral and detached judicial official rather than immediately complying with O'Brien's instructions.

facility was not dependent upon signing, and the agent signed the agreement as the principal's attorney-in-fact. In 2016, the principal filed a lawsuit alleging that the facility was negligent in providing him care and treatment. The lawsuit prompted the facility to file a motion to compel arbitration in accordance with the agreement that the agent signed upon admission. The principal responded that the agent exceeded his authority when he executed the agreement and that, therefore, it was not binding. At issue before the court is whether the powers granted to the agent under the principal's durable power of attorney are sufficiently broad to include the power to enter into pre-dispute arbitration agreements. Upon review of the Uniform Power of Attorney Act, how would you rule if you were the judge? *See* Golden Gate National Senior Care, LLC v. Dolan, 2019 WL 3047425 (Ky. Ct. App. 2019).

D. Guardianship

Uniform Probate Code (2019)

§ 5-102. Definitions.

* * *

(3) "Guardian" means a person who has qualified as a guardian of a minor or incapacitated person pursuant to appointment by a parent or spouse, or by the court. The term includes a limited, emergency, and temporary substitute guardian but not a guardian ad litem.

§ 5-301. Appointment and Status of Guardian.

A person becomes a guardian of an incapacitated person by a parental or spousal appointment or upon appointment by the court. The guardianship continues until terminated, without regard to the location of the guardian or ward.

§ 5-306. Judicial Appointment of Guardian: Professional Evaluation.

At or before a hearing under this [part], the court may order a professional evaluation of the respondent and shall order the evaluation if the respondent so demands. If the court orders the evaluation, the respondent must be examined by a physician, psychologist, or other individual appointed by the court who is qualified to evaluate the respondent's alleged impairment. The examiner shall promptly file a written report with the court. Unless otherwise directed by the court, the report must contain:

> (1) a description of the nature, type, and extent of the respondent's specific cognitive and functional limitations;

> (2) an evaluation of the respondent's mental and physical condition and, if appropriate, educational potential, adaptive behavior, and social skills;

> (3) a prognosis for improvement and a recommendation as to the appropriate treatment or habitation plan; and

(4) the date of any assessment or examination upon which the report is based.

§ 5-311. Findings; Order of Appointment.

(a) The court may:

(1) appoint a limited or unlimited guardian for a respondent only if it finds by clear and convincing evidence that:

(A) the respondent is an incapacitated person; and

(B) the respondent's identified needs cannot be met by less restrictive means, including the use of appropriate technological assistance; or

(2) with appropriate findings, treat the petition as one for a protective order under Section 5-401, enter any other appropriate order, or dismiss the proceeding.

(b) The court, whenever feasible, shall grant to a guardian only those powers necessitated by the ward's limitations and demonstrated needs and make appointive and other orders that will encourage the development of the ward's maximum self-reliance and independence.

(c) Within 14 days after an appointment, a guardian shall send or deliver to the ward and to all other persons given notice of the hearing on the petition a copy of the order of appointment, together with a notice of the right to request termination or modification.

§ 5-314. Duties of Guardian.

(a) Except as otherwise limited by the court, a guardian shall make decisions regarding the ward's support, care, education, health, and welfare. A guardian shall exercise authority only as necessitated by the ward's limitations and, to the extent possible, shall encourage the ward to participate in decisions, act on the ward's own behalf, and develop or regain the capacity to manage the ward's personal affairs. A guardian, in making decisions, shall consider the expressed desires and personal values of the ward to the extent known to the guardian. A guardian at all times shall act in the ward's best interests and exercise reasonable care, diligence, and prudence.

(b) A guardian shall:

(1) become or remain personally acquainted with the ward and maintain sufficient contact with the ward to know of the ward's capacities, limitations, needs, opportunities, and physical and mental health;

(2) take reasonable care of the ward's personal effects and bring protective proceedings if necessary to protect the property of the ward;

(3) expend money of the ward that has been received by the guardian for the ward's current needs for support, care, education, health, and welfare;

(4) conserve any excess money of the ward for the ward's future needs, but if a conservator has been appointed for the estate of the ward, the guardian

shall pay the money to the conservator, at least quarterly, to be conserved for the ward's future needs;

(5) immediately notify the court if the ward's condition has changed so that the ward is capable of exercising rights previously removed; and

(6) inform the court of any changes in the ward's custodial dwelling or address.

In re Maher

New York Supreme Court, Appellate Division, 1994
207 A.D.2d 133, 621 N.Y.S.2d 617

Friedmann, J.

On this appeal—which appears to represent a case of first impression at the appellate level—we are asked to consider the propriety of a determination by the Supreme Court, Kings County (Leone, J.), embodied in a judgment entered October 8, 1993, that the respondent, Francis E. Maher, was not incapacitated as that term is defined in the recently enacted Mental Hygiene Law article 81. Based upon this determination, the court dismissed, with prejudice, the petition for a guardian for the respondent's property which had been brought by Francis E. Maher, Jr., the respondent's son. Since the court properly applied the standards and carried out the legislative intent of Mental Hygiene Law article 81, we now affirm.

* * *

On December 11, 1992, the respondent, attorney Francis E. Maher, suffered a stroke which left him with right-sided hemiplegia and aphasia. He was admitted to St. Luke's-Roosevelt Hospital where, on December 12, he underwent surgery, *inter alia,* to evacuate a hematoma from the frontal portion of his brain. For some time after the operation, the respondent remained partially paralyzed and aphasic, although occasionally he was able to speak a few words and to move a bit on his right side.

By order to show cause dated December 17, 1992, the appellant commenced a proceeding pursuant to Mental Hygiene Law article 77 for the appointment of a conservator. On December 17, 1992, the Honorable Sebastian Leone, Justice of the Supreme Court, appointed Ronald M. LaRocca, Esq., as temporary receiver, and Margaret M. Bomba, Esq., as the guardian ad litem, for the respondent. The guardian ad litem filed a report dated January 4, 1993, wherein she stated that due to the respondent's physical condition "he is presently incapable of managing his own business and financial affairs", and she recommended the appointment of a conservator of his property. The guardian ad litem objected to the appointment of Ronald M. LaRocca as conservator because of a "perceived conflict of interest"—due to the fact that LaRocca also represented a hospital that owed the respondent considerable sums in attorneys' fees for services rendered in past litigation. By order dated January 20, 1993, the Supreme Court permitted LaRocca to withdraw as temporary receiver and appointed the appellant and Elizabeth Maher, the respondent's sister and for many years his office manager, as temporary receivers pending the conservatorship hearing, upon the posting of an undertaking in the sum of $1,000,000 with an authorized surety company. LaRocca subsequently became the attorney for the appellant in the instant proceeding.

On March 31, 1993—the day on which the respondent executed a power of attorney naming the appellant as his "attorney-in-fact"—the temporary receivers advised the court that the respondent's condition had "improved dramatically" and that the appellant wished to discontinue the proceeding. The guardian ad litem joined in the application, and the court granted the request orally, directing the parties to settle an order withdrawing the petition.

However, according to the appellant, on the very night of the withdrawal petition, namely March 31, 1993, the respondent's condition abruptly deteriorated, and he began to behave in an irrational and abusive manner. At about this same time, the respondent also declared his intention to marry Ms. Helen Kelly, an attorney formerly associated with his law firm, whom he had been seeing since shortly after the death of his first wife in March of 1992. It was the guardian ad litem's considered opinion that the respondent's agitation was provoked by his sons' attempts to isolate him from Ms. Kelly and other friends, as well as by their refusal to permit him access to funds of any kind.

On May 7, 1993, the appellant announced his intention to go forward with the conservatorship proceeding, based on his allegation that the respondent had become "confused and irrational". On May 19, 1993, the respondent revoked the previously issued power of attorney in favor of the appellant, and executed a new power of attorney in favor of Irwin F. Simon, an attorney who had done per diem work for the respondent's law firm for many years. The guardian ad litem submitted her interim report dated May 20, 1993, along with a proposed order to withdraw the petition. The appellant promptly opposed the guardian ad litem's motion to dismiss, and requested a hearing to explore the need for the appointment of a conservator. The guardian ad litem submitted a "Supplemental Report" on June 1, 1993, defending herself against the appellant's charges of bias, and again urging the dismissal of the petition.

On June 1, 1993, the respondent disappeared from the home that he had shared with the appellant and another of his sons. On June 17, 1993, the respondent married Ms. Kelly.

At the outset of the hearing, which was held on June 21, 1993 and July 16, 1993, the proceeding was converted, with the consent of all parties, to one for the appointment of a guardian for property management under Mental Hygiene Law article 81. At the hearing, testimony was taken from the respondent's sister, Betty Maher, two of his sons, George and the appellant, his speech pathologist, Susan Sachs, and Dr. Valerie Lanyi, a rehabilitation specialist who had treated the respondent at the Rusk Institute, and who had seen him in consultation as recently as June 10, 1993.

Testifying for the respondent were the respondent himself, and his wife, Mrs. Helen Kelly Maher. At the conclusion of the hearing, the court found that the appellant had not carried his burden of proving by the requisite clear and convincing evidence that (1) the respondent was incapacitated, and (2) a guardian was necessary to manage his property and financial affairs.

* * *

The Legislature enacted Mental Hygiene Law article 81 (L 1992, ch 698), effective April 1, 1993, to remedy the perceived deficiencies in Mental Hygiene Law former articles 77 and 78, which had authorized the appointment of a conservator for the property or a committee for the person, respectively, of individuals whose ability to care for their property was substantially impaired or who were adjudged to be incompetent.

Former Mental Hygiene Law former article 78, the committee statute, required a finding of complete incompetence. That statute provided no guidance regarding what constituted incompetence, no standard governing the type of proof required to establish incompetence, and no specification respecting the range of powers assumed by a "committee of the person". However, a finding of incompetence resulted in a complete loss of civil rights and the accompanying stigma of total incapacity. Because of this stigma and loss of civil rights, the judiciary became increasingly reluctant to invoke article 78. This reluctance, together with the statutory preference for a conservator which appeared in both Mental Hygiene Law former articles 77 and 78, resulted in the virtual abandonment of the committee procedure (Koppell and Munnelly, *The New Guardian Statute: Article 81 of the Mental Hygiene Law*, 65 NY St BJ [No. 2] 16 [Feb. 1993] [hereinafter Koppell and Munnelly]).

Mental Hygiene Law article 77, the conservatorship statute, enacted in 1972, allowed for the appointment of a conservator for property only. While certain language in article 77 regarding the "personal well-being" of the conservatee suggested the possibility of using conservators of the property to exercise authority over the person of the individual, the needs of the population to be served by guardianship statutes proved so varied that the relief ostensibly offered by article 77 simply did not in fact afford either the authority or the flexibility necessary to address them all (Koppell and Munnelly, *op. cit.*).

On April 30, 1991, the Court of Appeals decided *Matter of Grinker (Rose)* (77 NY2d 703), holding, *inter alia*, that Mental Hygiene Law article 77 did not authorize a court to grant to a conservator the power to commit the conservatee to a nursing home. Such power to so significantly displace personal liberty, the Court explained, can be granted only pursuant to Mental Hygiene Law article 78, the committee statute, "with its full panoply of procedural due process safeguards"*(Matter of Grinker [Rose], supra,* at 710). That decision, although it clarified the respective reaches of articles 77 and 78, reinstated the courts' earlier dilemma. It further left without recourse the majority of incapacitated individuals who, although somewhat handicapped, were not hopelessly incompetent, and who, notwithstanding their need for varying degrees of assistance with their personal affairs as well as with property management, were not prepared utterly to relinquish in exchange therefor a lifetime's investment in integrity, autonomy, and dignity *(see,* Mental Hygiene Law § 81.01).

* * *

In response to this predicament, in 1992 the New York State Law Revision Commission proposed the creation of a single statute to replace Mental Hygiene Law articles 77 and 78. The projected legislation envisioned "a new type of guardianship proceeding based on the concept of the least restrictive alternative — one that authorizes the appointment of a guardian whose authority is appropriate to satisfy the needs of an incapacitated person, either personal or financial, while at the same time tailored and limited to only those activities for which a person needs assistance. The standard for appointment under this new procedure focuses on the decisional capacity and functional limitations of the person for whom the appointment is sought, rather than on some underlying mental or physical condition of the person. The proposal encouraged the participation of the allegedly incapacitated person in the proceeding to the greatest extent possible" (Koppell and Munnelly, *op. cit.,* at 17).

As a threshold matter, the new legislation emphasizes that "it is desirable for and beneficial to persons with incapacities to make available to them the least restrictive form of intervention which assists them in meeting their needs", while at the same time permitting them "to exercise the independence and self-determination of which they are capable". Such intervention was therefore to be "tailored to the individual needs of that person", taking into account "the personal wishes, preferences and desires of the person", and affording the person "the greatest amount of independence and self-determination and participation in all the decisions affecting [his] life" (Mental Hygiene Law § 81.01).

In exercising its discretion to appoint a guardian for an individual's property (the focus of the instant proceeding), a court must make a two-pronged determination: first, that the appointment is necessary to manage the property or financial affairs of that person, and, second, that the individual either agrees to the appointment or that the individual is "incapacitated" as defined in Mental Hygiene Law § 81.02 (b) (Mental Hygiene Law § 81.02 [a]).

As to the first prong, "the court shall consider the report of the court evaluator [heretofore the guardian ad litem, although with certain significant differences, as laid out in Mental Hygiene Law § 81.09] . . . and the sufficiency and reliability of available resources [*e.g.,* powers of attorney, trusts, representatives and protective payees] . . . to provide for personal needs or property management without the appointment of a guardian" (Mental Hygiene Law § 81.02 [a] [2]; § 81.03 [e]).

As to the second prong, a determination of incapacity must be based upon clear and convincing evidence that the person is likely to suffer harm because he is unable to provide for property management and cannot adequately understand

and appreciate the nature and consequences of such inability. The burden of proof is on the petitioner (*see,* Mental Hygiene Law § 81.02 [b]; § 81.12 [a]). In reaching its determination, the court must give primary consideration to the functional level and functional limitations of the person, including an assessment of the person's ability to manage the activities of daily living related to property management (*e.g.,* mobility, money management, and banking), his understanding and appreciation of the nature and consequences of any inability to manage these activities, his preferences, wishes, and values regarding management of these affairs, and the nature and extent of the person's property and finances, in the context of his ability to manage them (Mental Hygiene Law § 81.02 [c]; § 81.03 [h]).

Even if all of the elements of incapacity are present, a guardian should be appointed only as a last resort, and should not be imposed if available resources or other alternatives will adequately protect the person(*see,* Law Rev Commn Comments, reprinted in McKinney's Cons Laws of NY, Book 34A, Mental Hygiene Law § 81.02, 1994 Pocket Part, at 241–242).

* * *

Upon our review of the record before us, we are satisfied that the Supreme Court properly assessed the evidence in accordance with both the letter and the spirit of the new Mental Hygiene Law article 81.

Contrary to the appellant's contention, the clear and convincing evidence in the hearing record establishes only that the respondent suffers from certain functional limitations in speaking and writing, but not that he is likely to suffer harm because he is unable to provide for the management of his property, or that he is incapable of adequately understanding and appreciating the nature and consequences of his disabilities. Indeed, by granting a power of attorney to Irwin Simon, and by adding his wife as a signatory on certain of his bank accounts, the respondent evidenced that he appreciated his own handicaps to the extent that he effectuated a plan for assistance in managing his financial affairs without the need for a guardian.

Several witnesses testified to the respondent's ability to understand what he was told and to make his wishes known demonstratively. For example, the respondent's sister testified that she believed that her brother understood her when she provided him with information about the office. The appellant himself conceded that he routinely discussed collection and related business matters with the respondent, and that the respondent had regularly indicated his satisfaction with the appellant's management of his law firm's affairs. Dr. Lanyi, the physician in charge of the respondent's rehabilitation, expressed her doubt that at the time of his discharge from the Rusk Institute in mid-March 1993, the respondent could have managed his checkbook as he had formerly done, but opined that he was nonetheless, even at that time, aware of the magnitude of the sums he was spending. Moreover, according to Dr. Lanyi, when she last saw the respondent on June 10, 1993, her patient appeared to understand everything she said to him or asked of him, noting that on that occasion he had consistently responded to her remarks and inquiries in a prompt, calm manner, with appropriate words or gestures. The respondent's speech therapist, too, documented a steady improvement in her patient's ability to comprehend and respond to the tests she administered. Generally, the consensus among all witnesses was that the respondent had made, and was continuing to make, dramatic progress in his ability to comprehend information and to express himself—as well as in his mobility, which seemed essentially restored to normal—since the initial cerebrovascular episode.

Moreover, the court, which was in the best position to observe the respondent throughout the hearing, remarked that he reacted fittingly to the proceedings—even to the point of making it clear to his attorney and the court when he felt that certain questions or answers were objectionable. The court was further persuaded that the respondent knew the correct responses to the questions put to him on the stand, although he was not able verbally to express them. * * *

Although the appellant tries to distinguish the foregoing cases on the ground that the assets at issue were far more modest than the very substantial estate involved here, we do not find the size of the property involved, standing alone, to be dispositive. Rather, in the matter before us, there has been no showing that the respondent has lost the ability to appreciate his financial circumstances, or that others have taken control of his affairs without his comprehension or rational supervision. There has further been no demonstration of any waste, real or imminent, of the respondent's assets. There is an absence of proof that the respondent's chosen attorney and his wife (who is also an attorney) are incapable of managing the property at issue in accordance with the respondent's wishes.[1] Under such circumstances, the appellant has failed to demonstrate the need for a guardian under the standards enunciated in Mental Hygiene Law article 81.

The court did not err in excluding from evidence certain "tests" or "demonstrations" of the respondent's inability to expatiate on the meaning of a complicated legal text, to write checks in differing amounts to different payees, to separate and count diverse kinds of currency, and to explain his execution of two successive powers of attorney. The court was already well aware of the respondent's difficulty—due to his expressive aphasia and apraxia—in verbally communicating his understanding of the questions posed to him, and in writing or counting numbers clearly—although he could make himself understood to those to whom he could demonstrate nonverbally. Therefore, such "tests" would not have served to inform the court about the material issue before it—namely, whether the respondent appreciated the nature and consequences of his alleged inability personally to manage his property, and that he could suffer harm as a result *(see,* Mental Hygiene

---

1. It is further worthy of note that there has been no serious allegation, let alone demonstration, that either Ms. Kelly or Mr. Simon—two individuals with whom the respondent had long been acquainted *(cf., Matter of Ginsberg [Ginsberg],* NYLJ, Jan. 3, 1992, at 27, col 6, *supra)*—used fraud, duress, or undue influence on the respondent in order to bring about either his marriage or his execution of a second power of attorney.

Law § 81.02 [b]). As the evidence sought to be elicited would merely have distracted the court from the main point at issue, the court properly exercised its discretion in denying the admission of that evidence *(see, Harvey v Mazal Am. Partners,* 79 NY2d 218, 223–224; *People v Acevedo,* 40 NY2d 701, 704–705; *Clark v Brooklyn Hgts. R. R. Co.,* 177 NY 359, 361; *Riddle v Memorial Hosp.,* 43 AD2d 750, 751; Richardson, Evidence §§ 134, 136 [Prince 10th ed]).

The court was similarly justified in refusing to allow the appellant's expert, Dr. Gannon, who had never examined the respondent, to testify to the respondent's alleged incapacitation based upon his appearance in the courtroom. As the court correctly ruled, the appellant could not compensate for his failure to request a timely psychiatric examination of the respondent by permitting Dr. Gannon to draw professional conclusions about the respondent in such an improper setting and under such stressful conditions. Dr. Gannon was also correctly precluded from testifying to the respondent's competence based upon his review of the respondent's hospital records, which the appellant's counsel had subpoenaed to his office on May 24, 1993, pursuant to his client's power of attorney, some five days after that power of attorney had been revoked. There is further no merit to the appellant's contention that the respondent had waived his physician-patient privilege by permitting the appellant's witness, Dr. Lanyi, to testify "full[y]" to her assessment of his inpatient condition, because the record reveals that Dr. Lanyi relied only upon her own notes during the hearing, and at no point consulted the respondent's charts from St. Luke's-Roosevelt Hospital or the Rusk Institute.

Finally, the hearing court erred in admitting into evidence the report of the court evaluator because, although present at the hearing, the court evaluator did not take the stand and submit to cross-examination *(see,* Mental Hygiene Law § 81.12 [b]). We conclude that this error was harmless, however, in view of the fact that the court expressly based its decision upon its own observations of the respondent during the proceedings, and upon the testimony of the various witnesses. Moreover, the record amply supports the Supreme Court's conclusion that the appellant failed to establish by the requisite clear and convincing evidence the respondent's need for a guardian of his property under the standards enunciated in Mental Hygiene Law article 81, independently of the improperly admitted court evaluator's report *(see, e.g., Berger v Estate of Berger,* 203 AD2d 502; *Matter of Wieczorek,* 186 AD2d 204; *Matter of LoGuidice,* 186 AD2d 659, 660; *Turner v Danker,* 30 AD2d 564).

Therefore, the judgment is affirmed insofar as appealed from.

O'Brien, J. P., Joy and Krausman, JJ., concur.

Ordered that the judgment is affirmed insofar as appealed from, with costs.

Notes

The appointment of a guardian, as distinct from a durable power of attorney, results from a judicial determination that, first, a court has jurisdiction to appoint a guardian, *see* Uniform Adult Guardianship and Protective Proceedings

Act § 203 (2007), and, second, an individual met the definition of incompetency under the state code. *See, e.g.,* Davis v. Cuyahoga County Adult Protective Services, No. 77116, 2000 WL 1513752 (Ohio Ct. App. 2000) (holding that appointment of a guardian was consistent with due process when it was demonstrated that an individual was incapable of taking proper care of himself or his property); Desiree C. Hensley, *Due Process is Not Optional: Mississippi Conservatorship Proceedings Fall Short on Basic Due Process Protections for Elderly and Disabled Adults*, 86 Miss. L.J. 715 (2017). There remains a presumption that the proposed ward possesses capacity at the start of any proceeding. *See, e.g.,* Holmes v. Burchett, 766 So. 2d 387 (Fla. Dist. Ct. App. 2000) and that incapacity must be proved with clear and convincing evidence. *See, e.g., In re* Carole L., 26 N.Y.S.3d 133, 135 (N.Y. Supreme Ct. 2016). Any evaluation of incapacity must be performed by a professional with expertise appropriate for the allegation of incapacity. *See, e.g.,* Matter of Bailey, 771 S.W.2d 779 (Ark. 1989) (holding that the state's statutory requirements were not met for an adjudication of incapacity).

A guardian is empowered by the court to manage the estate of an incompetent to accommodate the "best interest" of the incompetent. Alternatively, a court will permit a guardian to utilize a "substituted judgement" approach, approximating what the incompetent would have done in similar circumstances. *See, e.g., In re* Guardianship of John J.H., 896 N.Y.S.2d 662 (N.Y. Surr. Ct. 2010) (holding that guardian could not sell ward's artwork and donate proceeds to charity); *but see In re* Trott, 288 A.2d 303 (N.J. Super. Ct. Ch. Div. 1972) (holding that guardian could transfer assets of the incompetent to donees by gift); Lawrence A. Frolik & Linda S. Whitton, *The UPC Substituted Judgement/Best Interest Standard for Guardian Decisions: A Proposal for Reform*, 45 U. Mich. J.L. Reform 739 (2012). The alternative for "substituted Judgement" is doing what the guardian considers to be in the best interest of the incapacitated person. *See* Unif. Prob. Code § 5-314(a) ("A guardian at all times shall act in the ward's best interest and exercise reasonable care, diligence, and prudence.").

State statutes often require guardians to report to the court on an annual basis, reporting on the status of any ward for whom the guardian is responsible. *See, e.g., In re* Mark C.H., 906 N.Y.S.2d 419 (N.Y. Surr. Ct. 2010); Karen E. Boxx & Terry W. Hammond, *A Call for Standards: An Overview of the Current Status and Need for Guardianship Standards of Conduct and Codes of Ethics*, 2012 Utah L. Rev. 1207; Unif. Prob. Code § 5-317. Reports: Monitoring of Guardianship (2019).

The excerpt concerning Brooke Astor that follows is illustrative of a guardian's criminal mismanagement. On June 21, 2013, Mr. Marshall, then 89 years old, entered Fishkill Correctional Facility, 70 miles north of New York City, but was paroled in August of the same year due to documented health issues that could not be addressed in prison. Russ Buettner, *Brooke Astor Son is Paroled*, N.Y. Times, Aug. 23, 2013, at A21. Mr. Marshall died on November 30, 2014, at the age of 90 years old.

MERYL GORDON
MRS. ASTOR REGRETS: THE HIDDEN BETRAYALS
OF A FAMILY BEYOND REPROACH

(2008)

[A]t the age of 105, Brooke Astor had passed away at her Westchester County home, Holly Hill. For nearly a century she had presented herself to the world as a woman with a good-natured and witty persona, keeping secrets and sorrows at bay. But as her life began to draw to a close, her dreams grew more vivid and disturbing; imaginary intruders pursued her. In her last year, she was dangerously fragile and affected with a *Merck Manual* of ailments. A voracious reader and the author of four books, she had lost the ability to speak in full sentences but could still communicate using gestures or facial expressions. . . . Even near the end, keeping up appearances still mattered, as she clung to her sense of dignity.

[At the death of Vincent Astor, Brooke Astor's husband, in 1959], Brooke became a rich woman, with $2 million in cash, $60 million in trust for her benefit, and valuable real estate, including the couple's New York apartment, Ferncliff, and the houses in Maine and Arizona.

Id. at 4.

Notes

Brooke Astor—at one time, one of the wealthiest women in the United States, and certainly one of the most notable matriarchs of New York society—died in 2007, amidst a civil and criminal dispute concerning her son's conduct as her guardian and conservator. The suit against Anthony D. Marshall had been initiated by his own son, Philip Marshall—the grandson of Brooke Astor—who had charged his father with elder abuse, alleging that his father permitted his grandmother to live "in squalor amid peeling paint and was being deprived of medical care." MERYL GORDON, MRS. ASTOR REGRETS: THE HIDDEN BETRAYALS OF A FAMILY BEYOND REPROACH, 40 (2008). Philip requested that his father be removed as guardian and replaced with Annette de la Renta, a long-time friend of his grandmother. "Her bedroom is so cold in the winter that my grandmother is forced to sleep in the TV room in torn nightgowns on a filthy couch that smells, probably from dog urine. [His father] has turned a blind eye to her . . . while enriching himself with millions of dollars." *Id.* at 41. On October 8, 2009, a jury convicted Mr. Marshall on charges that he stole tens of millions of dollars from [his mother] as she suffered from Alzheimer's disease in the twilight of her life. John Eligon, *Mrs. Astor's Son Guilty of Taking Tens of Millions*, N.Y. TIMES, Oct. 9, 2009 at A1. Mr. Marshall, then 85 years-of-age, was convicted of fourteen of the sixteen counts brought against him; the crimes ranged from possession of stolen property to grand larceny. When the suit against Mr. Marshall was brought by the district attorney, the statement made to the press stressed that the indictment was meant to send a message: "It happens fairly frequently that a son or daughter or grandson will steal from their parent or grandparent . . . . That's why these cases are important, because we want the public to know that if you take advantage of an elderly person with diminished capacity, you're going to get prosecuted." Meryl Gordon, Mrs. Astor Regrets: The Hidden Betrayals of a Family Beyond Reproach, at 269 (2008).

Problem

Three adult sisters petitioned the court to name one of them as the guardian for their mother, who, they allege, exhibited negative behavior, including unreasonable desires and wishes, such as living in a large urban environment and volunteering at the American Museum of Natural History. The daughters assert that this behavior results from a stroke the mother suffered eight years ago and the prodding of the mother's male occupational therapist. Overall, the mother does not recognize the perils of her desires, thereby exhibiting paranoid, unrealistic, and somewhat delusional behavior. This behavior, together with the difficulty the mother has in performing the activities of daily living, such as bathing, dressing, and performing household tasks, suggests that the mother needs to have a guardian appointed to care for her. Based on the Uniform Probate Code provision provided and the holding of the *Maher* decision, if you were the judge before whom the parties appear, what test would you employ in determining whether to grant the guardianship petition of the daughters? *See* Matter of Judith T., 58 Misc. 3d 747, 67 N.Y.S.3d 447 (2017).

E. Conservatorship

Wayne M. Gazur & Robert M. Phillips
Estate Planning: Principles and Problems
(2d ed. 2008)

> In some states the term "guardian" encompasses protection of an individual's body and welfare (*e.g.*, daily care and educational and medical decisions) as well as management of the individual's finances. [Nonetheless] we will use the modern bifurcated structure of the [Uniform Probate Code] in which the protector of the individual's body and welfare is a "guardian" and the manager of the individual's finances is a "conservator."

Id. at 153.

> If the parents have left more than trivial amounts of property to their minor children a conservator will often be required to manage the property and make payments to the guardian for their care and expenses or to others for the benefit of the children. Third parties such as life insurance companies often refuse to make disbursements to a minor unless a conservator has been appointed. Under the UPC there is a specified order in which the court must consider otherwise qualified persons to be a conservator.

Id.

> While the guardian and the conservator may be separate persons, clients often designate the same individuals to serve in both capacities. This makes sense in some situations, but there are some drawbacks. First, the guardian is usually chosen for protective and nurturing characteristics and may not possess the money management and recordkeeping skills required of a conservator. Second, if the guardian's household is of much more modest wealth than the ward's the ward's higher standard of living in dress, entertainment, and education may create friction with the guardian, the guardian's children, and so forth. Granted, this friction cannot be avoided by using a separate conservator, but not doing so can invite abuses (*e.g.*, the ward foots the bill for everyone on excursions) that might be avoided if the two function are separated. That said, in some situations, not naming the guardian also as the conservator could be taken as an insult.

Id. at 154.

Uniform Probate Code (2019)

§ 5-401. Protective Proceeding.

Upon petition and after notice and hearing, the court may appoint a limited or unlimited conservator or make any other protective order provided in this [part] in relation to the estate and affairs of:

(1) a minor, if the court determines that the minor owns money or property requiring management or protection that cannot otherwise be provided or has or may have business affairs that may be put at risk or prevented because of the minor's age, or that money is needed for support and education and that protection is necessary or desirable to obtain or provide money; or

(2) any individual, including a minor, if the court determines that, for reasons other than age:

(A) by clear and convincing evidence, the individual is unable to manage property and business affairs because of an impairment in the ability to receive and evaluate information or make decisions, even with the use of appropriate technological assistance, or because the individual is missing, detained, or unable to return to the United States; and

(B) by a preponderance of evidence, the individual has property that will be wasted or dissipated unless management is provided or money is needed for the support, care, education, health, and welfare of the individual or of individuals who are entitled to the individual's support and that protection is necessary or desirable to obtain or provide money.

§ 5-403. Original Petition for Appointment or Protective Order.

(a) The following may petition for the appointment of a conservator or for any other appropriate protective order:

(1) the person to be protected;

(2) an individual interested in the estate, affairs, or welfare of the person to be protected, including a parent, guardian, or custodian; or

(3) a person who would be adversely affected by lack of effective management of the property and business affairs of the person to be protected.

* * *

§ 5-413. Who May Be Conservator: Priorities.

(a) Except as otherwise provided in subsection (d), the court, in appointing a conservator, shall consider persons otherwise qualified in the following order of priority:

(1) a conservator, guardian or the estate, or other like fiduciary appointed or recognized by an appropriate court of any other jurisdiction in which the protected person resides;

(2) a person nominated as conservator by the respondent, including the respondent's most recent nomination made in a durable power of attorney, if the respondent has attained the age or 14 years of age and at the time of the nomination had sufficient capacity to express a preference.

(3) an agent appointed by the respondent to manage the respondent's property under a durable power of attorney;

(4) the spouse of the respondent;

(5) an adult child of the respondent;

(6) a parent of the respondent; and

(7) an adult with whom the respondent has resided for more than six months before the filing of the petition.

* * *

§ 5-418. General Duties of Conservator; Plan.

(a) A conservator, in relation to powers conferred by this [part] or implicit in the title acquired by virtue of the proceeding, is a fiduciary and shall observe the standards of care applicable to a trustee.

(b) A conservator may exercise authority only as necessitated by the limitations of the protected person, and to the extent possible, shall encourage the person to participate in decisions, act in the person's own behalf, and develop or regain the ability to manage the person's estate and business affairs.

(c) Within 60 days after appointment, a conservator shall file with the appointing court a plan for protecting, managing, expending, and distributing the assets of the protected person's estate. The plan must be based on the actual needs of the person and take into consideration the best interests of the person. The conservator shall include in the plan steps to develop or restore the person's ability to manage the person's property, and estimate of the duration of the conservatorship, and projections of expenses and resources.

(d) In investing an estate, selecting assets of the estate for distribution, and invoking powers of revocation or withdrawal available for the use and benefit of the protected person and exercisable by the conservator, a conservator shall take into account any estate plan of the person known to the conservator and may examine the will and any other donative, nominative, or other appointive instrument of the person.

Notes

State statutes often use the terms "conservator" and "guardian" interchangeably, although the Uniform Adult Guardianship and Protective Proceedings Act (2007) and the Uniform Probate Code distinctively assign property management to a conservator and personal decisions concerning a ward to a guardian. There may be additional parties with responsibility over a ward—for example, a person able to make personal health care decisions for the ward, often nominated under a health care directive. Such medical decision-making authority is not part of the list of powers given to a guardian by state statute. *See, e.g., In re* D.L.H., 2 A.3d 505 (Pa. 2010) (holding that guardians may not refuse life-preserving medical treatment on behalf of an incompetent person who is not faced with an end-stage condition or permanent unconsciousness). In addition, if a competent person executed a durable power of attorney, the holder of that power is responsible to the guardian appointed by the court. *See, e.g.,* Estate of Ellis, 23 So. 3d 589 (Miss. Ct. App. 2009). A principal giving a durable power of attorney may provide a preference when, and if, a court subsequently appoints a guardian or conservator. *See, e.g., In re* Guardianship and Conservatorship of Parkhurst, 243 P.3d 961 (Wyo. 2010). However, any choice must be established to be in the best interest of the incompetent person. *See, e.g., In re* Iwen, No. CX-02-1777, 2003 WL 21007240 (Minn. Ct. App. May 6, 2003).

F. Health Care Decisions

Every state has enacted legislation allowing a competent adult to authorize health care decisions, thereby allowing a person to decline additional health care, among other things, even if this should result in death. Indeed, Congress has decided that every patient admitted to a hospital receiving federal funds must be advised of his or her right to sign a health care directive. *See Patient Self-Determination Act, Omnibus Budget Reconciliation Act of 1990*, Pub. L. No. 101-508, § 4751, 104 Stat. 1388, 1388-204 (Requirements for Advance Directives) (codified in scattered sections of 42 U.S.C. §§ 1396a(a)(58) & (w) (2015)). Please note that declining additional health care is not comparable to "causing or aiding a suicide," as that term was discussed in Washington v. Glucksberg, 521 U.S. 702, 117 S. Ct. 2258 (1997). In that decision, the Court held that Washington's prohibition of assisted suicide does not violate the Fourteenth Amendment's liberty interest as it extends to a personal choice, by a mentally competent, terminally ill adult, to commit physician-assisted suicide. The state's prohibition is rationally related to its interest in preserving life, protecting the integrity and ethics of the medical profession, protecting the most vulnerable in society from coercion, and erosion of the ban on voluntary euthanasia.

The Supreme Court of Montana has ruled on whether physician assisted suicide may be prosecuted as homicide and, in the alternative, whether the practice violates public policy. Baxter v. State, 354 Mont. 234, 224 P.3d 1211 (2009). The decision involved a retired truck driver who was terminally ill with lymphocytic leukemia, with diffuse lymphadenopathy. *Id.* at 237–38, 224 P.3d at 1214. The legal issue was whether the state's homicide statutes could be used to prosecute the physicians who had provided the man with a lethal dose of medication, to be self-administered at the time of the patient's choosing, the effect of which would be to cause his death. *Id.* at 237, 224 P.3d at 1213–14. Instead of focusing on whether the dying man had a right to die with dignity under the state's constitution, the court focused its opinion on "whether the consent of the patient to his physician's aid in dying could constitute a statutory defense to a homicide charge against the physician." *Id.* at 239, 224 P.2d at 1215. The court held that consent to physician aid in dying, provided to terminally ill, mentally competent adult patients, is not against public policy. *Id.* at 240, 224 P.2d at 1214. Instead, the Montana Rights of the Terminally Ill Act "confers on terminally ill patients a right to have their end-of-life wishes followed, even if it requires *direct* participation by a physician through withdrawing or withholding treatment." *Id.* at 244, 224 P.3d at 1215 (emphasis in original). The court distinguishes physician assistance from mercy killing or euthanasia, holding that, under physician assistance, the physician is not intending to kill the patient, but instead, is providing assistance to a patient's autonomous decision to self-administer drugs that will cause his or her own death. *Id.* at 247, 224 P.3d at 1219. The state statute mandates such cooperation; indeed, a physician's failure to give effect to a terminally ill patient's life-ending declaration is a crime. *Id.* at 246, 224 P.3d at 1219. There was a strong dissent, arguing that the statute upon which the majority based its opinion — the Montana Rights of the Terminally Ill Act — was enacted to protect physicians when they withhold or withdraw life-sustaining treatment, not when they knowingly provide treatment that will result in the death of patient. *Id.* at 269, 224 P.3d at 1233. The fact that the patient takes the medication at a time of his or her choosing does not lessen the impact of providing the means by which the patient will die. *Id.* at 275, 224 P.3d at 1237. "Thus, the law accommodating a patient's desire to die of *natural* causes by withholding treatment does not, as the Court posits, support a public policy in favor of the deliberate action by a physician to cause a patient's *pre-natural*, or premature, death." *Id.* at 276, 224 P.3d at 1237.

In 1994, Oregon became the first state to legalize physician-assisted suicide with the passage of the Oregon Death With Dignity Act. OR. REV. STAT. §§ 127.800 et seq. (2019). *See also* Gonzales v. Oregon, 546 U.S. 243, 126 S. Ct. 904 (2006) (upholding state statute). The Act differs from the approach permitted by the Montana legislation. In Oregon, a physician is exempt from civil or criminal liability if the physician prescribes a lethal medication for a terminally ill patient, but the patient must make multiple requests, notify any next-of-kin of the action, and wait for two waiting periods.

Increasingly, states are enacting physician-assisted suicide statutes. Washington legislation permits physician-assisted suicide in a manner similar to Oregon. *See*

WASH. REV. CODE §§ 70.245.010 *et seq.* (2019). Similar to Oregon's statute, Washington's statute permits an adult, who is a resident of the state and has been determined by the attending physician, and also by a consulting physician, to be terminally ill, to be prescribed medication that will cause death. Both physicians must conclude that the patient is suffering from an incurable terminal illness that will result in death within six months. The patient must voluntarily express his or her wish to die and then request the medication that will result in terminating life in a humane and dignified manner.

Vermont has enacted an assisted suicide statute—the Patient Choice at End of Life, 18 Vt. Stat. Ann. §§ 5281–5292 (2019). The legislation grants immunity to any physician "if the physician prescribes to a patient with a terminal condition medication to be self-administered for the purpose of hastening the patient's death and the physician affirms by documenting in the patient's medical record that" fifteen conditions have been met. The fifteen conditions involve a patient's request, while fully capacitated and knowledgeable, and while the patient has a terminable condition. Similar to the Oregon and Washington statutes, the Vermont statute provides that the patient must make two oral requests and one written request of the physician, with requirements for documentation and witnesses to the requests. Vermont also has waiting periods between when the physician receives the requests and when the prescription may be filled.

The California legislature passed legislation permitting assisted suicide, and the governor signed the bill into law in October 2015. Similar to other state laws permitting assisted suicide, the California law has requirements of adulthood, state residency, a terminal diagnosis, a waiting period, multiple requests to a physician, and various determinations that a physician must make before prescribing life-ending drugs. *See* End of Life Option Act, CAL. HEALTH & SAFETY CODE § 443 *et seq.* (2019).

For an analysis of physician assisted suicide, see Zachary A. Feldman, Comment. *Suicide and Euthanasia: The International Perspective on the Right to Die*, 104 CORNELL L. REV. 715 (2019); Samuel D. Hodge, Jr., *Wrongful Prolongation of Life—A Cause of Action That May Have Finally Moved Into the Mainstream*, 37 QUINNIPIAC L. REV. 167 (2019); Frederick R. Parker, *Palliative Sedation and the Louisiana Natural Death Act*, 79 LA. L. REV. 1103 (2019); Mark Storslee, *Religious Accommodation, The Establishment Clause, and Third-Party Harm*, 86 U. CHI. L. REV. 871 (2019); Lois Shepherd, *The End of End-of-Life Law*, 92 N.C. L. REV. 1693 (2014); Paul T. Menzel & Bonnie Steinbock, *Advance Directives, Dementia, and Physician-Assisted Death*, 41 J.L. MED. & ETHICS 484 (2013); Barbara A. Noah, *The Role of Race in End-of-Life Care*, 15 J. HEALTH CARE L. & POLICY 349 (2012); Brian H. Bix, *Physician Assisted Suicide and Federalism*, 17 NOTRE DAME J.L., ETHICS & PUB. POL'Y 53 (2003); Cass Sunstein, *The Right to Die*, 106 YALE L.J. 1123 (1997); Kevin P. Quinn, *Assisted Suicide and Equal Protection: In Defense of the Distinction Between Killing and Letting Die*, 13 ISSUES L. & MED. 145 (1997); Washington v. Glucksberg, 521 U.S. 702, 117 S. Ct. 2258 (1997) (state's prohibition of assisted suicide does not offend a liberty interest under the Fourteenth Amendment). For cases pertinent to the litigation involving family members, see *In re* Guardianship of Schiavo, 792 So. 2d 551 (Fla. Dist. Ct. App. 2001); Norman L. Cantor, *Twenty-Five Years After Quinlan: A Review of the Jurisprudence of Death and Dying*, 29 J.L. Med. & Ethics 182 (2001).

Often a state statute will refer to "living wills." These are written directives of the principal, requesting to be allowed to die a "natural" death, without the necessity of providing extraordinary medical procedures to prolong life. The importance of these statutes is that they insulate the physician or a medical establishment against civil or criminal liability. *See, e.g.,* Brooke M. Benzio, *Advance Health Care Directives: Problems and Solutions for the Elder Law and Estate Planning Practitioner,* 26 St. Thomas L. Rev. 37 (2013); Joseph Karl Grant, *The Advance Directive Registry or Lockbox: A Model Proposal and Call to Legislative Action,* 37 J. Legis. 81 (2011); Ohio Rev. Code Ann. § 2133.11 (2015); 755 Ill. Comp. Stat. § 35/7 (2015). For additional commentary on health care directives, see Jeffrey A. Schoenblum, 2008 Multistate Guide to Estate Planning, at Table 7 (detailing state variations).

Health care directives are a recent phenomenon, and there is great variation among state requirements. The Uniform Health-Care Decisions Act (1993) has been enacted in a few states. Other states have different requirements, thus necessitating careful preparation of instruments. Without the written instrument, reliance will be upon what the court defines as "clear and convincing evidence" of intent. Consider the following.

Uniform Health-Care Decisions Act (2019)

§ 2. Advance Health-Care Directives.

(a) An adult or emancipated minor may give an individual instruction. The instruction may be oral or written. The instruction may be limited to take effect only if a specified condition arises.

(b) An adult or emancipated minor may execute a power of attorney for health care, which may authorize the agent to make any health-care decision the principal could have made while having capacity. The power must be in writing and signed by the principal. The power remains in effect notwithstanding the principal's later incapacity and may include individual instructions. Unless related to the principal by blood, marriage, or adoption, an agent may not be an owner, operator, or employee of [a residential long-term health-care institution] at which the principal is receiving care.

(c) Unless otherwise specified in a power of attorney for health care, the authority of an agent becomes effective only upon a determination that the principal lacks capacity, and ceases to be effective upon a determination that the principal has recovered capacity.

(d) Unless otherwise specified in a written advance health-care directive, a determination that an individual lacks or has recovered capacity, or that another condition exists that affects an individual instruction or the authority of an agent, must be made by the primary physician.

(e) An agent shall make a health-care decision in accordance with the principal's individual instructions, if any, and other wishes to the extent known to the agent. Otherwise, the agent shall make the decision in accordance with the agent's determination of the principal's best interest. In determining the principal's best interest, the agent shall consider the principal's personal values to the extent known to the agent.

(f) A health-care decision made by an agent for a principal is effective without judicial approval.

(g) A written advance health-care directive may include the individual's nomination of a guardian of the person.

(h) An advance health-care directive is valid for purposes of this [Act] if it complies with this [Act], regardless of when or where executed or communicated.

Notes

Every state permits citizens to make a heath care directive. Some call it a living will, some specify the use of a power of attorney for health care, and some allow family members or friends to make health care decisions if they become incapacitated. In many ways, the uniform act parallels federal legislation. *See, e.g.,* PATIENT SELF-DETERMINATION ACT, 42 U.S.C. § 1395cc(f)(1)(C) (Medicare); 42 U.S.C. § 1396a (w)(1)(c) (Medicaid). The 1993 legislation is an effort to create some uniformity to assist a very mobile population seeking certainty in varying locations. Nonetheless, not all states comply with all of the provisions of the legislation. For example, compare the California legislation, *infra*, with the essential elements of the uniform act. The goals of the uniform act, as described in the Prefatory Note, are the following:

First, each competent adult, or a designated agent, has the right to make all medical care decisions concerning his or her care;

Second, the uniform act addresses every aspect of health care;

Third, the uniform act emphasizes simplicity; instructions may be written or oral, neither witnesses nor acknowledgment is required, and a form is provided;

Fourth, the wishes of the principal are paramount, and if unknown, an agent must act in the best interest of the principal and in accordance with the values and wishes of the principal. Furthermore, a guardian may not revoke an incapacitated principal's health directive without court approval;

Fifth, health care institutions must comply with the health care directive of the principal unless compliance violates conscience, quality of care, or applicable health care standards;

Sixth, the legislation provides a procedure for resolution of disputes.

California Probate Code (2019)

§ 4701. Statutory form.

The statutory advance health care directive form is as follows:

Advance Health Care Directive

(California Probate Code Section 4701)
Explanation

You have the right to give instructions about your own health care. You also have the right to name someone else to make health care decisions for you. This form lets you do either or both of these things. It also lets you express your wishes regarding donation of organs and the designation of your primary physician. If you use this form, you may complete or modify all or any part of it. You are free to use a different form.

Part 1 of this form is a power of attorney for health care. Part 1 lets you name another individual as agent to make health care decisions for you if you become incapable of making your own decisions or if you want someone else to make those decisions for you now even though you are still capable. You may also name an alternate agent to act for you if your first choice is not willing, able, or reasonably available to make decisions for you. (Your agent may not be an operator or employee of a community care facility or a residential care facility where you are receiving care, or your supervising health care provider or employee of the health care institution where you are receiving care, unless your agent is related to you or is a coworker.)

Unless the form you sign limits the authority of your agent, your agent may make all health care decisions for you. This form has a place for you to limit the authority of your agent. You need not limit the authority of your agent if you wish to rely on your agent for all health care decisions that may have to be made. If you choose not to limit the authority of your agent, your agent will have the right to:

(a) Consent or refuse consent to any care, treatment, service, or procedure to maintain, diagnose, or otherwise affect a physical or mental condition.

(b) Select or discharge health care providers and institutions.

(c) Approve or disapprove diagnostic tests, surgical procedures, and programs of medication.

(d) Direct the provision, withholding, or withdrawal of artificial nutrition and hydration and all other forms of health care, including cardiopulmonary resuscitation.

(e) Make anatomical gifts, authorize an autopsy, and direct disposition of remains.

Part 2 of this form lets you give specific instructions about any aspect of your health care, whether or not you appoint an agent. Choices are provided for you to express your wishes regarding the provision, withholding, or withdrawal of treatment to keep you alive, as well as the provision of pain relief. Space is also provided for you to add to the choices you have made or for you to write out any additional wishes.

If you are satisfied to allow your agent to determine what is best for you in making end-of-life decisions, you need not fill out Part 2 of this form.

Part 3 of this form lets you express an intention to donate your bodily organs and tissues following your death.

Part 4 of this form lets you designate a physician to have primary responsibility for your health care.

After completing this form, sign and date the form at the end. The form must be signed by two qualified witnesses or acknowledged before a notary public. Give a copy of the signed and completed form to your physician, to any other health care providers you may have, to any health care institution at which you are receiving care, and to any health care agents you have named. You should talk to the person you have named as agent to make sure that he or she understands your wishes and is willing to take the responsibility.

You have the right to revoke this advance health care directive or replace this form at any time.

* * * * * * * * * * * * * * * * *

PART 1
POWER OF ATTORNEY FOR HEALTH CARE

(1.1) DESIGNATION OF AGENT: I designate the following individual as my agent to make health care decisions for me:

_____

(name of individual you choose as agent)

_____

(address) (city) (state) (ZIP Code)

_____

(home phone) (work phone)

OPTIONAL: If I revoke my agent's authority or if my agent is not willing, able, or reasonably available to make a health care decision for me, I designate as my first alternate agent:

_____

(name of individual you choose as first alternate agent)

_____

(address) (city) (state) (ZIP Code)

_____

(home phone) (work phone)

OPTIONAL: If I revoke the authority of my agent and first alternate agent or if neither is willing, able, or reasonably available to make a health care decision for me, I designate as my second alternate agent:

_____

(name of individual you choose as second alternate agent)

_____

(address) (city) (state) (ZIP Code)

_____

(home phone) (work phone)

(1.2) AGENT'S AUTHORITY: My agent is authorized to make all health care decisions for me, including decisions to provide, withhold, or withdraw artificial nutrition and hydration and all other forms of health care to keep me alive, except as I state here:

_____

_____

_____

(Add additional sheets if needed.)

(1.3) WHEN AGENT'S AUTHORITY BECOMES EFFECTIVE: My agent's authority becomes effective when my primary physician determines that I am unable to make my own health care decisions unless I mark the following box. If I mark this box [ ], my agent's authority to make health care decisions for me takes effect immediately.

(1.4) AGENT'S OBLIGATION: My agent shall make health care decisions for me in accordance with this power of attorney for health care, any instructions I give in Part 2 of this form, and my other wishes to the extent known to my agent. To the extent my wishes are unknown, my agent shall make health care decisions for me in accordance with what my agent determines to be in my best interest. In determining my best interest, my agent shall consider my personal values to the extent known to my agent.

(1.5) AGENT'S POSTDEATH AUTHORITY: My agent is authorized to make anatomical gifts, authorize an autopsy, and direct disposition of my remains, except as I state here or in Part 3 of this form:

_____

_____

_____

(Add additional sheets if needed.)

(1.6) NOMINATION OF CONSERVATOR: If a conservator of my person needs to be appointed for me by a court, I nominate the agent designated in this form. If that agent is not willing, able, or reasonably available to act as conservator, I nominate the alternate agents whom I have named, in the order designated.

PART 2
INSTRUCTIONS FOR HEALTH CARE

If you fill out this part of the form, you may strike any wording you do not want.

(2.1) END-OF-LIFE DECISIONS: I direct that my health care providers and others involved in my care provide, withhold, or withdraw treatment in accordance with the choice I have marked below:

[ ] (a) Choice Not To Prolong Life

I do not want my life to be prolonged if (1) I have an incurable and irreversible condition that will result in my death within a relatively short time, (2) I become unconscious and, to a reasonable degree of medical certainty, I will not regain consciousness, or (3) the likely risks and burdens of treatment would outweigh the expected benefits, OR

[ ] (b) Choice To Prolong Life

I want my life to be prolonged as long as possible within the limits of generally accepted health care standards.

(2.2) RELIEF FROM PAIN: Except as I state in the following space, I direct that treatment for alleviation of pain or discomfort be provided at all times, even if it hastens my death:

_____

_____

(Add additional sheets if needed.)

(2.3) OTHER WISHES: (If you do not agree with any of the optional choices above and wish to write your own, or if you wish to add to the instructions you have given above, you may do so here.) I direct that:

_____

_____

(Add additional sheets if needed.)

PART 3
DONATION OF ORGANS AT DEATH (OPTIONAL)

(3.1) Upon my death (mark applicable box):

[ ] (a) I give any needed organs, tissues, or parts, OR

[ ] (b) I give the following organs, tissues, or parts only.

_____

(c) My gift is for the following purposes (strike any of the following you do not want):

(1) Transplant

(2) Therapy

(3) Research

(4) Education

PART 4
PRIMARY PHYSICIAN (OPTIONAL)

(4.1) I designate the following physician as my primary physician:

_____

(name of physician)

_____

(address) (city) (state) (ZIP Code)

_____

(phone)

OPTIONAL: If the physician I have designated above is not willing, able, or reasonably available to act as my primary physician, I designate the following physician as my primary physician:

_____

(name of physician)

_____

(address) (city) (state) (ZIP Code)

_____

(phone)

* * * * * * * * * * * * * * * * *

PART 5

(5.1) EFFECT OF COPY: A copy of this form has the same effect as the original.

(5.2) SIGNATURE: Sign and date the form here:

_____

_____

(date) (sign your name)

_____

_____

(address) (print your name)

_____

(city) (state)

(5.3) STATEMENT OF WITNESSES: I declare under penalty of perjury under the laws of California (1) that the individual who signed or acknowledged this advance health care directive is personally known to me, or that the individual's identity was proven to me by convincing evidence, (2) that the individual signed or acknowledged this advance directive in my presence, (3) that the individual appears to be of sound mind and under no duress, fraud, or undue influence, (4) that I am not a person appointed as agent by this advance directive, and (5) that I am not the individual's health care provider, an employee of the individual's health care provider, the operator of a community care facility, an employee of an operator of a community care facility, the operator of a residential care facility for the elderly, nor an employee of an operator of a residential care facility for the elderly.

First witness Second witness

_____

_____

(print name) (print name)

_____

_____

(address) (address)

_____

_____

(city) (state) (city) (state)

_____

_____

(signature of witness) (signature of witness)

_____

_____

(date) (date)

(5.4) ADDITIONAL STATEMENT OF WITNESSES: At least one of the above witnesses must also sign the following declaration:

I further declare under penalty of perjury under the laws of California that I am not related to the individual executing this advance health care directive by blood, marriage, or adoption, and to the best of my knowledge, I am not entitled to any part of the individual's estate upon his or her death under a will now existing or by operation of law.

_____

_____

(signature of witness) (signature of witness)

PART 6
SPECIAL WITNESS REQUIREMENT

(6.1) The following statement is required only if you are a patient in a skilled nursing facility—a health care facility that provides the following basic services: skilled nursing care and supportive care to patients whose primary need is for availability of skilled nursing care on an extended basis. The patient advocate or ombudsman must sign the following statement:

STATEMENT OF PATIENT ADVOCATE OR OMBUDSMAN

I declare under penalty of perjury under the laws of California that I am a patient advocate or ombudsman as designated by the State Department of Aging and that I am serving as a witness as required by Section 4675 of the Probate Code.

_____

_____

(date) (sign your name)

_____

_____

(address) (print your name)

_____

(city) (state)

Wendland v. Wendland

Supreme Court of California, 2001
26 Cal. 4th 519, 28 P.3d 151

WERDEGAR, J.

In this case we consider whether a conservator of the person may withhold artificial nutrition and hydration from a conscious conservatee who is not terminally ill, comatose, or in a persistent vegetative state, and who has not left formal instructions for health care or appointed an agent or surrogate for health care decisions. Interpreting Probate Code section 2355 in light of the relevant provisions of the California Constitution, we conclude a conservator may not withhold artificial nutrition and hydration from such a person absent clear and convincing evidence the conservator's decision is in accordance with either the conservatee's own wishes or best interest.[1]

The trial court in the case before us, applying the clear and convincing evidence standard, found the evidence on both points insufficient and, thus, denied the conservator's request for authority to withhold artificial nutrition and hydration.[2] The Court of Appeal, which believed the trial court was required to defer to the conservator's good faith decision, reversed. We reverse the decision of the Court of Appeal.

* * *

On September 29, 1993, Robert Wendland rolled his truck at high speed in a solo accident while driving under the influence of alcohol. The accident injured Robert's brain, leaving him conscious yet severely disabled, both mentally and physically, and dependent on artificial nutrition and hydration. Two years later Rose Wendland, Robert's wife and conservator, proposed to direct his physician to remove his feeding tube and allow him to die. Florence Wendland and Rebekah Vinson (respectively Robert's mother and sister) objected to the conservator's decision. This proceeding arose under the provisions of the Probate Code authorizing courts to settle such disputes. (Prob.Code, §§ 2355, 2359.) * * *

Following the accident, Robert remained in a coma, totally unresponsive, for several months. During this period Rose visited him daily, often with their children, and authorized treatment as necessary to maintain his health.

---

1. While this case was under submission following oral argument, the parties informed us the conservatee had passed away. Rather than dismissing the case as moot, we chose to retain the case for decision. We have discretion to decide otherwise moot cases presenting important issues that are capable of repetition yet tend to evade review. * * * [Citations omitted]. This is such a case. The case raises important issues about the fundamental rights of incompetent conservatees to privacy and life, and the corresponding limitations on conservators' power to withhold life-sustaining treatment. Moreover, as this case demonstrates, these issues tend to evade review because they typically concern persons whose health is seriously impaired.

2. At the time of these proceedings, Robert was receiving food and fluids through a PEG (percutaneous endoscopically placed gastronomy) tube.

Robert eventually regained consciousness. His subsequent medical history is described in a comprehensive medical evaluation later submitted to the court. According to the report, Rose "first noticed signs of responsiveness sometime in late 1994 or early 1995 and alerted [Robert's] physicians and nursing staff." Intensive therapy followed. Robert's "cognitive responsiveness was observed to improve over a period of several months such that by late spring of 1995 the family and most of his health care providers agreed that he was inconsistently interacting with his environment. A video recording * * * of [Robert] in July 1995 demonstrated clear, though inconsistent, interaction with his environment in response to simple commands. At his highest level of function between February and July, 1995, Robert was able to do such things as throw and catch a ball, operate an electric wheelchair with assistance, turn pages, draw circles, draw an 'R' and perform two-step commands." For example, "[h]e was able to respond appropriately to the command 'close your eyes and open them when I say the number 3.' . . . He could choose a requested color block out of four color blocks. He could set the right peg in a pegboard. Augmented communication[5] was met with inconsistent success. He remained unable to vocalize. Eye blinking was successfully used as a communication mode for a while, however no consistent method of communication was developed."

Despite improvements made in therapy, Robert remained severely disabled, both mentally and physically. * * * The same medical report summarized his continuing impairments as follows: "severe cognitive impairment that is not possible to fully appreciate due to the concurrent motor and communication impairments . . ."; "maladaptive behavior characterized by agitation, aggressiveness and non-compliance"; "severe paralysis on the right and moderate paralysis on the left"; "severely impaired communication, without compensatory augmentative communication system"; "severe swallowing dysfunction, dependent upon non-oral enteric tube feeding for nutrition and hydration"; "incontinence of bowel and bladder"; "moderate spasticity"; "mild to moderate contractures"; "general dysphoria"; "recurrent medical illnesses, including pneumonia, bladder infections, sinusitis"; and "dental issues."

After Robert regained consciousness and while he was undergoing therapy, Rose authorized surgery three times to replace dislodged feeding tubes. When physicians sought her permission a fourth time, she declined. She discussed the decision with her daughters and with Robert's brother Michael, all of whom believed that Robert would not have approved the procedure even if necessary to sustain his life. Rose also discussed the decision with Robert's treating physician, Dr. Kass, other physicians, and the hospital's ombudsman, all of whom apparently supported her decision. Dr. Kass, however, inserted a nasogastric feeding tube to keep Robert alive pending input from the hospital's ethics committee.

---

5. "Augmented communication" refers to communication facilitated by a so-called yes/no board, a machine that pronounces the words "yes" and "no" when corresponding buttons are touched.

Eventually, the 20-member ethics committee unanimously approved Rose's decision. In the course of their deliberations, however, the committee did not speak with Robert's mother or sister. Florence learned, apparently through an anonymous telephone call, that Dr. Kass planned to remove Robert's feeding tube. Florence and Rebekah applied for a temporary restraining order to bar him from so doing, and the court granted the motion ex parte.

Rose immediately thereafter petitioned for appointment as Robert's conservator. In the petition, she asked the court to determine that Robert lacked the capacity to give informed consent for medical treatment and to confirm her authority "to withdraw and/or withhold medical treatment and/or life-sustaining treatment, including, but not limited to, withholding nutrition and hydration." Florence and Rebekah (hereafter sometimes objectors) opposed the petition. After a hearing, the court appointed Rose as conservator but reserved judgment on her request for authority to remove Robert's feeding tube. The court ordered the conservator to continue the current plan of physical therapy for 60 days and then to report back to the court. The court also visited Robert in the hospital.

After the 60-day period elapsed without significant improvement in Robert's condition, the conservator renewed her request for authority to remove his feeding tube. The objectors asked the trial court to appoint independent counsel for the conservatee. The trial court declined, and the Court of Appeal summarily denied the objectors' petition for writ of mandate. We granted review and transferred the case to the Court of Appeal, which then directed the trial court to appoint counsel. (Wendland v. Superior Court (1996) 49 Cal.App.4th 44, 56 Cal.Rptr.2d 595.) Appointed counsel, exercising his independent judgment (see generally Conservatorship of Drabick (1988) 200 Cal.App.3d 185, 212–214, 245 Cal.Rptr. 840 (Drabick)), decided to support the conservator's decision. (Because the conservator's and appointed counsel's positions in this court are essentially identical, we will henceforth refer solely to the conservator for brevity's sake.)

The ensuing proceeding generated two decisions. In the first, the court set out the law to be applied at trial. The court found no "clear cut guidance" on how to evaluate a conservator's proposal to end the life of a conscious conservatee who was neither terminally ill nor in a persistent vegetative state. Nevertheless, drawing what assistance it could from cases involving persistently vegetative patients (Drabick, *supra*, 200 Cal.App.3d 185, 245 Cal.Rptr. 840; Barber v. Superior Court (1983) 147 Cal.App.3d 1006, 195 Cal.Rptr. 484 (Barber)), the court held the conservator would be allowed to withhold artificial nutrition and hydration only if that would be in the conservatee's best interest, taking into account any pertinent wishes the conservatee may have expressed before becoming incompetent. The court also determined the conservator would have to prove the facts justifying her decision by clear and convincing evidence. A decision by a conservator to withhold life-sustaining treatment, the court reasoned, "should be premised on no lesser showing" than that required to justify involuntary medical treatment not likely to cause death. On this point, the court drew an analogy to Lillian F. v. Superior Court (1984) 160 Cal.App.3d 314,

206 Cal.Rptr. 603, which requires clear and convincing evidence of a conservatee's inability to make treatment decisions as a prerequisite to involuntary electroconvulsive treatment. Finally, the court held the conservator would bear the burdens both of producing evidence and of persuasion. "[F]inding itself in uncharted territory" on this subject too, the court explained that "[w]hen a situation arises where it is proposed to terminate the life of a conscious but severely cognitively impaired person, it seems more rational . . . to ask 'why?' of the party proposing the act rather than 'why not?' of the party challenging it."

The trial generated the evidence set out above. The testifying physicians agreed that Robert would not likely experience further cognitive recovery. Dr. Kass, Robert's treating physician, testified that, to the highest degree of medical certainty, Robert would never be able to make medical treatment decisions, walk, talk, feed himself, eat, drink, or control his bowel and bladder functions. Robert was able, however, according to Dr. Kass, to express "certain desires. . . . Like if he's getting tired in therapy of if he wants to quit therapy, he's usually very adamant about that. He'll either strike out or he'll refuse to perform the task." Dr. Kobrin, Robert's neurologist, testified that Robert recognized certain caregivers and would allow only specific caregivers to bathe and help him. Both Dr. Kass and Dr. Kobrin had prescribed medication for Robert's behavioral problems. Dr. Sundance, who was retained by appointed counsel to evaluate Robert, described him as being in a "minimally conscious state in that he does have some cognitive function" and the ability to "respond to his environment," but not to "interact" with it "in a more proactive way." * * *

Robert's wife, brother and daughter recounted preaccident statements Robert had made about his attitude towards life-sustaining health care. Robert's wife recounted specific statements on two occasions. The first occasion was Rose's decision whether to turn off a respirator sustaining the life of her father, who was near death from gangrene. Rose recalls Robert saying: "I would never want to live like that, and I wouldn't want my children to see me like that and look at the hurt you're going through as an adult seeing your father like that." On cross-examination, Rose acknowledged Robert said on this occasion that Rose's father "wouldn't want to live like a vegetable" and "wouldn't want to live in a comatose state."

After his father-in-law's death, Robert developed a serious drinking problem. After a particular incident, Rose asked Michael, Robert's brother, to talk to him. When Robert arrived home the next day he was angry to see Michael there, interfering in what he considered a private family matter. Rose remembers Michael telling Robert: "I'm going to get a call from Rosie one day, and you're going to be in a terrible accident." Robert replied: "If that ever happened to me, you know what my feelings are. Don't let that happen to me. Just let me go. Leave me alone." Robert's brother Michael testified about the same conversation. Michael told Robert: "you're drinking; you're going to get drunk. . . . [Y]ou're either going to go out and kill yourself or kill someone else, or you're going to end up in the hospital like a vegetable—laying in bed just like a vegetable." Michael remembers Robert saying in response, "Mike, whatever you do[,] don't let that happen. Don't let them do that to me." Robert's daughter Katie remembers him saying on this occasion that "if he could not be a provider for his family, if he could not do all the things that he enjoyed doing, just enjoying the outdoors, just basic things, feeding himself, talking, communicating, if he could not do those things, he would not want to live."

Based on all the evidence, the court issued a second decision setting out its findings of fact and conclusions of law. Specifically, the court found the conservator "ha[d] not met her duty and burden to show by clear and convincing evidence that conservatee Robert Wendland, who is not in a persistent vegetative state nor suffering from a terminal illness would, under the circumstances, want to die. Conservator has likewise not met her burden of establishing that the withdrawal of artificially delivered nutrition and hydration is commensurate with conservatee's best interests, consistent with California Law as embodied in Barber [, *supra*, 147 Cal.App.3d 1006, 195 Cal.Rptr. 484] and Drabick, *supra* [, 200 Cal.App.3d 185, 245 Cal.Rptr. 840]." Based on these findings, the court granted the objectors' motion for judgment (Code Civ. Proc., § 631.8), thus denying the conservator's request for confirmation of her proposal to withdraw treatment. The court also found the conservator had acted in good faith and would be permitted to remain in that office. Nevertheless, the court limited her powers by ordering that she would "have no authority to direct ... [any] health care provider to remove the conservatee's life sustaining medical treatment in the form of withholding nutrition and hydration." (See Prob.Code, § 2351.) * * *

The conservator appealed this decision. The Court of Appeal reversed. In the Court of Appeal's view, "[t]he trial court properly placed the burden of producing evidence on [the conservator] and properly applied a clear and convincing evidence standard. However, the court erred in requiring [the conservator] to prove that [the conservatee], while competent, expressed a desire to die in the circumstances and in substituting its own judgment concerning [the conservatee's] best interests...." Instead, the trial court's role was "merely to satisfy itself that the conservator had considered the conservatee's best interests in good faith...." This limited judicial role, the Court of Appeal concluded, was mandated by section 2355, as interpreted in Drabick, *supra*, 200 Cal.App.3d 185, 245 Cal.Rptr. 840. While acknowledging the trial court had already found the conservator had acted in good faith, the Court of Appeal nevertheless declined to enter judgment for the conservator. Instead, the court remanded to permit the objectors to present any evidence rebutting the conservator's case-in-chief. Finally, recognizing that an amended version of section 2355, effective on July 1, 2000, might "be a factor upon remand," the court determined the new law did not affect the outcome. We granted review of this decision.

* * *

The ultimate focus of our analysis must be section 2355, the statute under which the conservator has claimed the authority to end the conservatee's life and the only statute under which such authority might plausibly be found. Nevertheless, the statute speaks in the context of an array of constitutional, common law, and statutory principles. The Law Revision Commission, which drafted the statute's current version, was aware of these principles and cited them to explain and justify the proposed legislation. Because these principles provide essential background, we set them out briefly here, followed by the history of the statute.[8]

* * *

One relatively certain principle is that a competent adult has the right to refuse medical treatment, even treatment necessary to sustain life. The Legislature has cited this principle to justify legislation governing medical care decisions (§ 4650), and courts have invoked it as a starting point for analysis, even in cases examining the rights of incompetent persons and the duties of surrogate decision makers (e.g., Drabick, supra, 200 Cal.App.3d 185, 206, 245 Cal.Rptr. 840; Barber, supra, 147 Cal.App.3d 1006, 1015, 195 Cal.Rptr. 484). This case requires us to look beyond the rights of a competent person to the rights of incompetent conservatees and the duties of conservators, but the principle just mentioned is a logical place to begin.

That a competent person has the right to refuse treatment is a statement both of common law and of state constitutional law. In its common law form, the principle is often traced to Union Pacific Railway Co. v. Botsford (1891) 141 U.S. 250, 251, 11 S.Ct. 1000, 35 L.Ed. 734, in which the United States Supreme Court wrote that "[n]o right is held more sacred, or is more carefully guarded, by the common law, than the right of every individual to the possession and control of his own person, free from all restraint or interference of others, unless by clear and unquestionable authority of law." Applying this principle, the high court held that the plaintiff in a personal injury case was not required to submit to a surgical examination intended to reveal the extent of her injuries. (Ibid.) Courts in subsequent cases relied on the same principle to award damages for operations performed without the patient's consent. The landmark case is Schloendorff v. Society of New York Hospital (N.Y.1914) 211 N.Y. 125, 105 N.E. 92, 93, in which Judge Cardozo wrote that "[e]very human being of adult years and sound mind has a right to determine what shall be done with his own body; and a surgeon who performs an operation without his patient's consent commits an assault, for which he is liable in damages." We adopted this principle in Cobbs v. Grant (1972) 8 Cal.3d 229, 242, 104 Cal. Rptr. 505, 502 P.2d 1, adding that "the patient's consent to treatment, to be effective, must be an informed consent." Most recently, in Thor v. Superior Court (1993) 5 Cal.4th 725, 21 Cal.Rptr.2d 357, 855 P.2d 375, we held that the common law right of

8. The current version of section 2355 governs this case. It took effect on July 1, 2000, and defines the powers of conservators in California from that day forward. A trial court's order limiting a conservator's powers, like an injunction, defines the rights of the parties in the future and is subject to modification based on changes in the law. In such a case, a reviewing court applies the law in effect at the time it renders its opinion. (Hunt v. Superior Court (1999) 21 Cal.4th 984, 1008, 90 Cal.Rptr.2d 236, 987 P.2d 705; Tulare Irr. Dist. v. Lindsay-Strathmore Irr. Dist. (1935) 3 Cal.2d 489, 527–528, 45 P.2d 972.)

a competent adult to refuse life-sustaining treatment extends even to a state prisoner; we thus absolved prison officials and medical personnel of any duty to provide artificial hydration and nutrition against the will of a quadriplegic prisoner who needed such treatment to survive.

The Courts of Appeal have found another source for the same right in the California Constitution's privacy clause. (Cal. Const., art. I, § 1.) The court in Bartling v. Superior Court (1984) 163 Cal.App.3d 186, 209 Cal.Rptr. 220 held that a competent adult with serious, probably incurable illnesses was entitled to have life-support equipment disconnected over his physicians' objection even though that would hasten his death. "The right of a competent adult patient to refuse medical treatment," the court explained, "has its origins in the constitutional right of privacy. This right is specifically guaranteed by the California Constitution (art. I, § 1). . . . The constitutional right of privacy guarantees to the individual the freedom to choose to reject, or refuse to consent to, intrusions of his bodily integrity." (Id. at p. 195, 209 Cal.Rptr. 220.) To the same effect is the decision in Bouvia v. Superior Court (1986) 179 Cal.App.3d 1127, 225 Cal.Rptr. 297, in which the court directed injunctive relief requiring a public hospital to comply with a competent, terminally ill patient's direction to remove a nasogastric feeding tube. "The right to refuse medical treatment," the court wrote, "is basic and fundamental. . . . Its exercise requires no one's approval. It is not merely one vote subject to being overridden by medical opinion." (Id. at p. 1137, 225 Cal.Rptr. 297; see also Rains v. Belshé (1995) 32 Cal.App.4th 157, 169, 38 Cal.Rptr.2d 185, Drabick, *supra*, 200 Cal.App.3d 185, 206, fn. 20, 245 Cal. Rptr. 840, Keyhea v. Rushen (1986) 178 Cal.App.3d 526, 540, 223 Cal.Rptr. 746, Foy v. Greenblott (1983) 141 Cal.App.3d 1, 11, 190 Cal.Rptr. 84 [all describing, albeit perhaps in dictum, the competent person's right to refuse medical treatment as protected by the state constitutional right to privacy].) * * *

Federal law has little to say about the competent person's right to refuse treatment, but what it does say is not to the contrary. The United States Supreme Court spoke provisionally to the point in Cruzan v. Director, Missouri Dept. of Health (1990) 497 U.S. 261, 110 S.Ct. 2841, 111 L.Ed.2d 224 (Cruzan). At issue was the constitutionality of a Missouri law permitting a conservator to withhold artificial nutrition and hydration from a conservatee in a persistent vegetative state only upon clear and convincing evidence that the conservatee, while competent, had expressed the desire to refuse such treatment. The court concluded the law was constitutional. While the case thus did not present the issue, the court nevertheless acknowledged that "a competent person['s] . . . constitutionally protected liberty interest in refusing unwanted medical treatment may be inferred" (id. at p. 278, 110 S.Ct. 2841) from prior decisions holding that state laws requiring persons to submit to involuntary medical procedures must be justified by countervailing state interests. The "logic" of such cases would, the court thought, implicate a competent person's liberty interest in refusing artificially delivered food and water essential to life. (Id. at p. 279, 110 S.Ct. 2841.) Whether any given state law infringed such a liberty interest, however, would have to be determined by balancing the liberty interest against the relevant state interests, in particular the state's interest in preserving life. (Id. at p. 280, 110 S.Ct. 2841.)

In view of these authorities, the competent adult's right to refuse medical treatment may be safely considered established, at least in California.

The same right survives incapacity, in a practical sense, if exercised while competent pursuant to a law giving that act lasting validity. For some time, California law has given competent adults the power to leave formal directions for health care in the event they later become incompetent; over time, the Legislature has afforded ever greater scope to that power. The former Natural Death Act (Health & Saf.Code, former § 7185 et seq., added by Stats.1976, ch. 1439, § 1, p. 6478, and repealed by Stats.1991, ch. 895, § 1, p. 3973), as first enacted in 1976, authorized competent adults to direct health care providers to withhold or withdraw life-sustaining procedures under very narrow circumstances only: specifically, in the event of an incurable condition that would cause death regardless of such procedures and where such procedures would serve only to postpone the moment of death. In findings accompanying the law, the Legislature expressly found "that adult persons have the fundamental right to control the decisions relating to the rendering of their own medical care" (id., § 7186) and explained the law as giving lasting effect to that right: "In recognition of the dignity and privacy which patients have a right to expect, the Legislature hereby declares that the laws of the State of California shall recognize the right of an adult person to make a written directive instructing his physician to withhold or withdraw life-sustaining procedures in the event of a terminal condition." (Ibid.) In 1991, the Legislature amended the law to permit competent adults to refuse, in advance, life-sustaining procedures in the event of a "permanent unconscious condition," defined as an "irreversible coma or persistent vegetative state." (Health & Saf.Code, former §§ 7185.5, 7186, subd. (e), added by Stats.1991, ch. 895, § 2, pp. 3974–3975, and repealed by Stats.1999, ch. 658, § 7.) Intervening legislation also enabled a competent adult to execute a durable power of attorney authorizing an agent to "withhold[ ] or withdraw [ ] . . . health care . . . so as to permit the natural process of dying," and to make other health care decisions, in the event of the principal's incompetence. (Civ.Code, former § 2443, added by Stats.1983, ch. 1204, § 10, p. 4622, and repealed by Stats.1994, ch. 307, § 7, p.1982.)

Effective July 1, 2000, the Health Care Decisions Law (Stats.1999, ch. 658) gives competent adults extremely broad power to direct all aspects of their health care in the event they become incompetent. The new law, which repeals the former Natural Death Act and amends the durable power of attorney law, draws heavily from the Uniform Health Care Decisions Act adopted in 1993 by the National Conference of Commissioners on Uniform State Laws. (See 2000 Health Care Decisions Law and Revised Power of Attorney Law (March 2000) 30 Cal. Law Revision Com. Rep. (2000) p. 49 [preprint copy] (hereafter California Law Revision Commission Report).) Briefly, and as relevant here, the new law permits a competent person to execute an advance directive about "any aspect" of health care. (§ 4701.) Among other things, a person may direct that life-sustaining treatment be withheld or withdrawn under conditions specified by the person and not limited to terminal illness, permanent coma, or persistent vegetative state. A competent person may still use a power of attorney for health care to give an agent the power to make health care decisions (§ 4683), but a patient may also orally designate a surrogate to make such decisions by personally informing the patient's supervising health care provider. (§ 4711.) Under the new law, agents and surrogates are required to make health care decisions "in accordance with the principal's individual health care instructions, if any, and other wishes to the extent known to the agent." (§ 4684; see also § 4711.)

All of the laws just mentioned merely give effect to the decision of a competent person, in the form either of instructions for health care or the designation of an agent or surrogate for health care decisions. Such laws may accurately be described, as the Legislature has described them, as a means to respect personal autonomy by giving effect to competent decisions: "In recognition of the dignity and privacy a person has a right to expect, the law recognizes that an adult has the fundamental right to control the decisions relating to his or her own health care, including the decision to have life-sustaining treatment withheld or withdrawn." (§ 4650, subd. (a) [legislative findings].) This court made essentially the same point in Thor v. Superior Court, *supra*, 5 Cal.4th 725, 740, 21 Cal.Rptr.2d 357, 855 P.2d 375, where we described "the [former] Natural Death Act and other statutory provisions permitting an individual or designated surrogate to exercise conclusive control over the administration of life-sustaining treatment [as] evidenc[ing] legislative recognition that fostering self-determination in such matters enhances rather than deprecates the value of life."

* * *

The ultimate focus of our analysis, as mentioned at the outset, must be section 2355, the statute under which the conservator claims the authority to end the conservatee's life. The statute's history indicates that the Law Revision Commission, which drafted the current version, was aware of and intended to incorporate some, but not all, of the Drabick, *supra*, 200 Cal.App.3d 185, 245 Cal.Rptr. 840 court's construction of the former statute.

* * *

In 1990, the Legislature repealed and reenacted former section 2355 without change while reorganizing the Probate Code. But in 1999, section 2355 changed significantly with the Legislature's adoption of the Health Care Decisions Law (§ 4600 et seq., added by Stats.1999, ch. 658). That law took effect on July 1, 2000, about four months after the Court of Appeal filed the opinion on review. Many of the new law's provisions, as already noted, are the same as, or drawn from, the Uniform Health-Care Decisions Act. (See 30 Cal. Law Revision Com. Rep., *supra*, p. 49.) Section 2355, as a statute addressing medical treatment decisions, was revised to conform to the new law.

The main purpose of the Health Care Decisions Law is to provide "procedures and standards" governing "health care decisions to be made for adults at a time when they are incapable of making decisions on their own and [to] provide [ ] mechanisms for directing their health care in anticipation of a time when they may become incapacitated." (30 Cal. Law Revision Com. Rep., *supra*, p. 6.) The core provision of the new law, which comes directly from the Uniform Health-Care Decisions Act, sets out uniform standards for the making of health care decisions by third parties. The language embodying this core provision now appears in statutes governing decisions by conservators (§ 2355), agents (§ 4684), and surrogates (§ 4714). This language is set out below in italics, as it appears in the context of section 2355: "If the conservatee has been adjudicated to lack the capacity to make health care decisions, the conservator has the exclusive authority to make health care decisions for the conservatee that the conservator in good faith based on medical advice determines to be necessary. *The conservator shall make health care decisions for the conservatee in accordance with the conservatee's individual health care instructions, if any, and other wishes to the extent known to the conservator. Otherwise, the conservator shall make the decision in accordance with the conservator's determination of the conservatee's best interest. In determining the conservatee's best interest, the conservator shall consider the conservatee's personal values to the extent known to the conservator.* The conservator may require the conservatee to receive the health care, whether or not the conservatee objects. In this case, the health care decision of the conservator alone is sufficient and no person is liable because the health care is administered to the conservatee without the conservatee's consent. For the purposes of this subdivision, 'health care' and 'health care decision' have the meanings provided in Sections 4615 and 4617, respectively." (§ 2355, subd. (a), as amended by Stats.1999, ch. 658, § 12, italics added.)

* * *

This background illuminates the parties' arguments, which reduce in essence to this: The conservator has claimed the power under section 2355, as she interprets it, to direct the conservatee's health care providers to cease providing artificial nutrition and hydration. In opposition, the objectors have contended the statute violates the conservatee's rights to privacy and life under the facts of this case if the conservator's interpretation of the statute is correct. * * *

The conservator asserts she offered sufficient evidence at trial to satisfy the primary statutory standard, which contemplates a decision "in accordance with the conservatee's ... wishes...." (§ 2355, subd. (a).) The trial court, however, determined the evidence on this point was insufficient. The conservator did "not [meet] her duty and burden," the court expressly found, "to show by clear and convincing evidence that [the] conservatee ..., who is not in a persistent vegetative state nor suffering from a terminal illness would, under the circumstances, want to die." To be sure, the court made this finding under former section 2355 rather than the current version—and not because the former statute expressly called for such a finding but under the belief that case law required it. (See ante, 110 Cal.Rptr.2d at p. 418, 28 P.3d at p. 156.) But the finding's relevance under the new statute cannot easily be dismissed: The new statute expressly requires the conservator to follow the conservatee's wishes, if known. (§ 2355, subd. (a).)

The conservator argues the Legislature understood and intended that the low preponderance of the evidence standard would apply. Certainly this was the Law Revision Commission's understanding. On this subject, the commission wrote: "[Section 2355] does not specify any special evidentiary standard for the determination of the conservatee's wishes or best interest. Consequently, the general rule applies: the standard is by preponderance of the evidence. Proof is not required by clear and convincing evidence." (30 Cal. Law Revision Com. Rep., *supra*, p. 264.) We have said that "[e]xplanatory comments by a law revision commission are persuasive evidence of the intent of the Legislature in subsequently enacting its recommendations into law." (Brian W. v. Superior Court (1978) 20 Cal.3d 618, 623, 143 Cal.Rptr. 717, 574 P.2d 788.) Nevertheless, one may legitimately question whether the Legislature can fairly be assumed to have read and endorsed every statement in the commission's 280-page report on the Health Care Decisions Law. (Cf. Van Arsdale v. Hollinger (1968) 68 Cal.2d 245, 250, 66 Cal.Rptr. 20, 437 P.2d 508 [describing the inference of legislative approval as strongest when the commission's comment is brief].)

The objectors, in opposition, argue that section 2355 would be unconstitutional if construed to permit a conservator to end the life of a conscious conservatee based on a finding by the low preponderance of the evidence standard that the latter would not want to live. We see no basis for holding the statute unconstitutional on its face. We do, however, find merit in the objectors' argument. We therefore construe the statute to minimize the possibility of its unconstitutional application by requiring clear and convincing evidence of a conscious conservatee's wish to refuse life-sustaining treatment when the conservator relies on that asserted wish to justify withholding life-sustaining treatment. This construction does not entail a deviation from the language of the statute and constitutes only a partial rejection of the Law Revision Commission's understanding that the preponderance of the evidence standard would apply; we see no constitutional reason to apply the higher evidentiary standard to the majority of health care decisions made by conservators not contemplating a conscious conservatee's death. Our reasons are as follows:

At the time the Legislature was considering the present version of section 2355, no court had interpreted any prior version of the statute as permitting a conservator deliberately to end the life of a *conscious* conservatee. Even today, only the decision on review so holds. The court in Drabick, *supra*, 200 Cal.App.3d 185, 245 Cal.Rptr. 840, as we have seen, found sufficient authority in the statute to confirm a conservator's decision that artificial hydration and nutrition was not in the best interest of a *permanently unconscious, persistently vegetative conservatee.* The Drabick court, however, expressly limited its decision to cases involving conservatees in the same medical condition and stated that its reasoning was, in some unexplained way, predicated on such facts. (Id. at p. 217, fn. 36, 245 Cal.Rptr. 840.) While the conservator embraces Drabick in other respects, the authoring court, she writes, "was flat-out wrong to limit the applicability of [section] 2355, of its statutory analysis, and of its constitutional insights to permanently unconscious conservatees as these limitations ignore the plain language of the statute as well as logic." To the contrary, by limiting its decision in this way the Drabick court thereby avoided the constitutional problem we confront here, namely, the propriety of a decision to withhold artificial nutrition and hydration from a conscious conservatee who, while incompetent, may nevertheless subjectively perceive the effects of dehydration and starvation. (See ante, 110 Cal.Rptr.2d at p. 426, 28 P.3d at p. 163)

In amending section 2355 in 1999, neither the Legislature, nor the Law Revision Commission in its official report to the Legislature, alluded to the possibility that the statute might be invoked to justify withholding artificial nutrition and hydration from a conscious patient. The conservator sees evidence of specific legislative authority for such a decision in the findings that accompanied the Health Care Decisions Law, but we do not. These findings, which first entered California law as part of the former Natural Death Act (Health & Saf.Code, former § 7185.5; see ante, 110 Cal.Rptr.2d at p. 423, 28 P.3d at p. 160), were revised and recodified in the new legislation as Probate Code section 4650.[11] The Law Revision Commission in its report accurately explained the proposed change in the findings as follows: "The earlier legislative findings were limited to persons with a terminal condition or permanent unconscious condition. This restriction is not continued here in recognition of the broader scope of this division and the development of case law since enactment of the original Natural Death Act in 1976." (30 Cal. Law Revision Com. Rep., *supra*, p. 61.) From this history, the conservator deduces that the commission, and by inference the Legislature, intended to give conservators the power she has sought in this case to end a conscious conservatee's life. Considering, however, the subject's importance and potentially controversial nature, it seems extremely unlikely that the Legislature intended to regulate the subject through the deletion of a few limiting words from a legislative finding. In any event, the commission's reference to "the broader scope" (*ibid.*) of the new law more plausibly refers simply to the fact that the new law, unlike the former Natural Death Act, permits a competent person to provide by advance directive for virtually all aspects of his or her future health care rather than, as previously, simply

---

11. Section 4650, in full, currently provides as follows:
"The Legislature finds the following:
"(a) In recognition of the dignity and privacy a person has a right to expect, the law recognizes that an adult has the fundamental right to control the decisions relating to his or her own health care, including the decision to have life-sustaining treatment withheld or withdrawn.
"(b) Modern medical technology has made possible the artificial prolongation of human life beyond natural limits. In the interest of protecting individual autonomy, this prolongation of the process of dying for a person for whom continued health care does not improve the prognosis for recovery may violate patient dignity and cause unnecessary pain and suffering, while providing nothing medically necessary or beneficial to the person.
"(c) In the absence of controversy, a court is normally not the proper forum in which to make health care decisions, including decisions regarding life-sustaining treatment."

the withdrawal of life support under narrowly circumscribed facts. (See ante, 110 Cal.Rptr.2d at p. 423, 28 P.3d at p. 160.) Certainly the commission's reference to "the development of case law" since 1976 cannot be understood as suggesting that conservators may end the life of conscious patients. At the time the commission wrote, no California case had addressed the subject. Moreover, of the four cases the commission cites, two involved competent patients (Bouvia v. Superior Court, *supra*, 179 Cal.App.3d 1127, 225 Cal.Rptr. 297; Bartling v. Superior Court, *supra*, 163 Cal.App.3d 186, 209 Cal.Rptr. 220), and two concerned patients in persistent vegetative states (Drabick, *supra*, 200 Cal.App.3d 185, 245 Cal.Rptr. 840; Barber, *supra*, 147 Cal.App.3d 1006, 195 Cal.Rptr. 484); none involved withdrawal of life support from a conscious but incompetent patient. One also finds in the commission's lengthy report, albeit in a different comment, the cryptic statement that the amended version of section 2355 is "consistent with . . . Drabick." (30 Cal. Law Revision Com. Rep., *supra*, com. to § 2355, p. 263.) But Drabick was expressly limited to patients in persistent vegetative states. (Drabick, *supra*, 200 Cal.App.3d 185, 217, fn. 36, 245 Cal.Rptr. 840.) Consistency with Drabick on this point does not support the conservator's position. For all these reasons, we are not convinced the Legislature gave any consideration to the particular problem before us in this case. The prefatory note and comments to the Uniform Health-Care Decisions Act are also silent on the point.

Notwithstanding the foregoing, one must acknowledge that the primary standard for decisionmaking set out in section 2355 does articulate what will in some cases form a constitutional basis for a conservator's decision to end the life of a conscious patient: deference to the patient's own wishes. This standard also appears in the new provisions governing decisions by agents and surrogates designated by competent adults. (§§ 4684, 4714.) As applied in that context, the requirement that decisions be made "in accordance with the principal's individual health care instructions . . . and other wishes" (§ 4684) merely respects the principal-agent relationship and gives effect to the properly expressed wishes of a competent adult. Because a competent adult may refuse life-sustaining treatment (see ante, 110 Cal.Rptr.2d at p. 420, 28 P.3d at p. 158 et seq.), it follows that an agent properly and voluntarily designated by the principal may refuse treatment on the principal's behalf unless, of course, such authority is revoked. (See, *e.g.*, §§ 4682, 4689, 4695 [providing various ways in which the authority of an agent for health care decisions may be revoked or the agent's instructions countermanded].)

The only apparent purpose of requiring conservators to make decisions in accordance with the conservatee's wishes, when those wishes are known, is to enforce the fundamental principle of personal autonomy. The same requirement, as applied to agents and surrogates freely designated by competent persons, enforces the principles of agency. A reasonable person presumably will designate for such purposes only a person in whom the former reposes the highest degree of confidence. A conservator, in contrast, is not an agent of the conservatee, and unlike a freely designated agent cannot be presumed to have special knowledge of the conservatee's health care wishes. A person with "sufficient capacity . . . to form an intelligent preference" may nominate his or her own conservator (§ 1810), but the nomination is not binding because the appointment remains "solely in the discretion of the court" (§ 1812, subd. (a)). Furthermore, while statutory law gives preference to spouses and other persons related to the conservatee (id., subd. (b)), who might know something of the conservatee's health care preferences, the law also permits the court in its sole discretion to appoint unrelated persons and even public conservators (*ibid.*). While it may be constitutionally permissible to assume that an agent freely designated by a formerly competent person to make all health care decisions, including life-ending ones, will resolve such questions "in accordance with the principal's . . . wishes" (§ 4684), one cannot apply the same assumption to conservators and conservatees (cf. § 2355, subd. (a)). For this reason, when the legal premise of a conservator's decision to end a conservatee's life by withholding medical care is that the conservatee would refuse such care, to apply a high standard of proof will help to ensure the reliability of the decision.

* * *

In this case, the importance of the ultimate decision and the risk of error are manifest. So too should be the degree of confidence required in the necessary findings of fact. The ultimate decision is whether a conservatee lives or dies, and the risk is that a conservator, claiming statutory authority to end a conscious conservatee's life "in accordance with the conservatee's . . . wishes" (§ 2355, subd. (a)) by withdrawing artificial nutrition and hydration, will make a decision with which the conservatee subjectively disagrees and which subjects the conservatee to starvation, dehydration and death. This would represent the gravest possible affront to a conservatee's state constitutional right to privacy, in the sense of freedom from unwanted bodily intrusions, and to life. While the practical ability to make autonomous health care decisions does not survive incompetence,[13] the ability to perceive unwanted intrusions may. Certainly it is possible, as the conservator here urges, that an incompetent and uncommunicative but conscious conservatee might perceive the efforts to keep him alive as unwanted intrusion and the withdrawal of those efforts as welcome release. But the decision to treat is reversible. The decision to withdraw treatment is not. The role of a high evidentiary standard in such a case is to adjust the risk of error to favor the less perilous result. The high court has aptly explained the benefits of a high evidentiary standard in a similar context: "An erroneous decision not to terminate results in a maintenance of the status quo; the possibility of subsequent developments such as advancements in medical science, the discovery of new evidence regarding the patient's intent, changes in the law, or simply the unexpected death of the patient despite the administration of life-sustaining treatment at least create the potential that a wrong decision will eventually be corrected or its impact mitigated. An erroneous decision to withdraw life-sustaining

---

13. Except, of course, when a person has before incompetence left legally cognizable instructions for health care or designated an agent or surrogate for health care decisions.

treatment, however, is not susceptible of correction."[14] (Cruzan, *supra*, 497 U.S. 261, 283, 110 S.Ct. 2841, 111 L.Ed.2d 224; see also In re Martin (1995) 450 Mich. 204, 538 N.W.2d 399, 409–411 [requiring, under Michigan law, clear and convincing evidence of a conscious but incompetent conservatee's desire to refuse artificial nutrition and hydration].)

In conclusion, to interpret section 2355 to permit a conservator to withdraw artificial nutrition and hydration from a conscious conservatee based on a finding, by a mere preponderance of the evidence, that the conservatee would refuse treatment creates a serious risk that the law will be unconstitutionally applied in some cases, with grave injury to fundamental rights. Under these circumstances, we may properly ask whether the statute may be construed in a way that mitigates the risk. "If a statute is susceptible of two constructions, one of which will render it constitutional and the other unconstitutional in whole or in part, or raise serious and doubtful constitutional questions, the court will adopt the construction which, without doing violence to the reasonable meaning of the language used, will render it valid in its entirety, or free from doubt as to its constitutionality, even though the other construction is equally reasonable. [Citations.] The basis of this rule is the presumption that the Legislature intended, not to violate the Constitution, but to enact a valid statute within the scope of its constitutional powers." * * * [Citations omitted]. Here, where the risk to conservatees' rights is grave and the proposed construction is consistent with the language of the statute, to construe the statute to avoid the constitutional risk is an appropriate exercise of judicial power.

* * *

The "clear and convincing evidence" test requires a finding of high probability, based on evidence """"so clear as to leave no substantial doubt" [and] "sufficiently strong to command the unhesitating assent of every reasonable mind." '" (In re Angelia P., *supra*, 28 Cal.3d 908, 919, 171 Cal.Rptr. 637, 623 P.2d 198; accord, Sheehan v. Sullivan (1899) 126 Cal. 189, 193, 58 P. 543.) Applying that standard here, we ask whether the evidence the conservatee would have refused treatment under the circumstances of this case has that degree of clarity, bearing in mind that what we are asking, in essence, is whether the conservatee would actually have wished to die.

On this point the trial court wrote: "[T]he testimony adduced focuses upon two pre-accident conversations during which the conservatee allegedly expressed a desire not to live like a 'vegetable.' These two conversations do not establish by clear and convincing evidence that the conservatee would desire to have his life-sustaining medical treatment terminated under the circumstances in which he now finds himself. One of these conversations allegedly occurred when the conservatee

---

14. The court in *Cruzan, supra*, 497 U.S. 261, 110 S.Ct. 2841, 111 L.Ed.2d 224, upheld Missouri's choice of an evidentiary standard; the court did not purport to impose that standard as a matter of federal constitutional law. No such question was presented. Nevertheless, the court's pertinent observations on standards of proof have persuasive value on a question we must decide under California law.

was apparently recovering from a night's bout of drinking. The other alleged conversation occurred following the loss of conservatee's father-in-law, with whom he was very close. The court finds that neither of these conversations reflect an exact 'on all-fours' description of conservatee's present medical condition. More explicit direction than just 'I don't want to live like a vegetable' is required in order to justify a surrogate decision-maker terminating the life of . . . someone who is not in a PVS [persistent vegetative state]." We agree with the trial court's assessment of the evidence. That assessment is essentially in accord with the only case directly on point, in which the Michigan Supreme Court found no clear and convincing evidence of a desire to refuse treatment under very similar facts. (See In re Martin, *supra*, 450 Mich. 204, 538 N.W.2d 399, discussed ante, 110 Cal.Rptr.2d at p. 435, 28 P.3d at p. 170 et seq.) We add to the trial court's assessment only that Rose acknowledged Robert did not describe the precise condition in which he later found himself (see ante, 110 Cal.Rptr.2d at p. 419, 28 P.3d at p. 157) and that, while experts dispute the consistency and accuracy of Robert's responses to questions, it is difficult to ignore the fact that he declined to answer the question "Do you want to die?" while giving facially plausible "yes" or "no" answers to a variety of other questions about his wishes. (See ante, 110 Cal.Rptr.2d at p. 419, 28 P.3d at p. 157 et seq.) On this record, we see no reason to hold that the evidence does not support the trial court's finding.

* * *

Having rejected the conservator's argument that withdrawing artificial hydration and nutrition would have been "in accordance with the conservatee's . . . wishes" (§ 2355, subd. (a)), we must next consider her contention that the same action would have been proper under the fallback best interest standard. Under that standard, "the conservator shall make the decision in accordance with the conservator's determination of the conservatee's best interest. In determining the conservatee's best interest, the conservator shall consider the conservatee's personal values to the extent known to the conservator." (*Ibid.*) The trial court, as noted, ruled the conservator had the burden of establishing that the withdrawal of artificially delivered nutrition and hydration was in the conservatee's best interest, and had not met that burden.

Here, as before, the conservator argues that the trial court applied too high a standard of proof. This follows, she contends, from section 2355, which gives her as conservator "the exclusive authority" to give consent for such medical treatment as she "in good faith based on medical advice determines to be necessary" (§ 2355, subd. (a), italics added), and from the decision in Drabick, *supra*, 200 Cal.App.3d 185, 200, 245 Cal.Rptr. 840, which emphasized that a court should not substitute its judgment for the conservator's. The legislative findings to the Health Care Decisions Law, the conservator notes, declare that "[i]n the absence of controversy, a court is normally not the proper forum in which to make health care decisions, including decisions regarding life-sustaining treatment" (§ 4650, subd. (c)); similarly, the Law Revision Commission has explained that "[c]ourt control or intervention in this process is neither required by statute, nor desired by the courts."

(30 Cal. Law Revision Com. Rep., *supra*, com. to § 2355, p. 264.) Based on these statements, the conservator argues the trial court has no power other than to verify that she has made the decision for which the Probate Code expressly calls: a "good faith" decision "based on medical advice" and "consider[ing] the conservatee's personal values" whether treatment is "necessary" in the conservatee's "best interest." (§ 2355, subd. (a).) The trial court, as noted, rejected the conservator's assessment of the conservatee's best interest but nevertheless found by clear and convincing evidence that she had acted "in good faith, based on medical evidence and after consideration of the conservatee's best interests, including his likely wishes, based on his previous statements." This finding, the conservator concludes, should end the litigation as a matter of law in her favor.

The conservator's understanding of section 2355 is not correct. To be sure, the statute provides that "the conservator shall make the decision in accordance with the conservator's determination of the conservatee's best interest." (§ 2355, subd. (a), italics added.) But the conservator herself concedes the court must be able to review her decision for abuse of discretion. This much, at least, follows from the conservator's status as an officer of the court subject to judicial supervision. While the assessment of a conservatee's best interest belongs in the first instance to the conservator, this does not mean the court must invariably defer to the conservator regardless of the evidence.

In the exceptional case where a conservator proposes to end the life of a conscious but incompetent conservatee, we believe the same factor that principally justifies applying the clear and convincing evidence standard to a determination of the conservatee's wishes also justifies applying that standard to a determination of the conservatee's best interest: The decision threatens the conservatee's fundamental rights to privacy and life. While section 2355 is written with sufficient breadth to cover all health care decisions, the Legislature cannot have intended to authorize every conceivable application without meaningful judicial review. Taken to its literal extremes, the statute would permit a conservator to withdraw health care necessary to life from any conservatee who had been adjudicated incompetent to make health care decisions, regardless of the degree of mental and physical impairment, and on no greater showing than that the conservator in good faith considered treatment not to be in the conservatee's best interest. The result would be to permit a conservator freely to end a conservatee's life based on the conservator's subjective assessment, albeit "in good faith [and] based on medical advice" (§ 2355, subd.(a)), that the conservatee enjoys an unacceptable quality of life. We find no reason to believe the Legislature intended section 2355 to confer power so unlimited and no authority for such a result in any judicial decision. Under these circumstances, we may properly construe the statute to require proof by clear and convincing evidence to avoid grave injury to the fundamental rights of conscious but incompetent conservatees. (See ante, 110 Cal.Rptr.2d at p. 433, 28 P.3d at p. 169 et seq.)

We need not in this case attempt to define the extreme factual predicates that, if proved by clear and convincing evidence, might support a conservator's decision that withdrawing life support would be in the best interest of a conscious conservatee. Here, the conservator offered no basis for such a finding other than her own subjective judgment that the conservatee did not enjoy a satisfactory quality of life and legally insufficient evidence to the effect that he would have wished to die. On this record, the trial court's decision was correct.

* * *

For the reasons set out above, we conclude the superior court correctly required the conservator to prove, by clear and convincing evidence, either that the conservatee wished to refuse life-sustaining treatment or that to withhold such treatment would have been in his best interest; lacking such evidence, the superior court correctly denied the conservator's request for permission to withdraw artificial hydration and nutrition. We emphasize, however, that the clear and convincing evidence standard does not apply to the vast majority of health care decisions made by conservators under section 2355. Only the decision to withdraw life-sustaining treatment, because of its effect on a conscious conservatee's fundamental rights, justifies imposing that high standard of proof. Therefore, our decision today affects only a narrow class of persons: conscious conservatees who have not left formal directions for health care and whose conservators propose to withhold life-sustaining treatment for the purpose of causing their conservatees' deaths. Our conclusion does not affect permanently unconscious patients, including those who are comatose or in a persistent vegetative state (see generally Conservatorship of Morrison, *supra*, 206 Cal.App.3d 304, 253 Cal.Rptr. 530; Drabick, *supra*, 200 Cal.App.3d 185, 245 Cal. Rptr. 840; Barber, *supra*, 147 Cal.App.3d 1006, 195 Cal.Rptr. 484), persons who have left legally cognizable instructions for health care (see §§ 4670, 4673, 4700), persons who have designated agents or other surrogates for health care (see §§ 4671, 4680, 4711), or conservatees for whom conservators have made medical decisions other than those intended to bring about the death of a conscious conservatee.

The decision of the Court of Appeal is reversed.

GEORGE, C.J., KENNARD, J., BAXTER, J., CHIN, J., BROWN, J., concur.

Notes

These are difficult decisions. Often parents challenge the decisions of spouses and domestic partners of their children, as was evidenced in the *Wendland* decision. More frequently, challenges involve nutrition and hydration, and an appropriate standard of proof when there is no written health-care directive. In 2004, the Supreme Court of Florida ruled on a case that involved a husband seeking to withhold nutrition and hydration to his wife of fourteen years—Theresa Schiavo. She did not have a health-care directive, but the husband petitioned the guardianship court to authorize termination of life-prolonging procedures. The husband argued that his wife, who suffered cardiac arrest and was in a persistent vegetative state for eight years, with no hope of improvement, would not choose to continue constant nursing care with hope of a miracle. Rather, he argued, she would want a natural death to occur so her family could go on with their lives. The guardianship court allowed for the cessation of nutrition and hydration, but the wife's parents objected, arguing that new medical evidence indicated potential improvement of their daughter; they asked that life support continue. The guardianship court nonetheless rejected the parents' argument, holding that there was clear and convincing evidence that the woman maintained on total life support would want to discontinue all nutrition and hydration. *See In re* Guardianship of Schiavo, 780 So. 2d 176, 177 (Fla. 2d Dist. App. 2001). The parents appealed, and the Florida court affirmed, denying relief to the parents, stating:

> But in the end, this case is not about the aspirations that loving parents have for their children. It is about Theresa Schiavo's right to make her own decision, independent of her parents and independent of her husband. . . . It may be unfortunate that when families cannot agree, the best forum we can offer for this private, personal decision is a public courtroom and the best decision-maker we can provide is a judge with no prior knowledge of the ward, but the law currently provides no better solution that adequately protects the interests of promoting the value of life.

In re Guardianship of Schiavo, 851 So. 2d 182, 186–87 (Fla. 2d Dist. App. 2003).

After the court's decision to remove the nutrition and hydration tube, the tube was removed on October 15, 2003. On October 21, 2003, the Florida legislature enacted a statute that allowed the governor of the state broad powers to issue a one-time stay to prevent the withholding of nutrition and hydration if the patient has no written advance directive, the court finds the patient to be in a persistent vegetative state, the patient has had nutrition and hydration withheld, and a member of the patient's family has challenged the withholding of nutrition and hydration. *See* TERRI'S LAW, FLA. STAT. ANN. § 744.3215 (2004). The nutrition and hydration tube was then reinserted. But one year later, the Supreme Court of Florida ruled that the legislature's enactment of the statute encroaches upon the power of the judicial branch, thereby violating separation of powers. *See* Bush v. Schiavo, 885 So. 2d 321 (Fla. 2004). The court held:

> In enacting [the statute], the Legislature failed to provide any standards by which the Governor should determine whether, in any given case, a stay should be issued and how long a stay should remain in effect. Further, the Legislature has failed to provide any criteria for lifting the stay. This absolute, unfettered discretion to decide whether to issue and then when to lift a stay makes the Governor's decision virtually unreviewable.

Id. at 334.

In concluding, the court stated:

> The trial court's decision regarding Theresa Schiavo was made in accordance with the procedures and protections set forth by the judicial branch and in accordance with the statutes passed by the Legislature in effect at

that time. That decision is final and the Legislature's attempt to alter that final adjudication is unconstitutional as applied to Theresa Schiavo.

Id. at 337.

Subsequently, the U.S. Supreme Court declined to hear an appeal brought by the government in January 2005. One day before Terri Schiavo's feeding tube was to be removed at the request of her husband, a Florida circuit judge granted a motion for a temporary stay, which was requested by Terri Schiavo's parents, who claimed that the husband was not acting in Terri Schiavo's best interest. However, the stay was subsequently lifted, and the feeding tube was removed on March 18, 2005. In response, the U.S. Senate and House of Representatives deliberated overnight and passed emergency legislation "for the relief of the parents of" Terri Schiavo. The President signed the legislation — the Schiavo Bill — on March 21, 2005. The legislation provided for injunctive relief to safeguard the right to continued medical treatment. Despite this, the federal district court declined to issue relief. The parents appealed to the Florida Supreme Court and the U.S. Supreme Court, but both declined to intervene. Terri Schiavo died on March 31, 2005. *See* Laura Stanton, *The Battle Over Terri Schiavo*, Wash. Post, Apr. 1, 2005, at A13. Terri's husband, Michael, and her parents, the Schindlers, have published books describing the events surrounding the withholding of life support from Terri. *See* Michael Schiavo & Michael Hirsh, Terri: The Truth(2006); Mary Schindler, Robert Schindler, Suzanne Schindler Vitadamo & Bobby Schindler, A Life That Matters: The Legacy of Terri Schiavo(2006).

Problem

A sixteen-year-old boy suffered multiple injuries in an automobile accident but was conscious when medical help arrived to take him to the local hospital. He told the emergency technicians that he was a Jehovah Witness and did not want to receive a blood transfusion. Upon arrival at the hospital, he reiterated this, and his mother and father confirmed his objection to a blood transfusion. The boy underwent surgery without the transfusion, but throughout the next 36 hours, his blood level declined and doctors became increasingly concerned about his survival. Finally, the surgeon contacted hospital officials and attorneys to alert them to the possibility that the boy may not survive much longer. Immediately, the hospital petitioned the local court for the appointment of a guardian ad litem to provide legal permission for the blood transfusion. The court held its hearing at the hospital the next day and garnered testimony from the physicians concerning the health of the boy and the consequences involved. The boy's family was not notified of the hearing or its order. Upon the completion of the testimony, the court appointed a guardian ad litem, who then gave permission for the blood transfusion. When the transfusion was completed, the boy recovered and was soon discharged from the hospital. The parents have now filed a tort petition alleging substantive and procedural due process violations for a deprivation of the parents' and child's liberty interest in freedom from interference with familial relationships. The hospital asserts that it acted as a result of a genuine medical emergency and in connection with judicial approval. If you were the judge who ordered the hearing concerning the appointment of the guardian ad litem for the boy, what would be the focus of your inquiry? *See* Novak v. Cobb County-Kennestone Hosp. Auth., 849 F. Supp. 1559 (U.S. Dist. Ct. N.D. Georgia 1994).

G. Interment of the Body

Cohen v. Guardianship of Cohen

Fourth District Court of Appeal of Florida, 2005
896 So. 2d 950

WARNER, J.

The brother and sister of the deceased, Hilliard Cohen, appeal the probate court's order requiring the burial of the deceased in a Florida cemetery, where he could be buried next to his wife of forty years, instead of the family cemetery plot in New York. Hilliard's 1992 will contained a request to be buried in the family plot, but his wife and others testified that he wished to be buried in Florida where his wife could also be buried. Because we conclude that the provisions of the will are not conclusive, we affirm the court's refusal to enforce the burial instructions in the will under the evidence presented in this case.

Hilliard and Margaret Cohen were married for forty years at the time of his death. They had four children together, and she had two from a previous marriage. Hilliard was Jewish and Margaret was not. They celebrated some religious holidays with the family, but they did not belong to a temple, nor did the children regularly attend services. Hilliard never had a bar mitzvah ceremony. The Cohen family had a family plot in Mount Hebron Cemetery, a Jewish cemetery in New York, purchased by Hilliard's grandfather. All of Hilliard's family and their spouses were buried there. Hilliard and Margaret lived in New York until 1998 when they moved to Florida.

After relocating to Florida, Hilliard began to have health problems. Around 1999, Hilliard told Margaret that he wanted to be buried in his family plot in Mount Hebron with her. However, in May of 2001, when Hilliard went into the hospital, he and Margaret first discussed being buried together in Florida.

Hilliard's brother and sister, Ivan and Cressie, were close to him, but they did not have a good relationship with Margaret. As a result, Hilliard would visit with them in Arizona and New York after he moved to Florida. In February 2002, Ivan took Hilliard to a doctor in Arizona, who diagnosed him with dementia and Parkinson's disease. Later that year, while visiting Cressie in New York, he executed a durable power-of-attorney, naming Ivan as his agent. When Hilliard returned to Florida, Margaret would not allow Ivan or Cressie to see Hilliard, necessitating them to obtain a court order permitting visits.

In May of 2003, Margaret filed a petition to determine Hilliard's incapacity, alleging that Hilliard suffered from various diseases, including dementia and Alzheimer's. A subsequent petition for appointment of a guardian was filed. In the course of those proceedings, Hilliard met with the attorney ad litem appointed to represent him. Hilliard told the attorney that he did not want a guardian but expressed no preference as to who should be appointed if he were declared incompetent. He also told the attorney that he was aware of the rift between his siblings and his wife and felt caught in the middle. A physician who examined Hilliard testified that during the examination Hilliard expressed the sentiment that he wished to be buried in Florida with his wife.

Ivan also filed a petition to be appointed Hilliard's guardian, based upon the durable power-of-attorney. However, while both petitions were pending, Hilliard died.

Shortly before Hilliard's death, Ivan produced a will that Hilliard had apparently executed in 1992 in New York, in which he directed that he be buried in "a traditional Jewish burial in our family plot in Mount Hebron Cemetery, Flushing, Queens, N.Y." In that will, he appointed Ivan as executor. The will also left only the statutory minimum to Margaret. Ivan testified that at the time Hilliard executed the will he was angry with Margaret because he believed she was having an affair. When Margaret found out about the will, she asked Hilliard about it. He denied ever executing a will, saying that he had signed something in New York regarding Cressie's house.

After Hilliard's death, Margaret planned to have Hilliard cremated, as they had discussed before his death. They chose cremation due to financial considerations and because Hilliard was angry with his brother. Prior to the cremation, Ivan sought a court order to enforce the burial provisions of the will. During a hearing to prevent the cremation, Margaret changed her mind after hearing a rabbi testify that it was against Jewish law. She then wanted a burial in Florida as they had discussed, where she could be by his side like she "ha[d] been the last forty years."

The trial court held two evidentiary hearings regarding the disposition and burial of the deceased. In addition to the testimony of Margaret, Ivan, and Cressie, a rabbi testified as to Jewish burial customs. He explained that: a) Cremation is prohibited under Jewish law and would not be considered a traditional Jewish burial; b) Jewish tradition is that husbands and wives are buried together as long as the wife is Jewish; c) Some Jewish cemeteries allow a non-Jew to be buried but not in the confined Jewish cemetery area; and d) More recent traditions allow Jews who are married to non-Jewish spouses to be buried in the same cemetery but not in the exclusive restricted area. The family plot in Mount Hebron was in the Jewish restricted area; therefore, Margaret could not be buried there. Finally, Hilliard's daughter testified that he had expressed a desire to be buried with his wife in Florida.

The trial court determined that the will was ambiguous as to Hilliard's intent because it stated that Hilliard wanted a "traditional Jewish burial," yet his wife could not be buried in Mount Hebron with him. Because the will was ambiguous, the court considered the extrinsic evidence and determined that Hilliard's true intent was to be buried alongside Margaret. The court therefore ordered Hilliard to be buried in the Florida cemetery.

This case presents an issue of first impression in Florida. The question presented is whether a deceased's testamentary burial instructions are binding upon the court or may be disregarded when the testator has made a subsequent oral statement of desire as to his final resting arrangements. The parties and the trial court considered the issue as though it was necessary to find an ambiguity in the will in order to vary its terms by the oral statements of the deceased. We instead affirm the trial court's ruling, adopting the majority view that provisions in a will regarding burial instructions are not conclusive of a testator's intent, and the trial court may take evidence that the testator changed his or her mind regarding disposition of his body.

The common law recognized no property right in the body of a deceased. *See Jackson v. Rupp*, 228 So.2d 916, 918 (Fla. 4th DCA 1969). In the absence of a testamentary disposition, the spouse of the deceased or the next of kin has the right to the possession of the body for burial or other lawful disposition. *Kirksey v. Jernigan*, 45 So.2d 188, 189 (Fla.1950).

Where the testator has expressed his exclusive intention through the will, the testator's wishes should be honored. For instance, in *Kasmer v. Guardianship of Limner*, 697 So.2d 220 (Fla. 3d DCA 1997), the testator directed that his body be cremated. The executor of the will refused to follow that direction for reasons of conscience. The court concluded that the testamentary language was controlling, and the executor was required to fulfill the testator's directives. 697 So.2d at 221. However, *Kasmer* was not a case where the testator indicated a change of mind as to the disposition of his body subsequent to the execution of the will. * * *

We have found no cases in Florida or across the country in which a testamentary disposition has been upheld even though credible evidence has been introduced to show that the testator changed his or her mind as to the disposition of his/her body. In Florida, as in New York, a will is construed to pass all *property* that the testator owns at death. *See* § 732.6005(2), Fla. Stat. As set forth above, the testator's body is not considered property. Therefore, just as in New York, a directive in a will regarding the disposition of a body does not have the same force and effect as do provisions directing the disposition of property. We therefore conclude that a testamentary disposition is not conclusive of the decedent's intent if it can be shown by clear and convincing evidence that he intended another disposition for his body.

To hold otherwise could cause untoward results. *Nelson v. Schoonover* is an example. There, the wife had resided in Ohio when her will was made but subsequently moved to Kansas with her husband. Obviously, burial in Ohio would have taken her away from her family. A more common occurrence might be the execution of a will during marriage indicating a burial location with the spouse. A subsequent divorce would make following such a direction impractical and not in accordance with the testator's intent.

Our current society is exceedingly mobile. One might live in several states during a lifetime. A provision made in a will that is not revisited for many years may not reflect the intent of the testator as to the disposition of his or her remains. A direction for the disposition of one's body should not be conclusive when contrary and convincing oral or written evidence of a change in intent is present.

In this case, the deceased executed a will in 1992 requesting burial in his family's plot in New York. However, six years later he and his wife moved to Florida. He spoke of burial plans with his wife, as well as his daughter, and expressed a desire to be buried with his wife. At first, he wished to be buried with her in New York. Later, he agreed to burial with her in Florida. Hilliard's desire was also expressed to a doctor who examined him. Although his statement to the doctor may be discounted because he was being examined for competency, it was consistent with his prior statements that he wished to be buried with his wife. In all of his verbal expressions on this matter, Hilliard expressed a desire for burial in a place where his wife of forty years could also rest upon her death. This could not occur if he were buried in the family plot in Mount Hebron.

The trial court heard the evidence and weighed its credibility. "It is not the function of an appellate court to substitute its judgment for that of the trial court by reevaluating the evidence presented below." *State v. Melendez*, 392 So.2d 587, 590 (Fla. 4th DCA 1981). The trial court was aware of the heavier burden to disregard an express term of the will. Even where the standard that must be met is a clear and convincing evidence standard, "[O]ur task on review is not to conduct a de novo proceeding, reweigh the testimony and evidence given at the trial court, or substitute our judgment for that of the trier of fact." *In re Adoption of Baby E.A.W.*, 658 So.2d 961, 967 (Fla.1995). A trial court's determination will be upheld if it is supported by competent, substantial evidence. *Id.*

It is a sorrowful matter to have relatives disputing in court over the remains of the deceased. In this case in particular, there is no solution that will bring peace to all parties. We express our sympathies to both sides in their loss, which must be magnified by these proceedings. Cases such as this require the most sensitive exercise of the equitable powers of the trial courts. We are confident that the experienced trial judge exercised his power with due regard for the serious and emotional issues presented. We find no abuse of the discretion afforded to the trial court.

Affirmed.

POLEN and HAZOURI, JJ., concur.

Notes

Testamentary burial instructions are not binding upon a court or the surviving family members. As expressed in the *Cohen* decision, courts may disregard any stipulations made by a decedent in a Last Will and Testament or *inter vivos* instrument.

Often tasked with resolving disputes among surviving family members, some courts note that a human body is not property and should not be governed by the same rules applicable to chattel. Instead, courts often look to the inherent equity of the case appearing from all of the attending facts and circumstances. *See* McRae v. Booth, 938 So. 2d 432 (Ala. Civ. App. 2006) (ordering an immediate burial of the mother, over the objection of her two disputing children). Once the body has been interred, probate courts retain broad powers to administer the estate, such as ordering a deceased man's estate to exhume his body for genetic testing in response to a claimant's credible claim of paternity. *See, e.g,* Estate of Kingsbury, 946 A.2d 389, 2008 Me. 79 (2008). There are many instances of celebrities and family disputes over their remains, once they have died. *See, e.g.,* Mary Catherine Joiner & Ryan M. Seidemann, *Rising From the Dead: A Jurisprudential Review of Recent Cemetery and Human Remains Cases*, 45 Ohio N.U. L. Rev. 1 (2019); Frances H. Foster, *Individualized Justice in Disputes Over Dead Bodies*, 61 Vand. L. Rev. 1351 (2008) (describing, among others, the dispute over the body of baseball star Ted Williams); Thomas H. Robinson, *Stop! Are You Sure You Want to Throw Grandpa's Body Away?*, 63 Miami L. Rev. 37 (2008); Ann M. Murphy, *Please Don't Bury Me in That Cold Cold Ground: The Need for Uniform Laws on the Disposition of Human Remains*, 15 Elder L.J. 381 (2007); Russell E. Haddleton, *What To Do With the Body? The Trouble With Postmortem Disposition*, 20 Prob. & Prop. 55 (Nov./Dec. 2006).

Uniform Probate Code (2019)

§ 3-701. [Time of Accrual of Duties and Powers].

The duties and powers of a personal representative commence upon his appointment. The powers of a personal representative relate back in time to give acts by the person appointed which are beneficial to the estate occurring prior to appointment the same effect as those occurring thereafter. Prior to appointment, a person named executor in a will may carry out written instructions of the decedent relating to his body, funeral and burial arrangements. A personal representative may ratify and accept acts on behalf of the estate done by others where the acts would have been proper for a personal representative.

II. Entitlement Programs

A. Social Security

Blanche Weisen Cook
Eleanor Roosevelt: Volume 2, The Defining Years, 1933–1938
(1999)

The year 1935 opened with such promise that ER [Eleanor Roosevelt] proclaimed it an "epochal" year.... Initially social security legislation included work security, which was to be federally administered and not subject to the whims of state control where regional habits threatened race equity. . . . On 17 January, FDR (Franklin Delano Roosevelt] presented his social security package, which included unemployment compensation, old-age benefits, federal aid to dependent children "through grants to states for the support of existing mothers' pension systems and for services for the protection and care of homeless, neglected, dependent, and crippled children," and federal aid to state and local public health agencies, with a strengthened Federal Public Health Service. . . .

Id. at 233–34.

Only old-age insurance was the direct responsibility of the federal government, paid for by payroll taxes shared by employer and employee. By 1 January 1937, "Social Security" numbers were assigned to 38 million workers, now entitled to a secure old age.

Id. at 282.

In a series of 5–4 decisions, with Justice Owen Roberts reversing himself, the Supreme Court finally upheld progressive and New Deal legislation. . . . On 24 May [1937], the Social Security Act was allowed. Suddenly the Court acknowledged that Congress and state governments had the power to protect the interest of the people.

Id. at 460.

Social Security is a federal insurance program based on taxes paid by an employee and employer, and is a means to provide retirement and/or disability benefits to an insured or his or her dependents. Application for retirement benefits may be made online at: http://www.ssa.gov/applytoretire. Social Security is not "needs based" as is Supplemental Security Income (SSI), which provides benefits based on age, disability, and inadequate resources and income. Employees and employers pay a combined tax rate of 7.65% on wages, up to earnings of $118,500 for 2015. *See* Internal Revenue Service, *Topic 751 — Social Security and Medicare Withholding Rates,* http://www.irs.gov/taxtopics/tc751.html. This tax is divided between old-age and disability benefits and the Medicare benefits to which an employee is entitled. Thus, 6.2% is for old-age and 1.45% is for Medicare. Once an employed person qualifies for Medicare and enrolls in Part B, *see supra,* an additional $104.90 (for 2015) is withheld from any Social Security payment to pay for Medicare Part B. Self-employed persons must pay 15.3% of what they earn, up to $113,700 of income (2013 amount).

As of December 2013, there were 63,169,000 beneficiaries of Social Security, Supplemental Income, or both. *See* Social Security Administration Online, *Fast Facts & Figures About Social Security, 2014,* http://ssa.gov/policy/docs/chartbooks/fast_facts/2014/fast_facts14.pdf. Benefits received from Social Security totaled more than $863 billion, accounting for 38% of income for 90% of elderly persons. *See* Social Security Administration, *Social Security*

Basic Facts, http://www.ssa.gov/news/press/basicfact.html. Among the recipients of Social Security, 66% or 41,717,000, were 65 or older, and the average monthly benefit as of December 2013 was $529. *See* Social Security Administration Online, *Fast Facts & Figures About Social Security, 2014,* http://www.ssa.gov/policy/docs/chartbooks/fast_facts/.

- BENEFITS: Benefits are not assignable during life or at death. Retirement benefits may be collected at age 62, but benefits will be higher for those waiting until 67. Medicare coverage, not the same as Social Security, is fixed at age 65 regardless of when a worker elects to take Social Security. Benefit estimates for an eligible individual may be found online at: http://www.socialsecurity.gov /mystatement/; or at www.ssa.gov/estimator/.

- ELIGIBILITY: Eligibility for Social Security payments comes from having earned a sufficient number of quarters paid into the system or from being in a dependent relationship with someone eligible for benefits. Subject to specific rules, the following persons may be considered dependent and eligible: surviving spouses, divorced spouses, unmarried minor children, parents of minor children who are dependent on eligible persons, and disabled children. To be fully insured a worker must have accumulated 40 quarters (ten years), but they do not have to be consecutive quarters. To compute the number of quarters sufficient to qualify, *see* Social Security Administration, http://www.ssa.gov /OACT/COLA?OC.html.

- APPEALS: Persons representing applicants in benefit disputes may have their fees paid either through: (1) a separate agreement with the client, which is approved and filed with the Social Security Administration; or (2) from the client's award and the person agrees to accept the lesser of $6,000 or 25% of the award; or (3) a federal judge may award a higher fee. *See* 42 U.S.C. § 406(a)(2) (A). Claimant Representatives, http://www.ssa.gov/representation/.

Lawrence A. Frolik & Bernard A. Krooks
Planning for Later Life
154 Trusts & Ests. 21 (July 2015)

At 62, your client can claim his Social Security retirement benefits. Of course, if he does, he permanently reduces them by 25 percent compared to the amount he would have received at his full retirement age, currently 66. If your client waits until he's 70 to claim benefits, the amount rises by 32 percent, at 8 percent for each year he defers. At 70 there is no reason to delay further because the amount is set for life — except for possible annual cost-of-living increases. For many, deferring claiming Social Security past 66 makes sense.

Id. at 21–22.

For commentary on Social Security as an entitlement program, see, *e.g.*, Kevin Sigler, *When to Take Social Security Retirement Benefits*, 35 No. 2 J. OF COMPEN. & BENEFITS ART. 6 (2019); Naomi Cahn, *The Golden Years, Gray Divorce, Pink Caretaking, and Green Money*, 52 FAM. L.Q. 57 (2018); Neil H. Buchanan, *Social Security is Fair to All Generations: Demystifying the Trust Fund, Solvency, and the Promise to Younger Americans*, 27 CORNELL J.L. & PUB. POLICY 237 (2017).

B. Medicare

"Briefly stated, Medicare, Title XVIII of the Social Security Act, 42 U.S.C. §§ 1395-1395ccc, is a federally-run program, enacted in 1965, to provide financing for medical procedures for certain disabled individuals and people over 65 years of age. 42 U.S.C. §§ 426(a), 1395c." Rehabilitation Association of Virginia v. Kozlowski, 42 F.3d 1444, 1446 (4th Cir. 1994). The Medicare program does not provide medical treatment; instead it subsidizes health insurance with federal funds to pay for medical treatment. Medicare benefits are divided into four parts:

PART A. Hospitalization: Technically Part A establishes eligibility requirements for all of Medicare's benefits. In addition, Medicare Part A provides full or partial payment for reasonable and necessary medical care provided in: (1) hospitals; (2) skilled nursing homes; and (3) hospice care. 42 U.S.C. § 1395y(a)(1).

- Hospitalization must be based on a doctor's prescription specifying that the enrollee requires care that can only be provided in a hospital and the hospital's utilization review committee does not disapprove. Coverage is limited to a specified number of days, and a co-pay will be required after a specified number of days.

- Skilled nursing homes are entitled to Medicare if an enrollee completed at least three days at a hospital and then is admitted within thirty days following discharge from the hospital. The enrollee must be certified by a physician as needing skilled nursing care,and the care must result from the same cause as that treated in the hospital, and rehabilitation must be required daily. 42 C.F.R. § 409.31(a)-(b). Treatment is skilled if it is inherently complex or because of risks posed by complications. 42 C.F.R. § 409.32(a)-(b). Any patient is limited to one-hundred days of treatment in the skilled nursing home, and at some point a co-pay will be charged.

- Hospice care includes active pain management, counseling services, respite care, and services to the extended family. 42 C.F.R. § 418.202. The enrollee must be certified as terminally ill, with a life expectancy of less than six months, and this conclusion must be supported by written medical documentation. 42 C.F.R. § 418.22(b). Hospice benefits are provided up to 90 days but may be extended for another 90 days. Thereafter, benefits are extended for 60 day periods, but there must be a face-to-face meeting between the physician and the patient no more than 30 days prior to the third extension of the benefit period; subsequently, similar meetings are required 30 days prior to any recertification. 42 C.F.R. 418.22(a)(4).

PART B. Physicians and Healthcare: Unlike Part A, Medicare Part B is optional and requires the payment of a premium for all enrolled beneficiaries. Primarily, Part B covers physician services and related elements such as diagnostic tests, medical equipment, ambulance, outpatient physical and speech therapy, home care, prosthesis, and prescription drugs needed for actual treatment. 42 U.S.C. § 1395y(a)(1)(A). Excluded from coverage are eyeglasses, dental care, and long-term custodial care, although some of these items may be provided through enrollment in Medicare Advantage plans. Beginning in 2011, in part because of the Affordable Care Act of 2010, certain preventive measures and screenings became available for services that the U.S. Preventive Services Task Force recommends for seniors. 42 U.S.C. § 1395-x(ddd)(3).

PART C. Medicare Advantage Plans: Medicare Advantage plans permit private insurance companies to offer coverage to Medicare enrollees to provide benefits associated with Medicare. To attract enrollees, the insurance companies often provide benefits not covered by Medicare. The insurance companies agree to accept from Medicare an annual dollar amount for each person enrolled in Part A and Part B. In return, the insurance companies provide benefits to the enrolled, often at lower copays, in a similar fashion to a health maintenance organization (HMO) or a preferred provider organization (PPO). Each insurance carrier must accept Medicare applicants living in the plan's service area, and the carrier must publish policies and benefits, and provide for administration, as with any other insurance program. The Affordable Care Act of 2010 froze the 2011 payments made by Medicare to the private insurance companies offering advantage plans. In addition, the Affordable Care Act mandated that, by 2014, insurance companies must demonstrate that at least 85 percent of every dollar the company receives is spent on direct care and not on administration, marketing, or profit.

PART D. Prescription Drug Coverage: Prescription drug coverage became available to enrollees with the enactment of the Medicare Prescription Drug, Improvement and Modernization Act of 2003. There is a yearly deductible and then coinsurance payments of 25% of the cost of the medications, up to 25% of the cost of the medications. For overall prescription drug regulations, see 42 C.F.R. Part 423. Part D prescription drug coverage will not pay for all types of medications, and there are additional restrictions on dosage levels and the use of generic drugs. If an enrollee seeks to use a non-approved medication, any exception must be based on a doctor's certificate stating that no other approved drug will be as effective as the one being requested.

Notes

For commentary on the different aspects of Medicare coverage, see, *e.g.*, Mark Miller, *Medicare: The Next Frontier*, 159 Trusts & Ests. 52 (July 2019); Ann Connelly, Kathleen Healy, Hale Melnick, James Roosevelt, Jr., *A New Look at Medicare Advantage: What Lawyers Need to Know to Advise or Contract with Medicare Advantage Plans*,

12 J. HEALTH & LIFE SCI. L. 1 (2018); Lee B. Staley, *A Drug's Worth: Why Federal Law Makes it Hard to Pay for Pharmaceutical Performance*, 98 B.U. L. REV. 303 (2018).

RAYMOND C. O'BRIEN & MICHAEL T. FLANNERY
LONG-TERM CARE: FEDERAL, STATE, AND PRIVATE OPTIONS FOR THE FUTURE
(1997)

The health status of the elderly has been improving constantly with the concomitant increase in the percentage of the population that is becoming elderly.* * * The present increase in the elderly population is small compared to that which is expected in 15 years. The newcomers to the elderly population now are those who were born during the depression, which accounted for the lowest birth rate in the country's history. But by 2010, the elderly population will be flooded with baby boomers reaching retirement age.* * *

[T]he number of elderly is rising,* * * and those who comprise the elderly population are living longer. For example, in 1900, total life expectancy was approximately 37 years.* * * When social security was founded in 1935, life expectancy at age 65 was only 12.6 years.* * * In 1950, it was 13.9 years, and this figure increased to 17.2 years in 1989.* * * This figure will increase to as high as 21.3 years by the middle of the twenty-first century, when it is estimated there will be 392 million people inhabiting the United States.* * * Because of continuing advancements in medical technology and its ability to prolong life,* * * [in] 2000, there [were] 10 million more Americans over age 65 than there were in 1980.* * *

Id. at 16–17.

When Medicare was created [more than] 30 years ago, it was designed "to cover acute but not chronic care—the heart attack patient in the hospital, for example, not the [Alzheimer's] patient in a nursing home."* * * As of 1988, Medicare extended its services to include catastrophic illnesses.* * * Nevertheless, protection against the increasing costs of catastrophic and long-term health care under Medicare is minimal.* * * In fact, since 1986, "[o]lder persons [have paid] a larger portion of their income for health care than they did before Medicare was enacted."* * *

Medicare's hospital insurance is available at no cost to everyone who is entitled to Social Security.* * * Still, in 1987, Medicare costs were approximately $67 billion.* * * By the year 2040, this figure could rise as high as $200 billion.* * * Under the catastrophic health insurance plans of this country, however, less than 3 percent of Medicare's 31 million beneficiaries receive help with the care they need.* * * In 1985, Medicare paid only 1.7 percent of all nursing home bills, and private insurance covered less—0.8 percent, while 51.4 percent was paid out-of-pocket by consumers.* * *

Id. at 35–36.

C. Medicaid

Unlike Social Security and Medicare, Medicaid is a joint federal-state coopera-tive program governed by federal law and state regulations. Medicaid originated in 1965 to provide medical care to the elderly, blind, and disabled poor. Each state is permitted to administer its own program as long as the state regulations do not conflict with federal Medicaid regulations. Such a system creates diversity among the states, often precipitating different eligibility or benefit provisions. Age is not a factor as it is with Social Security and Medicare; rather, the only consideration is whether the applicant meets the state's financial, elderly, or blind eligibility require-ments. Overall, the following apply:

FUNDING: The federal contribution towards each state's Medicaid expenses may not be less than 50 percent or more than 83 percent.

ELIGIBILITY: The federal Centers for Medicare and Medicaid Services (CMS) supervises each state's administration, but each state is individually responsible for: (1) eligibility standards; (2) scope of services; (3) duration of services; (4) payment for services; and (5) administration of services. Eligibility depends on each state's financial criteria. There are no deductibles or copayments, but once an individual qualifies, the enrollee will be reviewed annually to maintain eligibility. In addition to financial eligibility, states must provide Medicaid to those who are "mandatory categorically needy" and those who are "categorically needy." Included in the lat-ter category are certain infants, low-income children, certain disabled adults, and recipients of state supplementary payments.

BENEFITS: Medicaid coverage is not limited to a set number of days, as is the case with Medicare. Medicaid will often pay for services not covered under Medi-care, such as vision, dental, and medical supplies. In addition, there are the follow-ing advantages and disadvantages:

(1) Coverage includes non-skilled nursing home care — custodial care — for an indefinite period of time. Long term care may include nursing homes, assisted living facilities, and in-home care.

(2) Persons considered elderly and poor may benefit most from Medicaid through use of medications and long-term nursing home care, which is considered custodial rather than skilled. If a person qualifies for Medicaid and Medicare, Medicaid may pay for all premiums, copays, and deductibles associated with Medicare.

(3) Physicians and facilities providing medical services participate in Med-icaid in a manner similar to participating in an HMO or a PPO. Likewise, enrollees may be denied a particular physician or a medical service because the provider does not participate in Medicaid.

(4) The Patient Protection and Affordable Care Act of 2010, through its reform of healthcare, expands home and community based services and increases the number of persons eligible, permitting access for persons with

incomes of up to 300% of the federal poverty level. *See* 42 U.S.C. 1396n(i) (6) (as amended by ACA § 2402(b)).

III. Long-Term Housing Payment Options

A. Self-Pay Option

Russell N. Adler, Peter J. Strauss & Regina Kiperman
America's Long-Term Care Crisis
153 TRUSTS & ESTATES 44 (July 2013)

Forty million Americans (13 percent of the population) are over the age of 65; by 2050, this number is projected to more than double to 88.5 million (20 percent). In addition, 5.7 million Americans (1.8 percent) are over the age of 85; by 2050, this number is projected to more than triple to 19 million (4.4 percent). Fifty percent of individuals over 85 will need assistance with daily functioning, and their home care can cost from $55,000 to $75,000 a year and up to $180,000 annually for nursing care. This is both a national and an individual crisis—most middle income families can't afford these costs, and a large segment of American society is being financially devastated.

. . .

[Long term care] insurance is designed to cover LTC costs not covered by Medicare. For those who can afford it and who can meet medical underwriting criteria, these policies offer a viable option for financing (in whole or in part) LTC at home or in a nursing home. Indeed, having a policy may preclude the need for Medicaid planning or, in some cases, allow planning through divestiture because the policy benefits could cover costs during a period of ineligibility.

Premiums for LTC insurance depend on age, geographic location, the amount of coverage desired, exclusion period chosen and whether an inflation rider and waiver of premium rider are purchased. Benefits are payable when a licensed health care practitioner certifies that the insured is unable to perform at least two of five activities of daily living (usually toileting, bathing, ambulating, feeding and dressing) without substantial assistance for a period expected to last at least 90 days.

Id. at 45.

Bernard A. Krooks & Lawrence A. Frolik
The Graying of America
154 TRUSTS & ESTS. 11 (Jan. 2015)

The Affordable Care Act, for all its benefits, doesn't pay for any LTC [Long Term Care]. Neither does Medicare, which, at best, may cover short-term rehabilitation under very limited circumstances. Medicare provides no coverage whatsoever for custodial care, such as for individuals who need help in getting in and out of bed, dressing, bathing or with other activities of daily living. Thus, we aging Americans are either forced to fend for ourselves and pay for LTC out of pocket (either privately or through insurance) or rely on Medicaid, which was originally intended to be a program for the very poor.

B. Long-Term Care Insurance Option

Lawrence A. Frolik & Bernard A. Krooks
Planning for Later Life
154 Trusts & Ests. 21 (July 2015)

Medicare pays for acute care, not LTC. Medicare may pay for up to 100 days in a nursing home (with significant copays for days 21 to 100), but that's it. After that, your client is on his own. With a nursing home costing between $6,000 and $20,000 (in some states, the cost can actually exceed $20,000) a month, your client needs to plan for how he'll pay for it should the need arise. And, it may well arise because over a third of those 80 and older suffer some degree of dementia, and many others suffer from chronic physical conditions that necessitate LTC. There are generally three ways to pay: (1) LTC insurance; (2) out of your client's income and savings; and (3) Medicaid. LTC insurance is expensive and not for everyone. Another form of "insurance" is to move to a continuing care retirement community (CCRC) that provides a range of housing, including independent living, assisted living and skilled nursing care. Many CCRCs charge a high admission fee — $300,000 to $1 million is common — but part of that fee helps pay for the increasing level of care provided to residents whose monthly fee doesn't increase, even if they have to move into the CCRC's skilled nursing facility. CCRC fees and what they provide vary greatly, so your client needs to shop around before he commits.

Id. at 23.

Thomas J. Pauloski
Financing Long-Term Care Expenses
152 Trusts & Ests. 22 (Sept. 2013)

Under most [insurance] policies, the payment of benefits is triggered by an insured's cognitive impairment or inability to perform, without substantial assistance, at least two ADLs [activities of daily living]. . . . [Policies] take two basic forms. Indemnity policies simply pay a specified daily amount on a triggering event, regardless of how much the family actually pays out for LTC. In contrast, reimbursement policies cover the actual costs incurred. In either case, stand-alone LTC insurance is "classic" insurance—policyholders who don't use some or all of the policy benefits pay for those who do. Thus, in financial terms, policy holders who collect substantial benefits usually reap a windfall, and those who don't often incur a substantial opportunity cost due to premiums paid and investment returns that those dollars would have yielded.

Id. at 23.

Gregory D. Singer & Michael Schmid
The Financial Sweet Spot for Long-Term Care Insurance
153 Trusts & Ests. 48 (July 2014)

There are additional variables that investors will want to assess in making the decision about whether LTC insurance might improve the probability of sustaining lifetime spending. These factors include:

- Age of the individuals. Starting younger can lower the premiums and ensure insurability. On the other hand, starting older, if the individual is still healthy, may reduce the overall cost of insurance.
- Number of individuals in the household for which LTC is a possibility.
- Family health and longevity history and how long the individual might have to stay at a LTC facility.
- Cost of LTC in the area where an individual resides.
- Expected living expenses during retirement and as a percentage of the portfolio.
- Anticipated future inflation, generally, and for LTC, in particular.
- Wealth transfer objectives.

Id. at 51.

C. Medicaid Spenddown Option

Lopes v. Department of Social Services
United States Court of Appeals, Second Circuit, 2012
696 F.3d 180

LOHIER, Circuit Judge: . . .

The [Medicare Catastrophic Coverage Act of 1988 ("MCCA")] requires States to consider the resources of both the institutionalized spouse and the "community spouse" in determining the former's eligibility for Medicaid benefits. 42 U.S.C. § 1396r–5(c)(2)(A). The MCCA also requires States to exclude certain community spouse funds and assets from the calculation of total resources. First, it provides that "[d]uring any month in which an institutionalized spouse is in the institution . . . no income of the community spouse shall be deemed available to the institutionalized spouse." 42 U.S.C. § 1396r–5(b)(1). Second, it excludes specified assets, such as the couple's home and one automobile, from counting against the eligibility of the institutionalized spouse. 42 U.S.C. § 1382b(a). If, after these exclusions, the community spouse's resources still exceed a pre-determined "community spouse resource allowance," the institutionalized spouse is ineligible for Medicaid benefits until the excess resources are depleted. 42 U.S.C. §§ 1396r-5(c)(2)(B), 1396r-5(f)(2)(A). In determining eligibility for benefits under the MCCA, the States must use criteria that are "no more restrictive than the methodology which would be employed under the supplemental social security ['SSI'] program." 42 U.S.C. § 1396a(a)(10)(C)(i). . . . When Lopes filed her husband's application for Medicaid benefits, the applicable "community spouse resource allowance" was approximately $180,000. . . .

Shortly before Lopes filed her husband's application for benefits, her liquid assets exceeded the community spouse resource allowance by about $160,000. Seeking to reduce her resources to below the protected amount, Lopes purchased an immediate single premium annuity with a premium of $166,878.99 from The Hartford Life Insurance Company ("The Hartford"). The annuity contract, which was governed by Connecticut law, provided for monthly payments of $2,340.83 over a period of approximately six years. At Lopes's election, the annuity contract contained an "Assignment Limitation Rider," which provided:

> This contract is not transferable. The rights, title and interest in the contract may not be transferred; nor may such rights, title and interest be assigned, sold, anticipated, alienated, commuted, surrendered, cashed in or pledged as security for a loan. Any attempt to transfer, assign, sell, anticipate, alienate, commute, surrender, cash in or pledge this contract shall be void of any legal effect and shall be unenforceable against [The Hartford].

Lopes requested a letter from The Hartford clarifying the import of the Assignment Limitation Rider. The Hartford confirmed that "neither the Annuity Contract, nor any periodic payments due thereunder can be cashed-in, sold, assigned, or otherwise transferred, pledged, or hypothecated [due to the Assignment Limitation Rider]." . . . Lopes submitted the application for Medicaid benefits thirteen days after purchasing the annuity. Because the Department of Social Services's Uniform Policy Manual ("UPM") § 4030.47 provides that, for purposes of determining benefit eligibility, "the right to receive income from an annuity is regarded as an available asset, whether or not the annuity is assignable," the Commissioner sought to determine whether Lopes could sell her annuity income stream to a third party notwithstanding the Rider. Although a third party, Peachtree Financial, appears to have been willing to purchase the payment stream for approximately $99,000, Lopes maintained that the annuity was a "fixed income stream[,] . . . not an asset that she [was] required to" liquidate. In May 2010 the Commissioner told Lopes that her husband was ineligible for Medicaid benefits because she had "failed to apply for or try to get assets which may be available to [her] family." . . .

We review the grant of summary judgment *de novo* and "will uphold the judgment if the evidence, viewed in the light most favorable to the party against whom it is entered, demonstrates that there are no genuine issues of material fact and that the judgment is warranted as a matter of law." *McGullam v. Cedar Graphics, Inc.,* 609 F.3d 70, 75 (2d Cir.2010) (quotation marks omitted). Because the material facts are not in dispute here, we consider only whether the annuity is non-assignable and, if so, whether it is income or a resource. . . . [footnote omitted]. The language of the relevant regulations, as clarified in the POMS and in HHS's amicus brief, convinces us that the income stream from Lopes's annuity is properly considered income, not a resource, because the annuity is non-assignable. . . .

As noted above, the SSI regulation that differentiates between income and resources provides that a community spouse's asset is a resource "[i]f the individual has the right, authority or power to liquidate the property, or his or her share of the property." 20 C.F.R. § 416.1201(a)(1). The Assignment Limitation Rider strips Lopes of both the right to assign her payments under the annuity, by providing that "[t]he rights, title and interest in the contract may not be transferred," and the power to assign her payments, by providing that "[a]ny attempt to transfer, assign . . . [or] cash in . . . this contract shall be void of any legal effect. . . ."[2] Under Connecticut law, this language suffices to make the annuity non-assignable. *See Rumbin v. Utica Mut. Ins. Co.,* 254 Conn. 259, 757 A.2d 526, 535 (2000) (holding that a general provision prohibiting assignment eliminates a payee's "*right* to assign, but not his *power* to do so," and that the latter may be eliminated only through "express language to limit the power to assign or to void the assignment itself"). . . . The Commissioner nonetheless submits that the owner of a non-assignable annuity has the effective "right, authority or power" to liquidate the asset, as long as there is a prospective purchaser for the payment stream. We cannot agree. We recognize that the SSI regulations do not specifically address the status of a "non-assignable" annuity like the one Lopes purchased. But one SSI regulation, 20 C.F.R. § 416.1121, supports the classification of the payment stream from such an annuity as income:

> Some types of unearned income are . . . [a]nnuities, pensions, and other periodic payments. This unearned income is usually related to prior work or service. It includes, for example, private pensions, social security benefits, disability benefits, veterans benefits, worker's compensation, railroad retirement annuities and unemployment insurance benefits.

20 C.F.R. § 416.1121. Section 416.1121 makes clear that payments from an annuity can constitute "unearned income." The provision also generally classifies various non-assignable income streams (social security benefits, disability benefits, and so on) as income, without regard to the existence of a prospective purchaser. These income sources are analogous to Lopes's annuity in both their payment structure and their non-assignability.

---

2. Although the regulation also references the "authority" to liquidate an asset, 20 C.F.R. § 416.1201(a)(1), the Commissioner does not argue that Lopes has the "authority" to assign the payments, as distinct from having the "right" or "power" to do so.

The Commissioner points to additional SSI regulations that appear to say that if an individual liquidates a resource before applying for benefits, the receipts from the liquidation are still a resource. For example, the Commissioner cites 20 C.F.R. § 416.1207(e), which provides: "If an individual sells, exchanges or replaces a resource, the receipts are not income. They are still considered to be a resource." 20 C.F.R. § 416.1207(e); *see also* 20 C.F.R. § 416.1103(a) (providing that "what you receive from the sale or exchange of your own property is not income; it remains a resource"); 20 C.F.R. § 416.1103(c) (providing that "[r]eceipts from the sale, exchange, or replacement of a resource are not income but are resources that have changed their form," and using as an example: "[i]f you sell your automobile, the money you receive is not income; it is another form of a resource"). In particular, the Commissioner contends that Lopes's annuity qualifies as a resource under these regulations because Lopes converted her excess resources into a non-assignable annuity shortly before she sought benefits.

We reject the argument for the following reasons. Unlike §§ 416.1201(a)(1) and 416.1121, which apply more specifically to the issue in this case and guide more explicitly our consideration of whether Lopes's annuity is a resource, the regulations upon which the Commissioner relies do not address whether the "converted" form of Lopes's assets—the non-assignable annuity—qualifies as a resource. *See United States v. Torres-Echavarria*, 129 F.3d 692, 699 n. 3 (2d Cir.1997) ("The operative principle of statutory construction is that a specific provision takes precedence over a more general provision."). Instead, they establish only that if Lopes had converted a resource to cash, those cash proceeds would also be a resource. Nor do these regulations establish that Lopes's annuity is a resource merely because it existed in the form of cash shortly before she applied for Medicaid. The Medicaid program categorically excludes certain assets, such as a home and one automobile, from consideration as resources. 42 U.S.C. §§ 1396r–5(c)(5) & 1382b(a). How recently those assets were purchased appears not to matter in determining whether they should be excluded from the relevant pool of resources.[3] Accordingly, that Lopes converted cash to an annuity shortly before applying for Medicaid is irrelevant to whether the annuity, in its current form, qualifies as a resource under the applicable SSI regulations. . . .

The POMS is a set of guidelines through which the Social Security Administration "further construe[s]" the statutes governing its operations. *Clark v. Astrue*, 602 F.3d 140, 144 (2d Cir.2010). We have held that POMS guidelines are entitled to "substantial deference, and will not be disturbed as long as they are reasonable and consistent with the statute." *Bubnis v. Apfel*, 150 F.3d 177, 181 (2d Cir.1998). But we have declined to defer to the POMS where "the plain language of the statute and

---

3. The regulations account for the possibility that, even while receiving benefits, an individual may trade resources that count against Medicaid eligibility for resources that do not, affecting her benefits eligibility status for the following month: "If, during a month . . . an individual spends a resource or replaces a resource that is not excluded with one that is excluded, the decrease in the value of the resources is counted as of the first moment of the next month." 20 C.F.R. § 416.1207(c).

its implementing regulation do not permit the construction contained within the manuals." *Oteze Fowlkes v. Adamec*, 432 F.3d 90, 96 (2d Cir.2005). . . . As relevant here, the POMS provides that "[a]ssets of any kind are not resources if the individual does not have . . . the legal right, authority or power to liquidate them (provided they are not already in cash). . . ." POMS § SI 01110.15 (emphasis added). This provision strongly supports the District Court's conclusion that the payment stream from Lopes's non-assignable annuity is income. As discussed above, notwithstanding the existence of a prospective purchaser for the payment stream, the Assignment Limitation Rider divests Lopes of the legal right and the power to direct that the payor pay the annuity benefit directly to a third party. *See Rumbin*, 757 A.2d at 531, 535. . . . We conclude that POMS § SI 01110.15, which is reasonable and consistent with § 416.1201(a)(1) and therefore entitled to deference, supports Lopes's argument that the payment stream is income. . . .

In its amicus brief, HHS makes two persuasive arguments that support the District Court's and Lopes's interpretation of the SSI regulations. First, it interprets § 416.1121, § 416.1201(a)(1), and POMS § SI 01110.15 as classifying income from non-assignable annuities as just that—income. Second, it explains that this interpretation coheres with the policy goals of Medicaid—in particular, protecting community spouses from impoverishment by permitting them to retain some of their assets, while recognizing that couples must apply a fair share of their combined resources toward the cost of care before receiving benefits. . . . HHS further notes that its interpretation of the income/resource distinction is consistent with the treatment of annuities in the [Deficit Reduction Act of 2005 (DRA)]. The DRA provides that, so long as annuities are disclosed in Medicaid applications and name the State as the remainder beneficiary, the placement of assets in an annuity will not be considered a suspect "transfer of assets" exposing an applicant to certain penalties.[5] 42 U.S.C. §§ 1396a(a)(18), 1396p(c)(1)(A), 1396p(e)(1). It further provides that these disclosure requirements apply "regardless of whether the annuity is irrevocable or is treated as an asset." 42 U.S.C. § 1396p(e)(1). That the DRA has disclosure requirements for irrevocable annuities, but does not categorically classify them as resources or designate their purchase as an impermissible transfer of assets, supports HHS's view that Congress has not demonstrated an intent to exclude all annuity payment streams from being treated as income. *See James [v. Richman*, 547 F.3d [214,] 219 (3d Cir. 2008)] ("Congress provided a detailed set of rules governing transactions that it considered suspicious, and the purchase of an annuity is not among them.").

HHS's position as articulated in its amicus brief accords with our reading of the relevant regulations and POMS guideline and is consistent with both Medicaid's

---

5. Under the DRA, if a couple disposes of any assets for less than fair market value during a specified "look-back" period, the institutionalized spouse becomes ineligible for Medicaid benefits for the length of time that those assets could have covered his or her medical costs. *See* 42 U.S.C. § 1396p(c)(1)(A).

policy goals and the DRA. We attach some persuasive value to HHS's views, which in any event only bolster our conclusion that Lopes's annuity payment stream qualifies as income. . . . We therefore hold that the payment stream from a non-assignable annuity is not a resource for purposes of determining Medicaid eligibility. In doing so, we now join those of our sister circuits that have addressed the same issue. *See id.* at 218 (holding that even if the community spouse "has the *de facto* ability to effect a change in ownership," a non-assignable annuity "cannot be treated as an available resource"); *Morris v. Okla. Dep't of Human Servs.*, 685 F.3d 925, 932–34 (10th Cir.2012) (concluding that entitlement to receive non-assignable annuity payments is income, and not a resource); *see also Hutcherson v. Ariz. Health Care Cost Containment Sys. Admin.*, 667 F.3d 1066, 1069 (9th Cir.2012) (noting that "the Medicaid statute allows the community spouse to purchase an annuity . . . allowing the spouse to convert his or her assets, which are considered in determining the institutionalized spouse's eligibility, to income, which is not considered" (citation omitted)). . . .

For the foregoing reasons, the judgment of the District Court is AFFIRMED.

Notes

Medicaid will pay for long-term skilled nursing care, outpatient treatment, medications, acute medical care, and long-term nursing home residential care. *See* 42 U.S.C. §§ 1396 *et seq.* But to qualify for Medicaid payment: (1) an applicant must be categorically needy, (2) an applicant must be medically needy because medical costs far exceed income or assets, or (3) the applicant's assets and income must be less than a minimum level. Often, persons seeking to obtain Medicaid benefits will attempt to "spenddown" assets and reduce income so as to qualify. These spenddown attempts often seek to transfer assets to relatives or friends. To protect against attempts by applicants to spenddown assets and qualify for Medicaid assistance, Congress passed a series of laws to find assets and use these assets to pay for long-term care. *See, e.g.*, Medicare Catastrophic Coverage Act of 1988, Medicare Catastrophic Coverage Repeal Act of 1989, the Omnibus Budget Reconciliation Act of 1993, the Deficit Reduction Act of 2005, and the Patient Protection and Affordable Care Act of 2010. The effect of this legislation was the following:

BONAFIDE SPENDDOWN ITEMS: Eligibility for Medicaid long-term care will depend on meeting income and resource limits. Spenddown is the process of reducing both income and resources, and the general rule is that Medicaid applicants do not have to count income or resources that are "converted" to exempt assets. Among these exempt assets are the following: (1) a home, up to the limit imposed by the Deficit Reduction Act of 2005; (2) home improvements, up to the limit imposed by the Deficit Reduction Act of 2005; (3) new home furnishings; (4) a new automobile; (5) a new home mortgage or paying the existing home mortgage to increase the community spouse resource allowance; (6) a funeral contract; and (7) a life insurance contract, up to the limit imposed by the Deficit Reduction Act of 2005.

INELIGIBLE SPENDDOWN ITEMS: If an applicant gives away items within five years of applying for Medicaid long-term care, a transfer penalty will result. *See* 42 U.S.C. § 1396p(c)(1)(A). Any transfers outside that five year period are unimportant for eligibility purposes. The Deficit Reduction Act of 2005 mandates that the total amount of disqualifying gifts be calculated by adding them together and then dividing by the state's divisor, which is based on the average monthly cost of long-term care in that state. The resulting number represents the number of months of ineligibility that will begin to run in the month in which the applicant is otherwise eligible for Medicaid long-term care. Among the ineligible spenddown items are the following: (1) any unauthorized annuity; (2) any unauthorized loan; (3) a life estate in which the purchaser does not reside in the purchase for at least one year; (4) disclaimer of an inheritance or other property right; (5) waiver of a statutory election against an estate plan of a deceased spouse, *see, e.g., In re* Estate of Cross, 664 N.E.2d 905 (Ohio 1996); (6) the exercise of an intervivos power of appointment in favor or a third party; (7) failure to exercise a Crummey trust right to withdraw corpus that is not exercised; (8) the value of any assets sold below fair market value; and (9) withdrawal by another joint owner of any jointly held account.

The *Lopes* decision from the Second Circuit offers an introduction to both spousal protection envisioned by the Deficit Reduction Act of 2005 and approved annuities, which have become increasingly popular methods by which married couples may safeguard the financial viability of a supporting spouse and permit the other spouse to qualify for Medicaid assistance. For further commentary on Medicaid spenddown as a means of qualifying for Medicaid, see, *e.g.,* Bernard A. Krooks & Lawrence A. Frolik, *The Graying of America*, 154 Trusts & Ests. 11 (Jan. 2015); Raymond C. O'Brien, *Selective Issues in Effective Medicaid Estate Recovery Statutes*, 65 Cath. U. L. Rev. 27 (2015); Craig J. Langstrast, Lanitra Harris, and James M. Plecnik, *Annuity Strategy When Spouse Needs Nursing Home Coverage*, 41 Est. Plan. 25 (2014); Russell N. Adler, Peter J. Strauss & Regina Kiperman, *America's Long-Term Care Crisis*, 152 Trusts & Ests. 44, 47 (July 2013); Sean R. Bleck, Barbara Isenhour & John A. Miller, *Preserving Wealth and Inheritance Through Medicaid Planning for Long-Term Care*, 17 Mich. St. U. J. Med. & L. 153 (2013); Thomas J. Pauloski, *Financing Long-Term Care*, 152 Trusts & Ests. 22 (Sept. 2013).

Index